IRELAND IN THE TWENTIETH CENTURY

Tim Pat Coogan is one of the best known figures in Ireland. Author, broadcaster and former editor of the *Irish Press*, he has written several books, including *The Troubles* and *The IRA*; the pioneering study, *Ireland Since the Rising*; *On the Blanket*; *Wherever Green is Worn*; and a number of others including his bestselling biographies of *Michael Collins* and *De Valera*.

Praise for Tim Pat Coogan's previous book, *Wherever Green is Worn*:

'A journey into our own psyche . . . Tim Pat Coogan has dug, Heaney-like, into the past while opening doors to faraway places.' Frank McCourt

'When Tim Pat Coogan does things, he tends to do them definitively . . . So it's no great surprise to find that his long-awaited account of the Irish Diaspora is the most far-reaching and comprehensive study of that phenomenon ever written.' *Books Ireland*

'[It] is an intellectually ambitious work, the result of great energy, imagination and painstaking detective work. Tim Pat Coogan manages to find 'the story' in about every country he has visited. This volume will stand as a challenging and controversial work on the Irish diaspora . . . It is a big book on a big topic. Don't just read it. Buy it and reread it.' *The Irish Times*

'The definitive story of the Irish abroad.' *Ireland on Sunday*

'Amusing, interesting and often absorbing . . . Peppered with the kind of Irish humour that can make you laugh out loud.' *Guardian*

Ireland in the Twentieth Century

Tim Pat Coogan

arrow books

Published in the United Kingdom by Arrow Books in 2004

3 5 7 9 10 8 6 4 2

Copyright © Tim Pat Coogan 2003

The right of Tim Pat Coogan to be identified as the author of this work
has been asserted by him in accordance with the
Copyright, Designs and Patents Act, 1988

First published in the United Kingdom by Hutchinson in 2003

Arrow Books
The Random House Group Limited
20 Vauxhall Bridge Road, London SW1V 2SA

Random House Australia (Pty) Limited
20 Alfred Street, Milsons Point, Sydney,
New South Wales 2061, Australia

Random House New Zealand Limited
18 Poland Road, Glenfield,
Auckland 10, New Zealand

Random House (Pty) Limited
Endulini, 5a Jubilee Road
Parktown 2193, South Africa

The Random House Group Limited Reg. No. 954009

www.randomhouse.co.uk

A CIP catalogue record for this book is available
from the British Library

Papers used by Random House are natural,
recyclable products made from wood grown in sustainable
forests. The manufacturing processes conform to the
environmental regulations of the country of origin.

Typeset in Times New Roman by
MATS, Southend-on-Sea, Essex

Printed and bound in Great Britain by
Cox & Wyman Ltd, Reading, Berks

ISBN 0 09 941522 4

To my own children, Thomond, Jackie, Olwen, Tom, Rachel and Clara, and to all the children of the Twenty-first Century – may they learn from the Twentieth

CONTENTS

ILLUSTRATIONS

PREFACE

As with the world generally, the changes in Ireland throughout the twentieth century were vast, politically, economically, and in the field of religion. This last had a greater significance in the world of politics and sexual morality than in most other countries. Ireland entered the twentieth century as a slumbesmirched colonial backwater, a provider of cheap food and cheap labour to her imperial neighbour, and left it as a sovereign country, a respected member of the EU and the UN. Where the nations of the world were concerned, Ireland, though a small country, was like Ulysses, not least but honoured of them all.

This outline picture is an accurate one, but it is an outline overlooking much in the way of detail concerning tragedy, lost opportunities, emigration, poverty, bloodshed and death. Much of the latter could have been avoided had a pattern, which was coming ominously close to repetition as this was being written, not been followed by English decision-takers between the mid-1880s and the period 1916–21. Put bluntly, that pattern consisted of ignoring the democratically expressed wishes of an overwhelming majority of the inhabitants of the island of Ireland in favour of a colonial oligarchy and the possibilities which supporting this oligarchy offered the Conservative Party for wresting power from the Liberals.

The decision to bypass the ballot box and support the thesis of the Conservative leadership that Ulster would fight, and Ulster would be right, led to many protests in arms by Irish Nationalists, from which the country emerged, after some 50 years of recuperation from the wounds of rebellion, civil war and partition into two states: today's 26-county Republic of Ireland and the Six Counties of North-Eastern Ireland erroneously known as 'Ulster', a term which rightly belongs to the original nine-county province of Ulster from which the Six Counties were sundered. If football can be said to be a game of two halves, the same can certainly be argued to hold good for Ireland in the first and second parts of the twentieth century. The early part was a tale of the high heroic gradually diminishing into one of old men incapable of leaving, or leading, from positions of power. Whatever powers of innovation the survivors of the civil war generation possessed drained out of them during the 1940s and 1950s in both of the island's political entities north and south of the border.

The results were backward-looking, stagnation, the story of old wrongs being kept alive so as to be manufactured into an ersatz political plasma. It was a grim irony that, in the Republic, one of the main scandals of the latter part of the twentieth century concerned the insertion of diseased blood products into the physical veins of Irish citizens. Until the late 1950s and early 1960s, many of Ireland's leaders could fairly be accused of doing the same with political philosophy.

The Republic became an emigration-drained land wherein poverty, priest and publican dominated and occasionally the gunman reached in his holster for a solution to the problems of partition. The Six Counties became a political slum, an unjust, resentful, sectarian, one-party statelet wherein fundamental democratic rights such as one man, one vote, did not apply. Britain failed to exercise her responsibility to ensure that the same standards applied to 'the UK overseas' as to 'the UK mainland' and the statelet's paraphernalia of unjust laws became the envy of the Boers. Violence and bloodshed were the inevitable outcome. In the first half of the century there were sporadic outbursts of IRA activity then, from the sixties onwards, a sustained, ugly convulsion of death and destruction that lasted for nearly thirty years until the IRA ceasefire of 1994. The grudging and slow acceptance of the opportunities presented by the ceasefire, by both the Conservatives and the Unionists, and an increasing unsureness of touch by the current Labour Government, meant that, as this was written, the jury was still out on the issue of whether we are to have a long-term settlement or a possible return to violence.

Where the Republic was concerned, from the sixties onwards, as Ireland opened to newer worlds, those of the EEC, television, improved educational facilities, and the second Vatican Council, the story becomes one of a distancing from two forms of colonialism, Mother England and Mother Church. There were many false starts, and wrong turnings. Emigration was not brought under control until the 1990s, and who can say that the events of 11 September 2001 have not set in train shockwaves which will re-open this distinctively Irish wound. But overall, despite the appalling spread of corruption in the wake of prosperity, progress was made towards realising at least some of the aspirations of those, like the 1916 leaders, who dreamed that a free and independent Ireland would also be a prosperous and caring one, with a distinctive Irish identity of its own.

I believe this identity exists, to be found in terms of personality not solely of language; though language, music and traditional forms of dance, design and song all play their part, as does climate, and, until towards the close of the century, so does a distinctively Roman Catholic formation in school, church and home. But, I believe there is something in those whom Yeats termed the 'indomitable Irishry' which transcends both language and religion, and harps back to a Celtic ancestry for its source. A nation on the run cannot be expected to pause to create works of art on canvas or in bronze, and this for many years caused people to say that the Irish had no visual sense; but this was proved not to be true when circumstances improved so that the running could stop. Creativity in fields other than the portable ones of the oral tradition began, with spectacular success in the field of rock music for example. So does the contemporary period of prosperity with all its vexations and crude, grasping, corrupt materialism offer a plateau on which new cathedrals of the mind can be built, old blueprints re-examined, not to the old authoritarian gods of conformity and a pietistic hypocrisy, but to something more vigorous and true. For both Church and State the challenge is to harness the Irish caring impulse, which yielded her unique missionary tradition, to the needs of a better educated world with different perspectives on the spheres of economic, political and sexual morality.

Movements apart, two men may be regarded as the ratchets on which the Irish Republic swung: the civil servant, Ken Whitaker, and the politician, Seán Lemass. They set in train the policies of economic concentration and of looking into the outside world for new opportunities that changed backward-looking Ireland to outward-looking Ireland. The men and the momentum which they brought to Irish society threw out many babies with the bathwater. In some spheres, that of public morality, for example, the story is a sorrowful decade of the Rosary. A list not of ten Hail Marys, but of ten tribunals investigating Irish veniality which appears as an appendix, illustrates all too clearly what I mean.

In other spheres, particularly the problem of the six north-eastern Irish counties, the story has been a bloody one oscillating between troughs of atrocity and peaks of hope. The highest of these, which offered the possibility that the troughs might never again re-occur, was the Good Friday Agreement, involving all the parties to the Irish dispute, which was signed in 1998. But the hopes have not been realised. In such a complex situation, it is not possible simply to point a finger and say all the blame lies over *there*, pointing to one party or another to the dispute. But it is both fair and accurate to say that a major part of the difficulty has been the unwillingness of the Ulster Unionists to accept change and the transition to proper democracy which the Good Friday Agreement offers. They appear to be like the Bourbons who forgot nothing and who learned nothing. As the world moves on, they still cry 'Ulster says no', ignoring the stark realities of demographic change. The figures for the 2001 census, though massaged by Whitehall so as to prevent frightening the horses in the street, could not hide the reality that for the first time in the existence of the statelet the Protestant population had slipped below the 50 per cent mark.

Increasingly, British policy has tended to tilt towards the dwindling Protestant and Unionist majority. A cardinal tenet of the Good Friday Agreement was Britain's declared intention to withdraw from sovereignty in Ireland and to allow the contending parties to resolve their difficulties between Irish men and women. Instead, in a vain attempt to shore up the fortunes of David Trimble, the Official Unionist Party leader, and to keep both Sinn Féin and Ian Paisley's Democratic Unionist Party (DUP) at bay, Britain has consistently intervened on the side of the remnants of its colonial oligarchy in Ireland, the ineffectual and increasingly dissension-torn wing of Unionism led by Trimble. The democratic Assembly set up by the Good Friday Agreement has been suspended, and worse, in an effort to ward off David Trimble's internal enemies, scheduled elections have been postponed *sine die*. No doubt it would be mightily inconvenient for Whitehall, and indeed for Dublin, if Sinn Féin and the DUP were, as appears inevitable, to emerge as the dominant groupings in the Six Counties. But there is a word for such inconvenience. It's called democracy, part of the mechanism for dealing with the detritus of empire.

Tony Blair told the American Congress that he was sure that history would forgive him and George Bush for invading Iraq. Perhaps, but certainly, as this book goes to press, a huge Irish diplomatic effort was in progress, trying to reinstate elections for late 2003. Ireland will not forgive Mr Blair should it fail. Nature abhors a vacuum, and if the Sinn Féin leaders cannot make good on their promise that political progress can be made via the ballot box rather than the bomb, then – the virulence of the Irish physical-force tradition being what it is – the protective political covering which, though fraying, is still encasing that tradition will be yet again eaten through.

Another problem which Ireland does not confront, or even acknowledge, is that of its diaspora. The Irish worldwide are one of the globe's success stories, emerging from slum, swamp-draining, coal-mining, brawling, and boozing illiteracy, literally to the scents of the rose garden of the White House in the case of John F. Kennedy. But the only group which overlooks its potential is the Irish Government. The diaspora is neither cherished nor mobilised. After the Twin Towers, Ireland can no longer afford that luxury. Only one American Congressman in five holds a passport, and the American continent is so vast and its media so poor that relatively few Americans either know, or have reason to know, a great deal about the world in which most of us live. As a result, the great lobbies, the industrial military complex, the Israelis, the oil companies, the Cubans, the British, all exercise a powerful influence on American foreign policy and hence on world events. The Irish are potentially one of the greatest of all the groupings which could be assembled. At census time in America alone, forty-three million people give their ethnic origin as Irish. That resource should be respected, and mobilised, by Dublin. In today's world, the Irish must do more with their heritage than organise a booze-up every St Patrick's Day and congratulate themselves on the amount of American companies which have set up in Ireland. Now that the EU has been enlarged, many of these companies can just as easily relocate to Eastern Europe, and at far less cost. Some have already begun to do so.

But above all, to cherish the diaspora is to acknowledge, as to some degree Dublin governments have begun to do with Irish artists, that it is necessary to make an active affirmation, to today's diaspora as to those who have gone ahead, that it is composed of people of substance, intellectually and spiritually as well as economically. The Irish are no petty people, as their survival and success through the ups and downs of the turbulent twentieth century amply illustrate. But after 11 September 2001, the cant about a New World Order has come to possess an uncomfortable degree of truth. A terrible beauty has not been born but something terrible has emerged. Though Ireland itself has emerged from the twentieth century with more pluses on balance than minuses, the minuses exist. To make progress in the twenty-first century, Ireland, a mother nation, will have to turn for help to her children abroad, as well as to those at home.

ONE

GRASPING THE ORANGE NETTLE

(PRE-1916)

'Ulster will fight and Ulster will be right.' In a very real sense the two states into which modern Ireland is divided at the time of writing grew out of that statement. The words were uttered at a public meeting by a senior British Conservative, Lord Randolph Churchill.[1] Along with telling his audience that they would be right to fight, he gave Ulster Unionists a pledge that if the Liberal Prime Minister, Gladstone, attempted to introduce Home Rule to Ireland, 'There will not be wanting to you those of position and influence in England who are willing to cast in their lot with you, whatever it may be, and who will share your fortune and your fate.'

The meeting, held on 22 February 1886 in the Ulster Hall, had been advertised in the *Belfast News-Letter* as a 'conservative demonstration – a monster meeting of conservatives and Orangemen'. Certainly Irish Nationalists would argue that the meeting's outcome was monstrous. At the risk of appearing to mix political metaphors it may be said that the Orange element took Churchill's speech as a green light for political demonstrations – Belfast style. Protestant–Catholic rioting had been a feature of the city's life since 1813, but 1886 still stands out as a particularly bad year for sectarian violence. In a summer of discontent some 32 people were killed, 371 injured, and much property destroyed.

In the coded language of such documents, the report of the commission set up to inquire into the riots listed amongst their causes 'the sudden and unexpected advance of the Home Rule question'. In helping to trigger that dementia, Churchill had acted quite deliberately. Six days before he made his speech in Belfast he had written to his friend Lord Justice Fitzgibbon saying he had 'decided some time ago that if the GOM went for Home Rule, the Orange card would be the one to play. Please God it may turn out the Ace of Trumps, and not the two.'

Churchill's prayers were answered. Gladstone, the GOM, did introduce a Home Rule Bill for Ireland, and the Orange card turned up trumps. A number of Liberal Unionists, led by Joseph Chamberlain and Lord Hartington, sided with the Conservatives, and the Bill, which incidentally only proposed a very limited form of self-government within the British Empire, was heavily defeated. Nevertheless, in the subsequent general election Ireland returned 86 Home Rule members against 17 Unionists. By way of illustrating the

1

essentially party-political (and of course undemocratic) nature of the Tory campaign against Home Rule, it might be noted that, in the period of crisis engineered by the Conservatives' opportunism – from 1886 until the 1916 rising brought the issue to another plane – from a pool of 103 Irish seats, Unionists never won more than 23.

Given the size of that majority, one might reasonably enquire: if the Irish were so overwhelmingly in favour of independence from Westminster, what were they doing sitting there in the first place? The short answer is that the bulk of the Irish representation – that is, its Catholic and Nationalist component – would not have been there had history not consigned them to seats in the House of Commons in London rather than an Irish parliament in Dublin. The situation had its origins in the policy of plantation, the settling of Protestants from England and Scotland on land confiscated from the native Irish Catholics; in particular the settling in the north-eastern province of Ulster, during the reign of James I, of Lowland Scottish Protestants.

A high percentage of these came from the English–Scottish border region where hostility to one's neighbours and the custom of 'reiving' (cattle rustling) were the norm. Hardy and ruthless, these Presbyterian settlers were well prepared for the challenges of farming with one hand resting on a plough and the other on a musket. These skills, honed in Ireland, would later stand the descendants of the 'Scotch Irish' in good stead, after they emigrated to America and began cultivating land wrested from the Indians. Pawky in their humour and pious in their Presbyterianism, these planters may accurately be thought of as 'children of wrath' rather than of love. They lived, moved and had their being like settlers the world over, constantly mindful of the possibility that one day the indigenous people might rise against them and seize back their land.

However, they, and the Protestants of the north-east generally, could also fairly be regarded as enjoying a far greater prosperity than existed in the rest of the country, particularly after 1700. Not only did they hold their farms on far less onerous terms than those available to Catholics; they also profited when an influx of Huguenot refugees helped to galvanise the linen industry. William of Orange commissioned Louis Crommelin to modernise this particular industry, because unlike the Irish woollen trade, or for that matter the shipping and cattle trades, all of which were taxed out of existence as a result, there was no jealousy from English competition. The introduction of ship-building to Belfast during the nineteenth century added to the generation of wealth. Unfortunately it also added to the sectarian bitternesses as Catholics poured into the city, and elsewhere in the region, in pursuit of job opportunities.

The employment situation was on such a scale that at the time of Churchill's speech Belfast had grown to a city of around 230,000 people from the mere 37,000 recorded in the census taken only 60 years earlier, in 1821. The Belfast Riots Commission of 1886 commented on the districts whence the rioters came in terms which would still have been applicable a century later, in 1986:

The extremity to which party and religious feeling has grown in Belfast is shown strikingly by the fact that the people of the artisan and labouring classes . . . dwell to a large extent in separate quarters . . . the great thoroughfare of Shankill-Road . . . is an almost purely Protestant district; and the parties referred to in the evidence as 'the Shankill mob' are a Protestant mob. The great Catholic quarter . . . consists of the thoroughfare known as the Falls-Road . . . the 'Falls Road mob' are therefore a Catholic mob . . . a spirit has grown up . . . which has resulted . . . in 1857, 1864 and 1872 . . . of disturbances and long continued riots.

When the Home Rule crisis first broke, Belfast looked like a red-bricked provincial British city. The Protestant burghers who guided its destinies thought like Mancunians. They saw Belfast as being allied economically to Manchester, Liverpool and Glasgow. In Ireland they regarded northern cities such as Derry and Portadown as the proper centres for investment, not Dublin in the rural and predominantly Catholic south. So much of Ireland's taxable capacity lay in the north that, as the crisis deepened, Unionist apologists would claim that two-thirds of the country's customs revenue was generated by Belfast. It would not be inaccurate to think of industrialised Ireland as lying within the ambit of the northern cities mentioned, an area which, at the time of writing, is referred to by the Unionists as 'Ulster' and more accurately by the Nationalists as 'the Six Counties': Antrim, Armagh, Derry, Down, Fermanagh and Tyrone. The actual province of Ulster consists of nine counties. To the foregoing should be added Donegal, Cavan and Monaghan, but, as we shall see, when the crunch came, the Unionists shied away from the prospect of governing them because they contained too many Catholics.

So much for the economic and religious reasons which accounted for 17 Unionists taking their seats in the House of Commons. The military and political factors which drove the 86 Home Rulers into the mother of parliaments chiefly dated back to two events in the last decades of the eighteenth century.

One was the formation of the Protestant Volunteers at Dungannon in 1782 by a number of able and far-sighted landed gentry led by Henry Grattan. The corps was ostensibly formed to defend Ireland from the revolutionary influences flowing from the turbulence in America and France. But the Volunteers' primary mission was to defend the commercial interests of the ruling Protestant Ascendancy class, as it was known, in the face of English discrimination against Irish economic life as a whole.

The Ascendancy was not the only section of Irish society with reason to complain. As in England itself, Catholics had suffered under the Penal Law Code, which, although lately somewhat relaxed, had through the century particularly enervated the majority Catholic Irish population by forbidding it property, education, or advancement in government. The Presbyterians too were discriminated against by the Anglicans for refusing to join the Established Church. Many emigrated to America as a result.

Standing under arms, the Volunteers demanded, and got, an Irish parliament in Dublin in 1782. Knowing the unease with which imperial England was likely to view the growth of an independent and possibly powerful Ireland, which could be used as a back door by a hostile power such as France, the Volunteers were careful to stress their loyalty to the Crown, proclaiming at their formation that 'a claim of any body of men other than the King, Lords and Commons of Ireland to make laws for this Kingdom is unconstitutional, illegal and a grievance'.[2] However, they also passed a resolution drawn up by Grattan, declaring that:

> we hold the right of private judgement in matters of religion to be equally sacred in others as in ourselves . . . as men and as Irishmen, as Christians and as Protestants, we rejoice in the relaxation of the Penal Laws against our Roman Catholic subjects, and we conceive the measure to be fraught with the happiest of consequences to the union and prosperity of the inhabitants of Ireland.

The new parliament did generate some happy consequences. Independence set in train the creation of a degree of prosperity and cultural activity. The Protestant Ascendancy flourished and a small Catholic middle class emerged.

However, the parliament did not address the grievances of the Catholic majority. The man generally regarded as the founder of modern Irish republicanism, Theobald Wolfe Tone, a Protestant lawyer, took up the cudgels on behalf of 'that large and respectable class, the men of no property'. As the problems of the Presbyterians also remained unsolved, many of them supported Tone when in 1791 he and a group of Protestant gentlemen founded the Society of United Irishmen in Belfast. The aim of the United Irishmen, in Tone's words, was to forget past differences and unite 'Catholic Protestant and Dissenter'. Unlike Grattan's Volunteers, with their fidelity to 'Kings, Lords and Commons', the French- and Thomas Paine-inspired United Irishmen subscribed to Tone's doctrine of breaking 'the connection with England, the never failing source of all our political evils'. Tone argued that the best time to attempt such a break was when England was preoccupied with a foreign war, and succeeded in enlisting the aid of French forces in an attempt to put his arguments into practice.

Unfortunately for him and the United Irishmen, the French fleets were delayed by bureaucracy and bad weather, and the policies of the authorities goaded the rebels into premature and ill-organised revolt in 1798. One of the principal forces used to incite rebellion was the Orange Order, which actively worked to prevent the union of Protestant and Catholic which the United Irishmen were trying to promote. The Order was formed amongst militant Protestants after a clash in 1795 between Protestants and Catholics over land near Loughgall in County Armagh. It took its title from William of Orange, who had defeated the Catholic and French forces under James II at the Battle of the Boyne in 1690, thus establishing both the Protestant Ascendancy and the Orangemen's annual feast day of 12 July, which at the time of writing still commemorates the Boyne victory.

4

At the risk of oversimplifying a complex and highly charged situation, it might be said that amongst British decision-takers there were two views of the disorderly situation in Ireland. There was that of the British Commander-in-Chief, Sir Ralph Abercromby, who felt that the Irish landlord class were ignorant, tyrannical bigots and that the condition of the British army was, in his own words,'disgraceful ... formidable to everyone but the enemy'.[3] Opposing this analysis, General Gerard Lake believed that the landlords were correct in denying any concession to their rebellious Catholic tenants and that heavy-handed methods should be used to snuff out disaffection. London favoured Lake, who succeeded Abercromby and went on to become a viscount. The Irish 'gentry' and their militias were unleashed. Hostile troops were billeted on the people. Militias indulged in rape and murder and devised new tortures to punish real or suspected rebels. One such torture was 'pitch capping', which entailed first shaving the victim's hair, then placing a linen 'cap' filled with pitch on the unfortunate's head and setting it alight.

A few Catholic United Irishmen replied in kind. At Scullabogue, in County Wexford, Protestant prisoners were massacred and a barn filled with women and children was burned to the ground. A British army equipped with cannon and muskets thus received an added incentive to slaughter opponents armed mainly with weapons such as pikes and scythes. As Thomas Pakenham has noted: 'In the space of a few weeks, 30,000 people, peasants armed with pikes and pitchforks, defenceless women and children ... were cut down or blown away like chaff as they charged up to the mouth of the cannon.'[4]

The 1798 rebellion ended in disaster for the United Irishmen. Tone died in jail after cutting his own throat so as to cheat the hangman. The Presbyterians fared so badly at the hands of the authorities that, amongst those who survived, emigration soared, and those who remained would never again contemplate any large-scale alliance with the Catholics. For the moment, 'the men of no property' sank even deeper into poverty and despair, though Tone's doctrines remained a source of inspiration for physical-force republicanism.

Irish political nomenclature acquired the term 'unionist' in the aftermath of the 1798 rebellion. The British used the uprising as an excuse to suppress Grattan's parliament by the Act of Union of 1800. Henceforth the Irish electorate would return its representatives to London, not Dublin. Cooke, the Under-Secretary in 1799, summed up the rationale for this step in classic 'realpolitik' terminology:

> By giving the Irish a hundred members in an Assembly of six hundred and fifty they will be impotent to operate upon that Assembly, but it will be invested with Irish assent to its authority ... The Union is the only means of preventing Ireland from becoming too great and too powerful.[5]

The Act of Union was pushed through with the aid of bribes, peerages and pressures of all sorts. And it achieved its aim, depriving Ireland of real political power and destroying Dublin's briefly flowering artistic, economic and political life. Robert Emmet's ill-fated attempt at rebellion in 1803 cost him and many of his followers their lives and left Ireland with little beyond the epitaph of his ringing declaration from the dock that his memory should not be written until Ireland had taken her place amidst the nations of the earth. Catholic Ireland became prey to mismanagement and absentee landlordism. Sex being one of the few pleasures left to the peasantry, the population continued to rise inexorably, with disastrous consequences. Writing in 1839, Gustave de Beaumont noted that 'the land in Ireland is covered with a number of petty cultivators, between whom it is divided into portions of five, ten and twenty acres'. He went on to pose ominous questions: 'But in a country where the land is the sole means of existence, what is the fate of those to whom land is wanting? What becomes of an ejected tenant . . . ? What is to become of his children?'[6]

The great famine of the 1840s, when the peasantry's staple, the potato, failed, answered de Beaumont's question. The famine was not only an outcome of the policy of depriving the Irish of the ability to address their own problems, it also provided the opportunity for a degree of social engineering, in that it allowed landlords to clear an uneconomic tenantry off their over-subdivided holdings. In 1835, de Beaumont accompanied his better-known companion, Alexis de Tocqueville, on a tour of Ireland, before which the young French noblemen recorded an illuminating conversation between Nassau William Senior and John Revans, two of the more knowledgeable men in London on Irish affairs.[7] Revans was secretary of the Royal Commission of 1832–40, the recommendations of which became the basis of the 1834 Poor Law, and Senior, an economist, was also a member of that commission. Their description of Irish conditions is worth more than most of the myriad volumes of explanations, polemics and propaganda which the famine elicited:

SENIOR: To what do you principally attribute the poverty of Ireland?

REVANS: To a landlord system that profits from the intense competition of labourers [for land] to exact from the farmers an excessive rent. From the moment a farmer begins to make a profit, the landlord raises the price of the lease. The result is that the farmer is afraid to make improvements, for fear of being taxed by his master for a much higher sum than his improvement would be worth to him, and he confines himself strictly to subsisting.

SENIOR: Do you think that a good poor law would by its nature diminish this evil?

REVANS: Yes, by diminishing the competition of labourers and by putting the common man in a position to lay down, up to a certain point, the law to the proprietor of the soil.

SENIOR: Is the poverty as great as they say?

REVANS: The poverty is horrible. The people live only on potatoes and often they lack them.

SENIOR: The number of children is very great?

REVANS: Yes. It has been observed that the poorer they were the more children they had. They believe that they have nothing more to fear. They marry in despair and try to forget the future.

SENIOR: What is the state of morality in Ireland?

REVANS: This requires a great deal of explanation . . . There is not a people more gentle than the Irish when the moment of anger has passed. They forget offences easily. They are very hospitable. There is not an Irishman so poor that he does not share his last potato with someone who is in need. Crimes are very rare amongst them except theft, which occurs in order to subsist. They steal things that can be immediately eaten. There is the good side. Here is the bad: there is not a country where it is more difficult to obtain the truth from a man.

SENIOR: The spirit of party is very strong in Ireland?

REVANS: To a point where it would be almost impossible for you to conceive. It would take a foreigner ten years to understand the parties. Party spirit pervades everything, but particularly in the administration of justice. To tell the truth there is no justice in Ireland. Nearly all the local magistrates are at open war with Ireland. Moreover the population has no idea of public justice. In Ireland nearly all justice is extra-legal. Unless Englishmen are sent to serve as judges, it will remain the same there. The jury system is almost impracticable in Ireland.

SENIOR: Why do the Irish have such a great hatred for us?

REVANS: Above all because we have always sustained the Orangemen whom they consider as their oppressors.

SENIOR: Of what is the Catholic Party composed?

REVANS: Of nearly all the people. But very few wealthy and educated men are met with in this party, which has always been oppressed. That is a great misfortune.[8]

The general picture of despair painted by Revans, in particular his reference to extra-curricular justice, does much to explain the violence which the Irish peasantry sometimes showed to landlords, their agents, and each other. Overall, de Tocqueville's record of the Senior/Revans dialogue generally explains why the Irish peasantry were unable to withstand the loss of their potatoes a few years after the two men talked.

The famine furthered the strategic objectives of the Act of Union. Far from becoming 'too great and too powerful', Ireland lost one million of her population to starvation and a further million to emigration, much of it to America, where, as we shall see, the Irish Catholic swamped the Presbyterian tradition and, towards the end of the twentieth century, ultimately came to have a marked influence on developments in Ireland. The abortive and short-lived Young Irelanders' rebellion of 1848, born out of anger at the famine, also had a lasting effect on Irish developments. Firstly, it provided revolutionary continuity with 1798 and with Robert Emmet. Secondly, it provided the leaders who formed the Irish Republican Brotherhood, or Fenian movement (which will be discussed later), from which stemmed today's IRA.

Perhaps the greatest long-term evil arising from the loss of the Irish parliament was that it deprived the country of a forum wherein, through natural evolution, Protestant and Catholic, northern and southern Ireland would have come together. The beneficial consequences of such a meeting, both for the Orange and Green traditions themselves and for relationships with

England, can hardly be overstressed. As it was, the British tended to blame the Irish for exhibiting the consequences of the conditions they themselves had created in Ireland. In the post-famine era, during which thousands of disease-ridden, destitute Irish swarmed into the United Kingdom, existing anti-Irish prejudices flourished. The stereotype of the ape-like Irishman portrayed in *Punch* was given further force by the writings of influential British commentators. James Froude described the Irish as being 'more like tribes of squalid apes than human beings'. Charles Kingsley claimed the famine victims in the Westport workhouse were 'the acme of human swinery'. Thomas Carlyle favoured the ape-like comparison over that of swine, saying that during a tour of the west of Ireland, he was 'haunted by the human chimpanzees I saw along that hundred miles of that terrible country'.[9]

Matters which might have placed a different interpretation on events such as the famine were simply airbrushed out of history. For example, one of the most popular school texts, Robert Sullivan's *Geography Generalized*, published in 1850, roughly three years after the famine had passed its peak, claimed that:

> In 1847 a great potato famine occurred, caused by the almost entire failure of the potato crop. Since that distressing period Ireland has improved in every respect. To this desirable result many causes have contributed – such as emigration to the Colonies, the operation of the Encumbered Estates Act, and the extension of Education.[10]

Sullivan, an Irishman, also instructed Catholic Irish schoolchildren that as a result of the Ulster plantation 'great improvements were made in the laws and administration of justice'.

Even the most benign (towards the Irish, that is) British commentators either overlook or fail to grasp the deeply traumatic effect of British rule in Ireland. For example, as Jeremy Smith, one of the more authoritative and fair-minded analysts of Tory policy in Ireland, points out:

> Peel went far to appease Irish Catholic sentiment. In 1829 he steered Catholic Emancipation through the House of Commons, against much of his party and his own predilections. Later, during his 1841–46 ministry, he introduced the Charitable Bequests Act and increased the state grant to the Catholic seminary of Maynooth. Clearly, then, a strain of Toryism believed Union carried a Christian obligation to bring justice as well as order to Ireland, and to alleviate legitimate grievances.

However, it did not appear to dawn on Smith that the fact that the famine broke out during Peel's ministry might have lessened Irish appreciation of the Charitable Bequests Act. Certainly there was little in the way of bequests and less of charity once the Tories had successfully laid a parliamentary ambush for Peel. The changes which the new administration brought included the placing of Irish famine relief in the hands of Charles Trevelyan in the Treasury. Almost his first act was to cancel shipments of grain for Ireland which Peel had been surreptitiously organising. He had to be surreptitious because the Tory landlords, wishing to maintain the high tariffs on imported corn, were opposed to any cheap grains being imported into either Ireland or England. The harsh and insensitive manner in which Trevelyan subsequently discharged his duties, combined with the conditions already described, ensured that a potato shortage became a famine.

The Trevelyan/Tory legacy helps to explain why great numbers of the schoolchildren instructed in Mr Sullivan's analysis clearly did not agree with it. Sixteen years after the publication of the *Geography*, there occurred in Canada and in Ireland the events known as the Fenian uprisings. The Irish Republican Brotherhood, popularly called a Fenian movement after the legendary band of Irish warriors, was an oath-bound secret society. Modelled on similar continental organisations, it was founded in 1858 by survivors of the 1848 revolt living in Ireland and America. In Ireland the movement was led by James Stephens; in America, where a sizeable proportion of its members had fought on both sides of the American Civil War, by John O'Mahony. O'Mahony was the architect of the Canadian invasion plan whose objective was to pressurise the British into conceding Irish independence. The idea initially caused a split in the American movement, and subsequently a sensation throughout North America and the British Empire, when, in 1866, a wing of the Fenians, significantly describing themselves as the Irish Republican Army (IRA), under Colonel John O'Neill, actually crossed into Canada and defeated a British force at the Battle of Ridgeway. The following year, the Stephens-led wing of the movement planned a large-scale rising in Ireland. The Fenians were able to call on a substantial pool of manpower, including Irishmen serving in the British army, but spies and informers delivered sufficient advance warning to the British to enable the authorities to snuff out the movement before it ever got off the ground. However, as we shall see when we come to examine the Fenian brotherhood's role in the 1916–23 era, isolated Fenian activities over the next decades kept the doctrines of Tone, Emmet and the physical-force tradition alive.

By contrast, a tradition which the Fenians helped to kill was that of having Irish Catholics pay tithes to maintain the Protestant clergy. This custom had led to much bitterness. Although Daniel O'Connell's mass movement for Catholic emancipation, the precursor of the massive civil rights demonstrations of the 1960s, secured its aim in 1829, the custom of tithe payments remained, and led to a veritable tithe war during the 1830s. An ameliorative measure passed in 1838 ended active hostilities over the tithes issue, but it remained an irritant in the Irish body politic which had the effect of heightening sectarian tensions, not merely in the north, but throughout Ireland.

The landlord–tenant relationship was already exacerbated through the tenant having to pay rent to a non-improving landlord who was either a Protestant who had seized the land from a Catholic or a Catholic who had turned Protestant to keep the property. The tithe system directed some of this animosity directly at the respective clergy. De Tocqueville described the relationship between a Protestant minister and a Catholic parish priest in Mayo as 'open war': 'They attacked each other in the newspapers and in the pulpit in very bitter style.' The priest, many of whose parishioners were starving, 'was on chilly terms at least, if not quarrelling with the large local landlords', but was regarded with a respect bordering on reverence by his flock. De Tocqueville felt that if the Catholic clergy generally received state aid (Maynooth did receive a grant) it might help relationships. However, when asked if the Church would not gain by accepting state aid for the building of churches and the endowment of clergy, he replied in terms which explain how men like him held that respect for generations thereafter:

> If I preach today peace and patience, I am believed . . . but if they could see in me an agent of the state, what weight would my opinion have? . . . We would lose by the change . . . It is in the people that the root of beliefs is found. It is they who firmly believe in another world because they are unhappy in this one; it is they whose simple and naive imaginations lead them without reserve to faith. Any religion that will wander away from the people, Sir, will loose its principal support . . .[11]

In his portrayals of the two characters, both of them good men, de Tocqueville, who could fairly be regarded as an exemplar of the best type of what today would be termed 'investigative reporter', was in fact describing the clash of the two kinds of colonial cultures out of which modern Ireland emerged: Mother England and Mother Church. On one side was the Church of the Brontës, or if one likes of imperial England, in which the squire and his relations showed all their proper stations; on the other that of the people who inhabited the novels of Charles Kickham or the pages of William Carleton's *Irish Peasantry*.

The priest lived 'in a little house with four windows in the front and two stories'. His church was 'a small building, roughly built of stone . . . it had neither vault nor ceiling, the floor was of beaten earth, the altar was of wood, the walls had neither paint nor pictures . . .' The minister lived in a 'Handsome house . . . in the middle of a garden of flowers'; his church was 'small gothic' built of 'cut stone . . . Inside the church. Stove. Carpet. Pews. Two or three rich landlords. Many servants.' The Catholic school was 'very wretched', containing only one room and no seats. It had 30 pupils taught by a 'man of middle age, barefooted, who taught scholars in rags'. But 'there existed a fervour for work that is not always found in the wealthy English universities. The next generation will not resemble that which we see,' prophesied the priest. He passionately believed in education, and in a free press for highlighting injustices. 'All his passions, all his ideas, clearly tended to democracy,' said de Tocqueville whom the priest invited to dinner and to spend the night.

By contrast the Protestant minister, who had 'just returned from Italy for his health', turned out to be an 'amiable man with very distinguished manners' whose sermon on 'moral obligations was very well composed'. He also invited de Tocqueville to his home, though he could not offer him dinner as he was dining that night with 'the Lord'. He also apologised that his daughter could not play the piano for the visitor because it was a Sunday. The minister believed that education had to be 'directed in a certain way to be good'. The press, he felt, could lead people 'astray'. He believed in the need for an aristocracy, for a national Church, for a clergy richly endowed by the state. De Tocqueville's notes showed him speaking of the 'Incapacity of the people in general and above all the Irish people to govern themselves. Savages.'

These brief extracts speak volumes about the difficulty of trying to accommodate the two conflicting worlds and systems in a small country governed uncomprehendingly and often unsympathetically from afar.

A word might be said here on the perception of the Irish as savages which the Protestant clergymen held so strongly. A mention has been made of the 'violence' of the Irish peasantry. It existed in strange counterpoint fashion alongside the docility of that same peasantry in the presence of their priest which de Tocqueville also noted. Around the time that de Tocqueville visited Ireland, faction fighting was still a serious problem. Groups sometimes fought on behalf of their parishes against other parishes, and sometimes as a result of class warfare. Scholars dispute as to why faction fighting occurred when it did, in the early part of the nineteenth century, becoming less intense in the 1830s, as the effects of the new Royal Irish Constabulary began to be felt throughout the countryside. It may have been that it had its origins in a general disrespect for law and order as experienced by the peasantry, or it could have been a reflection of the widespread impoverishment of a society wherein 'the big house' had once dispensed some measure of relief. After the union, the flight of capital and patronage to England dried up these wellsprings of benignity. Such fighting may simply have been a manifestation of nineteenth-century gang warfare, or in celebrated cases such as the conflict between the 'Caravats' and the 'Shanavasts', a symptom of class tension, the Caravats being representative of the labouring class, the Shanavasts of the wealthier farmers. The battles between the two classes raged in parts of Leinster and Munster for several years in the earlier part of the century. Humphrey O'Sullivan, a diarist of the period, noted, of Callan, County Kilkenny: 'If it ever was "Callan of the ructions" it certainly is now for cursed crowds on either side of the King's River are throwing stones at each other every Sunday and holiday night. The Caravats on the South side.' And later in the year, on Ascension Thursday: 'a holiday' . . . The Ballingeary Shanavasts came to Callan. Caravats attacked them. But the Shanavasts put the Caravats to flight in their own town. Two were badly injured, a Shanavast and a Caravat. This is bad behaviour on a solemn feast day!'[12]

Similar violent outbreaks between representatives of different counties occurred later in the century in America when the great canals were being built by the Irish. These pitched battles were extremely violent, employed a variety of weapons and sometimes involved several hundred men on either side.

11

While this form of violence probably had much of its roots in the disturbed and unjust political and economic soil of the nineteenth century, it should be borne in mind as a contrast to the image of a supine Catholic peasantry meekly accepting its fate which the de Tocqueville memoir suggests.

Another form of militancy which could be considered when comparing the outlook of the two types of clergy which de Tocqueville described is contained in the career of the celebrated Cardinal Paul Cullen, which might be taken as a paradigm of the operations of the second colonial influence which shaped Ireland's destiny in the nineteenth and twentieth centuries: that of Mother Church. Cullen, a former rector of the Irish College in Rome, was so able that it is said that had Pius IX died a little earlier, he would have become Pope. He was sent by Rome to Ireland as a legate in 1850, and as Archbishop of Dublin he both reformed and transformed the Irish Church according to Rome's wishes. He added a new dimension to the term 'ultramontane', introducing discipline and a standardisation of worship according to Roman specifications, and sparking off what the Irish American historian Emmet Larkin termed a 'devotional Revolution'. In other words, Cullen promoted practices such as confession-going, novenas, rosaries and pilgrimages, and stamped out activities such as heavy drinking and the playing of erotic games at wakes.

The disturbed state of Ireland following the Reformation had left the Irish Catholic hierarchy in such a weakened condition that the Roman Congregation for the Propagation of the Faith (Propaganda Fide) exercised a good deal of direct influence there, and a combination of this factor – which persisted until Rome introduced changes in 1908 – and Cullen's great abilities made the country a world centre of missionary activity. The Vatican established a vast theological extractive industry in Ireland, siphoning off an incredible amount of Irish energy into the Church. Cathedrals and seminaries arose in commanding positions from Newfoundland to Sydney Harbour. Devoted Irish nuns and priests travelled everywhere in the English-speaking world, establishing schools, churches, hospitals and Roman Catholic influence. Cullen's personal reach extended to Australia, Canada, Newfoundland and the United States. Apart from the clerical formation which he put in place in Ireland, and his influence on the educational system, which ensured that the Irish Church was the template which was replicated throughout the world, cousins of his became bishops in Brisbane, Bathurst and Maitland, and his nephew, Patrick Moran, the Archbishop of Sydney, later became a cardinal and the most important cleric in Australia.

Like the question as to the origins of the faction-fighting custom, Cullen's career poses one of the great 'ifs' of Irish history. If the Act of Union had not throttled political and economic progress, would an independent Ireland have deployed the energies which instead went into the Church to create a vibrant secular society many scores of years before she finally set about this task in the latter part of the twentieth century? What we do know is that the clash of Protestant and Catholic cultures often became a clash of arms. In 1869, in the wake of one such clash, the Fenian excitements, the House of Commons moved to remove one cause of dissension, passing Gladstone's Act ordering the disestablishment of the Protestant Church in Ireland. The removal of this irritant (for Catholics) is one of the reasons why Catholic–Protestant animosities in southern Ireland subsided to a far lower pitch than that which obtained in the north. O'Connell was successful in securing Catholic emancipation, but the grail of repeal of the Union was denied him and he died in Italy a broken man, at the height of the famine.

The 1870s saw other men and movements pick up the cudgels in the constitutional campaign to secure repeal. The Protestant lawyer Isaac Butt founded the Irish Home Rule League in 1870, and four years later became leader of the Home Rule Party in the House of Commons. Butt introduced the tactic of obstructionism, whereby the Irish MPs delayed legislation and harassed the Government. However, the outnumbered Irish parliamentarians were unable to secure any substantive relief measures for Ireland. A total of 28 bills which sought to improve Irish conditions were rejected between 1870 and 1880. Bad harvests threatened to bring famine to the country once more. It was averted by the activities of two men in particular, Michael Davitt and Charles Stewart Parnell, and by one of the earliest and most successful organised women's movements, the Ladies Land League, led by Anna Parnell, a sister of Charles Stewart.

Michael Davitt was an ex-Fenian who, until the advent of Seán Lemass some eighty years later, deserves to be regarded as the Irish leader who delivered the most tangible benefits to his people. As a youth Davitt lost an arm in an industrial accident, and later served a jail term for Fenian activities. In 1877 he began what became known as the 'Land War', organising tenants to campaign against excessive rents by first refusing to pay them, then offering the landlord what was considered a reasonable rent, and if, and generally when, he refused it, paying it into a fund which helped to support tenants if, and generally when, they were evicted. The first target chosen was one Canon Burke, a Catholic clergyman in Mayo, who was forced to reduce his rents. But this was not the circumstance which aroused the Vatican's displeasure at the Plan of Campaign, as it was known. British diplomacy caused a papal fact-finding delegation to be sent to Ireland in 1887, and the following year, more mindful of Rome's interests within the British Empire than of those of Irish peasants, the Vatican sparked a furious reaction from Irish Catholics by issuing a Papal Rescript denouncing the Plan. Even the Irish hierarchy, notoriously subservient to Rome, were markedly unenthusiastic about the decree. The war spread throughout the country, producing Coercion Acts, filling the jails and giving a new word to the English language: boycotting. The name derived from a Captain Boycott, a landlord who had the dubious honour of being the first man to have people refuse to serve him in shops, help with farm work, or even speak to him or acknowledge his presence on the street. Any farmer who took land from which the previous occupant had been evicted was also boycotted. The campaign on the ground was assisted by money collected amongst the Irish in America.

In London, Charles Stewart Parnell guided the political battle in the House of Commons, having succeeded Butt as leader of the Home Rule Party. Under Parnell, there began what was known as the New Departure, whereby Davitt's Land League, the Fenians and the Irish Parliamentary Party came together in pursuit of Home Rule. Parnell further developed Butt's tactics of obstruction, and made it plain that he would ally the Irish votes with neither the Conservatives nor the Liberals, but would strive to hold the balance between them, so as to further his objectives. In 1881, in a notable example of what became known as the 'carrot and stick policy', the British seized over 1,000 prisoners, including Davitt and Parnell, and declared the Land League illegal. At the same time, an improving Land Act was passed, the precursor of many such measures.

In the wake of Parnell and Davitt's imprisonment, 'Captain Moonlight' ruled the Irish countryside. Agrarian outrage proliferated and Gladstone was forced to take steps to relieve the situation. The prisoners were released, and a new Lord Lieutenant and Chief Secretary, both of them sympathetic to Ireland, were appointed. But in that calamitous pattern which has so often bedevilled Anglo-Irish relationships, disaster followed good intent. The new Chief Secretary, Lord Cavendish, and the Under-Secretary, Thomas Burke, were stabbed to death in the Phoenix Park in Dublin immediately upon Cavendish taking up his appointment. The drastic Crimes Act of 1882 virtually placed Ireland under martial law. It was the fifty-seventh Act specifically aimed at disaffection passed since the Union.

Nevertheless, although the fall of Parnell also hastened the end of the Plan of Campaign, an inexorable progress towards both the Home Rule and land issues continued. While the stick continued to be wielded in the form of packed juries, evictions, and zero-tolerance police activities, the land question showed continuing signs of improvement. As a result of an exercise in what became known as 'constructive unionism', various ameliorative policies were introduced, including the Local Government Act of 1898, and the setting up of a Board of Agriculture and Technical Instruction. The Congested Districts Board was established specifically to bring assistance to the poverty-stricken western areas of the country. This beautiful but barren region had become overpopulated partly as a result of Cromwell's policy of offering owners of good land in other parts of the country a choice of going to either 'hell or Connaught'. The Wyndham Land Act of 1903 put the seal on a series of Acts which largely removed the land issue from the Irish political agenda. Government loans were extended to tenant farmers in the form of annuities, to be repaid over lengthy periods (up to 70 years). These loans, which were supplemented by a direct bonus to landlords, enabled the tenantry to buy out their holdings and create a peasant proprietorship.

Land reform also helped to create a circumstance which would have a direct bearing on the creation of political change in Ireland: population growth. Economic improvement had the effect of keeping an unusually high proportion of young Catholics, who would otherwise have had to emigrate, at home in Ireland. Apart from there being more money available for them, there was more cultural and educational sustenance also, and an increased sense of Nationalist and Catholic identity was spreading throughout the country.

The Irish Christian Brothers, founded in 1803 by Edmund Ignatius Rice, the son of a family of well-to-do farmers from Callan, County Kilkenny, had a significant effect on the development of modern Ireland. Along with imparting a general education, they lent a markedly Nationalist character to their training, in contrast to that of the Catholic schools for the well-to-do. These, chiefly the Jesuits' Clongowes Wood College, the Holy Ghost Fathers' Blackrock College, and later the Dominican Fathers at Newbridge, County Kildare, and the Vincentians at Castleknock, County Dublin, sought to prepare Irish Catholics for the upper reaches of the British administration, or for positions in the law, medicine and the army throughout the Empire. Consequently a more anglified tone permeated their classrooms and playing fields, where rugby, cricket and tennis were played, rather than the Gaelic games of hurling and Gaelic football, which were favoured by the Brothers.

The Brothers were not trying to foment revolution or the spread of Wolfe Tone's doctrines, but they were consciously trying to inculcate a love of Irish culture, its language, its history, its songs, in an era when official textbooks encouraged Irish schoolchildren to thank God for being born 'a happy English child' and contained passages such as: 'On the east of Ireland is England where the Queen lives; many people who live in Ireland were born in England, and we speak the same language and are called one nation.'[13]

In school, as in parliament, colonial policy aimed at anglicising the Irish, and stressing the superiority of the Anglo-Saxon race. This superiority, it may be noted, was widely accepted as an article of faith by those responsible for education in Ireland. Writing to the Under-Secretary at Dublin Castle, Alexander McDonnell, Resident Commissioner of National Education, remarked *inter alia*: 'The Celtic mind, it may be said, though perhaps inferior in the long run, especially for practical purposes, to the Anglo-Saxon, is much more rapid in its early development.'[14]

It was said at the time of Catherine the Great that any truth in Russia was like a spark hurled into gunpowder. Given the history of British rule in Ireland, it was inevitable that the Brothers' teachings should recall the Russian saying. Reliable Irish authorities have taken the analogy further. Dr C.S. Andrews, who participated in the 1916 Rising and later became one of Ireland's most senior civil servants, and who was educated by the Brothers, later wrote:

> Without the groundwork of the Christian Brothers' schooling it is improbable that there would ever have been a 1916 Rising, and certain that the subsequent fight for independence would not have been successfully carried through. The leadership of the IRA came largely from those who got their education from the Brothers, and got it free.[15]

The historian F.X. Martin pointed out that:

The leaders who emerged in 1916 and the subsequent years were largely past pupils of the Christian Brothers' Schools ... Due recognition has not yet been given to the Irish Christian Brothers for their part in the nationalist struggle, particularly for their unqualified support of the Gaelic revival.[16]

The Gaelic revival to which Martin was referring could be said to have begun with the foundation of two organisations in particular: Douglas Hyde's Gaelic League, which he founded in 1893, and the Gaelic Athletic Association, (GAA), begun by Michael Cusack in 1894. The former brought people of all ages and both sexes into classes where they learned the Irish language and Irish dances, and acquired an interest in Irish history. The Gaelic Athletic Association revived Irish games such as hurling and Gaelic football; indeed the hurling stick became a symbol of militant national identity, being carried in demonstrations to such an extent that even during the phase of Anglo-Irish hostilities which concluded (hopefully) in the era of the Good Friday Agreement it was known as 'the Tipperary rifle'.

In a different sphere, that of Irish writing in the English language, writers, poets and playwrights of all sorts were also helping to forge a heightened consciousness of being Irish. The Abbey Theatre staged the plays of Lady Gregory, J.M. Synge and W.B. Yeats. Few independence movements in the world can be said to have been so strongly influenced by the work of a theatre and its playwrights as was the Irish one by the Abbey. One expert said of Yeats:

His early plays, for instance, had the effect of converting to the National movement certain young men, amongst them some poets and writers associated with the literary movement, who later died securing the political independence of their country from England in 1916. One of the members of the seven-man Supreme Council of the IRB which had planned that famous Insurrection, tells me that he himself entered the political movement of the day after he saw the opening performance of Yeats's *Cathleen ni Houlihan* in April, 1902, prior to which he 'never had a political thought'.[17]

In the *Leader* magazine, D.P. Moran, its editor, developed the idea of what he called 'Irish Ireland'. These athletic and cultural developments so popularised the concept in all its manifold forms that the period came to be referred to as one of a 'Celtic dawn'. The logical outcome of all this self-conscious Irishness, of course, could have been, and should have been, constitutionally achieved self-government as desired by the majority of Irish nationalists, and not the revolution which the denial of that aspiration inevitably led to.

True this 'dawn' did not rise on an altogether beauteous landscape. The slums in Dublin were appalling. In a survey conducted in 1910, some 20,000 families were found to be living in one room each. A Poor Law Commission report for that year found that in a survey conducted amongst 1,254 families, wage scales were between five shillings and a maximum of £3 a week. Not surprisingly, infant mortality was far higher than in London, 142 per 1,000 compared to 103. Alcoholism was rife; it was discovered that 46,574 women and 27,999 children were observed passing through the portals of 22 Dublin pubs which were kept under survey for a two-week period. Alcohol-induced insanity was a commonplace, and insanity overall was estimated at 63.5 per 1,000. In such conditions, crime flourished. Crimes like rape and murder were nearly five times as common in Dublin as elsewhere in the country.

The slums of Dublin were in fact one of the worst remaining scars of the Act of Union. The great Georgian mansions of the departed nobles who had fled to London after the Irish parliament was suppressed had been acquired by rack-renting landlords, and in the years before 1916 had come to hold one-third of the population of the city. Population density sometimes rose to 800 people to the acre, with as many as 100 occupants in a single room. As one indignant chronicler has written: 'The living conditions of many tenement dwellers were hellish.'[18] Unfortunately, as we shall see, the tumult and shouting which accompanied the unfolding of Irish history for much of the earlier part of the century did nothing to alleviate these conditions, and they were still present, albeit to a lessening degree, at the outbreak of World War II. The conditions of the poor, however, very rarely captured the imagination of either writers or their readers.

What did catch the attention of some commentators, particularly those with a political agenda, were the more attractive aspects of Irish society. The unionist historian Paul Bew has pointed out that between 1861 and 1911, the percentage of Catholic barristers and solicitors rose from 34% to 44%, and that of doctors from 35% to 48%.[19] But this still left the Catholics, who comprised four-fifths of the population of the island of Ireland, with something of a professional mountain to climb. The French writer Paul Dubois observed in 1908 that:

In the Privy Council there are only 7 Catholics as against 50 Protestants, of the 18 Judges of the High Court only 3 are Catholics . . . of the 68 Resident Magistrates only 19 are Catholics, of the County Court Judges only 7, of the 37 County Inspectors of Police only 4, and of the 124 District Inspectors of Police only from 20 to 30.[20]

In general the Catholics held the lower positions in the civil service. The custom was to transfer them to England, leaving the higher positions to Protestant Loyalists. Yet outside the northern province of Ulster, sectarianism in Ireland had lost much of its virulence. In the north, where land reform made less of an impact than in the south and west, because the Protestant community already owned most of the land and capital, the advance of the Catholic professional classes was slower. In Antrim, there were only two Catholic doctors as opposed to 65 Protestants (Presbyterians, Methodists and Episcopalians); in the law, there were nine Catholic barristers and solicitors as opposed to 62 Presbyterians and Methodists and 22 Episcopalians.

Along with this imbalance, indeed because of it, fear of the Catholic population existed lest the situation might some day be rectified by violent means. Paul Bew cited a telling memoir of an outstanding Presbyterian figure, the Reverend John McDermott, a former moderator and a liberal and enlightened Unionist, who said of his Catholic fellow Antrim men:

> All oppressed people hug to themselves the memory of past wrongs and the hope of future vengeance. Such memory and such hope are their solace and their refuge. I know of peasants even in Antrim who possess carefully treasured maps, as much as 200 years old, on which are marked the lands that are still theirs. The lands may have been confiscated for rebellion, they may have been sold for a good price, they may have passed from class or family to another according to any of the common and natural chances and changes. But these later incidents are wiped out. All that is remembered is the old ownership. This recording spirit exists in the people all over Ireland; and there are churches and buildings marked down in the same way as the plots of land. It is certain that out of this feeling trouble will proceed.[21]

It was, however, from the Protestant ranks, not the Catholic, that trouble proceeded when John Redmond moved to settle the last great outstanding political demand of the Catholics – Home Rule. The logical outcome of the growth in Catholic and Nationalist economic well-being and cultural and athletic independence of spirit was political independence also. At Westminster, it seemed not only logical but inevitable that this fact would be given legislative recognition. In 1912 the Liberals were in power, and dependent for that power upon the support of the Irish Parliamentary Party. The Prime Minister, Herbert Asquith, and his friend and ally Augustine Birrell, the Chief Secretary for Ireland, were both convinced Home Rulers. Moreover, though no such conviction existed on the Conservative side of the argument, the Tories were in a far weaker position to impede Home Rule than they had been in Randolph Churchill's time. As a result of their incautious opposition to a Liberal budget, the House of Lords had lost the power of veto. Under the Parliament Act of 1911, a Bill which passed through the Commons for three consecutive sessions automatically became law. Even apart from this change, a qualitative alteration had taken place in the House of Lords also, as the Liberals had created a number of Liberal peerages so as to dilute the Conservatives' representation.

On one level the Liberal and Irish Parliamentary Party calculation that at this time Home Rule must surely pass proved correct. On 11 April 1912, Asquith moved the Home Rule Bill. Having been voted down by the House of Lords on two occasions, the Bill was passed in the House of Commons on 25 May 1914, by a majority of 77 votes. In normal circumstances, it should then have received the royal assent and become law. However, normal circumstances did not apply. What did transpire was one of the greatest convulsions in English parliamentary history. Vast changes had taken place during the Victorian age. It was said that the sun never set on the British Empire. Britain led Europe in coal production, the building of railways, and the production of iron. By the time Asquith introduced the Home Rule Bill, the Liberals had come up with the revolutionary concept of taxing the rich, via levies on land and the creation of increased death duties, which paved the way for social reform and measures such as the National Health Insurance Act.

However, in one respect, British society remained unalterably against change. The Tories were still bitterly opposed to Home Rule for Ireland, and they were, if anything, even more prepared than they had been in Randolph Churchill's day to excite dementia, to the extent in fact of flirting with treason. Writing in July 2000, Jeremy Smith judged that:

> The Ulster crisis was, to a greater extent than previously thought, manufactured by the Conservative leadership. Conservative leaders chose to make the issue of Ulster an acute political problem, after 1912, for English domestic electoral reasons. The intention was to force the government into an election upon an issue with which Tories believed they could sweep the country and so return them to office. To achieve this their leaders engaged in extreme rhetoric, personal abuse, they legitimated and sanctioned recourse to armed resistance, and attempted all manner of parliamentary trickery. They also encouraged King George V to enter the political game, interfered with the loyalty of the army and raised funds to help build a paramilitary force in Ireland. More dramatically, they actively thwarted any settlement of the Irish issue, either along federal lines or around the exclusion of Ulster, sponsored by Carson and the Ulstermen from 1913 onwards, that could well have formed the basis of an agreement with Asquith. In other words, the Tory leadership resisted closure to the Home Rule crisis, deliberately perpetuating the imbroglio until the government caved in and granted an election. Indeed, Bonar Law's choice to fight Home Rule on Constitutional grounds and demand an election, made a settlement more difficult because it shifted attention from the specific details of the bill, where a compromise could be brokered, onto more open-ended and abstract questions about the legality of the bill itself.[22]

There were many strands to the Conservatives' stated philosophy, the primary one being the attainment of power. There was also the belief that the concession of Home Rule, and a breach in the Union, would result inevitably in the break-up of Empire and the perception of Ireland as a lawless place, ruled by priests. The Irish Unionists also had a certain influence. The Irish Ascendancy class in the south, who were well represented in the House of Lords, had exercised leverage on the Conservative Party at constituency level through the Irish Loyal and Patriotic Union. There was also the block vote in the House of Lords of the influential Ulster Unionist peers, and the strength of the Orange Order and the Ulster Unionist Clubs Association. This body actively laid plans for civil war, should Home Rule be introduced. As early as 1910, the UUC's leader, F. H. Crawford, had brought in some 2,000 weapons. When the Tories were again defeated in a general election in January 1911, the reaction of Sir James Craig, who would later emerge as Northern Ireland's first Prime Minister, was to urge Crawford: 'I am strongly of the opinion that the fishing rods should be got in as secretly as possible . . . My great fear is that the game will be up before anything is done. It is a mere matter of time.'

It is sometimes argued that the Ulster Unionists were merely taking a leaf out of the Nationalists' book, and doing as Nationalists had traditionally done, threatening war and land agitation in order to obtain reform. But there was another powerful emotion at work on the Conservative and Unionist side: religious feeling. Ireland was not merely a backward nation whose rebellious inhabitants should rightfully regard themselves as being in the loyal and subsidiary position laid down for them in the schools' texts. It was also a *Catholic* nation, liable to interact with other Catholic races should opportunity offer. His biographer, R. Blake, quotes Andrew Bonar Law, who succeeded Arthur Balfour as leader of the Conservative Party, as spelling out the sectarian factor in a conversation with Prime Minister Asquith on 15 October 1913:

> At bottom, one of the strong feelings in England and Scotland was Protestantism, or dislike of Roman Catholicism, and that if Protestants from Belfast were actually killed, then in my belief, the effect in Great Britain would be not only that the Government would be beaten, but that they would be snowed under.

Bonar Law's boyhood was spent in frugal circumstances in Canada, where his father, a widower, was a Free Presbyterian minister. He was then brought to Scotland by an aunt, Janet Kidston, a member of a wealthy merchant banking family, to be raised and educated. Bonar Law was a teetotaller who was said to care nothing for art, music or scenery, but to have been heavily influenced by his reading of Thomas Carlyle. He was said never to have 'asked for favours, and therefore never expected to be asked for them'. In 1877 his father's health broke down, and he returned from New Brunswick to his native Ulster (he came from Coleraine), where his son visited him every weekend. Bonar Law's interest in Ulster may be said to have begun.

Paul Bew has settled on a letter of Bonar Law's containing what Bew describes as an 'important passage' which 'at root explains Bonar Law's conviction, a conviction which did not leave him when other "imperial" considerations of security were apparently satisfied'.

> The real reason why in my opinion the Ulster question should be kept to the front is that, whether the cause be religious (or not) and I do not think it greatly matters, the population there is homogeneous and determined to be treated in the same way as the citizens of the United Kingdom. In my opinion, from every point of view, they have the right to take that attitude. Suppose three quarters of Ireland were of the exact class of which the Ulster minority is composed and suppose that there in the rest of Ireland were one quarter of the population who looked with horror upon the idea of being governed by Orangemen and demanded the right to continue under the control of the British parliament. In that cause, whatever the reason, I should think their claim was just.[23]

The passage is certainly 'important', though not in the way Bew suggests. What it does do is illustrate the fundamental hollowness of the Unionist case. The population was not homogeneous and there were centuries of sectarian strife to prove it was not. Bonar Law himself frequently said that the Ulster issue was a religious question. And beyond both those points lay the fact to which the Unionist/Tory cause never adverted: democracy. A majority of the people of Ireland had voted for Home Rule.

Under Bonar Law, using the sort of logic highlighted by Bew, the Conservatives deliberately wove a tapestry of defiance and illegality, at bottom not so much to keep the Irish Catholics from falling into the power of the French, but to put an end to their own continual loss of power. The party had been voted out in 1892, in 1895, in 1906, and were again in the wilderness as Asquith moved his Home Rule Bill in 1912. As a result, according to the sympathetic, but objective, historian of unionism Patrick Buckland: 'Unionists, furious with frustration at their continued exclusion from power, were thus willing to adopt almost any means to defeat the Liberals and return to power.'[24]

Bonar Law began his campaign against Asquith's Home Rule Bill on 8 April 1912 in Belfast, by presiding over a 'wedding of Protestant Ulster with the Conservative & Unionist Party'.[25] Overhead there fluttered what was claimed to be the largest Union Jack ever woven – it measured 48 by 25 feet. Seventy English, Scottish and Welsh MPs were present, and the Church of Ireland Primate of all Ireland and the Moderator of the Presbyterian Church led the huge audience in prayer. Bonar Law excited his audience by recalling the heroism of the Protestants who had successfully withstood the siege of Derry by Catholics, saying:

> Once again you hold the pass, the pass for the Empire. You are a besieged city. The timid have left you; your Lundies have betrayed you; but you have closed your gates. The Government have erected by their Parliament Act a boom against you to shut you off from the help of the British people. You will burst that boom. That help will come, and when the crisis is over, men will say to you in words not unlike those used by Pitt – you have saved yourselves by your exertions, and you will save the Empire by your example.[26]

He subsequently moved on to make what Asquith termed 'A declaration of war against constitutional Government' at Blenheim on 24 July:

> We regard the Government as a revolutionary committee which has seized upon despotic power by fraud. In our opposition to them we shall not be guided by considerations or bound by the restraints which would influence us in an ordinary constitutional struggle. We shall take the means, whatever means seem to us most effective, to deprive them of the despotic power which they have usurped and compel them to appeal to the people whom they have deceived. They may, perhaps they will, carry their Home Rule Bill through the House of Commons and I repeat here that there are things stronger than parliamentary majorities . . . Before I occupied the position which I now fill in the party I said that, in my belief, if an attempt were made to deprive these men of their birthright – as part of a corrupt parliamentary bargain – they would be justified in resisting such an attempt by all means in their power, *including force* [author's emphasis]. I said it then, and I repeat now with a full sense of the responsibility which attaches to my position, that, in my opinion, if such an attempt is made, I can imagine no length of resistance to which Ulster can go in which I should not be prepared to support them, and in which, in my belief, they would not be supported by the overwhelming majority of the British people.[27]

With encouragement like that, the Ulster Unionists set about playing their part in frustrating the introduction of Home Rule with an understandable enthusiasm. They chose as their leader a man of whom the poet Padraic Colum said: 'his demeanour was that of a joyless man going on a joyless errand'. This was the Unionist MP for Trinity College, Dublin, Edward Carson, who had a successful career as a Crown Prosecutor behind him in Ireland, and an even more successful career at the English Bar before him, appearing in such celebrated cases as the rehabilitation of the cadet George Archer-Shee, the Winslow boy, and the destruction of Oscar Wilde. But it was his Irish activities which most clearly marked Carson's political philosophy. The condescension and contempt which characterised his assault on the idea of Home Rule for Irish Catholics had been honed by his period of service as the legal hammer with which Arthur Balfour attempted to smash Irish resistance to the Crown – and support for the Plan of Campaign – during his period as Irish Chief Secretary 1887–91. Balfour, who became known as 'bloody Balfour', partly because of his general attitude towards Irish nationalism and partly because of outrage generated by police firing on a crowd at Mitchelstown in 1887, was one of the principal architects of Tory policy in Ireland for decades. He succeeded his uncle, Lord Salisbury, as Conservative Prime Minister, 1902–5. In many ways he may fairly be remembered as the man who left the world with two of its most enduring trouble spots: the Middle East and Northern Ireland. He supported the Zionists in their demand for a Jewish homeland in Palestine (the Balfour Declaration of 1917), while at the same time being party to assuring the Arabs that if they revolted against the Ottoman Empire they would be given independence. His support for Carson and the Unionists had its inevitable outcome in partition. His successor at the Foreign Office, Lord Curzon, considered him to be an evil and dangerous man who presided over a regime marked by 'lamentable ignorance, indifference and levity'.[28]

Carson was one of Balfour's principal lieutenants: Balfour said of his expertise in securing convictions: 'I made Carson and he made me.' Carson's own principal lieutenant was James Craig, he of the fondness for fishing rods, and a millionaire whiskey distiller. Either distinction would have qualified him for advancement in Unionist political circles, but it was his support and backing for Carson which was the significant factor in his securing of the hearts and minds of Ulster Unionists. It was at Craig's family seat, Craigavon, that Carson read what might be termed the Unionists' foundation document and declaration of war – the Ulster Covenant. It was based on the old Scottish Covenant, and read thus:

> Being convinced in our consciences that Home Rule would be disastrous to the material well-being of Ulster as well as the whole of Ireland, subversive of our civil and religious freedom, destructive of our citizenship, and perilous to the unity of the Empire, we, whose names are underwritten, men of Ulster, loyal subjects of His Gracious Majesty King George V, humbly relying on the God whom our fathers in days of stress and trial confidently trusted, do hereby pledge ourselves in solemn covenant throughout this time

of threatened calamity to stand by one another in defending for ourselves and our children our cherished position of equal citizenship in the United Kingdom, and in using all means which may be found necessary to defeat the present conspiracy to set up a Home Rule Parliament in Ireland. And in the event of such a parliament being forced upon us we further solemnly and mutually pledge ourselves to refuse to recognise its authority. In sure confidence that God will defend the right we hereto subscribe our names. And further, we individually declare that we have not already signed this covenant. God save the King.[29]

The Covenant was subsequently signed by 471,414 people. These included law lords, civil servants, soldiers and uniformed police. A little-commented-on feature was that Protestants living in the three counties of Ulster which were later to be included in the Irish Free State, and not the six-county statelet controlled by Protestants which ultimately emerged, were also induced to sign the Covenant. This put them in the unfortunate position of having taken an oath *not* to live under a national government, and yet been forced to do so by the action of the Unionist leaders who had induced them to take the oath in the first place. It may be noted that despite the oath, these Protestants formed an industrious and valuable component of their unsought-for state. To show that the signatures implied more than mere moral force, Carson and his henchmen also formed a Protestant Volunteer Force amongst the signatories of the Covenant. Carson used a loophole in the law which stated that if the signatures of two justices of the peace were obtained from their area of jurisdiction, then armed drilling and preparations for war could go forward, providing 'that the object was to render citizens more efficient for the purpose of maintaining the Constitution of the United Kingdom as established'. The manner in which Carson intended to maintain the constitution became clear on 24 September 1912. On that day, he became chairman of the Central Authority of the Provisional Government of Ulster. The Authority set up a Military Council, and made preparations to constitute itself as the illegal Government of Ulster if Home Rule was introduced.

Carson was completely open and explicit about the nature of his defiance: 'The Volunteers are illegal, and the Government know they are illegal, and the Government dare not interfere with them.' He said of his behaviour that he 'did not care tuppence whether it was treason or not'. He made such statements in the knowledge that, apart from Balfour and Bonar Law, his supporters included Waldorf Astor, the Duke of Bedford, Sir Edward Elgar, Rudyard Kipling, Lord Milner and Lord Rothschild. From the sectarian politics which made Liverpool practically a colony of Ulster Unionism, there stepped forward F.E. Smith, whose very public toings and froings at Carson's rallies led to his being nicknamed 'Galloper Smith'. More importantly, he would later become Attorney General and be created a viscount. He was also created an honorary Orangeman following a speech he delivered on his birthday, which, by a particularly fortuitous coincidence for a Conservative MP with a constant eye on Liverpool's Orange vote, fell on 12 July.

In his speech, Smith deliberately set out to exacerbate his audience's feelings towards Irish Nationalists:

You compose a section of the community of which even your opponents have never denied that it is prosperous, law-abiding and loyal. You have, it is true, avoided the method of calling attention to your grievances which for generations has distinguished your political opponents; you have maimed no dumb animal, you have shot no woman, you have stabbed no Sunday School child. [Cheers.] Your claims, therefore, on the present Government are obviously small in comparison with those of the men who dictate Mr Asquith's policy.[30]

He went on to tell his Orange listeners that they were correct to mistrust 'the Nationalist members', and that the establishment of a Home Rule parliament 'would be disastrous both to Ulster and the Empire'. 'You know,' he went on, 'that the spirit of ascendancy, of sacerdotalism and persecution is as active and virulent in their ranks as it was active and virulent when your forefathers met and drove theirs in rout at the battle of the Boyne . . .'

In his speech, Smith struck a note which was sounded by Conservative apologists for the Unionist cause throughout the crisis. If the Unionists did not get their way by peaceful means, then:

you will, in my judgement, be entitled to forget the community which has driven you forth, and to combine in opposition to the community which claimed your allegiance as the fruit of a corrupt and abominable bargain . . . the crisis has called into existence one of the supreme issues of conscience amid which the ordinary landmarks of permissible resistance to technical law are submerged . . .

Thus the issue was transformed from being one of responding to the democratically expressed wishes of the people of Ireland through the ballot box to one of preventing loyal Protestant citizens of the Crown being cast into an exterior darkness ruled by ravenous servants of Rome. This portrayal was most memorably depicted in a poem written by Rudyard Kipling:

> The blood our fathers spilt
> Our love our toils our pains,
> Are counted us for guilt,
> And only bind our chains.
> Before an Empire's eyes,
> The traitor claims his price.
> What need of further lies?
> We are the sacrifice.
>
> We know the war prepared
> On every peaceful home,
> We know the hells declared
> For such as serve not Rome –
> The terror, threats, and dread
> In market, hearth, and field –
> We know, when all is said,
> We perish if we yield.

Believe, we dare not boast,
Believe, we do not fear –
We stand to pay the cost
In all that men hold dear.
What answer from the North?
One law, one land, one throne.
If England drive us forth
We shall not fall alone.

These airs on an Orange theme of defiance were unwelcome to constitutionalists and dismaying in particular to proponents of Home Rule. But
they were not unwelcome to those who saw themselves as contemporary
Fenians, and upholders of the physical-force tradition. One of them, a gifted
polemical journalist and biographer of Michael Collins, Piaras Béaslaí, has
left a telling description of how the nearly dormant Irish Republican Brotherhood viewed Carson's cavortings:

> In an Ireland doped into an unlimited patience, and credulity, an unlimited confidence in
> its Party Leaders, and in the British Liberal government, and a confident expectation of
> Home Rule, came Sir Edward Carson to save the situation for the Physical Force Party.
> He, more than any man, is responsible for the events which have created the Irish Free
> State. He defied law, appealed to force; he preached the doctrines which led to the
> founding of the Irish volunteers – and the amazed Irish people, with their pathetic faith in
> the infallibility of their Party leaders, and the honesty of the British Government, saw that
> Government recoil before the bluff of the 'Ulster Volunteers'. They found threats of
> physical resistance by a minority accepted as a successful argument against justice to a
> majority. They found that the rifles and parading of the 'Ulster Volunteers' were
> jeopardising the long-expected Home Rule Act. Here was the opportunity of the IRB (the
> Irish Republican Brotherhood).[31]

Prior to Carson's eruption on to the national stage, there had been precious
little opportunity for the IRB to take any action to further its goals, nor within
its ranks was there sufficient strength to do so. Fenianism appeared to be
largely a thing of Ireland's romantic, revolutionary past, kept alive in ballad
or fireside tale, and by occasional 'Fenian outrages'. These included the killing
of a policeman in Manchester in an unsuccessful attempt to rescue the Fenian
leader Colonel Kelly. Three Manchester Fenians, Allen, Larkin and O'Brien,
were hanged as a result, and passed into folklore and balladry. Apart from
invading Canada, the Fenians snatched prisoners from jail in Western
Australia, and let off dynamite in London. One of these dynamiters, Thomas
Clarke, having served a 15-year sentence in the barbarous jail conditions of
the time, which drove many of his fellow prisoners mad, went to America for
some years, where he became a friend of the principal Fenian leader, John
Devoy. Devoy united the Fenians under the banner of Clan na Gael, and
would later be a moving spirit behind the 1916 rebellion of which Clarke
would become the father figure.

When Clarke returned to Ireland in 1907, the Irish political landscape appeared very unsuitable terrain for rebellion. The IRB had become better known for its literary figures than its revolutionaries, John O'Leary and Charles Kickham being well-known writers whose example had led W.B. Yeats to become an IRB man. The movement had become a thing of old men lifting a glass to bygone heroes, or attending annual commemorations of revolutionary figures. However, in the early part of the century, a more militant note began to be sounded amongst Irish Nationalists. A Quaker, Bulmer Hobson, and a Catholic, Denis McCullough, revived the memory of Grattan's Volunteers by founding a group called the Dungannon Clubs in Belfast. The Clubs were avowedly separatist and Republican, but though they condemned recruitment to the British armed services or to the Royal Irish Constabulary, they preached friendship to the Orangeman. Hobson and McCullough approved of certain of the policies of a man who will shortly be described in more detail, Arthur Griffith, the founder of Sinn Féin (Ourselves Alone). The policy which appealed to the separatists was his argument against sending Irish MPs to Westminster: 'Ireland has maintained a representation of 103 men in the English Parliament for 108 years . . . the 103 Irishmen are faced with 567 foreigners . . . Ten years hence the majority of Irishmen will marvel they once believed that the proper battle-ground for Ireland was one chosen and filled by Ireland's enemies.' But young men and women of the Béaslaí-Hobson-McCullough school found Arthur Griffith's Sinn Féin policy to be something like the curate's egg: good in parts. The part which those who espoused traditional Fenian values found least good was Griffith's monarchism and his opposition to physical force. He did not believe that Ireland had the strength either to launch a successful war against England or withstand the inevitable retaliation which would follow any militant action.

Griffith was one of the most influential Irish political thinkers of the twentieth century. A printer by trade, he was also a brilliant journalist, who could have had a lucrative career in American journalism had he not chosen instead to remain in Ireland, living on the margins of poverty in order to further his political ideals. A man of the highest integrity, he stepped down in favour of Eamon de Valera as president of Sinn Féin, rather than face a leadership challenge which he could easily have won, not out of timidity but because of his deep-seated belief that the Sinn Féin movement should not become overly identified with one man, as had Home Rule and the Irish Parliamentary Party with Parnell collapsing as a result in the wake of Parnell's own collapse. He was a founder member of the Celtic Literary Society, and was active in the Gaelic League and, for a time, the IRB. In 1897 he went to live in South Africa for about eighteen months and sided with Boer aspirations towards a republic.

While Griffith consciously walked in the footsteps of Irish political leaders of the Republican, democratic school, such as the Young Irelanders or Parnell, he also advocated the idea of a dual monarchy for Ireland and England, and brought new European exemplars to the notice of the Irish public: the Hungarian Francis Deak, with his policy of passive resistance, the

German economist Frederick List, with his doctrines of self-sufficiency. To this day, Republicans continue to cherry-pick from Griffith's basic ideas. The contemporary Republican/Fenian movement also rejects physical force (currently) and monarchism, styles itself Sinn Féin, preaches self-sufficiency and abstention from the British parliament, and consciously tries to advance Griffith's idea of attempting to solve Irish problems with a basically Irish approach. The wings of Fenianism, which continued to uphold the physical force tradition, the Continuity IRA and the Real IRA, nevertheless supports Griffith's other teachings.

At the first Sinn Féin convention, in Dublin on 28 November 1905, Griffith told his audience, only about one hundred in all, that the basis of his policy was 'national self-reliance'. The previous year he had published his major work, *The Resurrection of Hungary: a Parallel for Ireland,* in which, while advancing the principle of dual monarchy, he also noted that Hungary 'won her independence by refusing to send members to the Imperial Parliament at Vienna or admit any right in that parliament to legislate for her'. That idea, abstentionism, would strike deep roots in Ireland. The precise meaning of the term Sinn Féin has frequently been the subject of controversy, but as is so often the case in Ireland, or indeed in revolutionary situations anywhere, it is what an idea or a slogan signifies to its hearers that counts, rather than its dictionary meaning. The longevity of Arthur Griffith's party in Irish politics is perhaps best explained by the following translation from a poem by the founder of the Gaelic League, Douglas Hyde:

> Waiting for help from France, waiting for help from Spain; the people who
> waited long ago for that, they got shame only.
> Waiting for help again, help from America, the lot who are now waiting for it,
> my disgust forever on them.
> It is time for every fool to have knowledge that there is no watchcry worth any
> heed but one – Sinn Féin amhain – Ourselves Alone!

One of those who doubted the efficacy of Griffith's constitutional approach was Thomas Clarke. His little tobacconist shop in Dublin's Parnell Street became a meeting place for the IRB, which co-opted him on to its Supreme Council. Following Clarke's co-option, the IRB founded a newspaper, *Irish Freedom,* and appointed a full-time organiser, Seán MacDermott, who was also the editor of the paper. These two steps began a policy of steady infiltration of Irish Ireland movements such as the Gaelic League and the Gaelic Athletic Association, the establishment of Fianna Eireann, the Republican boy scout movement, and a build-up in the quality of the Brotherhood, which by 1912 is estimated to have been some 2,000 strong. In the previous year, there had been a split in the movement between the 'forward' party led by Clarke, MacDermott and others, and older Fenians of the Kickham-O'Leary school, which left the 'forward' men in control.

Compared to the strength of the forces which supported the Irish Parliamentary Party, and John Redmond's Home Rule policy, the IRB was a minuscule organisation. Yet underneath the surface of Irish political life, the tradition of famine and Fenianism made of the IRB a potentially powerful current, should anything happen to fray the parliamentary covering, which, like that on an electric wire, prevented dangerous sparks from escaping. As the Home Rule crisis reached its climax in 1914, the Conservatives and the Unionists finally frayed the covering.

The Unionists did not merely play the Orange card, they played the German one also. On 1 January 1913, Bonar Law said in the House of Commons that rather than be ruled by Irish Nationalists, the Ulster Unionists would 'prefer to accept the Government of a foreign country'. As we will see, this strange variation on the theme of 'loyalty' continued to be sounded almost to the day that the Great War broke out.

However, such utterances notwithstanding, leading figures in British society organised homes for Loyalist refugees from Ulster should war break out over Home Rule, and an indemnity fund of a million pounds was begun to assist the wounded or the widowed in the event of hostilities commencing.

Watching these developments, the IRB, through its propagandists, notably Padraig Pearse, who, as we shall shortly see, would emerge as the leader of the physical-force men, had begun making public appeals for the formation of a Nationalist volunteer corps. In July the IRB had taken a decision that such a body should be founded, but hesitated to be seen making the call itself. The philosophy behind the projected volunteer force was outlined by Pearse. It combined a declaration that the Green was as entitled to arm as the Orange with an assurance that the Green bore no ill will towards the Orange: 'Personally, I think the Orangeman with the rifle a much less ridiculous figure than the Nationalist without a rifle.' A little later he said: '. . . accursed be the soul of any nationalist who would dream of firing a shot or drawing a sword against the Ulster Volunteers in connection with this Bill [Home Rule author]. Any such action would be an enforcement of a British law upon an Irish population which refused it; would be a marshalling under the Union Jack.'[32]

By this time, the Ulster Unionists were generally believed to be armed with something in excess of 50,000 rifles and revolvers, and a quantity of machine-guns. The Unionist *Northern Whig* of 4 June 1913 claimed

> that importation of arms into Belfast has been going on regularly for more than a year and a half, ever since the Parliament Act broke down the bulwark which the House of Lords raised against Home Rule. A good many thousand of modern army rifles have been received and distributed during that period . . . Rifles – and not only rifles, but machine guns and a large quantity of ammunition – have reached Ulster from many sources and under many aliases.

Neither the membership of the UVF nor its leaders were inclined to argue that the soul of any Unionist who fired shots or drew swords against anyone who attempted to introduce Home Rule would be accursed. Militarism was in the air on all fronts, political, sectarian and social. In Dublin, the appalling slum conditions had finally led to a degree of violence arising from the great lock-out of 1913. James Larkin, who with James Connolly had founded the Irish Transport and General Workers Union, and the Irish Labour Party, had called a series of strikes in the city. A tramway strike led by Larkin precipitated wholesale industrial warfare with the Federation of Dublin Employers, led by the boss of the tram company, William Martin Murphy, the leading Dublin businessman of his time, who, amongst other ventures, controlled the *Irish Independent*.

Larkin and Connolly were two of the most remarkable men of their period. Both were the sons of Irish parents who had had to emigrate; both knew grinding poverty in their youth, Connolly in Edinburgh, and Larkin in Liverpool; both sought to enrich not merely the pockets of the workers but their cultural and political horizons also; and both came up against the dark lowering bigotry of Belfast in their efforts to bridge the sectarian divide and help Catholic and Protestant alike. In Belfast, as in Liverpool, the Orange Order was used by employers for political and economic advantage to stop workers from uniting in their own interests, and so kept wages down. Both men had an international dimension to their socialism: Connolly spent the years between 1903 and 1910 in America, where he became an active member of the Industrial Workers of the World, the 'Wobblies', and, like Larkin, a friend to political activists such as the Flynn family of New York, of whom Elizabeth Gourley Flynn became known as one of America's most prominent trade unionists. Connolly advocated the emancipation of women and one of his principal lieutenants was Countess Constance Markievicz. As Margaret Ward has pointed out, he regarded women, literally, as comrades in arms in the revolutionary struggle, whereas the Nationalists saw the various militant women's organisations which sprang up around this time purely as auxiliary groups providing support services to the fighters, who were visualised as being male only.[33] Significantly, when fighting did break out in 1916, Markievicz was one of the very few women known to have actually fired a gun, and she did so in the uniform of Connolly's Citizen Army, not with a women's corps.

A fine polemical journalist, Connolly made a powerful impact with his books *Labour in Irish History* and *The Re-conquest of Ireland*. Pungent phrases of his still have their place in Irish folklore: 'The Irish Peasant is a slave, and his daughter is the slave of a slave.' He advised the poor of Ireland that the great only appeared great because they, the poor, were on their knees – and he urged them to get off their knees.

The labour unrest of 1913 may justly be regarded as a precursor to the 1916 Rising itself. Murphy's forces dismissed any worker who joined Larkin's union and refused to re-employ them until they signed a declaration disavowing the IT&GWU. In a straightforward clash between capitalism and labour, a general lock-out was declared, and there were riots, sympathetic strikes, and a good deal of police brutality. In breaking up a meeting addressed by Larkin on 31 August, the police killed two men and a woman with their batons, and Larkin, unlike Carson, went to jail for using 'seditious language'.

The lock-out led to extreme hardship amongst the already near-destitute workers of Dublin. Food ships were sent by sympathisers in England, money came from the Continent, writers contributed polemics in support of the workers. One of the most memorable pieces was an open letter from George (A.E.) Russell to the employers of Dublin, whom he termed 'blind Samsons pulling down the pillars of the social order'. He wrote: 'You determine deliberately in cold anger to starve out one-third of the population of this city, to break the manhood of the men by the sight of the suffering of their wives and the hunger of their children.'

It might be remarked that the Dublin employers were not the only body to view the hunger of the workers' children in political rather than humanitarian terms. The Catholic Church intervened to prevent strikers' children being sent to godless England, lest along with physical nourishment they imbibed the sinful teachings of Protestantism. Under the pressures of both capitalism and the Church, the strike ended in failure in early 1914, but it left behind a significant military legacy – the Irish Citizen Army which was formed to protect the workers from the police. James Connolly, who, when the lock-out commenced, had been in Belfast organising the IT&GWU, returned to Dublin to give leadership, first to the strike and then to the Citizen Army, which was trained and organised by Captain J.R. White, a Protestant Ulsterman who had won the DSO during the Boer War and was a son of General Sir George White, the hero of the defence of Ladysmith. A gesture of Captain White's says more about the condition of the Dublin workers than any statistics could. He offered to give fifty pounds to buy shoes for the prospective soldiers of the Citizen Army, pointing out that the men's existing footwear was so broken and ill-fitting as to render marching impossible. If the men could not march, they could not drill. His offer was taken up and presumably added to, as approximately a hundred men were given decent footwear. As the Citizen Army drilled and marched, it imparted a background note of militarism to the Dublin debate on Home Rule.

The IRB's determination to bring this note to the fore found its opportunity in an article written in the journal of the Gaelic League, *An Claidheamh Soluis* (The Bright Sword), by the League's vice-president, Eóin MacNeill, Professor of Early Irish History at University College, Dublin. MacNeill proposed the formation of a body of Nationalist Volunteers, saying that if the UVF were arming and organising to defeat Home Rule, then the Nationalists should do likewise to prevent force being made the arbiter of the Home Rule debate. The IRB recognised that Pearse's formulation that the Nationalist without a rifle was more ridiculous than the Orangeman with one was becoming acceptable in respectable circles. The organisation immediately sent one of their leading members, the O'Rahilly, to meet with MacNeill. The O'Rahilly (the 'the' denotes chieftainship of an ancient Gaelic clan), a prominent Kerry business-man, had no difficulty in securing McNeill's agreement to the setting up of a committee to organise a volunteer corps. The committee was duly estab-lished,[34] with a leavening of poets, one of them Padraig Pearse. It also included leading IRB men such as Seán MacDermott, Eamonn Kent, Bulmer Hobson and Piaras Béaslaí.

Events moved swiftly. On 25 November 1913, less than a month after MacNeill's article appeared, a public meeting was held in the Rotunda, Dublin. It was an immediate success. Over 4,000 men enrolled in response to a manifesto read from the stage which claimed that the Volunteers were a response to the situation 'deliberately adopted by one of the great English political parties . . . to make a display of military force and the menace of armed violence the determining factor in the future relations between this country and Great Britain'.[35] MacNeill also delivered an unrealistically optimistic view of the Ulster Volunteer Force, which, while it completely underestimated the tone and temper of militant Ulster Protestantism, would nevertheless continue to be the official attitude of militant Irish republicanism to the time of writing. (It may be remarked *inter alia* that the degree of opposition to it in the ranks of loyalism would also appear to be the same.) MacNeill said:

> We do not contemplate any hostility to the Volunteer movement that has already been initiated in parts of Ulster. The strength of that movement consists in men whose kinsfolk were amongst the foremost and the most resolute in winning freedom for the United States of America, in descendants of the Irish Volunteers of 1782, of the United Irishmen, of the Antrim and Down insurgents of 1798, of the Ulster Protestants who protested in thousands against the destruction of the Irish Parliament in 1800. The more genuine and successful the local Volunteer movement in Ulster becomes, the more completely does it establish the principle that Irishmen have the right to decide and govern their own national affairs. We have nothing to fear from the existing Volunteers in Ulster nor they from us. We gladly acknowledge the evident truth that they have opened the way for a National Volunteer movement, and we trust that the day is near when their own services to the cause of an Irish Nation will become as memorable as the services of their forefathers.[36]

Practically speaking, this was fine-sounding but empty rhetoric. The Ulster Volunteer movement of course abhorred the idea of service to an 'Irish Nation'. Its warp and woof was British, Protestant, supremacist. But for many of the young men who enrolled in the Rotunda, joining the Volunteers was the crystallisation of an idea whose hour had struck. Their growing cultural, economic and educational awareness had inevitably, and naturally, sought a political outcome; a constitutional outcome at that. But for years now they had seen their legitimate political aspirations frustrated by seemingly uncontrollable, unstoppable forces. Now they had suddenly been given an opportunity to have a say of their own in the direction of events. Although writing from his own perspective, the man who had worked longest to bring about the Rotunda meeting, Tom Clarke, later accurately described its outcome:

> . . . there is an awakening, the slow, silent plodding, and the open preaching is at last showing results . . . Such an outpouring of young fellows was never seen . . . then the class

31

of fellows who are there – and the enthusiasm and the national note in the atmosphere – tis good to be in Ireland these times . . . hundreds of young fellows who could be interested in the national Movement, even on the milk and water side are in these Volunteers and are saying things that proves the right spot has been touched in them by the volunteering. Wait till they get their fist clutching the steel barrel of a business rifle and then Irish instincts and Irish manhood can be relied upon . . .[37]

Here it might be remarked that Irish womanhood could equally be relied upon but was not viewed as equal either by the Volunteers or indeed by those who led the women's equivalent of the Volunteer movement, Cumann na mBan, which was formed the following year, in April 1914. Its role was to *assist* the Volunteer movement, not to have a say in how the men's organisation spent its money, or formulated its policies. In 1915 Cumann na mBan's own president and most prominent member, Countess Constance Markievicz, addressing a group of women (the Irish Women's Franchise League) who felt that Cumann na mBan should demand equal status from the Volunteers as the price of their support, said: 'Today the women attached to national movements are there chiefly to collect funds for the men to spend. These Ladies Auxiliaries demoralise women, set them up in separate camps, and deprive them of all initiative and independence.'[38]

Amongst those who joined in the fervour of the moment was Eamon de Valera, who would go on to dominate Irish political life for many decades to come. This strange, semi-mystical, semi-disturbed, altogether political figure came from a background which may help to explain the complexities of his character. His official biography[39] claims that his parents were married in 1881 at St Patrick's Church, Greenville, New Jersey, but in fact no such wedding is to be found in the church records.[40] His baptismal certificate in St Agnes's Church, 61 East 41st Street, New York, states that he was born in the nearby foundling home, The Nursery and Childs Hospital, and that his mother was Catherine Coll and his father was Vivion De Valeros, an artist born in Spain. The original of this certificate, which is still retained at St Agnes's Church, where de Valera was baptised on 3 December 1882, was later altered by Vivion de Valera, his eldest son, who in his own handwriting altered De Valeros to de Valera, and Edward to Eamon. Eamon in fact was an Irish version of Edward, which de Valera only began using later in life, after he had joined the Gaelic League. His state birth certificate has also been altered. The original version, registered on 10 November 1882, refers to him as 'George de Valero'. Again, the father is stated to have been an artist, and to have been born in Spain. This certificate was changed, or in the official term 'corrected', on 30 June 1916, by Catherine Wheelwright. Catherine, the former 'Kate' Coll, from Bruree, had since married a Charles Wheelwright. The official story is that Vivion de Valera, the artist, had contracted TB and died shortly after he and Kate were married, and that that is why she was forced to send the infant de Valera back to Bruree to be reared by his family. However, even after marrying Wheelwright and establishing a home, Kate refused to bring

Edward back to the US. The alterations which Kate made to her son's birth certificate would appear to have been carried out shortly after the 1916 Rising, when she was seeking to establish his American citizenship to save him from the firing squads which claimed the lives of his fellow leaders of that rebellion.

A large percentage of those who enrolled in the Volunteers with de Valera were supporters of John Redmond, and genuinely believed that their action was, and would be seen as such by the authorities, no more than pointedly but nevertheless peacefully putting a little muscle behind the pro-Home Rule movement. They, and a sizeable segment of Nationalist Ireland, were considerably jolted when equally pointedly, but in stark contrast to the manner in which the Unionists' arming, drilling and preparing to set up an illegal government had been condoned, the Government issued a proclamation banning the importation of arms into Ireland. The difference in how Orange and Green preparations were regarded grew starker still a few months later, when the extraordinary saga known as the Curragh Mutiny was played out.

The British army was largely pro-Unionist, and received the strongest possible encouragement to develop that sentiment, even to the point of mutiny. Bonar Law, in a letter to Carson dated 8 September 1913, described a conversation he had had with Winston Churchill, who had been authorised by Asquith to sound him out, about how he and other highly placed Tories would actively encourage the army to refuse orders to enforce Home Rule in Ulster.[41] Bonar Law also went to the extent of raising with the King the possibility of the army refusing to obey orders. The King thereafter became noticeably cool towards the leader of His Majesty's Loyal Opposition.

In his authoritative study, Ian F.W. Beckett wrote:

> Although sometimes erroneously referred to as the 'Curragh Mutiny', rather than more appropriately as the Curragh 'incident', it remains one of the very few occasions in modern times when the British Army could be said openly to be challenging Civil Supremacy over the military in peace-time . . . There was widespread sympathy for the Ulster Loyalists . . . up stemmed from the Unionist instincts of the officer corps as a whole.
>
> There was also a 'widespread disinclination' among naval officers to take part in the coercion of Ulster. Such disinclination extended to the most senior ranks . . .[42]

Beckett notes an important factor in the army's attitude:

> Increasing impoverishment of the Anglo-Irish gentry had resulted in a high proportion of the class, especially younger sons, making the army their career. Moreover, then as today, Ulstermen were particularly numerous amongst army officers. To all these officers 'coercion of Ulster', as it came to be called, was profoundly repugnant.

An officer to whom Home Rule was particularly repugnant was Field Marshal Sir Henry Wilson, Director of Military Operations and later Chief of the Imperial General Staff. Wilson's life, a biographer of Bonar Law has judged, was 'devoted to the art of secret intrigue'.[43] Intrigue was the very fibre of his being. He was never more at home than in the atmosphere of plot and counter-plot and labyrinthine manoeuvre which prevailed in high army circles at this time. Wilson gave inside intelligence to the leader of the opposition (Bonar Law) to subvert the policy of the government he was sworn to serve. This was the private face of the army. The public face was that of Field Marshal Earl Roberts, 'the most beloved and respected soldier of his day, victor of the South African War . . . a violent opponent of Home Rule'.[44] It was Roberts who recommended General Sir George Richardson as Commander of the UVF, and who personally interceded with him to ensure that he took the post, thereby giving what was in effect an organisation formed to resist the Crown under force of arms, some priceless *cachet*.

These then were the men who were to help to pour the blood of a generation of young English and Irish men into the mud of Flanders, Ypres and the Somme. Yet assessing the carnage which put an end to the 'Curragh incident', a chronicler of the Ulster crisis would write that the World War I 'saved the Army', although in making that judgement he quoted a contemporary authority, Sir George MacMunn, who pointed out that that salvation had a price, and wondered: 'If General Sealy and Mr Churchill each offer little candles to the memory of William Hohenzollern for restoring the Officer cadre of the British Army and Navy, for them, even though it died in the process.'[45]

The army's role in the Home Rule crisis was one of the major causative factors in ensuring that, effectively speaking, peaceful progress towards Home Rule died also. Military memoirs of the period[46] make it clear that senior officers had taken part not only in bringing arms into Ulster, but also in laying plans whereby the UVF could, at a moment's notice, seize military installations in Belfast and elsewhere. By March 1914, the Government had become sufficiently worried at the drift of events to prepare to send troops from the Curragh in County Kildare in the south to Ulster to protect various strategic points. But on 20 March 1914, an alarming telegram was received at the War Office from the Commander in Chief of the forces in Ireland, General Sir Arthur Paget. Paget informed London that General Hubert Gough, who was himself from Ulster, and 57 officers of the 3rd Cavalry Brigade had let it be known that they would prefer dismissal to moving north. Gough was summoned to London by the Minister for War, Colonel John Sealy. Would it be court-martial or capitulation, was the question of the hour. It was to be capitulation. The weight of top-level army influence for the 'mutineers' became evident when Gough emerged from his encounter with Sealy with a document which concluded with a paragraph in his own writing stating that 'troops under our command will not be called upon to enforce the present Home Rule Bill on Ulster, and we can so assure our Officers'.[47] The paragraph had in fact been composed by Sir Henry Wilson, who was amongst those who had briefed Gough prior to his interview.

The net result of the Curragh Mutiny, or incident, however one terms it, in realpolitik terms, was that it made clear that the army could not be used to enforce Home Rule. This fact was glaringly underlined a month later, on the night of 24/25 April 1914, when a ship, the *Clyde Valley*, sailed into Larne harbour with a cargo of weapons from Germany for the UVF. Police and customs officials were held at gunpoint, but the army stood idly by as 35,000 rifles and five million rounds of ammunition were loaded into a cavalcade of waiting motor cars to be transported safely to various destinations within Ulster. The gun-runners' password was 'Gough'. The truth of Kipling's pledge to the Orangemen that 'we shall not fall alone' had been strikingly borne out.

The Government's reaction was to shrink from the prospect of civil war, and embrace instead the vision of partition as a means of reconciling the conflicting claims of Orange and Green. Less than three weeks after the gun-running, on 12 May, Asquith announced that the Government intended to introduce an Amending Bill to the Home Rule proposals, which would have the effect of excluding a portion of Ulster from the operation of Home Rule.

The idea of partition had floated above the conflict in a somewhat nebulous form since June 1912. During a debate on Home Rule, the Liberal Unionist T.C. Agar-Robartes had proposed that the Act should exclude Down, Antrim, Armagh and Londonderry. The Nationalists rejected this angrily, one speaker, William O'Brien, describing the proposal as 'an impossible and hateful one, both to Protestants and to Catholics'.[48] The amendment was defeated, and Nationalists regarded the proposal as being unserious, designed merely to wreck the Home Rule proposals. However, though a Unionist, Agar-Robartes was also a Liberal, who may have been testing the waters for Lloyd George.

While literally testing the waters two months later, at Marienbad, Lloyd George informed the Irish MP T.P. O'Connor in confidence that the Government had decided on partition. As O'Connor was a prominent member of the Irish Parliamentary Party, it is hard to believe that he did not inform his leader, John Redmond, of this important piece of news.[49] But throughout the crisis of the ensuing two years, Redmond continued to refuse to countenance any suggestion of partition. After the UVF gun-running, however, it was not possible to maintain a credible *non possumus* position.

As partition would become a recurring source of crisis from the period of the Home Rule debates up to the present day, it is important that the various steps towards the division of Ireland should be chronicled in some detail. The actual Home Rule Bill which Asquith introduced on 11 April 1912 was far from revolutionary. There was to be an Irish parliament consisting of the King and two houses: a House of Commons of 164 members, and a Senate of 40. The effective head of the envisaged Irish Executive was to be, not as one might expect the person at the head of the largest party to be returned by the electorate, but a Lord Lieutenant who would be nominated by the British Prime Minister. The Lord Lieutenant was to appoint ministers and senators, albeit ultimately on the advice of the Irish ministry, and the appointment of judges was also his prerogative. The army, navy, issues of peace and war, laws concerning other countries, and such important matters as customs and excise and taxation were all the concern of the British parliament which was to have the power to change or repeal any Act which the Irish parliament might pass. A certain amount of Irish representation at Westminster was to continue, although this was to be reduced from 103 to 42 MPs. The Bill also contained a provision to safeguard the position of Protestants in Ireland, which would have made it impossible for the parliament to discriminate on the grounds of religion, or to give any religion a favourite position. This pill, however, did not sweeten the measure for Carson. He argued that the points made in favour of Home Rule by the Nationalists could also be made by the Ulster Protestants, and said flatly that it would be impossible for Home Rule to be introduced against the wishes of 'Ulster', which at this stage of the debate still meant the historic nine counties, not the six it actually became.

It was during this debate, at the committee stage, on 11 June, that Agar-Robartes proposed the partition amendment which Carson supported. The following year, on 1 January, Carson took the partition issue a stage further, in the course of the speech in which he told the House of Commons that his followers would prefer 'the Government of a foreign country' to rule by Nationalists. He formally moved that the province of Ulster be excluded from the provisions of the Home Rule Act. Asquith, who throughout the debate had taken the position that a minority could not be allowed a veto over the wishes of the majority in Ireland, opposed the motion, which was defeated. Redmond also strongly opposed the Carson amendment, saying that Nationalists could 'never submit' to the creation 'for all time [of] his sharp, internal dividing line between Irish Catholics and Irish Protestants'.

However, Redmond's position was considerably undermined when Asquith, though still opposing partition, announced during the debates that before the Home Rule Bill could become law, a general election would have to be held. This was a surrender to the Conservatives' position that the issue was not one of peacefully introducing Home Rule to Ireland, but was between upholding the Union and the civil war which the fire-eating speeches of Carson and the Conservative leadership constantly promised outside the Chamber.

Outside the Chamber also, Nationalists in the area affected by the partition proposals registered their opposition to the proposals in striking fashion. A by-election occurred in Derry, and it is said that the dead, and certainly the dying, amongst the Nationalist electorate came out to vote for the successful Nationalist candidate, leaving the Irish representation at Westminster from the supposedly overwhelmingly Unionist province of 'Ulster' divided 17–16 in favour of the Nationalists. Despite, or more accurately because of, the Derry result, the Unionists' preparations to resist, described above, continued with renewed force.

On 4 August James Craig announced that: 'We may look for Home Rule in May, Civil War in June, the Union Jack being hauled down and trampled upon in July, and the smash-up of the Empire in August.' To avoid this dire prospect, the Unionists organised a major series of demonstrations, parades and meetings of every sort. It was at one of these, on 7 September, that Carson made the announcement that if Home Rule became law, an illegal government would be set up. 'I am told it will be illegal . . . of course it will. Drilling is illegal . . . The Volunteers are illegal, and the Government know they are illegal, and the Government dare not interfere with them . . . don't be afraid of illegalities.'

The Government's inactivity in the face of this gathering storm of treason was variously ascribed to Asquith's 'wait and see' philosophy in politics, and to his waiting for 'a favourable curve' in the course of events which he could take advantage of. But Asquith himself rather grandly glossed over his government's paralysis in his autobiography by saying: 'The Government abstained from criminal proceedings upon grounds of high policy.'[50] This 'high policy' was unquestionably influenced by an uneasy awareness of the situation brewing in the army and the navy. In the run up to the bursting storm of the Curragh Mutiny in March 1914, Bonar Law and his cohorts were actively considering a plan whereby the House of Lords would block the annual implementation of the statutory Army Act, so as to ensure that from 30 April the legal position would be that the United Kingdom did not have an army. Against this background, Asquith moved again on the partition front in the House of Commons on 9 March.

During a debate on the Home Rule Bill, he proposed an idea known as 'county option with a time limit'. With the four predominantly Unionist counties in mind, he proposed that any Ulster county which voted to do so by a majority of its parliamentary electorate could exclude itself from the operation of the Home Rule Bill for six years. By now Redmond's position had become so weakened that he agreed to the proposal. Nationalists would subsequently strongly criticise him for his 'weakness' during the Home Rule crisis. But, as Asquith himself pointed out, the oft-repeated contention that Redmond should have done more because the Liberals were dependent on him could very easily be turned on its head. Given the strength and ferocity of Conservative/Unionist opposition to Home Rule, and the extra-parliamentary lengths to which they were prepared to take that opposition, Redmond in fact was as dependent upon the Liberals as they were on him.

In the event, however, Redmond's concession on the county options idea had no practical effect. Carson rejected the proposal, saying: 'We do not want a sentence of death with a stay of execution of six years', and claiming that 'Ulster was ready for any exigency'. The Curragh Mutiny exigency presented itself a few days later.

Having backed down in the face of the army's mutinous demeanour, on 25 May the Government tacked an Amending Bill on to the Home Rule proposals. The amendment made it clear that part of Ireland would be excluded from the operation of Home Rule when the Bill received the royal assent. Redmond and his supporters voted for the Home Rule Bill, which then at long last passed the House of Commons. However, his support drew heavy and sustained fire from Nationalists. Prominent amongst these was William O'Brien, the veteran Nationalist leader who, with John Dillon, had led the Irish Parliamentary Party's opposition to Parnell. O'Brien had later founded the All-for-Ireland League, from the ranks of the more militant wing of the parliamentary party who opposed Redmond's conciliatory policy towards the Liberals, but were conciliatory themselves towards the Protestant Irish landlords, and drew support from this quarter from improving landlords like Lords Dunraven and Monteagle. O'Brien now led the League in abstaining from voting for what O'Brien bitterly described as an Act: 'born with a rope around its neck. It is not even intended to be enforced . . . We regard this Bill as no longer a Home Rule Bill, but as a Bill for the murder of Home Rule, such as we have understood it all our lives, and we can have no hand, act or part in the operation.'

Outside the House of Commons, Nationalist opinion was divided. Those who supported Redmond welcomed the passage of Home Rule with the lighting of bonfires – apparently without any realisation that they were also celebrating partition. However, Sinn Féin, the emerging Labour movement, and, of course, the IRB were implacably opposed to the partition idea. Recruitment to the Irish Volunteers mushroomed. In America, a Volunteer Fund Committee was set up under the chairmanship of a prominent IRB activist, Joseph McGarrity, who was born in Carrickmore in County Tyrone, one of the northern counties which would be partitioned from the rest of Ireland.

McGarrity's support for physical-force republicanism was such that his name would be used by the IRA many decades later, as a pseudonym on their announcements. When de Valera visited America on a mammoth propaganda tour in 1919, his principal allies in a feud which developed between him and the prominent Irish-American leaders John Devoy and Judge Cohalan would be McGarrity and his friend Dr Pat McCartan, also from Carrickmore.

The final act of this stage of the partition drama was played out a few days before the outbreak of a far greater exigency – the Great War. By then, matters had reached such a pitch that the United States Ambassador in Berlin reported that the German Department of Foreign Affairs was of the opinion England was so enmeshed in the Ulster situation that she would not go to war.[51] The Home Rule Bill became trapped in parliamentary gridlock. Though the Lords could not now reject it, they could, and did, pass a counteracting Bill, on 8 July. The partition proposals re-emerged, this time without the six-year county option, and envisaging the exclusion of not four, but the entire nine counties of Ulster from the operation of Home Rule.

Thus the British Government was now committed to Home Rule for all Ireland – and to a contradictory Amending Bill which only envisaged Home Rule for three of its four provinces. In an effort to break the deadlock, the King intervened. On 21 July, George V called a conference at Buckingham

Palace between the contending parties. It was chaired by the speaker of the House of Commons. The Government was represented by Asquith and Lloyd George, the Conservative and Unionist Party by Lord Lansdowne and Bonar Law, the Ulster Unionists by Carson and Craig, and the Irish Nationalists by Redmond and John Dillon. Churchill has left us his celebrated description of how, for days, the gathering toiled unsuccessfully through the muddy by-ways of Fermanagh and Tyrone. Not surprisingly, they failed to reach agreement, and this chapter of the partition saga closed in failure on 24 July. Asquith was in the act of reporting the Buckingham Palace Conference breakdown to the Cabinet when the wording of the Austrian ultimatum to Serbia was handed to the Foreign Secretary, Sir Edward Grey. In the memorable words of Churchill, 'The parishes of Fermanagh and Tyrone faded back into the mists and squalls of Ireland, and a strange light began immediately, but by perceptible gradations, to fall and grow upon the map of Europe.' War was inevitable, and as Carson himself later remarked, Home Rule had been rendered 'a nullity'.

Back in Ireland, Redmond had realised that the Irish Volunteers were a threat to his position and had forced them to co-opt 25 of his nominees on to the committee. The IRB had accepted this unwelcome development as being preferable to a public split with the Irish Parliamentary Party leader. However, the gathering pace of events made a split inevitable. Between parliamentary methods and physical-force methods there was as little room for compromise as there was between the goals of Orange and Green. And two days after the Buckingham Palace Conference collapsed the IRB had received a powerful boost to its ambitions.

On Sunday 26 July 1914, Erskine Childers, and a crew which included his wife Mary 'Molly' Osgood of Boston, and Mary Spring Rice, a daughter of Lord Monteagle, sailed into Howth and history, aboard the yacht *Asgard*. The *Asgard*'s cargo consisted of 900 German rifles. Childers was the son of a noted English oriental scholar, Robert Caesar Childers. He grew up with his mother's family, the Bartons, in Annamoe, County Wicklow. After graduating from Cambridge, he became a clerk in the House of Commons. His novel, *The Riddle of the Sands*, is said to have led to the strengthening of the British navy's North Sea Fleet because it gave such a realistic picture of a plot by the Kaiser to invade England across the North Sea.

Childers is one of the most tragic figures in Irish history: he was to die before an Irish firing squad during the civil war. He was a committed Home Ruler, and had become disenchanted with Britain's imperial policies during the Boer War. He readily agreed when he and another Irish yachtsman, Conor O'Brien, were approached by Mary Spring Rice, after the Larne gun-running, with the idea of sailing German arms into Dublin. Other prominent figures of the period who donated or helped to raise money for the project were the historian Alice Stopford Green, the humanitarian Roger Casement and the novelist Darrel Figgis.

Ironically enough, Childers and his two female accomplices set off for

Howth, some eight miles north of Dublin, on the Orangemen's feast day, 12 July 1914, and landed in broad daylight on a Sunday afternoon. Childers's rifles were followed a few days later (Saturday 1 August) by a consignment of 600 guns which were sailed to the Welsh coast aboard Conor O'Brien's *Kelpie*. Here they were trans-shipped to the yacht *Chotah*, owned by a Dublin surgeon, Sir Thomas Myles, and landed at Kilcoole on the Wicklow coast, about 17 miles south-east of Dublin.

The significance of the Howth consignment was tragically underscored by the Bachelors Walk incident, which occurred after the arms had been safely landed. Approximately 800 Volunteers were marching back to Dublin with the rifles when they were confronted by Assistant Commissioner Harrell of the Dublin Metropolitan Police, supported by a company of the King's Own Scottish Borderers. A bout of parleying and scuffling ensued, as a result of which the Volunteers managed both to hold on to their weapons and get away safely. However, as the Borderers marched back to their barracks, they were stoned by members of a hostile crowd which had gathered at Bachelors Walk. The soldiers fired into the crowd, killing four people and wounding 37. The sharp contrast between the behaviour of the British army towards a Dublin mob following a gun-running and that displayed towards the Ulster Volunteers during and after Larne was taken by Nationalists throughout Ireland as yet another manifestation of the fact that there was one law for Green and another for Orange.

However, the Bachelors Walk storm of reaction, intense though it was (and *ipso facto* of immense benefit to the IRB's cause), was overshadowed by the outbreak of world war a week later. As soon as Sir Edward had formally announced the war to the House of Commons, Redmond rose to assure the House that the British Government could with confidence withdraw all its troops from Ireland because the Irish Volunteers would co-operate with the Ulster Volunteers in protecting its shores. As Carson had already pledged the services of the UVF to the British, this was cheering news for the Foreign Secretary. Accordingly Sir Edward responded by saying: 'The one bright spot in the very dreadful situation is Ireland. The position in Ireland . . . and this I should like to be clearly understood abroad . . . is not a consideration among the things we have to take into account now.'

This was not the view of the IRB, and even Augustine Birrell, who liked and respected Redmond, judged that he had made a mistake. In the course of Redmond's obituary in *The Times*, Birrell wrote: 'His famous speech in the House of Commons was a mistake, though a noble one. He took the curve too sharply and did not carry the train with him.'

One of the factors which derailed the train was the fact that the Home Rule Bill had been placed on the statute book and given the royal assent, but at the same time (18 September) a Suspensory Act was passed postponing the operation of the Home Rule Act. Asquith told the House that the Bill would 'not come into operation until Parliament should have the fullest opportunity, by an Amending Bill, of altering, modifying, or qualifying its provisions in such a way as to secure at any rate the general consent both of Ireland and the United Kingdom'.

Whatever the verdict of the Orangemen might have been on this strategy of postponement, 'consent' was most definitely not forthcoming from the IRB who saw the war as an opportunity to follow Wolfe Tone's dictum that 'England's difficulty is Ireland's opportunity'.

Amongst the IRB men there was a sense of moral obligation to fight that is difficult to understand today. Many of these men felt a sense of shame at belonging to the first generation of Irishmen for 120 years not to have risen with arms in their hands. As they saw it, the opportunity of a rising during the Boer War had been missed, but the chance provided now by the war should not be passed by. Above all, their initiative in creating the Irish Volunteers had given them an army to rise with.

Accordingly, on or around 9 September 1914, at a meeting in the Gaelic League's premises at 25 Parnell Square, Dublin, the Supreme Council of the IRB decided that the war provided the opportunity for a rising, which was to take place if any one of the following conditions arose: if the British attempted to enforce conscription; if the Germans invaded Ireland; or if the war seemed to be ending. The rising was to be accompanied by a formal declaration of war on England, bracketed with the demand that Ireland would be represented at the peace conference following the war's end. Padraig Pearse, who had been co-opted on to the Supreme Council the previous July, was one of those present at the fateful meeting. He was also Director of Organisation in the Volunteers.

Patrick Henry Pearse was the barrister son of an Irish mother and an English father. He was born in Dublin in 1879 and educated at the Christian Brothers' School, Westland Row. He was well known in Gaelic League and educational circles, being the editor of the League's paper, *An Claidheamh Soluis*, and the creator of a large body of literary work in both Irish and English. He also ran an innovative, if debt-burdened, school for boys, St Enda's, at Rathfarnham in the Dublin foothills, to further his ideal of an Ireland not merely free, but Gaelic as well. It was during a fund-raising visit to America for St Enda's that he became enrolled in the IRB. Subsequently his oratorial and literary gifts led to his being appointed first President of the Irish Republic.

A speech of his delivered in 1915 over the grave of the Fenian O'Donovan Rossa at Glasnevin Cemetery in Dublin attracted widespread attention. It contained something of his philosophy that death could be life-giving:

Life springs from death: and from the graves of patriotic men and women spring living nations. The Defenders of this Realm have worked well in secret and in the open. They think they have pacified Ireland. They think that they have purchased half of us and intimidated the other half. They think that they have foreseen everything, but the fools, the fools, the fools! . . . they have left us our Fenian dead, and while Ireland holds these graves, Ireland unfree shall never be at peace.

In December he developed the theme further, writing of the war:

> the last sixteen months have been the most glorious in the history of Europe. Heroism has come back to the earth . . . the people themselves have gone into battle because to each the old voice that speaks out of the soil of a nation has spoken anew . . . Belgium defending her soil is heroic, and so is Turkey fighting with her back to Constantinople . . . The old heart of the earth needed to be warmed with the red wine of the battlefields. Such august homage was never before offered to God as this, the homage of millions of lives given gladly for love of country . . . war is a terrible thing and this is the most terrible of wars, but this war is not more terrible than the evils which it will end or help to end.

These Rupert Brooke-like sentiments were not uncommon amongst romantics on both sides of the Irish Sea at that stage in the Great War's history, before the grinding horror of the conflict became more generally understood. They attracted attention at the time, and amongst revisionists who examined Pearse's career posthumously, revulsion. But it is a mistake to regard them as Pearse's most influential writings. The thoughts he expressed in his poem 'The Rebel' were still motivating militant Nationalists in Northern Ireland more than four-score years after he penned these lines:

> And now I speak, being full of vision . . .
> And I say to my people's masters: beware
> Beware of the thing that is coming, beware of the risen people,
> Who shall take what ye would not give.[52]

The IRB took hard, practical steps to create a 'risen people'. A military council was set up to plan the proposed insurrection. The IRB had officers throughout the Volunteers and it was arranged that when the decision to rise was put into operation, these men would take their orders from Pearse and Seán MacDermott, and not Eóin MacNeill. The military council consisted of Pearse, MacDermott, Thomas Clarke and Joseph Plunkett. Later they would form themselves into a provisional revolutionary government with the addition of three other names, James Connolly, who took charge of the military operations during the Rising, Eamonn Kent and Thomas MacDonagh.

Eamonn Kent (Irish form, Ceannt) was born in County Galway in 1881. He played the Uilleann pipes, the Irish version of the bagpipes, and was a member of the governing council of the Gaelic League. Thomas MacDonagh was born at Cloughjordan in County Tipperary in 1878 and educated at Rockwell College, Cashel. A respected poet and critic, he was a lecturer in English at University College, Dublin, and taught at St Enda's. Curiously for a man who spent his life defending literary and political freedom of expression, one of his heroes was the Florentine monk Savanarola, known through history for his book-burning activities.

One of the most exotic, and most determined, of the revolutionaries was Joseph Mary Plunkett, whose two brothers, George and Jack, were to fight alongside him in the coming rebellion. All three were sons of the papal Count

Plunkett, whom the IRB sent to Rome on the eve of the Rising to inform the Pope of their intentions and to assure his Holiness that he had nothing to worry about, that the Rising was a purely nationalistic, not a socialistic affair, a sentiment which James Connolly for one would hardly have approved of. Plunkett was born in Dublin in 1887. With his taste for flowing cloaks, bangles and jewellery, he appeared an unlikely revolutionary, particularly as he suffered from practically continuous ill-health. But he had an educated, enquiring mind with a hard edge to it. He studied philosophy and science, and, like MacDonagh, was a poet; the two men helped to found and edit both the *Irish Review* and the *Irish Theatre*. But he also had a taste for conspiracy and revolutionary planning. It was he who gave Michael Collins a copy of Chesterton's *The Man who was Thursday*, and advised him to act on the Chief Anarchist's advice: 'If you don't appear to be hiding, nobody seeks you out.' It was advice which Collins was to follow with spectacular results. Plunkett was appointed Director of Military Operations in 1916.

Plunkett's plans were based on those of Robert Emmet for the short-lived insurrection of 1803. Main Dublin centres were to be seized and roads and railways cut off to prevent reinforcements reaching the city. The Rising's headquarters was to be the General Post Office (GPO) in Sackville Street, Dublin's main thoroughfare. After making a stand in Dublin, the rebels intended to move north to rendezvous with Volunteer units in Tyrone. The plans depended on a number of things which did not materialise: a sizeable shipment of German arms, possibly even artillery; a submarine; and the help of German officers. Plunkett's planning also envisaged that the segment of the Volunteers which had not followed Redmond would immediately rise in arms, and that as the fighting wore on, the Redmondite section would also join in.

One essential component of Plunkett and the IRB's planning which did work almost to the last fateful moment was that neither Redmond nor the nominal leader of the Volunteers, Eóin MacNeill, should be given any idea of what was going on.

Despite the Orangemen's activities, and those of the Conservative Party, coming against the appalling backdrop of the nineteenth century, with its famines, evictions and transportations, Irish public opinion was pro-British. Within the ranks of the Volunteers, a majority were in favour of recruitment to the British army. Ameliorative legislation and educational and economic improvement had had their effect. Moreover, there was a long history of Irish recruitment to British regiments. In addition, Germany was Lutheran, while 'plucky little Belgium' was not merely seen as Catholic, but as the home of Louvain, with its traditional Irish connections and its priceless collection of Celtic manuscripts which the German onslaught had destroyed. Despite Bachelors Walk, Redmond's pledge that Britain could in safety withdraw her troops from Ireland struck a chord of acceptance. Union Jacks abounded, as did white feathers for young Irishmen who did not join up. The press was almost unanimously pro-British and pro-recruitment. Almost: a strongly dissentient note was struck in one paper, Arthur Griffith's *Sinn Féin*:

Ireland is not at war with Germany. She has no quarrel with any continental power. England is at war with Germany, and Mr Redmond has offered England the services of the National Volunteers to defend Ireland. What has Ireland to defend, and whom has she to defend it against? Has she a native Constitution or a National Government to defend? All know that she has not. All know that both were wrested from her by the power to whom Mr Redmond offers the services of National Ireland. All know that Mr Redmond has made his offer without receiving a quid pro quo. There is no European Power waging war against the people of Ireland. There are two European Powers at war with the people who dominate Ireland from Dublin Castle. The call to the Volunteers to 'defend Ireland' is a call to them to defend the bureaucracy entrenched in that edifice.

Our duty is in no doubt. We are Irish Nationalists, and the only duty we can have is to stand for Ireland's interests, irrespective of the interests of England, or Germany, or any other foreign country.[53]

This was the view of both the MacNeill and IRB factions within the Volunteers. The gulf between these factions and Redmond's followers became unbridgeable within a matter of weeks of the war's commencement. On 20 September, Redmond made a recruiting speech at Woodenbridge in County Wicklow, urging his listeners to join in the war 'in defence of right, freedom and religion'. The MacNeill wing of the Volunteers immediately issued a statement:

Mr Redmond, addressing a body of Irish Volunteers on last Sunday, has now announced for the Irish Volunteers a policy and programme fundamentally at variance with their own published and accepted aims and pledges, but with which his nominees are, of course, identified. He has declared it to be the duty of the Irish Volunteers to take foreign service under a Government which is not Irish. He has made this announcement without consulting the Provisional Committee, the Volunteers themselves, or the people of Ireland to whose service alone they are devoted.

Having thus disregarded the Irish Volunteers and their solemn engagement, Mr Redmond is no longer entitled, through his nominees, to any place in the administration and guidance of the Irish Volunteer organisation.[54]

The Volunteers' numerical strength at this stage is open to argument. Paper strengths were not necessarily the same as the numbers who turned up for drill sessions. Overall numbers tended to fluctuate, rising during times of excitation, and falling when nothing seemed to be happening. But following the Woodenbridge speech, it is estimated that out of approximately 180,000 Volunteers, the vast majority followed Redmond, leaving the IRB with a potential army of only some 12,000 men.

However, Redmond was to receive a very poor reward for his recruiting activities and pledges of loyalty. Though he acted in good faith, believing that England would also keep faith and introduce Home Rule after the war, neither at the outset of the war, nor after it, was any indication given of the change in Conservative and Unionist attitudes which would have been necessary to bring this about. Redmond's son was one of the many Nationalists to be refused a commission. Nationalists were not allowed to form their own regiments as were Ulster Protestants, despite their recent history. In fact in his War Diaries, Lloyd George opined that a contemptuous public snub to Irish Nationalists by the Minister for War, Lord Kitchener, was a 'sinister order [which] constituted the first word in a new chapter of Irish history'. At a public gathering, Kitchener decreed that a banner embroidered with the Red Hand of Ulster be honoured, while one emblazoned with a harp was ordered to be taken away. The banner had been created for a Nationalist regiment which never materialised. What did materialise, however, a matter of some months later constituted a body blow for Home Rule.

On 19 May 1915, Asquith, under wartime pressures, reorganised his government so as to form a coalition with the Conservatives. It included eight Unionists. Bonar Law became Secretary of State of the Colonies, Carson became Attorney General, F.E. Smith Solicitor General. Birrell's judgement on the Unionists' inclusion in Cabinet was that it was 'impossible to describe or over-estimate the effect of this in Ireland. The steps seem to make an end of Home Rule.' Redmond was offered a seat in Cabinet, but by now his position had become so undermined that he turned it down, stipulating only that Birrell remain as Chief Secretary for Ireland. Yeats later made a comment which summed up what even moderate Dublin feeling on the appointments must have been at the time:

> I have been looking for a historical precedent for the remarkable fact that certain Englishmen who afterwards became Cabinet Ministers and in other ways rose to the highest positions in the State went over to Ulster some 15 years ago and armed the people at a time of entire peace and urged them, and are now urging them, to use these arms against us. I have found a historical precedent which establishes that it is an old custom of the British Government. I have found that Edmund Burke in the middle of the eighteenth century drew attention to a very remarkable item in the Estimates of the year. It was an item of so much money for the purchase of five gross of scalping knives, which scalping knives were intended to be given to the American Indians that they might scalp the French.[56]

Birrell had long realised that by caving in to the Tories and the Ulster rebels over the Curragh Mutiny the British were storing up trouble for themselves, writing: 'Politics often consist of balancing one set of grave evils against another set, and after consideration the Cabinet, with my concurrence, decided to leave it alone, although by doing nothing they almost negate their right to become a Government at all.'[57]

By 1915, Augustine Birrell's job had become 'odious and hateful' to him. He feared that the introduction of conscription would precipitate 'shipwreck and disturbances on a big scale in Ireland'. 'Ireland,' he said, 'is, I am sure, in a rotten state – ripe for a row, without leadership.' He had done his best to provide that leadership, benign leadership at that, being responsible for many of the improvements which had come about in Irish society over the previous decades. But he increasingly became ground between the upper and nether millstones of Conservative and Unionist defiance and Nationalist rebelliousness.

Piaras Béaslaí wrote of Birrell, years after he had resigned in disgrace:

> There exists a curious idea in England to this day that Mr Asquith and Mr Birrell were in some mysterious way responsible for the Insurrection of Easter Week. As one who was working tooth and nail to bring about an insurrection, I can testify that the biggest obstacle that we had to contend against was the cleverness of Mr Birrell's policy. The one thing that would have rallied support to our side was drastic coercion on the part of the English Government; but Mr Birrell cleverly contrived to appear as not interfering with us, while taking care that we were effectually silenced. The Editors of anti-English papers and pamphlets were not proceeded against; the papers were not officially suppressed; but, under the Defence of the Realm Act, the printers who produced them were liable to be closed down.[58]

The effect of the Defence of the Realm Act was to create a 'mosquito press'. Polemical and short-lived papers and pamphlets called *The Spark, Honesty, Scissors and Paste* fell victim to Dublin Castle censorship, even though *Scissors and Paste*, for example, only printed items which had already appeared in respectable publications. Neither *Irish Freedom* nor *Sinn Féin* was considered respectable, and were forced to close. Griffith's weekly *Nationality* was killed by the outbreak of the Rising itself. The Irish Volunteers' paper, *The Irish Volunteer*, had a good run because, in the view of the IRB, the Orangemen were only loyal 'not to the Crown but the half crown'. Consequently they had the paper printed by an Orange firm in Belfast. The effect of these publications on London decision-takers served to make Birrell's position even more uncomfortable. He ardently sought recruitment to the British army and could point to the fact that 150,000 Irishmen had joined up voluntarily. But this did not satisfy London proponents of conscription like Field Marshal Sir Henry Wilson. Apart from the Unionist and Protestant ideology of Wilson and so many other War Office figures which caused them to regard the Catholic Irish as shirking their duty to Empire, there was the pressure to supply more cannon fodder to make up for the appalling slaughter in the trenches, much of it caused by the incompetence of British generalship. Dublin supporters not merely of conscription but of a crackdown against the increasingly active Nationalists also urged Birrell to act.

But public opinion, while not in favour of rebellion, was proving itself as being not in favour of conscription either. The Unionists' behaviour had created antagonisms, and the death toll amongst the Irish Nationalists who had volunteered was beginning to have its effect. Men appearing on charges of making anti-recruitment speeches began to be acquitted, although Seán MacDermott received a six-month sentence for his crime. The reaction to the six-month sentence encouraged the IRB to flout another measure which the authorities in desperation brought in to punish those opposed to recruitment – deportation, from Ireland, a part of the United Kingdom, to another part,

England! When served with deportation orders the rebels ignored them, were brought to court and received sentences of three or four months which were reckoned to be a cheap price to pay for the popular indignation which the verdicts aroused.

By the time 1916 dawned, matters had probably reached a point where even if Birrell had cracked down, the trouble would have only been temporarily contained and would inevitably have flared up later. But a number of events in the early part of the year should have given even Birrell cause to re-examine the softly, softly policy. One was the setting up of a base for 'refugees', men like Michael Collins who, scenting rebellion in the air, had returned from England or elsewhere abroad to take part in whatever was brewing. The refugees were located at Larkfield, the Plunkett family home in Kimmage, where Collins was employed, ostensibly as a 'financial adviser'. Apart from financial advice, those present were able to obtain tips on handling weaponry and making bombs. These went off with sufficient unpredictability, one would have thought, to attract some slight curiosity on the part of a vigilant police force. Other Republican prologues to the swelling theme of revolution included a mock takeover of the entire centre of Dublin enacted by the Volunteers on St Patrick's Day. At Tullamore, the police and Volunteers exchanged gunfire after wrathful local Loyalists had attacked the Sinn Féin headquarters following a demonstration against an Irish regiment leaving for the war.

These events helped to convince both the Lord Lieutenant, Lord Wimborne, who had been appointed in 1915, and the GOC of the Irish Command, Major-General L.B. Friend, that trouble was coming and should be headed off. Friend ordered a raid on Liberty Hall, the headquarters of both the IT&GWU and the Citizen Army, but Birrell countermanded the attack, fearing it would spark off a larger disorder. He and the Under-Secretary, Sir Matthew Nathan, discounted reports of an imminent rising, even when these appeared in Sinn Féin correspondence captured by British intelligence. Most inexplicably, the Irish executive failed to act on reports from Admiral Hall, the British Admiralty intelligence expert, who had intercepted messages between Clan na Gael in New York and the Germans in Berlin. These reports spoke of shipping movements, which Dublin apparently interpreted as meaning between New York and Dublin, not Germany and Dublin. In his desire to protect his sources, Hall apparently did not sufficiently enlighten the authorities.

Talk of German involvement in the Irish situation had been in the air on the Orange side of the dispute quite openly in the wake of statements such as those made by Carson and Crawford. In fact, such remarks had prompted the Ulster Liberal Association to publish a pamphlet, *The Kaiser's Ulster Friends*. In both Berlin and Vienna, the Conservatives' and Unionists' apparent willingness to contemplate civil war created speculation that this threat would render Britain unable to fight in an external war.

A lunch which Carson had with the Kaiser in Hamburg in 1913 seemed to bear out this supposition. Carson agreed with the Kaiser that he was opposed to Home Rule because he refused 'to be ruled by the priests'. A month later, a military expert, General von Bernhardt, opined in the *Berlin Post* that 'It is not without interest to know that if it ever comes to war with England, Germany will have allies in the enemy's camp, who in given circumstances are resolved to bargain, and at any rate will constitute a grave anxiety for England, and perhaps tie fast a proportion of English troops.' The heading of the article, 'Ireland, England and Germany', made it quite clear who the 'prospective allies' were. Later in the year, on 14 November, the *Irish Churchman* stated confidently:

> We have the offer of aid from a powerful continental monarch who, if Home Rule is forced on the Protestants of Ireland, is prepared to send an army sufficient to release England of any further trouble in Ireland by attaching it to his dominion . . . and should our King sign the Home Rule Bill, the Protestants of Ireland will welcome this continental deliverer as their forefathers under similar circumstances did once before.

Certainly there appeared to be sufficient interest in Berlin in taking Belfast's temperature for von Kuhlmann, the Counsellor of the German Embassy in London, to pay an incognito visit to Unionists on 12 July 1914, just before the war's outbreak. The Nationalists' leader, John Dillon, later informed the House of Commons that von Kuhlmann's report had determined the Kaiser on going ahead with the war. As we have seen, this view seems to have been shared by the United States' Ambassador to Berlin who was quoted by Lord Riddell as reporting to Washington that the German Department of Foreign Affairs believed England so preoccupied by events in Ireland that she would not declare war.[59] A.T.Q. Stewart, a distinguished Unionist historian, writes that Austria too took note of the Irish situation:

> On the 26th of July, Dr E. J. Dillon, a special correspondent in Vienna, telegraphed his newspaper that one of the reasons why Austria expected a free hand in dealing with Serbia was that the British Government was absorbed 'in forecasting and preparing for the fateful consequences of its internal policy in regard to Irish Home Rule', which may, it is apprehended, culminate in Civil War.[60]

Clearly the Irish situation was taken into account in Berlin and Vienna, but whether it received the weight accorded to it from their differing perspectives by Orange and Green polemicists is a moot point. It seems more likely that the Germans, prior to the outbreak of war, were pursuing a general 'the enemy of my enemy is my friend' policy. For example, as the Ulster Volunteers' guns were being loaded at Hamburg, much larger quantities of weapons were being put aboard German ships to Mexico, where the Germans wished to make difficulties for the Americans.

Where the Green component in the 1916 drama was concerned, German assistance fell well below IRB expectations. Immediately on war's outbreak,

John Devoy and a Clan na Gael delegation met the German Ambassador to America, Count von Bernstorff and his military aide, the then Captain von Papen. Devoy told von Bernstorff that the IRB meant to use the war to stage a rising, leading to the setting up of an independent Irish government. To assist this objective, they sought German armament and the training of German officers. Von Bernstorff made the Irishmen feel that their representations had been sympathetically received, but in fact advised Berlin against acceding to the Irish request lest it play into the hands of American Anglophiles to the detriment of Germany. The von Bernstorff approach continued to influence German attitudes towards the Irish revolutionaries, although it took the IRB's principal emissary to Berlin, Roger Casement, some time to realise this.

Casement, born in 1864 to Ulster Protestant parents in County Antrim, had a distinguished career in the British Consular Service, for which he received both a knighthood and international recognition after he had publicised the brutal treatment meted out to native labourers in both the Belgian Congo and the Latin American Putumayo. His espousal of the Irish cause moved from the writing of poems and articles supporting the Irish language, to helping to provide guns for the revolutionaries and attempting to enlist German support for them into the bargain. For this he aroused a hatred in British decision-taking circles which was to lead him to the scaffold. In their zeal to have him executed, the British circulated his diaries to Irish and Irish American leaders, which revealed that he was homosexual.

Casement arrived in Berlin from New York on 31 October 1914, having travelled under an assumed name, and successfully evaded an attempt by the British Consul in Norway to have him murdered. On 27 December he concluded an agreement with the German State Secretary, von Zimmerman, which amongst other provisions allowed for the setting up of an Irish brigade drawn from Irish prisoners of war in Germany. The brigade proved a non-starter. With a handful of exceptions, the Irish prisoners refused to join, either out of unwillingness to betray their comrades in arms, or because back in Ireland their dependants were receiving allowances. Joseph Plunkett also visited Berlin in the wake of the Zimmerman agreement, and was promised a shipment of arms. These were to arrive in Ireland the following spring, as were the promised German officers, and even an expeditionary force armed with artillery. The effect that these prospects had on the IRB planners, who did not have even one machine-gun at their disposal, can readily be imagined. But time would show that German support was to lie more in the realm of the imagination than the practical.

One of Casement's more lasting achievements was the foundation with Joseph Gaffney of a German-Irish Association. The Association, though it attracted the support of several leading political and military figures, amongst them the legendary air ace, Baron von Richthofen, was more culturally than militarily orientated. One of Casement's closer German friends was Kuno Meyer, who held the Chair of Celtic Studies at the University of Berlin. He had been a close ally of Douglas Hyde's in the fight to retain Irish on the Irish school curriculum, and set up a highly successful Irish Studies institute in Dublin. The formation of the Association, on 13 February 1916, elicited a message from the Kaiser which epitomised the German attitude towards Ireland: sympathy and all action short of meaningful support. It said: 'His majesty follows the struggle for liberation in brave Ireland with interest and lively sympathy, in the awareness that the German sword has led many a nation to liberty.'

However, German swords would prove to be in short supply. Actual German help was to fall well short of what the Irish envisaged. A shipment of arms was sent at the time agreed, Easter 1916, but no training officers, no expeditionary force. The Irish compounded the effects of these disappointments in two ways, one knowingly, the other unwittingly. The IRB decided the arms landings should be postponed from Maundy Thursday until after the Rising had actually begun, on the date selected, Easter Sunday. The reasoning was that an arms shipment arriving before the Rising began would tip off the British and allow them to strike first. Unfortunately, the British were already tipped off. Admiral Hall's team had succeeded in cracking the German codes, and were fully aware of every communication between the German Embassy in Washington and the Foreign Office in Berlin. Dublin was in fact informed that 'a Rising had been planned for Easter Eve', but this was where imprecision and a lack of liaison between the naval and military authorities set in. As was noted earlier, the significance of the fact that a ship was on its way to Ireland was not properly assessed.

But the Irish too were to suffer a damaging self-inflicted wound. Austin Stack, the local IRB commander, failed to organise the display of two pre-arranged green lights which were to have guided the German ship, the *Aud*, to the spot where the arms were to be landed on Tralee Bay. To compound this failure, three radio experts sent by Michael Collins to Kerry, charged with destroying the Government's radio station at Valentia and setting up the IRB's own transmitter with which to guide the German ship safely to anchor, took a wrong turning and drove off Ballykissane pier, near Killorglin. All three men drowned.

On the afternoon of 20 April, the *Aud* arrived off Inishtooskert Island in Tralee Bay after an epic voyage past British warships, masquerading as a Norwegian vessel. After nightfall, the captain, Karl Spindler, sailed further into the bay and began signalling the shore, but no green lights winked back. Eventually British warships descended on him, and he was ordered to Queenstown (Cobh), where he scuttled his ship, sending it to the bottom together with 20,000 rifles, 10 machine-guns, 1,000,000 rounds of ammunition, and all the hopes of the Irish revolutionaries for a successful rising. Worse was to accompany the *Aud*'s sinking. Roger Casement was also captured. He had returned to Ireland aboard a German submarine, the U19, which left Germany two days after the *Aud*. He had not come to further the Rising, however, but to call it off. He had discovered that the Germans were not sending artillery, or men, to Ireland, and realised that any uprising was doomed to failure.

For some reason, the submarine commander, Lieutenant Weisbach, the man who sank the *Lusitania*, made no effort to contact the *Aud*, although the ship came quite close to him. Instead he decided, not having sighted any green lights either, to put Casement and his two companions, Robert Monteith of the Dublin Brigade and Daniel Bailey, one of the few prisoners Casement had succeeded in recruiting to the ill-fated Irish Brigade, into a collapsible boat and let them make their own way to the shore as best they could. None of the three were oarsmen. The boat was inevitably overturned by the heavy surf which habitually breaks on Banna Beach. Casement almost died from hypothermia and was discovered, recovering from his ordeal, hiding in a nearby ruin known as McKenna's Fort.

Meanwhile, back in Dublin, further disasters were befalling the IRB's plans. Bulmer Hobson, the Volunteers' secretary, discovered that Volunteer units throughout the country were preparing to go to war on Easter Sunday. Hitherto Hobson, like MacNeill, had had no idea that anyone was contemplating using the Volunteers in an offensive rather than a defensive capacity. Accordingly, as the U19 fruitlessly cruised Tralee Bay, he got MacNeill out of bed to warn him of what was happening. MacNeill was appalled, and, stopping only to change into outdoor clothes, had Hobson drive him to Pearse's home, where a blazing row ensued. MacNeill warned Pearse that he intended to do everything he could short of ringing up Dublin Castle to prevent a half-armed force being called out for a hopeless, bloody encounter with a modern army. Tempers cooled somewhat later in the morning, after Pearse had got MacDermott and MacDonagh out of bed to go with him again to MacNeill to defend and explain their action.

MacDermott succeeded in talking MacNeill around to the IRB's way of thinking by using two arguments. One was the realpolitik position that the IRB was the de facto controller of the Volunteers, and could hold a rising whatever MacNeill ordered. The second and clinching argument was that there was now no way of avoiding hostilities anyway because of the arms landings in Kerry, which MacDermott mistakenly believed had gone ahead successfully. MacNeill sighed and decided: 'Well, if we have to fight or be suppressed, then I suppose I'm ready to fight.' He then got dressed for the second time that night, shook hands with Pearse and invited everyone to stay for breakfast. The Pearse–MacNeill accord was short-lived. Bulmer Hobson was kidnapped by the IRB. A prominent Volunteer leader, the O'Rahilly learned of the kidnapping and, brandishing a revolver, descended upon Pearse telling him that anyone who attempted to kidnap him would have to be a 'quicker shot'.

The altercation between the O'Rahilly, a respected Kerry businessman and a prominent Gaelic Leaguer, and Pearse encapsulated what might be termed the practical and the poetic positions on the wisdom of a rising. The O'Rahilly was appalled at the prospect of inevitable failure and loss of life, and in forthright terms denounced Pearse's arguments as being those of a poet and an idealist. This is exactly what they were. As the plans for the Rising caved in on him, Pearse did not waver one iota from the position he had taken up at the outbreak of the war when he said that:

> The European war has brought about a crisis which may contain, as yet hidden within it, the moment for which the generations have been waiting. It remains to be seen whether, if that moment reveals itself, we shall have the sight to see and the courage to do, or whether it shall be written of this generation, alone of all the generations of Ireland, that it had none among it who dared to make the ultimate sacrifice.[61]

The O'Rahilly then called on MacNeill, who was already in a disturbed state of mind, having read an item in the morning papers which stated that a man had been captured in Kerry after landing from a German submarine. MacNeill began writing a series of countermanding orders to be delivered to Volunteers throughout the country, telling them that no rising was to take place, no matter what instructions to the contrary they received. Late that afternoon, Easter Saturday, the O'Rahilly returned to his home in the company of two Kerry Volunteers, who made him aware of the identity of the captured man and the sinking of the *Aud*. Although a rising was now obviously hopeless, a final argument in St Enda's concluded with Pearse telling MacNeill: 'We have used your name and influence for all their worth. Now we don't need you any more. It's no use you trying to stop us. Our plans are laid and will be carried out.'

The men parted angrily, with MacNeill, still hoping that his intervention would bring home to the IRB the folly of a rising, giving Pearse until ten o'clock that evening to call it off. When ten o'clock came with no word from Pearse, MacNeill sent the O'Rahilly on an extraordinary journey throughout Ireland to deliver and disseminate his countermanding orders. He then personally arranged the publication of the following in the *Sunday Independent*:

> Owing to the very critical position, all orders given to Irish Volunteers for tomorrow, Easter Sunday, are hereby rescinded, and no parades, marches, or other movement of Irish Volunteers will take place. Each individual Volunteer will obey this order strictly in every particular.

When Pearse, Connolly, Clarke and the other members of the provisional government read the *Sunday Independent* the following morning, they realised, if they had not done so before, that the position was completely hopeless. However, their arguments centred not on for or against calling off the Rising, but on whether to postpone or not postpone. Clarke was in favour of going ahead that day, calculating that once fighting broke out in Dublin, Volunteers outside the city would join. Pearse and MacDermott disagreed. Connolly finally gave the casting vote in favour of a rising, beginning at noon the following day, Easter Monday, 24 April 1916. They had no illusions as to what they were doing. They knew their lives were forfeit. After the vote was taken, Clarke told Béaslaí: 'MacNeill has ruined everything, all our plans, I feel like going away to cry.' And as the rebels moved off the following morning from Liberty Hall, Connolly told William O'Brien, his successor as leader of the Irish Transport and General Workers Union: 'Bill, we're going out to be slaughtered.'

Anyone looking at the Volunteers' armament would have agreed with Connolly's assessment. Apart from a few modern Lee Enfield rifles, bought from British Tommies, a handful of Italian rifles, and the Howth guns which Childers had sailed in, their weapons ranged from the pathetic to the ludicrous. Some carried pikes, as used by the insurgents of 1798. These were a type of hooked spearhead, well adapted to slashing the reins of horses but useless against rifles. The heavy German Mauser rifles dated from the 1870s and only fired a single shot. These too were much inferior to the standard issue British Lee Enfield. The bullets were of the explosive or dum-dum variety, which created terrible exit wounds that were to be a contributory factor to the Volunteers' post-Rising popularity.

The Volunteers also carried crowbars, pickaxes and sledgehammers. Much of this weaponry was transported on horse-drawn carts; some in the O'Rahilly's motor car. The old-fashioned gallantry of the man was such that, having done all he could to call off the Rising during the previous 48 hours, he turned up at Liberty Hall saying: 'Well, I've helped to wind up the clock – I might as well hear it strike.' Another of the Volunteers' leaders, Joseph Plunkett, got out of his sickbed to join in the Liberty Hall proceedings. He had recently been operated on for glandular tuberculosis, and had to be helped out of bed and dressed by his aide, Michael Collins. With typical Irish raillery, instead of pondering on Plunkett's ghastly complexion, the O'Rahilly's gesture, the scarcity of arms or the enormity of what they intended to do, the Volunteers in Collins's vicinity proceeded to give him a 'slagging' over his resplendent appearance – he was wearing a Volunteer officer's uniform.

The rag, tag and bobtail army included a hansom cab and two motorbikes, and Roddy, Connolly's 15-year-old son. As midday approached, the lad marched after his father up Abbey Street, across O'Connell Street and into the GPO, to create a right-angled turning point in Irish history, away from Home Rule and towards republicanism, albeit, let it be said, a very Irish form of republicanism where women's role in the scheme of things was concerned. Cumann na mBan were not involved in the mobilisation plans, but immediately on hearing of the rebellion's outbreak bravely turned up at the various rebel-held strongpoints offering their services, only to be told initially to go home.

The GPO was easily taken. It was a bank holiday; much of the British army officer corps were at the Curragh Races, and the few soldiers present, like the rest of Dublin's population, were in a relaxed holiday mood, with nothing more serious in mind than the purchase of stamps. It being an Irish revolution, four actions of great symbolic significance then ensued. In one, Michael Collins discovered that, given their meagre armament, some Volunteers had preferred other means of fortification for the fighting that lay ahead and had come equipped with two tierces[62] of stout. Collins had these poured away, declaring: 'They said we were drunk in '98. They won't be able to say it now.' No one who witnessed his successful emergence from that episode can have been surprised at the subsequent series of miraculous escapes from capture and death which were to characterise his short, blazing career.

The second symbolic act was the hauling down of the Union Jack over the GPO and its replacement, by Gearóid O'Sullivan, the youngest Volunteer officer in the building, with two potent emblems. One was the customary green Irish flag, emblazoned with a golden harp but now accompanied by the extraordinary legend 'Irish Republic'. The symbolism of the other is almost as unfulfilled today as it was in the cauldron of the GPO. It was the flag of today's Irish Republic, the tricolour: green for the Gaelic and Irish tradition, orange for the Unionists, and white for peace between them. It had been given to the Young Irelanders, in place of the arms they had hoped for, by Lamartine, the poet and politician, in a gesture more redolent of politics than poetry.

The third piece of symbolism was the most significant of all. It was the reading of a document which was to cost its signatories their lives – the 1916 Proclamation declaring an Irish republic.

Poblacht na h-Eireann
The Provisional Government of the Irish Republic
To the People of Ireland

Irishmen and Irishwomen: in the name of God and of the dead generations from which she receives her old tradition of nationhood, Ireland, through us, summons her children to her flag and strikes for her freedom.

Having organised and trained her manhood through her secret revolutionary organisation, the Irish Republican Brotherhood, and through her open military organisations, the Irish Volunteers and the Irish Citizen Army, having patiently perfected her discipline, having resolutely waited for the right moment to reveal itself, she now seizes that moment and, supported by her exiled children in America and by gallant allies in Europe, but relying in the first on her own strength, she strikes in full confidence of victory.

We declare the right of the people of Ireland to the ownership of Ireland and to the unfettered control of Irish destinies, to be sovereign and indefeasible. The long usurpation of that right by a foreign people and government has not extinguished the right, nor can it ever be extinguished except by the destruction of the Irish people. In every generation the Irish people have asserted their right to national freedom and sovereignty: six times during the past three hundred years they have asserted it in arms. Standing on that fundamental right and again asserting it in arms in the face of the world, we hereby proclaim the Irish Republic as a Sovereign Independent State, and we pledge our lives and the lives of our comrades-in-arms to the cause of its freedom, of its welfare and of its exaltation among the nations.

The Irish Republic is entitled to, and hereby claims, the allegiance of every Irishman and Irishwoman. The Republic guarantees religious and civil liberty, equal rights and equal opportunities to all its citizens, and declares its resolve to pursue the happiness and prosperity of the whole nation and of all its parts, cherishing all the children of the nation equally, and oblivious of the differences, carefully fostered by an alien government, which have divided a minority from the majority in the past.

Until our arms have brought the opportune moment for the establishment of a permanent National Government, representative of the whole people of Ireland, and elected by the suffrages of all her men and women, the Provisional Government, hereby constituted, will administer the civil and military affairs of the Irish Republic under the protection of the Most High God, Whose blessing we invoke upon our arms, and we pray that no one who serves that cause will dishonour it by cowardice, inhumanity or rapine. In this supreme hour the Irish nation must, by its valour and discipline, and by the readiness of its children to sacrifice themselves for the common good, prove itself worthy of the august destiny to which it is called.

Signed on Behalf of the Provisional Government,
Thomas J. Clarke
Scán MacDiarmada
Thomas MacDonagh
P.H. Pearse
Eamonn Ceannt
James Connolly
Joseph Plunkett

After Pearse had finished reading, Connolly shook his hand, saying, 'Thanks be to God, Pearse, that we live to see this day.'

The fourth piece of symbolism occurred later in the day. A Cumann na mBan delegation finally managed to contact the IRB leaders in the GPO and wrest from them a mobilisation order which recalcitrant rebel commanders around the city agreed to accept in all cases but one. Throughout the week, Eamon de Valera refused point blank to allow any women to join his men. Elsewhere, throughout the fighting, the women cooked, acted as nurses, carried dispatches, and showed by their contribution and demeanour that they were conscious of taking part in an event of significance.

It cannot be said that Dubliners showed a similar sense of history. L.G. William Redmond-Howard, a nephew of John Redmond, who witnessed the scene, said:

There was practically no response whatever from the people; it seemed the very antithesis of the emancipation of the race, as we see it, say, in the capture of the Bastille in the French Revolution . . . Instead of eagerly scanning the sheets [of the Proclamation] and picking out the watchwords of the new Liberty, or glowing with enthusiastic admiration at the phrases or sentiments, most of the crowd bought a couple as souvenirs – some with acute business instinct that they'd be worth a fiver each someday, when the beggars were hanged.[63]

Just before the rebels burst into the GPO, the man in charge of it, Sir Hamilton Norway, the Secretary of the General Post Office, received a phone call from the Under-Secretary for Ireland, Sir Matthew Nathan, summoning him to Dublin Castle for a meeting with the Castle's military intelligence officer, Major Ivor Pierce. At long last, the British had decided that a rising was imminent and a crackdown had to be initiated. Ten minutes after Norway left his office, the rebels entered it. As he was signing the necessary orders in the Castle, the rebels attacked it. The British now knew the exact time of the Rising's commencement.

The senior British officer in Ireland at the time (General Friend had taken the weekend off to go to London), General W.H.M. Lowe, had a total of some 4,650 men at his disposal when the Rising broke out. The bulk of the troops were in the Curragh Camp, County Kildare. An additional thousand were sent from Belfast and further thousands arrived within days from England. The troops were armed with machine-guns and artillery. With no doubt unconscious symbolism, the first 18-pounder to be deployed was at Grange Gorman Lunatic Asylum. Equally lunatic was the first British military response – a cavalry charge down Sackville Street, under the waiting guns of the GPO. However, lunacy was not the sole prerogative of the British. Including the Citizen Army, the insurgents had just 1,200 troops at their disposal, and no artillery or machine-guns. One result of the paucity of manpower was that the Castle, which was largely undefended, was not seized by the rebels after the initial attack.

A number of strongpoints were captured along with the GPO: the South Dublin Union, James's Distillery, Jacobs Biscuit Factory, the Four Courts, St Stephen's Green, and Boland's Bakery, plus two attendant vantage points, Clanwilliam House, and number 55 Northumberland Road. Lowe's response to the seizures was to begin driving wedges between the principal rebel strongpoints. One ran from Kingsbridge, the south's major railway station, to Dublin Castle, and down Dame Street to Trinity College. A cordon was thrown around the GPO and the Four Courts in order to cut off the rebels' headquarters from their other Dublin positions.

By the end of the week, these arrangements proved to be successful. Apart from their lack of armaments, lack of manpower meant that the IRB failed to take a number of strongpoints which would have been invaluable to them and, as a consequence, were equally valuable to the British. Amongst these were the Crown Alley Telephone Exchange, Trinity College, and the Shelbourne Hotel, which overlooked the flower beds and ornamental lake of St Stephen's Green which were seized by Michael Mallin and Constance Markievicz, a piece of strategic thinking which can hardly have contributed to a dispelling of trust in female militarism within the ranks of the Volunteers. However, though the rebels were speedily driven out of this easily enfiladed position, they commandeered the College of Surgeons building, which also overlooked the Green, and fought bravely and effectively until ordered to surrender.

The fighting was almost solely confined to Dublin, although a few isolated engagements took place outside the city. The Fingal area of North County

Dublin was dominated by a mobile party of some 50 Volunteers, led by Thomas Ashe and Richard Mulcahy. This squadron was to be the precursor of the IRA's 'flying columns' which were used in the subsequent Anglo-Irish war. The men had bicycles, and Ashe himself possessed a motorbike. Apart from capturing the small towns of Donabate, Garretstown and Swords, Ashe's men took part in an engagement at Ashbourne in County Meath in which 11 members of the RIC were killed and a number wounded. There was also a shoot-out at Castlelyons in County Cork where the three Kent brothers, David, Richard and Thomas, held off a party of soldiers and police, their mother loading and reloading the rifles for them. The Kents only surrendered after Richard had been killed and David severely wounded.

However, the confusion and countermanding which had gone on before the Rising began meant that neither in Cork City nor in Limerick, both vital to Plunkett's plans, did the Volunteers take action. In both Galway and Wexford minor actions occurred, resulting in the taking of the town of Enniscorthy and the taking to the hills in Galway of a group of volunteers led by Liam Mellows, without hostilities occurring in either place. In County Louth, north of Dublin, the rebels also captured an RIC barracks in Castlebellingham.

These seizures would hardly have provided the springboard for the emergence of the contemporary Irish Republic were it not for the manner in which the rebels fought in Dublin. Apart from the GPO itself, a couple of other areas deserve particular mention. One of these was the Mount Street Bridge area, which became known as the Irish Thermopylae through a combination of the manner in which the insurgents fought, and the British army's complete disregard for the casualties inflicted on the Tommies. On the very first day of the Rising, Easter Monday, the Volunteers served grim warning of what was to come on a corps of middle-aged Home Defence veterans who, unknown to the Volunteers, were unarmed. They had been on manoeuvres with unloaded rifles at Kingstown (now Dun Laoghaire) six miles away when news of the Rising broke. Following the slaughter of the veterans, the Volunteers made it a rule not to fire on men, even uniformed ones, who could not defend themselves. But later in the week, after reinforcements were landed at Dun Laoghaire, the Sherwood Foresters were deliberately marched into the Mount Street Bridge area once more. Even when casualties mounted, and the troops' commanding officer sought permission simply to by-pass the area and march into Dublin by another route, General Lowe forbade the diversion and ordered that the strongpoint be taken at all costs. Thus a tiny handful of Volunteers killed or wounded four officers and 215 'other ranks'. Half the total British casualties were sustained in the Mount Street Bridge area.

De Valera took no direct part in the action. His command post at Bolands Mill lay some hundreds of yards to the east. But the fact that the Irish Thermopylae occurred in his area, and that the Volunteers involved were under his command, coupled with the fact that he was the only commandant to survive 1916, later contributed greatly to his mythical stature. He excited such loyalty that it was only when the fiftieth anniversary of the Rising was being commemorated in 1966 that some of the survivors of Boland's Mills made public the fact (in interviews with the journalist Max Caulfield for his book *The Easter Rebellion*) that he had suffered a temporary nervous breakdown and had been forced to rest.

The end of the fighting was a foregone conclusion. Cut off from the rest of the country, confronted by vastly superior forces, many of them Irish units like the Dublin Fusiliers, and even ex-Volunteers who had answered Redmond's recruiting call, the rebels had no chance of success. But their desperate resistance later became a factor in the Nationalists' success. British artillery shells turned the centre of Dublin into an inferno. At night, people took to the hills around the city to watch the flames, and in their light could clearly see Nelson on his pillar from a distance of 10 miles.

Eventually, after holding out until Saturday, the rebels were forced to vacate the now blazing GPO and escape under heavy fire into nearby Moore Street. By then, the heat inside the GPO had become so intense that when hoses were aimed at its barricades to prevent them igniting, the water immediately turned to steam. By now, also, Connolly had been badly wounded in the ankle and was in great pain. The O'Rahilly was killed in the final charge from the GPO; his last act before lapsing into unconsciousness was to write a note to his wife explaining why he had taken part in the Rising. Many other acts of defiance would also shortly pass into Irish folklore.

Connolly had asked a young Volunteer, Seán Heuston, to hold the Mendicity Institute for four hours, to enable the Four Courts area to be fortified. Heuston held it for 50, and the defence of the Four Courts/North King Street area itself would also pass into legend for other reasons, not all of them concerned with heroism, as we shall see.

Neither legend nor folklore were to the forefront of the rebels' minds that Saturday afternoon in April 1916. After making a fruitless attempt to negotiate with Lowe, Pearse was forced to sign an unconditional surrender note, which was eventually accepted by the rebel garrisons around the city.

The Rising had killed, or badly wounded, about 1,350 people. Some 61,000 square yards of building were destroyed at an estimated cost in the values of the day of some £2,500,000. The centre of Dublin was burned out, and close to a third of the city's population was on public relief. Throughout the Rising, the shortage of food and of gas had created great hardship. Widespread looting had added to the anger of the population.

However, General Sir John Maxwell, who was sent over from London to assume overall command of operations, becoming a sort of de facto military governor, soon began to swing the pendulum of popularity back towards the rebels. Having issued a proclamation in which he said that he 'found it imperative to inflict the most severe sentences on the organisers of this detestable Rising, and on the Commanders who took an actual part in the actual fighting', he soon translated words into action.

On 3 May, Pearse, Clarke and MacDonagh were shot. Twelve other executions followed at intervals until the 12th, when public opinion forced their halt. Amongst those shot were some of the men who had fought most bravely: Seán Heuston, for example, and Edward Daly, who had commanded the North King Street area, which Heuston had been protecting. Daly had ordered that the Volunteers' meagre rations be shared with captured British soldiers, and at risk of their lives had his men put out fires which he feared would spread and place civilians at risk. North King Street received a poor return for Daly's chivalry; 15 civilians were deliberately shot in the area by members of the South Staffordshire regiment. Documents kept secret from the public until the year 2001 later revealed that the authorities felt that had the incidents occurred in England, the soldiers responsible would have been tried for murder, but that overall responsibility for the shootings was largely attributable to an order of Lowe's that no prisoners be taken.[64]

Other executions which helped to sway public opinion were those of Joseph Plunkett, who was married to his fiancée, Grace Gifford, in his cell, ten minutes before being shot; Willie Pearse, who had taken no part in the planning of the Rising, and was shot merely because he was Padraig Pearse's brother; and James Connolly, whose wounds were so serious that he had to be strapped into a chair to face the firing squad. Connolly's last words to his wife were: 'The Socialists will never understand why I am here. They will all forget I am an Irishman.' Before he died, he prayed: 'Father forgive them. They know not what they do.'[65]

In the wake of their executions, the last words and the unflinching demeanour of the condemned men had the effect of making many people 'remember that they were Irishmen'. But not immediately.

TWO

AFTERMATH AND CIVIL WAR

(1916 TO 1922)

In the immediate aftermath of the Rising, the anger directed at the rebels by the citizens of Dublin was such that prisoners' recollections of the period contained statements like: 'If it weren't for the fact that we were so strongly guarded by British troops, we would have been torn asunder by the soldiers' wives in the area.'[1] More civilians had been killed than the combined total of the British and Irish military casualties. Some 2,000 people had been wounded, and for the citizens of Dublin, the period had been one of food and gas shortages, looting and terror. The soldiers' wives, 'separation women' as they were known, because they received separation allowances while their men were at the front, were simply more abrasive in their reaction than the rest of the population. The Rising was of course condemned by press and pulpit. The Bishop of Ross, Dr Kelly, summed up the sentiments of many members of the hierarchy by describing the rebellion as 'a senseless, meaningless debauch of blood'. The *Irish Catholic* echoed the Bishop's tone, declaring the Rising 'as criminal as it was insane . . . traitorous and treacherous'. The Protestant Archbishop of Dublin went a step further, writing to *The Times* on 4 May, to urge the Government that 'This is not the time for amnesties and pardons; it is the time for punishment, swift and stern.'

The two leading secular newspapers, the *Irish Times* and the *Irish Independent*, went further, siding with the Protestant Archbishop. The *Irish Times* declared that 'the rapine and bloodshed of the past week must be punished with a severity which would make any repetition of them impossible for many years to come'. The *Irish Independent*, owned by William Martin Murphy, Connolly's adversary in the great lock-out, called for Connolly's execution, although without naming him. On 10 May, the paper printed an editorial article which noted that some of the leaders were still awaiting sentence (these included Connolly), and went on:

> When, however, we come to some of the other ringleaders, instigators and formentors not yet dealt with, we must make an exception. If these men are treated with too great leniency, they will take it as an indication of weakness on the part of the Government . . . let the worst of the Rebels be singled out and dealt with as they deserve.

The Unionists of Dublin signed a memorial, protesting against any step which would interfere with the commanders-in-chief of the forces in Ireland (i.e. to carry out executions), and the operation of martial law. The Dublin Chamber of Commerce demonstrated its loyalty to both the Crown and the half crown by writing to Buckingham Palace protesting its loyalty and its abhorrence at the Rising. The Chamber went on to blame the Irish Executive for what had happened, saying that 'the carnage could have been avoided were it not for the gross and imponderable laxity, long continued' of the Irish Government. Therefore, the Chamber argued, the Imperial Treasury should repay 're-building costs, etc'.

However, other more prescient comments began to be heard. The rebellion had not even ended when the *Glasgow Observer* (29 April 1916), while condemning the bloodshed and destruction, went on to say:

> No Irish Nationalist should grovel to his British neighbour over what happened in Dublin on Monday. It was simply the consequences of what happened earlier at Larne when the associates and followers of Sir Edward Carson flouted and defied the law of the land, held up its legal guardians and engaged in military operations. . . . Hand in glove with them in the lawlessness was Mr Bonar Law, now a Coalition Minister and Sir F. E. Smith, then Carson's 'galloper', now Attorney General for England. The Carsonite Rebellion, for that is what it was, was not merely tolerated and utilized by the whole Tory Party . . . Larne begat Dublin.

As tales of the Rising, the destruction, the gallantry, the looting, were still spreading throughout a startled country, news of the executions of some of the leaders began to spread also. The sounds of the firing squads began to be heard shortly after the gunfire of the rebellion died away. They soon drowned out the sound of the critics of the Rising. A sharp and very public divergence from the attitude of the bishops quoted above occurred with the publication of an angry letter from the Bishop of Limerick, Dr Edward O'Dwyer, to General Sir John Maxwell on 17 May. Maxwell had written to the Bishop complaining of the Nationalist activities of two of his priests. The Bishop replied:

> . . . you appeal to me to help you in the furtherance of your work as military dictator of Ireland. Even if action of that kind was not outside my province, the events of the past few weeks make it impossible for me to have any part in proceedings which I regard as wantonly cruel and oppressive. You remember that Jameson raid, when a number of buccaneers invaded a friendly state and fought the forces of the lawful government.
>
> If ever men deserved the supreme punishment it was they. But officially or unofficially the influence of the British Government was used to save them and it succeeded. You took care that no pleas for mercy should interpose on behalf of the poor young fellows who surrendered to you in Dublin. The first information which we got of their fate was the announcement that they had been shot in cold blood.
>
> Personally I regard your action with horror, and I believe that it has outraged the conscience of the country. Then, the deporting of hundreds, and even thousands, of poor fellows without a trial of any kind seems to me an abuse of power, as fatuous as it is arbitrary, and altogether your regime has been one of the worst and blackest chapters in the history of the misgovernment of this country. I have the honour to be, sir, your obedient servant.
>
> Edward Thomas, Bishop of Limerick.

The executed men were tried before military courts held in camera, and the first the public knew of the trials was when the news of their executions was announced. There were 15 in all, spread out over nine days until public opinion called a halt. By the time Roger Casement was executed on 3 August, when all danger from the rebellion was long since past, England was already losing the propaganda war.

A commission of inquiry into the cause of the Rising found the mandatory scapegoats. Birrell was accorded most of the responsibility, and his political career came to an end. The Under-Secretary, Sir Matthew Nathan, was also censured, but he later went on to a distinguished career in the public service. Maxwell too suffered. He was refused the rank of full general, which he had held in Egypt, and transferred to a dead-end job as GOC, Northern England. A military man, he had been placed in a position created by politicians, encouraged to take a firm hand, and then blamed when he did so. In his time in Ireland, he developed a grasp of the situation and an affection for the people. In June, he made an assessment that:

> Though the Rebellion was condemned it is now being used as a lever to bring on Home Rule, or an Irish Republic. There is a growing feeling that out of Rebellion more has been got than by constitutional methods, hence Mr Redmond's power is on the wane . . . It is becoming increasingly difficult to distinguish between a Nationalist and a Sinn Féiner . . . If there was a General Election, very few, if any, of existing Nationalist MPs would be re-elected so there is a danger that Mr Redmond's party would be replaced by others perhaps less amenable to reason.[2]

Maxwell concurred with the *Glasgow Observer*'s judgement, saying that the basic cause of the outbreak was the latitude allowed to Carson and the Ulster Volunteers. He advocated the installation of an executive which would 'meet a warm-hearted people half way in addressing grievances'. Amongst these latter he included absentee landlordism and the appalling poverty of Dublin which 'could easily be prevented'.

Had his advice been taken, it would have prevented much of what was now to befall.

By the end of the summer, news of the prisoners' fortitude in the face of death had spread. James Connolly had been in such pain from his wounds that he had to be given morphine to enable him to sleep. He was woken up to be told he would be shot at dawn. At his last meeting with his family, he patted his distraught wife on the head and said, 'Don't cry Lilie, you'll unman me.' Joseph Plunkett's last moments on earth also passed into folklore. Already dying, following an operation on his neck for tuberculosis, he was married by candlelight to Grace Gifford on the morning of his execution. Soldiers stood by with fixed bayonets as an officer ticked off the seconds of the ten minutes allotted to the couple to be together before Plunkett was taken out to be shot. Pearse's last words to his court-martial were: 'You cannot extinguish the Irish passion for freedom. If our deed has not been sufficient to win freedom, then our children will win it by a better deed.'[3]

Theories as to what form that 'better deed' might take began to circulate amongst the prisoners rounded up in widespread swoops in the wake of the rebellion. Too widespread. People who were in no way connected with the IRB or Physical Force went into camp or jail either on the word of an informer, because they were members of the Gaelic League, or for any of the myriad reasons that motivate panic-stricken police forces in the aftermath of a catastrophe. In all, some 2,500 were arrested. Initially the prisoners were scattered throughout a variety of British prisons of which Dartmoor and Lewes became the most prominent. A prisoner-of-war camp was established at Frongoch, near Bala, in north Wales. This became the principal 'Republican University' of the period. Men with professional qualifications and men with no education were brought together in a ferment of new books, ideas and interchange which provided revolutionary graduates who would change the course of Irish history.

Michael Collins, the best known of those, began to reorganise the IRB in the camp, using the wide variety of inmates to ensure that the doctrines of Wolfe Tone would be carried to the four corners of the land when internment ended. The IRB was structured on a cell system wherein only the cell, or circle, leader knew all the members, and how to make contact with the circle above him. Collins was elected head of the Frongoch IRB cell. Later he would become president of the Supreme Council, in effect the boss of the entire brotherhood. He was thus ideally placed to implement the theories he began to evolve in the wake of the Rising concerning a new form of warfare, that of the urban guerrilla, and the 'flying column' based on the methods of the Boer farmers under the famous South African guerrilla leader, de Wit. The insurgents became guerrillas by night and returned to their farms by day. It had become obvious to Collins that while the Rising had kept faith with the past, and with Wolfe Tone's doctrine of striking at England while she was preoccupied with the Great War, and was certain to go down in history as one of the most gallant of the Irish revolutionary tradition's long litany of gallant failures, that was all it was: failure, another sorrowful decade of the Rosary. 'Static warfare', the seizure of a fortified building or mountain, from which the rebels could eventually be blasted by superior man- and firepower, did not bring victories.

In Frongoch also, the 'Republican University' saw the setting of one of those stern tests of the human spirit which, in the coming decades, would provide martyrs, inspiration and eventually political gain for the physical force school: a hunger strike. The strike broke out over the prisoners' refusal to give their names to the authorities, both to frustrate attempts to find out who was who in the revolutionary movement and to prevent the prisoners from being conscripted. The hunger strike and press publicity interacted with the swing in public opinion, particularly in America, which forced the British to reconsider their Irish policy to such an extent that on 21 December an amnesty was declared, and the Frongoch men were released.

By this time, Irish America had become a factor in the situation. A descendant of Robert Emmet's brother, Dr Thomas Addis Emmet, had set up a relief fund in the wake of the Rising, which was patronised by tycoons of industry, bishops, archbishops and Irish men and women of every walk of life. The British were desperate for American aid; the 'saving of the British army' alluded to earlier was being achieved by the terrible blood-letting at Verdun and elsewhere. But the British Ambassador to Washington, Sir Cecil Spring Rice, informed the Cabinet that the Irish in America 'have blood in their eyes when they look our way', as a result of the executions.[4] Spring Rice went on, 'I do not think we can count on American help, perhaps not even on American sympathy . . . the attitude towards England has been changed by recent events in Ireland . . . If we are able in some measure to settle the Home Rule question at once, the announcement will have a beneficial effect here.'

As 1916 was an American presidential election year, Spring Rice's and similar advice had to be heeded. Lloyd George was given the problem of accommodating the Nationalists' demand for Home Rule in the face of the Unionists' opposition to it. The scheme he devised and the effect it had was later described by the old Irish Party leader, William O'Brien, as 'an unhappy instrument' to which 'must be traced the responsibility for all the years of disappointment, bloodshed, and devastation that were to follow'.[5] It is no exaggeration to say that the Lloyd George proposals are still having unhappy consequences as this is being written. But it is also true to say that all they did was to give written acknowledgement to what had been in his mind when he gave T.P. O'Connor a bad case of depression at Marienbad. Briefly, what happened was that at the end of May 1916, Lloyd George gave both Carson and Redmond proposals for immediately bringing into operation the postponed Home Rule Act of 1914, but for the 26 counties only. Antrim, Armagh, Derry, Down, Fermanagh and Tyrone, the six north-eastern counties which increasingly became known as 'Ulster' – though as already mentioned, the province of Ulster also includes Donegal, Cavan and Monaghan – were to be excluded for an indefinite period. The proposed Bill was to

remain in force during the continuance of the war and a period of twelve months thereafter; but, if Parliament has not by that time made further and permanent provision for the Government of Ireland, the period for which the Bill is to remain in force is to be extended by Order in Council for such time as may be necessary in order to enable Parliament to make such provision.

Carson of course had not the slightest intention of allowing the six counties to come under the sway of Dublin, and had poured scorn on the idea of 'a sentence of death with a stay of execution' – though any form of Home Rule for Ireland was unwelcome to the Unionists, partition, if it had to come, also had to be permanent. John Redmond, however, believed that this would not, and could not, be the case and publicly denied a report in the *Irish Times* that partition was intended to be permanent, and that Lloyd George had given

Carson a guarantee to this effect: 'that statement is an absolute lie . . . the proposals are temporary and provisional. If they were not, I would oppose them.'

It was not the first time that Redmond had been hoodwinked. The covering note which Carson had received with his copy of the proposals contained the following from Lloyd George: 'We must make it clear that at the end of the provisional period Ulster does not, whether she wills it or not, merge in the rest of Ireland.'[6] As Redmond discovered that he had been deceived, and as this realisation sank in more widely amongst Nationalists already turning from Redmond's party, he withdrew his assent to Lloyd George's 'unhappy instrument' on 24 July. The electoral vacuum deepened, and Ireland continued to be governed, or at least administered, by the executive located in Dublin Castle.

However, within a few weeks of the Frongoch prisoners' release, there was a by-election in North Roscommon, and Count Plunkett, father of Joseph, and of George and John, still in jail in England, announced that he would stand. Apart from his family connection with the Rising, he was the object of increased public sympathy at the time, because on 20 January, the Royal Dublin Society, then dominated by freemasonry, expelled him due to his sons' activities.

The increasing support for the 1916 men was demonstrated by Plunkett's victory. He defeated his Irish Parliamentary opponent almost two to one, by 3,002 votes to 1,708, and after his election announced that he was going to abstain from Westminster. By now, Plunkett, and those like Michael Collins who campaigned for him, were referred to generally as 'Sinn Féiners'. But there was a dichotomy in the views of the forces loosely grouping under the Sinn Féin banner. A meeting at the Mansion House on 19 April found great difficulty in harmonising the views of Sinn Féin, Labour, the Volunteers and Count Plunkett's personal followers. Collins, and those who thought like him, were in favour of that part of Griffith's policy which espoused abstention and self-sufficiency. But they shared neither his opposition to violence, nor his recognition of the British Crown. The more socialist-minded remembered Connolly's injunction to his men to 'hold on to your rifles'. Connolly was keenly aware that the Nationalists and the Socialists had different agendas. However, the various strands agreed to entwine on a number of basic issues: abstention, the sending of a delegation to the peace conference after the war, which America had just entered, and the contesting of another by-election in May 1917 in Longford.

By now, Michael Collins was reorganising the Volunteers, the IRB and Sinn Féin, under cover of his post as secretary to the Irish National Aid fund set up by Tom Clarke's widow, Kathleen. He was establishing links with Clan na Gael in New York, and building up IRB contacts in the United Kingdom in the major Irish centres, Glasgow, Liverpool, London and Manchester. As part of the Sinn Féin thrust, he was strongly in favour of contesting the Longford by-election, which was to have considerable significance both through its outcome and by virtue of the fact that it would appear to be the first occasion on which Collins and de Valera differed on a major policy issue. De Valera wrote from Lewes jail that 'As regards the contesting of elections question, it is so extremely dangerous from several points of view that most of us here consider it unwise.'[7]

Collins and his cohorts went ahead and enthusiastically fought a winning campaign for another Lewes jail candidate, Joseph McGuinness, a member of a prominent Longford family. De Valera's stated objections were said to be twofold: fear of a loss of face for the men of 1916 should the candidate be defeated; and a refusal to acknowledge the British parliament. However, as he disregarded these arguments when he was chosen shortly afterwards as a by-election candidate himself, it is legitimate to speculate that his real objection to the McGuinness selection was that, as the sole surviving commandant of 1916, and the prisoners' leader in Lewes jail, he felt that his reputation entitled him to have been selected to contest Longford. As it was, McGuinness narrowly won (by only 37 votes) with the aid of one of the most effective election posters in Irish electoral history. It showed a man in prison uniform, and an inscription reading: 'Put him in to get him out'.[8]

The election of a convicted criminal posed serious problems for the British Government. Count Plunkett's victory could be seen as being due to a sympathy vote, but McGuinness's triumph had repercussions on Irish American sentiment. In an effort to placate Irish and Irish-American public opinion, Lloyd George set up a convention in Dublin to 'recommend a settlement of the Irish problem'. The convention proved to be a non-starter when it met on 25 July. Sinn Féin were allocated 5% of the membership, but Griffith refused to attend a convention whose delegates were nominated by the British Government, and announced that he would only go if the delegates were elected by the Irish people. However, another initiative connected with the convention had better-received and more far-reaching effects. On 15 June, in order to create 'a favourable atmosphere for the Irish Convention', Bonar Law announced that the remainder of the 1916 prisoners were to be released unconditionally. Had there been any remaining doubts about the change in post-Rising sentiment, the return of the Lewes men dispelled them. Frank Thornton's account of his return to Dublin a little over a year since he had departed it was literally the direct opposite of the atmosphere following the Rising:

> . . . there was a terrifically enthusiastic crowd on the pier at Dun Laoghaire . . . We were escorted to our carriages on the train and when we arrived at Westland Row our real trouble started . . . the crowd nearly tore us asunder. Every man was trying to carry some other man out to the coaches outside . . . We were carried out to the open brakes outside Westland Row and escorted through the city by a huge crowd of people up to Fleming's Hotel in Gardiner Place. Here a royal feast awaited us . . . we were back in Dublin with a determination. The surrender of 1916 was only a breathing space between that and the commencement of war proper for the freedom of the country.[9]

'The commencement of war proper' began immediately, with the prisoners affixing their signatures to an address to the President and Congress of the United States containing a quotation from President Wilson's recent ringing address concerning 'the right of each people to defend itself against external aggression, external influence . . .' A second important step in the war was the selection of de Valera to contest the by-election in East Clare, caused this time by the death in action in France of John Redmond's brother, Major William Redmond. De Valera, all reservations about contesting elections cast aside, stepped triumphantly on to the national stage, on 10 July, defeating his Irish Parliamentary Party rival by 5,010 votes to 2,035. Apart from de Valera's emergence, the by-election was also significant for the fact that, for the first time since the Easter Rising, the Volunteers publicly appeared as a uniformed disciplined force who not only acted as election workers, but kept order during both candidates' meetings. This last was a notable demonstration of moral force – the Volunteers were armed only with sticks – during a particularly heated election contest. A month later, another 1916 veteran, W.T. Cosgrave, won Kilkenny for Sinn Féin in a further by-election. Sinn Féin were on the march.

But so too were the Volunteers. Sinn Féin's stated aim was the restoration of 'the King, Lords and Commons', whereas the Volunteers stood for the Republic declared in the 1916 Proclamation. However, in the self-sacrificing manner which characterised his career, when a Sinn Féin convention was held in the Mansion House on 25 October 1917, Griffith announced that he was retiring in favour of de Valera, 'a soldier and a statesman'. Accordingly, de Valera became president and Griffith vice-president of the organisation which Griffith had founded. Two days later, at the GAA's premises at Jones's Road, Drumcondra, de Valera was also elected president of the Volunteers. Collins became director of organisation, and a number of IRB men were placed in key controlling positions on the Volunteer executive. As a result of these manoeuvrings, de Valera obtained support from both Sinn Féin and the Volunteers for the following policy declaration: 'Sinn Féin aims at securing the international recognition of Ireland as an independent Irish Republic. Having achieved that status, the Irish people may, by referendum, freely choose their own form of government.'[10]

However, the road towards that 'international recognition' was getting progressively stonier. There had been one notable Sinn Féin/Volunteer casualty in the month preceding de Valera's election as president. On 25 September, Thomas Ashe, one of the heroes of 1916, died after forcible feeding in Mountjoy Jail. He had been on hunger strike for political status. Clad in a Volunteer uniform, his body lay in state at the Mater Misercordiae Hospital, and was visited by some 30,000 people. In their greatest public display of strength since the Rising, the Volunteers took over the city for the funeral. At the graveside, Collins made a short, ominous speech, following the firing of three volleys by Ashe's colleagues: 'Nothing additional remains to be said. That volley which we have just heard is the only speech which it is proper to make above the grave of a dead Fenian.'[11]

Dead Fenians there would be in plenty before long, but the most important death after Ashe's was that of the Irish Parliamentary Party leader, John Redmond, in the following March. The cynicism and political chicanery with which his Conservative and Unionist opponents had greeted his sincere efforts to find a peaceful solution to the Anglo-Irish issue were a poor reward for his years of parliamentary endeavour. In retrospect, his espousal of the cause of recruitment to the British army seems both naive and ill-judged, and certainly helped to send thousands of young Irishmen to their deaths. Even his friend Augustine Birrell judged that he had 'taken the curve too soon'. The conscription issue and Redmond's fate, drowning in a tide of pro-Sinn Féin sentiment, a shattered, disillusioned figure, would henceforth stand as an awful warning for Irish Nationalists when faced with the prospect of trusting English statesmen.

However, in the latter part of 1917, through 1918 and beyond, the activities of British statesmen held out little prospect that they would win the trust of any Irish Nationalist. The question of conscription hung over Ireland, and over the efforts of the British Government to find a solution to the Irish problem. Bloodbaths like those at the Somme, a macrocosm of the slaughter of young Tommies at Mount Street Bridge a few weeks earlier, made the military desperate for new sources of cannon fodder. With a breathtaking disregard for the manner in which the Home Rule Bill had been obstructed by Unionists and their sympathisers, like himself, Sir Henry Wilson told the Cabinet in October of 1917 that with Europe 'in anguish', Ireland 'had no real grievances' but that actual rebellions and seditious acts were being promulgated.

The last statement was certainly correct. There were still people alive who remembered the famine, a burning issue in the folk memories of the people. Sinn Féin became alarmed at the rate with which food was being exported from the country because of the war, and introduced illegal policies of its own to encourage tillage. Cattle were driven off land, especially in the west, and Sinn Féin supervised its use. Landlords were supposed to receive rent from the tillers of the soil, but whether practice equalled the theory is decidedly a moot point. What is certain is that the cattle drives and the subsequent ground-breaking became the subject of much local excitation, some of which spread to Sinn Féin headquarters, which became alarmed at the socialistic character of the land seizures and issued a directive condemning them. The British issued directives of a more draconian nature. As the Volunteers were also carrying out raids for arms, it was declared illegal to carry arms in Clare, Galway or Tipperary, while Clare was also declared a military area which no one could enter or leave without a passport. Other Sinn Féin activities included seizing animals destined for export, slaughtering them and selling them to local butchers, the proceeds then being passed on to their owners.

Trying to contain Sinn Féin, grapple with the conscription issue, and at the same time come up with a solution to the Home Rule crisis which would satisfy both Unionists and Nationalists, and mollify Irish-American opinion, proved an impossible task for a British Cabinet now heavily Conservative and Unionist in membership. The Foreign Secretary, Viscount Grey, argued that an improvement in American sentiment was dependent on a solution which he expected to come on the basis of 'separate treatment' for Ulster, i.e. partition.[12] He reminded the Cabinet of how damaging the extraordinary latitude extended to Carson's illegal activity appeared in Washington:

> They regard it as unfair that Carson should have been allowed to import arms into Ulster from Germany. Arms which were to have been used against the policy of the British Government. They regard it as very unfair that these arms should not have been seized or molested, while arms used by Nationalists are seized . . . They also point to the fact that Carson has twice been taken into the Cabinet . . . and that the other day the first announcement in the American papers that the Cabinet was considering a new Irish policy contained the statement that Carson had been called into consultation with the Cabinet.[13]

The Irish Cabinet Committee,[14] which was set up (on 11 April 1918) to draw a Home Rule Bill for Ireland, was in favour of Ireland as a whole being granted dominion status, but the Government, in the words of Arthur Balfour, was 'unalterably averse to granting independence from any of its parts',[15] and did not concede that Ireland, all Ireland, had a 'separate national existence'.[16]

However, Balfour, who may be taken as the authentic view of unionism at the Cabinet table, differed sharply from Grey. Too intelligent a man to attempt to evade reality, he conceded that despite all that had happened, the Unionists had not won the argument. 'I admit that for many reasons, amongst which the British party system is not the least important, the Unionist policy has not succeeded . . . The only really workmanlike alternative to preserving the Union is the excision from it of the south and west of Ireland . . .' Though both he and Grey, albeit from different viewpoints, conceded the principle of partition, Balfour differed sharply from the Government's attitude towards the Unionists:

> On the one hand, they make it as easy as possible for Ulster to join itself with the rest of Ireland in forming a 'dominion' state. On the other hand, they give it no power whatever to remain what it is, and as I think ought to be, an integral part of the UK.
> . . . is it tolerable that we should take by force from our loyal fellow countrymen for no better reason than that they should live in the same island with those who proclaim their disloyalty in every quarter of the world.

The Government finally decided to square all these conflicting viewpoints by simultaneously issuing Home Rule proposals and introducing conscription to Ireland. The attempt fell at the first hurdle. As indicated earlier, the convention which Lloyd George set up to placate Irish-American opinion had very little credibility because its members were nominated by the British Government, and it was boycotted by Sinn Féin. However, it was to this body rather than its own Irish Cabinet Committee, containing some of the most important British politicians of the day, that Lloyd George now turned. The convention reported on 5 April 1918, proposing a parliament for Ireland, which would have only those powers that the British supervening parliament decided it should have. Until it did so, the Irish Assembly would have no control over customs, the postal service, the army or the navy. A minority report proposed a form of dominion Home Rule, as it was called, which would in effect have given Ireland less than the autonomy enjoyed by the existing dominions. Moreover, 40% of the seats in the lower house were to be allocated to Unionists, although it will be recalled that the actual number of Irish seats won by the Unionists had never exceeded 23 out of 105. In view of the mountainous upheavals over Home Rule, these proposals obviously constituted something of a legislative mouse. But with a monumental disregard for Irish public opinion, the British bracketed them with an announcement that the Military Service Act was to be introduced to Ireland, and on 16 April, 11 days after the convention reported, pushed the Military Service Bill through the House. The Bill did more damage to the Act of Union than Daniel O'Connell, the Fenians and Parnell combined ever did. The Irish Parliamentary Party reacted by withdrawing from the House of Commons, thereby ending a tradition of Irish representation which had lasted for 118 years.

Irish public opinion went into convulsions. On 18 April a meeting representative of every strand of Nationalist opinion was convened in the Mansion House under the chairmanship of the Lord Mayor, Laurence O'Neill. The meeting agreed to publish two statements drawn up by de Valera. The first declared: 'Denying the right of the British Government to enforce compulsory service in this country, we pledge ourselves solemnly to one another to resist conscription by the most effective means at our disposal.' It was agreed that this pledge would be made available for signature at church doors the following Sunday. The second statement, which was handed to the newspapers immediately, also called for resistance, but went on to say ominously that: 'The passage of the Conscription Bill by the British House of Commons must be regarded as a declaration of war on the Irish nation.' Having agreed the two statements, the meeting then appointed an All Party Delegation to drive to Maynooth, where the Irish Catholic hierarchy was meeting, to call on the bishops to issue an anti-conscription statement. Their lordships did so in the following terms: 'We consider that conscription forced in this way upon Ireland is an oppressive and inhuman law which the Irish people have a right to resist by every means that are consonant with the law of God.'

This statement had an enormous effect, and the Mansion House pledge collected vast numbers of signatures from every Catholic church gate in the country. The agitation was of immediate benefit to Sinn Féin. The party had recently begun losing by-elections in Nationalist areas of northern Ireland because the Unionists voted for Irish Parliamentary Party candidates. But following the Mansion House meeting, the Irish Parliamentary Party withdrew its candidate for by-election in County Offaly, and the Sinn Féin candidate was returned unopposed. A week after the by-election, the entire country, with the exception of Belfast, was closed down by a one-day general strike called by Labour. It was quite obvious to any observer that Ireland was going over to Sinn Féin, horse, foot and artillery, but far from abandoning its plans for conscription, the Government accelerated them. It began by reshuffling its Irish Executive so as to remove any vestige of pro-Nationalist sentiment. Lord Wimborne could hardly have been accused of being over-infected with that particular virus, but he was replaced by Field Marshal Lord French, who was given the title Lord Lieutenant-General and General Governor of Ireland, which had obvious resonances of military rule. The Chief Secretary, Henry Duke, was replaced by Edward Shortt, General Sir Frederick Shaw replaced Sir Bryan Mahon at the Military Command, and various other changes followed. The British were gearing up for hostilities. Sir Henry Wilson recorded in his diary that 'Lloyd George impressed on Johnny [Lord French] the necessity of putting the onus for first shooting on the rebels.'[17] To this end, the provisions of the Defence of the Realm Act (DORA) were liberally applied, to prohibit not only militaristic displays such as drilling, and the bearing of arms, but also Irish language classes, Gaelic football matches, Irish dancing competitions, and even athletic competitions.

A pretext for targeting Sinn Féin itself came on 12 April with the capture of Joseph Dowling, a member of Casement's Irish Brigade, who had been landed off the Galway coast by a German submarine. Apparently it was intended that he would set up lines of communication between Sinn Féin and the Germans. But he was a low-level emissary who only managed to establish communication with the wares of the public house in which he was captured shortly after landing. The British used his capture, however, to generate a wealth of propaganda concerning a supposed 'German plot', and on 17 May launched a series of arrests of Sinn Féin leaders. Collins learned of the impending swoop in advance, and warned those concerned, including de Valera, not to go home. His advice was not heeded, and amongst those picked up were de Valera, Arthur Griffith, Count Plunkett, William Cosgrave, Tom Clarke's widow Kathleen, and Countess Markievicz. The German plot arrests had two important consequences. First, they effectively left the running of Sinn Féin and the Volunteers in the hands of Collins and his friend Harry Boland, an equally militant IRB man; and second, they removed de Valera from the Irish scene at a crucial period, thus weakening his first-hand appreciation of events and both literally and figuratively placing distance between him and Collins. The Danton and Robespierre of the Irish Revolution were setting off on separate courses which would ultimately lead to destruction.

Faced with the uproar in Ireland, the British Government hesitated to introduce either conscription or Home Rule for the rest of that year. The signing of the Armistice removed the first, but not the second, issue from the table. A general election followed the ending of the war on 14 December, and

Sinn Féin won 73 out of 105 seats, gaining a majority in all but four counties, Antrim, Derry, Armagh and Down. The Irish Parliamentary Party was wiped out, falling from 80 to six seats. Unionists won only 315,394 votes out of a total of 1,526,910, roughly the same four-fifths majority for Home Rule which had existed since Gladstone's day. The difference was that this time Nationalist Ireland had not merely voted for Home Rule, which Britain found great difficulty in contemplating; they had voted for an All Ireland Republic, completely independent of England. Even though much of the vote cast had been for peace, not war, in gratitude because of Sinn Féin's opposition to conscription, which had kept sons and loved ones at home, conflict now became inevitable.

In the heady atmosphere of the moment, violence and bloodshed appeared remote, however. When the first meeting of the Dail, described as the 'Parliament of the Republic of Ireland' was held in the Mansion House, Dublin, on 21 January 1919, the atmosphere was such that the *Times* correspondent wrote: 'The proceedings throughout were orderly and dignified, not a word being uttered that could produce ill-feeling.' Orderly and dignified the proceedings certainly were, but a better analyst of the Irish scene than the gentleman from *The Times* would have found considerable potential for ill-feeling in the proceedings.

To begin with, that first Dail, which was presided over by the Nationalist Cathal Brugha, who had been left for dead during 1916 but somehow survived his wounds, held a roll-call which included the Unionists who had been returned to Westminster in the general election. This list included names like Carson and Craig, who of course would not have touched the Dail with a forty-foot bargepole. Nevertheless, they were solemnly declared to be '*as lathair*' (absent). So too were Irish Parliament Party representatives including Captain W. Redmond and Joseph Devlin. Of the Sinn Féin MPs, 40 were declared to be either '*ar dibirt ag gallaib*' (deported by the foreigner) or '*fé ghlas ag gallaibh*' (jailed by the foreigner). Collins and Harry Boland were absent also, arranging, as we shall see, to spring de Valera from an English prison, and in fact only 28 Sinn Féiners were marked present.

But this quorum made a declaration of independence, sent a message to the free nations of the world and adopted a democratic programme which contained provisions which some of the Sinn Féiners (including Collins) were later to find 'too socialistic'. The programme declared that 'all right to private property must be subordinated to the public right and welfare', and that citizens were entitled to have 'an adequate share of the produce of the nation's labour'. However, it was not the Socialist but the Nationalist components of the declaration of independence and the message to the free nations which one would have thought would have set the alarm bells ringing for the *Times* correspondent. The former stated:

We the elected representatives of the ancient Irish people in the National Parliament assembled do, in the name of the Irish nation, ratify the establishment of the Irish Republic and pledge ourselves and our people to make this Declaration effective by every means at our command.

We ordain that the elected representatives of the Irish people alone have power to make laws binding on the people of Ireland, and that the Irish Parliament is the only Parliament to which that people will give its allegiance.

We solemnly declare foreign government in Ireland to be an invasion of our national right which we will never tolerate, and we demand the evacuation of our country by the English Garrison.

The message to the free nations of the world was equally inflammatory. It called

upon every free nation to uphold her national claim to complete independence as an Irish Republic against the arrogant pretensions of the England founded in fraud and sustained only by an overwhelming military occupation and demands to be confronted publicly with England at the Congress of Nations in order that the civilised world, having judged between English wrong and Irish right, may guarantee to Ireland its permanent support for the maintenance of her national independence.

By a notable, and eerie, coincidence, as these documents were being made public, a party of Volunteers held up a party of RIC who were escorting a load of gelignite at Soloheadbeg, County Tipperary, and deliberately shot two of the policemen dead. Perhaps not surprisingly, from a combination of this shooting, which might be taken as the commencement of a new phase of the Anglo-Irish struggle, and the meeting of the first Dail, the public from then on began to refer to the Irish Volunteers first as the Irish Republican Army, and then as the IRA.

The application of the Defence of the Realm Act kept the prisons filled, and presented a corresponding challenge to Collins and his friends to organise jail breaks. Some of these were so audacious that in one, from Mountjoy jail, 20 prisoners made their way over the walls via a rope ladder, while five others with their hands in their pockets apparently clutching revolvers held up the warders. Later it was discovered that the 'revolvers' were in fact spoons, and the resultant publicity benefited the Sinn Féiners enormously. Further publicity came from a riot led by Austin Stack in Crumlin Road jail, Belfast. The Republicans barricaded themselves into a wing of the prison for a fortnight, having first laid in food and water. Meanwhile outside, Orange mobs threatened sectarian riots in reprisal. As prison contests often do, the Crumlin Road protest ended in a victory for the prisoners. It was agreed that a Volunteer, John Doran, would be regarded as a political prisoner, and placed with Stack and the others rather than the criminal prisoners. Even when prominent Republican prisoners were transferred to English jails for safety, Collins managed to get them out. Six prisoners escaped from Strangeways Prison, while Volunteers held up the traffic to allow them to climb down the ladder in safety.

The effect of all these raids and rallies was to temper the spirit of the younger Volunteers. 'Irish classes' being held around the country were in fact Volunteer training camps, at which Republican commanders like Dick McKee, the officer commanding the Dublin Brigade of the IRA, turned farm labourers into guerrillas. The change in spirit which the efforts of the Volunteers had on recruits was a crucial factor in the coming struggle. During de Tocqueville's visit, he had commented to a priest on 'the admiral virtue' of a starving people in seizing neither the grain nor the animals belonging to the local landlord. The priest replied:

> You must have no illusions, Sirs. Religion doubtlessly counts for much in this patience; but fear counts for even more. This unfortunate population has been so long a butt for so cruel a tyranny, it has been so decimated by the gibbet and transportation, that all energy has finally left them. They submit themselves to death sooner than resist. There is not a population on the continent that in the face of such miseries would not have its Three Days.[18]

The dissipation of that fear from the formation of the Volunteers onwards through 1916, and in the period of reorganisation that followed, was what made the IRA campaign of 1919–21 possible. The Volunteers moved from the nearly unimaginable step of taking on the RIC, to the British army, in heavily garrisoned areas where traditionally police and army were regarded as being omnipotent. The unemployed Volunteers were badly armed and 'on their keeping'; in other words dependent on the local population for food, shelter and clothing. An authenticated story[19] of the period records how two IRA leaders, Seán Treacy of Tipperary, and Michael Brennan of Clare, having spent time in jail under DORA, decided that henceforth they would carry arms and fight to the death if necessary to resist arrest. As this obviously involved taking on the British Empire, the two men decided to check the financial resources available to them to further their combined onslaught. Brennan had one shilling and sixpence, Treacy fourpence. Nevertheless, Treacy was one of those who fired the fatal shots at Soloheadbeg a few days later.

Initially not everyone on the Sinn Féin side wanted to go to war. Figures like de Valera, Griffith and Darrel Figgis realised that there was a difference between widespread public support for the Nationalists and condoning the shooting of detectives. At this stage, *circa* early 1919, Collins was engaged in a variety of activities, organising a national loan and overseeing the development of both the Volunteers and Sinn Féin itself. He was also working on the creation of an elite hit squad, whose job would be to assassinate spies, informers and political detectives; in a word, building up the unique network ranging from railway porters to policemen, to typists in Dublin Castle, to contacts in the higher echelons of the civil service, which was to make him the world's first urban guerrilla leader, or, in modern nomenclature, terrorist.

But while Collins, Boland, McKee and those who thought like them believed that Ireland stood to gain more from a general state of disorder than from political activity, de Valera succeeded in imposing his contrary view-point on the firebrands.

The prison escape of the period which attracted most attention had been that of de Valera himself on 3 February 1919 from Lincoln jail. Collins organised that a key be smuggled in in a cake, and de Valera and two other prominent prisoners, Seán McGarry and Seán Milroy, were able to walk out under cover of darkness.

However, de Valera became involved in controversy with his colleagues almost from the moment he left the jail. He had decided while in prison that the best thing he could do was go to America and publicise the Irish cause there. Collins and the rest of the Volunteers GHQ thought that this would be disastrous and represented as cowardice. It was decided to send Cathal Brugha to the safe house in Manchester where de Valera was hidden after the escape, in order to persuade him that if he must go to America, he should at least first come to Ireland, so that the publicity value of his escape would be maximised. Eventually de Valera agreed to this and Collins had him hidden in the gate lodge of the Archbishop of Dublin's house in Drumcondra. Here he occupied himself by drafting a statement for the peace conference in Paris. Collins meantime, characteristically without consulting his colleagues, was busy arranging a huge public welcome for de Valera. The centrepiece of this was intended to be a presentation of the keys of the city to de Valera by the Lord Mayor at Mount Street Bridge, the defence of which had done so much to enhance de Valera's fame.

Understandably, de Valera liked the idea and prepared a strongly worded speech for the occasion. The speech was destined never to be delivered. An influenza epidemic was raging at the time, and this, combined with the publicity surrounding de Valera's escape, decided the authorities, after a prisoner had died in jail, that the best thing to do was release all the Sinn Féin prisoners, including Arthur Griffith. The return of Griffith and the others precipitated an acrimonious meeting of the Sinn Féin executive at which Darrel Figgis brought the political wing of the leadership directly into conflict with the 'forward' party led by Collins. Figgis demanded to see the minutes of the executive, which had sanctioned the Mount Street reception. Collins told him bluntly that he had made the decision in Sinn Féin's name only. The real authority had been 'the proper body, the Irish Volunteers'.[20]

Though he didn't know it at the time, Collins was here highlighting a dilemma which would confront Irish Nationalist politics throughout the century, the relationship of a militant second authority with a constitutionally elected Sinn Féin. On this occasion, the constitutionalists won. In a letter de Valera accepted the validity of their fears that the planned reception would lead to violence: 'I think you must all agree with me that the present occasion is scarcely one on which we would be justified in risking the lives of citizens. I am certain it would not . . . We who have waited know how to wait. Many a heavy fish is caught even with a fine line if the angler is patient.'

De Valera's standing may be judged from the fact that the Dail now elected him its president, with the Irish title of Priomh Aire, which means First Minister in English. However, when he got to America, he was described as 'President of the Irish Republic', which was easier for Americans to understand, but which was to prove a Laocoön-like toil at a crucial juncture in Irish history some years later, as we shall see. De Valera appointed a Dail ministry in which Collins was Minister for Finance, Arthur Griffith Home Affairs, W.T. Cosgrave Local Government, Countess Markievicz Labour, Eóin MacNeill Industries, and Robert Barton Agriculture. The Dail showed itself to be somewhat ahead of its time in appointing Markievicz, the first woman in Europe to be so honoured, and was considerably ahead of British opinion in its decision to open what were termed 'embassies' in France and Washington, with Seán T. O'Kelly and Dr Pat McCartan as 'ambassadors'. Collins was authorised to launch a national loan of £1,000,000. This he managed to do throughout the ensuing period of warfare, although the British had declared the loan illegal. Collins also held a variety of other positions, in both Sinn Féin and the Irish Republican Brotherhood, all of which demanded a great deal of time and energy.

Another decision of the Dail, which was carried unanimously, was to have literally fatal results. De Valera proposed that 'members of the police force acting in this country as part of the forces of the British occupation and as agents of the British Government be ostracised socially by the people'. MacNeill seconded the motion, saying: '. . . the police in Ireland are a force of spies. The police in Ireland are a force of traitors, and the police in Ireland are a force of perjurers.' Collins then had himself smuggled into detective headquarters in Brunswick Street by Eamonn Broy, a detective in Dublin Castle, and spent the night going over secret police records, to study how the force of spies and perjurers might be combated. He made the simple but profoundly important discovery that everything the ordinary police force recorded of a political nature then wound up in the hands of a relatively small group of detectives attached to the 'G Division' or Political Section of the Royal Irish Constabulary. Collins realised that if these men were eliminated, the intelligence-gathering system would be paralysed. As he said himself, 'the new man could not step into the dead man's shoes *and* his knowledge'. Accordingly, on 9 April 1919, he ordered that a number of G men be approached by Volunteers, and warned of the consequences which would follow if they continued their intelligence activities. Several of the detectives took the hint, but others did not, and on 30 July the warnings progressed to shootings with a fatal attack on a well-known Dublin detective, 'the Dog' Smith, near his home in Drumcondra.

The reaction of the authorities was to ban Sinn Féin and with it, on 12 September, the Dail. Bad days lay ahead.

One of the main theatres of the propaganda war which the Irish and British now found themselves engaged in was America. As we have seen, de Valera was so keen to avail himself of Irish-American support that he wanted to go straight to America following his jail escape, and had to be persuaded to pay a visit to Ireland first. Having spent a few months at home, he eventually left for the US in June 1919 and did not return until Christmas 1920. The importance of America was fully recognised by the Nationalists. On 12 April 1919, the Dail passed a motion proposed by Michael Collins.

> The elected Parliament and Government of the Irish Republic pledge the active support of the Irish Nation in translating into deed the principles enunciated by the President of the US at Washington's Tomb on 4th July, 1918, and whole-heartedly accepted [by America]. We are eager and ready to enter a World League of Nations based on equality of rights, in which the guarantees exchanged neither recognise nor imply a difference between big nations and small, between those that are powerful and those that are weak. We are willing to accept all the duties, responsibilities and burdens which inclusion in such a League implies.[21]

The most important source of recognition was Washington, and when President Wilson passed through London on his way to the peace conference in Paris, which hoped to create a new world order and instead led to the Treaty of Versailles and World War II, a Sinn Féin delegation which included Collins made an unsuccessful effort to hold a meeting with the President. Wilson argued that peoples had a right to live under governments which they themselves chose. But as Margaret MacMillan has pointed out:

> [he] had no sympathy for Irish nationalists and their struggle to free themselves from British rule. During the Peace Conference he insisted that the Irish question was a domestic matter for the British. When a delegation of nationalist Irish asked him for support, he felt, he told his legal adviser, like telling them to go to hell. His view was that the Irish lived in a democratic country and they could sort it out through democratic means.[22]

Given the importance of the Irish in America, and of course his own basic empathy with the rights of small nations, Wilson was prepared to make a distinction between his antipathy towards the Irish-American leaders whom he suspected of being pro-German, and the situation in Ireland itself. But his advice in Ireland tended to come from Anglo-Irish sources, Sir Horace Plunkett, the chairman of the Irish Convention, and the writer Sir Shane Lesley, a landowner, patron of the arts and cousin of Winston Churchill. However, he did send an emissary, George Creel, to Ireland, who met with Collins and other Sinn Féin leaders before briefing the President on conditions.[23] Creel's verdict was that the strength of the Irish-American lobby was such that an Irish settlement had to be found. He thought that dominion status on the lines of either Australia or Canada was the best solution, as Home Rule would no longer satisfy Irish nationalism. He felt (rightly) that Lloyd George was not to be entirely trusted over Ireland and that if prevarication and delay set in, 'sentiment in Ireland and America will harden in favour of an Irish Republic'.

Evidence of the truth of Creel's assessment came shortly after he reported to the President. The House of Representatives passed a resolution sponsored by Thomas Gallagher of Illinois, saying 'That it is the earnest hope of the Congress of the United States of America that the Peace Conference now sitting at Paris and passing upon the rights of various peoples will favourably consider the claims of Ireland to self-determination.' The demand for Irish representation in Paris put the President in something of a cleft stick. Britain had been his staunch ally in the recent war, and Wilson needed equally staunch support now to further his post-war aims, one of which was a strong League of Nations with America at the helm. Had he achieved this position, Wilson fully intended to try to advance Ireland's claims for self-determination. However, ill health and changes in American politics frustrated his hopes.

Irish hopes were to be frustrated also. By way of backing up the Gallagher resolution, which, though trumpeted by de Valera as an instruction to Wilson to support Ireland's claim, never received Senate approval, an Irish delegation met Wilson in New York on the night the resolution passed in the House of Representatives. The meeting took place in a bad atmosphere. Wilson had agreed to meet the delegation on condition that the Clan na Gael leader, Daniel Cohalan, withdrew from it. Wilson had a number of scores to settle with Cohalan. One was the fact that Cohalan had campaigned against his nomination for the presidency at the 1912 Democratic convention. Another was Cohalan's German contacts in the run-up to 1916. Above all, as he told the delegation, he could not intervene as they wished in Britain's domestic policy. The delegation was acting on resolutions passed at a huge Irish race convention held in Philadelphia the previous month (22 and 23 February). One of these resolutions which did find a degree of favour with Wilson was the appointment of an Irish delegation to the peace conference in an attempt to secure a hearing for Ireland.

But the visit to Ireland of three men, prominent Irish-Americans chosen to report to Wilson on the delegation issue, so annoyed the British that in the event no Irish delegation was allowed at the conference. The three were Frank P. Walshe, a lawyer who had been joint president of Wilson's War Labour Conference Board, Michael J. Ryan, a leading Philadelphia lawyer, and Edward F. Dunne, the Governor of Illinois and a former mayor of Chicago. Before going on to Paris, the three men went to Ireland for a 10-day visit (beginning on 3 May) during which they addressed the Dail and received a rapturous welcome throughout the country. A contemporary description of their reception in Galway records that when the men appeared, 'We cheered 'til we were hoarse. I remember less of what they said than of what they meant to us, something outside of Ireland herself and working for her freedom.'[24]

The Unionists took a correspondingly opposing view of the Americans' visit and the speeches they made. The Lord Mayor of Belfast refused to meet them. London took its tone from Belfast rather than Galway. Even the King pressed Lloyd George to demand from Wilson 'a disavowal of the action of these American citizens'.[25]

By the time the three men reached Paris, the damage was done. Although he had poured cold water on Irish-American aspirations to be received at the peace conference, Wilson had subsequently worked assiduously to secure a right of audience for the Irish, and in fact had very nearly succeeded when the storm generated by the Americans' Irish visit burst. He told the three men: 'We were well on the way to getting Mr de Valera and his associates over here, we were well on the way, when you made it so difficult by your speeches in Ireland that we could not do it . . . it was you gentlemen who kicked over the applecart.'[26]

He was pressed by the Irish-Americans to reconcile his attitude with his celebrated statement to Congress of 11 February 1918 that 'national aspirations must be respected; peoples may now be dominated and governed only by their own consent. Self-determination is not a mere phrase. It is an important principle of action which statesmen will henceforth ignore at their peril.' The beleaguered President was by now feeling the repercussions of his words in countries as far apart as Africa, India and Korea, and he made the famous reply: 'You have touched on the great metaphysical tragedy of today.'

The Irish-Americans, like Sinn Féin, opposed Article 10 of the Covenant of the League of Nations, which stated that 'The High Contracting Powers undertake to respect and preserve against external aggression the territorial integrity and existing political independence of all State members of the League. In case of any such aggression, the Executive Council shall advise upon the means by which this obligation shall be fulfilled.' Metaphysics aside, it was certainly a tall order to expect Wilson to act in accordance with this Covenant, and at the same time support a self-proclaimed Irish Republic, which Great Britain did not recognise, in disrupting the territorial status quo of the United Kingdom. Wilson summed up his dilemma succinctly: 'We are utterly at a loss how to act in the matter without involving the Government of the United States with the Government of Great Britain in a way which might create an actual breach between the two.'[27] Apart from this difficulty, he also had to contend with the hostility to the League of Nations which existed in America amongst both Irish-Americans and his other political opponents. A resolution from which the Sinn Féiners took heart passed by the Senate on 6 June expressed sympathy with the aspirations of the Irish people 'for a Government of their own choice' and asked that the Irish be admitted to the peace conference. But the resolution was a sham designed merely to make trouble for Wilson and the League of Nations. One of its principal supporters, the influential Senator Lodge, informed the British Embassy in Washington that he was in fact not in favour of an independent Ireland.

In the face of these complexities, pressurising the White House into supporting Sinn Féin in its pursuit of the grail of an Irish Republic was obviously a somewhat fraught process which demanded the utmost tact and diplomacy if it were to have any remote chance of succeeding. Sinn Féin's president, Eamon de Valera, now took up the cudgels in a manner lacking in either tact or diplomacy. His dream of getting to America began to come true on Sunday 4 June, when Collins arranged for him to cross the Irish Sea on the mailboat from Dun Laoghaire to Holyhead, thence to be smuggled aboard the liner *Celtic* as a stowaway to New York. His first press statement (on 23 June) contained an attack on Wilson, and declared: 'I am in America as the official head of the Republic, established by the will of the Irish people in accordance with the principle of self-determination.' It continued:

> We shall fight for a real democratic League of Nations, not the present unholy alliance which does not fulfil the purposes for which the democracies of the world went to war. I am going to ask the American people to give us a real League of Nations, one that will include Ireland.
>
> I well recognise President Wilson's difficulties in Paris. I am sure that if he is sincere, nothing will please him more than being pushed from behind by the people for this will show him that the people of America want the United States Government to recognise the Republic of Ireland.
>
> That is the reason I am eager to spread propaganda in official circles in America. My appeal is to the people. I know if they can be aroused government action will follow. That is why I intend visiting your large cities and talking directly to the people.

De Valera, in his subsequent career, did not always adhere to his stated intentions. But in the case of his American tour, which was to last for some 18 months, he certainly did 'spread propaganda', securing massive publicity for Ireland's case, even if he failed in his aim of proving to the White House that Americans wanted 'the United States Government to recognise the Republic of Ireland'.

We will return to de Valera's peregrinations, insofar as these were to have a bearing on the attitudes he was to display at critical junctures in Ireland's history subsequently. But for the moment, let us take up the thread of how, back in Ireland, Sinn Féin went about persuading the British to recognise an Irish republic.

To begin with, in either June or July of 1919, in the wake of de Valera's departure, some of the leading Republicans elected Collins as president of the Supreme Council of the IRB. In this role, he was regarded as the real president of the Republic, and the influence of the IRB in the battle over the type of settlement which was to emerge from the fast-approaching period of strife would prove decisive. The British, like Wilson, were facing deeply conflicting policies in attempting to come to terms with Sinn Féin's demands. Enough has been said about imperial attitudes, Conservative chicanery, and the determination of Unionists to resist Home Rule, to make clear what these conflicting currents were. But, as pressure from the deteriorating situation in Ireland itself and the need to placate Irish-American sentiment grew on the British Government, the Irish Committee of the Cabinet was finally driven to draw up a report as to how matters might be resolved. It may be remarked that the report, which was circulated in great secrecy, could have spared both Irish and British a great deal of agony had it been acted upon promptly, and in the spirit in which it was written. It said that the Committee found that

> in view of the situation in Ireland itself, of public opinion in the Dominions, and in the United States of America, they cannot recommend the policy either of repealing or of postponing the Home Rule Act of 1914. In their judgement it is essential, now that the war is over, and the Peace Conference has dealt with so many analogous questions in Europe, that the Government should make a sincere attempt to deal with the Irish question once and for all.[28]

However, there were serious obstacles to the successful conclusion of the 'sincere attempt':

> On the one hand the Government was committed against any solution which would break with the unity of the Empire. On the other, it was committed that Ulster must not be forced under the rule of an Irish Parliament against its will. The first condition therefore excludes any proposal for allowing Ireland, or any part of Ireland to establish an independent Republic. The second again precludes them from again attempting what has so often failed in the past, the establishment of a single parliament for all Ireland on the lines of the Home Rule Acts of 1886, 1893 and 1914.

Clearly, any solution which the Committee could come up with was going to be a long way short of the 32-county republic to which Sinn Féin aspired, and so it proved. The Committee, on 24 November, recommended to the Cabinet that in effect Ireland should not get a republic either north or south, but that it should get partition. There were to be two parliaments, one in Belfast, one in Dublin, linked under the Crown by a Council of Ireland. Neither parliament would have the power to conduct foreign affairs or decide on such matters as what was treason, or the conferring of dignities. At least some of the Committee's members made the offer of the two parliaments purely for public consumption, in the certain expectation that Sinn Féin had been made an offer it could not accept. F.E. Smith, by now Lord Birkenhead, said:

> I assent to this proposed Bill as effecting an ingenious strengthening of our tactical position before the world. I am absolutely satisfied that the Sinn Féiners will refuse it. Otherwise in the present state of Ireland I could not even be a party to making the offer, for I believe the Sinn Féiners, if they accept their parliament, would use it only for the purpose of forwarding separation.[29]

However, despite these reservations, and the related fact that the Home Rule proposals found no favour with Nationalists, the British pressed ahead with their proposals, and the 'Better Government of Ireland' Bill was introduced in the House of Commons on 22 December 1919. The Bill would trundle through the House throughout 1920 and culminate in the setting up of a parliament in Belfast on 22 June 1921. Behind this bald statement of fact there lies a chapter of unnecessary and largely irrelevant horror. Irrelevant that is to the inevitable working out of the corollary to the constitutional path which Britain had embarked upon. The introduction of the Government of Ireland Bill facilitated the setting up of another parliament, in Dublin, which would give effect to partition, which was the realpolitik of the Bill. Less than a month after the introduction of the Government of Ireland Bill, on 15 January 1920, local government elections were held in Ireland under the authority of the Castle. Of the 206 councils contested, 172 went to Sinn Féin, with the Six Counties of Northern Ireland providing the bulk of the remainder which voted Unionist. Thus, though neither the Irish Nationalists nor the British acknowledged the fact, a de facto, if not a de jure, partition of the country was well under way.

Throughout 1920, however, the British and the Irish fought a brutal war which embittered Anglo-Irish relations for a generation and introduced new terms of horror to the Anglo-Irish nomenclature. 'Bloody Sunday', 'Black and Tans', 'murder gangs', 'assassination', 'reprisal' were the words and deeds which earned 1920 the description 'The Year of Terror' in Irish history. The Sinn Féin members elected to the new councils formed after the 15 January elections cut their links with the Castle, declared their allegiance to the Dail, and along with the creation of 'Sinn Féin courts' set about establishing an administrative and legal framework independent of the British. At the same time, Sinn Féin's militant arm, the IRA, stepped up its attacks on the British, burning barracks, shooting police, soldiers and informers. The British counter-insurgency tactics included undercover hit squads which carried out reprisals that claimed the lives of prominent Sinn Féiners like the Lord Mayor of Cork, Tomas MacCurtain.

As the war intensified, powerful military voices were raised on the British side, demanding that the burden of the opprobrium of much that was happening be lifted from the soldiers of the military, by giving the hostilities the appearance of a 'police war'. Sir Henry Wilson had his own proposal. He advocated the drawing-up of lists of prominent Republicans and 'shooting by roster'. He reasoned that if Sinn Féiners were to be murdered, then the Government should be seen to do the murdering. Not surprisingly, the Field Marshal's diary records that when this proposal was put to the Prime Minister, Lloyd George 'fairly danced'.[30] However, two new forces were introduced to Ireland. One was the Black and Tans, drawn from the ranks of ex-servicemen. Their name came from the colour of their uniforms, a combination of khaki and police clothing. The men were paid 10 shillings a day and more or less given a free hand, to shoot, loot and carouse as they wished in their allotted task. This was described in the Castle's 'Weekly Summary', as 'making appropriate hell' for the rebels. Churchill is believed to have been behind the formation of the second corps, the 'Police Auxiliary Cadets'. These were drawn from the ranks of ex-officers and paid £1 a day, and proved themselves to be an even more ruthless and devastating body than the Black and Tans.

Around 200 unarmed civilians, some of them women and children, were killed by Crown forces, either deliberately or as a result of indiscriminate firing. Towns like Limerick, Fermoy, Thurles, Kilmallock, Kilcommons and Lismore were shot up by these police. Part of Cork city was burned, and the town of Balbriggan in North County Dublin was subjected to a particularly notorious sacking. A factory, some 49 houses and four public houses were burned, and two civilians were shot after a fight in a pub in which two Black and Tans were fired at. The burning of Balbriggan was probably unauthorised, but much other destruction of property was carried out as part of the 'frightfulness' policy, as it was termed, deliberately carried-out reprisals formulated by the Cabinet on 31 May 1920 so that 'Irish men were made to feel the effect of the campaign of murder and arson along economic channels'.

Torture became an accepted, and widely used, tactic by the Castle authorities. It was equally denied by British spokespersons, notably Sir Hamar Greenwood, whose stentorian denials of misbehaviour on the part of Crown forces led to a new definition of lying: 'telling a Hamar'. Lloyd George made a memorable speech at the Guildhall, London, on 9 November, which summed up the Government's official attitude to what was happening in Ireland: 'We have murder by the throat . . . we had to re-organise the police. When the Government was ready, we struck the terrorists and now the terrorists are complaining of terror.'

But even though 'frightfulness' became an acceptable, if oft-denied, policy, the British were constrained by public opinion from putting forth their full strength. Residual sympathy for the Irish cause stemming from the latitude allowed to the Unionists and the events of 1916 was strong in many places, notably in Irish-American circles. World sympathy for the Irish was excited by episodes such as the death of Terence McSwiney, who had succeeded Tomas MacCurtain as Lord Mayor of Cork, after 74 days of hunger strike, and the execution by hanging of the 18-year-old Kevin Barry. Barry was an IRA Volunteer who was captured after an ambush which was intended only to take rifles from a party of soldiers went wrong and three Tommies were shot. The fact that he had been due to sit a university examination on the morning of the raid but decided that he had time to squeeze in the 'op' first lessened support for the 'murder by the throat' argument.

In the far-away Punjab, 250 men of the First Battalion of the Connaught Rangers created world headlines when they laid down their arms in protest against what was happening in Ireland. The subsequent courts-martial and death sentences added to the publicity, although ultimately only one soldier, James Daly, was executed.

The IRA's assassination campaign and the tactic of ambushes by flying columns, which successfully adapted the Boers' hit-and-run tactics to Irish conditions, tied up some 50,000 soldiers, and made war zones of several key areas in the south, Dublin, Cork, Clare, Longford, Limerick, Mayo and Tipperary. The RIC were effectively driven out of their barracks, and survived only in fortified towns.

How unsafe the towns were in reality was shockingly demonstrated on Sunday 21 November 1920, Bloody Sunday, when Collins's men shot 19 soldiers, who included the leaders of the British counter-insurgency effort, at eight different addresses in Dublin. The men were roused from their sleep, shot in front of their wives and mistresses, or put standing against a wall for execution. At the risk of digression, it might be noted by way of illustrating the subsequent development of the Anglo-Irish relationship that amongst the assassins that terrible morning were Seán Lemass, who subsequently became Ireland's most constructive prime minister, and Mick O'Hanlon, whose son Hugh became a cabinet minister in an Irish government and whose grandson, Ardal O'Hanlon, is one of the most popular comedians on British television. Later that day, the Tans and auxiliaries shot up Croke Park, where Dublin were playing Tipperary at Gaelic football. Rifle and machine-gun fire killed 14 spectators, and injured hundreds more. Although the British tried to pass off the 'Park shooting' as being a return of fire at 'desperate characters' amongst the Tipperary crowd, and Sir Hamar Greenwood professed to the Cabinet to be at a loss as to why the British soldiers were shot, the Castle authorities and Lloyd George knew otherwise. Collins had effectively crippled the British undercover operation in Ireland, and significantly, the day after Bloody Sunday, Lloyd George stressed to Patrick Moylette, the IRB representative, with whom he was in contact at the time, that the police feelers should continue.

The British had also reorganised the administrative front. Some of England's more distinguished civil servants were sent to the Castle, notably Sir John Anderson, later Lord Waverly, Mark Beresford Sturgis, whose diaries constitute the most valuable record of the last days of British administration in Dublin, and Alfred Cope. Cope was in fact Lloyd George's personal man in the Castle, the civil servant most responsible for establishing and maintaining contact with Sinn Féin. He organised *sub rosa* meetings with Collins and other Sinn Féin leaders to such good effect that Unionist elements in the Cabinet reacted angrily by passing resolutions that no servant of the Crown should have contact with Sinn Féin.

Peace negotiations in Ireland probably do not run any less smoothly than they do elsewhere, it only appears that they do. Approaching Christmas 1920, Lloyd George's post-Bloody Sunday resolution to stay on the peace path was considerably weakened by three separate happenings in Ireland. The first was a report of a discussion at Galway County Council on 3 December of a resolution, which was not passed by the six members of the (normally 32-strong) council present, calling on the Dail to sue for peace. This was followed by the publication in the press of a letter from Roger Sweetman, the Sinn Féin deputy for Wexford North, calling for a conference of public bodies to draw up peace proposals. The impact of the Galway and Wexford happenings was heightened by a telegram from the Vice-President of Sinn Féin, Father Michael O'Flanagan, to Lloyd George, saying that Ireland was willing to make peace, and asking him what steps he proposed. At this stage, Lloyd

George had been holding discussions with Dr Joseph Clune, the Archbishop of Perth, whose nephew, Conor, had been murdered by Crown forces. Clune had been put in touch with Collins by Archbishop Daniel Mannix, whom the British had sent a warship to intercept as he approached Ireland on a liner some time earlier. The intervention of these highly placed clerics had given the peace discussions some significance, but this evaporated in the face of the Galway/Flanagan/Sweetman developments. Lloyd George told Clune that taken together, the three incidents constituted 'the White Feather, and we're going to make these fellows surrender'.[31]

It is difficult to know to what extent Lloyd George's personal convictions or those of the Unionist and Curragh Mutiny factors governed Irish policy at this stage. Obviously the Tory/Curragh viewpoint was still strong at Cabinet, and certainly after a two-day meeting on 29 and 30 December 1920, the British Government decided to continue with the policy of 'frightfulness'.[32] Four generals from the Irish campaign (Boyd, Macready, Strickland and Tudor) calculated that another four months of campaigning at the current rate of progress would bring victory, and argued that a truce would give Sinn Féin a chance to regroup, particularly in its intelligence operations. Sir Henry Wilson opined that 'the decent peasant' was basically on the side of the Government, and would be lost to the British if a truce were declared, because this would send the peasantry into the arms of Sinn Féin. He was in favour of applying martial law to the entire country. This, he believed, would induce 90% of the Irish electorate to the British way of thinking.

These military appreciations are worth recording because they show how fundamentally out of touch with the reality of the situation the military leaders were. Although the Irish situation had all the outward appearances of a military campaign, on the IRA's side it was basically a secret services war. There was never the remotest possibility of the IRA defeating the British army. Once a truce was declared, far from being an unalloyed plus for the Republicans, it deprived them of their most important weapon, secrecy. This was a factor that governed Michael Collins's cautious approach to peace feelers. Wilson's recommendation of course would have had the effect of replicating the consequences of Maxwell's executions policy after 1916 on a grander scale.

However, though the Cabinet decided in effect at the 29–30 December meeting to long-finger the truce option for several months, the talk of peace had one important result – it caused de Valera to reintroduce himself to Ireland.

To understand de Valera's behaviour immediately on returning to Ireland, as well as during the subsequent discussions with Lloyd George, the negotiation of the Anglo-Irish Treaty which laid the foundation for today's Irish Republic, and the futile and tragic civil war which broke out over the Treaty's provisions, it is necessary to know something of how he acted during his long sojourn in the United States, and to bear in mind that he was away throughout a lengthy and significant period of hostilities, which inevitably lessened his grasp of the realities of the conflict. His time in America closely resembled the curate's egg. On the publicity front, he certainly heightened awareness of the Irish situation. An Irish-American historian, Francis M. Carroll, assessed the publicity side of his tour as follows:

> De Valera spoke before State legislatures, conferred with Governors, was given the freedom of several cities, and received two honorary doctorates . . . always, he addressed large public audiences . . . perhaps de Valera's travels throughout America, more than any other event since the 1916 Rising, dramatised for the American people the dimensions of the Irish struggle.[33]

But other entries have to be recorded on his balance sheet. His ego was such that he found it impossible to work with the principal Irish-American leaders, Daniel Cohalan and John Devoy, declaring that he realised early on in his trip that big as America was, 'it was not big enough to hold the judge and myself'. He also clashed bitterly with Devoy over the latter's coverage of his tour in his newspaper, the *Gaelic American*. Devoy's tactic of printing a large picture of Michael Collins under the heading 'Ireland's fighting Chief', and making pointed comparisons between Collins fighting in Ireland and de Valera campaigning from the Waldorf Astoria Hotel was a particular *casus belli*. In addition, there were serious policy differences over an interview de Valera gave to the *Westminster Gazette* in which he suggested that a British version of the Monroe doctrine could result in Ireland achieving a position analagous to that of Cuba vis-à-vis America. How much de Valera understood about Cuba's actual vassal state relationship with America is a moot point.

What is certain is that he pursued policies which led to a split in the principal Irish-American organisation, the Friends of Irish Freedom, headed by Cohalan, and the setting up of his own organisation, the American Association for the Recognition of the Irish Republic. The fraught atmosphere generated between de Valera and his adversaries may be gauged from the following account of one 'acrimonious in the extreme' confrontation in the Park Avenue Hotel which went on for ten hours. It is taken from a letter to a friend written by the Irish-American shipping magnate John P. Grace:

> . . . De Valera's attitude was one of infallibility; he was right, everybody else was wrong, and he couldn't be wrong . . . Bishops and priests, Protestants and Catholics, aged men born in Ireland and young men born here worked for those ten hours to bring President de Valera to the point of amenability . . . I beg to repeat that not having seen him before, as for those ten hours he unfolded himself, I thought the man was crazy.[34]

But these internal disputes did not reach a wider public, before whom de Valera pursued four objectives: raising money, defeating the League of Nations; securing the recognition of the Irish Republic, and having himself recognised as the policy-maker and spokesperson for Irish policy, by both the Irish-American leadership and the American public. He certainly raised a lot of money. Franklin D. Roosevelt, then an up-and-coming New York lawyer, advised him on the issue of 'bond-certificates', which raised a total of $5,123,640 to help Ireland achieve its freedom. But, in the same manner in which de Valera saw the Irish cause as being personified and controlled by him, he seemed to regard this money as being his to direct. Only half of it was remitted to Ireland to help the war effort; the rest remained in New York banks, and, as we shall see later, de Valera eventually succeeded in getting control of enough of it to enable him to found a newspaper empire in Dublin, the Irish Press Group.

De Valera's attacks on the League of Nations of necessity placed him in opposition to President Wilson, whose Scots Presbyterian ancestry and pro-British attitudes hardly disposed him towards Irish nationalism in the first place. But de Valera compounded his differences by his attitude to the two presidential conventions which occurred during his American tour. At the Republican convention in Chicago, which selected Warren Harding, leading a delegation of his own, he submitted a plank to the Resolutions Committee calling for the recognition of an Irish republic. It was turned down by 11 votes to one. Instead the Committee adopted a milder resolution submitted by Cohalan. This called for 'recognition of the principle that the people of Ireland have the right to determine freely, without dictation from outside, their own Governmental institutions, and their international relations with other States and peoples'. This was narrowly accepted by the Committee (seven votes to six), but de Valera deliberately sabotaged it, saying he wanted a republican plank. The Resolutions Committee, faced with two feuding delegations, decided that the best solution was to have no Irish plank. De Valera made no bones about his motivation in acting as he did. He wrote to Arthur Griffith, saying that he had undermined Cohalan so that people would not think that the judge was 'the power behind our Movement – the man to whom they would have to go. Were I to allow myself to appear thus as a puppet, apart from any personal pride, the Movement would suffer a severe blow.' The movement had suffered, and was to suffer again. When the Democratic convention was held shortly afterwards in San Francisco, de Valera again attended and again failed to persuade the Democrats to adopt a resolution on Ireland.

To follow de Valera's labyrinthine machinations further would take us too far from our story at this stage. Suffice it to say that finding peace initiatives were in train, he had Collins smuggle him across the Atlantic once more, this time to Dublin, where on his return his first major initiative was an attempt to get Collins out of Ireland to the United States.

To return to the progress of the peace negotiations, apart from the Clune initiative mentioned earlier, these had gathered force with the publication (on 8 October 1920) of a letter to *The Times* from Brigadier General Cockerill MP, suggesting that a conference be held 'of fully accredited pleni-potentiaries, representing Ireland and Great Britain, equal in number and untrammelled by restrictive instructions and empowered by means of negotiation to make the best peace possible'. The Brigadier also proposed a truce and an amnesty. It was following the publication of this letter that the Sinn Féin emissary, Patrick Moylette, a London-based Irish businessman, contacted Lloyd George to say that the Cockerill proposals could form the basis for peace. At this stage, several important bodies and individuals were also active on the peace front. Important newspapers like the *Manchester Guardian*, the *Daily Herald* and *The Times* condemned the policy of frightfulness on the same day that the Cabinet met the generals responsible for Irish military policy (29 December 1920). A British Labour Party commission published a report on Irish conditions which said that the auxiliaries and the Black and Tans were 'compelling the Irish people – men, women and children – to live in an atmosphere of sheer terrorism'. The Irish Self-Determination League, headed by Art O'Brien, continually made the same point, as did Lord Henry Cavendish-Bentinck's 'Peace with Ireland Council', which represented English Catholics. Some of the leading writers of the day, including Belloc, Chesterton and Shaw, were also raising their voices on the side of the Irish.

The Roman Catholic Church played an important role in the securing of peace. Archbishop Clune's activities have been indicated earlier. The overall importance of the Church to the Irish situation had been adverted to by the principal English civil servant at the Cabinet meetings which decided to continue with the 'frightfulness' policy. Sir John Anderson's view was that the influence of the Church would probably turn out to be the most important factor in determining the outcome of the struggle. His Irish visit over, Clune called on Pope Benedict on his way back to Australia to discover that British diplomacy had been instrumental in the drawing up of a papal condemnation of violence in Ireland in which the staff of St Peter fell most heavily on the backs of Sinn Féin. However, Clune strongly remonstrated with Benedict, giving his own first-hand experiences of Black and Tan savagery in Ireland, as well as the calibre of the Sinn Féin leaders, in particular Michael Collins, and succeeded in obtaining a postponement of the papal pronouncement. Individual Irish bishops, notably Cohalan of Cork, had condemned the IRA, Cohalan going so far as to threaten excommunication to those who took part in ambushes, kidnappings or murder. But a papal onslaught was another matter, and it was conveyed to His Holiness from both the Irish and American hierarchies that neither Ireland nor America would tolerate the sort of condemnation which was envisaged.

Weighing up these factors, the papacy turned to the source which the British would have least favoured for Irish opinion-sounding, the outspoken Archbishop Daniel Mannix of Melbourne. Mannix was invited to provide a draft of the sort of pronouncement he felt the situation called for. He both did this and suggested to the Pope that he make a public contribution to the American White Cross, which was providing relief in Ireland. It might be remarked here, *inter alia*, by way of illustrating the extent of sympathy in America towards Ireland, that this organisation, whose activities drew support from, amongst others, President Harding, raised some $5 million, quite apart from the sums secured by de Valera. The money was actually spent on relief, Collins having guaranteed that none of it would go towards IRA purposes. The Pope agreed to this suggestion, and when his pronouncement on Ireland appeared on 22 May 1922, it clearly bore a Mannix imprint:

> We are most especially concerned about the condition of Ireland. Unflinching even to the shedding of blood in her devotion to the ancient Faith and in her reverence for the Holy See she is subjected today to the indignity of devastation and slaughter . . . neutrality . . . by no means prevents us from wishing . . . that a lasting peace . . . may take the place of this terrible enmity . . . we do not perceive how this bitter strife can profit either of the parties, when property and homes are being ruthlessly and disgracefully laid waste, when villages and farmsteads are being set aflame, when neither sacred places nor sacred persons are spared, when on both sides a war resulting in the deaths of unarmed people, even of women and children, is carried on. We exhort English as well as Irish to calmly consider . . . some means of mutual agreement.[35]

The British were furious, delivering a protest of their own to the Vatican at the placing of 'HMG and the Irish murder gang on the foot of equality'. But the view from the throne of St Peter of what was occurring in Ireland was not altogether dissimilar to that from the throne of England. King George V, as indicated earlier, in the days of the Ulster crisis, had not taken altogether kindly to the activities of the leader of his loyal Opposition. Bonar Law was not happy with Irish events either. Sir James Craig, Carson's successor as leader of the Unionists and now Prime Minister of 'Ulster', had invited His Majesty to open the new parliament in Belfast. But the King, mindful of the fact that he had Catholic as well as Protestant subjects in Ireland, feared that this might 'look like a deliberate affront to the South'. He conveyed his fears to the Prime Minister of South Africa, General Smuts, who had been invited to Windsor on 10 June, 12 days before the King was due to speak in Belfast.

Smuts then produced for the King the draft of a speech which took King George's intervention beyond the partisan gesture of opening a small subordinate parliament, and became a message of peace addressed to Ireland, the Dominions and America. Smuts was concerned at the situation in the Pacific, and saw the solution to British defence problems in the drawing together of America and Japan. An imperial conference was impending and Smuts, whom Lloyd George invited to address the Cabinet, pointed out that a solution to the Irish problem would improve the atmosphere both at the Conference and in America. The Cabinet, which was unaware either that Smuts had prepared a draft for the King, or that Lloyd George, who shared his opinions, had already seen and approved the speech, agreed to a peace initiative. This was a dramatic reversal of earlier policy because Arthur Balfour had also drawn up a draft for the King which was practically a declaration of war on Ireland.

Accordingly, in Belfast on 22 June, King George delivered a speech which deserves to be set against an unfortunately long litany of occasions when intervention in Ireland by the Crown had less benign results:

I speak from a full heart when I pray that my coming to Ireland today may prove to be the first step towards the end of strife among her people, whatever their race or creed. In that hope I appeal to all Irishmen to pause, to stretch out the hand of forbearance and conciliation, to forgive and forget, and to join in making for the land they love a new era of peace, contentment and goodwill.

It is my earnest desire that in Southern Ireland, too, there may, ere long, take place a parallel to what is now passing in this hall, that there a similar occasion may present itself, and a similar ceremony be performed. For this the Parliament of the United Kingdom has in the fullest measure provided the powers. For this the Parliament of Ulster is pointing the way . . .[36]

Though the militarists and the Tories had temporarily carried the day with the Cabinet, the King's voice, echoing in the wake of the other peace initiatives which had gone before, had its effect. Although Unionist-minded Tories like Sir Hamar Greenwood objected to the abandonment of the 'frightfulness' policy, Lloyd George acted on the King's speech, sending a public appeal to de Valera suggesting a peace conference, so that 'the King's appeal for reconciliation, for peace in Ireland, shall not have been made in vain'. He offered de Valera and anyone he wished to bring with him to England safe conduct, and proposed a meeting between Craig and de Valera.[37]

Both de Valera and Craig reacted to the initiative in the same way, by pouring cold water on it. De Valera replied to Lloyd George on 28 June: 'We most earnestly desire . . . a lasting peace, but see no avenue by which it can be reached if you deny Ireland's essential unity and set aside the principle of self-determination.' He also sent a letter to Craig, addressing him as *'a chara'* (friend), written in terms which guaranteed that Craig would not see him as a friend:

A Chara, the reply which I, *as spokesman for the Irish nation* [author's italics], shall make to Lloyd George will affect the lives and fortunes of the political minority in this island, no less than those of the majority.

Before sending that reply therefore, I would like to confer with you and to learn from you at first hand the views of a certain section of *our* people of whom you are representative.

I am confident that you will not refuse this service to Ireland, and I shall await you at the Mansion House, Dublin at 11 a.m. on Monday next in the hope that you will find it possible to attend.

Lady Craig's reaction to the letter was that 'for sheer impertinence it could hardly be beaten'. Craig's own attitude was summed up more diplomatically in a remark he made to the British civil servant Mark Sturgis to the effect that he would 'sit on Ulster like a rock. Let the PM and Sinn Féin settle it. He was satisfied with what he had got.'

Apart from the totally divergent viewpoints of the two Irish leaders on 'essential unity', various other issues obstructed the rash of peacemaking which now broke out. Interestingly enough, one was the question which, at the other end of the century, after the Good Friday Agreement of 1998, also threatened the peace settlement: the issue of IRA arms. A retarding factor in the 1920 dialogue between the British and Sinn Féin was a demand by the military that a condition of a truce must be that the IRA surrender its weapons.

A truce was, however, declared on 11 July 1921. It did not come a moment too soon. On the one hand, the British had plans for the introduction of full-scale martial law throughout the country, which would have entailed increasing British military strength by 300%. On the other, Collins was on the verge of another, far greater Bloody Sunday-style operation, in which upwards of 100 British agents, auxiliaries and Black and Tans were to be mown down. Half an hour before the operation was due to be launched, word came from Lloyd George that he wanted to open peace negotiations. The mood throughout Dublin lightened immeasurably. General Macready was cheered to the echo as he arrived at the Mansion House to arrange truce details.

One man who did not join in the cheering was Michael Collins. His view was that 'once a truce is agreed, when we come out in the open, it is extermination for us if the truce should fail . . . we should be like rabbits coming out of their holes'.[38] Even though he had plans in train for wiping out enemy agents, and the Dail Cabinet had adopted his strategy to declare war 'on anyone who either supported or dispensed English law in Ireland after a certain date', he knew that the IRA was strained to the utmost, and that in agreeing to a truce his principle weapon, secrecy, was gone. And he had other reasons for foreboding, which caused him to write the following sombre note apparently only two days after the truce was agreed:

> Agreement is a trifling word or so I have come to look on it as such. At this moment there is more ill-will within a victorious assembly than ever could be found anywhere else except in the devil's assembly. It cannot be fought against. The issue and persons are mixed to such an extent as to make discernibility an utter impossibility except for a few.[39]

The 'issue and persons' which made 'discernibility an utter impossibility' was the underground campaign which de Valera had been carrying on against Collins with the aid of Collins's two principal adversaries in the Cabinet. On his return from America (on 23 December 1920), de Valera had been met off the boat by two prominent IRB men, Tom Cullen and Batt O'Connor. He asked them how things were going, and when Cullen replied, 'Great, the Big Fellow is leading us, and everything is going marvellous', he grew visibly angry, and, banging his hand on the ship's rail, replied, 'Big Fellow! We'll see who's the Big Fellow.'[40] He translated this statement into action by writing to Collins on 18 January 1921, directing him to go to America, where he would take orders from Brugha. The reaction within the IRB and the Volunteers' GHQ to this proposal was such that de Valera had to quietly abandon the suggestion. Both by his own ability, and because of press publicity, Collins had come to symbolise the entire struggle against the British. As we have seen his energy was such that along with running his intelligence service, he directed the floating of a Dail loan so efficiently that it achieved the target set; he effectively ran the Sinn Féin political machine while the other members of the Sinn Féin Cabinet were in jail, carried out the work of Minister for Finance in the underground government, and as president of the IRB directed the work of that organisation.

Brugha and Stack, on the other hand, while admired for their bravery, scored low marks for efficiency. In 1916, Stack, having failed to organise a successful arms landing in Kerry, then cycled to the police station, where Casement was being held, to try to obtain news – and was promptly arrested. Collins angered him by publicly throwing down a sheaf of papers in front of him one day, and telling him in the hearing of others that his adjectival department (Ministry of Home Affairs) was an adjectival 'disgrace'. Brugha's animosity towards Collins was more deep-seated; like Stack, he resented Collins's interference in the running of his department, the Ministry of Defence, but he was jealous of Collins into the bargain. A contemporary of both men judged that 'Cathal Brugha hated Collins like poison. It was pathological . . . Brugha was Minister for Defence but he never did anything. He was not able, but he was never on the run. He continued to work as manager for Lalor's candle factory on Ormond Quay . . . Collins was so energetic that he had usurped many of Brugha's functions: he sure was hated by him . . .'[41]

However, as he had done in the US, with Joseph McGarrity and Patrick McCartan, in his war with Cohalan and Devoy, de Valera traded on the differences of opinion between Collins and the two men by becoming friendly with Brugha and Stack. Even though Collins had been acting President of Sinn Féin while he was in America, he appointed Stack as his President designate, thus not only studiedly demoting Collins, but doing so for a man proven to have far less ability. He also agreed to preside over an inquiry called for by Brugha into Collins's handling of Volunteer funds. After a deeply embarrassing airing of Brugha's charges, during which Collins wept openly, de Valera was forced to pronounce that 'it is quite clear that these charges are groundless'.[42] A further continuing source of dissension between de Valera and Collins was de Valera's espousal of 'static warfare'. On his return from America, he informed the IRA leadership that the ambushes and assassinations were having a bad effect on American public opinion, and wanted instead to stage a battle once a month involving a corps of around 500 Volunteers. Knowing that this would have resulted in the Volunteers being wiped out, even more easily than they had been subdued in 1916, Collins fiercely resisted the idea, but in the end had to give in to de Valera's pressure to stage one spectacular major 'static warfare' assault, the destruction of James Gandon's handsome Dublin Customs House.

The operation, on 25 May 1921, attracted worldwide publicity, and could be accounted a propaganda success. Moreover, as the building was the seat of

Irish local government administration, its destruction paralysed unpopular activities such as income tax collection. However, it was a military disaster, which, had it been replicated on any scale, would have speedily destroyed the IRA. Six Volunteers were killed, 12 wounded, and some 75 of the best members of the Dublin Brigade were arrested. This outcome was not an unexpected one for Collins at least, as ammunition was in such short supply that some of the Volunteers going into action had only four or five rounds each. But, while the Customs House losses and the Brugha feud weighed with Collins, the most immediate source of his despondency as he penned his depressed letter during the euphoria and optimism which followed the declaration of the truce was a calculated and very obvious snub which de Valera had just delivered. He had gone to London with a delegation to meet Lloyd George, but had pointedly left Collins out. His excuse was that he did not want to give the British opportunities of taking photographs of him, which they would of course have had ample opportunity of doing had Collins agreed to go to America.

Ignoring Collins's protests, de Valera not only left Collins at home, but took Austin Stack with him in the delegation, which also included Arthur Griffith, Robert Barton, Count Plunkett and Erskine Childers. Once in London, de Valera left his delegates out of the talks, and conferred alone with Lloyd George in several lengthy meetings spread out over a number of days. De Valera apologists have tended to gloss over the significance of these lengthy meetings, but it cannot be gainsaid that at the conclusion of them there was not the remotest possibility that de Valera was not fully briefed on what was on offer from the British side: a 26-county state with a simulacrum of dominion status in that the southern state could have an army but no navy, and Britain was to be given whatever facilities she might require in time of war. It might be noted here that de Valera himself would later demonstrate to the world, during World War II, how much substance there was in the amount of sovereignty conceded by the Treaty, and how little in this concession on facilities. Above all, partition was to be recognised. The existing powers and privileges of the parliament of Northern Ireland were not to be 'abrogated except by their own consent'. These powers and privileges were very considerable, and there was not the remotest possibility of any willing abrogation of them by the Unionists.

Before continuing to follow the path of the de Valera–Lloyd George negotiations, it is essential to have some understanding of how the 'Ulster' situation developed as the peace talks gathered force. Over the previous year and a half, it had become clear, to the initiated at least, that what the Protestant leadership of Northern Ireland was aiming at was in fact an Orange state. On 17 February 1919, the Irish Committee had recommended to the Cabinet that 'The whole of the Province of Ulster should be included in the Northern Parliament. The Committee consider that a Northern Parliament consisting of the nine counties in Ulster is more likely to lead to the ultimate union of the whole of Ireland than if the Northern Parliament was composed of Six Counties only.' That continued to be the majority opinion, not only within the Committee, but in the Cabinet throughout 1920 and afterwards. Even a dedicated imperialist like Birkenhead, becoming irritated at the provincialism of the Unionist leader, Lord Londonderry, sharply pointed out to him: 'The admitted circumstances that if the political considerations allowed it, the economic and financial interests of Ireland would be greatly benefited by Union, however long postponed.' A peaceful, and united, Ireland, given defence – particularly naval defence – and security considerations, was obviously in Britain's best interests. A reading of the Cabinet proceedings for December makes it quite clear that British Cabinet policy *as a whole* favoured a united Ireland as the ultimate goal.[43]

However, the Unionists and their advisers were at work. On 19 December the Unionist sympathiser Worthington-Evans told the Cabinet that the Ulster leaders were doubtful whether the northern parliament of Ireland would be able to govern Northern Ireland where there was a Nationalist majority, and greatly preferred that the scheme should be limited only to the six Protestant counties. The Cabinet was also informed that Craig had proposed

> the establishment of a Boundary Commission to examine the distribution of population along the borders of the whole of the Six Counties, and to take a vote in those districts on either side of and immediately adjoining that boundary in which there was no doubt as to whether they would prefer to be included in the Northern or the Southern Parliamentary area.

Ironically, Craig would subsequently react vehemently against the idea of a Boundary Commission, and it would recur later in the 1920s, as a vehicle of Nationalist aspirations for the shape of the Six Counties rather than Unionist ones, aspirations which, as we shall see, were destined not to be fulfilled. The main problem with the Six Counties through the course of the century would not be the shape of its boundaries, but Protestant mistrust of a large Catholic minority within them. In fact, the minority constituted the majority in Counties Fermanagh and Tyrone, and in the city of Derry. But from the outset, the Orange leaders made it abundantly clear that the main thrust of their energies in setting up and running the new state would be directed at preventing that large and inconvenient Catholic minority from ever taking control within the Six County area.

At the 19 December 1919 Cabinet meeting, while it was argued that the new state should include the whole of Ulster, Unionist spokesmen carried the day. The Cabinet minutes show that it was acknowledged 'That the jurisdiction of the Northern Parliament over the whole of Ulster as a geographical unit was more logical and in many ways easier to defend in Parliament.' But the realpolitik of the situation was summed up in the statement that it was 'generally felt that it was even more important to get a scheme which, even though theoretically less perfect, would meet with general acceptance'. The reality of the 'theoretically less perfect' conditions and the identity of those with whom they would meet 'with general acceptance' were well understood at the Cabinet table. Some of the Conservatives sitting at that table were privately colluding with the Ulster Unionists in securing that 'acceptance'.

The Cabinet had proposed that the Ulster statelet should have an upper house weighted in favour of the Catholics so as to prevent discrimination against them. But a Cabinet meeting held on 3 November 1920 which both Balfour and Bonar Law attended was informed that 'Sir Edward Carson and the Ulster members were strongly opposed to a second chamber for the Northern parliament and would use the whole weight of their opposition to endeavour to defeat the proposal.' No second chamber emerged, nor was the British proposal that the new state should elect its representatives by proportional representation acceptable to the Unionists. The Ulster Volunteer Force had not been formed to defeat Home Rule, only to have it introduced by the back door via electoral systems and upper chambers. In fact, many of the UVF were drafted into a new special constabulary known as A, B and C Specials. The Specials were necessary, in Craig's words, in order to create 'A system of organised reprisals against the rebels, mainly in order to defeat them, but partly to restrain their own followers from acts which are regrettable and in a large measure, ineffective.'[44]

Both the civil and military arms of British administration in Ireland opposed the Specials' formation. Anderson wrote directly to Bonar Law, joining Macready in his opposition to 'the rumour that the Government contemplate recognising the Ulster Volunteers in any form', a course which Anderson warned would exacerbate 'Party and religious feeling' throughout Ireland. But to no avail. The Specials were duly formed and paid for by the British taxpayer, despite the opposition of both the Liberal and Labour parties, and two of the most prominent civil servants connected with the Irish issue, Lionel Curtis and Tom Jones, who pointed out that 'The whole of these Specials are Protestant . . . The British Government has armed and is paying for that force, but without question the Government of Northern Ireland controls it . . . The British Government has armed and is paying for forces which, it is told by the one who controls them, will in certain eventualities be turned against itself.'

Craig, the controller of the Specials referred to, had warned Lloyd George that should the British try to enforce proposals which the Unionists did not agree with, such as the Boundary Commission, the Specials would be used in the resistance. However, while in the event they were not used against the forces of the Crown, they were widely used against Catholics in a manner described by General Ricardo, one of the founders of the original UVF, who had become disenchanted with both his creation and its offspring:

The 'B' Head Constable . . . goes to the leading local nationalist . . . He tells him that they have arms and mean to patrol at nights . . . the nationalist is shown a list with his name at the top and is told that if any 'B' man is touched, the list will be attended to from the top. This is not an effort of the imagination but is not an uncommon arrangement.

Given the nature of these steps to preserve Protestant hegemony in Northern Ireland, and the fact that the truce which allowed de Valera and Lloyd George to confer had arisen out of the King's speech marking the opening of a parliament in Northern Ireland – to say nothing of the deep-seated attitudes which had led to the opening of that parliament under the terms of an Act of Parliament passed by the House of Commons the previous year – it is obvious at this remove that a *de facto* partition of the country had occurred by the time de Valera got to London. Nevertheless the Nationalists generally neither accepted nor adverted to this fact. It was not until 9 April 1922 that Michael Collins would publicly admit the significance of the Government of Ireland Act, the 'Partition Act', as the Nationalists referred to it. Speaking at Wexford, Collins said: 'It is my own very strong view now that we should have refused to negotiate a Peace until that Act of Usurpation had been written off.'[45] But by then, as he admitted, the acceptance of partition was an inescapable part of the settlement arrived at. Craig, however, was under no misapprehension as to the significance of the Act. He greeted the opening of the de Valera–Lloyd George talks by saying: 'It now merely remains for Mr de Valera and the British people to come to terms regarding the area outside of which I am Prime Minister. I go back to Ireland to carry on the practical work of Government.'[46]

De Valera responded to this statement by writing to Lloyd George complaining that the claim that he only spoke for the area outside the north was 'wholly inadmissible'. Before going on with the talks, he sought from Lloyd George 'a definite statement as to whether your Government is in agreement with Sir James Craig, and intends to support his view'. No such definitive statement was forthcoming. Lloyd George fended off de Valera's letter by replying: 'I am responsible neither for Sir James Craig's statement to the press, to which you refer, nor for your statement, to which Sir James purports to be a reply.' Nevertheless, de Valera continued his meetings with Lloyd George, from which not surprisingly the Craig-leaning proposals on partition emerged.

At first, de Valera maintained that the proposals were so unacceptable that he could not bring them back to Dublin. However, having left them lying on Lloyd George's table, he then sent a messenger around to collect them, but told his colleagues that the British had forwarded them. Having spent several hours, over a period of days, talking tête-à-tête with Lloyd George, de Valera, more than any man in Ireland, was aware of the almost visceral detestation of the concept of a republic existing in the England of the time. Lord Longford, who knew Lloyd George, summed up both his attitude towards Ireland and the pressures on him to steer clear of any Republican headline-setting, either where English public opinion was concerned or, for example, in either Egypt or India. He wrote that Lloyd George could

talk to perfection the jargon of nationalist aspiration . . . He believed in the paramount necessity of settling the Irish question . . . but . . . he was a politician, not a philanthropist or international philosopher ... His own reputation was endangered anyway by negotiations. It would be blackened inevitably by the consequences of another recourse to war, but it would be destroyed once and for all by any surrender that Parliament judged one of principle, say for Ireland to retain her Republic.

However, de Valera and, let it be said, the other Sinn Féin leaders, pressed along the Republican path as though British resistance to the idea did not exist. When the Dail met to discuss the British proposals, on de Valera's return from his talks with Lloyd George, the first business was to elect him President of the Republic. Collins in fact wrote out the speech in Irish for the proposer of the presidential motion, Seán MacEoin. What had been American usage was now to be Irish practice. It is easy nowadays to view such shadow-boxing as being dangerously unrealistic in the circumstances. But the Republican ideal was deep-seated, within both Sinn Féin and the IRA, whose membership had taken an oath to uphold a Republic. Before the truce, Collins gave newspaper interviews in which he said he believed that the effort which had led to Dominion status being considered would result in the concession of a Republic. And amidst rank-and-file Sinn Féiners and members of the IRA, the idea of a Republic was invested not merely with political, but religious overtones. After Bishop Cohalan had pronounced his decree of excommunication on IRA members who took the lives of Crown forces, an IRA chaplain wrote a strongly dissenting letter for the benefit of the Volunteers:

An excommunication ... may be inflicted only for the external and grievous (or mortal) violation of the law (Canon 2242) ... kidnapping, ambushing and killing obviously would be grave sins or violation of the law. And if these acts were being performed by the IV as private persons (whether physical or oral) they would fall under the Excommunication.

But they are doing them by and with the authority of the State – the Republic of Ireland. And the State has the right and duty to defend the lives and property of citizens and to punish even with death those who are aiming at the destruction of the lives or property of the citizens or itself. It has moreover a right and duty to protect by every means in its power the liberty of the State and its citizens against the Army of Occupation of a Foreign Power unjustly present in the country.

Hence these acts performed by the IV, the Army of the Republic, are not only not sinful but are good and meritorious.

Thus, having taken life, believing such activity to be 'good and meritorious', and of course risked their own lives in the process, to sustain the Republic declared at Easter 1916 and reaffirmed by the first Dail, the predominantly young Sinn Féin/IRA membership viewed the idea of a Republic in a manner which, when the moment of truth came, presented many of them with a severe crisis of conscience. But it cannot be pretended that from the moment negotiations began in July, the British did anything other than point out to the Irish the incompatibility of Republican aspirations with imperial realities. As late as 18 September, Lloyd George was warning de Valera that 'conference between us is impossible' if de Valera continued to assert a right to begin negotiations on behalf of an independent state:

> From the very outset of our conversation I told you that we looked to Ireland to own allegiance to the Throne, and to make her future as a member of the British Commonwealth. That was the basis of our proposals, and we cannot alter it. The status which you now claim in advance for your delegates is, in effect, a repudiation of that basis.

Further correspondence between the two men concluded with an agreement to open full-scale negotiations on a basis that clearly ruled out the Republic. Lloyd George's said:

> His Majesty's Government ... cannot enter a conference upon the basis of this correspondence. Notwithstanding your personal assurance to the contrary, which they much appreciate [de Valera had written to Lloyd George saying: 'We would have thought it as unreasonable to expect you, as a preliminary, to recognise the Irish Republic, formally or informally, as you should expect us, formally or informally, to surrender our national position'] [author], it might be argued in future that the acceptance of a conference on this basis had involved them in a recognition which no British Government can accord. On this point they must guard themselves against any possible doubt ... The position taken up by His Majesty's Government is fundamental to the existence of the British Empire and they cannot alter it. My colleagues and I remain, however, keenly anxious to make in co-operation with your delegates another determined effort to explore every possibility of settlement by personal discussion ... We, therefore, send you herewith a fresh invitation to a conference in London on 11 October, where we can meet your delegates as spokesmen of the people whom you represent with a view to ascertaining how the association of Ireland with the community of nations known as the British Empire may best be reconciled with Irish national aspirations.

De Valera's response was as follows:

> We have received your letter of invitation to a Conference in London on October 11th 'with a view to ascertaining how the association of Ireland with the community of nations known as the British Empire may best be reconciled with Irish national aspirations'.
>
> Our respective positions have been stated and are understood, and we agree that conference, not correspondence, is the most practical and hopeful way to an understanding. We accept the invitation, and our Delegates will meet you in London on the date mentioned 'to explore every possibility of settlement by personal discussion'.

The two positions on a Republic being so diametrically opposed, and having been demonstrated repeatedly to be so opposed since de Valera had met Lloyd George in July, de Valera was now faced with an insuperable diplomatic problem in attempting to reconcile them. How was he to face the challenge? Quite simply, is the answer. He would not face it. He would leave it to Michael Collins to do so. The history of de Valera's activities in America and in the months which followed his return to Ireland has been indicated. As we now approach a period in which events transpired which literally continue to affect both Ireland and, to a degree, England as this is being written, I find myself recalling two memorable observations about men and affairs. One was by the great Australian historian Manning Clark, who counselled that the writing of history should always be illuminated by the light of pity; the other was by an Irish lawyer, Con Lehane, who, speaking of his time as a political activist, told me once: 'I only realised when I got into the Dail that in politics the worst attrition comes from your own side.' Learning what was now to befall, readers may feel it appropriate to apply both Clark and Lehane's dictums to de Valera and to alter the word 'pity' in Clark's to 'charity'.

Collins felt that as a soldier his place was back in Ireland, making preparations lest the truce break down. Of the many indications of his reluctance to accept the poisoned chalice of London, one, the recollection of Batt O'Connor, who had been instructed by de Valera to talk his friend Collins into going, will suffice:

> I will never forget his agony of mind. He would not sit down, but kept pacing up and down the floor, saying that he should not be put in that position. It was an unheard-of thing that a soldier who had fought in the field should be elected to carry out negotiations. It was de Valera's job, not his.

Apart from Collins himself, Arthur Griffith and W.T. Cosgrave also wanted de Valera to go, but with the support of Robert Barton, and, inevitably, that of Brugha and Stack, de Valera was able to use his casting vote in the Cabinet to ensure that he stayed at home. Cosgrave actually proposed a motion to the Dail that the President should accompany the delegation, as chairman, because of his experience in negotiations, and the fact that he had met Lloyd George recently. The British delegation would be led by their head of state, but the Irish were 'leaving their ablest player in reserve'. Speaking on the motion, Collins said bluntly that he didn't want to go, and that he felt de Valera should do so. However, de Valera argued that his experience had taught him that Collins would be vital to the delegation. Of himself, he said he would go, but as President he was 'the symbol of the Republic'. The symbol had to be kept untouched, so it would not be compromised by any arrangements which it might be necessary for the plenipotentiaries to make. His prestige was such that his arguments carried the day and Cosgrave's motion was defeated.

The actual delegation comprised Collins, Griffith, Barton, Eamon Duggan and George Gavin Duffy. Erskine Childers was the official secretary. Brugha and Stack had been invited to go but had turned down the invitation, and unlike Collins, de Valera did not subject them to any pressure to change their minds. He later told Joseph McGarrity that he had deliberately constructed a delegation which contained divisions within its ranks. He had expected Griffith and Collins to accept the Crown, but reasoned that Barton, and in particular his cousin Erskine Childers, would oppose them. Duffy and Duggan he scornfully dismissed as mere legal padding, chosen for their training as solicitors. He said that he had not chosen Brugha because he would have caused rows, and that Griffith and Collins would not work with Stack. What de Valera envisaged was the Cabinet at home hanging on 'to the delegation's coat-tails'. He claimed that the final 'tug-of-war' would come over a concept of his own – external association. Ireland was to be recognised as an independent state, with an external association to the British Commonwealth. Not surprisingly, Barton would later record a remark of de Valera's at the time which made a lasting impression on him: 'We must have scapegoats.' Collins too was under no illusions about de Valera's machinations. He wrote to a friend: 'I was warned more times than I can recall about the One. And when I was caught for this delegation, my immediate thought was of how easily I had walked into the preparations. But having walked in, I had to stay.' An inauspicious background indeed for a group of men chosen to conduct literally historic negotiations concerning the future of their country.

Against this divided delegation, the British fielded what was probably the most formidable political team assembled in the country's history. Lloyd George himself, Birkenhead, Austen Chamberlain, who had succeeded Bonar Law as Conservative leader, and Winston Churchill. The other British negotiators included the Attorney General, Sir Gordon Hewart, the Secretary of State for War, Sir Lamington Worthington-Evans, and Sir Hamar Greenwood, the Chief Secretary of Ireland. Behind them were the resources of the Empire's civil service, in particular two outstandingly brilliant individuals, Tom Jones and Lionel Curtis. All these men were imbued with the attitudes of the imperial England of the day. The idea of a Republic was anathema to them, and even talking to Sinn Féiners was an extremely dubious exercise for most of them. There were no handshakes before the two delegations sat down. Lloyd George swept the Irish to their side of the table and introduced the parties, thus deftly avoiding a more formal set of introductions which would have involved the credentials signed by de Valera, which depicted them as already possessing a degree of independence which the British did not acknowledge. The British side was keenly aware that their presence at Downing Street exposed them to great suspicion and political danger from their followers. But they did have one tremendous overriding advantage, the tradition of British statescraft. Robert Barton has left a description of the opening of the negotiations:

> We Irishmen were nervous and ill at ease, it was our first introduction to Diplomacy. The English were at home, and confident in surroundings where they had met and out-manoeuvred or intimidated their opponents in a hundred similar struggles. On the walls hung portraits of past Prime Ministers, the builders of Britain's Empire. Opposite to me was the portrait of Sir Robert Walpole and beneath it sat Winston Churchill.[47]

However, though on the face of it the encounter between the two delegations would appear to have been a complete mismatch, the force of Collins's energy, intelligence and personality was such that he and Birkenhead, whose earlier incarnation as Carson's 'galloper' has been described, achieved an extraordinary friendship. Birkenhead would later become Carson's principal adversary in the House in arguing successfully for the settlement that was eventually reached. Griffith, though less flamboyant, older, and almost worn out by his exertions for his country, was also a formidable intellect, and proved himself to be both an imaginative and a steadfast negotiator. He was the nominal leader of the delegation, but realising his limitations of age and health, in characteristically self-sacrificial fashion, he allowed Collins to become the effective leader, the person who took on the major share of the negotiating, drafting, sub-conferences, etc.

Both sides saw value in the sub-conference approach which Collins and Griffith proposed, as, apart from the fact that smaller committees have larger work rates than big ones, it enabled both the British and the Irish to sideline diehard elements in their respective delegations. Where the Irish were concerned, the sub-conference ploy effectively knocked out much of the force of de Valera's stratagem of building division into the delegation. This did not mean that the Irish did not keep Dublin informed. Every week, at least one member of the delegation returned to Dublin to make a progress report. Collins in particular returned almost every weekend.

Apart from his racking negotiating work, he was also, while labouring for peace, preparing for war should the negotiations break down. Secret arrangements were made for an aeroplane to stand by throughout the negotiations to fly him out of London at short notice. He continued, as president of the IRB, to attend to the detail of the running of that organisation, whose power was demonstrated in telling fashion at one notable juncture in de Valera's on-going campaign to place himself unassailably ahead of Collins, and in charge of both the political and military wings of Sinn Féin. Collins defeated de Valera over the 'New Army' controversy which erupted on 25 November, as the London negotiations were nearing conclusion. During the previous March, he had influenced the IRB to alter its constitution so as to fall in with de Valera's wishes. The Supreme Council of the IRB regarded itself and its president as the real government of Ireland. But de Valera, who disliked the IRB, argued that in order to give legitimacy to the Volunteers' activities, the IRA should be seen to be controlled by the Dail. Collins agreed to this at the time, since the move lessened the force of British propaganda efforts to depict the IRA as merely a lawless bunch of assassins.

Now, however, in November of 1921, with Collins enmeshed in negotiations, de Valera proposed to mark the anniversary of the founding of the Volunteers in 1913 with the creation of a 'New Army'. What this meant was that the existing army, both men and officers, were to take an oath of loyalty to the Dail, which effectively speaking meant an oath of loyalty to de Valera. The officers' commissions were to be contingent on them taking this oath. Even though the negotiations were in progress, de Valera had arranged that a Cabinet meeting be held, including the members of the Cabinet who were in the delegation, to conclude the arrangements for this manoeuvre. When Collins, who kept the IRB apprised of developments throughout the negotiations, received his invitation to the meeting, he mobilised the IRB.

Consequently, when de Valera, who also attempted to place Stack on the GHQ staff, 'as Brugha's ghost', summoned the GHQ men to announce his proposals, he found that none of them were in favour. The meeting broke down with de Valera giving vent to a fit of the temper which had so dismayed John Grace in New York.[48] Rising excitedly, he pushed away the table in front of him and, half screaming, half shouting, said: 'Ye may mutiny if you like, but Ireland will give me another army' and dismissed them all from his presence.

When he cooled down, de Valera acknowledged the unlikelihood of his being provided with another army, and that it would be madness to attempt to force change on an unwilling GHQ staff at such a critical juncture. The New Army proposals were dropped. But de Valera advised that the new commissions be accepted.

Not surprisingly, back in London, Collins had written earlier in the month:

> (4 November) . . . Not much achieved, principally because PM [Lloyd George] recognises our over-riding difficulty – Dublin. Plays on that. On the other hand we fight every word, recognising that to betray ourselves would mean disaster for us.
> G [Griffith] said, 'What do we accept?'
> Indeed what do we accept? If we accept at all it will be inferred as a gross betrayal or a similar act of treachery. What have we come for? I ask myself that question a dozen times a day.

To judge from the notation of subsequent exchanges between the two men, and the record of what transpired later, they were never fully illuminated as to what they had come for. But what they accepted, after weeks of exhaustive argument, and even more exhausting trips back and forth across the Irish Sea, may be studied in full in the Articles of Agreement in the Appendix, or the Treaty, as it is generally referred to in Ireland. In summary, the document created of the 26 counties an Irish free state with dominion status, recognised partition, and contained the following oath to be taken by members of the parliament of the Irish Free State:

> I . . . do solemnly swear true faith and allegiance to the constitution of the Irish Free State as by law established and that I will be faithful to HM King George V, his heirs and successors by law, in virtue of the common citizenship of Ireland with Great Britain and her adherence to and membership of the group of nations forming the British Commonwealth of Nations.

Clearly, the Republic had slid off the radar screen. Like radar itself, the British had yet to invent an acceptance of republicanism. Before signing the document, the delegates made a last journey to Ireland, Collins arriving in

Dun Laoghaire aboard a delayed ferry, after a sleepless night, to confront not one but two meetings, one of the IRB and the other of the Dail at the Mansion House. He had to consult with the IRB during a lunchtime break in the extremely fractious and confusing encounter at the Mansion House and evidently succeeded in obtaining the brotherhood's general acceptance of the proposed treaty's provisions, albeit with some reservations over the oath and partition. No records of this meeting exist, but as subsequent events tend to prove, we will shortly be able to make an educated guess as to what arguments eventually swayed the IRB to Collins's side. Nor do we have full accounts of what transpired at the Mansion House meeting.

Brugha was unalterably opposed to the document, the signing of which he said would split the country. In reply Griffith told Brugha that he would not sign the document, but would submit it to the Dail 'and if necessary to the people'. He also said that the country would not fight on the allegiance issue and that the Dail was the body to decide for or against war. Although Griffith was speaking to Brugha, not de Valera, de Valera later claimed that it was Griffith's promise not to sign without returning to Dublin which decided him against joining the delegation. From the differing versions which emerged we know that de Valera objected to the oath and the Ulster provisions, but thought that with amendments the document might be made acceptable. If the amendments were not forthcoming, he said, the delegation should let the British know 'they were prepared to face the consequences, war or no war'. To this day, confusion exists as to what sort of an oath de Valera would accept. Collins, Childers, de Valera himself, and the official notetaker at the conference, Colm O'Murchadha, all gave differing interpretations of what he said. De Valera, in fact, ultimately gave three differing definitions in all. But one thing he was quite clear about, as he later told the Dail, was that he 'did not give, nor did the Cabinet give, any instruction to the Delegation as to any final document which they were to put in'.

One might imagine that de Valera would have sought to cloud the fact that he sent back to London at that historic juncture with such imprecise instructions a set of negotiators who, apart from the overriding political considerations, on a personal level would have given their lives for him during the war which had barely ended, but he regarded this exercise in 'cute hoorism' as of such significance in exculpating him from all responsibility for the delegation's actions that he told the Dail (on 14 December): 'I say that there is nothing in type that I ever saw taken back to London that represented my views. There were certain verbal things . . .'

The differences at the meeting and within the delegation itself were symbolised by the fact that the delegates went back to London that evening (3 December) on separate boats. Collins and Griffith sailed together from Dun Laoghaire, Barton, Duffy and Childers from Dublin. Back in Dublin, O'Murchadha recorded the meeting as deciding that the delegates were to carry out their original instructions with the same powers. But the existing oath could not be subscribed to and the Cabinet was prepared to face war as a result. Griffith was to say the document could not be signed, but to try to break on Ulster. Before the Treaty was signed, Lloyd George briefed his Cabinet on what had gone on in Dublin. He told his colleagues that 'the division of opinion which had manifested itself among the Irish Representatives in London, also existed in the Irish Cabinet'. He noted that the rejectionists were in the majority and that they had submitted counter-proposals. But he went on to make the significant observation that 'The document contained no counter-proposals regarding Ulster, from which it would appear that no Sinn Féin objection would be forthcoming to the proposals regarding Ulster.' Thus, the shadow of the oath, and not the substance of the dismemberment of the country, was to constitute the basis for war, a war in which one of Collins's principal generals, Seán MacEoin, reckoned that his troops had one rifle for every fifty men, and in which Collins knew his formerly lethal secret service was now exposed and impotent. Whatever hope that had ever existed of Griffith getting away with the Ulster ploy speedily evaporated when negotiations resumed. Gavin Duffy blurted out that the Irish difficulty lay in 'coming into the Empire'. The British withdrew and the talks temporarily broke down.

It was a time of extreme tension. For the first time since the truce had come into operation, the British put armed patrols on the streets of Dublin, stopping and searching civilians. Armed men also showed up in the streets outside the houses in London where the delegates stayed. The Irish delegates were confused and angry. Neither Collins nor Griffith liked the proposed treaty, but Collins was mindful of how Home Rule had been lost through sudden changes in circumstance, such as the Phoenix Park murders. Moreover as he noted in one of his tête-à-têtes with Griffith early in negotiations: 'The advantages of Dominion status to us, as a stepping stone, to complete independence are immeasurable.' He added that even if 'we were to go back to Dublin tomorrow with a document which gave us a Republic', he doubted that such a document would find favour with everyone.

Griffith had agreed with him, while worrying that even if the Dail did ratify any agreement, 'a certain amount of power is still in the hands of those we know will be against anything which treats of Empire status'. However, while gloomily noting the certainty of opposition to any agreement which the delegation could hope to conclude, Griffith went on to face the nub of the matter: '. . . sooner or later a decision will have to be made and we shall have to make it – whatever our position and authority'.

Decision time had now arrived. Griffith arranged through the British civil servant Tom Jones for a meeting between Collins and Lloyd George, at which the pair reached an agreement that the talks would recommence, although neither man conceded anything of substance. But it appears to be the inescapable logic of the situation that, faced with deviousness in Dublin and the prospect of securing his own army from London, Collins, possibly for some weeks before this, had made up his mind to use the treaty as a stepping stone to gain his long-term objective of a united Ireland.

Accordingly, several hours of high theatre now ensued in which Lloyd George finally killed any lingering hopes the Irish may have entertained of making a stand on Ulster by producing a letter from Griffith, based on a memorandum which Griffith had been given by Jones earlier in the talks. In substance Griffith developed the memorandum into an assurance that he would be prepared to agree to a formula recognising the Crown and a free partnership with the British Commonwealth, in return for guarantees on that mystical entity 'essential unity'. Armed with this assurance, Lloyd George had subsequently overridden diehard opposition to his treaty policy at a crucial Unionist meeting in Liverpool. When confronted with the document, which he had obviously forgotten, Griffith honoured his commitment, although by then of course the 'essential unity' of his country was long gone, pledging that though his colleagues refused, he would sign the proposed agreement. His demeanour so impressed his opponents, who very well understood what opprobrium he would face in Dublin, that Austen Chamberlain afterwards said: 'A braver man than Arthur Griffith I have never met.' By now, Lloyd George was aware that Collins intended to sign, and that Barton was the one most likely to resist, and he staged a *coup de théâtre* for the young former British army officer's benefit. Having declared with great seriousness that anyone who did not sign the agreement would have the responsibility for war on their shoulders, he produced two letters, saying that he had to communicate with Craig that night:

> Here are the alternative letters which I have prepared, one enclosing the Articles of Agreement reached by His Majesty's Government and yourselves, and the other saying that Sinn Féin representatives refuse the Oath of allegiance and refuse to come within the Empire. If I send this letter, it is war – and war within three days. Which letter am I to send? Whichever letter you choose travels by special train to Holyhead, and by destroyer to Belfast. The train is waiting with steam up at Euston. Mr Shakespeare is ready. If he is to reach Sir James Craig in time we must have your answer by ten p.m. tonight. You can have until then but no longer to decide whether you will give peace or war to your country.

In fact, all Lloyd George was committed to doing was sending a copy of the proposals to Craig. And as for the details concerning the waiting train and the civil servant Shakespeare, Barton was not to know that the Prime Minister had, earlier in his meeting with Collins that morning, promised to allow more time for consideration of the proposals. To his credit, Barton did not break, and it took several hours of persuasion from his colleagues in a separate conference before he agreed to sign. The British delegation had begun to fear that the Irish were not going to return to Downing Street when they eventually did turn up. By that time the Auxiliaries had returned to the streets of Dublin. The signatures which removed them were appended at 2.30 on the morning of 6 December 1921. Birkenhead turned to Collins after signing and said: 'I may have signed my political death warrant tonight.' Collins replied: 'I may have signed my actual death warrant.' He had.

At the moment of the Treaty's signing, de Valera was staying in the home of a leading businessman and Sinn Féin supporter, Stephen O'Mara, in Limerick. He had been on a tour of inspection of army units with, amongst others, Cathal Brugha, and Richard Mulcahy, the Chief of Staff. Mulcahy took the phone call from Gearóid O'Sullivan, a member of the GHQ staff, informing the party that a Treaty had been signed. De Valera refused to come to the phone to hear what O'Sullivan had to say. He may very well have received a phone call at the O'Mara house himself. In a letter to the author, Etienne Rynne, whose father, Mulcahy's aide, was also present in the house, said:

> My father always said, and I even recall him saying it to de Valera himself over the phone, when the latter rang my father in 1969 to check on the matter [de Valera was having his authorised biography written at the time], that he seemed to remember a tall figure, most likely de Valera, taking the phone call, as also did his sister, Mary, who was also staying in Strand House at the time.[49]

De Valera, however, maintained that he had no idea that the Treaty had been signed, and that he only learned something of its contents at 7.30 on the evening of 6 December, when he was shown a copy of the *Evening Mail* by Brugha and Stack, just before he presided over a Dante commemoration ceremony in the Mansion House. This contention beggars belief. Firstly, it is impossible to imagine that Mulcahy did not impart some details of the O'Sullivan phone call to the group waiting agog for news from London in the O'Mara household. It is simply not credible that in a country like Ireland, where news and gossip travel with something approaching the speed of light, merely by using word of mouth, such important political intelligence would not have been communicated to de Valera before 7.30 p.m. It is also inconceivable that he would not have had someone, probably Childers, in London keeping him informed. Phone lines between London and Dublin were buzzing that day. Moreover, as de Valera boarded the train to Dublin from Limerick later that morning, news boys were selling papers, containing details of the Treaty's signing, in and around the station. In Dublin de Valera drove across the city to spend some time in Rathgar and later went back to Greystones, in County Wicklow, before the Dante ceremony. In those (pre-electronic media) days the city would have been dotted with newspaper sellers and posters advertising one of the most avidly followed news stories of the era.

De Valera's initial reaction closely resembled his attitude to the Irish plank which Cohalan had secured at the Republican convention in America. Not being his resolution, it was rejected. He later described the delegates' signing of the Treaty as 'an act of disloyalty to their President and to their colleagues in the Cabinet such as probably without parallel in history. They not merely sign the document, but in order to make the "fait accompli" doubly secure, they published it hours before their President or colleagues saw it.' The signing rather than the contents of the Treaty was the greatest sin. While the delegates were still on their way home from London, de Valera called a meeting of the other three Cabinet members in Dublin, Brugha, Stack and W.T. Cosgrave, and announced that he intended to sack the three members in London (Barton, Collins and Griffith). He knew that Brugha and Stack would support this move, and knowing the respect in which he was held by the mild-mannered Cosgrave, was confident of his backing also. However, Cosgrave astounded him by stipulating that Collins & co. should be heard before any action was taken against them. Suddenly, from being four against the three signatories, de Valera found the odds had shifted in the opposite direction. Accordingly, a full Cabinet meeting was scheduled for the following day.

Hitherto, the de Valera–Collins rivalry, and the subsidiary antipathy of Brugha and Stack towards Collins, had remained hidden from the public at large. But as the people cheered the largely undigested Treaty document, taking it as copper-fastening the peace, de Valera moved to bring the divisions into the open, and with them the possibility of war. He ordered the publication of the following statement before the meeting of the Cabinet:

> In view of the nature of the proposed Treaty with Great Britain, President de Valera has sent an urgent summons to the members of the Cabinet in London to report at once, so that a full Cabinet decision may be taken. The hour of meeting is fixed for 12 o'clock noon tomorrow. A meeting of the Dail will be summoned later.

The meeting was predictably acrimonious and confused, a rerun of the meeting at the same venue before the Treaty was signed. The main thrust of de Valera's attack on the Treaty was that the delegates had not referred it to him before signing. He claimed that he would have gone to London himself had Arthur Griffith not promised him that he would consult him before signing. Barton, who had shown in London that he deplored the absence of a Republic and the presence of the oath in the Treaty to a greater extent than most, counter-attacked with an argument which probably expressed the feelings of all the signatories. De Valera, he said, had created the situation by refusing to go to the talks himself, and his 'vacillation' was the root cause of the problem. Barton voted with Collins, Griffith and Cosgrave against de Valera, Brugha and Stack in preventing the Treaty from being summarily rejected and instead calling for a meeting of the Dail, which had appointed the plenipotentiaries to decide the issue.

Temporarily foiled, de Valera confided to Childers that he intended to gain his objectives by courting 'extremist support'. He began his campaign to secure this support by following up his earlier message to the press with a longer statement, one considerably more damaging to the prospects of securing a peaceful outcome to the Treaty debate.

> You have seen in the public press the text of the proposed Treaty with Great Britain. The terms of this agreement are in violent conflict with the wishes of the majority of this nation as expressed freely in the successive elections during the last three years.
>
> I feel it my duty to inform you immediately that I cannot recommend the acceptance of this Treaty, either to Dail Eireann or the country. In this attitude I am supported by the Ministers of Home Affairs and Defence.

A public session of Dail Eireann is being summoned for Wednesday next at 11 o'clock. I ask the people to maintain during the interval the same discipline as heretofore. The members of the Cabinet, though divided in opinions, are prepared to carry on the public services as usual.

The Army as such is, of course, not affected by the political situation, and continues under the same orders and control. The great test of our people has come. Let us face it worthily without bitterness and above all, without recriminations. There is a definite constitutional way of resolving our differences – let us not depart from it, and let the conduct of the Cabinet in this matter be an example to the whole nation.

De Valera knew that despite his own objections and those on whom he counted for 'extremist support', like Brugha, Stack, and the more doctrinaire members of the IRA, the public at large did not share his views. In fact, when the Dail debate commenced (on 14 December), he conceded that if a plebiscite were held, the people would accept the Treaty. However, his attitude was, as he stated at another stage of the debate, that 'no-one is going to bind me here by a majority rule'. He succeeded in having the debate transferred from public to private session so that the press, and hence the public, were kept in the dark as to what was going on, and he also attempted to have a proposal of his own brought forward as the basis for a new treaty, Document No. 2, as it came to be popularly known. This document, a version of his external association ideas, which the plenipotentiaries had put to the British only to have them rejected out of hand, contained mention of neither a Republic nor an oath. It provided that 'for the purposes of the Association, Ireland shall recognise his Britannic Majesty as Head of the Association'. During the debates, de Valera admitted that Document No. 2's provisions on partition were 'practically the same as the Treaty provisions', containing an 'explicit recognition of the right on the part of Irishmen to secede from Ireland'. Of the Treaty's own provisions on partition, he admitted (on 14 December) that he did not know how they could be gone back on 'except to make a declaratory statement in the beginning that we don't recognise the right of any part of Ireland to secede, still for the sake of so and so we are willing to accept it'. The problem, he said, was 'not the Ulster question' but a 'fight between Ireland and England'. One of the most extraordinary features of the, at times vicious, debate was that this order of priorities was widely accepted. The intangibles of oaths and republics took centre stage. De Valera deliberately made use of woolly, superficially sentimental language to confuse his critics. Speaking on 14 December in private session, he said:

There are differences that may be regarded as shadows, but they are more than shadows – the things that matter for us. If to the crown and His Majesty's ministers in this country these things are not shadows to them; but the Irish Army and the Irish Ministers if they are mere shadows, why should they be grasping for the shadows, and why should not we? I wanted to clear these shadows because they meant an awful lot. We have the country supporting definite proposals. It will be the mischief to get the British out of the position they are in.

The tangible fact that the country was 'supporting definite proposals' – those contained in the Treaty, was glossed over. So, incredibly, was the tangible fact that co-religionists and fellow Irishmen and women were being murdered daily, and that part of the island had been removed from the purview of the Dail. These things were scarcely adverted to, even though, in retaliation for the attacks, the Dail was supporting a boycott of Belfast manufactures. One deputy, a Belfastman, Seán MacEntee, speaking on 16 December in private session, did base his opposition on the issue of partition, saying that the Treaty created 'the title deeds for a fortress of Orangeism and Unionism that will hold Ireland for England as surely as Gibraltar holds the Mediterranean for them'. But in general partition was so largely airbrushed from the exchanges that an observer might be forgiven for concluding that deputies were giving tacit acceptance to the fact that partition had been accepted as a fait accompli by an assembly which, for all its divisions, was largely drawn from outside the Six County region and knew very little about the area concerned.

De Valera used his extraordinary prestige both inside and outside the Chamber. Outside it, by attempting to pressurise individual deputies into voting his way, and by making yet another attempt to influence the army GHQ, which failed, as had his 'New Army' initiative. Inside it, the Dail record shows that he made 250 interruptions, and that his contributions to the debate came to a total of 39 pages as compared to 20 for both Collins and Griffith. Out of all this welter of argument and filibuster, de Valera's net arguments may be summarised by quoting two of his statements. First:

> I am against this Treaty because it does not reconcile Irish national aspirations with association with the British Government . . . I am against this Treaty, not because I am a man of war but because I am a man of peace. I am against this Treaty because it will not end the centuries of conflict between the two nations of Great Britain and Ireland. [The Treaty is] absolutely inconsistent with our position; it gives away Irish independence; it brings us into the British Empire; it acknowledges the head of the British Empire, not merely as the head of an association but as the direct monarch of Ireland, as the source of executive authority in Ireland.

In the second statement he said that he was:

> . . . captaining a team and I felt that the team should have played with me to the last and should have got the chance which I felt would put us over and we might have crossed the bar in my opinion at high tide. They rushed before the tide got to the top and almost foundered the ship.

Both in the debate and subsequently he continued to argue that Griffith's undertaking to Brugha at the 3 December meeting was the reason he had not gone to London.

Collins dealt with the captaincy argument by commenting that de Valera was 'a captain who sent his crew to sea, and tried to direct operations from dry land'. And the contention about Griffith's pledge to Brugha weighed little with public opinion against the fact that he had had several opportunities to join the delegation, indeed had been repeatedly pressed to do so, in the months which had elapsed since he first met Lloyd George. In all, the wearisome debate continued for 13 days in private and public session, with a break for Christmas, until 7 January 1922. In the course of the debate it became clear that 'extremist support' was not enough. Press, pulpit, big business (what there was of it), the bigger farmers, most of the labour movement, and the public at large supported the Treaty. It offered tangible benefits like the prospect of founding an Irish army and police force, acquiring fiscal autonomy, and losing the Black and Tans.

Against these gains Document No. 2 held little attraction. It was too abstruse for the man in the street and too soft on the Republic for the extremists whom de Valera wished to woo. On the other hand, public reaction was clearly with Collins after he said of the Treaty:

In my opinion it gives us freedom, not the ultimate freedom that all nations desire and develop to, but the freedom to achieve it . . . we have stated we would not coerce the North-East. We have stated it officially. I stated it publicly in Armagh and nobody has found fault with me. What was the use talking big phrases about not agreeing to the partition of our country. Surely we recognise that the North-East corner does exist, and surely our intention was that we should take such steps as would lead to mutual understanding. The Treaty has made an effort . . . to deal with it on lines that will lead very rapidly to goodwill and the entry of the North-East under the Irish Parliament.

Collins's analysis of the partition issue will require revisiting at a later stage because of both what he said and what he did not say. But it touched a chord with the southern electorate. A much deeper chord echoed to his vision of freedom to achieve freedom, the concept of using the Treaty as a stepping stone to complete autonomy. So much so that, during the Christmas recess, 24 county councils passed resolutions supporting the Treaty, largely it is said at the instigation of W.T. Cosgrave. Collins's problem lay not with the public but within the Dail, and, to a degree, was of his own making. As the 1918 election had approached it was he, along with Harry Boland, who had chosen 'forward'-minded candidates to stand for Sinn Féin. These deputies' views were more radical than the people they represented. In addition Boland, who had been in America with de Valera, was now opposed to Collins, who, apart from political divergence, had compounded the differences between the two men by becoming engaged to the woman Boland had hoped to marry, Kitty Kiernan. Apart from the support of figures like Brugha, Stack and Childers, de Valera was backed by a formidable group of woman deputies, Madame Markievicz, Mary MacSwiney, a sister of the dead hunger striker Terence MacSwiney, Padraig Pearse's mother Margaret and Tom Clarke's widow Kathleen. Thus de Valera, it was said, had the support of the 'women and Childers' party. It was not enough.

On 7 January 1922, one of the most important votes in Irish history was cast. The Dail voted by 64 votes to 57 to accept the Treaty. By seven votes, the people's representatives had accepted the foundation document on which independent Ireland was subsequently built. Three days later, de Valera attempted to interrupt the building process by forcing a decision on his own resignation, which could be represented as a second vote on the Treaty. However, though he succeeded in whittling the Treaty majority down to two votes (60–58), he lost again. This time he made clear the seriousness of the implications of his refusal to be bound by parliamentary majority. He left the Chamber in protest after the vote, followed by his supporters. The following day he gave a press conference at which he said: 'We will continue every resistance against outside authority that has been imposed on the Irish people. We have a perfect right to resist by every means in our power.' 'Even by war?' asked a surprised reporter. De Valera replied: 'By every means in our power to resist authority imposed on this country from outside.'[50]

In effect this left the country without a government. The deputies who remained elected Griffith to succeed de Valera and appointed the following Cabinet: Michael Collins, Finance; Gavin Duffy, Foreign Affairs; W.T. Cosgrave, Local Government; Kevin O'Higgins, Defence; Eamon Duggan, Home Affairs; and Richard Mulcahy was appointed to the vital Defence Ministry. These young men faced a daunting political and economic landscape. The split in the Dail was replicated in the army. Important GHQ and rural officers were anti-Treaty because, as Liam Lynch, the most influential southern commander, said, they had 'declared for an Irish Republic and will not live under any other law'.

There wasn't very much law to live under. Normal policing had broken down. The Black and Tan war and the reprisals policy had caused enormous economic destruction. Huge tracts of land lay uncultivated, and all this in a country which was already so poor that five years earlier the first essential step towards creating a revolutionary army had been to buy footwear for the shoeless would-be soldiers. This very poverty motivated some IRA men to continue the struggle. They had fought in rags with nearly empty weapons and equally empty bellies for a Republic, and they felt that a continuation of their efforts would bring one as assuredly as it had a dominion. Also, just as in 1916, the 'gallant failure' philosophy was strong. The motivation for fighting had been to continue the tradition of a rising in every generation, not the expectation of actually winning. That was something which the Irish physical-force tradition had little experience in coping with. And this was only in the south. In the north, as we shall see, sectarian warfare was claiming hundreds of lives, and organised pogroms drove some 23,000 Catholics from their homes. As events in the south were confusing enough, however, developments in the Six County area will be dealt with separately.

Under the terms of the Treaty, a provisional government had to be formed to take over the British administrative machine until such time as the government of the free state envisaged by the Treaty was actually set up. This government formally came into being on 14 January and subsumed the

Cabinet formed in the wake of the de Valera walkout, including some other prominent Sinn Féiners, Eóin MacNeill, P.J. Hogan, Joe McGrath, Kevin O'Higgins and Fionan Lynch. Collins became chairman of the Government, Griffith held on to the role of president of Dail Eireann, while de Valera continued to try to obstruct the implementation of the Treaty by remaining outside the provisional government along with his followers. However, the de Valera-ites, as members of the Dail, continued to turn up at the Mansion House, and put down questions, challenging provisional government actions.

One of Collins's arguments in favour of the Treaty was that the test of who won the war was left in charge of the battlefield. The most tangible proof of the truth of this came less than a week after de Valera walked out of the Dail. Dublin Castle, the seat of British administration in Ireland, was handed over to the Irish, Collins taking the salute. Two days later, on 18 January, a major split in the IRA was temporarily averted when a four-man council, two pro- and two anti-Treaty, was set up to ensure that 'the Republican aim shall not be prejudiced' until a convention representative of the army could be held. In favour of holding a convention were Rory O'Connor, Liam Lynch, Liam Mellows, Oscar Traynor and Seán Russell. Had they got their way in early February, it is probable that the obvious open split would have caused the British to halt their evacuation. As it was, the setting up of the watchdog council meant that, until the pace was forced by the Republicans and a convention held in March, the British were handing over barracks to both pro- and anti-Treaty forces.

On the political front, Collins also sought to stave off a split by agreeing with de Valera that the Treaty not be voted on at an extraordinary Sinn Féin Ard Fheis, which was held on 21 February to formulate policy in the wake of the passage of the Treaty in the Dail. Apart from avoiding a split, Collins avoided an embarrassing defeat, for the Sinn Féin delegates had considerably more radical views on the Treaty than had the country at large. De Valera for his part would have suffered an even more embarrassing larger-scale defeat had an election been called and the issue put to the public.

Collins hoped that the means of avoiding the threatened splits would be found in the wording of the new constitution which the Treaty demanded. The constitution committee, of which he was the chairman, held its first meeting in Dublin on 25 January 1922. Collins took the final decisions on the recommendations of the committee, which he charged with drawing up 'a true Democratic Constitution'. Meaningfully, he also directed that it be 'easy to alter as the final stages of complete freedom were achieved'. He directed that as the oath was already included in the Treaty, it should be left out of the constitution, which should not suggest that any power in Ireland derived from the Crown, nor contain mention of a governor general. The constitution was to guarantee Ireland's equality of status with the nations of the world, not merely within the British Empire. Much of what he hoped to achieve by producing such a constitution was negated by Lloyd George's insistence that the British would have to have sight of it before it was published. But he did succeed in persuading Lloyd George not to hold up the process of ratifying the Treaty until the constitution was drafted, because delay could mean the collapse of the provisional government under the anti-Treaty-ites' pressure.

Convinced of the urgency of the situation, the British introduced the Irish Free State (Amendment) Bill on 9 February. Churchill pushed the Bill through the House in the teeth of diehard opposition, and Birkenhead piloted it through the Lords so swiftly that it received the royal assent on 31 March. Both Churchill and Birkenhead, despite his earlier pro-Unionist activities, deserve credit for playing a significant role in the re-creation of an independent Ireland. Had such celerity been achieved with the Home Rule Bill, both Britain and Ireland would have been spared much anguish.

While the provisional government was attempting to set up a new state, and a new army and police force, the anti-Treaty IRA was raiding for arms, money and transport all around the country and, where possible, setting up independent fiefdoms of its own. Pro-Treaty newspaper editors were threatened with death, and in some cases their printing presses smashed. In Dublin the *Freeman's Journal* and in Clonmel the *Nationalist* suffered this treatment.

Anti-Treaty forces took over the city of Limerick, and Collins and Mulcahy, realising that the army they were building was not yet strong enough to force the IRA out, agreed to an arrangement whereby both pro- and anti-Treaty forces withdrew from the city. Within the provisional government, while Collins was reluctant to use force against his former comrades in arms, hardline figures such as Kevin O'Higgins regarded this agreement as drawing a line in the sands of toleration; giving in to mutineers must come to an end. Rory O'Connor, who had been best man at Kevin O'Higgins's wedding but was now leading the anti-Treaty forces, turned up the heat by going ahead with the arrangements for the army convention which the Collins/Mulcahy faction had hoped to avoid. The provisional government were forced to ban the convention, but O'Connor not only insisted on holding it, on 26 March, but gave a disturbing press conference into the bargain.

Asked if he intended to set up a military dictatorship, he replied: 'You can call it that if you wish.' As the public knew very little of the divisions within the IRA, this statement naturally set alarm bells ringing. But worse was to follow. The convention discussed resolutions which included 'the declaration of a dictatorship which would . . . overthrow the four Governments in Ireland opposed to a Republic – viz: Dail Eireann, Provisional Government, British Government and Northern Government'. It also heard of the necessity for the suppression of newspapers (after which the *Freeman's Journal* was wrecked, because of its convention reportage), and of preventing the development of the new army, police force, and court services. The convention's distaste for the rule of law was underlined by an outburst of bank and post office raiding, a seizure of whatever state revenues were available, which included everything from excise duties to dog licences, and interfering with the mails. The prosecution of the boycott against Six County manufactures was intensified. On 14 April, Rory O'Connor crossed the Rubicon. Along with seizing a number of centres in Dublin which had either Masonic or *ancien regime* associations, such as the Kildare Street Club, he and his colleagues struck at the very heart of the Irish legal system, taking over the Four Courts in Dublin and making it their headquarters. The 'humiliating fact' of the situation which their activities created throughout the country had already prompted Michael Collins to say at a meeting in Wexford that 'Our country is now in a more lawless and chaotic state than it was in the Black & Tan regime. Could there be a more staggering blow to our National pride and our fair National hopes.'

The answer was, there could be and there would be many more blows. On the political front, the objective of the provisional government was to buy time to hold the election called for by the Treaty, when the new constitution was ready, and to develop and maintain the institutions of state against the onslaughts of their opponents. Violence was clearly inevitable, but for a time Collins's reluctance to proceed against his former comrades was sufficiently mirrored in the ranks of the Republicans, or the 'irregulars' as the provisional government spokespersons described them to stave off the inevitable. Arthur Griffith showed notable courage in insisting on going to Sligo to speak on Easter Sunday (16 April), despite the fact that his meeting was proclaimed by the irregulars, who filled the streets of the town with armed men. Griffith arrived in an armoured car surrounded by armed soldiers. The leader of the anti-Treaty forces, Liam Pilkington, recognising that if he attempted to enforce the ban on Griffith's address he would be giving the signal for a war of brother against brother, allowed the meeting to pass off peacefully. Kilkenny was less lucky a few weeks later. Heavy fighting broke out over a period of two days, and the provisional government forces took 150 prisoners.

Still, sufficient of the Collins/Pilkington spirit of restraint persisted within the IRB for a final attempt at reconciliation to be made within the ranks of the fighting men. Liam Lynch, Tom Hales, Seán O'Hegarty and Florrie O'Donoghue were disturbed by the anti-democratic tendencies of the Four Courts men. Apart from Rory O'Connor himself, these included Ernie O'Malley and Liam Mellows. The Lynch group eventually joined with Collins's men, on 1 May, in issuing a statement, co-signed by the anti-Treaty men (Seán O'Hegarty, Humphrey Murphy, Florrie O'Donoghue and Tom Hales), calling for a closing of ranks in the face of 'the greatest calamity in Irish history'. Remarkably the statement conceded that a majority of the people wanted the Treaty. It also called for an agreed election, and the forming of a government which would have 'the confidence of the whole country'.

O'Connor for one had no confidence in the peace initiative and immediately issued a public disavowal of the statement as 'a political dodge intended to split the Republican ranks'. One of the aims of the statement signed by the pro- and anti-Treaty men had been 'Army unification', and towards that end an 'executive' had been set up consisting of three nominees from each side, who continued to meet and uphold some sort of a truce in the face of an ever-rising tide of bank robberies. These were on such a scale that one nationwide swoop on the Bank of Ireland's branches netted some £230,000, a huge sum in the money values of the time. 'Army unification' proved a chimera when O'Connor's men demanded that they be allowed to appoint the army chief of staff, and on 15 June O'Connor and O'Malley formally repudiated the six-man talks. They made their position crystal clear at a meeting described as 'an Executive Convention' in the Four Courts three days later. The resolution before the gathering was 'that this Executive Council of the IRA hereby decide . . . the only means of maintaining the Republic is by giving the English 72 hours notice to evacuate the country'. By way of winning friends and influencing people into supporting this objective, O'Connor's group proposed 'The destruction of all barracks occupied by our troops, the attacking present port positions held by the English troops. The striking at English forces . . . wherever possible in areas which the pro-Treaty troops occupy so that they may be brought into collision with English troops.'

The fact that such activities would also bring the anti-Treaty forces 'into collision' with the vast majority of the people did not trouble the anti-Treaty leaders, notably de Valera. He had greeted O'Connor's seizure of the Four Courts with a proclamation on 16 April which declared: 'Young men and young women of Ireland, the goal is at last in sight. Steady altogether; Ireland is yours for the taking. Take it.' Privately, when waited upon by a Labour Party delegation, which urged him to act to prevent civil war, he declared that the 'majority have no right to do wrong'.[51] In the wording of the Irish colloquial expression, de Valera 'lost the run of himself' on his return to Ireland from America insofar as he allowed his ego and jealousy of Collins to govern much of his policy. But from the time of the Treaty's signing, in his pursuit of 'extremist support', he seems to have undergone a sort of emotional and political impairment similar to that he displayed at earlier moments of crisis in his career, notably during 1916, and in his jousts with the Irish-American leaders.

His acclaim for O'Connor's seizure of the Four Courts was no isolated act. It followed a set of what became known as 'wading through blood speeches' which he had delivered the previous month. At Dungarvan on 16 March he said:

> The Treaty . . . barred the way to independence with the blood of fellow Irishmen. It was only by civil war after this that they could get their independence. If you don't fight today, you will have to fight tomorrow; and I say, when you are in a good fighting position, then fight on.

The following day, he piled Pelion upon Ossa. At Carrick-on-Shannon, he told a gathering which included hundreds of armed IRA men that:

> If the Treaty was accepted the fight for freedom would still go on; and the Irish people, instead of fighting foreign soldiers, would have to fight the Irish soldiers of an Irish Government set up by Irishmen. If the Treaty were not rejected, perhaps it was over the

bodies of the young men he saw around him that day that the fight for Irish Freedom may be fought.

He then travelled to Thurles, where again many in his large audience carried weapons openly, and having repeated the foregoing, said:

> If they accepted the Treaty, and if the Volunteers of the future tried to complete the work the Volunteers of the last four years had been attempting, they ... would have to wade through Irish blood, through the blood of the soldiers of the Irish Government, and through, perhaps, the blood of some of the members of the Government in order to get Irish freedom.

The following day in Killarney, he stated that:

> If our Volunteers continue, and I hope they will continue until the goal is reached ... then these men, in order to achieve freedom, will have, I said yesterday, to march over the dead bodies of their own brothers.

Challenged on these utterances (by the *Irish Independent*), de Valera said that the paper's criticisms showed 'criminal malice' and gave as a rationalisation for his speeches the fact that they were an answer to those who said that the London Agreement gave 'freedom to achieve freedom'. A few weeks later, the Four Courts having been seized, the Labour Party delegation met him in an attempt to head off disaster. One of the delegates, Senator J.T. O'Farrell, said afterwards:

> The only statement he made that has abided with me since as to what his views were was this: 'The majority have no right to do wrong'. He repeated that at least a dozen times in the course of the interview, in response to statements made to him to the effect that the Treaty had been accepted by a majority, and that consequently, it was his duty to observe the decision of the majority until it was reversed. He refused to accept it on the grounds that the majority had no right to do wrong.

He had an opportunity during an abortive peace conference (on 29 April) called by the Catholic Archbishop of Dublin, Dr Byrne, between himself, Brugha, Collins and Griffith, to retract his 'wading through blood' speeches, but chose not to take it. Collins, responding to Brugha, who had called him and Griffith British agents, said: 'I suppose we are two of the Ministers whose blood is to be waded through?' Brugha replied, 'Yes. You are two.'[52] But de Valera made no effort to deny Brugha's statement. He refused to entertain Collins's suggestion that a plebiscite be held on the Treaty, whereby people would record their opinion when walking through certain gates or barriers erected at churches. He also refused to co-operate in ensuring that the election, which under the Sinn Féin Ard Fheis pact was now scheduled for 16 June, would be intimidation free, saying that 'Republicans maintain that there are rights which a minority may justly uphold, even by arms, against a majority', and sought instead a six-month postponement of the election, so that 'time would be secured for the present passions to subside'.

Members of the provisional government Cabinet, Griffith in particular, saw this postponement attempt not as an effort to allow passions to subside, but as a ruse to provide further opportunities for bank robberies. However, a few weeks later, on 20 May, Griffith's patience was tested to the utmost when Collins made an extraordinary, and undemocratic, effort to reach out to his adversary by means of an electoral pact worked out by Harry Boland. The idea was that both pro- and anti-Treaty candidates would form a coalition panel of candidates, the two sides having a number of seats equivalent to their existing strength in the Dail. After the election, Cabinet seats in the government would be apportioned on the basis of election results. The thinking behind the pact was that it would remove the Treaty as an issue from the election. But it was a non-starter which appalled Griffith to such a degree that his friendship with Collins never recovered fully. It cut across the interests of other parties, such as Labour and the farmers, and violated the provisions of the Treaty whereby every member of the provisional government was bound to accept it in writing.

It also appalled the British. Knowing something of what was in the wind, Churchill wrote to Collins a few days before the pact was concluded, warning that

> It would be an outrage upon democratic principles and would be universally so denounced ... Your Government would soon find itself regarded as a tyrannical junta which having got into office by violence was seeking to maintain itself by a denial of constitutional rights.

However, Collins was moved less by Churchill's opinion than by that of former friends like Lynch, O'Connor and Hales. He was prepared to go to almost any lengths to avoid drawing the sword against his former comrades. But he was in a desperate position, caught between British pressures that he uphold the Treaty, and *inter alia* suppress rather than make concessions to the Four Courts men, and the impossibility of squaring the circle between Republican demands and those of imperial England. The Northern Ireland situation usually attracted the least attention of all the problems of the time from historians, but in fact it was the source of the worst violence of the era, and this was Collins's most controversial policy of the period. Faced with a tale of mounting horror in the north, he had entered into a most unconstitutional *sub rosa* agreement with the Four Courts executive to launch an armed offensive into the Six Counties in support of the beleaguered Six Counties Catholics. Collins's motive in entering into this illegal agreement was twofold. First, he sought to defend the Catholics, and second, he hoped by so doing to secure Republican support, particularly northern Republican support, for the Treaty. But whether the Treaty would have survived British and Unionist outrage had his secret pact been discovered is a moot point. The Treaty, of course, specifically recognised the existing Six County state. We will return to the situation in Northern Ireland later. For the moment continuity demands that we follow developments in the south, and in London.

Civil war in Ireland became inevitable between the last few days of May and the holding of the Irish general election on 16 June. As drafted, Collins's constitution would certainly have satisfied the aspirations of all but the most extreme Republicans, but the combination of the pact between Collins and de Valera and the contents of the constitution was too much for Lloyd George and Churchill, the two British statesmen with whom Collins concluded the fateful negotiations on both. Churchill bluntly told Collins that his policy of 'surrender' to the Republicans had exposed him and the other Treaty signatories to a 'fierce scrutiny of our actions', and declared that the proposed constitution was 'of a Bolshevick character'. Lloyd George pronounced the draft constitution as being so far from the expected Canadian model as to be a 'setting up of an Independent Republican Ireland'. He said that the proposed constitution only dealt with the Crown 'under conditions very derogatory to its dignity. The Court, which constitutes the Empire, was expressly excluded . . . The British Empire was ruled out from the making of Treaties altogether . . . the Constitution was a complete going back on the provisions of the Treaty.'

Churchill had warned Collins that the British were 'just as tenacious on essential points – the Crown, the British Commonwealth, no Republic, as de Valera and Rory O'Connor. And we intend to fight for our points.' And fight they did. Collins's draft constitution was ruthlessly altered. The Treaty's oath of allegiance became mandatory on members of the Irish parliament. The legislature itself consisted of the King and two Houses. Parliament could only be summoned and dissolved in the name of the King. His Majesty's representative in Ireland, the Governor General, could negate any Bill that the two Houses passed, because his signature was required before a Bill became law. As the right of appeal to the Privy Council from the Irish Supreme Court was included, the Privy Council thus became a superior court to any in Ireland. And the preamble to the constitution included a statement that the Articles of Agreement had the force of law and any law passed or amendment made under the constitution deemed repugnant to the provisions of the Treaty became 'absolutely void and inoperative'.

Collins became so emotional during the negotiations that Lloyd George described him as being 'just a wild animal, a mustang'. The British accused Collins of creating the situation which had arisen in Dublin by refusing to confront O'Connor, and condemned the conclusion of the pact with de Valera. Collins argued that without the pact an election could not be held. He became so heated that during one meeting, which Lloyd George described as being of 'great gravity and of a menacing character', he repeatedly told the British Prime Minister that he was willing 'to give Ireland back as a present' and from his general demeanour allowed the

British to deduce that he supported what the IRA were doing in the Six Counties.

However, the Irish side did slightly better over the north. Collins handed over to Lloyd George a dossier on atrocities committed against Catholics, and Griffith argued that the British tactic of arming the B Specials was 'akin to arming the East End'. On this point, Lloyd George agreed with Griffith, demurring only to the extent of saying: 'the Fascisti in Italy would be a more exact analogy'. Eventually, after much heated exchange, Lloyd George decided to yield to Collins's demands for an inquiry into the Six County murders. He told the Cabinet that he was afraid that Collins was trying to manoeuvre him into a break over Ulster, not the constitution. He admitted that the British record in Northern Ireland was bad. They had armed Protestants and allowed Catholics to be murdered with impunity. However, he felt that if the break was to come on the issue of a republic versus the monarchy, then world opinion would support England. Accordingly, he decided to meet one of Collins's requests that an inquiry be set up into the Ulster atrocities, and Craig was brought to London to be informed of the proposal, which, as we shall see, ultimately came to nothing.

Having failed to get the constitution he wanted, Collins, who had joined in a public appeal with de Valera (on 6 June) to support the pact, finally repudiated it two days before the election. Speaking in Cork, he said in a prepared speech, which was printed in all the important newspapers the next day:

> You are facing an election here on Friday and I am not hampered now by being on a platform where there are Coalitionists. I can make a straight appeal to you – to the citizens of Cork, to vote for the candidates you think best of, who the electors of Cork think will carry on best in the future the work they want carried on. When I spoke in Dublin I put it as gravely as I could that the country was facing a very serious situation. If the situation is to be met as it should be met, the country must have the representatives it wants. You understand fully what you have to do, and I depend on you to do it.

De Valera had been aware that the constitution had run into severe difficulties with the British. His paper, the Childers-edited *Poblacht na hEireann*, had printed a commentary on the fact. But by this stage he had come to realise that his 'extremist support' policy had backfired on him. Those who thought like Rory O'Connor were moved by the traditional rhetoric of the Irish physical-force movement, not that of Eamon de Valera, and moderate support had been outraged by his 'wading through blood' speeches. Accordingly, de Valera did not risk any breach of the pact, from which he stood to benefit more than the pro-Treaty side, by attacking the constitution as he had done with the Treaty. Whether that oft-referred-to entity, the Plain People of Ireland, would have been greatly moved by the constitution's terms one way or another is a matter of speculation. By the time the election was held, the concerns of the average person were with the economic situation of the country, spreading disorder, and the looming spectacle of civil war.

The election results mirrored these concerns. Overall, the pro-Treaty parties won a huge majority, 486,377 votes to 132,162.[53] Although the Collins/ Griffith party lost 8 seats, it won 58 to de Valera's faction's 36. The Labour Party won 17 seats, the Farmers' Party 7, there were 6 Independents and 4 Unionists. But the counting of votes had barely concluded when the election results were completely overshadowed by the assassination of Sir Henry Wilson on 22 June. Wilson was shot because of his activities on behalf of the Unionist administration in Northern Ireland. The British assumed that he had died as a result of orders from O'Connor, rather than Collins, who seems in fact to have been responsible. The Conservatives, who had been increasingly coming to view the Treaty as a sell-out to gunmen, were incandescent. Churchill's policy came under even fiercer scrutiny. He told the House of Commons:

> The presence in Dublin, of a band of men styling themselves the Headquarters of the Republican Executive is a gross breach and defiance of the Treaty. The time has come when it is not unfair, premature or impatient for us to make to the strengthened Irish Government and new Irish Parliament a request in express terms that this sort of thing must come to an end. If it does not come to an end, if through weakness, want of courage, or some other less creditable reason it is not brought to an end and a speedy end, then it is my duty to say, on behalf of His Majesty's Government, that we shall regard the Treaty as having been formally violated, and we shall take no steps to carry out or legalise its further stages, and that we shall resume full liberty of action in any direction that may seem proper, or to any extent that may be necessary to safeguard the interests and the rights that are entrusted to our care.

Collins initially reacted by growling, 'let Churchill come over here and do his own dirty work'. But he knew that the sands were running out. It was profoundly irritating, having just received a large electoral mandate in support of the Treaty, to be put in the position of seeming to act at the behest of the British. But it was becoming increasingly clear by the hour that if he didn't act, the British would. On the other hand, the fact that law and order was breaking down so rapidly, and his colleagues were becoming increasingly urgent in their demands that the Four Courts men be suppressed, also called for action. Both hands were finally forced when the provisional government arrested a prominent Four Courts man, Leo Henderson, who was in the act of commandeering transport from a Dublin garage for use in the north. The Four Courts men regarded this as a breach of the *sub rosa* agreement with Collins to attack the north, and retaliated by kidnapping the Deputy Chief of Staff of the National Army, Ginger O'Connell. A day later, 28 June 1922, the Four Courts garrison was served with an ultimatum either to immediately vacate the building and surrender its arms, or else face military action. The ultimatum was ignored and, with two howitzers borrowed from the British, the new Irish army began shelling their old comrades. Civil war had formally begun.

Once it did so, the result was a foregone conclusion. A majority of the people were with the Government, and the anti-Treaty forces were badly led and confused in their strategy. In six weeks, the provisional government took Cahir, Cashel, Clonmel, Dundalk, Limerick, Sligo, Tipperary, Tuam and Waterford. The difficulty of breaking through the strong Republican defences of Cork, Tralee and Westport was met by the simple expedient of surprising the attackers with seaborne landings. Some serious fighting did occur in County Limerick, chiefly around Limerick City, and at Kilmallock and Newcastle-West. But the anti-Treaty forces, being less well armed and far fewer in number than those of the newly created Free State Army, were forced to adopt guerrilla tactics which soon rebounded against them. The destruction of Irish life and property by Irish forces in obvious contravention of the will of the people as expressed at the ballot box created widespread alienation, even of devout Republicans.

The strain of it all finally caught up with Arthur Griffith. On 12 August 1922 he died of a brain haemorrhage. In London on the same day, the two men who had shot Wilson at Collins's behest, Reginald Dunne and Joseph O'Sullivan, were hanged. Ten days later, Collins himself died in an ambush in his native County Cork. The leader of the ambush, Tom Hales, during the Black and Tan war had resisted appalling tortures rather than betray Collins and his friends. W.T. Cosgrave succeeded Collins as head of government. With Collins gone, there were no scruples in Cabinet about prosecuting a war against former colleagues. Kevin O'Higgins summed up the Cabinet's attitude in a famous phrase. 'The Government,' he said, 'was simply eight young men standing amidst the ruins of one administration with the foundations of another not yet made, and with wild men screaming through the keyhole!'[54]

Following a meeting between de Valera and Richard Mulcahy, who succeeded Collins as Chief of Staff of the Free State Army, the Government decided to put an end to the screaming by the most ruthless means possible. A Monsignor Ryan of San Francisco had brought the pair together against the tenor of Cabinet policy, which was setting its face against peace initiatives which led nowhere. However, this peace initiative also led nowhere. Mulcahy, who was a shorthand notetaker, records in his papers that de Valera said: 'Some men are led by faith and some men are led by reason, but as long as there are men of faith like Rory O'Connor taking the stand that he is taking, I am a humble soldier following after them.'[55]

In the wake of the meeting, Mulcahy recommended to the Cabinet that the civil war could only be ended by a drastic stepping up of the attrition against the irregulars. One of the most drastic pieces of legislation ever seen in Ireland was the result, an Emergency Powers Act which made it possible for the Government to execute irregulars for any act of war it chose. One of the first marked down for doom was Erskine Childers, who had been captured in possession of a small revolver given to him by Michael Collins. In order to prepare public opinion for his death, four rank-and-file Volunteers arrested some time earlier in possession of weapons were executed by firing squad on 17 November.

Childers died with great nobility on the 24th, after shaking hands with each member of the firing squad. On the night before his execution, he advised his twelve-year-old son, also Erskine, never to do or say anything that would cause bitterness. It might be remarked here that the son's observation of this advice was one of the factors that subsequently carried him through public life so successfully that eventually he would succeed de Valera as President of Ireland. But there was little else of nobility in what followed. In December 1923, when the civil war had ended, the Garda Siochana compiled a report for the Executive Council detailing crimes committed by either serving or demobilised members of the Free State Army between 1 July and 31 December.[56] The IRA reacted to the Government's draconian policies by issuing a list (on 30 November) containing the names of a number of people who were targeted for death in retaliation. Apart from journalists and judges, every member of the provisional parliament which had voted for the emergency powers measure was included.

On 7 December, the day after the Free State constitution came into operation, thereby formally inaugurating a new Free State legislature with Cosgrave as president of its executive council, two members of the new parliament were fired on. One, Seán Hales, one of Collins's closest friends, a brother of Tom who led the ambush which killed Collins, was shot dead. The other, Padraig O'Maille, deputy chairman of the Dail, was wounded. The Free State Government reacted by executing four of the Four Courts leaders, who had been in custody for several months: Rory O'Connor, Liam Mellows, Richard Barrett and Joseph McKelvey.

Reprisal begat counter-reprisal: Kevin O'Higgins's father was shot dead in his home some days later; the seven-year-old son of a prominent IRB man, Seán McGarry, died when the McGarry home was set on fire. Arson also destroyed some of the most valuable and historic homes in the country as the irregulars targeted pro-Treaty senators and land-owners. Priceless libraries and collections of art vanished along with a part of Ireland's architectural heritage in this wave of attacks. But the blows which took longest to recover from were those delivered at that sense of community which is so vital to the fabric of a nation. As the war turned increasingly bitter, and the irregulars were forced to rely more and more on the guerrilla tactics used in the Black and Tan war, deeds were done which infected Irish public life for a half-century.

When eventually the shooting ended, and political life resumed, however falteringly, each side focused on the horrors perpetrated by the other to the exclusion of its own. The Free Staters were maddened by the loss of life and destruction, above all the loss of opportunities offered by the Treaty, caused by the irregulars. The irregulars merely shot a soldier, or bombed an 'economic target'. The Free Staters buried a colleague, and counted the cost of trying to repair an invaluable rail link like the Mallow bridge linking Dublin with Cork. Reprisals followed, sometimes of a barbaric nature. In remote Kerry, for example, far from the discipline which could be expected to be exerted by GHQ, amidst the favourable guerrilla terrain provided by that lovely area's narrow roads and high mountains, ghastly things were done. At Ballyseedy, after a group of Free State soldiers were ambushed and shot dead, a group of irregulars were chained together and put to work dismantling a barricade which the Free Staters had mined, with results which can be imagined from the saying: 'There were fat crows about Ballyseedy.'

THE NORTH

As these events were unfolding, a similar if not worse chapter was being written in the north. Over the years, a twofold convention developed amongst northern commentators concerning what happened in Northern Ireland. On the one hand these events were viewed as somehow unconnected to what was happening in the south, and on the other were somehow sanitised and made less real than they were. It will be quite clear to readers from what follows that a sustained attempt was made to drive thousands of Catholics from their homes and workplaces. Some historians tend to use the term 'pogroms' in inverted commas, as though this in some way lessened, or questioned, the impact of what occurred. One historian, applying some statistical yardstick of his own, has gone so far as to suggest that what happened in Northern Ireland in the period under review did not justify the use of the term, as what befell the Catholics did not satisfy the criteria for constituting a pogrom. Evil, like beauty, lies in the eye of the beholder.

It can be said with certainty, however, that the man at the epicentre of the Unionist agitation, Edward Carson, on at least one notable occasion used the same sort of emollient language towards Catholics that Pearse and O'Neill used about the Orangemen – with precisely the same lack of relevance to the reality of the situation. Speaking to the meeting of the Ulster Unionist Council at which he formally relinquished his leadership (on 4 February 1921), Carson told his audience:

> From the outset let us see that the Catholic minority have nothing to fear from a Protestant majority. Let us take care to win all that is best among those who have been opposed to us in the past. While maintaining intact our own religion let us give the same rights to the religion of our neighbours.

However, the reality of how life was lived, or rather death inflicted, in the north is contained in the following description of events by the distinguished Unionist historian A.T.Q. Stewart:

> ... the Treaty had turned the attention of terrorists to Northern Ireland, where, in the terrible year of 1922, attacks and outrages, aggravated by outbreaks of sectarian rioting, claimed the lives of 232 people, including two Unionist MPs. In London on 22nd May 1922 Carson's friend Field-Marshal Sir Henry Wilson was murdered by the IRA on the steps of his home in Eaton Place, only a few doors from Carson's house.[57]

The Stewart quotation does give an indication of the bitterness which the Treaty generated in the Six County area, which, while it settled for an Orange version of Home Rule, would really have preferred to have Ireland as a whole remain part of the United Kingdom, not merely the Six Counties. There was a sense of scales falling from eyes, a resentful acceptance of the fact that the Ulster Unionists had only been pawns in a Conservative game. This sense of betrayal, leading to a feeling of Orange Sinn Féin-ism, ourselves alone, amongst the rulers of the new Orange statelet, was articulated by Carson in the speech he made to the House of Lords on the signing of the Articles of Agreement:

> At that time I did not know, as I know now, that I was a mere puppet in a political game. I was in earnest. I was not playing with politics. I believed all this. I thought of the last thirty years, during which I was fighting with others whose friendship and comradeship I hope I will lose from tonight, because I do not value any friendship that is not founded upon confidence and trust. I was in earnest. What a fool I was! I was only a puppet, and so was Ulster, and so was Ireland, in the political game that was to get the Conservative Party into power.

Given Carson's long acquaintanceship with the Conservatives, his intimate dealings with them at the highest levels, including at the Cabinet table, one can hardly accept that he remained unaware of the Tories' motives in supporting the Unionists, until some of them signed a treaty with Sinn Féin. What is certain is that his activities, coming on top of the ancient rancours of Northern Ireland, had helped to bring death and destruction to the north and to Ireland for several years before the Treaty was signed.

For example, a *Daily News* correspondent, Hugh Martin, reported that on the weekend of 20 August 1920, he found that 5,000 Catholics had been driven out of the shipyards of Belfast, and that thousands of Catholics had been forced from their homes in the Ballymacarrett and Crumlin Road districts of Belfast as part of 'a deliberate and organised attempt, not by any means the first in history, to drive the Catholic Irish out of North-East Ulster, and the machinery that was being used was very largely the machinery of the Carsonite army of 1914'. This bad situation was made immeasurably worse after District Inspector Swanzy of the RIC, who was found guilty by a coroner's court of participating in the murder of the Mayor of Cork, Tomás MacCurtáin, was shot dead in Lisburn on 22 August 1920, by order of Michael Collins.

The Catholics of Lisburn were driven out of their homes en masse, and hundreds of homes were burned in Bangor, Banbridge, Belfast and Lisburn. There were scores of deaths, and over a million pounds' worth of property damaged. Martin wrote: 'Since the early days of the German invasion of Belgium, when I witnessed the civilian evacuation of Alost and the flight from Ostend, I have seen nothing more pathetic than the Irish migration.'

That was not how Sir James Craig saw matters. Although the Unionists had mobilised under Carson to prevent Home Rule being introduced to Ireland's 32 counties, not to end up witnessing it being introduced to the six they ended up with, they were sternly intent on holding on to what they had been given. Far from criticising the UVF for the activities described above, Craig, addressing a UVF gathering in Belfast, asked: 'Do I approve of the action you boys have taken in the past?' Then he answered his own question, 'I say yes.'[58] His answer formed part of a strategy which the Unionist leaders were implementing at the time to tighten their grip on the Six Counties.

In the first place, as we have seen, the Orangemen had succeeded in securing a six-county state which they could control, rather than the nine-county one which they had been offered but which contained too many Catholics. In the second, the Unionists, led by Carson, had taken a step which rather vitiated the sentiments he had expressed to the Ulster Unionist Council concerning Catholics. Just four months earlier, he had blocked a Cabinet proposal to give 'Ulster' an upper house weighted so as to safeguard Catholic interest. Thirdly, as noted, on 3 November 1920, the Cabinet was informed that 'Sir Edward Carson and the Ulster members were strongly opposed to a second chamber for the Northern Parliament and would use the whole weight of their opposition to endeavour to defeat the proposal.'[59]

The Unionists also knocked out another proposal aimed at giving fair play to the Nationalists, the introduction of proportional representation to the area. But the most important step followed Craig's public declaration of approval for the Ulster Volunteers' actions in shooting Catholics and driving them from their homes: the formation of the B Specials. Sir Basil Brooke, who later became a Six County prime minister, had begun organising UVF men into a vigilante corps to curb Sinn Féin activities in his native Fermanagh. Carson argued formally that it was important that such a force be organised, lest it take matters into its own hands and thus come into conflict with British forces. In fact, there was little likelihood of this happening, as British agents like the celebrated Captain Hardy[60] were organising them into undercover murder gangs, exactly as Hardy's successors were to do later in the century. But Balfour backed Craig when he submitted a memorandum to Cabinet, complaining about Catholic influences in the RIC, and demanding the immediate formation of a special constabulary from within the UVF.[61] If it were not forthcoming, the memorandum warned, Unionists would: 'See what steps can be taken towards a system of organised reprisals against the rebels, mainly in order to defeat them, but partly to restrain their own followers from acts which are regrettable and in a large measure ineffective.'

Balfour and other highly placed Tories backed the idea, and the formation of the Specials was duly announced on 22 October 1920, even though Britain's top military and civil experts on the ground in Ireland, General Macready and Sir John Anderson, both strongly opposed the idea, which Anderson pointed out correctly would intensify 'Party and religious feeling'. The Specials were of course exclusively Protestant. They subsumed into their ranks existing militias such as the 'Cromwell Clubs' which had been set up in Belfast for the specific objective of terrorising Catholics by ambushes, shootings and midnight visits.[62] The Specials and those who organised them did not fully accept the truce declared in Dublin in July 1921, and felt free to take whatever action they saw fit to, as they saw it, curb Sinn Féin or IRA activities. But the body which was to generate the most controversy, part of which was still having its effect as this was being written, was a creation of Sir Henry Wilson's, the Royal Ulster Constabulary.

On retirement from the army, Wilson had been returned unopposed as the Unionist candidate for North Down on 21 February 1922. He was appointed military adviser to the northern government on 14 March and given carte blanche by Craig to do whatever he thought necessary in turning the Six Counties into Fortress Orange.[63] Wilson deemed it necessary to disband the RIC, which Unionists like the Minister for Home Affairs, Dawson Bates, thought contained too many Catholics. The new armed police force, a marked contrast with the unarmed Garda Siochana being set up at the same time in the south, was conceived not as a regular police body, but as a counter-insurgency one, seen by the Unionists as part of 'their' law and 'their' order. For reasons of public relations, a number of positions in proportion to the number of Catholics in the Six County area were set aside for Catholics.

Not unsurprisingly, these were not taken up. The new force contained many recruits who joined up wishing to be ordinary policemen. But it also contained murder gangs headed by men like a head constable, who used bayonets on his victims because it prolonged their agonies, and as a matter of principle he did not believe in giving his victims an easy death.[64] Brown Street Barracks, at the foot of the Protestant Shankill Road, was infamous for housing 'a number of notorious murderers'. As Bishop Joseph MacRory told a meeting of the North-Eastern Advisory Committee,[65] at which Michael Collins was present, the most notorious of the murderers were District Inspector Harrison and Detective Inspector Nixon. Nixon's counter-insurgency activities found such favour with his superiors that he was able to refuse to turn up at an identification parade at Brown Street Barracks after witnesses claimed they had seen him at the site of a number of murders in the Catholic area of Arnonn Street. The most terrible atrocity attributed to Nixon was the slaughter of the menfolk of the MacMahon family, in which a Catholic publican, his three sons and a barman were murdered. One of the tragedies of Northern Ireland in the twentieth century, particularly in its closing decades, was the fact that the character and reputation imparted to the RUC, at its origins, would cause many members of the force to be shot by the IRA for the sins of its founding fathers, and helped to prevent many Nationalists from ever regarding the force as anything other than a partisan one set up to maintain Orange hegemony.

As the fears and hatred generated by the actions of individuals within the RUC can be said to have had their influence on events which occurred in the late twentieth century, one can imagine the effect they had at the time. One of the people who reacted adversely to happenings like the MacMahon murders was Michael Collins. He adopted a frankly duplicitous policy towards the state whose existence he had endorsed in the Treaty, telling his Cabinet colleagues that 'non-recognition of the Northern Parliament was essential – otherwise they would have nothing to bargain on but Sir James Craig'.[66]

Collins had a number of reasons for acting as he did. He succeeded in convincing a number of opponents of the Treaty to vote for it by using the argument 'The British broke the Treaty of Limerick, and we'll break this Treaty too when it suits us, when we have our own army.'[67] Many of his most senior colleagues, like Eóin O'Duffy, whom he regarded as his successor, were authorised to use the same argument at IRA gatherings around the country. Thus, under pressure from de Valera on the political front, and Rory O'Connor on the military one, Collins was driven to get support for the Treaty in the south by promising to negate one of its essential provisions in the north. He unleashed a battery of measures directed at destabilising the Six Counties. The 'non-recognition policy' included such measures as paying Catholic national schoolteachers in the north out of secret service funds, to ensure that a Nationalist curriculum would be taught; obstructing co-operation between government departments north and south; and, as the situation of Catholics in Northern Ireland deteriorated, arming the IRA, against whom he was prosecuting a war in the south, so as to facilitate the launching of a campaign against the Orangemen. One of the most spectacular incidences of this campaign was the mass kidnapping (on 7 February 1922) of some 42 Orangemen, who were brought across the border to be held in southern centres as hostages against the release of a group of prominent IRA prisoners held in the north.

These activities were of course grossly at variance with Collins's position as head of the provisional government, but they were consistent with the oath he had taken on joining the IRB to create an all-Ireland Republic. Collins was after all now president of the IRB. However, even in this role, it is doubtful whether he would have acted as he did had the pressures on him not mounted north and south. Immediately on the Treaty's passage, a representative of the provisional government, Diarmuid Fawsitt, was sent north to find out how the northern government viewed relations with the south. Fawsitt reported a few days later (on 13 January 1922) that the north wanted 'understanding and co-operation with the South' but that no formal steps could be taken until after the meeting of the Ulster Unionist Council scheduled for the 27th of the month. Collins was shortly to find out, as would his successors in government in Dublin, many decades after he had died, that like the RUC, the influence and actions of members of the Unionist Council were to have more bearing on the outcome of events than the attitude and commitments of elected Unionist leaders.

Without waiting for the Council meeting, Collins met Craig in London at the Colonial Office, where Churchill had become chairman of the Provisional Government of Ireland Committee, which replaced the Cabinet's earlier Irish Committee. Although the meeting took place against a background of continuing outrage directed at Catholics in Northern Ireland, which Collins informed Craig he could stop if he and his Cabinet had a mind to, the atmosphere was friendly. Both men had agreeable personalities and the pair got on so well that a five-point agreement was reached. It called for a conference of elected representatives 'for all Ireland' to draw up a constitution guaranteeing northern autonomy. The Boundary Commission was to be scrapped and Collins and Craig were to work out the boundary between them. Collins promised to call off the Belfast boycott and Craig agreed to get the Catholic workers who had been driven out of employment reinstated. The two men also promised to meet again to thrash out that perennial Irish issue – the question of Republican prisoners in northern jails.

Collins's principal motivation in signing the Treaty was to get control of the 26 counties, an army, civil service, Dublin Castle and much of the substance of independence, and then to move on, by fair means and foul, to securing a 32-county Ireland utilising these assets. Generally speaking, he mistrusted the British with whom he had to deal, with some exceptions, such as Birkenhead, whom he came to like. In particular he had no illusions about Lloyd George, who during one heated exchange had confirmed Collins's assertion that had he fallen into British hands during the war of independence, the Prime Minister would have sanctioned his hanging. Nevertheless, on one basic component of the Treaty concerning Northern Ireland, the Boundary Commission, Collins had reason to believe that it would give Tyrone, Fermanagh and part of Derry, Armagh and Down to the south. Lloyd George did nothing to disabuse him of this interpretation in the concluding stages of the Treaty negotiations, and in fact stated in the House of Commons:

> There is no doubt, certainly since the Act of 1920, that the majority of the people of the two counties prefer being with their Southern neighbours to being in the Northern parliament. Take it either by constituency or by poor law union, or, if you like, by counting heads, and you will find that the majority in these two counties prefer to be with their Southern neighbours . . . if Ulster is to remain a separate community, you can only by means of coercion keep them there and, although I am against the coercion of Ulster, I do not believe in Ulster coercing other units.[68]

As we shall see, Lloyd George would later publicly go back on this interpretation. Privately he assured Craig that the Boundary Commission would only make the most minute alterations to the border, and was assured in return by Craig, who of course had come up with it in the first place, that the whole idea of a Boundary Commission was now repugnant to both him and his followers.[69]

However, Collins, who was not party to the private exchanges between Lloyd George and Craig, apparently felt secure enough about the outcome of his meeting with Craig to assure a delegation of northern Nationalists whom he met in Dublin on 1 February – the day before he was scheduled to meet Craig in Dublin for a progress report on their London deliberations – that large sections of the Six County area would be transferred to the south. It was not to be. The Unionist Council had been so hostile to the boundary proposals that Craig had had to give an assurance that there would be no change in the existing Six County area. The All-Ireland conference idea was not even discussed. When Collins produced maps for Craig, showing how much territory would be ceded to the south under the terms of the Boundary Article of the Treaty, their meeting broke up. Collins was now in an extraordinarily difficult position, torn between the machinations of de Valera, the increasing intransigence of the Unionists, and his emotional attachment to his former comrades-in-arms like Rory O'Connor, with whom he was prepared to go to almost any lengths to avoid a break. Emotionally too he empathised with the sufferings of the Catholics in Northern Ireland, which he felt an obligation to relieve. At the same time, he knew that his primary responsibility was to give the people whom he represented, the electorate of the 26 counties, what they most desired: peace. He knew that the majority of his Cabinet colleagues regarded this as their main priority also. With the exception of Mulcahy – the others were Griffith, Eóin MacNeill, Kevin O'Higgins, Patrick Hogan, Ernest Blythe, and W. T. Cosgrave – the Six Counties was well down on the agenda after the need to crush the irregulars before the situation in the south got out of hand. The Free State had to be built today; the north could be addressed tomorrow.

Nevertheless, Collins did what he could within these limitations to influence the fate of northern Catholics. The risks he took were incredible. The IRA prisoners whose threatened execution prompted the mass kidnappings were actually reprieved the night the kidnappings occurred. But in an initiative of his own, Collins had independently attempted the murder of the two hangmen deputed to carry out the executions. Two members of his squad were sent to England and actually called at the hangmen's homes, only to find that the men had left for Ireland. However, the tensions unleashed by the kidnappings led to the shooting of four B Specials in Clones, as they stopped in Monaghan en route to Enniskillen in County Tyrone. Amongst other retaliations the Orangemen bombed a Catholic playground in Belfast, killing six school-children.

It was after this atrocity that Collins introduced his scheme for paying teachers who refused to accept the authority of the Six County Government. For their part the British responded to the kidnappings and their aftermath by halting troop withdrawals from the south and by setting up a border commission (on 16 February) which was supposed to control activities along the border. The commission's membership was made up of British, B Special and IRA observers, and proved to be ineffectual, as the Unionists refused to co-operate with it. The B Specials had been increasingly coming back into the picture, having been dispensed with by the British on the signing of the truce in Dublin in July. But the Unionists and their Tory allies in London saw to it that the British resumed payments to the B men as part of Wilson's re-organisation of the north's security forces.

Collins protested to Churchill that the payments made the British Government 'directly responsible for the situation in Belfast' and warned that events in Belfast were creating pressures on the provisional government which were 'well nigh overwhelming. It is no exaggeration to say that the very existence of the Treaty will be gravely threatened.'[70] Collins was not exaggerating the pressures. The split in the south was replicated in the north also, with the votes of pro-Treaty supporters in the southern border counties being particularly important. These people were generally more active in their sympathies towards the northern Nationalists than inhabitants of counties further from the conflict. Like the Nationalists in the Six Counties, the issue for the nine counties of Ulster was not so much abstractions concerning the oath as whether Michael Collins or his adversaries would be most likely to come to the aid of the beleaguered Nationalists.

Collins took a major step towards staking his claim to be trusted by the Nationalists, and to be correspondingly distrusted by the Orangemen, had they known what he was doing, by backing the formation of a Northern Military Council under the command of Frank Aiken, who would eventually end up as Chief of Staff of the anti-Treaty forces opposed to the provisional government. His deputy was Seán MacEoin, who, in the flux of the time, would become one of the principal generals engaged in crushing the anti-Treatyites. But for the moment, on the north, both pro- and anti-Treaty supporters united to further the objectives of the Council: to prevent the Belfast government from consolidating its position under the 1920 Government of Ireland Act, and to protect the Catholics of Northern Ireland. A policy directive of Richard Mulcahy's made the objectives of the Council absolutely clear: 'The general aim underlying all operations in Carsonia is to disorganise the economic structure of the territory and to make the hostile inhabitants realise that aiding and abetting the activity of the Enemy does not pay.'[71]

In an attempt to throw the British off the scent, Collins swapped some of the military equipment he had received from London for weaponry held by anti-Treaty IRA men. The rifles and ammunition were then smuggled across the border. One of the gun-runners was Seán Haughey, whose son Charles would one day become an Irish prime minister. Collins also organised the setting up of a Belfast Guard. The payments for the Guard and its officers, a total of £216 per week, gives an indication of the minuscule forces available to the Nationalists compared to their adversaries. Most of the Guards' energies went into protecting Catholic districts which were under continuous attack. Evidence given to the Northern Advisory Committee into the murders of Catholics stated: 'There is little difference between these murders and the murders carried out in various parts of Ireland by the Black & Tans, except that in nearly all cases in Belfast, the bodies were mutilated.'[72] Most of these murders were attributed to police gangs.

The MacMahon murders in particular prompted a response from London. Another meeting between Collins and Craig was organised. This second meeting took place in a far less cordial atmosphere. Collins blamed Craig for failing to uphold his commitments under the earlier pact between the two men, and with a sublime disregard for his *sub scriptum* involvement with northern Republicans, said it was 'an outrage' for Craig to suggest that the south had anything to do with bombing and sniping attacks in the north. The two men differed fundamentally on Collins's interpretation of the boundary clause in the Treaty. Clause 12 stated that the boundary was to be determined in accordance with the wishes of the inhabitants insofar as these were 'compatible with economical and geographical conditions'. But Craig said that Collins's maps constituted a 'predatory attack on Ulster'. The reality of these exchanges was that Craig was at the time preparing to withstand that attack by pushing through the Representation of the People Bill (No. 2) in the northern parliament. The effect of this legislation would be to gerrymander the counties Tyrone and Fermanagh, so that it would be almost the end of the century before the wishes of the Catholic inhabitants of these areas came to be electorally expressed.

Nevertheless, in an exercise of the politics of 'because I wish it to be, therefore it is', Churchill caused the first paragraph of the agreement which was eventually achieved between the two men to read: 'Peace is today declared.' The agreement (20 March) called for the policing of Protestant and Catholic areas by police of the respective religions; the setting up of an advisory committee of Belfast Catholics to assist Catholic recruiting to the Specials; a joint committee of Protestants and Catholics to investigate complaints of intimidation; a cessation of IRA activity; further meetings of the Boundary Commission. Persons expelled from their homes were to be encouraged back by the advisory committee. Half a million pounds was voted for relief works in Belfast, two-thirds for Protestants and one-third for Catholics, and political prisoners imprisoned for crimes committed before 31 March were to be released.

This all seemed very reasonable in London, but in Belfast it was a different matter. In parliament, Unionist spokesmen were hostile. On the ground a spate of grisly murders occurred following the publication of the agreement, including the Aron Street killings attributed to DI Nixon and a group of his colleagues from Brown Street Barracks. At a meeting of the northern government, Wilson pointedly asked Craig: 'Who is governing Ulster, you or Collins?'[73] General Solly Flood simply refused to give the advisory committee any say in the reform of the B Specials. He regarded the committee, some of whose members were in the IRA, as a device to gain information about the security forces. By the beginning of June, the committee had collapsed through a combination of violence and a lack of co-operation. Some members of the committee were arrested, and the homes of members, including those of priests, were shot up.

In retaliation, the IRA launched an offensive throughout the north. It began on 18 May and was virtually snuffed out by the end of June. During that time, over a million pounds' worth of Unionist property was destroyed by fire. Most of the destruction occurred in Belfast, where the death toll was heaviest also. In the month of May, there were 63 deaths in the city, of whom 40 were Catholic. Amongst the Protestants killed was the Unionist MP W.J. Twaddell, after whom Belfast's Twaddell Avenue was named. Twaddell was shot because of his involvement with Loyalist paramilitary groups and his inflammatory speeches. Other prominent Unionists who suffered through having their property destroyed were the speaker of the Six County parliament, Sir Hugh O'Neill, and the Conservative MP Captain Ronald MacNeill. One of the worst atrocities of the period was directed at a group of Unionist farmers in South Armagh on 17 June. Some farms were burned, and amongst the dead were a farmer and his wife, a father and son, and two single men.[74]

The short, bloody campaign never had the slightest chance of success. Churchill agreed to the plans of Wilson and Solly Flood which called for additional British troops to be sent into the area (there were some 9,000 in all) and the heavy arming of the B Specials and the RUC. Craig demanded and was given additional money and armaments: some five million pounds sterling; and 23,000 rifles, 15,000 bayonets, quantities of Lewis and Vickers machine-guns, and other equipment such as mortars, grenades, uniforms and tents. There were in all some 48,000 Specials, and British officers were sent to Ulster to train them. Units of the army and navy were also dispatched. The weakness of the IRA in contrast may be gauged by these extracts from a report to GHQ in Dublin on the strength, or lack of it, of the IRA in Belfast, which at the time, two months after the May offensive began, was the only IRA unit still capable of putting up any sort of a fight.

Strength of Brigade – 800 men
Armament: 181 rifles and 11,600 rounds of ammunition. 308 service revolvers and autos, 7,400 rounds of ammunition. 5 Thomson guns and 1,220 rounds of ammunition.

Engineering material:	156 detonators
	12 stone war flour
	20 lbs cheddar [Home made explosives]
	12 lbs gelignite
	20 ft time fuse
	Enemy strength in area:
British military:	5,500
RUC:	2,650
Specials:	26,680
Total:	34,830

The enemy are continually raiding and arresting; the heavy sentences and particularly the 'floggings' making the civilians very loath to keep 'wanted men' or arms. The officers are feeling their position keenly. Recently a number of men were rounded up and detained in custody. The mother of one of the boys when bringing him food shouted out, in the presence of Crown forces, the name of local o/c and made a tirade against him for misleading her boy into this movement.

As I have mentioned before the economic position is very acute. To give a rough idea there are 171 married men with 405 dependants and 346 single men with 936 dependants.

These figures are taken from cards returned by each company and where there were two brothers the number of dependants was divided. To relieve the situation it would require a grant of say £500 per week.

The men are in a state of practical starvation and continually making applications for transfer to Dublin to join the 'Regular Army' . . . under the present circumstances it would be impossible to keep our Military Organisation alive and intact, as the morale of the men is going down day by day and the spirit of the people is practically dead.

Churchill's viewpoint was that

the prime and continuing cause of all the horrors which have taken place in Belfast is the organisation of these two divisions of the Irish Republican Army in Northern territory and the continuous effort by extreme partisans of the South, to break down the Northern Government and force Ulster against her will to come under the rule of Dublin.[75]

He had earlier given tangible support to the Unionists by ordering military action in their support in two border disputes involving a sliver of Fermanagh which touched Free State territory. One portion of the sliver, Pettigo, was bisected by the border so that it ran through a number of houses, the bulk of which lay in the Free State. Beleek was in the Six Counties, overlooked by a fort on the Free State side. After Specials had commandeered a house in Pettigo, there was an exchange of fire between the Specials and provisional government troops, in which one Special was killed and the rest put to flight. Two days earlier, Churchill had told the Committee of Imperial Defence's Sub-Committee on Ireland that in order to protect Ulster from invasion, he wanted plans drawn up immediately so that 'All our means of exercising pressure on Southern Ireland should be applied at once . . . We must act like a sledge-hammer so to cause bewilderment and consternation amongst the people in Southern Ireland.[76] The sledgehammer was duly brought down on Pettigo. Churchill sent in 1,000 heavily armoured troops and a howitzer battery with instructions to inflict the greatest possible casualties on 'the enemy'. The resultant shelling emptied Pettigo of civilians, and managed to kill three Free State soldiers and one Special.

The son of the man who had decreed that Ulster would fight and Ulster would be right had given tangible evidence that he believed in the correctness of his father's dictum.

While the situation in the north was deteriorating, relationships in the Liberal–Conservative coalition were also worsening, and plans were afoot amidst right-wing Conservatives to create a new right-wing party. Lord and Lady Londonderry were active in this movement, which had the support of a number of peers, including Lord Salisbury and Lord Northumberland, as well as leading Unionists like Carson and Ronald MacNeill. Sir Henry Wilson, a strong supporter of the idea, was regarded as a likely leader of the new grouping. The Collins–de Valera pact gave Wilson the opportunity of stepping up his onslaught on the coalition for being 'increasingly inclined to work with the King's enemies'.[77] Churchill was equally opposed to the pact, telling a delegation of Catholic businessmen from Belfast that it doubled the power of evil and halved that of good, in that it doubled the power of Wilson.[78] He told the delegation that 'you are being tortured by Wilson and de Valera'.

. However, Churchill did make a gesture of concession towards alleviating the Catholics' plight by putting pressure on Craig to agree to one of Collins's principal demands, the setting up of a commission of inquiry into what was happening in Northern Ireland. However, the Minister for Home Affairs, Dawson Bates, who had been chosen because of, rather than despite, his notoriously anti-Catholic attitudes, wrote to Craig strongly opposing the idea, saying: 'To set up an outside Tribunal to enquire into the action which it is found necessary from hour to hour and to justify or condemn it would strike at the very roots of Government.'[79] Armed with this letter, Craig vetoed the inquiry, but made a suggestion to Churchill and Lloyd George, with which they agreed: the sending to Belfast of a government officer to decide on the merits or de-merits of holding an inquiry.

The man chosen, Colonel Stephen Tallents, was widely welcomed by the Unionists, and duly produced the recommendation they wanted, namely that there should be no public inquiry because 'it would lead to a revival of propaganda about matters that are best forgotten'.[80]

Tallents was aware of the highly delicate political milieu in which he was operating, and was aware too that with the coalition under extreme pressure from Unionists and right-wing Conservatives, the production of a report which would prove that the south was implicated in incursions into Ulster territory might bring down the Government. Consequently, he stated that 'I am not aware of any responsible suggestion that the Provisional Government have promoted active measures by the IRA in Northern Ireland against the Northern Government.' A statement which was clearly at variance with the vast mass of evidence[81] compiled by Solly Flood and others as part of the research he conducted for his report, which was never published. Tallents did, however, recommend that 'future consideration' be given to the fact:

> ... that the system employed in the Agreement of inviting Mr Collins virtually to act as the representative of a minority in the territory of another Government both encouraged the Catholics in the North in their policy of non-recognition of the Northern Government and exasperated Sir James Craig's supporters.

He was rewarded for his discretion by being appointed permanent Representative of the British Government in Belfast.

However, Tallents did provide a great deal of information privately to his superiors, in which he made it quite clear that all was not well with the Unionists' administration.[82] He found that 'the Government has failed to perform the elementary duty of guaranteeing life and property'. He was highly critical of the Specials, whom in a first draft he described as 'disgusting', later toning down this term to 'disquieting' for the purposes of his report. He was highly critical of the fact that Craig and Solly Flood had been allowed to set up a force of 48,250 armed paramilitaries, costing nearly five million a year, saying 'a weapon is being forged which in time of crisis might be most dangerously used by other hands than those who now control it'. He also thought that Dawson Bates was so bad that he was 'an asset' to the Republicans.[83]

The assassination of Wilson in London on 22 June, at Collins's instigation, brought matters to a head north and south of the border.[84] The coalition swayed in a gale of right-wing outrage that may be gauged from the anti-Treaty *Morning Post* editorial, which stated that 'Mr Lloyd George, Mr Austen Chamberlain, and Mr Asquith all shared in the murder of Sir Henry Wilson and are bedabbled with the stain of his blood.' Lloyd George wrote to Collins stating:

> The ambiguous position of the Irish Republican Army can no longer be ignored by the British Government. Still less can Mr Rory O'Connor be permitted to remain with his followers and his arsenal in open rebellion in the heart of Dublin in possession of the Courts of Justice, organising and sending out from this centre enterprises of murder not only in the area of your Government but also in the Six Northern Counties and in Great Britain. His Majesty's Government cannot consent to a continuation of this state of things and they feel entitled to ask you formally to bring it to an end forthwith . . .
>
> I am to inform you that they regard the continued toleration of this rebellious defiance of the principles of the Treaty as incompatible with its faithful execution. They feel now that you are supported by the declared will of the Irish people in favour of the Treaty, they have a right to expect that the necessary action will be taken by your Government without delay.[85]

As we have seen, 'necessary action' was taken, and a civil war commenced which was to claim the lives of both Collins and O'Connor. In death Wilson had a more profound effect on creating hostilities in Ireland than he had achieved in his lifetime. He was followed to his grave by his two assassins, both ex-servicemen, Reggie Dunne and Joseph O'Sullivan, who had lost a leg at Ypres. Both men went to the scaffold without implicating anyone else in their deed.

The civil war in the south, combined with the IRA's weakness in the north, forced Collins into calling off the northern IRA campaign. He told a meeting of Officers from the northern IRA divisions in Portobello Barracks, Dublin, on 2 August:

> . . . with this Civil War on my hands, I cannot give you men the help I wish to give and mean to give. I now propose to call off hostilities in the North and use the political arm against Craig so long as it is of use. If that fails, *the Treaty can go to hell and we will all start again*.[86] [Author's emphasis]

His audience's recollections of the meeting certainly indicate that they believed he sincerely intended to do everything within his power to encourage non-recognition of the northern government and active resistance to its functioning, and if this did not succeed in destabilising the northern administration, adopt the option of force. Writing to Churchill a week after the Portobello meeting, Collins took strong exception to the passage of the Local Government Bill, which had just been passed, which he viewed as 'a sentence of death or expulsion on every Catholic in the North'.[87] He pointed out that the British had insisted on introducing proportional representation in 1919 to safeguard minorities everywhere in Ireland, 'but particularly where they most needed it, in the North-Eastern counties'. The Bill just passed, however, restored the system of gerrymandering which had obtained prior to 1919. Churchill argued that Collins's arguments against gerrymandering were invalidated by 'the continuing refusal of the Catholic minority to recognise the Northern Government'.

Faced with such attitudes, and examples of indiscriminate firing by the British military – in particular one which claimed the lives of two teenage girls at Edenappa, near the Jonesboro–Louth border – Collins's inclination was to reach for the sword. He wrote to Cosgrave after the Portobello meeting, saying of the Edenappa shootings:

> I am forced to the conclusion that we have yet to fight the British in the North-East. We must by forceful action make them understand that we will not tolerate this carelessness with the lives of our people . . . It is not individuals who are in charge of shooting parties or 'Hold-Up' parties that are the guilty ones. The guilt lies with the high authorities, and we must face that.

He followed this up with a memo to GHQ on 7 August which gives further evidence that he was considering a resumption of hostilities against the north once the civil war ended: 'At the present moment I think we ought to be making every possible effort to develop intelligence systems in North-East.'[88] However, little more than a fortnight after writing that, Collins was dead. He was 31 years of age, and in his last days torn by pressures from every part of the political and military compass. What this extraordinary man might have achieved had he lived must necessarily be a matter of speculation. Would a period of respite following his successful prosecution of the civil war have given him time to reflect and to direct his incredible physical and intellectual energies towards nation building and statesmanship, or would he have continued with his plans to destabilise the Six Counties, thereby perhaps generating a second and even more destructive civil war, this time between north and south?

All we can be certain of are two things: that a majority of his Cabinet colleagues clearly feared the latter outcome; and that his death, combined with that of Arthur Griffith, removed from the pro-Treaty side qualities of leadership, imagination and political philosophy which were not replicated for the rest of the century. Arguably and ironically, a case could be made, as we shall see, that the man who would demonstrate qualities of leadership of the order of Collins and Griffith came not from the ranks of their colleagues, but was their principal opponent, Eamon de Valera.

The day after Collins was buried, his Cabinet colleagues circulated to government members a memorandum drawn up by Ernest Blythe and Michael Hayes which completely overturned his policy. It became not only that government's policy, but the policy of virtually every subsequent 26-county government.

As soon as possible all military operations on the part of our supporters in or against the North-East should be brought to an end . . . The line to be taken now and the one logical and defensible line is a full acceptance of the Treaty. This undoubtedly means recognition of the Northern Government and implies that we shall influence all those within the Six Counties who look to us for guidance, to acknowledge its authority and refrain from any attempt to prevent it working.

. . . Nothing that we can do by way of boycott will bring the Orange party to reason . . . Their market is not in our territory. Our boycott could threaten the Northern ship-building industry no more than a summer shower would threaten Cave Hill . . . the same may be said of the linen industry . . . pressure must be absolutely normal and constitutional. The use and threat of arms must be ruled out of the dispute . . .

The events of the past few months have done much towards fixing the Border where we cannot consent to its being fixed. It is full time to mend our hand . . . Payment of teachers in the Six Counties should immediately stop . . . We should stop all relations with local bodies in the Six Counties. Catholic members of the Northern Parliament who have no personal objection to the Oath of Allegiance should be urged to take their seats and carry on a unity programme . . . precautions should be taken to prevent border incidents from our side. Any offenders caught by us should definitely be handed over to the Northern authorities . . .

Catholics in the North . . . should be urged to disarm 'on receiving satisfactory assurances from the British'. Prisoners in the North should be requested to give bail and recognise the courts. The outrage propaganda should be dropped in the twenty-six counties.

Heretofore our Northern policy has been really, though not ostensibly, directed by Irregulars. In scrapping their North-Eastern policy we shall be taking the wise course of attacking them all along the line . . . The belligerent policy has been shown to be useless for protecting the Catholics or stopping the pogroms. There is of course the risk that the peaceful policy will not succeed. But it has a chance where the other has no chance. The unity of Ireland is of sufficient importance for us to take a chance in the hope of gaining it. The first move lies with us.

At the time of writing, the 'unity of Ireland' has yet to be achieved, because while the new provisional government policy did help to bring about an end to the grosser forms of violence, the effects of the discrimination and gerrymandering which Collins railed against are still with us, although the democratic deficit has, as we shall see, been very considerably reduced. For so long as they could maintain their hold, the Orangemen, inspired by the events described, did so, living in a political and psychological laager in which the rancours of centuries and the playing of the Orange card combined to create a sense of encirclement by hostile forces akin to that felt by the Boers or the Israelis. For those who wished (and still wish) to maintain such fears for political advantage rather than encourage co-operation between Protestant and Catholic, or between Dublin and Belfast, the events of 1919–22 sowed dragons' teeth.

An equally large and malignant crop was sown in the south during the same period. As the civil war wore on, the pressures on the Republicans increased almost hourly. On 4 October the Executive Council decided to seek the assistance of the Catholic hierarchy in putting down the irregulars. The previous day, the Council had announced an amnesty for 'Every person [engaged in insurrection against the State] who on or before the 15th day of October 1922 voluntarily delivers into the possession of the National forces all firearms, arms, weapons, bombs, ammunition and explosives, and all public and private property now unlawfully in his possession.'[89] Anyone failing to take advantage of this amnesty, and who was found to be in contravention of its terms, would be brought before military courts and risked execution. The bishops agreed to the Government's request. A pastoral letter was issued on 10 October, which urged that the amnesty offered be accepted. But it then went on to warn that those engaged in warfare against the provisional government would 'not be absolved in confession, nor admitted to Holy Communion'. Mindful of the example of the chaplain to the Cork Brigade whose letter has been quoted, they warned that priests who disregarded the sanction of withholding sacraments would be 'guilty of the gravest scandal'.[90] Any priest who encouraged the revolt against the Government would be suspended. Kidnappings and the killing of soldiers were no longer 'good and meritorious acts'.

This edict, which was strictly enforced by the majority of priests throughout the country, gave a cloak of moral authority to the provisional government in carrying out its executions policy. The Republicans, understandably, viewed it with great bitterness, saying that the bishops had issued their opponents with a licence to kill. And it has to be conceded that that would appear to be how W.T. Cosgrave viewed the pastoral letter. On 18 November 1922, he wrote to Archbishop Byrne of Dublin, turning down the Archbishop's request that he should release Mary MacSwiney, who was on hunger strike in Mountjoy. The previous day Cosgrave and his Cabinet had sanctioned the execution of four Dublin lads who had been caught with guns. The executions, though Byrne didn't know it, were in preparation for the execution six days later of the much higher-profiled Erskine Childers. The Free State authorities didn't want to begin their reprisal policy with Childers, whose lawyers were still fighting his case. In the course of his letter to Byrne, Cosgrave said that the Government was preparing to act 'In the spirit of the solemn teaching of our highest moral authority and recalling in the grave words of the Pastoral letter of the 11 October, that in all this, there is no question of mere politics, but what is morally wrong, according to the divine law.'[91] The Archbishop was being given a belt of his own crozier.

However, without attempting to pursue the theological arguments on either side of the case, it can be said that the hierarchical and clerical condemnations proved a potent barometer of public opinion which, when taken with the increasing military weakness of the Republicans, made the ending of the civil war to all but the most obdurate a question of when, not if. An authoritative assessment of the Republicans' strength in their stronghold in southern Ireland, as compared with that of their opponents, was:

> ... the relative strengths in the 1st Southern Division area at the time were: IRA, 1,270; Free State, 9,000. In the Southern Command area, which included the counties of Cork, Kerry, Limerick, Clare, Tipperary, Kilkenny, Carlow, Wexford and about half of Galway, 6,800 IRA men were opposed by 15,000 troops. In the whole country IRA strength did not exceed 8,000 at that time, and against them the Free State authorities had built up a force of at least 38,000 combat troops. The possession of barracks, armoured cars and artillery emphasised the overwhelming Free State strength.[92]

Politically, de Valera's external association pony had proved itself a nonstarter. The principal IRA leader, Liam Lynch, wrote to him angrily, saying: 'Your publicity as to sponsoring document no. 2 has had a very bad effect on the Army, and should have been avoided. Generally they do not understand such documents. We can arrange peace without referring to past documents.'[93] Lynch's note could have been taken as expressing the views of rank-and-file IRA men. The views of de Valera's opponents in high places, particularly the hierarchy, were even more scathing. Their lordships fired another broadside in the wake of their October edict in their Lenten pastorals: that of Cardinal Logue (*Irish Independent*, 12 February 1923) contained the following:

> Never before in the world's history did such a wild and destructive hurricane spring from such a thin, intangible, unsubstantial vapour. The difference between some equivocal words in an oath; the difference between internal and external connection with the British Commonwealth; this is the only foundation I have ever seen alleged. Men versed in the subtleties of the schools may understand them; men of good, sound, practical common sense shall hardly succeed.

In a clear attack on de Valera's motives, the Cardinal went on: 'There may be other foundations – pride, jealousy, ambition, self-interest, even mere sentimentality; but if they exist they are kept in the background.' But though his arguments were unappreciated, de Valera himself was by now far from being 'in the background' in the ranks of 'the irregulars'. A week after the Bishop's pastoral, he had secured the IRA's agreement to issuing a statement drawn up by himself, stating that he had been called upon 'to resume the Presidency and to preserve a Government which shall preserve inviolate the sacred trust of National Sovereignty and Independence'. A week later, de Valera formed a 'government' which regarded itself as the second Dail.[94] His long, slow climb back to the power he had left behind him when he walked out of the Dail after the Treaty vote had begun.

By the time he had formed his 'government', de Valera realised that the first essential towards any sort of political progress was an ending of the civil war. However, Liam Lynch remained obdurately set on continuing the struggle. Lynch had in fact been captured by provisional government forces at the start of hostilities. Knowing that he had quarrelled with the Four Courts men, and assuming therefore that he was in favour of peace, the Executive Council decided to release him. By April, even Lynch had come to realise that the position was hopeless, but had decided to cling on for some more days in the vain hope that artillery would reach the irregular forces from Italy. It never did, and Lynch was fatally wounded on 10 April while crossing the Knockmealdown Mountains. He was succeeded by Frank Aiken.

Apart from being active in the Collins-sponsored covert action against the Six Counties, Aiken had built up a formidable record as commander of the Fourth Northern Division of the IRA during the Anglo-Irish war. He had initially tried to prevent the civil war, and in the flux of the period ended up by becoming one of its principal prosecutors. However, he was also a realist. Having been elected Chief of Staff on 20 April, he saw to it that the meeting which elected him passed a resolution empowering 'the Government and Army Council to make peace with the Free State Authorities'. De Valera subsequently contacted two prominent members of the Free State Senate, Senators Jameson and Douglas (Jameson's name had been at the head of the list of senators whom the IRA had planned to assassinate) with a view to opening negotiations between himself and Cosgrave.

The senators refused to act as negotiators but consented to become intermediaries. Cosgrave also refused to negotiate, but used the intermediaries to pass on surrender terms to de Valera. These included acceptance by de Valera of the principle that political issues should be settled by a majority vote, and agreement to a surrender of arms, which would be arranged 'with as much consideration as possible for the feelings of those concerned'. Cosgrave also promised to allow a 'clear field for Mr de Valera and his followers, provided they undertook to adhere strictly to constitutional action'.

De Valera produced his own conditions. These included the abrogation of the oath, and the 'assigning to the Republican forces at least one suitable building in each province, to be used by them as barracks and arsenals, where Republican Arms shall be stored, sealed up, and defended by a specially pledged Republican guard'. He proposed that after an election the arms would be reissued to their owners. Another of his conditions indicated his long-headedness. He proposed in effect that the monies which he had collected while in the States, 'the funds of the Republic', which the provisional government had caused to be frozen, should be released 'for peaceful efforts in support of the Republican cause'.

Understandably, quite apart from the arms issue, Cosgrave was neither prepared to tear up the Treaty, which abrogating the oath would have entailed, nor hand over millions of dollars to de Valera. He told Jameson and Douglas to tell de Valera 'no talk, no negotiations, unless there is a surrender of arms'. In the words of Kevin O'Higgins, the provisional government's attitude was 'this is not going to be a draw, with a re-play in the Autumn'. De Valera realised the game was up. He arranged with Frank Aiken for the final blowing of the whistle. On 24 May, he and Aiken issued two statements. Aiken's contained a solution to the problem of surrendering arms: 'Comrades! The arms with which we have fought the enemies of our country are to be dumped. The foreign and domestic enemies of the Republic have for the moment prevailed.'

De Valera's said:

> Soldiers of the Republic, Legion of the Rearguard: The Republic can no longer successfully be defended by your arms. Further sacrifice of life would now be vain and a continuance of the struggle in arms unwise in the national interest and prejudicial to the future of our cause. Military victory must be allowed to rest for the moment with those who have destroyed the Republic. Other means must now be sought to safeguard the nation's right.
>
> You have saved the nation's honour, preserved the sacred national tradition, and kept open the road of independence. You have demonstrated in a way there is no mistaking that we are not a nation of willing bondslaves.
>
> . . . The sufferings you must now face unarmed you will bear in a manner worthy of men who were ready to give their lives for their cause. The thought that you still have to suffer for your devotion will lighten your present sorrow, and what you endure will keep you in communion with your dead comrades, who gave their lives and all those lives promised, for Ireland.
>
> May God guard every one of you and give to our country in all times of need sons who will love her as dearly and devotedly as you.

The civil war was over.[95] But as in the north, the new state had been born in bloodshed and hatred, which would affect political, economic, cultural and social progress for many years into the future.

THREE

FROM BLOOD TO BOOK-KEEPING

(1923 TO 1939)

The days of the high heroic were over, and the dull, grey business of balancing the books, of making the new Irish Free State work, resemble nothing so much as the cleaning up of a house after what was intended to be a massive and joyous party ended in violence and destruction. Figures quoted in the Dail for the period August to February 1922–3 put the number of reported cases of arson and armed robbery at 1,502. Internally, the civil war had cost the state some £47 million. These figures remind me of a radio programme I took part in with the late Dermot Morgan, who played Father Ted in the cult TV series. We were supposed to be having a serious discussion about the prison regime at Portlaoise jail. But before the panellists began their debate, a tape of Morgan's was played over, in which the audience heard him saying: 'There are people in here who would cut your throat in a church and smile. There are criminals and murderers and rapists – and then there's the prisoners!'

Professor Tom Garvin has noted that from the Republican side there came 'looting, house burning, land-grabbing and, occasionally, rape'.[1] In the absence of a police force, 'uncontrollable gangs of young men roamed at will and burned out unionists, shop-keepers, and those they regarded as either political anathema or agrarian enemies'. On top of the damage caused to the infant state by the Republicans, there was that carried out by the National Army. A meeting of the Executive Council held on 22 December 1923, when the civil war still had some months to run, was told in a police report that members of the National Army, which of course had mushroomed so quickly that not only had many undesirables found their way into its ranks, but discipline had had but little time to take root, were responsible for, or were suspected of being responsible for:

60 per cent of murders; 28 per cent of raids, hold-ups, robberies and larcenies involving the use of guns; 43 per cent of manslaughters; 21 per cent of attempted murders; 31 per cent of armed attacks on houses; 20 per cent of robberies with arms and 50 per cent of rapes, indecent assaults and other sexual offences.[2]

The figures for civil war deaths are disputed, but a total of around 4,000 is widely quoted. In 1923–4, 30% of national spending was devoted to defence.

142

Borrowing money to help the new state was no easy matter. It is on record that the 'banks' reluctance to accommodate the new Government left something of a sour taste in Cosgrave's mouth'.[3] As ever, some bankers demonstrated their pinstriped lineage to the Unrepentant Thief and banks took advantage of the disturbed situation to indulge in profiteering and to charge higher interest rates than their British counterparts. What these factors[4] added up to was a fairly desperate effort to defend the Irish currency and keep the new ship of state afloat. For the internal bills were not the only ones the Free State had to face. Externally too, there were costs stemming from the very nature of the independence struggle, as W.T. Cosgrave explained in a well-known letter which he wrote to Judge Cohalan the year after the civil war ended.[5] In it he pointed out that the very fact of fiscal independence from Britain generated hostility to Ireland, because the steps the Irish took to improve their economy inevitably impacted on British profits. No English political party therefore had 'anything to gain from any dispensation of justice much less favours' to the new state. The Irish population had declined over the previous 50 years and trade was 'much of a kind which spells prosperity for a few, and poverty and insecurity for the many'. In attempting to rectify this situation, the new government equally inevitably incurred the hostility of vested Irish interests as well as British ones, with consequent implications for the stability of the fledgling state.

Cosgrave was writing to brief Cohalan on the need for propaganda in the US concerning a crisis that would shortly bear down on the Free State Government: the outcome of the Boundary Commission's deliberations, which we will shortly examine. But even before the Boundary Commission crisis broke around the Government's head, there were more immediate problems to be dealt with. De Valera had decreed that his followers should not be allowed to emigrate unless granted a permit to do so. The IRA had enforced this policy during the Anglo-Irish war, and thus built up a large pool of manpower in the country. In addition, de Valera vetoed the destruction of arms in return for an amnesty. He reasoned that so long as guns remained in IRA hands, the Free State authorities would not crack down too harshly on the Republicans for fear of starting the civil war afresh.

But the retention of weapons meant that the authorities did continue to raid and arrest IRA supporters. Speaking in the Dail, Kevin O'Higgins stated that in some counties there were persons elected to the Dail 'but who have not yet, so far, taken advantage of that honour, leading armed gangs of robbers'. The already swollen prison population went up. In July 1923 there were more than 11,000 prisoners, of whom 250 were women, in custody, many without trial. To legalise their continued detention, the Government used its majority to force through a Public Safety Bill on 2 July, and then on 3 August an Indemnity Bill to protect its forces from suits brought as the result of the harassment of Republicans. Apart from the stated objectives of these measures, the Government was setting the scene for the holding of a general election on 27 August. The purpose of the election was to secure for the

Government a new and stronger mandate to counter the arguments of de Valera and his supporters, who claimed that the Government was not a legitimate one, but a usurping junta which had failed to deliver on the promises of the undemocratic pact between de Valera and Collins before the previous year's election, which – no matter what the electorate decided – was intended to return a coalition government, in which de Valera and a number of his colleagues would have held power.

When the election was declared, de Valera and most of the 87 Sinn Féin candidates who went forward were on the run. De Valera therefore decided to have himself arrested in a blaze of publicity, and made a public announcement that he would address a meeting in Ennis, County Clare, on 15 August, Our Lady's Day. He duly made his way to Clare, and succeeded in getting on to the election platform before he was recognised, and arrested by a party of soldiers. In jail, de Valera was almost as big a problem for the Free State authorities as he had been at liberty. It proved very difficult to gather evidence to sustain a charge against him in court, particularly as his objective in getting himself arrested was to create a trial not merely of himself 'but of the whole system which brought the Free State into existence'. In other words, to rerun the Treaty debates in that most favourable of Irish political environments, from the dock. In the end, these considerations decided the authorities not to bring a charge against de Valera, and he was ultimately released in July 1924. But it was the result of the election which gave the Government most pause for thought.

De Valera himself secured a massive majority in the Clare election, recording almost double the vote of his rival, Eóin MacNeill, who stood for Cumann na nGaedheal, as the Government party now called itself. His followers also did well. The constituencies had been revised so that the number of seats went up from 128 to 153, and the Government had expected to win the bulk of the new seats. In the event, they only secured five to Sinn Féin's eight. Overall, the results were as follows:

Cumann na nGaedheal	62
Sinn Féin	44
Farmers' Party	15
Labour	14
Independents	17

The result was partly due to a revival of sectional interest politics, as the vote for Farmers, Labour and Independents indicates. But it was partly a reaction against the executions and the numbers in prison. Moreover, the fact that a ceasefire had been declared meant that the large number of people who were Republican in outlook but had hitherto been repelled by IRA violence could now support the de Valera-ites. De Valera's presence on the Sinn Féin side was, of course, an incalculable asset. With the deaths of Collins and Griffith, he now literally towered over the other figures on the Irish political scene, both physically and in terms of reputation.

The death of Collins had an effect on a major crisis for the Free State Government which occurred while de Valera was still in prison, the so-called army mutiny. It was a mutiny in the sense that some orders were disobeyed and arms went missing from various barracks around the country. But it was a bloodless affair. The mutineers never fired a shot and there were no courts-martial or firing squads, an acknowledgement both of the contribution many of those concerned had made in the war of independence, and of a fact which was recognised, without being acknowledged, namely that much of the mutinous spirit involved was distilled rather than intellectualised. The Collins factor in the mutiny stemmed from the fact that some of his close intelligence colleagues, notably Liam Tobin, Charlie Dalton, Tom Cullen and Frank Thornton, all senior officers in the new army, came to believe that his 'stepping stone' policy towards a united Ireland was being abandoned, that 'pro-British elements' were being advanced, and that far from pressing on towards a 32-county republic, the Free State was becoming an end in itself. There was also the fact that the army was being reduced from its peak total of 40,000 to some 20,000 officers and men. And there was some rivalry between the Tobin/Dalton grouping, who had organised 'an old IRA' faction within the army to counter Mulcahy's revival of the IRB. Mulcahy was also acting under Collins's influence. He wished to keep Collins's Republican approach alive in the officer corps, though not to the extent of encouraging mutiny, which some of the officers appeared to contemplate.

The enforced retirement of a group of officers who had taken part in the Anglo-Irish war prompted the serving of an ultimatum on the Government on 7 March 1924 by the Tobin/Dalton grouping, demanding the suspension of demobilisations and the abolition of the Army Council. Joseph McGrath, who had acted as an intermediary between the Tobin/Dalton group, who felt that Collins's ideals were being lost sight of, and the Government, resigned from the Government, but secretly worked to bring the crisis to an end. Tobin and Dalton were induced to send a letter of apology to Cosgrave, recognising the principle of civil control over the army. Cosgrave in turn gave the mutineers a few days to surrender and return all commandeered arms.

However, before this could happen, a group of senior officers, acting on their own initiative, surrounded Devlin's Hotel in Rutland Street, Dublin, where the mutineers were holding a meeting, and arrested them. Mulcahy was not informed of the arrests until after they had taken place. The following day, he was asked for his resignation by O'Higgins, who was acting head of government in the absence of Cosgrave, who was ill. The general opinion of the time was that O'Higgins took advantage of the 'mutiny' to vent a long-standing antagonism towards Mulcahy. Mulcahy, though he had ruthlessly crushed the IRA, was the most Republican member of the Free State Cabinet. The 'mutiny' marked the end of any surviving influence of the IRB in the army. The heads of a number of senior officers also rolled. Ultimately, the 'mutiny', as Dermot Keogh has noted, cost the resignations of 'two Ministers, three Major Generals, seven Colonels, nearly thirty Commandants, forty

Captains, and nineteen Lieutenants'.[6] However, though some of the men were undoubtedly unjustly dismissed, and for a time the affair was deeply troubling to both Government and public alike, high standards of army efficiency and discipline were maintained, and the fledgling army, along with the unarmed police force, the Garda Siochana ('guardians of the peace'), became one of the pillars of the new state.

The setting up of an unarmed police force in the midst of a civil war was a particularly notable achievement. In some parts of the country, lawlessness was such that in extreme cases an attempt by police to perform a normal duty such as enforcing the licensing laws took, in my father's words, 'more heroism than an ambush against the Black and Tans'. Weapons abounded and men who might not have been particularly noticeable for their activities during the Tan war could sometimes be found in pubs armed in equal measure with revolvers and whiskey, daring all-comers to deal with them. An episode in the life of both my father, who at the time was Deputy Commissioner of the Gardai, and Michael Joseph Conneally, in Oranmore, County Galway, on 23 February 23 1923, says much about the conditions of the time. My father was 24, and Conneally 23. A former member of the IRA serving under Seán MacEoin, in Roscommon, Conneally had been one of the first to respond to an appeal by Michael Collins to join the new force, and was the first recruit into the Kildare Training Centre in February of 1922. He and three other members of the fledgling force were assigned to Oranmore on 27 October 1922. Here they found that the accommodation assigned to them was 'so terrible' that they were delighted to find a young married couple, in need of money, who were prepared to allow them 'two rooms upstairs' in their semi-detached house.

These rooms became both their bedroom and the police station. At least notionally so, because between October and February the young Gardai were not supplied by Dublin with either pay or furniture of any sort. They made do with orange boxes and kept the station records in a biscuit tin. The general atmosphere in the area was Republican and anti-Treaty, and the Gardai were under instructions not to go out alone. They indicated their presence on arriving in Oranmore by going to mass in full uniform, and serving mass when called upon to do so, also in uniform. But in the absence of pay, they were driven to working for local farmers to earn money, and lived on food parcels and subventions from home. By these means they earned enough to pay a little rent to what Conneally termed 'the very brave young couple', one of the few families in the district who would have been willing to house them. Then, on the morning of 23 February, Deputy Commissioner Coogan arrived unexpectedly to carry out an inspection.

In the kitchen of the young couple's house, he found the wife busily engaged in making butter. Helping her with the churning was a fine-looking young man dressed in Garda trousers and shirt, who resolutely kept his back turned on the Deputy Commissioner. The duties of a Garda are many, but they do not include the making of butter. Accordingly, his gaze fixed on a spot approximately six inches to the left of the young man's left ear, my father enquired of the woman if she had any idea as to how the station party might be contacted. The housewife opined that she had, and the Commissioner courteously took his leave after asking her to be good enough to inform the men that Deputy Commissioner Coogan would be returning to the 'barracks' at 1 p.m. to conduct an inspection.

The 'inspection' consisted of my father sitting on a pile of newspapers, using the biscuit box as a desk, with four smartly uniformed Gardai (including Michael Conneally, whom he strangely failed to recognise from his earlier visit that day) standing before him, as he took careful note of how much pay they were owed and what furniture and fittings they required to perform their duties. He thanked them for 'holding on' and, promising that they would have everything they needed within a few days, took his leave after giving the young men what Conneally termed 'the best advice I ever got in the force': 'Start talking to the people. Stay with the people. Never stop talking to the people.'

Two days later an escorted army lorry made its way into Oranmore carrying all the required furniture and the Gardai's back pay. Later that year, the fruit of that inspection was seen after the general election of August 1923 had been held, and the Oranmore party had been transferred to Athenry to supervise the proceedings. Local Republican elements had vowed that the votes would never get to Galway for counting, and lined up outside the building where the votes were gathered into steel boxes, armed with horse whips to prevent them being transferred into cars or lorries. Conneally sized up the situation and, telling his comrades, 'We'll only get one chance at this', had the boxes loaded into the well of a sidecar. Then, with Gardai sitting on either side of the car to protect the boxes, the group made an unexpected, and successful, emergence from the yard at the back of the building, galloping through the flailing, but off-balance horsewhippers, relatively unscathed, 'while the local parish priest roared out encouragement to the IRA from a window in the Presbytery!'.

Understandably, de Valera was not a popular figure in the Conneally household, but a footnote to the Oranmore saga indicates something of the calibre of Conneally and some of those who helped in the creation of the institutions of the new state. In August 1975, Conneally, now a widower, was living in retirement with his daughter Maureen in Dublin, when he saw in his newspaper that de Valera's funeral cortège would pass outside their home next day. He astounded Maureen by getting up early and putting on his best suit and a black tie. Then he stood at the street gate for some hours until the coffin approached. As it passed, he shrugged off the years, and, drawing himself upright, delivered an impressively formal salute. Later that day, on one of the few occasions when she did so, Maureen questioned the reasons behind an action of her father. He replied: 'I paid my last respects to an old comrade who went wrong.'[7]

The outcome of the second major crisis to afflict the state in 1924 was not so satisfactory. The Boundary Commission pot had been simmering away from the time of the signing of the Treaty under Article 12, which gave the government of Northern Ireland the choice to opt out of the Free State within a month, thereby both continuing the Government of Ireland Act in force, and setting up the mechanism for a Boundary Commission, which was to be

a Commission consisting of three persons, one to be appointed by the Government of the Irish Free State, one to be appointed by the Government of Northern Ireland and one to be appointed by the British Government, shall determine in accordance with the wishes of the inhabitants, so far as may be compatible with economic and geographic conditions, the boundaries between Northern Ireland and the rest of Ireland, and for the purposes of the Government of Ireland Act, 1920, and of this instrument, the boundary of Northern Ireland shall be such as may be determined by such Commission.

Coping with the pressures of the civil war, while at the same time trying to keep the Irish exchequer solvent, knowing that there were many in high places in the ranks of Torydom, Unionism, and the British civil service dealing with Ireland who would not be sorry to see Irish independence collapse in bankruptcy, who in fact would accelerate the process if they could, had left neither Cosgrave nor his government with much time to progress the setting up of the Boundary Commission. Where Northern Ireland was concerned, the policy of the Dublin Government up to 1924 could, not unfairly, be termed one of activity without movement. A North-East Boundary Bureau was set up which engaged in research into propaganda over the north. Its principal figure, Kevin O'Shiel, a government law officer, inherited something of Collins's Janus-faced policy approach to the north, in that he found himself preaching peaceful approaches, but at the same time having to advise his government that any form of united Ireland policy would involve the Government in working with Sinn Féin in the north, while it harassed its supporters in the south. The old Irish Parliamentary Party, represented by Joe Devlin, was in favour of entering the northern parliament. The Janus-faced approach forced the Dublin Government to support Sinn Féin in the Westminster elections of November 1922 in an attempt to defeat Devlin.

After the election, on 7 December, the Six County parliament formally departed the Free State, but, rather than proceeding to co-operate in the setting up of the Boundary Commission, which, according to Article 12 of the Treaty, should have accompanied this step, Craig declared the Boundary Commission *ultra vires*.[8] Dublin was loath to challenge Craig on this interpretation too forcefully, because Lloyd George had fallen from office, largely over the Treaty settlement, and had been replaced by Bonar Law. There was every reason to believe that with the Unionists' champion ensconced at Westminster, any boundary settlement arrived at would be distinctly unpopular with northern Catholics, and the shock waves thus generated might bring down the Dublin Government. However, Dublin did appoint a representative to the Boundary Commission in July 1923, and made provision for propaganda on the Boundary Commission issue. The installation of Ramsay MacDonald's government in December 1923 seemed, in Free State eyes at least, to offer some prospect of progress. But the following year (on 10 May), Craig refused to appoint a commissioner from the Six Counties to the Boundary Commission.

The refusal placed Dublin in a delicate position. As Cosgrave wrote to Cohalan, the cost of the civil war and British commercial rivalry meant the Free State administration at that juncture was 'more costly and less efficient than it was in the British Occupation period'. Therefore:

> We now enter into this Boundary Commission proceedings with all these weighty considerations against us. We have no friends. People in USA, England, Scotland, France and elsewhere are friends of Ireland, but for the people immediately responsible for the Government of Ireland they have little or no use . . . many in Ireland have the same views . . . We can tolerate criticism from without, but it is largely built on misgivings within . . .

After directing Cohalan's attention to the facts of tampering with Article 12 and making the Boundary Commission subject in advance to the decisions of politicians or statesmen, Cosgrave made the point that the Treaty was not the instrument signed by Collins and Griffith:

> . . . I would direct your attention to the arbitrary selection of six parliamentary counties for the constitution of the Northern Government. The British Government made that selection. The Irish people were not consulted and did not accept it . . . Article XII was specially designed to secure that people were not placed under a Parliament against their will.
>
> If it be contended that Nationalists in Tyrone, Fermanagh, Derry, Armagh are only to be used as filling-in stuff to enable those against Irish unity to maintain a parliament, it is not a valid excuse. They have their legitimate national rights which neither Birkenhead, Lloyd George, Sir James Craig nor anyone else has a right to take from them . . . .

However, Birkenhead, Lloyd George, Craig and many others in high places were busily engaged in arguing that these rights should be taken away. The reason that Cosgrave wrote to Cohalan to ask his help in drumming up support in the US in the first place was that Balfour had just released a letter to the press which Birkenhead had sent him in March 1922. In it, Birkenhead had interpreted Article 12 as meaning that the Six Counties would remain under Unionist control. The wasteful debate amongst the Irish over the chimera of the oath facilitated Birkenhead in arriving at this interpretation. It had been pointed out to Griffith on the eve of the final fatal wrangle with de Valera over the oath on 3 December 1921 that the clause was too vague and left too much power to the Commission itself. John O'Byrne, a legal adviser to the Treaty delegation, had suggested to Griffith that electoral units should be specified. Griffith saw the point, but correctly doubted whether at that stage it would be possible to get agreement on the clause. Neither he nor Collins addressed the boundary issue during a meeting 'obsessed with the question of the Crown'.[9]

Thus Birkenhead was able to say of the Boundary Commission: 'I have no doubt that the Tribunal, not being presided over by a lunatic, will take a rational view of the limits of its own jurisdiction, and will reach a rational conclusion.'[10] Lloyd George supported the Birkenhead conclusion, the day after the letter appeared (8 September 1924). He said Birkenhead's was 'the only responsible interpretation of that important clause' and summed up the boundary controversy as being 'a Sectarian quarrel in a corner of Ireland'.

The Boundary Commission controversy provided an excellent example of a British policy approach to Ireland with which the Irish both had been and would become increasingly familiar. On the one hand, Northern Ireland was dismissed as being a problem for the intractable Irish, but on the other, the Tory antiphon was sounded: 'Ulster will fight and Ulster will be right.' Some days after Lloyd George's letter appeared (on 27 September) another Treaty signatory, Sir Lamington Worthington-Evans, made a speech at Colchester in which he was reported in the press as saying:

> It was not intended that there should be large transfers of territory . . . If by any chance the Commissioners felt themselves at liberty to order the transfer of one of these counties nothing would induce the Ulster people to accept such a decision and no British Government would be guilty of the supreme folly of trying to enforce such a decision.

With such orchestration in progress, the prospects of the Boundary Commission resolving the partition issue were minus zero. However, at the time of the Cosgrave/Cohalan correspondence, both the Dublin and London governments were acting as though the Commission was a thing of substance. By an agreement dated 4 August 1924 between Cosgrave and Ramsay MacDonald, the British and Irish governments moved in response to Craig's refusal to appoint a commissioner. The Treaty was amended to allow the British Government to appoint the north of Ireland representative. He was J.R. Fisher, a prominent Orangeman and former editor of the *Northern Whig*. The British also appointed the chairman of the Commission, Justice Feetham, a South African. The Free State's nominee was Eóin MacNeill, who at the time was Minister for Education in the Cumann na nGaedheal Government.

Between November 1924 and July 1925, the Commission took evidence from hundreds of witnesses, and received a large number of written submissions from interested parties. The general opinion amongst Nationalists was that the south would lose no territory and that the northern statelet would end up so truncated as to be no longer viable. Fermanagh and Tyrone were expected to be returned to the Free State, along with a large portion of South Down. This certainly was the opinion in Cosgrave's department,[11] though whether Cosgrave himself was so sanguine is debatable. Dublin took an active part in an election which Craig called on 3 April 1925. Cosgrave sanctioned the sending of money and organisers northwards to campaign for Nationalists. The mood of expectation was summed up by the Nationalist candidate, who claimed that the next election in Tyrone and Fermanagh would be for the Dail.[12] The actual election result was a more accurate barometer of things to come. The Nationalists won only 12 seats. The storm broke on 7 November 1925, with a leaked report in the *Morning Post* of what the Commission intended to propose. In a nutshell, the three northern counties with the largest Catholic representation, Derry, Fermanagh and Tyrone, were to stay under Unionist control, and though the actual acreage which was to be transferred from one side to the other in border areas actually favoured Dublin – 183,000 acres to Dublin, 49,242 to Belfast – the Free State stood to lose quite a substantial portion of Donegal. It is said that Kevin O'Higgins, the strongman of the Government, fainted after reading the *Morning Post* report. He had good reason to. One of the more trusted Free State army officers, General Joseph Sweeney, who had staunchly supported the Government during the army mutiny crisis, drew up plans to prevent the handover of his native Donegal, in which he was supported by many other senior army officers. There was dismay in the ranks of the Gardai also.

There had been a controversy within the force the previous year spearheaded by my father, Deputy Commissioner Eamon Coogan, when the Government, in a move which had resonances of the disputes over the RUC badges which were still continuing as this was being written, proposed to change the monogram of the Gardai insignia, from GS, meaning Garda Siochana na hEireann (the civil guards of Ireland) to SE, for Saorstat Eireann, the Free State, in other words the 26 counties. My father, who was in charge of the force at the time, as the Commissioner, General O'Duffy, was in America, spoke for the officer corps when he argued successfully for the retention of the GS insignia, saying:

> We who are looking ahead, look upon the guard as the Civil Guard of Ireland and not of any portion thereof. To treat the Guard as a portion of Ireland rather than a Guard for the entire country would be, to my mind, a great mistake. . . . Surely it is not seriously suggested that we must change our badges in order to make it clear that we are a police force for only 26 counties of Ireland.

The officers argued that if there was any objection to the title 'Garda Siochana na hEireann', there was still more objection to the title 'Royal Ulster Constabulary' which they felt would be more appropriately styled 'Royal Six Counties of Ulster Constabulary'. Sentiment on the unity issue was therefore widespread and deep-rooted on both sides of the political divide in southern Ireland. Eóin MacNeill resigned from the Commission, amidst a storm of criticism which suggested that he should have gone before letting matters get to that stage.

But this was as nothing compared to the reaction in Belfast. Craig announced that he would no more hesitate than he had done in 1914 'to fight in the open against our enemies who would take away the loved soil of Ulster from any of the Loyalists who would want to remain there'. And the *Belfast Newsletter* (16 November 1925) quoted another Unionist Member of Parliament as saying that 'if certain things happen . . . the Prime Minister and the members of the Government will hand in their resignations and take the field'. The 'certain things', apart from the transfer of acreage, envisaged a limited population transfer also. The Free State was to receive 31,319 people, 27,843 of them Catholic, the rest Protestant. Northern Ireland was to get 7,594 people, of whom the majority, 4,830, were Protestant. With civil war threatening in the north, and de Valera deriving priceless propaganda in the south, Cosgrave had no option but to repair to London, where he signed a tripartite agreement on 3 December with Craig and the British Prime Minister, Stanley Baldwin. The principal provisions of the agreement were:

1. The boundary between north and south remained unaltered.
2. The Free State was released from its liabilities under Article 5 of the Treaty for its share of the public debt of the United Kingdom, and for war payments.
3. In effect, the Council of Ireland which was technically in being under the Government of Ireland Act, was abolished.

The Dublin Government also succeeded in having the original Commission report suppressed so that the gory details would not give further aid and comfort to its enemies. Prior to the negotiations, O'Higgins had warned Baldwin that the Irish Government's position was so delicate that if the report were published, and if Dublin did not secure an advance on the *Morning Post*'s terms, de Valera would come to power. In the circumstances Cosgrave termed the settlement, which of course recognised the existing border, 'a damned good bargain', and said that he had succeeded in getting what he wanted from England: 'a huge 0'. In addition to the financial provisions, some 30 IRA prisoners, held in northern jails since the time of Collins's border offensive, were released.

The financial provisions were rooted in Article 5 of the Treaty settlement, which said:

The Irish Free State shall assume liability for the service of the Public Debt of the United Kingdom as existing at the date hereof and towards payment of war pensions as existing at that date in such proportion as may be fair and equitable, having regard to any just claims on the part of Ireland by way of set-off or counter-claim, the amount of such sums being determined in default of agreement by the arbitration of one or more independent persons being citizens of the British Empire.

The Irish had dragged their heels on the question of having an imperial arbitrator adjudicate on their claims, which some estimates put at £300 million on the basis of British over-taxation in Ireland. The British demand was of the order of £175 million, which was the cost of the compensation they had had to pay for damage caused by Crown forces during the Anglo-Irish war. The British also sought compensation from the Irish for the cost of recompensing Unionists whose property had been damaged. This came to some £5 million. The Irish had agreed to a 10% increase in the compensation payments and a contribution to the war debt, even though this meant in effect that it was they who had to pay for the havoc the Auxiliaries and the Black and Tans had wreaked upon them as part of Lloyd George's reprisal policy. One financial loose end which remained unaffected by the Boundary Commission settlement was that of the land annuities. These annuities were paid by Irish farmers in repayment of the loans which the British Government had raised to buy out landlords during the era of the land settlement. As we shall see, the land annuities issue lay like a rake hidden in the long grass of Anglo-Irish relationships, waiting to be trodden on and smite both governments between the eyes at a later date.

In addition to the attrition from de Valera and his followers, Cosgrave's government had faced trouble in its own ranks throughout 1925. Repercussions flowed from the army mutiny crisis in the form of a new party being formed by Joseph McGrath from the ranks of the Government's deputies. This party, known as the 'National Party', contributed to the holding of nine by-elections in the month of March. In these, the Sinn Féin vote went up and two Sinn Féiners won seats, giving the party a total of 48 seats in Leinster House. These seats all had one thing in common: they were empty. The party still considered itself bound not to recognise the Free State parliament, holding that they had been elected not to a parliament stemming from the Treaty, but to the second Dail, which had never been dissolved. The futility of the empty seats policy was graphically illustrated on 3 April 1925.

DE VALERA BREAKS WITH THE IRA

Since the ending of the civil war, the IRA had not merely remained in being, but had reorganised and was increasingly coming into conflict with the forces of the state. The Government reacted by forcing through a draconian public safety measure, the Treasonable Offences Act, which provided for deportation and the death penalty. Many of the Government's own supporters opposed the Bill, as did the Labour Party and other groupings. In fact, only 30 deputies voted to legalise the measure. Had Sinn Féin been present the Government would have been defeated. Within the ranks of Sinn Féin, the debate on abstention grew in intensity. Meanwhile, the economic situation was worsening. What few jobs there were in the public service went to supporters of the Government. De Valera's prohibition on Republicans leaving the country was swept aside in a tide of emigration, much of it to America. The boundary issue caused a second grouping to break away from the Government under a former Cumann na nGaedheal deputy, Professor Magennis, who set up a short-lived party, Clann Éireann, the Children of Eireann. The children were soon to be orphaned. The party disappeared at the next general election, but it cost Cumann na nGaedheal a couple of deputies and one senator.

Ever since his release from prison, de Valera had been aware that abstention was not a fruitful policy. He and his followers might propose, but the public disposed. Sinn Féin had attempted to persuade the public not to support a loan of ten million pounds sterling which the Government sought for purposes of reconstruction – much of it being necessitated by the destruction caused or sanctioned by de Valera and his supporters – by warning that the Sinn Féin 'government' would not accept any liability for the loan. However, the loan was oversubscribed, mostly by small investors. A month after he was set free, therefore, de Valera convened a meeting of Sinn Féin deputies, those returned both at the previous general election and to the second Dail. He persuaded the gathering, held on 7 and 8 August 1924, to set up what he termed 'a council of state', known as 'Comhairle na dTeachtai' (Council of Deputies). Grandly ignoring the inconvenient fact that there was a democratically elected government sitting in Leinster House running the state, the formal mission statement of the role of the Council and second Dail was set out as follows:

> For formal acts on a count of continuity . . . it would be wiser to regard the second Dail as the *de jure* government and legislature. But the whole body of elected members, including those just returned, should act as the Council of State and be the actual government for the country.[13]

The council of state idea was not as impracticable as it might appear. Theologically, it put blue water between itself and the second Dail, thus somewhat loosening the second Dail's grip on the Sinn Féin deputies' imagination. But more importantly, from de Valera's point of view, it established him, not the second Dail, as the source of authority. A week after the Sinn Féin meeting, he travelled again to Ennis to speak on the anniversary of his arrest a year earlier. Surrounded by an IRA guard, he drew laughter and cheers with his opening remarks: 'I would disappoint a number here if I were not to start by saying, "Well as I was saying to you when we were interrupted . . .".' But, literally under the noses of the IRA guard, behind the laughter, the cheers and the excitement, he continued as he had done a week earlier, and began laying down a course away from 'extremist support':

> Things may be forced on us, we may temporarily have to submit to certain things, but our assent they can never have . . . Don't forget for a moment that there is a vast difference between patiently submitting, when you have to, for a time, and putting your signature to a consent, or assent to these conditions.

Thus, while seeming to declare that he would never sign his affirmation to the oath, he was laying a marker that an entry to the Treaty-established parliament was not impossible. At the same time, having avoided the partition issue during the Treaty debates, indeed indicated a willingness to accept it, he now began shuffling the cards so that partition became the major weapon in his armoury. He told the Ennis meeting that his reason for entering politics was to prevent partition. A week later, in Dundalk, a border town, he said the reason for not entering Leinster House was that it was a partition parliament. But he really grabbed the headlines with the partition issue during the general election held in Great Britain and Northern Ireland on 29 October 1924. He stood for South Down and was arrested for defying an exclusion order. On 1 November he was sent to prison for a month in solitary confinement. He won the South Down seat and, more importantly, Sinn Féin's vote went up in the south in a set of by-elections held in November. Tentative negotiations with the Labour Party leader, Thomas Johnson, showed him that the Labour Party could be counted upon for support in bringing about social change. The Boundary Commission contretemps, coming on top of the foregoing developments, made it a question of when, not if, de Valera would enter the Dail.

He reacted to the announcement of the signing of the tripartite London agreement by issuing a statement claiming that when he met Lloyd George in 1921, he 'broke with him on this policy of Partition; and had Mr Griffith acted as I had believed he meant to act, he too would have broken on Partition'. This statement overlooked the fact that in Document No. 2, de Valera had specifically ruled out force against the Unionists, and went on to confirm them in their position by offering them 'privileges and safeguards not less substantial than those provided for in the Articles of Agreement for a Treaty signed in London on December 6th 1921'.

The IRA was not unaware of the subtle alterations in de Valera's policy. Several leading members were uneasy about the influence that de Valera was exerting on Frank Aiken, and feared that they were in danger of being led into supporting Leinster House. The issue came to a head at an IRA convention held in Dalkey, County Dublin, on 14 November. Peadar O'Donnell, who, in addition to his IRA activities, was a well-known author and a Socialist, had become increasingly disenchanted with Sinn Féin's preoccupation with the second Dail and the oath, and wanted the IRA to concentrate on Socialist objectives. Accordingly, he moved the following resolution:

> That in view of the fact that the Government has developed into a mere political party and has apparently lost sight of the fact that all our energies should be devoted to the all-important work of making the Army efficient so that the renegades who, through a coup d'état, assumed governmental powers in this country be dealt with at the earliest possible opportunity, the Arm of the Republic sever its connection with the Dail, and act under an independent Executive, such Executive be given the power to declare war, when, in its opinion, a suitable opportunity arises to rid the Republic of its enemies and maintain it in accordance with the proclamation of 1916.

During the discussion on this resolution, Aiken was challenged by George Plunkett, Count Plunkett's son, as to his intentions on entering Leinster House. When Aiken admitted that discussions had taken place on entry if the oath was removed, the meeting erupted. The O'Donnell resolution was passed overwhelmingly, Aiken and his supporters were dismissed, Andy Cooney was elected Chief of Staff, and the IRA became a law unto itself independent of political control from de Valera. But de Valera thus also became independent of the IRA. On 9 March 1926, at a Sinn Féin emergency Ard Fheis, he proposed a resolution that 'Once the admission Oaths of the twenty-six and six county assemblies are removed, it becomes a question not of principle but of policy whether or not Republican representatives should attend these assemblies.' However, Mary McSwiney and Austin Stack supported an amending resolution proposed by Father O'Flanagan: 'That it is incompatible with the fundamental principle of Sinn Féin to send representatives into any usurping legislature set up by English law in Ireland.' This passed narrowly and was put to the meeting as a substantive motion. It was defeated by two votes, 179 to 177, with 85 abstaining.

In a demonstration of de Valera's enormous prestige, O'Flanagan and McSweeney then sponsored a motion expressing 'the deep love and gratitude which each member feels for the man who is described by one delegate as the greatest Irishman of the century'. This passed by acclamation. However, de Valera was not swayed. As he had done in America when opposed by Cohalan and Devoy, and in Ireland when defeated by Collins and Griffith over the Treaty vote, he intended to set up his own organisation. He told the Ard Fheis, 'this is the opportune time and I realise that the coming General Election is the time . . . I am from this moment a free man . . . my duty as President of this Organisation has ended . . .'

In making for the 'coming General Election', de Valera – apart from his towering prestige – had two important strings to his bow, influence in the two major spheres of Irish international interest, Rome and America. Where Rome was concerned, he had a twofold objective: he wanted to find out how the Church generally would react to him if he were to enter mainstream politics; and he wanted to confer with some sympathetic and highly placed clergy on his proposed new course of action. The Rector of the Irish College, Monsignor John Hagan, and Archbishop Daniel Mannix of Australia were particular friends of his. Mannix visited Rome in 1925, and was sounded there by Hagan on the abandonment of abstention and entry to the Dail. Mannix felt that abstentionism could be contemplated, providing that there was no split in Sinn Féin.

De Valera himself visited Rome, dressed as a priest, and consulted with Hagan and others. Hagan's analysis was: 'may not the present situation be likened to a ship carrying Ireland and its fortunes, but managed by a crew of mad men who were driving the vessel straight on to the rocks, while the doomed passengers refused to step in and pitch the mad men overboard, on the pleas that even that much contact with them would soil their hands'. Fortified by what he had heard in Rome, de Valera returned to Dublin and, disregarding Mannix's caveat about avoiding a split, proposed the motion at the Sinn Féin Ard Fheis which led to his severing his ties with that organisation and setting out to form his own new party.

The new organisation which de Valera formally launched on 16 May 1926 in the La Scala Theatre, Dublin, was Fianna Fáil, the Warriors of Destiny. De Valera explained that the name had been chosen to symbolise: 'A banding together of the people for national service, with a standard of personal honour for all who join as that which characterized the ancient Fianna Eireann, and a spirit of devotion equal to that of the Irish Volunteers of 1916–21.' The Fianna were the Irish Samurai, and the term 'Warriors of Destiny' had sometimes been applied by Irish speakers to the Volunteers instead of the more common 'Oglaig na hEireann', the Irish Army.

The new party would prove itself to be one of the most durable and powerful Irish institutions of the twentieth century. It managed to combine a patina of 'national service' and 'a spirit of devotion' with a smoke-filled backroom skulduggery which could not have been bettered in Mayor Curley's Boston. Its stated objectives were Republican and it moved the partition issue to the premier place in its objectives:

> ... re-uniting of the Irish people and the banding of them together for the tenacious pursuit of the following ultimate aims, using at every moment such means as are rightfully available:

> 1. Securing the political independence of a united Ireland as a Republic.
> 2. The restoration of the Irish language and the development of a native Irish culture.
> 3. The development of a social system in which, as far as possible, equal opportunity will be afforded to every Irish citizen to live a noble and useful Christian life.
> 4. The distribution of the land of Ireland so as to get the greatest number possible of Irish families rooted in the soil of Ireland.
> 5. The making of Ireland an economic unit, as self-contained and self-sufficient as possible – with a proper balance between agriculture and other essential industries.

In his address to the La Scala gathering, de Valera sounded grace notes which would be the leitmotiv of Fianna Fáil for many years, rhetorically nodding towards the IRA and Republican heroes of the past, while acting constitutionally. The day chosen to launch the new party was that of Childers's execution. Not long before, a prominent Republican, Jack Keogh, had been rescued in an IRA jail break. In the course of his speech – to wild applause – de Valera said:

> When a military commander is given a task, he feels it his first duty to 'appreciate' or judge the situation correctly ... I am willing to wager that when the boys who rescued Jack Keogh the other day undertook their task, they ... started I am sure by finding out all they could about the conditions of his detention. They were then able to prepare their plans wisely ... we must act similarly in our political task.

He told his audience:

> It is vain to think that the natural aspirations of Irishmen for the liberty of their country are going to be stifled now. If the road of peaceful progress and natural evolution be barred, then the road of revolution will beckon and will be taken. Positive law and natural right will be involved in the old conflict. The question of minority right will be again bloodily fought out.

I have never said, and I am not going to say now, that force is not a legitimate weapon for a nation to use in striving to win its freedom . . . But a nation within itself ought to be able to settle its polity so that all occasions of civil conflict between its members may be obviated . . . This eternal menace of civil war was concealed in the womb of England's Greek gift of the 'treaty'; and, of all the duties which this nation owes itself, the duty which at this moment is paramount is the duty of seeing that this menace is not passed on to the coming generation . . .

The complex relationship between Fianna Fáil and the IRA requires separate treatment and will be discussed in the chapter detailing the IRA's history. Before dealing with this most indigenous of Irish phenomena, it is time to turn to de Valera's major theatre of external activity, the USA. Where his domestic political rivals were concerned, de Valera can be said to have won the propaganda war in America hands down. After his triumphant tours of the States in 1919–20, where most Irish-Americans interested in Irish affairs were concerned, de Valera *was* Ireland. As soon as Fianna Fáil was safely launched, he moved to cash in some of this enormous store of political, and financial, capital.

He arrived in New York on 5 March 1927, and again was received like a superstar. People literally fought to be admitted to meetings at which de Valera would be introduced in the sort of ringing terms with which he was welcomed to a huge gathering in Boston:

The man who fought in the streets of Dublin for the independence of Ireland. We welcome you as the man who accepted the sentence of death proudly and who when that sentence was commuted fought and defeated the English in their prisons. We welcome you as the man who coming from jail unbroken rallied the Irish nation to the success of 1918 . . .

Not surprisingly, his plans to collect money for the new party were hugely successful. Even before his coast-to-coast tour (it lasted until 1 May) involving all the major American cities and centres of Irish interest had time to take effect, it is recorded that New York alone had collected $25,000 by 29 March.[14] Apart from the money he was directly responsible for collecting, de Valera had another source of funding in view, one which was to have a significant effect on his eventual rise to power in Ireland. This was the $3 million portion of the bond drive which he had left in New York banks after his return to Ireland at Christmas 1920. At the time of the Treaty split, he had agreed with Collins 'that this money should not be used for Party purposes'. But he now set about making blatant, and strenuous, endeavours to get control of the money for 'party purposes'.

During the Anglo-Irish war, as well as the money de Valera raised externally in America, Collins had successfully floated an internal loan in Ireland. In 1922, the provisional government claimed the balance of this internal loan. De Valera, however, objected, in his capacity as trustee. He claimed that the money had been subscribed to maintain the Republic and was not transferable. On 31 July 1924, a Dublin High Court Judge, Judge Murnaghan, found in the Government's favour. The decision was upheld by the Irish Supreme Court on 17 December 1925. Part of the motivation for de Valera's 1927 visit to America lay in his determination to prevent the New York monies fetching up in the Free State's coffers, as the provisional government wished. The Cosgrave administration had successfully applied for an injunction to prevent the New York banks from handing over the money to de Valera, and followed this up with an application to the New York Supreme Court seeking to be declared the rightful owners of the money as the legitimate successor to the Republican Dail.

However, apart from the objections of de Valera's front organisation, the 'Bond Holders Committee', to this proposition, there was a third contestant in the field – the New York banks argued that the money should properly be returned to the original shareholders. The centrepiece of de Valera's first month of his 1927 tour was a three-day appearance in the New York Supreme Court, before Mr Justice Peters, who, as we shall see, ultimately found in favour of the bank's viewpoint the following May. On 1 May 1927, de Valera left Boston, to the cheers of thousands, aboard the appropriately named SS *Republic*. The election which he had had his eye on since the time of his break with Sinn Féin occurred on 9 June. It was a torrid affair, literally fought out in many cases between men who had opposed each other in a civil war a few years earlier, but from the start of the campaign, Fianna Fáil's was the glamour team.

Apart from de Valera's own dominance of the scene, the Cosgrave Cabinet consisted of tired men, worn out by the trauma of the civil war, and the subsequent attrition of trying to run a new state while contending with the activities of such formidable adversaries as de Valera and the IRA in the era of the Wall Street Crash. In addition to the funds de Valera had raised in the US, Fianna Fáil also had the benefit of the drive and organisational talent of men like Seán Lemass and Gerald Boland, who, building on the old Sinn Féin organisation which had swept the polls in 1918, were able to forecast almost to within a vote the support for the new party in every town and village in the country. Organisational ability was backed by the infusion of energy which many members of the IRA brought to the campaign. Young, enthusiastic men and women campaigned for Fianna Fáil with as much zeal as if they were fighting an action in the field. In those days it was difficult to tell at what point a Fianna Fáil *cumann*, or branch, became an IRA flying column at night. In this welter of energy and excitement, with a scent of change in the air, the existing Sinn Féin party, which de Valera had left, was brushed aside.

The result of the poll was as follows:

Cumann na nGaedheal	47
Fianna Fáil	44
Labour	22
Independents	16

159

Farmers' Party	11
National League	8
Sinn Féin	5

A Fianna Fáil election slogan had been 'Fianna Fáil is going in', and on the basis of the figures, many people assumed that with the assistance of independents, not only would Fianna Fáil go into the Dail, it would go into government. But the hurdle of the oath still remained. As his authorised biography made clear, de Valera knew that neither he nor his deputies would be admitted to their seats without taking it. Nevertheless, ever mindful of publicity, in the presence of a vast crowd, he presented himself at the Dail with his supporters, claiming that he had legal opinions that he could not be prevented from entering because of the oath. However, the official in charge of proceedings, Colm O'Murchadha, said that he could, and that he would be excluded unless he complied with 'a little formality' on the signing of the book in which the wording of the oath was contained. When de Valera made it clear he was not going to comply, O'Murchadha had the Dail chambers locked, and after a well-rehearsed display of spontaneous indignation, de Valera withdrew to carry out plans B and C.

Plan B was the taking of a high court action by Seán Lemass and Seán T. O'Kelly seeking a declaration that the expulsion was illegal. Plan C was a recourse to the initiative provisions of the constitution. Article 48 provided that a referendum on a proposed constitutional amendment would have to be held if a petition signed by 75,000 voters were presented to the legislature. In the circumstances of Irish public opinion at the time, de Valera would have been fairly certain of obtaining the 75,000 signatures in the first place, and in the second, carrying the referendum, as the idea of voting to retain an oath to the British Crown was not exactly calculated to enthuse the public. However, before the matter could be put to the test, a tragedy befell. As he walked to mass on Sunday 12 July 1927, Kevin O'Higgins was assassinated, by three IRA supporters acting on their own initiative. One of them, it was established years later, was in fact a member of Fianna Fáil, Timothy Coughlan.

This fact, which would of course have had an effect on de Valera and Fianna Fáil akin to that of the Phoenix Park murders on Parnell and the Home Rule campaign, was not known at the time, and de Valera's was one of the most vehement of the condemnations elicited by the murder. Although reeling from the shock of O'Higgins's killing, coming on top of an exhausting and traumatic election campaign and result, the Cabinet responded in resolute fashion. Cosgrave firstly refused the offer of an all-party coalition proposed by the leader of the Labour Party, Thomas Johnson, and then moved to head off both the further attacks which the police and army intelligence foretold, and indeed a backlash from within the security forces, amongst whom O'Higgins was deeply respected, if not always liked.

Cosgrave then introduced a number of very drastic public safety measures which practically took away civil liberties for any organisation deemed to be involved in seditious or treasonable activities. The use of military courts with powers to invoke the death penalty was envisaged. The second measure was an Electoral Amendment Bill, which would have required election candidates to sign an affidavit that they would take both their seats and the oath if elected. Failure to do so would result in disqualification. The third removed the initiative and referendum clauses from the constitution. The writing was now on the wall for de Valera and Fianna Fáil. Two prominent Fianna Fáil deputies who read it, Dan Breen and Paddy Belton, promptly took the oath and entered the Dail. Dan Breen was a famous gunman, one of those who had fired what are often described as the first shots of the Anglo-Irish war in the controversial Soloheadbeg ambush in which two RIC men were shot dead. Now, metaphorically, he had fired highly significant shots across de Valera's bows. Though he formally reacted by expelling the pair from the party, de Valera knew that if matters were allowed to drift Breen and Belton were clearly not going to be the only ones prepared to pass under the yoke of the oath.

After much vacillation and consultation with other parties, chiefly the Labour Party under Tom Johnson, and the National League, which attracted the support of large numbers of Irish ex-servicemen, under Captain Redmond, a son of John Redmond, the old Irish Parliamentary Party leader, de Valera issued the following statement to the press:

> It has . . . been repeatedly stated, and it is not uncommonly believed, that the required declaration is not an oath; that the signing of it implies no contractual obligation, that it has no binding significance in conscience or in law, that in short it is merely an empty political formula which Deputies could conscientiously sign without becoming involved, or without involving their nation, in obligations of loyalty to the English Crown.
>
> The Fianna Fáil Deputies would certainly not wish to have the feeling they are allowing themselves to be debarred by nothing more than an empty formula from exercising their functions as public representatives, particularly at a moment like this. They intend therefore to present themselves at the Clerk's office of the Free State Dail 'for the purpose of complying with the provisions of Article 17 of the Constitution', by inscribing their names in the book kept for the purpose, amongst other signatures appended to the required formula. But, so that there may be no doubt as to their attitude, and no misunderstanding of their action, the Fianna Fáil Deputies hereby give public notice that they propose to regard the declaration as an empty formality and repeat that their only allegiance is to the Irish nation, and that it will be given to no other power or authority.

De Valera returned to the Dail accompanied by Frank Aiken and Dr James Ryan, who had been the doctor to the rebels in the GPO, to confront O'Murchadha once more. This time he read out a prepared speech in Irish, saying:

> I want you to understand that I am not taking any Oath nor giving any promise of faithfulness to the King of England or to any power outside the people of Ireland. I am putting my name here merely as a formality to get the permission necessary to enter among the other Teachtai that were elected by the people of Ireland, and I want you to know that no other meaning is to be attached to it.

O'Murchadha responded that these remarks were no concern of his; what he wanted was de Valera's name in a book. De Valera took a copy of the Bible, which was lying on the book of signatures, and placed it at the far end of the room. He then signed the book, covering the wording of the oath with some papers. He said later that he had signed 'in the same way that I would sign an autograph in a newspaper. If you ask me whether I had an idea what was there, I say "yes", but it was neither read to me, nor was I asked to read it.'

His first act on entering the Dail was to join with Labour in demanding that the Electoral Amendment Bill be suspended pending a referendum. However, he subsequently abandoned the idea of gathering the necessary signatures (one-twentieth of the registered voters) for a petition which should have accompanied the demand, and the Bill passed into law, having served its purpose before it entered the statute book. Once he had entered the Dail, the electoral arithmetic almost allowed de Valera to seize power. He joined with Labour and the National League in agreeing to form a coalition government. On 16 August, the Labour leader, Thomas Johnson, moved a vote of no confidence in the Government. But some of his opponents pulled off a very Irish coup. A former Unionist, Major Bryan Cooper, a Sligo man, joined with Bertie Smylie, who became a famous editor of the *Irish Times*, in plying a third Sligo man, Alderman John Jinks, a National League deputy, with drink and political advice in equal measure. The advice was to the effect that the ex-servicemen who supported Redmond's party had not returned Jinks to the Dail to install de Valera in power. The alcohol ensured that Jinks accepted the advice, and he entered not the voting lobbies of Dail Eireann, but the next train back to Sligo.

The vote was a tie and the chairman gave his casting vote in favour of the Government. Buoyed up by this success, the Government went on to win two pending by-elections, emboldening Cosgrave to call a general election for 15 September. The result was as follows:

Cumann na nGaedheal	62
Fianna Fáil	57
Labour	13
Independents	12
Farmers' Party	6
National League	2
Independent Labour	1

The Alderman Jinks episode resulted in the good Alderman being laughed out of politics, and in the Cosgrave government ruling for another five years. The five years were of benefit to Fianna Fáil inasmuch as the party, which Seán Lemass conceded at the time of the oath-swallowing exercise was 'pretty raw', gained valuable experience in parliamentary procedure. Hitherto, its field of expertise had lain in organising to dislodge its opponents from power, not in exercising it. The five-year parliamentary apprenticeship helped to ensure that when Fianna Fáil did take over, it made a remarkably good job of government. This is not to say that the Cosgrave administration did not deserve high praise. Apart from the obvious, towering fact that the Free State's first Government ensured that that state would be a democracy, and forged an unarmed police force, a loyal army and a largely corruption-free civil service in the midst of a civil war and its hostile aftermath, the Cosgrave administration did other good things.

COSGRAVE'S GOVERNMENTAL RECORD

The Ministers and Secretaries Act of 1924 set up government departments on such a sound basis that the system thus created still operates at the time of writing. The police, army and judicial systems have also stood the test of time. An energetic Minister for Agriculture, Patrick Hogan, oversaw a variety of improvements in Irish agricultural production which boosted exports to Britain. The improvements included an Arterial Drainage Act, which did something to cope with the perennial scourge of flooding, and the creation of the sugar beet industry. Despite the anti-interventionist utterances of some ministers, the administration also made a start on slum clearance and new housing construction, making grants of some £300,000 available. One of its most courageous initiatives was an effort to restrict the sale of alcohol, whereby drinking hours were curtailed and on three national feast days it was banned altogether, Christmas Day, Good Friday – and St Patrick's Day! As the Dublin Dog Show was one of the few places drink could be obtained on the national saint's day, one result was that canine veneration reached heights unequalled anywhere else in Europe.

The administration's fidelity to the principle that agreements, once entered into, should be upheld, principally in the case of the Treaty; its efforts to maintain friendly relationships with Britain, and with the northern statelet, even when these were not reciprocated; its concern to balance the books and take a conservative approach to social problems: all this provided an unending supply of ammunition to the de Valera-ites, who claimed that the party was pro-British and anti-worker and small farmer. Sometimes government spokespersons provided this ammunition themselves, as for example when Patrick McGilligan became Minister for Industry and Commerce in 1924. McGilligan, who after the murder of Kevin O'Higgins became the outstanding figure of the Cosgrave administration, was called upon to speak in a Dail debate (10 October 1924) on the appalling unemployment situation.[15] Statistics for the period are the subject of much controversy, but through the 1920s the figure seems to have hovered constantly in the 75,000 to 100,000 region. In the course of the debate, during which mention was made of the fact that a little boy had died from starvation on a Dublin street, he stated that 'you cannot take measures this year which may lead to more people going hungry next year'. At this the Labour leader

Thomas Johnson interjected: 'But if they die this year?' prompting McGilligan to make a rejoinder which was taken down, distorted and used against him by his political adversaries in the court of public opinion to prove that Cumann na nGaedheal was indifferent to starvation amongst the unemployed: 'There are certain limited funds at our disposal. People may have to die in this country and may have to die through starvation.' He made it clear that he did not wish to see this happen, but later on in the debate replied to an opponent that

> If it is said that the Government has failed to adopt effective means to find useful work for willing workers, I can only answer that it is no function of Government to provide work for anybody. They can try and develop tendencies, and can try and set the pace a bit, but it is not the function of the government to provide work.

McGilligan's approach permeated the Cosgrave administration. Mention has already been made of the class structure of the Irish educational system: for the sons of clerks, labourers, small farmers – the Christian Brothers; for the professional classes and the sons of well-off farmers – schools like Blackrock College, run by the Holy Ghost Fathers, and the Jesuit-run Clongowes. The Christian Brothers boys' jibe against their Clongowes rivals was that these wealthy farmers' sons were like the cream produced on their farms – rich and thick! The reality was that many of these young men were outstandingly able and capable of what they had been originally trained for, take a leading role in the running of the British Empire. Instead, history dictated that they find themselves running a post-revolutionary government, trying to work free of British influences, while at the same time being dubbed pro-British by their domestic political opponents. They were not pro-British but they were conservative.

The most revolutionary of all the Cumann na nGaedheal founding fathers, Michael Collins, described the democratic programme of the first Dail as being 'too socialistic'. Based on the Proclamation of 1916, the social provisions of the programme were derived from drafts prepared by Thomas Johnson, who at the time was secretary of the Labour Party, and William O'Brien, the trade union leader, not because their socialistic cast of mind was shared by the leadership of Sinn Féin, but because most of the Sinn Féin leadership was not available for the drafting process as a result of the 'German Plot' swoops. Most of the Cumann na nGaedheal Cabinet would have agreed with Collins and shared Kevin O'Higgins's assessment of the aspirations of the democratic programme as being 'largely poetry'. On social issues, their Catholic upbringing left them deeply imbued with the principle that 'the poor ye shall always have with you' and their more recent experiences with the belief that, politically, the opportunity to build a new Irish state would only come around once.

Their top-hatted style made it comparatively easy for Valera and his colleagues to depict the Cosgrave team as West British, even though de

Valera himself had of course been educated at, and taught in, Blackrock, the prestigious Holy Ghost college. Ex-Clongowes men in the first Cumann na nGaedheal Government included McGilligan (Industry and Commerce, External Affairs), Kevin O'Higgins (Justice), Paddy Hogan (Agriculture), John Marcus O'Sullivan (Education), and Kevin Burke (Lands). These men were almost uniformly able, but they were young and, initially, inexperienced in government practice, and heavily dependent on civil service advice. As was the case in many of the new nations which emerged from under the lion's paw, this civil service was, together with all the other institutions of the new state, British-inspired. Many of the officials who held office at the time of the Free State takeover elected to either retire or to transfer to Northern Ireland or Britain, but the parliamentary system and local government administration continued to follow British models. Once the Free State was set up, the Government largely dispensed with the Sinn Féin courts and returned to the British legal model, retaining only the Sinn Féin concept of circuit courts. The Irish and British legal systems had been identical since the seventeenth century, with Irish barristers practising in British courts, where the pickings were better than in Ireland, and English judges receiving Irish appointments. Neither the enactment of specifically Roman Catholic legislation in the twenties, nor the constitutional tinkerings of de Valera in the thirties fundamentally altered either courts, codes, or methods of practice. For the public at large the law remained, like the Ritz Hotel, open to everybody.

However, the new state did attempt, and achieve, some political and administrative innovation. Even as the Black and Tan war reached a climax, the revolutionaries had been attempting to think, and act, constructively. Their efforts are worth at least a fleeting examination as they shed light both on the thinking of the Sinn Féin leadership and on the conditions prevailing in the country at the time. Increasingly throughout 1920, the Sinn Féiners had attempted to take over local government functions, including the collection of rates. This meant considerable difficulty and dangers for those involved, as apart from the chaotic wartime conditions, there was the physical danger of what might befall Sinn Féin administrators engaged in what the Auxiliaries and the Black and Tans regarded as subversive activity punishable by death. Different Sinn Féin luminaries reacted in contrasting ways to the situation. Kevin O'Higgins, according to Professor Mary Daly, 'emerges as both unrealistic and intolerant, with little understanding of the pressures facing local Councils or officials'.[16] Cosgrave, however, with his background in county council work, was both more understanding and effective. He argued that 'persons appointed to public positions and definite terms must have some security of tenure'; he rejected the American precedent where the election of a new president led to the appointment of a new set of officials.[17] Like Sinn Féin generally, Cosgrave sought to have it accepted that appointments made under Sinn Féin's aegis should be based solely on merit, and not on either IRA service or local influence.

To this end, the underground Dail directed in 1921 that a number of inspectors be appointed, three of them women. (Inspectors formed the key supervisory grade in the existing British local government system.) One of these was my father, who, in November 1921, conducted an examination in Killarney to select a secretary for the county home. During the examination, three armed and masked men entered the examination hall, ordered both my father and the candidates into another room and confiscated the exam papers, warning that anyone who spoke about the affair would 'pay the penalty'. The raiders explained that they felt it 'unfair to allow shirkers and slackers to secure positions whilst men were suffering in jail'. My father stayed up most of the night setting alternative papers, and the exam continued the next day. However, Kerry is Kerry. The successful candidate was leant on by a member of the committee appointed by Kerry County Council to run the county home and 'asked' to withdraw in favour of an ex-internee who would come second. He did so, and the ex-internee got the job.[18]

Perhaps understandably, my father informed his superiors that he was 'thoroughly sick and disgusted with Kerry', where, he complained, 'hidden forces' were blocking his efforts at reforms. He wrote:

> I had to report before the apathy of public bodies towards reforms and their reluctance to co-operate with me in effecting tangible reforms. For aiming at the latter, I have been accused of being too materialistic. Incidentally, I must say, therefore to such people as my accusers the constructive policy of this Department is too materialistic and lacks the finer qualities and ideals of those more progressive reformers in Kerry who have spent their time since 22 June last building castles in the air from the County Council offices.[19]

Behind that light-hearted memo there lies the tragedy of the civil war in Kerry. When the military as opposed to the administrative forces of the Free State arrived in Kerry to enforce Dublin's rule, fierce local pride ensured that they were received not only with obstruction, but with blood-letting. The consequent reprisals left wounds which had not fully healed at the time of writing.

When Cumann na nGaedheal assumed office, a popular phrase of the day was that 'Ireland had as many Boards as would make her own coffin.' The various crises in the Anglo-Irish relationship had resulted in a jumble of systems of control. Some bodies were responsible to the Chief Secretary for Ireland, who was always a member of the British Cabinet, some to Whitehall, some to local authorities of varying degrees of autonomy.

The Ministers and Secretaries Act of 1924 tidied up this situation and became in effect the statutory basis for Irish central administration throughout much of the century. The Act divided up the existing agencies into eleven departments each under ministerial control. It also laid down the regulations governing the relationships between ministers and departments, and provided for the creation of an Attorney General and for junior ministers, known as parliamentary secretaries, who were responsible to the Dail but were not Cabinet members. A less durable experiment was that of 'extern ministers'. These, seven in number, were appointed to the Executive Council, in effect the Cabinet, because of some administrative or technical expertise, and were responsible to the Dail rather than the Executive Council. The idea, based on Swiss practice, was to get away from the all-pervasive British influence. But the experiment was discontinued, by constitutional amendment, in 1927 after the inevitable clash between the political and the technocratic approaches had led to public disagreements between an extern, J.J. Walshe, and the Cabinet. Walshe, a protectionist, fell out in particular with the able and far-seeing Minister for Agriculture, Patrick Hogan, a devotee of free trade. A local government version of the extern experiment, the 'county manager' system, proved more successful. The innovation was both an attempt to break from British models, by following the American example of city managers, and an effort to replace amateur committees with professional expertise. Needless to say this innovation when introduced first, in Cork, in 1929, aroused much opposition because of the threat it posed to the ambitions of corrupt individuals anxious to line their pockets by means of local politics.

A peasant people scarred by poverty, absentee landlordism, war and civil war must have prompted many a would-be reformer sent from Dublin to ponder the words ascribed to Odysseus as he prepared to leave Ithaca: 'I meet and dole unequal laws unto a savage race.' For example the Roscommon town commissioners were probably only more culpable in degree rather than kind compared to other local bodies. In 1924 it was discovered that the chairman, town secretary, assistant secretary and two commissioners were employed by the *Roscommon Messenger*. The commissioners had ordered the building of some local housing units whose tenants included several other *Messenger* employees, town commissioners and even the builders who put up the houses. There was no public lighting because the commissioners had not paid the gas company, and the position regarding rate collection and other public services such as sewerage was deplorable.

But the manager system stood the test of time and ultimately became the norm for all local authorities. One of the reasons that it did so was because of the Local Appointments Commission, set up in 1926 to vet candidates for appointments within the local government system and recommend its nominees to the authority concerned. The work of the Commission both helped to remove many such appointments from the grasp of local interests and saw to it that some able men became county managers, their role being to prepare budgets and initiate major schemes for which the relevant councils voted yea or nay.

However, despite successes in local government, it is probably not surprising that a combination of the 'Made in England' ethos, which was imported, and some peculiarly Irish, domestically developed attitudes meant that the new state made little progress in what would on the surface at least have appeared to be two priority areas, given the Government's revolutionary background. One was the Irish language, and the other the status of women.

167

While the Government did make some, admittedly unsuccessful, efforts at achieving the former, it is possible to argue that it actively worked to downgrade the latter. The disturbed state of the country as the Irish took the reins of government in their own hands meant that there was little time or resources for promoting Irish. It was made a compulsory subject in schools and for the public service, but this served to spread hostility rather than affection for the language, because it was badly taught, due to a shortage of teachers, and people like Michael Conneally, for example, found difficulty initially in sitting promotional examinations. English was the spoken language of the country, despite the work of the Gaelic League and the enduring popularity of the Irish games, hurling and Gaelic football. The Government engendered hostility, rather than enthusiasm, in the legal profession, for example, by stipulating that lawyers should have a knowledge of the language at a stage when there were no relevant textbooks. The new government contained some notable Irish scholars – Eóin MacNeill and John Marcus O'Sullivan were Cumann na nGaedheal Ministers for Education – but the shine was rubbed off the joyous badge of identification which the language had been to many young Irish people, pre-independence, by the censorious, killjoy attitude which soon began to permeate the new state as Christ and Caesar got down to the business of sharing the spoils of independence. Women were a principal casualty in the share-out. In the first Dail, Constance Markievicz (Labour) had been the first woman minister in Europe, but de Valera, as part of his manoeuvrings against Collins, had subsequently (August 1921) created a smaller, decision-taking Executive Cabinet, from which she was excluded, although she retained Cabinet rank. It was downhill politically for women thereafter. Between 1922 and 1937, when de Valera introduced a constitution which copper-fastened the belief that women's place was in the home, only nine women held places in the Dail and Senate. The Dail deputies were usually the widows or relatives of famous figures in the war of independence, such as Kathleen Clarke, Tom Clarke's widow, and Michael Collins's sister, Margaret Collins-O'Driscoll. They, and the moral climate of the day, did not deem it appropriate that they speak out on issues such as divorce or contraception. The day proved to be a long one. Not until 1979 would another woman (Maire Geoghegan-Quinn) be appointed to a Cabinet post.

The 1916 Proclamation had guaranteed 'equal rights and equal opportunities to all its Citizens' and promised to cherish 'all the children of the nation equally'. Mother Church helped to put a speedy end to those heretical aspirations. As late as 1971, the authority on Irish Church–State relationships, J.H. Whyte, could correctly point out that the Church had 'carved out for itself a more extensive control over education in Ireland than in any other country in the world'.[20] Almost a half-century earlier, as Ireland recovered from its post-civil war hangover, the position of women under this celibate, male-enforced control was equally accurately described as follows by Aine McCarthy:

The prevailing gender ideology was given religious endorsement by the Roman Catholic Church, which emphasised the 'natural' female virtues of obedience, servility and self-sacrifice for women and repressed the reality of female sexuality. At the same time, there was an undercurrent of obsession with women's bodies as a source of sin, by which was meant sexual misconduct.[21]

Such attitudes were buttressed by the economics of rural Ireland. The famine had imparted a culture shock to Ireland which manifested itself in a mistrust of early marriage, and often of marriage at all, because the institution increased the numbers of those vulnerable to a sudden economic downturn. Moreover, economics also dictated that the subdivision of farms amongst the sons of the family was to be avoided. Therefore it became the norm that one son, usually the eldest, got the farm, and the others either emigrated or did not marry. Female emigration from Ireland reached higher levels than in other countries, almost equalling that of men. Part of this outflow was economically induced, part a desire for sexual freedom and intellectual enrichment. I conducted a study of the Irish diaspora in the last year of the twentieth century,[22] and I found in several countries that I visited that while many women complained of loneliness, and a loss of their heritage, particularly if they had emigrated to England, on balance a majority found that emigration had been an enabling experience when contrasted with the restrictive atmosphere which prevailed in Ireland.

One Irish characteristic which an authoritarian Church bolstered was the attitude of specifically Irish, as opposed to clerical, authoritarianism, which permeated Irish society until well into the latter quarter of the century. Somehow, the Irish had managed to combine the practice of democracy, freedom of expression, and an independent judiciary with a strongly autocratic style of authority. In the early days of the new state, de Valera's followers found it natural to refer to him as 'The Chief'. At the end of the century, their successors found it equally natural to refer to his inheritor as leader of the largest political party in the state, Mr Charles J. Haughey, as 'The Boss'. Members of the hierarchy were keen that not only their authority, but that of the heads of families, should be upheld. Bishop O'Doherty of Galway, who shared the general episcopal antipathy towards dancing and the exposure of the young Catholic men of Ireland to the temptations of womanhood, advised fathers that 'if your girls do not obey you, if they are not in at the hours appointed, lay the lash upon their backs. That was the good old system, and that should be the system today.'[23]

The Bishop, and his colleagues, may have been conditioned in their approach to the linked issues of dancing and the need to uphold parental authority by the rise in the illegitimate birth rate in the first years of the state (from 2.6% in 1921–3 to 3.5% in 1933–4).[24] At all events, their lordships issued a pastoral in 1927 which summed up the hierarchy's view of the dangers threatening Ireland:

These latter days have witnessed, among many other unpleasant sights, a loosening of the bonds of parental authority, a disregard for the discipline of the home, and a general impatience under restraint that drives youth to neglect the sacred claims of authority and follow its own capricious ways . . . The evil one is ever setting his snares for unwary feet. At the moment, his traps for the innocent are chiefly the dance hall, the bad book, the indecent paper, the motion picture, the immodest fashion in female dress – all of which tend to destroy the virtues characteristic of our race.

Their lordships did not confine themselves merely to issuing pastorals. They actively exerted their influence to ensure that as Mother England vacated the corridors of power, Mother Church took them over. A series of Catholic laws, or laws designed to bolster Catholic attitudes, were enacted by the Free State Government, beginning with the Censorship of Films Act of 1923. Under it, a film censor was appointed who could cut a film, or refuse a licence, if he felt it to be 'subversive of public morality'. The Catholic viewpoint on divorce was strictly enforced. Before independence, a person living in Ireland who wanted a divorce got one by having a private Bill introduced at Westminster. This system was altered so that the Bills would be presented to the Dail instead. Three such Bills were presented, but Cosgrave put through a motion, in 1925, which forbade the introduction of any more, saying: 'I consider that the whole fabric of our social organisation is based upon the sanctity of the marriage bond and that anything that tends to weaken the binding efficacy of that bond to that extent strikes at the root of our social life.'[25]

This essentially Catholic view of Irish society was challenged by the poet W.B. Yeats, who made a magnificent speech in the Senate, pointing out the injustice of such a measure to Irish Protestants within the confines of the 26 counties, and the appalling effect it would have on those in the six north of the border with whom the Free State claimed it sought unity, but to no avail. Ireland free was going to be Ireland Catholic. It was also going to be Ireland sober if the new puritans could make it so. Liquor Acts were introduced in 1924 and in 1927 which tried to cut down on drinking by reducing pub opening hours, and also trying to cut the number of pubs in the country.

Any Irish Catholic who wished to use literature to take their minds off an unhappy marriage or their restricted ability to alleviate either this condition or any of the other trials of life in the new state by means of a drink or a visit to the cinema speedily found their choice of reading material severely curtailed also, by the Censorship of Publications Act 1929. Not only did the board which the Act set up have the power to ban any book or periodical, because it was 'indecent or obscene', the Act also prohibited the dissemination of literature which advocated birth control, and formed the basis for legislation which ultimately outlawed contraception altogether. Women took very little part in the birth control debate which, as Mary Clancy has pointed out, had a subtext: 'A significant desire to extend control over aspects of women's lives in general. Not least was the disapproval shared by a number of deputies regarding the reading material enjoyed by girls and women.'[26]

In these years, the Church took steps to extend its own control by further tightening its grip on the educational system. Some commentators have tried to explain the introduction of sectarian legislation into a state whose founders had paid with their blood to make it a republic as being due to the fact that as Catholics the Cumann na nGaedheal legislators would have wanted this kind of legislation anyhow, without being leant on by the bishops. In aid of this proposition one could point to the fact that Cosgrave, speaking as a member of the Cabinet of the outlawed first Dail, when it was obviously necessary to attempt to establish Sinn Féin's credentials for orthodoxy with the hierarchy, made two (unsuccessful) proposals which, though uttered in Dublin, were clearly designed to be heard in Rome. He proposed, during a debate in February 1921, 'a theological board or upper house to the Dail which would decide whether any enactment of Dail Eireann were contrary to faith or morals or not'. By way of buttressing this cheerless proposal for Protestants in the proposed new Ireland, he also suggested that a guarantee be given to the Pope that: 'the Dail will not make laws contrary to the teachings of the Church'. However, to argue that the Catholic legislation brought in by Cumann na nGaedheal was merely a result of the Dail's religious outlook overlooks the inconvenient fact that it was the bishops' death grip on the Irish educational and thought-moulding process which produced that kind of legislator and legislation. That was why the bishops fought for educational control in the first place, and continued to fight for it in the new state. The one aspect which lay more or less outside the Church's influence was technical education, which was ostensibly controlled not by the clergy but by local authorities. In practice, however, the local committee which ran these schools generally had a priest as chairman. In 1930, a Vocational Education Act allowed for an increase in the spread of technical education. But Cumann na nGaedheal formally[27] assured the hierarchy that vocational education would remain just that and would not be allowed to develop in competition with the Church-controlled system. The cobbler really would stick to his last.

All of this political activity on the part of the Church of course had a definite aim in view: the creation of a system wherein Catholic parents would be inculcated to produce large numbers of children who would uphold the doctrines of the Church at home, and when, not if, many of them were driven to emigrate, would spread the Church's power base internationally. But with an eye to women in particular, the Church defined its ideals in more emollient terms. In 1924, the Jesuit Father Edward Cahill, whom de Valera would later consult during the drafting of his constitution, said of the role of the state towards women:

> The duty of a Christian State [is] to remedy, by prudent legislation, the abuses which have driven an excessive number of women into industrial employment outside the home . . . In a Christian State women should be excluded even by law from occupation unbecoming or dangerous to female modesty. The employment of wives or mothers in factories or outside their own household should be strictly limited by legislation. Girls should not be employed away from their homes or in work other than domestic until they have reached a

sufficiently mature age, so that they be not exposed too soon to external dangers to their modesty.[28]

It should not surprise us therefore that the Cosgrave government systematically eroded women's rights. In 1924 and in 1927, legislation was enacted restricting women's right to serve on juries. In 1925, women's right to sit for every civil service examination was limited. The trend thus begun was continued under de Valera. In 1932, compulsory retirement was enjoined on women teachers who got married, and this ukase was subsequently extended to the civil service. In 1935, the state took power to restrict the employment of women in industry. All this legislation would be reflected in the 1937 constitution.

One of the most important, if not the most important, British institutional legacies to Ireland was the influence of the Treasury on the philosophy of the Irish Department of Finance, which has the same relationship with the Irish Government as has the Treasury with the British. Other departments may propose in their estimates, but it is the Department of Finance which disposes in its pronouncements to the Minister for Finance on departmental estimates. The influence of the Department of Finance is felt in every other department and hence in all state planning. This of course does not absolve ministers from their prerogative, and obligation, of controlling and directing policy, but the potential for stagnation, or innovation, in the hands of the secretary of the Department of Finance throughout the entire Irish system, as we shall see, only became obvious to the Irish public some decades after Cumann na nGaedheal had ceased to exist and the dynamic T.K. Whitaker had come to power.

Some historians, notably J.J. Lee, have attributed much of the Britishness or Treasury-style philosophy of the Irish Department of Finance to C.J. Grigg, who had become a friend of Cosgrave's and was loaned to the Irish Government by the British Board of Inland Revenue to set up the new Irish civil service. When Grigg returned to London, the top civil servants whom he left behind him to run the key Irish Department of Finance were cast in the British Treasury mould, one of a predominant negativity towards proposals for increasing state expenditure and a strong predilection towards balancing the books at all costs. These were Joseph Brennan (also a Clongownian), who became secretary of the department, and J.J. MacElligott, the Assistant Secretary, who later succeeded Brennan.

However, the men were already moulded and cast in their attitudes well before Grigg arrived. Brennan's ability had been acknowledged by Warren Fisher, the British expert sent over to examine the workings of Dublin Castle in the post-1916 era. The point is that though the Castle administration functioned badly it functioned as a unit of the British civil service and, unlike the new army and police forces which were green-field starts, the British-style civil service continued after independence, much like the letter boxes which received a coat of green paint through which the crowns were still visible.

It is arguable that both Brennan and MacElligott were prepared to take risks, had they been given forceful and imaginative leadership. MacElligott fought in 1916 and Brennan, a man of legendary character and integrity, had taken extraordinary risks while still working in Dublin Castle for the British. Unknown to his masters, he supplied Collins with position papers which Collins was able to use to great effect during the Treaty negotiations. However, Ernest Blythe, the Free State Minister for Finance, could be forceful, but one could accuse neither him nor his Cabinet of having fallen prey to imagination. In fact Professor Lee has argued that the founders of the Free State 'waged a coherent campaign against the weaker elements in the community'. This ensured that 'the poor, the aged, and the unemployed' all felt 'the lash of the liberators'. To substantiate this judgement Lee could validly point to the Government's aversion to building houses for the poor. Despite the appalling housing conditions, only 14,000 were built from public monies between 1922 and 1929. However, the passage of time and the economic circumstances of the period have combined to make the provision of 2,000 houses a year less paltry than it appears on the surface. For while it would be of little comfort, or relevance, to anyone hoping for a local government-provided house in the 1920s, the fact is that with the full force of the so-called Celtic Tiger economy behind it, the Government in charge of running the state as the new (twenty-first) century dawned had again reverted to producing only 2,000 such houses a year. The Cumann na nGaedheal Cabinet's enthusiasm for cutting blind and old age pensions cannot be made to appear even remotely humane by any comparison, however. Beginning with the 1924 budget, Cumann na nGaedheal cut pensions from £3.18 million in 1924 to £2.54 million in 1927. Opposition pressure eventually forced some restoration of the cuts in 1928, but by the time of the 1932 general election these pensions were still below those obtaining in 1924 and the pensions issue provided an important campaign weapon for de Valera.

Overall government expenditure was reduced from £42 million in 1923–4 to £24 million in 1926–7. Income tax was lowered, but the Government did not intervene to ensure that the capital thus produced did anything other than gather meagre deposit rates in Irish banks, or be exported abroad. The Irish exported some £195 million in 1926–7 and only attracted in around £73 million. The banking system itself did much to endorse the British Treasury-style approach. A banking commission set up under Cumann na nGaedheal in 1926 found that the Free State 'is now and will undoubtedly continue to be, an integral part of the economic system at the head of which stands Great Britain'.

For all his anti-British rhetoric and his protestations about Irish independence, de Valera did little to distance himself from this view. Years later (1934), when he was in power, he too established a banking commission:

> to examine and report on the system in Saorstat Eireann of currency, banking, credit, public borrowing and lending, and the pledging of credit on behalf of agriculture, industry

and the social services, and to consider and report what changes, if any, are necessary or desirable to promote the social and economic welfare of the community and the interests of agriculture and industry.

Thus the way was seemingly prepared for a shake-up of the extremely conservative Irish banking system in which the dominant Bank of Ireland played a role akin to that of a central bank.

However, one Saturday shortly before the commission was announced, de Valera unexpectedly summoned the startled Governor of the Bank of Ireland, Lingard Goulding, to Government Buildings and informed him of the impending announcement in such a way as to make it clear that he was only setting up the commission under pressure from his party. He felt that a report was therefore required, but that no alteration to the system was necessary. To ensure that no radical change would come about, he presented Goulding with a list of the proposed commission members, one of whom is thought to have been Maynard Keynes. In Goulding's own words, the list was 'modified by the removal of several names'. Not surprisingly when the commission reported in 1938 it found in favour of the status quo. Equally unsurprisingly, de Valera accepted the report. The 'made in England' brand continued to be the favoured one in the Irish financial marketplace for several decades more.

One major exception to the Cumann na nGaedheal Government's policy of non-intervention in the economic sphere was in sponsoring the brainchild of an Irish engineer, Thomas McLoughlin, the Shannon electricity scheme at Ardnacrusha in County Limerick, which was constructed in the years 1925–9. The Government set up the Electricity Supply Board (ESB) to produce and generate electricity throughout the state. Apart from being the first major public investment of the new state, the scheme proved to be a test, which the Government passed successfully, of its ability to face down commercial and trade union opposition as strongly, some would say ruthlessly, as it had put down its political foes during the civil war. The existing private electricity providers, mostly Unionists, opposed the scheme, and suggested an alternative initiative for the River Liffey. There was also opposition to the fact that the contract to build the generating station was given to a German firm, Siemens. Construction was delayed by a bitter strike amongst the building workers, who wanted higher wages. It was equally bitterly, and successfully, resisted by the Government.

Nevertheless, despite all this constructive work, the support of former Unionists and the 'made in England' style of its civil service helped to create a pro-British aura which de Valera exploited mercilessly and successfully. In later life pictures of the tall, top-hatted figure of de Valera became for Ireland the epitome of dignified elder-statesmanship, but in his advance towards power he managed to make of the top hat a potent propaganda weapon against Free State ministers. He derided their formal attire of 'this wonderful tall hat, this most capacious and highly respectable tall hat'. And in its early years as a party and in government the badge of a Fianna Fáil public figure became a felt hat which literally and metaphorically sat more easily on the head of an average Christian Brothers boy than did a 'topper'.

W.T. Cosgrave, however, was an above-average Christian Brothers boy who presided over his Clongownian Cabinet with courage and common sense. He lacked the flamboyance of many of his contemporaries but his background as a hero of 1916 and a Dublin county councillor stood him in good stead as he kept one eye on the mettlesome steeds who propelled his Cabinet, and the other on both the petit bourgeoisie who supported his administration and on the Church. Cosgrave epitomised the Irish working-class Catholic brand of patriotism which was deferential and independence-seeking at the same time. The Irish struggle and the state which emerged from it was, by both tradition and empiricism, republican in character. But conceivably it could just as easily have ended up as a monarchy. Griffith's early vision of Sinn Féin embodied a king, Lords and Commons, and even the most advanced Irish Republicans went along with the concept to the extent that Pearse, Plunkett and Clarke discussed the possibility of having a German prince as head of the proposed Irish state. Their candidate was Prince Joachim, the youngest son of Kaiser Wilhelm II. De Valera too later flirted with the idea of a monarchy. Count Lucena Hugo O'Donnell told me that after taking power in 1932, de Valera raised with his great-grandfather, the then Duke of Tetuan, the idea of restoring a monarchy in Ireland. As a descendant of one of the great earls, the Duke would have been an obvious candidate for the post, which in the event never materialised.

However, the fact that these suggestions were mooted illustrates the fact that Irish republicanism was overall more of a concept of freedom, of the right to manage one's own affairs, than a doctrine. Certainly a majority of its adherents would not have subscribed to Voltairean notions of 'godless republicanism', particularly if the bishops objected! De Valera, although he frequently demonstrated in political manoeuvrings that he had swallowed Machiavelli whole, in his private thoughts and utterance was a far more honest and casuistry-free figure than he appeared to be in public. A remark of his to his son Vivion, who later retold it to me, both illustrates this quality and provides a telling summing up of the Cosgrave administration's tenure in office. Vivion and he were in a car together, some time after de Valera had come to power, and Vivion made some standard Fianna Fáil criticisms of Cumann na nGaedheal. De Valera surprised Vivion by cutting him off and waving a forefinger, exclaiming, 'Yes, yes, yes. We said all that . . . but when we got in and saw the files . . . they did a magnificent job, Viv.' The dun, insular practicality of the early Irish political leaders (a practicality which was carried on by their successors) was epitomised by one of Cosgrave's opening remarks on taking office as leader of the provisional government: 'Our foreign policy, other than commercial, would be a matter of no importance.' Yet it was in the foreign policy arena that the urge towards independence won out over merchant caution. For it was in the international sphere that the Cosgrave administration proved itself to be far from 'pro-British'. Ironically enough, Cosgrave's son Liam eventually became a minister for Foreign Affairs. The new state joined the League of Nations in 1923, and despite strong British objections succeeded in having the Treaty registered with the League the following year, thus strongly advancing the claim of those who saw the Treaty not as an internal matter for Britain and the Commonwealth, but as an international agreement between two sovereign powers. Acutely conscious of the effect of this on the Dominions, the British argued forcefully, but unsuccessfully, with Cosgrave that 'the action of the Free State Government raised questions of very great Constitutional importance between the component parts of the Empire . . . the Treaty was not, in their opinion, an instrument proper to be registered . . .' The British claimed that the League had no role in 'the relations *inter se* of the various parts of the Commonwealth'.

But the Irish pressed ahead with the establishment that year of another notable diplomatic bridgehead. The first Dominion Ambassador to Washington, Professor T.A. Smiddy, was accepted by the Americans as the first 'Minister Plenipotentiary'.

As part of its policy of removing British governmental influence from the new state's affairs, the Irish wore down strong British opposition to their getting direct access to the King, and, as a corollary, to securing the right to have state documents authenticated not with a British seal but with the great Seal of the Irish Free State. McGilligan scored another diplomatic first when, on 19 March 1931, he was received at Buckingham Palace by the King without having to go through a British minister. He also secured the royal signature to a treaty concluded between the Irish Free State and Portugal, and stamped it with the great Irish seal. This apparently symbolic act had the practical effect of ending the British Government's power in law to pass judgement on any proposed action by the Irish which could have cut across the existing rights of either the United Kingdom or its dominions.

From the outset, the Irish political and diplomatic representatives punched well above their weight. The Irish politicians very early on made a discovery which they did not talk about publicly, and which was also to cause surprise when encountered by de Valera and his associates a decade later. Namely, that the reality of the ability of British statesmen could sometimes fall well below the level of their public images. During the Imperial Conference held in London in 1930, Desmond Fitzgerald wrote wonderingly to his wife that MacDonald and Thomas (the British delegates) were 'so badly briefed' that he and Patrick McGilligan ended up 'acting as general advisers to the whole lot'. A few years later (at the 13th session of the League of Nations in Geneva during September 1932), Joseph Connolly, who was accompanying de Valera, spent an evening with Ramsay MacDonald and Sir John Simon, after which he declared himself

Worse than bored. I had the staggering realisation that this man who had been entertaining me was the Prime Minister of Britain, and that his attendant henchman was

Foreign Secretary. The former was either tired and exhausted, or a completely spent force, and his Foreign Secretary was a 'yes man' politician keeping in step without marching.

As Fitzgerald wrote to his wife, that sort of thing gave the Irish 'a sense of confidence'. Along with Fitzgerald and McGilligan, the Cosgrave government in its early years also had, prior to his murder, the services of the remarkable Kevin O'Higgins. His men were backed up by three outstanding civil servants, Diarmuid O'Hegarty, who was in effect secretary to the Government, Joseph P. Walshe (another Clongowian), who deserves to be regarded as the father of the Department of External Affairs, and E.V. Phelan, an Irish civil servant with the International Labour Office at Geneva, who put both his position and expertise at the service of his country at a number of crucial junctures.

Ironically, two of the Cosgrave administration's most important international achievements would ultimately prove to be of the greatest assistance to de Valera. One was the election of Ireland to the Council of the League of Nations (on 17 September 1930). The more important of the two was the passing into law of the Statute of Westminster (on 11 December 1931), which gave effect to the resolutions of the Imperial Conference of 1930. The path to this was begun by Kevin O'Higgins at the Imperial Conference of 1926. These efforts were built on by his successors at succeeding Commonwealth fora, and it is acknowledged that it was the Irish who played the largest part in the drawing up of the Statute. It contained the following:

1) No law made by the Parliament of a Dominion shall be void and inoperative on the grounds that it is repugnant to the law of England, or to the provisions of any existing or future Act of Parliament of the Parliament of the United Kingdom, and the powers of the Parliament of a Dominion shall include the power to repeal or amend any such Act, order rule or regulation in so far as the same is part of the law of the Dominion.
2) The Parliament of a Dominion has full power to make laws having extra-territorial operation.
3) No future Act of Parliament of the United Kingdom shall extend to a Dominion unless it is expressly declared in that Act that the Dominion has requested and consented to its enactment.

No one was more aware of the potential of these provisions for Ireland than that arch-Imperialist and co-father of the Treaty, Winston Churchill. He realised that if the Statute of Westminster passed into law, then the Dail could repudiate anything it wished in the Treaty, including the oath. On 20 November 1931, he supported an amendment by the Unionist Colonel Gretton which would have prevented this and other evils, including the repeal of the Free State constitution, creating, in Churchill's term, an 'inexpressible anomaly'.

The Free State Government was disturbed by the reaction to the Gretton amendment, which read as follows:

Nothing in this Act shall be deemed to authorise the legislature of the Irish Free State to repeal, amend or alter the Irish Free State Agreement Act, 1923, or the Irish Free State Constitution Act, 1922, or so much of the Government of Ireland Act, 1920, as continues to be in force in Northern Ireland.[29]

Cosgrave sent a letter to the British Prime Minister setting forth Dublin's apprehensions, which Baldwin took the unusual step of reading into the House of Commons record:

I . . . am greatly concerned at Mr Thomas's concluding statement that the Government will be asked to consider the whole situation in the light of the debate. I sincerely hope that this does not indicate any possibility that your government would take the course of accepting an Amendment relating to the Irish Free State.

. . . the happy relations, which now exist between our two countries is absolutely dependent upon the continued acceptance by each of us of the good faith of the other . . . the Treaty is an agreement that can only be altered by consent.

. . . there seems to be a mistaken view in some quarters that the solemnity of this instrument in our eyes could derive any additional strength from a parliamentary law. So far from this being the case, any attempt to erect a statute of the British Parliament into a safeguard of the Treaty would have quite the opposite effect here, and would rather tend to give rise in the minds of our people to a doubt as to the sanctity of this instrument.

The House listened to Cosgrave rather than Churchill or Gretton. The amendment was defeated by 360 votes to 50. This meant that the situation had moved on from the point where the British had objected to the Irish registering the Treaty with the League of Nations to one where they had acquiesced in recognising it as a bilateral international agreement. Britain's right to intervene in Ireland under British law was gone. The benefit of the freedom of manoeuvre which this conferred on Irish diplomacy, however, redounded to the credit not of Cosgrave but of Eamon de Valera. Two months later, the Dail was dissolved, and de Valera succeeded Cosgrave.

De Valera in Power

The sort of successes which the Free State administration had achieved in the international field, though immensely significant, were not those which weighed with the man or woman in the street. Seán and Mary Citizen were more immediately affected by the domestic aspects of Cumann na nGaedheal's policy, which, in the run-up to a general election, included cuts in pensions for the blind and the elderly, and an announcement that the Government intended to balance the books by cutting the pay of both the Gardai and teachers. The hostility of the teachers was compounded by the declaration that married women would no longer be allowed to teach. There was nothing new in this approach by Cumann na nGaedheal.

There was far more buzz and imagination about the Fianna Fáil package. De Valera proposed to remove the oath and to retain the land annuities in the state treasury. He said that the monies involved could be used to relieve farmers of rates, and to lower taxation. He claimed that the monies payable under the ultimate financial settlement towards RIC pensions etc., bore more heavily on the Irish people than did 'the burden imposed on the German people by war reparations'. Until this burden was removed, he claimed, economic recovery was impossible. On the economic front, he made a far greater impact than did the Cumann na nGaedheal policy of laissez-faire, arguing repeatedly that 'You must actively interfere. We hold, unlike the Ministers opposite, that active interference is necessary by the Ministry, if we are going to get the country out of the rut in which it is at present.'[30] The de Valera shopping basket also contained attractive promises to help both agriculture and industry under protection. A preference was to be sought on the British market for Irish agricultural produce in return for Irish purchases of the British machinery needed to build up agriculture and industry. The threatened cuts of the Cumann na nGaedheal Government throughout the public service were mitigated by a promise not to cut the pay of those on the lower rungs of the scale. And the impression that Fianna Fáil was more concerned with Irish culture than its opponents was furthered by a promise to save the Irish language and the inhabitants of the Gaeltacht from emigration.

On paper, there was no contest between the two programmes. Fianna Fáil's election manifesto, compared to that of Cumann na nGaedheal, seemed a kind of mini New Deal. But the election was about more than manifestos. There was a tremendous political energy in the atmosphere, deriving in part from the activities of the IRA, and in part from those of de Valera and his supporters, which to many of his opponents either appeared to be, or could be represented as, the two sides of the one coin. As stated earlier, the evolution of the IRA and of Fianna Fáil to their ultimate parting of the ways will be discussed later. Here it can be said that from the period of the reorganisation of the IRA following the end of the civil war, to the victory of Fianna Fáil in 1932, the IRA and the Free State security authorities were engaged in what, in military terminology, might be classed as low intensity operations. Murder, intimidation of juries, allegations of police brutality, and constant agitation about IRA prisoners were a staple diet of the newspaper readers of the period. A former colleague of mine, whose first childhood acquaintance with the IRA occurred when the police came to his school to arrest one of the teachers in connection with the shooting of Kevin O'Higgins, described the impact of the IRA on his political thinking subsequently:

> From that moment until the late 1940s the IRA was a background to any thinking I might do on politics. It was the Mafia; it was truth; it was cruelty; it was justice – you didn't know what and this shifting assessment of their place in Irish life was one which most people shared.
>
> You couldn't escape the shadow of Republicanism and the IRA in Dublin of the late 1930s. They weighed heavily on the nation; they were powerful and whatever the reality – menacing.[31]

The IRA can be said to have helped de Valera defeat Cosgrave in three ways: through the land annuities affair, the 'Release the Prisoners' campaign, and by straightforward campaigning. The origins of the land annuities issue has already been described in the Anglo-Irish context. The IRA became involved when the IRA leader and novelist Peadar O'Donnell discovered that his neighbours in Donegal were being served with summonses because of the annuities. Arrears of annuities had built up, in some cases stretching back as far as 1916. O'Donnell and Colonel Maurice Moore, the former Volunteer training officer, organised a campaign to help people hide their cattle to prevent them being seized by bailiffs. Not only were people encouraged not to pay arrears of annuities, but Moore and O'Donnell urged them not to pay any annuities in the future. The annuities agitation spread, and became a popular plank in Fianna Fáil's manifesto. The average IRA member or supporter had a similar outlook and social background to that of Fianna Fáil supporters: small farmers, labourers, tradesmen, people who in another country would probably have been involved in the Labour Party. IRA members, and members of the women's wing of the movement, Cumann na mBan, being energetic, and highly politicised, were extremely valuable election workers. Numerically, these workers were not a negligible factor; police estimates of the time place IRA membership at around 30,000.

The 'Release the Prisoners' campaign was fuelled by the IRA's custom of refusing to recognise the courts, as the organisation did not acknowledge the state which set them up, a custom which guaranteed that at any given time there were a particularly large number of prisoners for whom release was demanded. Given Irish history, the issue of Republicans in jail is always a potentially fissionable one. In 1931, both the IRA and the Government upped the ante on each other over this time-honoured source of dissension. The law and order situation deteriorated so badly that in order to curb the IRA, the police resorted to what was known as the 'cat and mouse tactic'. Suspects were picked up for a few days, released, and then picked up again. A number of IRA men took successful actions against the state for wrongful arrest, thus weakening the efficacy of this tactic. Meanwhile, those prisoners in jail came into increasingly abrasive contact with the warders. Outside the jails, a number of murders had occurred, and an interview by the IRA leader, Frank Ryan (*Daily Express*, 24 August 1931), in which he justified these, decided the Government on drastic action.

On 20 October 1931, the IRA and its political offshoots were banned, as were a group of left-leaning organisations such as the Friends of Soviet Russia, which, in the conditions of the time, were adding a scare of the Red variety to that of the Green one being generated by the IRA. The Government threw a scare of its own into the ranks of the militants by bracketing this prohibition with the introduction of a special powers tribunal, consisting of five military officers, to bolster the courts' weakness in dealing with subversives.

While welcoming, if he did not always acknowledge, IRA help, de Valera also took a particularly important step to help himself before the 1932 general election. This was the foundation of his own newspaper, the *Irish Press*, in September 1931. In that pre-television age the paper had an enormous impact. A leading member of Fianna Fáil, Joseph Connolly, who also became a director of the paper, described it:

> The new paper gave an added impetus to the already considerable growth of Fianna Fáil all over the country. While it adhered firmly to its motto of 'The Truth in the News', it was nevertheless frankly a Party paper and as such was zealous in spreading the gospel of Fianna Fáil ... it was the necessary coping stone to all the speeches, lectures and propaganda of the movement.[32]

The other two national daily papers published in Dublin, the *Irish Independent* and the *Irish Times*, had been frankly hostile to de Valera from the time of the civil war onward, and from that time de Valera had turned his thoughts to getting a propaganda organ of his own. The question of how to control the bond money, which for some unexplained reason he left behind him in New York, had been present in his mind for years before the case came for judgement before Mr Justice Peters. Even as the arguments over ending the civil war still raged, and the guns still rang out, he kept his eye on the ball. As we have seen, the surrender terms which he offered to Cosgrave, and which were rejected (on 8 August 1923), included 'That the funds of the Republic, subscribed in the US and elsewhere, and at present sealed up by Injunction, shall be made available immediately for peaceful efforts in support of the Republican cause.' In 1927, while he was conducting inconclusive coalition talks with the Labour leader, Thomas Johnson, he stipulated that the proposed governmental programme should 'Immediately make provision for the discharging of the full national obligation towards the subscribers to the External Loan of the Republic, adding for the purpose the necessary sum to the balance now being returned by the receiver appointed by the Supreme Court of New York State, and thereby establishing National Credit.'

Establishing a national newspaper would have been nearer the truth. Earlier in 1927, Judge Peters had found, as was expected, that whatever monies were at that stage on deposit in the banks should be returned to the original bond subscribers, after all expenses had been met. This meant in effect 58% of the face value of the bonds. Anticipating this verdict, de Valera had the bond holders circulated, asking them either to endorse the cheques which the Peters judgment would shortly place in their hands, and send them to him, or to legally assign the bond certificates to him, so that he could set up a newspaper which would combat the prevailing journalistic ethos in Ireland, which he described as follows:

> The existing daily press is consistently pro-British and imperialistic in its outlook. In foreign affairs it invariably supports British policy and strives to arouse hostility against all possible rivals of Great Britain, not excepting the United States. During the European

War it was the main vehicle of lying British propaganda and was the sole agency in luring young Irishmen into a war in which 50,000 of them lost their lives.

Not surprisingly, given the reputation which de Valera had built up in the US, huge sums of money were turned over to him. In addition to obtaining funds by these means he also launched a fund-raising campaign in Ireland following the formal incorporation of a company, Irish Press Ltd, on 4 September 1928. Two hundred thousand ordinary shares were offered to the public at £1 each. Members of Fianna Fáil both bought shares themselves and enthusiastically promoted their sale to others.

The American subscribers regarded the paper as a sort of an outcropping of the national struggle, a desire to see Ireland free to which they had subscribed their bond monies. In Ireland, as Connolly's comments on the nature of the paper indicated, it was regarded as a party organ. But in fact it was de Valera's private fiefdom. The board of directors consisted of seven prominent Irish businessmen and a controlling director, Eamon de Valera. The articles of association described his role:

> The Controlling Director shall have sole and absolute control of the public and political policy of the company and of the editorial management thereof and of all newspapers, pamphlets or other writings which may be from time to time owned, published, circulated or printed by the said company . . .
>
> The Controlling Director can: appoint, and at his discretion remove or suspend all editors, sub-editors, reporters, writers, contributors of news and information and all such other persons as may be employed in or connected with the editorial department and may determine their duties and fix their salaries and/or emoluments. Subject to the powers of the Controlling Director the directors may appoint and at their discretion remove or suspend managers, editors.

To further the national-appearing character of the paper, Margaret Pearse, mother of the executed 1916 leader, was selected to press the button which started the rotary presses rolling to produce the first edition on 5 September 1931.

It would not be long before the paper was playing a vital role in a general election campaign which its founder would win the following February. The election was called not because the Government was in a strong position; in fact it was facing unpopularity when the Dail was dissolved on 29 January 1932, because the wages of Gardai and teachers had just been cut. Electorally speaking, it would have been better to have called the election at the end of the summer, but what weighed with Cosgrave was the impending approach of the 31st International Eucharistic Congress, which was held in Dublin in June 1932. The pious Cosgrave felt that the rough and tumble of a brawling Irish election would not be a seemly spectacle for the hordes of bishops, cardinals, monsignori and clergy of all sorts who descended upon Dublin in an outburst of fervour – or Roman Catholic triumphalism – only witnessed at one or two other occasions in the century (the Marian year ceremonies of 1955, or the

Pope's visit to Ireland in 1979). In the event, the Eucharistic Congress proved an important milestone in the respectabilisation of de Valera and Fianna Fáil. The pictures of Fianna Fáil luminaries associating daily with some of the most senior clergy in the world were an invaluable offset to the taunts of communism and closet IRA-ism which the party had to endure both in the run-up and during the election.

De Valera hadn't waited either for the launching of the new paper or for the election campaign to ensure that his name was kept before the public. As we have seen, two years earlier, on 5 February 1929, he had returned to Belfast, to speak at a GAA/Gaelic League function, knowing that the exclusion order served against him was still extant. As expected, he was arrested as soon as he reached the border, and duly reaped the publicity bonanza of a month in jail. The arrest provided the pretext for a huge protest meeting in Dublin at which Seán MacEntee made the ringing declaration that 'Fianna Fáil was working for the day when the Republican flag would fly over the Six County Parliament'.[33] He continued: 'Let the grass grow on the streets of Belfast. Let the mills be silent . . . The people who built up Belfast were not Irish, but English and Scottish, and they would not be Irish until the people of the South showed them they were stronger than they.'

In addition to this bitter, fiery rhetoric from his supporters, de Valera turned election meetings, particularly rural ones, into pure theatre. He would enter a country town, studiedly late, to whet the waiting crowds' appetites, on a white horse, wearing a long black cloak, preceded by a guard of honour of men carrying lighted sods on pitchforks. His meeting would very probably be punctuated by cheering, occasional fist-fights, interjections from hecklers, and an air of excitement that made his bandwagon irresistible. As the election neared, the *Irish Press* published front-page cartoons depicting his opponents as being in the grip of the Freemasons, the Unionists, and the British. Fianna Fáil threw other ingredients into the heady mix of its electoral stew. It promised to increase tillage, in an attempt to make the country self-sufficient in wheat, oats and barley. Though the Irish climate is not ideal for growing cereals, the implementation of this promise proved to be invaluable some years later when World War II broke out. The party also promised to reduce taxation, create new jobs in industry, put up the wages of agricultural workers, and provide affordable housing for working-class families. In contradistinction to the penny-pinching of Cumann na nGaedheal, Fianna Fáil promised to extend state pensions, and to create employment in the building industry by substituting Irish-produced goods for imported British ones.

Against this, Cumann na nGaedheal's plans to balance the books and uphold law and order cut but a pallid picture. In fact, the law and order issue backfired on the Government. Less than two weeks before the election, the editor of the *Irish Press*, Frank Gallagher, was hauled before a military tribunal, charged with seditious libel. He had run a series of articles detailing the treatment of IRA prisoners and suspects by detectives and warders. The case ran right up to polling day, and over 50 witnesses gave evidence which bore out the truth of Gallagher's articles. Both editor and paper were fined £100 – the day *after* polling – but the prosecution costs were refused. It was one of the most rewarding fines in electoral history anywhere. The lurid evidence rocketed the sales upwards from around 75,000 copies daily to 115,000. The effect on voters was summed up by a Fianna Fáil deputy who said, in the course of another Dail controversy involving the *Irish Press*: 'The *Irish Press* settled Cumann na nGaedheal.'

On 16 February 1932, Cumann na nGaedheal lost nine seats in the election, while Fianna Fáil's total went up to 72, its vote having increased from 35.2% to 44.5%. The final tally of seats was as follows (with pre-election strengths in brackets):

Fianna Fáil	72 (56)
Cumann na nGaedheal	57 (66)
Independents	11 (13)
Labour	7 (10)
Farmers' Party	4 (6)
Independent Labour	2 (2)

Labour had had a split and its leader, Tom Johnson, had been defeated. The new leader, William Norton, agreed to support Fianna Fáil on the basis of its social and economic programme. He also extracted a promise from de Valera that he would not victimise senior Garda officers, and de Valera held a meeting subsequently with the Garda commissioner, Eoin O'Duffy, and the head of the Special Branch, David Nelligan, to assure them that they would not have anything to fear if they served the Government in a professional manner. In the event, however, both they and a number of other senior Garda officers, including my father, either resigned or found themselves subject to what nowadays would be termed 'constructive dismissal'.

On Tuesday 9 March 1932, de Valera became President of the Executive Council. Dublin had been rife with rumour that efforts would be made to prevent him and his colleagues from entering the Dail. Many of the prospective ministers carried revolvers as did de Valera's son, Vivion. However, the rumours proved to be unfounded, though they had their basis in events which will shortly be discussed when we come to chart the rise and fall of the Blueshirt movement and de Valera's parting of the ways with the IRA. Apart from the Labour Party, de Valera received the support of three of the Independents, one of them James Dillon, a son of the old Irish Parliamentary Party leader, John Dillon, who later became one of de Valera's principal adversaries. Cosgrave did not stand for the presidency of the Executive Council when the vote was called, and de Valera won by 81 votes to 68. His Cabinet was as follows: Vice-President and Minister for Local Government and Public Health, Seán T. O'Ceallaigh; Minister for Finance, Seán MacEntee; Minister for Industry and Commerce, Seán Lemass; Minister for

Agriculture, Dr James Ryan; Minister for Lands and Fisheries, Patrick J. Ruttledge; Minister for Justice, James Geoghegan; Minister for Defence, Frank Aiken; Minister for Education, Thomas Derrig. De Valera retained the External Affairs portfolio for himself. There would shortly be important negotiations in London, and this time he would go to them in person.

We now enter on a period of radical change in Ireland. De Valera and most of the Cabinet he nominated on his first day in power would govern Ireland for 16 unbroken years, and subsequently intermittently after that. In his first tumultuous years in office, de Valera would remove the oath of allegiance and the office of the Governor General, fight a ruinous economic war with Britain, destroy his extra parliamentary rivals to left and to right (the IRA and the Blueshirts), introduce a new constitution, and make good on many of his election promises in the social, economic and industrial spheres. The obverse side of the medal of these successes was that, in so doing, he underlined the futility of the civil war and the rejection of the Treaty, because ironically his very successes emphasised the validity of Collins's stepping-stone argument. In fact, when he moved in the Dail to remove the oath, he acknowledged this himself, although in such a way as to counter his opponents' arguments against his action:

> They proposed the removal of the article of the Constitution which provided for appeals to the English Privy Council . . . The basis of their argument was that the status of the Free State was not fixed at a special period and kept there, and the fact that we had advanced was given recognition to, not very long ago, when the Statute of Westminster was passed . . .
>
> When the Treaty was being put before the old Dail, one of the arguments put forward in favour of it was that it gave freedom to achieve freedom. Are those who acted on that policy now going to say that there is to be a barrier – and a perpetual barrier – to achievement? Let the British say that if they choose. Why should any Irishman say it, particularly when it is not true?

Before introducing the Bill (on 20 April 1932), which the Statute of Westminster made possible, de Valera had been sparring with J.H. Thomas, the British Secretary of State for Dominion Affairs, whom he had directed the Irish High Commissioner in London, J.W. Dulanty, to inform that the oath was not mandatory under the Treaty. Thomas's reply next day (on 23 March 1932) had been that the oath was an integral part of the Treaty. Significantly, Thomas also raised the question of the land annuities which de Valera had not done in the directive he had given Dulanty. On the annuities, Thomas stated that

> the Irish Free State Government are bound by the most formal and explicit undertaking to pay the land annuities to the National Debt Commissioners, and the failure to do so would be a manifest violation of an agreement which is binding in law and in honour on the Irish Free State, whatever administration may be in power, in exactly the same way as the Treaty itself is binding on both countries.

185

In a manner reminiscent of the de Valera–Lloyd George correspondence which preceded the Treaty, further exchanges continued across the Irish Sea, during which de Valera shelved the question of the annuities and maintained his position on the oath in the Dail. The opposition argued that his failure to negotiate with the British on the oath issue might expose the state to British reprisals of some sort, and upheld the sanctity of existing agreements. But they were in the unenviable position of having to oppose de Valera for implementing their policies, and subsequently not merely in the oath controversy, but in other matters involving Anglo-Irish relations, this stance left them vulnerable to the charge of being pro-British while de Valera was upholding national interests. The Bill passed into law on 19 May 1932, with Labour support. However, in a move which was to rebound on its members' heads, the Senate used its powers of delay, and the Bill did not pass into law until May of the following year, during which time another election was held. This gave de Valera plenty of time and opportunity to decide on how best to dispose of the turbulent priests in the upper chamber.

However, his annuities campaign was subject to other and more serious delays. The annuities continued to be a bone of contention between the two countries from 1932 to 1938, generating economic warfare between the Free State and England, and creating a situation in which a considerable amount of violence occurred in Ireland. After de Valera had challenged Thomas on the British assertion that the Irish had undertaken to pay the land annuities, Thomas replied (on 9 April 1932), pointing out that the ultimate financial settlement of 1926, which, as we saw, arose out of the Boundary Commission decisions, was based on the agreement of 12 February 1923, between the British and Irish governments. This settlement contained a provision that 'The government of the Irish Free State undertake to pay to the British government at agreed intervals the full amount of the annuities accruing from time to time under the Irish Land Acts, 1891–1909, without any deduction whatsoever on account of income tax or otherwise.'

De Valera had not been aware of the existence of the ultimate settlement. He had begun his campaign on the basis of legal advice that the annuities payments were not legally binding. The 1926 document had allowed the Six County Government to retain similar annuities. However, Thomas's reference to a 1923 agreement initiated a search, and the Irish civil service eventually turned up the agreement in a file marked 'secret'. The agreement was apparently concluded at a time when London had the Free State over a barrel as a result of the civil war. Secret the documents certainly were. De Valera's enquiries revealed that the Cosgrave government had apparently initially refused a British request to have the document published in connection with a court case heard in 1925. Agreement was only granted on condition that the section dealing with the land annuities was pasted over. As late as 1931, the Cosgrave administration had taken steps to conceal the existence of the document from its own lawyers. Physically speaking, de Valera told the Dail, the document was 'literally in tatters, half pages, parts of pages not typed, interlineations and so on. Honestly I never saw a contract of any kind presented in such a form. There is not even an Irish signature to it.'[34] Apparently Cosgrave had signed the British copy.

De Valera argued that even had the 1923 agreement been ratified, which it had not, it only rendered Ireland liable for payments which had not been cancelled by the 1925 Boundary Commission settlement. Apart from the strength of this argument, de Valera also had a base in Irish public opinion, which recognised that the annuities issue arose because of previous confiscations of land. The emotional and symbolic aspects of the British–Irish exchanges were heightened by the fact that Irish public opinion also took note of the fact that de Valera wrote on behalf of the Government of the Irish Free State, whereas Thomas on behalf of the British wrote to 'His Majesty's Government in the Irish Free State'. De Valera won further kudos by demanding that Britain send Cabinet ministers to Dublin to state Britain's case. In a notable break with custom two ministers duly arrived (on 7 June), Thomas and Lord Hailsham, the Minister for War. Whatever worries there were in Dublin about the implicit threat contained in the sending of a minister holding that particular folio, the audacity of de Valera contrasted well with the timid behaviour of the Cosgrave administration, which always went to London for ministerial meetings. In fact, it is widely believed that Cosgrave had urged the British to take a strong line with de Valera over the annuities and oath issues, and that this was responsible for a tough statement from Thomas (on 11 May 1932), stating that if the Treaty were abrogated by the removal of the oath, the British would make no further agreements with Dublin.

De Valera finally wound up negotiating not merely with Cabinet ministers but with the British Prime Minister, Ramsay MacDonald, the Lord Chancellor and the Attorney General, on 16 July 1932. The discussions were acrimonious and unfruitful. British accounts quote de Valera as threatening them with trouble from Irish miners in the Lancashire coalfields. The meeting ended with a walk-out from de Valera. The annuities were not paid on the following day. The British retaliated, as they had said they would, with the imposition of a 20% levy on Irish imports into the UK. The Irish responded with similar levies on British exports to Ireland. To understand the enormity of this turn of events, it should be remembered that at the time, Britain accounted for approximately 96% of Irish exports. Yet despite the fact that at one stage during the controversy de Valera declared that the British market was gone for ever, incredibly enough the economic war worked in his favour. At its commencement even his most loyal and efficient minister, Seán Lemass, was horrified. He sent de Valera a memo warning him that the country was facing a crisis 'as grave as that of 1847 [the worst year of the great famine] and I feel strongly that our present efforts are totally inadequate to cope with it'.

De Valera had begun moving up the popularity stakes with the less well off by increasing public spending in the first year in which he was elected by approximately 20%, from £24 million to £29 million. In those days, £5 million bought a lot of popularity when spent on things like unemployment benefits, blind and old age pensions, housing, roadworks, healthcare, and the provision of free milk for schoolchildren. In addition, agricultural rates were cut, and subsidies cushioned the effect of the lost British exports of butter, cattle, eggs and pig meat. For smaller farmers, the reduction of the annuities and the funding of arrears for three years were welcome gestures. The bigger farmers, those hit by the increased tariffs, were largely Cumann na nGaedheal supporters. Their complaints at being left with unsaleable calves which had to be sent unprofitably to the slaughterhouse were balanced by the reaction of the poor, amongst whom the resulting free meat was distributed.

In addition to the poorer classes, Fianna Fáil, largely through the efforts of Seán Lemass, developed a burgeoning constituency amongst the entrepreneurial class. In de Valera's first year in office, 43 different categories of imports had levies imposed on them. Ultimately, this combined policy of protection and subsidies was found to be deficient for the public at large. The newly created entrepreneurs took advantage of protection and the absence of competition to give the home market a combination of shoddy services and equally shoddy goods. Doles and subsidies helped to spread a dependency culture, particularly in the west, where Fianna Fáil built up a huge following. In the poverty-stricken Irish-speaking districts, the various doles, including hand-outs for speaking Irish, were manna from heaven, but hardly calculated to encourage initiative.

Though he broke sharply with his Cumann na nGaedheal opponents on relationships with England and on economic policies, externally de Valera continued on the path set by the Cosgrave administration. The Irish were accorded by rota both the presidency of the Council of the League of Nations and the acting presidency of the assembly for the 13th session of the League at Geneva in September of the first year of de Valera's taking office. His first speech to the assembly, delivered on 26 September 1932, was independent-minded, and widely praised:

> Out beyond the walls of this Assembly there is the public opinion of the world, and if the League is to prosper, or even survive, it must retain the support and confidence of that public opinion as a whole . . . People are becoming impatient and starting even to inquire whether the apparently meagre, face-saving results of successive League conferences and meetings justify the burden which contributions to the League Budget, and the expense of sending delegation after delegation to Geneva, impose upon the already overburdened national taxpayer . . . there is a suspicion abroad that little more than lip-service is paid to the fundamental principles on which the League is founded . . .
>
> Ladies and gentlemen, the one effective way of silencing criticism of the League, or bringing to its support millions who at present stand aside in apathy or look at its activities with undisguised cynicism, is to show unmistakably that the Covenant of the League is a solemn pact, the obligations of which no state, great or small, will find it possible to ignore.

The *New York Times* thought that the speech and the manner in which de Valera presided over the debate on the potentially explosive issue of

Manchuria 'unquestionably made him the outstanding personality of this session'. In order to silence criticisms that excessive nationalism of the sort that de Valera himself preached had helped to bring the League to its low ebb, he returned to the theme of the League's future a few days later (on 2 October), saying that he spoke 'not as an enemy of the League, but as one who wishes the League to be strengthened and developed as the best visible means of securing peace among the nations and of solving the major political and economic problems which face the world today'. Thus were his anti-League utterances in America *circa* 1919–20 put behind him and the Irish tradition of maintaining an individualistic stance in international affairs maintained.

Back in Ireland, his policy of hostility towards symbols of British power continued. Along with his campaigns against the oath and the annuities, de Valera publicly declared war on the Governor General. Privately he had already assured the IRA leadership that as part of his programme for the re-publicisation of the state, he intended to downgrade the office. The assault commenced at a function in the French legation on 23 April 1932. As soon as the Governor General arrived, the two Fianna Fáil ministers present, Frank Aiken and Seán T. O'Ceallaigh, ostentatiously left. The Governor General, James MacNeill, was of course the man from whom 'His Majesty's Government in the Irish Free State had received its seal of approval', and MacNeill wrote a vehement letter of protest to de Valera, seeking an apology, which de Valera refused to give. Further acrimonious correspondence was exchanged over an invitation from MacNeill to some dignitaries to stay with him in the vice-regal lodge during the Eucharistic Congress.

MacNeill had sought clarification in advance as to how the Government would regard his issuing such invitations. However, de Valera delayed in giving him an answer until after MacNeill had committed himself to inviting his guests. Then the Department of External Affairs let it be known that the Government regarded the issuing of the invitations as an embarrassment. MacNeill wrote to de Valera on 24 May, protesting at the delay in letting him know where he stood, with the result that de Valera delivered two further snubs. Neither MacNeill nor his party were invited to a glittering state reception in Dublin Castle. He was invited to a civic reception given by the Lord Mayor at the Mansion House, but the Government refused to allow the army band to play there. Waiting until the Congress was over, MacNeill wrote again to de Valera, warning that unless he got his apology the correspondence would be published. Writing in reply, de Valera forbade him to publish the letters.

On 10 July, MacNeill disregarded the instruction by sending the correspondence to the newspapers. Warned of its arrival in the *Irish Press* offices, de Valera then took a strange decision for a newspaper publisher, one which put a question mark against the *Irish Press*'s motto, 'the truth and the news'. He sent the police around to other newspaper offices, threatening repercussions if the letters were published, and succeeded in intimidating them into silence. When the letters appeared in the British papers, de Valera then tried, and failed, to prevent their Irish editions being distributed. Following their publication in England, de Valera relaxed his ban, and the full correspondence appeared in the Irish dailies on 12 July, an appropriate, if unfortunate, date, given the significance of the correspondence for the Orangemen.

Using the direct route to the King which his predecessors in government had established, de Valera caused a submission to be made on 9 September 1932, asking that MacNeill's appointment be terminated and that the Irish Chief Justice, Hugh Kennedy, be allowed to carry out his functions until a successor was appointed. The King suggested a compromise, that MacNeill be allowed to stay on for some weeks (his term of office expired anyhow on 3 February 1933), in that he should resign, not be forced out. After seeing the King himself, MacNeill eventually did resign, but on 1 November, two weeks later than de Valera had wished him to. De Valera's plans hit a further snag when Kennedy objected to taking the necessary oaths. He told de Valera: 'If the Chief Justice, or if a group of Judges, were to be constituted, the King's agent in the Saorstat [state], I believe that the prestige of the Courts would be greatly damaged, and they would be exposed to a species of attack which would seriously shake, if not destroy, their authority.'[35]

The Dominions Office also objected to any procedure which might have allowed the Chief Justice to act without taking the oaths. The dispute rumbled on, with the British objecting to a proposal from de Valera that one way out of the problem would be to establish a commission consisting of the chairmen of the Dail and the Senate, and himself. To the British, de Valera was part of the problem, not the solution, and the suggestion that he might in some way act as Governor General was vetoed.

Eventually, after Kennedy had resisted further pressure from de Valera to take on the job, the problem was solved by a suggestion from Kennedy himself, namely that the Governor General's office should be an ordinary one in which an 'officer with a bureau' would transact business away from the trappings of the 'sham court' atmosphere of the grand vice-regal lodge.[36] A new Governor General was appointed. Donal O'Buachalla, a retired shopkeeper, was installed in a modest Dublin house, with a salary of only £2,000 a year, as compared to MacNeill's £24,000. Again taking advantage of his predecessor's success in attenuating the British links, de Valera directed that the signet seal used was that approved by the King for use in the Irish Free State.

But de Valera's utilisation of his Irish opponents' actions for his own purposes was as nothing to the manner in which he turned the annuities dispute to his own advantage. With an eye to American public opinion, Neville Chamberlain, the British Chancellor of the Exchequer, announced on 15 December 1932 that Britain would make her war debt payments to America on time, despite the fact that parliament would have to be asked to sanction a supplementary estimate, necessitated in part by the loss of the Irish annuity payments. At the time a number of other European countries were defaulting on their war debts to America and the British gesture met with a very favourable response, the *New York Times* running a particularly glowing story which said that the Irish losses had helped to run up a debt of some £21 million for Britain. De Valera, however, riposted by announcing that Ireland intended to repay in full the bond loan which he had raised in America, even though its terms had stipulated that it would not be repayable until Ireland became an independent republic. Any bondholder who had applied for a refund as a result of the Peters case was to get $1.25 per bond held. Anyone who had got their 58 cents was now to get a further 67. The total amount involved was some £1.5 million.

However, when the Loans and Finance Bill which gave effect to this provision was debated (on 5–6 July) in the Dail, uproar broke out when Desmond Fitzgerald revealed that the *Irish Press* was almost bankrupt, owing a total of £100,000, according to figures released at the paper's annual general meeting a few days earlier. But because of the number of bonds which had been turned over to him as a result of his manoeuvre in setting up the newspaper, de Valera would now receive £100,000 if the Bill went through. Fitzgerald accused him of placing a huge charge on the taxpayer so that he might get a percentage for himself. Cosgrave pointed out that there was no necessity for the taxpayer to pay anything. The Peters decision had denied the state's title to the bonds and therefore neither their benefits nor their liabilities accrued to Ireland. Batt O'Connor, who had helped Michael Collins to hide the monies raised by the loan in Ireland, at the risk of his own life (he buried gold ingots under his kitchen floor), pointed out that he had subscribed more to the loans than either de Valera or any of his colleagues in government with no thought of gain, and added:

> The indecent haste about it is that you want to get control of the money to help you out of your difficulties with your daily paper . . . Think of the conditions of the farms . . . the cutting of the salaries of teachers and the civil servants . . . now you pass a Bill to pay £1.5 million . . . put country before party politics and a party newspaper.

There was much more in this vein from the opposition and equally bitter bluster and recrimination from the Government side. All in all it was an unedifying and embarrassing affair, but in the end numbers told. The Bill went through, the debate went largely unnoticed in America, where Roosevelt was amongst those who congratulated plucky little Ireland for paying its debts, even when it did not have to, and the *Irish Press* was saved for God, de Valera and Fianna Fáil, although not necessarily in that order.

The *Irish Press* secured, the governor generalship devalued, de Valera now moved on to deal equally effectively with the Blueshirt and IRA controversies.

The Blueshirt upheaval could be said to have its origins in the civil war, and partially in both the hostility of Fianna Fáil/IRA activists to the Cumann na nGaedheal administration, and in an optical rather than a substantive relationship to the growth of shirted movements in the European continent.

191

Insofar as the public awareness of Fianna Fáil's relationship with the IRA and the party's commitment to constitutionalism were concerned, a succession of statements by Fianna Fáil leaders, including de Valera himself, gave every indication that the two organisations were opposite sides of the same medal, and that constitutionalism was a lightly worn garment. For example, speaking in the Dail (12 March 1928), Seán Lemass said:

> Fianna Fáil is a *slightly* constitutional party. We are open to the definition of a constitutional party, but before anything we are a Republican party. We have adopted the method of political agitation to achieve our end because we believe, in the present circumstances, that method is best in the interests of the nation and of the Republican movement, and for no other reason. Five years ago the methods we adopted were not the methods we have adopted now. Five years ago we were on the defensive, and perhaps in time we may recoup our strength sufficiently to go on the offensive. Our object is to establish a Republican government in Ireland. If that can be done by the present methods we have, we will be very pleased, but if not, we would not confine ourselves to them.[37]

The attitude of Fianna Fáil towards the Dail and towards Cumann na nGaedheal was one of studied hostility. the *Nation*, the Fianna Fáil journal which preceded the setting up of the *Irish Press*, stated the attitude of the party to the Dail on 23 February 1929:

> We entered a faked parliament which we believed in our hearts to be illegitimate and we still believe it; and we faced a junta there which we did not regard as the rightful Government of this country. We did not respect, nor do we now, such a Government or such a Parliament . . . Our presence in the 'Dail' of usurpers is sheer expedience, nothing else.

By way of underlining these sentiments, Seán T. O'Ceallaigh made a reference in the Dail a few days later to the Cumann na nGaedheal Minister for Defence as the 'so called Minister for Defence', and two weeks after that, de Valera himself made what many in Fianna Fáil and the IRA regarded as the definitive pronouncement on the legitimacy of the state:

> I still hold that our right to be regarded as the legitimate Government of this country is faulty, that this House itself is faulty. You have secured a *de facto* position. Very well. There must be some body in charge to keep order in the community, and by virtue of your *de facto* position, you are the only people who are in a position to do it. But as to whether you have come by that position legitimately or not, I say you have not come by that position legitimately. You brought off a *coup d'etat* in the summer of 1922 . . .
>
> If you are not getting the support from all sections of the community that is necessary for any executive if it is going to dispense with a large police force, it is because there is a moral handicap in your case. We are all morally handicapped because of the circumstances in which the whole thing came about. The setting up of this State put a moral handicap on everyone of us here. We came in here because we thought that a practical rule could be evolved in which order could be maintained; and we said that it was necessary to have some assembly in which the representatives of the people by a majority vote should be able

to decide national policy. As we were not able to get a majority to meet outside this House, we had to come here if there was to be a majority at all of the people's representatives in any one assembly . . .

As a practical rule, and not because there is anything sacred in it, I am prepared to accept majority rule as settling matters of national policy, and therefore as deciding who it is that shall be in charge of order . . .

I, for one, when the flag of the Republic was run up against an Executive that was bringing off a *coup d'etat* or afterwards, as long as there was an opportunity of getting the people of this country to vote again for the Republic, I stood for it.

My proposition that the representatives of the people should come in here and unify control so that we would have one Government and one Army was defeated, and for that reason I resigned. Those who continued on in that organisation which we have left can claim exactly the same continuity that we claimed up to 1925. They can do it . . .

You have achieved a certain *de facto* position, and the proper thing for you to do with those who do not agree that this State was established legitimately, and who believe that as a matter of fact there was a definite betrayal of everything that was aimed at from 1916 to 1922, is to give those people the opportunity of working, and without in any way forswearing their views, to get the Irish people as a whole again behind them. They have the right to do it. You have no right to debar them from going to the Irish people and asking them to support the re-establishment, or if they so wish to put it, to support the continuance of the Republic.

The Executive have been trying to use force, and have been using it all the time. If they are going to meet force by force, then they cannot expect the co-operation of citizens who wish that there should not be force.[38]

De Valera's statement that those who continued in the IRA could claim the same continuity that Fianna Fáil had been claiming up to 1925 gave IRA recruits a sense that the IRA was a legitimate organisation with its roots in Irish history,[39] but did little to assure Cumann na nGaedheal supporters that Fianna Fáil was a responsible body. When Cosgrave introduced the military tribunal, de Valera's response (on 14 October 1931) was: 'These men are misguided, if you will, but they were brave men anyhow. Let us have the decent respect for them that we have for the brave.'

Against a backdrop of these sort of speeches, and Fianna Fáil and IRA violence at election meetings, a group of ex-army officers convened a meeting at Wynn's Hotel in Dublin six days before the general election of February 1932. Opinions differ on whether this meeting was held for the purpose of trying to prevent de Valera taking power, or because of worries that the incoming administration would cut or remove the pensions of its civil war opponents. The attendance included such prominent Cumann na nGaedheal figures as General Mulcahy, and Dr T. F. O'Higgins, a brother of Kevin O'Higgins. A further meeting was held on St Patrick's Day at which a group known as the Army Comrades Association was formed to act as a benevolent association for ex-servicemen by lobbying for work for them in county councils and so on. Fianna Fáil, however, were mindful of the rumours which had circulated prior to de Valera's taking office concerning likely resistance to that happening. Conversations had taken place amongst some police and army officers, with General Eóin O'Duffy in particular to the fore, suggesting that Fianna Fáil be kept out. These suggestions did not find favour in either the police or the army. The officer corps in both organisations had fought a civil war to maintain democracy against de Valera and his supporters and, distasteful and worrisome though they found the prospect of his taking power, they were not going to jeopardise democracy now by espousing his principle that the people had no right to do wrong. Moreover, the normal processes of ordinary living were taking effect; most of these men had departed the world of revolution not merely for nation building, but for marriages, mortgages, school attendance, taxes and bill paying. The Army Chief of Staff transferred a number of disaffected officers who might have agreed with O'Duffy, and Cosgrave issued a strong denial that there was any question of interference with the will of the people expressed through the ballot box, although privately, I understand, he decided that if he won the election, O'Duffy would be shifted from his post as Commissioner of the Gardai.

However, rumour and suspicion, bred of civil war animosities, continued to spread. Practically de Valera's first act on taking office was to direct the release of the IRA prisoners from Arbour Hill Military Prison. The Ministers for Justice and Defence, James Geoghegan and Frank Aiken, went to the jail within hours of being appointed and spoke to each prisoner in his cell. The prisoners were released on 10 March 1932; the banned IRA newspaper *An Phoblacht* was republished 48 hours afterwards, and Saor Eire, a proscribed political grouping, was deemed to be no longer unlawful. More importantly, the military tribunal was suspended.

THE BLUESHIRTS

On 13 March the IRA held a big demonstration in Dublin's College Green to welcome home the prisoners. Men paraded in military formation and Cumann na mBan appeared in uniform and Sam Browne belts. The feelings of the IRA towards Cumann na nGaedheal were summed up for me once by a friend of mine, Con Lehane, a prominent Republican, who later became a well-known Dublin solicitor. Mellowed by the time we came to know each other, he still recalled: 'I felt a tremendous release. It was a marvellous thing, we really hated those buggers. It was great to see them out.' One of the released prisoners, Seán McGuinness, publicly articulated these feelings at the demonstration in harsher terms. He said of the outgoing administration that they were: 'a menace to Society and the independence of Ireland, and it behoved all Republicans to unite and wipe out that menace at all costs'. The Army Comrades Association (ACA) was founded a few days later. As we shall see, de Valera, far from colluding with the IRA, was secretly trying to get the organisation to abandon force. But Cumann na nGaedheal adherents did not know this. Their attention focused on statements like that of Seán MacBride who told the meeting which McGuinness addressed that the IRA would not disband, and intended to continue towards its objectives. Proof that it had not disbanded came the following June when the Wolfe Tone commemoration ceremonies at Bodenstown in County Kildare were attended by some 15,000 IRA marchers.

Throughout the year, statements in *An Phoblacht* and by IRA spokespersons conveyed a direct threat to Cumann na nGaedheal speakers' right to be heard. In successive issues (15 and 22 October), *An Phoblacht* decreed that 'Free speech and the freedom of the press must be denied to traitors and treason mongers.' On 10 November a public meeting in Dublin was told by two of the leading members of the IRA, Frank Ryan and Peadar O'Donnell, that this was indeed IRA policy. Ryan said: 'No matter what anyone says to the contrary, while we have fists, hands and boots to use, and guns if necessary, we will not allow free speech to traitors.' O'Donnell added: 'The policeman who puts his head between Mr Cosgrave's head, and the hands of angry Irishmen, might as well keep his head at home.'

As if to encourage the Gardai to follow this sort of advice, another act of leniency by de Valera towards the IRA also had its effect on Cumann na nGaedheal fears. The Gardai were urged to go easy on the IRA, the Cumann na nGaedheal policy of coercion was abandoned, and within the force it became difficult to obtain sanction to bring charges. In addition to this, some members of the IRA began jostling Gardai in the street, or in strongly Republican areas like Kerry and Galway started giving orders to Garda sergeants in isolated villages. So far as the more unsophisticated Republicans were concerned, their side had won the 1932 election, and now they could tell the police what to do. Initially, de Valera's own actions fuelled the Gardai's fears. Conor Foley has described[40] an incident shortly after de Valera's election, while he was playing to the gallery of 'extremist support'. On a victory tour in Skibbereen in County Cork, the Gardai had assembled to greet him on one side of the road, while the IRA had drawn up its guard of honour on the other. De Valera paused in front of the IRA group, took their salute, and entered the town, completely ignoring the small group of police.

It also became difficult for the police to obtain convictions against IRA men in the courts. On 14 July 1932, in the Dublin Circuit Criminal Court, a jury found Gerald Dempsey, an IRA officer, not guilty of the illegal possession of guns and ammunition. He refused to recognise the court, and said the weapons had been stolen from him. On hearing the jury's findings, the judge commented: 'How you regard that verdict I don't know. Possibly you have the same contempt for it I have.' He then sentenced Dempsey to three months for his refusal to recognise the court. *An Phoblacht* called for his release, and three days later James Geoghegan, the Minister for Justice, made an order setting Dempsey free.

Some Gardai took matters into their own hands, and the month after the Dempsey case, two prominent IRA men, George Gilmore and T.J. Ryan, were badly beaten up by detectives in County Clare. The men involved were suspended following an inquiry which also provided a pretext for the removal of David Nelligan as head of the Special Branch. He had taken up a collection for his suspended subordinates, and as a result was transferred to a non-job in the Land Commission with a notation on his file 'not to be considered for promotion'.

The IRA and the ACA started coming into conflict when the 'no free speech for traitors' policy was put into operation, and the ACA began providing bodyguards to Cumann na nGaedheal speakers. An additional, and very Irish, source of conflict arose towards the end of 1932, when a senior executive of the English brewing company Bass made some anti-Irish comments. The IRA riposted by destroying a lorryload of Bass, raiding pubs and smashing windows, and the Dublin vintners applied to the ACA for protection. Subsequent movements of Bass took place with ACA bodyguards.

In the midst of this uproar, de Valera took a step which significantly added to his freedom of manoeuvre. The land annuities had provided the catalyst for the formation of a new political party on 6 October 1932. It was called the Centre Party, and it was led by James Dillon and Frank McDermott, an ex-British army officer and a New York banker. The party was largely supported by the bigger farmers on whom the annuities dispute fell heaviest. McDermott, who became the leader of the new party, argued that partition could only be solved when normalcy returned to Dublin–London relationships. He made a point which found wide acceptance that whatever one might say about leaving or staying in the Commonwealth, there was nothing to be said in favour of remaining in it while suffering the drawbacks of being outside. At the time there was a general feeling that the times called for the creation of a more powerful new party from all the existing opposition parties on a basis of friendship with England and independence within the Commonwealth.

The Lord Mayor of Dublin convened a meeting in the Mansion House on 28 December 1932 at which leading professional men passed a resolution endorsing the idea. Watching the political pressure cooker heating up, and becoming increasingly irked by his reliance on the Labour Party, de Valera was moved to take action when J.H. Thomas, the Dominions Secretary, made a speech on the annuities issue in which he questioned de Valera's right to act for the whole Dail, when he only represented 72 members out of 153.[41]

De Valera riposted by announcing a general election at a dramatic midnight press conference four days after the Mansion House meeting. During the election campaign, he successfully invoked the party's caring attitude to the poor, and its economic initiatives, all of which, he said, had its justification in 'the encyclicals of either Leo XIII or the present Pontiff'. The election, on 24 January 1933, resulted in a gain of five seats for Fianna Fáil. The election campaign was of course fiercely fought, possibly the most violent of the century. The ACA, which by now was claiming a membership of some 30,000, was often the only force which allowed a hearing for de Valera's opponents. Responsible Garda officers and politicians of the period whom I interviewed many years later told me that either through deliberate policy or shortage of resources, there simply were not enough Gardai at meetings to secure a hearing for Cumann na nGaedheal or Centre Party spokespersons in the face of IRA/Fianna Fáil supporters' opposition. A senior Garda officer, Superintendent Moore, who had been a sergeant at the time, once told me a story about a famous meeting of Cosgrave's in Cork which was broken up by Fianna Fáil and Republican extremists:

> I had been sent there, and I only had a couple of men with me. The meeting was hot. We were completely outnumbered. We'd have been lynched if we tried getting a hearing for Cosgrave. Ned Cronin came up to me and said, 'Are you going to do anything to stop this?' I pointed to my two guards and said, 'What can I do?' and Ned said, 'Well, I'll do something.' With that, he went back into the middle of a crowd where one fellow was shouting his head off, and he picked him up and came out of the meeting with the man held over his head.

Cronin was to be one of the principal figures in a new movement, the National Guard, which was set up later in 1933 under the leadership of General O'Duffy, who was sacked by de Valera a few days after he won the general election of February 1933. Eamon Broy, Michael Collins's old informant in the Castle, who had been appointed to succeed David Nelligan, another of Collins's principal informants, as head of the Special Branch, took over as Garda Commissioner as well. De Valera also ordered the arrest of the deputy head of the Special Branch, Inspector E.M. O'Connell, and an army colonel, Michael Hogan, a brother of the former Minister for Agriculture. They were charged under the Official Secrets Act. The country was ablaze with rumours that they and O'Duffy were planning a coup, that de Valera intended to set up a dictatorship or at best was intent on purging the Gardai of all who had been zealous against Republicans in the previous decades. The arrests turned out to be but smoke in a bottle when the charges were read out in court. Apparently, some information about subversive organisations gathered by the Special Branch had been passed to James Hogan, a brother of Michael Hogan. James Hogan, a professor of history at Cork University, and a theoretician of the right, had used the information in anti-de Valera articles and in a famous pamphlet, 'Could Ireland go Communist?' He argued that it could, that de Valera was the Irish Kerensky who, by weakening Cumann na nGaedheal, would bring about a takeover by the IRA and the Communists.

Both men were acquitted, and O'Duffy, against whom no charges were brought, and who refused to continue on in government service in another unspecified post but on his existing salary, became something of a martyr in the eyes of wide sections of the public. *An Phoblacht* had been demanding that he be sacked for months and there were suspicions that he had been sacrificed as a result of Fianna Fáil's fellow-travelling with the IRA. This fact, and his organisational abilities, led to his being offered the leadership of the ACA on 20 July 1933. Since the previous April, at the suggestion of Ned Cronin, a former Commandant in the Free State army, who became Secretary of the

ACA, the organisation had adopted a blue shirt as its uniform. The stated reason for this was to avoid unfortunate errors in the usage of knuckle-dusters as an aid to the enforcement of the democratic right of free speech at public gatherings. However, when O'Duffy took over, the ACA, along with changing its name to the National Guard, adopted not only the blue shirt, but the one-armed 'Hitler salute'. The new organisation promised that 'illegalities will not be tolerated, physical drill will be practised only as a means of promoting good health, character and discipline'. However, the National Guard struck a militant note from the start. The *United Irishman* newspaper of 12 July 1933 said: 'If a comrade is subjected because of his membership of the Association to gross abuse, his reply should be a swift blow or series of blows.'

Writing in the same journal, a correspondent, 'Oghnach', suggested that Blueshirt audiences when greeting their leaders should imitate the Nazis, and 'give three sudden staccato bursts of mass cheering, each burst consisting of one sharply ejected syllable ... the word may be Hale (Hail), pronounced sharply, or it may be Hoch (Up)'. One of the secretaries of the ACA, Professor M. Tierney, wrote: 'The corporate state must come in the end to Ireland as elsewhere', and his fellow secretary, Professor James Hogan, also wrote a widely read series of articles which were later reprinted in the best-selling pamphlet 'Could Ireland go Communist?', mentioned above. Apart from civil war animosities, which brought the IRA and the Blueshirt movement into conflict at public meetings, there were two other reasons for strife, one overt, the other covert.

The overt issue was a by-product of the economic war. The bigger farmers, incensed at finding their cattle practically unsaleable, began to refuse payment of their land annuities. To counteract this, the Government brought in the Land Act of 1933 under which a warrant issued by the Land Commission was substituted for legal proceedings. Over 400,000 of these warrants were lodged in the 12 half-year periods beginning in November/December 1933 and ending in May/June 1939. Some £2.5 million was collected through them. Sometimes cattle were seized from the farmers to pay for the arrears and then sold at sales which were protected by armed police. The purchasers were generally jobbers, some acting on behalf of the Government, some of whom gave fictitious names and bought the cattle for practically nothing because butchers and ordinary farmers refused to buy cattle sold under these conditions. These sales, as we will see, were the cause of at least one particularly tragic and controversial incident.

The covert source of conflict was described by a man who should have known, Maurice Twomey, who was at the time Chief of Staff of the IRA. Writing to Joe McGarrity in America, Twomey described the real influence at work in creating some of the disturbance:

The fact is that the opposition is spontaneous and that these attacks are largely made by members of the Fianna Fáil organisation and active supporters of Fianna Fáil. As a matter of fact we have ordered Volunteers not to take part as units in these attacks, while saying that if there is opposition they should, of course, join in with others who resent the preaching of treason and surrender. But the point is that Fianna Fáil leaders are using the commotion their own followers are largely responsible for creating to attack us.[42]

Publicly, de Valera did not concede that he or his government were fomenting or tolerating disturbances for their own ends. His comment on the attacks on Blueshirt meetings was: 'It is up to the Government to see that opportunities for free speech are given. But the Government cannot possibly make people or causes popular.'[43] His public reaction to the formation of the National Guard was to immediately take a strong law and order line by revoking all firearm certificates. These had been issued fairly liberally after the murder of Kevin O'Higgins. Amongst the public figures who carried legally held firearms were O'Duffy and the former Cumann na nGaedheal ministers. But following de Valera's order of revocation, the homes of former ministers were visited by police who collected the revolvers over the weekend of 30 July. No move was made to seize the IRA's illegally held arms. But two days later de Valera told the Dail that O'Duffy was aiming at a dictatorship, and that the Government would not tolerate private armies. Challenged by James Dillon, in the light of that statement, to define his attitude towards the IRA, de Valera replied that there was now no need for the IRA because the oath had been removed, and it was merely a matter of time before this was generally realised. However, 'the National Guard was not a body which had any roots in the past, not a body which can be said to have a national objective such as the IRA can be said to have'.

To his own supporters at least, de Valera appeared to be justified in this attitude by an announcement of O'Duffy's. He declared that he intended to hold a march to government buildings on Sunday 13 August to lay a wreath at the Cenotaph on a lawn there. He said that his intention was to revive a custom, practised by Cumann na nGaedheal, and discontinued by Fianna Fáil, of laying wreaths in memory of Collins, Griffith and O'Higgins. De Valera used the analogy of Mussolini's marching practices, and banned both the parade and the National Guard. In addition, he revived the military tribunal and, overnight, recruited an armed cadre of police known as the 'S' branch. This consisted mainly of Fianna Fáil supporters who had fought against the O'Duffy-ites in the civil war. I interviewed some of the survivors of this corps, and they assured me that the first they heard of it was when they were knocked up by police in the small hours of the morning and asked if they would like to join. They admitted frankly that so far as they knew, their principal qualification for getting the invitation was that they could shoot straight. The new unit became known as the Broy Harriers after the Commissioner of Police, Eamon Broy, who, as we have seen, had once been one of Michael Collins's principal informants in the Royal Irish Constabulary. It was an apprenticeship which Broy put to good use under de Valera.

The country held its breath to see whether the Harriers would have reason to course their prey if O'Duffy decided to defy the ban. Anxiety levels would probably have been higher had it been generally known that the army council of the IRA planned to ambush the marchers as they passed along Dublin's Westmoreland Street. However, at the last moment, O'Duffy decided to cancel the march, and bloodshed was averted. But his intervention on the political scene gave a new impetus to political forces which had been gathering for some time. Cumann na nGaedheal decided to join with the Centre Party and with the National Guard in the formation of a new party, the United Ireland Party, popularly known by its Irish name, Fine Gael. The leader of the new party was General O'Duffy, and the National Guard was renamed the Young Ireland Association in order to get around the governmental ban. Cosgrave continued as the parliamentary party leader of the new grouping, as O'Duffy did not hold a Dail seat.

The Dail was not the arena for the struggle between the right-wing forces of the new grouping, who were supported by the bigger farmers, by ex-Unionists and by some business and professional people, and what might broadly be termed the left, Fianna Fáil, Labour and the IRA. Uproar broke out all over rural Ireland. Not only did the sales of seized cattle become the focus of riots; so did the roads leading to them, as they were trenched and trees and telegraph poles felled. Public meetings resembled nothing so much as a revival of the traditions of Donnybrook Fair and faction fighting. Mention has been made of the bitterness of the civil war in Kerry. Memories of that period came alive again in October when a Fine Gael convention was held in Tralee. A full-scale riot broke out in which O'Duffy was struck on the head with a hammer as he and Cronin were attacked in the street. O'Duffy's car was burned out, and during the convention a Mills bomb was thrown at a skylight only to bounce harmlessly off some wire netting.

Anti-Blueshirt feeling was so strong in Kerry that after 12 IRA men were sentenced to jail terms of from four to six months each for their part in the attacks, de Valera had to travel to Tralee to ward off a split in the Fianna Fáil organisation, and demands for the release of the prisoners. At the Fianna Fáil Ard Fheis (on 8 November), he adroitly turned criticism directed at him for not being Republican enough against his accusers by saying:

> . . . we cannot have it both ways, and I am afraid there are in our organisation a number of people who would like to have it both ways. They want to be free to criticise us themselves, but they want to deny that right to other sections of the people. Now, you cannot have that.

However, he continued to hold his hand, in public at least, in confronting the IRA as an organisation, and concentrated his main attention on the Blueshirts. The Young Ireland Association was banned, and police raided the homes of United Ireland supporters and the party headquarters. The raids yielded some political ammunition for Fianna Fáil. A letter from an O'Duffy supporter addressed to a British Conservative MP, which was read out in the

Dail on 30 November 1933, showed that there were tensions developing between Cosgrave's party and the newer members of the Blueshirt alliance. But the most damaging ammunition used against the Blueshirts was supplied by O'Duffy himself.

At the time, in the wake of the Eucharistic Congress, religious fervour reached a peak of intolerance. Bishops condoned the setting up of vigilance committees to ensure that Ireland did not turn Communist. Cardinal Logue, the leading member of the hierarchy, said that: 'Like a plague, bolshevism seems to be spreading. It is time that all of us should feel called upon to prepare ourselves for this trouble that seems to be coming.'[44]

The coming trouble was prepared for by causing it, as rightists fell on known IRA men and left-wingers. Against this backdrop, O'Duffy went on what the literary editor of the *Irish Press*, M.J. McManus, described as 'A raging tearing campaign throughout the country, enlisting recruits, using fascist symbols and the fascist salute, announcing to the people that the object of his Movement was to save the country from Communism.' The Blueshirt flag, he declared, would soon be flying beside the tricolour on government buildings.

All this certainly gave the impression that continental fascism had made an appearance in Ireland. And Fianna Fáil and the left were at pains to draw that analogy. The *Irish Press* was probably the most formidable foe which the Blueshirts encountered. The paper sent reporters around the country in O'Duffy's wake to report what he actually said at public meetings, as opposed to the decorous press releases which emanated from party headquarters. But while the General and his movement certainly looked and sounded fascist, all this leaves out the Irish dimension that after a convivial welcome what Eóin O'Duffy might say in Knocknagoshel might bear relationship to the speeches prepared for him by the temperate theoreticians at party headquarters. And above all, there had been a civil war, and there was an economic war which was maddening large sections of the farming community.

De Valera continued to turn the screw on the Blueshirts. After lawyers for the United Ireland Party reacted to the banning of the Young Ireland Association by changing its name to the League of Youth, and then won a High Court action on the grounds of free speech, declaring the new organisation lawful, de Valera had O'Duffy and some of his colleagues arrested at Westport on 17 December. The arrests and detention were declared illegal by the High Court on the 21st, but O'Duffy was immediately served with a summons calling upon him to appear before the military tribunal on charges not merely of belonging to two unlawful associations, the National Guard and the Young Ireland Association, but of incitement to murder de Valera. However, the Government failed to make the charges stick. The High Court further undermined the tribunal by declaring that it was a court of limited jurisdiction and that it was not exempt from prohibition.

Buoyed up by these successes, one of Fine Gael's leading lawyers, John A. Costello, exultantly declared in the Dail on 2 February 1934 that the

Blueshirts would be 'Victorious in Ireland ... [as] the Blackshirts were victorious in Italy ... the Hitler shirts ... victorious in Germany.' Like many in Fine Gael who were not fascists, but who allowed themselves to be carried away in the enthusiasm of the moment, Costello, who would one day become prime minister, was unwittingly giving priceless ammunition to his opponents to be used against his party. Even at the time of writing, there are many in Fianna Fáil who gleefully refer to Fine Gael as the 'Blueshirts'.

Later in the month, the Blueshirt–IRA hostility turned particularly nasty. On the 11th, the home of a Blueshirt supporter in Dundalk was bombed after he had given evidence before the military tribunal, identifying men who had robbed him of United Ireland Party funds. The man's mother was killed in the explosion and two of his children were badly injured. A judicial inquiry was sought into this explosion by W.T. Cosgrave, who tabled a motion to this effect in the Dail, but it was voted down by Fianna Fáil. Cosgrave made a statement in the Dail that detectives had kept watch on a house in Dublin, No. 44 Parnell Square, in which he alleged a meeting was held to give instruction in the handling of a landmine, which was to be exploded the following day, the day of the Dundalk bombing. De Valera continued his war of attrition against the Blueshirts. On 23 February, he introduced the Wearing of Uniform (Restriction) Bill. The Bill prevented the use of badges, uniforms or military titles in support of a political party, and the carrying of weapons, including sticks, was also declared illegal. In an attempt to get around the High Court strictures on the military tribunal, it contained a provision that offences under the proposed law could only be tried by district courts. There was to be no appeal to the High Court. The Bill went through under the guillotine on 14 March, many of the Fine Gael deputies attending the chamber in their blue shirts.

However, having got through the Dail, the Bill was then rejected by the Senate. So far as de Valera was concerned, the rejection brought down the avalanche on the Senate, and the following day (22 March) he introduced a Bill in the Dail to abolish it. Ironically, while this Bill would pass into law, that which precipitated it, the Uniforms Bill, was not required. O'Duffy's lack of political judgement on the one hand, and a particularly ugly outbreak of violence at a cattle sale in Cork on the other, helped to bring about an end to Blueshirt-ism. Local government elections were scheduled for the summer of 1934, and O'Duffy made the rash prediction that Fianna Fáil would lose 20 out of the 23 councils. In fact, the result was completely the opposite. Fianna Fáil won 20 of the councils, Fine Gael only three. Underneath all the *Sturm und Drang*, de Valera's social policy was attracting the vote. As with the IRA, people were prepared to give money to the Blueshirts, or to lend that most valuable of assistance to such movements, the 'friendly blind eye', but the vote was a matter for the head, not the heart.

The other blow struck against the Blueshirts came in response to an all too effective display of marksmanship by the Broy Harriers, at Marsh's Sale Yard in Cork City on 13 August. A police cordon, keeping a hostile crowd away from a sale of distrained cattle, was broken by a lorry containing 15 men armed with sticks. The cordon hastily re-formed, thus trapping the lorry and three or four spectators, who had followed it, inside the yard. However, the Broy Harriers opened fire on both the men and the lorry, and on the handful of spectators. Seven people were wounded and a 15-year-old boy was killed.

The boy's father subsequently took an action against three of the S-Branch members and the superintendent who was nominally in charge of the men. The judge, Justice Hanna, dismissed the charges against the superintendent, but awarded damages to the father and declared that the evidence in the case constituted a *prima facie* case of manslaughter. He added: 'These S-Men are not real Civic Guards. They are an excrescence upon that reputable body.' And he found that there was 'no justification for sending fusillade after fusillade of revolver shots into the men huddled in the lorry and at the three or four men running to escape'. The S-men's principal qualification, he concluded, was their ability to handle guns. De Valera disagreed. Two of the S-Branch members involved in the shooting were promoted to the rank of sergeant. No charges of manslaughter were brought, but an unsuccessful appeal against Hanna's judgment was mounted in the Supreme Court.

While many people, even outside the ranks of the Blueshirts, would not have agreed with de Valera's stance over the Marsh's Yard episode, a general feeling was growing in the country, particularly amongst the more conservatively inclined in Fine Gael, that things were getting out of hand. But instead of attempting to cool things down, five days after the shooting, O'Duffy turned the temperature up. At the League of Youth Congress which he presided over, on 18–19 August, a resolution was passed calling on farmers to withhold not only annuities, but rates as well. This brought the feelings of the conservatives within Fine Gael to a head. At a meeting of the party's national executive held shortly afterwards (on 31 August), James Hogan resigned and issued a statement saying that he had done so as 'the strongest protest I can make against the general destructive and hysterical leadership of the President, General O'Duffy . . . in politics I have found him to be utterly impossible. It is about time that the United Ireland party gave up its hopeless attempt of saving General O'Duffy from his own errors.'

Shortly after the Hogan resignation, on 21 September, O'Duffy was pressurised into resigning as chairman. He was also deemed to have resigned as director general of the League of Youth. O'Duffy, however, objected to this, and refused to accept the appointment of Cronin in his stead. The Blueshirt movement then split between the Cronin-ites and the O'Duffy wing. O'Duffy's section became known as the National Corporate Party, but the net effect of the internal disagreements was to severely damage both the strength and the reputation of the opposition. Cosgrave was re-elected leader of a much-weakened Fine Gael Party, and O'Duffy meandered off into a political tributary by organising a contingent to fight for Franco in the Spanish Civil War. Whether or not the Blueshirt eruption could be thought of as a truly fascist movement is a moot point. On the one hand, it looked like one, and at times acted like one, but the temper of the strongly individualistic Irish people and the cleavages of the civil war strongly militated against the growth of a united agrarian movement arising out of the annuities controversy. Moreover, there just weren't enough capitalists around to support a capitalist movement. The only native Irish institution which might have fuelled fascist leanings was the Catholic Church, whose authoritarianism could in some ways be compared to the underlying basis of fascism. To those who would argue that the Shirt-ist trappings, and the fact that the bigger farmers were in the Blueshirts, betokened the arrival of Hitlerism or Mussolini-ism in Ireland, it could just as easily have been counter-argued that if it were not for de Valera and his policies, and the presence of the IRA, Blueshirt-ism would never have been heard of.

The IRA

The IRA, however, most certainly would have, and it is time now to examine something of the history of that organisation in the 1920s and 1930s and its relationship with de Valera and Fianna Fáil. Both de Valera's domestic opponents and the British shared a common opinion that de Valera was hand in glove with the IRA. The British Prime Minister, Ramsay MacDonald, in a letter to the Archbishop of York, said of de Valera: 'He will do nothing except what is a step to an Irish Republic, and is undoubtedly a complete prisoner to the Irish Republican Army.'[45] However, the seemingly close and continuing relationship of Fianna Fáil and the IRA was more apparent than real. From the time of his sojourn in Bolands Mill during 1916, and its resultant toll on him, de Valera never showed any great personal appetite for the gun. Indeed, despite the many and varied objections which he put up against the Treaty, which placed him on the same side as the IRA, one could validly argue that it was not his republicanism, but his sense of outraged lèse-majesté at the Treaty having been signed without his authority that determined him in seeking 'extremist support'.

Once the civil war died away, no political practitioner of de Valera's acumen could have been under any illusion that physical force stood a chance of attracting widespread support – on either side of the border. North of the border the IRA's position is simply told. The forces deployed against the militant Republicans have already been described. These smashed the northern IRA far more comprehensively than the Republican forces were defeated in the southern civil war. It would remain in a weakened state in the Six Counties until a combination of circumstances and the old Tory–Unionist alliance breathed new life into the organisation in 1970. In a sense, the IRA of the 1920s could be said to have acknowledged the reality of its position in the north without adverting to it. After the civil war ended, a draft constitution was drawn up at a two-day meeting of the IRA in the Elliott Hotel in Harcourt Street, Dublin. The bulk of the constitution was taken up with organisational matters: how the army should be controlled, what were the powers of its executive, how its chief of staff should be appointed and so on. Its core objectives were stated to be:

A. To guard the honour, and maintain the independence of the Irish Republic.
B. To protect the rights and liberties common to the people of Ireland.
C. To place its service at the disposal of an established Republican Government which faithfully upholds the above objects.

The constitution also stipulated that the following oath of allegiance be taken by every member of the army:

I . . . do solemnly swear that to the best of my knowledge and ability I will support and defend the Irish Republic against all enemies, foreign and domestic, that I will bear true faith and allegiance to the same. I do further swear that I do not and shall not yield a voluntary support to any pretended Government, Authority, or Power within Ireland hostile or inimical to that Republic.

I take this obligation freely without any mental reservation or purpose of evasion – so help me God.

Over the years, the opposition of the Church to oath-bound secret societies led to new recruits not being asked to 'solemnly swear' but to make a 'declaration' of loyalty to the IRA. But what of the declaration of loyalty to a 32-county unitary state? It could be taken as implicit that the Irish Republic referred to above was that declared in 1916, and ipso facto that this applied to all 32 counties of Ireland; nevertheless, partition is not mentioned. The headquarters staff of the IRA were Frank Aiken, Dr Andrew Cooney, Maurice Twomey, Michael Carolan, Seán Russell, Jim Donovan, Seán Moylan, Seán Lemass, Tom Daly, Seán MacBride, Michael Price and Jim Killeen. These were all civil war veterans and men of above-average ability. Three of them, Aiken, Lemass and Moylan, would later serve as ministers in Fianna Fáil cabinets. A fourth, Maurice Twomey, could have done so had he wished. But with the exception of Frank Aiken they all came from south of the border and had little experience of the day-to-day reality of Six County life. They were also highly moral men. Critics of Dublin administrations, exasperated at what outsiders often perceive as a culpable failure to extirpate 'the Movement', as its members generally referred to the IRA, overlook this fact. Irish governments found themselves dealing with an armed second authority, which challenged their jurisdiction and sometimes carried out murders and robberies, though, unlike say the Mafia, not for personal gain, but did operate against a historical background, the deeply rooted Irish physical-force tradition. Moreover, as a contemporary readership had an opportunity to witness during the series of IRA hunger strikes which occurred during the Troubles of 1966–98, they were prepared to endure as well as to inflict for 'the cause'.

While the historical factor gave the IRA apologists one source of justification, by quoting Wolfe Tone, Pearse, the Fenians, etc., they also deployed religious and political arguments. Religiously, for those who condemned the movement's taking of life as being opposed to the Catholic Church's teaching, there was the ploy of quoting the Church's own teaching on the correctness of taking up arms in a 'just war'.

Politically, 'the Army', as its members were encouraged to refer to the IRA, pointed to the true source of authority in the country as being the Second Dail, not the usurping Free State parliament. 'After all,' Maurice Twomey remarked to me during an interview, 'it is recognised that there are governments in exile. That's how we see the Second Dail.' Twomey could have taken a ministerial position in the Free State parliament had he so chosen, as part of the inducements which de Valera offered the IRA in secret negotiations he conducted on taking office in an effort to get the movement to abandon force. Although he refused, and was subsequently jailed, de Valera continued to have a high regard for him. Not long before he died I was present at a meeting between Twomey and Vivion de Valera, who had succeeded his father as controlling director of the *Irish Press*, at which Vivion offered Twomey 'all the resources of the *Irish Press*' to enable him to produce the memoirs which I was trying to persuade him to write. Twomey, an old school Fenian of the 'tell them nothing' brigade, turned down the offer, but the fact that it was made indicates something of the regard in which he was held.

On 15 September 1926, when rumour and counter-rumour were in the air over the formation of Fianna Fáil, Cooney and Luke Dillon, secretary of the American Clan na Gael, came to an agreement which again defined the IRA's objectives. The agreement stipulated that the Clan would give its 'undivided support, physically, morally, and financially to Oglaigh na hEireann [literally meaning the Irish Army] to secure by force of arms the absolute independence of Ireland'. Again partition was not mentioned, and the theatre of operations in which the IRA sought 'absolute independence' therefore became not the severed Six Counties, under British rule, but the 26, which were already independent and whose government viewed the IRA's activities as jeopardising that sovereignty. Another fundamental problem for the organisation was that while it was by definition an army, and therefore used military means to gain its objectives, these means turned off a great deal of potential support. When the movement decided to put aside force and go political, as it did at several junctures in its history throughout the century, the inevitable 'force v. constitutional action' debate resulted in weakening splits. When the guns were exchanged for butter, some of the white-hot fire of 'the Cause' was inevitably lost, and up to the re-emergence of Sinn Féin in the 1980s, republicanism did not attract mass support. For those who continued with the gun, force always had its adherents, but on a small scale, and inevitably the use of guns created widespread revulsion against their users. The reason that Anthony Butler described the IRA as the perennial background to his thinking on politics, saying that 'it was the Mafia; it was truth; it was cruelty; it was justice', may be gauged from the following summary of some of the activities of the gun users.

In 1924, fatal incidents included the firing on a tender from Spike Island at Cobh, County Cork, in which a British soldier was shot dead as he came ashore with a party which included women and children, some of whom were also wounded. At Creg, County Tipperary, an IRA man resisted arrest, fatally wounding a member of the guards.

The following year, there was another fatal shooting in Claremorris, when a man coming home from a dance was fired on by members of the IRA. Later that year, massive publicity was generated for the IRA when an IRA party under George Gilmore and Jim Killeen was rescued from jail with 18 other prisoners.

In 1926, as part of its general anti-British campaign, the IRA cracked down on what it termed 'British propaganda films'. Cinemas were attacked and their managers warned that they would be 'drastically dealt with' for showing films like *Ypres* and *Zeebrugge*. In Clare, a Garda who was deemed to have taken undue interest in IRA activities was shot dead.

The following year, there were a number of shootings and the intimidation of jurors became widespread. A sergeant and two guards were shot by the IRA either in ambushes or in the course of raids on Garda stations. These sort of happenings, of course, generated strong feelings amongst the police, and well-founded charges of police brutality became a commonplace. De Valera derived much valuable publicity from the 'kicking cow' case, involving an IRA man, T.J. Ryan, in County Clare, who was beaten unconscious by colleagues of a murdered detective. The police, however, claimed that he had been 'kicked by a cow'. After the Minister for Justice, James Fitzgerald-Kenney, told de Valera, in the Dail (on 31 July 1929), that he accepted this explanation, the detectives became known as 'Fitzgerald-Kenney's cows'.

Another IRA activity of the period was the seizing of money-lenders' books and records. As the money-lenders were generally Jewish, these activities contributed to a feeling that the IRA was anti-Semitic, which they indignantly denied. The year also of course saw the murder of Kevin O'Higgins, and several shooting episodes and incidents of jurors being intimidated. The anti-British campaign took the form of tearing down Union Jacks from shops which displayed them on Armistice Day, particularly in the then pre-dominantly Protestant area of Dublin, the fashionable Grafton Street, Dawson Street and Dame Street. British Legion and scouting halls were also burned down throughout the year.

The years 1929 to 1931 saw a huge increase in the numbers of shootings and raids, and retaliatory action by the police. A campaign against jurors led to the setting up of the military tribunal. By that time, not only were jurors being intimidated whenever they sat in IRA cases, but in a number of cases they were shot, as were witnesses who had given evidence against the IRA. Guards and prison warders became commonplace targets for attack. The IRA paper, *An Phoblacht*, printed statements such as the following (on 20 June 1931), justifying such behaviour: '*An Phoblacht* states that members of the CID should be treated as "social pariahs". That treatment must be extended to . . . judges and district justices, to uniformed police, to every individual who is a willing part of the machine by which our Irish patriots are being tortured.' The 'pariahs' of 1931 included one Patrick Carroll of Dublin, thought to be a police spy, who was shot and had his head blown off by a hand grenade, and a Police Superintendent Curtin shot dead on the steps of his own house. Other targets for fatal attack of course were members of the IRA who turned informer. The legend 'spies and informers beware IRA' made its appearance in Ireland again, as it had done several times before during the Anglo-Irish war, tied to the neck of a corpse, John Ryan of Tipperary.[46]

Cosgrave created widespread public unease when he read out in the Dail the text of an interview given by Frank Ryan to a British newspaper. The interview made it quite clear that it regarded the members of the Government as being included amongst the 'pariahs'. After objecting to the use of terminology like 'murder' and 'assassination' in describing shootings such as the above, Ryan went on: 'The shootings to which you referred were not murder, they were acts of war. You must remember this, the Irish Republican Army is still at war with Britain. We regard the Free State Ministers merely as the agents of Britain.' He said that Superintendent Curtin had 'exceeded his duty. He went out of his way to persecute the IRA . . . The civil guard have no right to interfere in matters which don't concern them. If they ask for trouble they must not be surprised if they get it.' Justifying the death of John Ryan, he said that he had given evidence for Curtin, therefore he was 'nothing else than a traitor'. Carroll was described in similar terms. Ryan went on: 'Military organisation cannot tolerate spies or traitors. But let me tell you this – these things are not decided lightly. Decisions are made only with very great reluctance. Traitors must be punished, but there are fewer in our ranks than anywhere else.'

In view of the treatment meted out to them, the scarcity of traitors was hardly to be wondered at. But, eventually, the more political members of the IRA realised, as figures like de Valera, Aiken and Lemass had already done, that some form of political activity was preferable to the type of thing indicated above – and I say 'indicated' advisedly; the list gives but a fraction of the incidents of violence which occurred. At the instigation of a group which included Peadar O'Donnell, Seán Russell, David Fitzgerald, Michael Fitzpatrick and Michael Price, a new party, Saor Eire, was set up following a congress held in Dublin on 26 and 27 September 1931. Earlier in the summer (on 7 June) Peadar O'Donnell had stated that the days of active service were over for the present, and that the need now was for a Republican Workers Party, working for a 'Peasants Republic', and controlled jointly by peasants and workers. Saor Eire proposed:

To abolish, without compensation, landlordism in lands, fisheries and minerals.
To establish a State monopoly in banking and credits.

To create a State monopoly in export and import services and to promote co-operative distribution.

To make the national wealth and credit available for the creation and fullest development of essential industries and mineral resources, through Industrial Workers' Co-operatives, under State direction and management, workers to regulate internal working conditions.

The doom of Saor Eire was contained in the first sentence of its objectives. In practical terms, it meant taking land away from Irish farmers without compensating them. The unease of figures within the movement, like Maurice Twomey, a right-wing Fenian of the old school, who was also a dedicated Catholic, in addition to becoming chief of staff of the IRA, was shown in the 1932 IRA convention's resolution on Saor Eire: 'That we approve of Saor Eire. That the activities of Saor Eire be confined to an effort to educate the people in the principles of Saor Eire without publicly organising it as Saor Eire.' By this time, Twomey had good reason for his caution. Saor Eire, the IRA, Fianna Eireann, Cumann na mBan, the Friends of Soviet Russia, and other Communist-supporting organisations had all been declared unlawful, and the combined influence of the Eucharistic Congress and the Irish hierarchy was also telling against such bodies. The IRA would suffer guilt by association with leftist groupings, as we shall shortly see.

But initially, the approach of Fianna Fáil to the corridors of power appeared to herald a new dawn for the militant Republicans. As we have seen, prisoners were released, the military tribunal was abolished, and an IRA policy, Peadar O'Donnell's initiative on the land annuities, taken up by the Government. To a wide section of the public, certainly amongst the supporters of the Cosgrave administration, it seemed that the IRA and de Valera were hand in glove. The annual commemoration of Wolfe Tone at his grave in Bodenstown, County Kildare, is both an IRA show of strength and an opportunity (by analysing the speeches) for judging the policies of the movement. In 1931, Cumann na nGaedheal cancelled the special trains which are normally laid on for the occasion, and police prevented open militaristic display. But members of Fianna Fáil marched together in a body, and de Valera laid a wreath on Tone's grave. The speeches of de Valera, Lemass, O'Ceallaigh, etc., and many of the other episodes of seeming Fianna Fáil indulgence towards the IRA buttressed rather than weakened this impression. However, publicly, the IRA sounded a warning note. *An Phoblacht*, which had been banned by Cosgrave, was unbanned when Fianna Fáil took office, and on its reappearance contained an article by Maurice Twomey which said:

> Fianna Fáil declares its intention to chop off some of the imperial tentacles; every such achievement is of value and will be welcomed. Notwithstanding such concessions, the Irish Republican Army must continue its work, and cannot escape its role as the vanguard of the freedom movement.

At Bodenstown that year, Tom Clarke's widow, who was also a Dail deputy, laid a wreath on Tone's grave on behalf of the National Executive of Fianna Fáil in the presence of some 15,000 men arrayed in military formation. But Bodenstown watchers would have realised that all was not well in the relationship between the IRA and Fianna Fáil. Delivering the oration, Seán Russell quoted Wolfe Tone's denunciation of Grattan's parliament: 'Of all Parliaments beyond all comparison, the most shameful and abandoned of all sense of virtue, principle or even common decency.' Privately, de Valera, on taking power, had met with representatives of the IRA leadership on a number of occasions in an effort to get them to abandon physical force, and support his programme of removing the oath, the governor generalship, and so forth. He told the IRA that with these achievements accomplished, the declaration of a republic would only be a formality, that then there would 'only be partition left to deal with'. He pressed the IRA to disband, and accept the principle of majority rule. Not surprisingly, the IRA, as an organisation devoted to a 32-county Republican Ireland, baulked at that 'only'. They countered by reminding de Valera of his own record where majority rule was concerned. The majority had opposed 1916, supported the Treaty, and, amongst Republicans, opposed his break with Sinn Féin. Majority rule was okay in a free country, but Ireland was not free. De Valera was reminded that he was the man who had said that 'the people have no right to do wrong'.

The IRA's counter-offer to de Valera was that they should combine with Fianna Fáil against British aggression. Joseph McGarrity, who was still on good terms with de Valera at this stage, had a scheme whereby the Free State army's oath would be changed to pledge allegiance to the nation as a whole. This would mean that the IRA could join the army without any loss of principle – and take it over! McGarrity later wrote to de Valera saying:

> To be frank, it is apparent that an agreement between your forces and the forces of the IRA is a national necessity. They can do things you would not care to do or cannot do in the face of public criticism, while the IRA pay no heed to public clamour, so long as they feel they are doing a national duty.

In the early days of his first election victory, de Valera hoped, by getting a public declaration of support from the IRA for Fianna Fáil and his programme, that he could avoid having to rely on Labour support. He also tried to meet the objection to taking an oath alluded to by McGarrity in his plan to assist the IRA in taking over the army. He told the IRA that he planned to set up a national reserve which members of the organisation could join without taking an oath, but by making a declaration of support for the Government, and privately by supporting its campaign against what de Valera termed 'reactionary forces', Cumann na nGaelheal, the Senate and the banks. The IRA calculated correctly that a principle objective of the new National Reserve, which was duly set up as an adjunct to the National Army, was to draw off potential IRA recruitment and support. This was also the aim of another of his proposals which went into operation, a scheme whereby those who had fought against the state in the civil war received pensions as did those who had upheld it. Nevertheless de Valera continued to put out feelers, and even occasionally to meet with the IRA for approximately three years after taking office.

Even before O'Duffy was dismissed (on 18 February 1933), the army council of the IRA had called a general army convention to consider the political situation. After stating that 'the aim of the organisation was to assert the sovereignty and unity of the Republic of Ireland, in which the ownership of the means of production, distribution and exchange will be vested in the Irish people', the document convening the convention went on:

> At the last Convention it was decided not to take any action which would actively impede the newly established Fianna Fáil 'Government'. This decision governed to a great extent the policy of the Army Council, and every effort was made by the Council to avoid clashes. On the other hand, to put it mildly, not much assistance was given by the Fianna Fáil 'Government' in carrying out this policy; the police and the CID tried in many instances to provoke conflict. The Coercion legislation passed under the Cosgrave regime was not repealed – on the contrary in many cases it was actually used against Republicans, and thus we have witnessed the jailing of many of our comrades.

The document decided that the economic war was 'being used for the advancement of both British and Irish capitalism within our shores' and went on:

> It is the opinion of the Army Council that the policy of the Fianna Fáil 'Government' is bound to lead to widespread disillusionment amongst a great proportion of its republican supporters, and of the workers and the working farmers. One of the principal tasks of the Convention will be to decide whether such disillusionment can be availed of in the achievement of the aims of the Irish Republican Army.

However, the IRA moved to bring further 'disillusionment' down on its supporters by allowing itself to become embroiled in futile clashes with the Blueshirts, which both drew off its strength and inevitably brought the organisation into conflict with the police.

Apart from the tensions and divisions which clashes with the Blueshirts generated, the perennial debate of force versus constitutional action also led to splits within the movement. The left-wing element of the IRA became involved in two controversies in particular which helped to heighten left versus right divisions. Figures like Peadar O'Donnell, Michael Price and Frank Ryan decided to support the cause of James Gralton, a County Leitrim man who had become a naturalised American citizen but had returned to Ireland in 1932 to propagate communism. He hit on an ingenious method of disseminating his views – running free dances in a dance hall he owned. Not surprisingly, he drew large crowds; equally unsurprisingly, he aroused strong opposition amongst the puritanical Roman Catholic Irish clergy for whom communism, though distasteful, was a lesser evil than what Brendan Behan once termed 'mixed dances', those catering for men and women. After his hall had been fired into, Gralton was served with a deportation order (on 9 February 1933). He went on the run, but was eventually caught and deported. A public campaign to 'keep Gralton here' was mounted by a group which included the Revolutionary Workers Groups (in effect the Communist Party), and by figures like Captain Jack White, the founder of the Citizen Army, and Mrs Sheehy Skeffington, whose pacifist husband had been murdered in 1916 by a demented British officer.

Maurice Twomey, the IRA Chief of Staff, was unhappy at the IRA's involvement in the Gralton campaign, as was the Leitrim IRA leader, Seán O'Farrell, who, realising the extent of local feeling against communism, advised against involvement in the affair. Gralton's deportation helped to dampen down the left–right argument within the IRA, but before it had time to die away completely, the Connolly House fracas blew up, during February and March of 1933. A house in Eccles Street had been donated for use as a workers' college by Madame Despard, a sister of Lord French and a left-wing intellectual who moved in British Labour Party circles frequented by figures like Sir Stafford Cripps. Many of the workers who availed themselves of the Eccles Street facilities were left-inclined members of the IRA, but the tenants also included the Friends of Soviet Russia. Not far away, in Strand Street, was Connolly House, the headquarters of the Irish Revolutionary Workers Party. Gralton and the two houses became intertwined in the public mind after the Lenten pastorals bracketed the Gralton case with their condemnations of communism. A Jesuit preacher in Gardiner Street church, which is in the Eccles Street area, was particularly strong on the dangers which stalked Dublin streets. Groups of rightist youths, mobilised in an organisation known as St Patrick's Young Men's League, began marching in Dublin, occasionally stopping pedestrians to check on their religious practices (the wearing of medals and scapulars met with approval in their eyes). Religious fervour mounted throughout the month of March, and on the 27th, both houses were attacked and some damage caused. On the 29th, a mob gathered, looted Connolly House, and after doing what it could to wreck the place, set it on fire.

Charlie Gilmore, a member of a well-known IRA family, who attempted to defend the place, was arrested and charged with the illegal possession of firearms and the attempted murder of a police officer. Gilmore conducted his own defence and managed to get himself acquitted, but the IRA took umbrage because in the course of his defence he said that he had authority from them to defend the Communist building. A communiqué was issued to the *Independent* on 30 March by the IRA, denying that Gilmore had been authorised to carry a revolver. However, the officer who had given him permission to carry the weapon was his brother Harry, who publicly contradicted the IRA communiqué. He too was tried, this time by an IRA court-martial, and was also acquitted, even though he refused to sign a letter to the press exculpating the IRA of any taint of communism.

These incidents helped to bring about a split in the IRA. The left-wingers felt that the IRA was getting nowhere. It had become a 26-county-bound organisation which was frittering its strength in futile drillings and attacks on the Blueshirts. The right wing was concerned at being ground down by Fianna Fáil on the one hand and charges of communism on the other. The issue came to a head at a convention held in Dublin on 17 and 18 March 1934, at which O'Donnell, the Gilmores, Price, Ryan and Michael Fitzgerald lost by one vote, that of Maurice Twomey, a proposal to set up a new party. They immediately walked out and began setting one up anyway. It was launched at Athlone on 8 April and was known as the Republican Congress Party. The Congress proposed to contest elections and proclaimed itself 'in favour of the overthrow of all the existing political and economic machinery which at present holds this country and our people in subjection'. It said that its call was 'Workers and working farmers unite on to the Workers' Republic.' By this of course the Congress leaders meant an all-Ireland workers' republic, and in both parts of Ireland, north and south, the party did attract some support from the more leftist-inclined in the Labour Party, the trade unions and the Communist Party. While in the north of Ireland working-class solidarity proved to be of short duration in the face of sectarianism, the Congress was responsible for one notable act of concerted approach by both Protestants and Catholics. Some 200 members of the Congress volunteered to form the James Connolly battalion of the International Brigade, which fought for the Republicans in the Spanish Civil War. The battalion took part in some of the fiercest engagements of the war and suffered heavy losses. Thus in death and prison cell, in a foreign country, Belfast Protestants and Dublin IRA men achieved a unity that eluded them at home.

The riposte of the Army Council, printed in *An Phoblacht*, was to agree with the Congress's social and economic policies, but to condemn the drift towards constitutionalism:

> This Party will, in course of time, contest elections and enter the Free State Parliament. Inevitably it will follow the road which has been travelled by other constitutional Parties which, though setting out with good intentions, ended in failure. It is not very long ago since Fianna Fáil leaders told us that they wanted to go into the Free State Parliament only for the purpose of smashing it up, but they now hold this institution and the whole Free State machine as sacred.

The argument against constitutionalism would still be in use at the end of the century by spokespersons for the continuation of the physical-force tradition (the Real IRA) against support for the Good Friday Agreement of 1998. The Congress split led to a great deal of bad blood within the ranks of republicanism. Gilmore, O'Donnell and the others were court-martialled by Twomey's wing of the IRA, and expelled with ignominy *in absentia*. O'Donnell greatly angered the more theologically minded amongst the rightists with the levity with which he received the awesome verdict of an IRA

213

court-martial: he sent back word that as they had court-martialled him *in absentia*, they could carry out the sentence in his absence also. However, the Congress was not a long-lived creation. It attracted recruits like Connolly's children, Nora and Roddy, and Frank Edwards, a Waterford schoolteacher who became nationally known because the bishop of the diocese had him dismissed for joining the new movement and Edwards had the temerity to engage in public controversy with his Lordship. But the movement split after only a few months in existence. At a convention held in Rathmines Town Hall on 29 and 30 September, there were divisions between the founders over a proposal by Michael Price that the organisation should concentrate on joining in strikes, helping to resist evictions and contesting municipal and Dail elections. O'Donnell, Gilmore and Ryan thought that the hour had not yet come for such activities and that the thing to do was to infiltrate trade unions and political organisations with their supporters. It was a policy which the inheritors of the left-wing IRA tradition would put into effect following yet another split in the IRA in the 1970s.

In fact, all sections of the IRA showed a tendency to take a hand in strikes when these arose, and to co-operate in campaigns for the release of prisoners or in commemorating Easter week. But the right-left dichotomy proved impossible to bridge. Bodenstown became the scene of physical violence between the two sides in 1934 and again in 1935. The right-wing IRA actually attacked a contingent of Protestant Shankill workers, who had been brought to the grave of the founder of the United Irishmen who wished to unite Catholic, Protestant and dissenter. Their banner inscribed 'United Irishmen of 1934' was torn down. In 1935, the IRA Army Council ordered country units to attack Republican Congress contingents. Another order of the Army Council had brought the IRA into conflict with the Government earlier that year. On 22 March, the IRA intervened in a strike of Dublin transport workers when the army was called out by the Government in an effort to provide transport. A letter from the Army Council to the joint strike committee contained the following: 'The Army Council offers the services of the Army to assist in mobilising the maximum support for the Dublin transport workers in their struggle, and is prepared to send representatives to meet the Strike Committee for this purpose.'

The Government reacted the following day by rounding up some 44 members of the IRA and of the now greatly attenuated Republican Congress Party. The solicitor Con Lehane, a member of the Army Council, received 18 months from the military tribunal, and lesser sentences were handed down to others including the Cork IRA leader Tom Barry. Maurice Twomey, Seán MacBride, Michael Fitzpatrick and Seán Russell went on the run. However, the IRA continued to struggle towards some form of political expression, despite the continuing opposition of Maurice Twomey and his adherents. A new political party, Cumann Phoblachta na hEireann, was founded at a meeting in Barrys Hotel, Dublin, on 7 March 1936. It was stated that the new party would contest elections both north and south of the border, but if elected would not take its seats. Those who supported the formation of the new party included Seán MacBride, the former IRA Chief of Staff; Dr Andrew Cooney; Fiona Plunkett, a sister of the executed 1916 leader; Madge Daly, a sister of Kathleen Clarke, the widow of the executed 1916 leader Thomas Clarke; and Patrick MacLogan, who at the time was an IRA organiser and Nationalist MP for South Armagh.

However, Twomey continued to object to the formation of political parties, as did many in the Dublin brigade of the IRA, and these objections came to a head at a special IRA convention on 19 May at which Seán MacBride proposed that the new party should receive the backing of the IRA. Twomey and his supporters within the Dublin brigade, Claude O'Loughlin, James Coulton and Kevin Lawless, objected and walked out, saying that there was no difference between the MacBride proposal and that which had emanated from de Valera and led to the formation of Fianna Fáil.

The public's verdict on these internal IRA disputes may be gauged from the results of a poll held on 30 June. The highest vote secured by a Republican Congress candidate (George Gilmore) was 730 out of a total poll in his area of 32,617 votes. For Cumann Phoblacht na hEireann, Maud Gonne MacBride was the biggest vote-getter, with only 689 votes out of a total poll of 29,733.

With his enemies on the right now in disarray, de Valera decided that it was time to turn his attentions to the IRA. The final breach between Fianna Fáil and the IRA may be said to have been hastened by three incidents involving loss of life. The deaths were those of Roderick More O'Farrell, fatally wounded on 9 February 1935 at Edgeworthstown, County Longford; John Egan, shot dead in public in Mitchell Street, Dungarvan, on 26 April 1936; and Vice-Admiral Henry Boyle Townsend Somerville, killed at Castletownshend, County Cork, on 24 March 1936 at the front door of his home. This last death in particular created a public outcry. The Admiral was a brother of Edith Somerville, the co-author of *Some Experiences of an Irish RM*. He had been in the habit of giving references to any local lads who approached him for help in joining the British navy, and was shot on the orders of the local IRA commander, Tom Barry, not the IRA Army Council. Young More O'Farrell had intervened to prevent a group of IRA men taking away his father to tar and feather him as a result of a local land dispute. Shots were fired and the young man was fatally wounded. As the raiders had broken in on a convivial occasion, a dinner party, this shooting too, which again was not sanctioned by the Army Council, aroused widespread condemnation, particularly because of the unsatisfactory nature of the subsequent court proceedings. On 10 December, seven members of the IRA were discharged at the Central Criminal Court in Dublin, after the jury brought in a verdict of not guilty – *before* the evidence of the defence was taken. Gerald Boland, the Minister for Justice, later told the Dail (16 June 1936) that the case had not been heard before the military tribunal because a certificate could not be issued to empower the tribunal to adjudicate on the matter since the Minister 'could not conscientiously state that the crime was committed for the purpose of interfering with the machinery of Government or the administration of Justice'. The Egan killing *was* sanctioned by the Army Council, in the belief that Egan had turned state's evidence in a case in which the commander of the West Waterford battalion of the IRA, William O'Donoghue, had been sentenced to three months' imprisonment on a charge of illegal drilling.

Beginning three days after Egan's death, on 29 April, widespread swoops on IRA men commenced, netting most of the principal leaders in Dublin and Cork. Maurice Twomey subsequently received a three-year sentence from the military tribunal for membership of an unlawful organisation. The IRA was declared unlawful by order of the Executive Council on 18 June. Speaking in the Dail debate which preceded the banning, Gerald Boland made two statements which laid down what the policy of Fianna Fáil towards the IRA would henceforth be:

> ... the fact that these murders have occurred ... makes it clear that stern action must be taken against any organisation which claims to have the power of life and death over its members, or ex-members, or other citizens, or which claims that it is entitled to use force upon the community to compel obedience to its will. I now give definite notice to all concerned that the so-called Irish Republican Army, or any organisation which promotes or advocates the use of arms for the attainments of its object will not be tolerated ...

The next day he followed this up by saying:

> ... we smashed them [the Blueshirts] and we are going to smash the others [the IRA] ... if there are people who know where arms are, and their sense of civic duty will not encourage them to tell where they are, then if any form of reward is necessary to induce them to do so, we will give it ...

De Valera had abandoned the position which he had announced in the Dail a few years earlier, that Republicans who continued in the organisation which he had left could claim 'exactly the same continuity that we claimed up to 1925. They can do it . . .' Now they could no longer do it. As part of the tough new policy, the Government banned the Bodenstown commemoration which was scheduled for the day after the Minister's speech. All trains and buses heading for the commemoration were stopped. To heighten the sense of urgency, an aeroplane hovered overhead, and on the ground armed police and armoured cars were grouped. IRA men from Limerick who had seized a lorry in an attempt to get to Bodenstown were arrested and sentenced to nine months by the military tribunal. One of these, Seán Glynn, subsequently committed suicide in Arbour Hill Prison on 13 September. An inquiry into his death found that imprisonment had caused him to become depressed.

Glynn's suicide had a powerful effect on the Clann na Gael leader, Joseph McGarrity. He had been de Valera's closest and most influential ally in de Valera's first great American tour. His influence on the physical force school of Irish republicanism was such that in the 1970s IRA communiqués were still being signed with the pseudonym Joseph McGarrity. After Glynn's death, he wrote harshly condemning de Valera's treatment of the IRA,[47] and saying that IRA prisoners were 'so unmercifully treated in prison that young Glynn was found hanging dead in a cell in Arbour Hill Prison, Dublin . . . This was the last straw for me . . .' As we will see, McGarrity subsequently broke with de Valera and sponsored an IRA bombing campaign in England.

DE VALERA'S CONSTITUTION

Now it is time to turn to an examination of the device whereby de Valera hoped to convince both the IRA and the Irish public that the Republican objectives for which he had opposed the Treaty, and subsequently Cumann na nGaedheal, had in fact been achieved: his new constitution.

De Valera himself thought so highly of the constitution that he commented on one of its articles (1) that: 'I would be very glad indeed at the hour of my death to stand over it.'[48]

By 1936, he had effected such changes in the wake of the passing of the Statute of Westminster, and the alteration of the status of the Governor General, that the constitution had been altered very considerably from that of Michael Collins. In dropping the oath, de Valera argued that once it went, those Republicans who still withheld their recognition of parliament would drop their objections to the legitimacy of the state.[49] His constitution was intended to both further this improbable objective, and somehow, while representing a Catholic electorate, create the conditions which would make the state described in the constitution attractive to the northern Protestants. In fact, as its wording will make clear, parts of the constitution were guaranteed to offend not merely extremist Unionist sensibilities, but middle-of-the-road feelings also. Obviously the fact that the King (Edward VIII) was left out of the document was guaranteed to ruffle Unionist feathers. And in all honesty, one could hardly expect an intensely Protestant state to enthuse over a document which conceded a 'special position' to the Roman Catholic Church.[50] Article 2, as de Valera made clear, declared the national territory to consist of 'the whole of Ireland, its islands and the territorial seas'. Article 3 asserted the *right* to exercise jurisdiction over the whole national territory, but made it clear that pending the reintegration of said territories, the provisions of the constitution would apply only to the 26 counties. Speaking in the Dail, de Valera stated flatly that in the Articles referred to 'is claimed by the nation the whole of the national territory', but because '*at the moment*' Ireland was not in a position to make the will of the majority of the people effective throughout the whole island, the writ of the Dail stopped short at the border.[51] With the passage of time, it became clear that the Articles, while they provided some psychological solace for the beleaguered northern Nationalists, were of no practical relevance to the partition question, although as will be seen at a later stage, they caused some dismay to Nationalists when they were ultimately dropped as part of the Good Friday Agreement of 1998. What they did do, as will be described in the next chapter, was provide a pretext for Craig to declare a snap election which greatly strengthened his position.

The constitution drafting was begun in April of 1935 when de Valera instructed the legal adviser to the Department of External Affairs, John Hearne, to start writing a constitution incorporating the idea of external association. There were other drafters, most notably John Charles McQuaid, a Holy Ghost Father and President of Blackrock College, a noted educationalist but a man of very blinkered views concerning either Protestants or Jews. Another contributor of ideas was the conservative Jesuit Father Edward Cahill. De Valera also talked over his proposed constitution with Father Dennis Fahey, another Holy Ghost priest who, though a kindly man personally, was to become the driving spirit behind Maria Duce, an ultra-Catholic organisation with a disturbing streak of anti-Semitism. Fahey does not appear to have had any input into the final drafting of the constitution, but the spirit of McQuaid, who, largely as a result of his services to de Valera, later became the most conservative archbishop in the history of the Dublin Archdiocese, ultimately did come to permeate much of the constitution. Alarmed that Father Cahill, a man noted for his extreme views, might also influence the document, the Jesuit Provincial set up a committee of distinguished Jesuits to draw up a joint document, which was forwarded to de Valera by Cahill and then passed on to McQuaid. In general, therefore, it may be said with some confidence of de Valera's chosen theological trio that they were not picked for their empathy with the Protestant community of north-eastern Ireland.

De Valera notified the King of his intentions to introduce a Bill for the purpose of setting up a new constitution which, while 'establishing conditions for permanent peace and harmony' would abolish the office of Governor General and create that of President. The subsequent departure of the King from the throne both removed His Majesty from any involvement in de Valera's plans, and at the same time provided a context, because of the abdication crisis, which enabled de Valera to bring forward the constitution.

Under the terms of the Statute of Westminster, any alteration in law affecting a succession to the throne, or the royal styles and titles, required the assent not merely of the House of Commons, but of all the dominion parliaments. Therefore, as the abdication storm broke, the British Prime Minister, Stanley Baldwin, sent an emissary to Dublin (on 29 November), to sound de Valera's views on the alternatives the crisis posed for the British Cabinet:

1. That Mrs Simpson be recognised as Queen.
2. That she should not become Queen, but that there was no need for the King to abdicate.
3. That the King should abdicate in favour of the Duke of York.

De Valera opted for No. 2, on the basis that England recognised divorce. The other dominion prime ministers made their views known directly to the King, but de Valera merely asked the British emissary, Sir Henry Batterbee, to keep him informed of the King's intentions. He did not inform the British as to his own. Batterbee tried to find out through Joseph Walshe, the Secretary for the Department of External Affairs, and was blandly informed by Walshe that 'We are going to amend the existing Constitution so that the law would exactly express the realities of the Constitutional position in regard to the functions expressed directly by the King. The precise manner in which this is to be done, has not yet been determined.'

When the British found out that de Valera was not planning to summon the Dail for a week, Malcolm MacDonald, the Secretary for the Dominions, was deputed to ring him immediately to get him to convene parliament without delay. The British fear was that a week's hiatus would mean that the King would still be King in Ireland, thus creating the Free State an independent monarchy. However, on the same day that Walshe spoke to Batterbee, and MacDonald made his phone call, 10 December 1936, de Valera, who had had the necessary legislation prepared all along, telegrammed deputies to attend the Dail the next day, when he put forward two Bills under a guillotine motion. The first, the Constitution (Amendment No. 27) Bill 1936, had to pass through all stages between 3 and 11 p.m. The second, the Executive (External Relations) Authority Bill, had also to pass the following day. And pass they did, despite determined opposition from the lawyers with which Cumann na nGael abounded. The effect of new legislation was to get rid of the King, the Governor General and Article 1 of the Free State constitution, which recognised the state as 'a co-equal member of the Community of Nations forming the British Commonwealth of Nations'. The Prime Minister would henceforth be termed Taoiseach, or Chief, not President of the Executive Council. There was to be another office of President, the official head of state, elected by popular franchise, which though not entirely without power would in practice be a largely ceremonial title. Years later, in attempting to answer a question as to just what sort of a state the constitution made of the old Irish Free State, de Valera resorted to the use of several dictionaries and encyclopaedias to define the term 'republic'. As a result, he was thenceforth taunted with having created a 'dictionary republic'. However, though defining a republic created problems for him, he had no difficulty in coming up with a definition of the King. In Article 51 of the constitution, he was termed 'an organ':

> Provided that it shall be law for the Executive Council, to the extent and subject to any conditions which may be determined by law to avail, for the purposes of the appointment of diplomatic and consular agents, and conclusion of international agreements of any organ used as a constitutional organ for the like purpose by any of the nations referred to in Article One of the Constitution.

The purpose behind this circumlocution was to avoid difficulties over diplomatic representation. The Crown was retained for external purposes only.

The constitutional manoeuvrings illustrated the value to de Valera of his removal of the Senate. The External Relations Bill also went through without a hitch the following day. It retained a link of sorts with Britain and the Commonwealth because de Valera felt that might help in ending partition. It stated that:

> So long as Saorstat Eireann is associated with the following nations, that is to say, Australia, Canada and Great Britain, New Zealand and South Africa, and so long as the King recognised by those nations as the symbol of their co-operation continues to act on behalf of each of those nations (on the advice of the several Governments thereof), for the purpose of the appointment of diplomatic and consular representatives, and the conclusion of international agreements, the King so recognised may, and is hereby authorised to, act on behalf of Saorstat Eireann for the like purposes, as and when advised by the Executive Council so to do.

The passing of these two Bills cleared the way for the introduction of de Valera's new constitution. The Article governing the position of the Catholic Church caused a great deal of controversy behind closed doors, all of it, it could be argued, quite unnecessary because as the constitution he was replacing had not mentioned the Church, there was no need for de Valera's document to do so either. However, de Valera's civil war activities, which had provoked hierarchical displeasure, meant that he felt the need to show himself uncoo guid. The first draft of the religious provision read 'that the true religion is that established by our Divine Lord Jesus Christ himself, which he committed to his Church to protect and propagate as the guardian and interpreter of true morality. It acknowledges, moreover, that the Church of Christ is the Catholic Church.' The Church, said the draft, was 'a perfect society, having within itself full competence and sovereign authority, in respect of the spiritual good of man'.

This wording appalled the Republican-minded members of de Valera's Cabinet. One of them, Gerard Boland, correctly pointed out that the wording, if passed, would be equivalent to the expulsion from Irish history of Protestant patriots like Wolfe Tone, Robert Emmet, Parnell, and most tellingly, de Valera's former friend, Erskine Childers. Boland declared ringingly that such men would not have lived under a sectarian constitution, and said that he wouldn't live under it either.[52] De Valera was in contact with the Papal Nuncio, Pascal Robinson, ten times over the proposed definition. He had a particularly difficult encounter at the nunciature with Cardinal MacRory who wanted his wording in the constitution: 'The State, reflecting the religious convictions of 93 per cent of its citizens, acknowledges the Catholic religion to be the religion established by Our Lord Jesus Christ.' It would also of course have involved a going-back on the guarantees of fair and equal treatment which Arthur Griffith and the founders of the state had given to southern Unionists. De Valera sent Joseph Walshe to the Vatican to argue that if an attempt were to be made to embody in the new Constitution the full Catholic ideal, there would be an immediate outcry from the Protestant section of the population, and a bitter religious controversy might easily ensue . . . the Government would likewise be charged with having provided the occasion for a renewal of the bitter attacks on our fellow countrymen in Belfast . . . the Government would further be charged with having raised a new barrier to the reunion of our country.

Of course, any reference to Catholicism in the constitution was bound to provoke that sort of reaction from a section of unionism anyhow. While the Vatican's Secretary of State, Cardinal Pacelli, who later became Pope Pius XII, told Walshe that 'quite truthfully, according to the strict teaching of the Church, we were heretics to recognise any Church but the one true Church of Christ', unofficially the Vatican took a more relaxed view of de Valera's document. The Pope adopted a neutral attitude, neither approving nor disapproving of the final wording, but Pacelli let it be known that he was gratified by de Valera's use of the 'official title' of the Church. This is more than can be said for McQuaid, who was furious when he first learned that the constitution would not recognise Catholicism as the One True Church. However, the final form of the religious provision, Article 44 of the constitution, read as follows:

The State recognises the special position of the Holy Catholic Apostolic and Roman Church as the guardian of the faith professed by the great majority of the citizens. The State also recognises the Church of Ireland, the Presbyterian Church in Ireland, the Methodist Church in Ireland, the Religious Society of Friends in Ireland, as well as the Jewish Congregations and the other religious denominations existing in Ireland at the date of the coming into operation of this Constitution.

Before publication de Valera had the wording shown to the leaders of the Irish Protestant Churches and to the Jewish leader, Dr Isaac Herzog, none of whom objected. The constitution also specifically outlawed divorce, but guaranteed 'to every citizen freedom of conscience and the free profession and practice of religion', with a proviso that these be subject to public order.

The preamble to the constitution was also frankly theocratic. It stated:

In the name of the Most Holy Trinity, from Whom is all authority and to Whom, in our final end, all actions both of men and States, must be referred,
We the people of Eire,
Humbly acknowledging all our obligations to our Divine Lord, Jesus Christ, who sustained our fathers through centuries of trial. Gratefully remembering their heroic and unremitting struggle to regain the rightful independence of our Nation.
And seeking to promote the common good, with due observance of Prudence, Justice, and Charity, so that dignity and freedom of the individual may be assured, true social order obtained, the unity of our country restored, and concord established with other nations. Do hereby adopt, enact and give to ourselves this Constitution.

Articles 2 and 3 have already been described. Article 3, given in full, said:

Pending the re-integration of the national territory, and without prejudice to the *right* [author's italics] of the Parliament and Government established by this Constitution to exercise jurisdiction over the whole of that territory, the laws enacted by that parliament shall have the like area and extent of application as the laws of Saorstat Eireann and the like extra-territorial effect.

Again the fine Italian hand of McQuaid lay behind this article. The County Cavan-born Ulsterman felt as strongly on the partition issue as any Republican, and his influence on the constitution was far from being restricted to the religious articles. But not all Nationalists felt as did McQuaid. Some of the most trenchant arguments against putting in Articles 2 and 3 were advanced privately by the Secretary of the Department of Finance, J.J. MacElligott, a staunch Nationalist who had fought in the GPO. Articles 2 and 3, he said, seemed 'rather to vitiate the Constitution by stating at the outset what will be described, and with some justice, as a fiction'. He warned that the fiction would do nothing to help the unity of Ireland, rather the reverse. Claiming territory which did not belong to the state enshrined in the constitution a 'claim to Hibernia irredentia'. MacElligott argued that 'the parallel with Italy's historical attitude to the Adriatic seaboard beyond its recognised territory is striking, and in that case it is likely to have lasting ill-effects on our political relations with our nearest neighbours'.

De Valera was, however, unmoved by such arguments. He said that the Dail, on behalf of the nation, had a duty to assert a moral claim and right to such jurisdiction because there was no doubt that 'The vast majority of the people of this island would claim that the nation and the State ought to be co-terminous.' He was equally unmoved by the onslaughts of feminists on the constitutional provisions governing the family. Article 41 states:

1.1 The State recognises the Family as the natural primary and fundamental unit group of Society, and as a moral institution possessing inalienable and imprescriptible rights, antecedent and superior to all positive law.

1.2 The State, therefore, guarantees to protect the Family in its Constitution and authority, as the necessary basis of social order and as indispensable to the welfare of the Nation and the State.

2.1 In particular, the State recognises that by her life within the home, woman gives to the State a support without which the common good cannot be achieved.

2.2 The State shall, therefore, endeavour to ensure that mothers shall not be obliged by economic necessity to engage in labour to the neglect of their duties in the home.

3.1 The State pledges itself to guard with special care the institution of Marriage, on which the Family is founded, and to protect it against attack.

3.2 No law shall be enacted providing for the grant of a dissolution of marriage.

3.3 No person whose marriage has been dissolved under the civil law of any other State but is a subsisting valid marriage under the law for the time being in force within the jurisdiction of the Government and Parliament established by this Constitution shall be capable of contracting a valid marriage within that jurisdiction during the lifetime of the other party to the marriage so dissolved.

In considering the foregoing, it should be noted that de Valera had earlier introduced a Conditions of Employment Bill by which he acquired the right to restrict or exclude women working in industry in order to 'protect the interest of the male workers, who, without such restrictions, might have been swamped by lower paid women in the new industries'. This did away with the guarantee which had existed in the Michael Collins constitution, which stated (in Article 3), that 'Every person without distinction of sex, domiciled in the area of the jurisdiction of the Irish Free State, shall, within the jurisdiction of the Irish Free State, enjoy the privileges and be subject to the obligations of such citizenship.' Nor was de Valera's new legislation in line with the promises of the 1916 Proclamation: 'The Republic guarantees civil and religious liberties, equal rights and equal opportunities to all its citizens.'

De Valera was accused of having 'an innate prejudice against women anywhere outside the kitchen', and 'a fascist and slave conception of women as being a non-adult person who is very weak and whose place is in the home'.[53] One of his closest allies, the distinguished Protestant historian Dorothy Macardle, wrote to him saying: 'As the Constitution stands, I do not see how anyone holding advanced views on the rights of women can support it, and that it is a tragic dilemma for those who have been loyal and ardent workers in the national cause.' However, de Valera listened not to Macardle, but to McQuaid, who claimed that the feminists were 'very confused. Both Casti Connubi and Quadragesimo Anno [Papal Encyclicals] answer them.' The priest said that it was not correct to say that men and women had an equal right to work of the same kind. They had equal rights to *appropriate* work. McQuaid cited an argument which was frequently heard in Ireland up to the time when Pope John XXIII set up the second Vatican Council in the 1960s and, in the oft-quoted phrase of Harold Macmillan, 'a wind of change' began blowing through the musty halls of Irish Catholicism:

> The law of nature lays diverse functions on men and women. The completeness of life requires this diversity of function and of work. This is diversity, not inequality of work. In the desire to cut out unfair discrimination against women, diversity of work is being constantly confused with inequality of work.

McQuaid's attitude to women in the workplace also caused objections from Louie Bennett, who was secretary of the Irish Women Workers Union and one of the most respected figures in Dublin society. She took exception to Section 4(2) of Article 45, which said:

> The state shall endeavour to ensure that the strength and health of workers, men and women, and the tender age of children shall not be abused, and that citizens shall not be forced by economic necessity to enter vocations unsuited to their sex, age or strength.

This seemingly emollient language was attacked by Bennett as being:

The most indefensible in the Constitution. It takes from women the right to choose their own avocation in life. The state is given power to decide what avocations are suited to their sex and strength. It would hardly be possible to make a more deadly encroachment upon the liberty of the individual than to deprive him or her of this right.

However, as throughout the 1930s there were never more than three women in the Dail – from all parties – and they supported party policy rather than women's issues, such protests were attacked and disregarded. The Women's Graduate Association, which campaigned against the constitution, was condemned by the *Irish Press* in sectarian terms:

This group of university women are in actual revolt against the authority and teaching . . . of Pius XI. When they are attacking the terms of the Constitution, they are in reality assailing the weighty and deeply pondered words of the Sovereign Pontiff. They are deliberately placing themselves in opposition to the advice, the solemn exhortation, the paternal admonition given by the venerated head of the church, to all who would listen to his voice as to the position, the sphere, the duties of women in the world in which we live today.

The draft constitution was approved by the Dail on 14 June 1937, and de Valera dissolved parliament and announced a general election for 1 July, the same day that the constitution was to be voted on by the people. The economic situation was worsening by the hour. All but 9% of the country's exports still went to Britain, but their value, because of the economic war, had dropped by 50%. That year's trade deficit, Ir£20.7 million, was a record. In all, the economic war must have cost some Ir£47 million by the time it ended in 1938. Unemployment had also shot up alarmingly. Between 1931 and 1935 it rose from 28,934 to 138,000. Some of this rise was due to the fact that in order to qualify for the new doles introduced by the de Valera government, small farmers had to sign on at labour exchanges as unemployed. But by concentrating on the constitutional issue, de Valera kept the electorate's mind from this inconvenient fact as adroitly as he maintained that the constitution solved all the problems concerning partition and the Republican aspirations of the IRA.

In addition, the election was the first to be held under the terms of the constituency revisions decreed by a Cabinet committee which de Valera himself had set up after the 1933 election. The committee consisted of himself, Seán Lemass, Seán T. O'Ceallaigh and Jim Ryan. It abolished the six university seats, four of which had been in Fine Gael hands, and overall reduced the number of seats from 153 to 138. One of his principal opponents in the Dail, Frank McDermott, did not stand.

Despite the advantages conferred by the constitution's deflection of public attention from economic issues, and the constituency committee's revisions, de Valera did not do well at the poll. In party terms he lost his overall majority, falling from 80 seats to 69, and had to rely on Labour support. The constitution passed narrowly, by 685,105 votes to 526,945. Some 31% of the electorate did not vote, and spoiled papers were unusually high at approximately 170,000. It is thought that this result was contributed to by many Protestants either abstaining or spoiling their votes, thus ensuring the opposite result to which they intended, the passage of the constitution. This fact may or may not have had a bearing on de Valera's choice for the first holder of the office of President created by the new constitution: Douglas Hyde, the founder of the Gaelic League and a Protestant. The nomination was popular across the party divide, and he was declared to have been elected on 4 May 1938. By way of rendering unto Caesar, de Valera took him to the Phoenix Park after his election, ostensibly to inspect his new home, the old Vice-Regal Lodge, which had lain unoccupied since de Valera had got rid of James MacNeill, the then Governor General. However, the inspection completed, de Valera then conducted Hyde to another dwelling in the Phoenix Park, the home of the Papal Nuncio, Monsignor Pascal Robinson, who entertained his guests to afternoon tea.

The impetus given to the debate on women's rights by the constitutional controversy helped to bring about the formation of a specifically women's party in November of 1937, the Women's Social and Progressive League, with the objective of promoting the political, economic and social status of women. At the time, women were actively discriminated against in the workplace. Female primary schoolteachers had to resign at 60, thus losing their full pension rights. There were large pay differentials between male and female schoolteachers, as there were amongst civil servants and professional people generally. Women could not serve on juries, and in general de Valera's constitution reflected an ethos where a woman's place was seen as being the home. However, the time for feminism was not yet, and a general election held in 1938 was not a success for the Women's Party. Nor did it do any better in the one after that (in 1943), when again no feminist candidates were elected. However, de Valera and Fianna Fáil did do extremely well in the 1938 election, largely because he was able to claim, although he adroitly allowed others to do it for him, that in the words of his Tanaiste (deputy prime minister), Seán T. O'Ceallaigh: 'In the past six months, look how we whipped John Bull every time. Look,' thundered O'Ceallaigh, with perhaps unconscious regard for John Bull's gender, 'at the last agreement we made with her, we won all around us. We whipped her right, left and centre, and with God's help, we shall do the same again.'

The whipping and the agreement to which O'Ceallaigh was referring was the arrangement which de Valera came to with Neville Chamberlain, the British Prime Minister, on 25 April 1937, whereby the economic war was brought to an end, and Ireland got back the ports which had been ceded to Britain under the terms of the treaty of 1921. Possession of these ports enabled Ireland to stay neutral during World War II.

While the effects of the economic war fell most heavily on cattle-producing Irish farmers, it was not without impact on the British economy also. Britain did collect the lost annuities through increased tariffs but, as papers such as the *Manchester Guardian* and *The Economist* pointed out in increasingly critical tones, there was a fall-off in trade. De Valera heightened fears by indicating that this fall-off could increase. In the autumn of 1934 he let it be known that the Irish were thinking of replacing their British coal imports with coal from Germany and Poland. As we will see, this proposal was more aspirational than real where the Germans were concerned, but the British did not know this and fears of a serious loss to their coal industry led to a break in the diplomatic impasse. In January 1935 it was agreed that Britain would increase its cattle imports by one-third and that Ireland would increase its imports of coal from the United Kingdom. Later that year, at a League of Nations meeting in Geneva in October, Joseph Walshe delivered a message from de Valera to Sir Anthony Eden, the British Foreign Secretary, to the effect that Dublin would be receptive to an initiative from Britain on the ports issue and the ending of the economic war. The possibility of such an initiative occurring improved a little later when, as a result of a British general election, Malcolm MacDonald, a son of Ramsay MacDonald, replaced J.H. Thomas as Dominions Parliamentary Secretary. Thomas, and indeed many members of the Cabinet's Irish Situation Committee, including Ramsay MacDonald himself, had been openly hostile to de Valera. MacDonald senior was a friend of the prominent Unionists Lord and Lady Londonderry, and according to one Irish historian, the words 'lunatic', 'visionary', 'dreamer', and 'crank' were sprinkled through the letters, diaries, and minutes of the committee members as epithets describing de Valera, who was considered as great a troublemaker as Gandhi.[53]

However, young MacDonald (he was only 34 at the time) felt that it might be a good idea to tease out the approach Walshe had made to Eden. The Italian campaign in Abyssinia, and the fact that Hitler was rearming Germany, provided a backdrop against which it was clearly inadvisable that 'Ireland might become an enemy'. Accordingly, MacDonald obtained the permission of Stanley Baldwin, the new British Prime Minister, for a meeting with de Valera in the Grosvenor Hotel, London, as de Valera passed through the city en route to Geneva to visit an eye specialist. In order to keep the meeting a secret from pro-Unionist members of the Cabinet, like Lord Hailsham, a member of a family in which anti-Irish Nationalist sentiment was almost an article of faith, MacDonald was conveyed to de Valera's room by the Irish High Commissioner to London, J.W. Dulanty, via the tradesmen's entrance, through the kitchens, and up the servants' back stairs. The ensuing conversation proved as circuitous as the route taken to the meeting, but provided the basis nevertheless for further contact.

MacDonald secured from the Imperial Defence Committee a report which concluded that 'Provided improved relations are assured, despite the risks involved, it would be desirable to hand over the complete responsibility for the defence of the reserve ports to the Irish Free State.' However, little progress was made on the basis of this judgement between a meeting of the Irish Situation Committee on 12 May 1937, and 24 November of that year, when de Valera decided to overlook the difficulties which had arisen in the interim, and contacted Chamberlain, who had succeeded Baldwin as prime minister, through MacDonald, suggesting that the way to proceed was via inter-governmental meetings.

Hitherto, talks had foundered on the question of partition, and on British objections to de Valera's constitution. The Articles governing the King, Articles 2 and 3, and the implications of external association had all ruffled feathers. But MacDonald argued successfully that it was wiser to ignore these irritations rather than send the tortuous peace process off the rails. His approach was greatly furthered by Neville Chamberlain's appeasement policy. Chamberlain saw the necessity of having a friendly Ireland at his back as the spectre of an increasingly hostile Germany arose before him, and thought that in an Irish settlement 'the great gain would be that the attitude and atmosphere in Eire would be altered'. He opted for direct inter-governmental talks with de Valera and his ministers on outstanding issues. This time de Valera did not do as he had done during the Treaty negotiations and stay at home. He went to London with an Irish delegation, which included Seán Lemass, Industry and Commerce; Seán MacEntee, Finance, and James Ryan, Agriculture. Curiously, he did not bring the minister responsible for the ports, his close ally Frank Aiken, the Minister for Defence. One explanation for this is thought to be the fact that Aiken was generally regarded as the embodiment of the IRA tradition in the Cabinet. By leaving him at home and making frequent references to the danger of allowing concessions which might assist in an IRA recrudescence, de Valera may have been artfully adopting an argument of Michael Collins's that, instead of being sent to London to negotiate the Treaty, he should have been left in Dublin, depicted as a figure of menace, who would reject any compromise forced on the Irish delegation.

De Valera's team was confronted by Chamberlain himself; MacDonald; Hailsham; the Chancellor of the Exchequer, Sir John Simon; the Home Secretary, Thomas Inskip; the Minister for Agriculture, Stanley Morrison; the President of the Board of Trade, Oliver Stanley; and the Minister for the Co-Ordination of Defence, Sir Samuel Hoare. During the talks, which began on 17 January 1938, de Valera proceeded as though he believed partition to be the main issue, although, as we shall see later, he had in effect declared the border to be irrevocable, and abandoned the northern Nationalists to the tender mercies of the Unionists. De Valera also sought to induce Roosevelt to put pressure on Chamberlain to concede Irish demands. Roosevelt reacted by merely instructing the American Ambassador to the Court of St James, Joseph Kennedy, to inform the Prime Minister that he would be pleased 'if reconciliation could be brought about'.

After much fruitless talk across the table about partition, and much contro-versy away from the conference table concerning it, an agreement was finally reached on 25 April. Ireland got back the ports without conceding the defence agreement which the British had originally sought. Chamberlain, however, finally accepted a further judgement from his military advisers that 'it would be preferable to waive assistance on a formal undertaking which might be politically impractical for Mr de Valera to give, and which would not necessarily have any value in the event, by so doing we could secure a satisfactory agreement with Ireland'. Britain thus waived any rights which they could have claimed from Ireland during the war under the Treaty provisions. The British also agreed to forgo their demands that de Valera make some concession on allowing access to southern markets for Six Counties goods. De Valera declared that 'the six county Government had shown no inclination to treat the majority justly', and until it did so, he saw no reason why it should be presented with free entry into the main Irish market. Throughout the talks, he maintained that the Irish had no rights to give away and that they were merely recovering what had wrongfully been taken away from them. Neither did he make any concession on the 26 counties' ordinary protectionist duties. Only the penal duties imposed by both sides at the commencement of the economic war were removed, on a single payment of £10 million by the Irish.

In a letter to Chamberlain de Valera made a revealing comment about how he saw the two parts of Ireland: 'Our present Constitution represents the limits to which we believe our people are prepared to go to meet the sentiments of the Northern Unionists.'[54] Decoded, this meant the limits to which de Valera was prepared to go. He was not willing to take on the Church in drawing up some other constitution which might have conceded the Protestant liberty of the individual, even though in the talks he had thrown out a suggestion that the parties might explore the possibility of 'entry into the parliament here of the present representatives of the parliament in Dublin'. Thus in effect de Valera's vision of his state was a mirror image of Craigavon's 'Protestant parliament for a Protestant people'. The 26 counties were to form a Catholic state for a Catholic people, albeit a fairer and more benign one where minority faiths were concerned than the one in the north. However, to be fair to de Valera himself, the stated reasons he gave for his attitude appear to contain a certain prophetic ring when set against the Unionists' behaviour towards major peace initiatives later in the century, notably the power-sharing executive of 1974 and the Good Friday Agreement of 1998. He told Chamberlain:

> . . . on the plan proposed, Lord Craigavon and his colleagues could at any stage render the whole project nugatory and prevent the desired unity by demanding concession to which the majority of the people could not agree. By such means unity was prevented in the past, and it is obvious that under the plan outlined they could be used again.

De Valera's diplomatic successes angered the Unionists, whom Chamberlain placated by coming to an agreement with Craigavon which conceded benefits to the northern statelet on agricultural subsidies and increases in Northern Ireland's share of British armament manufacture. Dealing with Chamberlain direct was probably far more to Craigavon's taste than having to accept concessions from the hand of de Valera. As it was, as we shall see in due course, he was able to turn the Chamberlain–de Valera negotiation to electoral advantage. So too was de Valera.

Within two months of concluding the agreement, de Valera went to the country again, on 17 June. He secured 77 seats, which gave him a majority of 16 over all the other parties, thus enabling him to dispense with the services of Labour, and placing him in a position whereby he managed to remain in power for a further ten years, helped rather than hampered by the tensions arising from the outbreak of world war a little over a year later. He also used his increased parliamentary strength to launch an anti-partition campaign ostensibly designed to appeal to British public opinion, in reality to placate those within his own party who were disappointed at the lack of substantive progress on partition. Given de Valera's and Craigavon's positions on the issue, the campaign has to be evaluated as being for the optics rather than actuality. Nevertheless, with de Valera's backing, an Anti-Partition League was formed, and throughout 1939 much speechifying ensued before darker and all too real actors shouldered the League off the stage.

FOUR

OURSELVES (VERY MUCH) ALONE

(NEUTRALITY IN WORLD WAR II)

One of the ironies of de Valera's career was the fact that, for a man who prided himself on his own and his country's role in international affairs, nothing contributed so much to his reputation as his performance in removing both himself and Ireland from the international stage during one of the most important, and critical, periods of the twentieth century – World War II. Understandably his utilisation of the opportunities provided by the Treaty to keep Ireland neutral in that terrible conflict earned him both more praise and more criticism than came his way in the civil war era because of his opposition to the Treaty in the first place. One of his most implacable foes throughout the war years was a principal architect of the Treaty, the British Prime Minister, Winston Churchill.

He likened the giving up of the ports to handing back Malta to Italy and Gibraltar to Spain. In the course of the debate on the conclusion of the economic war he said in the House of Commons (5 May 1938):

> These ports are, in fact, the sentinel towers of the Western approaches, by which the 45,000,000 in this island so enormously depend on foreign food for their daily bread, and by which they can carry on their trade, which is equally important to their existence.
>
> We are to give them up, unconditionally, to an Irish Government led by men – I do not want to use harsh words – whose rise to power has been proportionate to the animosity with which they have acted against this country, no doubt in pursuance of their own patriotic impulses, and whose position in power is based upon the violation of solemn Treaty engagements.

Another even more influential opponent was the man who had advised him how to circumvent American laws in order to launch the bonds drive which he eventually utilised to fund the *Irish Press*, President Franklin Delano Roosevelt. As we shall see, when the parts they played are explained, the drama of Ireland's wartime years also had a talented cast of supporting actors, diplomats, intelligence chiefs, spies and politicians drawn from several different countries. But the Irish neutrality play, *Cathleen ni Houlihan Stands Aloof*, was very much the de Valera show, a show moreover in which he had the overwhelming approval of his Irish audience, which included a large number of his civil war enemies. While there were widespread doubts as to Ireland's ability to stay out of the war, and a general expectation that she

230

would inevitably be caught up in the hostilities, nevertheless there was an overwhelming desire to remain neutral if at all possible. On 23 October 1939, Sir John Maffey, who was in effect, if not name, the British Ambassador in Dublin, assessed Irish attitudes as follows:

> The policy of neutrality commands widespread approval among all classes and interests in Eire. It is remarkable how even the 'pro-British' group, men who have fought for the Crown and are anxious to be called up again, men whose sons are at the front today, loyalists in the old sense of the word, agree generally in supporting the policy of neutrality in the war.[1]

As we have seen, the new Irish state began carving out a position of independence for itself in its infancy, taking initiatives such as those involved in joining the League of Nations in 1923 and the subsequent endeavours at the various imperial conferences which led to the passing of the Statute of Westminster in 1931, despite Churchill's accurate warnings that this might lead to the Irish dismantling the Treaty. Apart from the steps taken by de Valera to validate Churchill's forecast in regard to the Treaty itself, the abolition of the oath and the office of the governor general, and the nullification of the provisions concerning the ports, which made a neutrality policy possible, he had continued in the Free State mode of seeking as much independence in international affairs as possible. In 1932, having been elected President of the Council of the League of Nations, he condemned the use of force in international affairs and demanded international respect and support for the covenant of the League. Later, despite the risk of domestic reaction to what might be termed support for communism, he advocated the admission of the Soviet Union to the League and, in the teeth of strong Irish clerical support for Franco, backed the League's policy of non-intervention in the Spanish Civil War. He also backed the use of sanctions against Italy because of its aggression in Ethiopia. The distinguished journalist and historian Robert Fisk has judged that his disillusionment with the League of Nations drove de Valera

> into the isolationist camp, a status that was best expressed by a policy of non-intervention and neutrality ... His disappointment accentuated a pragmatic, almost ruthless sense of self-preservation which he applied to Irish Government policy from then on with ever increasing severity. The failure of collective security brought about an introverted perspective which defined Eire's continued independence – and the future unity of Ireland – as the governing principles in all matters of foreign affairs.[2]

There is a large measure of truth in that assessment, but the Free State, and de Valera, were on an independent course from that of the United Kingdom, or any other country, long before the League entered its death throes. The decision to repossess the ports, which pre-dated the League's expiry, and made neutrality possible, had its roots in the Irish independence movement.

However, as the League disintegrated and war neared, de Valera made statements in the first part of 1939 which indicated that the Irish Government would stay neutral in any conflict. He followed up a broadcast to this effect, made in February of 1939, with a statement to the Dail in May that 'we believe that no other position would be accepted by the majority of our people as long as the present position exists'. The 'present position' was partition. In all his dealings throughout the war, be it with the British, the Americans, or even the Canadians, he stressed the impossibility of abandoning neutrality. He would never allow Ireland to be used as a base from which to attack England, but there would be no question of returning the Treaty ports to Britain so long as partition lasted. (It is of course a valid speculation that even had partition miraculously ended, some other reason for retaining the ports and maintaining neutrality would have been found.)

In fact it was partition, rather than the ports, which led to the first great public Anglo-Irish controversy of the war period, before the war had even started, in May of 1939. The actual bone of contention, as it would be on a second occasion, in May 1941, was conscription. The background was as follows. In between making the statements on neutrality referred to in the previous paragraph, de Valera saw Chamberlain privately at Chequers, on 25 March, following the German invasion of Czechoslovakia, and, having raised the partition issue and the treatment of the Nationalist minority by the Unionists, was rapped over the knuckles by the British Prime Minister, who reminded him that when, a year earlier, he had been offered the opportunity of easing the situation in Northern Ireland by giving trade concessions to the Unionists he had refused to do so, and since then 'had done and said many things which had embittered feeling in Northern Ireland and made things worse than ever; in fact, he had so conducted his affairs that he had not got a single friend in Northern Ireland'.[3] De Valera in his turn reminded Chamberlain of what had befallen John Redmond after he trusted the British over unity and pledged the support of his followers to the Empire in the coming war.

A month after that meeting, both men were embroiled in a very public controversy over partition generally and specifically the issue which had destroyed Redmond's career, conscription. The row, which Hitler gleefully seized upon for his own ends, broke out after the Unionists demanded that the provisions of the Compulsory Service Bill, reintroduced by Chamberlain on 26 April, should be applied to Northern Ireland, a proposition which was of course anathema to the Nationalist community. De Valera had been planning a trip to America, to open the Irish Pavilion at the New York Fair. There had been considerable anxiety in London and Washington that he might use the trip to try to stir up Irish-American agitation against Britain over the partition issue, and Roosevelt had issued instructions to set up a tête-à-tête with the Irish leader, after a formal White House dinner planned in de Valera's honour, at which he had hoped to persuade his old friend[4] to take a more emollient view of Britain's problems. However, the dinner never took place.

De Valera chose to make of the conscription issue a major demonstration of his neutrality policy. He cancelled his American trip, protested to the British Government 'in the strongest terms' (*Irish Press*, 3 May 1939) and issued a statement saying that, as under the constitution the Six Counties formed part of the national territory, the enforcement of conscription would be 'an act of aggression'.

The Irish hierarchy also condemned the proposal, Cardinal MacRory being particularly strong on his people's right to resist, as did the Irish Trades Union Congress and a host of other organisations and Nationalist political leaders. Such an outcry was entirely foreseeable. At that stage there was very little knowledge in Ireland of the true nature of Nazism, the memory of the Black and Tans was still fresh, and the Catholics of Northern Ireland felt they had been given more cause to fight against rather than for either the state which actively discriminated against them, or the British Government which sustained that state. It was as if in our day the Israelis were to attempt to enforce conscription on the Palestinians to fight for the Americans.

No one knew better than de Valera, whose ascent to becoming president of Sinn Féin and presiding over the deposition of John Redmond rested on the conscription issue, just how live and emotive the subject was in Ireland. He was also keenly alerted to the possibility that any attempt to enforce conscription on an unwilling Six County population might easily trigger a 1916 situation which could lead to a recrudescence of IRA strength and an overspill of northern reaction south of the border. Moreover he had spent much of his term in office trying to throw off imperial shackles. Capitulation on the conscription issue would nullify much of his activity in this area. Per contra for the Unionist leader, Craigavon, it was imperative that he show that 'Ulster' was as loyal as he said it was. He had spent his term in office trumpeting loyalty while at the same time seeking any economic or social benefits which accrued to the 'UK mainland' for his statelet. Now was his chance to prove that his loyalty was to the Crown, not, as the Nationalists sneered, to the half-crown. There were also concerns amongst Unionists that failure to introduce conscription could result in Catholics, whom it was presumed would not join up voluntarily, taking Protestant jobs.

However, other influences were coming to bear on the conscription issue. Roosevelt came under heavy pressure from Irish-Americans to do what he could to prevent conscription and, worst of all, Hitler joined in the cacophony. Roosevelt had sent an open letter to Hitler, asking him not to attack a number of countries (31 in all) including Ireland. Hitler replied on 28 April, saying that Roosevelt had

mentioned Ireland, for instance, and asks for a statement that Germany will not attack Ireland. Now, I have just read a speech by de Valera, the Irish Taoiseach, in which, strangely enough, and contrary to Mr Roosevelt's opinion, he does not charge Germany with oppressing Ireland but he reproaches England with subjecting Ireland to continuous aggression . . .

Hitler also pointed out that Britain had troops stationed in Palestine. In the circumstances, an enraged Craigavon received little joy when he saw Chamberlain in London on 2 May. Chamberlain frankly told the northern leader that the Cabinet were alarmed at the force field de Valera was generating over the issue, particularly in America, even though, as Lady Craigavon noted indignantly in her diary, 'Ulster affairs have *nothing* to do with him.' Significantly, Lady Craigavon also noted that the military authorities had advised against going ahead with conscription because of the problems trying to enforce it would create in the Falls Road. Chamberlain put it to Craigavon that in view of all the difficulties, if he really wanted to help Britain in its war effort, he would not press for conscription. The discomforted Ulsterman had no choice but to accept Chamberlain's wishes, even though some Unionist critics took the opportunity to attack him at Stormont, suggesting that he should resign, seeing that the British Prime Minister accepted de Valera's advice rather than his.

It was an important first step in de Valera's campaign to remain neutral. Later in the year he took other initiatives involving both sets of belligerents, beginning with the Germans. The German Minister to Dublin was Eduard Hempel, who had been an officer in the German army during World War I, and taken a doctorate in law before entering the foreign service in 1927. Hempel, with considerable justice, has generally been portrayed as being a career diplomat who believed from the outset that de Valera was sincere about maintaining neutrality, and that he would confront all comers in doing so, particularly his internal dissidents, the IRA. Hempel convinced Hitler of these facts, judging that de Valera was 'the only recognised political leader of larger stature'.[5] Hitler's own opinion of de Valera was also correct: he believed that for any policy to succeed where Ireland was concerned, de Valera's agreement was essential. This belief, coupled with Hempel's repeated insistence that the Abwehr should stay off his turf and desist from clumsy efforts to put German spies in touch with the IRA, in addition to the more compelling circumstance that the Germans were not in a position to invade Ireland successfully, induced the Nazis to decide that Irish neutrality should be respected. By way of encouraging this belief, the Irish at the war's outset also played the Irish-American card, Joseph Walshe informing Hempel on 26 August 1939 that Ireland wanted to stay neutral, unless she was attacked first, perhaps, he shrewdly indicated, by bombing. But, he assured Hempel, Ireland had no intention of concluding an Anglo-Irish alliance. The Irish-Americans would not favour such a tie-up and they could also be counted on to use their influence against any British attempt to invade Ireland. Implicitly of course they could also be counted on to oppose any German invasion. The Irish appreciation of the threat posed by the Luftwaffe would later prove to be soundly grounded, but the Irish policy stance was officially accepted by Berlin. Hempel was instructed by cable three days later:

In conformity with the previous friendly relations between the two countries, the German Government will refrain from all hostile activity towards Irish territory and will respect

234

Ireland's integrity provided that for her part Ireland will observe strict neutrality towards Germany. In the event of war against England the German Government will do its utmost to reduce to a minimum the resulting unavoidable disadvantage for Ireland and Irish trade. Germany is entirely clear as to the difficulties facing Ireland in consequence of her geographical position.[6]

Substantively this continued to be Germany's position throughout the war, although various low-grade German fifth column plans were attempted but little of substance was achieved. These attempts, which will be examined in context, had their origins in challenges to Hempel's analysis in the German Foreign Ministry. The authors of these challenges were powerful men, including the Foreign Minister, von Ribbentrop, and Woermann, the Under-Secretary of State, who drafted a memorandum on 10 February 1940 stating that 'by reason of their militant attitude towards England, the IRA is Germany's natural ally'. He also reasoned that as Fianna Fáil and the IRA were *ad idem* on the issue of Irish unification, the only difference between the two organisations was methodology.

Ironically, Hempel, regarded as the ultra-punctilious diplomat, who argued in favour of Irish neutrality and against underground intelligence ventures, was himself the architect of a number of intelligence initiatives which had serious consequences for the Allies. According to an authoritative work by a distinguished army officer, Colonel John Duggan, Hempel's information was behind the German successes in scotching the Dieppe raid in August 1942 and the Arnhem airborne landings in September 1944.[7] On 26 August 1939, de Valera took the initiative in Irish–German relationships by having Joseph Walshe contact Hempel to inform him of the ground rules which were to govern Ireland's neutrality and her attitude to Germany throughout the war.

Walshe informed Hempel that Ireland would remain neutral unless she were attacked, perhaps by bombs being dropped on an Irish town. But pointedly he indicated that the Irish Government did not expect this to happen. It would not be in the German interest, and above all, Irish-American influence, which was at the time strongly against an American–British alliance, would turn against the Germans. The Irish Government expected that because of the Irish-American factor the Germans would do everything they could to avoid violating neutrality. Walshe sought an understanding that in any German act of war against Britain, involving Ireland, suffering be kept to a minimum. The Irish sought a formal declaration from Germany which would disavow any aggressive intent, and express sympathy for Ireland and her national aims, mentioning if necessary Northern Ireland, and stating that Germany regretted Irish suffering and would attempt to keep this to the unavoidable minimum. Finally, Germany was urged to avoid interning Irish nationals in case of war. Three days later, Ribbentrop cabled Hempel, authorising him to make the declaration quoted above and in addition to tell de Valera that

In accordance with the friendly relations between ourselves and Ireland we are determined to refrain from any hostile action against Irish territory and to respect her integrity, provided that Ireland for her part maintains unimpeachable neutrality towards us in any conflict. Only if this condition should no longer obtain, as a result of a decision by the Irish Government themselves, or by pressure exerted on Ireland by other quarters, should we be compelled to safeguard our interests . . . in the sphere of warfare.

You are requested to deliver this statement in clear yet definitely friendly terms and in doing so you can refer (without expressly mentioning Northern Ireland) to the wide sympathy felt in Germany for Ireland and the national aspirations of the Irish people.

Hempel carried out his instructions, meeting with de Valera on 31 August 1939. After the meeting, he reported to Berlin that 'the Government's aim was to remain neutral', adding the highly significant proviso that in the circumstances the Irish would have to 'show a certain consideration for Britain which, in similar circumstances, they would also show to Germany'. Barring a few alarums and excursions, the Germans accepted this position for the duration of the war. As Joseph Carroll has noted: 'It was, after all, quite an achievement for German diplomacy. For one of the countries of the British Commonwealth headed by the king to remain neutral, and German diplomacy right through the war worked for the continuance of this state of affairs.'[8]

British diplomacy, on the other hand, worked (as did American and Canadian) throughout the war to achieve a discontinuance of this state of affairs. On paper, the British should have had no difficulty in achieving their objectives. Leaving aside Britain's strength and proximity to Ireland, Ireland's economic dependence on Britain was almost total. All Ireland's coal came from Britain, as did more than 90% of its iron piping and almost 80% of its cattle feed; the Irish relied on British shipping for most of its imports, petrol, timber, maize and wheat. Ninety per cent of Ireland's exports went to England; 50% of her imports came from there. On top of this trade dependence, almost all Ireland's foreign reserves (£200 million) were in British securities. Militarily speaking, the position was, if anything, worse. The Irish had four fighter planes, Gloster Gladiators, which were supplemented the year after war broke out by six Hawker Hinds, used as trainers. The other aircraft available to the Irish, for example, a few Walrus sea planes, would not have troubled either the Luftwaffe or the RAF. Naval preparations were almost nonexistent, reflecting the continuing Irish blind spot concerning the fact that Ireland is surrounded by water, with all the potential dangers and disadvantages this circumstance creates, in the development of a fisheries industry for example. Naval patrol vessels consisted of two former British gun boats, one of which had been used to shell the 1916 insurgents, and a handful of torpedo boats. The Irish army, of roughly 20,000 men, was equipped with rifles, machine-guns, and a few field pieces.

These were meagre enough resources with which to contemplate repelling a modern invader. But, following warnings from the Minister for Finance, Seán MacEntee, that an increase in defence spending would lead to an increase in taxation, the Government actually cut back on defence. On 1 December 1939, the Government decided to reduce the army strength by about 4,000 men. There was in addition an auxiliary local defence force of around 100,000 men. But there were only rifles for some 20,000 of these at the war's outset. An Irish army historian has judged that 'The country was almost defenceless when the Second World War broke out. The forces were inadequate and neither trained nor equipped for war. Defence matters were not taken seriously ... the financial position of officers and men was acknowledged to be unsatisfactory.'[9] The use of the word 'unsatisfactory' indicates the extent to which the English custom of understatement had taken root across the Irish Sea. For example, a common or garden private was supposed to be paid 14s. a week, which in today's currency would be something of the order of 70p. In fact, with deductions for social welfare payments, laundry and haircuts, actual take-home pay fell below 13s. When, with breathtaking generosity the Government sanctioned a rise of one shilling a week in 1942, only sixpence of this was paid there and then, with payment of the rest held over until the end of the war.

However, this military weakness was turned to good effect by de Valera. Firstly, the economies in defence spending meant that, although little good use was made of the monies saved, Ireland came out of the war relatively better off than other neutral countries with wealthier economies. Secondly, he made a strength out of his weakness by claiming that the only course open to him in the circumstances was neutrality. The country's military condition, however, was rather like de Valera's own physical condition at this stage. Blind, in his sixties, he possessed reserves of physical strength, will power and political initiative which made him a formidable opponent. In the same way, Irish soldiers fighting in the defence of their homeland against the backdrop of the Irish tradition of military prowess and expertise, particularly in guerrilla warfare, would have given a good account of themselves, although realistically the Irish could not have expected to hold out indefinitely against either an Allied or a German onslaught.

On the British side, the fortunes of war brought de Valera's greatest English critic back to the corridors of power: Winston Churchill returned to the Cabinet as First Sea Lord. The war was only two days old when Churchill began a search, not merely for the return of the ports, but into the entire basis of Irish neutrality. The pursuit of both objectives became increasingly pressing as German U-boats began sinking British ships, including (on 14 October) the prestigious battleship *Royal Oak* at Scapa Flow, in Scotland. U-boat successes (in the first two weeks of hostilities alone, the Germans sank 28 British ships) meant that the Irish ports in general, and in particular the sheltered anchorage at Lough Swilly in Northern Ireland, became highly desirable. The southern ports would have increased the British anti-submarine range by 100 or more miles, and forced the U-boat wolf packs under the surface to a far greater extent than the manner in which they were in fact able to operate. Throughout the war, several sightings of U-boat sinkings off the Irish coast were reported. These were severely practical considerations.

But psychologically and emotionally, the Treaty architect and imperialist Winston Churchill was completely at odds with the man he regarded as the Treaty wrecker and back-stabber of Britain, Eamon de Valera. After Sir William Malkin, the Foreign Office's law officer, had pointed out that if 'Eire' was to be regarded as a neutral, and if de Valera was 'determined to be really neutral, there is from the legal point of view no more to be said',[10] Churchill sent the Foreign Office the following rocket:

> So far as 'legality' counts the question surely turns on whether 'Eire is to be regarded as a neutral state'. If this is conceded then the regular laws of neutrality apply. But is the neutrality which Mr de Valera has proclaimed a valid condition, and on all fours with, the neutrality of, say, Holland or Switzerland?
>
> It is to this point that attention should first be directed. What is the international juridical status of Southern Ireland? It is not a Dominion. They themselves repudiate this idea. It is certainly under the Crown. Nothing has been defined. Legally I believe they are 'At war but Skulking'. Perhaps Sir William should examine this thesis.[11]

However, Sir Anthony Eden, who had moved to the Foreign Office, backed Malkin, saying of the law officer's report, 'I fear that it becomes every day clearer that it is scarcely possible for "Dev" to square neutrality with the grant of facilities for which the Admiralty ask. And at least 80% of the Irish people favour neutrality, altogether a pretty problem.'[12]

At this stage of the war Eden was not hostile to de Valera, at least not personally; the two men appear to have got on well with each other at League of Nations meetings. Certainly their relationship could be regarded as professional, and this approach permeated the philosophy of the man whom the Foreign Office chose to deal with de Valera personally for the war's duration. Sir John Loader Maffey had had a distinguished career before coming to Dublin. A graduate of Rugby (on being made a peer, he chose the title Lord Rugby) and Oxford, he had served as a political officer in India before being appointed Governor General of the Sudan in 1925 and then Permanent Under-Secretary for the Colonies in 1933. Throughout his career, he had acquired a host of honours and designations. None of the latter proved as difficult to define as did his Irish title. Before taking up his appointment, the British and Irish quarrelled as to whether he should be known as an ambassador or a minister.

The Irish wanted a full-blown ambassador, but the British baulked at the idea of appointing an ambassador to a country which it regarded as being part of the British Commonwealth. The Irish were worried about giving aid and comfort to dissentient Republicans by agreeing to any title which might seem to underline that status. However, the dispute was finally resolved on the basis of a British compromise that the envoy should be known as the 'United Kingdom representative in Eire'. De Valera accepted the wording, only after making the significant change of 'to' for 'in'. At the time, he was almost totally blind, and a little later, when he formally signed the Irish Cabinet minutes of the meeting which officially approved the Maffey appointment, he failed to note that whoever had typed them up had described Sir John as the 'British Diplomatic Representative in Ireland'.[13] The incident might be taken as symbolising Anglo-Irish relationships during the war years; it was not what was said that mattered in the end, it was what was done.

And so far as the British were concerned, the first thing to be done was to get de Valera to change his mind on neutrality. Maffey first saw de Valera on 14 September 1939. He wanted to discuss the Irish Government's memorandum containing the exclusions and stipulations concerning military activity that it intended to enforce on all belligerents, which the Irish High Commissioner in London, J. W. Dulanty, had delivered in London 48 hours earlier. The exclusions included the denial of the ports to the Royal Navy. Ireland's coastal waters and Irish air space were also declared no-go areas. De Valera, on the other hand, wanted (or said he did) to discuss partition, which he blamed for the fact that he had to contend with political enemies who were watching his every move to pounce on any gesture of rapprochement with the United Kingdom. At this meeting, de Valera began, as he continued to do throughout the war, by playing the Irish-American card with great finesse. As Maffey noted, while expressing 'great sympathy' for England, he managed to turn the conversation from the issue of confronting Nazism to the fate of John Redmond and the evils of partition. He asked Maffey to explain why the British did not curb Unionist injustices, and pointed out the advantages which would accrue from a United Ireland:

> ... the effect in America where the Irish element had ruined and would ruin any possibility of Anglo-American understanding! ... it was not a matter of religion. The petty tyrannies and oppressions now going on in Northern Ireland must lead to disaster. 'If I lived there', he exclaimed with heat, 'I should say "I'll be damned if I'll be ruled by these people". He went on to voice the fear that if the war went on for long, the danger of a physical clash between the rival forces in Ireland could not be averted ... 'My friends in America say to me "Why don't you take a leaf out of Hitler's book and work the Sudeten Deutsch trick in Northern Ireland?"'[14]

It will be noted in the foregoing that where the Irish in America were concerned, de Valera took an opposite tack to the one he used with Hempel in which he hinted at the possibility of utilising Irish-American sentiment on the German side. To the British, he indicated, however, that he was anxious to convert the sons and daughters of the diaspora to a pro-British line. After this meeting, Maffey informed London that 'the only line possible at present is to retain his good will and to render his neutrality as benevolent as possible'.

This in fact was roughly the line which the British took for the war's duration. Although there were junctures at which Churchillian fulminations and policy shifts aimed at securing Irish compliance, at the expense of forgoing goodwill – by resorting to devices such as a hostile press campaign and a severe economic squeeze – did seriously disturb relationships, the

British never attempted to change Irish neutrality policy by military means. Two other meetings with Maffey at this time are worth noting, as they set in train a series of *sub-rosa* defence arrangements between Dublin and London, which continued throughout the war. Maffey was sent back to see de Valera on 20 September 1939 by Chamberlain, who was becoming increasingly horrified at the shipping losses for which his handover of the ports was held to be at least partially responsible. He was also suffering from cancer, and before he died (in November 1940) became as hawkish towards de Valera as Churchill.

Maffey's brief was to give de Valera a letter from Chamberlain, outlining British fears about the issue of principle involved in a member of the Commonwealth becoming a neutral, and the linked issue of Irish bases (and coastal waters) having a damaging effect on British shipping. Maffey's reading of the letter to de Valera provided a basis for a number of suggestions from de Valera which were to prove of assistance to Britain throughout the war. British air crews who occasionally landed in Ireland, in Maffey's lyrical phrase 'like exhausted birds', were to be repatriated to Britain. German crews, however, would be interned. When U-boats were spotted, the Irish coastguard service would wireless this information uncoded, which meant in effect that, in de Valera's phrase, the information went out 'to the world'. De Valera also proposed the system whereby dumps of civilian clothing were established at Holyhead so that the thousands of Irish men and women who joined up during the war could change out of uniform before returning home. This procedure prevented the sight of khaki on Irish streets becoming the focus for anti-British sentiment. These concessions on Irish neutrality paved the way for a far wider range of co-operative measures which were introduced later in the war.

In May 1940, after a transmitter and other spying materials, including details of a German contingency plan for an airborne attack on Ireland, were found in a raid on the home of a Dublin businessman of German origin, de Valera officially informed the British that

> The twenty-six counties would fight if invaded by Germany and would call for assistance from Great Britain as soon as this appeared necessary.
> The British would not be invited until after fighting had begun. If they arrived before it, he could not be responsible for the political consequences.
> He was not under threat from internal dangers such as fifth columnists. All potential subversives were under surveillance.[15]

He followed this up by sending Joseph Walshe to London with the head of Irish military intelligence, Colonel Liam Archer, to give a number of assurances on policy and co-operation.[16] Instead of stressing the threat which the IRA posed to neutrality, because of partition, and the possibility that IRA grievances over partition might lead to serious German infiltration in Ireland, which was the line de Valera normally took when dealing with the British,

Walshe admitted that the IRA were not a serious threat. De Valera was prepared to deal ruthlessly with the organisation, Walshe said.[17] He added that 'the Government of Eire anticipated no difficulty in dealing with the IRA. In fact, the outbreak of specific disturbances were the kind of opportunity which they were seeking in order to crush finally the organisation.' As de Valera had allowed d'Arcy and McNeela to die on hunger strike the previous month, the assurances about ruthlessness carried weight.

The practical outcome of these meetings was that the British and Irish agreed to pool their information on all sorts of issues pertaining to the war effort. German and Italian official communications were routed through Britain; Shannon Airport was used by the British; British overflights of Irish air space and 'hot pursuit in Irish territorial waters' were sanctioned, as was the use of extra allegedly 'secret' transmitters in the British legation. There were also agreements about shared arrangements in shipping and petrol rationing, the joint purchasing of commodities and other matters which the British later took advantage of to put economic pressure on the Irish, apart from the continual supply of Irish man-, and woman-, power to the British war effort. This last, according to a note which the Secretary of the Government, Maurice Moynihan, appended to an Irish Government memorandum dated 24 May 1941, detailing Irish co-operation with the British, amounted to: '150,000 men to British bases. About 60,000 workers (men) had collaborated. We have 250,000 men in all our military forces, i.e. 400,000 in military defence of Ireland, and we could not do more if we were in the war, all our surplus production going to them.'[18]

There may be some debate concerning Moynihan's figures, but Irish assistance to Britain in the war years was unquestionably very considerable, and grew more so progressively as the pragmatic Irish decision-takers saw the war swing in the Allies' favour. However, the dichotomy between the military figures responsible for operational matters and the political leaders, Churchill in particular, which was to manifest itself throughout the war, was exemplified by the fact that as the operational arrangements were being successfully worked out in May and June of 1940, the British made a political overture aimed at getting de Valera into the war. London was motivated both by real and unreal considerations. The real were the very tangible string of German successes in Europe, and the continuing losses to U-boats. The unreal, a set of alarming reports about IRA Nazi activities in Ireland from Sir Charles Tegart, an Anglo-Irish graduate of Trinity College whose tenure as security adviser to the Palestinian police force, which had subsumed members of the Black and Tan corps into its ranks, had not inculcated any feelings of tenderness towards the Dublin regime. He wrote that 'the German gauleiters of Eire are already there . . . up to 2,000 leaders have been landed in Eire from German U-boats and by other methods since the outbreak of war'.[19]

This assessment was nonsense, but it found resonances with the dying Chamberlain, who felt that the Irish had betrayed the trust he had shown in handing over the ports, and of course with Churchill himself, who had become prime minister of the wartime coalition on 11 May 1940, just a matter of days before the Irish and British met to commence co-operation on operational matters. Churchill, who detested Malcolm MacDonald for his role in the ports handover, now chose him because of, not in spite of, his record as a de Valera appeaser, to make an offer to Dublin that neutrality should be forgone in return for an agreement on Irish unity. He had already tried and failed to get Roosevelt to send a flotilla of American vessels to Irish ports, as a warning against any German invasion. It was an election year, and Irish-American sentiment had to be taken into account. Pearl Harbor had not yet occurred, and the fires of isolationism would have been fuelled rather than quenched by what could be represented as an American aggression against Ireland.

The MacDonald mission, involving three meetings, lasted from 17 to 27 June. At the first meeting, MacDonald argued for an abandonment of Irish neutrality, saying that delaying until the Germans actually landed would give the German fifth columnists a chance to create such havoc as to render the Anglo-Irish operational plans nugatory. He wanted de Valera to invite British troops into Ireland to defend strategic areas. De Valera turned this down, arguing, correctly, that it would breach national unity. The day before meeting MacDonald, he had stood on a platform in Dublin flanked by the leaders of Fine Gael, W.T. Cosgrave, and of Labour, William Norton, appealing, successfully, for support for a nationwide recruiting drive for the Irish security forces. He had also set up a national defence conference on an all-party basis. It was really a fig-leaf body compared to a wartime coalition government, such as that which the British had created. But it was tangible evidence of the widespread support for neutrality which Maffey had reported finding shortly after coming to Dublin, and it made de Valera's refusal of MacDonald's offer sound more convincing. He asked instead that the British supply the Irish with arms so they could resist any German threat.

De Valera's response was not well received in London. Chamberlain, the former appeaser, was so angry that on this occasion it was Churchill who urged restraint when Chamberlain mooted the idea of taking back the ports by force.[20] MacDonald was sent back to see de Valera with a new offer:

> That there should be a declaration of a United Ireland in principle, the constitutional and other practical details of the union to be worked out in due course; Ulster to remain a belligerent, Eire to remain neutral at any rate for the time being, if both parties desired it, a joint Defence Council to be set up at once; at the same time in order to secure Eire's neutrality against violation by Germany, British naval ships to be allowed into Eire ports. British troops and aeroplanes to be stationed at certain agreed points in the territory, the British Government to provide additional equipment for Eire's forces, and the Eire Government to take effective action against the Fifth Column.[21]

De Valera objected to this on the grounds that if British troops arrived in Ireland without a German invasion, there would be trouble with the civilian population. He proposed instead that partition should end and that a united Ireland would then become neutral, with Britain and the United States guaranteeing that neutrality, and that American, not British, ships and troops should give effect to the guarantee. MacDonald turned this down, pointing out the difficulties of, amongst other things, creating an agreed constitution. However, when he returned to Dublin for his final joust with de Valera, he brought with him a document drawn up by Chamberlain which attempted to get around the constitutional difficulty. It stipulated:

1) A declaration to be issued by the United Kingdom Government forthwith accepting the principle of a United Ireland.
2) A joint body including representatives of the Government of Eire and the Government of Northern Ireland to be set up at once to work out the constitutional and other practical details of the Union of Ireland. The United Kingdom Government to give such assistance towards the work of this body as might be required.[22]

In return for this, the 26 counties were to enter the war, the ports were to be made use of, and British troops provided to guard them. There were also provisions about interning Germans and Italians, and British promises to furnish military equipment to the Irish 'at once'.

De Valera reacted by pointing out that Ireland was expected to enter the war immediately, whereas a united Ireland lay somewhere in the future. He also expressed the fear that if the Irish did as the British asked, the German reaction would be to bomb her savagely, so as to make an example to other neutrals. MacDonald concluded that de Valera was of the opinion that Britain was going to lose the war. The Irish Cabinet rejected the MacDonald overture, and de Valera, accompanied by Aiken and Lemass, conveyed the rejection to the English emissary. It was based on the fate of Redmond, episodes such as the Curragh Mutiny, and above all, the fear that no matter what the British proposed, the Northern Ireland Government would not agree. At this meeting, Lemass showed himself at least willing to tease out some possible line of compromise, whereas Aiken and de Valera took a resolutely negative line. Negativity was also the leitmotiv in Belfast. Chamberlain had sent a copy of the British proposals to Craigavon, who telegraphed a sulphuric reply: 'Am profoundly shocked and disgusted by your letter making suggestions so far-reaching behind my back, and without any pre-consultation with me. To such treachery to loyal Ulster there will never be a Party.'

Craigavon followed this up with a further telegram (on 26 June) saying: 'De Valera under German dictation and far past reasoning with. Stop. He may purposely protract negotiations til enemy has landed. Stop. Strongly advocate immediate naval occupation of harbours and military advance south.' It was 'not an inch' in both Dublin and Belfast, and that was how it stayed throughout the war. Indeed, the Unionists' anger at Dublin was such that, as we shall see, a toned-down version of Craigavon's proposals, i.e. the imposition of economic sanctions, was visited on the southern state.

Another grouping which also came to favour sanctions against the south was the Americans. Initially, both Roosevelt and the American minister in

Dublin were sympathetic to de Valera. But the diplomat concerned, David Gray, ended the war *persona non grata* with the Irish Government, and Roosevelt himself literally sent the crockery flying when Aiken visited him in the White House, and subsequently gave Ireland what he termed the 'absent treatment'. David Gray, who arrived in Dublin on 8 April 1940, was married to an aunt of Eleanor Roosevelt. He was 70 when he took up his appointment. He had been a journalist, a successful playwright, and had served in World War I as a liaison officer with General Mangin's army in France. He had also spent a year living in Castletownshend in County Cork, where he had taken a keen interest in de Valera's rise to power, and had commenced writing a book on Ireland, which was never published. Nor was a second volume, *Through the Green Curtain*, in which he took an even keener and far more hostile look at the Irish leader.

Many commentators have suggested that the American Ambassador's attitude to de Valera was purely personal, and that he was responsible for the deterioration in American–Hibernian relations. But his correspondence with Roosevelt,[23] and Cordell Hull, the Secretary of State, make it clear that Gray was completely *ad idem* with the American decision-takers on policy towards Ireland. Unlike Hempel or Maffey, he was not a professional diplomat, but a product of the American system whereby ambassadorships are conferred on people of means and either political, professional or business achievement. Their more direct American style often contrasts with that of their European counterparts, but on substance they rarely differ from official policies. On one occasion, after Gray had enquired of Roosevelt as to whether he should 'be careful' in laying down the American line, Roosevelt wrote back specifically telling him that he need not 'be careful'. In a sense, the antagonisms between de Valera and his Cabinet and those of the patrician Roosevelt and his circle were a rerun of those between Irish-Americans, including de Valera, and Woodrow Wilson. In both eras, the American presidents were enraged by the activities of 'hyphenated Americans', i.e. Irish-Americans, who, for historical reasons, were antagonistic towards White House attempts to bring America into war on the side of England against Germany.

Just as after America's entry into the 1914–18 war, Irish-Americans supported the war effort, and their leaders muted their criticisms of the British–US alliance, lest they be termed pro-German, after Pearl Harbor, Irish-Americans, though they continued to be largely sympathetic to Irish neutrality, abandoned their opposition to joining 'Britain's war', and rallied round the flag.

Roosevelt, who wanted to get rid of the political influence of the 'hyphen-ates', once wrote to Gray, indicating that he was in favour of providing a 'rude awakening' for Ireland, which had lived too long 'in a dream under the rule of a dreamer', so that Anglo-American relationships would no longer be disturbed by Irish-Americans.[24] He said: 'If and when we clean up Germany, I think that Mr Churchill and I can do much for Ireland and its future – and I think that he and I can agree on the method with due consideration of firmness and justice.'

Even now, 80 years after Gray and Roosevelt's correspondence, the conditions which govern American foreign policy have not changed fundamentally from de Valera's day. America is not a country, it is a continent, with an incredible variety of attractions and interests, so much so that cultivated, wealthy people can live rich and varied lives without ever leaving its shores. George and Martha Average American are generally content to leave foreign policy to the Washington decision-takers, with no greater concern than the possibility at the back of their minds that some inexplicable war in some hitherto unheard-of part of the globe may result in George Junior being sent home in a body bag. As this is being written, only approximately one-fifth of the membership of the American Congress holds a passport.[25] Consequently, apart from a relatively small group of policy-makers in Washington, American foreign policy is to a large extent in the hands of lobbies: the industrial-military complex, the Jews, the Cubans – and the Irish. The difference between the Irish and the others is that Irish political demands are opposed by another very large influential grouping – the British. Irish influence has on one momentous occasion proved stronger than that of the British Tories in influencing Bill Clinton's White House in 1994 to assist in bringing the IRA in out of the cold. This made possible a ceasefire in Northern Ireland, and ultimately led, in 1998, to the signing of the (American-brokered) Good Friday Agreement in Belfast.

In the early days of World War II, however, the isolationist Irish-Americans were directly at odds with Roosevelt's anti-isolationist, pro-British stance, opposing him directly over the lease-lend programme. An American official of the period penned an accurate assessment of the debate:

> The attitude of Ireland to the war is a crucial point in American public opinion with respect to the administration's foreign policy . . . up to now the public has gotten the impression that . . . lease lend aid [is being used] only as a sort of club to force Ireland into line with British policy . . . out of question to expect Irish to respond favourably.[26]

However, the official's recommendation for changing perceptions was overlooked. He argued that failure to include Ireland in the lease-lend arrangements was 'probably a mistake which should be rectified as soon as possible'. As a means of bringing home how isolation was viewed in Washington and London, an opposite course was followed: economic sanctions. These initially seemed to have been largely the brainchild of the Unionists, or at least one leading Unionist, Sir Wilfred Spender, the head of the Northern Ireland civil service. The Unionists of course had their own particular, Orange-tinted, view of Irish neutrality, seen through their prism of 'loyalty', and dislike of the southern state. Almost no description of the war years is complete without a quotation in whole or in part from the Belfast-born poet Louis MacNeice's sulphuric poem, 'Neutrality', in which he addresses 'the neutral island facing the Atlantic' off which 'the mackerel are fat – on the flesh of your kin'. Spender believed that those whom he held responsible for feeding the mackerel should be punished by a reduction in their own diet. On 9 November 1940, he wrote to the Chancellor of the Duchy of Lancaster, Lord Hankey, proposing economic sanctions against the southern state.

He wanted it brought home to the Irish that the loss of the ports 'would inevitably mean considerable hardships themselves'.[27] To this end he proposed the stopping of arms supplies, and a reduction in ships made available to Eire, on the basis that 'for every British ship which is lost due to the closure of the ports, the ship intended to bring imports into Eire should be diverted to a British port'. He pointed out that while there was severe rationing in the United Kingdom, petrol and a range of other products were readily available south of the border, and he followed this up with another letter to Hankey enclosing a copy of the *Irish Times*, which had 16 pages as compared to the six 'small pages of the *Daily Telegraph*'.[28] Spender turned the knife in the wound by adding:

> I am told that the tourist harvest in Eire is very good and that the brilliantly lighted towns which serve as such a useful landmark to the enemy airplanes in their attacks on Liverpool, and in their shipping prove a great attraction to those who have left the dimly lighted towns elsewhere.

These letters, which Hankey circulated, found their mark on 16 December. Sir Kingsley Wood, the Chancellor of the Exchequer, gave Churchill plans for restricting Irish shipping, cutting down, or cutting off, the export of food and goods of all sorts to Ireland, and freezing Eire's sterling balances. Wood also got his retaliation in first insofar as the propaganda war was concerned, by accompanying his proposals with a rationale for them: 'So long as we are subject to difficulties in the supply of certain things, we cannot in present circumstances go on giving Eire the generous share of them that we have so far allowed her.'[29] Churchill agreed, and shortly after Christmas, drastic petrol rationing was introduced in Ireland. Her bread supply turned dark, as wheat imports disappeared, and her tea pale as the ration of two ounces per person fell by half, and then to a half ounce per head, whereas Britain's remained at two ounces. Coal for domestic use disappeared, though it remained available in Britain where gas supplies for cooking were not curtailed, and though the soap ration was cut to four ounces per head per week, it was more than double that of the Irish one. As time passed, the screw was progressively tightened.

Coal needed to produce coal gas ran short, as did seeds, fertilisers and feeding stuffs, and a host of other products, leaving neutral Ireland materially worse off than belligerent Britain. The Irish met the shortfalls by a policy of improvisation. The self-sufficiency policies which de Valera promoted helped Irish farmers to increase the acreage under tillage. Wheat-growing shot up. Turf production was increased, and the industries established under protection went some way towards supplying clothing and footwear. Other forms of Irish improvisation also came into play. The efforts of the 'glimmer-man', the state employee who went around checking whether the rationed domestic gas supplies were being misused, were constantly frustrated by housewives who managed to cook food and boil kettles on tiny amounts of gas from taps which in theory should only have been used for specified periods. A combination of the sanctions policy and genuine wartime exigencies meant that the Irish lived out the war on the edge of a perpetual supply crisis.

For example, petrol supplies had almost run out when, on Christmas Eve 1941, a large tanker approached Dublin port only to discover that it was too heavy to clear the bar. It returned to Liverpool, to lighten the tonnage by discharging some of the cargo – and was sunk. As a result, the Irish petrol coupon was cut from two gallons to one-quarter of a gallon. The absence of petrol meant that gas-powered burners were sometimes used to power motor cars, albeit at very slow speeds. Very shortly their use gave rise to stories about drivers who used them to camouflage the fact that they were using black-market petrol such as the one about the Garda who stopped a motorist driving at high speed outside a country town. The motorist brazenly greeted the Garda: 'Hello, Guard, great things these gas yokes!' 'Yours is certainly great entirely,' replied the Garda. 'That's what I wanted to tell you. It fell off when you were going through Naas.'

But there was little of humour in the plight in which the 26 counties now found themselves, particularly in the vital areas of both shipping and armaments. Part of the problem was the Government's own fault – a lack of preparedness. As far back as 1935, civil servants in de Valera's own department had drawn up a memorandum warning of the consequences of a war. In plain language, the memorandum stated that 'the stoppage or serious curtailment of supplies of petrol and other fuel and lubricating oils would practically bring road transport in this country to a standstill in a short time'.[30] It also warned about what shortages of coal would do to rail traffic, and urged the Government to consider the development of wood- and turf-burning engines and the building of a factory to create the necessary spare parts. It warned also about what the lack of raw materials generally would lead to during a war. The memo's predictions were to be all too well borne out when war came, but were ignored by de Valera at the time of compilation.

As a result, the Irish made strenuous efforts to develop the bogs, and Dublin's Phoenix Park was transformed into a vast turf depot. But the absence of coal could not be so easily countered on the rail service. An oft told story[31] of the unreliability of the trains during the war concerns the guard who, after his train had broken down, walked along the track calling out: 'Who owns the bike in the guard's van?' When eventually a surprised passenger answered, 'I do' the guard told him: 'Get out and ride to the next town and ask for a new engine or we'll be here all night!'

The position arrived at in September of 1941 was no laughing matter. It was described in the Dail by a parliamentary secretary, Hugo Flinn:

We had cases where a couple of hundred empty wagons were sent off and simply did not arrive at their destinations. You had passenger trains which went out into the blue and remained in the blue. The end of it was that by the middle of October the railways had practically sat down, due to the amount and quality of coal.[32]

Another authoritative warning, this time on the vital area of air-raid precautions, made by Colonel J. J. O'Connell in a magazine article which was filed away in de Valera's department, was also ignored. Indeed, during 1939, the Cabinet urged that ARP expenditure be curtailed; for example, that no air-raid shelters were to be built outside Dublin.

Governmental policy at this time was a good example of de Valera's political acumen and financial meanness in action at the same time. Some indication of his preparedness for neutrality in the political sphere has already been given, the repossession of the ports being the prime example. And he met the war's outbreak by making 'the most extensive re-shuffle in the history of the independent Irish state'.[33] In the reshuffle he created two new departments, which were central to Ireland's neutrality during the war. One was the new Department of Supplies, with Seán Lemass at the helm, the other a Ministry for the 'Co-Ordination of Defensive Measures' which Frank Aiken took over. The conservative Seán MacEntee was moved to the Department of Industry and Commerce, and Seán T. O'Ceallaigh, equally conservative, but a less powerful personality, succeeded him as Minister for Finance. Paddy Rutledge took over from O'Ceallaigh at Local Government, and the hardline Gerry Boland, who was to become the nemesis of the IRA, succeeded Rutledge. Tom Derrig was given Boland's job at the Department of Lands, Oscar Traynor became Minister for Defence, and de Valera, who was already both Minister for External Affairs and Prime Minister, added the education portfolio to his remit. P.J. Little, the Chief Whip, became Minister for Posts and Telegraphs. The only man to retain his existing position was Dr James Ryan, the Minister for Agriculture.

The core of the reshuffle was the new authority which de Valera had conferred on Seán Lemass, whose responsibilities cut across other departments, and who in effect became the national improviser, creating new organisations to cope with needs as they arose, and somehow keeping the country limping along throughout 'the emergency'. Aiken's role was, in large measure, to prevent the country from realising how badly it limped, in his role as chief censor. He viewed neutrality, as he said in a famous memo, not as

he who is not with me is against me. In the modern total warfare it is not a condition of peace with both belligerents, but rather a condition of limited warfare with both, a warfare whose limits, under the terrific and all prevailing force of modern total warfare, tend to expand to coincide with those of total warfare. In cold economic and military fact it is becoming more and more difficult to distinguish between the seriousness of the two emergencies called war and neutrality ... A neutral perilously located in regard to the main belligerents may have to make more extensive use of censorship and other emergency powers than a belligerent situated a long way from the main theatre of war.[34]

And certainly the use Aiken made of censorship was extensive. Everything from bishops' pastorals to editorial comments, news reports, the comments of parliamentarians, had to be submitted to Aiken's department before publication, where the blue pencil was used copiously and rigidly (even on episcopal utterances) to ensure that the Irish public remained largely in ignorance of much of what happened throughout the war. Unlike the voluntary censorship practised by the papers in England, the Irish variety ensured that the people lived through the emergency, in the famous phrase of the historian F.S.L. Lyons, in 'Plato's Cave'. Although the Government was fully aware of what the Nazis were doing to the Jews in the Holocaust, or to Catholics in Poland and elsewhere, the public were not told. In addition to the press and radio, communication of all kinds, postal and telegraphic, was subject to censorship, phones being tapped and mail opened under the direction of one of the great spy masters of the age, Colonel Dan Bryan, who replaced Liam Archer as the head of G2, as military intelligence was known.

Apart from the censorship wall which protected the cave, there was of course the military defence perimeter, described above. But, as indicated, de Valera's tight-fistedness meant that this was far less well defended than it might have been. Not only did de Valera and his Cabinet decide that the army establishment was to be cut so as to achieve 'the smallest number of troops necessary to garrison fixed positions', it also decided that expenditure on ARP training was to be 'reduced to the lowest practicable level'.[35]

But even Plato's Cave resounded to the thunder of the German advance through Europe to the coast of France in the summer of 1940, and Cabinet meetings in May and June resulted in a much more realistic attitude being taken on the defence issue. By 1941, the Government had sanctioned increases in military strength to 42,000 and later to 50,000 men. The Cabinet also sanctioned the purchase of large numbers of heavy weapons, Bren guns, anti-aircraft guns, heavy artillery, aircraft even. The only problem was where to get them. The Irish flocked to the colours willingly, but those who could have armed them, the Allies, proved notably reluctant to do so, at least without concessions which would have ended Irish neutrality. Those who did offer arms, the Germans, were making an offer which, as we will see later, could not be accepted. Throughout the war, the Irish continuously entreated the Allies to supply them with weapons, and were, with some notable exceptions, almost invariably turned down. The penny-pinching of 1939 looks particularly short-sighted when it is realised that General Michael Joseph Costello completed a successful arms procurement mission to Washington in May 1939, during which he made firm arrangements to buy weapons. However, the Irish Government 'regarded the price of the weapons as exorbitant'.[36]

Both the British and the Irish must share the blame for the failure of an Anglo-Irish trade agreement to emerge from trade talks which took place between the Irish and British governments in 1940. The intention was to secure agreement on a wide range of issues, including shipping and exports between the two countries. The British were keen to maintain the preferential position for their exports to Ireland which had been agreed in the 1938 agreement that cost them the ports. But they also sought to prevent Ireland from pushing out the boat of economic independence generally, and in particular to prevent Irish profiteering on agricultural exports, as had happened during World War I. The Irish were represented by Seán Lemass and Dr James Ryan. Sir Anthony Eden led the British team. The British had agreed to meet Irish objections to what they termed low prices for agricultural produce by proposing a subsidy on cattle imports. This should have concluded the talks, which took place between April and December 1940. But this was a period when the war was taking a particularly serious turn for the British. Accordingly, as the talks apparently neared finality, the Irish chose to object to a part of the agreement which provided for port repairs and transshipment facilities for British shipping. Lemass and Ryan argued that the presence of British ships in Irish ports would be a breach of neutrality that would cause the ports to be attacked. The talks broke down on this issue.

However, even if they had not, it is doubtful whether the British would have honoured the agreement subsequently. Certainly, as part of the general sanctions policy, they broke another agreement on shipping which was made at the outbreak of the war. Lemass had been attempting to build an oil refinery at Dublin port, but was frustrated by the oil companies. However, the oil refinery project had resulted in Ireland having what was described as 'probably the most modern oil tanker fleet in the world when the war broke out'.[37] Though British-owned, the tankers were registered in Ireland. In a manner reminiscent of Chamberlain's handover of the ports to de Valera, de Valera himself transferred the tankers back to the British register without getting any concessions on fuel supply in return. Even if he had got them, it is doubtful whether the British would have honoured their agreement. Where shipping was concerned, the Allies' attitude towards providing facilities to convey goods to Ireland might be judged from the tone of a letter from Churchill to Roosevelt: 'Our merchant seamen, as well as public opinion generally, take it much amiss that we should have to carry Irish supplies through air and U-boat attacks . . . when de Valera is quite content to sit happy and see us strangled.'[38]

Of course, the publicity campaign which the Churchill government whipped up against neutrality played a large part in the formation of 'public opinion generally', and as we will see, far from sitting idly by while Britain was strangled, de Valera's government in fact sanctioned a high level of *sub rosa* co-operation with the Allies. But to worsen the effect of the denial of shipping facilities to Ireland, the British enforced the navicert system, which meant that in order to obtain a warrant or navicert, Irish ships had to call at British ports for examination on every voyage, be it to America or Greece, thus running the gauntlet of the German blockade, frequently with fatal results for the Irish crews. Some navicerts, which were stated to be a method of denying neutral shipping to the Germans, carried a stipulation as to routes, which sometimes added over 1,000 miles to a journey. The navicerts were later used to further harass the Irish, being subject to delay when required for Irish shipping. The harassment did not end there. Having secured a navicert, Irish ships travelling the Atlantic in convoy were generally allocated the most dangerous, outside positions. The seamen's dangers were added to by the decision of the Irish Government that if guns were provided by the Government, this would amount to a breach of neutrality, and Irish ships were attacked or sunk all through the war – by one set of belligerents or the other, though mainly by the Germans – with the loss of 135 seamen, quite apart from the deaths suffered by those who had joined the British navy. The lack of protection for individual seamen mirrored that of the overall Irish shipping position. The Irish Government, which had begun the war without an ocean-going merchant fleet, did not form a shipping company of its own until March 1941, when Irish Shipping was set up, mainly as a result of Seán Lemass's efforts. The fleet eventually reached a grand total of 15 ships, but their size may be guessed at by the fact that two chartered American Liberty ships, both of which were sunk, the *Irish Oak* and the *Irish Pine*, amounted to 20% of the fleet's carrying capacity. In all, some 20 Irish ships were lost, mainly the small coasters which ran the gauntlet of the Dublin–Lisbon–Dublin route.

Lemass's Department of Supplies was responsible for a whole range of enterprises born out of wartime exigencies. These included Grain Importers Ltd, Animal Feeding Stuffs Ltd, Fuel Importers Ltd, Oil & Fats Ltd, Timber Importers Ltd, and Tea Importers Ltd. After London insurance interests added their heightened demands to the general economic squeeze, the Insurance Corporation of Ireland was set up. But not all the squeezing was done by British interests. Irish banking interests too fulfilled the suspicion in some quarters that bankers owed their lineage to the Unrepentant Thief. One of the difficulties Lemass faced at the outbreak of the war was in providing credit for members of the Federation of Irish Manufacturers to finance increased purchase of stocks. The manufacturers needed credit, which in the first instance they sought from the Government, at workable interest rates. The Government passed the buck to the banks who resisted the approach, finally agreeing only after pressure from Lemass's department, and without reducing their rates of interest. This provoked a caustic comment from the department's 'historical survey': 'The Irish banks who, in 1938/39, would not advance money at 4 per cent to an Irish manufacturer for the purchase of raw materials, were at a later date prepared to gamble it for a mere 2 per cent on the survival of the British Empire by investing in British loans.'[39] Lemass took a hard line with black marketeers. In the three years 1941–3, he ensured that some 5,000 prosecutions were brought for breaches of the various rationing and distribution regulations.

By the end of the war, Irish Shipping had brought a million tons of cargo to Ireland, two-thirds of it wheat. Wheat remained in short supply throughout the war, although it was in this area that the Government achieved one of its greatest successes in self-sufficiency. Compulsory tillage orders brought the increase in wheat-growing from 21,000 acres in 1932 to 640,000 in 1944.

Experimentation of all sorts became the order of the day, the Government setting up a scientific research bureau, headed by scientists and an engineer.

One of the more notable experiments of the period, which did not become public knowledge, was conducted by Eamon de Valera's eldest son, Vivion, a major in the Irish army. Vivion, who had scientific as well as legal qualifications, was accorded facilities by the Irish army which might not have been available to any ordinary mortal. But as he thought that he could develop a substitute for rubber, he was given a laboratory in a remote part of the Curragh military camp, where he pursued his researches, known unflatteringly to his brother officers as 'Vivion's stinks'. An army unit was also placed at his disposal, headed by a particularly efficient NCO. However, despite these assistances, Vivion gradually came to realise that no matter what he did, there was one essential flaw to his product – it was porous. As this unwelcome realisation began sinking in, he also had to contend with the vexation of working without his customary complement of helpers, as one after another the soldiers allotted to him began departing on matrimonial leave. Were it not for the presence of his stalwart NCO, his morale would have cracked altogether. Then, *horresco referens,* his trusty subordinate deserted, and was arrested, like many another of his compatriots, trying to cross the border into the Six Counties to join the British army!

Shocked and angered, Vivion made no contact with his disgraced aide for some days, but then relented and decided that the man's earlier services at least merited some assistance, perhaps by way of defence at his court-martial. However, when he visited the detained man, he found that his only request was that he be allowed to remain in solitary confinement. One characteristic which Vivion had inherited from his illustrious father was a deep suspicion of human motives, and he conducted an investigation into the reasons for the man's unusual request. He found that, not knowing that Vivion's solution had developed the fatal flaw of being porous, the NCO had conducted an experiment of his own and discovered that when a large test tube was dipped in the solution, and allowed to dry, the coating apparently made a perfect condom. He had then sold these 'condoms' to his colleagues. Hence the spate of applications for marriage leave; hence the attempt to desert, from his comrades' wrath to the comparative safety of the British army.

A more serious attempt to supply Irish deficiencies occurred in March 1941. Aiken was sent to America to try to procure the arms and ships which could not be had from the British. Both Maffey and Gray thought the visit a good idea, because it would expose Aiken to the realities of American public opinion. Gray in fact furnished Aiken with several letters of introduction which Aiken left behind him. Aiken intended to see Roosevelt and other leading American decision-takers, but just as de Valera himself had done earlier in the century, he was also hoping to enlist the support of the Irish-American societies.

Back in Dublin, de Valera had authorised Walshe to inform Hempel that, while taking care to 'avoid the appearance of co-operation' with the Germans, he had instructed the Irish Ambassador in Washington, Robert Brennan, to, in fact, attempt that co-operation. Hempel cabled Berlin that Brennan's instructions were

> ... to make contact with Senators of Irish origin who are friendly to Germany, in order to take steps against the agitation against Irish neutrality ... Walshe indicated to me further that closer co-operation between the Irish element in the United States and the German element there, and also with the Italians, might be in the general interest, and he had also stated something like that to the Italian Minister. The Irish Government apparently believes that if the Irish element in the United States is properly used, it could constitute a powerful influence in our favour, likewise the Irish-American press.[40]

Mindful of the potential of Irish-American political clout, Ribbentrop instructed the German Embassy in Washington 'to cultivate as much as possible relations with the leading Irish there'. He was assured that contact had already been achieved and that 'considerable sums' had been spent in increasing the sale of the *Irish-American New York Enquirer*, and in making contact with the *Gaelic American* and other Irish-American journals. Understandably, this activity, coupled with Churchill's attitude to de Valera personally, and the Irish neutrality policy generally, was not a propitious background for Aiken's visit, which began on 18 March, just after lend lease had become law on the 11th. Aiken faced a hostile press conference immediately on landing, at which his declaration that he was neither pro-British nor pro-German was 'not well received'. Nor was he well received by Roosevelt. Just hours before Aiken and Robert Brennan were due to visit the President, Lord Halifax, the British Ambassador, got his retaliation in first. He informed Roosevelt that he knew 'from most secret sources' that Aiken was 'not alone anti-British but also hopes for, and believes in, German victory'.[41] As a result, Aiken walked into a barrage from Roosevelt, about statements he was supposed to have made in favour of a German victory, and about the need for Ireland to assist Britain.[42] Roosevelt's aide, Colonel Watson, was signalling the end of the interview when Aiken finally managed to get in a request for arms.

Somehow, he managed to persuade Roosevelt to make an offer of supplying the Irish with submarine-spotting aircraft. These would also have been of benefit to the British, because of the Irish habit of transmitting all sightings of submarines in 'clear', which was of considerable assistance to British submarine hunters. Aiken met the offer by saying that Ireland had nothing to fear from submarines, which was not of course correct, as German submarines did in fact sink Irish ships, but he wanted to make the point that Ireland's real fear was of invasion. He asked if Ireland would have Roosevelt's sympathy in the event of such aggression. Roosevelt replied, 'Yes, German aggression.' Aiken countered: 'Or British aggression.' This enraged Roosevelt, who shouted back at him, 'Preposterous!' Aiken riposted that if the idea was so outlandish, why therefore did the British not give a guarantee of non-aggression. Roosevelt again stated that what Aiken had to fear was German aggression, but Aiken replied, 'Or British aggression.' This enraged Roosevelt completely, and bellowing out another 'Preposterous' he seized the tablecloth on his desk and sent the crockery and cutlery, which had been laid for his lunch, flying all over the floor.

By way of assisting the Aiken mission, de Valera's traditional St Patrick's Day broadcast had contained an observation that by blockading each other, the belligerents were blockading Ireland. Delivered in Ireland, this statement was intended to be listened to in America, and Washington decided to bracket a response to de Valera's speech with one to Aiken's American tour. Gray was instructed to call on de Valera and tell him that he was going to be given two ships, but that the offer was being made to him, not Aiken, because

> as a result of the conversation which various officials of your Government have had with General Aiken, that the point of view of the latter ... would appear to be utterly lacking in any appreciation of the fact, which seems to your Government completely clear, that the future safety and security of Eire depends inevitably upon the triumph of the British cause.

Gray was further instructed to tell de Valera that America was pledged to support Britain, and to ask for a clarification of his blockading references in the St Patrick's Day speech. The US Ambassador pointed out to de Valera (whom he saw on 28 April) that the Irish were still importing three-quarters of what they had done in the same period the previous year – carried by British ships. Gray turned the knife in the wound by commenting that de Valera had 'made no contribution to the safety of British sea-borne commerce', and by pointing out, which was true at that point in the war, that a number of Irish vessels had been sunk by Germany, whereas Britain had never attacked Irish shipping. At this stage, de Valera did a mini Roosevelt, 'flushed angrily and shouted that it was impertinent to question the statements of the Head of a State'.

Gray's summation of the encounter was:

> The effect of a stiff attitude will be sobering. It is the only way to impress him that there are realities closing in on him. No one has ever taken this line with him. He always outmanoeuvred Chamberlain. I no longer hope to get anything from him by generosity and conciliation. He must be made to realise that it is possible that a situation is approaching, in which if it is essential to survival, his ports will be seized with the approbation of the liberal sentiment of the world, that he will have only the choice of fighting on the side of Great Britain or Germany.

Politically, Gray judged some years later, the exchange between the two men represented a watershed which 'marked a turning point in Irish-American relations. Washington at long last had begun to resent having its English policy made in Dublin. The recent "exchange of views" was a first step towards emancipation. For the next two years Mr de Valera made no more broadcasts to "our people in the United States".'[43]

Certainly, insofar as getting a pro-Irish, as opposed to pro-British, response on partition was concerned, 'English policy' prevailed for almost 50 years after the Gray–de Valera bust-up. Roosevelt began what he called 'absent treatment' towards de Valera to the point where he refused even to answer a Christmas card. For his part, de Valera decided to react as the Americans had done. He communicated his response to Gray not to the minister, but to the American Government. On 15 May, he turned down Roosevelt's offer of the ships, saying that the manner 'in which the offer is made, and the suggestion of implied conditions render it impossible for the Irish Government to accept. They cannot accept that the estimate of Mr Aiken's attitude and the criticism directed against him is just.'

However, Roosevelt outflanked de Valera by announcing at a press conference a couple of days later (20 May) that two cargo ships and half a million dollars for the Red Cross to buy food were on their way to Ireland. De Valera, who had not made his refusal public, caused a report to be placed in the *Irish Press* which, while it noted that no official comment was forthcoming from the Irish Government on Roosevelt's offer of the two Liberty ships mentioned earlier, mentioned that Aiken was in the United States seeking supplies. The implication was that the visit had yielded the ships. Roosevelt was evidently displeased with the Irish attitude, and the ships' handover was delayed throughout the summer, culminating in a refusal by Roosevelt (on 17 September) to sign a directive to the lend-lease authorities authorising the deal. It took intercession from John McCormack, the Democratic house leader, to get the ships transferred to Irish Shipping. Rechristened the *Irish Oak* and the *Irish Pine*, they were both sunk by German submarines, the *Irish Pine* on 28 October 1942, and the *Irish Oak* on 15 May 1943. De Valera did not protest to Germany over the sinkings and the Americans turned down any further requests from Dublin for ships on the grounds that the Germans were making war on Ireland, while at the same time using Ireland's neutrality against the United Nations. The Americans viewed the sinking of the two vessels as harming not only Ireland, but the United States which had lost the use of them, and argued that any further shipping transfers would have been subject to the same fate.

Roosevelt and de Valera would joust later in the war, most notably in the largely Gray-inspired 'American Notes' episode. But while the Aiken saga was still unfolding in America, a tragic event in Ireland underlined both the rationale behind the neutrality policy and the ever-present dangers of serious trouble erupting from the antagonisms of Northern Ireland. This was the carnage created by the German bombing of Belfast, which ironically was to trigger a huge controversy, not between Ireland and the Nazis but between Ireland, the Unionists and the Allies. Part of the controversy, and of the carnage, was caused by the same virus which had been at work in the southern part of the country as war approached – short-sightedness. Craigavon was of the opinion that the north's geographical position rendered it immune from German bombing, because the bombers would have to first traverse hostile

England and then cross the Irish Sea before they could unleash their lethal cargoes on the Six Counties. In making a pitch for rearmament contracts from the British Government, Stormont had assured London: 'it would hardly be possible to find in the United Kingdom any industrial area less vulnerable in time of war than Northern Ireland'.[44] A year later, in June 1939, a parliamentary secretary, Edmund Warnock, with responsibility to Dawson Bates, was still arguing that there was no need to follow the British example in forcing large-scale employers to build air-raid shelters. Belfast, he said,

> is the most distant city of the United Kingdom from any possible enemy base. It is 535 miles from the nearest point in Germany. An attack on Northern Ireland would involve a flight of over 1,000 miles. For aeroplanes of the bombing type, loaded, this is a very big undertaking. To reach Northern Ireland and to get back again the enemy aeroplanes must twice pass through the active gun, searchlight and aeroplane defences of Great Britain . . . In coming to Northern Ireland the attacking plane would pass over targets which would appear to be more attractive than anything the North of Ireland has to offer. Bearing these facts in mind, it is possible that we might escape attack altogether. But if Northern Ireland is attacked the above factors would suggest that at least we shall not be subject to frequent attack or to attack by large concentrations of enemy aircraft.[45]

Warnock actually returned shipments of fire-fighting equipment to Britain, saying they were not needed in Northern Ireland. As the war progressed, however, Craigavon became worried, and proposed that a committee be set up to advise what could be done to protect the population against air raids. But Dawson Bates argued against this idea, because it would put Stormont MPs 'in possession of information showing for example that we had not distributed gas masks on the scale we had promised, and that our shelter programme was far behind that of Great Britain'.[46]

The results of this were that air-raid precautions, i.e. the provision of either shelters or anti-aircraft weapons, were very badly neglected. When the Germans struck on the night of 15 April 1941, it is estimated that there were only seven aircraft batteries defending Belfast. The resultant death toll was horrendous. The authorities eventually placed the number at 745, but it could have been far higher. As Robert Fisk noted, 'even weeks afterwards, when the official casualty toll had risen above 700, corpses were being discovered in derelict houses, disembodied arms and legs, green with corruption, trapped in trees and in the guttering of roofs'.[47] As it was, the casualties were higher than those of the notorious Coventry raid which claimed 554 lives. If ever the Irish needed an argument in favour of neutrality, this was it. But de Valera's initial response was a notable breach of neutrality. He ordered the Dublin Fire Brigade to go north to help in putting out the fires. The gesture was appreciated at the time, as was the kindness shown to the thousands of refugees, both Protestant and Catholic, who poured across the border in panic, but the goodwill was not long-lasting.

In any other part of the United Kingdom, one would have expected the governmental response to such a calamity as befell Belfast on 15 April to run along the lines of evacuation of civilians, the provision of massively increased air-raid defences, and so forth, and to a degree these were undertaken, but only after some peculiarly Unionist reactions. As we shall see in more detail, Dublin too was bombed by the Germans a few weeks later, on 30 May, at a cost of 34 dead, some three times that number injured, and the loss of 300 houses. The predictable result was to increase the general desire to avoid further casualties by maintaining neutrality. But in the north the bombing of Belfast served to trigger off a confused attempt to uphold the status quo which could have resulted in further carnage and destruction, and which did have serious national and international consequences: a further attempt to introduce conscription. Its origins lay deep in the Unionist psyche. Cabinet records show that governmental meetings held after the tragedy devoted several hours to the question of how the large bronze statue of Edward Carson, which stood at the entrance to Stormont, could be protected against damage in the event of further raids. Before these confabulations had time to take effect, there were two further raids, on 4 and 5 May. The first raid killed 150 people, but unlike the 15 April attack, the bombs were concentrated not on civilians but on the shipyards and dock areas. Shipping was destroyed, water mains cracked, and the Harland & Wolff shipyard lost several months of production. In all, some 56,000 houses were damaged.

De Valera waited three days before expressing public sympathy with the Belfast victims. If he made any formal protest to the Germans, no record of it survives, but Cardinal MacRory did contact the German Ambassador, Hempel, and asked that Armagh, the ecclesiastical capital of Ireland, be spared. No official response came from the Germans, either to this suggestion or to one from Walshe that Derry should be left alone, but, remarkably, there were no more raids, although the Six Counties became increasingly bound up with the Allies' war effort. However, there was fallout. One of the consequences of the raids had been a nightly exodus (initially reaching almost 100,000 people, and then settling down for some weeks at an average of around 20,000) of panic-stricken Belfast citizens taking to the hills and the countryside around the city in anticipation of further bombs falling. Their plight was met in a notably uncompassionate fashion by the Stormont authorities. Dawson Bates, for example, in the course of presenting the scale of the requirement for billets to house the fleeing refugees, said: 'There are in the country probably about 5,000 absolutely unbilletable persons. They are unbilletable owing to personable habits which are sub-human. Camps or institutions under suitable supervision must be instituted for these.'[48]

But if the official human response to the nightly exodus was confused and lacking in focus, politically the analysis was sharper. The effect on the Government of the raids was to rekindle the fears of the thirties of some unity being achieved between Protestant and Catholic workers against the establishment. Now the poor of Belfast were voting with their feet against the government which had failed to protect them. There were also signs of a want of 'loyalty' towards the establishment. Fire-watchers were not turning out at night, or if they did, they did so unwillingly. Even in the immediate aftermath of the bombing, soldiers complained that as they laboured to pull the dead and dying from the rubble, crowds of able-bodied men stood idly by watching them. Industrial relations in the war industries became strained, and in the shipyards, workers refused to man the night shifts.

None of these manifestations of disaffection were new. Northern Ireland did make a notable contribution to the war effort, building 15,000 heavy bombers and 140 warships, some 123 merchant ships and 500 tanks. In addition, materials such as gun barrels, bayonets and parachutes were produced in large quantities. Perhaps unsurprisingly, food was also produced at a proportionately higher rate than in any part of the United Kingdom. Northern Ireland, after all, shares a fertile soil with her southern sister. North of Ireland servicemen contributed 4,735 lives in the many battles in which northern regiments fought with distinction. However, even before the major raid on Belfast, with its resultant exodus, the Stormont government had had cause to worry about the fact that there was 'no feeling of a quality of sacrifice throughout the country', in the words of John McDermott, the north of Ireland Minister of Public Security.[49] In the Stormont Cabinet's view, the way to generate this feeling was to introduce conscription! McDermott did concede that conscription would 'cause difficulties with the minority', but he felt that these would be less than those experienced during the earlier attempt to introduce conscription, and that in any event the advantages would outweigh the disadvantages. In fact, as the records of the period show, the only worry that the Cabinet had about the Catholic population of the island as a whole was that southerners did not take the jobs of conscripted Protestants. In reality, there was no possibility of this occurring. Of the 48,000-strong pool of manpower which conscription was expected to mop up, Catholics formed the bulk. Apart from the fact that the Catholics were largely unemployed, most Protestants were in 'reserve' jobs, and thus not liable for conscription.

All the contradictions of Ulster Unionist political and religious attitudes came under strain because of wartime conditions. On the one hand, the Protestant churches complained to both the Stormont and the British authorities about the provision of Sunday entertainments for the troops, because 'the sanctity of the day of rest and worship . . . is regarded among the citizens of Ulster generally as essential to the highest interests of the nation'.[50] On the other hand, the rate of venereal disease amongst the troops was the highest in the United Kingdom.[51] It was not the VD statistics, however, which curtailed the rate of enrolment in His Majesty's Forces during the war, but a shared reluctance on the part of both Protestants and Catholics to join up. Protestant reluctance was put down to a folk memory of the slaughter at the Somme during World War I, and the fear that if Protestants did join up, Catholics might take their jobs. Catholics, on the other hand, regarded the police with more hostility than they did the Germans, and felt no compulsion to serve under a Crown which they saw as the symbol of the unjust system they laboured under. And the Unionists took active steps to encourage Catholics in their belief that the defence of the Six Counties was in fact a buttressing of Orange defences.

The Ulster Defence Volunteers, set up by Craigavon as a local defence force, was effectively the B Specials under another name. So few Catholics were enrolled that a group of serving and ex-British army and navy officers, including General Gough, who had spearheaded the Curragh Mutiny, and Sir Shane Leslie, Churchill's cousin, signed a protest to Churchill denouncing the B Specials' enrolment as being 'pregnant with many evil consequences'.[52] Another 'evil consequence' of Unionist rule was unemployment. Harold Wilson reported to his Cabinet that:

> At the end of fifteen months of war . . . Ulster, far from becoming an important centre of munitions production, has become a depressed area. While other areas of similar size and industrial population have played an increasing part in war production, Ulster has not seen the construction of a single new factory. At the same time orders placed with existing firms (shipbuilding yards excepted) have been on an exceedingly meagre scale. [Northern Ireland's unemployment figures were] roughly equal to the percentage unemployment in Great Britain in 1932 . . . the worst year of the great depression. It would be difficult to find a more striking index of depression than this.[53]

Wilson made the telling observation that when a batch of 'Go To It' posters similar to those displayed in the 'UK mainland' were put up as part of the war effort, employers asked that they be suppressed because 'they would only cause discontent, owing to the absence of anything to which a loyal and willing population might go'. Part of the unemployment problem was not the Unionists' fault; the war had created a collapse in the linen industry, throwing some 20,000 women out of work. But certainly where industrial initiative was concerned, Belfast and the north generally had fallen on evil days compared to the era of industrialists like William Pirrie, who had built up the ship-building industry in Belfast's heyday. One of the Unionists' stratagems for cutting the unemployment figures was to send workers to Britain by the thousand.

But the absence of work was not the only problem confronting Unionist decision-takers. Even when war work was made available, letters intercepted by the censors show that it was carried out with a good deal of delay and dishonesty.[54] A complaint by a Protestant to a friend lamented that work rates amongst his colleagues were such that 'there is no earthly chance of our winning the war when so many only concern themselves over what they can make out of it without much effort'.[55] Other letters speak of workers being told to slow down if they attempted to do an honest day's work, and of the hardest part of the job in Belfast shipyard being 'killing time'.

The workers were not alone in their slack-jawed approach to the war effort. Other censored letters refer to managements spinning out the work by forcing their workers to go slow. One writer alleged that the main concern amongst the management at Short and Harland's aircraft factory seemed to be 'taking advantage of the present emergency to build up the place for peace-time production, and don't seem to give a damn about wartime production'. Strikes were commonplace. In one, during 1942, 18,000 craftsmen struck over pay, causing Churchill to express his surprise and annoyance to the north of Ireland Prime Minister, J.M. Andrews.[56] As many as 6,000 men were prosecuted for illegal strikes, and many were sent to prison. The shortage of skilled labour was such that the Stormont authorities issued work permits to between 6,000 and 7,000 citizens of Eire to work in the Six Counties, where many of them recorded with astonishment how little work they were expected to do.

Accordingly, the German air raids helped to create a sense of urgency concerning the deficiencies and indiscipline in the northern system, and when the British Government responded positively on 20 May 1941 to Stormont's ideas on introducing an 'equality of sacrifice' into the Six Counties, the Unionist Cabinet immediately telegraphed London that it was

> emphatically of opinion that conscription should be applied to Northern Ireland. It considers that in this matter a common basis for the whole of the United Kingdom is just. It further considers, particularly in the light of recent heavy enemy attacks, that the principle of equality of sacrifice and service underlying conscription is essential to promote the degree of corporate discipline which is necessary if our people are to withstand the tide of total war and play their full part in the national effort.[57]

Decoded 'corporate discipline' meant nipping potential concerted opposition to the ageing Unionist Government in the bud. But the Cabinet seriously underestimated the reaction of Nationalists to the nipping process. The fat hit the fire almost as soon as Churchill acted on the Unionists' telegram, the day it arrived (21 May), and announced in the House of Commons that the introduction of conscription to Northern Ireland was under consideration. In Ireland, both Christ and Caesar immediately protested. De Valera sent John Dulanty, the Irish High Commissioner, to Downing Street to convey his alarm and anger, and received a couple of Churchillian broadsides for his trouble. In the first (on 22 May) Churchill told Dulanty that if Nationalists wanted to 'run away' across the border, they could do so. To which Dulanty replied that the Irish were not noted for running away, particularly when they fought the English! To his credit, Churchill immediately conceded that the Irish were 'one of the world's finest fighting races'. But he thought it wrong that they were not on the side of the world's freedom fighters because of the 'ignoble fear of being bombed', and he pointed to the damage caused to prospects of Irish unity by the spectacle of the northerners fighting alongside the British while the southerners stood aloof. In a remarkably candid statement about his former prime minister, he told Dulanty: 'You should tell your Government that we are fighting for our lives, and owing to the imprudence of Mr Chamberlain, we are denied the use of the ports which were given you.' The ports provisions in the Treaty had been Churchill's own, and it was obvious that he still deeply resented their abrogation in particular, and that of the Treaty in general. The casting aside of the Treaty, he said, meant that 'since that date he had drawn the sword'.[58] He told Dulanty that the Irish were only staying out of the war because they thought Britain would lose, and that he expected that de Valera intended to do Britain as much harm as he could in the United States.

Dulanty was actually an old friend of Churchill's, but he got nowhere with him on the conscription issue. He had an even worse reception when he returned to Downing Street four days later with a message from de Valera which said:

> The conscription of the people of one nation by another revolts the human conscience . . . an act of oppression upon a weaker people . . . The Six Counties have towards the rest of Ireland a status and relationship which no Act of Parliament can change. They are part of Ireland. They have always been part of Ireland, and their people, Catholic and Protestant, are our people . . .

De Valera's biographers described the reaction to this claim on both the Protestants and Catholics of the north as one of Churchillian fury. He threw the text to one side and marched up and down the room, first threatening that if de Valera wanted a public answer to his message, he would give it in terms that would 'resound about the world'. He then denounced what he termed 'broken faith' over the Treaty. Ireland, he said, had lost her soul. Dulanty quoted him as saying that when he thought of John and Willie Redmond, of Kettle – one of the best minds Ireland had produced in recent times – 'When he thought of their courage and valour his blood boiled.' In the boiling process, Dulanty and his attempts at interjection were simply swept aside.

Churchill's rage, however, was that of a man who knew that he had lost this particular round of the never-ending Anglo-Irish encounter. Back in Ireland, there was all-party unity in opposition to the conscription proposal, with Fine Gael and Labour supporting de Valera.

Where the representatives of Christ were concerned, Cardinal MacRory led the charge for the Catholics of Northern Ireland, issuing a very strongly worded statement in which he warned that any attempt to impose conscription would be a disaster. He was joined in his protest by trade unionists and by Protestant members of the Labour Party. After failing with Churchill, Dulanty was instructed to call on Herbert Morrison to warn that there would be serious trouble if conscription were introduced. Resistance by northern Nationalists would be intense, and could overspill across the border. Hunger strikes could be expected, and a rise in support of the IRA, much as had happened in John Redmond's day when the British also went for conscription in Ireland. The Redmondite parallel was underscored when in the north Nationalist politicians drew up a pledge to be signed by Catholics which basically consisted of the same wording as that issued by the Catholic bishops during the 1918 conscription crisis. Signatories pledged themselves

261

'solemnly to one another to resist conscription by the most effective means at our disposal, consonant with the law of God'.

On the wider stage, both David Gray and the Canadian Prime Minister urged that the conscription idea was highly dangerous. Gray's personal view was that he would 'like to see them all drafted and put in the front line'; however, he warned the State Department that the introduction of conscription would 'seriously hamper the Opposition on which we must rely'.[59] Gray, while resenting de Valera's marshalling of Irish-American forces opposed to Roosevelt, had no compunction about making use of Irish opposition to de Valera. However, in view of Irish-American sentiment, he cabled the State Department that:

> Opposition leaders yesterday informed me that conscription without a conscientious objector's clause for minority Catholic nationalists will constitute a major irretrievable and probably fatal political blunder at this time and play directly into de Valera's hands with grave possibilities for American interests. They predict draft riots, the escape of draft dodgers to Southern Ireland who will be acclaimed as hero martyrs by three-quarters of the population and the fomenting of trouble by Republicans and Fifth Columnists. The clearest headed leader predicts that de Valera will seize the opportunity to escape from economic and political realities by proclaiming himself the leader of the oppressed minority and with the blessings of the Cardinal will rouse anti-British feeling and call a Holy War. I think it a very likely prediction. All classes of opinion here unite in condemning the move as calamitous . . . a repetition of the same fatal blunder made during the last war. Unless Britain is prepared from a military point of view to seize the whole country it appears to be madness . . . Eighty thousand Irish volunteers in [the] British Army will be disaffected. A Government, a popular majority and an army inclined to be friendly to Britain rather than to the Axis will become definitely hostile, possibly giving active aid to Germany . . .[60]

A copy of this went to London via Maffey, and another, minus the criticisms of him, was given to de Valera. He initially approved of it, but later in the day had a confrontation with Gray over the reference to the escape clause for Catholic objectors. He said that his government could not concede the right of another government whether in Ulster or elsewhere to conscript Irishmen. Gray noted this with some 'astonishment',[61] saying that de Valera had raised no objection to the clause when first shown the document, and pointing out that the issue at hand was not a discussion on partition. According to Gray's notes, the following exchange then occurred:

> DE VALERA: I didn't really note the clause, or grasp its significance.
> GRAY: Do you mean to take the position that Orangemen cannot conscript themselves?
> DE VALERA: Why should they? They can volunteer.
> GRAY: Some volunteer, and others need to be conscripted.
> DE VALERA: Don't say that; it's not true.
> GRAY: It is true. You rule this country. You are far and away its most powerful man and you have to take responsibility for what it thinks.
> DE VALERA: That is not so.
> GRAY: Are you trying to tell me that you insist on bringing up partition in principle in this

emergency and refuse to compromise in the interest of humanity and to save bloodshed?
DE VALERA: No, but I cannot ignore the conviction of the Irish people.[62]

It is ironic to find de Valera and the Unionist leaders taking a different view of the willingness of Orangemen to volunteer to demonstrate their much-vaunted 'loyalty'. Whether he really believed in his assessment of their eagerness to answer the call of Empire or not, however, is not the point. His joust with Gray was an underlining to the Americans of the point he had already made to the British in his telegram to Churchill: 'Catholic and Protestant are our people ...' Vehemently as the Unionists would have contested this point, neither they nor the British attempted to dispute the assessment which ultimately torpedoed the conscription proposals, that of the Unionists' own chief of police, the Inspector General of the RUC, Lieutenant Colonel Charles Wickham. Incredibly it seems the Northern Ireland Prime Minister, Andrews, had not consulted Wickham before a crucial meeting with Churchill and his advisers on 24 May in London. But Herbert Morrison, whom Dulanty had apparently lobbied with some success, asked the police chief for his opinion. Wickham blew the Unionists' arguments out of the water.

It is extremely doubtful if conscription has the whole-hearted support of either section of the population and there is considerable danger that it will drift into a local political issue and the main fact be overlooked that once the Bill is passed each individual must obey the law regardless of the attitude of his neighbour. It will fall more heavily upon the Roman Catholic section than the Protestant because a greater proportion of the latter are in reserved occupations, a fact which has already been exaggerated by Nationalist speakers.
... active organisation to resist it will commence at once in every parish and will not cease if a Bill is introduced and passed into law. Many will cross the Border but from those who remain wide resistance to the enforcement of the Act may be expected. This in the first instance will be demonstrated by failure to register. It will then be necessary for the Police to carry out arrests to which resistance may be expected even down to the use of firearms ... conscription will give new life to the IRA and will attract into its ranks many who today are keeping well clear of it. It will provide it with a new strength and prestige which may last for a long while after the War is over. Further sectarian feeling will be embittered on both sides which will increase the risk of Protestants adopting the attitude that they go only if the Roman Catholics are taken.[63]

Whether Wickham produced such a flatly contradictory opinion to that of his political masters out of the blue during a vital top-level meeting in Downing Street, or whether he was acting under instructions from Andrews, is a moot point. Years later, Sir Basil Brooke, who was to succeed Andrews as prime minister, and who accompanied him to London for the crunch meeting, told me in confidence that he felt that despite the objections, conscription could have been put through. He said that Andrews had shown weakness, but he asked me not to record his observation at the time (I was researching the first edition of my IRA book in 1966), as 'the family would be upset'. Interestingly enough, he also said that his real worry about the south was that de Valera might abandon the neutrality policy and come into the war, which would have made it 'nearly impossible for us to stick out against a united Ireland after the war'. Whether or not his assessment was right, one would never accuse the Orangemen of a lack of willingness to confront that possibility!

Where the conscription proposal was concerned, Churchill obviously decided that the Ulster leadership was buckling and opted for the Wickham assessment. He agreed that the American Ambassador to the Court of St James, John Winant, should send the following message to the US Secretary of State, Cordell Hull:

> The Ulster Government has weakened considerably over the weekend and consequently the Cabinet is inclined to the view that it would be more trouble than it's worth to go through with conscription. No immediate decision will be taken and in the meantime the less made of the affair the better.[64]

He followed this up with an announcement in the House of Commons, on 27 May, that: 'It would be more trouble than it was worth to enforce such a policy in Northern Ireland.' There were no cheers in Stormont however. Andrews's critics charged him with having less influence than de Valera in London, and the failure over conscription was a factor in his subsequent overthrow by Brooke.

De Valera's proprietorial attitude to the Six Counties involved him in some further sparring with Gray and the American administration during 1941. Acting on reports that American technicians were building a base in Derry to help in the defence of Iceland, de Valera asked Gray if this was true. The matter was of concern to him because 'while he recognised the de facto occupation of that part of Ireland, he could not waive Irish rights of sovereignty over it'.[65] Gray however refused to discuss partition, and suggested that the matter be raised through the Irish Embassy in Washington.

Roosevelt's reply to Gray's letter informing him about the de Valera approach confirmed the growing hostility towards de Valera in Washington:

> It is a rather dreadful thing to say but I must admit that if factories close in Ireland and there is a great deal more suffering there, there will be less general sympathy in the United States than if it had happened six months ago. People are, frankly, getting pretty fed up with my old friend Dev.[66]

The hostility got a more public hearing when de Valera again questioned reports about the presence of American military personnel in Derry, after the *Daily Mail* carried an article on 13 October that American marines were now protecting the 'Icelandic' installations. America was preparing for a large-scale landing of troops at the Derry base, but Pearl Harbor was still some months away, and as America had not yet officially entered the war, Roosevelt had no intention of informing de Valera of this crucial area of

American military planning. The Derry base was central to US operations in Europe, its value far outweighing anything that the Six Counties contributed by way of men or matériel to the war effort. In fact, had Derry not been available, the Allies would probably have seized the ports and invaded southern Ireland.

Accordingly, after an approach made through the Irish Embassy in Washington concerning the *Daily Mail* report was simply ignored, a formal request for information from de Valera, delivered in Washington on 6 November, drew a very frosty response from Roosevelt. In the course of his enquiry, de Valera had stated that 'the restoration of the integrity of the national territory of Ireland' was 'the primary political aim of the majority of the people of Ireland'. Roosevelt's reply, however, said curtly:

In as much as the enquiry contained in your communication under acknowledgement relates to territory recognised by the Government of the United States as part of the United Kingdom . . . the enquiry in question should be addressed by the Irish Government to the Government of the United Kingdom.

And there the matter rested for a few months. But the day after Pearl Harbor was attacked, 'the Government of the United Kingdom' unexpectedly addressed an enquiry to the Irish Government. De Valera was made aware of its approach by telephone at 1.30 on the morning of 8 December. Maffey had a message for him from Churchill which wouldn't wait until daybreak. In view of the Pearl Harbor attack, de Valera thought that he could be about to be informed that the ports were to be seized. Accordingly, he woke up the Chief of Staff, Major General Dan McKenna, and the Secretary to the Government, Maurice Moynihan, and warned them to stand by for any eventuality. Churchill's message to de Valera read: 'Now is your chance. Now or never. "A nation once again." I am very ready to meet you at any time.'

De Valera concluded that this meant that now there was an opportunity for him to take action leading to the end of partition. He didn't agree that the time was propitious and, above all, he didn't want to meet Churchill. He had avoided meeting him at all the earlier crisis points of the war. His memoirs drily state: 'I didn't see any basis of agreement . . . This agreement might leave conditions worse than before.'[67] Nor did he see any reason why he had been got out of bed to receive such a missive. At first sight 'a nation once again' would appear to have contained an offer of unity, but in fact Churchill was referring to the fact that this was the song of the old Irish Parliamentary Party, for whose leading figures he had expressed admiration to Dulanty during the conscription crisis. De Valera pointedly decided not to reply to Churchill for another two days to indicate to the British Prime Minister 'that he saw no point in being awakened out of his sleep'.[68] In his reply, de Valera thanked Churchill, and suggested that Lord Cranborne be sent to Dublin where he might achieve 'a fuller understanding of our position here'.[69] Cranborne and de Valera duly met on the 16th, but there was no meeting of minds on either partition or neutrality, nor on a suggestion from de Valera that the Irish might supply more food to the British – if the price was right! Neither were any British arms forthcoming.

Pearl Harbor accelerated the American military preparations in Northern Ireland, and large-scale troop landings commenced shortly after the Cranborne visit, on 26 January 1942, as part of Operation Magnet, as the Irish section of the overall landing of some one and a quarter-million US troops in the United Kingdom was known. De Valera met the initial arrivals by sending a protest to Washington on 6 February which, after a summary of the history of partition, restated his constitutional claim to Northern Ireland:

> The people of Ireland have no feelings of hostility towards, and no desire to be brought in any way into conflict with, the United States. For reasons which I referred to a few weeks ago, the contrary is the truth, but it is our duty to make it clearly understood that no matter what troops occupy the Six Counties, the Irish people's claim for the union of the whole of the national territory and for supreme jurisdiction over it will remain unabated.

This provoked a dusty answer, authorised by Roosevelt, which, without directly adverting to de Valera's claim, made it clear that Northern Ireland was regarded as part of the United Kingdom. Moreover, it contained a pretty strong hint that Ireland might be left out in the cold when the inevitable post-war peace process took place.

> The decision to dispatch troops to the British Isles was reached in close consultation with the British Government as part of our strategic plan to defeat the Axis aggressors. There was not, and is not now, the slightest thought or intention of invading Irish territory or of threatening Irish security. Far from constituting a threat to Ireland, the presence of these troops in neighbouring territory can only contribute to the security of Ireland and of the whole British Isles, as well as furthering our total war effort.
> . . . At some future date when Axis aggression has been crushed by the military might of free peoples, the nations of the earth must gather about a peace table to plan the future world on foundations of liberty and justice everywhere. I think it only right that I make plain at this time that when that time comes the Irish Government in its own best interest should not stand alone but should be associated with its traditional friends, and among them, the United States of America.[70]

Roosevelt underlined the inadvisability of the 'stand alone' policy by continuing his personal 'absent treatment' of de Valera, but there were no further serious disagreements between Dublin and Washington for approximately two more years, until the 'American Note' storm broke. The military reality was that, as an American OSS officer wrote: 'Eire was a significant help to the Allies and was neutral in name only – a fact known to the Germans and the Japanese.' The Irish army liaised closely with both the British and the Americans. The officer who commanded British troops Northern Ireland, General Sir Harold Franklyn, liaised closely with the Irish General Chief of Staff, Lieutenant General McKenna, who kept de Valera fully informed of what was said at their meetings. By way of further co-operation, de Valera appointed his son, Vivion de Valera, as liaison officer to Franklyn. Nevertheless, Roosevelt and Gray, at a political level, continued to consider ways in which the influence of the Irish could be eliminated from American politics.

Roosevelt was completely supportive of Gray in his general attitude towards de Valera and the Irish, although he didn't act on some of the Ambassador's more explosive suggestions. For example, after the failure of the Cranborne mission, Gray wanted all petrol supplies to Ireland cut off as a punishment for not supplying Britain with more food. He also wanted to put an end to the practice of allowing unarmed neutral ships to sail in American convoys. Had the Americans decided to invade, he had plans drawn up for the establishment of a puppet government. Seizure of the ports was to have been accompanied by a mass drop of leaflets from 'a great flight of planes'. If the leaflets didn't convince the public of the rightness of American actions, and the Irish fired on American troops, 'A few well-placed bombs on the Irish barracks at the Curragh, and in the Dublin area, would be the most merciful way of shutting off opposition.'

But while Roosevelt, no doubt mindful of the assistance which was being rendered to the Allies *sub rosa*, did not fall in with such suggestions, he made it clear that he was fully behind Gray on the political front, e.g. the removal of the 'hyphenates' from the American body politic. Some months after the American troops landed in the north, he wrote to Gray, on 16 September 1942, in flattering and supportive terms:

Several people who have come back from, or passed through Ireland, have told me what a perfectly magnificent job you are doing. I did not have to be told that because I knew it, for the very simple fact that you have not given me the remote shadow of a headache all these years.

Roosevelt went on to describe how he had recently applied the 'absent treatment' policy to one of de Valera's friends in America: 'A typical professional Irish American – came in to tell me about the terrible starvation among the people of Ireland. I looked at him in a much interested way and remarked quietly, where is Ireland?' However, while Roosevelt was obviously keen to see the end of the 'professional Irish-Americans', he also had a broader objection to de Valera's policy, telling Gray:

I do wish the people as a whole over there could realise that Dev is unnecessarily storing up trouble because most people over here feel that Dublin, by maintaining German spies and by making all the little things difficult for the United Nations, is stirring up a thoroughly unsympathetic attitude toward Ireland as a whole when we win the war. That is a truly sad state of affairs.[71]

The thinking revealed by the Roosevelt–Gray exchange, and in particular the idea that Dublin was a centre for German influence, was to lead to the American Note crisis nearly two years later.

The first sparks in the controversy were struck at a dinner held in Claridges Hotel, London, a few months after Roosevelt wrote to Gray. The dinner was hosted by the American Ambassador to Britain, John Winant, and the guests included Gray; a future prime minister of England, Clement Attlee, then Minister of State for the Dominions; the Home Secretary, Herbert Morrison; Lord Cranborne, then Minister for the Colonies; and Maffey. The object of the dinner party was to discuss the removal of the thorn of Anglo-Irish relations from the flesh of both the British lion and Uncle Sam. It was agreed that the ending of partition was highly desirable, but that of course the north could not be coerced, and that Ireland must never be used as a base from which to attack England, which was the one solid guarantee that de Valera had given. But the British ministers were suffering from the strain of their war work and had little else to offer apart from a general distaste for Ireland. Consequently, when Maffey suggested that, whatever happened in the long term, it would be desirable in the short term to call for the removal of the Axis diplomatic representatives in Dublin, the idea was seized upon.

Seized, but not acted on. At another high-level social gathering that month (on the 29th), a lunch hosted by Churchill at Downing Street at which both Gray and de Gaulle were guests, Gray was informed by Churchill that while the ports would have been valuable earlier on in the war, things had now progressed to a stage where the war could be won without them. Again Gray developed his thesis on the need for removing the hyphenates from the Anglo-American equation. The idea of doing something to lay a marker on Ireland continued to circulate between the British, the Americans and the Canadians. Like the British, the Canadians were unhappy, or at least the Canadian High Commissioner in Dublin, John Kearney, was, at the prospect of de Valera reaping post-war benefits such as Commonwealth preference or UN membership, after having stayed out of the war. Finally, Gray drafted a lengthy memo for the State Department on 14 May 1943, recommending that de Valera be made a request which he could not concede: an Allied demand for the ports.[72] Gray wanted de Valera on the record for the time when the Irish societies, which he expected de Valera to manipulate, came to life again after the war. He said:

> The important thing from the view-point of Anglo-American co-operation is to bring to the notice of the American people the unfair and destructive policy of the de Valera politicians at the time when British and American interests are essentially the same and to obtain a verdict of American disapproval which will remove the pressure of the Irish question from Anglo-American relations.

The memo was well received by Roosevelt who passed it on to the Secretary of State with a note saying:

I think Mr Gray is right in his desire to put de Valera on record. We shall undoubtedly be turned down. I think the strongest fact is that we are losing many American and British lives and many ships in carrying various supplies to Ireland, without receiving anything in return or so much as a 'Thank you'.[73]

However, no diplomatic note emanated for some time. Unknown to Gray, there was opposition from both American and British decision-takers to his suggestion. The OSS, like the military in England, were quite happy with the way Irish neutrality was working in practice as opposed to precept, and Carter Nicholas, the Irish desk officer at OSS headquarters in Washington, worked to 'block a strident note on the issue of Irish neutrality which was being sought by Minister Gray'.[74] Nicholas's man in the American Embassy in Dublin, Ervin Marlin, had reported that contrary to what Gray said, Irish counter-intelligence was of such a high calibre that there was no question of threat from Axis agents. When Gray found this out, he asked for Marlin's recall. The British for their part had lost their appetite for the ports on military grounds, as the tide of war was now flowing against the Germans, and commercially there were suspicions that if the ports fell into American hands, so too would Irish markets which were traditionally exploited by the British. There was also a consideration which Gray acknowledged that despite de Valera's convincing demonstration of the state's sovereignty, there were elements in the British establishment which were 'reluctant to recognise Eire as not a Dominion and under British tutelage'.[75] In addition, as Gray also conceded, very few members of the Cabinet, with the exception of Churchill and Herbert Morrison, appreciated de Valera's role in influencing Irish-Americans and felt that as long as he was not actively stirring up trouble, there was no need for the British and Americans to do so either.

However, the approach of the Normandy landings gave the note issue an extra dimension of urgency in Allied eyes. Accordingly, it was decided to revert to Maffey's original suggestion about removing the Axis diplomats, while retaining Gray's initial objective, thus getting de Valera on the record as an Axis collaborator, while at the same time continuing with the highly desirable *sub rosa* military co-operation. The notes were presented on 21 February 1944 by Gray, and the following day by Maffey.

Unknown to the two diplomats, de Valera had already taken steps to curb the Germans' activities. Hempel is thought to have used the embassy transmitter to send reports to Germany which resulted in the destruction of American shipping (the *Iroquois* in September 1939 is certainly attributed to Hempel, and there are suspicions that other ships may have met their fate through his reportage). In addition, the transmitter is thought to have been used to send weather reports, which enabled three German warships, the *Prinz Eugen*, the *Gneisenau* and the *Scharnhorst*, to escape through the English Channel from Brest in February 1942. De Valera warned Hempel after the ships' escape that either he stop using the transmitter altogether or it would be transferred to the custody of the Irish Department of External Affairs.

Hempel himself was not keen on the transmitter's use, and unsuccessfully petitioned Berlin to allow him to stop the weather reports.[76] But Berlin found the reports too valuable to discontinue, and even after de Valera's warning, Irish intelligence discovered that broadcasts were being made from the coastal town of Bettystown, not far from the border.

De Valera decided to crack down on the broadcasts after the Germans parachuted two Irishmen into County Clare on spying missions on 16 and 19 December 1943. Both were apprehended within hours of landing but the fact that they were provided with transmitters as part of their spying equipment sealed the fate of the one in Hempel's possession, and it was placed in a safe in a Dublin bank on 21 December. For added security, the Irish and the Germans each held a set of keys, both of which were needed to open the safe, which meant that it could not be opened except in the shared presence of Irish and German officials.

Gray was unaware of the German transmitter's fate, and the note he handed to de Valera referred both to the transmitters found on the men captured in Clare, and to the one presumed to be in the German legation. But de Valera was fully aware of the real purpose behind the notes, and decided to counter-attack by treating them as though they were the precursors to an invasion. Speaking in Cavan on 27 February, he said: 'At any moment the war may come upon us and we may be called upon to defend our rights and our freedom with our lives. Should the day come, we will all face our duty with the traditional courage of our race.' All army leave was immediately cancelled, and the leisurely air which had begun to permeate neutral Ireland vanished immediately as bridges were mined, guards were placed on airfields and other strategic positions, and the local defence units were mobilised and armed. Before either Gray or Maffey had had a chance to contact the Canadian High Commissioner, John Kearney, to brief him, de Valera called him in, treated him to an angry lecture and asked for his help in getting the notes withdrawn.

Judicious leaks about the serving of the notes and the Irish military preparations guaranteed that the notes became a *cause célèbre* in both American and British newspapers. De Valera's position on the notes, for the benefit of the Canadians, was that they were an Irish version of the Chanak incident involving the Dominions.[77] He was fully aware that there was no question of an Allied invasion. A formal statement to this effect was given to the Irish Ambassador in Washington, Robert Brennan. However, the State Department official warned that while there was no ultimatum, or invasion, envisaged, de Valera would have to fear 'the wrath of American mothers' if the Axis mission led to the deaths of their sons. Apart from the formal guarantee that no American aggression was contemplated, which Roosevelt had promised Brennan during the stormy Aiken interview two years earlier, but had not followed up on until now, Kearney was cleared by his own superiors to go back to de Valera and assure him that no invasion was envisaged.

Gray also called on de Valera to confirm what had been told to Brennan in

270

Washington, but de Valera shifted the thrust of his response to focus on the State Department official's remark about the wrath of American mothers, and the implications of having the comment entered on the official record. In his formal written reply to the American note, delivered on 7 March 1944 by Brennan in Washington, de Valera expressed surprise at such a portentous note being addressed to his government in view of the friendship between the Irish and Americans, and of the 'uniformly friendly character of Irish neutrality in relation to the United States'. The Irish Government felt that

> The American Government should have realised that the removal of representatives of a foreign state on the demand of the Government to which they are accredited is universally recognised as the first step towards war, and that the Irish Government could not entertain the American proposal without a complete betrayal of their democratic trust. Irish neutrality represented the united will of the people and parliament. It is the logical consequence of Irish history and of the forced partition of national territory.[78]

The texts of the American and British notes were published simultaneously on 11 March, and made world headlines. For a day or two, the initiative rested with the Allies, they had at least succeeded in their ambition of getting de Valera on the record. But in the Anglo-Irish relationship, the path of true misunderstanding never runs smooth. The Normandy landings were imminent, and as part of the military preparations the Allies had been considering the curtailment of communications with Ireland, lest somehow word of what was contemplated reached Berlin via Dublin. Reports that a decision to proceed with the curtailment was imminent appeared in British newspapers on 13 March. Worse, suggestions were made that economic restrictions were also in prospect.

These reports were naturally viewed in Dublin as being related to the notes crisis, although the Allied planners had not intended this. However, Churchill made a speech on 14 March which made it appear that the travel restrictions *were* part of the notes démarche. Speaking in the House of Commons, he revealed that the notes were American-originated and delivered with British support. He went on to say that steps had been taken to minimise the security risks posed by the presence of German diplomats in Dublin, and added that

> these measures must be strengthened, and the restrictions on travel announced in the press yesterday are the first step in the policy designed to isolate Great Britain from Southern Ireland, and also to isolate Southern Ireland from the outer world during the critical period which is now approaching. I need scarcely say how painful it is to us to take such measures in view of the large numbers of Irishmen who are fighting so bravely in our armed forces and the many deeds of personal heroism by which they have kept alive the martial honour of the Irish race. No one, I think, can reproach us for precipitancy. No nation in the world would have been so patient.[79]

Churchill's speech had the effect of delivering de Valera's Chanak option for him. The Canadian Government immediately cabled London stating that the recent developments concerning Ireland are matters of high concern to all the members of the Commonwealth . . . We were not consulted in advance of the attempts to secure the removal of the Axis representatives, nor were we informed of your intentions concerning travel restrictions . . . if Ireland is moved to leave the Commonwealth, this is a matter of serious moment to us.[80]

In far-away South Africa, Dr Malan, on behalf of the opposition, sent de Valera a telegram of support. During a debate on the Irish issue, Malan followed this up by telling Prime Minister Smuts that Eire had the right to control its own external affairs and to remain neutral, even though Britain had gone to war.

The Allies began to back-pedal. Roosevelt told London that he didn't want sanctions imposed, and Gray condemned a proposal of Cordell Hull's that a further note be sent denying either that the American Government had been misinformed, or that the issue was one of 'Ireland's right to remain neutral'.[81] The goal posts were rapidly moving from the original target of 'getting Ireland on the record'.

Churchill was enraged at what he perceived as a softening of the American attitude, and wrote to Roosevelt:

> Gray's lead in Ireland had been followed by us and it is too soon to begin reassuring de Valera. A doctor telling his patient that medicine prescribed for his nerve trouble is only coloured water is senseless. To keep them guessing for a while would be much better in my opinion. I think that we should let fear work its healthy process, rather than allay alarm in de Valera's circles. In that way we shall get a continued stiffening up of the Irish measures behind the scenes. At the moment these are not so bad as to prevent a leakage.[82]

But as Maffey noted, the failure to foresee that the planned restrictions should be disassociated from the notes issue meant that the 'British and American Governments are now on different courses. American Notes have fallen into the background. American Minister has given the Eire Government every assurance that there is no intention of following it up in any way . . .'[83] The affair ended on 27 March, when, despite Churchill's objections to 'reassuring de Valera', Maffey was instructed to call on the Irish leader to assure him that the planned communication curtailments, and any shipping deficiencies, were purely temporary and of a military character, divorced entirely from the notes. Both Gray and Maffey later judged that despite the hiccup over communications, the note affair was a great success, a triumph over what Gray termed an 'ugly group of bad hats' who ought to be told to 'go sit on a tack'.[84]

However, it was de Valera who proved to be the ultimate beneficiary. Internally, he took advantage of the publicity generated by the serving of the notes to call a snap general election, which he won handsomely (on 30 May), thereby completely reversing a growing trend in domestic unpopularity that had seen him take a drubbing in another general election, held only a year

ABOVE LEFT: *The persistence and danger of the underlying Irish physical-force tradition, fuelled by the partition issue, was graphically illustrated on the fiftieth anniversary of the 1916 Rising when IRA sympathisers blew up Nelson's Pillar in O'Connell Street, Dublin.*

ABOVE RIGHT: *In the same year it appeared that old animosities had been buried as de Valera shook hands with the British officer to whom he surrendered after the Rising, Captain Hitzen (left)*

LEFT: *The humanitarian Sir Roger Casement who was executed by the British in 1916*

ABOVE: *John Redmond inspecting Irish Volunteers. Because he pledged the Volunteers to fight for Britain in the Great War, in the unfulfilled hope of gaining Home Rule, in return he and his party were destroyed politically.*

BELOW LEFT: *Eamon de Valera presides over a meeting of the first Dail in the Mansion House, Dublin*

BELOW: *Dan Breen,
who, with Seán
Tracy, fired the fatal
shots which began
the Anglo-Irish War
of 1919–21 as the
first Dail held its
first meeting*

ABOVE: *A grim-faced Michael Collins
strides past a little boy, Alphonsus
Culliton, after returning from the
Funeral Mass of a group of his soldiers
who had been killed during the Civil
War. Culliton was fourteen at the time
the picture was taken. Collins had
falsified his age, on discovering that the
lad had run away from a broken home,
so that he could join the Army and had
him placed in the care of a former
member of the Squad, Tom Keogh,
who like Collins died in the Civil War.
The boy was subsequently raised
by the Army.*

ABOVE: *Irish Parliamentary Party leader John Dillon (left) and Joseph Devlin who later led the Nationalists of Northern Ireland. Dillon's son, James, later became one of the Dail's most outspoken figures and leader of Fine Gael.*

ABOVE: *W.T. Cosgrave, President of the Executive Council, effectively Prime Minister of an Independent Ireland*

ABOVE: *Dubliners celebrate the Centenary of Catholic Emancipation in 1929*

BELOW: *A once common architectural style, the thatched cottage, is now rarely encountered. This one survives at Rush, Co. Dublin.*

ABOVE: *This was how most Dubliners got their coal and turf delivered in the first half of the century*

ABOVE: *Shem the Penman… The man who changed twentieth century literature, James Joyce.*

BELOW: *The original Abbey Theatre, pictured in 1935 as Seán O'Casey's 'The Plough and the Stars' was being staged. It burned down in 1951. A larger theatre designed by Michael Scott opened on the fiftieth anniversary of the Rising in 1966.*

ABOVE: *Two of Ireland's favourite Englishmen, Hilton Edwards and Michael MacLiammoir outside the Gate Theatre which they founded in 1928. It became a Mecca for stars such as Orson Welles and James Mason.*

ABOVE: *The clash of the ash… One of the all-time greats of hurling Christy Ring of Cork (left) pulls on a ball against the legendary Wexford hurler Bobby Rackard during an encounter at Croke Park, Dublin. Ring was so accurate that he could ring a doorbell across a street with a well-struck ball.*

BELOW: *Poet Patrick Kavanagh*

ABOVE: *Playwright Samuel Beckett*

BELOW: *Signing in and signing off, the end and the beginning of an era?… In fact, de Valera was signing the instrument which dissolved the Dail in 1965, bringing about Lemass' last election. De Valera outlived Lemass by several years.*

LEFT: *A once famous Irish institution, now no more: an Irish Hospitals Sweepstakes draw in progress during the 1930s*

RIGHT: *John A. Costello (left) leader of the two inter-party governments of the 1950s with Liam Cosgrave, son of the first Irish Prime Minister after independence, who himself later also became a Prime Minister*

BELOW: *During 'The Emergency', as World War II was referred to in Ireland, curious onlookers gather in 1940 to inspect the small concrete structure on the left. It was one of the first air raid shelters Dublin had seen. Note its size in comparison with the Church of Adam and Eve on the right and the Four Courts rotunda across the Liffey.*

LEFT: *T.K. Whitaker, an architect of change*

ABOVE: *The Irish Chekov, playwright Brian Friel*

BELOW: *Ireland's finest contemporary novelist, John McGahern*

BELOW: *Nobel laureate, poet Seamus Heaney*

earlier, which had left his government in a minority position. The reason for the unpopularity was simple enough: life in Plato's Cave was not lived merely in ignorance, it was lived in discomfort and very often in poverty. The celebrated Mayor of Boston, James Michael Curley, once memorably described his childhood by saying, 'Life was grim on this corn beef and cabbage riviera.' It was grim in the many homes of the poor in wartime Ireland also, with this difference: they couldn't afford corn beef. The grimness was added to by the fact that there was a major outbreak of foot and mouth disease in 1941. This led to the widespread slaughter of livestock and restrictions on people's movements which included the cancellations of one of the few remaining sources of enjoyment left to the people – GAA matches. Inflation, shortages, the rationing of petrol and essential foodstuffs, and restrictions of all sorts added to the tribulations of living in a depressed economy. Even for those lucky enough to have the protection of a trade union, the war had provided the excuse for some pretty repressive anti-union legislation, which Seán Lemass had attempted to blunt, achieving some satisfaction with the trade union leadership if not always with the rank and file.

What had happened was that a strike of municipal workers which began in Dublin during January 1940 had virtually paralysed the city, and as it spread, threatened imports and exports also. The workers had demanded a rise of 8s. a week. The city manager offered 3s. 9d., but the Government intervened, reducing the offer to 2s., and maintained a hard-faced attitude until the strike was settled. In its wake, the initial reaction of some members of the Cabinet, notably that of Seán MacEntee and his civil servants in the Department of Industry and Commerce, revealed the basically authoritarian attitudes which permeated government on both sides of the border. MacEntee's department's response was in some way a mirror image of the way the Unionists over-reacted to the pressures of war by attempting to dragoon their citizens by means of conscription. As Dr Dermot Keogh has noted, MacEntee's department drafted a bill which proposed the following:

> When strikes threatened essential public services, the government was empowered to declare a state of emergency. Employees were to be listed and called upon, in the name of the people, to perform the services. A refusal could mean dismissal, fine or imprisonment; loss of social welfare and pension rights might also ensue. Traders were to be disbarred from providing goods to the said individuals. There were also other draconian proposals regarding incitement or picketing and a minimum of one month's notice for a strike was necessary. There was also a proposal to issue a licence to all associations of workmen and employers engaged in setting wages or negotiating conditions. Upon receipt of a fixed sum of money.[85]

These Orwellian propositions ran into opposition from the Attorney General, on the grounds of constitutionality, and at the Cabinet table, chiefly from the Department of Finance and above all Lemass, who made counter-proposals which were accepted in May 1941. These centred on lightning strikes and a wage standstill. The latter was introduced under the Emergency Powers Act, and the trade unions were further controlled by the Trade Union Act of 1941. However, Lemass continued in negotiation with the Trades Union Congress leaders, as a result of which a new Trade Unions Bill was introduced the following year, removing some of the more onerous provisions of the previous legislation. Part of Lemass's motivation lay in the fact that he, unlike some of his Cabinet colleagues, still retained some of the early Fianna Fáil affinity with Labour. Part was less altruistic: a general election was looming in 1943 and in several constituencies Fianna Fáil deputies depended on Labour transfers. Knowing the mood of the electorate, de Valera tried and failed to avoid this by having the life of the Dail prolonged but, scenting blood, the opposition rejected this ploy and the country went to the polls on 22 June 1943.

After a campaign bedevilled by petrol shortages and embittered by MacEntee's attacks on Labour, which were later blamed for deflecting many of the much-needed transfers away from Fianna Fáil, de Valera's party dropped 10 seats, to 67, and Labour rose from 9 to 17. Clann na Talmhan, the farmers' party, won 14 seats and independents 8. However, a tiring Fine Gael fell from 45 seats to only 32, thereby allowing Fianna Fáil to carry on as a minority government, a situation which de Valera found particularly irksome for what commentators would come to regard as 'the natural party of government', immune to diseases to which lesser political bodies were prone – such as joining coalitions as Fine Gael had proposed to the other opposition parties during the election.

Apart from consigning de Valera to the unaccustomed role of minority Taoiseach, the campaign was notable for eliciting what is probably de Valera's most quoted speech, that concerning 'comely maidens'. In one sense, this is the political equivalent of identifying W.B. Yeats as the man who wrote the poem 'The Lake Isle of Inisfree'. But in another, this much derided (and defended) St Patrick's Day message, delivered on the fiftieth anniversary of the Gaelic League, contains much of what de Valera marketed as his brand image to an electorate which found that image appealing, in those halcyon pre-television days. It also contained a tacit admission that he had not been able to give reality to the image. He said:

Acutely conscious though we all are of the misery and desolation in which the greater part of the world is plunged, let us turn aside for a moment to that ideal Ireland that we would have. That Ireland which we dreamed of would be the home of a people who valued material wealth only as the basis of right living, of a people who were satisfied with frugal comfort and devoted their leisure to the things of the spirit – a land whose countryside would be bright with cosy homesteads, whose fields and villages would be joyous with the sounds of industry, with the romping of sturdy children, the contests of athletic youths and the laughter of comely maidens, whose firesides would be forums for the wisdom of serene old age. It would, in a word, be the home of a people living the life that God desires that man should live.[86]

He cited Thomas Davis, who had spoken of the development of Irish natural resources such as harbours, rivers, bogs and mines, and 'the still more important development of the resources of the spirit'. For de Valera, the most important of these was the Irish language. But he did touch base with reality to the extent of saying:

> For many the pursuit of the material is a necessity. Man, to express himself fully and to make the best use of the talents God has given him, needs a certain minimum of comfort and leisure. A section of our people have not yet this minimum. They rightly strive to secure it, and it must be our aim and the aim of all who are just and wise to assist in the effort. But many have got more than is required and are free, if they choose, to devote themselves more completely to cultivating the things of the mind, and in particular those which mark us out as a distinct nation.

As Professor Joe Lee has commented in his inimitable fashion:

> The response to the dream was depressing. Urban workers wanted higher wages. Farmers wanted higher prices. The election result did not enhance the market value of comely maidens. Female favours filled no pockets. As the Fianna Fáil nag trotted up to the starting tape for the 1944 election, 'comely maiden' was unceremoniously dumped out of the saddle, and 'rural electrification' plonked in her place as a better bet to brighten up the countryside.[87]

Apart from the unhorsing of Comely Maiden and the favourable publicity derived from the American note issue, de Valera also reaped the benefit of a split in the Labour Party which reversed the gains of the previous year and checked the growth of the party for decades. In January, a long-simmering hostility between James Larkin and William O'Brien, who had succeeded Larkin as leader of the Irish Transport and General Workers Union, had resulted in the Labour Party splitting into Larkinite and O'Brien factions. O'Brien founded a new party, National Labour, from amongst the deputies whom the IT&GWU sponsored. He also withdrew the union from both the Labour Party and the Irish Trades Union Congress, saying that Labour had become infiltrated by Communists, code for Jim Larkin and his son James, both of whom had won seats in the 1943 election. Fianna Fáil and MacEntee in particular were only too delighted to ensure that the Catholic electorate were fully informed about the red scare. On top of this, Fine Gael, by now an exhausted remnant of the old Cumann na nGaedheal, had lost its leader. William T. Cosgrave had resigned from politics and General Richard Mulcahy, who succeeded him, for a time did not even have a seat in the Dail and led the party from the Seánad, which of course meant he was debarred from contributing to debates in the all-important lower chamber. The other potential leader, James Dillon, a man of principle and a gifted orator, had been forced to resign from Fine Gael because he opposed neutrality, an incident which says all that is required concerning the depth of bi-partisan

275

feeling across the Irish parliamentary spectrum in favour of neutrality. All these factors combined to give de Valera a sizeable majority when he called a snap election on 9 May 1944, catching the weakened opposition completely off guard and becoming Taoiseach of a majority government again on 9 June.

His total of 76 seats was 14 more than all the other opposition parties combined could muster. Fine Gael dropped again, winning only 30 seats, Clann na Talmhan fell to 11. Independents went up one to nine, but Labour won only eight seats and National Labour four. In addition to this success, the Normandy landings, which occurred a week after the election, largely removed de Valera's major worries concerning his neutrality policy. Largely but not completely.

Roosevelt died of a brain haemorrhage almost a year after the American note controversy, on 12 April 1945, and de Valera and the Irish people paid tributes to the fallen leader. Gray was particularly moved by de Valera's own tribute to Roosevelt in the Dail, and by the stream of condolences which poured into his office from both members of the Government and people in all walks of life. However, the moment of appreciation soon passed. Gray returned to the charge against the Axis diplomats shortly after Roosevelt died (on 30 April 1945). Having failed to ensure that what he termed 'Axis war criminals' would not be given asylum in Ireland after the war, he demanded that the keys of the German legation be handed over to him to prevent the Germans destroying archive material which he claimed contained intelligence on submarine warfare. De Valera treated him to some of the instantaneous procrastination for which he was famous, and riposted by saying that the matter was one for his legal advisers, and no definitive answer could be given there and then. He was courteous, but Gray reported that he was evidently angered and 'grew red'.[88] This did not displease Gray as he judged that once more the Irish Government was on the record for refusing to co-operate 'in a friendly and non-legislative way'.[89]

The anger which Gray's visit to de Valera generated may have had a bearing on a remarkable step by de Valera two days later. On learning of the death of Hitler, he called on Hempel 'to express condolences'. Both Boland and Walshe tried to dissuade him, accurately forecasting the thunderstorm of criticism which the visit would bring, as the contents of the Nazi death camps were being revealed to the world's media at the time. De Valera's response to the criticism was contained in an *aide-memoire* on the incident which he sent to Robert Brennan in Washington:

> I have noted that my call on the German Minister on the announcement of Hitler's death was played up to the utmost. I expected this. I could have had a diplomatic illness but, as you know, I would scorn that sort of thing . . . So long as we retained our diplomatic relations with Germany, to have failed to call upon the German representative would have been an act of unpardonable discourtesy to the German nation and to Dr Hempel himself. During the whole of the war, Dr Hempel's conduct was irreproachable. He was always friendly and inevitably correct – in marked contrast to Gray. I certainly was not going to add to his humiliation in the hour of defeat.[90]

He also advised Brennan that his action was not to have any significance attached to it 'such as connoting approval or disapproval of the State in question, or of its head'. This was not how Maffey for one saw it.[91] He cabled London that he felt de Valera had taken 'a very unwise step . . . stung perhaps by . . . the request for . . . the German archives before VE Day'. As Maffey noted, the ending of censorship meant that the Irish public suddenly became aware of the scale of Nazi atrocities, and that as a result after de Valera's visit 'a sense of disgust slowly manifested itself'. De Valera was rescued from the disgust by an unlikely source: Winston Churchill.

In the course of his victory speech, on 13 May, Churchill had spoken of the desperate straits in which England had found herself in the early days of the war, when German U-boats came within an ace of slashing the Atlantic arteries through which pumped American aid. He said:

> This sense of envelopment which might at any moment turn to strangulation, lay heavy upon us . . . Owing to the action of Mr de Valera, so much at variance with the temper and instinct of thousands of Southern Irishmen who hastened to the battle-front to prove their ancient valour, the approaches which the southern Irish ports and airfields could so easily have guarded were closed by the hostile aircraft and U-boats. This was indeed a deadly moment in our life, and if it had not been for the loyalty and friendship of Northern Ireland we should have been forced to come to close quarters with Mr de Valera or perish for ever from the earth. However, with a restraint and poise to which, I say, history will find few parallels, His Majesty's Government never laid a violent hand upon them, though at times it would have been quite easy and quite natural, and we left the de Valera Government to frolic with the Germans and later with the Japanese to their heart's content.[92]

De Valera's reply, on 16 May, was probably the most eagerly awaited statement made by any Irish statesman of the twentieth century. Streets emptied, pubs and dances fitted with loudspeakers filled. In home and in hospital, crowds gathered around whatever radio set was available. After a lengthy preamble in Irish and English, in which he charted the course of the war (and particularly thanked the Irish speakers who had helped to save the country from its dangers!), he came to the point:

> Certain newspapers have been very persistent in looking for my answer to Mr Churchill's recent broadcast. I know the kind of answer I am expected to make. I know the answer that first springs to the lips of every man of Irish blood who heard or read that speech, no matter in what circumstance or in what part of the world he found himself. I know the reply I would have given a quarter of a century ago. But I have deliberately decided that it is not the reply I shall make tonight.
>
> Allowances can be made for Mr Churchill's statement, however unworthy, in the first flush of his victory. No such excuse could be found for me in this quieter atmosphere . . . Mr Churchill makes it clear that in certain circumstances he would have violated our neutrality and that he would justify his action by Britain's necessity. It seems strange to me that Mr Churchill does not see that this, if accepted, would mean that Britain's necessity would become a moral code and that when this necessity became sufficiently great, other

people's rights were not to count . . . this same code is precisely why we have the disastrous succession of wars . . . shall it be world war?

It is indeed fortunate that Britain's necessity did not reach the point where Mr Churchill would have acted. All credit to him that he successfully resisted the temptation . . . By resisting his temptation in this instance, Mr Churchill, instead of adding another horrid chapter to the already bloodstained record of the relations between England and this country, has advanced the cause of international morality an important step – one of the most important, indeed, that can be taken on the road to the establishment of any sure basis for peace.

Mr Churchill is proud of Britain's stand alone, after France had fallen and before America entered the war. Could he not find in his heart the generosity to acknowledge that there is a small nation that stood alone, not for one year or two, but for several hundred years against aggression, that endured spoliations, famines, massacres in endless succession, that was clubbed many times into insensibility, but that each time on returning consciousness took up the fight anew, a small nation that could never be got to accept defeat and has never surrendered her soul?[93]

Cheering broke out all over the country when he finished, and was continued in the Dail the next day. When he entered the Chamber, he was given a standing ovation. Maffey summed up the response in a memorable, albeit rueful comment to Sir Eric Machtig, the Dominion Office Permanent Under-Secretary: 'Phrases make history here.' He correctly judged that Churchill's incursion into the china shop had presented de Valera with the opportunity to escape 'from the eclipse which had closed down on him and the Irish question . . . Mr de Valera assumed the role of elder statesman and skilfully worked on all the old passions in order to dramatise the stand taken by Eire in this war'.

Such, in outline, was the main course of the Irish relationship with the Allied powers during 'the Emergency'. That with the Germans, who actually inflicted casualties and death on the Irish, and fought not for democracy but for one of the most evil creeds man has known, was paradoxically much smoother. Part of the reason lay in the fact that Germany of course was further away than the United Kingdom, and part in the skilful diplomatic performances of both de Valera and his team, principally Walshe and Boland, and the German Ambassador to Ireland, prior to as well as during the war, Eduard Hempel, who was formally termed the Minister Plenipotentiary for the Third Reich to Ireland.

We have already seen something of the limited extent of Irish Nationalists' contact with Germany during World War I. It could be argued that the Howth guns, and the hope of German assistance, were powerful ingredients in setting off the 1916 explosion, and arms smuggling from Germany continued at a significant level during both the Anglo-Irish war and the Irish civil war. But after 1916 both the Irish and the Germans developed separate reasons for caution in their dealings with each other. In April 1918 a former member of Casement's brigade, Joseph Dowling, was dropped off a submarine on to an island in Galway Bay and arrested. Nevertheless, as we have seen, the British used his arrest as a pretext to announce the discovery of a 'German plot' which justified the arrest of much of the Sinn Féin leadership, including Griffith and de Valera. Later that year (on 11 October), a more substantive reason for distrust of German militarism occurred not far from Dublin Bay when the ferry the *Leinster*, linking Dun Laoghaire with Holyhead in Wales, was torpedoed, killing 501 passengers. It has been suggested that this sinking was responsible for upsetting secret peace negotiations, begun only a week earlier, by Chancellor Prince Max of Baden, and thus contributed to a prolongation of the war and further useless slaughter.

After the war it was the Germans who became wary of the Irish. German strategy for escaping the more onerous provisions of the Treaty of Versailles rested on hopes that the British might rein in the vengeful instincts of the French, and the British had objected to an audience for Sinn Féin at the Paris peace conference, declaring Dail Eireann a threat to security. Subsequently Sinn Féin sent the solicitor Gavan Duffy, a son of Sir Charles Gavan Duffy, the former Young Irelander and Prime Minister of Victoria, to Berlin to plead the Irish case, but the most tangible result of his visit was a memorable dinner given by the German Irish Association which was enlivened by a remarkable speech in Irish delivered by the Celticist Professor Julius Pokorny, of the University of Berlin. The Reichstag turned a deaf ear to a plea for recognition from the Dail. However, Sinn Féin did manage to get an office opened in Berlin that year (1921) with the help of the German Irish Association, which had come alive after the war with the help of Pokorny and some of his students, among them Nancy Wyse-Power, who ran the office. In 1921 also the Dail sent two representatives to Berlin. First John Chartres, a former British civil servant who was one of Collins's advisers during the Treaty negotiations, and subsequently Charles Bewley, who was destined to return as the Free State's Ambassador, only to depart from Berlin during the 1930s in a welter of controversy. By then Bewley had become an admirer of the Nazis and a rabid anti-Semite. He was replaced by Cornelius Duane in 1923. None of these figures was able to achieve anything of note either politically or economically in the face of Germany's inflationary problems and her official attitude towards the United Kingdom. When, in 1922, the committee drafting the Irish constitution asked the German Embassy in London for a copy of the Weimar constitution, Berlin's response to the Embassy referred to the UK's Irish policy and stated that 'Any direct contact of official bodies with representatives of the Irish people are, as far as possible, for the time being to be avoided.'[94]

Unofficial contact in the arms trade, however, survived official disfavour, and Robert Briscoe, who later became Dublin's first Jewish Lord Mayor, Seán MacBride, a son of the executed 1916 leader John MacBride, and Charles McGuinness, a sailor and Republican, busied themselves to such good effect in this area that during the early twenties, despite the Versailles Treaty, a substantial flow of German arms reached Ireland. One shipment, in November 1921, was estimated at 1,500 rifles and 1.7 million rounds of ammunition.[95] When the Troubles subsided, the trio maintained links with

Germany, Briscoe setting up sizeable trading contacts, and McGuinness buying one of the first ships of the Free State's infant merchant fleet, the *City of Dortmund*. MacBride and another prominent IRA man, Donal O'Donoghue, attended the Congress of the Anti-Imperialist League in Frankfurt in 1929; Peadar O'Donnell represented left-wing IRA thinking at the European Small Farmers Congress in Berlin a year later. The writer Francis Stuart, who was married to MacBride's sister Iseult, was prominent in German literary circles and, his writings apart, was well known for his propagandising on behalf of Irish independence. As we shall see, music, Celtic and Irish language studies by German scholars also provided fertile ground for German-Irish contact. Sport and adventure too played a part. German teams competed in the Dublin Horse Show and both Germany and Ireland thrilled to a shared German-Irish aviation feat in 1928, the first east–west transatlantic crossing, from Baldonnel, County Dublin, to Newfoundland. This reverse version of Lindbergh's exploit was carried out by two German aviators, Baron von Huenfeld and Captain Kohler, and the Irishman Colonel James Fitzmaurice.

Other factors which helped to build a favourable image of Ireland in Germany were Heinrich Boll's widely read *Irish Diary* and the fact that sections of Irish and German opinion had a residual shared mistrust of international treaties stemming from the Anglo-Irish Treaty and Versailles respectively. Successive Irish governments evinced sympathy towards Germany over the war reparations issue. Cumann na nGaedheal announced that it wanted no share in the reparation money, and de Valera's policy was that the payments should be cancelled altogether. Both countries had passed through experiences which had bred a heightened sense of national culture and of patriotism. However, on the bread-and-butter issues of trade there was less goodwill. The Shannon hydro-electric scheme project resulted in an imbalance in the Irish–German trading relationship which illustrates both the disparity and the scale of the volume of trade. Between 1924 and 1930 Irish exports to Germany rose by 500%, amounting to a total of £237,981 in 1930. Irish imports from Germany, however, rose from £744,580 in the same period to £1,329,931.

The economic war with Britain made Dublin disposed towards increasing this trade, but the Nazis carried on the policy of a cautious approach towards Ireland for fear of offending Britain, which in addition was seen as being more closely related in Aryan and Germanic origin than the Celtic Irish. Consequently a major deal which the British feared would result in a loss to their mining industry never materialised. The Irish had proposed that the Germans build another massive power plant, this time on the Liffey, which was to have been fuelled by German coal. Eventually, however, the cost of German rearmament, necessitating an increase in foreign currency, led to the signing of an Irish–German trade agreement in 1935. While this initially fixed the ratio of imports to exports at 3:1, the ratio was subsequently expanded to 3:2. The Germans drove a hard bargain. Cabinet records for 1937 show that the

Irish Government gloomily considered the prospect of having to export cattle to Germany at prices which would not cover the cost of transportation. Nevertheless, exports to Germany rose from £66,408 in 1933 to £912,269 in 1938. Imports from Germany rose from £1.3 million to £1.5 million in the same period.

The ending of the economic war and the outbreak of the global shooting one largely removed trade considerations from the German–Irish equation. Not so political relationships. These may be said to have formally begun with the appointment in 1929 of Professor D.A. Binchy as Irish Minister to Germany, hitherto the Irish Free State had been represented by the British Ambassador. At British insistence, Binchy, a distinguished academic, was officially known not as 'Irish Minister', but 'Minister for the Irish Free State'. His appointment got off to a heart-stopping start. He was waiting outside President Hindenburg's office to present his credentials when he discovered that he had left them in his hotel room, thereby necessitating one of the all-time great diplomatic sprints. The incident was symbolic of Binchy's stay in Berlin. He did not like the Germans and Hitler in particular. He resigned in 1932, and was succeeded the following year by Charles Bewley, who had meanwhile become the Free State's First Minister to the Vatican. A Wykehamist, Oxford graduate, and member of the Irish Bar, he was as enamoured of the Nazis as Binchy was not. On the eve of war, de Valera recalled and demoted him, forcing him into resignation.

Binchy's counterpart was Dr Georg von Dehn-Schmidt, who, prior to 1929, dealt with Irish affairs as the German representative in Liverpool. He took his tone from the general forelock-tugging German diplomatic attitude to things British, and was condescending and dismissive towards the new Irish state, perhaps influenced in his approach by his friendship with the pro-British editor of the *Irish Times*, R.M. Smylie. When in 1928 he was approached by the Irish Department of Defence with a view to supplying German-style helmets to the Irish army, von Dehn-Schmidt snubbed the approach, claiming that it breached trading regulations. As a result, an order for 5,000 German-style helmets was subsequently executed by the British firm Vickers! Von Dehn-Schmidt was appointed to Bucharest in 1934. Prior to leaving Dublin, he paid a courtesy call on the Papal Nuncio and was photographed kissing the Nuncio's ring. The then curator of the Irish National Museum was the Celtic scholar Adolf Mahr, who had succeeded another German, Dr Walter Bremer, as director of the Irish branch of the Nazi propaganda organisation *Auslands-organisation*. Mahr caused the photograph to be reproduced in the Nazi paper *Sturmer*. Hitler saw it, and immediately terminated von Dehn-Schmidt's ambassadorial career.

Von Dehn-Schmidt's successor, Wilheim von Kuhlmann, also a career diplomat, was troubled by ill health. In addition, his mother died in a fire at his home in Cabinteely, County Dublin. His tenure in office was unsettled by some demonstrations against Nazism. Irish public opinion was swinging against Germany, influenced by the Nazis' attitude towards the Catholic

Church. These antipathies accelerated after the publication (on 14 March) of Pope Pius XI's encyclical *Mit Brennender Sorge*, on the state of the Catholic Church in Germany. Regrettably, as we shall see shortly, Irish public opinion was but very slightly concerned with the plight of the Jews. Von Kuhlmann died in 1937. During his illness, his place was taken by one Schroetter, who also had to contend with the activities of the *Auslandsorganisation*, which apparently succeeded in causing the German Foreign Ministry officially to describe him as the 'unattached legation Counsellor charged with temporary representation of the legation', rather than as *chargé d'affaires*, which the newspapers termed him.

Thus when Hempel, a career diplomat whose principal activities hitherto had been looking after the Foreign Ministry's furniture, fixtures and properties abroad, took up his appointment in 1937, there was a fairly robust German presence in Ireland, accompanied by a good deal of intrigue, and some anti-German feeling to be contended with. In addition to the *Auslands-organisation*, there was the inevitable Nazi party cell, and a thriving German Club which catered to German businessmen and met regularly in the Red Bank restaurant. Moreover Hempel had to reckon with the fact that the other personality at the German Embassy, Henning Thompsen, was a member of the S.S. Hitler personally briefed Hempel on the Irish situation, and impressed him with his knowledge of Irish affairs.

For a time, Hempel's reports to Berlin had to contend with the influence of Bewley, who told his audience that de Valera was pro-British, and not the committed neutral whom Hempel described. De Valera had intended to replace Bewley with Dr Tom Kiernan, a former director of Radio Eireann, and a Celtic scholar, whose wife was the colourful Delia Murphy, a well-known ballad singer. However, de Valera's concern to keep the link with the Commonwealth, because he thought it would help towards eventual unity, meant that his credentials would have had to be signed by the King, and this, on the outbreak of war, presented a difficulty. In the event, the Irish legation in Berlin was run from 1938 to 1943 by its First Secretary, William Warnock, a Protestant graduate of Trinity College, who was only 28 when he took up his appointment. The German Foreign Ministry was not best pleased at having to deal with a junior, but somehow Warnock, unaided, managed to contain the fallout in Berlin from de Valera's neutrality balancing act until it proved possible to appoint one of Ireland's most experienced diplomats, Cornelius Cremin, as minister in 1944.

At the time of Hempel's coming to Dublin, the Germans had a plentiful supply of intelligence on Ireland and on the Irish. The construction of the Shannon hydro-electric scheme had brought a stream of German technicians and engineers to work for Siemens in Ireland, and as the examples given above indicate, German nationals were to be found involved in various branches of Irish economic and cultural life. For example, Oswald Muller-Dubrow, the director of Siemens-Schuckert, as well as being chairman of the German Association in Dublin, was deputy leader of the *Auslandsorganisation*. The

German Academic Exchange Service was headed by Helmut Clissmann, who became a close friend of the IRA leader Frank Ryan, in whose company he told me he often 'pulled the shirt off a Blueshirt's back'. The fact that the Blueshirts were supposed to be the Irish fascists and thereby the natural allies of the Third Reich, was outweighed by Clissmann's relationship with Ryan, which of course also provided him with a unique insight into Irish revolutionary politics. It was Clissmann who first introduced Hempel to Seán MacBride. Apart from Mahr at the National Museum, the Germans also had Colonel Fritz Brase, who was director of the Irish Army School of Music. Brase was told by the authorities that he must give up either the *Auslandsorganisation* or his directorship. He chose to stay at the School of Music, and when he retired he was succeeded by another German, his deputy Captain Sauerzweig.

Approximately 40 of the outstanding members of the German community, including those mentioned above, returned to Germany after war broke out (on 11 September) and it is popularly said that the Germans later regretted their departure because they would have been a source of invaluable information in Ireland. But in the first place they were given posts of Irish interest in Germany: Clissmann was in military intelligence, the Abwehr; Mahr went to the Foreign Ministry's Cultural Division; and other academics who had been in Ireland, like Dr Ludwig Mulhausen, became involved in Celtic studies or in Goebbels's propaganda machine in the English-speaking section of Radio Europe. Hempel reported to Berlin that he found that both in governmental and Irish language circles, the use of the Celtic scholars, who sometimes broadcast in Irish, drew praise for this, the first international recognition of the Irish language. The best-known war-time English-language broadcasters from the station were Francis Stuart, whose interests, and broadcasts, were literary rather than propagandist, and William Joyce, popularly known as Lord Haw Haw, whom the British executed after the war, claiming that as he had held a British passport (which he acquired under false pretences) for nine months of his Berlin sojourn, he therefore owed allegiance to the Crown and was guilty of high treason.

The second and more important consideration concerning the German colony in Ireland is the fact that despite the exodus at the beginning of the war, there were still some 560 German nationals living in Ireland at the end. So whether all or any of these engaged in espionage activities, the potential was certainly there.

Intrigues, departures and the outbreak of war, however, did not cloud Hempel's vision. A month after the war began, on 7 October, he sent back an assessment of the Irish situation which, in effect, became the German policy towards Ireland for the course of the war. He said that neutrality had the support of the vast majority of the population, despite the undermining effect of certain pro-British circles. The Irish army stood ready to defend neutrality against all comers; the IRA was scarcely a factor. There was some anti-German feeling because of the Russo-German pact, and the invasion of Poland. The Irish Catholic Church supported the Government's neutral position, despite Poland. There was a strong anti-British undercurrent, and the attitude of the Government to Hempel was 'definitely friendly'. As a consequence, he advised that Germany should continue to support Irish neutrality, because it symbolised the loosening ties of Empire which could have an important knock-on effect in America, India and the Dominions.

Despite a broad acceptance of the Hempel analysis, elements in both the Abwehr and the Foreign Ministry itself tried, against Hempel's wishes, at various stages in the war, as we shall see, to make use of the IRA, on the basis of the IRA's own dictum, Wolfe Tone's 'England's Difficulty is Ireland's Opportunity'. Hempel's own boss, Ribbentrop, the Reich Foreign Minister, was responsible for appointing Edmund Veesenmayer, a *coup d'état* specialist, to foment a rebellion in Ireland, despite Hempel's accurate judgement that the IRA was not strong enough to achieve any lasting success which would justify either alienating the Dublin government or throwing it into the arms of London. Hempel himself was at the receiving end of a notable Irish manoeuvre to avoid alienating Berlin.

Immediately after the successful German advance through Belgium and Holland (on 10 May 1940), Maffey called on de Valera and urged him to abandon neutrality in the face of the 'maniacal force' unleashed on the world. De Valera turned him down on the old grounds of partition and of fear of extremist reaction to neutrality's ending. Maffey counter-attacked that given leadership, the extremists would respond to 'a better call'. But, he said, 'Mr de Valera held to his narrow view. He seems incapable of courageous or original thought and now on this world issue and in every matter he lives too much under the threat of the extremist . . . not a strong man and his many critics here know that well . . .'[96]

At the risk of divergence, it is worth noting here that Hempel by contrast would come to the conclusion that de Valera was a strong man, the strongest Nationalist leader in fact, and the man whose support was essential for any policy in Ireland to succeed. Words like 'lunatic', 'impractical', and 'dreamer' did not figure in his dispatches. The Maffey–de Valera exchange ended with de Valera refusing either to abandon neutrality, or to accede to Maffey's request that the German legation be closed. He told Maffey that if the British would cease stalling Irish requests for arms, the Irish would be well able to defend themselves, and so ensure that no attack could be mounted on England from Irish soil. However, the one crumb of comfort de Valera did give Maffey was a hint that he would depart from neutrality to the extent of publicly criticising the German onslaught on Belgium and Holland.

De Valera duly went to Galway where, away from such minor distractions as the importunings of Churchill and Maffey, he attended to the serious business of choosing a Fianna Fáil candidate for a by-election. During the proceedings he made the following comments:

I was at Geneva on many occasions . . . The representatives of Belgium and the representatives of the Netherlands were people that I met frequently, because we co-operated not a little with the northern group of nations. Today these two small nations are fighting for their lives, and I think I would be unworthy of this small nation if on an occasion like this, I did not utter a protest against the cruel wrong which has been done them.

As this was de Valera's first public condemnation of Germany, the Allied representatives were delighted. David Gray wrote to de Valera to congratulate him on his 'brave and explicit' statement, but got no reply. Had he known of the gloss put on the Galway speech for German consumption he would have understood why. When Hempel called to the Department of External Affairs to protest, he was told by F.H. Boland 'in an apologetic manner' that the department had not had an opportunity of vetting the speech delivered by de Valera! In Berlin Warnock also spoke in a 'similarly apologetic manner' and added 'that Ireland wished to maintain neutrality towards all Powers and said personally that Ireland, in the last war against England, had struck too early. This mistake would not be repeated. In view of the German success the question, however, was whether Ireland would not come too late.'

The idea that de Valera, who was his own Foreign Minister, would have either allowed someone to vet his speech or permitted a junior diplomat to make such highly charged observations, in such a delicate situation, was of course preposterous, but the Galway incident passed off without any further repercussions. One reason it did so was that on the heels of Warnock's communication to the German Foreign Office, the Irish police in Dublin discovered that they had considerably more reason to complain to the Germans than had the Germans to the Irish. A raid on 22 May on the home of a Dublin businessman, Stephen Carroll Held, whose father was German, found that there was a German spy in Dublin. The spy himself, one Captain Hermann Goertz, prudently disappeared out the back door as the police came in the front. But he left behind him some £20,000 in cash, a parachute, a radio, and, most worrisome of all, the bones of a plan for a German invasion of Ireland. Plan Kathleen, as it was known, called for a German sea-landing near Derry, and IRA support for German invasion across the border into southern Ireland.

The plan was a figment of German spying imagination, but it did not appear so at the time when the evidence against Held was read out in court. This evidence was compounded by the publicity surrounding the appearance of Francis Stuart's wife in court. Goertz had landed by parachute in County Meath, and had made his way across country on foot to the Stuart home in Laragh, County Wicklow, the address of which had been given to him in Berlin by Francis Stuart. Iseult Stuart had bought some civilian clothes for Goertz and these were easily traced following the Held raid. A combination of the fact that she was the daughter of Major John MacBride and Maud Gonne, to say nothing of being Seán MacBride's sister, led to her acquittal, but Held vanished behind bars. Berlin was worried about the publicity given to the two cases. Censorship was relaxed to allow the court proceedings to be reported, and Hempel was directed by Woermann, Director of the German Foreign Ministry's Political Division, to deliver the following message in Dublin:

> We considered it important to inform the Irish Government once again that our sole object in the struggle was England. We believed that Ireland, whose enemy through history was known to be England, was fully aware that the outcome of this struggle would also be of decisive importance for the Irish nation and the *final realisation of its national demands* [author's italics]. Given this situation we believed that we could also count on the greatest possible understanding from the Irish Government, despite its neutral attitude, even if Ireland might in some ways be affected by our measures.

Hempel was also instructed to show a glimpse of the mailed fist beneath this velvet glove, a warning that episodes like the Held/Stuart affair should not be made the occasion of press publicity. At this stage, the war was swinging markedly in Germany's favour, and during Hempel's visit to Joseph Walshe, the Irish diplomat expressed 'great admiration for German achievements' – the same 'achievements' against which de Valera had been protesting a little earlier. Well had Hempel himself judged early in his Irish sojourn that there was a tendency in Dublin 'to say pleasant things' which they thought you wanted to hear. Ribbentrop now took a hand in the 'pleasant things' business. Learning of the Malcolm MacDonald visit to Dublin, and the offer of Irish unity, he instructed Hempel (on 11 July) to stress that all Germany wanted in the Irish context was a maintenance of neutrality. His dispatch read:

> Accordingly it is an utterly unreasonable suspicion that we might have the intention to prepare to use Ireland as a military base against England through a so-called 'fifth column' which besides does not exist. If the British Government in dealing with the Irish Government makes use of the idea of a union of Northern Ireland with Southern Ireland, it is evident that this is only a sham which is only engaged in for the purposes of manoeuvring Ireland out of her neutrality and drawing her into the war.

In fact Ribbentrop was lying through his teeth. His telegram was an example of the sort of Nazi duplicity about which small countries like Ireland, which did not manage to remain neutral throughout the war, learned to their cost. For Ribbentrop personally authorised a number of efforts at starting fifth column type activities in Ireland. Probably the most important of these was the ill-fated 'Operation Dove'. This was agreed at a meeting in Berlin on 5 August 1940 between Ribbentrop, Admiral Canaris, Chief of the Abwehr, the *coup d'état* specialist, Dr Veesenmayer, and Lieutenant Colonel Lahousen, who had experience of inciting minorities to rebellion, and it involved smuggling the IRA leader, Seán Russell, out of America and into Ireland. Russell had gone to the US prior to the IRA bombing campaign in England, leaving his ill-prepared subordinates to carry on their disastrous operations. He had been served with an expulsion order by the Americans, but managed to remain at liberty in America through the influence of Clan na Gael. Hempel became aware of moves to smuggle him into Germany and advised against IRA involvement, prompting the overriding memorandum from Woermann stating that the IRA were Germany's 'natural ally'.

Around the same time, friends of Frank Ryan in Germany, Helmut Clissmann and Dr Jupp Hoven, succeeded in persuading the Abwehr that it would create a good impression in Ireland to use German influence in having Frank Ryan, Clissmann and Hoven's IRA friend of the thirties, released from jail in Spain. Ryan had been captured during the Spanish Civil War and escaped death by a hair's breadth. After his whereabouts became known, the publicity attaching to his case caused de Valera to arrange through the Irish Ambassador in Madrid, Leopold Kearney, for the services of a Spanish lawyer to defend Ryan. Most of those captured with Ryan were shot, but his sentence was commuted to life imprisonment. A combination of Hoven and Clissmann's efforts and the intercession of the Irish Government resulted in the Spanish authorities handing Ryan over to the Germans.

In Berlin, he was reunited with Russell, who agreed to take him back with him to Ireland on a German U-boat. Ribbentrop disliked the Irish in general, and Russell in particular, but nevertheless he had agreed to the placing of a U-boat captained by Commander Von Stockhausen at Russell's disposal to take him back to Ireland on a mission which it was hoped would create trouble for the British. As Russell had been given sabotage lessons during his German sojourn, it is more likely that his efforts would have resulted in trouble for the Irish. But in the event these came to nothing. Russell died in Ryan's arms aboard the submarine 100 miles off the Galway coast on 14 August, apparently from a perforated ulcer. He was buried at sea with full military honours, wrapped in a German flag. Ryan, who was in poor health following his traumatic imprisonment in Spain, knew nothing of Irish conditions at that stage, nor what Russell was supposed to be doing, and returned with the submarine to Germany. He died alone and deaf in a sanatorium at Dresden Loschwitz, on 10 June 1944.

After the war, Goertz, who poisoned himself rather than be returned to Germany, wrote a series of articles for the *Irish Times*, in which he drew a pen picture of the IRA, whom Russell had been attempting to reach, which was far from flattering. Goertz had managed to stay at liberty for a year and a half before being captured, and jailed. He owed his freedom not to the IRA, but to a network of sympathisers. In fact, there is some mystery about his survival at large for so long in wartime conditions. A number of senior Irish army officers were able to make contact with him during this period, to sound out German intentions towards Ireland, so it is at least possible to speculate that somebody in authority watched over him for a time. Goertz described the IRA, in the course of his *Irish Times* series, published posthumously in August 1947, as follows:

> The IRA had become an underground movement in its own national sphere, heavily suppressed by men who knew all their methods. Inside the IRA, nobody knew what game

was really played, not even their leader. Their internal means of communication were as primitive as boys playing police and brigands. They got no further than the open message in the sock of a girl. And what messages! There was no code – they did not want to learn the most simple code, they preferred to sacrifice their men and women. They had not a single wireless operator; they made no attempt to learn messages discipline, their military training was nil. I once said to one of them whom I admired for his personal qualities: 'You know how to die for Ireland, but of how to fight for it you have not the slightest idea.' In spite of the fine qualities of individual IRA men, as a body I considered them worthless.

This was also Hempel's view of the organisation. Nevertheless, at least during the early part of the war, the Germans persisted with the 'natural ally' theory. In 1939, one Oscar C. Phaus had been directed by the Abwehr to establish contact with the IRA. He did so by approaching one of the IRA's most inveterate foes, General O'Duffy! However, he did manage a meeting with Maurice Twomey and the Army Council, after which Seamus O'Donovan, again a figure with a Clongowes background – he taught science there – was appointed the principal IRA–Nazi link. O'Donovan, an engineer with the state electricity company, the ESB, was responsible for much of the planning of the IRA's bombing campaign in England. There were initial difficulties between him and the Abwehr, after the German customs strip-searched his wife because she was carrying what was considered to be an illegal packet of cigarettes. But eventually the Germans made arrangements through O'Donovan for supplying the IRA with money, a transmitter and courier routes. Little of value passed from the IRA to the Germans via the transmitter, which was eventually seized by the Gardai in the raid which, as we shall see, led to the imprisonment, hunger strike and death of two IRA men, Tony d'Arcy and Jack McNeela.

Nor did the handful of other spies whom the Germans managed to land in Ireland get very far. One was a former strongman in a circus, Ernest Webber-Drohl, who managed to spend about a month at liberty after being landed by a submarine in January 1940. Karl Anderson, who was landed in Kerry in June, was picked up in Dublin the following day. Three others landed in Cork in July from a yacht, including an Indian. The two Germans with him had little chance of escaping detection as they set off from Baltimore making enquiries about the way to Dublin, some 175 miles away; his presence in wartime Ireland ensured that the trio's period at liberty was measured in hours rather than days. A handful of other agents were landed from U-boats or parachuted into Ireland, but none succeeded either in escaping speedy capture or in sending anything of value back to Germany, even though the fulminations of Churchill and Gray at times made it appear that Ireland was crawling with Nazi spies.

While clumsy German spying attempts were an embarrassment to the Irish Government and a threat to neutrality, a more deadly threat was contained in Woermann's telegram to Hempel indicating that Ireland 'might in some ways be affected by our measures'. She was, grievously, from the air and at sea.

The official Standing War Orders from Grand Admiral Karl Dönitz to submarine commanders, stated that

> basically Irish ships also come under the neutrality regulations . . . In addition, for political reasons, Irish ships and also at times Irish convoys are not to be attacked within the blockade zone if they are seen to be such. However there is no *special obligation* to determine neutrality in the blockade zone.[97]

The Germans certainly displayed 'no special obligation' towards Irish shipping or ships bearing Irish cargoes. In theory, ships bearing Irish markings or ships whose cargoes had been notified to the Germans and would remain in Ireland were not to be attacked. In practice, however, U-boats do not seem to have exercised any great diligence in discovering whether or not their targets were destined for neutral Ireland. One memo from Warnock to the German Foreign Ministry covering June and July of 1940 cites the sinking of one Finnish and four Greek ships carrying grain destined for Ireland. And specifically Irish-registered ships which were bombed, mined or torpedoed included the *Munster*, the *City of Limerick*, the *Isolada*, the *Glencullen*, the *Glencree*, the *Kyleclare*, and the *Kerry Head*, which, like most Irish ships, was painted with huge tricolours and had 'Eire' written on its side in letters 20 feet high. The RAF occasionally mistakenly attacked Irish ships also, as in the case of the off-course *Kerlogue*, which was strafed in the Bay of Biscay and for which the British refused to take responsibility, although London did agree to ex gratia payments to Irish sailors wounded in the attack. Until the fortunes of war unmistakably swung in the Allies' favour, the Irish tended to soft-pedal in their responses to German attacks, and it was not until a German plane sank the *City of Bremen* off the Cork coast on 2 June 1942 that, as one commentator put it, the time for 'bowing and scraping passed' and a vigorous protest was mounted.[98]

Apart from the shipping attacks, the Germans, or at least Ribbentrop, displayed a mulish attitude to the Irish over two issues: one the supply of captured British arms to de Valera, and the other a demand that extra personnel be supplied to the German Embassy. This last may have had a tragic and brutal outcome, causing bombs to fall on Ireland. It was also virtually the last act in the drama of German overtures towards Ireland, both diplomatic and hostile which continued throughout much of 1940.

This was the year of maximum pressure for the Irish. Emergency plans were made for getting de Valera and a hand-picked team of leading politicians and officials out of the country to America on a sea plane from the airport at Foynes on the River Shannon. If there was room on the plane, it was proposed to take the Irish gold reserves along too, a proposal which presumably would have had a limiting effect on the number of those travelling. It was in 1940 also that de Valera ordered that all records of discussions with foreign diplomats held in the Department of External Affairs were to be destroyed. He feared that in the event of an invasion, the Germans might use these later as a justification for their action, as they had done in Holland. The pendulum of anxiety swung continuously from fears of an Allied invasion, or at least a British one, to the threat of a German thrust, with Britain reeling from the ferocity of the U-boat onslaught against the Atlantic convoys. Churchill complained about the loss of the ports in the House of Commons on 6 November, saying that it was a 'most heavy and grievous burden and one which should never have been placed on our shoulders, broad though they be'. This was the trigger for the unleashing of a press campaign in England and America against Irish neutrality. Even George Bernard Shaw joined in:

> If I were in Churchill's place I should put it more philosophically. Instead of saying I will reoccupy your ports and leave you to do your damndest, I should say – 'My dear Mr de Valera, your policy is magnificent but it is not modern statesmanship. You say the ports belong to Ireland; that is what you start from. I cannot admit it. Local patriotism with all its heroic legends is as dead as a doornail today. The ports do not belong to Ireland; they belong to Europe, to the world, to civilisation, to the Most Holy Trinity, as you might say [a satirical reference to the Irish constitution], and are only held in trust by your Government in Dublin. In their names we must borrow the ports from you for the duration. You need not consent to the loan, just as you did not consent to the Treaty; and you will share all the advantages of our victory. All you have to do is to sit tight and say: "I protest!" England will do the rest. So here goes.'[99]

De Valera responded to Shaw via the associated press and to Churchill in the Dail (on 7 November) in what some of his supporters regard as the best speech of his life. In the course of it he said:

> I want to say to our people that we may be – I hope not – facing a grave crisis. If we are to face it, then we shall do it, anyhow, knowing that our cause is right and just, and that if we have to die for it, we shall die for that good cause.

A combination of these exchanges and the obviously orchestrated press campaign caused the Germans to think again about Ireland, and Hempel was instructed to tell de Valera that a British attack would automatically place Ireland in a front alongside Germany. Hitler and Ribbentrop conferred, and the question of supplying captured British arms to the Irish was considered. The question of actual German involvement was ruled out. A German contingency plan, Operation Green, was prepared in August 1940 whereby as part of the overall Operation Sea Lion, as the planned invasion of England was known, a diversionary landing would be made in Ireland, involving some three divisions arriving on the beaches of Waterford and Wexford. There was also a German plan prepared by General Kurt Student, commander of the German 11th Airborne Corps, for a paratroop attack on Northern Ireland. Student suggested to Hitler that the best date for such an attack would be the anniversary of the 1916 Rising in April 1941. It was as well for Ireland that this plan never materialised, as Student and his men showed their mettle in 1941 when they captured the strongly held island of Crete from the British.

In fact, one of the mysteries of the entire war period is why the Germans did not continue their attacks on Northern Ireland after the Belfast bombings. It is known that through Walshe de Valera had representations made to Hempel suggesting that Derry be spared on the basis that it was strongly Nationalist, and that there was nothing of military value there, apart from some shirt factories. Hempel is known to have supported this suggestion and the one from Cardinal MacRory asking that Armagh be spared as the ecclesiastical capital of Ireland. In the event, Derry was left alone, although it was one of the most vital bases of the entire Allied war effort.

The British too had their contingency plan for Germany's invasion of southern Ireland, Plan W, which envisaged them fighting alongside the Irish army after they crossed the border. It says much for the reality of Irish–Allied co-operation that while the politicians were jousting, and sponsoring, a virulent anti-Irish Press campaign, the military authorities on both sides had made preparations which included the provision of small tricolours for the British soldiers which they were supposed to wave to identify themselves as friendly when they crossed the Irish border. Other concrete displays of friendliness included the fact that crashed Allied airmen were regarded as being on non-operational flights and eventually found their way back to their units, whereas German military, air or sea personnel cast up on Irish soil were interned for the duration of the war, albeit in fairly lenient conditions.

However, the atmosphere continued to be fraught as the Battle of Britain raged, and Germany appeared invincible. Walshe, for example, is known to have believed that a German victory was inevitable. In vain did de Valera urge the British to let the Irish have arms. In an interview with Maffey on 17 July, he made it clear that while at the beginning of the war the Irish had stood ready to resist aggression from England, they had changed to planning to ward off a German invasion instead. He cited all the steps taken by the Irish to co-operate with the British, but pointing to British lack of response to Irish requests for arms, and the spying activities of British intelligence despite this co-operation, warned that the Irish army now expected to have to contend with a British rather than a German invasion.

Maffey's record of the interview noted that de Valera asked:

> Why will you not trust us? If you think we might attack the North I say with all emphasis we will never do that. No solution there can come by force. There we must now wait and let the solution come with time and patience. If you think the IRA will get the arms, I can assure you that we have no fifth column today. There is no danger in that quarter.
>
> Give us help with arms and we will fight the Germans as only Irishmen in their own country can fight. There is no doubt on which side my sympathies lie. Nowadays some people joke about my becoming pro-British. The cause I am urging on you is in the best interest of my own country and that is what matters most to me.

As a result of this communication, the British War Cabinet took a slightly more emollient view of Dublin's situation, and while refusing to give a public guarantee not to invade Ireland, it did agree after some quibbling to the supply of some military equipment, chiefly for anti-aircraft purposes. With a tendency towards farce which is never wholly absent from Anglo-Irish relationships, the equipment also included a supply of British-style steel helmets – to replace the German-style ones which the Irish had been forced to obtain from the British! However, the Churchill–de Valera exchanges of November apparently rekindled German interest in the Irish situation, and a number of initiatives were undertaken both at a military and political level. The military appreciation was not promising.

General Warlimont, Deputy Chief of the Wehrmacht High Command Operations Staff, told the Foreign Ministry (on 14 November) that aerial landings on Ireland were impossible, because supplies could not be guaranteed. The most that the Germans could do would be to concentrate German submarines around the ports, which it was expected the British would seize, and direct the Luftwaffe's attention towards the ports also. Warlimont's arguments were supported on 3 December by the commander-in-chief of the German navy, Admiral Raeder, who said that Germany simply didn't have the naval strength to carry out a successful sea landing in Ireland should the British invade.[100] Ireland had no fortified bases or anchorages, and the Germans could not hope to create these in time for a successful amphibious landing. Geography also precluded a seaborne invasion, as the coasts of Wales and Cornwall menaced the German approaches and supply lines. Airborne activities were ruled out on the grounds of Irish weather conditions, and the inadequacy of Irish airfields for German requirements. In fact, all the conditions pointed to the inevitability of creating a German version of Dunkirk should a German invasion take place.

However, the Raeder analysis did leave open the possibility of the Germans making occasional sorties into Irish waters to land supplies of armaments, with Irish co-operation. Ribbentrop directed Hempel to sound out de Valera on a proposal to supply a significant amount of captured British weaponry. Compared to the tiny amount of arms which the Irish had been able to prise out of Britain's grudging hands, the list of proffered war material was mouth-watering. It included 550 machine-guns, 10,000 rifles, 1,000 anti-tank rifles and 46 field guns, together with the requisite ammunition for this lethal largesse. But it was of course an offer which the Irish had to refuse. There was not the remotest possibility that such large-scale landings could be made without the British learning of them. The discovery of this particular 'German plot', with a world war raging, would have created a reaction that would have overshadowed those which had already occurred in Irish history with disastrous consequences.

Hempel realised this, but Ribbentrop was far from understanding. He ordered Hempel to tell de Valera that the much-vaunted Irish preparations to resist a British attack could not be all that serious if the Irish would not accept German arms to help withstand it. De Valera, however, turned away this feint by observing that the German general staff could be relied upon, with typical German thoroughness, to take whatever steps appeared necessary in the event of a British invasion.

Parallel with the military overtures, Ribbentrop had been exerting diplomatic pressure to have the staff at the German legation in Dublin increased. It appears that Warlimont, in the course of his assessment, had mooted the possibility of sending civilian meteorologists to Ireland, and that the Germans also felt it desirable to send 'an official or officer experienced in military reconnaissance'. Hempel was instructed to inform Dublin of a proposal to fly this new staff to Rineanna (later expanded and developed into Shannon Airport) on Christmas Eve. The proposal made initially to Boland at External Affairs struck the Irish like a bombshell. Boland's initial reaction was to tell Hempel that only the Government could give permission for the landing and that he did not think it would be forthcoming. The position was complicated by the fact that de Valera was in hospital for an eye operation. But Hempel made it clear that the matter was seriously regarded in Berlin. He told Boland that this was the first request Germany had made, and that it was being refused, and, having failed with the diplomat, went on to press his case with the Irish deputy prime minister, Seán T. O'Ceallaigh. He also temporised, and the matter was brought to de Valera's attention in hospital.

Hospitalised or no, de Valera ordered that if the Germans landed, they were to be arrested immediately. It later emerged that they could not have done so anyhow, because obstacles had been placed along the runway. However, the army was placed on alert, and the officer in charge of the southern command, Major General Michael Costello, was ordered to arrest the Germans. Rumours abounded, and it was widely believed that the alert was issued because a British invasion was expected. But General Dan McKenna, the officer in charge of the Irish army, who knew the source of the alert, later told the journalist Joseph Carroll that for him it was the most worrying moment of the war.[101]

In the event, a German plane did show up over Rineanna on Christmas Eve morning, and, presumably having inspected the inhospitable runway, flew away again. Before examining what appeared to be the consequences of the fruitless flight, it is worth noting that there was this much substance to the rumours of a British invasion: following Churchill's House of Commons speech, the British, at Churchill's insistence, began implementing the shipping and commodity squeeze already referred to. The Germans proceeded to add their mead of discomfort to these unpleasant proceedings.

Hempel and de Valera had a confrontation over the Rineanna incident on 27 December. In the course of it, Hempel spoke of 'the gravity of the situation', stating that he was confining himself to his instructions, and would 'not speak about possible concrete consequences of a negative Irish attitude'. These consequences would appear to have been felt a few days later. A series of inexplicable German bombing 'mistakes' occurred in various Irish counties on 1 and 2 January 1941. Bombs fell in Carlow, Drogheda, Kildare, Wexford and Wicklow. Hitherto, the only other German bombing incident had been at Campile, County Wexford, the previous August. Further German bombs fell in Dublin on 25 and 31 May 1941. The second raid killed 20 people, wounded

150 more, and destroyed several houses in the North Strand area. This raid was later said to have occurred because the British had discovered a method of deflecting the beams used to guide German bombers, so that planes intended for English cities wound up over Dublin, but no such explanation could be advanced in the case of the earlier raids, which seem inextricably linked with the turning down of Ribbentrop's overtures. These raids ceased as the Germans abandoned Operation Sea Lion in the wake of the successful RAF campaign in the Battle of Britain, and turned their attention instead to Operation Barbarossa, the invasion of Russia. Apart from comparatively minor irritations, such as the Allies notes controversy, Ireland had avoided the dangers of war.

One challenge which the war posed for consciences everywhere was the treatment of the Jews. Ireland did not face it well. Earlier in the century, there had been some significant outbreaks of anti-Semitism, chiefly in Limerick, as the result of inflammatory preachings by a Redemptorist priest, Father John Creagh, director of the Arch-Confraternity of the Holy Family, in January 1904. In Belfast in the thirties some complaints were made to the IRA alleging Jewish extortion in money-lending dealings and hire purchase arrangements for what was claimed to be shoddy furniture. These complaints resulted in Jewish traders being made temporarily unwelcome in some Catholic districts. In all, census reports put the total number of Jews in the country at the turn of the century as being just under 4,000. But Father Creagh perceived a major threat from Jewish money-lenders:

> They have made Limerick their headquarters, from which they can spread their rapacious nets over the country all round. When they came here first, they had to carry their packs upon their shoulders. Now they can afford to have horses and traps to carry their goods, and they can go long distances by train, and succeed in making the farmers their dupes as well as those living in the towns ... I do not hesitate to say that there are no greater enemies of the Catholic Church than the Jews ...[102]

The agitation which followed this and other utterances of Creagh resulted in a boycott of Jewish traders, and several prominent Jewish families left Limerick as a result of abuse and in some cases actual violence. To their credit, Irish leaders like Michael Davitt and John Redmond spoke out against the boycott, and Father Creagh. But Arthur Griffith's *United Irishman* commented:

> We are glad Father Creagh has given the advice he did. We trust he will continue to give it. We have no quarrel with the Jews' religion; but all the howling of journalistic hacks and the balderdash of uninformed sentimentalists will not make us, nor should it make any honest man, cease to expose knavery, because the knavery is carried on by Jews.

The Creagh controversy had become a distant memory by the time Hitler came to power, and protests in Dublin against the Reich were well supported when organised in 1933 by the Chief Rabbi, Dr Isaac Herzog, who later became Chief Rabbi in Israel and father of Chaim Herzog, a future president of Israel.

Robert Briscoe (1894–1969) was a prominent and well-respected member of the Fianna Fáil party, who continuously spoke out against anti-Semitism. Unfortunately two of his opposition fellow TDs, Patrick Belton and Oliver Flanagan, were amongst those to whom he had to address himself. Belton had been active on behalf of Franco during the Spanish Civil War, and Flanagan, a younger man, made his entry into Irish politics during the 1943 election campaign on a confused programme of what he termed monetary reform.

This was in part inspired by the right-wing, anti-Jewish ideas of Father Fahey, the Holy Ghost priest who sought to influence de Valera over the constitution. Like Flanagan, who later told me that he regretted his early anti-Jewish utterances,[103] Fahey was mouthing popular prejudices without any real knowledge of what was going on in the concentration camps. But the attitude of de Valera and his government, who did know, was one of sympathy which stopped well short of actual support for victims of the Holocaust. At an international conference at Evian-Les-Bains in France, called by Roosevelt in 1938, Irish policy was laid down. Effectively, the country was closed to refugees. The Irish representative, Frank T. Cremins, said that Ireland did not have enough land to satisfy the needs of its own people. Thousands of Irish had to emigrate each year, therefore Ireland would make 'no real contribution to the settlement of refugees'. This internationally expounded position was enshrined in a Department of Justice memorandum which made specific reference to Jews. It stated:

> It is the policy of the Department of Justice to restrict the immigration of Jews. The wealth and influence of the Jewish community in this country, and murmurs against Jewish wealth and influence are frequently heard. As Jews do not become assimilated with the native population, like other immigrants, there is a danger that any big increase in their numbers might create a social problem.[104]

The first sentence of the foregoing was later changed to read 'The immigration of Jews is generally discouraged.' At various meetings and discussions on this memorandum, and others which it elicited from other departments, Irish refugee policy acquired a more liberal tone than the Justice memorandum suggested. A minute of 15 December said that

> The Taoiseach explained the attitude of the Government as being that our policy towards this problem should be liberal and generous, due regard being had to our own interests in regard to certain matters, such as employment, foreign relations and the necessity for excluding undesirable persons. Subject to the necessary safeguards in these respects we should be as helpful as possible and we should try positively to give asylum to aliens seeking refuge in existing circumstances.

De Valera was quoted as saying that he 'emphasised the necessity for a positive and liberal policy. Financial considerations should not be allowed to present an insuperable difficulty.'

And at various junctures throughout the war, one could point to representations made to the Germans on behalf of individual Jews by Irish diplomats as indications that de Valera did as requested in a telegram sent to him in December 1942 by Isaac Herzog, with whom he had enjoyed friendly relations during Herzog's Dublin stay, even to the extent of conferring with him about the proposed constitution. The telegram read: 'Revered friend please leave no stone unturned to save tormented remnant of Israel doomed alas to utter annihilation in Nazi Europe.'[105] However, the reality of what was actually done when separated from the rhetoric appears paltry and totally inadequate in the face of the horrors of the Holocaust. In his fine book on the Jews in twentieth-century Ireland,[106] Dermot Keogh summed up the position with both accuracy and restraint: 'It remains very difficult to calculate the number of Jews allowed into Ireland during the war years. Whatever the number – and it may have been as few as sixty – it was insignificant for the six years of war known officially in Ireland as "the Emergency".'

That sixty looks increasingly accusing when contrasted with de Valera's very public stand against the Allied bombing of Rome which he took following the destruction of Monte Cassino as fascism began crumbling in Italy. His biography makes much of the fact that he appealed to the belligerents in March 1944 to save 'this great centre of Christian Faith and Civilisation'. De Valera was subsequently thanked in an address of gratitude signed by hundreds of leading Italian intellectuals, saying: 'the memory of this noble gesture on the part of Ireland's Prime Minister will pass on also to future generations'. By then of course Germany was trembling on the brink of defeat and his stance won him considerable popularity with the influential Irish clergy. Where the less influential Jewish community in Ireland was concerned, de Valera's lack of public condemnation of Hitler's barbarism to their people was compounded by his inexplicable visit of condolence to the German legation. To them, as to many others, the neutrality policy had taken a step too far.

Was Irish neutrality that harmful to the cause of democracy? Obviously, an honest answer must include some recognition of the fact that the curtailment of operating range which the loss of the ports enjoined on the British navy had to have a bearing on the loss of life and shipping off the Irish coast. But the ports were not as strategically vital as Churchill claimed. Nor indeed were they anything like the main cause of British losses. With the fall of France and Norway, British supply lanes along the south-west coast of Ireland became vulnerable to attack by German bombers based in France, which then flew on to Norway to refuel. It is true that, as James Dillon wished, the provision of fighter bases on the Irish west coast for the RAF could have intercepted these bombers, but if the British couldn't guarantee the safety of the ports (or indeed of Belfast), it is difficult to see how they could have prevented German bombers from expunging any such bases before they became operational. The real cause of the shipping losses was a breach in British security. The Germans had cracked their naval codes during a visit by the Royal Navy to the Red Sea, as part of the futile League of Nations sanctions programme in 1936. The British do not appear to have discovered this until the summer of 1943, by which time the Germans had sunk 11.5 million tonnes of shipping in the North Atlantic.

Replying in the Dail to a hostile critique of Irish neutrality in the *New York Times* by Professor Comager,[107] de Valera quoted a spirited defence of the neutrality policy by one of his political enemies, Henry Harrison, a former Parnellite, who, while de Valera and his colleagues were fighting in 1916, was winning a Military Cross with the British in France. Harrison had also attacked Comager, who had said that Ireland had 'missed out somehow on the greatest moral issue of modern history'. But Harrison's reply deals tellingly with that charge.

> You proclaim that the Irish people have 'missed out somehow on the greatest moral issue of modern history' . . . Presumably when Britain and France declared war upon the Axis in September 1939, 'the greatest moral issue in modern history' came into being but Russia continued to 'miss out' on it until Hitler invaded her territory in June, 1941, and America herself 'missed out on the greatest moral issue of modern history' for two and a quarter years until December 1941, when Japan struck her the assassin blow at Pearl Harbor. These two great leviathan Powers were no voluntary crusaders leaping into the arena in unreflecting and disinterested enthusiasm for high moral principle. They remained neutral when Denmark and Norway, Holland and Belgium, Jugoslavia and Greece were, in turn, ravaged and enslaved. They fought because they had to, because they had no choice left, because they were attacked, because being attacked, they needs must fight or submit to a conqueror's yoke. And little Ireland was not attacked. That is the difference. That is the sole difference. For there is nothing more certain than that Ireland also would have fought back if she had been attacked.

George Bernard Shaw also came to admire the Irish stance and to admit that he had misjudged de Valera, saying 'that powerless little cabbage garden called Ireland wins in the teeth of all the mighty powers'. The garden produce motif is not inappropriate. In summing up the Irish position during the war years, I am reminded of a description of the Irish by a French acquaintance of mine: 'For all the hospitality and the friendship, the drinking and the jokes, and the songs, the Irish have a very hard core – like a peach.' De Valera's successful prosecution of neutrality was a peach of a diplomatic achievement. In the words of A.J.P. Taylor: 'The Government of Eire remained implacably neutral, despite much British and American prodding.'[108]

FIVE

STORMONT: A BODY IMPOLITIC

THE ORANGE STATE'S FIRST DECADES

Through sins of omission the British Government and by sins of commission the Unionist establishment created in six counties of north-eastern Ireland a statelet which, while allegedly part of the United Kingdom with all the privileges and responsibilities involved, in practice exhibited a close resemblance to South Africa under apartheid, the principal difference lying in the fact that discrimination was carried on in the name of religion rather than colour. In her book *The Catholics of Ulster*,[1] Marianne Elliott quotes from Brian Moore's novel, *The Emperor of Ice Cream*, to illustrate the mindset of a middle-class reader of the Catholic-catering *Irish News* during the 1930s and 1940s. Moore's character

> read the newspaper as other men play cards, shuffling through a page of stories until he found one which would confirm him in his prejudice. A Jewish name discovered in an account of a financial transaction, a Franco victory over the godless Reds, a hint of British perfidy in international affairs, an Irish triumph on the sports field, an evidence of Protestant bigotry, a discovery of Ulster governmental corruption: these were his reading goals.

Not surprisingly, Moore had emigrated from such a background, to Canada, by the time he wrote his novel. Not surprisingly either, the attitude of his character epitomised that of many Catholics. Whereas in the south, despite the enormous influence of the Catholic clergy and hierarchy, a combination of the Republican tradition of not differentiating between Protestant and Catholic in the common name of Ireland, coupled with the new state's requirement, and inclination, to win the allegiance of former Unionists, meant that the Government tried to make Protestants welcome in government, civil service, army and the professions, the opposite was true in the north. Making due allowance for the fact that the Unionists would have had to be superhuman not to have been filled with feelings of the deepest apprehension at their laagered situation on the island of Ireland as a whole, wherein they faced an overwhelmingly Catholic majority outside their border, and a sizeable Catholic minority inside it, nevertheless they had one vital power which they chose not to use – the power of initiative. They had the option of extending the hand of friendship to the

Nationalist community but chose instead to establish a regime wherein Catholics were actively and strenuously discriminated against from the outset.

The sustained chorus of 'Ulster will fight and Ulster will be right', coming against a backdrop of centuries of clashes between natives and settlers, from the time of Gladstone's Home Rule Bill onwards, created a situation where, to put it bluntly, dementia became the Unionists' most valuable electoral lode. It was mined industriously and continuously, allegedly to safeguard Ulster from 'the hells prepared by Rome'. The Unionist establishment, comprising the Protestant landowner, industrialist and professional man, with the aid of the Orange card, managed for several decades to achieve the twin goals of denying Catholics a position of respect within the Six Counties, and at the same time dividing the working class along religious lines so that the contagions of socialism or trade unionism were largely inoculated against. On a rhetorical level, the supremacist tradition of Protestantism versus Catholicism was continuously trumpeted in statements from the Unionist leadership, which would have rung in the ears of Moore's newspaper reader and thousands like him. For example, the attitude of the northern decision-takers to the Catholic civil servants who had been transferred by Dublin Castle to Belfast after partition may be gauged from a comment by a Unionist minister, Sir Edward Archdale, in 1925:

> A man in Fintona asked him how it was that he had over 50 per cent Roman Catholics in his ministry. He thought that was too funny. He had 109 on his staff and so far as he knew there were four Roman Catholics. Three of these were civil servants turned over to him, whom he had to take when he began.[2]

Dawson Bates, however, made Archdale seem positively liberal. He 'had such a prejudice against Catholics that he made it clear to his Permanent Secretary that he did not want his most juvenile clerk, or typist (if a Papist), assigned for duty to his ministry'.[3] His reputation amongst Catholics was such that it was popularly believed that he slept with a revolver and a copy of the Special Powers Act under his pillow.

Speaking at a 12 July rally in 1933, Sir Basil Brooke, who later became Prime Minister, said that:

> There were a great number of Protestants and Orangemen who employed Roman Catholics. He felt he could speak freely on this subject as he had not a Roman Catholic about his own place. He appreciated the great difficulty experienced by some of them in procuring suitable Protestant labour but he would point out that Roman Catholics were endeavouring to get in everywhere. He would appeal to Loyalists therefore, wherever possible, to employ good Protestant lads and lassies.

The following March Brooke amplified his philosophy:

I recommend those people who are Loyalists not to employ Roman Catholics, 99 per cent of whom are disloyal; I want you to remember one point in regard to the employment of people who are disloyal . . . You are disfranchising yourselves in that way . . . You people who are employers have the ball at your feet. If you don't act properly now, before we know where we are we shall find ourselves in the minority instead of the majority. I want you to realise that, having done your bit, you have got your Prime Minister behind you.[4]

Asked to repudiate Brooke in the Stormont parliament the following day, James Craig, who in 1927 had been created the first Viscount Craigavon, retorted: 'There is not one of my colleagues who does not entirely agree with him and I would not ask him to withdraw one word he said.' A month later, Craigavon went further, making the ringing declaration: 'I have always said that I am an Orangeman first and a politician and a member of this parliament afterwards . . . All I boast is that we have a Protestant parliament and a Protestant state.'[5]

The statements quoted above scored into the consciousness of Catholics, and underlined for them how fundamentally unwelcome they were in the Protestant state. Resentment and reaction naturally followed, sometimes expressed in the ghetto mentality of the Moore character, sometimes in IRA violence, more often in despair and the sullen acquiescence of the defeated. From the breakdown of the Collins–Craig pact, the northern government continued to strengthen its hand. The old RIC was disbanded a few days after the pact was signed, and from 4 April the new paramilitary force, the Royal Ulster Constabulary, took over. Its composition was intended to be 2,000 ex-RIC men and 1,000 A Specials. It had been envisaged that half of the RIC men would be Catholic, but less than half of the projected number of Catholics came forward, their quota being made up from the ranks of the Specials. At this stage both Protestants and Catholics had good reasons for their fears and angers. An observer at the inaugural meeting of the North-Eastern Advisory Committee,[6] which was held in Dublin on 11 April, would have gained a good insight as to what these were.

Michael Collins chaired the meeting, which was attended by several members of his Cabinet, a number of northern bishops and priests, some northern Sinn Féiners, and members of the IRA. It did not include any representatives of the more constitutional-minded Nationalists, politicians like Joseph Devlin and his followers, who represented the strain of the old Irish Parliamentary Party in Northern Ireland, moderate propertied Catholicism. Collins's friend, Bishop MacRory, described the plight of the Catholics, hounded out of their workplaces and penned into ghettos which were fired on nightly by the Specials. The conditions were such that, in order to move about, even by day, without being shot while venturing into the streets, Catholics had tunnelled through the walls of their back yards and sometimes their houses.

One of MacRory's suggestions for coping with these conditions was that Catholics should recognise the new police force. This would at least have the benefit of placing arms in the hands of some 1,000 Catholics. The subtext of much of the contributions to the meeting was not about how the new state might be recognised and worked with, but how it could be destroyed. Richard Mulcahy told the meeting: 'I take it that under the terms of the Treaty we recognise that Parliament in order to destroy it . . . to carry out all its terms will completely unify the country and destroy the Northern parliament.' Nobody contradicted him. Collins himself read from documents which made it clear that he was hoodwinking the northern authorities in the matter of paying primary schoolteachers.

On the educational issue the clerical representatives made it clear what their priorities were: to retain control of their schools. Archdeacon Tierney said: 'We have come here merely to attend to the national aspect of things . . . what I would suggest is that schools under Catholic managers would get the right to adopt the programme and timetable of southern Ireland. If we get that, I will close with them at once.' In the event, Catholic schools would develop a separate ethos and, for example, teach the Irish language and Irish history, whereas Protestant schoolchildren learned British history. We will return to the educational system later. Suffice it to say at this juncture that the relationship between the two churches which de Tocqueville had encountered the previous century had not fundamentally altered where Northern Ireland was concerned.

Kevin O'Higgins, with his usual uncomfortable honesty, drew the meeting's attention to the fact that, as a result of some unsanctioned IRA activity in the south, carried out by way of supporting the Belfast boycott, some Unionist property was being destroyed, and that this was giving the northern Orangemen grounds with which to justify their violent behaviour. Things were to get worse shortly after the meeting was held. On 25 April, in the Bandon district of County Cork, an IRA commandant was shot dead as he called on a Protestant-owned house. By and large Protestants were not attacked by the IRA in the south, though there had been a few isolated killings of Protestants in Kerry and elsewhere for which the only motivation that could be adduced was the religious one. However, following the Bandon incident in the one major outburst of sectarianism in either the Anglo-Irish war or the civil war, ten innocent Protestant men were shot in reprisals. Griffith and Collins denounced the killings, and the dead IRA officer's successor called in arms and ensured that no further Protestant killings occurred. However, the incident naturally raised fears in the Protestant community of Northern Ireland.

Nor would Protestants have been reassured if they could have heard the discussion which followed O'Higgins's intervention at the North-Eastern Advisory Committee meeting. One northern delegate, Dr Russell MacNabb, argued in favour of the destruction of property, remarking that there had been 'some beautiful fires in Belfast each night'. The underdog bites at the testicles. MacNabb was referring to the fact that some one million pounds' worth of Protestant-owned property had been destroyed in the summer of 1922.

Between 10 and 25 May alone, there were 41 big fires in Belfast, costing some half a million pounds. Outside Belfast, Shanes Castle, Randalstown, the ancestral home of the Speaker of the Northern Ireland parliament, Colonel O'Neill, was amongst a number of other mansions, mills and railway stations destroyed.

Collins's response to MacNabb on the policy of incendiarism was: 'I know for a good many months we did as much as we could to get property destroyed. I know that if a good deal more property was destroyed . . . I know they think a great deal more of property than of human life.' He then asked one of the two crucial questions raised at the meeting. Speaking to the northerners he said: 'The whole thing is, what *is* proposed?' The second question was raised by Bishop MacRory and addressed to the southerners. He asked: 'Can you protect us?' No answer was forthcoming to either question. But the bloody reaction was all too clearly visible in Northern Ireland. May and June were particularly bad months in Belfast. The Specials and murder gangs such as the Ulster Protestant Association made shooting galleries of the Catholic ghettos. The UPA was one of the more notorious of several pseudo-gangs set up by the British military establishment in co-operation with the Unionists to combat the IRA from 1920 onwards. Normally these gangs consisted of British soldiers, often under the control of an officer, members of the RUC, and ex-UVF men and B Specials.

They usually operated under cover of darkness, assisted in carrying out assassinations in reprisal for IRA activities by the poor quality of Belfast's street lighting. In an effort to curb the guerrillas and their support, they would burst out of cars, with blackened faces, or prowl mean, curfewed, silent streets in stockinged feet to shoot some – often dubiously chosen – target, or hurl a hand grenade through a window. If a gang were spotted, the inhabitants of the district would join in a long-drawn-out keening howl, 'M-U-R-D-E-R-R-H', accompanied by a custom which, like the gangs themselves, reappeared in Belfast during the 'troubles' in the later part of the century, banging bin lids, pots or pans against the pavement.

One of the earliest childhood memories of Michael Traynor, who grew up during these happenings and later joined the IRA as a result, was of going with some other boys to view the bodies of three IRA Volunteers who had been shot as a reprisal for the deaths of three Auxiliaries. Crosses had been cut into their feet and foreheads and

They had small black holes in their heads . . . I remember the MacMahon murders, we didn't think that especially brutal for the time. I remember we thought that throwing hand grenades into the bedroom of two elderly sisters on St Patrick's night in Thompson St was far worse because there was an awful job cleaning up afterwards with feathers and bits of bedding and pieces of flesh all splashed around the room. That was done by the Specials.

The UPA were described in a police report as 'having been formed by well disposed citizens' but becoming dominated by the 'Protestant hooligan element'.[7] Their 'whole aim and object was simply the extermination of Catholics by any and every means'. They 'entered thoroughly into the disturbances, met murder with murder, and adopted in many respects the tactics of the rebel gunmen'.

Apart from the well-disposed citizenry behind the UPA, the rulers of the new state also had at their disposal some 16 battalions of British troops, and nearly 50,000 police and Specials. It is doubtful if the IRA at any stage exceeded 8,500. Apart from numerical weakness, the IRA also faced a battery of laws, in particular the Northern Ireland Special Powers Act, which allowed for the death penalty, internment and flogging. This fearsome piece of legislation remained in being throughout most of the century, even at times when all threat of IRA violence had ceased. Its draconian powers were so highly esteemed by other repressive regimes that John Vorster, then the South African Minister for Justice, commented, as he introduced a swingeing new Coercion Bill in the South African parliament in April 1963, that he 'would be willing to exchange all the legislation of that sort for one clause of the Northern Ireland Special Powers Act'.[8]

Some defenders of unionism, such as Patrick Buckland, have argued that

law enforcement was not as severe and brutal as hostile critics of Northern Ireland have liked to suggest . . . The Special Powers Act was a legitimate response to the problem of maintaining law and order. It had been urged on Craig by the army, which was loath to use its powers under the Restoration of Order in Ireland Act; it was less far reaching than the British Act – and subsequent anti-terrorist laws in the South; and Craig only reluctantly authorised the use of the new powers.

This was not the view of the British Council of Civil Liberties. After the Act had been in place for over a decade, following a period of savage rioting in the thirties, it issued a report which said:

Firstly, that through the operation of the Special Powers Act contempt has been begotten for the representative institutions of government.

Secondly, that through the use of the Special Powers, individual liberty is no longer protected by law, but is at the disposition of the Executive. This abrogation of the rule of law has been so practised as to bring the freedom of the subject into contempt.

Thirdly, that the Northern Government has used Special Powers towards securing the domination of one particular political faction and, at the same time, towards curtailing the lawful activities of its opponents . . . The Government's policy is thus driving its opponents into the way of extremists.

Fourthly, that the Northern Irish Government, despite its assurances that Special Powers are intended for use only against law-breakers, has frequently employed them against innocent and law-abiding people, often in humble circumstances, whose injuries, inflicted without cause or justification, have gone unrecompensed and disregarded.

In addition to the foregoing measures, internment was introduced. A prison ship, the *Argenta*, was moored in Belfast Lough. It has been argued that the purpose of internment was economic and political rather than military. Denise Kleinrichert has quoted survivors of the *Argenta* as saying that there were fewer than half a dozen IRA activists aboard, but that there were men who had had good jobs which within weeks of their arrests went to Unionists. 'The internment was about an empowered Government confiscation of education, jobs, financial resources, security and personal freedom. Professional businessmen and Sinn Féin leaders were in the group interned which interrupted the establishment of a nationalist presence to formulate policy related to the Boundary Commission.'[9]

A good deal of the information laid against the more than 600 men and women (the women were lodged in Armagh jail) picked up in internment swoops on and after 22 May 1922 was collected by local Specials who probably confused political activism with IRA activity. Catholics claimed that if they blessed themselves they were liable to be interned! But whatever the motivation for internment, a combination of the pressures brought to bear on the Nationalist community meant that by the end of 1922, the IRA was virtually wiped out in the Six Counties, and the new state felt strong enough to abandon its policy of 'the enemy of my enemy is my friend' and to crack down on Loyalist as well as Republican violence, the UPA being one of the organisations which was broken up and its members jailed. By the end of 1924, internment was ended and a curfew which had remained in operation in Belfast was temporarily done away with, though it reappeared in Catholic areas several times in the ensuing decades.

In its early days, the new parliament held its meetings in Belfast City Hall, albeit between increasingly long periods of suspension. It then took a lease on the Presbyterian Assembly's training college near Queen's University, and by 1932 the new state had become secure enough to have built an imposing new parliament building at Stormont, where, at the time of writing, the northern assembly continued to meet. By that time, apart from the security measures, the Unionists had taken a number of other steps which made their control of the political system virtually impregnable.

In 1920, Nationalists controlled 25 local councils in the north. By 1924, the Unionists had whittled this down to two (out of a total of approximately 80). This is how it was done. Dublin Castle handed control of local government to the new Belfast parliament on 21 December 1921, and the northern Ministry of Home Affairs circularised local authorities, informing them of the change and requesting their co-operation. Tyrone County Council reacted by writing to refuse recognition to the northern government, supporting instead the Dail in Dublin. The police were promptly ordered to take control of the council's offices, and the Local Government (Emergency Powers) Bill was put through the Belfast parliament, enabling the Ministry for Home Affairs to dissolve rebellious councils and appoint in their stead a commission to carry out their duties.

Fermanagh County Council behaved as Tyrone had done and on 21 December passed a resolution stating that they, in view of the expressed desire of a large majority of people in this county, do not recognise the partition parliament in Belfast and do hereby direct our secretary to hold no further communications with either Belfast or British local government departments, and we pledge our allegiance to Dail Eireann.

Again the RUC were sent around, and a commission replaced Fermanagh County Council. The same procedure was followed where other Nationalist-controlled councils, town commissioners, boards of Poor Law guardians and so forth were concerned. By way of underlining the new order of things, the commissioner appointed to Armagh and Keady urban councils, Colonel Waring, was an officer in the B Specials. But the state did not put its trust merely in symbolic appointments. Before 1922 ended, the Local Government Bill had passed into law both abolishing proportional representation and making a declaration of allegiance to the Crown and to the Government obligatory on all officials. A combination of protests from Dublin and a recognition that an important minority safeguard was being destroyed caused a temporary withholding of the royal assent, which a resignation threat from Craig soon removed. The Orangemen then moved to set up a judicial commission under Sir John Leech, KC, to delineate new local government boundaries.

The Nationalists boycotted Leech's work, partly out of outrage at the destruction of proportional representation, and partly because of the speed at which he worked, allowing councils only a week or a fortnight to supply proposals to him. Above all, Nationalists believed that Leech and the PR manoeuvre were both irrelevant because the Boundary Commission would inevitably do the right thing by them. They were to be sadly disillusioned. On 12 July 1923 the Unionist MP for Fermanagh and Tyrone, William Miller, spelt out the reasons why with more accuracy than sensitivity: 'When the Government of Northern Ireland decided to do away with proportional representation the chance that they had been awaiting for so long arrived and they took advantage of it . . . they divided the country in the way they thought best.'[10]

The way 'thought best' was simplicity itself. In areas with a Nationalist majority, the wards were redrawn so that it took a huge Nationalist majority to win a seat, thus eating up Nationalist votes. However, Unionist areas required but a small majority to get elected. The Local Government Bill aided this process by restricting the franchise to rate-payers and their wives. The poorer Catholics who did not pay rates thus lost the vote. In order to see how this operated in practice, no better example can be given than Derry, known to Unionists as 'the Maiden City' because its defences were not penetrated during the siege of Derry, 1688-9. Thus the city acquired a symbolic importance for the Unionists. It had held out against external forces. It must not be allowed to yield to internal ones. The problem was that Derry was overwhelmingly Catholic, by a majority of two to one. However, the Local Government Bill countered the Catholics' numerical superiority so effectively that more than 40 years later, appropriately enough in the anniversary year of the Rising, 1966, Derry's 10,274 Protestants still effectively controlled its 20,102 Catholics. What the Local Government Bill did not achieve initially was added to over the years by boundary revisions which divided the city into three electoral wards. The restricted franchise, limited to those who paid rates, disenfranchised some 6,000 Catholics, and the subsequent carve-up resulted in the following division of local government – i.e. county council – seats.

South Ward	North Ward	Waterside Ward
11,185 voters	6,476 voters	5,549 voters
10,047 Catholics	2,530 Catholics	1,852 Catholics
1,138 Protestants	3,946 Protestants	3,697 Protestants
8 (Nationalist) Councillors	8 (Unionist) Councillors	4 (Unionist) Councillors

Apart from the obviously undemocratic nature of the gerrymander the system gave rise to various other evils. Poverty was an obvious one. Phil Coulter's line in his song 'The Town That I Loved So Well', 'where the men on the dole played a woman's role', accurately describes the situation of much of Derry's male, working-class population. 'Green children' were another symptom of the situation. The Catholic Church's opposition to birth control meant that there was a plentiful supply of cheap labour available amongst children, also known as 'half-timers', who worked half their time in the shirt factories, the other half at school. Tiredness and malnutrition accentuated their slum pallor. With rough-handed kindness, the Christian Brothers enabled many of the children to survive by administering a daily table-spoonful of cod-liver oil. But apart from poverty, which existed amongst Protestants also, one of the worst aspects of the system where Catholics were concerned was the mistrust it engendered in the idea of the vote being an instrument of change. None of the gerrymandered councils which the Unionists wrested from the Nationalists were ever returned to Nationalist hands, and thus Catholic voters gave up going to the polls, leaving the Unionists an uncontested run at elections. The system also created hardships for the Protestant working class.

As local government authority houses gave their occupants a vote, it became important to the Unionists that houses did not fall into the wrong hands. And the 'wrong hands' were many. Even though the Unionists controlled the councils, the majority eligible for local authority housing were Catholic. Faced with this dilemma, Omagh Rural Council, Unionist-controlled but presiding over a population which was 62% Catholic, wrote to the Unionist Chief Whip at Stormont[11] asking for advice on some method which would allow the allocation of houses to Unionists without benefiting Catholics:

> We would point out that in certain districts cottages are required by Unionist workers but we hesitate to invite representations as we know there would be a flood of representations

from the Nationalist side and our political opponents are only waiting the opportunity to use this means to outvote us in divisions where majorities are close.

The problem was eventually solved in Omagh as it was in other strongly Catholic areas by the simple expedient of building no houses for anybody, Catholic or Protestant. Decades later, the poor quality of the Six Counties housing stock would prove to be a potent weapon in the hands of Ian Paisley, as he successfully assailed the Unionist landowning and professionalist ascendancy with stentorian complaints about 'dry closets' (i.e. outside lavatories) on behalf of his working-class Protestant supporters.

The discrimination in housing, coupled with the gerrymandering approach, had the intended effect – it stopped the Catholics' higher birth rate from threatening Unionist hegemony. Statistics show that between 1937 and 1961, the Catholics, with one-third of the population, provided a majority of those who emigrated from the Six Counties, a total of 90,000 out of 159,000.[12]

Another tactic used by the Unionists to discourage existing Catholic families from continuing in local authority housing was to refuse to carry out repairs. In 1945, the Northern Ireland Government's own survey showed that 30% of all houses in the state needed to be replaced. In Catholic areas such as County Fermanagh, the figure frequently rose over 50%.

Some commentators on Northern Ireland aver that if the Catholics did not exactly deserve what befell them, they were in part at least the arbiters of their own misfortune through not having entered wholeheartedly into the running of the new statelet from the outset. Describing the early days, Marianne Elliott writes:

> Nationalists boycotted the new Northern Ireland parliament when it opened at Belfast City Hall on 22 June 1921, as they did every other state body including the crucial Leech and Lynn Committees (set up to decide on the future structure of local government and education). The policy of abstention was disastrous, particularly in these early days when things were still open to change. It also absolved the Unionists from blame for the developing bias, since they could legitimately claim that Nationalists had been given the opportunity to influence developments, but refused, and by so refusing simply proved their disloyalty.[13]

Abstention certainly is a sterile policy, even at its lowest; it flouts Lyndon Johnson's famous dictum that it is better to be in the tent with one's enemies pissing outwards than to have them on the outside pissing in. Obviously abstention removed Catholics from even sighting distance of the levers of power, but one may search the Unionist record exhaustively without finding much evidence that they were ever 'open to change' either during the period when the state was being founded or subsequently. Certainly the abandonment of abstention either in the twenties or later in the century did not elicit a generous response from a majority of Unionists. So far as the Catholics were concerned, they had voted for Home Rule, had seen democracy flouted, experienced the activities of murder gangs, and were given no indication by

Protestant decision-takers that joining the new state at its inception would lead to kindlier days ahead. Their unrealised hopes lay in the findings of the Boundary Commission. In fact, given the history of Orangeism, and the nature of the Orange state which it produced, it would have required not one but ten Nelson Mandelas to have bridged the gulf between the two traditions. The declaration which new members of the Orange Order are expected to make is explicitly anti-Catholic:

> Do you promise, before this Lodge, to give no countenance, by your presence or otherwise, to the unscriptural, superstitious, and idolatrous worship of the Church of Rome? And do you also promise never to marry a Roman Catholic, never to stand sponsor for a child when receiving baptism from a priest of Rome, nor allow a Roman Catholic to stand sponsor for your child at baptism? And do you further promise to resist, by all lawful means, the ascendancy, extension and encroachments of that Church; at the same time being careful always to abstain from all unkind words and actions towards its members, yea, even prayerfully and diligently, as opportunity occurs, to use your best efforts to deliver them from error and false doctrine, and lead them to the truth of that Holy Word, which is able to make them wise unto salvation?

From giving 'no countenance' to the idolatrous was but a short step to giving them nothing. All that the adjuration 'to abstain from all unkind words' towards Catholics meant in practice was that the Order's spokesmen used relatively polite language when outlining its discriminatory employment policies towards them. A Grand Master of the Orange Order, Sir Joseph Davison, explicitly stated these at a big Orange demonstration:

> When will the Protestant employers of Northern Ireland recognise their duty to their Protestant brothers and sisters and employ them to the exclusion of Roman Catholics? It is time the Protestant employers realised that whenever a Roman Catholic is brought into employment it means one Protestant vote less. It is our duty to pass the word along from this great demonstration and I suggest the slogan should be: Protestant employ Protestants.[14]

To understand the 'clout' which such sentiments carried it should be borne in mind that the ruling Unionist Council in 1966 contained 712 delegates. Of these, 122 were nominated by county grand lodges of the Orange Order. By the end of the century, this block vote had grown, as the Council itself neared the 900 mark, to around 160 members.

Apart from permeating every area of Unionist political life, including having a major say in the selection of candidates, the Orange Order was, and is, a powerful force in the civil service and in the professional life of the state. One of the most significant underlinings of the Order's position in Northern Ireland society occurred less than two months after the opening of the new parliament. In August 1922, Dawson Bates personally sanctioned the creation of a specific Orange lodge for the RUC, and underlined the importance he attached to it by addressing its first reunion the following year. This sort of involvement of the Order in politics drew Catholic criticism which was echoed in liberal circles in England, and as a result, open political involvement by the Order was officially discouraged. Unofficially the phrase 'in lodge' came to have a very particular significance where Northern Ireland Protestantism was concerned. The Catholics by contrast developed all the dark, brooding resentments of the defeated and the unjustly treated, occasionally contributing to the injustice by either refusing to go forward for state appointments, on the grounds that it was useless for Catholics to apply for such positions, or on the other hand, treating the handful of particularly able Catholics who managed to slip through the system as Uncle Toms. J.J. Campbell, the editor of the *Irish News*, who became a Nationalist MP and tried to co-operate with the system by taking his seat, became popularly known amongst Catholics as 'Judas Campbell' as a result.

This attitude persisted in the Six Counties right up to the eve of the formation of the co-ordinated civil rights movement which lit the spark that led to the conflagration that eventually destroyed Unionist hegemony. As late as 1964, a prominent Catholic layman, G.B. Newe, wrote (in *Christus Rex*) attacking the attitude of Catholics to serving on the various health and welfare committees:

> We seem to be not at all interested in either the existence or the work of such committees. Often it is alleged that these committees are carefully selected by 'the powers that be' so that we, who are an important section of this community, are deliberately excluded from their counsels. Even if it could be proved that this is so, *is it the whole story?* Can we *honestly* say that we are eager to assist the community in this kind of work? If we do take part, are we found to have the qualities required in these fields? Are we good 'stayers', really and sincerely interested in the good of *all* members of the community, including that vast majority who are not of the same faith as ourselves? ... In the great majority of instances, a Catholic boy appears for interview with, not a chip on his shoulder, but a blinking log! Many Catholic youngsters are predisposed to failure, and the attitude is, to a great extent, cultivated in the schools, and in some schools in particular. I fear that it is said openly: 'Because you are a Catholic you are not likely to get a job.'

The society Newe was writing about was not a happy one. Publicly, the middle classes, both Catholic and Protestant, interacted easily enough with each other at tennis and golf clubs, but privately, both sides knew a secret war raged against and to defend the status quo. The lodge expected the Protestant auctioneer to ensure that the Protestant business, farm or property did not fall into Catholic hands. The Sodalities, the Knights of Columbanus and Opus Dei, expected their adherents to be equally vigilant in defending Catholic interests. It was taken as a given that even if no actual hostilities broke out around the time of the 'twalfth', during the marching season, Protestants would draw apart from Catholics. Neighbours walked on either side of the street in the weeks immediately prior to the celebrations, and those who could afford to do so amongst the Nationalist community took their holidays in July. It was a well-recognised, though unacknowledged, fact that the southern

Irish tourist season, particularly in the west of Ireland and in Donegal, began with the annual Catholic exodus from Northern Ireland around the time of the 12th. The Protestants did not feel it necessary to leave their homes or go on holiday for the annual Catholic celebration of Our Lady's Day in mid-August, but it too provided its coolnesses, and the occasional riot. At working-class level, the currents of discrimination and of a consequent resentment ran deep and virulently.

Statistics for government employment under Unionist-controlled county councils give an indication of the situation.

	No. of non-manual Government employees	No. of Catholics	Catholics as % of employees	Catholics as % of population
Antrim	257	19	7.8	22
Armagh	129	16	12.5	46.5
Derry	206	16	7.8	43
Down	294	56	19	30
Fermanagh	53	5	9.4	55.4
Tyrone	156	18	11.5	55.3
Total	1,095	130	11.9	34

Bad as they are, these statistics do not give the full flavour of the pettiness which accompanied public employment policies. For example, in 1942, the town clerk of Barrow-in-Furness, a Protestant English gentleman, W. Allen, was appointed town clerk of Belfast. However, before the well-qualified Allen could take up the post, it was discovered that his wife was a Catholic. Ministerial approval for his appointment was withheld, and the job went to someone else. Such incidents added to the weight of the 'blinking log' on the shoulders of schoolboys described by G. B. Newe.

Both Catholic and Protestant schoolboys found it difficult to reach the sort of *modus vivendi* which might have lightened the weight of the log because of the structure of the educational system which the new state inherited and perpetuated. The bulk of the Irish educational system north and south of the border was denominational. On the Catholic side, bishops, priests and laity held a role, evolving from the type of priest and education structure described by de Tocqueville during his visit to nineteenth-century Ireland, which had been fought for and moulded by the Church. For the greater part of the twentieth century a teacher could not be appointed or dismissed without the local bishop's sanction. Most secondary schools were controlled by religious orders. Higher education too had been a denominational battlefield since the founding in 1592 of Dublin University, generally known as Trinity College Dublin, as a bastion of Protestantism in Ireland. In 1845, as the famine raged, Sir Robert Peel set up the three Queen's Colleges of Belfast, Cork and Galway. The Irish hierarchy, taking its tone from Pope Pius IX, condemned these as 'Godless colleges'. The Irish hierarchy also played a part in Cardinal Newman's attempt to set up a counterbalancing Catholic university in 1854.

Local opposition to the great English clergymen, and British governmental refusal to recognise its degrees killed the Catholic university project. Gladstone endeavoured to meet the conflicting demands for Irish university education in 1881 by setting up the Royal University of Ireland to organise examinations for the students of the three Queen's Colleges, and to confer degrees. University College Dublin was founded the following year by the Jesuits. Augustine Birrell made possible the setting up of an Irish National University in 1908 which embraced the four colleges and recognised some degree courses in Maynooth. All these steps had been accompanied by fierce debate between spokespersons for the emerging Catholic middle class, its clergy, representatives of the Protestant ascendancy, advanced Nationalists who wanted Irish on the university curriculum and reactionary elements in the British Government.

The educational issue was therefore a well-trodden battlefield by the time partition was introduced. Sniper fire, it might be remarked, was intensified by the deplorable papal Ne Temere decree of 1908, which applied to 'mixed marriages', i.e. marriages between a Catholic and a non-Catholic. This stipulated that the non-Catholic had to agree that any children of the union would be brought up Catholic. The decree both caused friction within marriage, and, throughout the century, provided a number of *cause célèbre* cases in which one partner or the other left the marital home, taking the children with them to be brought up in the religion of the parent. The decree proved a fertile source of propaganda for Unionist apologists, and was often pointed to by them as a symptom of papal bigotry which had led to a decline in the Protestant population in southern Ireland. Certainly in Northern Ireland, at least, the decree resulted in children attending schools with a very different tradition to that of their Protestant parent. Those traditions, like the schools themselves, were fixed in their polarity by what transpired at the setting up of the Six County state.

To be fair, education was one area in which the Unionists made a promising start. The Minister for Education, Lord Londonderry, was considerably more enlightened than the general run of his fellows. He wanted an educational system which would be both better funded and less sectarian than the existing one. Accordingly Craig agreed to the establishment of a committee headed by Robert Lynn MP to decide on how education should be organised in the new state. Lynn's committee recommended a break with the denominational system which had obtained under the British. It suggested that financial packages be introduced to encourage the churches to transfer their schools to the state. These schools would not give religious instruction, nor question the religion of anyone appointed to a teaching post. For its time (and place) these were far-reaching and far-seeing proposals. They were embodied in an educational bill which the new parliament passed during May 1923. However, they aroused strong opposition on both sides of the denominational divide. We have seen how, in his discussions with Michael Collins over the plight of Catholics in Northern Ireland, Archdeacon Tierney kept his eye on the ball to maintain control in and of Catholic schools. His attitude was that of the northern bishops who pressured Joseph Devlin, the Nationalist leader, and his colleagues to enter parliament to defend their educational interests. Recognition of the northern statelet was a very small gnat to strain at compared to swallowing any proposals which might threaten their control of the hard-fought-for Catholic school system.

On the other side of the fence, the General Assembly of the Presbyterian Church condemned the new proposals and teamed up with both the Church of Ireland and the Methodists in pressuring Craig to demand changes which would allow Bible instruction in schools, and the right to appoint teachers by a denominational management. The Protestant churchmen were supported by the Orange Order, which set up a special committee to lobby for these rights.

The Protestant churches ended up getting the best of both worlds. As Patrick Buckland notes: 'changes in 1925 and 1930 produced a system effectively endowing Protestantism and discriminating against Catholics, particularly by providing for compulsory simple Bible instruction'. Those schools which transferred to the state system got the grants which accrued with the change. In addition, they were given positions on the management committees, and Bible instruction was made a part of the curriculum so that the state schools effectively became Protestant schools. The Catholic Church, which opposed Bible teaching, remained outside the system, which now provided Protestant schools with more money than Catholic ones. The Bishop of Down and Connor, Daniel Mageean, condemned the outcome as being

> against all principles of justice and equity . . . We form a large portion of the population, and have more children attending primary elementary schools than any other religious denomination. We ask for no privilege, but we claim equality of treatment with our fellow citizens and we demand our rights.

Thus, for all these reasons and many more too wearisome to relate, the Catholics were driven to an undue reliance on their clergy and their Church, which ultimately, towards the close of the century, they were able to turn to advantage, ironically as the Church began to lose its grip on its followers. As the Irish had already found in America after the famine had created an acceleration in emigration, the tradition of community involvement and community activity, when translated into politics, was a powerful factor in the sudden surge of Nationalist strength which manifested itself in the last decade and a half or so of the century.

On both sides of the religious divide the clergy were an important factor in the organisation of political parties. On the Catholic side, the priest did not openly stand in politics as became the custom with Protestants. It was not unusual for a Protestant clergyman to become an MP, or even a minister, this tradition being most notably upheld in the case of the Reverend Ian Paisley who, as we shall see at a later stage, towards the end of the century would found his own political party and become a Member of Parliament in three assemblies (Stormont, Westminster and the European parliament). Catholic clergy tended to remain more in the background, their role being to nominate candidates, a potent unstated recommendation to the electorate as to whom they should vote for. Given the education levels which obtained in the north and the leadership position of priests in the Catholic community over the centuries, such clerical influence was perhaps inevitable, but for decades it was a factor in underpinning the sectarianism of Six County politics.

By 1925, the more enlightened Nationalist politicians, particularly Joseph Devlin, who had been a leading figure in the old Irish Parliamentary Party, had come to realise that whatever their feelings about the new state, remaining out of its parliament was no way to attempt to cure its ills. 'Wee Joe' Devlin was a man the Unionists could have done business with, had they wanted to. A convinced constitutionalist and one of the most effective Catholic parliamentarians of his day, he incurred great hostility from Sinn Féin through his efforts to persuade Nationalists to accept partition as part of the Home Rule settlement on offer after 1916. A bachelor, greatly admired by women, he was noted for his charity and for the fact that he had a personal power base through his presidency of the Ancient Order of Hibernians, a more benign version of the Protestant Orange Order. By 1925, apart from Devlin's own predilections, the Church, the Catholic business community and middle class, and the Dublin establishment were all moving to a position of resigned acceptance of the Six County statelet. Moreover, the national issue was beginning to recede in importance in the face of the growth of the social one.

The new state was marked by deplorable housing conditions, and some 48,000 unemployed. Labour did well in the 1925 Stormont elections held on 3 April. Three Labour candidates were elected from Belfast: Jack Beattie, who topped the poll in Loyalist East Belfast; Sam Kyle in North Belfast; and William McMullen, a Protestant, who was elected in the predominantly Catholic West Belfast constituency, on transfers from Joseph Devlin. In 1924, Sinn Féin had contested northern elections, putting forward candidates like de Valera and Mary MacSwiney from southern Ireland. De Valera got in, but the Nationalists overall suffered from the Sinn Féin intervention. Knowing that Sinn Féin's presence would split the Nationalist vote, the Devlinites did not take part in the contest, but the eight Sinn Féin candidates won only 26,257 votes compared with 104,716 in 1921. It was obvious that the Catholics were not prepared to risk a rerun of the violence they had already experienced by supporting extremist candidates.

Seeing this, and the growth of Labour, Devlin decided that the abstentionist policy should be ameliorated, at least in part. After Craig declared an election in 1925, a Nationalist convention was held in Belfast on 21 March. It included the outgoing Nationalist MPs in the Belfast parliament, a prominent ex-Westminster Nationalist MP, Cahir Healy, who had actually been interned by the Unionists, and a substantial representation of local politicians and Catholic business and professional men. Women, whether Protestant or Catholic, did not figure largely in Northern Ireland politics. One of the few tributes to Nationalist women's contribution in the political arena was the left-handed one paid by a military adviser to the Unionist Government who judged that 'Cuman na mBan is the most dangerous organisation with which we have to deal'!

The convention decided to contest the election with the proviso that MPs returned for areas likely to be affected by the report of the Boundary Commission should delay their decision on whether or not to take their seats until after the report. However, MPs who came from areas which the Boundary Commission's findings obviously would not affect, for example the strongly Protestant areas of Belfast and County Antrim, could take their seats. The Nationalists did well, winning 10 seats and 91,452 votes, a rise of some 50% on their 1921 showing. But Sinn Féin did badly, winning only two seats and 20,615 votes. The odour of sulphur was obviously distasteful to the Catholic electorate.

However, the odour of socialism was even more unwelcome to the Unionists. When the new parliament met on 14 April, Labour became the official opposition, and began a campaign to highlight not the divide between north and south, but that between rich and poor, which cut across Protestant–Catholic boundaries. Though small in number, the Labour MPs, as they had earlier done in the south, almost immediately showed signs of becoming an effective opposition. Too effective for both Unionists and Nationalists. Not wishing to have their clothes stolen while they bathed in abstentionist waters, pending the outcome of the Boundary Commission's report, Devlin and another Nationalist MP, T.S. MacAllister, took their seats. After the signing of the Boundary Agreement in December 1925, three of the remaining Nationalists did likewise. The others, mainly from Fermanagh and Tyrone, who had expected their area to be transferred to the south, were bitterly disappointed by the Boundary Commission's findings, and remained outside the parliament for another two years.

The drift towards abandoning abstention was greatly accelerated by two unrelated happenings. One was that in the south, a massive headline had been set by de Valera's abandoning this policy and entering the Dail. But secondly, and the second was like unto the first, the Unionists, seeing the dangers of a Labour Nationalist alliance across the sectarian divide, were moving to abolish the minority's last electoral safeguard in the Six Counties. On 12 July, Craig had taken the occasion of an Orange demonstration to announce that he was going to abolish proportional representation for parliamentary elections as he had already done in local government ones. As a biographer has pointed out, Craig

> disliked a system which allowed the return of Independents and Labour members who placed as much emphasis on bread-and-butter issues as on the border question, and who might, therefore, mislead electors into voting for a united Ireland . . . the abolition of PR in parliamentary elections was designed to clarify the issue between Unionism and nationalism.

314

Craig himself was candid about his motives:

> What I want to get in this House, and what I believe we will get very much better in this
> House under the old-fashioned plain and simple system, are men who are for the Union
> on the one hand, or who are against it and want to go into a Dublin Parliament, on the
> other.[15]

The Nationalists, both Sinn Féin and the Devlinites, organised themselves into a National League of the North, which was strongly Catholic and middle class, but which attempted to breathe fresh air into the fetid atmosphere of Six County politics. Speaking at the formation of the League (on 28 May 1928), Devlin told his audience:

> The Nationalist members of the Northern Parliament were absolutely united in aims and
> policy . . . they had no means other than the Northern Parliament for making their voices
> heard. Before setting out, they had consulted the Northern bishops and secured their
> approval . . .
> They wanted to bury old differences. Things were changing. There was a fresher
> atmosphere in Belfast; the masses of the people were now friendly; politics were no longer
> a cause for men hating each other.

However, things were not changing in the optimistic manner Devlin described. PR was abolished, and Craig increased his seats from 32 to 38 against a combined total opposition of 14. But it was the composition of the opposition that counted. The abolition of PR meant that under the straight vote system, Labour and Catholic candidates came into a sectarian conflict which the Catholics won. William McMullen was defeated in West Belfast by a National League candidate, Richard Byrne, a Catholic slum landlord whom Devlin detested. During an unsuccessful meeting with McMullen before the election, in which he appealed to the Labour man to stand down, offering him a seat in the Senate as an inducement, he spoke openly of Byrne as an 'old pisspot'. However, the basic sectarianism of Six County politics drove Devlin to support the 'pisspot', who had been proposed and seconded by priests. In addition to these nominations, an organisation called the Catholic Union directed its members to support Byrne on the grounds that 'Catholic representation is required to defend Catholic interests, especially on the education question'. Once in parliament, Byrne upheld the wishes of his sponsors, declaring: 'It is our duty in this Parliament . . . to look after the interests of the faith to which I am proud to belong.' The growing alliance between Nationalists and Labour was checked, and the Unionist strategists got what they wanted, a straight fight in parliament between Protestants and Catholics, which the Catholics had no chance of winning.

Outside parliament, the 'hungry thirties' really were just that. In Belfast in particular 'green children' were particularly numerous. But the Unionist ascendancy was so secure that it could blithely go ahead with measures such as cutting unemployment benefits while lavishing expenditure on the new parliament building, which was opened in 1932. Speaking at the opening, Devlin said:

> The fundamental principle of citizenship and of all Christian or humane law is either work or maintenance for the people . . . The people are not responsible for unemployment. Their masters are responsible for it. The conditions of industry today are due to causes over which the working people have no control whatsoever.[16]

Although he was speaking at the opening of a new parliament which ought in theory to have heralded the dawn of a new era, he went on sombrely to forecast the end of parliamentary attendance by Nationalists, saying:

> I believe this is the last time we shall meet in this House. Well thank God for that. My colleagues and I who represent democracy have no reason to rejoice at the years we have been here . . . You had opponents willing to co-operate. We did not seek office. We sought service. We were willing to help. But you rejected all friendly offers. You refused to accept co-operation . . . You went on the old political lines, fostering hatreds, keeping one third of the population as if they were pariahs in the community, refusing to accept support from any class but your own and relying on those religious differences and difficulties so that you could remain in office for ever.

The actual breaking point came two months later, during a debate on the budget, when the Speaker ruled that Cahir Healy could not discuss the services reserved to Westminster. As these represented £10 million of the £11½ million budget, the Nationalists made up their minds that there was no point in continuing, and walked out, leaving parliament with a three-man opposition, Jack Beatty, Labour, Thomas Henderson, Independent Unionist, and another Independent Unionist, ex-District Inspector J. W. Nixon, notorious for being the former leader of a *sub rosa* RUC murder gang. Parliament that year had a six-month summer recess, and when it met again, Beatty threw the mace at the Speaker and walked out accompanied by Henderson, saying, 'I absolutely refuse to sit in this House and indulge in hypocrisy while the people are starving outside.'

Parliamentary opposition in Northern Ireland, if it had not died, had certainly gone into a coma. As the *Irish News* said of what had befallen the attempts of men like Devlin and Healy to make the system work:

> Whenever they rose to address the House the Prime Minister and other Ministers and many of their followers retired ostentatiously and deliberately to the smoke-room. This wilful rudeness to the minority's representatives was repeated in their dealings with the people who comprised that minority. They were denied every possible right: the stamp of scorned inferiority was stamped on the brows of one third of the area's population, and they were allowed no say whatever in guiding the destinies of the country in which they lived and for whose welfare their regard was at least as sincere and deep as that of those who had placed them in subjection.[17]

Abstentionism had not proved efficacious for the northern Catholics, but neither had offering the hand of co-operation to the Unionist establishment. From the outset the Government was representative not merely of Protestantism, but of property. Apart from a calculated move to keep the Protestant working class in line which saw two tradesmen appointed to relatively minor posts (a parliamentary secretary and assistant whip), in the first government the Cabinet consisted of landowners, big businessmen and wealthy lawyers. The Unionist MPs, with four exceptions out of 40, were also prominent business people, members of the professional classes, or landowners. The Senate included five peers and two baronets. Craig's grip on his party was such that, towards the end of his life, he rarely held Cabinet meetings and took lengthy holidays at will, and his wife treated the Cabinet Secretary, Colonel Spender, like a superior class of butler, ordering him for example to ring up Fortnum and Mason when stocks of marmalade ran low. The Unionist establishment was not the milieu in which to breed affection for socialism or an empathy with the condition of the unemployed, of whom there were many throughout the Six Counties.

During the 1920s the Unionist focus on the Boundary Commission issue helped to divert attention from the unemployment situation which, in the Six Counties, was met by attempting to apply a peculiarly Belfast solution to a Northern Ireland problem. In September 1925, when it was estimated that there were some 64,000 out of work, 38,000 of them in Belfast, parliament had to be recalled to vote extra money to deal with the situation. However, in voting the money, parliament added stringent new regulations to its disbursement, which had the effect of lighting a fuse which exploded in 1932. Unemployment benefit was only paid to workers who could pass a tough means test and prove that they had been in work, paying state contributions, over the previous two years. Of course, many of the most needy had been out of work for well in excess of two years. Moreover, men on the dole who were offered a job in England which they would not, or often could not, take for family reasons were struck off, because they failed the test of 'genuinely seeking work'. It has been claimed that the basic unemployment figure of some 64,000 was increased by another 14,000 through the application of the regulations. In addition to these Dickensian ukases, the Belfast authorities made a change in the regulations covering outdoor relief from those obtaining in England, where if a man or woman was struck off the register they got supplementary benefit. Most applicants in Belfast got not a cash benefit, but a benefit in kind. The only alternative left to the poor, the workhouse, was rendered so unattractive that many chose to remain outside, half starving but free. Inmates had to wear workhouse clothes, families were split up, and one of the rules stipulated that everyone had to be in bed by eight each evening.

These conditions provoked widespread agitation, but the Government, acting through Dawson Bates, contained the situation through a liberal use of the Special Powers Act, and the batons of the RUC, until unrest was further defused by a combination of an improvement in trade in the years immediately following 1926, and the authorities agreeing to pay outdoor relief to the heads of families.

However, trade conditions worsened again following the Wall Street Crash, ushering in an era which saw a massive rise in unemployment, possibly as many as 100,000, for the Six County area as a whole. Again Belfast was hardest hit, containing nearly half the total unemployed, and, ominously for a continuation of working-class support for the Unionist establishment, a high percentage of these came from the shipyards. Between them, the two yards, Workman Clark and Harland & Wolff, had employed 20,000 men in the mid-twenties. By 1933, this had fallen to a total of only 2,000 men, and the Workman Clark yard was forced to close in 1934.

For the first time in living memory, the 'apprenticeship culture' of Belfast's skilled working class had suffered a serious blow. No longer did life consist of leaving school early to follow father, uncle or brother into a secure job in the yards. Now the skilled Protestant worker and the unskilled Catholic labourer were equally unemployed. The unemployed received lower relief rates than those which obtained in Britain, where a married couple with one child received approximately £1. 7s. a week, and perhaps additional benefits such as a rent allowance. In Belfast, however, a couple – and a couple meant a married couple – received only 12s. for one child, and with four or more a maximum of £1. 4s. a week. A couple with no children got only 8s. a week. Furthermore, the money was not simply handed over. In order to qualify, the husband had to do a minimum of two and a half days' work on the outdoor relief schemes, which largely consisted of road and pavement repair. Single men got 3s. 6d. a week if they worked on these schemes, otherwise they got nothing. Nothing was what widows, orphans and single women received. For them, the only state option was the workhouse. Otherwise it meant life with relations, if they had any, or prostitution.

Deaf and blind to the plight of such people, the Belfast Board of Guardians (on 20 September 1932) refused a proposal by a Nationalist councillor, James Collins, that relief grants for the winter should be supplemented by a payment of 10s. a week to help to buy fuel, and keep a roof over the heads of the unemployed. In the face of these conditions, a sort of socialist backlash occurred. What were known as revolutionary workers' groups (RWGs) began springing up. The RWGs organised an outdoor relief workers' committee which drew support from the trade unions, although it encountered opposition from the unions' leadership and from the Labour Party. The committee decided to strike against the relief work system, and on Monday 4 October sent pickets from one work site to another, closing them all down. A huge meeting (possibly attended by as many as 50,000) was held at the Customs House steps, demanding work, not charity. The meeting was addressed by Jack Beatty, who had distinguished himself a few days earlier by throwing the parliamentary mace at the Speaker in protest at the conditions he was seeking to redress. The other speakers included James Collins and Harry Diamond, from the Nationalist side, two Marxists, Tommy Geehan and Betty Sinclair, from the RWGs, and significantly, an 'Independent Unionist', Alderman Pierce. The protestors demanded payments of 15s. 3d. for a single man, and, in a demonstration of political correctness, Belfast style, 13s. 6d. for a single woman. They also wanted an end to the means test, the task work system and the payments of benefit in kind. The sanction imposed by the protestors was a novel one. Hundreds of single men descended on the workhouse, demanding to be admitted. As it cost more than 16s. a week to keep a person in the workhouse, the authorities became worried, particularly as the marches to the workhouse were accompanied by huge crowds. Fierce rioting broke out when the RUC attempted to clear the streets with their batons.

The authorities reacted by offering to increase relief payments by 50% and doing away with the benefit in kind system. However, the RWG leaders rejected the increase as inadequate, and called for mass demonstrations and bonfires on 10 and 11 October. The demonstrations were banned, but meetings went ahead anyway, and again there were baton charges and hand-to-hand fighting. In the Catholic Falls Road area, the police augmented their batons with revolver- and rifle-fire, killing one man and wounding several others. The Falls inhabitants retaliated by trenching and barricading side streets. A fellow anger doth make us wondrous ferocious, and rioting also broke out in the Protestant Shankill Road area, spreading to several parts of the city. A remarkable feature of the Protestant uprising was the fact that during it the IRA, which had effected a degree of reorganisation, secretly gave some of their meagre stock of weaponry to the Protestants to defend themselves against the security forces. An IRA leader of the time told me: 'We put guns into the hands of Orangemen for use against the B Specials.' More publicly, earlier that year as 12 July approached, the Army Council had attempted to reach across the sectarian divide by issuing a call to 'the men and women of the Orange Order' which included the following:

Fellow Countrymen and Women,

The fact is that we are quite unaware of religious distinctions within our Movement. We guarantee you, you will guarantee us, and we will both guarantee all full freedom of conscience and religious worship to the Ireland we are to set free.

Do you not see yourselves queued shoulder to shoulder outside the Unemployment Exchanges waiting for the 'Dole', that crumb which the exploiters throw to the exploited of different religions? In these vital matters your religion or your membership of the Orange Order counts for nothing, nor does Catholicism to the unemployed and starving Catholics in Southern Ireland.

The fact is that the religious feelings of the masses of both Orangemen and Catholics are played on and exploited by the Imperialists and Capitalists the more surely to enslave them.

The Protestant rioting was short-lived, however, and in a concerted effort to disrupt the incipient growth of working-class solidarity, the police literally concentrated their fire on the Catholic areas, using their armoured cars to smash through barricades and making scores of arrests. Councillor James

Collins and his son were forced by the police to work all through a rainy night taking down barricades.

By now, the official trade union leaders had become alarmed at the violence and, *inter alia*, the growing influence of the RWGs, and with the leaders of the protest either in jail or on the run they stepped into the breach to offer negotiations. These were accepted with alacrity by the Government, and new relief rates were agreed. A couple with one or two children now got £1 4s. a week, with three or four children £1 8s., and with over four £1 12s. A married couple with no children ascended to a pound a week. But all payments were made in cash and the payments net was widened to allow single persons living on their own to receive benefits. The strike and the demonstrations ended, and Tommy Geehan, a Catholic, hailed the outcome:

> What we have achieved is in direct contradiction to those who said that the workers could not unite and could not fight, and the past fortnight will be recorded as a glorious two weeks in the history of the working-class struggle. We saw Roman Catholic and Protestant workers marching together and on Tuesday last we saw them fighting together. As a result poverty and destitution have been swept away and homes will be made brighter for many of the unfortunate workers.

However, elections held in Belfast the following January and May, for the Corporation and Poor Law guardians, gave the lie to Geehan's optimism concerning Catholic and Protestant workers' solidarity. Geehan himself won a seat but Labour overall lost ground, losing their last seat in the dock ward in the Corporation contest, and in the Poor Law elections succeeding in taking only one seat. None of the candidates put forward by the outdoor relief workers' committee won any, and the Unionists emerged, despite the turmoil of the previous year, with a total of 29 seats. The Nationalists won four and Labour one.

So far as Northern Ireland politics were concerned, the lasting deposit of the outdoor relief rioting and strike was the impetus it gave to the Communist Party and the far left generally in terms of the need for working-class solidarity. But it was an idea that had to wait more than 30 years before achieving a degree of lasting fruition in the takeover by the left of the IRA. Left-wing ideology received a short-term boost the year after the strike ended, when the northern railways went on strike over a proposal to cut wages. The strike was significant because it affected the union movements both north and south of the border, and in England the two main railway unions (the NUR and ASLEF) viewed Belfast as a laboratory wherein the wage cut experiment, if successful, could then be implemented in England also.

The strike was extremely bitter. The employers brought in blacklegs, including students, who were paid more than double what it was intended to pay the rail workers (less than £2 a week). Trains were stoned, and in one case derailed, with the loss of two lives. Northern railway buses were included in the strike, being escorted in the north by RUC armoured cars and in the south by the Irish army and the Gardai. The violence spread to both sides of the border, as the stoning of lorries and buses and the sabotaging of rail lines became commonplace. The strike proved a shot in the arm for the almost dormant IRA, which fired at some strike-breaking lorry drivers on 28 February 1933. In an ensuing shoot-out with the RUC, an RUC man was shot dead. These incidents enabled the Unionist establishment to characterise the strike as being fomented by Communists and the IRA in what Craig, now Lord Craigavon, termed an 'insidious attempt by Nationalists, Communists and Socialists to betray Ulster into an All Ireland Republic'.[18] After further violence, including the bombing of a bus with a Garda escort in Dundalk on 16 March, a settlement was agreed. By its terms, union members' pay was cut by 7.5% on 1931 levels. They agreed to make no further wage claims for two years, and to forgo holiday pay for 1933. As the railwaymen were overwhelmingly Protestant, Craig's tocsin about Nationalists and Communists being in collusion to further the goal of an all-Irish Republic was understandable. In furtherance of their demands, the Loyalists had shown themselves willing to accept the help of the Catholic southerners, revolutionary groups such as the RWGs and, most remarkably, the IRA.

But alongside the growth of this working-class solidarity, with its implications for the future of sectarian politics in the Six Counties, a more traditional Ulster Protestant reaction had also taken shape in the form of the Ulster Protestant League (UPL). The UPL's attitude towards Catholics was defined as: 'Neither to talk with, nor walk with, neither to buy nor sell, borrow nor lend, take nor give, or to have any dealings at all with them nor for employers to employ them nor employees to work with them.' The activities of the UPL, angry meetings, provocative marches, helped to push up sectarian temperatures throughout the north, and on St Patrick's Day 1932, a parade by members of the Ancient Order of Hibernians was fired on in Derry. The following June, more serious widespread rioting occurred. All over the north, buses and trains carrying Catholics to and from the Eucharistic Congress in Dublin were attacked. Following an Orange rally in Dungannon, in August, a Loyalist mob looted and wrecked Catholic pubs. It was in this climate that Craig, Sir Basil Brooke, and Sir Joseph Davison made their statements about Orangeism and the employment of Catholics quoted earlier in this chapter, Craig going so far as to put down an amendment supporting Brooke when the Nationalists proposed a censure motion. The amendment, which was passed, said: 'The employment of disloyalists . . . is prejudicial to the state, and takes jobs away from Loyalists.'[19]

It was against this unpromising background that the Republican Congress movement invited the Shankill Road workers to march to Bodenstown on 17 June. The Belfast men carried banners with slogans like 'Wolfe Tone Commemoration, 1934, Shankhill Road, Belfast Branch. Break the connection with capitalism.' However, they were set upon by the anti-Congress faction of the IRA, and the grave of Wolfe Tone, who had attempted to unite Protestant, Catholic and Dissenter, became a battleground in which the seeds of working-class solidarity were trampled underfoot. Violence increased throughout 1935. Catholics were beaten up, a Catholic publican was shot dead, and the Silver Jubilee of King George V was made the occasion of an outburst of Loyalist triumphalism, in which another publican was shot, and there was constant firing into Catholic districts. Parts of Belfast were again placed under curfew, and in Catholic areas tunnelling between houses and back yards resumed so that Catholics could pass through without being fired on in the streets.

The UPL demonstrations created such mob violence that – following the shooting of a 15-year-old girl on her way to mass – on 18 June, all parades in the Six Counties were banned. The Orangemen promptly held their parade in Protestant York Street in defiance of the ban, while the RUC stood idly by. Davison, the Orange Grandmaster, commented that he did not 'acknowledge the right of any Government, Northern or Imperial, to impose conditions as to the celebration'.[20] Three days later, Dawson Bates removed the ban. From then until 12 July, there were sustained attacks on Catholic areas. The 12th itself provoked the most violent reaction of the year. As the Orange parade passed through Catholic areas of Belfast, fighting broke out in a number of places. The worst trouble occurred in the evening at Lancaster Street, a Catholic area near the Loyalist heartland of York Street. There is some dispute as to who fired first. The Protestants say the Catholics did, the Catholics that shooting occurred only after Protestant mobs began wrecking Catholic homes. What is not disputed is the result. The Orangemen, tired after a day's marching and drinking, exploded in fury after a Protestant was shot dead and another wounded. In the succeeding days, more Catholics were shot or beaten to death, homes were wrecked and Catholics were driven out of employment, and, after the RUC failed to intervene when Loyalist mobs attacked the Short Strand area, the army was called out and shot two Protestants.

In all there had been 11 murders, two attempted murders, 574 cases of criminal injury, 367 cases of malicious damage and 133 cases of arson. Some 2,241 Catholics were evicted, and hundreds more lost their jobs.

The reaction of the British Government when asked to intervene in these happenings in a part of the United Kingdom was that of Pontius Pilate. British liberal opinion, as exemplified by the *Manchester Guardian* and the National Council for Civil Liberties, blamed the anti-Catholic speeches of Orange politicians and decision-takers for the rioting and destruction. The Orange Order had taken a prominent part in a boycott of Catholic businesses, and the National Council for Civil Liberties had an observer in Belfast during the riots. He was Ronald Kidd, the Council's secretary, who wrote to Baldwin demanding that an inquiry be held into the 'abusive authority by the Northern Ireland Government'.[21] He did not get it. A group of Nationalists headed by the Catholic Bishop of Down and Connor helped to mobilise cross-party support for a private meeting of over 100 British MPs at Westminster, at which Kidd and a group which included trade union leaders, priests, and other

Nationalist speakers described the rioting. After listening to the damning evidence, the MPs voted in favour of a resolution calling on the Government to hold an inquiry.

However, the call only served to elicit a policy statement on behalf of the British Government which was destined to be repeated for decades. Turning down the inquiry request, Baldwin replied to the chairman of the meeting, J.R. Clynes MP, saying: 'This matter is entirely within the discretion and responsibility of the Government of Northern Ireland, and for fundamental constitutional reasons, the possibility of holding an Inquiry by the Imperial Government is completely ruled out.'[22] This 'hands-off' attitude by London was a major factor in the build-up of pressure within the northern statelet which finally burst in August 1969 with violent results which have not died away at the time of writing.

While the rioting and bitterness persisted, the Nationalist leader, Joseph Devlin, and his followers had been casting around for some effective political response. Catholic sentiment generally was increasingly anti-Stormont and pro-abstentionist. Support for the IRA and Sinn Féin was growing. Devlin travelled south to hold talks with de Valera, from whom he received little help. De Valera refused his request to grant seats in the Dail to him and Cahir Healy. Devlin later contacted leading Republicans with a view to uniting the Nationalist forces under his banner on a policy of abstentionism. But his initiative failed. A combination of hierarchical pressure and an approaching election forced Devlin and his followers to abandon abstentionism and return to Stormont in October of 1933 in an attempt to uphold the Catholic position on schools. But the return made no impression on the Unionists' impregnable majority at Stormont, and Devlin died a disillusioned man in January 1934. As he lay dying, prayers were in progress at his bedside when Senator James Gyle, an independent Unionist, called to pay his last respects. As a result, Gyle was suspended from the Orange Order for seven years. The episode in microcosm exemplified the tribulations Devlin had undergone in his un-successful attempt to introduce reform and normal parliamentary democracy to the Orange statelet.

After Devlin's death the Nationalists virtually disintegrated. In the words of Cahir Healy, who succeeded him as the Nationalists' most prominent spokesman, the MPs and their followers saw 'little use in playing politics with people who do not possess even the most elementary notion of justice or fair play'.[23] Only two Nationalist MPs, Richard Byrne and T.J. Campbell, attended Stormont with any regularity – although all took the oath of allegiance to King George VI after Edward VIII abdicated in 1936, and drew their salaries. The two non-party Nationalist candidates, Anthony Mulvey and Patrick Cunningham, elected to Westminster in November 1935, did not attend the parliament during the ensuing ten years. Attendance by Nationalists at Stormont became so sporadic that when George Leeke, the MP for mid-Derry, died in 1939, the writ for a by-election was not moved and the seat remained vacant for a further six years.

After the 1938 election, effectively speaking, the Stormont opposition was carried on by two Labour representatives, Jack Beatty and Paddy Agnew. Craig's Unionists handily shrugged off an internal challenge from a group of middle-class Protestant businessmen styling themselves Progressive Unionists. The Progressive Unionists were far less sectarian than the Craig echelon of the party, and wanted action in areas such as unemployment, house-building, and the agricultural sector. By now, unemployment had reached 90,000, but at the beginning of the year de Valera's moves to resolve the annuities question, and the wording of Articles 2 and 3 of his new constitution, gave Craig the opportunity of holding an election on the partition issue. That took care of Progressive Unionism. As a historian of Unionism, J. F. Harbinson, commented: 'Just as the sensational novelists of the early 19th century introduced apparitions to deter their characters from rash or criminal enterprises, so the invocation of political phantoms was expected to deter Protestant voters from supporting Unionist dissidents.'[24]

Ironically the 'phantoms' were just that, chimera. De Valera had not the slightest intention of getting involved in the concerns of Northern Ireland in any meaningful way. At the Fianna Fáil Ard Fheis of 1936 he had successfully opposed a motion by a prominent Fianna Fáil figure, Eamonn Donnelly, from Armagh, to allow 'the elected representatives of North East Ulster to sit, and vote in Dail Eireann'. When Craig called the election de Valera did not contest his own northern seat, thus underpinning the policy of abstention.

Although de Valera put up Craig's blood pressure by giving a press conference in Dublin, on 13 January, before going to London for the ports talks, at which he announced that partition would be on the agenda, and subsequently, during the talks, gave interviews in the same vein to the *New York Times* and the *Manchester Guardian*, his media comments were merely a negotiating tactic to give him leverage in the substantive issues of the ports and the annuities. The tactic worked insofar as it startled Chamberlain, who admitted after the first day of talks that he had 'never contemplated . . . any lengthy discussion on partition'. De Valera had earlier conceded to Malcolm MacDonald, the Dominions Secretary, that 'the partition solution would have to wait', but indicated that he might at a later stage embark on a publicity campaign on the iniquity of the northern situation. When a delegation of Nationalist MPs descended on him during the London talks he contacted the *Irish Independent*, asking the paper not to connect him with the northerners. The delegation spent a fruitless day in talks with him, not knowing that he had already sanctioned a briefing to the *Irish Independent*'s political editor, Patrick Quinn, which, Quinn cabled to Dublin, 'clearly shows he [de Valera] is accepting settlement – with partition shelved'.

Shelved it was, but the talks enabled Craig successfully to play the Orange card one last time. He died on 24 November 1940. How little of substance, or merit, that card brought to the society he ruled over for so long was conceded in an assessment of his career by a sympathetic biographer:

No serious or sustained attempt was made to overcome the admittedly daunting difficulties facing Northern Ireland. The result was that the country became saddled with a ramshackle system of government, and a whole range of services, such as health, housing and education, remained underdeveloped in comparison with the rest of the United Kingdom. The economy continued to decay. And the divisions between Catholics and Protestants became more pronounced and institutionalised.[25]

SIX

REPUBLICANS FALL AND RISE, CROZIERS FALL AND IRELAND LOOKS OUTWARD

At the commencement of World War II, Ireland, as seen through the eyes of various actors in the Anglo-Irish drama, appeared as follows. To the British, a troublesome back-door neighbour, half in and half out of the Commonwealth, which, though it had got its ports back, could hopefully be relied upon to allow them to be used if war came, and to co-operate in other ways also. This of course, as we saw, was not the opinion of Winston Churchill, whose outrage at the ports handover during the war was at least consistent with the views he expressed on learning of Chamberlain's action.

There was the official view of de Valera, that his constitution had solved the Republican issue and provided a long-term basis for the solution of the partition problem. Then there was the IRA view, that de Valera had failed to achieve either objective; and there was also the view of many an Irish family and individual, which ought to have commanded most attention, but did not: that of the unceasing flow of emigrants, who remained unaffected by any of the foregoing, and daily watched sadly as the hills of their lovely, uncaring land faded behind the wake of the ships taking them to England for jobs unavailable to them at home.

But for the moment it was the IRA view which commanded most attention. Just before German bombs began to fall on London from aeroplanes, the IRA began setting them off in the streets.

What happened was that within the IRA a series of splits and personality clashes had led to Seán Russell becoming Chief of Staff. Russell was the IRA emissary who had unsuccessfully negotiated with de Valera in April of 1935 on the possibilities of IRA–Fianna Fáil co-operation. De Valera had wanted the IRA to give up their weapons and stand down 'the army'. Russell had offered to co-operate with Fianna Fáil for five years from the date of the talks providing that de Valera would agree to declare a republic at the end of the period. According to Joseph McGarritty's diary, de Valera turned down this offer, saying 'you want it both ways'.[1] McGarritty had decided to break with de Valera after the death of Seán Glynn, which he said was 'the last straw for me', and in his diary refers to de Valera's policy, and scathingly to that of the northern government to the IRA: 'Craigavon and de Valera at least agree on one thing, and that is that all those known to be Republicans must be jailed or hanged.' Accordingly, he turned from being one of de Valera's closest friends and supporters to encouraging and financing Russell's plan to move IRA activities away from Ireland to where he thought they properly belonged, on the English mainland.

As a former quartermaster of the IRA, Russell had supporters within the movement who believed his claims (made in the *Daily Mirror* on 14 August 1936) that the IRA had 'splendidly military forces in Ireland, with cleverly hidden arsenals . . . a secret army of Irish men', and 'quantities of ammunition and other war material in England. Our airforce may be small, but it is reasonably efficient. When hostilities start, we shall certainly send planes to bomb England.' This was all sheer nonsense.

The secret army consisted of a handful of half-trained young men, short of weapons and largely ignorant of English conditions. One of them, Paddy McNeela, told me that before they set off they were addressed by Maurice Twomey, who advised them to keep up their religion and not to lose their Irish accents. McNeela came from Ballycroy in County Mayo, where not going to mass would be unthinkable, but where first-hand knowledge of English society was as rare as an encounter with an atheist. While engaged in the campaign, McNeela became fond of the English people of his own age whom he met, and told me wonderingly: 'They didn't seem to know anything about Ireland.' That statement could well have been taken as the *leitmotiv* for many in Ireland and England in the decades that followed. However, imbued with the Republican philosophy, McNeela and his colleagues were vastly impressed when, on 8 December 1938, the *Wolfe Tone Weekly* announced that the IRA Army Council now had the authority of 'the Government of the Republic of Ireland' from the 'Executive Council of Dail Eireann'. In other words, in its own eyes the Army Council had taken over from the second Dail as the legitimate government of Ireland. To the IRA, just as de Valera had claimed at one stage, the authority of the Dublin parliament now lay outside that assembly, and Russell thus had authority for his actions. The bombing campaign began formally on 12 January 1939, when the IRA issued an ultimatum addressed to, amongst others, the British Prime Minister, the North of Ireland Government, Hitler and Mussolini, demanding the immediate withdrawal of all British armed forces stationed in Ireland. Four days later, the British army not having moved, another proclamation, this time written by McGarritty and signed by the members of the Army Council (Stephen Hayes, Peadar O'Flaherty, Laurence Grogan, Patrick Fleming, George Plunkett and Seán Russell), called on the Irish at home and in exile 'to assist us in the effort we are about to make in God's name, to compel that evacuation and to enthrone the Republic of Ireland'.

The proclamation was largely disregarded, but its seriousness was underlined by a series of explosions which immediately followed. Russell's plan had envisaged the destruction of property, not the taking of life, but a bomb planted in a busy Manchester Street gave a 27-year-old fish porter, Albert Ross, the unsought distinction of being the first person to die in the campaign.

Over the next 15 months, bombs were set off in letter-boxes, public lavatories, railway cloakrooms, telephone boxes, post offices, and business premises of all sorts. In addition, crowded cinema audiences were thrown into panic by the use of tear-gas. The worst single incident occurred on Friday 25 August 1939 in Coventry, when a psychopathic bomber, realising that his bomb was due to go off shortly, left the bicycle bearing the explosives parked in a crowded street. It killed five people, and injured some 50 others, some of them very badly.

Long before Coventry, both British and Irish governments cracked down on the bombers. The British reacted by rounding up scores of IRA suspects, but de Valera was the first to bring in legislative measures against the IRA. On 14 June, the Offences Against the State Act was passed, setting up special courts composed of army officers. The IRA was declared an unlawful organisation and the annual pilgrimage to Bodenstown was banned, ending in a riot when some members of the IRA tried to force their way through army and police cordons.

A month later, on 24 July, the Home Secretary, Sir Samuel Hoare, introduced the Prevention of Violence (Temporary Provisions) Bill in the House of Commons, claiming that the IRA campaign was 'being closely watched and actively stimulated by foreign organisations'. The new law gave the Home Secretary the power to issue expulsion orders against suspects trying to enter the country. It relaxed the regulations under which search warrants could be issued, and gave the police power to arrest and detain suspects for five days without warrants. Introducing the Bill, Hoare told the House that by that date, 66 members of the IRA had been convicted and that tons of potassium chlorate, a quarter-ton of aluminium powder, 1,000 detonators, 1,500 sticks of gelignite, seven gallons of sulphuric acid and a quantity of ferrous oxide had been seized. In all there had been 127 terrorist attacks, 57 of them in London. But no air force, no secret army. What there were aplenty were innocent victims. Apart from those killed or injured or executed, like Peter Barnes, who, with Frank Richards (alias McCormick), was hanged because of the Coventry explosion though in fact he had had very little to do with it, hundreds of Irish workers with no contact with the IRA were expelled back to Ireland, and IRA prisoners were sometimes badly beaten up in jail.

The futile campaign, which scarcely amounted to a pinprick to the overall British strength and resolution compared to the country's experiences in Hitler's blitz, presented de Valera in particular with a difficult situation, not for its strength but because of the threat which it posed to his plans to keep Ireland neutral in the war which was obviously looming. On 2 September, the two houses of the Oireachtas (Dail and Seánad) declared a state of emergency: '. . . arising out of the armed conflict now taking place in Europe, a National emergency exists affecting the vital interests of the State'. The emergency powers gave the Government control of almost every aspect of Irish life: supplies, tillage, transport, censorship, military affairs – and the putting down of the IRA. On the face of things this should have been relatively easy. The IRA no longer had a figure of de Valera's stature encouraging the young people of the country to support the organisation. And even though the memory of the Black and Tans was too recent for the public to contemplate joining the war on England's side, neither was there any widespread support for activities which might jeopardise neutrality. The Special Branch was reorganised, as was military intelligence. And there were frequent arrests of IRA men. Similar swoops occurred in the north, where on 22 December a particularly large operation netted a haul of some 34 IRA men.

But if there was no great active support for the IRA, there was some sympathy. On 7 December a *nolle prosequi* was entered in the case of a hero of the Anglo-Irish war, Patrick McGrath, who went to death's door on a hunger strike that provoked widespread public debate and many private representations to de Valera. A week earlier Justice Gavan Duffy had evinced judicial sympathy for a claim by an IRA prisoner that his arrest was unconstitutional by granting him an order of *habeas corpus*. This decision, ironically based on de Valera's own constitution, resulted in the release of 53 other IRA prisoners also. Then, on 23 December, the IRA crossed, or were induced to cross, a bridge too far.

This was the Magazine Fort raid in the Phoenix Park, Dublin, which resulted in the IRA seizing the bulk of the Irish army's ammunition. The fort was badly guarded, a gate which should have been locked was left open, and, taking advantage of the laxity, the IRA got away with over a million rounds of ammunition, which required some 13 lorries to transport. Years after the raid, rumours circulated in Republican circles that the Government was aware of the planned raid and that the Magazine Fort was in fact an Irish version of Pearl Harbor. Certainly the attack gave the Government the excuse it needed to go to war. Over that Christmas, all army and police leave was cancelled and roadblocks were set up, with the result that from St Stephen's Day onwards, the ammunition began to be recovered. Approximately one lorryload remained undiscovered. But like Pearl Harbor, the aftermath was to be of greater significance than the raid itself. On 4 January, with parliament's determination strengthened by the fatal shooting of a policeman in Cork the day before, the Dail met for an emergency session, and passed a measure which allowed the Government to introduce detention without trial.

This alarmed the President, Douglas Hyde, who convened a meeting of the Council of State to advise him whether or not the act should be referred to the Supreme Court to test whether it was repugnant to the constitution. After meeting with the Council, he decided to refer the Bill, and it hung in legal limbo until the court decided on 9 February that it was valid, whereat Hyde signed it. The Bill duly became law and ultimately proved successful in combating the IRA, albeit not without some initial difficulties. Throughout 1939, there had been a number of IRA raids and attempts at prison breaks, which had increased police vigilance and hence arrests, with a consequential increase in prison numbers. As IRA prisoners in jail traditionally regard prison as simply another battlefield in which the war is to be carried on, the prisons thus became an increasing source of tension. The traditional IRA claim is for its members to be treated not as common criminals but as political prisoners. In the first week of March 1940, some very savage fighting broke out in D Wing of Mountjoy jail in Dublin, after prisoners barricaded themselves in to prevent two of their members being taken to court. In furtherance of the political status demand, police and warders successfully broke down the barricades. But the IRA had another and more powerful weapon to hand – hunger-striking.

Hunger-striking had been decided upon as a weapon in the political status fight for several months before the Mountjoy riot, and had proved a successful tactic in a country which, at least in part, owed its independence to the publicity generated during the Anglo-Irish war by the hunger strikes of figures like Thomas Ashe and Terence MacSwiney. Hunger-striking elicited a powerful resonance in public sympathy. As a result, several IRA men had their sentences quashed after going on hunger strike prior to February of 1940. As the Minister for Justice, Gerard Boland, said in the Seánad:

> We have got to deal with a very delicate problem ... A prominent member of the Opposition said to me in private – I mention no names and I hope I am breaking no confidence; this was a man who had taken very strong action against these people – that, in his view, we were not entitled to let these people die on hunger strike because, due to our attitude and general policy towards these people in the past, they were entitled to believe that if they went on hunger strike, we would let them out. Things like that had to be borne in mind, but I can assure this house that we are not going to let people take the law into their own hands, and that we shall not be prevented from detaining them ... There is no question of ruthlessness or rigour, but I am sure that there is going to be insistence that everybody in this country will obey the law.

However, when seven IRA men went on hunger strike on 25 February 1940 they were met with both rigour and ruthlessness. Wartime censorship prevented their cases getting much publicity, and two of the strikers, Tony d'Arcy and Jack McNeela (a brother of Paddy's) were allowed to die.

The inquest on d'Arcy found that he 'died of inanition secondary to cardiac failure while on hunger strike', but added a rider that 'immediate action should be taken with regard to the five men at present on hunger strike and in a serious condition. We desire to express our sincere sympathy with the widow, relatives and friends of the late Anthony d'Arcy on their bereavement.' The inquest on McNeela shortly afterwards also caused controversy. The Reverend John J. O'Hare, a Carmelite priest, gave evidence that he had seen the prisoners on the day of McNeela's death and conveyed instructions to them from IRA headquarters to call off the strike. The controversy arose when he said, as he had done at d'Arcy's inquest, that he could have had the strike called off three weeks earlier if de Valera or Boland had allowed him to see the prisoners. Boland entered the box in an effort to deny the allegations, but was subjected to a severe cross-examination from Seán MacBride, who had left the IRA after the enactment of de Valera's constitution and become a successful lawyer.

In fact the surviving prisoners did come off their hunger strike because of the priest's message, which came from Stephen Hayes, the IRA Chief of Staff, and told them they had got what they had struck for, namely political status. One of the prisoners, Michael Traynor, described to me the aftermath of the strike. The prisoners got a poached egg on toast, tea with milk and sugar, and a dose of hydrochloric acid to replace their digestive juices. The acid treatment lasted for a week. After every meal the prisoners could see the blankets rising above their bloating stomachs. Traynor told me: 'I looked like the woman that gave birth to the quintuplets in Mexico.' He was at the time of our talk (1966) the owner of a successful grocery business in Dublin's Upper Leeson Street. But he made a remark as we sat at dinner in his comfortable dining room which was chilling both in its simplicity and in its implications for the continuation of the IRA tradition. Waving at a besilvered sideboard, he said: 'Of course I'd give all this up in the morning if the IRA wanted me to.'

In 1940, having come off the strike, the IRA discovered that it still hadn't got what it wanted. The Hayes message proved to be unfounded. Instead of getting political status, the prisoners were served either with internment orders, or, if they had been sentenced to prison, with notification of the length of their jail sentences. In retaliation for the hunger-striking deaths, the IRA let off a bomb at the headquarters of the Special Branch, and fired on two policemen. De Valera went on the radio to announce that the IRA, having 'set the law at defiance, the law will be enforced against them. If the present law is not sufficient, it will be strengthened, and in the last resort, if no other law will suffice, then the Government will evoke the ultimate law, the safety of the people.'

He had come a long way from his civil war defence of the militant Republicans, and even further from his dismissal of majority opinion: 'The people have no right to do wrong.' He also had the support of his then opponent, W. T. Cosgrave, who said after the broadcast that Fine Gael would not contest two forthcoming by-elections, lest the contest might give rise to a belief that 'lack of support was due to the action which the Government, in recent months, had taken in connection with order in the State'.

Nevertheless, a series of other IRA activities throughout the summer decided de Valera that the existing laws were too weak to deal with the situation. On 16 August 1940, the Government deleted the right of appeal against findings of the military tribunal from the Emergency Powers Act. From that date, the tribunal was enjoined with the 'imposition and the carrying out of the sentence of death, and no appeal shall lie in respect of such conviction or sentence'. The Government also hit at the IRA by drawing off its source of manpower in the setting up of a local security force. Some 133,000 men were enrolled in this throughout the country.

But the military tribunal remained the Government's principal weapon. The deletion of the right of appeal was occasioned by the fatal shooting of two detectives. The men arrested after the shooting affray, Patrick McGrath and Thomas Harte, were executed on 6 September, after both the High Court and the Supreme Court rejected their appeals. In all, 27 IRA men were either executed or died on hunger strike or of illness brought on by imprisonment in jails in England and Ireland, north and south, during the war years.[2] For the last execution, that of Charlie Kearns, in Mountjoy jail in December 1944, de Valera dispensed with the use of firing squads and brought over an English hangman. This may have been because the calibre of some of the condemned men, notably George Plant, executed in Portlaoise in 1942, was such that army personnel of the period to whom I spoke recalled being repelled and disturbed at having to conduct such executions. The method of securing the evidence necessary for the death sentence would hardly have passed muster in peacetime conditions. In the case of Plant, two IRA men who had given evidence against him later withdrew their statements and the case collapsed. However, de Valera's government then altered the legal code by issuing an Emergency Powers Order on 30 December 1941. Under this, it became legal to use a statement, including one made by the accused, even though it was later withdrawn, or the person who made it had died or was not present at the trial. The Order went on to provide that if a military court decided that it should not be bound by any rule of evidence, either of military or common law, then the court could not be bound by such a rule. The rescinded statements made against Plant were then admitted to evidence and used to execute him.

De Valera himself was placed in an extraordinary position by his executions policy. For while he was bringing down the iron fist on the IRA in the south, he found himself in something of the same position as his old rival, Michael Collins, who, by crushing the IRA in the Free State, was forced to assist them in the Six Counties, albeit surreptitiously. De Valera, however, was driven to do so publicly. When six IRA men were condemned to death in the north for the shooting of a policeman, he was forced to join in the appeals for a reprieve, which ultimately succeeded in having all but one of the condemned men spared.

The death of Plant was in fact brought about by an action of the IRA itself – the forcing of a confession from Stephen Hayes, a chief of staff of the IRA, whom subordinates suspected of being an informer. Ground between the security forces north and south of the border, some of the northern IRA men began to feel that the litany of disasters befalling the IRA were in fact caused by an informer. The fortunes of war brought Seán McCaughey south, where, with his fellow Tyrone man, Eoin MacNamee, and a group of other northerners, it was decided that Stephen Hayes was passing on information to a fellow Wexford man, Dr James Ryan, the Minister for Agriculture, Thomás Derrig, the Minister for Education, and others, some of it through a member of the Special Branch, James Crofton. Hayes, who always protested his innocence,[3] was kidnapped by the IRA and interrogated over a period of two months, during which a confession was dragged out of him. At this remove, it is obviously impossible to establish the truth or otherwise of the confession, but one of the strange features of the affair was that apparently an offer was conveyed to McCaughey that the life of an IRA man awaiting execution in Portlaoise jail, Richard Goss, would be spared if Hayes was released. McCaughey turned it down and Goss was duly executed (on 9 August 1941).

Plant, who was executed the following March, died as a direct result of the Hayes confession. It stated that another IRA man, Michael Devereaux, had been shot by the IRA as an informer, and gave details of his shooting, which led to the arrest and execution of Plant. Hayes managed to escape shortly before he was due to be shot, and was subsequently given five years' penal servitude. Crofton, the Special Branch man, also got a five-year sentence, having been arrested while trying to get a German spy, Hermann Goertz, out of the country on a fishing boat. The Hayes confession, coming against a backdrop of vigorous government crackdown on the IRA, the use of draconian special powers, internment and censorship, destroyed the morale of the organisation in the south, and the IRA remained virtually crushed for the duration of the war.

It scarcely fared much better in the north. Here too internment was introduced, and a section of the internees, those held in Derry jail, rioted on Christmas Day 1939. The treatment of the prisoners after the riot elicited a good deal of sympathy in Nationalist areas. And for a period in 1940, the IRA gave the appearance of possessing considerable strength, setting up a pirate radio station, staging arms raids, bank raids, and gun battles with the police. However, conditions in the north were, if anything, more repressive than in the south. For example, in addition to their jail sentences, IRA men were frequently lashed with a cat o' nine tails. The conditions in which the men were held were sometimes far worse than those which obtained in the south, particularly on the *Al Rawdah*, a prison ship in Strangford Lough. The authorities were forced to move the men off the ship because of the adverse publicity which it generated.

By the time American troops landed in the Six Counties in 1942, the IRA was still sufficient of a threat for the Americans to make contact with the organisation through the head Catholic chaplain to assure the Republicans that they had nothing to fear from the troops. Like de Valera, the IRA had protested against the landing of the Americans without consultation. The American contact with the IRA was prudently withheld from the Unionists, as Sir Arthur Hezlet commented in his history of the B Specials, it 'would have caused a major political upheaval with the Northern Ireland Government'![4]

At this stage, the IRA had a significant Protestant component, led by John Graham, who amongst his other duties edited the IRA newspaper *Republican News*. Most of them had come into the IRA via the Ulster Union Club, an organisation headed by Captain Denis Ireland, a Protestant who sought to establish a forum for discussions on nationalism, Protestantism and the identity issue. The discovery of the activities of Graham and his colleagues' activities had a terminal effect on Captain Ireland's hopeful initiative. The duress of the circumstances led to the foundation of an IRA Northern Command, headed by Hugh McAteer, which decided, on 25 March 1942, to launch a campaign in the north. According to a statement captured by the police and published in the *Belfast Newsletter*, the command decided

> that military action be taken against the enemy forces in the six-county area by Oglaigh na hEireann [the IRA], reinforced by the entire resources and equipment of the army in the 26-county area, by sabotage of war industries and enemy military objectives by a semi-military force.[5]

Of course by this stage the IRA had almost no 'resources and equipment' in the 26-county area. However, it was relatively strong in the north, particularly in Belfast, and began to flex its muscles in preparation for the campaign. A policeman was shot in Dungannon on 3 April, and a major incident occurred two days later on Easter Sunday. An IRA party fired on an RUC patrol car, in the Clonard area of Belfast, not with lethal intent but as a diversion to draw the police away from an Easter commemoration parade being held on the Falls Road, in defiance of an official ban. However, police pursued the gunmen into a house in Cawnpore Street, and in the course of a shoot-out an RUC man was killed and the leader of the IRA party, Tommy Williams, was arrested.

All six IRA men were condemned to death. A huge reprieve movement sprang up. Despite all the violence of Northern Ireland, no Republican had previously been executed in the Six Counties. Now the prospect of six hangings convulsed Nationalist Ireland. Seán MacBride spearheaded the protest, collecting over 200,000 signatures for a reprieve petition. Huge meetings were held, addressed by a wide spectrum of community leaders, including Denis Ireland, Jim Larkin, and even members of Fianna Fáil. De Valera became alarmed at the prospect of trouble erupting, in the wake of the northern authorities behaving towards the IRA as he was doing in the south, and interceded with the British and the Americans to put pressure on for the exercise of clemency. David Gray, the American Minister, was not pleased, and wrote to de Valera at the height of the agitation (on 27 August 1942) saying that he and others found themselves 'embarrassed at the pressure exerted here on the Northern Government'.[6] However, the Ambassador was shrewd enough to advise his government that 'some measure of clemency is probably expedient. The British and Canadian representatives here hold the same opinion. Hanging six for one would shock public opinion.'

In the event, the pressure told. Only one IRA man was hanged, Tommy Williams. Amongst the five reprieved was Joe Cahill, who went on to become one of the best-known figures in the Provisional IRA. Even with the passage of time, the hanging of Williams stands out as an appalling incident in the blood-stained history of Northern Ireland.

It is accepted that the manner of taking the statements from all of the accused would not stand the test of a normal court, and deserved to be regarded as on a par with the legal manipulations of de Valera's military court in the south. Leave to appeal to the House of Lords was refused and the

Minister for Home Affairs, William Lowry, declined to receive a deputation of Nationalist parliamentarians to even discuss the case. But it was the behaviour of the crowds on the night before Williams's hanging and on the morning of his death that really became etched into the folklore of Belfast. On one side of the street Catholic women knelt in prayer. On the other, a crowd of Protestants sang Orange songs and shouted obscenities. Just prior to, and during, Williams's execution, the Protestants sang 'God Save the King', followed by 'There'll Always be an England'.

Thereafter the IRA went steadily downhill in the north as it had in the south. In September of that year, John Graham and David Fleming were arrested after a fierce shoot-out in a house on the Crumlin Road. After their capture, the RUC found a secret room containing a radio transmitter, some revolvers, a host of office equipment and several thousand copies of the *Republican News*. This effectively ended the IRA's publicity campaign, but one final act of defiance occurred the following Easter Sunday, 25 April 1943, when Hugh McAteer and Jimmy Steele, two leaders of the Northern Command, who earlier in the year had escaped from Crumlin Road jail, took over the Broadway Cinema on the Falls Road. They stopped the film, and went on stage to read a statement from the Army Council and the 1916 Proclamation. The incident created a sensation, as 1916 commemorations were banned at the time and the effect was compounded by the reading being referred to on German radio. By the end of the following year, the IRA was virtually defunct. One of the few IRA leaders still at liberty, Seamus 'Rocky' Burns, was shot dead by the RUC in Belfast in February, and Seán Doyle, a 16-year-old volunteer, died in a training accident in April. At the end of the year, the Stormont authorities were sufficiently confident of their ascendancy to disband the Home Guard, and cut the numbers of the B Specials to pre-war levels. However, the northern government still kept its internees under lock and key, although the southern government released the men held in the Curragh in November 1944.

The Curragh had played a central role in both crushing and enlightening the IRA. Early riots there were put down quite brutally, one internee, Barney Casey, being shot dead, and the rest settled down to the long slog of wartime confinement. During their stay in the camp, many of the internees came into contact with what might be termed 'higher education' for the first time. Dr Roger McHugh, who later became Professor of English Literature at University College Dublin, and Martin O'Cadhain, who subsequently became Professor of Irish at Trinity College, both conducted classes for the inmates, as did others with a teaching background. Splits and demoralisation set in over issues like the Stephen Hayes confession, and the efforts of a dedicated Communist, Neil Gould, to spread Marxist doctrines. The prisoners attempted to keep up their spirits by study, games, and the exercise of humour, such as christening the lavatories 'Gerry Boland', after the harsh Minister for Justice. But as indicated earlier, even Boland acknowledged that the IRA posed so little threat by 1944 that the internees were released.

However, as in Northern Ireland, the Dublin Government continued to hold convicted prisoners, and one of these was to figure in one of the two acts of bloody-mindedness which, more than anything else, contributed to the putting of Fianna Fáil out of power in 1948.

The prisoner was Seán McCaughey, who died in dreadful circumstances in Portlaoise jail. Portlaoise differed from the Curragh, or Arbour Hill or Mountjoy, in that Republican prisoners were not allowed to wear their own clothes, and had to don convict uniform. On being transferred to the prison in September 1941, McCaughey, like the other IRA prisoners who had preceded him, refused to wear prison clothes. This resulted in him being placed in solitary confinement, wearing nothing but a blanket. Solitary confinement was rendered particularly solitary by having an empty cell on either side, while the warders wore rubber soles so that no sound percolated to the captives, who were not allowed to leave their cells for any reason, even to go to the lavatory. In 1943, some relaxations to this regime were introduced. Prisoners were allowed out of their cells to converse with each other in a large cell for an hour mornings and afternoons. They were also allowed to receive a newspaper per week and a letter per month. During the four and three-quarter years McCaughey spent in Portlaoise, he remained naked, apart from his prison blanket, and received no visitors. Finally, on 19 April 1946, when the war was well over, and the IRA was clearly no longer a threat, he went on a protest hunger strike.

There is a conflict of evidence as to what he intended to achieve. His stated objective was release, which the Government refused. However, comrades of his whom I interviewed said that the authorities were fully aware of the fact that his objective was to be transferred to the Curragh, and that had this been done, he would have come off the strike. However, when, five days into the strike, the authorities showed no signs of budging, McCaughey ratcheted up the protest by refusing to accept water as well as food. He died after 17 days. His inquest afforded Seán MacBride the opportunity of cross-examining the prison doctor. In the course of this examination, he asked the doctor: 'If you had a dog, would you treat it in that fashion?' The doctor answered simply, 'No.'

The atmosphere in the coroner's court was extremely tense, and there was a very large Special Branch presence. MacBride told me afterwards that he had never felt so nervous in a courtroom and was never quite sure whether or not he was going to be prevented from carrying on, or even arrested. However, he managed to make a telling interpolation into the reporter's transcript of the proceedings, which heightened the effect of the doctor's admission throughout the country. The reporters were not certain whether or not the various emergency powers laws would be used to prevent them reporting what was said, and there was no question of course of amendment, change, or the provision of a colour piece in their copy. But MacBride approached the reporters' table and asked them whether they wanted to check anything with him. Grateful for the opportunity, one of the reporters[7] read over his notes, and asked if any change should be made. MacBride suggested one insertion, in brackets so that what appeared in the paper read as follows: 'Dr Duane (after a pause): No.'

That change literally gave Republicans around the country a pause for thought. In the year before McCaughey's death, the latent strength of republicanism in the country had been illustrated during a presidential election occasioned by the decision of the aged Douglas Hyde not to seek a second term in office. The Fianna Fáil candidate, Seán T. O'Ceallaigh, defeated Fine Gael's Seán MacEoin, but on the first count, the independent Republican candidate, Dr Patrick McCartan, who had been one of the most important Clann na Gael figures in America during the post-1916 period, got 212,834 votes. A second example of bloody-mindedness on the Government's part was to give Seán MacBride the opportunity of substantially increasing this Republican total.

This second example was the hard-faced reaction to a strike by primary teachers, members of the Irish National Teachers Organisation (INTO). The details of the strike, which largely centred over when, and how much, an award should be paid, were complex. But here it should be understood that probably no group in the country were more pro-Fianna Fáil and its aims than the INTO – before the strike. I remember one devoted Fianna Fáil teacher telling me that he turned against de Valera after discovering that he was earning less than a cleaner in a public lavatory. Apart from their poor overall pay, the teachers had suffered inexplicably from a derisory award made by the Government in 1944. Civil servants received cost-of-living bonuses which ranged from 7s. 9d. to 23s. per week. But the teachers were only given one shilling a week. Even after the war, the Government behaved towards the teachers as if the wartime wage standstill was still in place, and the Dublin INTO teachers went on strike on 20 March 1946. The strike lasted until the end of October, leaving a great deal of emotional scar tissue in its wake, in political, educational and even Church circles. The National Conference of Bishops had declared its support for a rise in teachers' pay in 1944, and the Archbishop of Dublin, Dr John Charles McQuaid, supported the teachers to the extent of writing to the union's secretary, T. J. O'Connell: 'Your Organisation must have no doubt that the clerical managers of the city and the religious superiors have full sympathy with the ideal of a salary in keeping with the dignity and responsibility of your profession as teachers.'[8]

This letter was published in the papers on 20 March 1946. However, in one of the few recorded instances in which the Government stood up to McQuaid, the Archbishop was snubbed when he offered to mediate in the dispute. De Valera spelt out the Government's attitude at the Fianna Fáil Ard Fheis on 6 September:

> The great difficulty where Government or parliament are concerned is to get them to say 'no' when they believe in their hearts it is 'no' they should say in the common interest. Do you think it pleased us to have the standstill order in regard to wages? I assure you it did not . . . It would be a great mistake to think that they could isolate one body of public

servants and give them increases and that they could deny the demands of other public servants.

Further bad blood was injected into the dispute because some religious orders, in response to governmental urgings, took children affected by the strike into their schools, particularly those run by brothers. Orders of nuns, however, proved more responsive to the wishes of the teachers. The strike finally came to an end after McQuaid had again intervened, and after the Government came in for much unfavourable publicity following a demonstration at the All-Ireland Football Final at the end of September in which demonstrating teachers were batoned by Gardai.

McCaughey's plight, and that of Republican prisoners generally, had led to some organised protest amongst Republican sympathisers, and after his death the protesters made common cause with the teachers, the Teachers Club in Parnell Square being a focal point for anti-government meetings. Out of these there grew a new political party, Clann na Poblachta (Clan of Republicans). The circumstances were extraordinarily like those obtaining when Fianna Fáil was nearing power. Apart from the bitterness at the treatment of McCaughey and the other blanket protesters in Portlaoise jail, there was the question of their being held in the first place. Just as in 1932, the cry 'release the prisoners' was to play a part in a change of government. One of the first acts of the new Minister for Justice, Seán McEoin, in fact would be to do just that.

However, the social conditions were also appalling and the impact of economic policies followed by, or forced on, the state during the war was still powerful. At the time, appropriately enough 4 July, Independence Day, 1946, that a group of Republicans met in Barrys Hotel, in Gardiner Street, Dublin, to decide on the formation of Clann na Poblachta (they included Seán MacBride, Con Lehane, Jim Killeen, Michael Fitzpatrick and Peadar Cowan), the wartime wage standstill was still in force. Bread rationing had been reintroduced following a series of bad harvests. The butter ration was reduced from four ounces to two. Fuel and other vital materials were still hard to come by. The closure of industry had added to the unemployment totals. Despite high emigration, there were some 70,000 out of work, and there was still residual fear that this total would rise if the war's ending resulted in Irish emigrants returning in their thousands from England. Ireland's industries at the time consisted mainly of brewing, distilling, wool and linen weaving, and agricultural produce.[9] Practically speaking, the state had no industrial base. The 26 counties constituted a small, open, island economy, vulnerable to all the international economic winds that blew. Most of her exports went to Britain, and costs were added to by the fact of having to transport goods to and from the country by sea.

Seán Lemass had foreseen post-war difficulties as far back as 1942, and recommended that the Government set up an economic planning committee consisting of the secretaries of the departments most concerned, agriculture, finance, industry and commerce. However, de Valera reacted negatively to this proposal, setting up instead a triumvirate of himself, Lemass, and a conservative, Seán T. O'Ceallaigh, the Minister for Finance, who could be guaranteed not to take any stand not favoured by de Valera or the equally conservative, and very powerful, Secretary of the Department of Finance, J.J. MacElligott. As a result, the committee frequently contented itself with literally rubbishy business, such as the state of Dun Laoghaire's refuse.[10] Lemass also tried to create a Ministry of Labour, but de Valera vetoed this too,[11] as he did Lemassian proposals for a full employment policy, which he modelled on the 1944 British White Paper on Full Employment. He argued that 'a Full Employment Policy is practicable . . . it is in line with modern economic thought . . . it involves no departure from democratic principles'. However, Lemass's ideas involved a fundamental departure from Fianna Fáil principles.

From the outset, the party's aims had included semi-mystical attachment to the concept of an Ireland which was largely rural and independent of the rest of the world. Launching the party in 1926, de Valera had stipulated that its goals would include the development of

> A social system in which, as far as possible, equal opportunity will be afforded to every Irish citizen to live a noble and useful Christian life. The distribution of the land of Ireland so as to get the greatest number possible of Irish familiies rooted in the soil of Ireland. The making of Ireland an economic unit, as self-contained and self-sufficient as possible – with a proper balance between agriculture and the other essential industries.[12]

One of Lemass's proposals was that if farmers did not work the land efficiently over a number of years, then the state should step in with compulsory purchase. He argued that 'only a limited number of families can be settled on the land, on economic holdings, and policy must be directed to ensuring that ownership be confined to persons willing and capable of working them adequately'. However, this was anathema to his Cabinet colleagues, particularly those with a rural background. James Ryan, the Minister for Agriculture, warned that if land were to be taken from inefficient farmers in sufficient quantities to have an impact on output 'there would be danger of serious agitation and public disturbances'. There would also of course have been serious disturbance amongst the small farmers who constituted the bedrock of Fianna Fáil support.

Lemass was that extraordinary being, a practical patriot. A city man and a businessman of drive and initiative, he saw no virtue in an Ireland that was not only bog-bound but Gaelic as well. He believed that the state should take a hands-on approach towards creating employment and industrialisation. Some of his schemes were far-fetched. His Ministry of Labour, for instance, would have introduced thoroughly undemocratic restrictions on the free movement and sale of labour. But by 1943, Lemass could see clearly that Fianna Fáil's protectionism had outlived its usefulness. An independent economist, James Meenan, writing in *Studies*, had pointed out that 'industrial protection has not resulted in a reduction of imports':

It has brought greater employment which, being increasingly urbanised, seeks an improving standard of living, which in its turn must increase our demand for other imports. In other words, industrial protection has increased not diminished our need of imports. It has consequently increased our need of exports to pay for those imports . . . each addition to the tariff wall is an additional burden on the exporting industries. The dilemma cannot be evaded.[13]

Lemass did not shrink from tackling the issue posed by the fact that import substitution had increased the demand for raw materials. But de Valera did. He was reluctant to attempt to correct trade imbalances, particularly in the years immediately after the war's end, by changing from protectionism to freer trade and a greater reliance on exports, and turning agriculture from the basis for an ideologically unrealistic vision of Ireland into an industry capable of making a contribution to rectifying the problems of unemployment, and facing up to those caused by industrialisation and urbanisation.

In an aide-memoire to de Valera on the position of agriculture, the influential Professor Smiddy, his economic adviser, wrote that 'the most striking feature of Irish agriculture since 1926–27 has been its static condition . . . there are some fundamental forces at work which render agriculture so inelastic . . . price, legislation and educational influences'. But agriculture was central to Irish economic policy. Smiddy judged that there was 'no economic or social problem of more importance for the welfare of the community and the maintenance of our standard of living than increased agricultural efficiency'. He bolstered this argument by pointing out that agriculture employed 49% of the population, and provided 30% and absorbed 59% of the revenue.[14]

But de Valera did not see agriculture as an 'industry'. To him the term 'increased agricultural efficiency' struck a discordant note compared to 'country life' and 'the land' which were the terms he used to describe rural Ireland in a keynote policy address:

To make country life more attractive, as far as the Government can do it, is the aim they have in mind, if they can achieve it by any means . . . we have, at some loss, brought industries as near to the land as possible. We have tried to prevent the overgrowth of large towns by doing everything we could to get industries established outside larger centres, where they would naturally grow, because if there was an economic urge people would go to the larger centres. We try to keep them in the country . . . the departure from the country areas, which is common to us and to other countries is, from our point of view, a national evil and a social loss.[15]

The 'most serious of all' the impediments to the creation of an Irish rural Arcadia was, de Valera said, 'the late marriage rate'. To remedy this evil, he said he would like to see 'a thumping good tax on bachelors' because, he said, people 'want to be too well off'. As this expedient was not proceeded with, for examples of the scale and quality of the innovations which *were* introduced to bring home to the population the attractions of the country, and thereby stem the outflow from it, we may turn to one policy failure and one success, the Clonlast experiment and the introduction of children's allowances. Both probably owe their conception not to de Valera but to James Dillon. The road to Clonlast, a bog near the town of Portarlington, began with a speech of Dillon's in the Dail.[16] In it he struck a chord with de Valera when he suggested that Roosevelt's Civilian Construction Corps offered a blueprint for coping with a 'curse' which was ruining decent young men and undermining parental authority, namely the effects of 'the dole for unmarried men in rural Ireland'. The American corps numbered about 300,000 youths, drawn from urban areas, who, living in work camps under good leadership and supervision, had made a noticeable contribution to the American economy, building roads, clearing wasteland and planting hundreds of millions of trees. De Valera had the Dillon suggestion examined, was impressed by the corps record of achievement, and, moving with unaccustomed speed, saw to it that an Irish version of Roosevelt's scheme was given the green light within two months of Dillon's speech.[17]

As a result, 174 unemployed urban youths were 'volunteered' to take up duties at a work camp in Clonlast, where, due to the 'departures from the country areas', the Turf Development Board was finding it impossible to get local labour. However, the gallant 174 did not turn their thoughts towards Clonlast with the same enthusiasm which motivated the young Americans who had taken part in Roosevelt's New Deal experiment. To begin with, they only came into the Irish scheme as a result of their dole being withheld. Even with this compulsion, the widespread perception amongst Dublin's slum-dwellers that countrymen, and in particular bog men, were apt to eat their young persuaded 106 of the 'volunteers' that, even without the dole, they were better off staying in Dublin than standing like Ruth amidst the alien turf. Eleven were rejected on health grounds and only 50 actually made it to Clonlast. By the end of the first week, 30 of these had given up. It is thought that approximately only nine of the original 174 managed to survive their green Siberia for any length of time.[18]

The Government explanation for the failure of the scheme, delivered in the Dail by Hugo Flinn, the Secretary of the Civil Service Economic Committee, who had been charged with its organisation, also contained a rationalisation for it: 'largely to ascertain whether or not we could, in Clonlast and other places, reconstitute and recondition these men and give them a chance in life'.[19] Flinn, a Cork TD and a parliamentary secretary, was one of the best brains in Fianna Fáil, therefore his grasp of the realities of life as it was lived by the poor, as opposed to being theorised about, was probably better than that of his average Cabinet colleague. Eamonn McKee, a perceptive student of the period, accurately summed up the implications of the Flinn defence of the Clonlast experiment: 'That the turf camps were a haven for ex-IRA men, fallen priests and the flotsam of the Ireland of 1930s and 1940s, and displayed a disturbingly high rate of VD, gave this idea of the rejuvenating quality of work on the bog a profoundly naïve and facile quality.'[20]

Dillon proposed the introduction of children's or family allowances in the Dail (on 30 March 1939) to alleviate the danger that 'poverty and starvation will destroy our government'. The Catholic newspaper the *Standard* was receptive to the idea and consulted with Professor Smiddy, who recapitulated de Valera's thoughts in a memo in which he indicated that he understood that he would be considering a system of allowances which would 'be made of such an amount as to be sufficient to keep the family in the [*sic*] frugal living when the bread winner is unemployed, and such an allowance to be a substitute for the existing dole'.[21] It was clear from the outset therefore that the allowances envisaged would be small. In fact when they ultimately emerged they were tiny, 2s. 6d. per week for the third[22] and subsequent children, but the amount of time and temperament expended on bringing this mouse to birth through the mountain of obstruction raised by bureaucrat and politician was colossal. It took from the spring of 1939 to that of 1944 to bring the scheme to fruition. And this, let it be remembered, was a policy which de Valera *supported*; the fate of those he opposed calls for imagination rather than description. At least one commentator has suggested that part of the delay was caused by the fact that the civil servant who initially had responsibility for administering the necessary background research was Brian O'Nolan, who at the same time was commencing the literary career which would bring him worldwide fame under the pseudonyms Flann O'Brien and Myles na Gopaleen.[23] In fact O'Nolan was the best placed amongst the *dramatis personae* involved in the children's allowances performance to understand what was involved. One of the great comic genius's unsung achievements was the fact that, out of what for most of his life was a very meagre income, he supported numerous brothers and sisters and would probably not have taken a civil service post had his father not died.

In the event, an interdepartmental committee set up to examine the issue took two years to make a report. But it reported in favour, saying that economic reform of the Irish system to provide the able-bodied with decent wage levels would be more desirable than the proposed 'palliative', but that 'as matters stand . . . we consider that family allowances should be adopted to mitigate the effect of one of the chief causes of poverty in the economic system'.[24] On the face of it, one might have assumed that this recommendation coming from a high-ranking committee, which included two Department of Finance mandarins, O. J. Redmond and T.K. Whitaker, would have been all that a favourably minded Taoiseach would have required to nod the proposal through. However, the nature of de Valera's death grip on his government and party has to be understood.

Partially for reasons of empathy, but also to maintain his absolute control, unthreatened by wearisome debates, potential splits and unwelcome publicity, de Valera restricted consideration of major policy matters to a small circle of ministers, Aiken, Lemass, MacEntee and O'Ceallaigh. Generally speaking, this charmed circle could be thought of as being enclosed within another circle, the restrictive influence of the Department of Finance, which in real terms meant MacElligott and his close advisers. De Valera's exhausting style of conducting his chairmanship of his close circle involved allowing his associates to have their say, without challenging him directly, and to wear each other down until, like a skilled fly-fisherman, he chose the moment to strike. In the case of the children's allowance issue, Aiken was supportive from the outset, in principle. He also thought that the system should be such as to enable the abolition of unemployment assistance and the consequent closure of labour exchanges.[25] MacEntee was hostile, because he felt that the scheme would undermine parental authority. In a memo to de Valera, he argued that 'without the firm exercise of such authority, a peasant economy such as ours, based on the patriarchal principle, cannot exist'.[26] A secondary consideration, of course, was that, along with the patriarchical principle, the peasant electorate might cease to exist for Fianna Fáil. O'Ceallaigh too was hostile, opposing the proposal from the outset on the grounds that there was:

> no apparent need for stimulation unless it can be shown that a higher rate of natural increase is desirable. This would seem to be a task of some difficulty in a state of affairs marked by a high rate of emigration, a large number of unemployed, and a generally low standard of living.[27]

The fact that the allowance proposal might have something to do with raising the said low standard of living did not appear to occur to O'Ceallaigh. Even on the eve of its being accepted as government policy, he was still issuing warnings about the dangers of the socialisation of children, the destruction of charitable institutions, and the undesirability of the removal of such tried and trusted incentives to work as hunger, or the fear of hunger.[28] Lemass was supportive from the outset, as he normally was with any improvement in social policy, and MacElligott, despite the recommendations of his subordinates, remained hostile. Taking advantage (legitimately) of the fact that the Minister for Finance was opposed, MacElligott wrote to Maurice Moynihan, the Secretary to the Government, asking him whether he could 'clear up' the dichotomy between the Minister's policy (and at this stage Tanaiste, or deputy prime minister) and the fact that the Cabinet had just directed Lemass to draw up the headings of a Bill, giving effect to a measure which the Minister opposed.[29] MacElligott's guarded use of language was an appeal to de Valera's famously conservative instincts, code for: 'Does the Taoiseach really want this spendthrift scheme to become law?' De Valera's oracular response to the serpentine MacElligott was of the 'a flat maybe' school. It said

> that it was not proposed to vary or add to the terms in which the decision was recorded. It was remarked however, that the direction for the preparation of the heads of a Bill would naturally be interpreted as implying that the Government was prepared in principle to adopt a scheme of children's allowance.[30]

Between this sort of somewhat less than ringing endorsement, and the harrying fire of senior colleagues, it is not surprising that another year was to elapse before Lemass was able to stand up in the Dail (on 23 November 1943) to begin shepherding a Bill through the Dail to introduce the principle of family allowances, supplementary to other allowances, on a non-contributory basis and without a means test. In view of the trench warfare that had gone before, it is interesting to note that Lemass prefaced his explanation of the Bill by saying: 'so general has been the approval given to the principle of the establishment of a children's allowance scheme that it might at first appear unnecessary for me to speak here or to defend or to justify the principle of the measure'.[31] Not the least instructive feature of the children's allowances saga is the fact that the Lemassian preface forcibly underlines the principle that one should always be wary of accepting ministerial statements at their face value.

But the overall point to be made about the relationship of the children's allowances issue to the general economic state of the country is that this mini-drama was played out, in the influential cabal of the ruling party, under the unseeing gaze of an ageing Taoiseach, whose sight was so bad that all written materials had to be read to him, generally by his private secretary, Kathleen O'Connell, who had been with him since his early loan-raising days in America. He was a blind Taoiseach, whose attention moreover was frequently distracted by being required to perform functions such as signing the occasional IRA man's death certificate, by Dun Laoghaire refuse disposal, or by dealing with representations made to him by various emissaries on behalf of personages such as Adolf Hitler, Winston Churchill, Franklin Delano Roosevelt, and the most Reverend John Charles McQuaid, DD, Archbishop of Dublin.

One of de Valera's most frequently quoted speeches, that containing his 'comely maidens' reference, was made on St Patrick's Day 1943, as the Clonlast and children's allowances sagas were nearing their end. It has been depicted variously as his core policy utterance, his vision of the Ireland that should have been, or, as Professor Lee argues, the epitome of his 'truly profound ignorance of economics'.[32] But it could also be taken as a public lament, and acknowledgement, that his vision was as impractical as Clonlast, and as peripheral to the reality of living as the level of children's allowances. The tragedy is that having come to the conclusion that the dream was a chimera, he stayed at the centre of Irish political life for another 16 years, during which time millions of his fellow countrymen either lived in poverty or emigrated. De Valera knew better than most political leaders of the twentieth century how to get and hold power, but the question of what to do with it was beyond him.

Wartime exigencies and de Valera's conservatism meant that none of Lemass's Beveridge-like suggestions for dealing with post-war conditions bore fruit. Ireland slowed down intellectually and economically. Fianna Fáil's housing drive, which in 1938–9 had been a torrent reaching 17,016 houses annually, had slowed to a trickle of 2,480 in 1943–4. An apologist for the Government might have pleaded wartime conditions to explain the fall-off, but the total for state-aided houses built in 1947 was inexcusable: a miserable 1,108, at a time when one of the best brains in the Department of Finance, Patrick Lynch, estimated that the housing requirement was 110,000 new dwellings.[33] The results could be seen in slum, dole queue, and emigrant ship. There was therefore fertile ground prepared for Clann na Poblachta to till. The new party proposed a variety of attractive-sounding policies. It promised to increase employment through introducing state employment schemes in areas such as fishing and forestry. Emigration was to be ended, slums abolished, and decent housing provided. The railways were to be electrified, as was society generally by other innovations such as the introduction of a minimum wage, the enhanced provision of credit and improvements in the field of social security. Another scheme which would prove to be of immense electoral advantage was a proposal to eliminate tuberculosis, which was taken up by one of the recruits to the new party, a young doctor, Noel Browne. In those days, TB carried a stigma far greater than AIDS does today, and was referred to as a 'delicacy'. Whole families were wiped out, particularly in the inner cities, where tenements were popularly known as 'coffin boxes' because of the prevalence of TB in their dark, noxious surroundings.

In addition to the inertia of a government which had spent 16 uninterrupted years in office, there was a whiff of scandal in the air. In one case, a prominent Fianna Fáil supporter, Dr F.C. Ward, who controlled a lucrative bacon-curing business, was forced to resign as a junior minister (Parliamentary Secretary). De Valera set up a tribunal inquiry into his affairs on 7 June 1946, after receiving a letter detailing a list of alleged transgressions, from another doctor. The tribunal largely cleared Ward of the charges, which centred on local government corruption in County Monaghan. But it did find that both Ward and his fellow directors had 'not brought to account for income tax purposes' payments they had made to themselves, and were forced to pay up to the Revenue Commissioners.[34] De Valera attempted to lessen debate on the Ward issue by only announcing the tribunal's findings a quarter of an hour before the Dail rose for its summer recess in 1946. However, as the opposition speaker, Dr T.F. O'Higgins, of Fine Gael, said: 'The country has for too long been the paradise of profiteers exploiting the consumers, but the reaction is setting in, public opinion is awake.' A reaction *was* setting in and for Clann na Poblachta, which was getting off the ground that month, the Ward affair was a godsend.

The godsend was added to the following year by controversy over the sale of Locke's Distillery. There were a number of bidders for this old established whiskey-producing firm in Kilbeggan, County Westmeath, when it was put up for sale in 1947, but it went not to Irish interests, but to an international consortium who in the event did not come up with the necessary down payment on the company. The directors of the company had been mixing in Fianna Fáil circles, and had in fact involved a Fianna Fáil senator, and auctioneer, William Quirke, in their dealings. It was Quirke who became suspicious and notified the police, leading to the deportation of one of the consortium, Alexander Maximo, who apparently committed suicide by jumping off the mailboat while being taken back to England, in the company of two Gardai, to face criminal charges. Two others, a Swiss, Georges Eindiguer, and an Austrian called Saschsell, also left, or were thrown out of the country, as a result of the police inquiry. De Valera also set up a tribunal to inquire into the Locke's affair, because Oliver Flanagan, the independent TD for Laois/Offaly, who had joined Fine Gael, raised the issue in the Dail. Under cover of privilege, he made lurid allegations against de Valera, Gerry Boland, Seán Lemass and de Valera's son, Eamonn, which the tribunal found to be utterly without foundation. The report published on 18 December 1947 found Flanagan guilty of giving 'untrue evidence', 'being uncandid', and being guilty of 'complete irresponsibility' and 'extravagant recklessness'.

However, as a speaker in the Dail said, 'the people of the country disagreed with the Tribunal'.[35] Flanagan topped the poll in a general election held two months later. A new spirit was gripping the electorate, a combination of Fianna Fáil's lengthy sojourn in power, its staleness, the attractive new programme and new faces in Clann na Poblachta, and the drive and initiative of two groupings in particular, the Republicans and the teachers, was proving irresistible. Fianna Fáil attempted to affect the issue of the election by introducing an Electoral Amendment Bill in 1947. The constituencies had not been revived since 1935, but since then the population had fallen. However, instead of reducing the number of Dail deputies, the Electoral Amendment Bill increased it from 138 to 147, and changed the number of three-member constituencies from 15 to 22, thus favouring Fianna Fáil over smaller parties. It may be remarked *inter alia* that this demonstrated that Fianna Fáil had little to learn from the Unionists when it came to gerrymandering. However, the Electoral Amendment Bill was not enough. Having lost two by-elections in October of 1947, one of which was won by Seán MacBride, the leader of Clann na Poblachta, de Valera called a general election for 4 February 1948. Despite the Bill, Fianna Fáil's seat total fell to 68, a loss of 8. Clann na Poblachta won 10 seats, and, were it not for the Fianna Fáil gerrymander, could have had 19, based on the proportion of votes it secured. Fine Gael only gained one extra seat, a total of 31. The two Labour parties, the official Labour Party and National Labour, commanded 19 seats between them, Clann na Talmhum 7, and there were 12 independents.

After the election, it turned out that the truism that there are two sides in politics, an inside and an outside, was as valid as ever. The parties of the opposition came together to form an inter-party government. Despite the fact that much of the motivation for founding the party and opposing Fianna Fáil had stemmed from de Valera's wartime's executions policy, Clann na Poblachta was able to abolish the memory of Fine Gael's much greater total of civil war executions. However, MacBride did stipulate that Richard Mulcahy should not become Taoiseach, and John A. Costello, a prominent barrister, was chosen instead.

NEW PARTY, OLD PROBLEMS

MacBride, and the emergence of Clann na Poblachta, having provided the catalyst for the change in government, naturally caught the eyes of both the public and, to a degree, of subsequent historians. But three other figures were to exert a considerable influence on the inter-party government. Two of them were scarcely known to the public at large. These were Alexis Fitzgerald, a Fine Gael solicitor, and Patrick Lynch, a Department of Finance mandarin who differed sharply from the prevailing wisdom in that temple of orthodoxy. Lynch believed in the John Maynard Keynes analysis of the economic system, and he and Fitzgerald were to exert a marked influence on the new Minister for Finance, Patrick McGilligan. Both men saw a role for central government in public investment and the development of the economy, ideas which were to permeate through the new administration's economic strategy.

The third influential figure in the incoming administration was James Dillon, who returned from his neutrality-imposed isolation to the forefront of Irish politics with his vigour and idealism still intact. In a memorable speech he both brushed off Fianna Fáil's anxieties about inflation, and summed up the economic rationale of the inter-party government.

> No appeal to financial rectitude will induce this government to purchase a reputation untarnished in a financier's estimate by the expenditure of the life of a single child of any citizen of this state. We intend here and now, so far as resources and manpower will allow, to eliminate the school calculated to destroy the health of children learning in it; to obliterate the slum and to establish citizens of this country in tolerable homes; to build such sanatoria as may be required to control tuberculosis in this country; to provide such hospital accommodation as will ensure that no poor person will want for the attention which may mean the difference between life and death.[36]

The new government was soon to be involved in two major controversies, one over the perennial national issue, the other a Church–State clash, and throughout its existence it was involved in a perpetual wrestling match with the economy, which, had the Church–State issue not arisen first, would probably have felled it a little later anyhow.

The national issue was the first to arise. In the immediate aftermath of the election, both de Valera and Costello made political capital out of partition and the relationship with England. Having been defeated at home, de Valera, reckoning correctly that Seán MacBride would now don the electoral cloak of partition, set off on a world tour beginning in America on 8 March 1948, and then moving on through Australia, New Zealand and India. Far from succeeding in removing the hyphenates from the American political scene, de Valera's wartime policy appeared to do him more good than harm. The tone of his American reception was set in New York, which 'staged the biggest parade since the one celebrating the end of the war'. Once more, he was received by mayors, governors, cardinals, and civic dignitaries of all sorts, including President Truman and the architect of the Marshall plan, George

Marshall – despite the fact that de Valera's wartime activities meant that back in Ireland, his countrymen were receiving a far lesser share of Marshall Aid than they might have done. But it was an election year in America, and the Democrats needed the Irish-American vote. De Valera was cheered to the echo in Detroit when he said:

> We refused to fight in World War I for what they called the freedom of small nations because our territory was occupied by Britain and we resented the injustice. We could not have been expected to fight in World War II unless we were attacked. Our territory was still occupied by Britain, and the injustice continued . . . you cannot ask a small nation to fight with you for justice when you are inflicting an injustice on the small nation.[37]

But back at home, the inter-party government which had ousted him was attempting to remove the arrow of partition from his quiver. The chosen method was to repeal the External Relations Act. To say that the constitutional position of the 26 counties was anomalous at this stage would be to understate the case. At the end of the war in which Churchill had had to fumingly accept that Ireland, though half in the Commonwealth, was also effectively speaking half out, de Valera had been forced to indulge in some verbal gymnastics in the Dail as to the exact status of the country. Possibly inspired by David Gray, James Dillon had enquired (on 11 July 1945): 'Are we a Republic or not, for nobody seems to know?' De Valera had given him short shrift with his answer: 'We are, if that is all the Deputy wants to know.' However, a few days later, he apparently decided that that was not all that Dillon, or the great Irish public, should know on the subject, and he took the opportunity of having to speak on the External Affairs estimate to define the status of the 26 counties. He said that in order to spare deputies the labour of looking up references, he had done so himself, and proceeded to quote the definition of a republic from a variety of dictionaries and encyclopaedias. It was this debate which offered humorists the opportunity of christening the state a 'dictionary republic'.

But de Valera also made one other fundamental point, saying of the External Relations Act that it was 'a simple statute repealable by the legislature and not of fundamental law'. It has been said that in his own mind he was becoming dissatisfied with the working of the Act, which had not provided for any meeting of minds between the north and the south, as he had claimed it would do. His official biography says that he had told Maffey that his mind was turning towards a Republic (hence the production of the dictionaries) and repeal, but that he was holding off in order to allow the British time to once more bring forward the concept of a Council of Ireland which had been contained in the original Government of Ireland Act, only to be thwarted by the Unionists.

The Council did not materialise, but Clann na Poblachta did, and given its Republican antecedents, it was not surprising that in its first year of office, not long after de Valera had returned from his triumphal tour, William Norton, who was the deputy leader of the inter-party government, mentioned in the Dail (on 6 August) that it would be a good idea for 'national self-respect' if the External Relations Act were to be speedily abolished. Just how speedily it was to go took everyone by surprise. Speaking at a meeting of the Canadian Bar Association in Ottawa, one of the least republican figures in the Cabinet, at least in public perceptions up to that moment, the Taoiseach, John A. Costello, denounced the Act as being 'full of inaccuracies and infirmities'. A week later, in the course of a press conference, he confirmed a report in the *Dublin Sunday Independent* (on 5 September) that the Government was planning to repeal the Act.

Various reasons have been advanced as to why Costello should have acted so precipitously in far-away Canada. Some say that the report in the *Sunday Independent* forced his hand, others that he and Mrs Costello were offered some official slights in Ottawa. At a banquet the toast of the President of Ireland was not proposed, but one to the King was. Worse, Costello had to sit in front of a replica of the great gun 'Roaring Meg', which the Protestants of Derry had used to withstand the siege of the Catholics. It was said the gun was placed there deliberately at the wish of Earl Alexander, the Governor General and a fervent Orangeman and Unionist.

At all events, the Secretary of the Department of External Affairs, Freddie Boland, who had drafted Costello's speech to the Bar Association, without reference to the External Relations Act, was astounded by the announcement, and phoned his minister, Seán MacBride, to inform him what had happened. By chance, MacBride was dining with Maffey at the time in a Dublin hotel, and Boland's call considerably enlivened the subsequent discourse. However, MacBride later claimed that the decision to repeal the Act was a Cabinet one, taken before Costello departed, the implication being of course that the impetus for the declaration came from Clann na Poblachta. There was considerable controversy[38] between MacBride and another inter-party minister, Noel Browne, who would shortly figure in an even greater controversy, as to whether or not the decision was a Cabinet one. Browne denies that it was, and certainly there is no Cabinet record of such a decision. For his part, Costello denied that his announcement was merely a reaction to slights, and averred that it was a considered Government decision.[39]

Whatever the truth of the decision to abolish the Act, it had harmful consequences, some of which persist to this day. Given his background, de Valera had no option but to support the abolition of the Act, and with the Dail unanimous, the Republic of Ireland Act was signed into law by the President on 21 December 1948, although its coming into operation was held over, and did not take effect until Easter Monday (18 April) the following year, the anniversary of the 1916 Rising. This was not the only republican initiative taken by Clann na Poblachta. Two seats in the Senate were allocated for citizens of Northern Ireland. One of these was Denis Ireland, the founder of the Irish Union movement, as a consequence of which he was cordially detested by the Unionists, and the other was Liam Kelly, a physical-force

Republican from County Tyrone, who subsequently led armed attacks on the north.

Unsurprisingly, therefore, the Unionist establishment viewed the new Dublin government and its activities with the greatest suspicion. Following the signing into law of the Republic of Ireland Act, Sir Basil Brooke, the Northern Prime Minister, summoned up the demons once more and declared a general election for 10 February. Costello met his announcement by calling an all-party meeting in the Mansion House, Dublin, to decide on how 'assistance can be given to the anti-partition candidates contesting seats at the General Election in the six NE counties'. It was decided at the meeting (on 25 January) that a public subscription be opened to fund an anti-partition drive. The Anti-Partition League founded as a result of this decision published a mountain of literature on discrimination and gerrymandering, and sent anti-partition speakers, including Denis Ireland and the famous Cork IRA leader, Tom Barry, on propaganda tours of England and America. The anti-partitionists also chose the date of the northern election to make the announcement that Easter Monday would see the coming into force of the Republic of Ireland Act.

Had Basil Brooke written the script himself, he could not have hoped for better. The 'political phantoms', the Republicans, were once more threatening 'Ulster'. The Labour Party was wiped out, and the Unionists were returned to power over the Nationalists with the same majority they had enjoyed in 1921, 42 seats to 12. But the worst was yet to come from the point of view of Dublin. Following the election, the Unionists switched their attention to lobbying the Labour Government in London, and as a result of Dublin's severance of its link with the Crown, a far stronger one was forged between Belfast and London. On 3 May 1949, Clement Attlee, the British Prime Minister, introduced the celebrated 'Unionist guarantee', as part of the Ireland Act:

> It is hereby declared that Northern Ireland remains part of Her Majesty's dominions of the United Kingdom and it is hereby affirmed that in no event will Northern Ireland or any part thereof cease to be a part of Her Majesty's Dominions and the United Kingdom without the consent of the Parliament of Northern Ireland.

Effectively speaking, to the time of writing, this guarantee, which was embodied in succeeding legislation after the British removed the Stormont parliament in 1972, created a veto on political progress, no matter how ardently this might have been desired by a majority in the two islands, unless the Unionists agreed, a result, it may be otiose to observe, which Clann na Poblachta had not foreseen. At this stage, it is probably necessary to point out that despite its Republican patina, the inter-party government was very far from being a collection of ravening radicals, a fact which will become abundantly clear when we come to consider the so-called Mother and Child controversy which brought the Government to an end in a clash involving both the medical profession and the Church. But the Government did show a certain radicalism in its approach to the economy that initially set it apart from its predecessor.

The inter-party government's 1950 budget, the first capital budget in the state's history, was the new administration's much-trumpeted instrument of change. The budget provided £11 million for food subsidies, £13.4 million for social service and employment schemes, £14 million for housing, £6.26 million for agricultural development, £4.75 million for electricity development and £2.25 million for improving the phone service. Further millions were put aside for developments in forestation, health, development of bogs and transport. All this called for sizeable borrowings: some £31 million on top of an increase in the state's debt from £116 million to £157 million in the first year of the inter-party's term of office.[40] The Minister for Finance, McGilligan, told the Dail that the intention of the new government's programme was not to generate state revenues, but to fix the gaps created by years of under-investment. The healthy creditor position of the country would guarantee that the money would be available to finance the programme, and the improvement to the state would therefore 'lighten the effective charge for the service of the debt which is being incurred in years to come'.[41] There were two sources of revenue available to the Government: liquidating its external assets and availing itself of the American resuscitation programmes for Europe. Both carried with them the risk of increasing inflation. However, McGilligan, while admitting 'that there was a danger of inflation', argued that this would be 'offset to the extent that domestic output of consumer goods and domestic savings increase and external assets are repatriated in the form of imports'.[42]

Costello also pooh-poohed inflationary risks, stating, on one occasion, that there was 'so much more to justify the effort than the comforting thought that in the long run we will all be dead'.[43] The noises emanating from the Fine Gael-led coalition were more like those from a socialist party, and the Department of Finance and the central bank reacted with anger, anxiety and disbelief at what had befallen the party of financial rectitude. MacBride and Clann na Poblachta were clearly in the driving seat. MacBride's contribution to the budget debate in fact was to regret that national capital development on a larger scale was not taking place, whatever this boded for the assets of the country held in sterling.[44] But Lemass was not merely scoring party political points when he warned in the Dail (on 9 March 1950) that the future was being mortgaged. He argued that the overall economic situation would deteriorate and that 1952 would be Ireland's zero hour. He felt that the Minister for Finance was leaving trip wires behind him for a successor to fall over.

Events certainly bore out both forecasts. The spectres at the feast which Lemass probably had in mind included the fact that Ireland was tied to an English economy which was being buffeted by the effects of a world war, the loss of an empire, wars and rumours of wars (it was the era of Korea). Domestically, the Irish industrialists weaned on protection and the extraction of the highest profit margins possible for the least possible value were not large enough economically or psychologically to develop an export trade to the area

351

that mattered most, America. Irish trade remained joined to the British economy like a Siamese twin. The single most important item, in the single most important Irish industry, agriculture, was the cattle trade. Prices here were fixed to those obtaining in the British market by an Anglo-Irish trade agreement of 1948, which was a plus for Irish farmers because of the higher prices prevailing in Britain, but the tie-in represents the reality of the Irish trading pattern. McGilligan was of course just as aware of these factors as Lemass. His was the hand priming the pump which was pushing up the level of imports, and creating a repatriation of external assets which, instead of generating increased exports, was creating a boom in domestic consumption not matched by significant increases in production. A man of the right who had made the notorious remark that people might have to die of starvation in Ireland, he was now forced to bring in a budget designed to appeal to the left.

Perhaps unsurprisingly, he reacted in an unusual manner for a Minister for Finance – he went missing. A fascinating piece of research by Eamonn McKee amongst Joseph Brennan's papers turned up a handwritten note which the amazed, and outraged, Brennan had written to himself concerning the difficulties which he and, in particular, MacElligott were having in trying to make contact with the Minister for Finance.[45] McGilligan did not turn up to a government meeting on 21 April 1950, which was a Friday, nor to one which followed on the Monday. On the Tuesday, Brennan noted that McGilligan

> did not attend the Central Bank meeting, the budget is due next week and he had to lie in wait to catch his M/F [sic] . . . if he turns up. MacElligott went to the Dail on the chance of the M/F being present and squatted in the M/F's row there. M/F appeared there 3.30 after questioning was taken aback to see MacElligott but stayed for a talk until 6 p.m.

McGilligan did turn up for divisions but not for a government meeting at eight p.m., even though the other ministers waited an hour and 45 minutes for him. In his memoirs, Noel Browne describes the influence of McGilligan over his colleagues:

> In a Cabinet room full of dull, earnest and dutiful plodders, Paddy McGilligan was an intriguing and polished anachronism. When he entered that room, always late, with five or six three-inch thick briefs under his arm, we all had to curb an inclination to stand to attention; the 'headmaster' had arrived. McGilligan impressed people with his sharp-edged Derry accent and the seemingly limitless range of his dialectical and intellectual skills.[46]

Budgeting for an inter-party government seemingly lay outside McGilligan's 'limitless range'. Brennan noted that MacElligott had told him that McGilligan was 'both sick and disappointed'. McGilligan frequently absented himself from his office on the grounds of indisposition, and indeed his appearance at a government meeting, to which he turned up late, did suggest ill-health. However, MacElligott's sympathy with his minister's condition evaporated somewhat on being told later in the day that McGilligan had been seen dining at Jammets, in those days the best restaurant in Dublin, in the company of his wife and the American minister. Brennan, too, was annoyed at McGilligan's utilisation of the Rooseveltian technique of 'absent treatment', and in fact offered his resignation in the summer after the budget, but was persuaded to stay on by Costello, whom he met, appropriately enough, at the Galway Races.

The coalition was in fact engaged in a vast gambling exercise, in which the favourite on which its wagers were placed was the skittish Marshall Aid. This financial steed almost refused to leave the paddock at the first outing, that at which Irish officials attended a meeting of the Foreign Relations Committee of the US House of Representatives in January 1948 to hear Assistant Secretary of State William Thorpe outline Ireland's case for receiving aid. F.H. Boland, Secretary of the Department of External Affairs, afterwards commented on Thorpe's presentation: 'A more deplorable performance would be hard to imagine.'[47] Thorpe did not distinguish between the state of Ireland's balance of payments and its ability to meet European import needs. Failure to secure imports from Europe would have meant that Ireland would have had to turn to dollar areas, thus incurring a deficit with the US. This inauspicious start was compounded by the attitude of the Irish Department of Finance to the whole question of Marshall Aid.

The Department of Finance attitude was that if sterling were convertible, Ireland 'would consider it altogether unjustifiable to look for a single cent of grant in aid from the US or any other country'. In fact, 'it was necessary to inquire whether there was not some arrangement by which we could avoid the indignity of accepting US aid'.[48] Finance saw the European Recovery Programme as a means to promote European, and in particular British recovery. T.K. Whitaker had a more well-founded objection to the local currency counterpart funds, saying that these 'provided a standing temptation to Governments to incur expenditure without due regard to the economic consequences'.[49] External Affairs, however, had it in mind to resist everything except this temptation. MacBride intended to get control of as much US aid as he could to make up for years of stagnation, and to further the aims of his party. He was clear from the outset that his target was aid, not a loan, telling a press conference:

> Inasmuch as our exports to the Western Hemisphere are negligible, we would have no means of repaying any dollars which the US might be kind enough to offer to us. Hence it appears to me that we may find ourselves unable to avail of ERP aid if it be by way of loan ... Unless the loans were solely in respect of capital equipment, designed to create new exports to the dollar market, we would have no means of meeting the obligations that the loan would involve. I doubt whether Ireland would be prepared to undertake obligations that it knows it could not meet.[50]

MacBride was aware of residual hostilities towards Ireland in decision-taking Washington as a result of neutrality, and he and his officials met with the Permanent Director of the European Affairs Department, Hickerson, on 20 May 1948, to test his response towards the question of aid for Ireland. It was hostile.[51] MacBride tried to inject the partition issue into the conversations, but Hickerson replied that the State Department wanted to maintain the border, partly because of Ireland's neutrality, partly out of friendship towards its wartime ally, Britain, and partly because the US had 'every reason to count on the use of bases in that area in the event of need. I am sure you will agree that this is a powerful argument for this Government's favouring the continued control of Northern Ireland by the UK.'[52]

Hickerson was no lone voice. Another senior official, Wayne Jackson, advised the responsible official, Harry Clement of the ECA Irish desk: 'Don't give the Irish any grant'; and opined that the Irish were 'difficult' and 'impossible' and 'pretty nearly everybody who had anything to do with the Irish got "sucked in" and ended up wearing green neckties'.[53] Jackson was voicing the State Department/David Gray attitude towards the Irish custom of regarding the State Department as being inhabited by British sympathisers, and by-passing them and their institution to make representations to politicians susceptible to the Irish-American vote. The State Department was also enraged at the Irish 'using the hospitality of a friendly power to undermine another friendly power', i.e. lobbying the US against partition. Against the background of neutrality, the Irish thus had something of a mountain to climb insofar as officialdom in post-war Washington was concerned.

Aid was out of the question, Ireland's creditworthiness was unquestionable, and the State Department averred that there was 'no over-riding international political consideration which would warrant preferential treatment towards the Irish. We feel therefore that a decision should be made on an economic basis in comparison with other countries.'[54] Of course, Irish creditworthiness stemmed from neutrality. The enforced savings of the wartime years had increased external reserves. This meant that Ireland could certainly be judged as creditworthy in terms of sterling, but she had little or nothing in the way of dollar holdings. During the 1948 Anglo-Irish trade talks, the British Chancellor of the Exchequer, Sir Stafford Cripps, stunned the Irish by informing them that as from the following June, Ireland would no longer be able to draw dollars from the sterling pool. Britain, of course, was at the time grappling with the problems of the austerity programme necessitated by her loosening grip on empire, post-war economic difficulties, and her diminishing share of the world's trade. Ireland's assumed prosperity was not so much a reflection of reality as an inability to spend money on imports.

Thus when MacBride visited Washington, he knew that his country did not have access to the sterling area's dollar reserves, that access to foreign currency could largely be determined by Whitehall, and that if the Irish turned down dollars in any form, even by way of loan, they could hardly then go to the British to ask them to dip into their diminished dollar pool. Even if they could get dollars from the British, the Americans would be even more reluctant to allow the Irish dollar aid, while at the same time she made up her dollar deficits from the British dollar pool. A loan it had to be. Nevertheless, the Irish persisted with some dubious stratagems in order to convince Washington that they were conforming with European Co-operation Administration regulations. Irish official policy was that they entered the Marshall Aid arrangements available, 'provided however that that should not be taken to mean that articles of an obviously unnecessary or luxury character might be imported freely'.[55] The use of the word 'obviously' is said to have originated with MacBride, and Irish civil servants translated it as that devious mind intended – to get around the ECA tests of availability and essentiality. The ice skated over by the MacBride formula was so thin that a Department of Finance memo of the period stated:

> The government ruling had not been disclosed because it conflicts with the assumptions on which the European Recovery Programme is based as well as with the exchange control policy of the sterling area of which we are a member. Thus we have been forced to adopt a sort of masquerade, professing to the British that we are spending dollars only on essential goods and tacitly leading the ECA to believe that our Exchange Control screens dollar applications by reference to the test of availability.[56]

In his seminal work, *The Irish Department of Finance, 1922–58*,[57] Professor Ronan Fanning gives a magisterial overview of the unfolding of the Marshall Aid drama. Nothing in it is more dramatic than the telling of the last act, which curbed MacBride's influence on the inter-party government's policy, and returned direction of the Government's finances from the hands of the Department of External Affairs to those of the Department of Finance. MacBride's Republican desire to escape economic dependence on Britain was the motivation for his ice-skating. But the link with sterling meant that should a strain come on the ice in the form of a British devaluation, then his reliance on expansion based on dollar loans would create not only cracks but black holes. The holes opened on Saturday 17 September 1949, when the British formally informed Dublin that sterling was to be devalued. Just as he would do later as the Mother and Child Scheme crisis reached a climax, MacBride had recourse to some forensic histrionics. He sat in a chair in an office at the Department of External Affairs (Iveagh House, the handsome building donated to the Irish state by the Guinness family), surrounded by other members of the Cabinet, and subjected Department of Finance officials to a prosecutorial inquisition which was as bizarre, gruelling and lengthy as it was ultimately useless. Apparently MacBride believed that the sterling balances held by Irish investors could be used to threaten the British with their repatriation. But there was no way that an Irish government could force its citizens to repatriate their own money. However, despite this extraordinary performance, which as Dr Fanning points out 'began at two o'clock in the morning', nothing that an Irish politician could do to Dublin civil servants was going to intimidate the British Chancellor of the Exchequer. The link with sterling meant that no matter how much huffing and puffing was done, if Britain devalued, then Ireland had to do so also – and pay more for the dollar loans which underpinned the budgets of 1950 and 1951.

Thus the Marshall Aid saga had far-reaching consequences for Ireland. There were firstly the improvements which the dollar loans effected in afforestation, telephones, electricity supplies and land reclamation. James Dillon, the Minister for Agriculture, did not succeed in his stated objective of 'drowning Britain in eggs', but he did manage to reclaim approximately a million acres of land in the west of Ireland. While admittedly some of the money was wrung out of the begrudging hands of the Irish bankers, the heady scent of dollars in the air had a bearing also on the fact that the inter-party government built ten times as many houses in 1951 as Fianna Fáil managed in 1947, a total of 11,305. Another positive outcome was a governmental realisation of the fact that the inefficient, often family-owned Irish industries had neither the will nor the expertise to penetrate the American market. This ultimately led to the setting up of Coras Trachtala, the Irish Export Board.[58] But there were downsides. Dollar spending continued to underpin the budgets of 1950 and 1951, thus storing up a day of reckoning which would be dictated along classical Department of Finance lines. It was recognised that although the inter-party government's hopes were not realised, henceforth central government could and probably would take responsibility for growing the economy. With this in mind, T. K. Whitaker persuaded MacElligott to set up a section within Finance, with himself at the head, that would examine 'all aspects of capital expenditure in the context of general economic, financial and monetary policy'.[59] In other words, as MacBride's star waned, that of finance came into the ascendant once more.

This restoration of power would ultimately have the happiest of consequences for the Irish economy, but initially it would steer it through a vale of tears. In a celebrated memo to MacElligott, pondering the lessons of Marshall Aid, and the introduction of capital budgets, Whitaker wrote in favour of:

> a realisation that if houses, electricity development, afforestation, and all the other forms of capital expenditure are desired by the commuity, the desire should be expressed in the form of preferring these things to other . . . of turning over to the state some of the money now being spent on non-essential consumer goods so that the state can carry on with its capital programme without causing too much inflation. If the public wish to spend now rather than save and the state also deems it wise to spend now largely on works that confer social benefits or whose economic fruits are slow to appear, the result must be that which our balance of payments show . . . purchasing power spilling over and being absorbed by surplus consumer imports.[60]

This doctrine would be swallowed whole, added to, and acted upon in the framing of the Fianna Fáil budget of 1952, with disastrous effects for the Irish economy throughout the whole of the ensuing decade. However, Fianna Fáil's return to power was facilitated not so much by the economic situation, but by the Church–State clash which inextricably became bound up with the public's perception of the inter-party government's handling of matters temporal and ecclesiastical.

It was an irony of ironies that Clann na Poblachta should have fallen over a clash with the Church. Practically MacBride's first act on the day of his by-election victory (on 29 October 1947) was to deliver to Archbishop John Charles McQuaid a letter which said:

> I hasten, as my first act, to pay my humble respects to Your Grace and to place myself at Your Grace's disposal. Both as a Catholic and as a public representative I shall always welcome any advice which Your Grace may be good enough to give me and shall be at Your Grace's disposal should there be any matters upon which Your Grace feels that I could be of any assistance. It is my sincere hope that Your Grace will not hesitate to avail of my services should the occasion arise.[61]

And when the Clann's influence proved decisive in putting Fianna Fáil out of office, MacBride's obsequious tone was continued by the Cabinet as a whole. After the first Cabinet meeting following the election in February 1948, the new government sent a telegram to the Pope which probably said all that needs to be said about the depth of religious feeling, the strength of Catholicism, and the fear of being perceived in any way anti-clerical in the Ireland of the year of our Lord 1948. The telegram declared that the new government would

> repose at the feet of Your Holiness the assurance of our filial loyalty and of our devotion to Your August Person as well as our firm resolve to be guided in all our work by the teaching of Christ and to strive for the attainment of a social order in Ireland based on Christian principles.

Despite this fairly comprehensive avowal of faith, the Taoiseach, John A. Costello, when involved in the Church–State controversy three years later, would still find it necessary to issue a Catholic version of William Craig's Declaration of Protestantism, saying: 'I am an Irishman second: I am a Catholic first' when it came to the teachings of the Church vis-à-vis state policy. Not surprisingly, therefore, although the inter-party government did make some significant breakthroughs in health and in the industrial sphere – notably in the treatment of TB and the setting up of the Industrial Development Authority – initially its main sphere of activity was in Catholic Action. As the new government began finding its feet, the Communists were taking over in Czechoslovakia and threatening to do so in Italy, where elections were to be held on 17 April. In Rome, Joseph Walshe had an audience with the Pope, in the course of which he told the pontiff that the Government, as well as the people, would regard it as the greatest moment in our history if He deigned to make Ireland the Home of the Holy See, for the period of persecution, if and when it came. For this offer He expressed his deepest gratitude and went on to say, 'Ireland is the only place I could go to – only there would I have the atmosphere and the sense of security to rule the Church as Christ wants me to rule it.'[62]

Following the meeting Walshe met with MacBride in Paris and, convinced that Ireland was, in Walshe's words, 'of supreme importance as a Catholic bulwark in Europe', MacBride contacted the Papal Nuncio to Ireland, Cardinal D'Alton, and Archbishop McQuaid to initiate a national fund-raising campaign for the Italian Christian Democrats. The Irish hierarchy fell in with the suggestion and McQuaid, who had already raised almost £20,000, took the unusual step of going on Radio Eireann to issue an appeal because 'The issue now being fought in Italy is as vital for peaceful Ireland as it is for every land where the name of Christ, Our Lord is still revered.'[63] Money flowed in. The Knights of Columbanus gave £5,000, McQuaid himself £2,500, as did a body less associated with devotion to the Spirit than to spirits, the Licensed Vintners Association. MacBride himself, alas, could only manage what he termed a 'small sum'. But de Valera and O'Kelly, possibly because they had been in office far longer than MacBride, sent a 'generous contribution' and a 'handsome cheque' respectively to help defeat the Communists. Defeated they duly were, McQuaid comparing the Christian Democrat victory to that of the Crusaders at the Battle of Lepanto. The Irish Crusaders' contribution would not have been as significant as it was had the ever-efficient Walshe not intervened to ensure that their money did not go through the Vatican Bank. For all his Holiness's concern about martyrdom at the hands of the Communists, the rate of exchange offered by the bank was far less than that available through the Banca di Roma, which meant that were it not for Walshe's intervention, the Irish contribution to the Christian Democrats would have been very much lower than it actually was.[64]

In considering the amounts raised to defeat communism in Italy, it is instructive of the attitudes of the time to compare the amounts raised to combat an evil nearer to home – that of emigration. Seven years after the Christian Democrat appeal, the Irish government of the day having washed its hands of the problem, the English Cardinal Griffin launched a fund to build an Irish Centre in Camden Town, north London, with a donation of £1,000. His Irish opposite number, Cardinal D'Alton, gave £250, McQuaid £500, and there is no record of either 'generous cheques' or even 'small amounts' from De Valera, O'Kelly, MacBride and company. It might also be legitimately observed as symptomatic of the Vatican's own attitudes towards Ireland, as opposed to the often-expressed papal appreciations of Irish piety and support, that while McQuaid's efforts were acknowledged by Dr Luigi Gedda, the head of the Italian civil movement which opposed the Communists, the Vatican newspaper *L'Osservatore Romano* only mentioned McQuaid's contributions over a month after his monies arrived in Rome, and then only after Walshe had raised the matter with the Vatican.

Although MacBride began his tenure in office as Foreign Minister apparently more zealous to further the interests of Rome than Dublin, he was in fact an international-minded man, who by the end of his career would have been awarded both the Lenin and Nobel Peace Prizes – the latter because he was a co-founder of Amnesty International, the former because he frequently stood up to the Americans during his career at the UN which followed his active participation in Irish politics. The whiff of sulphur which he brought to Irish public life through his association with the IRA, his charm, and his French-accented English made him for a time an exotic and compelling figure, rivalling de Valera in popularity. Also, though Archbishop McQuaid would not have approved, one historian's description of MacBride that 'although he was a married man, [he] was also known to be fond of women, especially when in Paris, found a resonance in the real Irish psyche to be found lurking behind the cloak of piety'.

Women were also fond of MacBride and extremely loyal to him. Louise O'Brien, who for a time had her own flat in MacBride's family home, Roebuck, in Dundrum, County Dublin, worked for him as his secretary in the Department of External Affairs without receiving any pay. She was not part of the department's establishment, but MacBride, who had a phobia about British intelligence activities, was not prepared to trust the secretarial assistance available to him, and in fact began his tenure as minister by telling the secretary of the department, Freddie Boland, that he wanted a list of the British agents working in there! Some commentators have tended to mock MacBride's caution in this regard, but apart from the well-known truism that the fact of being paranoid does not mean that people are not out to 'get' one, the history of Ireland past and present affords substantial reason for Irish politicians to be mindful of British intelligence-gathering. As this was being written, for example, a highly placed figure in the Irish Special Branch told me of his (and his colleagues') mistrust of MI5, who they had discovered had bugged the branch's headquarters in Harcourt Street, Dublin. MacBride in fact was a more cultivated version of a type frequently found in the IRA leadership.

Before being regarded as friends or enemies, patriots or subversives, Republicans or Nationalists, members of the IRA even, such figures, it has to be realised, have to be recognised as conspirators. A principal progenitor of the Irish state was the architect of the Treaty, the outgoing, wrestling, ebullient Michael Collins. He should also be regarded as one of the great conspirators of the twentieth century, the man who broke the British Secret Service in Ireland. MacBride was an extremely devious and complex man. Charles J. Haughey once described him to me as being 'as crooked as a ram's horn'. And a disgruntled colleague has left this vivid portrait of him:

> Of medium height, round-shouldered, he looked frail, indeed positively consumptive. But when he stayed near us in Connemara during an Attlee–Noel Baker visit in 1949, he was

seen when swimming to have a surprisingly powerfully-built body. He appeared always as the 'well dressed lawyer', wearing conservative, dark, well-cut suits. Overall he had a gaunt, cadaverous appearance and his sallow complexion gave him a Mediterranean look. His curved crescent-shaped nose suggested a distinctly Middle Eastern appearance, and left an impression of foreignness. He would have modelled for a powerful Epstein head of a man who had suffered much. The mouth was well-shaped, thin-lipped, and obstinate – a dangerous man to cross! His rare smile was a momentary muscular response, as used by a well-mannered diplomat; it did not infuse a sense of warmth, nor was it ever completely reassuring.[65]

But behind the conniving and scheming, MacBride was a straight-up Irish Republican, devoted to the goal which had claimed his father's life in 1916, a 32-county Irish republic. He never received a penny for the majority of the IRA cases he defended both during and after the war, and, despite his international career, amassed very little capital. However, he was sincerely devoted to the cause of Irish unity, although some commentators have criticised his methodology. Professor Keogh for example has described his 'posturing on NATO' as being 'as gauche as it was naïve', because it 'introduced a note of crude horse-trading into high diplomacy', and Boland found that he could not work with him, transferring to London as the Irish Ambassador to the Court of St James after two years of Clann rule.

One would have thought that the brutal realpolitik of Cold War European and world politics was the embodiment of extremely crude horse-trading. MacBride and the inter-party government entered the European arena when it was indicated to Ireland in an aide-memoir from the American minister who had succeeded David Gray, George Garrett, that membership of NATO was open to Ireland. However, the inter-party government, largely because of MacBride, continued the de Valera argument against breaching neutrality: Ireland could not join NATO because 'Six of our North Eastern counties are occupied by British forces against the will of the overwhelming majority of the Irish people.'

Dillon, now Minister for Agriculture in the inter-party government, continued to argue in favour of lining up alongside the Allies, as he had done during the war, but MacBride and those who thought like him were convinced that the issue of joining NATO should be made conditional on a move to end partition. However, the Americans' wartime experience had convinced them of the wisdom of maintaining partition so that the northern bases might be secured. Thus the continued American response to Dublin was that partition was a matter between Britain and Ireland, and that NATO was being created because of new security problems, not old political ones. Neutrality thus continued to be a cardinal point of Irish international policy, which periodically created debate for the remainder of the century, particularly when questions of military alliances within the EEC arose. MacBride helped to smooth Ireland's path on the road to European Union through his constructive attitude to the Council of Europe, which was set up in 1949, and which he urged should be enlarged to include Spain and Portugal; and despite

Ireland's absence from the side of the Allies during the 'Emergency', he managed to prise a modicum of Marshall Aid from Washington's grip.

The sums involved ($18 million in grants and $128 million in loans) were nothing like those available to countries which had fought in the war and had suffered devastation as a result. Nor were they anything like what MacBride was hoping for (somewhere in the region of £120 million in aid). But while Marshall Aid did not result in the setting in train of any great dynamism, which might have helped to lift the Irish economy and culture out of its depressed, censorship-ridden post-war existence, it nevertheless represented approximately half of the total state investment made during the new government's term of office.

Moreover, MacBride did manage to get control of the Marshall Aid grant for his own department, rather than the Department of Finance. This enabled him to give some stimuli to culture, setting up a Cultural Relations Committee, which supported the arts. The inter-party government also commissioned a report from Dr Thomas Bodkin on the state of the arts in Ireland, which ultimately resulted in improvements to the National Museum and the National Library, and in the introduction of legislation which led to the setting up of an Arts Council, albeit after Fianna Fáil had returned to office in 1951. Another brainchild of MacBride's was an Irish News Agency, which was set up with the somewhat contradictory aims of providing objective news, countering anti-Irish propaganda and attracting foreign investment. Its first managing director (appointed in March 1950) was Conor Cruise O'Brien. The INA never succeeded in establishing itself and was wound up by Fianna Fáil in 1951.

The inter-party government also deserves to be remembered for the foundation of the Industrial Development Authority, which ultimately, after some initial teething problems, laid foundations which at the time of writing have resulted in Ireland's becoming one of Europe's top centres of inward investment. Unfortunately, such is the ingratitude of political memory, the Government is probably better known in folk memory for another piece of inward-looking political activity, which resulted in the immortal Battle of Baltinglass and demonstrated that where Ireland at least is concerned, the more governments changed in Dail Eireann, the more they stayed the same on the ground. Clientilism, jobbery and skulduggery remained the reality of parish-pump politics.

James Everett of Labour, who had become Minister for Posts and Telegraphs in the inter-party government, decided not to confer the altitudinous position of sub-post-office holder on the acting incumbent at Baltinglass, a Ms Helen Cook. Ms Cook's family had run the post office there for nearly a century, and it was expected that its transfer into her name – she was running it for a sick aunt – would be automatic. However, Everett decided to transfer the post office to a local, a publican and shopkeeper called Michael Farrell.

Noel Browne said of Everett that

his sole interest in life was to remain a Dail Deputy and a member of the County Council, which he did until he died . . . he attended Cabinet meetings assiduously, taking no part in discussions, except when an item came up concerning Wicklow in any shape or form . . . he had little time for Cabinet meetings compared to the supreme importance of meetings of Wicklow County Council.

For Jim Everett it was not in government buildings in Merrion Street, but in Wicklow town that the real business of the state was transacted.

As a result of his transaction of business in Baltinglass, County Wicklow exploded in uproar. Alternative postal services were set up. Telegraph poles were cut down. There were mass public protest meetings, and whenever the Gardai set out from Dublin to implement the change from the Cook premises to those owned by Farrell, Fianna Fáil spies in Dublin Castle informed the locals of their approach so that roadblocks and protests made their task impossible. Finally, in January of 1951, the issue was diffused by the reinstatement of Ms Cook. No such solution, however, was possible in the Church–State clash which helped to bring down the coalition government later that year, destroying the Clann na Poblachta Party in the process, and returning Fianna Fáil to power.

Before detailing the encounter between Church and State, it is worth noting that, although the Church was in an extraordinarily powerful position in Ireland, under Fianna Fáil a tradition had grown up whereby outside the fields of education and health, strong-minded ministers, including de Valera himself, would stand up to individual bishops when the battlegrounds were favourable. Two examples in particular of this tendency may be given: the case of the Commission of Vocational Organisation, in 1944; and the clash between Seán MacEntee, then Minister for Local Government, and Dr Dignan, Bishop of Clonfert, which also began in 1944.

MacEntee took violent exception to proposals which Dr Dignan had made on national health insurance in a pamphlet which the bishop published in 1944, and denounced the bishop publicly. A vigorous letter-writing controversy ensued from which the socially concerned bishop emerged victorious. The bishop's sin in MacEntee's eyes was his denunciation of the Poor Law system as reeking with 'destitution, pauperism and degradation', which of course it was. It was MacEntee who had appointed Dignan, a staunch Fianna Fáil supporter, to the chairmanship of the National Health Insurance Society and whether he felt that a tool had turned in his hand, or because he was a doctrinaire member of the poor-ye-shall-have-always-with-ye school, MacEntee replied to the bemused bishop with a viperish eccentricity. The controversy did not result in any seminal change in Irish society, but it did show that where some Fianna Fáil personalities were concerned Caesar was occasionally prepared to take off the gloves with Christ at least for a few, inconclusive rounds.

The idea of vocationalism had attracted attention in Irish intellectual Catholic circles throughout the thirties following the publication of the Papal

Encyclical Quadragesimo Anno, which condemned equally the notions of organising society on either communistic or materialistic lines. De Valera personally would have had no quarrel with the papal thesis, but politically he found little to enthuse about in the prospect of having a vocational body set up in Ireland to, in effect, tell him what to do. Accordingly, he adapted a tactic used by the British to his own purposes: he would kill Rome rule by kindness, or at least circumvent the wishes of Irish vocationalists. As we have seen, he had killed off the first Irish Senate, not with kindness but with ruthlessness, because it had attempted to interfere with his legislation. But he appeared to give the principle of vocationalism a degree of statutory recognition in the manner in which he designed the 60-strong Senate which came into being under the 1937 constitution.

Forty-three of the senators were allegedly to be drawn from vocational interests, six were to be elected by the universities, and 11 by the Taoiseach of the day. Article 19 of the constitution specified that if the Oireachteas so decided, the 43 could be elected 'by any functional or vocational group, or association'. But the preceding article of the constitution, Article 18, set up another mechanism for electing the 43. Five panels were created. Election to the panels took place from the ranks of county councillors and TDs. This meant that the panels which elected the senators were in reality stuffed with party-political hacks. From the time he took power in 1932, de Valera used the scalpel rather than the bludgeon to cut out opposition to Fianna Fáil, in the army, the Gardai, the civil service and the professions. As Professor Lee has observed in his monumental work on Irish politics and society,[66] de Valera initially resisted the cruder pressures from his supporters that he should dismiss pro-Treaty civil servants and army officers. Instead, files were opened on political adversaries, promotions were blocked, life became less pleasant for many who had served under the old regime, as de Valera

> encouraged the gradual growth of an insidious, if initially discreet, spoils system in the army, the police, the judiciary, and the state sponsored bodies. He devised an electoral system for the Senate that invited corruption, and responded to pleas for reform by delicately holding his nostrils. Like his countrymen in general, he combined a rigid concept of private morality with a more selective one of public morality.... he had a highly refined capacity for self-deception.[67]

This capacity sustained de Valera for several years of the Senate's functioning, even though elections to it quickly became a by-word for corruption. At the conferences which followed the 'vocational' appointments to the Senate, in 1938 and again in 1943, the Association of Municipal Authorities publicly condemned the bribery which marked Senate elections. But de Valera rejected the condemnations in the Dail, and privately fended off pleas for reform from two of his most important ministers, MacEntee and Jim Ryan.[68] He did concede that 'some Senators have been elected through corrupt practices, through bribery'[69] after a former chairman of Dublin

Council, John A. Corr, received a three-month jail sentence for bribery and perjury. But overall, his policy of stifling rather than attacking the corporate urge continued.

In 1938, he agreed to suggestions that he set up a commission on vocationalism under the chairmanship of the prime bully amongst the Irish bishops, Michael Browne of Galway, known as 'cross Michael', and not merely because his signature was always accompanied by an episcopal cross. The commission's report, drawn up by a Jesuit, Father E.J. Coyne, was published in August 1944. It envisaged a totally new form of Irish society, one in which interventionism on a grand scale would bring about massive changes in the economic and social spheres. Participation by the public in decision-taking was to be fostered through a National Vocational Assembly. The report had its flaws, many of them, a principal one being that it did not explain how the vocational assembly would function alongside another body set up by the Irish people, known as the parliament, Dail Eireann. Moreover, Father Coyne's criticisms of the existing structures of government and civil service of course created a minefield of opposition, and, despite the report's august parentage, it withered on the vine. De Valera did not have to attack the report; as Professor Lee noted: 'The official mind did not so much confront as simply squash the challenge.'[70]

CHURCH VERSUS STATE: THE MOTHER AND CHILD OF ALL BATTLES

What has passed into Irish political folklore as 'the Mother and Child Scheme Affair' was a more serious, and sanguinary, business. The clash may in part have been prompted by the earlier Church–State rows described above, a sense that politicians were getting a little too uppity. But, ostensibly at least, it had its origins in a Health Bill which Fianna Fáil had initiated before going out of power in 1948. By now, a new generation of civil servants had either risen or were rising to the decision-taking echelons of the public service, where they were both proving themselves a force for innovation in some key areas, notably health, and supplying the initiative which most of the political leadership of the time lacked. At the Department of Health, figures like Dr James Deeny, the Department's Chief Medical Adviser, were conscious both of the changes in healthcare in England, flowing from the Beveridge Plan, and of newer trends in European Catholic social policy. They were also aware of health statistics such as the fact that infant mortality amongst the poor of Dublin was 133 per 1,000, compared with 29 per 1,000 amongst the better-off. A new Health Bill showing their influence was introduced in 1945 which proposed to curb the spread of infectious diseases, and to provide improved services for mothers and children. However, the Bill faltered when the junior minister responsible for piloting it through the Dail, Dr Con Ward, Parliamentary Secretary at the Department of Local Government and Health, was forced to resign. It was taken up again in 1947 by Dr James Ryan, who had been appointed Minister for Health and Social Welfare at the beginning of the year. Its radical proposals included providing public authorities with powers to declare certain diseases infectious, and to sequester the carriers from the public, particularly where TB and VD were concerned. Children with infectious diseases were to be kept from school, or public places. But it was not these draconian and isolationist positions which attracted the publicity, but a provision which sought to provide mothers and children with free medical care.

These provisions had survived the initial onslaught from the Church and public representatives about giving the state power to inspect individuals medically and to curtail their movement. Some of these objections were literally nit-picking, for Fine Gael's Dick Mulcahy attacked the fact that a child could be prevented from going to mass because it had nits in its hair.[71] But others were more serious. The Conference of Superiors of Convents Secondary Schools objected to the compulsory medical inspection of adolescent schoolgirls by doctors, and the Archbishop of Dublin, John Charles McQuaid, wrote to de Valera conveying the hierarchy's fears:

> The unusual and absolute power of medical inspection of children and adults, by compulsory regulation, and, if needs be, by force, is a provision so intimately concerned with the rights of parents and the human person, that only clear-cut guarantees and safeguards on the part of the Government, can be regarded as an adequate protection of those rights.[72]

De Valera soothed McQuaid's fears by arranging to have Dr Ward call on him. At their meeting, Ward promised McQuaid that at the committee stage of the Bill, he would introduce amendments, copies of which he later submitted to the Archbishop. These provided for the exemption of the schools for the better-off from inspection by state medical officers, and of pupils who had got a certificate from their own doctor. McQuaid accepted these amendments to the Bill, many of whose other features he praised. The opposition continued to attack the Bill as being totalitarian, with strong resonances of Nazism. But the Powerful Purple Ones remained silent throughout both the drama of Ward's departure and the reintroduction of the Bill in 1947 by Dr James Ryan. Ryan had also consulted with McQuaid, and, as a result of their conversations, had made further alterations to the Bill.

Speaking in the Dail, Ryan made it clear that the keystone of the arch of the Bill was the introduction of new services for mothers and children free of charge. But no one in the Dail, or the hierarchy, either objected or waved a crozier as the Bill passed into law in August 1947. However, James Dillon had a challenge mounted in the courts to test for constitutionality the provision compelling schoolchildren to undergo medical examinations. Then, on 13 October, a date which those with a taste for omens subsequently invested with significance, the hierarchy wrote to de Valera objecting to the proposed Bill on a number of grounds: 'The empowerment of public authorities to provide for the health of all children, to treat their ailments, educate them in regard to health, educate women in regard to motherhood and provide all women with gynaecological care.' The bishops said that for the state to claim such power was 'Entirely and directly contrary to Catholic teachings, the rights of the family, the rights of the Church in education, the rights of the medical profession and of voluntary institutions.'

By now, some rumblings had also been received from doctors expressing much the same sort of opposition to socialised medicine which the Beveridge Plan had had to surmount in England. Another unspoken objection was the fact that if the state began directing their activities, it would also gain an insight into their income tax returns. However, de Valera met the bishops' letter with an outburst of instantaneous procrastination and did not reply to their Lordships until 16 February 1948, two days before his departure from office. He let it be known that the delay was caused by the fact of the Dillon action and sent their Lordships a copy of a memo from Ryan's department which stated that

> Their Lordships may be assured that the Government, both in their legislative proposals and in administration, have constantly in mind, not only the State's function as guardian of the common good, but also the respect which is due to the fundamental personal and family rights.

De Valera thus avoided the risk of a 'belt of a crozier' for himself or his party during an election campaign, but the Ryan Bill was left lying like a rake in the political long grass waiting for an unwary passer-by to tread on it and be disastrously smitten between the eyes. That passer-by was to be Dr Noel Browne.

Browne became a minister the day he entered the Dail as a newly elected Clann na Poblachta TD. At 32, he was the youngest minister in the history of the state. A survivor of TB, which had claimed the lives of his father, mother and two sisters, and of grinding degrading poverty in his youth, he literally owed his professional training to kindly Chance. After his father's death, his terminally ill mother sold their house and few belongings, and sailed for England from Ballinrobe, where the family were never 'visited by any public official or person or substance other than the rent collector. No member of a religious order, nun, priest, or brother, came near the house to see if we needed help. Life in Ireland then was completely unconcerned with and uncaring for the poor.'[73]

In England, a series of flukes and friends bestowed on the young Browne a good education culminating in a spell at the Jesuit Beaumont College. Here he was fortunate to be asked by one of the Jesuits to look after another Irish boy, Neville Chance, who had joined Beaumont from Clongowes. Unlike Irish Cabinet makers, the Jesuit feared that Clongowes might have made the lad a trifle uncouth, and asked Browne, whom he judged had 'anarchistic tendencies',[74] to look after him. The ensuing friendship with Neville Chance led to the Chance family taking Browne to live with them, and sending him to Trinity College Dublin, to train as a doctor.

Browne once described himself to me[75] as a 'Socialist and a Catholic. I believe that the Sermon on the Mount says all there is to be said about socialism.' In view of what befell his political beliefs at the hands of his supposed allies, one presumes that he was referring to the Beatitudes rather than the verses which prophetically warned of the dangers of building a house on sand: 'And the rain fell and the floods came and the winds blew: and they beat upon that house. And it fell; and great was the fall thereof.'[76] Browne first encountered these allies while working at Newcastle Sanatorium in County Wicklow during the period when Clann na Poblachta was being formed. One of his patients was a journalist, Harry Kennedy, who was a friend of Michael Harnett, a close associate of MacBride, with whom he had appeared at McCaughey's inquest and in a number of IRA trials. Harnett and Kennedy introduced Browne to MacBride, who decided that he would make a good candidate, and that his views on the eradication of tuberculosis would form a valuable plank in the new party's programme. Not surprisingly, therefore, one of Browne's first official acts as Minister for Health was to visit Portlaoise jail to inspect the place of McCaughey's death. He found: 'McCaughey's cell deep underground, a truly awful place in which to die, hungry or not'.[77] In later life he would make the improvement of prison conditions a priority. By then, however, he had become a member of Fianna Fáil and de Valera blocked his proposals. Browne had more success with his first major campaign, the eradication of TB, and the implementation of a hospital-building programme which had been part of the stock in trade of political promises almost since the foundation of the state, but had not been acted on.

However, a combination of Browne's energetic new broom and the vision and hard work of civil servants like Deeny put through a massive programme in a very short space of time. It involved £30 million worth of building and upgrading to provide some 7,000 new hospital beds. Hitherto, health ministers had only used the interest on the capital which the state derived from the Irish Hospital Sweepstakes, some £100,000 a year. But Browne liquidated the capital itself and pledged the expected future income for another seven years. The result was an explosion in the building of clinics, hospitals and sanatoria. Some of Browne's critics alleged that the building of sanatoria was unnecessary, because of the discovery of the BCG inoculation. But somebody has to get the credit for the fact that TB death rates plummeted from 123 per 100,000 in 1947 to 73 per 100,000 in 1951, and continued to fall thereafterwards, earning for Browne the sobriquet in Dublin slumland of being 'the man who gave us the free TB'.

However, 1951 was also the year that Browne finally trod on the rake. Concurrently with his TB programme, he had sought to further the Mother and Child Scheme, although, curiously, it appears that for some time no one had made him aware of the bishops' shot across de Valera's bows. But when, on 25 June 1948, he announced to the Cabinet that he intended to progress the Ryan project, no one objected to the fact that the scheme would be free and not means-tested. A decision was taken to delete the clauses on providing advice to women on motherhood after James Dillon, who had been returned to favour in Fine Gael, and was now Minister for Agriculture, had taken exception to them. Browne went ahead with a publicity campaign, which in retrospect seems to have been inevitably destined to arouse medical opposition. Its central theme was 'No Doctors' Bills'!

The doctors had already sounded the tocsin warning against this idea. On 16 January 1946, the Private Practioners Group of the Medical Association decided the following:

> The provision . . . of free ante-natal and maternal services as well as free attendance on school children, all apparently irrespective of social class, might easily prove a serious source of concern to practitioners . . . For this reason it was proposed that the central council (of Irish Medical Association) in dealing with the minister designate, should ask that a means test be applied before any free medical attendance is made available.[78]

The Irish Medical Association began to make known its opposition. In Cabinet, the Association had a powerful lobbyist in the person of Dr Tom O'Higgins, a brother of Kevin O'Higgins. Some commentators have suggested that what befell subsequently was caused, not by the bishops' opposition to the Mother and Child Scheme, but by that of the medical profession. Eamonn McKee, from whose article[79] the private practioners' resolution given above was quoted, has powerfully argued this case. Others have tried to portray the hierarchy as being a tool of the doctors, but the reality is that while some doctors were bitterly opposed to 'socialised medicine' and its potential for backslidings from the teaching of the One True Church, to say nothing of the possibility that their incomes might be affected, the record bears the interpretation that the Church, and in particular John Charles McQuaid, the Archbishop of Dublin, was the main architect of the Mother and Child Scheme's destruction. A handwritten note of McQuaid's recording what had transpired in a meeting between himself and the Taoiseach, John A. Costello, on 5 April 1951 states that McQuaid made it clear to Costello that 'the Bishops detested socialistic state medicine'.

In the early part of 1950, Browne and McQuaid corresponded about the Bill without acrimony, and the McQuaid papers in the Dublin Archdiocesan records indicate that some source other than Browne, at a high level in the Department of Health, was also keeping McQuaid informed of what was going on.[80]

The Archbishop decided to obtain expert advice, and a doctor[81] nominated to study the matter for him reported that Browne's proposed Mother and Child Bill, as it would always be popularly known, had met the objections which had been raised by the bishops to the original Ryan proposals of 1947. However, Browne had been displaying an unwelcome independence in dealing with archepiscopal will. He had annoyed McQuaid by going against his wishes that nurses who were also in religious orders should be exempted from night duty at St James's Hospital. Browne had ruled that if lay nurses could do night work, so could nuns, thus leading to the withdrawal of the sisters from the hospital. His reputation as a 'Communist' was enhanced when he became the only minister who didn't visit Rome for the Holy Year ceremonies in 1950. Reading a *Sunday Independent* report in September 1950 giving details of the expected Mother and Child Bill, McQuaid therefore decided to jettison his medical expert's advice and reach for his crozier.

On 10 October, one of McQuaid's secretaries rang Browne telling him that His Grace wanted to see him the following day at the Archbishop's Palace[82] in Drumcondra. Up to now, Browne had not been aware that in Dublin the Minister went to the Archbishop, not vice versa. Put simply, at this stage in Irish development, John Charles McQuaid was the most important man in Ireland. De Valera was out of office, and even in it, as we have seen, he hesitated to take on this extraordinary figure, who, in his role and attitudes, exemplified much of the texture of Irish Catholicism and explains the dominance of that religion in Irish society. McQuaid was born in Cootehill, County Cavan, on 28 July 1895. A week later his mother, the former Jane Corry, died, and his father, Dr Eugene McQuaid, had the melancholy task of signing her death certificate. McQuaid was brought up by a stepmother whom the doctor married a little over a year later, and not until his teens did he realise that Agnes was not his mother. It was a large household. The McQuaids adopted two children, and added to their existing family of John and his sister Helen another four children. While there was not a great deal of money in the house, being a doctor's son in Cootehill clearly set McQuaid in a patrician mould. It also set him in an anti-Protestant one. He grew up in the era of the Home Rule crisis, a time when Orange bands and Hibernian ones made the streets of Cootehill loud with their respective cacophonies. McQuaid was a student in Clongowes, where he had been transferred from Blackrock College, when he learned from another pupil that Agnes was not his mother. The news seems to have affected him powerfully – when his father died, McQuaid had him buried with his mother, not his stepmother – and he spent the summer holidays not at home, but with a schoolfriend in Belfast. This was the summer of 1912, when Bonar Law and the Conservatives were exciting the Orangemen to frenzied heights in the Home Rule agitation, and, as John Cooney has shown in his invaluable biography of McQuaid, this left him with a lifelong suspicion of Protestants in general, and northern ones in particular.

He had been happy with the Holy Ghosts, and in 1913 became a Holy Ghost novice at Kimmage Manor, County Dublin, determined at the age of 18 to become a saint, and convinced that the road to that exalted state was one of mortification, and a denial of the urgings of the flesh. His MA thesis, for which he won first-class honours, was on Seneca, the Roman sage whose life led him to write:

> It is a great sign of strong virtue to abstain from pleasure when the crowd is wallowing in filth, to be sane and temperate when it is vomiting and drunk. But it is a much greater sign not to withdraw from the crowd nor mingle with it in all things. We can be merry without debauch.

McQuaid had need of philosophy during the civil war when his brother Dean, a doctor, was shot by some of de Valera's supporters in an ambush in County Mayo, and took three slow, agonising days to die. He never allowed Dean's death to embitter him, and as we have seen, and will see later, became a friend and confidant to both de Valera and his political opponents. He was ordained in 1924, and studied in Rome with a view to becoming a biblical scholar. One of his abiding memories of this period was of a visit to the tower where Thomas Aquinas had been imprisoned. He wrote that this was where Aquinas's 'fiendish enemies had tempted his chastity and where, in the hour of his triumph, God's angels had girded him in sign of the gift of perpetual virginity'. McQuaid's later career certainly bore out his belief that threats to chastity were indeed 'fiendish'.

His Roman studies were interrupted by being recalled to Blackrock, where he became Dean of Studies, and later the most famous president in the history of the college. Even in my time there, stories about him were legion. None of them portrayed him as an aloof tyrant, but a remarkable educator and an approachable man with a sense of humour. However, the college folklore also made it clear that in Blackrock, as in his later incarnation as Archbishop, John Charles McQuaid kept sacred the vow he had taken at ordination: 'to uphold those principal dogmatic truths which are directly opposed to the errors of this time'. He firmly believed that the Catholic religion had to reach into every aspect of its practitioners' lives. One of the Catholic organisations which sought to further 'the kingship of Christ on Earth' was An Rioghacht, the League of Christ the King, founded in his first year as Dean at Blackrock, whose membership included Eamon de Valera. Not only were Christ and Caesar hand in glove, they wove the gloves. Another organisation to which McQuaid belonged was the Knights of Columbanus, in which doctors figured prominently, including Dr Stafford Johnson, probably McQuaid's closest lay friend, and a host of other medical confidants with whom McQuaid liaised regularly on issues such as ensuring that Catholic doctors got jobs in hospitals ahead of Protestants. Apart from this circumstance, McQuaid's influence in the medical world was enormously strengthened by the influence of religious orders of nuns and priests in the Irish hospital network. Anyone wishing to become, or remain, a consultant would have been ill-advised to take up any position opposing that of the Archbishop of Dublin.

McQuaid's influence in Irish political circles was unrivalled. Mention has already been made of his work on the constitution. He also had a role stemming from the wide-ranging Cabinet reshuffle de Valera made at the beginning of the war. What was not generally realised at the time was that the education portfolio which de Valera retained for himself was in part at least entrusted to McQuaid. In his capacity as chairman of the Catholic Headmasters Association, McQuaid was in charge of 'work which de Valera wanted done but could not oversee personally'. This included the introduction of various changes which de Valera wanted made in school texts, particularly in Irish and English.[83] But de Valera had a greater task in mind for his Blackrock College friend. The ailing Archbishop of Dublin, Edward Byrne, died in February 1940, and de Valera set about installing McQuaid in the archdiocese. He had already been successful in getting two of his nominees installed in other dioceses, Dr Michael Browne in Galway, and Father Neil Farren in Raphoe, but he encountered unusual difficulties with Dublin. One was the fact that when, as they were required to do, the cathedral chapter presented the Nuncio, Pascal Robinson, with the list of three priests from which a successor to Byrne might be selected, McQuaid's name was not on it. The second difficulty concerned the Papal Nuncio's influence. Although the Nuncio supported McQuaid's candidacy because, as a result of Byrne's long illness, clerical discipline and church affairs generally had suffered in the Dublin archdiocese, and McQuaid's legendary prowess as an administrator made him an obviously good choice to tighten the reins, his influence almost came to nought. For while de Valera's diplomats in Rome were lobbying the Vatican, no word of support came from Robinson.

However, it then transpired that Robinson's dispatches had been lost en route to Rome. Their content was subsequently cabled to the Vatican and in November McQuaid's appointment was confirmed, thus making him the only bishop of his time to be appointed from a religious order. He was ordained to the episcopacy on 27 December in the pro-cathedral in Dublin, without any experience of pastoral work, but with a very finely honed touch for the levers of power.

He also had more practical concern for the poor and the emigrants than most people in Ireland at the time. In his first year of his episcopate he set up the Catholic Social Services Conference which co-ordinated the work of the great number of charitable organisations existing in the city and did help to alleviate the condition of many needy people. The following year (1942) he set up the Social Welfare Bureau which helped emigrants and their families, and throughout his career behaved like a man who believed that he has a duty to care for the poor.

However, when Browne entered the forbidding redbrick pile of the Archbishop's house in Drumcondra, apart from having committed the sin of receiving his education at Trinity College, an institution which McQuaid regarded as a place of mortal sin to be avoided by Catholics, he was also trespassing on an arena of the mind in which the main lay and Catholic actors behaved not so much as separate characters, but in supportive roles to the main drama. It was not a suitable stage for an English-educated Irish intellectual who confused socialism with the Bible. But, Browne averred, he was further disconcerted when, in a preliminary tête-à-tête, McQuaid's opening conversational gambit turned out to be the topic of child prostitution, informing Browne that 'the little child prostitutes charge sixpence a time'. Not a lot of people knew that. However, he was considerably more disconcerted when McQuaid then led him to another room occupied by the Bishop of Galway, Michael Browne, and the Bishop of Ferns, James Staunton, and proceeded to read out a letter from the hierarchy which was about to be sent to the Government. It was a declaration of war:

> The powers taken by the State in the proposed Mother and Child Health Service are in direct opposition to the rights of the family and of the individual and are liable to very great abuse. Their character is such that no assurance that they would be used in moderation could justify their enactment. If adopted in law they would constitute a ready-made instrument for future totalitarian aggression.
>
> The right to provide for the health of children belongs to parents, not to the State. The State has the right to intervene only in a subsidiary capacity, to supplement, not to supplant. It may help indigent or neglectful parents; it may not deprive 90 per cent of their rights for 10 per cent necessitous or neglectful parents. It is not sound social policy to impose a State medical service on the whole community on the pretext of relieving the necessitous 10 per cent from the so-called indignity of the means test.
>
> The right to provide for the physical education of children belongs to the family and not to the State. Experience has shown that physical or health education is closely interwoven with important moral questions on which the Catholic Church has definite teaching.
>
> Education in regard to motherhood includes instruction in regard to sex relations, chastity and marriage. The State has no competence to give instruction in such matters. We regard with the greatest apprehension the proposal to give to local medical officers the right to tell Catholic girls and women how they should behave in regard to this sphere of conduct at once so delicate and sacred.
>
> Gynaecological care may be, and in some other countries is, interpreted to include provision for birth limitation and abortion. We have no guarantee that State officials will respect Catholic principles in regard to these matters. Doctors trained in instruction in which they have no confidence may be appointed as medical officers under the proposed service, and may give gynaecological care not in accordance with Catholic principles.

This was no mere belt of the crozier. It was an episcopal salvo which would have the ultimate effect of destroying Browne's political career, wrecking Clann na Poblachta, and bringing down the coalition government. Perhaps had Browne, a 'difficult man', been 42 instead of 32 when he entered Cabinet, and acted with more circumspection, the result might have been different. It would certainly have been very different had Browne received more support from his Cabinet colleagues, or possessed the necessary political guile to secure it. But in the event, he became embroiled in an extraordinary chapter in Irish history in which his leader, Seán MacBride, turned on him, and his Taoiseach, John Costello, actively colluded with McQuaid against his fellow Cabinet member. The McQuaid papers validate John Cooney's judgement that the Archbishop acted 'with the kind of advisory authority customarily vested in a Cabinet Secretary'.

Costello continuously briefed McQuaid on Cabinet discussions of the issue. The relationship between Taoiseach and Archbishop was such that the Government's final statement of acceptance of the hierarchy's condemnation of one of its own minister's proposals was drafted by McQuaid. When Browne ultimately resigned, and made a powerful speech in the Dail outlining his position, McQuaid's papers reveal that it was he who assisted Costello, a distinguished lawyer, in drawing up a rebuttal.

The main outlines of the tragedy which followed Browne's meeting with the Bishop are easily told. But before doing so, it should be noted that it was a tragedy not merely for Browne, for Irish political development, for the poor of Ireland, but also for the Church, which stored up for itself a reservoir of hostility which is probably only finally overflowing (on the issue of paedophilia) as this is being written. After his encounter with the bishops, Browne met the Irish Medical Association later in that fateful month of October, this time at the Department of Health, not on the doctors' turf, and at an angry meeting hurled down a gauntlet by rejecting their proposal that his scheme should embody a means test. The IMA held a ballot which boomeranged on them. To the question 'Do you agree to work a Mother and Child Scheme which includes free treatment for those who could pay for themselves?' the answers were 'yes' 78%, 'no' 22%. These results (announced on 23 November) were made worse for the IMA by the fact that the turnout was only 54%, allowing Browne to claim that only a fraction of the medical profession opposed him.

However, one vote carried considerably more weight than the findings of any IMA poll. That vote was McQuaid's, and his influence on the hierarchy was such that it probably counted for as much as the remaining 25 members of the Bench of Bishops. McQuaid was fully aware that the Cabinet did not share Browne's assessment of the irrelevancy of the IMA's attitude. He knew that Costello and two other members of the inter-party government, William Norton and Tom O'Higgins, had by-passed Browne and were negotiating directly with the IMA. He wrote to Bishop Browne of Galway on 9 December:

> Negotiations are being conducted since the result of the Doctors' Referendum was made known, between the Doctors and the Taoiseach and with the Tánaiste. These are confidential talks. Time and silence are proving very helpful. I prefer not to write what I know, but my information is most reassuring from the very commencement of my own negotiations.

As a result of these negotiations, it was agreed that the doctors would come up with their own scheme, while keeping within the general parameters of the Act, and that they would formally propose to the Government that the state would give mothers £5 towards paying for their medical treatment. Browne continued to make speeches in defence of his proposals, which put up episcopal and medical temperatures, and added to the fires of controversy which by now were raging amongst the public at large, where Browne commanded a good deal of public sympathy, albeit of the sort of the French observer who, observing the Charge of the Light Brigade, remarked '*C'est magnifique mais ce n'est pas la guerre.*' McQuaid was sure enough of his sources to be able to tell the hierarchy standing committee (on 16 January 1951):

> The Bill is not Government policy. Not a single Minister wants it, except Dr Browne. The Taoiseach has affirmed twice in public that he will not stand for State medicine. To me he has given the assurance that whatever the Church declares to be right in respect of the

Mother and Child Health Service will be unequivocally accepted by him, even if the Minister had to resign or the Government fall. In fact, the Minister is the greatest single embarrassment that the Government endures.

McQuaid was able to tell the bishops that the Taoiseach had assured him that he intended to force Browne to answer the hierarchy's objections in writing, and then send Browne's response to their Lordships for their adjudication, the results of which the Taoiseach would then put to his Cabinet colleagues. McQuaid recommended to his own colleagues that they await the results of these colloquies before taking any action, saying:

> I do not consider it advisable to give Dr Browne and the Clann the chance of going to the country on the basis that the Bishops destroyed the Mother and Child Scheme for poor women and children.
>
> But I am convinced that, even at that risk, we may yet be obliged to break the certain introduction within our country of Socialist State medicine. I have already broken Dr Browne's scheme to socialise the Cancer Services: and my success so far, I say so far, gives excellent ground for hoping that we can break the free-for-all Mother and Child Scheme.[84]

McQuaid was indeed on 'excellent ground' from his point of view, and it was the unfortunate Browne who prepared it. The Minister had not made a formal reply to the hierarchy since his October meeting the following year. He always averred after his Drumcondra meeting that he had satisfied their Lordships' objections in the discussions which followed McQuaid's reading of their letter. The point at which this belief could no longer be sustained, or argued, came on 8 October 1951. After finally breaking off negotiations with the IMA (on 5 October), Browne sent a copy of the booklet 'Mother and Child', containing the details of the scheme, with a short covering note saying he was going ahead with its introduction. Before the booklet dropped on McQuaid's desk, Browne had already conveyed his intentions to the newspapers. It is virtually certain that even if he had sent McQuaid a formal reply five months earlier, it would not have reduced the Archbishop's determination to prevent the introduction of 'Socialist State medicine' to the country. But for Browne to pointedly send no more than a booklet with what could be interpreted as a discourteously brief 'take it or leave it' note containing information already in the public domain was asking for trouble.

By now the dogs in the street were aware that several of Browne's ministerial colleagues, including his party leader, Seán MacBride, were angered at his informing the press of his plans before telling them, and the papers were speculating that his resignation was imminent. McQuaid guaranteed that it was. On the afternoon of the booklet's arrival he sent hand-delivered copies of his response to both the Taoiseach and Browne:

> I welcome any legitimate improvement of medical services for those whose basic family wage or income does not readily assure the necessary facilities. And, if proof be needed of

my attitude, I may be permitted to point to many actions of my Episcopate, in particular the work of the Catholic Social Service Conference founded by me, more especially in Maternity Welfare services.[85]

And then the boot went in:

Now as Archbishop of Dublin, I regret that I must reiterate each and every objection made by me on that occasion [11 October] and unresolved, either then or later, by the Minister for Health. Inasmuch as I was authorised to deal with the Taoiseach, on behalf of the Hierarchy, I have felt it my duty to send to the Taoiseach today for his information a copy of this letter. I shall report to the Hierarchy at its General Meeting the receipt today of your letter, with enclosed pamphlet.

Browne made no reply to this. Costello, however, assured McQuaid by return that 'your Grace's views will receive respectful and earnest consideration' and in writing instructed Browne to placate the bishops:

I have no doubt that all my colleagues, and in particular yourself, would not be a party to any proposals affecting moral questions which would or might come into conflict with the definite teaching of the Catholic church. Having regard to the views expressed in the letters received from the Hierarchy I feel that you should take steps at once to consult their Lordships so as to remove any grounds for objection on their part to the Mother and Child Health Service, and find a mutually satisfactory solution for the difficulties which have arisen.

Browne, however, kept up a stubborn rearguard action, avoiding replying to the hierarchy and demanding funds from Costello to fight the doctors, declaring that he could 'break them', not knowing, as the McQuaid papers reveal, that Costello and McQuaid were keeping each other fully informed of what was happening. McQuaid knew that Browne was continuing to argue within Clann na Poblachta that only the 'political bishops', and in particular McQuaid himself, 'the chief political Bishop', were opposed to his scheme, which Bishop Dignan of Clonfert assured him, as did other theologians, was not in conflict with Catholic teaching.

Browne sought a declaration of support from MacBride, which it seems might have been forthcoming had not Costello warned MacBride that if a public statement were made, Fine Gael would reject it and say that Browne's scheme was not public policy. When Browne attempted to issue a statement via the Government Information Bureau saying that his scheme was Government policy which he was going to implement, no matter what influential persons were opposed, Costello ordered the bureau not to issue the statement, warned Browne that the scheme was not Government policy, and phoned McQuaid (on 21 March) to brief him on what had happened. Browne now understood, if he had not done so before, just how influential were the persons opposed to him. He decided to visit Canossa the following day and phoned

McQuaid for an appointment.[86] After the by now almost mandatory telephone conversation with Costello before taking action, McQuaid made time in the busy schedule of an Irish primate on Holy Thursday to talk with the distracted Browne, who still attempted to convince the Archbishop (without success) that he thought he had met all the bishops' objections during their first encounter, the previous October.

McQuaid was having none of it, and the following points taken from his notes of the meeting explain the position he adopted when Browne asked him if he thought the scheme was contrary to Church teaching:

> I said in my view it was undoubtedly contrary to Cath. Teaching, but I added that I was only one Bishop. In my opinion, it was contrary to Catholic teaching in that:
>
> a. State arrogated to itself a power in respect of education not properly its own.
> b. The rights of parents were not respected.
> c. Free for all scheme was an unjust tax. For a tax must be reasonably necessary in view of the common good. This tax could not be so regarded. I added that I was only one bishop, not the hierarchy.

This last disingenuous observation by McQuaid possibly had a bearing on Browne's next move. He set off around the country, to Galway, Wexford and Armagh, to try to influence Bishops Browne and Staunton, whom he had originally met with McQuaid, and Cardinal D'Alton. His useless peregrinations recall the hopeless buzzings of a bluebottle trapped in a jam jar. The dignatories he called on were maintaining a hierarchical position, not merely a McQuaid one, though it was McQuaid who drafted the hierarchy's formal rejection of Browne's scheme. On 1 April, an appropriate date, McQuaid, on the eve of the hierarchy's meeting in Maynooth, appended a covering note to the draft reply, saying:

> On our side we have the Doctors of the country and every member of the Government. If now we reject this particular Scheme, we shall have saved the country from advancing a long way towards socialistic welfare. In particular, we shall have checked the efforts of Leftist Labour elements, which are approaching the point of publicly ordering the Church to stand out of social life and confine herself to what they think is the Church's proper sphere.

The checking of 'Leftist Labour elements' commended itself to their Lordships as a worthy objective, and on 4 April, the hierarchy authorised McQuaid to write to the Government expressing formal disapproval of the Browne scheme:

> The Hierarchy must regard the Scheme proposed by the Minister for Health as opposed to Catholic Social Teaching ... In this particular scheme the State arrogates to itself a function and control, on a nationwide basis, in respect of education, more especially in the very intimate matters of chastity, individual and conjugal.

To make assurance doubly certain, McQuaid called on Costello the following day, and the pair went through the statement line by line to ensure that the bishops' condemnation of socialistic state medicine was fully understood. There had been reports that Browne might get support from the Labour movement for his proposals and possibly from Clann na Poblachta. But where the Labour Party was concerned, the influence of the chairman, William Davin TD, a member of the Knights of Columbanus, nipped incipient sympathy for Browne in the bud. In the case of the Clann, MacBride attempted to have it both ways. A national executive meeting of the party censured Browne but passed a motion supporting his scheme.

When Browne first read the bishops' letter pronouncing on his scheme (on 6 April), he attempted to portray it as carrying less import than it appeared to, judging that 'It is alright. The Bishops have not condemned the Scheme on the grounds of morals.' Browne was being advised throughout the crisis by a theologian friend, who led him to believe that he could afford to disregard an episcopal condemnation of social teaching, though not of morals. When Costello conveyed Browne's response to McQuaid by phone, McQuaid, however, made it clear to the Taoiseach for the benefit of the Cabinet that 'The letter was a definite, clear cut, and forthright condemnation of the Scheme on moral grounds. Catholic social teaching meant Catholic moral teaching in regard to things social.'

Browne continued to fight a rearguard action, even though every other member of the Cabinet accepted the bishops' letter. He arranged a public meeting in the Mansion House, designed to attract the attendance of two classes who were anathema to Archbishop McQuaid: Trinity College intelligentsia and the Labour left. The irony of such a meeting being necessitated in the Mansion House, where the first Dail had declared its independence of one colonial power, Mother England, did not apparently disturb McQuaid and Costello when they met at the Archbishop's house on 7 April. The purpose of the meeting graphically illustrated how the other colonial power, Mother Church, now controlled Ireland's destiny. The representatives of Christ and Caesar worked together on the reply to the hierarchy's letter which the Cabinet was to send.

Not unsurprisingly, the Government's reply was well received. McQuaid wrote to Costello the following day, saying that he felt

> permitted to anticipate the formal reply of the Hierarchy by expressing to you as Head of the Government my deep appreciation of the generous loyalty shown by you and your colleagues in graciously deferring to the judgement of the Hierarchy concerning the moral aspects of the particular Health Scheme advocated by the Minister for Health.
>
> In view of the clear attitude of the Hierarchy I may be allowed to express my conviction that the decision of the Government to proceed to formulate another scheme consonant with Catholic principles will receive the very welcome support of the Bishops.

Browne meanwhile had received a very unwelcome lack of support from his party. He was excoriated by MacBride during a rerun of his devaluation performance with the Department of Finance civil servants. Browne himself described the treatment he was subjected to as a 'Kafkaesque'[86] 13-hour cross-examination at a meeting of the Clann leadership which voted by 48 votes to four against him. Former active IRA men who had stood up to the Church for their beliefs turned against Browne because of MacBride's accusations that Browne's contempt for the rank and file Clann membership was such that he referred to the Republicans as 'illiterate gunmen'. Browne was anti-physical-force republicanism, and repelled by IRA activity such as the organisation's flirtation with Nazism. But the fraught meeting's real significance lay in the manner in which it underlined the wide gulf which existed between the Clann's core republicanism and Browne's socialism, the dichotomy between those who had joined the new party as a means of putting Fianna Fáil out of office, and traditional Irish Catholicism. For the future of his party, MacBride would have been better advised to support his stormy petrel minister and lead the Clann out of government in defiance of the brandished croziers. Even in those days of clerical oppression, there was still extant a strong Irish tradition of 'taking our religion from Rome, and our politics from home'. As it was, his only course of action following the meeting was to call on Browne to resign, which he did on 10 April. Browne, however, refused to die in silence, and gave copies of his correspondence with Costello and McQuaid to the *Irish Times*.

Commenting on the controversy, the paper made a judgement which found particularly strong acceptance in Protestant circles, particularly north of the border: 'The most serious revelation, however, is that the Roman Catholic Church would seem to be the effective Government of this country.' Had the editorial writer been privy to a conversation between Costello and McQuaid later that day, he might have been tempted to alter that 'would seem to be' to 'is'. Costello wanted to inform the Archbishop of Browne's statement of resignation in the Dail, to which he had to reply. Archbishop and Taoiseach together went over the form the Taoiseach's rebuttal should take, McQuaid authorising Costello to publish all the letters which had passed between them. Notwithstanding all this, Costello later gave an interview on Radio Eireann (on 27 April 1951) in which he said: 'There was not the slightest pressure by the Catholic Church to bring about the downfall of Dr Noel Browne as Minister for Health in the first coalition government.' To paraphrase Lewis Carroll, words mean what people choose them to mean.

The Government had suffered a mortal blow to its prestige, and fell within a matter of weeks on an issue unrelated to the Mother and Child controversy, the price of milk, which caused three of the Clann na Talmhan deputies to turn against the Government. De Valera was back in power the following month. Clann na Poblachta lost eight of its ten seats. Browne was returned as an independent, as were three of his supporters, Peader Cowan, Jack McQuillan and Dr Michael Ffrench O'Carroll, who polled twice as many first-preference votes as MacBride, who only got in on the last count, having headed the poll three years earlier.

The difference between the monolithic, tightly disciplined Fianna Fáil Party led by the father figure of de Valera and the motley collection of loosely disciplined parties which made up the inter-party government was illustrated in the manner in which the Mother and Child issue was finally put to bed. Ryan returned to the task of getting his Bill into law, and duly ran into difficulties with both the doctors and McQuaid in July 1952, when he published his White Paper. It proposed to assist mother and child for only six weeks after birth, and was to be free for only the very poorest. A nominal contribution, unspecified, was to be sought from the better-off. At the time of the White Paper's publication, de Valera was receiving treatment in Utrecht, Holland, for his blindness. McQuaid succeeded in having a committee of the bishops appointed to deal with Ryan and the proposed Bill. He was the committee's chairman. McQuaid contacted Lemass, who put Ryan in touch with the Archbishop. Initially, McQuaid had high hopes that Lemass's accommodating attitude during their meeting meant that there would be little difficulty in reaching a settlement. But Ryan indicated that he intended to take a holiday before meeting the Archbishop, thereby causing McQuaid to scent a lack of respect in the air, and to inject a note of urgency into the proceedings, seeking a meeting with the Secretary of the Department of Health in Ryan's absence. Ryan interrupted his holiday to call on the Archbishop.

At this meeting, McQuaid informed the Minister of the episcopal committee's existence, told him that the proposed Bill was too close to Browne's scheme for comfort, and suggested that Ryan should take care not to run into trouble. At a subsequent meeting between the two, in the presence of Bishops Browne and Lucey, McQuaid drew attention to what he termed 'the offensive portions of the proposed legislation', saying that the provisions on motherhood and infant care were contrary to the constitution and Catholic moral teaching, which saw the family providing for its own requirements. At the bishops' meeting in Maynooth on 14 October, McQuaid was deputed to act for the hierarchy in the matter, having stressed that he was keen to avoid a public conflict between Church and State.

The IMA rejected the Government's proposals, and McQuaid weighed in to demand that Lemass 'accord full weight to the most serious moral objections that I have brought to the notice of the Government'. He also wrote to the Papal Nuncio, Archbishop O'Hara, contrasting the attitude of Costello's government with that of de Valera's. Whereas the former was not concerned about the liberals and the Protestants, de Valera would steer clear of hierarchical consultation lest its discovery 'bitterly antagonised the North of Ireland Protestants, whom Mr de Valera always considers, in the hope of being able to remove partition'. Given Fianna Fáil's civil war past, and its defiance of the bishops at that time, McQuaid judged that while

the outward courtesies will be accorded, the inner spirit of sympathetic and open collaboration with the Hierarchy will be missing from a Fianna Fáil Government. Not that anti-Catholic measures may be expected from men who faithfully practice now the

Faith, but . . . a definite liberalism is always present. In my opinion, that liberalism must be incessantly watched. And what I particularly fear is the effect on the rising generation of an attitude which would successfully oppose the Hierarchy on the present Mother and Infant Scheme.

De Valera knew nothing of this letter, but he knew a great deal about the bishops, and about McQuaid in particular. Accordingly, from Utrecht, he instructed Lemass to read the bishops' original objections to the 1947 Act, and also to take on board a speech by Archbishop Kinnane, which dealt with the rights of bishops. It contained the following:

Subject to the supreme magisterial authority of the Holy See, Bishops are the authentic teachers of faith and morals in their own dioceses. And their authority includes the right to determine in case of doubt whether faith and morals are involved, so that one cannot evade their authority by the pretext that they have gone outside their proper sphere.

To make sure that there would be no 'case of doubt', de Valera directed that Lemass circulate the two texts to every member of the Cabinet and obtain from McQuaid a draft containing his objections to the Ryan Bill and the requirements to satisfy these. Lemass and Ryan were scheduled to meet with the bishops on 10 December, but before the meeting could take place, circumstances were altered by the appointment of de Valera's old schoolmate, John d'Alton, as a cardinal. McQuaid was informed by a friend in Rome that he could be assured that d'Alton's appointment was purely political. The Vatican fully realised that McQuaid was the leading contender for the red hat, but, McQuaid's friend wrote, he had been informed by Ireland's Ambassador to the Vatican, Joseph Walshe, that the reason for d'Alton's elevation was 'an attempt to conciliate the North and emphasise the unity of Ireland'.[87]

What the Ambassador, who had taught McQuaid during his term in Clongowes, did not tell the Archbishop's friend was that he had personally lobbied against the red hat coming to Dublin, on the grounds both of emphasising that though Armagh lay under British rule, Ireland was one, and of McQuaid's character. Walshe did not mention de Valera's anger over the teachers' strike and McQuaid's opposition to the Government on the issue. Instead he reminded the Vatican that McQuaid had made constant difficulties over precedence whenever the Nuncio attended the pro-cathedral and warned that if he became Cardinal the Nuncio would have 'endless difficulties in every sphere of his activities owing to this deplorable weakness in John's character, already so well known to the Holy See'.[88] Not unsurprisingly, McQuaid missed a good deal of the celebrations for d'Alton's elevation. He represented Ireland at the Eucharistic Congress in Sydney, but before he left for Australia he received drafts of the proposed Mother and Child Bill from Ryan and raised no objection to any of them.

Ryan duly introduced the Bill on 26 February, including a provision for a means test for better-off women, not expecting any further difficulties with the bishops. However, in McQuaid's absence, the hierarchy met at Maynooth on 13 April, and the meeting decided to oppose the Bill, beginning by sending a letter to the Government and to the national newspapers, excepting the *Irish Times*. The bishops' objections travelled over familiar ground, claiming that the Bill trespassed on the rights of individuals and fathers to provide for their own health requirements. Mothers' rights were similarly infringed since the state was to take responsibility for the treatment of all mothers in childbirth. The Bill was also objectionable in that it exposed patients to having to accept treatment from 'men who are embued with materialistic principles or advocate practices contrary to the National law'. Decoded, this last meant Protestant doctors. When this missive landed in the *Irish Press* offices, Vivion de Valera had it brought at once to the attention of his father.

De Valera immediately set the wheels of the Establishment turning. The President, Seán T. O'Ceallaigh, contacted Cardinal d'Alton who came from Armagh to Dundalk to meet secretly with de Valera, who succeeded in having the bishops' letter withdrawn. It is understood that one of the arguments he used at this meeting was that the bishops' theological arguments could be challenged in Rome by an outstanding theologian. This was probably Cardinal Browne, a Dominican, who was also a brother-in-law of Seán MacEntee. D'Alton shrank from a public confrontation with the de Valera-led Fianna Fáil Cabinet. But another secret meeting was convened between Government representatives and a team from the bishops' side in the President's residence, Aras an Uachtaráin, in the Phoenix Park. At this conclave, the bishops secured the changes they required in Ryan's proposed legislation. McQuaid, on his return from Australia, improved the shining hour at the hierarchy's meeting at Maynooth on 25 June. He agreed that the bishops' condemnation should be formally withdrawn and that the Phoenix Park pact should stand, but only on condition that the bishops gain a further foothold in the medical world. From then on, public hospitals were to be opened to the University Medical Schools for clinical teaching. This, in effect, gave the Church a say in deciding who should carry out such teaching. But de Valera agreed to the change after a further meeting in Aras an Uachtaráin on 7 July, and on the following day, the report stage of the Bill, Ryan duly incorporated the thoughts of Chairman McQuaid into it, but without giving any indication to the Dail of the presence of the Archbishop's fine Italian hand in its drafting.

The difference between the behaviour of de Valera and his party in the presence of raised croziers and that of the inter-party government was that Costello and his men fell on their faces before the empurpled might, whereas Fianna Fáil only fell to its knees, and then in secret. Had the Mother and Child Scheme rumpus not been conducted so publicly, and had de Valera not been in Utrecht when some of the preliminary meetings with the bishops occurred, it is unlikely that the situation would have been allowed to escalate to the point it did. As it was, the Browne and Ryan Health Bill controversies marked a high-water mark in the development of hierarchical authority in

Ireland. There would be many occasions on which Church and State would differ, and religious controversies of all sorts throughout the remainder of the century, but the bishops never attempted, or were allowed, to show their power so nakedly again.

DE VALERA BACK IN POWER

De Valera's official biography applauded the manner in which during the Mother and Child debate 'de Valera kept a tight rein on his followers. He took no part in the debate apart from a disdainful "I think we have heard enough" . . . The row was left to the disputants. Tactically, it was the shrewdest way.'[89] The shrewdest unquestionably, but also arguably the most ignoble. Shrewdness and ignobility marked the profiting of de Valera and his party from the controversy as a result of the 30 May 1951 election, which saw Fianna Fáil gain only one seat, making a total of 69. Nevertheless, he was able to form a government with the aid of four independents, supporters of Browne, who had sat as one in the few weeks which had elapsed between the débâcle of his resignation and the holding of the election. Clann na Poblachta almost disappeared, with only two seats (a loss of ten). MacBride's former Clann deputies, Cowen, Ffrench O'Carroll and McQuillan, all opposed him and were returned with higher polls than he. Fine Gael profited from Dillon's performance as Minister for Agriculture, and won nine extra seats. Labour dropped three seats despite having healed its split the previous year, and Clann na Talmhan dropped one of its previously held seven seats.

It was morning-after optimism, and Fianna Fáil's first budget certainly underlined this fact as the Department of Finance moved to cut down what it saw as the *fleurs de mal* sowed by Marshall Aid. The Whitaker prescription quoted earlier, that the state should get hold of 'some of the money now being spent on non-essential consumer goods so that the state can carry on with its capital programme without causing too much inflation', was about to be put into effect by the Minister for Finance, Seán MacEntee. Predictably, Lemass opposed retrenchment and argued in favour of retaining the capital programme. As a result, relationships between himself and MacEntee deteriorated to a point where the two men travelled to London for inter-governmental talks in 1952 on separate days.[90]

Apart from pressures from the Department of Finance, the Government also had difficulties with the British and with the Irish banks. The British wanted Ireland to keep in step with the sterling area policies. These in effect would have meant imposing such stringent restrictions on the Irish economy as to push up emigration and unemployment levels. Another bone of contention between the Irish and the British was the question of Irish coal imports. Britain had not kept to an agreement to supply Ireland with coal, and as a result American coal imports had added $16 million to Ireland's dollar deficit. The banks proposed an interest rate rise of as much as 1.5%,[91] but de Valera countered this by confronting the banks' standing committee (on 18

March 1952) with a heavyweight delegation led by himself, and including Aiken, Lemass, MacEntee, MacElligott and Moynihan.

De Valera warned of 'the widespread repercussions which, in their opinion, must follow an increase in bank rates'. Lemass suggested that perhaps the banks might use some of their profits to avoid the proposed increase! In the event, the banks, with 'considerable misgiving', settled for lower increases than had been envisaged. Overdraft rates went up from 5% to 6%, not 6.5% as planned. As an indication of the profit margins of Irish banks, even in straitened times, deposit rates for sums under £25,000 rose by a half per cent to 1.5%, and for sums over £25,000 to 2%. It was not a good backdrop against which to introduce a deflationary budget. But MacEntee persisted and introduced (on 2 April 1950) one of the earliest and harshest budgets in the history of the state. Practically every necessity of life was taxed or increased in price. Bread, butter, tea, sugar, beer, spirits, tobacco, petrol, motor vehicles, all were taxed. Food subsidies were removed and income tax was increased by a shilling in the pound. MacEntee argued that without the imposition of his hair shirt, a balance of payments deficit of £50 million would be run up by the end of the year.

However, this was special pleading and owed more to Finance's desire to curb the inter-party government's expansionist philosophy than the reality. As a prudently anonymous Patrick Lynch pointed out in the *Leader* (2 August 1952) if one based one's assessments on the volume of imports, rather than on their value, it would become apparent that the level of imports had shown a steady decline since April 1951. Moreover, the Department of Finance, in preparing its White Paper for the budget, had excluded tourist receipts. Had these been included, they would have shown that the country had managed to pay for 52% of its imports by exports in 1950, and not the third which the White Paper claimed.

So far as agriculture was concerned, there was a return to the 1930s policy of protection and subsidy, with wheat and sugar beet receiving government price supports. Frequently these led to surpluses, which in effect meant that the Irish taxpayer subsidised overseas buyers as the surpluses frequently had to be sold abroad at a loss. Needless to say, the economy stagnated. Very few businesses expanded; even fewer new factories were built. The cost of living continued to rise and emigration reached levels not seen in Ireland since the days of the land war in the nineteenth century.

This hard-hearted exercise in political book-keeping was defended by de Valera as a 'coming back from the riotous holiday to the sober everyday work . . . the morning after the night before'. He had taken a vow of poverty and the public were enjoined to keep it: 'These sacrifices can be summed up in not having extravagant notions, in not attempting things that are clearly beyond our means, but in adopting our means to the end and the end to the means.'[92] In real terms, what Fianna Fáil and the Department of Finance mandarins wrought in 1952 meant an 'end to the means' of living in their own country for some 400,000 Irish men and women over the course of a decade towards the end of which emigration ran at over 80,000 a year. Not until Whitaker went back to the drawing board, some seven years later, and produced a new economic blueprint, coupled with de Valera's long-delayed resignation and Lemass's equally long-postponed succession, did the clouds of economic gloom lift over Ireland. Needless to say, the tenure in office of Fianna Fáil after the budget was both unhappy and unproductive. Another general election followed in May 1954 when, as in 1951, independents withdrew their support.

The result of the 1954 election was another inter-party government, with John A. Costello once more at the helm as Taoiseach, but this time with a gain in seats from 40 to 50. The new inter-party government comprised three parties, Fine Gael, Labour and Clann na Talmhan, with Clann na Poblachta borrowing a concept from de Valera – external association, that is to say, supporting the Government with its small, but vital, total of three seats. The post of Minister for Finance was turned down by the first two choices, Patrick McGilligan, who instead elected to become Attorney General, and John O'Donovan, a former official with the Department of Finance, before the third choice, Gerald Sweetman, accepted it. Sweetman was a brash country solicitor, with a high opinion of his own talents, not always shared by his contemporaries. John O'Donovan, the Government's Parliamentary Secretary, commented: 'When Sweetman took office he knew nothing, after six months he thought he knew everything.'[93] He certainly knew how to deflate an already flat economy, meeting balance of payments difficulties by imposing a set of swingeing import levies on a wide range of products in March and July 1956. These resulted in a small trade surplus the following year, but created massive political reaction. Employment fell, particularly in the building trade. There was more emigration and large-scale protest marches. The most predominant Irish emotion of the period was depression. School-leavers and university graduates had a stark answer when asked what they were going to do with their careers: 'I'm going to join the 80,000.'

But Sweetman took one decision which would help to lift the depression: on 30 May 1956 he appointed T.K. Whitaker Secretary of the Department of Finance, at the age of 39. This appointment leapfrogged Whitaker over more senior colleagues, and up-ended the custom whereby promotion depended largely on length of service, rather than ability. Although for most of his career Whitaker had apparently toed the conservative party line insofar as MacElligott and the department were concerned, he had taken a degree in economics, and the Marshall Aid experiment, coupled with the growing crisis in the economy, had changed him from being a disciple of the Finance school of thought, which saw the department's role as being one of accounting, to a force for development. In 1950, he had persuaded MacElligott to place him in charge of a new think tank within Finance which in effect became the source of policy formation.

When Whitaker took over, the situation in Finance and in Government was, as he put it:

We were drifting along. Nobody was long enough there to accept full responsibility for things. There were quite a number of external crises: the Korean War, the British economy in difficulty and our own balance of payments in deficit. I suppose you can always excuse things, but there was no continuity or responsibility in government for the launching of any comprehensive programme.[94]

Whitaker saw the need for stopping the rot whereby Ireland was falling behind the rest of western Europe. It was obvious that free trade was on the way, bringing with it increased competition and an end to protection. The need was to create jobs in industry and the services, thereby necessitating a shift from agriculture. But the first major shift to follow Sweetman's appointment was in governmental power. The IRA had become active again, and Clann na Poblachta was experiencing difficulties in remaining in government with Fine Gael, which was reacting with traditional antipathy towards the Republicans' activities. Clann na Poblachta, on the other hand, owed much of its support to men who had been active in the IRA throughout the 1930s and 1940s. At the same time, Sweetman's policies were creating problems even for his own Fine Gael Party.

The economic and the IRA questions interacted. A crunch meeting of the Fine Gael Cabinet members was held in the offices of the party leader, Richard Mulcahy, at the Department of Education on 25 January 1957, to discuss the forthcoming budget. Sweetman announced that he intended to cut out food subsidies, causing four of the most influential Fine Gael members to threaten to resign: Liam Cosgrave, a son of the Minister for External Affairs; Tom O'Higgins, Minister for Health; Patrick McGilligan; and John O'Donovan. Though the meeting adjourned without a vote, the mood of the moment was that the Government was sure to fall. Either Sweetman would resign, or he would not, thus causing his colleagues to do so. Either way, a general election seemed inevitable.

It was, though not in the way the Fine Gaelers foresaw. As the ministers met, Clann na Poblachta's executive was also in session (over the weekend of 25–27 January 1957). The executive was discussing an order of Costello's to the Gardai earlier in the month, directing the arrest of members of 'illegal organisations', code for the IRA. The decision was that MacBride should withdraw parliamentary support from the coalition. MacBride argued, unavailingly, that the motion was ill-advised because de Valera could be expected to take more severe action against the IRA. Events were to prove him correct, but he followed his party's directive by introducing a motion of no confidence in the Dail on 29 January 1957, on the grounds that the Government had been deficient in its approach to both partition and the economy. By this time many of the senior figures in Fine Gael were becoming tired of politics and wanted to get back to their professional lives, in particular the large proportion of lawyers in Fine Gael wanted to resume their lucrative practices. The Clann vote aborted the Fine Gael Cabinet members' discussion on Sweetman's proposals. The most senior figures, Costello, Dillon,

McGilligan and Mulcahy, voted for an immediate general election. The younger men, Liam Cosgrave, T.F. O'Higgins and the Minister for Local Government, Patrick O'Donnell, voted to stay on. The seniors carried the day, and Costello decided not to face the vote of no confidence. Instead he sought, and received, a dissolution from the President, resulting in a general election on 5 March.

Fianna Fáil won 77 seats, Fine Gael slipped back to 40, Labour lost seven and Clann na Poblachta two, one of them Seán MacBride's. From being the party that appeared to be about to do what Fianna Fáil had done for the country in 1932, the Clann now virtually slumped into oblivion. The Republican quotient in Irish politics, however, showed its durability, with Sinn Féin winning four seats. De Valera moved swiftly to snuff out any prospect of a Sinn Féin resurgence by doing as MacBride had warned, introducing internment and co-operating with the Unionists in crushing the IRA so thoroughly that the organisation had virtually disappeared by the time the Unionists breathed life into it once more during the latter part of the 1960s.

WHITAKER'S NEW DEPARTURE

By 1957 Cathleen ni Houlihan herself was badly in need of a kiss of life. The election had taken place in a climate of despondency. The results of political inertia and economic mismanagement were summed up in the census returns for 1956. Despite the Catholic birth rate, in the five years from 1951 the population had fallen by 62,379. Overall the decline in the half-century from 1901 had been from 3,221,923 to 2,898,264. Emigration was the only option for the bulk of university graduates. A widely read set of critiques of Irish society, edited by John A. O'Brien, appeared to sum up the reality facing the country. It was called *The Vanishing Irish*. Against this appalling backdrop, two men of widely differing styles emerged to shape policies and events which would staunch the haemorrhage of emigration and lift Irish levels of morale and prosperity. The men were Seán Francis Lemass and T.K. Whitaker. If the acid test of public men is 'Was their country the better for their term in office?' both men may be adjudged to have passed with honour.

But in the aftermath of the 1957 election, such a verdict would have appeared remote. True, the new de Valera Cabinet contained some new faces. Neil Blaney from Donegal was appointed Minister for Posts and Telegraphs, Kevin Boland was appointed Minister for Defence, on his first day in the Dail, as a quid pro quo for getting rid of his father, Gerry. Death and the electorate also got rid of two other long-term Fianna Fáil stalwarts, Tom Derrig and Seán Moylan whom de Valera appointed to the Senate after he failed to gain re-election to the Dail. Moylan was also appointed Minister for Agriculture, but he only held the post for a few months before he too died in November 1957. The Cork hurling star Jack Lynch was appointed to the Department of the Gaeltacht which the previous administration had set up. De Valera was now 75. In his previous government (1951–4), he had relinquished the post of

Minister for External Affairs to Frank Aiken, who remained in office after the 1957 reshuffle. Lemass too maintained his portfolio of Industry and Commerce. But the key element in the Cabinet changes was the translation of Seán MacEntee to Health and Social Welfare, being succeeded in Finance by his predecessor, Jim Ryan, with whom Whitaker was about to strike up a close and fruitful relationship. A second consequence of the MacEntee/Ryan switch was that it clearly signalled that Lemass and his innovative policies had gained the ascendancy over the conservative and abrasive MacEntee, whose hair-shirt budget had contributed so much to putting Fianna Fáil out of office in 1954. Lemass was now de Valera's heir apparent, a position to which he should have been named ten years earlier.

As the new Cabinet assumed the reins of office, Whitaker worked in virtual secrecy to ensure that the reins twitched the almost inert filly, Cathleen ni Houlihan, into economic recovery. Apart from the externally administered nostrum of Marshall Aid, the filly had been subjected to five other remedies, four domestic and one other externally prescribed. This was the report of the New York-based consulting firm, IBEC Technical Services Corporation, which owed its parentage to the Marshall Plan. The European Co-operation Agency in Washington paid its dollar costs (roughly $100,000), the Irish Government its other expenses. IBEC, led by the American economist Stacy May, worked throughout the summer of 1951, interviewing and collecting data in Ireland, and issued a major survey: 'Industrial Potentials of Ireland: an Appraisal', in December 1952. Effectively speaking, Seán MacEntee binned the report. But some of its recommendations found a resonance with Whitaker, particularly those which stressed the need to concentrate on manufactured goods for the export market, the liberalisation of price controls, the encouragement of foreign investment, and the need for capital investment in plants and machinery rather than hospitals and government housing. IBEC also made a proposal that instead of exporting beef on the hoof to England, Ireland should slaughter and process at home. This seemingly obvious 'added value' concept was rejected by Whitaker, who thought it a 'strangely nationalistic idea . . . possible only if Ireland got away from the British subsidy system'.[95]

Similarly, Whitaker did not altogether take on board a major policy document put out by Fine Gael in 1953 'Blueprint for Prosperity'. Again, as in Fianna Fáil, this document masked a dichotomy in internal policy. Mulcahy and those who thought like him were against intervention. The 'Blueprint', a reprint of the 1953 annual conference speeches, quoted Mulcahy as pledging that the Fine Gael Party stood emphatically for keeping political influence and government interference out of industrial work. Costello, however, recommended the creation of a central savings office and the establishment of a capital investment board, to monitor public expenditure, and, daringly, sought to persuade the Irish banks to swap their overseas assets, chiefly sterling and UK Government IOUs, for Irish Government bonds. Costello also proposed that foreign investment be attracted by removing the barriers to such investments by the Control of Manufacturers Act. However, as we have seen, the opportunity which the 1954 general election offered for the implementation of these proposals was wasted, and led instead to Sweetman's levies.

Lemass next picked up the baton of government intervention by making what became known as his '100,000 jobs speech', on 16 October 1955, to party faithful at Clery's Restaurant in Dublin. While vague on specifics, the jobs speech envisaged the 100,000 jobs coming about due to a £67 million investment programme of government money and private savings. He also suggested that the banks' holdings in British pounds might be used to provide the lion's share of the proposed capital expenditure. Lemass spoke of the need to end the cycle of Irish savings being used to finance initiatives in Liverpool, rather than factories and places of employment in Dublin. Before delivering the speech, Lemass had studied the Italian Vanoni Plan, a 10-year economic recovery programme, which he got the Italian Embassy in Dublin to translate for him. The speech marked a break with Fianna Fáil's emphasis on partition and the restoration of the Irish language as being the main targets of achievement, and helped to bring the question of how to create prosperity further up the debating ladder. But it also aroused strong opposition from MacEntee and the right wing of the party.

Lemass later said[97] that he attempted to counter his opponents' arguments by saying that 'it would be politically wise for Fianna Fáil to try to restore the country's morale, regardless of the party in power and that there should be political debate on what measures might bring about the economic recovery'. He was correct on both counts. At this remove, it is almost impossible to recapture the spirit of depression and pessimism which pervaded Irish society during the mid-fifties. A famous *Dublin Opinion* cover cartoon of the period (September 1957), which Whitaker later credited with encouraging him in his own efforts, showed Ireland, Cathleen ni Houlihan, consulting a fortune teller whom she asks: 'Have I a future?' Costello, helped by his two polymath economists, Patrick Lynch and Alexis Fitzgerald – Lynch became a professor of economics and was later, rightly, regarded as one of the country's best economic brains, Fitzgerald, Costello's son-in-law, was one of the architects of the Industrial Development Authority, a law lecturer, and the head of the biggest firm of solicitors in Ireland – attempted a reply to Lemass. In a pamphlet 'Policy for Production', while worrying about the 'growing power of the state', he proposed that his former colleague Patrick Hogan's formula should be attempted – agriculture should become the motor force for developing the Irish economy. But Costello also argued in favour of new industrial incentives by way of taxation and government grants to encourage investment and new plant and factories. Some of these ideas were also taken up later by Whitaker.

MacBride also joined the economic debate in a memorandum which he circulated to his Cabinet colleagues, in late 1956: 'Brief memorandum on need for a 10-year economic development plan, and on method of formation.' MacBride's interest in economic planning had been stimulated by participation in a survey of the Italian, Turkish and Greek economies carried out by the OEEC. He called for a Government policy which would co-ordinate the work of the various departments in drawing up a plan which could be submitted to the OEEC, the International Monetary Fund and the World Bank for funding. He also suggested that Marshall Aid repayments be deferred. He suggested that a team of Irish economists be sent abroad to Europe to garner new ideas which could be applied in Ireland. Sweetman dismissed MacBride's initiative out of hand, but Costello referred it to his friend, John Vaizey, a Cambridge University Professor of Economics, for advice. However, before Vaizey replied, the Government fell.

The 1957 election campaign had very little to say on the issue of economic development. With the exception of Clann na Poblachta, the three major parties, including Labour, avoided mention of economic planning lest they be tarred with the brush of favouring enforced Stalin-like planning. MacBride's espousal of 'an agreed comprehensive long-term economic programme' did him no good at the polls and, as we have seen, he lost his seat. But Whitaker read the entrails correctly. He had studied French planning, and had seen what the Monet Plan had achieved, and he was aware of developments in the Common Market. If Britain joined, Ireland would have to follow, and protection would have to be jettisoned. The annual OEEC growth statistics showed clearly that Ireland was lagging behind in Europe. Ireland was the only country in Europe with a declining population and had the lowest per capita income in western Europe.

The return of Fianna Fáil meant that Whitaker now had a potentially sympathetic minister, James Ryan, to deal with, and less to fear from conservatives such as Seán MacEntee, whose hair-shirt budget led both to a loss of the finance portfolio, and a reduction in his influence. Whitaker took advantage of the change in government and the improving climate for innovative economic theories to set up an unofficial team within the civil service to draw up a plan for economic development. These men, Charles Murray, Maurice Doyle, S. Kissane, J. Dolan, M. Horgan, D. Lynch and T. Coffey, deserve as much credit as any government in Irish history for the turnaround that was subsequently wrought in Ireland. Whitaker made it clear to them from the outset that their normal duties would have to continue while they punched in the arduous hours which his project required. The team frequently worked at home in the evenings. By November of 1957, with some outside assistance from experts such as Dr Brendan Menton, they had produced a discussion document. But remarkably, Whitaker did not inform James Ryan, his minister, of his study until a few days before Christmas, some nine months after the work had begun.

Ryan had fought in 1916 and came from a prosperous Wexford farming family. But he still had enough 1916 courage and country contact with the realities of unemployment and emigration to make him responsive to initiative. Earlier in the year, he had circulated to his government colleagues a copy of a highly critical lecture by the economist Professor C.F. Carter which contained the following:

Income per head in the Republic is about 55% of that in the United Kingdom, but since the ratio is about 65% for the Province of Leinster, it must be less than half for the rest of the country . . . the Republic is falling further behind . . . Unique in the world, the Republic combines a large excess of births over deaths with a small and declining population . . .[98]

Whitaker's efforts offered the prospect of doing something about Carter's critique. Ryan was immediately enthusiastic and used his influence at Cabinet to get Whitaker the support he needed from other departments, such as Agriculture, and Industry and Commerce. More importantly, on 17 December, he placed Whitaker's proposals on the agenda of a Cabinet meeting in Government Buildings, at which de Valera was present.

By now de Valera was 76 and almost completely blind. Nevertheless, he remained in total control of both Cabinet and party, and his support was vital[99] to a furtherance of Whitaker's ideas. By an extraordinary intellectual sleight of hand, de Valera found that the Whitaker proposals were merely a continuation of long-established Fianna Fáil policy. The Government meeting decided, with de Valera's approval, that the Minister for Finance 'approve the proposals, submitted to him in the minute, for the preparation of a study'.[100] The minute, or the Whitaker Memorandum, as it was called, was a necessarily shortened version of his overall study. Whitaker gave an overview of the state of the Irish economy, and made a number of proposals aimed at promoting economic development, which stressed the need for choices, deciding on how revenue should be allocated to hospitals, schools, roads, and 'productive' investment. He warned about rising unemployment, a worsening balance of payments situation, and the need to be prepared for a forthcoming meeting of the World Bank.

But probably the most important factor which Whitaker stressed was the psychological one. The following year, in November 1958, a White Paper entitled 'Programme for Economic Expansion', and 'the Grey Book', as Whitaker's plan, 'Economic Development', was popularly known, because of its grey cover, were issued. The introduction to the Grey Book carried the following:

> There is a sound psychological reason for having an integrated development programme. The absence of such a programme tends to deepen the all too prevalent mood of despondency about the country's future. A sense of anxiety can be justified but it too easily degenerates into feelings of frustration and despair. After thirty-five years of native government people are asking whether we can achieve an acceptable degree of economic progress . . .

This was some indictment of a nation's progress, coming from the pen of its premier civil servant – a civil servant moreover who received, despite MacEntee's strenuous objections, the unique honour of having his plan published under his own name rather than as an anonymous government publication on official policy. The White Paper, which was also furnished to the World Bank, was circulated to both houses of the Oireachtas on 11 November 1958. The speed with which the Whitaker Plan became Government policy contrasts sharply with the glacial progress of the children's allowances proposal, an indication of what could be achieved when the resources of the civil service received political and departmental backing, rather than obstruction. Whitaker later said of the production of 'Economic Development':

> It was a kind of dawn in which it was bliss to be alive. There were a few small teams working on different aspects, such as industry and tourism. We worked into the night and were early to work, with real enthusiasm, the next morning. We were refreshed by our release from a purely negative role and the feeling that we were doing something constructive and worthwhile.[100]

There was remarkably little public debate about the Whitaker proposals. The Church stayed silent, possibly because Whitaker was shrewd enough to include in the foreword to the Grey Book a quotation from the Bishop of Clonfert, Dr Philbin, which he claimed had been a source of inspiration to him:

> We seem to have relaxed our patriotic energies just at the time when there was most need to mobilise them. Although our enterprise in purely spiritual fields has never been greater, we have shown little initiative or organisational ability in agriculture and industry or commerce. There is here the widest and most varied field for the play of the vital force that our religion contains.[101]

Moreover, the Grey Book spoke of programming, rather than of planning with its socialist overtones, and the fact that it was issued in Whitaker's name[102] meant that it was not denounced by the opposition as a party document. Its low-key launching also helped to curtail debate. Whereas the White Paper was circulated to all members of the Oireachtas, the Grey Book saw the light of day by having six copies of the document placed in the library of the Oireachtas. Shortly before it was published (on Saturday 21 November 1958), de Valera announced in the Dail that the Government had made an important decision:

> ... a programme envisioning public capital expenditure on an average of about £44,000,000 yearly. I do not think it would be desirable to go into this matter piecemeal. The Programme will be published in a White Paper soon. If the Dail requires to discuss it, an opportunity for doing that can be given.

The only deputy to raise any question about the programme was Noel Browne, and a document which marked a right-angled turning point in Irish economic affairs was accepted by the Dail without debate.

Press coverage was similarly muted. The Grey Book proposals were hardly revolutionary. Whitaker advocated that both individual and corporate taxes

391

be lowered. He also urged the banks and insurance companies to join with the state in making loans available for industry through the Industrial Credit Corporation and for agriculture through the Agricultural Credit Corporation. Where agriculture was concerned, he advised that subsidies to improve the greater use of fertilisers, for example, were preferable to price supports or guarantees. The major departure in the agricultural sphere from traditional Fianna Fáil policy was that Whitaker recommended that beef production rather than tillage should be encouraged. But the White Paper stressed that 'it is important that the tillage area be at least maintained'. It might be better for the national economy to put an end to unproductive farming methods, but what was such a paltry outcome compared to the overweening necessity for not putting an end to Fianna Fáil's rural vote? Where industry was concerned, Whitaker bluntly recommended abolishing protection, and the encouragement of foreign industrialists, who would not only bring capital to the country, but also much-needed expertise.

As indicated earlier, most of these ideas had been floating in the political ether for several years. The difference was that now they became Government policy. The results were dramatic in both psychological and economic terms. People came to believe that living conditions did not inevitably get worse. They could just as easily get better. National morale soared as a result of this simple but vitally important change in outlook. In the five years that followed the publication of 'Economic Development', GNP grew by just over 4% a year, unemployment dropped by a third, emigration fell to less than half of the average for 1954–61. Exports doubled, and by the end of the 1960s over 500 overseas firms had been encouraged to locate in Ireland. The population began to rise, and the volume of national investment almost doubled. Obviously, it can be argued that in the conditions of the global economy in the early sixties, Irish recovery would have taken place with or without Whitaker, but the fact is that this is speculation, and even though, as we shall see, planning eventually fell out of favour during the uncertain years following the OPEC oil price rises, the record, post-Whitaker, is there. So far as Irish public opinion is concerned, Whitaker was one of the great figures of twentieth-century Ireland. In fact, in November 2002, the committee of the prestigious People of the Year Awards named him Man of the Twentieth Century.

The Whitaker experiment was greatly furthered by the fact that at long last another great figure of the twentieth century came into his inheritance. During a Cabinet discussion on the Whitaker proposals, Lemass made a telling comment: 'I told you all these things. I put these ideas before you.'[103] He had indeed, and his chance to put them into operation came about on 14 January 1959, when de Valera announced his intention to retire as Taoiseach. A number of factors combined to force the decision. One was obviously de Valera's age and physical condition, another the fact that Seán T. O'Ceallaigh was due to retire as president later in the year, a third the irony that the *Irish Press*, which had done so much to put him in power, now added to the reasons why it became expedient that he should leave it.

What had happened was that of all people, Noel Browne was made a present of one *Irish Press* share. This entitled him to consult the *Irish Press* share records. He discovered that both de Valera and his son Vivion had been buying up shares since 1929. As the shares were not quoted on the Stock Exchange, their true value was not known, and the de Valeras had been able to make their purchases cheaply. Browne managed to put down a private member's motion (on 12 December 1958), which precipitated a Dail debate on the motion that de Valera:

> ... in continuing to hold the post of controlling director of the Irish Press Ltd while acting as Taoiseach ... has rendered a serious disservice to the principle of integrity in parliamentary government and derogated from the dignity and respect due to his rank and office as Taoiseach.

In the course of the debate, Browne damningly reminded the Dail that in an earlier debate de Valera had told the House that he had no financial interest in the *Press*, and allowed it to be thought that his shareholdings were of the order of 500 shares.[104] De Valera made an unconvincing defence of his position, denying that he had acted in a manner inconsistent with his duties as Taoiseach, and claimed that he only exercised a 'moral trustee-ship' over the company from which he derived no remuneration either as a director or a shareholder. This last could be accepted, as the paper never paid a dividend while de Valera was in charge. But as Browne took care to point out, the paper was worth over a million pounds, and had effectively become a de Valera family concern, with Vivion as managing director, and his brother-in-law on the board. This was hardly the outcome foreseen by the people who had originally subscribed money to a bond issue in order that Ireland might win her freedom. Nor was it foreseen still later when de Valera used his parliamentary majority to vote taxpayers' money towards the redemption of those bonds. Some of this money accrued to the *Irish Press* coffers. The embarrassing debate concluded after the Christmas recess on 14 January, when Fianna Fáil numbers ensured a defeat (by 71 votes to 49) for Browne's motion.

Apart from the embarrassment of the *Irish Press* issue, it was by now obvious that there could be no question of de Valera leading the party into the next general election. Rumours that he was about to step down had grown to such proportions that he had been forced to deny them at the Fianna Fáil Ard Fheis the previous November:

> I do not feel ill. I know I am hampered by the fact that I cannot read. This imposes upon me – it makes more difficult the many tasks that could otherwise be easy. But so long as this organisation wants me (if they do not want me, they can get rid of me very easily) and as long as Dail Eireann thinks I am doing my work and can do my work, then I stay.

But there was every reason why he would be an excellent standard-bearer for the party in the forthcoming presidential election, and after discreet conversation between top party loyalists, the much-respected Oscar Traynor, Minister for Justice, was chosen or, more likely, knowing the man's directness of approach, volunteered to make de Valera a suggestion he could not refuse. He should resign as Taoiseach and run for the presidency. Characteristically, the suggestion was conveyed in a manner that bore out the saying 'the darkest place is under the light': the conversation took place on the lawn outside Leinster House, where in full view but completely out of earshot, the two old comrades strolled and chatted, passing and repassing a memorial erected to the memories of Michael Collins and Arthur Griffith.[105]

De Valera informed the Fianna Fáil Party of his decision to retire, and of his availability to run for the presidency, on the morning of the Dail vote on Browne's motion. The result, in those pre-television days, was that the next day the newspapers majored on de Valera's historic decision, and correspondingly minored on the Browne-sponsored debate on the *Irish Press*. It was a triumph, both in news management and in the prevention of any party divisions. However, the subsequent presidential election only went partly according to plan. De Valera, with the willing co-operation of Fianna Fáil, had decided to use his own enormous prestige to make the election a springboard, not merely to Aras an Uachtaráin, but also for the abolition of proportional representation. He knew that, even with him at the helm, Fianna Fáil had only succeeded in winning an overall majority in four out of twelve general elections. With him gone, the unlovely prospect of coalition rule appeared to be the party's inevitable fate. He attempted therefore to get a Bill through the Dail which would allow him to secure an amendment to the constitution to drop proportional representation in favour of the first-past-the-post British system, which would have guaranteed huge majorities for Fianna Fáil as the largest party. However, the Bill ran into unexpectedly sturdy opposition, the Seánad rejecting it by a single vote, and subsequently exercising its powers of delay to prevent it coming into law for 90 days.

De Valera sought to redress this setback by having the vote on PR scheduled for the same date as the presidential election, 18 June 1959. The Fianna Fáil slogan was 'Vote Yes and Yes de Valera'. However, the plain people of Ireland voted Yes and No. De Valera went to the Phoenix Park, defeating his Fine Gael opponent, Seán MacEoin, by 538,000 votes to 417,636, but PR stayed. More importantly, Seán Lemass took over as Taoiseach. The Fianna Fáil parliamentary party meeting, held in the wake of de Valera's departure to the Park, was a foregone conclusion. Lemass was unopposed.

FOREIGN AFFAIRS

The post-World War II years were horizon-widening ones for Ireland. She attempted to join the UN in 1946 but the Russians used their veto to keep her out until 1955. However, the Irish did manage to join some important bodies under the UN umbrella: the United Nations Educational Scientific and Cultural Organisation, UNESCO, and the World Health Organisation, WHO. Ireland was a founder member of the Council of Europe, in 1949, and joined the UN in 1955 as part of a balancing act between the eastern and western blocs in which each agreed to nominations from the other side. A permanent mission to the UN was established in 1956. After the war, embassies were opened in several different countries throughout the forties, fifties and sixties. These included countries as far apart as Australia and Sweden (1946), Germany (1951) and Nigeria (1960).[106] Contact with the outside world also gathered pace in other ways, such as the establishment of Bord Fáilte, the Irish Tourist Board (in 1955), and the Shannon Free Airport Development Company (1959). There was even some official recognition of the fact that emigration existed, albeit in an effort to get the emigrants to come back to Ireland, however briefly, to spend their money by attending a specially designed annual festival known as 'An Tóstal'.

Wartime censorship disappeared, though the ludicrous variety sponsored by the Catholic Church remained, with distinctly harmful results. But despite this censorship, the fact that BBC programmes could be received on the east coast of the country, and that Penguin books were cheap and plentiful, meant that at home intellectual currents stirred, however sluggishly. Abroad, MacBride's activities at the Council of Europe were respected and helped to sustain that interest in affairs outside the country which is a characteristic of Irish public opinion. Throughout the period *circa* 1948–73, the independence of spirit which had characterised Irish international policy since the foundation of the state could be said to have continued. But, taking place as it did against the backdrop of a severely depressed economy, the horizon-widening process was painfully slow, and efforts to develop a new role for Ireland after the isolation of the forties had to be mindful of the old issue of partition.

The ineffectual banging on the partition drum rarely lessened under either the inter-party or Fianna Fáil governments of the late forties and fifties. Neither because of inclination nor party policy could MacBride, the leader of a Republican party, allow that essential political instrument to be muffled by letting it appear that Costello, who had actually declared a Republic, or de Valera, who inhabited a verbal Republic, were more Republican than he. But efforts to bring home British responsibility for Ireland's partition to post-war America and Europe were almost by definition doomed to failure from the outset when set against the admiration which the British role during the war had garnered for the United Kingdom. Where Irish foreign policy was concerned the first inter-party government laid down a line which Fianna Fáil did not markedly depart from for decades. MacBride made it clear that so long as partition lasted, Ireland could not join NATO[107] (the organisation is pledged to recognise existing borders), but this apart, both he and Costello made it abundantly clear that in the Cold War, Ireland was strongly anti-Communist. Addressing the House of Representatives, Costello declared:

'Communism, in our view, is a creed which confronts the established order of society with the most uncompromising challenge in history, a creed to which we are implacably opposed.'[108]

While the partition issue was cynically manipulated by some Irish leaders, de Valera in particular, it was, and remains, a genuinely raw issue and one which politicians had (and have) to be constantly careful about, as a small but significant and literally parish-pump issue which I witnessed in 1956 helps to illustrate. Various IRA activities were under way when Ireland joined the UN. Being largely cross-border affairs, these created little resonance in Dublin, particularly in the Dun Laoghaire area represented by Liam Cosgrave, the then Minister for External Affairs, which in those days had a large Protestant population, a relic of the time when the area, with its yacht and golf clubs, was a favourite haunt of British officers and Dublin Castle officials. It was the first year that an Irish delegation had been seated at the UN, and Cosgrave was speaking at a public meeting in the town hall to give his constituents a report which, in the Ireland of the time, was of considerable interest to a number of people, including myself. However, the meeting was temporarily sidetracked by a number of questioners from the floor who wanted to know why Cosgrave hadn't directed the UN to take action on partition. Cosgrave was in the middle of explaining the percentage of sittings taken up by the Palestine issue, decolonisation, and light matters such as the Cold War, the nuclear threat and so forth when a gentleman in his sixties arose to warn the Minister that 'Them things don't matter a damn. Your job is to get rid of that monstrosity, that relic of British imperialism at the bottom of Marine Road, and if you don't get rid of it yourself, it'll be blown up, and it won't be blown up by the new IRA – it'll be blown up by the old IRA.'

The 'monstrosity' was indeed 'a relic of British imperialism', a Victorian drinking fountain, under a latticed wrought-iron cupola, once common throughout the Empire. It was one of the last landmarks seen by the emigrants who were at the time shoaling out of Dun Laoghaire on the mailboat to England, as they headed for the gangway. At the time I dismissed the intervention both as a very good example of the reasons one should steer clear of political meetings, and as a piece of the irrelevant obscurantism which I hoped membership of the UN and kindred bodies would help to dispel. But over the years the fountain suffered many attacks, and was ultimately removed. However, as this book was being written, in the wake of the Good Friday Agreement of 1998, which, it was believed, had created an outburst of sanity in Anglo-Irish relationships, it was decided to renovate and replace the structure. By now, Liam Cosgrave, who fended off the heckler with humorous expertise, is an old man. The heckler has gone to his reward in the Great Republic in the Sky. But his successors have not – work on the monument's restoration was delayed because of threats allegedly made by the IRA. Nevertheless, finally, the Victorian monument seems to have been successfully installed through the implementation of 'an Irish solution to an Irish problem'. It has been painted a tasteful shade of green, with its adornments picked out in what might be taken for either gold – or orange! However, on the day of the official opening of the fountain (during June 2003) a group of concerned Republicans turned up to mount a spirited protest.

Though the fallout from partition continued to perturb Irish foreign policy to some degree, it has to be said that, despite the reservations of a section of the audience in the Dun Laoghaire town hall on that far-away summer night, accession to the UN did mark the opening of a new and creditable chapter in foreign policy, during which the Irish delegation punched well above its weight and was accorded a respect out of all proportion to the country's size and resources. In 1956, Ireland voted to condemn both the Anglo-French aggression in Egypt, and the Russian onslaught on Hungary. The Irish voice could generally be relied on to speak on the side of the angels on issues such as apartheid and decolonisation. Frank Aiken, who succeeded Cosgrave at the head of a remarkable delegation, in the words of one expert defined Irish foreign policy as accepting '. . . the obligations of the UN charter. To maintain a position of independence, and avoid becoming associated with particular blocks or groups as far as possible', and 'to preserve the Christian civilisation of which we are a part, and those powers principally responsible for the defence of the Free World'.[109] Aiken deserves to be remembered for taking the initiative which led to the creation of the only international statutory instrument aimed at limiting the spread of nuclear weapons: the Treaty for the Non-Proliferation of Nuclear Weapons, signed in Moscow on 1 July 1968, by members of the United Nations, including Aiken himself.

Aiken's plan, examined in the light of the contemporary crises over Iraq and North Korea, has a creditably prophetic air about it. He proposed a non-dissemination agreement to prevent the spread of nuclear weapons, principally by getting the existing nuclear powers to promise not to provide other countries either with such weapons or with the means to make them. Central to Aiken's plan was an insistence that non-nuclear powers should open their territories to international inspection. Speaking to the General Assembly (on 3 October 1963), Aiken suggested that in the event of conflict, a UN force should be sent to the war zone immediately to stabilise the situation, while the combatants were encouraged to the conference table under UN auspices. Though Aiken initially (before the political committee of the General Assembly in 1958) failed to get the support needed for his motion, the Irish resolution was adopted a year later (20 November 1959) with no votes against, and 12 states abstaining, for reference to the ten-nation disarmament committee, whence, via the Geneva disarmament conferences, it eventually found approval from both Moscow and New York in 1968. Speaking on its acceptance, Aiken managed to inject a note of sturdy independence into his speech of congratulation to the great powers: 'On behalf of the Irish delegation – which is not an automatic admirer of great powers – I wish to express our heartfelt gratitude to the Soviet Union and the United States for having overcome their differences and produced their draft treaty to stop the spread of nuclear weapons.'[110] In the years since, the hopes for the Aiken non-dissemination plan were of course diminished considerably as several other countries, amongst them India, Israel and Pakistan, acquired the Bomb. But the effect of the Irish initiative was not negligible; for example, it is worth noting that the proposal had a marked effect on the British Labour Party's nuclear policy of the sixties and early seventies.

During Aiken's time at the UN, Irish policies were condemned by the Americans as communistic, by the Russians as capitalist, by Franco's Spain as undemocratic, by South Africa, which denounced Ireland as 'an unfriendly Government', with the 'most unfriendly attitude at the UN', and by Beijing as emanating from 'lackeys of American imperialists'. So clearly the Irish were doing something right! But, apart from the fact that, given her size, there was always something of a *Mouse That Roared* dimension to Ireland's UN involvement, the high-wire activity on the East River also had a potential downside for domestic politics, if Aiken's policy could be translated at home into being pro-Communist or anti-American. This happened over the China issue. Although Ireland would jointly table (with Malaya) a resolution condemning Chinese aggression in Beijing, which was adopted (on 21 October 1959), she had blotted her copybook with the Americans two years earlier by sponsoring an Indian resolution which recommended that the question of the recognition of Communist China should be discussed.

The American reaction took the form of trying to cripple Aiken with a belt of a crozier. The Secretary of State, John Foster Dulles, secured a promise from the apostolic delegate to America that he would raise the matter with the Pope, and two of the most powerful American cardinals, Cushing of Boston and Spellman of New York, were incited to bring pressure to bear on the Irish minister. Spellman contacted the Irish Consulate in New York in advance of the vote to threaten: 'Tell Aiken that if he votes for Red China, we'll raise the devil.' The Cardinal was as good as his word. The diocesan press, the *Catholic Times*, and the *Brooklyn Tablet*, exploded in indignation, none of it well founded. The *Brooklyn Tablet*, for example, informed its readers that 500 young Irish people who had attended a music festival in Moscow had come home infected with communism, despite the fact that not one Irish visa had been issued for the festival. Aiken worsened the position, in American eyes, by following up his China recommendation with a proposal that there should be joint American–Russian troop reductions in Europe. He told me himself[111] that this suggestion was part of a wider policy which he felt was the most important raised by his country during his period at the UN, namely the 'areas of law concept'. Addressing the General Assembly on 30 September 1965, he defined an area of law as

an area in which a group of states will agree not to attack each other, to settle their differences peacefully and to restrict their armaments to police level, on the condition that the United Nations, backed by the nuclear powers, guarantees them against aggression from outside or inside the area.[112]

However, in 1957, his vision of a world containing wide areas which would be subject to the rule of international law met with little favourable resonance. Particularly in Europe. Every member of NATO which had an embassy in Dublin raised Aiken's suggestion with the Department of External Affairs, and Aiken was forced to back off on both the troop reduction and ultimately the China issue also, though he doggedly continued the fight for some years, under fire from right-wing American publications including the *New York Post*, the Jesuit periodical *America*, and Spellman's mouthpiece, the *Catholic News*. Eventually the clerical pressures caused Fine Gael to put down an opportunistic motion of no confidence in the Dail, despite the fact that under Cosgrave the party had committed itself to the view that the China issue should be discussed. Fianna Fáil weathered this mini storm by 78 votes to 38 on 28 November 1957, and Aiken went on to vote that the China issue should be discussed again the following year at the UN. In the course of his address to the General Assembly, he posed a question which came a little oddly from the lips of the man who had run the rigorous Irish censorship of the war years: 'Can the cause of freedom really be served by shirking discussion?'

One issue on which there were no U-turns was that of neutrality, and the joining of military alliances. In 1959, Aiken effectively said 'no' to NATO in straightforward South Armagh language: 'We will not go gunning for other people's freedom as long as we do not have our own.' His stance became an issue in the 1959 presidential election, causing Lemass to make a strongly supportive statement in the Dail (on 7 July). The various crimes against the fair name of Ireland alleged by the opposition included the fact that the Irish delegation to the UN had been following in the footsteps of Burgess and Maclean; was turning its back on the moral and spiritual values of the country, and there was clear evidence that the delegation was going communist: a Russian group had been invited to the Irish Consulate in New York. In the course of the debate, McGilligan observed that instead of 'hopping and hovering around the United Nations', Aiken should have been in Rome attending the obsequies of Pope Pius XII, to which Aiken replied with an eloquence that owed more to the tradition of the Dun Laoghaire fountain than that of the Athenians: 'If Deputy McGilligan had to climb on the bodies of his grandmothers and grandfathers for several generations to get a crack at Fianna Fáil, he would do it. He is a low type who would climb on the body of a dead Pope to have a crack at Fianna Fáil.'

But on 11 December 1961, Aiken effectively sided with the Americans after they had adroitly changed their stance on the China question. Hitherto the ostensible issue had been one of discussion, not recognition. But now the Americans confronted the Chinese with the question as to whether or not Beijing accepted previous decisions of the UN and recognised the UN charter. As the UN had already branded China an aggressor over Tibet, Beijing refused to give such guarantees. The refusal to recognise the UN charter enabled Aiken to vote with the Americans.

The vote came at a period when the Irish delegation was already coming under international pressure because of the actions of one of its former members, Dr Conor Cruise O'Brien, who was well recognised in New York and Dublin as being one of the architects of the China policy, in his capacity as head of the United Nations section of the Department of Foreign Affairs. The delegation also included Maire MacEntee, a distinguished poet, and daughter of Seán MacEntee, who later became O'Brien's wife, and Eamonn Kennedy, the department's African expert, who went on to serve his country at ambassadorial level in several important postings including Bonn and London. Ireland's permanent representative to the UN at this period was F.H. Boland, who became president of the General Assembly during the famous session of 21 September 1960, attended by, amongst other world leaders, Eisenhower, Macmillan, Nasser, Castro – and Khrushchev. Boland achieved worldwide prominence, when he was seen on television banging his gavel in a vain attempt to interrupt Khrushchev, who was accompanying his tirade against the West by pounding on his desk with his shoe.

O'Brien achieved even greater prominence during his term as UN representative in Katanga, which had seceded from the Congo. The Irish reputation in the UN, as a moderate, unaligned, albeit pro-Western country of impeccable anti-colonial credentials, aided by the fact that the UN Secretary General, Dag Hammarskjöld, liked his writings, particularly *Maria Cross*, a study of Catholic intellectuals, had resulted not only in O'Brien's appointment, but that of another Irishman, Lieutenant General Seán MacEoin, as commander-in-chief of the UN forces in the Congo. But the Congo operation turned sour. Ireland, which, in June 1959, had already sent a contingent of troops to the Lebanon as observers, dispatched a force of troops to the Congo on 27 July 1960 as peacekeepers. This was a historic moment, the first time (if one overlooks the IRA and Blueshirt forays into Spain during the 1930s) that Irish troops had actively served abroad. National pride was boosted by the fact that not merely had the world body asked the country to send troops (a mere nine days before they left), but they were serving in the cause of peace. However, on 22 November, news reached Dublin that ten Irish soldiers had been killed in an ambush at Niemba by Baluba tribesmen.

The sight of the coffins proceeding down O'Connell Street was one of the most memorable of the 1960s. It brought home to the Irish people the fact that the way of the peacekeeper really *was* hard. The ambush entered Irish folklore to the extent that for years afterwards, Gardai giving evidence against defendants in cases involving riotous behaviour were wont to inform the judge that their conduct 'was worse than the Balubas'. The Congo also claimed the lives of other Irish soldiers, of whom the most senior was Lieutenant Colonel Justin MacCarthy, Deputy Chief of Staff of the UN forces, who died in a car crash. Accordingly, when on 14 September 1961 a newsagency report reached Dublin mistakenly claiming that there had been huge Irish loss of life at Jadotville, during an action aimed at ending the secession of Katanga, the country went into shock, a shock which could have had serious isolationist repercussions, as there was a general election campaign in progress (the election was held on 4 October).

Aiken immediately flew to the Congo. Fortunately, however, the report proved to be erroneous, A company of the Irish 35th Battalion had been isolated without air support at Jadotville, and though the men fought bravely for four days, they were forced to lay down their arms, because the Katangese forces were able to cut off their water supplies, a contingency which had apparently not been foreseen and guarded against. Nor did the Irish foresee that the laying down of arms, which was part of a deal whereby the Katangese would also lay down theirs, would not be reciprocated by their adversaries. They were taken prisoner, but released after a ceasefire was agreed on 21 September. O'Brien became a casualty of the UN action, resigning on 1 December 1961 in a blaze of controversy.

That well-known Irish theatrical production *Uproar in the Dail* was mounted in the wake of the resignation. But the Government took the line that Dublin had no function in the matter; O'Brien had been an international civil servant at the time of his resignation. Lemass defended the decision to support the UN in the Congo against a not inconsiderable body of right-wing and clericalist opinion which sympathised with Katanga.

Overlooking the behaviour of the Belgian colonists, and Roger Casement's role in exposing these, figures like the redoubtable Dr Michael Browne, Bishop of Galway, stressed the great benefits brought to the Congo by Belgian administrators and Catholic missionaries, and took the line that Chinese and Russian infiltrators in Africa would be delighted to snap up rich pickings like copper and other minerals. Irish public opinion was sympathetic to O'Brien and the majority sided with Lemass, rightly taking the view that Belgium's precipitate withdrawal from the Congo, after years of rapacious exploitation, had created the situation which the UN were trying to control.

As Ireland moved towards the EEC, a seasoned Iveagh House veteran summed up for me the change which came over Ireland's foreign policy: 'Seán Francis [Lemass] said: "The UN stuff is great, but Jaysus, Frank, think of the economics!" ' A permanent mission to Brussels was appointed in 1966. Regardless of the exact terms used, it is a demonstrable fact that as EEC membership came nearer, the Departments of Industry and Commerce and Finance took over from Foreign Affairs, and international affairs increasingly became a matter of European affairs, although the Republic did continue to play a creditable role in international peacekeeping and in Third World aid. Where this last was concerned, the Irish role in terms of both the educational and the medical contribution of its missionaries and later its NGOs (Non Governmental Organisations) was also praiseworthy.

Along with the bullock, the Irish farmers developed a keen interest in strange economic animals such as 'the snake', and a marvellous invention called 'the green pound', which by some alchemy of Brussels transferred shifts in the value of sterling into the pockets of Irish farmers. Initially, the farmers were the main beneficiaries of the switch in external priorities. By 1978, farm incomes were double what they had been at the start of the decade. But EEC membership was to set in train a huge set of changes in Irish society which deserve to be regarded as being on the same scale of influence as the coming of Lemass and Whitaker, who of course did so much to make EEC membership possible.

The economic changes tower over everything; between 1994 and 1997, the Irish average growth rate was three to four times that of the EU countries, and higher also than the OECD average. But EEC membership also brought about important attitudinal changes in matters such as divorce, contraception, abortion, human rights, the status of women, and trade union activities. It could be argued, of course, that Irish starting points were so low on joining the EEC that there was no place to go but up. But upwards Ireland surely went. The average GDP growth during the 1970s was 4.9% compared to 3.2 % in the EU, and during the 1980s, apart from 1983 and 1986, the Republic of Ireland's growth rate was the fastest of any OECD country. One can indicate various turning points of great significance in accelerating and making possible this turnaround, for example the creation of a new industrial relations climate, and the bringing under control of the chaotic state of Irish public finances, *circa* 1986–8 (see page 000). But the principal factors may be taken as being a combination of internal developments, by, with or from EEC membership.

The quality of Irish education and the availability of a skilled labour force attracted inward investment. US investment in Ireland is 50% higher per capita than in the UK, and six times as high as in France or Germany. The sort of industry which US corporations mainly wished to site abroad, pharmaceutical and computer-related products, could be transported easily and the traditional arguments against investing in peripheral economies did not apply. This is why Ireland attracted so many of these industries, not merely, as some Irish commentators fondly believe, because of the success of the Irish Industrial Development Authority in beguiling corporate America. The IDA, a particularly efficient development agency by best-practice international European standards, certainly played a role. But there were other factors behind the birth of the Celtic Tiger. For example, as the only English-speaking country in the EU apart from Britain itself, full-bloodedly pro-European Ireland was a more attractive prospect for US investment, seeking a toehold in Europe, than a vacillating Britain. Ireland's favourable tax rates also played a role. But money alone does not make a society work – the billions which the British taxpayer has been forced to contribute to Northern Ireland, for example, have failed to produce a stable economic or political unit. Political independence, facilitating the choice of EEC membership, rather than relying on decisions taken in London, and developments such as investment in education and the putting of its own house in order encouraged the birth of the Celtic Tiger.

Its continuing health cannot rely too much on EEC membership. EU enlargement means the Brussels gravy train now has a great number of other stations to call at. Moreover, Ireland's wealthier east coast by the end of the century had achieved 104% of the European average income. The object of the cohesion funds from which Ireland benefited so greatly was to bring the poorer European states to a threshold of 75% of the European average income.

Many Irish commentators have expressed unease at the fact that Brussels was simply regarded as the place where the Irish got on the gravy train. But in Brussels itself I found Ireland, and its representatives, highly regarded and in many ways a model member of the European Club.[113] Ireland's commissioners in Brussels such as Patrick Hillery, who handled Ireland's accession negotiations, Ray McSharry and Padraig Flynn (all Fianna Fáil). were seen as being both diplomatic and effective. Peter Sutherland (Fine Gael) is remembered for handling complex trade negotiations with dexterity and aplomb. Foreign ministers, in particular Peter Barry, James Dooge and Garret FitzGerald (all Fine Gael), were mentioned with some admiration. Why Fianna Fáil commissioners should be regarded as doing particularly well when they got to Brussels, and on the other hand Fine Gael's politicians should be singled out as being somewhat more stylish, says something about the contrasting styles of the two parties. One sets store by what is actually delivered in the back rooms, be they smoke-filled or not; the other values presentational and representation skills. In fairness, both may be taken as having 'delivered' for Cathleen ni Houlihan. Both politicians and civil servants reacted in a manner which suggested that they were repossessing part of their heritage, rather than entering new and uncharted waters. As the history of Europe shows, it was a matter of pride with the Irish that Irish monks were once the educators and scholars of Europe – during the Carolingian era when Ireland earned the sobriquet of 'Island of Saints and Scholars', which some of her citizens worked so energetically to invalidate during the period under review. And later, in the 'Wild Geese' era, following the Battle of the Boyne, it was Irish diplomats and soldiers who manned the commanding heights of many of the European Catholic powers.

Where Irish civil servants and consultants were concerned, I also found that a consistently met with comment was 'the Irish punch above their weight'. A factor which would justify further research is the extent to which British attitudes towards Europe created a space for Ireland. The Irish were correctly perceived as being 'more European' than the British, and their political and diplomatic skills enabled them to achieve an influence out of all proportion to the size of the country. Irish trade union representatives in Brussels have also told me that they found they derived benefits in both status and assistance of various kinds from Britain's failure to capitalise on European membership. The main beneficiaries of the foregoing factors were the farmers. Apart from whatever came their way through the activities of civil servants, governments, and omissions on the part of British representatives in Brussels, even the least

Republican farmers demonstrated that they believed strongly that the term 'Sinn Féin' translated as 'ourselves alone'.

The famous farmers' march of October 1966 had a sub-text which fitted perfectly with activity in Brussels: 'Break out to break in'. What this meant in practice was that the more far-sighted farm leaders, such as the president of the National Farmers Association, Rickard Deasy, and the NFA secretary, Seán Healy, who listened to advice from the Irish Agricultural Institute, headed by Dr Tom Walshe, whose mantra was 'quality', wanted an outlet for beef other than the UK. In the mid-sixties, the backbone of Irish agriculture was beef. The cattle trade was ruled by jobbers, who controlled the open-air fairs at which cattle were sold, and who constituted a very powerful political lobby.

In the wake of the march, the NFA stepped up its contacts with European farm organisations like the Boerbond de Belge and the International Federation of Agricultural Producers. Contemporaneously, in an effort to break the jobbers' grip, and to end the colourful but unhygienic fairs which, in the morning, filled country towns with cattle, pigs and sheep, and in the afternoon left their streets filled with dung, the NFA dug into its own pockets to create a system of marts whereby livestock were auctioned publicly, and funded a meat-packing venture, Cork Marts IMP (Irish Meat Packers). The new emphasis on marketing and a more international approach benefited the farmers enormously. In 1986, the EEC farm support mechanisms yielded prices 100% higher than the world market norm to Irish farmers. Farm incomes rose by over 400% in the decade after Ireland joined the EEC. Land prices shot up astronomically to a point where land in Ireland, on the periphery of Europe, became dearer than it was in Holland, the centre of European agriculture. An ironic consequence of the boom of the seventies and early eighties was that Irish farmers began buying farms in the UK, where land prices were far lower than in Ireland, a novel method of 'breaking out' from under the lion's paw.

But, a downside of the boom, apart from the fact that irresponsible lending practices on the part of the banks encouraged wholesale debt, was that much of this improvement came about as a result of the pressure which the strength of the farmers, as an interest group, exerted on the Irish Government, which in turn extracted huge sums from the Common Agricultural Policy (CAP). The boom was interest-group led, not part of an overall Irish governmental strategy for the development of Irish natural resources. For an example readers are referred to the account of my conversation with Brian Lenihan on the potential for the marine (page 455). Ireland's incredibly fertile coastal areas contained an incalculable amount of the EEC's fish stocks, but in the absence of any development plan, Irish negotiators accepted a limitation on the Irish catch of 4.6% of the EEC total. The Irish fishing industry never achieved anything remotely approaching its potential. Even shell-fishing, which EEC membership would have encouraged, not limited, was neglected. The once clean waters of the bays around Ireland were allowed to become polluted to such an extent that as this was being written, the European Commission gave the Irish Government a deadline (17 April 2003) to explain why only 14 bays, out of 58, in which shellfish were cultivated were fit to be designated under the Quality of Shellfish Water Regulations. In 2002, the Irish Shellfish Association had appealed to the EU about the degradation of the water quality as a result of increasing pollution from urban centres, and bad sewerage controls. Far from assisting the shellfish industry, the Government had failed in its statutory duty to implement a European directive issued in 1979, the Protection of Shellfish Waters directive.

Here it might be observed that the Irish drive for industrialisation, foreign capital and all its consequential side effects meant that pollution was not confined to the shellfish industry. The mounting anecdotal evidence about the growing incidence of pollution acquired a sharper focus and environmental awareness was greatly heightened by a Homeric legal battle fought by a Tipperary farmer for most of the 1980s. Mary Hanrahan of Ballycurkeen became convinced that the inexplicable illness of her son, and amongst her livestock, was caused by emissions from the nearby chemical factory owned by the giant multi-national Merck, Sharp and Dohme and, after years of fruitless negotiation, brought an initially unsuccessful High Court action against the company in 1985.

As a result she was forced to put her 265-acre holding up for sale. However, being a forced sale no suitable bids were received. She managed to continue living in the farm, albeit in appalling conditions, while a considerable body of public sympathy built up for her plight, resulting in a number of lawyers and veterinary experts coming to her aid in an appeal to the Supreme Court which was decided in her favour on 5 July 1988.

But while the Hanrahan case can be regarded as a historic landmark in the struggle to keep Ireland green it has to be conceded that environmentally the hidden costs of progress continued to mount. One of the scandals of the last decade of the century was the discovery that the beautiful County Wicklow, 'the Garden of Ireland', adjoining Dublin had been besmirched by the creation of several illegal – and highly toxic – waste sites in disused quarries, and remote valleys. Per contra, while some members of the farming community allowed this to happen others closed off beauty spots by less harmful but still vexatious methods. With an eye to obtaining grants from the EU on the grounds that they are providing an environmental service by maintaining their lands, some property owners have been closing off walks and access to scenic areas, in an effort to put pressure on Brussels to concede their demands. The traditional Irish greeting to foreigners in Céad Míle Fáilte: a hundred thousand welcomes. But the access-denying attitude towards heritage, and a general greed in the tourist industry has contributed towards this saying being sometimes translated nowadays as the Frosty Fáilte.

A similar lack of foresight on the Government's part where Brussels was concerned very nearly created far more embarrassment than the fishing débâcle is unfortunately ever likely to. This was the handling of the Single

European Act (SEA), which laid the ground for the creation of Europe without many of the bureaucratic, fiscal and technical barriers, including frontier barriers, which obtained in the days of the Shellfish Waters directive. Sufficient has been said about the importance of neutrality in Irish foreign policy for it to be readily understood that when the SEA was signed into law by President Hillery on 24 December 1986, the concept of neutrality was not exactly a new one to Irish politicians and civil servants. But apparently the issue was overlooked in the rush to ensure that the public became convinced that the loss to Ireland of the principle of unanimity voting was enormously outweighed by the sweetener that the funds for the less developed regions were to be doubled. It did not stay overlooked for long.

On 9 April 1987, the Supreme Court found that the SEA was not an Act, but a treaty, the implementation of which would be 'inconsistent with the Constitution'. What had happened was that an agricultural economist, Dr Raymond Crotty, had sought and obtained a High Court injunction which delayed the Irish Government's ratification of the Act. The court agreed with Crotty's petition that the SEA was in conflict with the Irish constitution, and dismissed the state's appeal against this finding, saying that ratification would bind Ireland to engage actively in a programme which would 'impinge progressively on Irish sovereignty'. The result of this decision, delivered by Mr Justice Henchy, was that a referendum had to be held to amend the constitution. On 26 May, this passed by 755,423 votes to 324,977. The failure to foresee the effect of the constitution on the SEA, and as a result to arrange for the holding of a referendum before, not after, it had become law, was not the greatest example of foresight in the exercise of Irish foreign policy.

One could indicate other points in the period under review where the Irish system apparently took its eye off the ball at moments of national importance, or perhaps, more charitably, did not have the resources to keep an eye on all the balls in play. The most important of these was the Nice Treaty, which required two referenda before being accepted in 2002. The failure of the first (on 7 June 2001) was occasioned by apathy, because of a lacklustre governmental attempt to sell the treaty, which coalesced with a reaction amongst the public against ever-growing tales of corruption into a desire to teach the politicians a lesson. However, the teaching of the lesson, by a society which had benefited more, and been held up more, as a good example of EU membership than any other country, could have had the effect of delaying European enlargement. Only 32.9% of the Irish electorate turned out to vote. The result was 54% 'no', 46% 'yes'. Had the result stood, apart from its effect on the Poles, the Hungarians and the rest, this would have been seen in Europe as a disastrously insular piece of ingratitude, particularly as, regrettably, it has to be conceded, a not inconsiderable percentage of the anti vote was generated by racist attitudes towards the ever-growing influx of economic migrants and asylum seekers which Irish prosperity was attracting at the time.

As it was, the result created horror in some European circles. The French paper *Liberation* wondered how 'the Irish could be so ungrateful seeing that it owed its new found wealth to Europe' and concluded that 'The best pupils of the European class have spat in the soup.'[114] Blushingly, the Irish Government arranged for a second referendum, which was held on 21 October 2003. Before it, Polly Toynbee in the *Guardian* (18 October 2002) warned that if the Irish 'selfishly' voted 'no' again they would 'convulse Europe and be treated as a xenophobic pariah'. The enormity of the whole thing was such that the opposition parties joined in supporting a 'yes' vote. By now, in addition to disaffection with 'tribunalitis', there was additional, and widespread, anger amongst the electorate because in May another Fianna Fáil–PD coalition had been returned in a general election in which Fianna Fáil had brazenly promised there would be no cutbacks. Once back in power, however, the fiction that Ireland could remain insulated from the global downturn could not be maintained, and cuts became the order of the day. Nevertheless, despite this valuable electoral ammunition, opposition leaders, including figures like Garret FitzGerald, who came out of retirement to campaign, urged voters to reserve their justifiable anger against the Government for the approaching local government elections and support European enlargement. As a result of the improved campaign, both the turnout and the 'yes' vote went up. Turnout was 48% and the 'yes' vote was 62.89% of those who voted. But the need for a second referendum left a sour taste in many people's mouths, generating a widespread reaction that the Government had acted undemocratically, in effect telling the electorate that they could vote any way they wished so long as they voted 'yes'.

The size of the Irish spend on diplomatic activity is of course a limiting factor in generating a wider Irish awareness of complex international issues such as Nice. The Hillsborough accord, and what led up to it, is described elsewhere. A contributory factor to the lack of foresight on the SEA was the amount of time and political concentration which the Irish had at their disposal to devote to Irish-European affairs as opposed to matters Anglo-Irish. Sheer inexperience in international affairs also played a role as the spectre of conflict between Dublin and London raised its ugly head once more in the frenzied months that followed the outbreak of violence in Northern Ireland in 1969. Instead of attempting to reawaken the old Irish-American network, the Irish Government sent Patrick Hillery, the then Minister for Foreign Affairs, to the UN. Here the Irish were doomed to failure, given Britain's veto on the Security Council, but the British left nothing to chance. I happened to visit the UN not long after the Irish effort to get a UN initiative had failed, and experienced observers told me that the British had mounted the strongest lobbying campaign they had put on since the days of Suez. Voting strengths aside, any remote possibility which Dublin might have had of advancing its cause disappeared in the face of the argument that the British used with the American delegation in particular:

> This is a domestic Civil Rights issue. You have Civil Rights issues in your southern states. If you establish a precedent by sending a UN force to Northern Ireland, you could be

opening the door to having a UN force, including Chinese and Russian troops, along the banks of the Mississippi.

It would be decades before the Irish realised that mobilising the Irish in America to lobby the White House was far more efficacious than lobbying in the UN, an arena wherein Irish influence, if in reality it ever amounted to very much, had largely ended with the Aiken era. A combination of lack of foresight and of Government guilt over its lack of emigration policy resulted in at least one glaring oversight in the utilisation of potential American goodwill. The famous Speaker Tip O'Neill verified to me that he was only waiting for a call from the Irish Embassy in Washington to walk out on the floor of the Senate to obtain 'within five minutes' an exemption for Ireland from the 1965 Immigration Act that set up the quota system which, at the time of the SEA controversy, had created a severe problem for Irish 'illegals' in the US. As we will see, the resolution of this problem would later play its part in the resolution of the Northern Ireland problem. But here, all that needs to be said is that no call was made to O'Neill. A combination of a number of factors, including the old aversion to facing up to the problem, coupled with a belief which flourished during Seán Lemass's hopeful era of government that emigration was ended, meant that, having failed to provide them with jobs in the first place, Dublin contributed to serious problems for the Irish in New York, Boston, San Francisco and elsewhere in the US.

Before continuing with the story of the Irish in America, however, let us first finish with tracing their activities in Europe and elsewhere. In brief, the European experience can be summed up by saying that Europe was a Good Thing for Ireland. To give but a few examples, when Ireland joined the EEC, she was exporting goods worth £54 million to Germany. By the late nineties (1997), this figure had risen to £4.354 billion. In the same year, the Republic's exports to Italy had risen from only £18 million on accession to the EEC in 1973 to £1.149 billion. On accession, Holland bought goods worth £38 million. In the nineties, this figure had risen to £2.386 billion. As in the case of Europe generally, the balance of trade with these countries was in Ireland's favour. By the end of the century, Ireland was importing approximately only one-third as much as she exported to Europe. By that time also, Brussels' subsidies to Irish agriculture were in excess of £1.5 billion annually. Agri-business was responsible for about a third of Ireland's foreign earnings and some 340,000 jobs, but the net Irish contribution to farming was only £200 million.

Obviously this situation will change drastically as the effects of enlargement sink in. Another implication for the changes in Europe lies in the field of neutrality. It is very hard to see how Ireland will be able to avoid joining a Common European Defence Policy some time in the next decade. A first step in this direction has already been taken through Ireland's slipping quietly into the NATO-backed Partnership for Peace, as the century ended, without there being sufficient interest in this subject to call for a referendum to be held. A rapidly changing world is bringing pressure to bear on Ireland's once sacrosanct neutrality policy. The instances where preoccupation with other matters, in particular Europe and the north of Ireland, seemed to have distracted from concentration on other important affairs, such as the status of immigrants in America, appear to have been added to by a problem which became apparent in the build-up to war in Iraq. Little public attention had been paid to an ill-advised campaign, fuelled by the hubris generated by the Celtic Tiger performance, which had resulted in Ireland's having a place on the UN Security Council when the fatal vote was taken. This committed Ireland to a degree of support for the Anglo-American invasion of Iraq, which was deeply unpopular with the Irish public. But by then it was too late in the game to start paying attention to the handiwork of the individuals who had sought the Security Council seat in the first place. Whatever arguments one chooses to put up on the lines of 'never in, never win', the reality is that Ireland's military contribution to any conflict would be by definition minuscule. In the event, the mouse that had roared its way into the ranks of the big boys on the Security Council managed to evade the trap of involvement in the war because the Americans abandoned an attempt to get full UN support for a second resolution which would have legalised the invasion. But the fact that the Irish Government, constrained by lasting ties of blood and friendship as much as political and economic considerations with America, continued to give America landing rights at Shannon for the transportation of matériel and personnel throughout the war created serious divisions between opponents and supporters of the conflict.

This is not to say that Ireland has not played an honourable role in supplying military personnel for UN peacekeeping activities in various theatres of conflict: Cyprus, the Lebanon, and more recently the Balkans. Some eighty Irish peace-keepers have been killed over the years. The country also continues to play a constructive role under the United Nations Commission on Human Rights. Understandably, the Irish are noticeably active on religious intolerance issues, having the melancholy distinction of housing one of the world's laboratories for the study of such disputes in Ireland's six north-eastern counties. Another international field in which the Irish may feel some legitimate pride for their activities is that of the missionaries and NGOs. Although vocations had fallen considerably by the end of the century, there were still over 4,000 Irish missionaries working in the Third World, chiefly in Africa, but also in Latin America, the Philippines and elsewhere, including of course the developed world. No study of Australian or American history, for example, could be made without acknowledging the contribution of Irish nuns and priests to the development of those countries. Today, the missionary tradition is carried on by the NGOs. The major Irish aid agencies, Concern, GOAL, Trocaire, and others, though small by international standards, are highly regarded for their professionalism and commitment. It would be difficult to quarrel with a statement made by the Irish rock star Bono, in the course of accepting a humanitarian award of €100,000 to be spent at his discretion:

I'm going to give it to Concern and GOAL. These are two great, great organisations and €100,000 is a lot of money. In fact, it's 275 years' wages for most of the people that I represent when I'm doing this line of work. I've seen GOAL and I've seen Concern, and I've seen the way they work in Africa, and these people are real heroes. Much more than actors, much more than rock 'n' roll singers. These are real heroes out on the street, and they represent our country better than any of us here can this evening, and for them, they're getting the money. I want to thank them . . .[115]

The Irish missionary contribution to the Third World in the fields of education and healthcare is as significant as it is laudable. The basis for much of Africa's educational system, for example, was laid by Irish missionaries. Though the memory is fading somewhat as the twentieth century itself recedes, it is a demonstrable fact that many of Africa's revolutionary leaders who emerged in the post-colonial era of the 1960s owed their education to Irish religious. An Irish foreign policy mission statement issued towards the close of the century accurately summed up the Irish position by saying: 'Ireland's foreign policy is about much more than self-interest. For many of us, it is a statement of the kind of people we are.'[116] By way of putting money where mouths are, the statement is validated by the fact that Ireland is the only European country which, by the close of the century, was still consistently increasing its aid budget. While the UN target of 0.7% of GDP for developed countries' aid to the Third World has not yet been met, Ireland is pushing close to a target of 0.45%, and there is a genuine commitment in political and diplomatic circles to safeguarding the aid budget as much as possible in an era of economic downturn.

One arena in which Ireland continuously, for most of the century, failed to realise her diplomatic and political clout is that of Irish America. Here at times, particularly during some phases of the north of Ireland conflict, the attitude of Irish governments towards developing Irish America's political potential for assistance in solving domestic Irish problems was on a par with the approach to developing Irish fisheries. During the phase of Anglo-Irish conflict in the early part of the century Sir Auckland Geddes, a British ambassador to Washington, commented on 'the immense influence Irish men can exert on American politicians if they proceed wisely; and how ready American politicians are to withdraw themselves from that influence if they can find some colourable pretext for doing so'.[117] The curious point about the observation, which was as relevant at the end of the century as at the beginning, is that, particularly under Fine Gael administrations, it was the Irish in Ireland, not the 'American politicians', who sought to 'withdraw themselves from that influence', and it was the Irish-Americans themselves, albeit with the aid of a brace of notable Irish diplomats, who can fairly claim credit for much of the peace process.

The scale of the Irish contribution to America lies outside the scope of this book; I have written about it extensively elsewhere.[118] Here it is sufficient to say that at census time, some 43 million Americans acknowledge Irish ancestry, and people of Irish descent, or indeed origin, are to be found at every level of American decision-taking, political, financial, military, communication, education, show-business, whatever. Equally demonstrably, this ethnic heritage shows itself right across America in the friendship and interest in Ireland encountered by Irish visitors. Yet for most of the century, Dublin had a peculiarly cack-handed method of approaching this potential wellspring of support. Compared to the strength of the Israeli lobby, for example, the Irish-American lobby, if indeed one could properly describe it as a lobby, was minuscule. Even in the immediate aftermath of the serious disagreements which arose between Washington and Dublin over neutrality, de Valera encountered the most extraordinary manifestations of welcome and affection during a month-long visit he made to the US beginning on 8 March 1948. It is a matter of record[119] that hundreds of thousands marched in parades held in his honour in most American cities, being topped overall by Boston, where a million turned out. It was an election year, and the Geddes assessment was pointedly borne out in both Washington and New York. In the former, by his cordial reception by President Truman, and by George Marshall. In New York, although he had of course been born there, he was made an Honorary Citizen. The citation described him, despite all the bad things said about him during the war, as 'the boy from Manhattan who had made good in Ireland'.

The citation and the de Valera welcome encapsulate both the strength and weakness of much of what passed for Irish diplomacy in America, until virtually the last decade of the century. The Manhattan reference indicates something of the pride, and the interconnection, of the Irish in America with their country of origin. But the welcome was for de Valera; not any Irish leader, but the one who had been born in America, fought in an uprising and subsequently toured the continent extensively in the name of Ireland. When de Valera died, a great deal of the regard the Irish in America had for Ireland died with him. He had been regarded as the leader of the Irish in both Ireland and America. Kennedy's accession to the White House revived a great deal of the pride the Irish-Americans felt for their roots, and, more importantly, legitimised the position of Catholics in America. In the early sixties, 'no Irish need apply' signs were still a recent memory in WASP-owned corporations. The effect of the GI Bill of Rights was to combine with the Kennedy elevation to bring the Irish further up the prestige stakes.

But the response of Dublin to the improving status of the Irish was faltering and hesitant. The increasing focus on Europe left the American fields largely untilled. Irish diplomats dutifully did the rounds of the county associations (the Cork men, the Kilkenny men, etc.) at annual dinner or St Patrick's Day time. The attitude of some of them to attending functions such as the Communion breakfasts arranged by organisations like the Ancient Order of Hibernians may be judged by the reaction of one former diplomat who told me: 'Yes, I've gone to the breakfasts, and I have taken unto myself The Crumb.' Even commercial links such as tourism and the export of Irish products were tenuous enough. Tourism was largely a matter of a few flights

411

every so often from New York, organised by the Grimes Tourist Agency, and exports were confined to Waterford glass, Irish whiskey and Irish tweed. As the northern troubles worsened, the signals from Dublin to Irish America were at best confusing and at worst irritating.

The residual goodwill stemming from those parades held for de Valera was still there. But increasingly, the people who made the running in the States were sympathisers with militant republicanism. The Republican support group, NORAID, drew a certain amount of blue-collar support. NORAID was set up in the wake of the 1969 pogrom attempts following visits to America by prominent Provisional IRA leaders, who included Joe Cahill, Ruairi O'Bradaigh and Daithi O'Connell. In Congress it was left to an Italian American, Mario Biaggi, who was later sent to jail on corruption charges, to set up the 'Ad Hoc Committee' amongst congressmen and senators, which claimed to have 84 members. Biaggi was influenced by Father Seán McManus, a Redemptorist priest. McManus set up a lobby group in Washington known as the Irish National Caucus. Both were regarded with varying degrees of disgust in Ireland. The Unionists abhorred the former, and Dublin was decidedly underwhelmed by the latter. But no very coherent philosophy emerged from Dublin for perhaps the first 25 years of the conflict. Policy was aimed as much at curbing IRA sympathies as at furthering any discernible northern blueprint. 'Don't support the IRA, but do support the IDA' was about as far as direction went. The divisions in Fianna Fáil post-arms trial between hawks and doves, and the strongly anti-IRA but ultimately negative attitude of Fine Gael, all played their part. After internment was introduced, Ted Kennedy (speaking on 20 October 1971) called on the British to withdraw their troops from Northern Ireland. Jack Lynch was one of those who condemned him, saying with unusual vehemence that Kennedy did not know what he was talking about. The appreciation of Irish diplomats of the Irish associations was that they were divided and had little political clout, and that no one tried to do anything constructive about bringing the various strands together in a common objective, i.e. linking the associations, the Church, and corporate America in a push for peace.

As late as 1985, Charles Haughey, speaking at a dinner in New York held to launch the 'Friends of Fianna Fáil', a fund-raising organisation, said:

There has been a major failure of communication in recent decades. Conflicting and confusing signals have been coming from Ireland to the Irish in America. There has been no clear message on policy: no specifically enunciated national objectives behind which all right-thinking Americans could rally and to which they could give their unambiguous up-front support. More often than not the official message was negative, condemnatory and critical. Americans who wished only to offer genuine support and encouragement were met with suspicion, rebuff and disapproval. The time has come for all that to change and change radically. Where there was antagonism and suspicion we must now create a whole new atmosphere of constructive dialogue and co-operation as the basis for an effective, powerful Irish-American voice arrayed in legitimate support for clearly defined Irish national objectives – political, economic and cultural. Irish-American public opinion is a sleeping giant that must be awakened and fully motivated with a clear understanding of, and support for, Ireland's real and urgent needs.[120]

Haughey's statement was a fair assessment of the situation. But it is equally fair to say that, apart from the years of the Clinton presidency, not a lot was done by Dublin to generate 'an effective, powerful Irish-American voice'. Through his friendship with Ted Kennedy, John Hume was one of the first to see the potential value of American support, and from the time of the civil rights campaign onward, he targeted American political leaders rather than the county associations for assistance. But Dublin exercised its influence in such a diffused, negative fashion that a great deal of energy was dissipated through having the Irish Embassy network spend its time vetting speakers at Irish events, and trying to frustrate in their turn NORAID, the Ad Hoc Committee, and the Caucus. Relations between the Embassy and the largest Irish-American grouping, the Ancient Order of Hibernians, became so bad, for example, that during the hunger strike years, the chairman of the organising committee of the New York St Patrick's Day Parade, Judge Jim Comerford, hit upon a novel method of indicating public but discreet displeasure.

He caused the official programme, printed in authentic Kelly green, to carry amongst the list of dignitaries present only the title of the Irish Ambassador, not his name. The Ambassador, Seán Donlon, a Garret FitzGerald appointee, objected to NORAID being allowed to march in the St Patrick's Day procession, and every time a group carrying a NORAID banner approached the saluting base, he stepped down off the platform. When Haughey became Taoiseach in 1979, he attempted to move Donlon from Washington. In a move unprecedented in the history of the Irish Department of Foreign Affairs, Donlon, with the help of Garret FitzGerald, was supported by Tip O'Neill, Ted Kennedy and others, who conveyed 'regret' at Haughey's decision to the Taoiseach. Mass resignations from the foreign service were hinted at. Haughey caved in, and allowed Donlon to stay in America as ambassador. Under FitzGerald, Donlon subsequently became Secretary of the Department of Foreign Affairs, but resigned his post early in 1987, when it became apparent that Haughey would be returning to power. The Donlon–Haughey affair mirrored the tensions which split Irish America in the seventies and eighties.

Dublin was unenthusiastic about the 'MacBride principles' campaign, in which McManus, Biaggi, and like-minded supporters lobbied to have American investment in the Six Counties subject to conditions laid down by Seán MacBride, outlawing discrimination in employment practices. Lack of enthusiasm almost became open hostility in 1975, when, a week before Jimmy Carter's election, McManus succeeded in wresting from him a set of commitments on Northern Ireland. These included a statement that the Democratic Party was committed to Irish unity, and that America should play an active role in trying to resolve the conflict, and call for an international commission to be set up on Northern Ireland. All McManus was doing was, as the Americans themselves would say, using the system. It is normal practice during the primaries, and right up to the election itself, for interest groups to lobby presidential candidates to commit themselves to supporting various causes. The Irish Government, as in 1969, had not taken the chance of going the political route itself. However, in the wake of McManus's initiative, Dublin reacted to Carter's declaration by at first calling for a 'clarification' of his remarks, and then, reassured that the President of the United States did not actually intend sponsorship of the Provisionals, with the help of John Hume, belatedly set about securing the setting up of an organisation of its own, 'The Big Four' or, as it became popularly known, 'The Four Horsemen': Edward Kennedy, Hugh Carey, Patrick Moynihan and Tip O'Neill.

The Big Four were motivated by a shared concern over what was happening in Northern Ireland. But Dublin was mainly concerned to use them as a weapon against the IRA, and used the St Patrick's Day following Carter's inauguration to elicit from the Four Horsemen an appeal to 'our fellow Americans to embrace the goal of peace, and to denounce any action that promotes the current violence or provides support or encouragement for organisations engaged in violence'. The statement omitted any reference towards the British contribution to 'the current violence', and any impact it had was balanced by the annoyance it created amongst Irish-Americans at this omission. By now, a good deal of the Irish emigration to the US was coming from Northern Ireland Catholics, and neither they nor an Irish-American public not subject in its information flow to the restrictions of Irish broadcasting took kindly to this one-sided approach to the Irish problem. Dublin, however, was unmoved. The Four Horsemen had been brought together with a view to curbing IRA sympathies, not to bringing home to Whitehall a sense of its responsibilities.[121]

Dublin was fully aware of the dismissive attitude of the British to claims made on behalf of northern Nationalists, and to any intrusion by Ireland on the sacred turf of the Anglo-American special relationship. Years later, the man who became a lightning rod for much of the anger Irish-Americans directed at Dublin's divisive policies, Seán Donlon, revealed in the *Irish Times* the naivety with which Irish diplomacy approached the American political system, and the obstructions which the British placed in the way of that approach.

> We reckoned without the British influence and the skills of British diplomacy in exploiting to the full the special relationship between London and Washington. It took six months of patient and at times painful and bruising Irish diplomatic activity to overcome the many obstacles created by the British and to nudge the Carter administration into its new position . ... The episode also starkly illustrated a problem which Irish diplomats in the US have to deal with regularly; not only are they inevitably in confrontation with IRA supporters, but they are sometimes also in confrontation with the British, even when there are important shared objectives.[122]

I will leave it to readers to decide for themselves how it was, given Ireland's history, that Irish policy-makers set about influencing American political opinion without taking British influence into account. It would appear at this remove to have been the first matter to be considered in a campaign whose ultimate objective was to change British policy. But Donlon's remarkably frank analysis is also notable for its description of one of Dublin's self-inflicted wounds: 'Irish diplomats in the US ... are ... inevitably in confrontation with IRA supporters'. In fact, neither Irish diplomats nor Irish politicians would have had reason for much conflict with the IRA had they not tended to regard any expression of Nationalist opinion which did not automatically conform to Dublin's line, and a fuzzy and meandering line it frequently seemed, as being automatically supportive of the IRA. It was only when, guided tactfully in the background from Washington, in the late eighties and early nineties, by two outstanding Irish diplomats, Dermot Gallagher, the Ambassador, and Brendan Scannell, the Counsellor, who had also served in Boston, that a new generation of Irish-American activists found themselves able to mobilise in concert with active Sinn Féin supporters, in such a way that the peace process was advanced, and NORAID eventually sidelined. Nevertheless, the Carter initiative of 30 August 1977, to which Donlon adverted, did mark a watershed in American involvement in the Irish conflict. While making all the right noises about not getting involved with organisations which supported violence, and speaking encouragingly about job creation, Carter's statement did breach the principle of regarding Northern Ireland as a sphere of British influence in which America would not become involved. Carter declared: 'We support the establishment of a form of government in Northern Ireland which will command widespread acceptance throughout both parts of the country.' This was coded language for telling London that Washington wished to see it resuscitate a power-sharing initiative it had abandoned three years earlier.

From then on, substantive gestures towards Dublin's position emanated from the White House. In the wake of Thatcher's 'out, out, out' speech, Dublin managed to secure from Ronald Reagan a friendly nudge to her in the direction of the Anglo-Irish agreement, which the Americans also helped to further by allocating some $250 million towards investment in worthy Northern Ireland projects. In the event, the money proved to be the most lasting outcropping of the Carter initiative. The power-sharing suggestion was not taken up. But Congress did adopt a rider to the Aid Bill whereby Congress had to be assured that both the human rights position and that of the MacBride principles were satisfactory before the money was paid over. Congress would have gone further in 1977 had Dublin not successfully lobbied Tip O'Neill to abort an attempt by the ad hoc committee to hold congressional hearings on human rights abuses by the security forces in Northern Ireland. Just as in its lacklustre response to the Dublin/Monaghan bombings, Dublin decided that 'it was more important that the IRA be given no opportunity to enhance its credibility than that the British be criticised for their violations of Human Rights'.[123] This policy was sometimes taken to extreme lengths. Seán Donlon once wrote[124] to a Republican congressman,

Hamilton Fish, who had taken up the case of the Birmingham Six, questioning the credibility of Father Raymond Murray, who had interested Fish in the miscarriage of justice, by quoting to Fish the opinion of a Loyalist politician who had described Murray as interfering with the work of the security forces. This is being written at a time when the findings of the Stevens Inquiry have corroborated the work of investigative journalists like the BBC's John Ware, and Mark Urban, and even, dare I say it, some of my own writings,[125] which claimed that for several years, British security forces had been acting either individually or in concert with Loyalist murder gangs to kill innocent Catholics. But in the period under review, and right up to the millennium, it was official British policy to deny that such actions took place. Dublin's refusal to highlight these allegations, or even to pursue them in any meaningful way, even when they claimed the lives of Irish citizens, as in the case of the Dublin bombings, has to be regarded as contributing to the vacuum in which these murderous illegalities took place.

The passage of time did something to bring a degree of sophistication to Dublin's approach to Irish America. But the big change was generated within America itself by the Irish-Americans. The illegal immigrant issue took off amongst young Irish emigrants in the early eighties. One of them, Seán Minihane, has described[126] how he and another young Cork man, Pat Hurley, accidentally triggered a revolution amongst Irish-Americans by attending a meeting of the Cork County Association in New York during May 1987, at which they turned a meeting called to arrange the following year's St Patrick's Day festivities into a movement to get visas for themselves, and people like them. The movement, the Irish Immigration Reform Movement, was born four days later. It embraced young Irish men and women of every class and political persuasion. Utilising the traditional Irish political bent for creating political machines, the IIRM mushroomed into one of the most effective lobbies ever to descend on Washington.

Minihane and the others were backed by Irish-American congressmen who had shown an interest in the visa problem, like Brian Donnelly of Boston, who had already had some success in getting the quota of visas for the Irish increased by means of the Donnelly Bill, passed in 1986. Ted Kennedy lent his prestige and clout to another Bill sponsored by Congressman Bruce Morrison, of Connecticut. It passed in 1991. The cumulative effect of the Morrison and Donnelly Bills was to greatly increase the number of visas available not only for the Irish, but for other groups as well. A shrewd observer, and supporter of the IIRM campaign, Niall O'Dowd, publisher of the prestigious *Irish America* magazine, and of the weekly *Irish Voice*, decided that the IIRM phenomenon was too successful to be allowed to die with the passage of the Morrison Bill.

O'Dowd, who had emigrated from Ireland, had worked first in San Francisco, where he and Patricia Harty, who currently edits *Irish America*, had founded another newspaper, and from the time of the hunger strikes on had sought some means of progressing the Irish issue. The success of the

IIRM suggested to O'Dowd that the time was ripe for a new agenda which would enable Irish-Americans to do something for their country of origin without becoming involved in the never-ending dissension between Dublin and most of the existing Irish-American organisations. Even more importantly, it would enable congressmen and influential decision-takers to support such an agenda.

The new organisation was called Americans for a New Irish Agenda (ANIA). With the help of advice from Brendan Scannell, the Irish Consul General in Boston, O'Dowd put together a team of prominent Irish-Americans which included Chuck Feeney, the billionaire philanthropist and pioneer of the duty-free shops idea; Bill Flynn, one of New York's most prominent Irish-American businessmen, and chairman of the huge American Mutual Insurance corporation; the veteran civil rights activist Paul O'Dwyer; Ray Flynn, the mayor of Boston; Bruce Morrison, a former classmate of Bill Clinton; the prominent trade union activist Joe Jameson; and the Republican congressman Peter King. The initial policy of the ANIA was to try to get Washington to nudge London towards a settlement of the Irish issue, to have a peace envoy appointed to Northern Ireland, to implement the MacBride principles, and last, but far from least, to secure a visa to America for Gerry Adams. Again, as McManus had done, O'Dowd and his friends used the system. They studied the list of Democratic presidential candidates, decided that Bill Clinton was the most hopeful, and had a historic meeting with him at the Sheraton Hotel, New York, on 5 April 1992.

Clinton had been a student at Oxford during the birth of the Irish civil rights movement, and the treatment meted out to the peaceful marchers had aroused strong resonances of his own Arkansas experiences. He amazed the Irish delegation with his grasp of the Irish situation and his eagerness to do something to utilise the long-standing 'special relationship' with England to engage with the Irish situation rather than stand aside from it. Leaving the Sheraton after meeting with Clinton, Paul O'Dwyer turned to O'Dowd and said: 'If this guy does half of what he says he'll do, he'll knock their socks off.' The delegation was so impressed with Clinton that they formed another organisation, the Irish-Americans for Clinton–Gore. Ray Flynn became co-chairman of the Clinton campaign, and the other powerful founders of the ANIA and their friends became subscribers and backers. Clinton, as we will see later, did as he had indicated he would at the fateful Sheraton meeting, indeed far more, and the result was the Irish peace process.

However, while the Clinton episode might validly be held up as an example of the 'clout' of the Irish-American lobby, it could also be taken as an example of how much more could, and can, be done if the Irish American lobby remained organised with the direct supportive link to the Dublin Government. There was an element of luck in the IANIA's success. A number of ducks were in line, not least the presence of an unusually talented pair of Irish diplomats in Washington. Gallagher set up links with the Clinton White House and with Clinton himself, which were the envy of even the Israelis, and

Scannell proved to be a master strategist in providing advice and guidance to O'Dowd and his friends. However, the Irish diplomatic service is a human institution, subject to variations in talent. Not all Irish representation in Washington and on the Consulate network is of the Gallagher/Scannell class, and of course no matter how effective it proves itself to be at times, the Irish Embassy network is by definition a small one, operating with a fraction of the resources and personnel enjoyed by the British, for example.

After the Twin Towers atrocity, the world of international diplomacy changed radically, and it became clear that Ireland could no longer rely on the stop-go policies of the past, including the utilisation of the Irish diaspora, and in particular that in America, when circumstances required. Traditionally Ireland was able to bypass the State Department and the institutions responsive to British influence, or any other influence that Dublin wished to oppose by taking the political route, going direct to the Senator or the White House. In George Bush's dangerous new world order, one in which one American Congressman in five owns a passport, an accurate reflection of the amount of knowledge and interest which prevails generally in the United States where international affairs are concerned, the Irish need to take a leaf out of the Israelis' book, and get organised. America's policy towards other countries is largely influenced not by the average George and Martha, but by the great lobbies, the industrial military complex, first delineated by Eisenhower, the British, the Israelis, the oil companies, and, latterly, the Cubans. In this circumstance, with a potentially priceless resource to hand, Dublin's neglect of the Irish diaspora offers is not merely foolish, it is highly dangerous. In the contemporary world, a serious, sustained, tapping in to Irish American opinion must become a cardinal tenet of Irish foreign policy.

SEVEN

LEMASS: THE WINDOW-OPENER

(CIRCA 1959–65)

Compared to the stagnation and decay under de Valera, Lemass's brief tenure in office (1959–66) was astonishingly, refreshingly productive. He was like a man who inherited a potentially valuable house which had been allowed to run down, but who had thrown open its stifling shutters, seen what needed to be done, and set about doing it vigorously and largely successfully. The statistics of what grew from the Lemass/Whitaker era have been outlined in the previous chapter, but it is important as it were to put a human face on the facts, in order to grasp the magnitude of the change that came over Irish life from the sixties onwards. It was not all uniformly good; there are hidden costs to progress. But Lemass either originated, or presided over, a number of initiatives, in the fields of Anglo-Irish relationships, housing, Northern Ireland (where alas the shutters were slammed shut rapidly and disastrously by figures like Ian Paisley), Europe, and probably most importantly of all, in education, where the Lemass-inspired dynamism made possible the sometimes debatable achievements of what became known as the Celtic Tiger era. I remember an aphorism of Lemass's to the effect that the task of a leader was the 'release and canalisation of dynamism'. This he certainly did.

The average seaborne visitor to Dun Laoghaire today would enter this gateway harbour to Dublin and Ireland aboard a large, comfortable Stena Sealink car ferry. His fellow passengers would be either tourists, or Irish people returning to their native country for, or from, a holiday. The visitor would see a large yacht-filled harbour encircled by granite piers, a waterfront fringed with tall, brightly painted houses, some apartment blocks and a number of restaurants. In the distance a tide of (not all tasteful) modern development rises towards the lovely Dublin mountains. That is not how Dun Laoghaire appeared in the forties and fifties. Before the Lemass/Whitaker reforms kicked in, one got an all too accurate sense of Ireland by taking a walk down the East Pier in Dun Laoghaire in wintertime. Climate is still one of the most underestimated factors in assessing Irish statistics for depression, alcoholism and suicide. It was particularly so in the Ireland of the forties and fifties. Apart from what James Joyce accurately termed the 'snot green sea', the predominant colour of Dun Laoghaire was grey and depressing. Houses and doors were painted in dark colours, black or dark green for the doors, mostly peeling, dull plaster for the houses. Many of the people one

419

encountered were retired, unemployed, or filling in time before the Stena's precursor, the mailboat, moored across from the pier, took them to England. Poverty of both pocket and mind was almost a tangible thing. It reflected the lack of aesthetic sense, the haemorrhaging of intellect and of energy, symbolised by the battered black ferry which a disdainful British shipping company allocated to what was, for many, a dismal crossing of the Irish Sea towards a future of squandering their youth in the loneliness and false camaraderie of the doss houses and public houses of Camden and Kilburn; of lives lived in a milieu wherein the policeman's Black Maria was known as 'Paddy's taxi' and the money wrested from the 'subby' (sub-contractor) was thought of not as something to be put aside for a rainy day, or retirement, but for pissing down a pub toilet.

Emigration, and the relationship between Church and State, meant that the Irish cultural atmosphere was permeated by two blighting factors, acceptance and conformity. A generation grew up in which writers, or at least the better ones, either emigrated or lived out their lives in an aspic of poverty and alcohol, in a society drowning in velleity, in which the question asked of a writer's work was not 'Is it good or bad?' but 'Should it be banned?'

Artists were borne down by poverty, drink – and Dublin. This last was a combination of inertia, inwardness, begrudgery, conformity, lack of money and lack of international standards. A patron of the arts, John Ryan,[1] wrote in 1951 that: 'Ireland offers three prospects to the young writer of promise, poverty, obscurity and hatred.' I was once asked to write a biography of the painter Seán O'Sullivan, and discussed the idea with the writer and former revolutionary Peadar O'Donnell. O'Donnell scuttled the notion, pointing out, correctly, that through drink, Sullivan's early promise had degenerated into fashionable sketched likenesses of the great of Irish society of the time. 'The only thing you could do', he said, 'would be a case study of "Dublin and the Artist Destroyed".' In many ways, it would not be inaccurate to regard an Irish writer, until well into the sixties, as an Ishmael, his hand against every man, and every man's hand against him.

In *The Bell* (September 1951), the writer Anthony Cronin, whom fate would later place in a position to do a great deal for the arts in Ireland, declared:

> There is at present a disquieting lull in creative activity in Ireland and a lack of creative vitality in the generations now in their twenties or early thirties, giving cause for the fear that what the editor [*The Bell* was then being edited by Peadar O'Donnell] calls 'the Irish School of writing' may disappear altogether – or, as I would prefer to say, Ireland may be left altogether without a contemporary literature.

Three writers who could certainly be fitted into the Ishmael stereotype were Brendan Behan, Brian O'Nolan and Patrick Kavanagh. The published work which Behan has left us would scarcely merit his being included with the other two, but I do so in the belief that had he not been destroyed by alcohol, the writer of *The Quare Fellow*, *The Hostage* and *Borstal Boy* could have bequeathed a far richer oeuvre. Self-educated, a graduate of the 'Republican University' jail, he was also a product of the slums. His family was uprooted by the Fianna Fáil rehousing programmes out to one of the new council housing estates, where, because of the inexperience of the urban planners of the day, the newcomers found themselves dislocated, isolated, lonely, deprived of easily accessible shops or pubs, and surrounded by what Behan termed 'the black stuff they call clay'. They were a breed whose quick-cutting humour was as important to their survival as a good mother.

I was talking once to Stephen Behan, Brendan's father, about what I imagined to be the trauma of his son's having gone to the funeral of an IRA man shot by the Special Branch in controversial circumstances (as the man, Jackie Griffith, was on a bicycle when the police opened fire on him, it was alleged that he had cycled into an ambush, not an arrest) shortly after being released from internment, only to land himself back in jail almost immediately. Well lubricated, Behan had grabbed a revolver from a member of the IRA firing party, and opened up on a party of watching Special Branch men, for which he received seven years' penal servitude. 'Seven years!' I remarked wonderingly. 'Yeah,' replied the doting parent, 'one for every fucking yard he missed them by.'

Despite his inheritance of his family's famous sense of humour, his intuition and his facility for words, Behan found it difficult to face challenge of any sort without drink. It got him into the brawls, the headlines, and ultimately an early grave, much of the credit for his plays and his books due to his editors, and collaborators like the producer Joan Littlewood.

Patrick Kavanagh deserves to be regarded as the greatest Irish poet between Yeats and Heaney. *The Great Hunger*, *Tarry Flynn* and *The Green Fool* combined with his religious verse to present an authentic, unsurpassable and certainly unforgettable Portrait of the Artist as a Peasant in Mid-Century Catholic Ireland. It's fashionable, as this is being written, for survivors of his era to retell admiring anecdotes about his conversation and his eccentricities. But the observable reality of his existence in Dublin was of people drawing away from this strange, peering, shambling figure in buses or on the street. He lived under threat of being evicted from his flat by his landlord for non-payment of rent, being rescued at various stages by the generosity of friends, occasional royalties, the improbable friendship of the Archbishop of Dublin, John Charles McQuaid, and some journalism. One of the best-known anecdotes to survive the demise of the *Irish Press* concerns Kavanagh standing at the head of the stairs outside the office of the editor (before I occupied it, I'm happy to say), tearing up an article which he had failed to get published and muttering as he dropped the pieces over the banisters: 'Shite, pure shite, it's all pure shite.'

Of the three, O'Nolan probably suffered most in his public persona from the image of a bitter, drunken figure through whose veins coursed vitriol and alcohol in equal proportions. Yet O'Nolan was one of the kindest of men, as well as being one of the great comic geniuses of the twentieth century. He took up his civil service post largely to help his widowed mother with the rearing of his siblings (eight children) whom he supported until they began earning themselves. Otherwise he might have become an acknowledged writer, and a far less pressured one at that, far earlier in his career.

The question of what gives rise to alcoholism is a complex one. Whether O'Nolan's heavy drinking was caused by specifically Irish conditions, by the inner torments of the artist or by some other factor is obviously open to debate, but the fact is that drink formed a central and corrosive place in his life, and as it did with so many Irish artists, the effects of it tended to make Dubliners recoil from rather than warm towards one of the great figures produced by their city.

When his book *The Dalkey Archive* appeared (in 1964), I made arrangements with him to appear on an RTE programme called *Newsbeat*. He agreed to come on without any difficulty, but rang me back to say that he was very uncertain about this television business, and was afraid he'd dry up. I would have to attack him to goad him into doing justice to himself. A few hours later his wife also rang me to say: 'He is very good if he can be kept off the drink. But he won't do himself justice if he takes anything.' It was obvious that the great man was suffering from an acute case of stage fright at the prospect of a simple, low-key interview. Accordingly, I made arrangements with a cameraman to pick him up at 7.45 in the morning, and then collect me shortly afterwards so that we could proceed to the battlements of Cliff Castle Hotel, Dalkey, overlooking Dalkey Island, and one of the loveliest views in Ireland, do the interview and depart long before the bars would open at 10.30 a.m.

It seemed a foolproof arrangement, but at 8.30 a.m. I found myself fruitlessly walking up and down the road outside my house. At last a fairly distraught cameraman pulled up, seemingly without a passenger other than his son, who sat in the front. On looking through the back window, however, I saw a slumped figure in the back seat. The cameraman told me he had gone to O'Nolan's house as arranged to find the door opened by a resplendent, shining, shaved O'Nolan, clad in stylish grey charcoal pinstripe. The wife had prepared breakfast, and insisted that the cameraman and his son eat it. After about five minutes of pleasant conversation, O'Nolan excused himself and went to the lavatory. Time continued to pass pleasantly at the breakfast table, too pleasantly. Suddenly Mrs O'Nolan exclaimed, 'He's gone too long! Go up immediately and get him out.' The cameraman at first protested against the impropriety of disturbing a man in the lavatory, but ultimately gave in and dutifully banged on the door. Eventually it opened and O'Nolan stumbled out. Behind him a large empty bottle of Powers Gold Label Whiskey which had been hidden in the cistern rolled along the floor.

O'Nolan sat up when I opened the car door, and showed himself able to speak coherently, if somewhat indistinctly. So, after an exchange of pleasantries, I decided we'd go ahead with the interview. However, as the cameras were being set up, O'Nolan insisted that he'd have to have a drink before we began. I was known at the hotel, and even though it was still an hour and a half before opening time, I succeeded in getting him a whiskey, which he refused on the grounds that a) it was a small one, and b) I'd have to have one with him. I didn't drink spirits much in those days, and nearly gagged on the whiskey at that hour of the morning, but he swallowed his, a large one, in one gulp. The interview began with my vainly trying to follow his instructions about attacking him and at the same time get him to talk about the book. He had just got to the point of explaining that he was attempting to save the Church from itself, and that St Augustine had been big into buggery – this for a family audience of the Dublin of Archbishop McQuaid's heyday – when the wretched camera broke down. He refused to continue when it was repaired until I got another round, again large ones, which again he put away at a gulp, and we returned to St Augustine. I had just managed to elicit a few sentences about the book when Murphy's Law set in and the camera broke down again. Once more he demanded drink as the price of recommencing, and the waitress, flustered by his tone and demeanour, this time brought us two large gin and tonics, which she claimed was all she could find at that hour of the morning.

O'Nolan pronounced the change of drink didn't matter, 'It's all a grain base,' he said. Interview or no interview, I wasn't going to drink the gin, but he made no objection to drinking alone this time. Hitherto, I had associated drink with parties and celebratory occasions, and even now, nearly forty years later, I can still remember my recoil at watching the blue-tinged liquid passing through O'Nolan's almost equally blue, sucking lips. Somehow we got through the rest of the interview, managed to fend off further requests for drink on the pretext that the cameraman and I had to be back at RTE, packed up the gear, and were on our way five minutes before the hotel bar was officially due to open.

However, as we passed Searson's pub in Dalkey, there came a stentorian 'STOP. THEY'RE OPEN!' Ignoring our pleas that we had promised his wife to bring him home after the interview, he made his way into Searson's, and, the owner told me subsequently, remained there drinking continuously until he was decanted into a taxi at four o'clock in the afternoon. Needless to say, those who saw him that day (and probably the next as he battled with what must have been a horrific hangover) witnessed only the Ishmael side of the writer stereotype. By way of further underlining the nature of the climate of the time, I might add that I was congratulated on having taken part in a 'classic' by the programme's editor, who later became the state film censor, but as the interview could obviously not be shown,[2] and as I was on a freelance basis with RTE, I would not be paid.

The depressing appearance of Dun Laoghaire in the fifties, already referred to, was a direct consequence of the continuing mortal sin of all Irish governments before the Whitaker/Lemass era: the linked failure to do anything meaningful to either halt emigration or provide an education system to help create an economy which would have lessened emigration or provided those who could not remain in Ireland with the means of earning a living other than by unskilled labour. When something was done for the Irish emigrants in England, the opening of the Irish Emigrant Centre in Camden Town in 1955, as we shall see, it was little enough and owed more to the efforts of the English Church than an Irish government. The prevailing official attitude towards emigration for most of the state's existence can most charitably be described as one of ignorance. Emigration, like poverty, was generally held either to be the fault of those involved for deserting their country and its manifold attractions of mind and spirit, or a good thing under two headings, one stated, the other not. The stated one was that it spread the faith abroad to the inestimable benefit of the rest of the world's population, and of course, *inter alia*, the power of the Roman Catholic Church. The unstated one was that it provided a safety valve which drew off revolutionary tendencies.

The one major leader who consistently saw emigration in more realistic terms was Seán Lemass. In 1939, he said openly that the lack of solutions to economic problems had 'created a situation in which the very disappearance of the race was a possibility that could not be ignored'. Over the decades, he continually warned of the need to increase industrialisation, pointing out the obvious: 'The efforts we have made firmly to establish freedom here would be unavailing if we cannot secure our financial freedom as well.'[3] As the country's economic woes deepened, he bluntly stated: 'It is the survival of a nation that is involved now.' In order to understand the full significance of the changes Lemass put in train in both education and emigration, a brief examination of the history of both is necessary.

The opposition parties were as culpable as the Government in their skewed concerns, for the morals of female emigrants occupied decision-takers who should have been addressing the root causes of why the women left the country. The Fine Gael leader, James Dillon, contacted the Department of External Affairs in an unsuccessful attempt to get restrictions imposed on female emigration to protect women from the moral pitfalls which lay abroad.[4] In fact, though they often suffered terribly from loneliness, and a feeling of injustice that their heritage had been denied them, Irish women on balance, and particularly in America, found emigration to be an enabling experience.[5] But the loss to their country of origin was horrendous. Other European countries recorded emigration ratios of two males for every female. In Ireland, emigration of the sexes was roughly equal. The urge to get away from rural toil and stultification in particular was such that it was calculated that in Connacht, 42 out of every 100 girls aged 15 to 19 in 1946 had left five years later.[6]

A governmental commission on emigration which was set up in April 1948 eventually reported in May 1954. It found that of 25 countries surveyed, the Republic had the largest dependent group, i.e. aged below 14 and over 65. Noting the conservative and retarding effect of this dependency ratio, with its high preponderance of older people, the commission made a number of quite practical recommendations. These included the establishment of a land utilisation body, an export corporation and an investment council to decide public investment priorities, and the giving of old age pensions to small farmers if they transferred their holding to their children on reaching the age of 65. But it was this report which also contained the immortal statement that

> in general it may be said that those who remain single through selfishness, or through over-anxiety about the future, or for any other such reason – for instance, the woman who does not want to give up her independence or her job, or the man who does not want the burden of supporting a home – are failing in their duty to God, themselves and the race.[7]

There was a feeling abroad that a certain level of struggle, of the sublimation of self, of living just above the breadline was the norm, and that emigrating to get away from such conditions was somehow selfish. This idea crossed party boundaries. In a speech to the Dail on 2 June 1959, James Dillon said that 'a great deal of this talk about emigration is fraud, a great deal of this talk is dishonest, a great deal of the suggestion that emigrants are driven from this country by economic want is untrue'. Dillon went on to argue that people who were above the breadline norm, and who chose to emigrate, should not be classed as involuntary emigrants. The choice was theirs; the responsibility for their departure lay not with Irish society, but with the emigrants themselves.

As noted elsewhere, Alexis Fitzgerald was one of the best economic brains of his generation. Amongst his many activities was membership of the Commission on Emigration, quoted above. Fitzgerald submitted a minority report which included the following view of those who went abroad, written by someone who could be taken as epitomising the views of those fortunate enough to have remained at home in comfort:

> I cannot accept either the view that a high rate of emigration is necessarily a sign of national decline or that policy should be over-anxiously framed to reduce it. It is clear that in the history of the Church, the role of Irish emigrants has been significant. If the historical operation of emigration has been providential, Providence may in the future have a similar vocation for the nation. In the order of values, it seems more important to preserve the quality of Irish life and thereby the purity of that message which our people have communicated to the world than it is to reduce the numbers of Irish emigrants. While there is a danger of complacency, I believe that there should be a more realistic appreciation of the advantages of emigration. High emigration, granted a population excess, releases social tensions which would otherwise explode and makes possible a stability of manners and customs which would otherwise be the subject of radical change. It is a national advantage that it is easy for emigrants to establish their lives in other parts of the world not merely from the point of view of the individuals concerned whose horizon of opportunity is widened.

I can fairly claim that my travels around the world to research the history and contemporary position of Irish emigrants has given me, if not expert status, at least an above-average knowledge of how Irish emigrants managed to 'establish their lives' in other parts of the world. It was rarely easy and often traumatic, and though the contemporary picture of the Irish diaspora is an attractive one, it is a picture framed by the hardships of earlier generations. The often horrific history of the experiences of Irish emigrants in America is indicated by Martin Scorsese's film *Gangs of New York*, which, while distorted as to detail, is accurate in substance concerning the difficulties the Irish experienced through poverty, language barriers, nativism and religion. One of the reasons why President Kennedy received such a genuine outpouring of warmth and welcome on his visit to Ireland in 1963 was the largely nonverbalised acknowledgement of the fact that 'one of our own', whose ancestors had experience of violent stews like New York's Five Points, depicted in the film (and of similar areas of Boston and Chicago), had made it to the White House. In England, the centuries-old existence of anti-Irish prejudice was evidenced by boarding house signs (thankfully now vanished), reading 'No Irish, dogs or blacks'. Making all due allowances for aberrant behaviour on the part of the percentage of Irish who contributed to the undesirable impression, the fact is that the stereotypical image of an Irish emigrant which could be found amongst a section of what might be termed the English officer and gentleman class may be gauged from this memoir of the wife of a member both of that class and of a generation which would have been still alive when Fitzgerald delivered his judgement:

> In spotless white serge I sat in the railway carriage, waiting for the train to move . . . I felt quite cheerful and hopeful. A horrid-looking old man approached me, and said: 'Are you going to emigrate?' I put out an immaculate white shoe and silk-clad leg, and very nearly kicked him. Did I look like an Irish emigrant? I was quite speechless with wrath . . . Apparently I was deemed a potential emigrant. What an awful thought.[8]

Emigration was still an 'awful' subject during the 1950s, so much so that successive Irish governments did not give it any thought. The saga of the Irish emigrants in Birmingham during the 1950s may be given as an example. Because of the post-war boom, Irish emigrants had flooded into the British Midlands. It was reckoned that about 50,000 had concentrated in Birmingham, where conditions were so bad that sometimes as many as 50 men crowded into a small house, sleeping 15 to a room. In some places of accommodation, male shift workers occupied beds which at night were given over to girls. Sanitation was often conspicuous by its absence. Unfortunately, alcoholism, TB and gastroenteritis were all too frequently met with.

A report highlighting these problems was compiled by a young Irish social worker, Maurice Foley, and furnished to the Government in July 1951 by F.H. Boland, the then Irish Ambassador to the Court of St James. De Valera was advised that he could be 'put in a false position if he spoke in public about the contents of these reports unless some definite action had been taken by the government beforehand'.[9] He therefore took the precaution of writing (on 24 August 1951) to the Secretary of the Hierarchy, Dr Staunton, sending him a copy of the Foley report and stating that 'It refers in part to moral and religious aspects of the conditions in which some of these workers find themselves.' He went on to inform the hierarchy that he was instructing the Irish Ambassador to make 'suitable representations to the British government'. On the 28th, Boland duly handed a note concerning the conditions described by Foley to the Secretary of State for Commonwealth Relations. This enabled de Valera to claim that he had taken 'definite action', and the following day he made a speech about the issue at a Fianna Fáil function in Galway.

He began by extolling the virtues of the Irish monks who had brought civilisation to Europe in the Dark Ages, and said that Ireland's contemporary objective should be to work in the same spiritual field, not the material one. A prime method of doing this would be to restore the Irish language. With the essentials out of the way, he turned to what he termed the 'alarming dimensions' of emigration, which was then running at 40,000 annually, 50% more than it had been between 1936 and 1946. He then unblushingly informed his listeners in Galway, the principal city of the province of Connacht, whose female emigration statistics have been quoted above, that

> The saddest part of all this is that work is available at home, and in conditions infinitely better from the point of both health and morals. In many occupations, the rates of wages are higher at home than they are in Britain . . . an Irish worker's . . . conditions . . . are so unattractive that he prefers unduly long hours of overtime to a leisure which he cannot enjoy. There is no doubt that many of those who emigrate could find employment at home at as good, or better, wages – and with living conditions far better – than they find in Britain.

He then went on to describe the contents of the Foley report and said that 'the prestige of our people generally suffers by the suggestion that "anything is good enough for the Irish"'.

The Galway speech provoked angry reactions in both England and Ireland, where opposition spokespersons not unreasonably enquired why de Valera had not taken the same active interest in emigrant welfare during the preceding 16 uninterrupted years in office. But nothing tangible came of de Valera's posturings. The British did not reply to Boland's note. At the time, British workers were themselves living in appalling conditions and it was quite unrealistic to expect that special provision would be made for Irish workers to jump the housing queue.

The Church too had a vested interest in the housing of Irish workers. The Catholic clergy preferred to see the Irish corralled together, rather than dispersed into individual lodgings in English households, where, though 'materially better off, the atmosphere would often be destructive of spiritual values'.[10] This was code for keeping control of the Irish Catholics. The Department of External Affairs took it upon itself to take action after 20,000 Irish emigrants in England signed a petition asking the Government to help in the setting up of an Emigrant Information Centre in Birmingham. The grant the petitioners sought was rejected, but External Affairs prepared a memorandum which was read to de Valera on 5 January 1954. It proposed the establishment of an Irish community trust fund, to be financed by voluntary subscription, in Ireland and in Britain, amongst the emigrants themselves with the support of the Catholic clergy.

One paragraph of the original read: 'No Irish Government wished the Irish people to go to England, or could take responsibility for keeping them there; the Irish Government would, of course, be only too happy to look after them if they came home.' De Valera's reply deleted the reference to the Irish Government's happiness at the prospect of returning emigrants. He also altered 'The work of catering for the welfare of Irish workers in Britain would, however, to be effective and permanent, be done by the Irish in Britain with the help and co-operation of their English friends.' Both the 'however' and 'their English' disappeared. A more important amendment to the External Affairs drafts lay in the alteration of the following:

> The Minister pointed out to them that their request could not be granted but he promised to endeavour to have a fund raised by voluntary subscription in Ireland, which would be handed over to trustees, drawn from England, Scotland and Wales, who would administer it for the purpose of encouraging and assisting organisation among Irish people in Great Britain for social and welfare purposes.

What emerged was a definition of the amount of generosity de Valera was prepared to extend to the Irish emigrants in Britain:

> The Minister informed them that the Government could not undertake any responsibility for the financing of such a project. If, however, suitable trustees were appointed in Britain with a view to the raising of a fund by public subscriptions in that country and here, he would consider what might be done towards assisting in the collection of money in this country. The object of the fund would be to encourage and assist organisation among Irish people in Britain for social and welfare purposes.

To their credit, the English clergy showed a more generous spirit than did the Irish Government. After another wasted year, on 20 January 1955, Cardinal Griffin launched a fund to build an Irish centre in Camden Town. He donated £1,000, Archbishop McQuaid £500, and Cardinal d'Alton £200. The Irish Centre was finally opened on 25 September 1955. By then, de Valera was out of power, but the emigrant ships were fuller than ever.

What sort of conditions did they leave behind them? How were they equipped to fend for themselves when they got to England? The Fitzgerald quotation given earlier on emigration's value in preserving some notional 'quality of life' is of course a middle-class one, a Fine Gael one. However, the Fianna Fáil decision-taker's view was no different. Erskine Childers, a son of the executed Erskine Childers, showed himself to be equally out of touch with the realities of life when he wrote in tones of pained surprise to the then secretary of Fianna Fáil, not about the evils of emigration, but about the evils of the Fianna Fáil organisation which had just contributed to putting the party out of power after 16 years continuously in office. Many of the election meetings had been held indoors because of the bad weather, in what Childers termed 'appalling schools'. He proclaimed himself 'amazed at the appearance, the clothes, the absence of cleanliness among many of our own Fianna Fáil supporters who were teachers and whom I met during the elections; I was amazed too at the number who were obviously heavy drinkers'.[11]

Childers might not have been quite so amazed had he pondered the implications of a statement made by his leader, Eamon de Valera, concerning the importance of those 'appalling schools' both to the children who attended them, and to the teachers whom they helped to drive to drink. Speaking in the Dail, de Valera, who at the time held the education portfolio, said that 'for *nine out of ten* of our people, the primary school is their *only* educational experience'.[12] By way of confirming the accuracy of de Valera's statement, it might be pointed out that ten years later, in 1950, there were 464,000 pupils in primary schools, and only 7,900 in universities.[13] Far from proving itself the enabling and enriching process which the word education – from the Latin *educare*, to draw out – implies, for over 450,000 pupils annually the Irish educational system was a wasteland of unrealised hopes, undeveloped talent and opportunities denied. In addition, the curriculum which the pupils followed in primary school, which in many cases, probably a majority, meant until they were 12 (technically, children were supposed to remain in primary school until they were 14), devoted a large amount of time to the teaching of both Irish and the Roman Catholic catechism, which were hardly designed to prepare emigrants transferring from rural Ireland to industrial England. Moreover, the teachers who taught these unfortunates had their own built-in disabilities, described by the then Secretary of the Vocational Teachers Association, Charles McCarthy, as follows:

These young men and women were drawn from the most academically able in the country, but, certainly in the case of the men, from a remarkably limited social group. It appears to me that they came primarily from small farmers and small shopkeepers in the south and west, and in many cases had themselves left home as early as thirteen or fourteen years of age, attending first the preparatory colleges (which now fortunately have been dis-established) and also the diocesan colleges, all residential in character. From there they went to a residential training college which was conducted on remarkably authoritarian lines. What was intended to provide an opportunity for strong religious formation provided as well a golden opportunity to inculcate the principles of the romantic Gaelic culture, which had in the meantime become so dominant.

However, it would be almost impossible to overstate the amount of built-in resistance to change in the Irish education system which existed in the relationship between the Church, an extremely conservative department, and politicians, both government and opposition. Jack Lynch told me that when he took over as Minister for Education, he found his department was so stagnant that he had to 'kick civil servants out of the way to get anything done'.[14] The first Cumann na nGaedheal Minister for Education, Eóin MacNeill, who was 'widely recognised as the politician closest to the Catholic bishops, was likely to have been the recipient of their formal and informal observations on education policy in the new State; from September 1922, he was in a position to implement a policy which was in line with these observations'.[15] When MacNeill resigned over the Boundary Commission débâcle, he was replaced in 1926 by John Marcus O'Sullivan, who, though not as well known as MacNeill, was chosen by Cosgrave because 'he was assured of personal political loyalty, acceptability by the Catholic Church, and a prudence which would avoid any political embarrassment arising from the policies pursued'.[16]

That prudence continued to permeate both Cumann na nGaedheal and its successor, Fine Gael. Addressing the Conference of Convent Secondary Schools in June 1948, the Fine Gael minister in the inter-party government, Richard Mulcahy, described a proposed Council of Education as being a council 'which will recognise and proclaim the Catholic philosophy upon which our Irish system is based, the right of parents, the Church, the State'. He assured his hearers that the bishops had already given their sanction to the council and approved of the fact that it would be 'advisory, non-representative, and of no function in relation to the allocation of public funds'. Speaking in the Dail, Mulcahy defined his role as being 'a kind of dungarees man' whose function was to 'take the knock out of the pipes, and will link up everything'. One enters the realms of speculation here, but it seems fair to extrapolate from the climate of the time the inference that the links which Mulcahy sought to preserve were those between the vested interests in education, particularly between Christ and Caesar. In the wake of the Mother and Child fiasco, just before the inter-party government collapsed in 1951, he brought off a manoeuvre reminiscent of President Ronald Reagan's attempt to influence the future by packing the Supreme Court with extremely conservative nominees. He arranged with McGilligan, then Minister for Finance, that the outgoing secretary of the Department of Education, Michael Breathnach, who was due to retire that year, should be retained for two more years, and not only nominated Breathnach's successor, L. O'Muirithe, but O'Muirithe's successor, Tomas Ó'Ráifeartaigh, as well, thus influencing departmental policy until Ó'Ráifeartaigh retired in 1968.[17]

How did Lemass succeed in breathing change into these structures? The answer is that he proceeded, like bankruptcy, in two ways, gradually and suddenly. The bankruptcy illusion is not entirely inapposite, because de Valera's bankruptcy of policy, beyond a literally blind determination to cling to power, only left Lemass with some seven years of productive leadership in him. But when he did achieve office, he was fortunate in having two 'feelgood' factors going for him. Externally, personalities and events were to assist in both Lemass's task and the liberalisation of Ireland. For Catholic Ireland, the fact that Pope John would take over in the Vatican was to be of immense significance. In America, the emergence of John Fitzgerald Kennedy in the White House was a watershed for the Irish, both in the US and in Ireland. In America, his accession to power marked the triumph of the Irish over the forces of nativism and the WASPS. The effects of the GI Bill of Rights were to be seen in the growing numbers of second-generation Irish achievers in the professions. In Ireland, it was his style which counted, good-looking, young, elegant, professional, using nomenclature that made politics seem relevant to both the parent and the teenager with the guitar.

The guitar had a particular relevance in Ireland, because the sixties were the era in which the peculiarly Irish phenomenon of the fleadhs, festivals of traditional Irish music and song, impacted on the startled countryside. The word impacted is used advisedly. As the youth of the sixties poured out of the major centres to provincial towns like Mullingar in County Westmeath to enjoy the music, a combination of alcohol and the open air resulted in the Dionysian tradition prevailing over that of Savonarola. For youthful Ireland it was a case of Move over Woodstock. Arise Mullingar and take your place amidst the Nations of the Earth. Other forms of music also led to a lessening of Savonarola's shadow. The showband craze swept the country, and a number of star acts and performers like Dickie Rock, or Brendan Boyer and the Capitols, stepped on to first the Irish and then the international scene. Young people disported themselves in their tens of thousands as if the bishops' pastorals on the evils of dancing had never been issued. The coming of television, a relaxation of censorship, and an increase in prosperity all played their part.

Initially Lemass had to make haste slowly. De Valera hung on as long as he could. Although his resignation had been announced on 15 January, Lemass did not become Taoiseach until 23 June, after de Valera had been safely elected as President and removed to Aras an Uachtaráin in the Phoenix Park. 'Parked!' proclaimed a *Dublin Opinion* cartoon, showing him sitting on a bench in the park. The delay proved, if proof were needed, that it was the necessity to blanket the bad publicity from Noel Browne's *Irish Press* revelations that prompted de Valera's unusually early telegraphing of a political move.

For his part, Lemass telegraphed what his policy as Taoiseach would be in a keynote speech to the Dail on 3 June 1959, which was in effect a wake-up call to his party and the public:

> The historical task of this generation, as I see it, is to consolidate the economic foundations of our political independence. These foundations are not by any means firm enough to be certain of their permanency. The task of consolidating and extending them cannot be postponed. It has got to be done now or in the years immediately ahead of us. This, I believe, is the crucial period in our attempt to build up an Irish state which will be capable of maintaining permanent independence. If we fail, everything else goes with it and all the hopes of the past will have been falsified. But, if we succeed, then every other national problem, including particularly the problem of partition, will become a great deal easier of solution.

By way of smoothing Lemass's path, or more accurately, in an attempt to ensure that the departure of de Valera's towering presence from Fianna Fáil did not result in a similar fall-off in popularity, the improvement in the economic situation was utilised in the budget introduced by Jim Ryan. Not for him a MacEntee or a Sweetman hair shirt. Old age and blind pensions were increased, as were a range of other pensions in the military and public service, and income tax was cut by sixpence in the pound. This, and an improving economy, guaranteed a domestic feelgood factor, along with those taking shape outside the country. Nevertheless, Lemass felt it necessary to move cautiously when naming his first Cabinet. He later revealed that he would have liked to make Ryan Tanaiste, but felt it necessary to appoint MacEntee, the 'senior minister', code for 'senior critic', and equally importantly, a darling of the Fianna Fáil grassroots. He also had to be careful about Frank Aiken, whom one wing of the party saw as being more in the de Valera mould than the pragmatic, managing-director figure of Lemass. Accordingly, Aiken stayed in External Affairs.

Lemass did manage to bring in some new blood, partly by letting some of the old. The abrasive Gerald Boland was replaced in the Cabinet by his equally abrasive but less colourful son, Kevin. Dr Patrick Hillery, who had intended giving up politics to return to his Clare medical practice, had his arm twisted into taking over the hot potato education portfolio. Jack Lynch, one of the most famous hurlers of the century, was appointed Minister for Industry and Commerce. Another new face at the Cabinet table was Neil Blaney, the Donegal-born son of a Fianna Fáil founding father. The man who was to prove the most colourful, and abrasive, of them all, Charles J. Haughey, Lemass's son-in-law, was appointed Parliamentary Secretary to the Minister for Justice, Oscar Traynor.

According to Haughey himself, the fact that he was Lemass's son-in-law caused Lemass to give him a piece of advice rooted in his own experiences. He told him that as Taoiseach he was offering the job, and as his father-in-law he was urging him that he would be a fool to take it. It is probable that Lemass did say this, for although he had achieved much, Lemass had also been deeply wounded throughout his career by politically inspired gossip. His fondness for poker, in particular, had led to wildly inaccurate tales of gambling debts, which in turn were alleged to have made him susceptible to bribery and corruption. The reality is indicated by the fact that Lemass, on his retirement, never took a piece of paper with him. Nevertheless, no one was able to find anything in the files to accuse him of. But it is also true, and this could have been an early indication of Haughey's ambition and skill as a manipulator, that Lemass had wanted to appoint a rural deputy, Seán Flanagan, from Mayo, as Parliamentary Secretary, but the Dublin TDs objected and demanded a Dublin appointment. What, or who, sparked the demand is not clear, but Haughey got the break and Lemass subsequently altered the system of choosing parliamentary secretaries, which traditionally had been left to the parliamentary party, so that the Taoiseach appointed them henceforth.

Winding up the debate on the nomination of his governmental team, Lemass struck a note which was to be the *leitmotiv* of his term in office:

Personally, I believe that national progress of any kind depends largely upon an upsurge of patriotism – a revival of patriotism, if you will – directed towards constructive purposes. Patriotism, as I understand it, is a combination of love of country, pride in its history, traditions and culture, and a determination to add to its prestige and achievements.

These ideas were to be augmented by frequent use of terms like 'optimism', 'confidence', 'modernisation' and 'development'. But the idealistic Lemassian rhetoric was accompanied by a hard-headed, no-nonsense approach. For example, he also told the Dail, during the 1960 budget debate:

I am not at all sure that the main weakness in the Irish character, if there is any weakness at all, is an undue disposition to be sorry for ourselves. I personally hold the philosophy, which I think applies to nations as well as to individuals, that once you start getting sorry for yourself, you are finished.

From the outset Lemass was a convinced European, which both de Valera and many members of his party were far from being, because of a whole range of issues, a principle one being neutrality. Nevertheless, as a passionate poker player, he knew how to mask his hand, and told the Dail (in 1960) that it was too early to even think of joining Europe, and that a trade agreement concluded earlier in the year (on 13 April) with Britain was 'the keystone of our external trade structure'. No matter what emerged 'from discussions about European trade . . . the preservation of the chief characteristics of that agreement must be a main objective of that policy'. This statement, while being far more direct than anything de Valera would have said concerning the Anglo-Irish relationship, nevertheless served to stifle any criticism about a too precipitate advance into Europe, which to many a Fianna Fáil backbencher appeared on an intellectual map marked 'Here be Dragons', a place filled with strange beings like Socialists, Liberals, and people who used contraceptives and did not subscribe to the principals of patriarchy. It would not be until July 1961 that Lemass told the Dail that Ireland would apply to join the EEC, but even then he was careful to point out that membership would only follow on Britain's applying to join first. Lemass knew that if Britain went in, Ireland could not stay out, and that even if EEC membership did not materialise, the development of the European Free Trade Association (EFTA) meant that whatever happened in Europe, protectionism was finished, but the serum of this unpalatable truth had to be injected carefully into that large section of the Fianna Fáil body politic which had literally grown fat on protection.

As Lemass veered on, tacking towards the twentieth century, careful not to provoke mutiny amongst a crew that contained strong yearnings for the nineteenth, he was aided by the high degree of disorganisation and inefficiency which prevailed on the opposition benches. James Dillon, his wartime outspokenness forgiven, if not forgotten, had taken over as leader of Fine Gael on 22 October 1959. A week later Pope John assumed the papacy, but despite Dillon's ex-cathedra oratorical style, no link should be assumed between the two events. What had happened was that an inconsequential bout of soul-searching within the party following its defeat in the 1957 general election was given a new and sharper focus by Lemass's emergence at the head of Fianna Fáil. Fine Gael parliamentarians had a very poor attendance record at the Dail, certainly compared to the attention they gave to the lucrative careers at the bar followed by many of them. According to his biographer, Maurice Manning, whose more assiduous attendance record led to his being appointed the senate leader of Fine Gael, Dillon, for a time, considered appointing 'an informal Whip in the Law Library in an attempt to improve matters'.[18] The leader of the party had no secretarial or research facilities, and the public image of the party's Dail deputies was of a largely part-time collection of businessmen, farmers and lawyers who, if they did show up in the Dail, only did so after the day job was over.

Compounding all these manifest drawbacks was the fact that the party's leadership was split. Mulcahy was the party leader, but Costello was the parliamentary leader. Mulcahy was at this stage 72 years of age, and both wanted to retire and saw clearly the defects of the dual leadership situation. When he announced his retirement (on 17 October 1959) the front bench decided that his successor should be a full-time leader, both of the party and in the parliament. Costello, a popular figure with the majority within the party, although this did not include the forceful Gerard Sweetman, could have succeeded Mulcahy, but he was not prepared to give up his law practice. According to Manning, he sent a letter to a parliamentary party meeting, saying:

> My carefully considered opinion was, and is, that it is wrong in principle in a small democracy, where average incomes are low, that a leader of a party in opposition should necessarily be a person whose economic circumstances permit him to devote his whole time to party and parliamentary work. Others may legitimately hold different views, but it is not a matter on which to make a serious issue. My own circumstances are such as not to permit withdrawal from my professional practice.

He concluded that since a majority of his colleagues did not share this view, 'I should, as I do now, relinquish my position as leader of the opposition.' Dillon was subsequently elected by a considerable majority over the other leadership contestant, Liam Cosgrave, a son of W.T. Cosgrave. But as Manning notes drily: 'The voting figures were not announced [a tradition which Fine Gael still maintains], and the news release after the meeting indicated that Dillon's election had been unanimous; it failed even to mention the fact of Cosgrave's candidacy. It would not do, apparently, to let the public think that Fine Gael had engaged in anything as vulgar as an election contest.'

As readers can deduce for themselves, these gentlemanly proceedings did not indicate either a willingness or an ability on the part of the main opposition party for anything as vulgar as winning an election against the bare-knuckled Fianna Fáil Party. If anything, the position on the Labour benches was worse. The winds of change, and his age, caused William Norton to step down as leader on 26 February 1960, to be succeeded a week later by Brendan Corish as the leader of a party which John Horgan described as exhibiting

> many of the tendencies of a political organisation which had become very set in its ways ... the party could not hold a candle to its competitors in organisational, financial or professional terms. The party was not in fact organised at all in the accepted sense of the word, in that it had no central register of members, no income worth speaking of, and a tiny staff.[19]

Although Corish said at the party conference that year (in October) that Labour would 'weld together all progressive forces', and apparently proved that he meant what he said by teaming up with Noel Browne, the party then proceeded to shoot itself in the foot by guaranteeing that it would not be in a position to join with any force, progressive or otherwise. Unhappy with its experiences of inter-party government, Labour adopted a resolution guaranteeing that it would not join a coalition with either Fianna Fáil or Fine Gael, thus effectively excluding itself from a chance of sharing power, however diluted, and ensuring that for the next decade the Irish electorate could have any choice of government it wished, so long as it chose Fianna Fáil.

Within Fine Gael there were those, led by Declan Costello, a son of the former leader, who had been elected to the Dail in 1954, who sought to modernise the party. But as an election neared in 1961, they had made so little impact on the party's decision-taking process, or progress in developing distinctive policies, that Lemass was able to stigmatise the party with some justice as 'a lost tribe wandering in the wilderness, wandering around in circles', which would never get out of the wilderness until it had made up its mind to pursue definite policy objectives. The one policy different from those of Fianna Fáil which Fine Gael came up with before Lemass called a general election in September was a proposal to replace the compulsory element in teaching Irish. Henceforth, the emphasis was to be on inducement, rather than denying leaving certificates and matriculation certificates to students who failed Irish in these examinations.

The election was called in an atmosphere of some excitement. The power workers at the Electricity Supply Board had gone on strike, triggering off power cuts and an emergency recall of the Dail from its summer recess on 1 September so that legislation to force them back to work could be passed. A threatening situation immediately developed, because if striking workers were sent to jail, there would have been not only increased power cuts, but a general strike. However, this prospect concentrated minds wonderfully, and a frenzied bout of bargaining and an improved pay offer defused the situation on 7 September. Lemass went for the jugular and called an election the day after. But at that stage, the heat went out of both the labour situation and the campaign, and incredibly enough the main issue in the election turned out to be the Irish language. In the absence of de Valera, Fianna Fáil lost eight seats, while Fine Gael gained seven, and Labour four. Clann na Talmhan, the Farmers' Party, returned with two seats; Noel Browne and his colleague Jack McQuillan, now styling themselves National Progressive Democrats, held their two seats, Clann na Poblachta its one, and there were six independents. With Fianna Fáil down to 70 seats, Labour's decision to go it alone effectively decided who would govern. Four of the independents opted to support Lemass rather than face another election, even though Lemass made it clear that there would be no bargains, no deals as the price of their support.

Despite his reduced majority, Lemass had become Taoiseach in his own right, and was in a position to set about making major changes. He had already declared his intention to improve the education situation. Speaking in a debate initiated by Noel Browne on the linked issues of raising the school leaving age and making post-primary education available to children of all economic brackets, Lemass said that: 'The aim of government policy is to bring about a situation in which all children will continue their schooling until they are at least fifteen years of age.'[20] The sparks from the Mother and Child controversy were still flying, but already the new faces in Fianna Fáil were beginning to take a more independent line in matters which affected Church-inculcated attitudes. Jack Lynch began the process by rescinding the ban on married women teachers in 1958. A principal reason for its imposition, apart from the economic argument that a married woman having a husband to provide a livelihood should not keep an unmarried person out of a job, had been based on clerical objections to the unseemliness of having a pregnant woman in a classroom with impressionable children. Because of this objection, and any other handy stick which lay about to beat off change, the Secretary of the Department of Education, Tomas Ó'Ráifeartaigh, had been engaged in a fool's errand scuttling between the Government and the hierarchy for several fruitless months before Lynch, as he told me himself, became fed up and simply introduced the change, without suffering any crozier-induced repercussions. He also set in train a number of other reforms, restoring cuts in grants, and tightening up safeguards in the use of corporal punishment.

These incremental changes do not appear large today, but they marked a significant break with other holders of the office. Other 'new men' in Lemass's various Cabinets who followed in Lynch's footsteps as Ministers for Education, Dr Patrick Hillery, George Colley, Donough O'Malley and Brian Lenihan, introduced a series of reforms right across the educational spectrum, in primary schools, vocational schools, secondary schools and third level, and introduced innovations such as 'comprehensive schools'. One of the civil servants who exerted a considerable influence on educational policy at the time, Seán O'Connor, described the Lemass era to me: 'Lemass was a godsend. He brought in all these hungry young men, madly ambitious, out to make names for themselves, and they shook the place up.' A combination of the built-in conservatism of the Department of Education and the influence of the Church dictated that the governmental approach be slow and cautious. O'Connor told me that at the time the Department of Education was 'full of nuns and priests', too slow and too cautious for Lemass. On 20 May 1963 Hillery made a speech foreshadowing a wide-ranging set of reforms right across the educational spectrum. Much of what he indicated was to transpire, but not for several years and not until the number 13 proved a lucky one. On 13 July 1966, Lemass took a decisive step towards speeding up the pace of reform by appointing Donough O'Malley as Minister for Education. A Limerick engineer who in his day had been a first-class rugby player and who had set the seal on a middle-class education with the customary stint at Clongowes, O'Malley was a colourful character who built up a pyrotechnical reputation in his earlier years before he stopped drinking. A story told about him illustrates both something of this reputation and the quick-wittedness he brought to bear on his potentially explosive portfolio. A friend tackled him one day about reports that he had wrecked a fish and chip shop in the course of a fracas the previous night during which a woman had allegedly been kicked. O'Malley listened politely to the lurid tale, and then simply said: 'You're wrong. It wasn't me.' His friend was persisting that he had it on good authority that it was O'Malley when the future minister interrupted him, asking: 'How much damage was done?' 'A lot,' replied the friend, 'at least £500.' 'There!' O'Malley exclaimed triumphantly. 'I told you it wasn't me – if it was me it would have been at least £5,000!'

As O'Malley's predecessors from Lynch onward cautiously inched forward under the watchful eyes of the various vested interests in education, amongst whom none was more interested, or imposingly vested, than the ever-vigilant John Charles McQuaid, Archbishop of Dublin, a time bomb ticked away out of public gaze which had the potential to blow away the forces either of change, or of reaction. This was a committee established in 1962 by the economist Patrick Lynch, under the auspices of the OECD, to examine the Irish educational system. The committee's genesis lay in an OECD conference held in Washington in 1961 on 'Economic Growth and Investment in Education'. From it resulted a series of studies in a number of countries including Austria, Britain, Holland, Norway, Sweden – and Ireland. These wide-ranging studies were paralleled by similar projects in the underdeveloped countries of southern Europe under the Mediterranean regional project. This international background meant that in 1965, when Hillery took the bold step of publishing the Lynch Committee report, it could be presented not as the perverse brainchild of one aberrant figure, as the Mother and Child Scheme had been, but as part of the general move outward and upward necessitated by Ireland's decision to join the EEC.

In the event, the report, 'Investment in Education', proved to be of a significance to education comparable to Whitaker's on economics. Indeed, one could argue that its effects were more long-lasting, although one would hardly have happened without the other. The report convincingly demonstrated the failures in the existing system, highlighting the huge dropout rates and the inequality of educational opportunity, both geographical and economic. Children in remote areas, or in disadvantaged families, were far less likely to get an education than those sited in good educational catchment areas or in well-to-do families. The children of the social groups most beloved of advertisers, the ABC category, contributed 68% of those who sat the leaving certificate examination in 1963, and 85% of those who entered university. The report had generated much discussion and behind-the-scenes negotiation but not a great deal of concrete action by 13 July 1966, when Lemass decided that it was time to cut the Gordian knot and transferred O'Malley from Health to Education.

O'Malley, a tall, good-looking man, who generated a considerable force field, cut corners and cowed the bureaucracy; the conservative but mild Ó'Ráifeartaigh was understood at the time to have been almost terrified of him. O'Malley startled and thrilled the nation, just two months after he had been appointed, by announcing at a seminar hosted by the National Union of Journalists in Dun Laoghaire on 10 September that he was introducing a scheme to bring free secondary education within the reach of all, and a free transport system to facilitate children in accessing the scheme. Later, by way of good measure, he followed this up with a proposal to 'end an insidious form of Partition on our own doorstep' by merging Trinity College and University College in one multi-denominational university in Dublin. The audacity of O'Malley's 'full-frontal approach' may be gauged from the fact that at the time the bishops decreed that it was a mortal sin for a Catholic to attend Trinity without the permission of his or her Ordinary. One of the few shared facilities between Trinity and UCD was that of veterinary medicine at the Veterinarian College in Ballsbridge, Dublin. However, as in the view of Archbishop McQuaid, and other like-minded members of the hierarchy, the teaching of biology had a moral basis, the Trinity and UCD students studied their animals separately, so that those involved were said to study 'a Protestant cow', 'a Catholic cow', 'a Protestant horse', etc. Apart from the opposition of figures like McQuaid, the universities were themselves opposed to the merger and this idea ultimately foundered.

O'Malley slighted Lynch as Minister for Finance in making the 'free' education announcement, as it had not been discussed in Cabinet, nor had Cabinet sanction been obtained for his proposals. Whitaker too was horrified:

It is astonishing that a major change in educational policy should be announced by the Minister for Education at a weekend seminar of the National Union of Journalists. This 'free schooling' policy has not been the subject of any submission to the Department of Finance, has not been approved by the Government, has certainly not been examined from the financial (whatever about the educational) aspect, and therefore should have received no advance publicity, particularly of the specific and definite type involved in Mr O'Malley's statement.[21]

But the 'free' scheme announcement was part of the 'kicking civil servants out of the way' process which had Lemass's private support, as it accepted[22] that he had seen O'Malley's speech in advance. It is true that it is also suggested, notably by Lemass's biographer, John Horgan,[23] that O'Malley only gave Lemass a very general indication of what he intended to say. But it is also true that Lemass believed that as 'part of the art of political leadership ... one of the methods by which a head of a party or the head of government leads his party along a political line of action is to speak in public in favour of a line of action before the government or party has decided on it'.[24]

Although they generated immense controversy, what became known as the O'Malley Reforms also generated immense popularity. Great improvements were effected in the physical condition of what Childers had termed 'appalling schools'. Regional technical colleges were developed, and the groundwork for a mushrooming in the numbers receiving secondary education was established. For example, vocational schools, which hitherto had been largely technical schools, were transformed by allowing them to prepare students for the final school examination, the leaving certificate. Hitherto a barrier to their competing with Church schools had been enforced by only allowing them to offer classes up to intermediate certificate level. All this was not achieved without cost. Seán O'Connor described to me how, on the morning he was supposed to confront Archbishop McQuaid with the department's proposals for change in the secondary schools system, he suffered a heart attack. O'Malley himself actually died of a heart attack (in 1968). But somehow public episcopal opposition on the lines of the Mother and Child Scheme was avoided. The conventional political wisdom, certainly that conveyed by O'Malley's colleagues of the period, was that peace was preserved for a number of reasons: partly because the hierarchy realised that the bishops' power was something which could easily become diluted through overuse in the wake of the Noel Browne fiasco; partly because O'Malley was operating under a supportive Taoiseach and with a single strong party behind him, and partly too because, unlike the English public-school-educated Browne, who had come from a poverty-stricken background, O'Malley was from an assured, well-off family. Moreover, for all his urbane charm, he was also a smoke-filled-backroom brawler, whose sartorial style and political skills would, had he been born in America, have carried him into a high place in the rankings of the legendary Irish-American bosses stretching from the days of Tammany Hall to the Kennedy White House.

However, despite all these factors, the power of Mother Church was not that easily circumvented. The Trinity merger never went through, and the general assumption for this was that the staffs of the two colleges proved themselves more inclined to preserve their vested interests than to tear down an 'insidious partition' in Dublin. I noticed while talking to Seán O'Connor that while he did not venture any criticism of O'Malley, as befitted a loyal civil servant, he nevertheless pointedly gave most credit for the educational shake-up to Patrick Hillery, who had had the nerve to publish the 'Investment in Education' report, although it criticised his own department. This was something, O'Connor ventured, that 'no other Minister' would have dared to do. It emerges that the postponement of the merger and many of the concessions made to the Church in order to get the 'free' education scheme through may have stemmed not from O'Malley's resolution but from a want of it. A revealing document in the handwriting of John Charles McQuaid, dated 2 May 1967, throws a different light on O'Malley from that of the crusading minister normally portrayed. The document is McQuaid's personal note of what transpired between O'Malley and the bishops at what Dr McQuaid described as 'a delightful conference'.

McQuaid had given a lunch for the Bishops of Galway, Down and Connor, and for Professors Hogan and Tierney of UCD, at which the merger situation was discussed, and it was enthusiastically agreed that a single new university would be 'ideal, with TCD as we know it eliminated as far as possible, as a single identity'. With agreement reached, Hogan and Tierney withdrew, and at three o'clock, O'Malley and Ó'Ráifeartaigh arrived. The gathering was joined by the Bishop of Cork, and 'very explicit and friendly' discussions continued until 6.05 p.m. The Archbishop noted that it was 'a delightful conference', and that the Minister agreed 'again and again that there must be one university, and one authority, the Senate, while the Governing Body would be merely administrative'. McQuaid put it to O'Malley that his plan envisaged that 'Trinity, while it existed in name, was yet totally extinguished as we know it', and O'Malley admitted that that was his purpose.

McQuaid noted that while O'Malley 'did not minimise the subtlety, the intense activity of TCD, the very many difficulties to be overcome, especially at the beginning and for some years to come', he allowed that 'Trinity had to be preserved in name and identity', and that it would not be 'in any sense a corporate institute carrying out its ancient traditions and hostilities'. Not surprisingly, McQuaid's note says of this: 'We all agreed', but their lordships went on to express doubt about the 'optimism' which O'Malley expressed in thinking that 'in five years the commingling of students would have given the Catholic Irish a complete dominance' over Protestant students.

The bishops emphasised (and O'Malley agreed) concern about 'the Weak Irish Catholics who would show their tolerance by yielding to Protestants', the significance of the composition of the University Senate previously discussed at lunch emerging. O'Malley volunteered that he felt that 'the government and UCD nominees would outweigh TCD nominees'. The bishops agreed that the new Senate should have seven nominees each from Trinity and UCD, seven from the Government, and that McQuaid's idea of having the Lord Mayor and City Manager as ex officio members be adopted. McQuaid and the bishops were unanimous that it was 'all important' to site arts, 'the really formative subjects', meaning philosophy, literature and history, at UCD.

Therefore, in order to avoid 'fatal quarrels' between the two universities, O'Malley, not the universities, should choose where the various faculties should go. The bishops made it abundantly clear why they wanted the Minister to take this prerogative. McQuaid's note reads:

> I urged that as the Minister had declared his scheme which now must be accepted and which TCD knew well meant its extinction in its present exclusiveness, so he ought to declare where each Faculty is to be sited, always maintaining that Arts be sited in Belfield.

The Minister and Secretary agreed to the proposal with its prospects of extinction for Trinity College Dublin, and took leave of the bishops, with O'Malley saying that he 'only wished to do what we thought to be right'. As he accompanied this assurance with the promises to meet their lordships as often as they wanted, it is not surprising that McQuaid's note on what could have been an absolutely crucial meeting in Irish university history concludes: 'He could not have shown greater goodwill, good humour and realistic grasp of the difficult task before him.'

In the event, O'Malley's premature death and the administrative difficulties involved in pushing through the merger put an end to the bishops' hopes for the 'extinction' of Trinity, but McQuaid's note, each chiselled line exactly separate from the next, survives as an invaluable illustration of the realities of Church–State relations in Ireland 16 years after the Mother and Child Scheme controversy.

Apart from education, Lemass's reign was notable for two other major initiatives, one on Northern Ireland, the other on the EEC. Ireland applied to join the EEC on 31 July 1961, but ran into difficulties, largely because of the position on neutrality which remained officially what it had been under de Valera. So long as partition lasted, Ireland could not participate in a military alliance. However, as EEC membership became a real possibility, Lemass had to address the political implications of joining the Community. He did so with skill, determination and guile. No Americas Cup helmsman could have tacked, trimmed and, ultimately, sailed a winning course more successfully. He began from the traditional de Valera standpoint, by telling the Oxford Union that 'the removal of partition would make possible a fresh approach to consideration of the place of a reunited Ireland in the scheme of Western defence'.[25]

Much backing and filling later he had advanced along the course to a point where, at the Fianna Fáil Ard Fheis (on 10 January 1962) he successfully carried a motion in support of his EEC policy and, pointedly, the Government's 'approach to international affairs in general'. Addressing the Ard Fheis he said:

> Membership of the Common Market is open to those nations which accept the political aims which inspired it. A movement to political confederation in some form, is indeed a natural and logical development of economic integration. Henceforth our national aims must conform to the emergence, in a political as well as in an economic sense, of a union

of Western Union States, not as a vague prospect in the distant future but as a living reality of our own times.

Change the context and you change the problem! Decoded, this passage meant that the national aims of ending partition and of creating a self-sufficient, unitary state, as defined by Fianna Fáil at its inception, and the issue of confederation, long opposed by de Valera, were now being re-evaluated in the light of changing European conditions. These sentiments went down well amongst Ireland's prospective EEC partners without seriously ruffling feathers at home. Then, using the ploy which six years later would see O'Malley putting up blood pressure by announcing a huge departure in educational policy apparently without the full knowledge of the Taoiseach, Lemass had a sounding balloon launched the following month from an unlikely hand, that of the Minister for Lands, Micheal O'Morain. Speaking at a Fianna Fáil function in his native Mayo, where the issue of neutrality was, literally, somewhat remote, O'Morain stated that as between communism and freedom 'neutrality is not a policy to which we would even wish to appear committed'. In order to share the benefits of EEC membership, he said, 'It may be necessary for us to share any political decisions for the common good.'

The speech set the heather blazing, not merely for what had been said, but because, as the *Irish Times* pointed out, what appeared to be an important policy change was announced not in the Dail, but in far off Mayo. While the statements concerning NATO membership emanating from Irish governmental circles were read with approval in Europe and Washington, they resulted in tough questioning in the Dail. Lemass was conscious of the fact that he was under threat not merely from the opposition benches, but also from those in his own party who had always mistrusted him, largely because he was not de Valera, and from those who felt that what was involved was the slaughter of what, post-World War II, had become one of the party's most sacred of sacred cows, the neutrality policy.

But the poker-playing Lemass had one ace up his sleeve: unlike most of his critics, he literally knew what he was talking about. He had read the NATO Treaty and he was aware that there was nothing in it that forced the Republic to abandon its position on partition. After a month of controversy in the wake of O'Morain's test balloon, he was confronted in the Dail on 8 March 1962 by Jack McQuillan, who at the time constituted 50% of the Dail membership of Noel Browne's National Progressive Democrats Party, to state precisely what NATO membership meant. Did it mean that Dublin had to recognise partition as Lemass and de Valera had averred over the years, or did the recent noises emanating from Fianna Fáil mean that both gentlemen had been talking rubbish? Lemass batted the delivery to the boundary with the following disarming reply:

I confess I never read the text of the North Atlantic Treaty until it became necessary for me to do so when certain questions were addressed to me in the Dail regarding its provisions. I had no occasion to study it earlier. When I did read it however, and came across the article which had been interpreted over the years as implying that accession to the Treaty would involve some implication in regard to Partition, some undertaking to do nothing about Partition, I began to ask myself was it wise in the national interest that we should persist in forcing that interpretation on the Treaty article.

The relevant wording of the Treaty does of course imply the recognition of existing boundaries of member states – 'the territorial integrity' as it is termed – but as all it calls for in the event of a threat to said integrity is consultation amongst the parties, Lemass's dexterous use of language was justified. However, it was all love's labours lost, or at least postponed, when de Gaulle vetoed the British application in January 1963. 'A temporary setback and not . . . a final breach' was Lemass's reaction. (Ireland was eventually admitted to the EEC in 1973.)

Lemass placed the country on an EEC footing; tariff cutting, which had commenced just before the de Gaulle 'non', was continued. The setting up of two important committees deserves to be noted, as do two significant reports. The committees were the Committee on Industrial Organisation (CIO) set up on 30 August 1961, and the National Industrial Economic Council, inaugurated on 9 October 1963. The CIO's brief contained a central principle: 'Searching, uninhibited and objective surveys of industries are the only kind worth undertaking as a serious preparation to the realities of participation in the European Economic Organisation.' The small-scale nature of the Irish industrial arm at this stage may be gauged from the fact that one firm alone, Guinness, paid 25% of the excise duty raised in the country, and with 4,000 employees was Ireland's largest private employer. The series of reports which began to flow from the CIO commented adversely on the Irish industrial landscape. The committee found that Ireland suffered from excessive diversification, low standards of management and business methodology, even lower standards of design, and, in the wake of protection, a widespread unawareness of the lack of competitiveness of Irish industry and the requirements of competition and free trade. These findings resulted in a number of industries setting up 'adaptation councils' which resulted in the CIO's criticisms being addressed over time.

The National Industrial Economic Council was

> charged with preparing reports on the principles which should be applied for the development of the national economy, and for the realisation and maintenance of full employment at adequate wages and reasonable price stability, and reasonably long term equilibrium in the balance of external payments.

Its reports had a marked effect on national policy. Two which emerged in the Lemass era deserve mention: the report on manpower published in July 1964, and the report on economic planning published in June 1965. The former led to the setting up of a manpower authority with some idealistic and unattainable objectives such as a policy for giving workers job satisfaction, but also with some tangible goals which were met in the fields of training, vocational guidance, and adjustment to the inevitable dislocation caused by the drive to meet EEC requirements. For example, the small and inefficient Irish car assembly plant was an early casualty of EEC conditions. The report on economic planning effectively marked the beginning of the end for the 'programming' era, and emphasised the need for more detailed planning than anything seen before in Ireland. The report emphasised the obvious, but hitherto overlooked, and certainly unobserved, requirement for closer communication between employers and unions, and between industry and departments of state.

A principal concern of the Lemass era was the trade union movement. In the mid-sixties, there were some 100 trade unions in Ireland. Most of them were organised more along craft than 'industrial' lines. There was a good deal of poaching of membership, demarcation disputes, and difficulties between British-based unions and native Irish unions stemming from the setting up of the state. Irish unions had been set up in the unrealised expectation that the British unions would depart the scene as had the British army and civil service. The movement was further weakened by the dispute between William O'Brien and James Larkin, and by the border, which meant that many northern trade unionists joined either British unions or exclusively northern ones. However, from 1959, when the Irish Congress of Trade Unions (ICTU) was inaugurated, the trade union movement gained in cohesion and strength and became a major force to be reckoned with in all economic planning and development.

The glittering prospect of EEC membership fuelled expectations in the trade union movement, as it did in the rest of the economy, and initially Lemass helped to boost such expectations. He told the Dublin Chamber of Commerce that higher wages were not incompatible with competitiveness, and lectured employers whose idea of generating efficiency and competitiveness was 'limited to turning long faces to their workers when they propose wage increases'.[26] National wage agreements were negotiated between ICTU and the employers' association, the Federation Union of Employers (FUE), under the auspices of a national employer–labour conference. However, though wage increases multiplied, EEC prospects worsened, and in February 1963 the Government was forced to issue a White Paper, 'Closing the Gap', calling for wage restraint.

Domestic competitiveness had not increased, though tariffs continued to be cut, and imports to rise. Wage costs soared, rising by 17% in the period 1960–4. Emigration fell (from approximately 44,000 in 1961 to around 12,000 in 1964), thus creating a growing pool of manpower which was added to by the continuing flight from the land. Some 40% of the children of farmers left farming during the period 1951–61. This trend would continue to accelerate rather than decrease. A change in the method of calculating statistics by the Central Statistics Office turned up the inconvenient fact that employment, instead of showing a small increase in 1961 and 1962, as had hitherto been assumed, was in fact falling, and the requirement for new jobs by the end of the decade was nearly double what had previously been forecast, some 15,000 a year rather than the 7,000 or 8,000 projected.

Throughout the sixties there were strikes in practically every section of the economy: banking, the newspaper industry, the Electricity Supply Board, building, industry and the postal service. Industrial peace was not furthered by the introduction in the 1963 budget of a sales tax of 2½%, known as the 'turnover tax'. There was a pay freeze in the public service and a bus strike in the month in which the tax made its unpopular appearance.

Few people would have given Lemass much chance of achieving harmony in that climate. But after a protracted negotiation that continued through most of 1963, he succeeded in January 1964 in brokering a deal between trade unions and employers, one of the largest in the history of the state, 'the twelve per cent' as it became known. It was inflationary, but it helped Lemass to win two crucial by-elections, in Cork and Kildare, the following month. In Cork, a Fianna Fáil TD, John Galvin, had died, and in Kildare, Labour's William Norton had passed away. With the aid of a revitalised electoral machine powered by the new men, Blaney, Haughey and company, Fianna Fáil performed with all the ruthless efficiency of the early thirties and won both polls, the Kildare victory being especially significant as it gave Lemass an extra seat.

However, the approach towards the unions rankled with one old-guard Fianna Fáil minister, Patrick Smith, who took umbrage at efforts to resolve a two-month-old building strike which had broken out despite the 12% wage deal, and resigned, the first time in history that a Fianna Fáil minister had stepped down over a policy issue. Smith hoped to gain massive publicity by sending his letter of resignation to the press (on 7 October 1964) and calling a press conference. His letter stated that

> It is not necessary to go into any great detail on my reasons for taking this action since these have been repeatedly stated and discussed at one time or another at Government level. We all, I know, at one time or another made some effort to resist tyranny in all its forms, but when we are faced, as we are now, with not only a tyranny but a dishonest, incompetent one, matters become much more serious for the country. I say dishonest because of the utter disregard by the unions and their alleged leaders of the National Wage Agreement, entered into freely and generously, a few months ago, supposed to last for a period of two and a half years; incompetent because of the complete indiscipline of their union members and their own utter lack of leadership. Making agreements with such is a fraud. If proposals for such are recommended by the leaders, it is always a certainty that they will be rejected. If they are approved they are too weak even to try to enforce them.

Lemass, however, stole the headlines. Before replying to Smith, he reshuffled his Cabinet, moving Haughey from Justice to Agriculture, thereby transferring public interest from the dull, departing and very rural Smith to the urban Haughey, the personification of the new breed of Fianna Fáil politician whom I christened the Men in the Mohair Suits.

The Smith resignation had a significance beyond the fact that it was a first. On the one hand it highlighted something of a rural–urban divide in Fianna Fáil, partly occasioned by the fact that the farming community perceived Lemass as a city man with little interest in farming problems. Farming leaders felt, as did Smith, that unions were drawing off resources which should have gone to the country. On the other hand, the Smith resignation is a handy reference point for indicating the growth in a series of attitudes and activities which would later bedevil the Irish political system in general, and Fianna Fáil in particular: arrogance, corner-cutting, creeping corruption, and short-sightedness. A number of issues may be cited to indicate these trends, with which Haughey was, and would be, intimately connected.

In his maiden address to the Dáil, Haughey said that the trouble with Ireland was that 'too many people are making insufficient profits'. He opined that:

> It would be well for this country from every point of view – and particularly from the point of view of the weaker sections of the community – if our industrialists were put in a position where they could make adequate profits, which would ensure their continuation in business and their being able to finance further expansion.[27]

As Minister for Justice he showed both toughness and pragmatism in a dispute within the Garda Síochána that was to have far-reaching implications for both conditions and discipline in the force. Against Haughey's orders, Gardai gathered at the Macushla Ballroom in Dublin on 5 November 1961 to discuss a pay increase which had been refused. Haughey then had the names of many of those who attended taken down by officers stationed outside the ballroom. The Gardai retaliated by refusing to either direct traffic or issue parking tickets. Eleven of the leaders of this action were dismissed, and Haughey issued a statement saying that he would examine Garda complaints provided he received an assurance from the Commissioner that discipline had been restored throughout the force. That was the public, inflexible face of Haughey. Privately Mohammed went to the mountain – Haughey saw Archbishop McQuaid secretly and got him to intervene.

The issue was diffused when McQuaid, after taking soundings, announced that he was sure that matters could be resolved and discipline restored provided the Department of Justice carried out an investigation into the Gardai's claims. Haughey responded by having the dismissed 11 reinstated, and dropping disciplinary proceedings against others. He announced publicly on 13 November that the fact that a guarantee had been given by the Archbishop was good enough for him, and that he was satisfied that full discipline had been restored to the force. The ensuing years would yield many reasons for doubting that statement, but there can be no doubt that the influence of what in effect became the Gardai's trade union, the Garda Representative Body, was enormously strengthened.

Another nasty incident involving the Gardai occurred the following year.

One-way streets had recently been introduced in Dublin, and a Garda stopped Donough O'Malley driving the wrong way up O'Connell Street, obviously under the influence of drink. Somewhat flustered by the size of his unexpected catch, the embarrassed guard, James Travers, asked: 'Minister, did you not see the arrows?' 'Arrows?' replied O'Malley. 'I'm so drunk I couldn't see the fucking Indians.'[28] However, the humour went out of the incident following the resulting court case. Travers was transferred, and when he refused the clearly vindictive change in his duties he was told to choose between dismissal or resignation. He opted for resignation. The hearing of the case also had objectionable features. As had happened in other similar, potentially embarrassing cases, O'Malley's misdemeanour was heard outside the normal hours of court sittings, with no journalists present.

However, John Healy, a journalist whose career was later to intertwine with those of Haughey, O'Malley, and the mohair-suited section of Fianna Fáil, got wind of the case and wrote a story, accompanied by a double-column picture of O'Malley, which was printed in the last ever edition of the *Evening Mail*, which had run into financial difficulties. The edition subsequently became a collector's item. Healy had a burning sense of indignation at the neglect of his native Mayo by successive governments which had led to wholesale emigration and decay. He would subsequently write two minor classics about the depopulation process and the struggle for existence on a small western farm: *No Body Shouted Stop* and *Nineteen Acres*. He had a nose for new trends, and when he worked on the *Evening Press* in the late fifties and early sixties pioneered coverage of two developments which indicated that Irish society was at least becoming sufficiently affluent to allow a degree of leisure other than in conventional pastimes such as football and horse racing. These were angling and amateur drama, the latter involving as many as 700 groups in the annual All-Ireland drama competitions, the former introducing thousands of people to the realisation that the, at that time, unpolluted Irish coasts, rivers and lakes afforded some of the cheapest and best fishing in Europe.

Healy also introduced a new style of political journalism to Ireland. His 'Back-bencher' column in the *Sunday Review* contained an unprecedented formula of irreverence, inside information, gossip and pungent comment. When 'Back-bencher' transferred to the *Irish Times* under an outstanding editor, Douglas Gageby, who had also been Healy's editor at the *Evening Press*, it became a force in Irish political life, largely as a result of leaks (and subsequent publicity) to Healy by Haughey, O'Malley and Lenihan. Political journalism improved in all the newspapers and in the new TV station, thereby giving a new bite and openness to public debate. This process was greatly furthered by the proceedings of the Second Vatican Council, which was called by Pope John XXIII on 11 October 1962. Given the importance of religion in Ireland, the fact that cardinals and bishops were disagreeing openly over hitherto *verboten* subjects like sexuality, contraception, the role of the laity and episcopal authority had an extraordinarily potent effect. As in the political sphere, the effect was heightened by the fact that a new form of religious journalism had appeared. In the *Irish Times* and *Irish Independent*, two notable correspondents, John Horgan and Louis MacRedmond, reported on the Council in a forthright, lucid fashion which stimulated a new spirit of independence amongst thinking Catholics. Religious debate quickened also through the efforts of two outspoken Dominicans, Father Fergal O'Connor and Father Austin Flannery. Both priests appeared on television and wrote articles, both in the secular press and in religious journals such as *Doctrine and Life*, edited by Flannery, which pricked consciences over the lack of social justice in Ireland.

The new thinking even touched the hierarchy. In Kilkenny, a courageous and hard-working bishop, Peter Birch, influenced by the example of the French Canadian philosopher Jean Vanier, who set up hostels for the homeless, braved the conservatism both of his peers and of sections of the laity by setting up the Kilkenny Social Services Centre, involving young people in the care of the weak and disadvantaged within their community. Birch also encouraged the career of an Order of Mercy nun, Sister Stanislaus, whose work for the homeless both with him and subsequently with an organisation she founded, Focus Point, made her the Irish equivalent of Mother Theresa. The new mood in the country would be illustrated in a rather unpleasant role reversal when priests began to find themselves under attack from politicians. Both Flannery and O'Connor were criticised by Fianna Fáil ministers for raising uncomfortable questions about issues such as housing, a problem which no Irish government can be said to have dealt with completely satisfactorily throughout the century.

The post-war housing drive had reached its peak in the mid-fifties, with Dublin Corporation managing to build 4,784 houses in the year 1956–7. By 1961, a combination of the drive towards industrialisation, which resulted in foreign industrialists seeking houses for their workers, the accelerating flight from the land to the cities, and the demands of newly married couples had rendered the housing situation one of near crisis once more. The extent of the problem was drastically highlighted in the month of June 1963 when, over a ten-day period, three tenement houses in Bolton Street and Fenian Street – an ironic address in view of the Republican ideals of equality espoused by those whom the street was called after – collapsed, killing four people. Dublin Corporation was forced to evacuate 367 other houses which were in a dangerous condition, thereby putting 1,189 extra *families* on the housing list. The Government produced a White Paper, 'Housing Progress and Prospects', which set an annual target of approximately 13,000 new houses, which in fact was never met.

But out of the air of crisis there was born a number of initiatives which, to say the least of it, produced mixed results. A high-rise scheme at Ballymun, in the Dublin suburbs, had imaginative plans for a garden centre, swimming pools and other amenities. But while the high-rise buildings were commenced in 1965, work on the centre didn't begin until five years later. The high-rise buildings were eventually found to give rise to all the problems associated with such projects in other parts of the world, alienation, crime, aesthetic deprivation, and sheer hardship. If the lifts failed, which they frequently did, tenants, often elderly people or single parents, had to lug coal, groceries or babies up 10 or 15 flights of stairs. Other housing estates begun in the 1960s in Dublin, Limerick and Cork also suffered from design problems and lack of amenities, and over the years were plagued by crime and unemployment. One such housing development, the Kilbarrack Estate in north County Dublin, is the setting for Roddy Doyle's novels, *The Commitments, The Snapper* and *The Van*, in which Doyle's humour and his gift for catching working-class Dubliners' indomitable will to survive makes the fictional 'Barrytown' appear a lot more appealing than the reality. In later years, corruption and a flouting of the planning laws would make the housing issue one of the running sores on the Irish body politic.

But the principal source of street protest in the mid-sixties was not housing but Haughey's handling of the two major farm disputes. In the first, on 27 April 1966, the Irish Creamery Milk Suppliers Association (ICMSA) placed a picket on the Dail to further a demand for higher milk prices. The Government responded in Macushla fashion, and, of all pieces of legislation, utilised the Offences against the State Act, intended for use against armed subversives, to arrest the 28-strong picket. The ICMSA, led by John Feely, responded by increasing the size of the picket, with the result that 78 picketers were arrested the next day, and 80 more the day after. However, there was a presidential election campaign in progress at the time, and, despite the fact that Haughey, as Director of Elections, had managed to censor RTE's coverage of the Fine Gael candidate, T.F. O'Higgins, de Valera's candidacy was proving a lot less effective than expected. In view of the importance of the farmers' vote to Fianna Fáil, Haughey caved in and conceded price rises to the ICMSA.

De Valera squeaked in by a handful of votes. His opponent's campaign had been severely damaged by the lack of electronic coverage. Haughey had argued successfully with RTE that as de Valera's role as President placed him above politics, he would not be campaigning, and therefore to cover his opponent's campaign would be unfair. In fact, de Valera was 84 and nearly blind, and so could not have campaigned anyway. But RTE caved in to Haughey's pressure. Haughey then proceeded in effect to renege on the agreement by having his ministerial colleagues travel around the country, making announcements about forthcoming improvements, which were covered and helped to boost the Fianna Fáil campaign. Meanwhile, though de Valera did not actively campaign himself, much favourable publicity was generated for him by virtue of 1966 being the 50th anniversary of the 1916 Rising, and pictures of its most famous survivor at commemoration ceremonies were used liberally in both the print and electronic media. De Valera grandchildren making their first Holy Communions also provided valuable photo opportunities for their grandfather.

Haughey's news management interacted with another farmers' dispute later in the year. This time, the farming organisation concerned was the National Farmers Association (NFA), representing beef interests. Because of the setback on EEC membership, Irish beef exporters became heavily dependent on the British market, as, during April, the EEC raised tariffs on beef supplied from outside the Community. Again the presidential election played a part. As his biographer T. Ryle Dwyer has pointed out, instead of warning farmers of the inevitable fall in prices that lay ahead, Haughey had painted a rosy picture of the prospects for agriculture. The picture darkened suddenly when on top of the EEC tariffs, a British seamen's strike prevented the shipment of cattle to England. At the strike's end, a huge backlog of cattle had built up, creating a glut in the market. Demand for Irish cattle was further lessened when a credit squeeze prevented British interests from acquiring and keeping cattle long enough to claim subsidies.

None of this was Haughey's fault, but the NFA president, Rickard Deasy, angered at Haughey talking up the cattle industry at a time when he knew it was facing difficulties, used the NFA's annual general meeting in August to say harsh things about the Minister. Haughey riposted by cancelling a planned meeting with Deasy and other farm leaders, and made a bad situation worse the following month by telling the Dail (on 29 September) that in the face of falling prices, farmers should hold on to their cattle until the market improved. This was not how the NFA saw the situation. Their response was to tell their members to get out while the going was good, as prices would continue to fall. Understandably, RTE aired Haughey's comments, followed by the NFA statement. But Haughey flew into a tantrum at the *lèse-majesté* involved in a mere farming organisation's statement being carried in a manner which seemed to contradict his advice. He phoned RTE, had the statement deleted in subsequent broadcasts, and took his war with both Deasy and RTE a stage further by refusing to appear on one of the new, more outspoken political programmes, *Divisions*, to debate the cattle situation with Deasy.

RTE riposted by screening the programme with a reporter giving Haughey's side of the argument. Haughey was furious at the idea of anyone but himself explaining his own policy in his own way, and again protested to RTE, saying: 'I emphatically reject the right of any person not authorised by me to do so, to purport to outline the policy of this department.'[29] Had this principle been accepted, the national broadcasting station would of course have been debarred from giving any interpretation other than that of the politician concerned on matters of Government policy. At this stage, Lemass's resignation was only a matter of weeks away, and Haughey's hubris probably cost him his chance of succeeding him as Taoiseach. For, in order to force him to meet them, Deasy and a group of other NFA men set out on a 210-mile march to Dublin from Bantry in County Cork on 7 October. By the time the march reached Dublin on the 19th, it had swelled to huge proportions. But, following a rally outside Government Buildings, Haughey still refused to meet an NFA delegation. Deasy and eight of his colleagues retaliated by camping outside the Department of Agriculture for three weeks, until Lemass took a hand and brokered a deal whereby it was agreed that the incoming government would meet the farmers.

A further development in Irish politics around this time which deserves to be mentioned, and which also involved Haughey, was the foundation of a fund-raising organisation known as Taca (variously translated as meaning either 'a gift' or 'support'), which supporters of Fianna Fáil were invited to join on payment of £100 a year. Those who had joined were big businessmen, principally involved in the building industry and property development. The resultant suspicions of corruption formed an undercurrent in Irish political discourse, fuelled by a remark of George Colley's to a Fianna Fáil youth conference in Galway in May 1967, at which he told his hearers that they should not become 'dispirited if some people in high places appear to have low standards'. As Colley and Haughey were known to have fallen out, it was widely assumed that he was targeting Haughey. However, because of the Irish libel laws, such allegations and innuendoes remained an undercurrent, until, as we shall see, they flowed into full and unlovely view in the 1990s, when many prominent figures, including Haughey, found themselves before a number of judicial tribunals investigating corruption.

These developments would have appeared remote to the point of impossibility during the 1960s, however. Even though spin-doctoring and the manipulation of media to boost political image at the expense of the reality behind the myths had made their unwelcome appearance, a general trust in the political system and a belief in authority still existed. Although the times were changing, these factors continued to sustain Lemass and Fianna Fáil in the last days of Lemass's tenure in office. In 1963, politics and public life generally received a shot in the arm through the Kennedy visit, and some of the glow that spread through the country in the wake of the adoring crowds that greeted Kennedy wherever he went rubbed off on Lemass, who also received more favourable publicity when he paid a return visit to Kennedy in Washington a month before the President was assassinated. To this writer at least, the real significance of Kennedy's visit to Ireland, and the hopes unleashed by new men and new policies, lay in the episode of the Kennedy tree. He planted an oak in Aras an Uachtaráin, close to a mature towering oak which had been planted by Queen Victoria in the course of a visit during the famine which had impelled his ancestor, Patrick Kennedy, from Wexford to America at a time when the Aras was the Vice-Regal Lodge. As I stood beside the lithe, stylish young President as he planted the sapling, it seemed to me, as to Ireland in the sixties, that all things were possible, and that dreams could come true. However, the sapling died, and Kennedy was assassinated the following winter.

By way of further underlining the fact that new politics and new ideas were not to take root in Ireland just yet, despite the many manifest changes, there then burst on the public a thoroughly unpleasant little drama, with Frank Aiken cast in the role of villain. A combination of his civil war background and his admiration for Eamon de Valera led him to an unfortunate donning once more of the censor's robe which he had worn during the war. A booklet put out by the Department of Foreign Affairs, in March 1964, was found to have suffered an extraordinary distortion of the facts in its historical section. All mention of Cosgrave and Griffith was eliminated. Neither the foundation of the state nor that of the national parliament was mentioned; instead, the foundation of Fianna Fáil was trumpeted as the century's main political event. The only star figure of the 1920s political firmanent to twinkle was Eamon de Valera. As *Facts about Ireland*, in all other respects a good guide-book, was an official publication, of which 56,000 copies had been circulated, the historical omissions created widespread controversy before the booklet was withdrawn, after a heated Dail debate, rewritten and republished.

Yet Lemass's popularity held up, as a general election grew nearer and the economic situation suffered a nasty knock in October 1964. Harold Wilson came to power in Westminster at the head of a Labour administration, discovered that he had inherited a disastrous balance of payment situation from the Tories, and introduced a 15% imports levy. Given Ireland's near total dependence on the British market, the levy both served to worsen the Irish economic situation and underlined, if underlining were necessary, how dangerous it was for Ireland to be utterly dependent on her British trade. Lemass accurately described the levy as a breach of the 1938 Anglo-Irish Trade Agreement and a 'real body blow'.[30] By way of helping to improve Anglo-Irish relations, Wilson subsequently took a step which foreshadowed much of the cosmetic nature of British policy approaches towards Ireland when the north erupted later in the decade. In February of the following year (1965) he directed that Roger Casement's remains be removed from their prison resting place and returned to Ireland as Casement had wished. As some of the prisoners who were detailed to perform the unearthing of Casement's bones subsequently gave interviews in the media which indicated that no one had any accurate idea of exactly where the unfortunate patriot had been buried, and that the principal object of the exercise had been to put together a suitable skeleton, Dublin gallows humour had it that the remains, which were received in Ireland with great emotion at a dignified state ceremony in Dublin attended by his surviving comrades, including de Valera, were in fact those of the executed poisoner Dr Crippen.

The continuing ineptitude of the opposition parties apart, the factor which sustained the popularity of Lemass and Fianna Fáil as economic clouds gathered came from an unlikely source: Northern Ireland. Whitaker had met Captain Terence O'Neill, who had succeeded Basil Brooke as Prime Minister of Northern Ireland in 1963, at world bank meetings, and had become friendly with both O'Neill and his private secretary, Jim Malley, a former RAF ace. By 1964, when Wilson took over, it was obvious from Lemass's general demeanour and the tenor of his speeches on Northern Ireland that this friendship could be built on.

Lemass's basic approach was an irreproachably Fianna Fáil one:

First and foremost we wish to see the re-unification of Ireland restored. By every test Ireland is one nation with a fundamental right to have its essential unity expressed in its political institutions. The unit for self-determination is the whole country and we do not accept that a minority has the right to vote itself out of the nation on the ground that it is in disagreement with the majority on a major policy issue. We cannot and will not depart from that position. We hope that in time a climate of opportunity will be created in which the realisation of our national aim will be achieved in harmony and agreement. To that end it is our policy to develop closer and more neighbourly relations with Northern Ireland and to promote economic co-operation for the mutual benefit of both parts of the country.[31]

But in one of his first speeches on becoming Taoiseach, Lemass had told the Dail (in July 1959) that his approach would be one of achieving unity by consent. Later that year, addressing the Oxford Union in October, he had asked: 'Is it not common sense that the two existing communities on our small island should seek every opportunity of working together in practical matters for their mutual and common good.'[32] These remarks, and others like them, had fallen on stony ground where Brooke was concerned. But now Harold Wilson was sympathetic to a number of Lemass's ideas for co-operation in areas such as transport and power, and through both personal inclination and political awareness, O'Neill was also well disposed towards an improvement in Belfast–Dublin relationships. He realised that the Six County regime could benefit from some favourable publicity, particularly with the Unionists' traditional allies, the Tories, now out of office, and an unpredictable Labour Government installed in London. Even the Tories thought that the Unionists should have used Lemass's accession to power to improve relationships with the Republic. O'Neill also realised fully that in stretching out a hand to Dublin he was taking a very considerable risk that it might be chopped off, and that the sword would be wielded not from the southern but from his own side of the border. However, he took the risk, and thereby helped to quicken explosive forces for change which were already building up within his statelet.

The details of the historic Lemass–O'Neill meeting are well documented. Malley arrived in Whitaker's office on 3 January 1965 bearing an invitation to Lemass to visit Stormont, and went to visit the national gallery while Whitaker took the invitation to Lemass personally, who accepted it immediately. None of the ministers, including Aiken, with whom Lemass later consulted, raised any objection, and on the 14th, Lemass and Whitaker met Jim Malley at Killeen Customs Post, on the main Dublin–Belfast road between Dundalk in the south and Newry in the north, and drove with him to Stormont. O'Neill returned the visit on 9 February. Nothing was supposed to have leaked out before Lemass entered Stormont, but a group of people were at the entrance to throw snowballs at the entourage. This apart, the revelation that Lemass had gone north was greeted with equal measures of surprise and delight. The visits were enormously popular in the south, and initially received a general welcome in the north also. But presciently, O'Neill, as he subsequently pointed out repeatedly to interviewers, including the present author, replied to Lemass's remark, as both men made use of the Stormont Castle toilet facilities, that he would get into terrible trouble over the visit: 'No, it's I who will get into trouble.'

Many commentators have subsequently seized on a remark O'Neill made to Conor Cruise O'Brien to explain how his troubles came about. O'Neill told O'Brien that he suffered from a backlash amongst Unionists at Nationalists displaying tricolours and holding commemorations to celebrate the 50th anniversary of the 1916 Rising. A more important source of O'Neill's difficulty, however, lay in the small group of protestors who had received a tip-off about Lemass's arrival and were making known their displeasure as his car drove through the Stormont gates. Ian Kyle Paisley was just beginning to become well known.

In the course of an interview I conducted with O'Neill at Stormont in October 1965, well before the 1916 commemorations, he and Malley spoke of their fears about the damage Paisley could cause to plans for any improvement in north–south relations, or to a spread of the ecumenical spirit being fostered by the Vatican Council. Both men stressed the power of the Bible in Northern Ireland and the potent use Paisley made of that weapon, appearing both at protest rallies and on platforms with a copy clenched firmly in hand as he preached disaffection.

Paisley, and what he would wreak, lay ahead, however; the problems of the economy were to hand, and to prevent himself being swamped by them, Lemass used the popularity of his northern initiative to call a general election for 7 April 1965.

Unexpectedly, although the economy dominated the election campaign, it was not the major focus of political interest. This was created by a rebirth of political initiative on the part of Fine Gael. Declan Costello, operating almost single-handedly, succeeded in persuading the party to adopt a new blueprint, the Just Society.[33] His principal backer was Patrick McGilligan, whose reputation since the 1920s, and his remarks about starvation, had been somewhat unjustly cast in a light analogous to that of Marie Antoinette and the quotation attributed to her about eating cake. Dillon had been lukewarm about Costello's reforming ideas, which were energetically opposed by the conservative Gerard Sweetman, but Costello won the support of two future taosigh, Liam Cosgrave and Garret FitzGerald. At the time the latter was making a name for himself as a freelance journalist. As a result of Dillon's hesitancy, and opposition within the party, Costello's ideas were not adopted until well after the campaign had started.

On 18 March, Costello's blueprint, the Just Society, was formally launched as the party's election manifesto. The Just Society proposed a free medical service, control of the commercial banks' credit policies, an incomes policy which would both ensure the growth of incomes and guard against inflation, the establishment of a Department of Economic Affairs, more expenditure on housing and social amenities, improved treatment for the medically handicapped (a brother of Costello's was so challenged), improvements in the medical service which would include the abolition of a means test, and many other reforms, all of them predicated on the idea that 'equality of opportunity' was to be the goal of education. The ideas proved popular with the electorate, and would have proved more so had it not been for the divisions within the party, prompting Dillon to issue a statement on the day the Just Society was launched, reassuring the faithful that Fine Gael remained 'a party of private enterprise'.[34] The statement caused many members of the public to assume that Fine Gael had not really moved from the right, from being the vehicle of expression of big businessmen and big farmers, and also prompted Garret FitzGerald to decide against standing as a Fine Gael candidate.

The forces of opposition further shot themselves in the foot when Brendan Corish, the Labour Party leader, reiterated the party's no-coalition policy, thus effectively guaranteeing that Fianna Fáil would return to government again supported by independents. But while the 1965 election did not result in a change of government, it did result in a qualitative shift in Dail membership. The nature of Irish politics was such that it sometimes appeared that successful Dail candidates acquired testamentary rights to their seats. In an accelerating trend, out of the 37 by-elections fought between 1944 and 1961, ten were contested by close relatives of the former deputy. Of the six fought between 1961 and 1964, all were successfully contested by close relatives. But in the 1965 election, the shake-up was such that out of the total Dail membership of 144, only 24 had been TDs at the end of World War II.

The shake-up was so thorough that, although Labour gained six seats, both Noel Browne and Jack McQuillan lost theirs. Surveying the bleak electoral scene, Dillon, who was under no great pressure from his party because of the election result, decided it was time to go. He announced his intention on 21 April, almost immediately after the Dail had confirmed Lemass as Taoiseach by 72 votes to 67. Had he stayed on, Dillon himself would have been 67 by the time the next election was called, and, as he told his colleagues, the position of party leader called for a younger man. Liam Cosgrave was unanimously elected as his successor on the proposal of Sweetman, seconded by Michael O'Higgins. By now, Lemass too was feeling his age, despite the cocky sounds emanating from his Cabinet; after the 1965 election, 'Back-bencher' frequently echoed the Haughey/Malley clique's belief that the Cabinet was 'the youngest and best in Europe'.

This sort of remark accurately catches the 1965 government's spirit of hubris, preoccupation with image, and preoccupation too with the mohair-suited, urbanised philosophy of politics that in its haste not to be seen as backward-looking, also turned its back on things of value. I remember that year, before the election, interviewing Brian Lenihan, who was at the time the junior minister responsible for fisheries. The Irish waters at the time were probably the richest fishing grounds in western Europe. I asked him about the Government's plans for development, if we did secure EEC membership. His reply took the form of questions. Did I know exactly how many farmers there were in the country? No. He rattled off the hundreds of thousands plus, correct to the last decimal point. Did I know exactly how many fishermen, both whole and part-time, there were employed in catching fish? I did not know the exact number. He did. Eight thousand plus, correct to the last decimal point. 'There,' he said triumphantly, 'all put together including the teacher who goes out in the summer in the currach after a few salmon, they wouldn't elect one Fianna Fáil TD on the first count in a five-seat constituency!' I thought of his remarks many times in the years afterwards, particularly one night at the back of the Aran Islands when the Atlantic should have been pitch black. Instead it was lit up like a city by the lights of 65 French trawlers, which had come from L'Orient (as they did every year) to hoover up prawns. At the time of writing, the prawns, like all the other fish in the Irish Sea, have been fished to near extinction. But the fishing rights were bartered away to other EEC members in return for concessions to the powerful farm lobby. In the political calculation of the day, the farmers' numbers, not the long-term development potential of the fertile sea, was the prime concern.

In the wake of the election, Lemass too began making political calculations. Reports that his health was not good began to circulate. He was known to have suffered blackouts, and all around him the problems were beginning to multiply. By mid-1965, the balance of payments deficit was running at an annual rate of some £30 million. A letter of Whitaker's that year painted a graphic and gloomy picture:

> The economic situation is more serious than we have been admitting officially . . . We now have to increase the corrective measures. We should also, without being alarmist, be more forthright about the nature and extent of our problems. We would be deluding ourselves if we continued to make reassuring comments about their temporary nature, by highlighting the cattle shortfall and the British surcharge. There is a basic difficulty of a more lasting character and it is time we did something effective about it.[35]

Eventually, government cut-backs were instituted, and the banks were directed to introduce a credit squeeze. Employment fell, and it became clear that the targets of the Second Programme would not be met. The expected increase of 81,000 jobs proved to be wildly unrealistic, and in fact, in succeeding years, the Programme was quietly dropped. Worse, emigration had begun to climb again. An interesting sidelight, on both the state of the Irish economy, and the degree, or lack, of concern which Mother Church felt towards one of her most dutiful and generous children at this time, was the reaction of the Vatican to a feeler from Dublin. The Department of Finance raised the possibility that the Vatican might consider investing in Ireland, but Lemass was subsequently informed that the Irish Ambassador's investigations had revealed that the Vatican looked upon its investments in a purely commercial fashion.[36] Profitability and security were its guiding principles. Ireland's link with sterling, with its potential for the Irish economy to be

LEMASS: THE WINDOW-OPENER

harmed by any British devaluation, knocked the prospect of a Vatican investment in Ireland on the head. Papal problems aside, within his Cabinet, too, Lemass faced problems unfamiliar to the traditionally tightly disciplined Fianna Fáil Party. He had encouraged his young braves to carve out niches for themselves and to develop habits of initiative and independent thought. As a result, the gallop of the mettlesome mohaired warriors was proving difficult to rein in, and the party as a whole was developing a will of its own. In March 1966, the parliamentary party voted against Lemass's wishes to postpone the local government elections, out of fear that the prevailing economic climate would result in a caning for Fianna Fáil. In addition to all the foregoing, it was the 50th anniversary of the 1916 Rising.

At 67, Lemass realised it was time both to hand over to a new man, and to give him sufficient time to tackle the problems before another general election fell due. As he told his final press conference: 'The 1916 celebrations marked the end of a chapter; as one of the generation, this marked the end of the road for me.'[37] His decision was not generally welcomed within the parliamentary party. Aiken wanted him to stay on so that his nominee for successor, George Colley, who at the time was Minister for Education, would have time to build up a bigger following than Haughey, whom Aiken distrusted. Seán MacEntee, either because a full moon was in the offing, or for some other reason (Lemass had not reappointed MacEntee, then 76, to the Cabinet following the 1965 election), launched a vituperative attack on Lemass, saying that he was 'deserting in the face of the enemy' and that he had squandered the great heritage of Fianna Fáil which de Valera had left him. He too wanted Lemass to stay on for two more years, and urged him to follow the example of leaders such as Franco and Salazar![38] However, Lemass persisted in his resignation, and in the resultant party vote was succeeded by Jack Lynch by a margin of 59 to 19 over George Colley.

Lemass's contribution to Ireland was that he made possible a whole set of new directions, and a new spirit of optimism that prevented the 26 counties sinking into a sort of boggy, poverty-stricken papal state. As his biographer, John Horgan, has pointed out, he was a far deeper thinker than his image as the gruff managing director of Ireland Inc. would seem to suggest. One of his last acts as Taoiseach, if not the last, was to instruct the Economic and Social Research Institute to carry out research into people's behaviour in the new Ireland which he foresaw. He knew that the sort of idealistic nationalism which he and many of his colleagues had brought to public life was lessening in Irish society. Horgan quotes Desmond Fisher, former London editor of the *Irish Press*, who knew Lemass well, as saying:

He predicted great changes in Ireland before the end of the century – contraception and divorce being legalised and materialism becoming widespread because of growing prosperity. Back in 1962 these predictions seemed, at least to me, to be a bit daring. Up to a point, he welcomed changed social *mores*, but I felt that he was a bit pessimistic about a future in which some of the good qualities of the Irish people would be lost or diminished.

It was the first intimation I had got that there was a human being behind what appeared on the surface to be a politico-economic machine.[39]

By the end of the century, the appalling spate of scandals, court cases and tribunals arising out of the activities of some of the men, and the forces, which Lemass had unleashed on the Irish political scene would certainly have justified much of his pessimism. The position of his successor with regard to some of his colleagues and to the situation in the Six Counties would shortly give rise to both pessimism and a loss of 'good qualities'. Jack Lynch had only agreed to Lemass's suggestion that he go forward at the second time of asking, and after overcoming the resistance of his wife, Mairin, which had been the original cause of his rejection of the proposal. Two of his colleagues, Neil Blaney and Charles Haughey, had considered throwing their hats in the ring, but had withdrawn, at Lemass's instigation, when neither of them seemed likely to succeed. Too late they realised, Haughey in particular, that for the first time in the party's history a vote would be taken, and that in these circumstances, both men could have expected to make a respectable showing. The various tensions would interact within a few years to create another unprecedented situation, one in which Lynch would end up sacking both men and placing them, and others, on trial in a Dublin courtroom. To trace the circumstances which led to this, it is necessary to turn our attention once more to events north of the border.

EIGHT

THE GREEN FLICKERS OUT, THE ORANGE IGNITES

(HOW THE SIX COUNTIES EXPLODED)

What might be termed the constitutional Republican developments mentioned earlier, the saga of the rechristening of the Irish state as a republic, and the anti-partition campaign, form the background to the re-emergence of the IRA in the aftermath of World War II. Within the IRA itself, reorganisation had commenced from the ending of internment. The first significant IRA reunion occurred during the 1945 Bodenstown commemoration. Here a number of prominent Republicans, including Anthony Magan, a bachelor farmer from County Meath, and Michael Conway, who had been sentenced to death but reprieved at the last minute, spoke about the possibilities of reorganisation to individual IRA men who were attending the Wolfe Tone commemoration. Both Magan and Conway were deeply religious men of the old school of Irish Catholicism, bracketing Irish culture, patriotism and the Church in their motivating philosophies. Conway later became a Franciscan brother and Magan, who was to be interned a second time during the 1950s, occupied his time in custody by founding a thriving branch of the Legion of Mary.

Their efforts bore fruit to the extent the following year that a meeting was held on 9 March, in the Ardee Bar, in Ardee Street, Dublin, to discuss reorganisation plans. The police raided the meeting, picking up a number of prominent Republicans, including Cathal Goulding, John Joe McGirl, Peadar O'Flaherty and Patrick Fleming. Magan and Conway were also arrested subsequently. But this apparent setback turned into a springboard for the Republicans as documents seized by the Special Branch, which indicated that the IRA was stirring again, were read out in court and reprinted in the *Irish Press*, thus alerting sympathisers around the country to the fact that a new beginning was under way. The publicity surrounding the death of Seán McCaughey, the impetus this gave to the growth of Clann na Poblachta, the trial of a prominent IRA man, Harry White, who had been captured after several years on the run following an incident during the war in which a policeman was shot dead, and his companion, Maurice O'Neill, subsequently executed, all served to bring attention to bear on republicanism and the IRA.

Recruiting began again, drilling recommenced, as did the familiar IRA tactic of infiltrating GAA clubs, Irish language classes, debating clubs, and other such kindred bodies. The Sinn Féin Party came to life again and a newspaper, the *United Irishman*, was published in 1947. Pondering on the lessons of the war years, Magan directed that it be made known that the IRA had no hostile intent towards the Dublin Government. An IRA speaker, Christoir O'Neill, was empowered to state, during the Bodenstown address of 1949 that:

> The aim of the Army is simply to drive the invader from the soil of Ireland and to restore the sovereign independent Republic proclaimed in 1916. To that end, the policy is to prosecute a successful military campaign against the British forces of occupation in the Six Counties.[1]

This statement caused a certain amount of dissension in the ranks amongst those who wanted old scores settled against various agents of the Government for their part in the execution of Stephen Hayes as a traitor, or the wartime executions, or the harsh treatment of IRA prisoners. There was also a certain indiscipline in the 'army' at this stage which led to occasional bombings or the firing of shots at neighbours' houses. None of these led to any loss of life, but Magan cracked down on dissent and indiscipline, and ordered that the Army Council statement for Easter 1950 should declare that:

> In order that no excuse may be provided for using coercion and to define quite clearly that the Irish Republican Army has only one enemy, England, no sanction will be given for any type of aggressive military action in the Twenty Six County area.[2]

This principle would later be formally incorporated into the IRA's 'General Army Orders'. After a raid on Omagh barracks in October 1954, Standing Order Number Eight was worded as follows:

1. Volunteers are strictly forbidden to take any militant action against 26-County Forces under any circumstances whatsoever. The importance of this Order in present circumstances especially in the Border areas cannot be over-emphasised.
2. Minimum arms drill shall be used in training in the Twenty-Six County areas. In the event of a raid every effort shall be made to get the arms away safely. If this fails, the arms shall be rendered useless and abandoned.
3. Maximum security precautions must be taken when meeting. Scouts must always be posted to warn of emergency. Volunteers arrested during training or in possession of arms will point out that the arms were for use against the British Forces of Occupation only. This statement should be repeated at all subsequent Court proceedings.
4. At all times Volunteers must make it clear that the policy of the Army is to drive the British Forces of Occupation out of Ireland.[3]

This instruction remained in force for the rest of the century. Although the Gardai succeeded in inflicting more damage on the IRA, in terms of arrests and the prevention of raids, than did the RUC or the British army, the accepted custom for IRA men, even volunteers bearing arms, when apprehended by Gardai, was to 'go quietly'. The handful of Garda fatalities which proved the exception to this rule were either accidental, or individual acts of deliberate defiance of Army Council instructions. In fact, initially Magan and the IRA leadership of the late forties and early fifties favoured a policy of passive resistance in the Six Counties. Force was to be used only to protect those Nationalists, should the authorities crack down, who took part in an IRA-sponsored scheme to withhold rates. In fact, when the movement began advancing towards a more physical-force-favouring policy, something of a split developed. Michael Traynor wrote to the *United Irishman* (4 January 1949) saying that he was resigning because 'I would not be a party to organising the youth of Ireland to use force for the mere sake of using force'.

The principal leaders of the IRA at this time shared Traynor's reservations about force. Popularly known as 'the three Macs', these were Magan, Tomás MacCurtain and Padraig MacLogan. MacCurtain was a son of the Lord Mayor of Cork, Tomás MacCurtain, who was murdered by a counter-insurgency death squad during the Anglo-Irish war. He too had narrowly escaped execution for his involvement in a case involving the shooting of a detective during the war. MacLogan ran a public house in Portlaoise, which scrupulously observed the licensing laws. Like Magan, he was deeply religious, and kept his IRA documents in a home-made altar. These men and many like them in 'the Movement' wanted to end partition, and believed that Ireland would be better off for breaking the link with England. They favoured vocationalism, were impressed by the papal encyclical Rerum Novarum, and opposed the welfare state because they felt that it destroyed the rights of the individual, who should be free to decide his own economic situation.

However, these views and their war-induced caution about the use of physical force set them apart from the younger men who were coming into the movement, partly as a result of their own organising activities, partly because of the tradition in physical-force republicanism of staging a rising in every generation. As a result, there were three splits in the 1945–55 period, all of which resulted in attacks on the Six Counties, and ultimately forced the hands of the 'three Macs' into launching a large-scale but short-lived series of cross-border raids in 1956. A significant feature of this campaign in the light of what would happen later in the century was the fact that the leadership decided to cut Belfast out of its plans because it was felt that the IRA there was too weak to either protect the Catholics or launch any worthwhile campaign of its own. RUC intelligence was good, and even though hundreds of IRA volunteers could be turned out for a parade, Protestant–Catholic relationships had improved, largely as a result of shared wartime experiences. Moreover, the welfare state was making Nationalists less dissatisfied with the British links. And in a reversal of the war years, when northerners had come south to take over the IRA, the southerners now leading the movement decided that their campaign would take the form of attacking targets along the border, customs posts, police stations and army barracks, not an uprising in Belfast or Derry.

Nonetheless, the first major raid after the post-war reorganisation began was in Derry, on Ebrington Barracks, from which a quantity of arms was seized on 5 June 1951. A second arms raid occurred two years later, this time in England, on 25 July 1953, on Felsted School Officer Training Corps, Essex. Again the raiding party got away with a sizeable amount of armament. However, the arms were recovered and the raiding party's leadership was captured and sentenced to eight years' imprisonment, after police suspicions were aroused by a strange-looking van which drove through Bishop's Stortford with its windows obscured with strips of paper and whitening material. Amongst those arrested were two future chiefs of staff of the IRA, Cathal Goulding and Seán Stephenson, who later changed his name to Seán MacStíofáin. The raid and its aftermath did not generate much publicity or arouse much reaction in Ireland. However, this changed with the IRA's next major operation.

This was the raid on 12 June 1954 on Gough Barracks, Armagh, in which a substantial amount of arms was seized in a daring afternoon raid in which the IRA captured the sentry on duty at the main gate, installed a member of their own party in his stead and, while he marched up and down in approved military style, filled a lorry with arms and got away safely to County Meath, where the arms were dumped. An incident which occurred as the empty lorry was being driven back to Dublin indicates something of the attitude of the Clann na Poblachta-influenced government of the day.

Joseph Christle, who would later lead one of the splits in the IRA, ordered the driver to ram a squad car which pulled across the lorry's path. The squad car managed to drive out of the way in time, but later, when the lorry was being returned to the owner from whom it had been commandeered, two men in it were arrested and subsequently released. A Government statement said that nothing incriminating had been found. In fact, two revolvers had been seized. This raid provided a tremendous boost both to IRA morale and to recruitment. Another barracks raid later in the year, on Omagh Barracks, on 7 October, also generated much publicity, although it went wrong. This time, the sentry was not overpowered, because the IRA party which was supposed to have used knives to silence him hesitated to do so and instead attempted unsuccessfully to club him into insensibility. A number of raiders were captured and sentenced to long prison terms. But again the raid proved to be a publicity bonanza and two of the prisoners, Tom Mitchell and Philip Clarke, were elected to Westminster, though subsequently unseated as convicted felons.

Another unsuccessful IRA raid of the period was that on Arborfield Arms Depot in Berkshire on 13 August 1955. The raiders got away with five tons of guns and ammunition, but many of them, and all of the arms, were discovered within hours of the raid. This time the publicity was heightened by the howls of outrage in the British media at the discovery that the sentries on duty at the barracks were armed only with pickaxe handles. A group of British junior officers doing national service at Rhyl in Wales added to the Arborfield publicity two days after the raid by tying up a sentry at the Royal Artillery training camp and driving off with him in a lorry, pausing only to shout loudly at each other in simulated Irish accents. Coming on the heels of Arborfield, the Rhyl affair created a panic in Britain at the seeming prospect of a rerun of the 1939 bombing campaign. The Minister for War cancelled his holidays, Field Marshals conferred with the Prime Minister, Sir Anthony Eden, and emergency precautions of all sorts had been put into effect before the hoaxers confessed to their practical joke. The affair ended with the War Office issuing an apology to police and public for the trouble and inconvenience caused.

While these events were taking place, the IRA was suffering a good deal of trouble and inconvenience itself, arising from the familiar tendency of the movement to split. The Brendan O'Boyle split proves, if proof were needed, the continuing strength of the physical-force tradition in Irish-American circles. O'Boyle had joined the IRA while he was still a student at Queen's University, Belfast, in 1940. He was captured the following year, and took part in a mass breakout from Derry jail in March 1943. In the period of uncertainty which followed the ending of internment, he decided to form his own group. As he was coming to this decision, Clann na Gael was beginning to reorganise. A combination of FBI surveillance during the war and the fact that the Clann itself had suffered a split over the issue of whether some $30,000 it had accumulated should be spent on a monument to Seán Russell in Dublin, or kept until a new generation of IRA would arise in Ireland, meant that the organisation was in a weakened state when O'Boyle landed in New York in 1952 looking for funds. He knew little about Irish America and went to a meeting of the United Irish Counties Association in the mistaken belief that it would be physical-force minded.

However, he was recognised by a woman who had known him in Northern Ireland, and subsequently introduced to Harry Short from Armagh, who introduced him to other Clann na Gael leaders, notably Tadg Brosnan from Kerry. Eventually a committee was set up to raise funds, and it was agreed, in a break with Clann tradition, that O'Boyle would be placed in command of both his Irish group and the New York revolutionaries. In terms of what O'Boyle's initiative achieved, the story of his expertise in smuggling arms into Ireland makes more dramatic reading than did much of his border campaign. On one occasion, his contacts in the customs service enabled him to safely collect eight containers of arms at Cobh, where transatlantic liners bound to and from America traditionally call. However, communications in those days were not what they are at the time of writing, and O'Boyle didn't realise that there had been a ninth case addressed to him aboard. The ninth case made a round-the-world cruise before the liner docked at Cobh again, and a thunderstruck O'Boyle was phoned out of the blue to be informed that it was waiting for him. Somehow he managed to collect the case without its contents being discovered. But overall, the difficulties in communication and the hostility of the 'three Macs' hampered his campaign and the growth of his organisation. One day in July 1952, his movement was so diminished that to provide cover for an attempt to blow up Stormont telephone exchange, he had to utilise a neighbour and his wife, who, though not members of his group, had agreed to help him. At the last moment the neighbour's baby fell ill, and O'Boyle's wife Carmel volunteered to take the woman's place. Mrs O'Boyle got out of the car with the neighbour while her husband paused for a few seconds to prime the bomb. Something went wrong and the bomb went off prematurely, killing O'Boyle. Mrs O'Boyle was held but not charged, and though the Unionists refused to allow her to attend her husband's funeral, the authorities eventually acceded to a request from Cardinal D'Alton that she be released.

The Liam Kelly split also caused dissension within the IRA, but Kelly's activities resulted in more publicity, and criticism, for the Republicans' cause than almost anything else that happened during the 1950s, until a full-scale IRA campaign was launched in 1956. Kelly was a well-known figure in Northern Ireland, who had been elected to Stormont from mid-Tyrone in 1953, and subsequently sentenced to nine months in prison for sedition. On his release from prison, he wasted little time in building up his own military organisation, Saor Uladh (Free Ulster). He also led a political grouping called Fianna Uladh. His homecoming, to his native Pomeroy in County Tyrone, an area of strongly Nationalist and Republican sentiment, resulted in fierce rioting between supporters and the RUC. Kelly was also one of the two northern senators whom Seán MacBride had nominated to the Seánad, a fact which had a bearing on what followed an attack he led on Roslea RUC barracks, County Fermanagh, on 26 November 1955.

It was thought at the time of the raid, which began at 5.40 a.m. when a mine exploded against the barracks wall, that the main story of the episode was the fact that Sergeant Morrow, who lived in the barracks with his wife and two small children, had single-handedly driven off the raiders with the aid of his Sten gun, and that his colleague, Constable Knowles, who subsequently recovered, was hit seven times by bullets. But then the *Sunday Independent* published a report (on 28 November 1955) stating that one of the attackers had been killed in the raid and had been buried secretly in County Monaghan, following a coroner's inquest. The Government Information Bureau corroborated the fact that an inquest had been held on a man who had died of gunshot wounds, and that a verdict had been returned by a coroner's jury stating that there was no evidence to show how the injuries had been received. Then an *Irish Press* reporter, John Healy, managed to get a sensational interview with the coroner, 77-year-old Dr Thomas Leonard. Leonard revealed that he felt let down by the GIB announcement. He claimed that it had been agreed that no one who took part in the inquest was to talk. His story, which was subsequently verified, was quite extraordinary. The dead man, Connie Green, was an ex-British soldier. He died of his wounds later in the morning of the Roslea attack, having been attended by a local doctor and a priest. The doctor subsequently asked Leonard to hold an inquest, which he explained he could not do without informing the authorities. Later that day, a Garda superintendent called on Dr Leonard to advise him that he would be required for an inquest at eight o'clock that night.

Leonard was duly taken to a farmhouse, where he found the body of a 'fine-looking man' in a coffin, and a six-man jury already empanelled whom he swore in. The inquest was presided over by the superintendent and attended by a solicitor, a detective, the owner of the farmhouse and the doctor who had treated the man while he was dying. During the proceedings, detectives and uniformed Gardai guarded the house. A verdict that death was due to shock and haemorrhage was returned. Leonard made out a death certificate which contained no name of deceased, or any of the normal details such as marital status or occupation. In the age column, he wrote 'about thirty'. Green was buried the next day at Carrickroe cemetery, some 12 miles north of Monaghan, with the full rites of the Church. These extraordinary proceedings, which of course constituted a breach of both law and practice, created a storm of controversy both inside and outside the IRA.

What the public did not know was that Kelly had contacted MacBride with a view to having Green buried without an inquest. MacBride in turn contacted the Minister for Justice, who was now Michael Keyes. The upshot was that it was decided that an inquest would have to be held, but that it could be held in secrecy. Following Healy's revelations, the *Irish Times* published an interview with a barrister who summed up the implications of what had happened as follows:

> Let us take an extreme case. Suppose I and some friends of mine decided to commit a murder. Apparently all we have to do is to take out the victim, shoot him, and bring him to the nearest coroner for an inquest and then to a graveyard for burial. We don't even need to say who he was.

Northern misgivings were considerably sharper. The series of barracks raids had led to a heightened state of alert throughout the statelet, and Healy's explosive interview caused a heated debate at Stormont (on 29 November) during which the Minister for Home Affairs, George B. Hanna, announced the banning of Saor Uladh, and said that:

> The wisdom of our fathers in refusing to join with the South is evident when one considers the procedure at that inquest, which could not take place in any properly conducted community . . . I charge the Government in the South as being morally responsible for the raid.

Lord Brookeborough condemned the south, which had outlawed the IRA but was 'afraid to take action which any civilised country would take to prevent blackguards and scoundrels coming here to commit murder and create antagonism amongst the people'. Significantly, he revealed that he had asked the British Prime Minister to seek an extradition treaty with the Republic. Costello replied to him the following day in the Dail, condemning para-militarism and saying:

We must assert and vindicate the people's right to determine national policy and the right of the Oireachtas and the Government to maintain and to uphold the authority that reposes in them . . .

We are bound to ensure that unlawful activities of a military character shall cease, and we are resolved to use, if necessary, all the powers and forces at our disposal to bring such activities effectively to an end . . .

Significantly, however, he firmly rejected Brookeborough's extradition proposal, saying:

In order to prevent any future controversy or discussion on this point . . . there can be no question of our handing over, either to the British or to the Six-County authorities, persons whom they may accuse of armed political activities in Britain or in the Six Counties.

Fianna Fáil supported Costello in this position, as, predictably, did Clann na Poblachta.

The publicity – and pressure from the IRA, alarmed that Costello's statement indicated the approach of a crackdown – forced Kelly to publish a statement in the Fianna Uladh paper, *Gair Uladh*, on 16 December, accepting responsibility for the raid. The statement also revealed the difference between the IRA and Saor Uladh, saying:

Saor Uladh accepts the Constitution of the Republic enacted on 1st July 1937, and recognises that Oireachtas Eireann is the sole legitimate authority in Ireland.

Saor Uladh is organised solely in the Six Counties. Application of the laws enacted under the Constitution is by the Constitution itself restricted to the Twenty Six County area. It is apparent therefore that these laws are not applicable in the case of Saor Uladh.

The fact of the influence Kelly had been able to bring to bear in the staging of the secret inquest, before six jurors instead of the normal twelve, clearly showed that Saor Uladh was not just 'organised solely in the Six Counties', Kelly obviously did not feel bound by the laws of a state which had made him a senator. The statement, though it did not say so openly, indicated to those in the know that Kelly regarded the northern problem as one to be solved by northerners, with a support base in the north. Magan and the others, however, saw the north as a target to be attacked from the south, which was regarded as the IRA's safe haven and recruiting area. Kelly's campaign ultimately petered out because of lack of support in the north, and because the forces arraigned against him, the IRA and any combination of Republican groupings, were immeasurably stronger than anything the Republicans, with their limited organisation and arms supply, could muster. Kelly, for example, though he caused enormous political repercussions, probably never had more than 50 men under his command.

The IRA itself, however, although still ludicrously weak compared to the

Unionist and British forces, was a more formidable organisation, which proved itself able to put more than three times the total of Kelly's forces into the field, albeit for a very short time. One of the younger men who had joined the movement under the 'three Macs', Charlie Murphy, had become adjutant general of the 'Army', and with a group of other, younger, men, Ruairi O'Bradaigh, Tom Mitchell, Eamon Boyce, Joe Christle and Robert Russell, had built up a significant intelligence network and a far from insignificant military organisation. All these men shared a common interest in the Irish language and Irish history, and had joined the IRA through either a feeling for these subjects or family influence. Murphy, who had a particular aptitude for intelligence, and had managed to photograph the entire Special Branch, creating a card index system containing their names, addresses and telephone numbers, had become attracted to the IRA by the publicity surrounding the anti-partition campaign.

In April 1956, Murphy acquired a new colleague, Seán Cronin, a former Irish army officer, who had emigrated to America and returned to Ireland in October 1955, where he became a colleague of mine on the *Evening Press*. I was unaware as we sat together at the sub-editors' table that Cronin was also working his way up through the ranks of the IRA to join Murphy as one of the two key figures in charge of operations. It was Cronin who provided the blueprint, 'Operation Harvest', for an all-out onslaught on the Six Counties aimed at creating such widescale destruction of communications and military and civilian installations as to make the state ungovernable. Later, after Cronin had been captured and the document read out in court, reflecting on the fact that the man who wrote it had recently worked alongside me, I found the sub-editing of the court case the most blood-curdling copy I had handled in my hitherto uneventful journalistic career.

It fact, however, the document was totally unrealistic for two reasons. The principal one, which rapidly became evident after the IRA launched a concerted campaign on 12 December 1956, was their inability to sustain a large-scale campaign; the second was the Joe Christle split. Christle, who studied law, was an anarchic personality, possessing energy and leadership abilities, who had acquired a public reputation as a cyclist, and founder of the round-Ireland event, the eight-day Ras Tailteann. More privately, he was known in the IRA for being a daring operator. The conservative IRA leadership mistrusted his university student background and his flair for publicity. Moreover the need for secrecy kept Christle out of the small circle which knew that a campaign was being organised. Christle's pressure for a more 'forward' policy found a resonance amongst the younger activists in the movement, but aroused suspicions amongst the leadership that he was planning to take over the movement himself. He was dismissed in June 1956.

The dismissal provoked a split in the ranks in which most of the men on whom Murphy and Cronin had been relying for the planned campaign deserted to Christle. Between June and the December commencement of the campaign, as much energy went into trying to heal the split and get back the weapons Christle took with him as went into implementing 'Operation Harvest'.

In the meantime, Christle used some of the weapons to team up with Liam Kelly in launching a series of joint operations across the border. The largest of these was the first, on Armistice Day 1956, in which the group burned down customs huts all along the 150-mile length of the border. In all, Kelly and Christle probably mounted about a dozen raids, blowing up customs huts, B Special halls, bridges, telephone exchanges and the lough gates on the Newry canal. Christle in fact wanted to seize the town of Newry and hold it until the Irish army and/or the UN would be forced to intervene. Kelly, who was horrified at the prospect of loss of life amongst Catholics, vetoed this suggestion, as he did another of Christle's proposals, that the group should emulate EOKA's tactics of targeting British servicemen by planting bombs in bars and cafés frequented by the soldiers.

Kelly was a traditional Irish Nationalist who had little interest in who ruled Ireland, so long as it was free. Christle described himself to me as a revolutionary socialist who wanted to create a revolutionary situation by the judicious use of violence. In the end, luck, and Kelly's influence, helped to ensure that no lives were lost through the Christle–Kelly partnership which largely petered out after Kelly became disillusioned at the futility of their efforts and went to America without telling Christle.

The officially sponsored IRA campaign, directed by Magan, Murphy and Cronin, began in the small hours of the morning with ten more or less synchronised attacks involving some 150 men, in border areas from Derry to Down. The targets included the BBC transmitter at Rosemount, Derry; Gough Barracks, Armagh; Magherafelt courthouse; various bridges; and the inevitable B Specials hut (in Newry). The explosions and the ensuing gunfire gave the onslaught the appearance of being far more serious than it was. Charlie Murphy told me: 'The place looked like the Western Front. Bombs going off, flames, Very lights, guns, the lot.'

The ensuing denunciations were almost as loud as the bombs. The British Ambassador, Sir Alexander Clutterbuck, delivered an official protest in Dublin. Sir Anthony Eden made a strong statement in the House of Commons, and the Unionists reacted with equal measures of fury and efficiency. The Special Powers Act, which provided for arrest and internment without trial or warrants, was reintroduced on 15 December. Steps were taken to regulate the movement of traffic. Border roads were cratered, bridges blown up and the main arteries left untouched were guarded by large forces of police. The British army units in the north were placed on a state of alert, and 3,000 RUC men and 12,000 B Specials were mobilised. By the time the campaign officially ended in 1962, it had claimed the lives of 11 IRA men and six members of the RUC, cost £1 million in outright damage and £10 million in increased spending on police, military and B Specials. It also had, as we have seen, a direct bearing on the fall of the coalition government in Dublin. But though, throughout 1916, the confusion and uncertainty generated in

Dublin's approach to the IRA, brought about by the Clann na Poblachta factor in government, sometimes offered ammunition to the Unionists' claims that the coalition was soft on the IRA, it was in fact the Gardai who did most to ensure that the campaign never again reached anything like the pitch of intensity achieved on its opening night.

Nor could it have. The fundamental military philosophy behind the campaign was based on Anglo-Irish war books like Tom Barry's *Guerrilla Days in Ireland*, which told of daring raids and ambushes. But in Barry's day the IRA could generally rely on having several hours at their disposal in which to attack a rural RUC station. The 1950s IRA, however, had to contend with the effects of walkie-talkies and improved telecommunications, which brought reinforcements to the scene of an attack within minutes. The RUC were better armed; although the IRA possessed a number of Bren guns, these didn't always function properly, and when they did, they blasted off the IRA's scarce ammunition in such a short space of time that they were of little use in a sustained engagement. This was a factor in one of the most talked-about incidents of the entire campaign, the Brookeborough raid.

On New Year's Day 1956, an IRA patrol attacked the RUC barracks at Brookeborough, operating a Bren gun from the back of a lorry. The attackers had only three magazines for the weapon, which were speedily used up, and the man operating the gun, Seán South, was fatally wounded by fire from the upper windows of the barracks. A resolute defence by RUC Sergeant Kenneth Cordner, who was armed with a Sten gun, also claimed the life of another member of the attacking party, Fergal O'Hanlon, and wounded a number of others, including Daithi O'Connell, who would later become a founder and leader of the Provisional IRA. The party made their escape in the truck, two of whose tyres had been shot off, and whose tipper gears were destroyed, so that the dying, the wounded and those who had escaped injury were frequently hurled from one end of the truck to the other as it tipped up and down during the retreat. South and O'Hanlon were left in an open cow byre in a farmyard near Baxter's Cross, about five miles from Brookeborough. Neighbours were alerted to call a priest and a doctor, and the exhausted raiding party, most of them suffering from bullet wounds of varying degrees of seriousness, managed to cross the Slieve Beagh mountains into County Monaghan, where they were picked up by southern patrols.

The raid and the funerals of O'Hanlon and South unleashed a near tidal wave of emotion in the Republic. O'Hanlon was only 19, a popular figure in Monaghan, for whom he played Gaelic football, and South's character and personality had impressed everyone with whom he came in contact. Irish was his preferred medium of communication; he was deeply religious, an accomplished violinist and edited his own magazine, *An Gath*. The last words he wrote in the magazine's final edition (November 1956) were 'Jacta Alea Est! – there is an end to foolishness; the time for talk has ended.' The funerals of the two men brought thousands to the streets. O'Hanlon had a vast crowd in Monaghan; South's cortegè passed from Monaghan in the north, through

Dublin, where mourners from every walk of life, including prominent figures, walked behind the coffin, and on to Limerick, where it was met by a crowd of some 20,000, headed by the city's Lord Mayor. The following day, over 50,000 people attended the funeral. The numbers become even more remarkable when it is considered that as a result of the Suez crisis, petrol rationing was in force at the time. South and O'Hanlon had joined the pantheon of Irish marchers. To the time of writing, their memory is kept alive by one of the famous rebel ballads 'Seán South of Garryowen':

'Twas on a dreary New Year's day as the shades of night came down,
A lorry load of volunteers approached a Border town;
There were men from Dublin and from Cork, Fermanagh and Tyrone,
But the leader was a Limerick man, Seán Sabhat of Garryowen.

And as they moved along the street up to the Barrack door,
They scorned the danger they would meet, the fate that lay in store,
They were fighting for old Ireland's cause, to claim our very own,
And the foremost of that gallant band was Sabhat of Garryowen.

But the Sergeant foiled their daring plan, he spied them thro' the door;-
Then the Sten guns and the rifles, a hail of death did pour;
And when that awful night was past, two men were cold as stone;
There was one from near the Border and one from Garryowen.

No more he'll hear the seagull cry o'er the murmuring Shannon tide,
For he fell beneath the Northern sky, brave Hanlon at his side.
He had gone to join that gallant band of Plunkett, Pearse and Tone,
A martyr for old Ireland, Seán Sabhat, of Garryowen.

But though the emotions stirred by the Brookeborough raid touched a deep chord in the Irish rebel tradition, it proved to be a dangerous one for the IRA, despite all the sympathy and support the funerals elicited. Hitherto, a combination of Clann na Poblachta's influence and the Government's unwillingness to make martyrs out of the IRA had resulted in something of a blind eye being turned to their activities. Not long before the Brookeborough raid, after the IRA had attacked Lisnaskea Barracks on 13 December, police and army surrounded a house in Knockatallon, in County Monaghan, and, in the early hours of the morning, arrested a group of the raiders which included Charlie Murphy and Seán Cronin. After Murphy had obligingly dismantled a mine which the startled police came on in an upstairs room, the party were taken to Monaghan Barracks, together with a pile of incriminating captured documents. The IRA men had resigned themselves to long jail sentences when, to their astonishment, the police officer who had captured them, in the course of a phone call to Dublin to report his success, was overheard repeatedly saying in carrying tones: 'No, sir, they'd no ammunition!'

The IRA party were then told they were free to go. However, realising the way the wind was blowing, Cronin and Murphy refused to leave until taxis were provided for the main group, paid for by the police. Then Cronin and Murphy were driven to Dublin in a squad car, and walked up Emmet Road in Inchicore, where Murphy lived, in full American army battledress. After Brookeborough, however, things changed.

On 6 January, Costello made a statement on Radio Eireann saying that enough was enough. Three young Irishmen had been killed (as well as O'Hanlon and South, RUC Constable John Scally had been killed on a raid on Derrylin Barracks on New Year's Eve). Relationships between the Republic and Great Britain were deteriorating, and the authority of the Dail was at stake. The campaign could not be tolerated any further, and the police had been instructed to use the Offences Against the State Act to round up all known IRA men. In the days which followed, the police arrested dozens of activists, including the IRA leadership. In the swoop on Cronin's home, his blueprint for putting Operation Harvest into operation, entitled 'General Directive for Guerrilla Campaign', was captured. Even though the scale of activity contemplated by the document was completely unrealistic, apart from causing me sub-editing difficulties of an unusual nature, it provided a sobering antidote in the public mind to the emotion generated by the Brookeborough raid.

The campaign would stagger on for another few years. Occasionally the public would be jolted by news of an ambush, the blowing up of a customs post, or a disaster such as the explosion at Edentubber on the Louth–Down border in which a defective mine killed five Republicans in November 1957. But the crippling effect of Costello's crackdown was heightened by de Valera's return to power after Seán MacBride moved his motion of no confidence on 28 January 1957, castigating the Government for its 'failure to formulate and to pursue any positive policy calculated to bring about the unification of Ireland'. In the election which the vote precipitated, Sinn Féin won almost 66,000 votes, but frittered this advantage, which yielded four seats, because of the party's policy of abstention. De Valera reopened the Curragh internment camp, 60 men being rounded up on a single day, 8 July. By the time it closed again on 11 March 1959, 131 members of the IRA had been placed behind barbed wire. Many leading figures dropped out, including Murphy and Cronin, and, after a brief flare-up during 1961–2, the movement, riven by splits and dispirited at the failure of the border campaign, began turning its attention towards political rather than military activity. On 26 February 1962, the Irish Republican Publicity Bureau issued a statement announcing 'The Campaign of Resistance to British Occupation – all arms and other materials have been dumped and all full-time active service volunteers have been withdrawn.'

Not for the first time in the century, nor for the last, people drew the mistaken conclusion that the IRA was a thing of the past. In fact, the fifties and sixties would later prove to have been the testing ground in which many of the leaders of the Republican movement in the Troubles of subsequent decades were formed. Some of these were very lucky to escape the formative process. A leading member of the Provisional IRA, Kevin Mallon, with another young man, Patrick Talbot, was one such. He owed his life to Seán MacBride, who advised Murphy and Cronin – who had shelved IRA objections to recognising the courts, but had failed in their efforts to get a Dublin barrister to defend the pair – that no Unionist lawyer would take their case, no Nationalist one would have the necessary courage to do so, and the best thing to do therefore was to get an Englishman. He subsequently arranged for Elwyn Jones, later a Labour Attorney General, to defend the two 21-year-olds, who were charged with the death of Sergeant Ovens, who was blown to bits by a mine at Coalisland in County Tyrone. Jones's efforts ensured that the men received prison sentences rather than the death penalty, and they survived to be released when the campaign ended, their trial and the revelations about their treatment at the hands of the RUC having served to etch the Republican legend deeper into the Irish folk memory.

Although the Mallon and Talbot case was the most sensational of the period, another less famous one had a more lasting effect on the IRA and the Dublin Government's attempts to curb the organisation. In a case brought by a former Curragh internee, Gerard Lawless, before the Court of Human Rights, the Court ruled (on 1 July 1961) that it did not have to accept a member country's own opinion as to whether a state of emergency existed within that country sufficient to warrant internment. The Court itself was free to exercise its own judgement as to the extent of the internal crisis, and could rule on the measures adopted. The effect of the judgment was to prevent subsequent Irish governments from resorting to internment again during periods of IRA activity, and they had to use military courts instead.

THE NORTH – TOWARDS ERUPTION

As in the southern part of the island, the developments in the six north-eastern counties had their immediate origins in educational change. The Butler Education Acts of 1944, when introduced in England, applied to the 'UK Overseas' also and helped to create a new political culture amongst the Six County Catholics. In fact, one of the principal protest movements which preceded the outbreak of the Troubles arose out of an educational issue and was supported by both Nationalists and liberal Unionists. It stemmed from the findings of the Lockwood Committee on Higher Education published in February of 1965, which recommended that a new university should be sited at Coleraine in County Antrim, and not in Derry as had been widely expected. Derry already had a university college, Magee, a recognised college of the Queen's University, with 200 students. It had been supposed that this circumstance, combined with the fact that Derry, the second city of the region after Belfast, had a population of 54,000, whereas Coleraine only had 12,000, would make Derry the logical site. However, the Lockwood Committee did not have a Catholic in its membership, and what Catholics suspected became certainty when a Unionist, Dr Robert Nixon, Stormont MP for North Down, revealed that he had been informed by a member of the Cabinet that Unionists had taken a political decision, not an academic one, to site the new college at Coleraine.

The result was an unprecedented, if unavailing, action on 18 February, in which every Catholic school and business premises of any sort in Derry closed down, and a motorcade in which Unionists and Nationalists joined drove to Stormont, some 90 miles away, to deliver a protest. However, the Government carried a subsequent vote by 32 to 20, which nevertheless was one of the smallest majorities ever recorded at Stormont. The statistical basis of discrimination, the manner in which housing formed a vital part of the Unionist armoury in maintaining the apartheid statelet, has already been mentioned. At the time Derry was the worst example of both discrimination and gerrymandering. The Catholics formed two-thirds of the population. To counteract this, the Unionists deliberately ghettoised the communities so that the Catholics were herded into one area, the South Ward, and the Protestants into two others, the North Ward and Waterside. The two Protestant areas were allotted six councillors each, the Catholic South Ward, eight. Thus the Catholic two-thirds majority was converted into a one-third Protestant majority. To complete the disenfranchisement, the property voting system meant that only persons with a business or a home could vote in local government elections. Thus an adult Catholic, living with their parents, had no vote, as they were not a ratepayer. John Hume later recalled researching one of the mayors of Derry at the time, Sir Basil McFarland, who was also the Lord Lieutenant of the city.[4] Sir Basil owned seven limited companies which gave him six votes each. This, with his own vote, gave him a total of 43 votes. This was bad enough, but the Coleraine decision formed part of another Unionist development policy which, in the sixties, a better-educated Catholic population were finding increasingly irksome and unjust.

A definite pattern of discrimination against the predominantly Catholic western portion of the Six Counties, in favour of the Protestant-dominated east, became clearly discernible. In 1964, Derry's rail services were halved, so that that which served the county itself, and the counties of Fermanagh and Tyrone, was withdrawn, leaving the area with no trains. Also in 1964 (on 13 August), Geoffrey Copcutt, an English town planner who had been appointed to build a new town in County Armagh, resigned, saying that he felt that Derry should be developed as a priority on both environmental and strategic grounds. The Unionists, however, insisted that the new town, named Craigavon after their first prime minister, should be sited between the strongly Unionist centres of Lurgan and Portadown. Copcutt had argued that all that was needed was a 1,000-yard expansion of the towns' existing parameters to provide the population targets set for the new city. At the time, the Catholic birth rate meant that with roughly a third of the Six Counties population, the Catholics accounted for 48% of the total number of children attending primary schools. However, only five new Catholic schools were allowed for in Craigavon, which meant that even if Catholics did succeed in getting jobs in the new town, their children might not be guaranteed education.

Perhaps the clearest indication of Unionist intentions to withdraw to a kind of 'fortress Unionism' east of the River Bann lay in the findings of the Wilson Report. Professor Thomas Wilson, a Glasgow University academic, was conceived of as a northern version of Whitaker. He was appointed in October 1963 at the head of a team of government economists to produce a plan for economic development. His report was published in February 1965, and was adopted by the Government, thus guaranteeing that it would interact with the furore generated by the Lockwood Report. Wilson's job and investment targets were admirable. The former envisaged 65,000 new jobs over the next five years, the latter an investment of £900 million in education, housing and industry. However, with one exception, Derry, the ten growth centres stipulated in the report mostly fell within a 30-mile radius in the Unionist-dominated east. They were Antrim, Ballymena, Bangor, Carrigfergus, Carnmoney, Larne, Lurgan, Newtownards and Portadown.

The one power the Unionists possessed to break down the barriers of fear and resentment, of which the foregoing developments were the external sign, was initiative. However, when a Unionist prime minister, Captain Terence O'Neill, who succeeded Lord Brookeborough in March 1963, attempted to show initiative in dispelling old prejudices, his community destroyed him. O'Neill was a direct descendant of Sir Arthur Chichester, Lord of the Plantation of Ulster under James I; the O'Neill surname entered his family by marriage. He was part of the warp and woof of Ulster's Anglo-Irish landed aristocracy. Practically everyone related to him had held political office. His father had been the first MP killed in the 1914–18 war. O'Neill survived World War II, in which he served as a captain in the Irish Guards, but his two brothers were killed. A fundamentally decent man, of middle-rank political abilities, his career was bedevilled from the outset by the relentless hostility of the man he defeated, if that is the correct term, for the leadership. In those days, the Unionist system of appointing prime ministers had about as much, or as little, of democracy about it as that which obtains at the time of writing for the appointment of Roman Catholic bishops. The laity are not consulted (nor are the clergy), and the Papal Nuncio concerned forwards three names to Rome of possible candidates for the Vatican's final imprimatur. In the Unionist case, Brookeborough submitted three names to the Governor General: Sir John Andrews, a son of the former prime minister, and a nonentity; Brian Faulkner, Minister for Industry and Commerce; and Terence O'Neill, Minister for Finance. This was an advance on normal practice, in which only one name was submitted, but it is generally understood that Brookeborough wanted to blanket Faulkner's chances of succeeding him, so that his son, Captain John Brooke, would one day take over. Brookeborough, it is thought, reckoned that O'Neill, unlike Faulkner, would inevitably botch the premiership, and that this might create an opportunity for his lacklustre son to step into the breach.

O'Neill was appointed while Faulkner was out of the country in America, a fact which enraged Faulkner. In addition to Faulkner's enmity, O'Neill immediately had to cope with one of the two reasons for Brookeborough's resignation. One was unfounded: Brookeborough had developed a duodenal ulcer, and not cancer as he feared. The other was only too well grounded: anger at the economic situation, which had caused ten Unionist backbenchers to take the unprecedented step of signing a round robin calling for Brookeborough's resignation. In 1963, it is reckoned that 9.5% of the work-force were unemployed. By way of dealing with this situation, the Hall Committee, a British and Northern Ireland civil service body, issued a recommendation in 1963 which validates the saying that the dromedary was invented by the committee set up to design the horse. It suggested that the unemployed be encouraged to emigrate to the UK mainland, a nostrum which hardly spoke to the problems presented by the world decline in employment in the north's basic industries, agriculture, engineering, textiles and ship-building. In the first three, unemployment levels ran at some 40%. In the shipyards it approached 60%. Average weekly earnings overall were only approximately three-quarters of those in Britain, and almost one-third of the houses in the Six Counties area had no piped water, or flush toilets. This last factor would put an unusual but potent weapon in the armoury of another enemy who, in addition to Faulkner, would arise from the ranks of Unionism to challenge O'Neill – Ian Paisley, who was to generate a considerable following for his campaign against 'dry closets'.

Practically everything O'Neill did was inevitably doomed to bring him into conflict with some element of Unionism. As a representative of the Big House, and the landed gentry class, he aroused suspicions of being somewhat 'other' amongst the Presbyterian mercantile class which Faulkner was particularly well placed to exploit. Paisley represented the fundamentalist, deep Orange opposition to change of any sort, which either was, or could be represented as, 'soft' on Catholics or links with Dublin. Even O'Neill's initially successful attempts to improve the economic situation generated hostility. In attempting to implement the Wilson Report, the Republic's NIEC experiment was replicated, and an economic council was set up, including representatives of employers, government and labour. To facilitate this, O'Neill in effect recog-nised the all-Ireland Congress of Trade Unions (ICTU) by dealing with the Congress's northern committee. As Brookeborough had refused to recognise ICTU, because of its all-Ireland nature, O'Neill's gesture exposed him to attack from some quarters. On the investment front, his decision to accept Wilson's recommendations about attracting multinationals, while it met with considerable success – firms attracted to the Six Counties included ICI, Dupont, Enkalon, Goodyear and Courtaulds – had a political downside. The newer businesses did not respond, as did the old, to the institutionalising of discrimination in the workplace. The multinational employment practices were formulated with an eye to the balance sheet, not the political balance, and Catholic female employment began to rise, to the disquiet of the Orange Order and the Unionist establishment.

This disquiet was fanned by Faulkner and Paisley. Faulkner, like other Unionist politicians, had close links with the Republic, and yet, for political reasons, would on occasion warn against such connections. He attended St Columba's College in Rathfarnham, County Dublin, and much of the produce of his family shirt manufacturing business was sold in the Republic, where, apart from sales generated in the north, his company also for a time actually owned and operated a factory. But as Andrew Boyd has shown, Faulkner, when it suited him, followed the Brookeborough line that 'suggestions that the Ulster government should have direct trade negotiations with Eire constituted an effort to separate Ulster from the United Kingdom'.[5]

Lemass had suggested that the tariffs which the south had erected against the north should be dismantled, as part of a mini free trade agreement between north and south. London too felt that Belfast should be more open to overtures from Dublin, once Lemass took over from de Valera. The Home Office wrote to Stormont in February 1960, saying:

> There are political as well as economic arguments for going such distance as we can in reply to Mr Lemass. With the end of Mr de Valera's lengthy dominance of the Irish political scene, and the emergence of Mr Lemass, himself a business man, at the head of a more business-like administration, the political atmosphere in the South is changing. The metamorphosis will be neither rapid nor dramatic. But already there have been signs that the Dublin government are anxious to move away from the negative attitudes of earlier administrations.[6]

However, Brookeborough persisted in his attitude, telling the Unionist Party a couple of months later that 'the hand of friendship, and this brotherly embrace from Eire, would very quickly turn into a bear's hug'.[7]

Faulkner continued this attitude, even though by the mid-sixties I found that northern industrialists were welcoming what Sir Graham Larmor told me was 'a tremendous improvement' in north–south attitudes. He gave the south credit for 'interpreting tariff regulations in a new and intelligent way'[8] and he felt that Pope John also deserved praise for the change in attitudes he had helped to bring about throughout the Catholic world. In fact, however, the Orange Order had, as it continues to do to this day, served to frustrate attempts to democratise the Six County statelet. The electorate may wish for change within the Unionist Party, but key decisions are taken not by the party leadership, nor even by the Cabinet, but by the ruling Unionist Council. This nearly 900-strong body consists largely of members of the Order, who, to complete their domination, also exercise control through the nomination of a 160-strong block membership of the Council. But Faulkner continued in the Brookeborough vein, telling industrialists (in February 1966) that he was an upholder of 'the principles of the big drum'. The big drum should be beaten, the Union Jack waved, the border and the Orange Order maintained, because, as he said on another occasion, the Orange Order was 'the most democratic body in the world'.

Faulkner's rise to fame had been greatly assisted by his obeisance to the Orange Order, as Minister for Home Affairs in 1955. He sanctioned an Orange march through the Long Stone Road, a Catholic area of South Down, near Kilkeel, even though the march was deeply resented by Nationalists, who, by way of underlining their grievance, blew craters in the road two days before the march. However, not only did Faulkner provide the marchers with armoured cars, police dogs, and 600 armed police, he marched at the head of the procession himself on 12 July. To further make the point, he banned an Irish cultural demonstration which had been scheduled to take place in Newtownbutler, County Fermanagh, a few days later. In 1960, he reversed a decision made by his predecessor, W.B. Topping, who had banned an Orange parade through the strongly Nationalist area of Dungiven, County Derry, on police advice. After the march had been forced through Dungiven, supported by Orange lodges from all over the region, a leading member of the B Specials summed up the situation. The point of the exercise, he said, had been to show that Orange men could march where they liked, there was 'no such thing as a Nationalist district ... Dungiven has been restored to the Queen's dominions'.[9]

Thus Faulkner, from within the Unionist Party, had two strings to his bow as he took aim at O'Neill: his virulently Orange hue and his reputed business acumen, which he used both to gain publicity for successes in bringing foreign investment to the Six Counties, and at the same time to appeal to the fears of those who felt that the newer industries were lessening the ability of the Orange Order to influence employment policies. Employment policies aside, the Order, with its grip on the selection of Unionist candidates at constituency level, and its sizeable block vote on the ruling Unionist Council, was in a very strong position to influence overall political policy.

Outside the Unionist Party, O'Neill had to contend with the baleful influence of Ian Paisley, who did more than any other individual to halt reform and to send the statelet into turmoil. Paisley was born in Armagh in 1926. His father had been one of Carson's Volunteers, and the founder of his own Baptist church. But in politico-theological terms, Paisley's lineage went back to a previous century, to fundamentalist evangelical preachers like Henry Cooke or Hugh 'Roaring' Hanna, who guarded the pass against Catholicism from without and liberalism from within, and guaranteed that the strain of undiluted, neo-Cromwellian sentiment remained alive and virulent in the north's body politic. Within Unionist culture, no part of the core body of dementia remained as lucrative and productive of political as well as religious dividends throughout the period of the troubles as did Paisleyism. Part of the appeal lay in the man himself: a commanding presence, a dominating orator, a figure to turn to at a time of threatening change; part lay in the use of frankly sexual imagery. Paisley always portrayed Rome as the Roman whore, the scarlet woman, seeking to ensnare the innocent Protestant lad. He founded his own church, the Free Presbyterian Church of Ulster, when he was relatively youthful himself, only 25. He also founded the Ulster

Protestant Action group (UPA), which campaigned against the allocation of public housing to Catholics, and the giving of jobs to Catholic workers. Later, in 1966, he would found the *Protestant Telegraph*, a paper which gave a new dimension to the term 'hate creation', and the Ulster Protestant Volunteers. The UPV was organised by one of the *Protestant Telegraph*'s printers, who was also the secretary of another of Paisley's organisations, the Ulster Constitution Defence Committee, a sort of umbrella grouping of his various creations. The role of the UCDC and of the UPV in helping to create the situation which came to prevail in Northern Ireland was described in a government publication as follows:

> Fears and apprehensions of Protestants of a threat to Unionist domination and control of government by an increase of Catholic population and powers, inflamed *in particular* [author's italics] by the activities of the Ulster Constitution Defence Committee and the Ulster Protestant Volunteers provoked strong hostile reaction to Civil Rights Claims as asserted by the Civil Rights Association and later by the People's Democracy which were readily translated into physical violence against Civil Rights demonstrators.[10]

Paisley's anti-Catholicism had already made a name for him throughout the north when the Westminster election of 1964 gave him a chance to step on to the national stage. Divis Street, a typical dingy redbrick back street off the Falls Road, was the site of the Sinn Féin candidate Liam McMillan's election headquarters. A tricolour was displayed in the front window. Unionist attitudes to their Nationalist fellow citizens' sense of identity was that of the Long Stone Road variety. Properly speaking, there was no such thing as a Nationalist identity. In fact, under the Flags and Emblems Act, it was illegal to display the tricolour in public. But by 1964, a nondescript, inconspicuous area like Divis would not have been regarded by the police as being worthy of an enforcement of the Act. However, Paisley thought otherwise, and put up Belfast blood pressures very considerably by telling an overflow meeting at the Ulster Hall (on 27 September) that he was giving the police two days to remove the flag, or else he would lead a march to do it for them. He thus triggered the worst rioting seen in Belfast for 30 years. The trouble began the following day, when the police arrived in large numbers at Divis Street, broke into the Sinn Féin office, and removed the flag.

This incident, and the fact that the Falls dwellers expected Paisley's marchers to arrive, brought thousands of them on to the road. Cunningly, however, Paisley did not seek to confront them, but instead staged a rally outside the safely distant City Hall. Deprived of his appearance, the disappointed Falls Road crowd began setting fire to buses, the first time this happened during the Troubles. The bad feeling continued the next night, and rioting and baton charges broke out following a Sinn Féin meeting. Three days after the police had removed the flag, another tricolour went up in the Sinn Féin windows, and this time the RUC used pickaxes to smash their way into the building to seize the offending item. Ferocious rioting broke out as a result. Another 'first' in the wake of the bus burnings made its unwelcome appearance – the use of petrol bombs. On the Friday night, the authorities responded with water cannons, armoured cars, and riot police. Some 50 protestors fetched up in hospital in Belfast, and in Dublin Gardai were stoned when sympathetic crowds marched on the British Embassy. The rioting ended as a result of a compromise in which Nationalist leaders guaranteed the peace when the RUC stood back and allowed the tricolour to be carried openly at a Republican parade that Sunday.

All this seemingly mindless hostility to a flag being displayed in a street where very few people would have been aware of its presence had a practical objective. West Belfast is one of the more volatile constituencies in Ireland, and, given the employment situation, the Unionists had feared that their candidate, Jim Kilfedder, might lose to an opposition candidate. The rioting took care of that. Kilfedder headed the poll with 21,337 votes. McMillan got only 3,256. But the passions unleashed drove O'Neill, in a comment on the rioting, to say that 'today certain Republican candidates, many with backgrounds in the IRA . . . appear to be using a British election to provoke disorder in Northern Ireland'. The Prime Minister did not dare to say anything about Paisley, who had provoked the disorders. But Paisley had plenty to say about O'Neill. A month after the Lemass/O'Neill visits, he staged a huge demonstration outside the Unionist headquarters in Glengall Street, which intimidated O'Neill into calling off a planned function there. For the rest of 1965, and particularly in the following year, the anniversary of 1916, Paisley stalked the region, raising the ever-growing cry of 'O'Neill must go'.

It was said after O'Neill did go, a few years later, that his aristocratic remoteness and lack of empathy with the Nationalists were what caused his downfall, and to a degree there is truth in the charges. But in all fairness, it is difficult to see how even Nelson Mandela or Franklin Delano Roosevelt could have done any better in the perfervid circumstances of Northern Ireland. For, in addition to the ceaseless activities of Unionism's sleepless Cassius, Brian Faulkner, and the stentorian street politics of Ian Paisley, a belt of whose Bible was, in northern circumstances, more damaging than that of any Catholic bishop's crozier, O'Neill also had to cope with a recrudescence of the Ulster Volunteer Force that led to loss of life.

The new UVF was only a pale shadow of the old: 'a small group of Paisley supporters who, alarmed by his denunciations of the Unionist sell-out, had set up an armed organisation'.[11] The UVF's membership was predominantly working class. Its best-known leader was 'Gusty' Spence, who was an associate of Paisley's in the UPA. Spence was a shipyard worker, with a staunchly Unionist background and a term of service in the British army. Paisley-ite fervour and a detestation of republicanism, reinforced by Nationalist celebrations of the anniversary of 1916, led the UVF to commit the first killings of the Troubles. After a series of petrol bomb attacks on Catholic homes, they mistakenly killed an elderly Protestant woman, on

7 May 1966, in a petrol bomb attack on a Catholic pub beside her home. Then, on 22 May, the UVF issued a statement saying: 'From this day on, we declare war against the IRA, and its splinter groups. Known IRA men will be executed mercilessly and without hesitation.'

The problem was that the UVF of that period did not know many IRA men. Nor were there that many of them about. Nevertheless, on 27 May, a UVF squad set out to implement their public threat by shooting Leo Martin, known to be a prominent Belfast Republican. They failed to find him and instead shot the nearest Catholic to hand, John Scullion. He died on 11 June. Since Belfast was a small, closely knit city, the activities of the UVF and UPV were known over a wide area, so much so that a Labour MP, Tom Boyd, urged the Government to take action against both bodies. Nothing had been done, however, when three days later, Spence and his friends again decided to hit Martin. Once more he eluded them, and, as Irish revolutionaries of either Green or Orange hue are wont to do, the would-be assassins withdrew to drown their sorrows in a pub. The pub, in Malvern Street, was in a Loyalist district, off the Shankill Road, but it was also frequented by Catholics, who on the night in question included a group of off-duty Catholic barmen. As they left the pub, Spence's group ambushed them, fatally wounding one, Peter Ward. These killings forced O'Neill to take action, and with ironic symbolism he had to cut short a visit to the Somme, where the 1916 slaughter of the UVF was being commemorated, to return to Belfast to ban the contemporary UVF.

One has to go to America's Deep South, and the Ku-Klux Klan (which has a tradition of support by emigrant Ulster Orangemen), or to the deep recesses of Boer and Afrikaner ideology, for figures to compare with Paisley. Even the word loyalty had a peculiarly Ulster interpretation placed on it. Ulster Loyalists like Paisley would give their loyalty to leaders whom they perceived as being loyal to them, i.e. fellow supremacists. But the Unionists always felt, and feel, free to withdraw that loyalty from leaders whom they perceive as leading them astray. Both Paisley and Faulkner took advantage of this conditionality when it suited them to make common cause in attempting to undermine O'Neill. On 6 June, Paisley was again responsible for a major riot, when he led a march through the Catholic Cromac Square area of Belfast. Local residents who attempted to block the march wound up in hand-to-hand combat not with Paisley, but with the RUC. Paisley carried on with his demonstration and staged a rowdy rally outside the Presbyterian General Assembly. The Presbyterian Moderator, Dr Martin, demanded that the Government put a stop to Paisley's violent street theatre, but Faulkner supported Paisley, saying that the Moderator's request was 'an unwarrantable interference with the right of free speech and free assembly'. Faulkner's payback came shortly afterwards when Paisley addressed a meeting saying, 'Thank God for Brian Faulkner.'[12]

Paisley might also have muttered *sotto voce*, 'Thank God for 1916', because he was able to use the fact of the Nationalists celebrating the fiftieth anniversary of the Rising as a prime target for his activities for several months in that turbulent summer of 1966. He failed to force the Government to ban the various commemoration ceremonies held around Easter by the Nationalists, but he did succeed in having the B Specials placed on a state of armed alert all through the month of April, and in having a ban placed on trains coming from the south, bearing supporters of the 1916 ceremonies. He finally succeeded in his objective of securing that invaluable accolade of the political agitator, a short but significant jail sentence, when he refused to be bound to keep the peace for his activities outside the Presbyterian General Assembly, directed at what he termed the Presbyterians' 'Rome-ward trend'. The authorities unwisely brought him to court a few days after 'the twalfth', when marching fervour was still at its height. On 18 July, he refused to be bound to keep the peace for two years, and was duly incarcerated in Belfast's Crumlin Road jail. The jail thus became a focal point for riots as Paisleyite mobs clashed with the RUC. These mobs then went on a rampage through the city, seeking the traditional targets of Catholic businesses to break up. After two days of fierce hand-to-hand fighting, all further meetings and marches in Belfast were banned for three months. However, within the Unionist Party, Paisley's allies continued the onslaught on O'Neill. Desmond Boal, a barrister, who had been elected in 1961 with Paisleyite support, collected signatures amongst Unionist backbenchers, demanding that O'Neill must go. Faulkner invited Boal and some of his conspirators to a meeting in his house, but the petition came to nothing when O'Neill routed his critics at a Unionist Party meeting on 27 September.

One of the most important facts to be borne in mind concerning these turbulent years was that the violence almost exclusively originated from the ranks of Unionists. The first burnings, the first deaths, and, as we shall see, the first explosions, were all caused by 'Loyalists'. For most of the sixties, there was no IRA. Republicans did not fire a shot in anger until 1969, and then only in defence of Catholic districts or churches. The first British soldier to die in the Troubles was not shot until 1971. The IRA had become demilitarised after the 1962 ceasefire. The border campaign had received no support in Belfast, where the IRA had feared to take action anyhow, through being too weak to defend Catholics against the inevitable Protestant backlash, and in reality, it consisted of little more than a few sporadic attacks on RUC barracks and customs posts in border areas. The movement, which in the sixties was led from Dublin by a house painter, Cathal Goulding, had fallen under the influence of two Marxist Trinity College lecturers, Roy Johnston and Anthony Coughlan. Johnston had succeeded in getting himself appointed as a sort of education officer to the IRA, and his influence directed the Republicans towards the infiltration of trade unions, housing protests and agitations with local appeal, such as rows over fishing rights, or mining exploration. In a nutshell, the Marxist theoreticians who controlled the Republican movement for most of the sixties attempted a re-run of what the Republican Congress had tried in the 1930s. They infiltrated organisations which provided a useful cover for their activities, including the Dublin Action Housing Committee, set up because of the Dublin housing problems already discussed to campaign on behalf of the homeless. The 1916 commemorations helped to garner some support for Sinn Féin north and south, although in the north it was found expedient to use the term Republican Clubs, rather than Sinn Féin.

The left-wing orientation of political republicanism led to a two-day think-in, in August 1966, of people of differing religious and political outlook. The meeting which was attended by Cathal Goulding, took place at Maghera, County Derry, in the home of Kevin Agnew, a nationalist and a prominent Derry solicitor. Johnston's line, spelt out at the meeting in a paper read for him by Eoghan Harris, was that Northern trade unions should be infiltrated as a method for bringing Protestants and Catholics together. Given the reality of the state of Orange–Green relationships this was a somewhat unlikely tactic. The presentation was dismissed as 'embarrassing', by one of its hearers, the civil libertarian Professor Michael Dolley, of Queen's University. But on the second day of the think-in, another solicitor, Ciaran Mac an Ali, put forward a suggestion which helped to change the course of Northern Ireland's history. Mac an Ali advocated the formation of a broad-based civil rights movement. This idea was taken up, and the following January, in Belfast, a Northern Ireland Civil Rights Association was formed, based on the British National Council for Civil Liberties. Two of those who had taken part in the Maghera meeting were elected to NICRA's first committee, Agnew himself and Professor Dolley. The rest of the membership was of equal calibre and drawn from many walks of life. The chairman was a prominent trade unionist, Noel Harris, of the Draughtsmen and Allied Trades Association, the Vice-Chairman, Dr Con McCluskey, of whom more anon, the Treasurer was the leading Wolfe Tone Society member, Fred Heatley. Jack Bennett was appointed Information Officer. The rest of the committee were Betty Sinclair, a Communist, and a member of the Belfast Trades Council, Ken Banks, a colleague of Noel Harris; Paddy Devlin of the North of Ireland Labour Party, Joe Sherry of the Republican Labour Party, John Quinn of the Ulster Liberal Party, Robin Cole of the Queen's Young Unionist Group and Terence O'Brien, unattached. The committee did not include any persons with IRA links. This fact served to prevent Unionists discrediting the new movement as an IRA front, although this did not stop Paisley from subsequently using the slogan 'CRA=IRA'.

NICRA's demands were for 'one man, one vote', in other words, an end to the plural voting system in local elections, an end to discrimination, both in employment and in housing, and gerrymandering, the setting up of a mechanism to deal with complaints against the authorities, an end to the Special Powers Act and the disbandment of the B Specials. This shopping list of course was completely unacceptable to Unionists, and was to remain so. Many Nationalists too remained suspicious of NICRA, because of its left-wing component. At the time, the Nationalists, in fact all the opposition groupings, were divided, and, insofar as influencing Unionist policy was concerned, largely ineffectual. The North of Ireland Labour Party (NILP) was affiliated to the British Labour Party, and thus could attend Labour Party conferences but could not take part in debates. And while it could call on the support of some prominent British Labour Party members such as Stan Orme, Paul Rose, Kevin McNamara, Fenner Brockway, Geoffrey Bing and Lord Longford, the NILP was limited in the extent of the influence which it could exert on Labour Party policy towards Ireland.

It was even more limited in the extent to which it could hope to influence the Unionist Party, because it was always at risk of being ground between the upper and the lower millstones of Orange and Green extremism. In the 1949 election, the south's declaration of a Republic generated an Orange reaction which wiped out all of its nine candidates. By 1958 it had regained strength to the extent of holding four seats in the Stormont parliament, but lost the hearts and minds of the group of rising young Catholic radicals who had taken advantage of the Butler Education Acts in 1964, when, in a confused attempt to bridge the sectarian divide, the NILP voted with the more troglodyte wing of unionism to ban a proposal that Belfast Corporation should open its playgrounds to allow children to use the swings on a Sunday afternoon. Whatever hopes the NILP had of securing the support of the educated young Catholic figures who later emerged at the head of a civil rights movement, such as Bernadette Devlin, Michael Farrell and Eamon McCann, died at the locked playground gates. Terence O'Neill further eroded the NILP's support by targeting the party during the 1965 election campaign as being soft on the Union, thereby lopping off two of the seats gained in 1958.

The traditional Nationalist opposition at Stormont was conducted with a small 'o'. In the early sixties, the Nationalists were divided as to whether they should be in Stormont at all. Perhaps abstention was the better policy. But as the sixties wore on, new currents began stirring. In Dungannon in January of 1964, Dr Con McCluskey and his wife, Patricia, founded the Campaign for Social Justice on the basis of statistical research into the facts and figures of discrimination and gerrymandering. McCluskey's work provided Butler-educated young Catholic politicians like Austin Currie with hard information to hurl at their Stormont opponents. Even if these statistical missiles bounced harmlessly off a Brookeborough or a Faulkner, they nevertheless represented a departure from the traditionalist Nationalist policies of seeing the border as the principal political target. They also represented a qualitative shift. A Currie, or in particular a figure like John Hume, who would later dominate Catholic politics, could debate and articulate Catholic grievances with force and logic. The fact that most Nationalist representatives were unable to do this led to an important Nationalist meeting in Maghery, County Armagh, on 18 April 1964.

A Nationalist representative, James O'Reilly, had proved himself unable to match Brian Faulkner during a TV debate on what should have been the sure ground of discrimination. The Maghery meeting yielded a Nationalist political front, which involved rural Nationalists, Belfast representatives, and a group of Catholic graduates called National Unity, which had been set up some months earlier in an effort to formulate new Nationalist policies. National Unity was committed to the ideal of unification, but with the important rider that this was to be achieved through 'the consent of the people of Northern Ireland'. At the time, there was a custom whereby Nationalists contested Stormont, but left Sinn Féin free to contest Westminster elections. Neither wing of nationalism could claim to have made much impact on the Unionist monolith. The basic philosophy at the time was little more than Irish revivalism and a belief that somewhere down the line the Catholic birth rate would eventually solve the northern problem.

However, from Maghery onward, Nationalists began thinking more along the lines of the McCluskeys and the Campaign for Social Justice: reform within the system, an end to discrimination and gerrymandering, and a demand that as Northern Ireland was part of the United Kingdom, United Kingdom standards should apply in Belfast as in Bradford. On 2 June, the Nationalist Party chose Eddie McAteer from Derry as its leader. McAteer, a tall, distinguished-looking accountant, was a traditional Irish Catholic and a constitutionalist. His brother, Hugh, a Belfast travel agent, was a low-sized, unobtrusive man, and a former chief of staff of the IRA. In February 1965, following the Lemass–O'Neill meetings, Eddie McAteer accepted Lemass's advice that he should fully engage with the Stormont system by becoming the official leader of the opposition.

Thus, on the Nationalist side of the northern division, the pendulum swung strongly away from the old abstentionist policies and the sort of ambivalent attitudes towards force and the IRA best summed up by the attitude that 'you never know when you might need the pike in the thatch', to a general focus on the issues of the voting system, discrimination and gerrymandering. Along with new policies, there were new faces. In Derry, John Hume was acquiring stature for his work in the Credit Union Movement and the Derry Housing Association, and in St Columb's School as a teacher of French whose pupils achieved excellent exam results. Moreover, unlike the tongue-tied O'Reilly, he was a skilled orator, known for his prowess in the Columkille Debating Society. Also, though he had been a seminarian at Maynooth, Hume preached the unorthodox doctrine that one of the best things that could happen to Northern Irish politics would be 'the removal of the equation between Nationalist and Catholic'.[13] However, though in Northern Ireland a Hume might propose, it was the Orange element, and in particular Paisley and his cohorts, who disposed. Not only did Paisley copper-fasten the equation between Catholic and Nationalist, he also manufactured one between the newly formed civil rights movement and the IRA. 'CRA equals IRA' became one of his best-known catchphrases, along with 'O'Neill must go'. By now, the IRA was virtually demilitarised, and though some of its members did play a role within NICRA, they did so in a non-violent fashion, helping to keep the peace during demonstrations. After the formation of NICRA, many of the Republican Old Guard dropped out. As Hugh McAteer said to me, 'I just couldn't see myself walking up to an RUC barricade, and simply allowing the police to baton me.' A great many Republicans felt as McAteer did. They accepted that force had failed to remove the border, and that people were now more interested in butter than bombs. There was no role for the IRA. Ideologically, their focus was on sovereignty, on getting the British out of Ireland, and the idea of involving themselves in strikes and sit-ins was completely foreign to them. As a result of these attitudes, the IRA was to suffer a major split between the socially inclined and the traditionalists when serious rioting broke out all over the north in the summer of 1969.

Even though the civil rights marchers sang 'We Shall Overcome', not 'A Nation Once Again' or similar-style ballads, trouble was inevitable once they began to challenge the established order of things. I remember having a discussion with John Hume around this time, in the course of which he outlined his hopes for ultimate friendship and co-operation between Protestants and Catholics, and then added, 'But the Unionist will have to realise that, first, he has to take his foot off the Catholic's neck.' I got a sudden cold feeling as he spoke, because even though I knew that logically Hume was correct in his analysis, and I was only an uninformed Dubliner, it struck me that the whole purpose of the northern state was to keep the Unionist foot firmly down on the Catholic, and that any attempt to remove it would be fiercely resisted. But how fiercely few could have foreseen.

The first significant action of the civil rights movement was a sit-in at Caledon, in County Tyrone, caused by abuses in the housing system. At Caledon, as throughout the north, hundreds of Catholic families, some of them with over a dozen children, had their names inscribed uselessly on county council waiting lists. Ten-year waits were not unusual. But when an 18-year-old Protestant girl, the secretary to a prominent Orangeman, was allocated a house when she became engaged, two well-known Catholic families staged a sit-in. Numbers 9 and 11 Kinard Park, Caledon, were catapulted into the headlines. The squat lasted for nine months, and was given further publicity when the young Nationalist MP Austin Currie joined in, greatly to the rage of the Unionists, who felt that this was unacceptable behaviour for an MP, even a Nationalist one. The squatters were eventually evicted, amongst them a grandmother and a pregnant woman. The impact of the sit-in may be gauged from the fact that a granddaughter of the evicted granny, Anne-Marie Gildernew, at the time of writing is a Sinn Féin member of the Stormont Assembly. Her brother Martin was the baby whom the pregnant squatter, Geraldine Gildernew, was carrying.

The first major civil rights march took place on 24 August 1968, between Coalisland and Dungannon. Some 4,000 people took part, and for the first time the strains of 'We Shall Overcome' rang out across the fields of Tyrone. It had been intended that the march would conclude with a peaceful rally in Dungannon. But, in what became a pattern of collusive behaviour between Paisleyite and Unionist demonstrators of all hues, and the RUC, the authorities banned the civil rights rally because, it was said, as the Paisleyites had organised a counter-demonstration, violence might ensue. The August demonstration ended peacefully. But a group of left-wing Derry activists, led by Eamon McCann and Eamon Melaugh, decided to hold a deliberately provocative march in October, taking in a number of Protestant areas. The idea of Catholics marching in the first place was a bizarre and unwelcome one to Unionists. Marching was something the Protestants did as of right, not the Catholics. However, McCann and company were bent on confrontation and its resultant publicity. They reckoned that if the march went really well, and resulted in significant uproar, perhaps Stormont might collapse. Confrontation was guaranteed when, two days before the march was due to take place, on 5 October, the Minister for Home Affairs, William Craig, banned it on the grounds that the Protestant Apprentice Boys intended to march on the same route at the same time. Between the ban, and the fact that the Derry soccer team were playing that day, only 400 marchers turned up, but they proved more than sufficient to secure the publicity McCann wanted.

The RUC trapped the marchers between two cordons in Duke Street, and then batoned men, women and children indiscriminately. A water cannon was used, and the whole thing was recorded for television by RTE. Pictures of the Westminster MP Gerry Fitt with blood streaming down his face, a scalp wound caused by a baton, went around the world. That night, the Bogside in Derry's Catholic area erupted in riot for the first time. Civil rights groups were set up all across the Six Counties. Further marches and demonstrations took place, notably on 16 November, when some 15,000 people took part in another confrontation with the RUC in Derry. This march too had been banned, but it passed off peacefully, partly because of efficient stewarding and partly because members of the Derry Citizens Action Committee, which had organised the protest, were allowed through the police barriers, followed by some of their supporters, to hold a meeting in the Diamond, the heart of Derry's business area. However, though this particular meeting passed off without incident, the state of the Six Counties was such that it was obvious to observers that either reform came to the area, or revolution did. And there was no guarantee that if reform did come, as sought by the civil rights marchers, revolution would not break out on the Orange side.

Ultimately the problem was one for London, not Belfast. Under Section 75 of the Government of Ireland Act, 1920, London had responsibility for what transpired in the six north-eastern counties of Ireland, over which the Union Jack flew. But while Labour was more sympathetic to Nationalist grievances than were the Conservatives, the traditional allies of the Unionists, who took the Tory whip, there was no tradition at Westminster of governments of any stripe taking a hands-on attitude to the Six Counties; quite the reverse. The object of the partition settlement had been to get Ireland off the British political agenda. To ensure that it had stayed off since 1922, there had been a Speaker's ruling that matters relating to Northern Ireland could not be raised in the House of Commons. These fell solely within the purview of Stormont. Until the Troubles in Northern Ireland began bringing all too much attention to the area, the average amount of time spent in Westminster discussing the

Six Counties was less than two hours a year.There was a ginger group within Labour, the Campaign for Democracy in Ulster, which concerned itself with injustices in the Six Counties, and had perhaps 100 members. But there was also a strain in the Labour Party which was just as sympathetic to the Orange position as anything to be found amongst Unionists. In those days, the trade union block vote played a considerable part in Labour Party policies, and that block was heavily influenced by Scottish Presbyterians, men who empathised with the Protestant soccer team, Glasgow Rangers, not its Catholic counter-part, Celtic. Accordingly, the Wilson government's first response to the agitations taking place across the water in the UK overseas was not to get mixed up in it. James Callaghan, who, as Home Secretary, would ultimately find himself actively engaged in Belfast politics, told a London seminar that the Government didn't want to get involved because he and his colleagues knew that they were 'not welcomed by the Northern Ireland government'.[14] To implement reform, Callaghan said, Labour would have had to 'override the Northern government . . . we're not going to do that'.

When pressed to intervene in the House of Commons by Gerry Fitt, Harold Wilson replied:

> The question raises some very difficult issues because of the division of functions between the United Kingdom parliament and government and the Northern Ireland parliament and government. We are all aware that Hon. Members in more than one part of the House are very disturbed about certain things which go on. I am not taking sides in this because there are allegations and counter-allegations by one side or another within Northern Ireland.
>
> I do not believe that this is a matter to be dealt with in the manner suggested [setting up a Royal Commission to enquire into the workings of the Government of Ireland Act, author]. I think that the right thing would be for my Hon. Friend the Home Secretary and myself to have informal talks with the Prime Minister of Northern Ireland to see whether some of the difficulties which all of us recognise exist might be overcome in an informal way.[15]

That was in 1966. By 1968, however, Wilson was driven into 'taking sides'. It was no longer a matter of 'allegations and counter-allegations'. Speaker's rulings could no longer be used for shelter. On 4 November, O'Neill was received by Wilson in London. With him were two of his ministers, Craig and Faulkner. An indication of how matters stood between the Unionists may be gauged by the fact that Craig and Faulkner flew to London separately from O'Neill. Wilson's government had given the Unionists a chance to produce their own proposals for calming the situation. But as O'Neill revealed later, his colleagues refused to come up with any suggestions, and 'by their joint decision, we went naked into the Cabinet room', where they were forced to accept the package of reforms.[16] To accept but not to implement. This was the crucial weakness in London's policy. Instead of taking a hands-on approach to reform, matters were left in the hands of the weak and faltering Terence O'Neill. His heart was unquestionably in the right place, but his Cabinet colleagues were not. Effectively speaking, they stood on the same side as Paisley. While they did not publicly chant 'O'Neill must go', they did so privately, and openly stigmatised the civil rights movement as being an IRA front.

Before 5 October 1968, and the batoning of the Derry civil rights movements, the package which Wilson handed O'Neill would have seemed like manna from heaven to a majority of Northern Ireland's Catholics. It contained a promise to abolish the Special Powers Act, when it was safe to do so, to introduce a new system of housing allocation, and an end to the company vote. True, it was silent on the issue of giving the franchise to non-ratepayers. But, as the respected northern commentator Barry White wrote in the *Belfast Telegraph*, after the package was unveiled by O'Neill on 22 November (it had taken him that long, since seeing Wilson in London on the 4th, to get his Cabinet and party to agree even to the announcement of the reforms): 'In just 48 days since the first Derry march, the Catholic community has obtained more political gains than it had in 47 years.'

But the impact of these gains was to be speedily dissipated. Paisley and his henchman of the time, Major Ronald Bunting, used their counter-demonstration tactic on 30 November to cancel a major civil rights march which had been planned from Armagh. Shortly before the march began, the two men showed up in the city, accompanied by a cavalcade of cars containing men with cudgels and car boots full of stones. The RUC formula for preventing trouble was to ban the civil rights march. William Craig, the Minister for Home Affairs, who had unwillingly accompanied O'Neill to London to be acquainted with the reform package, issued a statement which was carried in the press on 3 December: 'One of these days, one of these marches is going to get a massive reaction from the population. Ordinary decent people have been at boiling point for some time. It's not just Mr Paisley.'

The following day, there was more trouble between Loyalists and civil rights marchers at Dungannon. It was clear that the situation was getting out of hand. On 9 December O'Neill made a notable effort to halt the slide to chaos, appearing on television to issue what became known as his 'Ulster at the crossroads' speech:

> Ulster stands at the crossroads . . . our conduct over the coming days will decide our future . . . These issues are far too serious to be determined behind closed doors or left to noisy minorities . . . For more than five years now I have tried to heal some of the deep divisions in our community. I did so because I could not see how an Ulster divided against itself could hope to stand . . .
>
> There are, I know, today some so-called loyalists who talk of independence from Britain – who seem to want a kind of Protestant Sinn Féin. These people will not listen when they are told that Ulster's income is £200 million a year but that we can spend £3,000 million a year only because Britain pays the balance . . . Rhodesia, in defying Britain from thousands of miles away, at least has an airforce and an army of her own. Where are the Ulster armoured divisions and the Ulster jet planes?

... Unionism armed with justice will be a stronger cause than Unionism armed merely with strength. ... What kind of Ulster do you want? A happy and respected province in good standing with the rest of the United Kingdom? Or a place continually torn apart by riots and demonstrations and regarded by the rest of Britain as a political outcast?

O'Neill came across as being strained, but utterly sincere. For a moment, it seemed that he would carry the day. Of his Cabinet colleagues, only Craig ventured public demur. O'Neill promptly sacked him, and demanded and got parliamentary backing from the Unionist Party of 29 votes to 0, with four abstentions. Press and pulpit rowed in behind him, north and south of the border. The civil rights marches were temporarily halted. He might just have averted anarchy, were it not for two points not mentioned in his speech. The first concerned his accurate statement about the cost to the British exchequer of running the Six Counties. But nothing was said about British intentions should the Unionists continue to refuse to give them value for their money. The saying 'the man who pays the piper calls the tune' was not current in London in 1968, nor with the exception of the year 1972, as we shall see, was it to be translated into action all through the Troubles. Money, billions of it, would be found to prop up the Unionist statelet. But no indication was ever given that British taxpayers' money would be withheld if standards of democracy as practised in Leeds or Bradford were not also upheld in Belfast. The other omission was to provide the reason for the spark which finally ignited a widespread explosion of violence: nothing was said about one man, one vote.

The People's Democracy was a student-led organisation which had its origins in the example of the student uprisings in Paris and Prague that year, and in reaction to the 5 October batonings in Derry. It was intended as a form of mass democracy without leaders. But, inevitably, it came under the influence of a group of student leaders, notably Michael Farrell and Bernadette Devlin of Queen's University, and Eamon McCann and a handful of his associates from Derry. They decided that as the behaviour of the police in Derry had been fully supported by the state, seeking reform within the system by asking questions in parliament, or protesting at Stormont, would get nowhere.[17] It would be necessary to expose the true nature of the state to the world. Insofar as Michael Farrell was concerned, O'Neill's omission of any reference to the key demand of the civil rights movement for one man, one vote meant that nothing had really changed, despite the London reform package, and that O'Neill's main objective was to defuse the civil rights movement.

Accordingly, the PDs decided to light a fuse of their own, a Six County version of the American civil rights march from Selma to Montgomery, Alabama. In place of generating a reaction to force the Federal Government in Washington to intervene, they would provoke a situation which would drive London to become involved. The PDs decision was opposed by other civil rights leaders like John Hume, Austin Currie and the Protestant Ivan

Cooper, who saw the proposed march from Belfast to Derry, via a number of Loyalist towns, as being dangerously provocative. However, on New Year's Day 1969, approximately 50 young demonstrators set off from City Hall, heading towards Derry and the history books. The marchers were attacked all along the way by organised groups armed with stones and clubs. The RUC's only intervention lay in preventing the marchers from walking through towns of their choosing, ostensibly to protect them. No effort was made to prevent a series of ambushes all along the route. As the students trudged on, increasingly bloodied, but determinedly unbowed, the pendulum of public opinion began swinging towards the marchers. Two final ambushes completed the swing from criticism to adulation.

At Burntollet Bridge, a few miles outside Derry, police and B Specials colluded in setting up an ambuscade several hundred strong. The students were attacked with iron bars, bicycle chains, clubs studded with nails, and stones. All of the demonstrators were injured to some degree, and a number were driven into the icy waters of the River Fahan. After recovering from this onslaught, the students were ambushed once more on the outskirts of Derry in the Protestant Irish Street. Again the police made no effort to intervene. But by now public opinion was so much in their favour that their former critics, Hume and Cooper, had organised a public reception for the students in Guildhall Square, and they limped into Derry to a heroes' welcome. After the reception, serious rioting broke out in the city, dying away after the pubs shut. But in the small hours of the morning, a drunken mob of RUC men entered the Catholic Bogside district, breaking windows and beating up any Catholics they came across. The police raid was the signal for the erection of the first barricade of the Troubles, and the creation of the first 'no-go area' in the Six Counties. After a week or so, Hume and Cooper succeeded in having the barricades taken down, but the slogan 'You are now entering Free Derry' appeared on the wall at the entrance to St Columb's Well Street, and was to remain there.

In the aftermath of what afterwards became known as the 'Burntollet March', London twisted O'Neill's arm into agreeing to the setting up of the Cameron Commission, under the Scottish High Court judge, Lord Cameron, to inquire into the violence of 5 October and subsequently, and 'to assess the composition and aims of those bodies involved in the current agitation, and in any incident arising out of it'. Decoded, this meant 'check out the Unionist allegations that all the trouble has been caused by the IRA'. The Commission sat in private with the assurance that the evidence given to it would not be used in prosecutions. Enraged at the temerity of an inquiry being held into the central questions for the Six Counties of Whose Law? And Whose Order?, Faulkner resigned on 28 January, being joined in his protest by another Cabinet colleague, William Morgan, the Minister for Health.

At this stage it should be pointed out that not every strain of Protestant political thought in Northern Ireland was of the bigoted nature of a Paisley, a Craig, a Faulkner or a Morgan. There have always been courageous individuals prepared to speak up for democracy from within the Unionist community. Ivan Cooper, who had lived and worked for a time in the Republic, has already been mentioned, and at this time, the new year of 1969, other prominent Protestants in Northern Ireland, for example Campbell Austin, the owner of what was at the time the largest department store in Derry, tried to lead their fellow Unionists to more liberal shores. The New Ulster Movement (NUM) sought the abolition of the B Specials and the setting up of a central housing executive and a community relations commission. The practical relevance of these proposals was demonstrated by the fact that they were all subsequently adopted, and whereas the NUM itself did not turn out to be the mass movement of 1969, it did give rise to the foundation the following year of the liberal Unionist Alliance Party, which attracted a not insignificant amount of professional support across the sectarian divide. However, it was the more illiberal section of unionism which spurred O'Neill into action in the early months of 1969. After a group of 12 Unionist backbenchers met in Portadown in the wake of Faulkner's resignation to demand that O'Neill should go, he decided to confront his critics and called a general election for 3 February.

The election campaign provided a vortex of new and old political thinking. Unionism fractured into two camps, pro- and anti-O'Neillites. Ranged against O'Neill were Paisley, Faulkner, Lord Brookeborough, Craig, Morgan, and many more hardliners. On the opposition side of the argument – by now it would not be accurate to automatically describe the opposition movement as Nationalist – there were the newer figures thrown up by the civil rights movement, who largely stood as independents, and left-wing personalities like Paddy Devlin of the NILP, and Gerry Fitt and Paddy Kennedy of the Republican Labour Party. The People's Democracy movement also put up candidates; Michael Farrell stood against O'Neill in his own Bann-side constituency. O'Neill was also opposed in the constituency by Paisley, and Farrell reasoned that if he could take sufficient votes from O'Neill to allow Paisley into Stormont, Harold Wilson would be forced to hotfoot it to Belfast immediately afterwards.

Paisley did do well, but O'Neill managed to hang on to his seat with a greatly reduced majority of only 1,400 votes. Of the 39 Unionist seats, pro-O'Neill candidates won 24, 10 were definitely opposed, and five waited to see which way the wind would blow. On the opposition benches, John Hume, Ivan Cooper and Paddy O'Hanlon had been elected as independents on a civil rights ticket, Hume felling Eddie McAteer, the former Nationalist leader, along the way. Though figures like Austin Currie, Gerry Fitt, Paddy Devlin and Paddy Kennedy had emerged from different stables, the emerging policy consensus on the opposition benches would be around a civil rights agenda. Outside the chamber, their opponents were also concerned about civil rights and the best means of preventing them.

Already the opposition inside Stormont to O'Neill had reached a pitch where his days were increasingly obviously numbered. His constitutional enemies within unionism struck him a serious blow on 22 April, when he moved to satisfy the civil rights objective of introducing one man, one vote for local government elections. His cousin, the Minister for Agriculture, Major James Chichester-Clark, reckoned, correctly, that the issue could provide him with a springboard for the premiership, and made himself a focal point for the anti-O'Neill lobby by resigning. Over the next three days, unconstitutional Loyalists also struck, and a series of explosions which had been in progress, directed at electricity installations, switched to attacking water pipes which supplied Belfast from the Silent Valley Reservoir in the Mourne mountains. The city was gripped with fear caused by rumours that the explosions formed part of a larger scheme aimed at depriving firemen of water when widescale Loyalist-initiated conflagrations took place. In the atmosphere of turmoil and mistrust, O'Neill resigned, on 28 April, less than a week after he had announced the introduction of one man, one vote.

Chichester-Clark had timed his resignation perfectly. He was appointed to succeed O'Neill, with the support of O'Neill himself, who acted to keep Faulkner out. But neither Chichester-Clark nor Faulkner, nor even Stormont itself, were destined to remain in power for long. 'Big Drum principles' now made a determined, but ultimately unsuccessful, attempt to impose themselves on 'Ulster', and this marked the stage at which the politics of Northern Ireland began to become part of the day-to-day concern of both Dublin and London. Derry and Belfast were the crucial cock-pit areas. The mood throughout the Six Counties was ominous and threatening, particularly in Derry. During the week of the 'twalfth', Samuel Devenney, a 42-year-old Catholic taxi driver, died of injuries inflicted by police who had broken into his house in William Street. The RUC were acting in the mistaken belief that some stone-throwing youths had taken refuge there, during rioting in April. His death gave an edge of anger to the fears of people in Derry at the approach of the Protestant Apprentice Boys March through the city on 12 August. In the weeks after Devenney's death, a group of old Republicans led by Seán Keenan set up the Derry Citizens Defence Committee to prepare for the march. At the beginning of August, there were savage riots in Belfast in the inappropriately named Unity Flats area. Reports of collusion between the RUC and Orange mobs added to Derry's fears and anger. A belief took hold that the Bogside area was in danger of being invaded, as had been the Unity Flats district, when the Apprentice Boys marched.

Material for erecting barricades was stored at all the entrances leading into the Bogside, and Irish history reversed itself as a new Siege of Derry was prepared with the Catholics in the defending role and the Unionists cast as attackers. After all that had happened, the Bogside was an explosion waiting to be detonated. Whether it was finally triggered by the Protestants' traditional gesture of contempt, the throwing of pennies on to Catholics from the old city walls, as the Catholics claim, or by Catholic youths stoning Protestant marchers as they passed Devenney's house, the result was the same. Centuries of antagonisms and decades of misrule came home to roost. Under a hail of stones from the Bogside youth, a mob of Apprentice Boys and police attempted to storm the Bogside. They were driven back by both brick-bats and the application of 'Big Drum principles'.

In order to corral the Catholic vote within the Bogside ward, to prevent it overflowing and tipping the balance in other areas of the city, the Unionists had built high-rise flats at Rossville Street, the entrance to the Bogside. The towering flats now became the Derry version of the GPO. A group of Derry teenagers climbed on to the roof and kept the mobs at bay with petrol bombs. Republican sympathisers immediately began subscribing money to keep the supply of petrol flowing. To counteract them, London gave permission for the first use of CS gas in the UK. The canisters of gas never reached the rooftop, of course, but the smoke drifted through the Bogside with serious effects for the elderly or those with respiratory problems. One of those who encouraged the Bogsiders to ignore the gas and keep stoning the police was the newly elected Westminster MP Bernadette Devlin. In all, the two-day battle resulted in over 1,000 people being treated for injuries in a makeshift hospital set up in a sweetshop by a local doctor, Dr Raymond McClean. More serious cases were taken not to the local hospitals but across the border. Sympathetic rioting broke out right across the Six Counties. Belfast was the worst affected, but Armagh, Coalisland and Dungannon also saw serious disturbances, so serious that the Republic was forced into taking action. The Irish army set up refugee camps, the largest of which, Gormanstown, on the main Belfast–Dublin Road, catered for some 6,000 people. In all, the rioting which originated in the week of 12 July, and quietened down somewhat in September, is said to have driven 1,800 Catholic and Protestant families out of their homes. Of these, the vast majority, 1,505, were Catholic. The severity of the dislocation was such that it was later calculated that in the period between the outbreak of the riots in 1969 and February 1973 over 60,000 people were forced out of their homes.[18]

South of the border the Bogside rioting helped to put in train the sensational events known as 'the Arms Trial Affair', which, as we shall see, convulsed southern politics. But for the moment, it is sufficient to record that in Dublin, Jack Lynch was driven to make a television broadcast which had serious repercussions. In the course of his speech, he said that the rioting was 'the inevitable outcome of the policies pursued for decades by successive Stormont governments'. The policies he proposed to pursue included the seeking of a UN force for the Six Counties; negotiation with London with the long-term goal of a united Ireland; a declaration that neither the RUC nor the British army were acceptable in the circumstances; and the setting up of Irish army field hospitals along the border to treat people injured in the riots who did not want to attend hospitals run by Stormont. This last statement, coupled with Lynch's comment that the Irish Government could 'no longer stand by and see innocent people injured, and perhaps worse', was widely interpreted in the north as indicating that the army personnel, said to be engaged in merely setting up field hospitals, might in fact be coming across the border.

However, it was the ferocity of the rioting itself, rather than concern at what Jack Lynch might do, that prompted London's reaction. Although the IRA was almost nonexistent at this stage, the Unionists sent an alarmist appeal to the Cabinet, saying that troops were needed because the Six Counties were in imminent danger of a large-scale IRA attack from across the border, according to a 'reliable source'. The Inspector General of the RUC, Anthony Peacocke, who signed the statement, said that the police could no longer control the situation, and were falling back to defend their barracks. At this stage, the police, far from retiring to their barracks, were actively engaged on the streets, supported by Protestant mobs, and the Stormont opposition had walked out following an announcement by the Deputy Home Affairs Minister, John Taylor, that he was mobilising 11,000 armed B Specials. However, whatever the location of the RUC, it was clear to London, as to any observer, that things were getting out of hand. The Cabinet finally decided that the situation called for the dispatch of troops to the province and for the taking over of security from the RUC by the army.

The soldiers arrived on 15 August 1969. At first the Bogsiders were delighted. A large force of armed B Specials had been sighted approaching the beleaguered area, and there were genuine fears that a massacre would ensue. The troops were greeted with cups of tea, and taken as a sign that the RUC had been defeated and the Bogsiders had won the battle. Bernadette Devlin and those who thought like her, however, had a different view. They correctly foresaw a day coming when Catholics and British soldiers would be at each other's throats. An armed soldier on the streets of a western European city is an unavoidably stark illustration of the fact that normal laws have either broken down or not been applied.

The passage of time has yielded Cabinet papers, memoirs, contributions to seminars, and interviews with participants that have since revealed the fears, hopes and constraints which preoccupied the decision-takers in Harold Wilson's government at the time, principally Wilson himself, James Callaghan, the Home Secretary and Denis Healey, the Minister for Defence.[19] There was an overall reluctance at getting involved at all, let alone accepting the necessary responsibility required to take full control of the situation and of the day-to-day application to detail required to push through reform and deliver ultimate stability. Wilson, more than most, correctly foresaw that once the troops went in they would be there for years, though even he did not foresee how long. The army itself had a phobia about becoming the piggy in the middle between Catholics and Protestants. It was an understandable reluctance, but nevertheless, as will become all too clear, the constant refusal in military terms to 'open a second front' completely undercut the prospects of a political settlement, or of the army being accepted as an impartial force, at vital moments in the conflict. Also there were junctures in the struggle at which the behaviour of the army made many people in Ireland wonder if it really supported Labour. Certainly it appeared more comfortable with the Tories, and was demonstrably given a freer hand by them than under the first Wilson administration. There was also a straightforward ignorance about the situation. Denis Healey, for example, the man in charge of the army when the troops were first sent in, argued against a takeover of Stormont on the grounds that it 'would put the British soldiers under pressure from the Republicans and the *Catholics* . . .'[20]

In the circumstances London opted for an unworkable formula. It sent in the troops, thereby accepting that law and order had broken down in the statelet; but at the same time, having seen what had happened to O'Neill when he attempted reform, it shrank from direct rule, deciding instead to work through the people responsible both for O'Neill's fall and for the said breakdown in law and order. By the time, a government later, that London came to the realisation that the Stormont experiment had been a disastrous error, and suspended the parliament, it was too late. A new force had arisen, the Provisional IRA, which saw the issue as one of sovereignty, not reform. The rise of the Provisionals will shortly be described in context, but for the moment let us examine the package which Wilson's Cabinet decided on. Security was transferred from the RUC to the military. It was agreed to disband the B Specials (although this fact was initially withheld from the Protestants). Steps were taken to begin reform of the RUC, and a top British civil servant, Oliver Wright, former ambassador to Denmark, was dispatched to Belfast as the British Government's representative in Northern Ireland, with a hotline to Harold Wilson. After a meeting between Wilson, James Callaghan and Chichester-Clark, a communiqué known as the 'Downing Street Declaration' was issued. It said that both London and the Northern Ireland Government were agreed that there should be 'full equality of treatment for all citizens', and that the 'momentum of internal reform should be maintained'. By way of evaluating that 'momentum', it may be noted that Wilson, in making the announcement of the declaration (on 19 August), let the cat out of the bag by announcing that the B Specials would be 'phased out'. Faulkner's response, as Minister for Home Affairs, appeared in the papers two days later. It said: 'There is absolutely no suggestion the USC will be disbanded. Let me make that crystal clear.' Where the quickening pulse of republicanism was concerned, the important paragraph in the declaration, aimed at calming Unionist fears, was the passage which said:

> Nothing which has happened in recent weeks in Northern Ireland derogates from the clear pledges made by successive United Kingdom governments that Northern Ireland should not cease to be a part of the United Kingdom without the consent of the people in Northern Ireland . . . The Border is not an issue . . .

The underlining of the fact that partition was to remain did not have the same immediate force as had the effects of the August burnings. But it did serve to reinforce the beliefs of some of the older Republicans, particularly a number who were actively engaged in defending the area around the Clonard Monastery off the Falls Road against a determined Loyalist effort to burn it down, that the Goulding strategy had been doomed to failure, and that a new departure, in an old direction, was both desirable and feasible in the new situation. The fighting around the Clonard area had been more horrifying than anything seen in Derry, and what made it worse, from a Republican standpoint, was that as a result of the doubts and hesitancies involved in the British army's deployment, which I have earlier adverted to, the army apparently showed up in a traditional partisan, pro-Loyalist role. A famous report of an Orange attack, in the *Irish News* of 19 April 1922, captured the role of the British army during the pogroms and inter-communal disorders of that period:

> The match and petrol men operated with as much freedom as if they had happened upon as many deserted 'shanties' in the American backwoods 100 miles from the nearest civilised settlement, and all the time scores of men wearing the King's uniform were quiet witnesses of the scenes of destruction and many scores were within hailing distance, while the occupants of an armoured car could almost warm their hands at the flames.

So far as the Clonard inhabitants were concerned, nothing had changed in the intervening 47 years, between the circumstances which gave rise to that report, and the experiences which they had just passed through. The RUC had used heavy Browning machine-guns, mounted on Shorland armoured personnel carriers, the noise of which alone had helped to spread panic in Catholic areas. In addition to the noise, the bullets which, of course, riddled the walls of the redbrick streets claimed the life of a nine-year-old boy, as he lay in bed. The Clonard area is both a repository of 1920s-style memories and, because it is an interface area, a seedbed of revolution, in which some of the most famous Republican families of the twentieth century lived and acted. Joe Cahill, who would emerge from there as a principal Provisional IRA leader, escaped the hangman's noose during World War II, as we have seen, for his part in the episode for which Tom Williams was hanged. The family of Gerry Adams's mother, the Hanaways, came from the Clonard area, as did many other noted Republicans.

On the night of 14 August, a large group crossed from the Protestant Cupar Street area, and attempted to burn down the Clonard monastery and the streets around it. The RUC made no effort to restrain the mobs, and refused to leave their barracks when entreated to do so by frantic Catholics. Individual RUC men, and sizeable groups of B Specials, were recognised amongst the mobs which attacked not only Clonard, but several other Catholic areas of Belfast, in particular the Catholic enclave of Ardoyne. But the mobs' greatest success came in the Clonard area. They succeeded in burning down one street, Bombay Street, before eventually being driven off, largely by the efforts of the locals, armed with sticks, stones and bottles. These forces were augmented by a small group of old Republicans like Liam Hannaway, Gerry Adams's uncle, who told me afterwards that he and his comrades were armed with somewhere between six and ten old weapons. One which has passed into the folklore of Belfast was a Wild West .45 Colt revolver with a defective chamber which could only be moved manually after a shot was fired.

In the defence of Bombay Street, a 15-year-old boy was shot dead. The monastery was ultimately saved, but through the efforts of the residents of the district, rather than because of troop deployment. Eye-witness accounts of the events of 14 and 15 August from several sources agree that the troops were marched past the beleaguered monastery, down Clonard Street, and on to the Falls Road several hundred yards from the monastery, and out of sight of Cupar Street, from which its assailants were emerging.[21] Apparently, the sort of alarmist and inaccurate assessment of the situation which the Unionists had given London in Peacocke's request for military assistance had led the army to believe that a major attack was going to be mounted on the Falls Road, not on the monastery behind them. Efforts to get the troops to advance towards the besieged monastery were met with a stock response: 'We have our orders.' Eventually the superior of the monastery, Father P.J. Egan, found a senior officer who agreed to help, and approximately two hours later, at about nine p.m., a group of soldiers took up position. Father Egan subsequently gave a celebrated account of what happened next. It included the following:

They [the troops] got into military formation and they charged down the street, charged the attackers. And the man in command shouted out an order to the assailants: 'Come out,' he said, 'with your hands up, and we'll not shoot.'

But the command was answered with a litany of obscenities, punctuated with uncomplimentary references to the Pope and Fenians and to the British Tommies. Instead of coming out with their hands up they shortly came out with guns blazing and petrol bombs being fired all over the place. More houses were set on fire and at their approach the soldiers turned and ran away. Well I have not heard, despite all this gun play coming from the area, I certainly have not heard that on the following morning police tenders pulled up at the houses of well-known leaders of the extreme Protestants, pulling them out of their beds and taking them into custody on the suspicion of their being illegally in possession of arms. I haven't heard that. And if you have heard it, I'd be very interested if you'd come and tell me, because, so far as I know, during fifty years of British rule in the Six Counties of Ireland that has never happened.

Again we are tempted to ask ourselves, was it perhaps people who were the possessors of legally held firearms that did the shooting on this occasion? But the supposition is too dreadful to pursue it. After retreating, the military soon reformed their ranks and they came down along these streets again and they took up their positions, some in Kashmir Road, and some in Waterville Street. But, undaunted by their presence, the attackers came along again with their petrol bombs and systematically, they went from door to door in Bombay Street, kicking in some doors and breaking in some windows, and throwing petrol bombs into the houses.

They stood outside the school, and in full view of the military, they broke the windows and threw bombs, fire bombs into the premises, into the school. Now, men, do not for one minute blame them. They had orders and their orders on this particular night were: 'Don't fire.' So they told me afterwards, because I was amazed at the performance and I asked them, and they told me their orders were not to fire. I do not blame these men who must act on their orders. But I certainly do blame the people who gave the information which resulted in the military getting that type of order.[22]

Not only did the residents of the Clonard district blame the people who gave the troops their orders for the Bombay Street burnings, and the death of young Gerard McAuley, a 15-year-old member of the IRA's youth wing, Na Fianna; they also blamed the IRA for failing in the traditional role of defenders. The letters IRA went up on gable walls as: Irish Ran Away and I Ran Away. The Catholic districts of Belfast were in a ferment. The debate between force and constitutional action was now swinging in favour of force. But for the moment, the initiative still lay with those who took their line from Dublin. The commander of the Belfast IRA, Billy McMillen, had been arrested during the riots, but his second in command, Jim Sullivan, was at liberty, and still had sufficient authority and respect to be supported in the setting up of the Central Citizens' Defence Committee in the immediate aftermath of the Bombay Street burning, on 16 August. The CCDC stood in the same relationship to the IRA as did the civil rights movement. IRA members were active in it, but so were a wide variety of other interests: the clergy, represented by Canon Padraig Murphy, a prominent Belfast parish priest; the left-wing MP, Paddy Devlin, and leading Catholic businessmen like Tom Conaty. The CCDC was mainly inspired by the fear that the Protestant mobs would return. It threw up barricades in Catholic districts, and organised welfare activities. It also organised patrols of the ghetto areas at night, because the absence of the hated RUC made for the presence of Catholic hooliganism, in addition to the threat of would-be assassins. As in any part of the world where a police force is used, not to maintain the peace, but to enforce 'our' law on 'them', some of the criticism directed at the RUC was unjust. Individual members of the force behaved with bravery and professionalism throughout the disturbances. So too on occasion did individual B Specials. But either body could expect as little general credit for this as could the IRA for the fact that, to my knowledge, individual members of the organisation have, on occasion, saved warders or security personnel from recognition, and certain death. However, the overriding fact, so far as the Catholics were concerned, is that unquestionably there was collusion by individual members of the force, who, for instance, were seen in some cases to abandon traffic control duties and vanish just before the Orange mobs arrived.

Of the homes and buildings damaged or destroyed in the rioting, 83% were Catholic-occupied. In all, the August riots claimed seven lives. Seven hundred and fifty people are reported to have been injured. But this total is probably far too low, given the number of Catholics who were known to have gone across the border for treatment.

Apart from the illegal barricades put up by Catholics, and sometimes emulated in Protestant districts also, the authorities, in an effort to get control of the security situation, put up a sort of mini Berlin Wall right across the Falls and Shankill districts in an effort to keep down incursions into either side. Unlike the Berlin Wall, the Belfast one still stands, and, tragically, over the years, has been strengthened and added to.

CCDC-type activities did not satisfy the aspirations of traditional Republicans, and on 24 August an important meeting took place between groups of leading Republicans from both north and south of the border. They included Daithi O'Connell, Seamus Twomey, Jimmy Steele, Jimmy Drumm, Billy McKee, Leo Martin, John and Billy Kelly, Joe Cahill and Gerry Adams. The upshot of the discussions was a decision that, beginning with the Belfast IRA leaders, McMillen and Sullivan, they would overthrow the Goulding leadership in Dublin. Their objective was a purely Republican one, to generate such turmoil that the British would be forced to introduce direct rule, and subsequently to concede the inevitability of a united Ireland. The plan went into operation the following month when McMillen was released from jail. He was confronted by an armed group led by McKee, who said they were taking over the movement because of its failure to protect the Catholics during the August burnings.

However, in the circumstances of the moment, he proved impossible to shift, because many of those who now wanted to oust him had already dropped out of the movement due to its Marxist tendencies; to the theologically minded IRA, it was anathema to hand over guns to people outside the movement. However, a compromise agreement was arrived at, which would have important implications for the future leadership of the movement, and lead to its being directed from Belfast, not Dublin. McKee and some of his supporters joined McMillen and Sullivan in a northern command, independent of Dublin. From then on, efforts were made to get in guns and support from any quarter from which it might be forthcoming, but for the best part of a year, this support was very slow to manifest itself.

There was a honeymoon period between troops and Catholics which lasted for several months, much to the chagrin of the reorganising IRA. The British gave tangible evidences of reform, and James Callaghan proved himself a master of public relations, being received with acclamation in the 'no-go' areas of Derry, and being generally popular in Belfast – with the Catholics. The Protestants were outraged and fearful at the changes which the upheavals brought in their train. Their hegemony was at risk. The Cameron Report, issued on 12 September 1969, found that the civil rights protestors were not simply IRA propagandists; there actually was something rotten in the state of Northern Ireland. The report found in favour of the Catholics in every major area of complaint: the absence of one man, one vote; discrimination in housing and employment; gerrymandering; the operation of the Special Powers Act; and the existence of the B Specials. It acknowledged that the frustration of Catholics at this state of affairs was justified. And it spoke about how Paisley's creations, the UCDC and the UPV, had worked to engender a situation that became 'readily translated into physical violence against civil rights demonstrators'.[23] If this were not bad enough, the report went on to state that its judgements had been borne out 'by decisions already taken by the Northern Ireland Government since these disturbances began'. Worse was to befall the Protestant community a month later. On 11 October, the Hunt

Report was published, recommending the abolition of the B Specials. On the same day, Callaghan issued a communiqué which promised improvement in the contentious areas of local government administration, the legal system, and policing. It also foreshadowed the setting up of a new housing authority, and said that the incitement to hatred laws would be overhauled.

So far as the Protestants were concerned, the abolition of the B Specials *was* an incitement to hatred. Callaghan rubbed further salt into Protestant wounds by replacing Peacocke, the alarmist RUC commissioner, who resigned on the publication of the Hunt Report, with Sir Arthur Young, a former London police commissioner. To the wrath and incredulity of the Unionists, Hunt also recommended that the RUC become an unarmed force. Other recommendations which were clearly designed to mollify the Protestants were overlooked. These included replacing the Specials with another less partisan (it was hoped, mistakenly) part-time military force, and the creation of an RUC reserve. Some of the most ferocious, and certainly most significant, rioting of the period ensued. The Protestant Shankill erupted in fury. Constable Arbuckle had the melancholy distinction of becoming the first policeman to be killed in the Troubles. He was shot by a Protestant sniper as Protestant mobs, waving Union Jacks, attacked the troops. They called for the restoration of the B Specials, and the departure of 'the English' back home. The only sounds of approval emanating from the mobs were slogans such as 'Paisley is our leader'.

The appointment of Sir Arthur Young, however, was received with acclaim by the Catholics. The climate improved so much that the barricades were taken down in Derry and in Belfast. They stayed down, even though in a ham-handed public relations gesture, of a sort that was to repercuss very badly upon the authorities the following year, the army drove a Real Live Catholic Bishop, as Dr Philbin, in whose diocese Belfast lay, was evidently perceived, in his purple regalia through the Falls area in an army vehicle to show that the dismantling had his blessing. Callaghan earned further Brownie points by appointing a Unionist, Dr Robert Simpson, as Minister for Community Relations (on 29 October). Simpson scored with the Catholic community by resigning from both the Masonic and the Orange Order, and becoming a minister. The following month, the publication of the Electoral Law Act (NI) on 24 November made it clear that the word about electoral reform was about to be made flesh – the Act provided for the introduction of one man, one vote in local government elections, and the abolition of the ratepayer qualification. Perhaps optimists, like the present author, dared to hope the Irish issue was at last about to be solved.

Alas, it was not to be. Events now moved at two levels, the visible and the unseen. The visible was the continued opposition of much of the Unionist community to the Labour Government's reforms; the hidden, the slow coming back to life of the Irish physical-force tradition, as manifested by the IRA. The immediate reaction of Belfast Republicans to the August burnings has been described. But continuing as though the letters IRA had never been translated as Irish Ran Away, the Dublin leadership stayed on the Marxist path and, meeting in secret, ratified a proposal to set up a National Liberation Front to embrace Sinn Féin and the Irish Communist Party, along with a number of other left-wing groups. In addition, the Gouldingites decided to drop the abstention policy, so that Sinn Féin representatives could take their seats, if elected, in the Dail, at Stormont, or at Westminster. As soon as the meeting was over, Seán MacStíofáin, who had been jailed alongside Cathal Goulding for his part in the Felstead arms raid in Essex, drove to Belfast where another gathering was in progress. It was to appoint him as Chief of Staff of the Provisional IRA.

The membership of the new Army Council included Ruairi O'Bradaigh, Daithi O'Connell, Patrick Mulcahy, Leo Martin and Joe Cahill. Their dissent from the Goulding–Johnston line became public knowledge on 11 January 1970, when Sinn Féin met in a Dublin hotel to ratify the abstention and NLF decisions. O'Bradaigh, O'Connell and MacStíofáin staged a walkout, followed by a large section of the audience, and made their way to the Kevin Barry Hall in Parnell Square where a 'Provisional Caretaker Executive' of Sinn Féin was set up. The use of the word 'provisional' by both the IRA and Sinn Féin owed its origins to the fact that the 1919 insurgents had also set up a 'provisional government'. The wing of the IRA which remained with Goulding termed itself the 'Official IRA', and used gum to affix Easter lilies to the lapels of its adherents. This eventually led to the Gouldingites being known as 'stickies', whereas the Provisionals, who used pins, became known as 'pinheads', or more generally as Provos, or 'Provies'.

THE ARMS TRIAL

Such in broad outline were the events which led to the birth of the Provisionals. They had emerged from the hatreds of Irish history, invasion, rebellion, famine, sectarianism, and more immediately the distillation of all these factors into the upheavals triggered in Northern Ireland by the Butler Education Act generation's attempt to solve old problems in a new way.

The 'Arms Trial' was the most significant and potentially the most destabilising political trial in the history of the century. It was set in train by the events of the 12th and subsequent days of August 1969. Dublin's decision-taking politicians were descended upon by distraught Nationalists seeking assistance, and not merely assistance in the form of money or rehousing. There was a general demand for guns to prevent what seemed the imminent slaughter of Catholics. As we have seen, the British Government viewed this threat so seriously that it took the distasteful step of sending in the army, accompanied by a future prime minister, James Callaghan, to carry out its disgracefully, and disastrously, neglected task of introducing democracy to 'Ulster'. Both collectively and individually, the Dublin Government also took the situation seriously from the Taoiseach, Jack Lynch, down. After Lynch's 'field hospitals' speech, the Minister for Foreign Affairs, Dr Patrick Hillery, was dispatched to New York in a futile effort to get the UN to send a peacekeeping force to the Six Counties. As Britain is a permanent member of the Security Council she had no difficulty in having the issue adjourned on 20 August. According to the UN Charter, no matter may be considered by the Security Council if one of its permanent members considers it to be of vital domestic concern. Dublin was fully aware of the possibility of this outcome before Hillery even boarded his plane, but the Government considered it essential that it be seen to take public action. It would subsequently become even more concerned to ensure that some of its other activities remained private, and to this day there is debate as to whether what happened should be viewed as official policy, or as the response of individual ministers to the sudden crisis.

Probably the best way to describe the situation within the Cabinet is that it was an unromantic triangle involving the two most forceful ministers, Neil T. Blaney and Charles J. Haughey, and the Taoiseach himself, Jack Lynch. In many ways, Lynch resembled his northern counterpart, Terence O'Neill. They were both fundamentally decent men caught up in a horrific situation, for which neither had either anticipation nor preparedness. To a degree both were compromise candidates for the position they held, and to a degree both existed in political cultures in which the backward glance, dogma and old prejudices were important. But there the resemblance ends. Lynch's constituency did not contain anything of the same quotient of dementia on which Unionist politics fed, and when the storm broke, Lynch was able to wait it out, showing inter alia a greater empathy with the man in the street, and more cunning and toughness than his enemies had supposed.

When the August crisis broke, Blaney was the figure in the Cabinet who, in both the public mind and in fact, had the greatest identity with the northern situation. He came from the border county of Donegal, from a strongly Republican family which had helped to set up Fianna Fáil. He was a legendary wheeler-dealer, whose personal political machine would have won the admiration of Tammany Hall. From across the political spectrum, people of all persuasions contacted Blaney in the wake of the rioting in Derry and Belfast. Haughey, per contra, had never been associated in the public mind with the north, and was thought of as the epitome of the business-orientated New Man of the mohair-suited wing of Fianna Fáil. However, he too had strongly Republican antecedents. His father had been a prominent IRA officer in Michael Collins's time, and more importantly, he was not a man to allow anyone in Cabinet, Blaney or anyone else, to outshine him on the north, or any other issue. There may have been a good deal of truth in the explanation given to me by a cynical, but knowledgeable, Fianna Fáil insider of how the 'Arms Trial' came about: 'Haughey wanted to make sure that he played outside Blaney. But he played so far outside him that he played himself into touch.'

The question addressed to the members of the triangle, as it was to the Cabinet, and to southern society as a whole, was: 'What are we going to do?'

To some northern Nationalists, the question meant 'What are we going to do to prevent ourselves being slaughtered in our beds?' To some members of Fianna Fáil, it meant 'Is this our chance to get back the Fourth Green Field? Do we invade, supply guns, humanitarian aid, appeal to the UN? What?' In the confusion and jostling for position that burst on the Dublin Government, the answer was a qualified yes, to all of the above.

Jack Lynch told me himself that he avoided the blizzard of phone calls and visits made to him on the night of 12–13 August by taking a sleeping tablet. But there was no avoiding the Cabinet's reaction on the morning of the 13th. The 'field hospitals' speech was drafted for him by his colleagues, something which had never happened to an Irish Taoiseach before, and the Hillery initiative to the UN was undertaken. A Cabinet sub-committee dealing with the north was set up, and Haughey, as Minister for Finance, was given authorisation to disperse funds for the alleviation of distress. Contingency plans were drawn up which, amongst other items, included an invasion of the north should the much-talked about Doomsday scenario arise. Army units were quietly deployed in Castleblaney, Cootehill, Dundalk and Cavan. The army suffered from a shortage of young officers – the average age of officers was 42 – and NCOs, and indeed of equipment of every sort, including ammunition. It is conceivable that a sudden incursion into Newry or Derry might have resulted in the seizing and temporary holding of these towns, but as the army only had enough ammunition for approximately 72 hours' continuous firing, nothing at all could have been done to alleviate the situation of Belfast Catholics, or indeed of those who lived any distance away from the border. If the Catholics were to be defended by military means, they would have to look to their own defences.

By way of at least partially meeting the problem, a £100,000 fund was set up which was supposed to be distributed by the Red Cross. But the northern-based Red Cross apparently objected to this, and a number of bank accounts were opened under various pseudonyms in Dublin. Some of this money was administered by Captain James Kelly, a rising star in Irish military intelligence. He had been on holiday in Derry when the Battle of the Bogside commenced, and his reports impressed his superior, Colonel Michael Hefferon, the head of military intelligence.

Throughout the ensuing months, everything that Kelly did was done with the full knowledge and consent of Hefferon, who also kept his minister, James Gibbons, the Minister for Defence, fully informed of what was going on. In subsequent court cases, it was revealed that Gibbons himself also spoke with Kelly, and at no time either directed, or suggested to him, that he should desist from his activities. These activities covered a wide range of contacts, including with people in Northern Ireland who would emerge as leaders of the Provisional IRA, and continental arms dealers, with whom Kelly arranged for the importation of arms paid for with Irish taxpayers' money. Haughey also saw to it that Kelly was given money to convene a meeting in Bailieborough, County Cavan, on the weekend of 4 and 5 October 1969, attended by prominent Republicans from all over Northern Ireland. The Republicans told Kelly that they needed the guns to protect Catholics when, not if, the Protestants descended on the Catholic ghettos again. The Doomsday scenario was very much to the fore at this juncture. But Lynch was increasingly showing himself to be a reluctant Taoiseach indeed, reluctant not only to engage in military activities, but even to acknowledge that events of a military nature were in train. He was uncertain a) what would the outcome be if he engaged in a trial of strength with Blaney and Haughey in Cabinet, and b) what would the reaction in the party be to a Taoiseach who could be represented as acting to prevent Catholics acquiring the means to defend themselves against Orange aggression in the north. Lynch did make a speech in Tralee which differed markedly in tone and content from Blaney and Boland's subsequent utterances on the north. Boland said that Britain was to blame for what was happening in the north. Blaney made a practice of stating that force was not ruled out on the part of the Irish Government as a means of ending partition. Lynch had said that he was not seeking the violent overthrow of Stormont and reiterated Lemass's approach of unity by consent.

Lynch finally jerked the reins with two public statements in quick succession. One occurred in the course of a radio interview on RTE on 28 December in which he said he had had 'a firm chat' with Blaney. After it, he said, Blaney understood 'that the members of the Government must adhere to Government policy. In fact he does.' Then, at the Fianna Fáil Ard Fheis, on 18 January, he again ruled out force, and challenged anyone in the audience to confront him to the contrary. No one did. Lynch went on to tell the Ard Fheis that it would have to be recognised that the majority community in Northern Ireland wanted to remain linked to Britain and refused proposals that Fianna Fáil should organise in the Six Counties. So far as the public face of Fianna Fáil policy was concerned, Lynch had judged the mood of the country perfectly.

Where the party's private initiatives towards Northern Ireland were concerned, Lynch's Hamlet-like indecision would cause the Secretary of the Department of Justice, Peter Berry, to say later: 'All this could not have gone on for several months without the knowledge of the Taoiseach, unless he was wilfully turning the blind eye.' But the blind eye could flicker into recognition at times. There is a record of a sulphuric conversation between Haughey and Berry over the arrest of a group of Derry men who had been receiving weapons training at Fort Dunree in County Donegal.[24] It emerged during the conversation that Berry had been acting on orders from Lynch. But the Cabinet sub-committee had hitherto apparently felt that such training came within its remit. The arrests, which put an end to the training programme, occurred between Lynch's rebuttal of Blaney and before his Ard Fheis speech, indicating that despite his indecision Lynch was groping towards a reassertion of his authority over his turbulent priests. However, even though after the Baliborough meeting Lynch was informed that a discussion had taken place at which it had been decided to try to put guns into the hands of those who had attended and the people in the north whom they represented, no action was taken.

Berry also came into conflict with Haughey over the events which brought the arms affair to public attention. The wing of security controlled by Berry, the Irish Special Branch, had received information alleging that Kelly, Haughey, his brother Jock, and a Belgian friend of Blaney's, Albert Luyks, were engaged in attempts to buy arms on the Continent and then to ship them to Dublin from Antwerp. Kelly had visited Germany in February and March 1970, buying weaponry which should have landed in Dublin aboard the *City of Dublin* on 25 March. Had this happened, Haughey had given instructions to Customs, in his capacity as Minister for Finance, that the arms were to be cleared without being inspected. However, British intelligence prevented the arms from being placed aboard the ship because no end-user's certificate had been provided.

This setback was countered by sending the resourceful Captain Kelly to Europe, where he arranged to have the cargo transferred to Trieste, and then had it switched to Vienna, whence it was to be flown to Dublin airport on a specially chartered plane. However, Haughey was tipped off that the Special Branch had been alerted to seize the cargo when it arrived at Dublin unless they received instructions to do otherwise. Berry later gave evidence that Haughey tried to get him to have it passed through with a guarantee that the arms would go straight to the north. However, Berry said that when Haughey phoned the Department of Justice, he was informed that, with the authority of the Minister for Justice, the cargo was to be seized if it landed. According to Berry, Haughey then said, 'I had better have it called off.' Whether the arms were originally intended to be stored south of the border and only issued to the northerners for defence when need arose, or to be sent directly, was a matter of some argument. I understand that one small consignment of armaments sent earlier did go north.

Berry, who had had an oft-times abrasive relationship with Haughey during the latter's term as Minister for Justice, had also discovered that Haughey had made contact with Cathal Goulding and discussed the northern situation with him. Berry supplied the Cabinet with a record of this meeting, but later he, and the Cabinet, accepted Haughey's explanation that the contact had been a casual one, of a sort that would have been unusual at other times, but was understandable in the extraordinary circumstances of the hour. The Goulding wing of the IRA do not appear to have received anything of significance in the way of support as a result of all this. A man through whom any monies paid over would have passed at this juncture told me that Goulding asked for £50,000, but received only £2,300. The whole question of arming northern Catholics had arisen after all because Goulding and company had turned away from the physical-force tradition. They did not appear to be willing to fight. The men who came to Balieborough did. This factor, as much as any question of distaste for 'reds' as opposed to 'greens', governed the choice of who Blaney and the others decided to support in the north. British intelligence of course was fully aware of what was going on from an early stage. A Captain Randall, whom Captain Kelly and Jock Haughey met in London, turned out to be a British agent, who would have been assassinated in Ireland were it not for Captain Kelly's intervention.

As a result of the divided counsels in Cabinet between hawks and doves, and because of Lynch's determined blind-eye policy, a factor which was to bedevil British attempts to curb the IRA in Northern Ireland played a role in the arms affair. In the north, MI5 and MI6 were engaged in a turf war for much of the conflict. The RUC Special Branch and the British army often failed to supply each other with information received by one or other. Scotland Yard, which was the traditional British anti-IRA force, was also isolated by MI5 in the turf wars. In the south there was an evident lack of liaison between the Departments of Defence and Justice. It has never been suggested that Colonel Hefferon acted other than correctly at any stage in the saga, and that therefore Gibbons was fully in the picture. Given Gibbons's generally friendly relationship with Lynch also, it is assumed that he kept his Taoiseach informed. Berry, however, revealed in court that he found it very difficult to get information to the Taoiseach. His minister, Micheal O'Morain, who took to drink under the strain of the affair, was quoted by Berry as saying that from the time of the Baliborough meeting onward, he had kept Lynch informed, but found it impossible to get him to take any action. Eventually, in the wake of the attempt to fly arms into Dublin airport, having taken the unusual, die-casting step of consulting with de Valera, Berry went directly to Lynch. He told Lynch what he knew about Blaney and Haughey's involvement in an attempted gun-running, and as he also informed him that he had consulted the President, Lynch realised that the time had come to act.

However, he was delayed in doing so for a week, because Haughey had sustained injuries, he claimed in a fall from a horse, which hospitalised him.[25] Lynch finally saw him in hospital on 29 April 1970. He made a statement in the Dail subsequently, in which he said that both Blaney and Haughey had denied 'in any way the attempted importation of arms'. He said that he had agreed to both men's request for time to consider their position. However, the pace was forced by Liam Cosgrave, who had been tipped off by a source thought to have originated with British intelligence. Cosgrave first tried to have the story printed in the *Sunday Independent*, but the paper refused to have anything to do with such a hot potato. Cosgrave then confronted Lynch, who in turn confronted Blaney and Haughey, seeking their resignations. When both refused, Lynch proceeded, as he was entitled to do under the Constitution, to ask President de Valera to remove them from office. The dismissals were announced in a Government statement at three o'clock in the morning of 6 May. Two of the sacked men's colleagues, Kevin Boland, and Paudge Brennan, Parliamentary Secretary to Boland, who had been Minister for Local Government, resigned in protest on learning of the news. As Lynch had also accepted the resignation of Micheal O'Morain 'on health grounds', the Fianna Fáil Government was thus rocked by a series of unprecedented departures, and the country by rumours that a coup d'état had narrowly been averted.

The Dail then went into an extraordinary continuous sitting that lasted for the best part of two days. But at the end of the marathon debate, during which fisticuffs were never too far away, Blaney, Boland and Haughey all voted with Lynch, as they did also at a Fianna Fáil parliamentary party meeting which unanimously upheld the Taoiseach's right to hire and fire as he chose. The principle that there are two sides in politics, an inside and an outside, had been thoroughly vindicated. Haughey and company had all demonstrated that they wished to be on the inside. Jack Lynch also wished to see them on the inside – of jail. Blaney, Haughey, Captain Kelly, the Belfast Republican John Kelly and Albert Luyks were all arrested and charged with attempting illegally to import arms into the state. The charges against Blaney were soon dropped. The others, however, were subjected to the ordeal of two trials. The first ended after the presiding judge, Andrias O'Kcefe, the President of the High Court, declared a mistrial after a defence lawyer accused him of unfairness. The defendants were furious, because it had become clear at that stage that the proceedings were going their way. If Gibbons, as Minister for Defence, had sanctioned the arms importation, then no question of illegality arose. And Gibbons had admitted that Captain Kelly had told him that he was planning to import arms, but that he, his political boss, had not told him to desist. Colonel Hefferon had been particularly damaging to the state's case. Although called as a prosecution witness, he revealed that Captain Kelly had at all times reported fully to him on his activities and that he in turn had informed Gibbons about the details of the planned arms importation. The arms he said were intended for 'the northern defence committees, in the event that a situation would arise where the government would agree to them going to them'. He had directed Captain Kelly to liaise with Haughey so that Haughey could sanction their importation without customs clearance being necessary. In the circumstances, many people in Ireland felt that O'Keefe had declared the mistrial to spare the Government the ignominy of losing the case.

But worse was to follow from the point of the Government's credibility in general, and Haughey's and Gibbons's in particular. A new trial opened on 6 October and the state tried to avoid calling Hefferon, but the presiding judge, Seamus Henchy, directed that he be recalled as a prosecution witness and that the defence could thus cross-examine him. Haughey averred that he was unaware of the exact contents of the cargo which was supposed to have come into Dublin initially on the *City of Dublin*, but as he had discussed its arrival with Gibbons, he assumed that whatever it was was legal. He also said that even though he had had the conversations referred to above with Berry, he remained unaware of the nature of the cargo. This appeared particularly difficult to understand in light of the fact that, as the Special Branch waited at the docks in the mistaken belief that the arms were aboard the *City of Dublin*, the group which was supposed to receive them, including Captain Kelly and John Kelly, discussed the arms shipments with customs officials, as they did later with officials at Dublin airport. Thus Customs and Excise, which is part of the Department of Finance, Haughey's department, was fully aware of the nature of the cargo which was supposed to be cleared through customs without hindrance.

Once again Hefferon, and this time Captain Kelly, were convincing witnesses, who impressed the court that they had acted as they had in the belief that they were doing their government's bidding. The Belfast Republican, John Kelly, received a prolonged burst of applause, in which at least one member of the jury joined, when he finished giving his evidence. In the course of it he said that he and the others being tried were charged as a 'matter of political expediency'. He said that everything he had done had been with the full knowledge of Gibbons 'and the government as a whole':

> I want to be very emphatic here, that we were coming from all parts of the Six Counties not to indulge in tea parties, not to be entertained, but to elicit in so far as we could what was the opinion of this government in relation to the Six Counties. We did not ask for blankets or feeding bottles. We asked for guns and nobody from Taoiseach Lynch down refused our request or told us that this was contrary to Government policy . . . I find it a very sad situation indeed that these institutions for which so much was sacrificed, which had been gained by such nobility, should be abused in this manner . . . There is no victory for anyone in these proceedings, my Lord. There is only an echo of sadness from the graves of the dead generations.

The result of the trial became a foregone conclusion when the judge summed up for the jury on 23 October 1970. Between Haughey, Berry and Gibbons, he said, someone had committed perjury. 'Either Mr Gibbons concocted this and has come to court and perjured himself, or it happened. There does not seem to me to be any way of avoiding a total conflict on this issue between Mr Haughey and Mr Gibbons.' After two trials and a hurricane of gossip and innuendo it took the jury about 45 minutes to return a verdict of 'not guilty'.

The amounts of money involved were minuscule; the amount of arms which did succeed in trickling through to Northern Ireland, to what was, at the time, an IRA controlled by the Officials, obviously had very little lasting impact on the situation there. Because of their left-wing orientation, the Officials are known at a later stage to have received large quantities of arms and ammunition from the Soviet Union,[26] but because of deficiencies in the Goulding/ Johnson leadership, and the irrelevance of trying to graft a left–right complexion on to the Orange–Green division, neither ideology, nor shipments, constituted the significant deposit of the attempt to take the IRA to the left. What did have a lasting effect was the infiltration technique which led to the shift in IRA policy. For several years, possibly for some decades, 'stickies' continued to infiltrate the trade unions, the media, particularly RTE, the civil service, and the Labour movement generally.

What really provided the bedrock of Provisional IRA support in Northern Ireland was not the manipulation of Dublin politicians, but a situation contained in an observation by a British army officer describing how Catholics got caught up in riots with fatal results in Northern Ireland, which contained an uncanny resemblance to the conditions described by General Maxwell which also had fateful consequences in 1916. Colonel Roy Jackson said that the chronic housing problems in Derry were a contributory factor in rioting in the city, adding:

> Although a generalisation, Catholics tended to have more children than Protestants and in 1970 there were usually not enough beds in all households to go round. The members of each household therefore often took it in turns to sleep and whilst the parents were sleeping the younger children were to be found walking the city; during riots they might attach themselves to the hooligan element.[27]

While Republicans might quibble with the description of themselves as 'the hooligan element', no one could disprove the truth of the Colonel's basic analysis. In the north, the Six Counties were a vast, dangerous lake of political petrol waiting for a spark to be dropped into it to explode. In the south, the situation did not explode, though the arms trial did have a number of outcomes. Haughey survived the disgrace of being put on trial and went on to become Taoiseach before being finally brought down by revelations that for much of his time in office his lavish lifestyle had been sustained by donations from wealthy businessmen. Blaney did not hold ministerial office again, but he had a successful career both as a member of the European parliament and as an independent TD. John Kelly, the Belfast Republican, later served six months on a charge of being a member of the IRA, and at the time of writing is a member of the Belfast Assembly. But Captain Kelly became the Irish Dreyfus through being forced into early retirement and being denied what had hitherto appeared to be a promising career. Colonel Hefferon had reached retirement age by the time he was called to give evidence and so it was generally assumed that no sanctions could have been, or were, imposed on him. But as this was being written, it emerged that documents discovered under the Freedom of Information Act showed that the prosecution had altered his original statement, made to Gardai in May 1970, detailing what he knew about plans to import arms into the Six Counties.[28] The alterations, in the words of the contemporary Minister for Justice, Michael McDowell, appeared to make Hefferon's statement 'more compatible with that of other prosecution witnesses and, in particular the testimony of James Gibbons TD'. In his unaltered statement Hefferon had given chapter and verse of who was involved in the arms importation plot and stated categorically that Gibbons was fully aware of what was being done, which would have undermined the state's case. It had earlier been discovered that a statement of Captain Kelly's had been similarly altered. What this means is that Colonel Hefferon's statement originally said that Captain Kelly had told Gibbons he was going to Germany to get arms for the north. But by changing 'him' to 'me' the

Colonel's statement was altered to make it appear that Kelly had told the Colonel, not Gibbons, what he was doing. Due process in the Republic had become infected by seepage from the northern contagions, and would continue to be so throughout the conflict. Phone tapping, and a turning of a blind eye to police excesses, became commonplace for much of the next 25 years.

Captain Kelly received a posthumous vindication. After years of struggling to clear his name, he died on 17 July 2003. On learning of his death, the Taoiseach, Bertie Ahern, took the unusual step of issuing an official statement saying that Kelly had honourably served his country. Ahern said: 'It is my belief that at all times during those difficult days in the early period of the Troubles, Captain Kelly acted on what he believed were the proper orders of his superiors . . . He was acquitted of all the charges laid against him. As far as the State is concerned, he was innocent of those charges.'

By coincidence Captain Kelly's funeral took place as the body of another Kelly was discovered, Dr David Kelly, whose death led to the Hutton inquiry. In their differing ways both stories illustrate what can happen to loyal servants of a state when their masters need a scapegoat.

Politically, of course, there was considerable short-term fallout from the arms trial. Lynch had to reshuffle his Cabinet, and ability was visibly sacrificed for dependability in many of the appointments. Kevin Boland, who resigned over the sackings of Haughey and the others, would hardly have been a minister in Fianna Fáil in the first place had his father not been one of the party's founding fathers. He proved to have neither the charisma nor the leadership qualities required for political success, when a party he founded, Aontacht Eireann (Republican Unity Party), petered out after a few years, after achieving very little beyond serving to keep the 'Arms Trial' before the public mind for somewhat longer than might have otherwise been the case.

NINE

DECADE OF DISSENSION

THE SOUTH AFTER 1969

In the mid-sixties, neither southern politics nor society contained any obvious hint of the tensions which would afflict government in the Republic from the period of the August 1969 burnings onward in Northern Ireland. Jack Lynch appeared to cruise effortlessly through the takeover from Lemass. The attendance at the first Ard Fheis that he presided over (in 1966) was strongly representative of the GAA, and delegates were only too delighted to welcome a Taoiseach who held six All-Ireland medals. Lynch's pleasant, deceptively self-effacing, modest demeanour did the rest. As yet, the hubris and ambitions of party colleagues like Charles Haughey were largely hidden. In fact, 'the youngest and best Cabinet in Europe' image fitted in rather well with that portion of the swinging sixties which Church and conservatism allowed to be (or were unable to prevent from being) swung in Holy Catholic Ireland, as the country was still being referred to in the classroom or pulpit. Haughey, who was given to telling people that he was the first *real* Minister for Finance the department had had, took over from Lynch. Blaney became Minister for Agriculture, Frank Aiken took off to the UN as Minister for Foreign Affairs. But, apart from a certain amount of reshuffling of other Cabinet posts, no great alterations took place following Lynch's accession to power. In May 1968, the death of Donough O'Malley created a by-election vacancy which set in train a mini-general election, as there were a number of other by-elections at around the same time. Fianna Fáil won all five, O'Malley being succeeded by his nephew, Desmond.

The Government's popularity was such that Fianna Fáil overreached itself in October by another attempt to remove proportional representation, which it coupled with a plan to change the number of TDs per constituency. The public correctly saw both proposals as having the same objective, the installation of Fianna Fáil governments in perpetuity. Both referenda were defeated by majorities of some 50% (657,898 votes to 423,496 against the proposal to abolish PR, and against the constituency alterations 656,803 to 424,185). As the economic problems which had contributed to Lemass's retirement hadn't gone away (the rash of strikes which afflicted the economy in the late sixties and seventies included one which closed the Republic's banks for lengthy periods in both decades, much to the amazement of the Europeans whom the

Irish were hoping to become partners with), one might have assumed that an election which Lynch called in June 1969 would have gone against the party, but two factors ensured that it did not.

Firstly, Labour unwisely continued with its go-it-alone policy, and secondly, Haughey introduced a blatantly election-slanted budget in the spring. This increased social welfare benefits across a wide range to the under-privileged, and I remember to my shame that the *Irish Press*, under my editorship, carried a banner headline describing the vote-buying exercise as a 'Share and Care Alike' budget. A combination of Lynch's personality, Neil Blaney's handling of the Fianna Fáil election machine, and the budget's timely display of Fianna Fáil's ability to wield together the industrialist and the widow dependent on children's allowances, returned Fianna Fáil with 75 seats, Fine Gael with 50 and Labour with 18. The Republic's political barometer appeared set fair. However, a few short months later, the August burnings took place in Northern Ireland, setting in train the events of the 'Arms Trial' described above, and for approximately two years, the good ship Fianna Fáil pitched and yawed uncertainly in some decidedly troubled waters.

In the immediate aftermath of his acquittal, Haughey gave a press conference on 23 October 1970 at which he said, 'I think those who are responsible for this debacle have no alternative but to take the honourable course which is open to them.' This was code for a sentiment which his supporters outside the court, and in bars around it, were expressing in chants which rose higher as the levels in pint glasses sank lower: 'Lynch must go.' However, Lynch did not go. He immediately began displaying something of the steel which helped to win those All-Ireland medals in one of the world's most demanding stick games, hurling. He had been in New York, addressing the United Nations, when Haughey spoke, but by the time he returned to Dublin three days later, he had orchestrated a welcome-home reception which would have done credit to a politburo photocall at the height of Stalinism. He was met at the airport by a solid phalanx of Fianna Fáil ministers, TDs and senators, all dutifully applauding as Lynch stepped off the plane. He followed this up by seeking and winning an overwhelming vote of confidence from the parliamentary party (70 to 3). On 10 November, he won a no-confidence debate on Gibbons in the Dail by 74 votes to 67. Despite Mr Justice Henchy's direction to the jury, as to the conflict of evidence between Haughey and Gibbons, Haughey (and Blaney) was amongst those who voted with the Government. Haughey still believed that Lynch must go, but obviously he wasn't going to go yet. Lynch also carried the day at the ugliest Fianna Fáil Ard Fheis in the party's history, held the following February. By this time, Boland's new party, Aontacht Eireann, was also taking shape, and there was a final outburst of bad feeling generated by the 'Arms Trial'. One of the high points of the Ard Fheis came when the normally controlled Paddy Hillery, his face contorted with fury, sprang to the microphone. He roared at the

surging delegates, some of whom were chanting 'Union Jack, Union Jack!':
'You can have Boland, but you won't have Fianna Fáil.' This sentiment
abided with the rank and file, and helped to explain why Boland failed to
make headway.

At the time, I was more interested in another statement from the platform,
a section of Lynch's speech which I had written, with an eye to quelling the
fears of Northern Protestants about Home Rule being Rome Rule. Referring
to the south's 'Catholic legislation', it said:

> ... times have changed. It was the great Protestant patriot Charles Stewart Parnell who
> said, 'No man may set a boundary to the march of a nation.' ... Where it can be shown
> that attitudes embodied in our laws and constitution give offence to liberty of conscience,
> then we are prepared to see what can be done to harmonise our views so that, without
> detracting from genuine values, a new kind of Irish society may be created equally
> agreeable to North and South.

It was not that agreeable in some quarters of the south. As Lynch delivered
these promises to an audience emanating equal measures of sulphur from the
'Arms Trial', and evidences of Guinness republicanism acquired at the bars,
more trouble descended. An early edition of the *Sunday Press* was delivered,
leading on a broadside from John Charles McQuaid against the idea of
legislative changes. Somehow he had got his hands on an advance copy of
Lynch's address. He followed this up with another onslaught a month later, a
letter read in every church in the Archdiocese. It warned against 'a disastrous
measure of legislation' to 'assist the unification of our country'. Such legislation, he wrote, would be 'an insult to our faith', a 'curse upon our country'.
John Charles McQuaid at least had no intention of advancing towards Irish
unity with a ballot box in one hand, and a condom in the other.

But times were changing. In less than a year, on 4 January 1972, John
Charles ceased to be Archbishop of Dublin. Whether he resigned or was
removed by the Vatican cannot be said with certainty at this stage. Certainly
when I called on him in retirement in his luxurious but lonely house in
Killiney, he did not give me the impression of being a happy man, although he
remained loyally silent on the events surrounding his departure. A year later
he died of a heart attack on 7 April 1973.

It was something of a watershed year in Irish society in many ways. Eamon
de Valera retired from the presidency and died two years later, in 1975. In a
mould-breaking election, he was succeeded by Erskine Childers, who for
many members of the Irish electorate became the first Protestant they had
voted for. Childers easily defeated Tom O'Higgins of Fine Gael. John
Charles McQuaid would not have welcomed that development. In fact, had
he not died in the spring of 1973 it is certain that another development that
year would have subjected his heart to very great strain. For in December
1973 the Supreme Court overturned a decision of the High Court which had
prevented a mother of four, Mrs Mary McGee, who could only have had

another child at serious risk to her life, from importing contraceptives. The appeal against the High Court's decision was made possible by financing from what, at first sight, may have appeared to be an unusual organisation to find in Holy Catholic Ireland, the Irish Family Planning Association – but not more unusual than the Irish Women's Liberation Movement which was also active around this time. One of its founders and moving spirits, the *Irish Press* woman editor, Mary Kenny, marked International Women's Day 1971 by sending Jack Lynch a pamphlet containing IWLM's aims. Her covering letter, on *Irish Press* note paper (a use never envisaged by the paper's founder, that lay Cardinal, Eamon de Valera, and which, when he learned of it, caused consternation to its then Editor-in-Chief de Valera's eldest son Vivion) invoked de Valera's constitution. She told Lynch[1]: 'Our basic aim, to begin with, is the implementation of the Constitution in its references to women.'

By way of implementing the changes which the IWLM wished to see introduced, Kenny and a group of her colleagues, most of them journalists, staged one of the publicity stunts of the century. They allowed it to be known that they were going with a group of women, many of them with babies, to Belfast, where they intended to purchase contraceptives, and then return with the dreaded condoms secreted in the babies' nappies, where the customs officials would be directed to find them. Media representatives from all over England and Ireland stood poised at Amiens Street station as the 'contraceptive train' pulled in, on 22 May 1971. Adding to the delights of the customs officers' searches, the libbers had fed the babies a generous amount of bottles on the journey from Belfast. The nappies were correspondingly well filled also, but to the disappointment of the waiting media horde, by pre-arranged decision the customs officials waved the women and their contraceptive babies through unsearched.

The changes that Mary Kenny and her colleagues in the IWLM sought were facilitated by entry to the EEC, which Ireland formally joined in 1973. Dr Hillery became Commissioner for Social Affairs. The economic benefits to farmers have already been discussed, but the benefits to Irish women in areas such as equal pay for equal work and ending discrimination against married women in the civil service and teaching professions were enormous also, both in economic and psychological terms. They also helped to provide the climate which led, ultimately, to the legalisation of contraception and divorce. In preparation for the implications of EEC membership for Irish women Lynch had set up a Commission on the Status of Women. In her letter, while complimenting the Taoiseach on this initiative, Mary Kenny crisply told Lynch:

> But of course it is the active and real changes that interest us most and one doesn't need to wait for the Commission's report to start removing some of the more glaring points of discrimination – starting possibly with the position of women in your very own Civil Service, would you believe?

'Active and real changes' in Irish society had been in train from the ending of World War II. Something approaching a welfare state had been laid down, and progressively throughout the seventies, the rights of the individual received more protection through a variety of legislation governing landlord and tenant relationships, hire purchase, consumer protection, restrictive practices, and also through the invocation of the constitution in the courts. As an expert on the period wrote: 'One successful constitutional action generated others' with the result that by the end of the seventies, a situation was arrived at wherein 'a week rarely passes in which constitutional issues are not being argued before the higher courts of the land'.[2] As we will see shortly, this development was to lead to one of the major constitutional crises of the seventies.

As Lynch's hold on the party tightened, and what happened in Belfast began more and more to interact with both London and Dublin, Lynch began cracking down on militant republicanism, increasingly free of criticism from ancestral voices within Fianna Fáil. In May 1972, the Special Criminal Court was re-introduced by Desmond O'Malley who, in the wake of the sackings and resignations caused by the 'Arms Trial', had become Minister for Justice at the age of 31. The Special Criminal Court provided for non-jury trials. Lynch closed down the Dublin office of Provisional Sinn Féin in October of 1972, and the following month Seán MacStíofáin was arrested and charged under the Offences Against the State Act. He announced that he would go on a hunger and thirst strike, which he managed to both sustain and circumvent, firstly by taking frequent showers and ultimately, when it became apparent that the Government was not going to release him, by contacting the IRA leadership who ordered him off the strike on 16 January 1973. By this time, his strike had created a great deal of publicity, partly because the IRA tried to rescue him from the Mater Hospital (and members of the raiding party were captured, and were themselves given long jail sentences) and partly because amongst those who visited him in hospital, albeit in more pacific manner, were Father Dermot Ryan, who had succeeded McQuaid as Archbishop of Dublin, and McQuaid himself.

Towards the end of November, another of Lynch's 'get tough' measures had the effect of convulsing the country. He introduced an Amendment Bill to the Offences Against the State Act, which gravely encroached on civil liberties. It permitted suspects to be sent to jail if a police superintendent stated in court that he believed them to be members of an illegal organisation. The Bill caused strong opposition in both Fine Gael and Labour to South African-style legislation, as it was termed. Patrick Cooney, who ironically would step into Desmond O'Malley's strong law and order role the following year, was particularly vehement in his opposition. It appeared that Fine Gael might split on the issue with the Cooney wing voting against the motion, and Cosgrave and those who thought like him, voting for the Government. Nevertheless, the conventional wisdom amongst political commentators was that the Government would not succeed in carrying the amendment, possibly

515

failing by only one vote, but failing nonetheless. A general election appeared inevitable.

Then, for the first time in the northern conflict, though not alas for the last, bombs suddenly exploded in Dublin. They went off outside Liberty Hall, and in nearby Sackville Place, killing two people and injuring 127, on the evening of 1 December. Fine Gael abstained, and Lynch won by 69 votes to 22. Who set off the bombs? No one was ever prosecuted for the fortuitous explosions, but inevitably Irish public opinion made British intelligence the prime suspect. The legislation was of the sort which the Heath government was pressing for at the time. Lynch followed up his crackdown by rounding up prominent members of Sinn Féin, including Ruairi O'Bradaigh, on 29 December.

The fact that he had a more or less clear run in office, once he mastered the turbulences of the 'Arms Trial' affair, may have prompted Lynch to misjudge the calling of a general election the following spring, on 28 February 1973, fifteen months before he would have had to go to the country. He may also have wished to go to the polls before some 140,000 young voters, of doubtful party allegiance, would come on the register later in the year as a result of a referendum held on 7 December 1972, which decided two issues: the removal of the clause governing 'the Special Position' of the Catholic Church in the constitution, and the reduction of the voting age from 21 to 18. Both may be taken as indicating the changes that were taking place in Irish society, but Lynch had hardly envisaged these including a change in government. The stated reasons for calling the election, which he gave in the Dail on 5 February, were that he wanted to end his minority situation in government, that he did not want to have a general election held at the same time as the forthcoming presidential election, and that he wanted the election out of the way before a border poll was held. But it is unlikely that Lynch factored into his consideration the one circumstance which was virtually guaranteed to put him out of office – Labour's abandonment of its 'no Coalition' stance.

It is virtually certain that, had the party not adopted this policy, it would have combined with Fine Gael to put Fianna Fáil out of office in 1969. Apart from the mere fact of helping to provide a credible alternative, there had been an influx to the party of high-profiled recruits such as Dr Conor Cruise O'Brien, whose name had remained before the public after Katanga, through his activities in universities as far apart as Ghana and New York, and David Thornley, a Trinity lecturer in political science, and an RTE personality, whom I would rate as one of the best brains of my generation. His premature death in 1978 was a real loss to Irish society. Another outstandingly able talent was Justin Keating, a veterinary surgeon who, like Thornley, had acquired a national profile as a current affairs broadcaster and commentator. The potential threat which these and other new faces in the Labour Party, such as the rising Trinity law lecturer and barrister Mary Burke (later to become internationally known by her married name, Mary Robinson), posed for Fianna Fáil in 1969, however, was nullified by a combination of the no-coalition policy and Jack Lynch's adroit use of 'red scare' tactics. Far too gentlemanly to mention the word communism, Lynch merely spoke mildly during the election campaign of 'alien ideologies'. A combination of Labour personalities openly advocating socialism, and a remark of Cruise O'Brien's that he would have preferred to see Ireland open an Embassy in Cuba, to some of the more traditional Catholic countries, did the rest. The passage of time, the result of the EEC vote, and the ever-present 'inside and outside' factor in politics meant that things were different in 1973 however. As soon as Lynch announced the election, it became evident that a coalition of Labour with Fine Gael was on the cards, and the two parties came together on a 14-point programme, which one historian[3] has described as 'not so much a programme as a string of platitudes pledging peace, social and economic reform, civil rights . . . etc.'. It certainly was a catch-all document, which aimed both at cashing in on the current agitation for women's rights, and at encouraging traditional Labour policies such as worker participation in state enterprises, reducing prices and unemployment, and increasing housing spending.

Moreover, the Labour-ites favoured proposals such as the introduction of a wealth tax, and of income tax for farmers, which had something of the same attraction for Fine Gael supporters as had holy water for the devil. However, the 'inside and outside' consideration took care of this difficulty, as it did of the inconvenient fact that Labour had combined with Sinn Féin to campaign against EEC entry which Fine Gael supported. Early on in the campaign, it became evident that the fatigue factor with Fianna Fáil, and the combined Fine Gael/Labour onslaught made a Fianna Fáil defeat inevitable. The Government party made a futile effort to stem the tide by introducing a shopping basket of electoral bribes a week before polling day. These included the abolition of rates, and an increase in social benefits. As befitting a man who had attempted to guide his party on a policy of butter before guns, where traditional republicanism was concerned, Lynch also promised to give families on social welfare a pound of butter per month, for virtually nothing (eight pence). As the party had feared it might, PR worked against Fianna Fáil at the election. Fine Gael and Labour votes transferred, and the coalition emerged from the election with 73 seats against Fianna Fáil's 69. There were two independents, Neil Blaney, who, like Charles Haughey, had headed the poll in his constituency, and Joseph Sheridan.

On 15 March, Cosgrave announced his new team. Garret FitzGerald, the rising star of Fine Gael since his election in 1969, was appointed Minister for Foreign Affairs, a move his critics felt was designed to keep him out of Finance, and the country. FitzGerald was generally regarded as being one of those whom Cosgrave had had in mind when he delivered a memorable broadside at unspecified critics within his own party at the Fine Gael annual conference in 1972. A keen huntsman he used the language of fox hunters to announce that his enemies, whom he termed 'mongrel foxes', would be rooted out and chopped. Finance went to Richie Ryan (FG), who never recovered from being labelled 'Richie Ruin' by the RTE television satirist, Frank Hall, who also happened to be a Fianna Fáil supporter. Mark Clinton (FG) became

Minister for Agriculture. Patrick Cooney of Fine Gael became Minister for Justice, a portfolio with which he proceeded to confound observers who had attributed liberal tendencies to him, because of his stance during the debate over the amendment to the aforementioned Offences Against the State Act, which had been brought to a close by the sound of exploding bombs. Brendan Corish (Lab), became Tanaiste and Minister for Health and Social Welfare, Justin Keating (Lab), Minister for Industry and Commerce, Michael O'Leary (Lab), Minister for Labour, Richard Burke (FG), Minister for Education, Conor Cruise O'Brien, (Lab), Minister for Posts and Telegraphs, Paddy Donegan (FG), Minister for Defence, James Tully (Lab), Minister for Local Government.

A combination of the individual ability of a majority of this Cabinet combined with the fact that Fianna Fáil had been in power for sixteen years should have guaranteed the coalition a successful term in office, and a good fighting chance of re-election for a second term. But it was not to be. A combination of factors, internal and external, put an end to the coalition after only four years. The economy suffered from the oil shock, and consequential rising inflation and unemployment. But the worst wounds are self-inflicted, and the blows which the Coalition managed to inflict on itself, generally arising from the Northern Ireland situation, though not exclusively so, eventually proved terminal. One of the most bizarre episodes of the Cosgrave administration's tenure was caused by Cosgrave himself.

During July of 1974, as a result of the Supreme Court decision in the McGee case, a measure was brought before the Dail by the coalition to regulate the law. As the matter involved was one of conscience, a free vote was allowed. To everyone's astonishment, Liam Cosgrave, the Taoiseach, and another member of his Cabinet, Richard Burke, a minister whose department, as readers who have perused the section of this book dealing with the education issue will have realised, had considerable dealings with the Church, crossed the floor to vote with Fianna Fáil. This was not what socialists had expected from their coalition partners. Nor did they anticipate the philosophical difficulties which the Government experienced over the wealth tax and farmer taxations proposal. The former was grudgingly introduced, but the latter in practice was evaded by the farmers.

But it was Northern Ireland which provided most of the tension and controversy which afflicted the coalition partners. The Government unquestionably faced a number of serious challenges originating from the northern situation. But it dealt with them through the use of the bludgeon rather than the rapier, Cosgrave in particular frequently giving the impression that anything his father and Cumann na nGaedheal could do to put down the IRA, he could do better. Two particularly emotional occurrences centred around the funeral of hunger strikers who died in British prisons. These were Michael Gaughan and Frank Stagg. Gaughan was the first hunger striker to die in an English prison since Terence MacSwiney, the Lord Mayor of Cork, some fifty years earlier. He was 24 when he died in Parkhurst jail on the Isle of Wight on 3 June 1974. A member of the Official IRA, he had been jailed for taking part in a London bank raid in 1971, which yielded a haul of only £530. As Gaughan had been on hunger strike since 31 March – demanding political status – his case aroused considerable publicity. His funeral in his native Ballycroy in County Mayo was a gigantic affair, over which banners waved, urging the public to 'support the IRA', a demand which, when seen on television, outraged Cosgrave. Therefore, when another hunger striker died two years later, Cosgrave was determined that the funeral should not be used to garner IRA publicity.

The hunger striker was Frank Stagg, who was also buried in County Mayo, at Leigue Cemetery, Ballina. Stagg had been on hunger strike with Gaughan but was ordered off the strike by the Provisionals after Gaughan's death. He went back on hunger strike two years later at Wakefield Prison, and died. As his remains were being flown back to Dublin airport, to be met by a Provisional IRA funeral party, Cosgrave ordered that the aeroplane be diverted from Dublin to Shannon, where the coffin was removed under the supervision of armed members of the Special Branch, taken to Mayo, and buried in a concreted grave. The Provisionals waited until the controversy died down, and then, under cover of darkness, dug up Stagg's remains and carried out his dying wish that he be buried in the adjoining Republican plot, to the accompaniment of prayers from a sympathetic priest.

The failure of the Sunningdale Agreement coloured the coalition government's policy towards the north. Cosgrave appeared to feel that the Unionists had won the battle and that the only thing to be done was to prevent the war spreading to the south. This last objective was one which the bulk of public opinion agreed with, whatever residual pockets of pro-IRA sentiment remained here and there in traditionally Republican areas, parts of Kerry, Mayo, the border counties, Laois, and Offaly in the south-eastern midlands, and Dublin itself. Overall, the core Republican vote rarely moved above 5%, except, as we shall see, at times of great excitation such as the hunger strikes. Nevertheless, the Unionists gave the Republic little thanks for its security efforts, which in percentage terms greatly exceeded those of Britain. Throughout the struggle, Unionist propagandists continually trumpeted the Republic as a safe haven and breeding ground for the IRA from which the Northern conflict proceeded, rather than owning it had its origins in Northern misrule. Though the Sunningdale Agreement fell, the Government, from 2 January 1974 onward, continued to uphold an agreement reached as a result of Sunningdale whereby suspects accused of murder in the north could be tried for the alleged crime within the Republic's jurisdiction. But the Northern authorities continued to prefer to make demands that the Republic extradite such suspects, rather than work the Sunningdale proviso.

Five episodes in particular helped to remove whatever velvet the coalition might otherwise have chosen to coat the iron fist it brought down on the IRA. One was the murder of a Fine Gael senator, another the Dublin and

Monaghan bombings, the third the murder of the British Ambassador, Christopher Ewart Biggs, and the fourth, the situation of riot and upheaval which prevailed in Portlaoise jail for much of the coalition's term in office. This stemmed from the traditional Republican demand for political status, and led to the murder of a guard in a booby-trapped cottage in Mountmellick, a town not far from the jail. The fifth was the kidnapping of the Dutch industrialist, Dr Tiede Herrema, in 1975, in order to secure the release of the British heiress, Rose Dugdale, who had been imprisoned for her part in an IRA raid on Sir Albert Beit's art collection at Russborough House, near Blessington, County Wicklow, which resulted in the seizure of art worth £8 million in the values of the time. Herrema was eventually released unharmed, in November 1975, after a 17-day police siege of a house in Monasterevin, County Kildare.

The Senator, Billy Fox, accidentally interrupted an arms raid at a house owned by a Mr Richard Coulson in County Monaghan, on 11 March 1974, and was shot dead by the raiders, who were from the Official IRA. There were in fact no arms in the Coulson house, and after an intensive manhunt, five men from the Clones area of Monaghan were sentenced to life terms of penal servitude the following June. Two months after the Fox murder, the Dublin bombing explosions went off, apparently timed to further the aims of the MI5-backed Loyalist strikers. A Yorkshire TV programme screened almost twenty years later, on 6 July 1993 as part of the *First Tuesday* series, named two dead undercover British officers said to have prepared the bombs. However, it is worth recording that both on the night of the bombings, and subsequently, I never heard any expressions of hatred or anger at either Britain or the Loyalists. The general mood was quite unlike the anger which followed the Bloody Sunday shootings in Derry. A frequently heard comment was 'this is what they've had to put up with in the north for years'. When Dubliners did gather in crowds both on the night of the explosions and subsequently, it was not to march on the British Embassy demanding revenge, but either to help with the rescue work, or to queue for hours at hospitals around the city to give blood.

However, the IRA did exact its own form of revenge two years later. The British Ambassador, Ewart Biggs, alleged to be an ex-MI6 operative, was assassinated in a meticulously planned operation, on 21 July 1976. A bomb was placed in a culvert under a by-road near the Embassy residence at Glencairn, in Sandyford, County Dublin, and detonated electrically from a field some 200 yards away. The IRA man whom the Gardai sought in connection with the explosion was also wanted in connection with the death of Garda Michael Clarkin at Mountmellick. This flagrant breach of Standing Order No. 8 was, as indicated earlier, an expression not merely of IRA anger at the situation in Portlaoise jail, but at the activities of what became known as the 'heavy gang'. This was a squad of Gardai which apparently had been given *carte blanche* in its handling of suspects. The rumours of heavy-handed treatment came to a head with the revelations[4] of what befell suspects in the Irish version of the Great Train Robbery, at Sallins, County Kildare, in March 1976 which netted the Provisionals some one million pounds.

As a result of widespread and rough-handed police swoops a group of young men who were members of the Irish Republican Socialist Party, not the Provisionals, were arrested and subjected to brutal treatment. The publicity generated by the affair eventually led to their release. One of them, Nicky Kelly, became the object of a famous publicity campaign. He had jumped bail and gone abroad while awaiting trial. As his fellow accused were subsequently released, he mistakenly thought it safe to come home and was promptly re-arrested. Dead walls all over the country became emblazoned with the slogan 'Free Nicky Kelly', after which, in some cases, the words 'with every packet of corn flakes!' were subsequently affixed by pranksters. However, the public did not find Kelly's treatment funny. He received a presidential pardon in 1992 and was ultimately awarded three-quarters of a million pounds compensation. One of the others was Osgur Brennacht. His father Deasun was at the time editing the IRA paper, *An Phoblacht*. He had formerly been Features Editor of the *Irish Press*. Embarrassed by what had befallen his son as a result of their action, one of the country's leading Provisionals contacted me and asked me to tell the Government who had really committed the robbery, which I did, but to no avail. During the coalition era the attitudes of the Irish authorities towards IRA suspects were not markedly unlike those which produced the Birmingham Six and Guildford Four cases.

The Portlaoise situation escalated until in 1977 a 47-day hunger strike occurred, led by Daithi O'Connail and Leo Martin, the unsuccessful attempt against whose life inaugurated the UVF campaign in the north. Portlaoise was the major centre for holding IRA men and the state of the buildings was not a great deal better than it had been during the war when de Valera allowed Seán McCaughey to die on hunger and thirst strike. Nor was the attitude of the authorities noticeably more enlightened. Prison officials told me that under the coalition they were under constant pressure to ensure that breaches of prison regulations did not occur. Prisoners were not to be allowed to form Provisional areas within the jail, or to have a command structure and concessions such as free association which would confer a *de facto* political status on them. Attitudes hardened as the IRA made an unsuccessful attempt on the life of the prison governor; and there was a successful jail break using explosives which had been smuggled in a box of Lucky Numbers sweets. (The prisoners knew which numbers were chocolates and which were explosives.) Another smuggling attempt failed when a woman visitor to the jail was caught passing a string to a prisoner, the end of which was attached to a contraceptive, filled with explosives, inserted in her person. These sort of incidents led to the banning of parcels of all sorts, and to visits being abruptly terminated or forbidden altogether. The loss of life which had led to the death of Garda Clerkin was added to when soldiers on duty at the jail shot dead a prisoner attempting to break out after an armoured bulldozer had been used in an attempt to break into the jail. For all these reasons, a sort of Clann na Poblachta voting renaissance occurred in the Republican community, and greatly assisted the swing towards Fianna Fáil in the February general election. Once in power, Fianna Fáil moved discreetly to defuse the situation. The Department of Justice adopted a more flexible attitude towards the prisoners, and the situation was gradually eased to a point where, although a judicial inquiry was refused, the national newspapers' editors were invited to visit the jail in November 1977. By then, the prisoners were back doing handicrafts, had their own areas within the prison, were wearing their own clothes, and the custom of strip-searching was all but a thing of the past. Under the Coalition, prisoners had been searched several times a day, the procedure involving manual parting of the buttocks and inspection of the testicles to check whether prisoners had explosives taped behind them (which had been known to happen). Outside the prison, security was as tight as ever, with soldiers patrolling and gun emplacements on the walls. Uniformed Gardai also augmented the warders inside the jail, but overall the steam had been released from the pressure cooker. The prisoners were being held, not humiliated. The Portlaoise situation may be taken as illustrating the differing stylistic approach of Fine Gael and Fianna Fáil towards containing the IRA. As we shall see, had the Fianna Fáil formula been followed in Northern Ireland, the history of Ireland would have been different.

In the Labour ranks, the IRA's greatest foe was Conor Cruise O'Brien, who saw the organisation as part of the Irish Nationalist culture which had to be cleansed of its atavistic infections. As Minister for Posts and Telegraphs, one of his principal targets for decontamination was RTE, which, as we have seen, Lynch also cracked down on. But speaking in the Dail during the rumpus over the sacking of the authority, when the then Minister for Posts and Telegraphs, Gerard Collins, was explaining that strict new guidelines were being introduced to govern the interviewing of members of Sinn Féin, O'Brien was one of the Government's sternest critics. He said:

> I do not think the Irish public would like to see RTE brought into line and being made the object of what the National Socialists used to call Gleichschaltung, co-ordination, being brought into line with the party, and being made transmission systems for the party's ideology . . . in any modern democracy the autonomy of radio and television is as vital as the freedom of the press.[5]

In office, however, O'Brien proved a far more vigorous gamekeeper than Collins had been, and went on to implement a ban on anyone from Sinn Féin appearing. O'Brien's target was wider than Lynch's. It could be argued that rigorous analysis from a penetrating mind like O'Brien's could only be of benefit to the body politic. The drawback to O'Brien's contribution was obvious. Censorship helped to denature the debate on the North, and by limiting discussion, helped to prevent a sense of urgency building up to help bring the carnage to an end. In the vacuum on discussion which the Coalition helped to deepen and prolong, the Provos were able to present themselves as being the only ones doing anything about the situation.

In O'Brien's case, his political trajectory ultimately took him from the ranks of the Labour Party to joining Robert McCartney's United Kingdom Unionist Party. He later resigned from the party after writing an article in the *Sunday Independent* suggesting that Unionists consider joining a United Ireland. The furore had been immense. Anti-McCartney Unionists displayed the article for the benefit of the TV cameras as McCartney spoke subsequently at Stormont. Existing tensions in the party were exacerbated. O'Brien resigned, he said, to avoid making these worse. But there were weakening upheavals and resignations anyhow. Accordingly, two months after the explosive piece appeared, O'Brien wrote another article (on 14 February May 1999) defending his position.

He said that the previous week-end he had received a standing ovation at a McCartney party gathering, although he had not retracted his original statement. This, he reminded readers had taken the form of suggesting that Unionists should consider 'voluntary incorporation into the Republic' in order to undermine Sinn Féin. Apparently entering the Republic would halt what he termed 'the castration of the RUC' at the hands of those who had murdered them.

O'Brien overlooked the fact that reform of the RUC was sought not merely by Sinn Féin, but by the RUC, Dublin, and the British Government. As to 'voluntary incorporation' I am simply at a loss to understand how a man of Dr O'Brien's experience could have imagined that the idea would have been well received by Unionists. Apart from his recent immersion in Unionist politics he had dealt with the Six Counties in his days as an Irish diplomat and he had been a Minister in the Dublin government which had to deal with the fall-out from the Unionists destruction of the 1974 power-sharing Executive. It collapsed over the Council of Ireland, a mere link, not 'incorporation'. However, in 1976, all this lay in the future. The attitude of the Coalition towards subversion was very much that of the Unionists before the Heath administration realised that a tough security policy, devoid of a political solution, was rapidly turning a potentially dangerous situation into a disastrous one.

In 1976, as the incidents chronicled above indicate, particularly the murder of Ewart Biggs, the situation in the Republic was not merely potentially dangerous, it was bad and getting worse – the month after Ewart Biggs was killed, five men blasted their way out of the basement of the Special Criminal Court in Green Street, Dublin. Accordingly, early in September, the Government decided to use the Offences Against the State Act to declare a state of emergency, and to introduce some draconian legislation. Under an Emergency Powers Bill, it was proposed to increase the length of detention for IRA suspects from 48 hours to seven days. With the 'heavy gang' in existence, few people felt that the extra five days would be devoted to improving IRA men's table manners. The army were given additional powers of search and arrest, and the penalty for IRA membership was increased from two to seven years. Allied to these changes, the Criminal Law Bill included a provision which aimed at increasing the control which the Government already had over RTE to the printed media. Section 3 of the Bill read:

> Any person who expressly or by implication directly or through another person or persons or by advertisement, propaganda, or any other means, incites or invites another person (or persons) generally to join an unlawful organization or to take part in, support or assist in its activities shall be guilty of an offence and shall be liable on conviction on indictment for a term not exceeding ten years.

In the circumstances at the time, Irish journalists, including myself, did not subject this passage to the scrutiny which should have been bestowed upon it. Everyone accepted the emergency legislation as a disagreeable but inevitable outcome of IRA violence, and it was expected that it would get through the Dail easily with little substantative opposition from Fianna Fáil. However, my attention became more sharply focused when I discovered that I was one of the section's targets. The *Washington Post* correspondent, Bud Nossiter, interviewed O'Brien about the proposed legislation, and discovered that it was intended to be used to 'cleanse the culture' of certain objectionable features. These included history teachers who glorified Irish revolutionary heroes, revolutionary ballads, and – letters to the editor of the *Irish Press*. Nossiter was somewhat startled when O'Brien opened a drawer containing cuttings of such letters. He said he did not intend to use the legislation against the authors of such offending missives, but against the editor of the paper concerned. Nossiter then proceeded to interview me on the subject, and I reacted by reproducing the interview, and printed a page filled with re-printed letters of the sort that had offended O'Brien. The result was a major media controversy, uproar in the Dail, and a spirited attack by Fianna Fáil on Section 3. The Government backed down, the Minister for Justice, Patrick Cooney, giving a commitment that the Bill was not intended for the prosecution of editors, and the offending section was altered to give effect to that commitment. Then the Emergency Powers legislation took another turn.

As mentioned earlier, Erskine Childers had succeeded de Valera as President in 1973. He proved to be a popular and vigorous successor, possibly too vigorous. As part of his drive to make the presidency more open to the people, he went about the country visiting schools, giving talks and attending functions of all sorts. While addressing the Royal College of Surgeons in Dublin, on the stresses of modern life, in November of 1974, he suffered a heart attack and died. It was decided that his successor should be an agreed candidate appointed without an election. The man chosen was Cearbhall O'Dalaigh, who had made legal history in 1946, when he became the youngest Attorney General in the history of the state, at the age of 35. He subsequently became Chief Justice, and played a notable part in the process of utilising the constitution to make changes in the courts which affected Irish life, as referred to earlier. He later became a judge of the Court of the European Community. But it is possible, in the context of the Emergency Powers legislation, that his career between 1931 and 1942 had a bearing on what was about to befall. In those years, O'Dalaigh, a noted Gaelic scholar, was the Irish editor of the *Irish Press*, and in the period under review, his brother Aengus was the paper's much-loved librarian. O'Dalaigh himself, who was also a deservedly well-loved figure, known despite his attainments for his courtesy and humility, took a keen interest in matters affecting freedom of the press, and from time to time sent me cuttings or photocopies of articles, or impending European legislation, which might have a bearing on the media.

The Irish President's duties and powers are not those of America or France, but he does have important functions. He formally appoints the Taoiseach and members of the Government, and summons and dissolves the Dail on the advice of the Taoiseach. He can also refuse a dissolution of the Dail in a situation where a Taoiseach has lost his parliamentary majority. Two of his functions in particular combine with the Emergency Powers legislation to create a major crisis. 1) As titular Head of the Armed Forces, their Commander in Chief, it is he who bestows commissions on cadet officers. 2) No Bill can become law without his signature, and the President can refer Bills to the Supreme Court to have them tested for constitutionality before he signs them. In the wake of the O'Brien controversy, on 24 September 1976, O'Dalaigh decided to refer the Emergency Powers Bill to the Supreme Court, to test whether it was 'repugnant to the Constitution', before becoming law. The courts subsequently found that it was not. The referral was O'Dalaigh's constitutional right and duty if he had any doubts about proposed legislation, but the law-and-order coalition's anger became public on 18 October. Speaking at the opening of a new canteen at Columb Barracks, Mullingar, the Minister for Defence, Patrick Donegan, referred to O'Dalaigh's 'amazing decision' to refer the Bill to the Supreme Court, and said that he was 'a thundering disgrace' to do so. 'Thundering disgrace' was the phrase reported, but there have been suggestions that something more earthy was used. The precise wording, however, was not the point, but the fact was that the Minister for Defence had criticised the Commander in Chief of the army in the presence of officers, some of whom had received their commissions from the President.

This was unheard of, and realising the extent of the gaffe, the Government issued an apology as soon as Donegan's utterances became known. But no move was made to either sack or transfer him. Cosgrave had not shown himself to be overly solicitous of O'Dalaigh's prerogatives in other areas, and seemed to regard him more as a Fianna Fáil nominee than the President of the country. Referring to earlier slights and snubs which he said he had received, O'Dalaigh told me himself that an invitation from the Vatican to attend the canonisation of Blessed Oliver Plunkett in Rome, addressed to the Head of State, was accepted by Cosgrave without any reference to the President. After Fianna Fáil had tabled an unsuccessful Dail motion aimed at forcing Cosgrave to sack Donegan, O'Dalaigh decided to resign from the presidency on 22 October, saying that he did so in order to preserve his own integrity, and the unassailable nature of the presidential office.

Following the inevitable bout of acrimonious party politicking over the débâcle, political wounds were bound up when Lynch and Cosgrave settled on another agreed presidential nominee, Dr Patrick Hillery, whose term as European Commissioner had just ended. But the memory of the controversy outlived its solution, and it would appear to have played some part in the electoral defeat of the Coalition the following year. What played a bigger part, however, were economic circumstances as the oil crisis removed some of the gloss from the gains made by farmers under the Common Agricultural Policy once EEC membership kicked in. The cost of paying for the Coalition's election promises also contributed to worsening the public finances, which had been approached for some years in a manner to anguish principled economists. Chief amongst these was T.K. Whitaker, who in fact had resigned his post as Secretary of the Department of Finance to become Governor of the Central Bank in 1969. One can merely speculate as to whether Charles J. Haughey's personality and budgetary policies played a part in Whitaker's resignation, as he was only 53 at the time. But it is certain that the trend of budgetary policy from Haughey onward was not one that Whitaker agreed with. In 1972, for the first time in the history of the state, Haughey's successor, George Colley, abandoned the practice of balancing the budget. Colley justified deficit spending by saying that the economy was running below capacity, and that: 'Unemployment is high. We lack the economic buoyancy required to tackle quickly and effectively the adaptation which membership of the EEC will demand.' Inflation rose, and between 1970 and 1972, national pay increases pushed up average workers' pay by 39%. The pay rise for 1974 was 29.4%. When oil prices quadrupled the following year, inflation rose to dangerous heights: 17% in 1974, and 21% in 1975. Unemployment also went up, from 71,000 in 1973 to 116,000 in 1977 – an election year.

The hot sun of an impending general election brought the adder out, though not the one envisaged by Shakespeare. The adding done in this case was carried out by the Coalition, and by Fianna Fáil. In the case of the former, James Tully, the Minister for Local Government, having done his electoral sums, drew lavishly on the example of both Kevin Boland and the Ulster Unionists in the matter of constituency revision, to produce what was popularly known as a 'Tullymander'. He increased the number of four and five-seater constituencies in rural areas where Fianna Fáil were strong. In the city, where Fianna Fáil traditionally did not perform well, he increased the number of three-seaters. These changes were designed to counter a small swing against the Government, which was all that the over-confident Coalition predicted. And had there been a small swing, the Government would have survived. But for all the reasons detailed above, a very large swing was in the making against the unsuspecting Government, and the 'Tullymander' backfired, producing a large majority for Fianna Fáil. Fianna Fáil contributed to its own success, with a 1977 version of its traditional policy of combining machine politics with shopping basket manifestos at election time. The party promised increased Government spending to promote industrial expansion and at the same time to abolish car tax and rates on houses. With an eye to the increased number of young voters now on the register, there were promises to concentrate in particular on eliminating youthful unemployment. These proposals were largely the brainchild of

Martin O'Donoghue, a Trinity Professor of Economics, whom Lynch subsequently appointed Minister of Economic Development and Planning, a newly created post. Fianna Fáil's machine muscle was added to by the youthful Seamus Brennan who succeeded the veteran party secretary, Tommy Mullins, and with two other new backroom boys, Frank Dunlop and Esmonde Smith, constituted the nucleus of a 'think tank' for the party, which favoured a technocratic approach to contemporary problems rather than that favoured by former party stalwarts such as Patrick Smith.

The result of the Coalition's old policies and Fianna Fáil's new approach was an unprecedented landslide for Jack Lynch, which caused Liam Cosgrave to resign shortly after the result became known, being succeeded by Garret FitzGerald. Fianna Fáil won 84 seats of the 148 on offer, and recorded 50.6% of the vote compared with 46.2% in 1973. Fine Gael took a hammering, losing 10 seats, from 53 to 43, it shared the vote falling from 35.1% to 30.5%. Labour lost three seats, amongst them that of Conor Cruise O'Brien. Patrick Cooney, the hardline Minister for Justice, was amongst the Fine Gael fallen. As the experienced Irish commentators Patrick Bishop and Eamon Maille observed: '. . . disquiet over the special legislation, exploited by Fianna Fáil, contributed to the coalition's defeat in the general election'.[6]

Labour lost Justin Keating, which surprised some commentators. It may be that his unexpected fall from popularity was due to having to preside over price increases, but equally it could be attributed to what the more Nationalist-minded regarded as his unduly anti-Republican questioning during the proceedings of a Dail committee established in the wake of the 'Arms Trial' affair in an ultimately futile attempt to get to the bottom of the matter. Although the prospect of EEC membership, which made US industrialists look favourably on the Republic as an investment centre, was central to the success of the Industrial Development Authority, he and the Managing Director, Michael Killeen, deserve an important part of the credit for Ireland's success in attracting foreign investment to the country. Keating's hope that Ireland would strike oil in its coastal waters was not realised, but a flow of inward investment was. This was achieved by a combination of a policy of tax and subsidy inducements, and by some very shrewd long-term planning which is still bearing fruit as this is being written. The IDA decided in 1973, as the EEC doors opened, to concentrate on two industries in particular, chemicals and electronics. These had the advantage of being high-end employment sectors, not being susceptible to cheap competition from the Third World, and had the added benefit for both the industries and Irish employment of providing outlets for the increasing number of university graduates being produced as a result of the educational breakthroughs of the sixties – breakthroughs which also facilitated the later explosion of American and Japanese computer companies coming to Ireland.

The 1970s were a period in which, helped by the CAP, Irish farmers and the Irish public generally worshipped at the shrine of both the bullock and the golden calf. At the level of the Minister for Finance and of the local country bank manager, the doctrine of spend now, pay later (sub-text: if at all) took hold. It was not unknown for a bank manager to visit Farmer Murphy in his farmyard with a message along the lines of: 'Aren't you the foolish man not to be taking advantage of a loan? Your man (Murphy's neighbour) is after building a new barn, *and* he's taken the wife and kids to the continent for a holiday.' 'Your man' might have received his dangerous holiday by way of a loan from the bank manager's rival branch of one of the major Dublin groups, and the Faustian suggestion to Farmer Murphy may have been based on irresponsible competition as much as on Government policy. But Government policy helped to drive up the debt burden. In the feckless climate of the period personal bank borrowings rose in the year 1977–8 by 45%

Colley's first budget (in February 1978) continued the deficit financing policy. He raised the deficit target to 6.2%, from 3.8%, and set the Exchequer borrowing target at 13% of GNP. The basis for this approach was the previous year's Fianna Fáil election manifesto which was converted into the White Paper, National Development 1977–1980.[7] Colley's budget speech took an optimistic view of the Irish economy. It spoke of Ireland's achieving growth at 'twice the EEC average', a 'dramatic fall in inflation', rising tourism revenues and rising employment levels. A paper issued by the new Department of Economic Planning and Development in 1978 spoke of 100% employment in 1983. T.K. Whitaker would later write scathingly about the 'chasm that has opened up between budgetary projections and actual results'. Characteristically he backed up his criticism with some devastating tables, two of which are reproduced here:[8]

Current Deficit (£ million)

Year	Budget Projection	Actual	Excess of Actual over Projection
1979	289	522	233 (81%)
1980	347	547	200 (58%)
1981	495	802	307 (62%)
1982	679	988	309 (46%)

Whitaker's comment on these figures was: 'The underestimation of current deficits, and consequently of the Exchequer borrowing requirement, has been so seriously disproportionate as to invalidate the whole budgetary exercise.'[9] The borrowing had occurred at a time when the economic climate was improving, thus pointing to debt reduction rather than increase. Whitaker's second table illustrated the growth of Government expenditure and how borrowing as a percentage of GNP had increased since the foundation of the state:[10]

Government Expenditure and Borrowing

Year	Current Expenditure		Capital Expenditure		Total Expenditure		Borrowing	
	£m	% GNP	£m	% GNP	£m	% GNP	£m	% GNP
1922	30	20	1	–	31	20	3	2
1950	77	19	25	6	102	26	23	6
1958	126	22	38	7	164	29	21	4
1972	665	29	251	11	916	40	151	7
1977	1,944	36	695	13	2,639	49	545	10
1982	5,897	50	2,000	17	7,897	67	1,945	16

Whitaker's severely under-whelmed comment on this performance was: 'The tendency for "getting and spending" by government to bulk ever larger in national activity has been common to many Western countries over this sixty-year span but nowhere, I believe, to a more marked degree than in Ireland.' By way of further underlining Whitaker's comment it might be remarked that, according to Department of Finance figures, the national debt rose from £4,220 million in 1977 to £10,196 million in 1981.[11] Other long-term adverse effects stemming from Fianna Fáil's 1977 electoral shopping basket were caused by the removal of rates. At the time of writing there is uproar around the country as various local authorities, starved for years of their ability to raise money to provide essential local services are being forced to re-introduce charges for water and refuse collection. Apart from the deterioration in local services, local initiative also suffered because of the enforced dependence on central financing and control. Local democracy was thus denatured and the tendency to look towards Dublin for everything was enhanced. One area in which the tendency to see Dublin as the centre of patronage (and with good reason) had a particularly harmful effect was the police force. In Dublin one day, I unexpectedly bumped into a country Garda sergeant whom I knew, and discovered that he was looking for a transfer and had come to town to ask for help in getting it from a minister who came from his district. The minister's department, Local Government, had nothing whatever to do with the Gardai, but for the sergeant and countless others like him it would have been unthinkable to have merely gone through normal Garda channels to further his request without seeking political assistance. His attitude did not merely have its origins in the 1977 general election, of course. Fianna Fáil had moved to appoint its own men ever since taking power in 1932, in both the Gardai and the army. As a result, Fine Gael had correspondingly acted to correct the balance when its comparatively brief periods in office allowed.

Edmund Garvey, the Garda Commissioner under the Cosgrave Coalition regime, was an important part of the law and order climate which prevailed at the time of the 'heavy gang'. But this was not what brought trouble on Garvey, who was what the Americans would describe as a 'straight arrow' cop. He tried to impose discipline not merely on the public but on members of his own force. This novel approach made him deeply unpopular in some quarters. The *Garda Review*, the Gardai's in-house journal, carried an editorial criticising Garvey in June 1976. His over-kill retaliation was to have the editorial referred to the Director of Public Prosecutions in an unsuccessful attempt to have the magazine's board charged with subversion and incitement to violence. As part of the vote-currying exercise during the 1977 campaign, certain Fianna Fáil canvassers seeking the votes of members of the force and their families – an important bloc in its own right – allowed it to be known that if Fianna Fáil were returned Garvey would depart. He was duly sacked on 19 January 1978, but the High Court ruled that his dismissal was null and void. The Supreme Court upheld the decision in March 1979 and Garvey was awarded costs and damages. He resigned with dignity the following month.

The case of Garda Travers, who had the misfortune to encounter Donough O'Malley driving in the wrong direction on the country's best-known street, has already been mentioned; another somewhat similar scandal occurred in the wake of the Garvey case. An attempt to transfer a Sergeant Tully in County Roscommon made national headlines after it was discovered that the transfer followed complaints by local Fianna Fáilers that Tully apparently suffered from the delusion that his role had something to do with upholding the law in matters such as after-hours drinking, the improper use of subsidised red diesel in private cars rather than in the tractors for which it was intended, and so forth.

But all of these matters paled into insignificance over the bugging affair which broke out a few years later. It involved both the tapping of journalists' phones and the conversations of a Fianna Fáil minister, and will be discussed in context during the examination of Haughey's regime. Having been caught up in the scandal, the Garda Commissioner of the day, Patrick McLaughlin, and an Assistant Commissioner, Joseph Ainsworth, both resigned after Fianna Fáil had been ousted from government. The Minister for Justice at the time of the scandal, Seán Doherty, subsequently gave an interview on the RTE *This Week* programme in which he dealt with suggestions that he had interfered with the work of Gardai:[12]

> I have not at any time stated that I would deny making representations on behalf of my constituents to the gardai or, indeed, to any public service body. It is my duty as a Dail deputy to communicate the views of my constituents to any particular area that I am requested to do so. I have done that in the past and I will do it in the future, and I make no apologies for doing it.
>
> The fact that I became Minister for Justice or Minister of State as I was in the past, doesn't necessarily mean that I have to be silent when it comes to my constituents. If that were the situation, they would have themselves with a Minister for Justice and lose themselves a TD. I am primarily a TD where my constituents are concerned – at a greater level I am Minister for Justice in the context of the national interest.

He agreed that he had made phone calls to individual Gardai at Gardai stations.

I have communicated to the gardai as I have to many other public service bodies on many occasions insofar as the views of my constituents need to be expressed to them. I make no apology for having done that and I will do it again.

When I represent my constituents it's at the bottom and that's in my constituency and I represent them as Seán Doherty, Dail Deputy.

A political scientist could explain Doherty's attitude, shared by many like him, using terms like 'rural, clientist political culture'. Looking at it from a historical perspective, however, one wonders how such attitudes would sit with the men who set up the unarmed police force in the middle of a civil war – men like Michael Connealy and his colleagues who braved horsewhips to ensure that the votes got to Galway safely from Athenry. Political interference, and strong-arm tactics such as those already described over the 'macushla revolt', were part of the reason for the members of the force coming increasingly to rely on their own trade union, the Garda Representative Association, and for a fierce 'tell them nothing' camaraderie that has resulted in police cover-ups and illegal behaviour which have gravely damaged the image of the force at the time of writing. To follow this development would, however, take us from our main narrative.

Put simply, the circumstances which allowed Seán Doherty to become a minister were two, the fall of Jack Lynch and the rise of Charles J. Haughey. The former was partly contributed to by the economic situation indicated above, partly by issues arising from Northern Ireland, and lastly, but far from least, by Haughey's continuing rivalry. As soon as the sparks from the Arms Trial had died away, Haughey had taken to what was termed the 'chicken and chips' circuit. A group of close associates, amongst them P.J. Mara, Liam Lawlor, and Owen Patten, took it in turns to drive him all around the country, attending Fianna Fáil functions, often leaving Dublin after their day's work was done, and returning in the early hours of the morning, after the function, only to repeat the performance the following evening. Gradually, Haughey's standing within the party improved and recovered to a point where Lynch had no choice but to appoint him as Minister for Health after the 1977 General Election. Haughey piloted through a measure, the Health (Family Planning) Bill 1978, which made contraceptives available 'to married persons or for family planning purposes'. However, he refused to make them 'freely available to everybody without any limitation of any kind'. The contraceptives were to be available only through chemist shops on a doctor's prescription. John Charles McQuaid might have died, and the McGee case might have necessitated a change in the contraception laws; nevertheless, by the time the Bill passed into law, Haughey was snapping at Lynch's heels in the succession race and he wasn't going to risk being put out of that race by a belt of the crozier like the one McQuaid aimed at Lynch after my exercise in speech writing.

The year 1979 was a black one for Jack Lynch. He faced elections for both the European parliament and local government on 7 June, with serious hostility from both trade unions and farmers because of the economic situation. In the spring, a potentially dangerous urban/rural divide had opened up between the unions and the Irish Farmers Association over a proposal in the 1979 budget to impose a 2% levy on farmers' sales. On the face of it, this was quite a reasonable impost. In the previous year, farmers' income tax had amounted to an average of 1% of their gross income – a glaring comparison with the tax paid by trade unionists: 16% for the average industrial worker. Moreover, as the flush of new cars, house extensions, and continental holidays indicated, farmers had been comfortably 'Brussels sprouting' for a number of years, to the envy of PAYE taxpayers. By 1979, however, the envy was slightly misplaced; the Brussels sprouts had withered somewhat. Over-production throughout the EEC because of the CAP meant that hand-outs from the Berlimont were less in 1978 than either farmers, or bank managers, had expected. In rural Ireland, many a farmer had cause to regret those visits to the farmyard by his friendly neighbouring bank manager. One began to hear rueful quotations of the old adage that 'a bank manager is a man who lends you an umbrella when the sun is shining, and takes it away when it's raining'. A rain of repossessions, credit-squeezes and plummeting farm values came upon the land. As a result, the farmers staged marches against the 2% levy throughout February. The trade unions riposted by staging even larger marches in March. Far more people marched in these on a single day than had turned out because of the Troubles in Northern Ireland over the whole decade. Paudeen was not so much fumbling in a greasy till as protesting at the prospect of only being able to buy yellow pack detergent for his hire-purchase washing machine.

Trade union resentment was heightened by the effects of the Government's decision to join the European Monetary System, absent Britain, in March 1979. This had the effect of breaking the link with sterling for the first time since the Act of Union, and linking the currency to the German mark. The presumption was that the fairly sizeable grants and loans available to Dublin from Brussels, to cushion the effects of the departure from sterling, would be accompanied by an outburst of self-discipline on the part of the Irish consumer and wage earner. Where in the Irish experience evidence was found on which to base this prediction, one does not know. The tables quoted above indicate the gap between presumption and reality. Nevertheless, the Government did attempt to take a hard line against wage demands, thereby further antagonising the trade union movement. A postal strike which broke out in February continued until June, by which time electricity charges had gone up by 20%, and Government and unions were girding their loins over a Cabinet proposal to hold wage increases to 7%. Not a good time to hold an election of any sort.

But Fianna Fáil compounded the inevitable impact of the economic situation with an ill-advised pre-election forecast that the party would win a majority of the 15 European parliament seats on offer. In fact, it won only five, and its percentage of the vote fell from 50.63% in the halcyon days of 1977 to only 34.68%. Murmurings against Lynch broke out in the ranks of

Fianna Fáil. Caucus meetings were held, and events took an even nastier turn on 27 August 1979, when the most important Irish political assassination of the decade occurred. At Mullaghmore, County Sligo, a Provisional IRA bomb blew up a boat owned by Lord Mountbatten, killing the Earl himself, his grandson, a local boy, and also fatally injuring Lady Brabourne. On the same day, at the gates of Narrow Water Castle, outside Warrenpoint in County Down, IRA bombs claimed the lives of 18 British soldiers. The subsequent gloating slogan on Six County Republican gable ends recalled the Bloody Sunday killings with appalling exultation: 'Thirteen dead, but not forgotten, we got eighteen, and Mountbatten.'

The fallout from the blasts damaged Lynch also. Having attended the state funeral for Mountbatten at Westminster Abbey, after which television pictures showed him visibly moved and borne down by a weight of accusatory ceremonial occasioned by assassins from his country, he later attended a difficult meeting with Mrs Thatcher, at which increased Anglo-Irish security co-operation was agreed. This provided further ammunition for the gathering hawks within Fianna Fáil who were preparing to fly at Lynch. Amongst these, the saying that the female of the species is more deadly than the male received an underlining when the sacred name of de Valera was invoked. At the annual Liam Lynch commemoration ceremony on 9 September 1979, Sile de Valera, the late President's granddaughter, spoke out against collaboration with the British. One of the concessions which Lynch had agreed to was the creation of an air corridor five miles or so into the Republic's territory along the border, so that by means of what was known as 'helli-telly', British helicopters in hot pursuit of IRA men could, in conjunction with the southern authorities, continue their hunt across the border. There were of course other obvious implications for intelligence-gathering flights, and the 'over-flights' issue became a live one within the party. One backbencher, Bill Loughnane, a popular Clare doctor and traditional musician, went so far as to call Lynch a liar over the issue. But feeling in the party against the over-flight concession was so strong that Lynch was unable to have Loughnane sacked. From my own experience of giving talks at different venues in the country at this time, which I have described elsewhere,[13] resentment at what was perceived as an intrusion by the British was widespread and genuine, even amongst Fine Gael supporters. Another aspect of the Mountbatten killing was also utilised to attack Lynch. He was criticised because he had not returned home from his holidays quickly enough after hearing the news. In fact, he had been unable to get a flight to Dublin from Portugal, but such niceties were of no consequence to his enemies.

Whether the anti-Lynch camp were responsible or not, the situation was complicated by a sudden spate of rumours which swept British and Irish media circles concerning the impending resignation of the President, Dr Patrick Hillery, because of an alleged affair, an unheard-of circumstance in the moral climate of the time. The rumours were made more embarrassing by the fact that they coincided with a visit to Ireland by Pope John Paul. It has been suggested that the coincidence was no accident: Lynch's enemies within the party wanted to ensure that Hillery was discredited and forced into resignation, so that there could be no question of his becoming Lynch's successor. Whether he ever intended to become such is a moot point. He told me himself, at the time he was offered the presidency, that he and his wife Maeve were considering going to work in the Third World. As far as challenging Lynch was concerned, his attitude was spelt out clearly. He volunteered without my pressing him that 'there is no other job for me in Irish politics, so long as Jack Lynch wants to remain Taoiseach'. However, the rumours built up to a point where a horde of tabloid journalists descended on Dublin. Several came into the *Irish Press* newsroom, seeking assistance, as they did in other newsrooms in the city. A couple of them even staked out a house in my area, following a tip-off that Hillery's alleged mistress lived there. Other stories had the lady located in Sandymount, Paris and Brussels. The only certainty is that no one ever succeeded in finding her.

As rumours reached a peak, there occurred an incident concerning which several inaccurate accounts have appeared. The following are the facts. Hillery asked to see the editors of the national newspapers, and a representative from RTE, to discuss how the story should be handled. It was understood that it was about to break in the Irish news and opinion journal, *Hibernia*. With millions of people about to turn out to greet the Pope during a visit which was known to be attracting worldwide TV attention, there was obviously a problem of national prestige involved. However, he stated categorically: 'I don't have a problem. I don't have a mistress. I don't even share one, like Mitterrand!'

He asked for advice as to what he should do. There was no question of suppressing the story. But, having witnessed the descent of the tabloid 'heavies' with my own eyes, I realised that to call a press conference would be to create a bear garden and that a simple press statement would not meet the case. Accordingly, I suggested that he agree to be interviewed by the political correspondents of the national daily papers and RTE. The journalists involved were all respected members of their professions who could be relied upon to both ask the hard questions and give the answers without distortion. The President and the other editors agreed. Seán Duignan, the RTE correspondent, broke the story on that evening's nine o'clock news, much to the relief of the *Irish Press* correspondent Michael Mills. Michael, a revered figure who was later appointed the country's first Ombudsman, had worked in the *Irish Press* during an era in which the words 'affair' and 'President' did not occur in the same context. He was so imbued with the political correctness of the period that he managed to write his story without mentioning that there was a woman involved! But the RTE disclosure enabled him to incorporate the fact into his report.

In the event, an unprecedented use of 'dirty tricks' in Irish politics did not spoil Pope John Paul's visit. Millions turned out to see him, probably the biggest crowd gathering a few hundred yards from Hillery's front door in the Phoenix Park for the open-air mass with which the Pontiff began his Irish tour which lasted from 29 September to 1 October. Some commentators have since judged that the papal visit helped to sustain Irish Catholicism in its old traditions, such as authoritarianism and resistance to change in matters such as contraception and divorce, for many years longer than would otherwise have been the case. This is certainly what it was intended to do, a sort of 1979 version of the Eucharistic Congress of the thirties. But in fact, under the surface, profound attitudinal changes were already at work in Irish society. When the papal encyclical condemning birth control, *Humanae Vitae*, was published in July 1969, there were already some 12,000 women on the pill. Predictably the Irish hierarchy loudly welcomed the encyclical, none more loudly than Archbishop McQuaid who trotted out a Maynooth professor of canon law, Dr P.F. Cremin, to a press conference to give theological backing to the papal directive. Dr Cremin did not have a lot to say on issues such as the economic, physical and psychological strains engendered by having overly large families. But he was reassuring on the subject of world over-population – a nuclear bomb could take care of that easily.[14] However, the Irish Family Planning Association, which has already been mentioned, was founded in the year *Humanae Vitae* was published. The Irish Womens' Liberation Movement's 'contraceptive train' pulled into Dublin two years later and the Dublin Well Woman's Centre was established in Dublin five years after the papal encyclical came out. Ireland was still deeply influenced by the slow-changing ethos of a strongly rural-based society in 1969 it is true, but two points concerning the Pope's visit probably give a truer picture of what Irish Catholicism's life was really like than any account of the admiring crowds which turned out for John Paul VI.

These accounts rightly focused on the extraordinary number of young people who turned out for the Pope's visit to Galway, but they failed to mention that a sizeable percentage of the said young men and women shared tents, sleeping bags and beds during the visit. Nor was it realised that the two Irish clerics most obviously connected with the papal visit in terms of organising ceremonies, leading singalongs and appearing on televison in the Pope's company were shortly to figure in internationally reported scandals. One, 'the young peoples' priest' Father Michael Clery, demonstrated his commitment to the company of young people by fathering two children on his long-term housekeeper and mistress. The other, Bishop Eamonn Casey, fathered a son with Annie Murphy, whose existence Ms Murphy detonated into the public consciousness some eighteen years later, causing Casey to leave Ireland in disgrace.

Although it was not realised at the time, the most lasting effect of the three-day visit was on Northern Ireland. It is fair to say that it may be regarded as the beginning of the peace process. In his speech at Drogheda, the Pope condemned the violence in Northern Ireland, saying:

... do not believe in violence; do not support violence. It is not the Christian way. It is not the way of the Catholic Church. Believe in peace and forgiveness and love; for they are of

Christ. On my knees I beg you to turn away from the paths of violence and return to the ways of peace.

This was the passage which got the headlines. But there was more in this speech than that, and more to its background. It was not realised at the time that the speech had been worked out between its author and Bishop (and later Cardinal) Cathal Daly, who was then Bishop of Down and Connor, and whose diocese encompassed strife-torn Belfast. Earlier that summer, Daly had visited Rome, where he stayed in the Irish College by night, making repeated trips by day to the Papal summer residence at Castel Gandolfo to go over drafts of the speech with the Pope and his advisers. It had been intended that the Pope would visit the Six Counties, but in the wake of the Mountbatten assassination this was cancelled. Even before the assassination it had been feared that the visit would be used by figures like Paisley to gain world publicity through demonstrating against the coming of 'anti-Christ'. Daly's text also directed a shaft towards those who had created the political vacuum in which the men of violence flourished. It said

> To all who bear political responsibility for the affairs of Ireland, I want to speak with the same urgency and intensity with which I have spoken of the men of violence. Do not cause or condone conditions which give excuse or pretext for violence. Those who resort to violence always claim that only violence brings about change. They claim that political action cannot achieve justice. You politicians must prove them wrong. You must show them that there is a peaceful, political way to justice. You must show that peace achieves the work of justice.

This passage was used by the redemptorist priest, Father Alec Reid, and Gerry Adams, who by now had gained the ascendancy in the Provisional movement, to open a dialogue with Bishop Daly himself, Cardinal O'Fiaich, and leading Irish politicians which ultimately led to the Good Friday Agreement of 1998. But in 1979 this prospect lay far in the future. No peace process was at work within Fianna Fáil. The hand of Lynch's enemies was strengthened by the loss of two by-elections in Lynch's home county of Cork. Lynch was weakened, too, by an admission he made at a press conference in Washington during a visit to America in early November, when he confirmed that he had given permission for over-flights. Hitherto the debate had centred on the issue of whether or not the air space commitment, if it existed, breached Irish sovereignty. By this stage, Lynch had had enough of controversy, and had decided to resign in the New Year anyhow. But in order to stymie Haughey's chances and advance those of George Colley, he brought forward his resignation announcement to 5 December 1979. However, Haughey had masked his hand as to the extent of his real support within the party, and he defeated Colley in the leadership contest by 44 votes to 38, even though distaste for him in some quarters was so strong that Aiken threatened unavailingly to resign if he was elected. A new and, on the whole, disturbing and unsatisfactory age in Irish politics was about to dawn. What should be the verdict on Lynch's era? To begin with, it should be remembered he was a widow's son from Cork, a city as far removed politically from the excitations of Belfast and its surrounding six north-eastern counties as it was geographically. His father had been a tailor, 'a poor man', as Lynch described him to me. He had seemed destined to make his way, via 'the books', as the route of study and scholarships was known at the time, via a law degree, to a reasonable, if not spectacular, career in the civil service, rather like that of his brother in the Church, who became a parish priest. Lynch's life-style was modest, as great a contrast to Haughey's ostentation as one could imagine. To take his call to the bar he had to borrow the money from a lawyer friend, the well-known Republican Con Lehane. Lynch himself was neither strongly Republican nor strongly for any Irish political party. In fact, he only declared himself firmly and unequivocally in favour of Irish unity well into the seventies, in 1975, long after the north had exploded, and then only because a prominent supporter of his, Michael O'Kennedy, one of the moderates of the party, had startled him by making a similar call a little earlier.

As one of the all-time great GAA players, he was head-hunted by both Fianna Fáil and Fine Gael, and only finally chose Fianna Fáil because he admired de Valera. He would have liked children, but he and his wife Mairin, who was one of his strongest political supporters, could not have any. When we discussed liberalising the contraception laws, his only objection was not fear of episcopal condemnation, but a certain unease at limiting other people's ability to bring life into the world, as he had been unable to do. Both his sporting and his Cork background showed in his speech patterns and in his attitude to politics. Brian Farrell, who was the anchorman of the special RTE programme mounted on the night of the 1973 election in which Lynch was driven from power for the first time, asked him what would be Fianna Fáil's attitude towards the incoming coalition. Showing absolutely no sign of bitterness in defeat, Lynch replied easily 'Sure, we'll give them fair play for a start anyway.' It would not be the worst of epitaphs to say that, whether or not he succeeded, Lynch attempted to bring fair play to Irish politics.

This is not something which Charles J. Haughey could lightly be accused of. He too was a widow's son. His father, Seán Haughey, like his mother, Sarah McWilliams, was from a strongly Nationalist area in Derry. Seán Haughey was a Collins supporter, and unlike those involved in the 'Arms Trial' affair, a successful gun-runner. When Collins launched his undercover IRA campaign against the Six Counties in May 1922, Seán Haughey was one of those who smuggled the rifles for the campaign across the border. Becoming an officer in the Free State Army, after the failure of the campaign, he later became a farmer, but had to give up on contracting multiple sclerosis. Sarah, a remarkable woman, managed successfully to rear her seven children, four boys and three girls, on the insignificant pension levels of the time, in the modest Dublin housing suburb of Donnycarney. Haughey was an outstanding student, and an athlete. Along with garnering scholarships, he played Gaelic football, hurling, and water polo. He was remembered from his student days for taking part in a counter-demonstration against Trinity College students who flew a Union Jack on the roof of the college to celebrate the news that Germany had surrendered and the war was ending. Haughey burned a Union Jack in retaliation, and a riot broke out as the police produced that indispensable adjunct to an Irish political demonstration – a baton charge. Haughey took law and accountancy degrees, and founded a successful accountancy firm with a member of the prominent Fianna Fáil political family, the Bolands. He and Harry Boland, Kevin's brother, set up Haughey, Boland & Company Ltd, in 1951. Earlier he had taken more significant steps, joining Fianna Fáil after his father died in 1947, and marrying Seán Lemass's daughter, Maureen, in 1951. After a number of unsuccessful attempts, he was elected to the Dail in 1957.

He articulated what might be termed his tent-pole philosophy in the Dail in the course of his maiden speech:

> The trouble with this country is that too many people are making insufficient profits. It would be well for this country from every point of view – and particularly from the point of view of the weaker sections of the community – if our industrialists were put in a position where they could make adequate profits, which could ensure their continuation in business and their being able to finance further expansion.[15]

This view would bring him both adulation and disgrace. Businessmen worshipped him, but, as revealed many years later when he had fallen from power, they also gave him large sums of money with which he sustained a spendthrift lifestyle involving Dom Perignon, Charvet shirts (custom-made in Paris at £600 a time) and riding to hounds. Haughey's career has always reminded me of the words of a senior Garda officer, describing how another prominent officer, with a seemingly glittering career ahead of him, had come to grief. 'He put on the red coat and he followed the hounds, and after a while you wouldn't know whether it was the hounds or the red coat that was tearin' at him.' Haughey was one of the most able men ever to enter Irish politics. In the course of his various ministerial posts, he cut through red tape and introduced several pieces of innovative legislation. I never knew a civil servant who worked with him, whether they liked him or not, who did not have the highest admiration for his intelligence, his work rate and his unparalleled ability to get things done. My own experience of him in this regard was that if I had occasion to ring him about anything, I never knew whether I would be told the thing was undo-able, and hung up on immediately, or it would be done instantly.

Haughey piloted through a huge amount of Bills, covering almost every field of Irish life while he was in the Department of Justice. His biographer, Dr T. Ryle Dwyer, lists more than two dozen pieces of legislation for which Haughey was responsible during his two and a half years in the Department of Justice alone. He is probably best remembered for smaller modifications which he made to the system in his term as Minister for Finance, during which he brought in the provision whereby artists – like bloodstock breeders – were not taxed on their earnings, old age pensioners could travel free on public transport during certain specified hours, and other small reliefs were given, including a certain amount of free units of electricity, and free television licences. It is said that after he was elected as party leader the ballot papers were burned, and that the resulting smoke set off the fire alarm in Leinster House.

Although neither Haughey nor most of the southern electorate realised it at the time, alarm bells were also ringing off-stage in the form of an extraordinary protest in the jails of Northern Ireland which would ultimately lead to a curtailment of his time in power. What he did realise, very speedily, was that his election had set alarm bells ringing on the opposition benches. When Haughey was nominated as Taoiseach (on 11 December 1979), Garret FitzGerald attacked him, saying:

> I must speak not only for the Opposition but for many in Fianna Fáil who may not be free to say what they believe or to express their deep fears for the future of this country under the proposed leadership, people who are not free to reveal what they know and what led them to oppose this man with a commitment far beyond the normal. . . . He comes with a flawed pedigree. His motives can be judged ultimately only by God, but we cannot ignore the fact that he differs from all his predecessors in that those motives have been and are widely impugned, most notably but by no means exclusively, by people within his own party, people close to him who have observed his actions for many years and who have made their human, interim judgement on him. They and others, both in and out of public life, have attributed to him an overweening ambition, which they do not see as a simple emanation of a desire to serve but rather as a wish to dominate, even to own, the state.

Several other parliamentarians criticised him also. Noel Browne described him as a cross between the former Portuguese dictator, Salazar, and Richard Nixon, going on to say: 'He has used his position unscrupulously in order to get where he is as a politician. He has done anything to get power; does anybody believe that he will not do anything to keep power?' However, the attacks did not prevent the Dail voting for Haughey. He became Taoiseach by 82 votes to 62. In fact, the onslaught brought him some sympathy, because the wounding speeches were listened to by his mother, Sarah, who was sitting in the public gallery with other members of the family. However, Haughey showed little sympathy to those who had opposed him in his days in the wilderness during and after the Arms Trial. Gibbons was dropped, as was Martin O'Donoghue, whose Ministry of Economic Planning and Development was also axed. Two other former ministers fell because they had been close to Lynch, Denis Gallagher, an honourable, Irish-speaking, west of Ireland Fianna Fáil stalwart of the old school, and another westerner of the younger school, Bobby Molloy, who would one day help to turn Haughey himself out of office. One of the most noteworthy appointments to Cabinet made by Haughey was that of Maire Geoghegan-Quinn, to whom he gave the Gaeltacht portfolio, formerly held by Gallagher, thus making Geoghegan-

Quinn the first Irish woman Cabinet Minister since the days of Countess Markievicz. Other new faces in Haughey's first Cabinet included Ray McSharry (Agriculture), Albert Reynolds (Posts and Telegraphs), who was to ultimately replace Haughey as Taoiseach, Michael Woods (Health and Social Welfare), and Patrick Power (Fisheries and Forestry). Haughey had no option but to retain his principal rival, George Colley, as Tanaiste, but he transferred him from Finance to Tourism and Transport. Michael O'Kennedy, whose support had been crucial to Haughey in the internecine party strife, became Minister for Finance in Colley's stead. Gerry Collins stayed in his old post of Department of Justice, Haughey's friend and ally, Brian Lenihan, was appointed to Foreign Affairs, and another Colley supporter, Desmond O'Malley, was also retained in the post he had held under Lynch, Minister for Industry and Commerce. His too was an appointment which Haughey would have cause to regret.

The new Cabinet got off to a bad start. Colley was reported in the *Irish Independent* on 19 December as saying that he and others saw Haughey as being someone who was 'dangerous, should have been blocked from the leadership and should be got out as soon as possible'. Privately, Colley informed his colleagues in Cabinet on the day that his comments appeared that Haughey had made an untrue statement to a press conference which he had given after his election.[16] In the course of the conference, Haughey said that Colley had given him assurances of loyalty and support. Colley, however, told the Cabinet that in view of the campaign waged against Lynch, he did not feel bound to give loyalty to Haughey. Colley followed this up by giving a press conference at which he revealed what he had said behind closed doors:

> I referred to Mr Haughey's ability, capacity and flair and I wished him well in the enormous tasks he was taking on. I did not, however, use the words 'loyalty' or 'support', which he attributed to me.

No Unionist, wedded to the principle of 'conditional loyalty', ever expressed his thoughts on support for a party leader so succinctly. Colley said that as the traditional loyalty normally given to the leader of the party had been withheld from Lynch, he was withholding 'loyalty to, and support for, the elected leader'. However, he magnanimously announced that he would support the Taoiseach 'in all his efforts in the national interest'. Thus praised with not so faint damns, Haughey commenced his troubled tenure in office. He went on television early in the New Year (on 9 January 1980) to tell the country that it was living beyond its means: 'In our present economic situation, it is madness to think that we can keep on looking for more money for less work.' He told the viewers that:

> We have been living at a rate which is simply not justified by the amount of goods and services we are producing. To make up the difference we have been borrowing enormous amounts of money, borrowing at a rate which just cannot continue.

Though nobody realised it at the time, this is exactly what he was doing himself in his private life. He owed the Allied Irish Bank approximately €1.4 million at this stage, and for more than a decade would continue to live beyond his means, being subsidised by huge donations from wealthy businessmen. How much these sums amounted to will probably never be known with accuracy, but tax settlements he made to the Revenue Commissioners as a result of two separate tribunals set up to investigate his finances are known to have amounted to €6,281,718.[17] Under him, Government spending also mushroomed in a number of areas. He introduced a presidential style to Irish government, making decisions himself which would normally have been left to individual ministers, and greatly increasing the size of his own Taoiseach's department, so that he could oversee his party colleagues' doings the more easily.

Inflation reached 20% and Haughey was forced to introduce a scheme to subsidise the interest owed by firms in trouble. There was unrest amongst teachers, car assembly workers, and in Aer Lingus, where planes were grounded for the month of June. In one way or another, Haughey intervened in all these disputes to see that they were settled, albeit over the heads, or behind the backs, of the relevant ministers. His decision to fund Knock Airport in County Mayo was a symptom of the rural/urban divide affecting the country at this time. In general, Dublin-based economists and civil servants thought the project was outrageous. Knock is the area in which the Blessed Virgin is said to have appeared at a local church. The parish priest of the area, Monsignor James Horan, built a Basilica on the site of this church, and it was he who succeeded in arranging that the Pope would come to Ireland mainly to open this in 1979. The Monsignor also thought that it would be a good idea to have an international airport built as well. While his plans may have been grandiose, and Dubliners scoffed at the proposal, it has to be acknowledged that the more modest airport, which Haughey's subsidies helped to make possible, was a priceless boon to the emigration-hit west. People living in Mayo and the adjoining counties were able to travel to England with particular ease, when compared to the hardships associated with the pre-airport days which often entailed long journeys to Dublin to catch a boat or plane. As times got better it was also an asset to the tourist trade.

With regard to Northern Ireland, Haughey both attempted to dispel the cloud of sulphur which hung over him so far as the British were concerned ever since the Arms Trial, and to reassure his own followers that his nationalist heart still beat strongly. At his first Ard Fheis after taking over from Lynch, he described the northern statelet as a 'failed entity'. He presented Margaret Thatcher with an Irish Georgian silver teapot when he met her for the first time at Downing Street on 21 May 1980. The pair got on well together, and it was agreed that they would hold further meetings on a regular basis, accompanied by their ministers when necessary. The communiqué issued after their May 21st meeting confirmed that there would be no change in the constitutional status of Northern Ireland without the consent of the majority, but included the comment from Haughey that it was 'the wish of the Irish government to secure the unity of Ireland by agreement and in peace'.

As we will shortly see, the prospects for either agreement or peace in Northern Ireland were precisely nil, because of the situation surrounding the 'dirty protest' which had broken out in Long Kesh. But Haughey, while making representations to Thatcher about the protests, continued to act in public as though a major breakthrough in Anglo-Irish relationships was on the cards. On 8 December 1980, an Anglo-Irish summit meeting was held at Dublin Castle between Thatcher, Haughey, and a top-level team of Irish and English ministers. On the British side, these included the Foreign Secretary, Lord Carrington, the Chancellor of the Exchequer, Sir Geoffrey Howe, and Humphrey Atkins, the Northern Ireland Secretary of State. Haughey was accompanied by his principal political adviser, Padraig O'hAnrachain, who had also served under de Valera, Lemass and Lynch. His ministerial advisers were Michael O'Kennedy and Brian Lenihan.

The meeting went well, and the communiqué issued afterwards reflected this fact. It spoke of the interests of the peoples of the two islands being inextricably linked, and pledged the two governments to the 'further development of the unique relationship between the two countries'. But the key phrase in the communiqué was the commitment of the two Prime Ministers when next they met in London to 'special consideration of the totality of relationships within these islands'. After the meeting, this phrase was used by Haughey and his spin doctors to indicate the possibility of a major breakthrough in the north, perhaps leading to an end to partition, never mind the Republican jail protest which by now had escalated into a full-blown hunger strike. In fact, the 'totality of relationships' phrase had first been used not by Haughey but by the British Ambassador to Ireland during the course of a dinner with O'hAnrachain.[18] The British certainly meant the 'totality' to include relationships in trade and security, but it was never envisaged as over-riding the wishes of the majority in Northern Ireland. The Castle meeting also included a commitment to joint studies of the northern problem, and to the setting up of an Anglo-Irish inter-governmental council. This provided for four committees, advisory, ministerial, official, and parliamentary, a four-tiered structure designed to improve the relationship between London and Dublin.

It might well have done so, had Haughey not oversold the Dublin Castle meeting in a way which indicated that a breakthrough on partition might be on the cards. Replying to a question of mine (on 21 March 1981) on a BBC Northern Ireland radio programme, Brian Lenihan interpreted the totality phrase as meaning that there would be a United Ireland within 10 years. He later stood over this interpretation publicly and enraged both Mrs Thatcher and Ian Paisley. Paisley held a rally at Stormont a few days later, which 30,000 protesters are said to have attended. On April Fool's Day he held late night rallies on a number of hillsides. Paisley and his supporters normally sang out of the same hymn sheet as the RUC, but at one of these rallies, at Gortin, there was an unusual outburst of violence between them.

Haughey and Mrs Thatcher also clashed, though behind closed doors. A member of the Irish delegation who accompanied Haughey to the first meeting held with Mrs Thatcher after the Lenihan interviews told me that she was furious. 'She thumped the table, and told him there was no question of a United Ireland.' Thus, far from Mrs Thatcher carrying Haughey to the dizzying heights of Irish unity, the Iron Lady's policies towards the north were in fact reaching the crisis which was to put Haughey out of office within a few months. In fact the only tangible result of Haughey's overblown use of the Dublin Castle summit was to provide Ian Paisley with an opportunity for publicity. He brought a son of Edward Carson's to the Six Counties, and with the sacred cloak of Carson's name thrown over his activities embarked on what he called a 'Carson trail' of rallies and speech-making. The real fallout from the North, the H-block controversy, was about to descend on the Republic's politics.

TEN

PAISLEY THE PARLIAMENTARIAN

A TURBULENT PRIEST IN POLITICS

In a by-election held on 16 April for Terence O'Neill's old Bann-side seat, Ian Paisley was returned to parliament for the first time; an associate of his, William Beatty, also won in South Antrim. Paisley had stood as a Protestant Unionist. His electorate did not trouble themselves overmuch with the fact that there was no other kind of Unionist on offer. What did disturb them was the fact that the B Specials were being disbanded in the month in which the by-elections were held, to be succeeded by the Ulster Defence Regiment (UDR), and, more damagingly, before the election (on 26 March), the Police Act laid impious hands on the RUC, setting up a police authority to rule over a civilianised, unarmed force. What the Protestants saw as hammer blows directed on their citadel continued to fall. On 29 May, the MacRory Committee on local government reported. It led to the appointment of area boards to control matters such as health education, and other such services, by government appointment, and not by the local Unionist county councillors.

How Unionists felt about these changes may be gauged from a vote of the Unionist Party a week after Paisley was elected (on 24 April) on the changes in housing policy. The party voted 281 to 216 against the housing policy changes. While housing reform, of course, carried a huge political overtone, because of the fact that it allowed more Catholics to live in the area, and also removed the property vote, it elicited nothing like the visceral response sparked by security issues, and these were now about to take centre stage. At this point, public sympathy in Nationalist areas generally lay with the British soldiers. They were still the saviours from the Orange mobs, still recipients of gratefully proffered cups of tea, and in London, Labour were clearly in favour of reform, and at least seemed to be attempting to bring it about, however well founded were forebodings on the ground at the prospect of a Unionist administration allowing it to actually take place. Opinions sometimes differ as to which was the most hard-line district in Belfast, Andersonstown, Ardoyne, Ballymurphy, Clonard, wherever. Ballymurphy, where Gerry Adams grew up, would certainly come to rank at, or very close to, the top. But even in Ballymurphy, in the wake of the August burnings, the IRA were initially deeply unpopular. The Provisional leadership, which began taking over the IRA after the August burnings, wanted to mobilise the Ballymurphyites, as they did the other flashpoint areas of Belfast, with a view first to demonstrating that they were 'the Defenders' against the Protestants, and secondly, when sufficiently strong, to moving against the British army. But the people of the district preferred, for some months, to rely on the army for defence.

Nothing did so much to undermine this reliance as did the controllers of the British army itself. The reluctance on the part of the generals to open a second front, that is, to treat the Catholics and Protestants impartially, played a part in what happened; the historical association of Protestant Ireland with the army, and particularly its generals and senior officers, also played a part; and the British regimental system had a role too. Soldiers are not policemen. At the best of times, putting an army on the streets is a risky business, particularly when its tradition is one of putting down uprisings in places like Aden, Cyprus, Borneo, Kenya or Malaya. Given Irish history, a British uniform on an Irish street is an irritant in the political oyster around which peril rather than pearl may be expected to form. Whereas the ordinary Tommy Atkins may be expected to make some form of human contact with fellow working-class citizens of the 'UK overseas', even if they do speak with funny accents, it is asking for trouble to put units like the marines or the paratroopers in among the shoppers and the potential stone-throwers. It is guaranteeing trouble to unleash Scottish regiments, which tend to be more of the Rangers than Celtic persuasion, into Catholic districts. The tradition of trouble almost invariably following in the wake of the passage of Scottish bands, around the twelfth, is well founded, because of their aggressive and sectarian behaviour. But, for reasons best known to the brass-hats, the Royal Scots Regiment was introduced to Ballymurphy, and very shortly afterwards came into abrasive contact with the locals.

Rioting broke out on 31 March. The locals say it was caused by the behaviour of the Scottish soldiers towards Catholic girls; the army that the Provisionals were behind it. What is certain is that against this troubled background, an Orange parade was allowed to march through the area. It was attacked by the Catholics. They in turn were attacked by the soldiers. The result was the most sustained, and savage, outburst of rioting and hand-to-hand combat seen in Belfast since the soldiers had first arrived the previous August. CS gas was used, as were bricks, stones, 'Tipperary rifles', bottles, and anything else that came to hand. More than three dozen soldiers were injured, and some hundreds of Catholics. The Provisionals attempted to come to the aid of the Ballymurphy people, but Gerry Adams drew a gun on the units which had been dispatched to the area by William McKee, and had them incarcerated in a house for the duration of the rioting. He did this not out of concern for the troops, but because he wanted the situation to develop into one where mass alienation of his neighbours occurred, and not merely a brief gun battle in which the small IRA party would have been easily overwhelmed. Over the ensuing months, Adams's tactic worked. The ferocity of the almost continuous fighting between the Ballymurphyites and the army made the area into one of Ireland's most heated hotbeds of militant republicanism. The army sometimes made as many as 1,500 house searches in a night, returning to the same house several times. The Adams home became a particular target, CS gas canisters being fired into the house so often that members of the family developed bronchial problems and speech defects.

The first six months of 1970 were not pleasant ones in Northern Ireland. The Protestant extremists continued to attack Catholic districts where they could. Catholics responded in kind. The Provisional IRA began to organise itself into battalions, and to acquire weaponry and training. Guns started to trickle in from America, and from all over Ireland. Shotguns, .22 rifles, machine-guns of the Black and Tan era vintage, all found their way across the border. Petrol bombs began going off with increasing regularity, then nail bombs, then gun battles were fought. At first these largely consisted of Protestants against Catholics. On 27 June, two controversial Orange parades were sanctioned. Inexplicably, one was again routed through Ballymurphy, the other through Ardoyne. The one in Ballymurphy predictably led to an outburst of bloody and prolonged rioting. But that in Ardoyne caused fatalities. Loyalist gunmen attempted to support their parading brethren when they were stoned by Catholics, but this time there was no 'Irish Ran Away' and no consequential burnings. The IRA shot and killed three of the Orange gunmen. The predictable Loyalist response was to attempt to burn down a church, St Matthews, in the Short Strand area, and with it as much of the Short Strand as they could manage. It appears that they could have managed quite a considerable amount: this small Catholic enclave is encircled by Protestant areas, and as has been well documented, the army and the RUC remained in their vehicles some distance from the Short Strand, and made no effort to interfere with the Protestant mobs.

However, a small IRA unit led by Billy McKee defended the church, and in the ensuing five-hour gun battle, in which McKee was badly wounded, one of his men and possibly as many as five of the attackers were shot dead.[1] The Loyalists were eventually driven into retreat. The Provisional stock soared – in Catholic ghetto areas. In Unionist circles, anger at having reforms imposed, and at the failure of the authorities to curb the IRA, increased exponentially. The few hundred Catholics who were known to be still working in the shipyards were driven out. But a more important form of reaction was now gathering. Protestant expressions of anger were beginning to fall on sympathetic ears. Just one week before the Ardoyne and St Matthews shootings, a general election had taken place in England which had returned a Conservative government, traditional allies of the Unionists, and upholders of the officer and gentleman class. Even though Labour had shirked its responsibility for reform, by passing the buck to Stormont, Wilson's administration had demonstrably tried to do something about Catholic grievances. The junior minister sent over from London to oversee the army, Roy Hattersley, had kept a firm hand on its operations. If water cannons were used, for example, Hattersley wanted to know why. He was replaced by the clever, but lazy and disdainful, Reginald Maudling.

Maudling's most celebrated contribution to Irish history is his much-quoted comment to an aide as he left Belfast, symbolically enough on the same day that he arrived: 'What a bloody awful country!' while demanding a large Scotch. However, a far more significant statement of Maudling's, also made on that first visit, was his off-the-record instruction to the British generals whom he met: 'It's your job to sort out those bloody people.'[2] 'Reggie', as his colleagues affectionately referred to him, might have appeared as no more than a well-meaning but ineffectual politician, given to playing bongo drums in London nightclubs at a time when Belfast was going up in flames. But well meaning or no, Maudling's descent on Belfast signalled the reinstatement of the traditional British approach to rebellious Irish nationalism. The Tories' corresponding friendship with the Unionists meant that the traditional Tory slogan for the Unionists now became 'If the Catholics fight, they will not be right'.

Accordingly, Maudling got his Scotch and the Catholics got the Scots: to be precise, the Black Watch, a regiment founded to put down the Catholic Highlanders during the Jacobite wars. Between 3 and 5 July 1970, there occurred what the Catholics saw as an indication of the new administration's attitude to them, the events known in Republican folklore as 'the rape of the Falls'. The 'rape', a brutal search and ransack operation in the Lower Falls area in the first week of July 1970, provided a significant turning point for Ireland: the first major accession of strength for the Provisional IRA. General Freeland, the GOC Northern Ireland, had issued a statement after the St Matthews siege warning that anyone seen carrying a gun was liable to be shot. Rioting initially broke out following the discovery of an arms cache belonging to the Official IRA in Balkan Street, stored there, though apparently army intelligence were not aware of the fact, because the McMillen/Sullivan wing wanted to avoid gunplay and to prevent the arms falling into the hands of the Provisionals. In the event, it was Freeland who fell into the arms of the Provos. He ordered 3,000 troops into an area that looks like Coronation Street and is in fact not a whole lot bigger than the setting for the TV series. The remit of the troops obviously went far beyond a simple arms search.

An attempt was made to teach the natives a lesson in what became more a ransack than a search operation. Houses were torn apart, holy pictures torn up, crucifixes thrown into lavatories. There was widespread pilferage. A curfew was imposed. People were instructed to stay in their homes by orders loudspeakered from a circling helicopter. The place was saturated in CS gas, which in that enclosed area had a particular effect on the young, the old and the asthmatic. The hand-to-hand fighting was probably the worst seen so far. Five civilians were killed, 45 injured and some 15 soldiers were treated in hospital. With that superb sense of occasion for which the officer and gentleman class have ever been noted in Ireland, General Freeland directed that this performance commence on the same day (3 July) that the Prevention of Incitement to Hatred Act was passed at Stormont. The coincidence helped to heighten a growing Catholic sense that many of the promised reforms were for the optics only. No searches took place in Loyalist homes in which, it was revealed later (in the *Sunday Times* of 28 March 1971), 73,000 licensed weapons were held. A custom initiated in the original UVF days pre-World War I, had resurfaced. Protestant Justices of the Peace had issued gun licences indiscriminately to their co-religionists under the guise of 'rifle clubs'. Weapons held by members of these alleged clubs ranged from hand guns to machine-guns.

To compound the sense of Catholic alienation, the army attempted to prove to Protestants that their appeals for a crackdown on the IRA were not falling on deaf ears, that the army *was* tough on Catholics. The method chosen was to drive through the supposedly cowed and pacified area with two Unionist ministers displayed as prominently as had been Bishop Philbin, one of the pair being Captain John Brooke, Lord Brookeborough's son. This was deemed acceptable behaviour, but when, a few days later, Dr Patrick Hillery, the Irish Foreign Minister, paid an unexpected visit to the area, the Unionists exploded in wrath. At Westminster, the British Foreign Secretary, Sir Alec Douglas-Home, also condemned the visit as a breach of diplomacy. But with the sparks from the arms trial affair still flying, and Haughey, Blaney and Co. yet to come to trial, Fianna Fáil was so angered by the 'rape of the Falls' that Lynch had to go further than responding to the army searches, with nothing more than a tour of inspection by one of his ministers. On 11 July, he made a broadcast aimed at reassuring the northern Nationalists. Acknowledging that it was to London they should look for redress of their grievances, he said, however, that Dublin was the 'second guarantor' in ensuring that their rights would be secured. The 'second guarantor' phrase gave some comfort to the Nationalist community, but it put the Unionist blood pressure up somewhere above the normal 12 July boiling point. Within the Unionist Party, sentiment was hardening by the hour. The pressures on the Minister for Home Affairs, Robert Porter, who was supposed to be in charge of law and order matters, were such that he resigned a month after the Falls Road curfew, revealing later that he had not been consulted about it. Chichester-Clark took the opportunity to placate those who said that he was not doing enough to curb the IRA by installing a critic of the reform programme, the right-wing John Taylor, in Porter's place.

Curiously enough, throughout this period, the army and the Provisionals had not come into any serious combat with each other. Fatalities arose between Protestants and Catholics, but it was not until February 1971 that the first British soldier was shot. John Taylor's hardline reputation had been borne out by an interview in the London *Times* in which he said: 'We are going to shoot it out with them. It is as simple as that.' In addition to Taylor's bellicose comments, the British had broken off negotiations which had been in progress between the IRA and the army (the IRA negotiators included Gerry Adams's uncle Liam Hannaway, his cousin, Kevin Hannaway, Proinnsias McAirt, Billy McKee, and Leo Martin, the man on whom the UVF had made the bungled assassination attempt which led to the first deliberate murder of a Catholic of the Troubles). General Anthony Farrar-Hockley named the IRA negotiators on television, and blamed them for the rise in violence.

Taylor's threat was borne out the next night, when a young Catholic was shot in the Ardoyne area by the army in the course of a riot. An IRA officer borrowed a machine-gun, which he did not know how to use, and fired at the soldiers, killing Ensign Robert Curtis of the Royal Artillery. Thus, on 3 February 1971, the unfortunate 20-year-old acquired the melancholy distinction of becoming the first British soldier to be shot in the course of the Troubles. More rioting ensued, spreading across Belfast and to Derry. The following day, Chichester-Clark went on television, his face visibly showing the strain of the situation, and made the ringing announcement that 'Northern Ireland is at war with the Irish Republican Army Provisionals.'

In the era thus ushered in, individual deaths and atrocities of such an appalling nature would occur that it seemed impossible that they could ever be forgotten. But in the passage of time, the horrors have blended into cold statistics. Later an attempt will be given to indicate something of the individual tragedies which occurred. Here it is important to describe the turning-point decisions and incidents which led to turmoil and death becoming the norm for a part of Ireland, and of the United Kingdom, for the rest of the century and indeed beyond. Where the Republicans were concerned, the Provisionals definitely emerged as the leading wing of the IRA after a feud which broke out in March, and was as much a turf war as an ideological one. The Officials intruded on Ballymurphy, to attack troops billeted in the Henry Taggart Memorial Hall. Enraged at the incursion, the Provisionals beat up a leading Official. More shootings and hostage-takings ensued, and on 8 March there was a major gun battle between the two sides, which the army gazed upon in delighted inactivity. After a leading Provisional, Charles Hughes, a popular figure, greatly respected for his courage, who ironically had come to the aid of Provisionals during the Falls Road curfew, was murdered by the Officials, a truce was arranged through the intercession of local clergy. This effectively left the Provisional IRA in command of Republican Belfast with the exception of an area in the Lower Falls.

As these events were unfolding, what might be thought of as the constitutional actors in the drama continued in their different ways to attempt to influence the situation. On the Unionist front, Chichester-Clark, and those ministers loyal to him, and these were becoming progressively fewer, attempted to do London's bidding, and introduced reform. But reforming Unionists when they appear are always an endangered species. On the plain grounds of administration, the Stormont civil service and the RUC were demoralised, disorganised – and distrusted. The army did not like the police, who under Sir Arthur Young were thought to be far too wimpish, exactly like London policemen in fact, which is why Jim Callaghan had appointed him in the first place. The British mandarins installed at Stormont didn't trust the

Unionist civil service, and ordered that their more secret communiqués were not to be shared with the natives. The sheer inefficiency of having a state which was sliding into anarchy being run by two masters, one of them across the Irish Sea, the other increasingly beleaguered in Belfast, also made for a paralysis of will in decision-taking. The main thrust of powerful and vigorous figures within the Unionist penumbra, like Craig, West, Paisley, Boal and Faulkner, lay not in furthering reform but in opposing it, and demanding instead that progress be made on the security front.Where the British were concerned, Maudling was a disaster. He wanted the army to sort out the situation, and did not appear to appreciate the need for reform, or if he did, he did not display the energy required to speed it up. Delays meant that while genuine efforts were made, events on the ground overtook them, and lost their impact on the Catholics while enraging the Unionists. For example, the RUC was in a state of such chaos that Sir Arthur Young resigned just three months after the Tories took over. Sir Arthur's resignation came a week after the RUC had agreed to becoming an unarmed force (on 15 September). Instead of having guns, they were supposed to use plastic bullets in riot situations. These had a range of 50 yards, and weighed five ounces, and were supposed to be fired at the ground so that they would ricochet against the legs of rioters. But, of course, panicky or vindictive officers frequently fired them directly at heads and chests, causing civilian fatalities. In any event, the disintegrating security situation soon put an end to the period of RUC disarmament, and the RUC fetched up with both its guns and the plastic bullets.

The Unionists fought the introduction of reform like a rearguard action in the field. Captain John Brooke demonstrated that he was his father's son, with the ringing declaration that Fermanagh County Council would only be reformed 'over his dead body'. The housing reform programme was, as we have seen, an absolute touchstone area where Catholics' trust in the reform programme was concerned. But Brian Faulkner dismissed complaints from the Catholics' political representatives about housing as being 'all part of a plot to discredit the established local authorities'. What this attitude meant in practice was illustrated in the Belfast High Court on 21 January 1971. The previous month, Dungannon County Council, situated in the same county (Tyrone) which had witnessed the first sit-in, in Caledon, over housing, had allocated 43 houses to Protestants, and only five to Catholics, poor progress towards reform after seven years. The High Court granted the Catholic applicant an injunction to prevent the council giving more houses to Protestants while he remained unhoused. Reform also stalled in the area of security. The new UDR to a large extent consisted of the old B Specials, and the corps increasingly became a handy training ground for Loyalist para-militaries. Brian Faulkner helped to ensure that they would have something to train with by refusing to crack down on the 'rifle clubs', with the result that by the end of the year, licensed weapons had risen from 73,000 to 110,000.

By now, the Six County statelet was both disintegrating and detonating. Behind the no-go-area barricades in Derry and Belfast, both Protestant and

Catholic paramilitaries controlled everyday life to a considerable degree. Whatever might be laid at the door of the RUC, their presence had at least helped to keep down ordinary crime and hooliganism. Inevitably, crime rates soared, and the danger to life and limb increased, as the numbers of young people running about with weapons multiplied. The IRA bombing campaign extended from targets such as RUC barracks and army posts to 'economic targets', which in effect meant business premises. The Protestant response was to demand tougher security. The word 'internment' began to be heard, as did demands for the death penalty, more troops, and an end to the no-go areas. Under pressure from the Paisley–Boal–Craig–West axis, Chichester-Clark teetered on the brink of resignation. He flew to London on 16 March in a vain attempt to have introduced the sort of security measures which the Unionists sought. All he succeeded in getting was an increase in troop numbers which brought the total number in the area at this stage to 9,700. The British were thus getting all the demerits of direct rule through an ever increasing involvement in the area, without any of the benefits.

But the fires of direct rule were burning ever closer. Dissatisfied with the result of his London visit, Chichester-Clark resigned and was succeeded by Brian Faulkner on 23 March 1971. He immediately set out to wrest from London what Chichester-Clark had failed to get, a swingeing security crackdown. Invited to the Cabinet committee set up to deal with the Irish eruption (known as GEN 42), he impressed on those present the need for internment and a raft of other measures which, if introduced, would have spread the conflagration into the Republic. He wanted the border sealed off, but not so much as to prevent one of his pet projects being put into effect: he wanted the army to send snatch squads into the Republic to seize suspected IRA men. The committee, which included the Prime Minister, the Home Secretary, the Foreign Secretary and the Chancellor, initially refused to sanction these measures, but Faulkner persisted with these urgings at subsequent meetings. Simultaneously, he also made some attempts at wooing Catholic support. It was a Janus-faced approach which was bound to fail.

On the one hand, he appointed someone who was not a Unionist to his Cabinet, as Minister for Community Relations, David Bleakley of the NILP, and he set up a number of parliamentary committees which, though they were intended to be consultative rather than representative, did offer two paid positions to Catholics as chairmen. This was bruited abroad as being an experiment in power-sharing. However, after announcing the committees, Faulkner and his ministers then drove to the headquarters of the inner circle of Orangeism, the Royal Black Institution, to explain how little his gesture meant in practice. He also refused to order the rerouting of the Derry Apprentice Boys march which had caused the Bogside rioting in 1969. Nevertheless, the Catholic opposition, as a whole, was prepared to give Faulkner a chance to continue along the Bleakley/committee route.

By now, the Catholic leaders had become better organised and more powerful. The month after the 'rape of the Falls', the Social, Democratic and

Labour Party was founded (on 21 August). It was led by Gerry Fitt, who had won a seat at Westminster in the June general election, which also saw two other prominent personalities emerge from the Catholic side to take former Unionist seats. Bernadette Devlin was returned for mid-Ulster, which did not prevent her serving a six-month sentence for throwing bricks at the RUC during the Bogside riots. Frank McManus, standing as a Unity candidate, won a seat in Fermanagh/South Tyrone. Ian Paisley showed the rising strength of fundamentalist Unionist sentiment by winning North Antrim. The new SDLP also included John Hume, Austin Currie, Ivan Cooper and Paddy O'Hanlon. The party aimed at the establishment of civil rights, Catholic–Protestant harmony, and co-operation with the south, which was envisaged as eventually leading to unity, albeit on a basis of 'Oh Lord make me good but not yet'. The SDLP also had, as a bow to its Socialist component, represented by the colourful Paddy Devlin, a radical programme of wealth redistribution. The SDLP offered the prospect of something new and constructive in Catholic politics which in better times could have led to rapprochement between Protestant and Catholic, but these were not the best of times. Circumstances dictated that the SDLP's first term at Stormont would last only until 8 July 1971.

Although Faulkner did not succeed in getting internment introduced at his first GEN 42 meeting, he continued to press for it. Violence was certainly increasing, but the reasons for it were more complex than either Faulkner, or ultimately the British, conceded. By now the activities of the British army were alienating more and more Catholics by the hour. I remember visiting areas like the Short Strand and the Ardoyne at around this time, and marvelling at the extent of the army presence on the streets. There appeared to be soldiers everywhere. Heavy armoured vehicles manoeuvred in little side streets by day and by night, making sleep almost impossible, and ordinary shopping excursions both difficult and hazardous. The soldiers showed a tendency to beat up any young Catholic male who crossed their path, and it was obvious from both the evidence of one's eyes, and that of priests, community workers and Nationalist politicians who lived in the area, that the British army was reverting to its traditional role in Irish affairs. Patrick Devlin, a Socialist, and a courageously outspoken enemy of the Provisionals, accurately summed up the effect of the army on Catholic opinion when he issued a statement after the troops had shot a Catholic youth, saying: 'With the restraining hand of Mr James Callaghan gone from the Home Office, General Freeland is reverting to the type of General that Irish people read about in their history books.'

There was more to the army's approach than mere mindless brutality. General Freeland's successor, Lieutenant General Sir Harry Tuzo, believed that he could contain the IRA without internment, by saturating Catholic districts with troops and capturing both IRA operators and their weapons. But this approach, particularly in the wake of the 'rape of the Falls', meant that the army in fact became the chief recruiting agent for the Provisionals. Many years later, a journalist who lived through much of the Troubles, Ed

Moloney, in a work which was quite hostile to Gerry Adams, and in no way sympathetic to the Provisionals, would write with accuracy:

> Just as Unionist obduracy had played the role of midwife to the new IRA, so the same need to placate Protestant extremism and prop up the Stormont government led Britain to take an increasingly tough line against the communities from which the IRA sprang. As that conflict worsened, the notion that as long as Unionists held power and were supported by Britain, Nationalists could expect no fair dealing gained more support and sympathy. The events of 1970 nourished the view that Northern Ireland was incapable of being reformed and that only its destruction could end the Nationalists' nightmare. For the first time in the history of the state, the extreme republican agenda and the IRA's violent methods were winning the allegiance of a sizeable section of the Catholic community. Unionists had created the Provos, and now they were sustaining them. Only in Ballymurphy had Republicans manipulated events; everywhere else there was no need to.[3]

Faulkner's sustenance of the Provos went into overdrive throughout the summer of 1971. His private arm-twisting of the British apparently gave him the confidence to make a statement on 25 May which presaged the ending of parliamentary opposition at Stormont. He said: 'Any soldier seeing any person with a weapon or acting suspiciously, may, depending on the circumstances, fire to warn *or with effect* without waiting for orders.' Acting in this spirit, the army shot dead two Catholics, Seamus Cusack and Desmond Beattie, on 8 July 1971, in Derry. The ensuing rioting was as violent as it was inevitable. John Hume, the local MP, called for an inquiry into the shootings, was refused, and on 12 July gave a press conference, announcing that the SDLP were withdrawing from Stormont. He said that to continue to support the parliament was not possible because 'there comes a point where to continue to do so is to appear to condone the present system. That point in our view has now been reached.' Fitt and Devlin, who were more Socialist than either Republican or Nationalist, had resisted similar pressures to withdraw from Stormont after army action had caused deaths amongst their constituents. But now they had no option but to support Hume in the setting up of what the SDLP termed 'an Assembly of the Northern people'. Having condemned the People's Democracy marchers on the grounds that their actions would incite violence, and then been driven to join in giving the marchers a heroes' welcome, Hume and company now found themselves calling for a radical departure of their own: a campaign for civil disobedience to include a rent and rate strike, and the withdrawal of Catholics from all public bodies.

Faulkner would later write of the shootings that 'Cusack might in fact have lived had not his friends, with obvious criminal mentalities, driven him several miles across the border to Letterkenny Hospital instead of to the nearby Altnagelvin Hospital in Londonderry.'[4] But his immediate instinct was to redouble his efforts to have internment introduced. There were several meetings of the GEN 42 committee in the immediate aftermath of the Beattie and Cusack shootings, which of course completely obliterated any vestiges of goodwill towards Faulkner's Catholic committee initiative that remained after his drive to the Orange elders, at which he pressed incessantly for internment. Faulkner was seized of the notion that internment was the answer to the north's problems, partially because he and his community felt that it was the way to deal with Nationalist uprisings, and partially because it was claimed to have worked during the 1956–62 IRA border campaign. In fact, it was not internment which ended the campaign, but the indifference, and sometimes the outright hostility, of the Catholics to the border 'incidents', as they were called. Belfast remained quiet.

With the Catholics withdrawn from Stormont, and disenchanted at the fate of their attempt at participative democracy, to introduce internment in 1971 was to play into the hands of the Provisionals. But on 5 August, a meeting of GEN 42 decided to go for Faulkner's solution. Amongst those who supported Faulkner at this crucial meeting were Sir Kenneth Bloomfield, the Under-Secretary to the Stormont Cabinet, and Howard Smith, who later became head of MI5, which, as we shall see, was to wield a continuously dark hand in Six County affairs. General Tuzo also backed internment on this occasion because, as he later explained, the IRA had set off some two tons of explosives in the three weeks ending 9 August 1971. It did not occur to the General that Gerry Adams and his friends might have been aware that internment was being contemplated, and wanted it introduced speedily before the British had time to get their intelligence in good working order.

This in fact was the case. The British had been making preparations for some months. RUC personnel had been trained at the British Intelligence Centre in Maresfield, Sussex, in the brainwashing techniques which the army had perfected in Aden, Cyprus, Kenya, and other sorrowful stepping stones out of Empire. An old prison ship, the *Maidstone*, was moored in Belfast harbour; a World War II airfield at Long Kesh, near Lisburn, and Magilligan prison, near Derry, were readied for internees. In the small hours of the morning of 9 August 1971, Operation Demetrius was launched. It proved to be an unmitigated disaster. A couple of weeks earlier, the British had conducted a trial run, a series of dawn raids which pulled in a few dozen suspects, and the Provisional IRA had been alerted to the approach of Demetrius. Some 350 detainees were picked up, most of them Officials, whom MI5 viewed as the potentially most dangerous wing of republicanism, because of the Cold War situation.

This apparently led the army to overlook the fact that the Officials were vainly trying to impose a ceasefire on their followers wherever and whenever possible. Another more damaging oversight was the fact that no Loyalists were picked up. The attempt by an army briefer to make a joke of this situation to journalists afterwards fell very flat indeed in the Catholic ghettos, particularly in Derry. The spin doctor protested, 'But we did arrest a Protestant – we arrested Ivan Cooper!' Along with Cooper, the army also picked up, and beat up, civil rights leaders like Michael Farrell of the People's Democracy. The army's intelligence, much of it supplied by the RUC, was appalling. They captured no Provisionals of note, and rounded up people whose worst crime was to fall out of favour with local RUC members who might have seen them at civil rights rallies.

It is difficult at this remove to recapture the sense of outrage which swept Nationalist Ireland as the selective nature of the round-up began filtering out in the days succeeding 9 August. The first riots of the Troubles had been triggered by Paisleyite activities. The first person to die in the Troubles had been burnt to death by a UVF petrol bomb. The first deliberate murders of the period had been carried out by the UVF. The first explosions had been the work of Paisley admirers, and the first policeman to be killed in the Troubles had been killed by Protestant rioters. Not surprisingly, a song, 'The Men Behind the Wire', written by Pat McGuigan, became a chart topper which has hardly been equalled since. It included the following verses:

> Armoured cars and tanks and guns
> Came to take away our sons
> But every man will stand behind the
>   Men behind the wire
> Through the little streets of Belfast
> In the dark of early morn
> British soldiers came marauding
>
> Heedless of the crying children
> Dragging fathers from their beds
> Beating men while helpless mothers
> Watched the blood pour from their heads
>
> Not for them a judge or jury
> Nor indeed a crime at all
> Being Irish means they're guilty
> So we're guilty one and all

As popular music often does, the spirit of defiance and of outraged nationality contained in 'The Men Behind the Wire' accurately mirrored the spirit increasingly to be met with amongst the Catholic community of the Six Counties. Mention has been made earlier of the significance of Pearse's term 'the risen people'. By now, in the Catholic ghettos of Belfast and Derry, and increasingly throughout other areas of the north as well, the Catholics were a risen people. They had learned that the unthinkable was possible, that they could stand up to the British army and to Stormont, and survive. They had graduated from the use of stones, to coffee-jar bombs, nail bombs, acid bombs, home-made explosives of all sorts, to the handling of guns, short arms and rifles. Now, in Pearse's words, they were prepared 'to take what you would not give'. What they wanted to take, and here a dichotomy emerges that would bedevil Nationalist politics for the next 30 years, was not civil rights, human rights, or reform within the system. Their main motivation was sovereignty, the expulsion of Britain from Ireland. All the other advances they saw merely as collateral benefits which would come automatically once their prime objective was secured.

Insofar as the military effectiveness of the swoop was concerned, the hollowness of Faulkner's statement on the day of internment was immediately exposed. He said: 'The security forces and the government feel that internment is working out remarkably well. It has exposed the gunmen.' Some of the gunmen in fact gladly exposed themselves. Joe Cahill, who had succeeded Billy McKee, who had been arrested, as OC of Belfast, gave a press conference at which he stated accurately that less than 10% of those picked up were members of the Provisionals, and that the Provos' capability had been unaffected by internment. Point was given to his remarks by the gun battles which were in progress all over the city at the time. Twenty-two people died in the three days after internment was introduced. They included a Catholic priest, Father Hugh Mullen, and the first member of the UDR to be killed, Winston Donnell. Protestant–Catholic rioting reached new levels of ferocity. Some 7,000 people were rendered homeless, most of them Catholics. But Protestants suffered homelessness also. In the Ardoyne area, Protestants who left their houses in the face of Catholic mobs set fire to some 200 homes, rather than see them fall into Catholic hands. A stepped-up IRA bombing campaign which accompanied all the foregoing, pointedly blew up the Unionist Party headquarters, along with a wide range of 'economic targets'.

Far from disabling the Republicans, the internment swoop created a tidal wave of support for the physical-force men, which increased the ranks of the Officials as well as the Provisionals, to an extent that the former were forced to abandon their defensive role. One of the factors which swelled recruitment were the increasing reports that torture was being employed at the interrogation centres set up to process the detainees. Names like Castlereagh RUC Barracks, and the army's Palace, Girdwood and Holywood Barracks passed into Nationalist folklore, as the techniques in which the British Ministry of Defence had trained its personnel throughout the summer were put into effect. Sustained and systematic brutality was used as an adjunct to internment both to gain information and to strike terror into the heart of Catholic communities, so as to render them unwilling to support the IRA. Detainees were softened up by being dropped out of helicopters which unknown to them were hovering only five or six feet above the ground, savaged by dogs and forced to walk over broken glass in bare feet and to run the gauntlet between rows of baton-wielding soldiers. For those deemed worthy of graduating to a higher plane of interrogation, there were the 'five techniques', which lasted for approximately a week. These comprised hooding, white noise, sleep deprivation, starvation diet, and standing all day spread-eagled against a wall supported only by the fingertips.

As knowledge about the interrogation techniques spread, they were taken up by the media, and Dublin was forced to complain. The British responded with the tried and trusted technique of setting up yet another committee of inquiry, this time under Sir Edward Compton. The detainees saw the setting up of the committee as a public relations ploy and refused to co-operate; only one of them gave evidence. This enabled Maudling to write a foreword to Compton's report saying:

> ... it is clear from the report that there were very few complaints, and those there were had, in the Committee's view, very little substance. The record of events reflects great credit on the security forces ... the Committee have found no evidence of physical brutality, still less of torture or brain-washing ... [5]

Compton's whitewash exacerbated rather than defused the situation, and the Irish Government were forced to take the matter further, to the European Court of Human Rights. On 2 September 1976, the court found that the interrogation techniques were a breach of the Convention on Human Rights, involving 'not alone of human and degrading treatment, but also of torture'. The British appealed this finding to the European Court of Human Rights, which (on 18 January 1978) ruled that the detainees had suffered 'inhuman and degrading treatment' but rejected the use of the word 'torture'.

Although for several years the violence in Northern Ireland would place the British and Irish governments in an awkward, tetchy relationship, internment and the events surrounding it did have the effect of forcing London to concede a greater role to Dublin than it had done at the time of the Hillery visit to the Falls Road in the wake of the search and ransack operation. Lynch was invited by Heath to a meeting with himself and Faulkner at Chequers the month after internment (on 27–28 September). But the meeting was to prove a microcosm of the difficulties arising from the priorities on either side of the Irish Sea. Heath (and of course Faulkner) saw the situation in security terms. He wanted Lynch to close the Provisionals' and Officials' Dublin head-quarters, censor RTE's reporting of the situation, and introduce British D-note-type restrictions on the printed media. Faulkner would have liked to see internment introduced in the Republic also. Lynch, however, required a more sensitive approach to security. In the wake of the Arms Trial affair, the intern-ment fallout was having an inflammatory effect on sections of his party, as was the British army's technique of cratering some cross-border roads. It was not uncommon at this stage for the army to crater roads which farmers on either side of the border used to transport livestock and machinery. Provisional Sinn Féin, sometimes led by a figure such as Ruairi O'Bradaigh, derived considerable publicity from this tactic by helping locals to fill in the craters, which, in a guerrilla warfare situation, were of very little value in preventing arms, or IRA men, slipping under cover of darkness, across adjoining fields at any one of a thousand points along a 150-kilometre border.

Thus, though the post-internment Chequers meeting was an important milestone in the Anglo-Irish relationship, at least in the sense that the Anglo component recognised the Irish interest in the situation, it did not immediately lead to any meeting of minds. But apart from furthering the strength of the Provisionals, the energies released by internment had a number of other effects which London had not reckoned on. Internment spurred the Provisionals to bring forward a policy document (released to the press on 5 September 1971), which sought to meet the Protestants' objections to an all-Ireland republic. This document, Eire Nua, proposed the setting up of four regional parliaments of which the northern one, Dail Ulladh (Ulster Dail), would assuage Protestant fears of a united Ireland because they would form 'a large part, possibly a majority' of it.

But the Protestants had their own methods of dealing with their fears, a mirror image of the IRA known as the Ulster Defence Association (UDA). The UDA emerged out of the same sort of conditions which existed behind the barricades in Catholic no-go areas. Protestants had been driven out of their homes, the B Specials had been disbanded, and Protestant vigilante groups were springing up everywhere in the wake of the dislocation and gun battles which followed internment. Towards the end of September, the UDA took to the streets, sometimes marching in a uniform which borrowed from the Provisionals' example: dark glasses, masks, combat jackets and balaclavas. It also enthusiastically embraced other Provisional activities, such as extortion, murder and sometimes simple thuggery. It developed links with the other Loyalist paramilitaries, and ultimately with the UDR. One of the UDA's most prominent leaders, Andy Tyrie, came from the New Barnsley area adjoining Ballymurphy, where many Protestant families were intimidated out of their homes by Ballymurphyites.

Another development within the ranks of Protestantism was the creation of the party which most members of the UDA probably voted for, that is, if they voted at all. With the help of Desmond Boal, Ian Paisley formed the Democratic Unionist Party (DUP) on 30 October 1971. Paisley's tenets included regarding the Pope as anti-Christ and the link with the United Kingdom as being in danger, not merely because of the IRA, but through the pusillanimity of the existing Unionist leadership, i.e. Faulkner, whom Paisley managed to stigmatise somehow by getting an extraordinary amount of venom into the description 'the shirtmaker'. The party described itself as being 'on the left on social issues'. This last translated in political terms into campaigning against 'dry closets'.

It was neither a pleasant nor a reassuring landscape, and one of those looking at it correctly divined that there were storm clouds gathering. Harold Wilson, speaking in the House of Commons, set out what became known as his '15 point plan'.[6] The central point of this was that the final settlement of the Irish question lay in unity, 'the aspirations envisaged half a century ago, of progressing towards a United Ireland'. Wilson pointed out that internment had completely changed the political situation, and that new initiatives had to be brought forward speedily because 'if men of moderation had nothing to hope for, men of violence will have something to shoot for'. Wilson was absolutely correct in his diagnosis. In the three years prior to Bloody Sunday, 30 January 1972, 210 people had been killed in the Troubles. In the 11 months after the shootings, 445 people lost their lives, and the total of bombs either planted or exploded had risen more than eight times to a total of 1,756. However, neither Wilson nor anyone else who heard or read his speech could have guessed where the single most infamous piece of shooting was shortly to come from.

The episode known as 'Bloody Sunday' (Bernadette Devlin, interviewed on television immediately after the shooting, evoked memories both of Michael Collins's era and of the Sharpeville massacre, saying: 'This is our Sharpeville. This is Bloody Sunday', and the name stuck) probably had a more damaging effect on Anglo-Irish relationships than had the original Bloody Sunday of 1920, which at least helped to accelerate progress towards peace talks. What happened in Derry on that January day helped to ensure more than two decades of subsequent IRA violence. The tough line which the British had been taking with the Nationalists on the advice of Brian Faulkner and his counsellors since the Tories had been returned to power in June 1970 resulted in a total of 14 deaths when paratroopers opened fire on unarmed civilians taking part in a march called to protest against internment (13 died on the spot, one later). The march had been banned in the general atmosphere of violence. In addition, a similar march a week earlier, which had been attacked by members of the 1st Parachute Regiment, who had used their batons with extreme brutality to deter civil rights marchers from staging an anti-internment protest at Magilligan Prison Camp, had raised temperatures in the city. The paratroopers' onslaughts on the demonstrators had only ceased when their own NCOs used their batons, sometimes breaking them, on the paras' heads.[7] Heath was made aware that the Parachute Regiment had been 'unnecessarily rough' at Magilligan, by the Cabinet Secretary, Sir Burke Trend, and was urged, apparently unsuccessfully, to review the activities of the regiment before it was moved to Derry. General Sir Michael Carver, the Chief of the General Staff, is on record as stating that he was informed by Heath that the Lord Chancellor, Lord Hailsham, had advised that it would be legal for troops to open fire on protestors. Because they were 'enemies of the Crown', they could be fired upon by the army, whether or not soldiers were being shot at. Carver replied that he could not 'under any circumstance, permit or allow a soldier to do that because it wouldn't be lawful'. The author Martin Dillon told the Bloody Sunday inquiry (the Saville Inquiry was established by the Prime Minister, Tony Blair, on 29 January 1998, into the events of Sunday 30 January, 1972)[8] that when he put Carver's allegation to Heath, during the course of a television interview, he was ordered out of the ex-prime minister's Salisbury home.

Fears about what might happen were not confined to the Nationalists. Colonel Roy Jackson, who was commander of the 1st Battalion of the Royal Anglian Regiment, which was based in Derry at the time of the march, told the Saville Inquiry that he told his superiors that he felt the paratroopers should not be used in Derry on the day of the march. However, he was informed by a senior officer, Brigadier Pat MacLellan, that the order to use the paratroopers came from 'the highest level', by which he understood government level.

There are very good grounds for the Brigadier's belief. A meeting of the Joint Security Committee which was held prior to the march heard General Sir Harry Tuzo, the north's GOC, argue that confrontation should be avoided and that a low-key strategy should be the order of the day. However, it seems that the meeting accepted Faulkner's view that it was the duty of the army to take a hard line with troublemakers.[9] Faulkner did not acknowledge that there was a civil rights, anti-internment component to the protests. To him they were 'republican demonstrations'. Just five days before Bloody Sunday, at a meeting of the Stormont Cabinet, he expressed satisfaction at the 'timely and effective intervention of the security forces' in the previous Sunday's marches (which included Magilligan). And so the paratroopers, the same men who had batoned the Magilligan demonstrators a week earlier, but this time armed with rifles, not batons, were sent into Derry. Major General MacLellan would later state[10] that his orders, for a very limited arrest operation carried out by soldiers on foot, were disobeyed, and that instead the paratroopers entered the Catholic Bogside area of Derry in force, backed up by armoured vehicles. Once there, they conducted not a limited arrest operation, but, in the words of Lord Saville, 'a running battle down Rossville Street', contrary to instructions. Whether or not word of the Security Committee's decision leaked or not cannot be stated with certainty. But it is at least curious that a rally called by Ian Paisley in furtherance of his well-known tactic of staging counter-demonstrations to civil rights marches, which was to have been held outside the Guildhall in Derry as the Nationalist demonstration went by, was called off.

What is certain is that in the wake of the shootings, Ireland's blood pressure went up north and south of the border. John Hume advised the Irish Department of Foreign Affairs that, if the Government wished, the Irish army could 'easily recruit 50,000 men from the North for the Army'. Probably one of the factors which helped to avert the issue of recruitment, or similar allied steps, was the fact that a mob burned down the British Embassy in Dublin in protest while the police stood by. The action, though destructive, and illegal, served to act as a kind of national safety valve. The Embassy burning alone probably would not have had this effect had Nationalist Ireland become aware at the time of the British Prime Minister Edward Heath's reaction to the shootings. In the immediate aftermath of the march, Heath took a blustering, headmasterly tone with Jack Lynch when the Irish Taoiseach phoned him on the night of the shooting. The transcript of the two men's conversation is too long to reproduce in full, but an extract from it gives something of the flavour of Anglo-Irish relationships at the time:

LYNCH: Lynch here. I am sorry to ring you at this hour but you will probably have heard the unfortunate news about Derry this afternoon.
HEATH: It is very bad news, yes.

LYNCH: Very bad news, yes. And from reactions received around the country at the moment it looks as if a very serious point has now been reached and the situation could escalate beyond what any of us would anticipate at this stage. I am told that, according to reports I received and checked on the spot, the British troops reacted rather beyond what a disciplined force might be expected to, and as you know, there were 13 killed and as many again injured . . .

HEATH: Well, now, as far as any accusations are concerned I obviously cannot accept that.

LYNCH: I assure you I can understand your point of view.

HEATH: I must also point out that this arose out of a march which was against the law, which was banned, you have always asked me to ban marches. Faulkner banned them last August and renewed the ban, as you know, for a year. Now this was done, and it is a policy which you have always urged, and we believe it was absolutely right for him to ban marches.

Now the people therefore who deliberately organised this march in circumstances which we all know in which the IRA were bound to intervene, carry a very heavy responsibility for any damage which ensued – a very heavy responsibility – and I hope that you would at least condemn the whole of that unequivocally and publicly.

LYNCH: Well I am waiting to get further clarification of the situation, but . . .

HEATH: So am I.

LYNCH: Well now, there is no indication at all that the IRA intervened before shots were fired from the British side. Now again you can disagree with that but this is the information I have got, and . . .

HEATH: I am not going to prejudge it.

HEATH: Well you know it is very difficult to accept a condemnation of Stormont for doing something which you yourself have requested, you have constantly requested. You spoke to me last summer that marches should be banned.

LYNCH: Because I think these marches are provocative.

HEATH: Well then, this was a provocative march today.

LYNCH: But the fact is that . . .

HEATH: And against the law.

LYNCH: Well it was a peaceful march up to the point when . . .

HEATH: It was against the law.

LYNCH: Yes.

HEATH: And it was provocative.

LYNCH: Yes. Well I admit . . . but on the other hand.

HEATH: Well I cannot therefore take this as a criticism of Stormont.

LYNCH: On the other hand, well the fact is that the whole thing arises as a result of the Stormont regime. It arises as a result of the . . .

HEATH: It arises as a result of the IRA trying to take over the country.

LYNCH: Well, we have no intention of letting them do that . . .'[11]

The difficulties the Tory attitude created for the diffident Lynch, trying to cope with upheavals both outside and inside his party, stemmed from the fundamental dichotomy of the approach by a Conservative Party bound by history, prejudice and expediency to the Unionists, and the situation as seen by either Heath's predecessor or by the Irish Prime Minister. Unionist misrule, constitutional change, were not the source of the problem. IRA violence was. However, as we shall see, Heath soon came to realise the deficiencies in the traditional Conservative approach, moving to take very radical steps to improve the situation. In the longer term, too, he became profoundly uneasy about the events of Bloody Sunday. After a period in which he declined to give interviews[12] on the subject, as pressures for an inquiry grew, he made an historic decision to appear before the Saville Inquiry[13] (on 20 January 2003), but evaded the question of responsibility. In the course of an abrasive exchange between himself and Michael Lavery QC, for the relatives of those shot on Bloody Sunday, Heath countered Lavery's attempt to find out who the British army was answerable to, by saying that the Government had no disciplinary force over the army, and offered to send Lavery 'the books' if he wished to examine the constitutional relationship between the Government and the army.

In the aftermath of the shootings, the constitutional arrangement which came under scrutiny was that between Whitehall and Stormont. As the Cabinet papers of the time reveal, a range of options was considered.[14] One of these was re-partition, which would have meant large-scale population transfers both within the Six Counties and across the border. It would have involved about 50,000 troops and the compulsory moving of about 300,000 Catholics. The resultant exclusively sectarian state would have been unstable and offered a better target for IRA action, as there would have been no Catholic enclaves to defend, and the Protestants of Derry, Fermanagh and Tyrone, who held most of the bigger farms and estates, would have been dangerously isolated. The unworkable contingency plan was one of a number of ideas put forward, and subsequently dropped, by the Cabinet in the months after Bloody Sunday. Heath reacted by attempting to hold the line on the PR front, as all over the world Britain took a drubbing in the media. Within a few days of the shootings, he called in a law lord, Lord Widgery, and, looking him in the eye as he told him that Britain was fighting a war on two fronts, one of them a propaganda war, asked him to conduct an inquiry into the shootings. Not surprisingly in the circumstances, the report, when it appeared, worsened rather than improved Anglo-Irish relationships.

The British were again angered by the activities of Dr Patrick Hillery, who set off on an international tour to win support for Dublin. Sir Alec Douglas-Home, the Foreign and Commonwealth Secretary, directed British embassies 'to take steps to offset any publicity hostile' to British interests. The Cabinet was also understandably exercised at the burning of its embassy in Dublin. As the crisis unfolded, the Government considered a range of sanctions against the Republic. These included immigration controls, obligatory identity cards for the Irish living in Britain, work permits, trade restrictions, and financial penalties of a serious nature, such as freezing the Irish sterling reserves. While many of the foregoing will have a familiar ring from the economic war/ neutrality period, other schemes considered indicate that the equally familiar, though unacknowledged, Dublin–London security co-operation also continued. The British considered ending the training of Irish naval and army cadets, and the Cabinet discussions revealed that the quid pro quo for the cadet training was the maintenance of a number of radio stations in the Republic, from whose existence the Irish security forces averted their official gaze.[15]

However, matters never came to the pass envisaged by the contingency planners. As the days passed, Heath got over his anger at Dublin and began training his fire on Belfast instead. He accepted Reginald Maudling's advice that the only way forward was via the suspension of Stormont, the imposition of direct rule, and some form of co-operation with Dublin. Sir Alec Douglas-Home went further, writing to Heath on 13 March warning him that there was no possibility of setting up a lasting framework which would keep Northern Ireland in the United Kingdom, and recommending a united Ireland as the long-term solution. Heath did not accept Douglas-Home's advice, and went instead for a formula based on a combination of the advice offered by Reginald Maudling and Oliver Napier, the Alliance Party leader. Napier urged him to move in such a way as to put the blame on Stormont and the Unionists.[16] He recommended that Heath inform Faulkner that he was taking over control of security, which would inevitably force Faulkner to resign. Heath was also prompted towards taking control of security by the result of an appeal against a fine imposed on John Hume and other civil rights leaders for taking part in a demonstration against the army. The Northern Ireland High Court found that legislation which permitted them to be fined contravened the Government of Ireland Act of 1920 which specifically prevented Stormont from legislating on matters affecting Crown forces. But the legislation under which Hume and the others had been fined had been drafted by Stormont, as an addendum to the Special Powers Act, in 1970. The effect of the judgement was that in carrying out Brian Faulkner's wishes, the British army had in fact been acting illegally between 1970 and 1972, which obviously had the most horrendous implications for actions such as the internment swoops and Bloody Sunday. In a panic, the Conservatives rushed through a *handwritten*[17] Bill, which passed both the House of Commons and the House of Lords in one day (23 February 1972), legalising the actions of the Government.

However, London realised that much more was needed to put the army on an effective footing. For Dublin to co-operate with London in putting down the IRA, it was obviously necessary to be able to demonstrate reform in the Six Counties. However, it speedily became apparent that Faulkner was not prepared to co-operate in the sort of reforms which the situation called for. He resisted Heath's suggestions that Catholics be brought into the Northern Ireland Cabinet, and argued that internment had worked. He told Heath on 4 February that the IRA had suffered 'a severe dislocation of command and communication systems', and that in Belfast the IRA was 'particularly short of leadership, experience and technical skill in the use of explosives'.[18] Had the conversation taken place in Belfast, it would probably have been punctuated by the sound of bombs going off, accompanied by the sound of sporadic gunfire, which would have cast a different light on Faulkner's claims. The Provisionals staged a grisly litany of bombings and shootings which demonstrated that they were short of neither 'technical skill', nor explosives. The worst of these was the bombing of the Abercorn restaurant in Belfast, in which two women were killed and 130 people suffered injuries which included the loss of limbs and eyes. Away from Belfast, the Official IRA, in revenge for Bloody Sunday, conducted a bungled operation at the Parachute Regiment's Aldershot headquarters. A bomb killed no paratroopers, but claimed the lives of five cleaning women, a Catholic chaplain and a gardener. The Officials also shot John Taylor, the hardline junior minister of Home Affairs, in the head. His life was saved because the RUC had secretly raided the IRA's arms dump, and 'duffed' the machine-gun used – by boring its barrel so that the bullets lost velocity.

. The mindset of Faulkner and his colleagues in the wake of Bloody Sunday recalls that of the Unionists after the Luftwaffe had bombed Belfast. A priority order of business for the Cabinet meeting after the bombing was to decide how best to safeguard Carson's statue against further attacks. Faulkner's corresponding Cabinet meeting, the Monday after Bloody Sunday, took a similar course. After a brief review of 'events in Londonderry on the previous day in which 13 civilians had been killed in riots, following an attempted Republican march in defiance of the government ban', a statement was issued 'stressing the dangers of defiance of the march ban'. The Cabinet then went on to discuss, amongst other matters, bar facilities in civil service canteens, the creation of a new fire authority for Northern Ireland, and the Employers Liability (Defective Equipment and Compulsory Insurance) Bill.

As Heath increasingly came to see Stormont not as part of the solution, but as the problem, the Unionists dug the hole deeper. On 16 February, Faulkner resisted greater participation by Catholics on the grounds that they would give aid and comfort to the IRA: '... intimations of impending radical changes can too easily bolster the standing and morale of that organisation'. At this stage, Catholics were resigning right, left and centre, not merely from Stormont, but from any public body to which they had been appointed. But the Unionists persisted in their intransigent attitude. On the very eve of the meeting with Heath, at which the British Prime Minister made Faulkner an offer he could not accept, Westminster control over law and order, the Unionist Cabinet decided to tell Downing Street that 'We are opposed to any measure to create by statutory means an entrenched position in the Cabinet for members of the Catholic community.' Faulkner was just as opposed as Carson and Craig had been to the introduction of proportional representation (PR). It was, he said, 'intrinsically unworkable'.

One of the reasons for Faulkner's defiance was the activities of the latterday Craig, William of that ilk, who, a week after Bloody Sunday, had founded the Ulster Vanguard Movement, into which he intended to subsume disaffected Unionists with a view to supporting the constitutional position, apparently by taking a course which one would have imagined would have had the opposite effect, tacking towards the shores of UDI (Unilateral Declaration of Independence). Even after Bloody Sunday, Vanguard sought further progress on the security front, code for putting down the papes. Craig, who was not known for opposition to the products of either grain or grape, was given to the use of threatening language. He told a Radio Eireann interviewer on 5 March that he could foresee a situation in which Loyalists might target Catholics as they had done in the 1920s: 'Roman Catholics identified in Republican rebellion could find themselves unwelcome in their places of work and under pressure to leave their homes.' At a rally in Belfast on 18 March he declared: 'We must build up dossiers on those men and women in this country who are a menace to this country. Because one of these days, if and when the politicians fail us, it may be our job to liquidate the enemy.' He had a habit of driving around to rallies, sometimes 50,000 to 60,000 strong, in an open touring car, attended by outriders, which did more to recall memories of Nuremberg than of Martin Luther King. This did not stop him attracting the support of a man who would later reluctantly accept (temporarily) what Faulkner had rejected, David Trimble.

However, Heath was not intimidated either by Craig himself or by Faulkner's use of the Craig-ite demonstrations to stall reform. Ironically, the biggest rally in which Craig and Faulkner were to participate occurred at Stormont on 28 March, the day the parliament met for the last time. The Napier formula had been applied. Faulkner had been called to London on 22 March, and told that his reform programme was inadequate and that London was taking over security. At first he apparently thought that Heath was bluffing, that no London government, particularly a Conservative one, would dare suspend Stormont. It took some hours to convince him to the contrary. Dumbfounded, he returned to Belfast where the next day he and his Cabinet resigned. On 24 March, Heath rose in the House of Commons to say:

> We were concerned about the present provision of responsibility for law and order between Belfast and Westminster whereby control remains largely with the Northern Ireland government, while operational responsibility rests mainly with the British army, and therefore, with the United Kingdom government. This responsibility is not merely domestic; it is a matter of international concern as well ... The United Kingdom government remained of the view that the transfer of this responsibility to Westminster was an indispensable condition for progress in finding a political solution to Northern Ireland.

The fruits of the 'Ulster will fight and Ulster will be right' policy had turned sour. The Conservatives had been driven to acknowledge that their Unionist allies had shown themselves so unfit to run a democratic parliament that the reins of government had to be taken away from them. Loyalist outrage at Heath's decision proved to be both short-lived and ineffective. Faulkner and Craig addressed a meeting approximately 100,000 strong from the balcony of Stormont, and later Vanguard, with the help of Billy Hull, a prominent Orange trade unionist, managed to stage a successful 48-hour strike, which shut off power and public transport. But overall, the Unionists had no option but to come to terms with the fact that if one declares oneself loyal to the

British Government, one therefore has little alternative to accepting its decisions, though the sincerity of this 'loyalty' might be debatable, it at least had the merit of keeping the cheques coming.

The British too had now to come to terms with an unpalatable reality – the continuing existence of the IRA, despite internment. In a remarkable series of undercover manoeuvres, a meeting was arranged between Daithi O'Conaill and Gerry Adams, and two Northern Ireland Office officials, Philip Woodfield and Frank Steele, an MI6 agent. Earlier in the year, O'Conaill and two other IRA leaders, John Kelly and Joe Cahill, had already held a lengthy secret meeting with another British political leader, Harold Wilson, who was on a visit to Dublin. When news of the meeting leaked, it greatly annoyed the Dublin Government, who saw such contact as giving aid and comfort to the IRA. The British were not seeking to comfort Messrs O'Conaill and Co., but they did give them a certain amount of aid in order to set up a meeting with William Whitelaw whom Heath had placed in charge of Northern Ireland to succeed Maudling. As part of the prior negotiations, the British made what would prove to be critical concessions to a group of hunger-strikers in Crumlin Road jail, led by Billy McKee, who had been fasting for 30 days. The strike was in pursuit of a demand for political status. This was conceded, and Adams was released from Long Kesh to take part in the talks. Woodfield reported favourably on Adams and O'Conaill, saying that they appeared to 'genuinely want a ceasefire and a permanent end to violence'. As a result of these and other meetings, a ceasefire was agreed to, and a historic meeting was arranged. For the first time since Michael Collins had negotiated with the British, an IRA party travelled under safe conduct to London to negotiate with members of the British Government, on 7 July 1972. The IRA delegation consisted of Seán MacStíofáin, Seamus Twomey, Ivor Bell, Martin McGuinness, Adams, O'Conaill, and a Dublin solicitor, Myles Shevlin, who kept the minutes for the Republicans.[19] The British team was led by William Whitelaw, and took place at the home of his junior minister, Paul Channon, in Cheyne Walk, Chelsea. While the meeting was undoubtedly momentous, there was no possibility of it ever achieving success at that stage. Tory backbench sentiment was such that even going some way to meet the wishes of the Dublin Government ran into difficulties. Jack Lynch remarked at around this time[20] that he had gleaned from the British Ambassador to Ireland, Sir John Peck, that the civil service were advising the British Government to move 'in the direction of a worthwhile political move, but it seemed to be killed on reaching Ministers who were influenced by the tough attitude of right-wing Tory backbenchers'.

For the Tory backwoodsmen, even the idea of talking to the IRA was anathema, never mind conceding to their demands, which included the following:

1. Britain to make a public declaration that it was for the whole people of Ireland acting and voting as a unit to decide the future of Ireland.

2. The British government to give an immediate declaration of its intent to withdraw from Irish soil, the withdrawal to be completed before 1 January 1975.
3. British troops to be withdrawn immediately from sensitive areas.
4. A general amnesty for all political prisoners in Irish prisons, all internees and detainees and all persons on the wanted list.
5. A suspension of offensive operations by the British army and an immediate end to internment.

Many years later, Whitelaw told me himself that the only long-term solution for Ireland was unity. We were attending a press reception at 10 Downing Street, but even then I noted that he dropped his voice and changed the subject as Margaret Thatcher approached. On 7 July 1972, all he was in a position to offer was reform within the system. He told the IRA men frankly that 'the Minority in the North have been deprived of their rights. I set myself the task of conquering this. You can give me some help in the matter.'

Not surprisingly, the meeting did not arrive at any substantive decision, but it was understood that the ceasefire would continue until 14 July, on which date the British would give their response to the IRA proposals. In the event, however, the ceasefire broke down on the 9th. It was the marching season, and tensions were high because the army had forced through an Orange march against the wishes of Nationalists in Portadown. Moreover, in Belfast, in the Lenadoon area of strongly Republican Andersonstown, a confrontation had built up between local residents and the army over a proposal to install homeless Catholics in some empty houses, which had once been Protestant homes. The UDA had announced that any Catholics entering the houses would be burned out, and a hostile Protestant crowd had gathered to enforce this ukase. The army appeared to be keeping the two sides apart until, in an incident captured on television, an army Saracen truck suddenly rammed a truck filled with the Catholics' furniture. O'Conaill eventually succeeded in reaching Whitelaw by phone, but Whitelaw told him that his information was that the IRA were attacking the army. The Lenadoon situation soon degenerated into chaos, and the ceasefire was over.

The ensuing spate of violence was the worst of the Troubles so far. The death toll for the month shot up to 95, the bulk of the victims being Catholics assassinated by Protestant death squads. In the week after the ceasefire broke down there occurred one of the most appalling atrocities of the entire period, the 'Bloody Friday' explosions of 21 July 1972. The Provisionals detonated 21 bombs in different locations, timed so closely together that, whether or not the subsequent IRA allegations that the police failed to respond to the warning calls were true or false, they would have been nearly impossible to deal with anyhow. Nine people died immediately and 130 were terribly injured. People all over the world were sickened by the resulting TV pictures showing parts of human bodies being shovelled into plastic bags. The failure of Cheyne Walk and the wave of revulsion at Bloody Friday decided the British on mounting the biggest military operation since Suez: Operation Motorman, which ended the no-go areas in Belfast and Derry. The operation involved 12,000 troops supported by tanks and bulldozers, but it was only a partial success. It succeeded in ending the no-go areas, but, as with internment, the Provisionals were expecting the swoop and no senior personnel were captured.

Apart from the fact that it set a precedent for talking to the IRA, the Cheyne Walk meeting, as we shall see, had a lasting effect on the north of Ireland situation which no one could have foreseen at the time. It helped to create the political status for IRA prisoners as a burning issue, a major source of Republican discontent and, ultimately, political success. Later that year (on 20 December), the report of a committee headed by Lord Diplock ensured that the numbers affected by the political status issue would be so large that they involved most parts of the Six Counties. Diplock recommended that the best way to deal with the problem of intimidation in cases involving terrorist crime was that 'Trials of scheduled offences should be by a Judge of the High Court or a County Court Judge sitting alone with no jury.' The recommendation to dispense with juries was adopted the following year, and prison totals shot up.

Lynch continued to chip away at Heath throughout 1972 at meetings held on the margins of talks aimed at getting both countries into the EEC, at the Munich Olympics, and at a particularly important working dinner held in Downing Street on 24 November. Initially, Heath was merely concerned to force Lynch's hand in cracking down on the IRA south of the border. However, Lynch warned Heath that even if the IRA were defeated temporarily, 'the kids on the streets who are already involved in the conflicts will be 18 and 19 years of age before too long, and trouble will inevitably break out again if there is no political solution'. He was also concerned, given the level of unemployment in the Republic, that a worsening of the northern situation would have the effect of increasing IRA recruitment. He urged the need for movement on internment. Sir John Peck, who played a useful hand in the British Embassy in Dublin, had advised the Department of Foreign Affairs to 'play the EEC card for all it was worth'. Lynch took up this refrain with a proposal that Dublin and London in the context of the EEC regional policy might conduct studies on the border area, west of the Bann, without actually considering the border itself. He also strongly pushed the idea of a Council of Ireland at the 24 November dinner. Heath saw virtues in the Council idea 'in the economic and social spheres, especially in the context of the Common Market'. But with typical condescension, he at first would only agree that Dublin could have 'consultation, discussion and contact' on the scope of the Council, not 'negotiation'.

However, Lynch continued to press him on the issue, and he later agreed to a 'significant advance on this position', an early meeting between Dublin and London officials to discuss the scope and functions of a Council of Ireland. Apparently part of the reason Heath's approach mellowed lay in the fact that earlier in the day Lynch had fired the governing body of RTE because it had allowed the broadcasting of the transcript of an interview with the IRA Chief of Staff, Seán MacStíofáin. MacStíofáin himself had been arrested (on 19 November) and sentenced to six months for IRA membership; for good measure, the reporter who interviewed him, Kevin O'Kelly, was given three months for contempt of court when he refused to identify MacStíofáin. By the time of the Downing Street dinner, MacStíofáin was on hunger strike, and the O'Kelly case had become such a cause célèbre that he had had to be released after a couple of days. Heath launched into a conversation on the problems governments faced with the electronic media, and confided to Lynch and the Irish Ambassador, Donal O'Sullivan, that 'he has his problems too, and would wish at times to be able to take the same forthright action against the BBC'. Clearly, the deceptively mild and guileless Lynch had achieved a piece of notable political scene-setting by sacking the authority just a few hours ahead of meeting the irascible Heath. But he had set the scene for reasons other than merely to please the British Prime Minister. O'Sullivan noted that Lynch argued for power-sharing 'with great candour and considerable force', stressing the need 'to avoid repeating the mistakes of the past'. The Irishman told his British counterpart that power-sharing within any Irish executive was a prerequisite for stability, as was the strong Council of Ireland with 'the possibility of evolution'.[21]

Apart from the Lynch–Heath encounters throughout 1972, both the SDLP and Whitelaw in their different ways had been edging towards new thinking on the north. The SDLP issued a policy document, 'Towards a New Ireland', which proposed that Britain and Ireland should share Northern Ireland's sovereignty, and took up the IRA suggestion that Britain should make a declaration that it intended to work for Irish unity. The SDLP paper was issued not long before a conference convened by Whitelaw at Darlington, on 24 September, which was attended by the Ulster Unionist Party, the Alliance Party, and the NILP, but not by the SDLP, because of the continued existence of internment, or by Paisley, because of the continued existence of the Irish Republic, to which Darlington might be a stepping stone. On 3 October, what might be termed the fruits of Darlington were seen, a North of Ireland Office discussion paper, 'The Future of Northern Ireland'. While the paper repeated the old guarantee that the area would remain part of Northern Ireland, so long as a majority of the people of Northern Ireland wished, it also nudged the Unionists towards taking a friendlier attitude towards the Nationalists: 'there are strong arguments that the object of real participation should be achieved by giving minority interests a share in the exercise of executive power'. The most significant part of the paper lay in the fact that it made a reference to 'an Irish dimension', pointing out that the Northern Ireland situation had to be viewed in conjunction with the south: 'A settlement also must recognise Northern Ireland's position within Ireland as a whole . . .' Where the British were concerned, a major incentive towards recognising Ireland as a unit lay in the prospect of 'concerted governmental and community action' against terrorism. Nevertheless, the Green Paper was the first occasion in which anything resembling the notion of an Irish dimension had emerged in an official NI document. After Darlington, it was announced that a referendum on the border would be held, followed by local elections under PR, and an observance of the principle of one man, one vote. The border poll was duly held (on 8 March 1973), and as it was boycotted by the SDLP (because of internment) and by the Provisionals and the People's Democracy, because they were the Provisionals and the People's Democracy, the poll was both low and a foregone conclusion. The poll in favour of unity was 6,463, against 591,000.

Undismayed, London published a White Paper shortly after the poll (on 20 March). It built on the foundations of the Darlington Green Paper, and on the discussion which had taken place on a Council of Ireland during dinner the previous November between Lynch and Heath. The functions of the Council were left purposely vague, but the mere fact that the idea of the Council was included in the White Paper made it a rock on which Unionists would unite to smash any prospects of agreement. The White Paper envisaged the Northern Ireland government consisting of a single-chamber, 78-seat assembly and an executive, under the Secretary of State, at Westminster. Elections were to take place under PR, and for the first time in the history of the northern statelet, power-sharing was to be imposed. The executive was 'no longer to be solely based on any single party, if that party draws its support and its elected representation virtually entirely from only one section of a divided community'. Another rock for the Unionists, and overall a document with which the Provisionals would not agree. Neither did the Orange Order. William Craig decided to found another Unionist party, the Vanguard Unionist Progressive Party, which had the support of the UDA and other Loyalist paramilitary groupings. This dubious company did not prevent Paisley's DUP from entering into an alliance with Craig when the Assembly elections were held on 28 June.

Craig put up 24 candidates, Paisley 16. Faulkner had 44. An alliance between John Taylor and Harry West put up 12, and there were various independent Loyalist candidates. When the votes were counted, the bottom line was that the anti-Faulknerite Unionists won a majority of the votes, a total of 235,873, which yielded 27 seats to Faulkner's 211,362 votes and 22 seats. The SDLP won 159,773 votes and 19 seats. One of the hopes, based on what exactly it is very difficult to say, given the circumstances at the time, was that that rarely met-with political animal, the 'moderate Unionist', would provide the cornerstone of the new Assembly. But out of its 35 candidates, the Alliance Party succeeded in returning only eight, with a total of just 66,441 votes. The NILP got only 18,675 votes, and won one seat. Thus, with the Provisional IRA providing the destructive, but real, motor force of the situation outside the walls of Stormont, and the anti-power-sharing Unionists inside it (to say nothing of their Loyalist paramilitary support outside), the initial prospects for the new Assembly appeared rather worse than those of the *Titanic* reaching port after the encounter with the iceberg. In the days after the election, the prospects worsened further. On 9 July, four of Faulkner's alleged pro-power-sharing followers turned up at a meeting called by the Orange Order for Unionists opposed to the White Paper. On the same day, a car crash claimed the life of one of his followers, and another ally, Nat Minford, was appointed Speaker of the Assembly. The net result was that when the Assembly met for the first time on 31 July, Faulkner's parliamentary party consisted of only 20 members.

Ironically, however, the fundamentally anti-democratic nature of the anti-power-sharing followers of Craig, Paisley, West and Co., provided a lifebelt for Faulkner. An outburst of hooliganism forced Minford to adjourn the session before any question of voting arose. Faulkner and the SDLP withdrew from the chamber, leaving behind a scene of chaos. Chaos reigned outside the chamber also. The Provisionals had marked the Darlington talks by blowing up Belfast's most prestigious hotel, the Russell Court, which cost some £2 million. They had also extended their operations to London, with a series of car bomb explosions (on 8 March 1973), and their increasing efficiency in other areas was underlined when the Provos themselves revealed that a soldier whom they had shot dead in Belfast the previous October had formed part of a British army covert operation run by the Military Reaction Force (MRF) behind fronts like laundries and massage parlours. The Provos revealed that it was not only the MRF who were operating in Northern Ireland; so too were the Special Air Services Regiment (the SAS). Both units had been responsible for a number of hitherto unattributed deaths. The Loyalist paramilitaries too continued to shoot Catholics, and sometimes to stab them to death. One of the most notorious killings was that of Senator Paddy Wilson and his friend, Irene Andrews, who were slowly knifed to death by the UDA's flag-of-convenience grouping, the Ulster Freedom Fighters (UFF). The numbers of prisoners interned and in jail was going through the roof, and a combination of the marching season and anti-internment demonstrations turned up the northern pressure cooker to boiling point. The situation was so bad that the haughty Heath finally decided that it merited his coming to Ireland, both parts of it, on 17 September. It was the first time that a British prime minister had visited the southern state since the Treaty.

Here it should be noted that in the south of Ireland he was received not by his old sparring partner, Jack Lynch, but by a new Taoiseach, Liam Cosgrave, who had come to power as a result of a general election held the previous February. We will return to the election and the course of events south of the border shortly. But for the moment, it is important to follow the fate of the most significant attempt to solve the problem stemming from partition since the days of the Home Rule crisis. Heath's visit broke the log jam. The Faulknerite Unionists, the SDLP and the Alliance agreed to form an executive. The SDLP agreed that there would be no change in the status of Northern Ireland for at least 10 years, when another border poll was envisaged. Finally, on 22 November, Whitelaw, who behind the scenes had performed miracles of arm-twisting and negotiation, announced the composition of the executive. It was to consist of 11 members: six Faulknerites, four SDLP and one Alliance. Brian Faulkner was to be the leader of the new Assembly, and Gerry Fitt his deputy. The details of the Council of Ireland were to be worked out at a conference at Sunningdale on 6 December.

The anti-Unionists' contribution to the Sunningdale conference was to start punch-ups in the Stormont Assembly with Faulkner's followers and break up the day's proceedings in disorder. The anti-Unionists did not restrict themselves to fisticuffs. Yet another anti-executive grouping was set up, the United Ulster Unionist Council (UUUC). This included Craig's followers in Vanguard, those of Taylor and West, and last but far from least, Paisley and the shadowy forces that swirled around him. It had been decided that there was no point in inviting the antis to Sunningdale, a civil servant-training college in Berkshire, because on the basis of their Stormont performances, they would have merely transferred the hooliganism from Stormont to Sunningdale.

There were other divisive forces playing about the Sunningdale talks. Fitt's heart was not in the Council of Ireland idea. Nor was that of Paddy Devlin. Both men were Belfast Socialists, more concerned with day-to-day problems such as getting houses for their constituents than with conceptual Nationalist thinking. They had come to have a certain sympathy with Faulkner's difficulties, and realised that the Council of Ireland was not a stick, but a heavy club for his enemies to beat him with. Moreover, sentiment against internment was so strong amongst Nationalists that four days before coming to Sunningdale, Fitt had had to assure the SDLP annual conference that the proposed executive would not function if internment continued. But probably the greatest single factor militating against the success of the power-sharing executive lay in the changing British political situation. Worried about the worsening economic situation (fuel prices were rocketing), and industrial relations problems, particularly with the miners, Heath suddenly plucked Whitelaw out of the Northern Ireland post on the eve of Sunningdale, and made him Secretary of State for Employment. He was replaced by Francis Pym, who knew nothing about the Six Counties, said virtually nothing throughout the Sunningdale conference, and certainly made no significant contribution to its outcome. Heath's decision to remove Whitelaw at that juncture indicated to many in Ireland, north and south of the border, that Ireland had a very low priority indeed with London.

Yet the talks yielded results: a two-tier Council of Ireland, a 14-man Council of Ministers, and a 60-member Consultative Assembly, half of which was to be drawn from the Dail and half from the Northern Assembly. All decisions were to be unanimous, and, initially at least, the Council's functions were restricted largely to economic and social co-operation. The thorny issue of reforming the RUC was fudged by allowing the Council of Ministers to be consulted on appointments to the police authorities north and south. An Anglo-Irish law commission was to be set up to address the problem of extraditing suspects from the Republic. For their part, the British undertook to start releasing internees, and to review the whole internment question.

The new executive took office on 1 January 1974. It consisted of Brian

Faulkner (Unionist), Chief Executive, Gerry Fitt (SLDP), Deputy Chief Executive, Herbert Kirk (Unionist), Minister of Finance, John Hume (SDLP), Minister for Commerce, Basil McIvor (Unionist), Minister for Education, Austin Currie (SDLP), Minister for Housing, Leslie Morrell (Unionist), Minister for Agriculture, Paddy Devlin (SDLP), Minister for Health and Social Services, Roy Bradford (Unionist), Minister for the Environment, Oliver Napier (Alliance), Minister for Law Reform, and John Baxter (Unionist), Minister for Information.

The first task of the executive was to convince the constituents of the various parties involved that words didn't mean what they said. They meant what the party said they meant. To Faulkner's followers, and foes, the Council was portrayed as meaning very little. To the SDLP, whose support was under threat from the Provisionals, the Council of Ireland was made to appear a stepping stone on the way to a united Ireland. Using this argument, the SDLP's Hugh Logue unwittingly presented Paisley with a whip of scorpions when, speaking at a debate at Trinity College Dublin (on 18 January 1974), he told a Republican heckler who had accused the SDLP of selling out on the national issue that 'The Council of Ireland is the vehicle which will trundle Unionists into a United Ireland.' On top of this, Kevin Boland took an action in the Dublin High Court, claiming that a commitment made by Dublin's delegates to Sunningdale was unconstitutional. It read: 'The Irish government fully accepted and solemnly declared that there could be no change in the status of Northern Ireland, until a majority of the people of Northern Ireland decided change in that status.'

Boland's action was dismissed (on 16 January 1974) by Justice Murnaghan, who ruled that the statement was no more than a statement of policy, and not in conflict with Articles 2 and 3 of the constitution. However, the pro-agreement Unionists had been arguing that one of the virtues of the Council of Ireland was the Irish Government's commitment, because for the first time it gave northerners a guarantee that their status could not be changed against their wishes. Boland's action and the Murnahan judgment therefore provided further anti-agreement ammunition for Paisley. Faulkner came under such pressure that he informed Dublin that unless the Republic repealed Articles 2 and 3, he and his followers would oppose the Council of Ireland. In order to help Faulkner survive, Cosgrave, who had no love for de Valera's constitution anyhow, gave him an assurance which without going so far as promising to drop the Articles, met the requirements of the situation. He told the Dail (on 13 March) that 'the factual position of Northern Ireland is that it is within the United Kingdom and my government accepts this as a fact'.

At the time, there were more things than Articles 2 and 3 to worry about. Amongst myriad IRA operations, a coach bombing on the M62 motorway in England killed nine soldiers and three civilians. Other bombings destroyed the Grand Central Hotel in Belfast, which was used as an army headquarters, and a number of properties in Armagh which alone cost over £1 million. By the end of May, the British army had suffered its largest death toll since the

Korean War, a total of 214 soldiers. In addition, 52 members of the RUC and 45 of the Ulster Defence Regiment were shot dead. For their part, the Loyalists attempted to drive Catholics from employment by shooting them going to and from work, and by bombing churches and pubs.

On the constitutional front, before this frightful litany had even got under way, the Ulster Unionist Council had begun the year by passing a motion rejecting the Sunningdale Agreement, on 4 January 1974. This forced Faulkner to resign, and to set up a new party, the Unionist Party of Northern Ireland. While he acquired new headquarters and remained as the Assembly's Chief Executive, his opponents in the party he had left commanded its electoral machine, the name 'Unionist Party' and the old Unionist Party headquarters. The Sunningdale Agreement was holed beneath the waterline. Nevertheless, some efforts were made to progress the Council of Ireland idea. On 1 February, members of the Dublin Government met at Hillsborough, the former headquarters of governors of Northern Ireland, and set up an Anglo-Irish legal commission to study the extradition question, and Belfast-Dublin contacts on policing and other matters continued. But whatever chance may have existed of patching the holes beneath the waterline in such turbulent waters disappeared on 28 February, when Ted Heath called a general election. Again, as he had done by recalling Whitelaw at a critical juncture, Heath underlined the low priority accorded to Irish affairs by brushing aside Francis Pym's protestations about what the election was likely to do to the fledgling Belfast Assembly. Had Paisley organised it, the timing could not have been worse for Faulkner. Bereft of a proper organisation, he could only field seven candidates. These polled only 94,331 votes and lost everywhere. Faulkner's former party, which viewed itself as the official Unionists, led by Harry West, did a pre-election deal with the United Ulster Unionist Council, whereby each grouping nominated only one candidate in each constituency. They won 11 seats, and 366,703 votes. The only SDLP figure to survive after the Westminster holocaust was Gerry Fitt, and he had a narrow escape. Albert Price took 5,000 votes, he was a well-known Belfast Republican, and father of the Price sisters, who had been arrested following the London bombings and were now on hunger strike, demanding that they be allowed to serve their sentences in the Six Counties.

Harold Wilson, who had far more interest in, and empathy with, the north of Ireland than did Ted Heath, was back in Westminster. But in Belfast, which was where getting Sunningdale to work really mattered, things went from bad to worse. On the pro-Sunningdale side, the SDLP support wobbled dangerously because, having called off the rent and rate strike, as they had to do on taking up office, the party then proceeded to penalise its followers who had done what they had been asked. Austin Currie made two announcements on 3 April which went down like a lead balloon. He declared that there would be no amnesty for those who had remained on the rent and rate strike after the SDLP's call-off, and in addition announced an increase in the amount which was to be deducted from the strikers' social welfare benefits, introducing a 25p a week collection charge. By the time Wilson got to Belfast on 19 April, working-class Nationalists were less concerned about what he had to say about supporting Sunningdale than what the SDLP had done to ensure lack of support for the rent strike.

Where working-class Loyalists were concerned, a conference called by the UUUC at Portrush, in County Antrim, a week after the Wilson visit, was of more significance than anything either Currie or Wilson had to say. This conference was attended by another prominent English politician, who seemed to see nothing incongruous in finding himself the star performer at a Unionist gathering openly acknowledged to include a large representation from the UDA, which, outside the conference, was known to be busily engaged in a sectarian assassination campaign. The politician concerned was the formidable Enoch Powell. With Powell's help, the conference called for a number of decisions which led to the final demise of the power-sharing executive. Portrush demanded that the executive be scrapped immediately, and that an election be called. The conference further demanded that the parliament that emerged from that election – and the voting figures for the Westminster elections indicate why they felt entitled to make a confident guess as to who would be in a majority in that parliament – would have security powers returned to it. The conference also wanted more resources devoted to both the RUC and the UDR. One of the groupings represented at Portrush which gave it the confidence both to make the foregoing demands, and to threaten strike action should Westminster not agree, was the Ulster Workers Council. This had been set up in the wake of a strike that was called after some Loyalists were interned early in 1973. The strike gave the UWC an insight into what might be achieved, and throughout the remainder of 1973, and the early part of 1974, they had quietly enrolled key trade union officials and workers in vital areas, notably the power stations.

The UWC did not have to wait long after Portrush to flex its muscles. On 14 May, anti-agreement Unionists failed to carry a motion opposing Sunningdale in the Stormont Assembly. The rejection was followed by the unveiling of yet another Loyalist organisation, the Ulster Army Council, an umbrella group for the various Loyalist paramilitaries. With the announcement of the UAC, there came briefings to journalists, at which it was made known that the UUUC would be supported by the Loyalist paramilitaries in organising through the Ulster Workers Council a stoppage of all essential services until such time as the Sunningdale Agreement was repealed. As a combination of Six County employment practices and a want of foresight on the part of the authorities meant that power supplies were in the hands of Protestants, the UWC thus literally had its finger on the switch of real power.

However, the strikers could have been faced down, as even anti-agreement Unionists objected to the thuggery which accompanied the strike, had London acted with resolution. It did not. Some of the strike leaders could not believe their luck. One of them, Glen Barr, has repeatedly said subsequently that had the strike been confronted early on, it would have crumbled. James Callaghan told me many years later that he believed that Sunningdale 'could have been and should have been seen through'. It could, of course, had the army been reliable. Merlyn Rees, who had become Secretary of State for Northern Ireland, proved himself irresolute as the British army and the undercover security services, notably MI5, proceeded to stage a 1970s-version rerun of the Curragh Mutiny. Loyalist paramilitaries took over the distribution of essential supplies such as petrol, and erected road blocks all across the Six Counties. People could not get petrol to drive to work without passes supplied by the paramilitaries, or permission to use the petrol to pass through the barricades without the paramilitaries' consent. As masked men armed with pickaxe handles enforced these conditions, the British army took no action. Photographs of the period show army and police personnel chatting with the strikers, while angry Catholics look on impotently. Sometimes the strikers enforced their will by methods other than displaying pickaxe handles. What were described as 'flying pickets', who were at the time wrecking pubs in the area, murdered two Catholic brothers in Ballymena.

The only time the army took an active part in the strike was the day before it ended, on 27 May, when, after the SDLP had threatened to resign if the troops did not act, the army manned 27 petrol stations. But at no time did the army show either the expertise or the willingness to take over the power stations. And at the time both the army and the Ministry of Defence made known their reluctance to deploy the resources which it was calculated would be required both to take on the Loyalists, and maintain the security situation. The army's inaction was compounded by the fact that the north of Ireland BBC was virtually an autonomous region, responsive throughout the strike to Unionist attitudes rather than those of Westminster to such an extent that a member of the Irish Government, Garret FitzGerald, a future Taoiseach, would later claim that the BBC was running 'a rebel station'. Certainly, as the strike gathered momentum, more and more recognised Unionist leaders decided that it was safe to jump on the bandwagon. Paisley, Craig, West, and representatives of several Loyalist paramilitary groups formed a co-ordinating committee to openly direct the strike.

How much a question of resources affected the decision, and how much reluctance to open a second front against the Protestants, and how much questions such as ancestral support for the Unionists and a dislike of Labour affected the army's attitude, are matters of conjecture. It is known that there had been difficulties involving the army and the Government over Rhodesia's UDI, and it later emerged that MI5 had been supplying Merlyn Rees's adversaries with information. Incidents such as Harold Wilson being booed by naval cadets are also well known. In these circumstances, even a stronger man than Merlyn Rees might have had difficulties in dealing with a strike. What is certain is that the belief that the army was a partisan force was copper-fastened on the Nationalist community. What happened over Sunningdale deepened and extended the Protestant–Catholic divide. The middle classes,

ABOVE: *Even in the days of puritanical censorship the 'Royalettes', who performed at the Theatre Royal until this Dublin landmark was demolished in 1962, were a highlight of the City's popular entertainment. The man in the centre is the comedian Cecil Sheridan.*

BELOW: *The first performance of the musical 'Riverdance' at the Point Theatre in Dublin in 1995 with Michael Flatley and Jean Butler (centre couple) in the leading roles. The musical went on to become one of the international smash-hits of the twentieth century.*

ABOVE: *They tried to bring North and South together… The Six County Prime Minister Captain Terence O'Neill (left) with the Republic's Taoiseach, Jack Lynch.*

RIGHT: *The smiling face of a rising young Six County preacher, Ian Kyle Paisley*

BELOW: *A clash of symbolism… Police remove a tricolour which was somehow affixed to Carson's statue at Stormont.*

ABOVE: *Symbolically far apart... Seated at a meeting of Jack Lynch's fractious Cabinet are Charles J. Haughey (far right) and James Gibbons (far left). Beside Haughey is Desmond O' Malley who later helped to found the Progressive Democrats Party in protest at Haughey's policies. Seated third from left is George Colley, Haughey's principal (and unsuccessful) rival to succeed Lynch.*

BELOW: *President Kennedy pays his respects at the graves of the executed 1916 leaders at Arbour Hill, Dublin, in June 1963. He was one of the most popular visitors to Ireland of the century. Five months later he was assassinated.*

LEFT: *Close encounters of the torrid kind… An incident during the 1995 all-Ireland Gaelic football semi-final.*

BELOW: *The famous Irish rugby international and later business tycoon Tony O'Reilly (right) with his fellow international Andy Mulligan in après match mode*

RIGHT: *Ireland's most famous traditional music group The Chieftains with their leader Paddy Maloney celebrate in 1984, on the 21st anniversary of their foundation*

LEFT: *In the shadow of the tiger… An accurate portrayal of the changes wrought in contemporary Ireland by the 'Celtic Tiger' era. Street football enjoyed by children in an area soon to be filled with traffic congestion as the building project indicated by the crane – and thousands like it all over – brought new life, and problems, to Dublin's sleepy back-waters.*

BELOW: *Appropriate attire for an Irish politician… Labour Party leader Ruairi Quinn, dressed as a Viking complete with battle-axe, takes part in a Wren Boys parade.*

ABOVE: *President Mary Robinson seen with Prince Charles on his first visit to Ireland in 1995*

ABOVE: *The Irish veneration of the horse is as much part of the culture as the weather and one of the most venerated horses of the twentieth century was the Cheltenham Gold Cup winner Arkle, seen here at the Dublin Spring Show of 1965 with his jockey Pat Taaffe, trainer Tom Draper and owner, Anne, Duchess of Westminster*

BELOW LEFT: *A rider who was also known for his appreciation of horse flesh, but who became unhorsed politically, Charles J. Haughey*

BELOW RIGHT: *President Mary McAleese*

ABOVE: *Albert Reynolds,*
the Peace Process Taoiseach

ABOVE: *The Fine Gael leader*
and Taoiseach, John Bruton

RIGHT: *Brian Faulkner, who, as Six County*
Prime Minister saw Stormont fall and the
Power-sharing Executive collapse

BELOW: *The Sinn Féin President,*
Gerry Adams (right), and the Sinn Féin
chief negotiator, Martin McGuinness (left),
with the Irish Foreign Minister,
Brian Cowen (centre)

ABOVE: *A somewhat fractured 'Yes'. Garret FitzGerald and John Hume (left) had to come out of retirement to help Taoiseach Bertie Ahern convince the electorate to vote 'Yes' in a second referendum on the Nice Treaty in 2002. The first had failed.*

LEFT: *Liberty Hall, the headquarters of Ireland's largest union, SIPTU, rises on the site from which James Connolly led out his tiny citizen army in 1916*

BELOW: *Pass the Peace Process parcel… Pat Cox, the Irish President of the European Parliament, gestures as Mark Durkan, the leader of the SDLP, looks down and David Trimble, the Ulster Unionist Party leader, appears to say, 'Who me?'*

who had hitherto managed to leave politics at the door of the golf club, separated on sectarian lines.

Wilson was out of sympathy with the strikers. He personally demanded that the Treasury, which had at first refused the request, provide him with the true cost of maintaining the Six Counties, and bypassing his normal speech writers, delivered a famous speech on television and radio on the evening of 25 May. In it, he condemned the effort to set up 'a sectarian and undemocratic state', from which one-third of the people would be excluded, and went on to deliver a broadside against those who benefited from the largesse of the British taxpayer, but who 'viciously defy Westminster, purporting to act as though they were an elected government, spend their lives sponging on Westminster and British democracy and then systematically assault democratic methods. Who do these people think they are?'

The next day, Unionists from every walk of life sported pieces of sponge on their lapels, and the strikers benefited from the wave of hurt pride which greeted Wilson's speech. But the hurt of Unionists, however real or feigned, was as nothing to that experienced in Dublin where, on 17 May, the worst day of the entire Troubles dawned. No-warning car bombs went off in Dublin and Monaghan, killing 33 people and wounding hundreds more. Over the years, suspicion has hardened into certainty that British undercover agents trained and equipped the bombers. The names of the British officers involved, as well as those of the paramilitaries concerned, are known. All have since died or been killed, either in Northern Ireland or in service abroad for the SAS. At the time of writing, a committee of inquiry under Mr Justice Barron is conducting the sworn public investigation into just who was responsible, and how far up the chain of command the decision to bomb Dublin was taken.

In the North the combined pressures inevitably took their toll. Light and heat supplies were gone. Water and sewage facilities were under threat. The strength of the Loyalist paramilitaries was such that a Faulknerite member of the executive's ministry, Roy Bradford, received a delegation from the UDA and UVF in his office at Stormont. After it, he broke with his colleagues and issued a statement to the papers urging that negotiations with the Ulster Workers Council begin. Rees refused to open talks, but on the same day, 28 May, Faulkner and his supporters resigned.

Such, in brief outline, was the history of the only really significant attempt to resolve the Irish issue for most of the Troubles. What happened between 1974 and 1994 filled many headlines, and many graves. But between the fall of Sunningdale and the Good Friday Agreement of 1998 which followed on an IRA ceasefire four years earlier, no meaningful effort to link London, Belfast and Dublin in a constitutional attempt to solve the crisis occurred.

ELEVEN

SINN FÉIN RE-EMERGES

While Haughey was conducting his laborious rise to power in the Republic throughout the seventies, the career of another figure affected by the violence in Northern Ireland also took off, that of one Gerry Adams. Adams's ascendancy, and that of other personalities later associated with him, like Martin McGuinness, had its origins in ceasefire negotiations which began on 20 December 1974 in a small hotel in Feakle, County Clare, through the intercession of a group of Protestant clergymen led by the Reverend William Arlow. Talks were held between the clergymen and an IRA team comprising most of the leading Provisionals of the day, Ruairi O'Bradaigh, Daithi O'Conaill, J.B. O'Hagan, Kevin Mallon, Jimmy Drumm, his wife Maire (who was subsequently murdered in her hospital bed by Loyalists), Billy McKee, Seamus Twomey and Seamus Loughran. The ceasefire was something of a curate's egg for the Provisionals. It was good in parts, small parts. On the one hand, it yielded tangible results such as the phasing out of internment, and the creation of 'incident centres', each with a hotline to Stormont. These were manned by Republican activists, and set up to monitor the ceasefire so as to avoid Lenadoon-like incidents arising. In effect they provided local centres of influence for the Provos. However, the cessation also had a seriously damaging effect on the organisation. The ceasefire era began at Christmas 1974, when the Provos institutionalised their custom of having an undeclared cessation of activities for the holidays. It broke down on 16 January, resumed on 9 February, and lasted for several months before disintegrating in October in an orgy of sectarian violence and feuding between the Provos and the Officials.

The talks between the British and Republicans were something of an open secret in Belfast. Ruairi O'Bradaigh, Billy McKee, Jimmy Drumm and Proinnsias MacAirt (Frank Caird) met British Foreign Office officials James Allan and Michael Oatley at various sites, principally in Derry, and at a house called Laneside owned by the British Government in Holywood, County Down, which is not only part of the so-called northern 'gold coast', but a centre of Orange and Unionist intelligence as well as economic strength. There was very little possibility of the talks yielding results. The IRA wanted a British declaration of intent to withdraw from Ireland, which the British, bound by the Downing Street Declaration, had no means, or intention, of delivering. The most the British can have hoped for from the talks was a reduction in the killings and an atmosphere of peace conducive to the functioning of a constitutional device which had been used without success in Ireland before, after 1916: a convention bringing all the parties together. This was held in the spring and early summer of 1975, but its futility was underlined by elections held on 1 May 1975, which anti-power-sharing Loyalists won by 47 seats to 31. However, enraged by the talks, the Loyalist paramilitaries, who may have also been used by MI5 in their turf war with MI6 which was involved in the talks with the IRA, began an outburst of sectarian slaughter. This was the era of the infamous 'Shankill Butchers', who operated out of the Lawnbrook Drinking Club in Belfast, which was also patronised by the RUC, but whose identities allegedly remained unknown for years during an orgy of killings carried out with knives, meat cleavers and other butchers' implements. The 'butchers' were finally put out of business in Belfast on 20 February 1979 when eight of them received 42 life sentences for 19 of the deaths for which they were held accountable.

The IRA responded with a murderous onslaught against the Protestant population, and the death toll of civilians by the end of 1976 was approximately 250 Catholics, and 150 Protestants, many of them at the hands of groups flying Republican flags of convenience. Provisional–Official feuding continued for some weeks in October and November of 1975, resulting in 11 deaths. These events facilitated the growth of Adams's influence, firstly amongst the prisoners in Long Kesh and then throughout the Republican movement as a whole. After the failure of the Cheyne Walk peace talks, he wound up back in Long Kesh, as he said in his book *Cage 11*, 'black and blue after being used as a punchbag in Springfield Road British Army Barracks and spending a few days in Castlereagh interrogation centre'.[1] He claims to have been the camp's 'most unsuccessful escapee'.[2] He made two attempts at escape and joined in a demonstration of the prisoners' 'heartfelt appreciation for being interned without trial by joining the sentenced prisoners in burning down the camp'.[3] As a result of his various activities, for a time he became 'an internee, a sentenced prisoner, and a remand prisoner, all at the one time'.[4] More importantly he became a centre for the expression of dissatisfaction at the outcome of the ceasefire talks, and the realisation that those who had thought that the talks would lead to a speedy end to the war were seriously mistaken. The prisoners were being offered major concessions in negotiations with the then prisoners' leader, David Morley, in the fields of educational and recreational facilities. There was also an extraordinary proposal that the British would create a sort of headquarters for terrorists by giving not only the IRA, but the UVF and the UDA, a premises in downtown Belfast, in Rosemary Street, where apparently it was expected that they would all cavort so gaily under the one roof that they would overlook both their own hostilities and the existence of British bugging devices. Some of the prisoners believed that a new era was dawning: for example, Morley was allowed out of Long Kesh to consult with IRA leaders across the border as well as in the Six

County area, and he was also provided with a gun to protect himself, supplied by the British.

But Adams remained sceptical. He began writing a series of articles under the pseudonym 'Brownie' in the Belfast Republican newspaper which, as his power grew, later amalgamated with the existing IRA newspaper, *An Phoblacht*. In these he criticised the policy direction taken by the movement, and promulgated the doctrine that, far from the ceasefires bringing peace, the IRA was in fact in for a long war. Adams was involved in the drafting of a speech which both stated this belief and hinted at resuming the forbidden path, which had led to the Officials–Provisionals split in the first place: political action. The speech was delivered by Jimmy Drumm, one of the ceasefire negotiators, at the 1977 Bodenstown commemoration of Wolfe Tone:

> The British government is not withdrawing from the Six Counties. Indeed the British government is committed to stabilising [them] and is pouring in vast sums of money . . . to assure loyalists and to secure from loyalists, support for a long haul against the IRA . . . a successful war of liberation cannot be fought exclusively on the backs of the oppressed in the Six Counties, nor around the physical presence of the British Army. Hatred and resentment of the army cannot sustain the war . . .

Along with facing political reality, Adams and his colleagues were also secretly confronting the military realities of the period, which were that the lengthy detention periods under the legislation introduced by the British, and the interrogation methods employed, were yielding a flood of information which was enabling the RUC to seriously damage the IRA's capability to wage any sort of war, long or short.

The result was twofold: the Green Book, the IRA compendium manual of both theological justification for its actions, and a series of dos and don'ts for resisting interrogation; and the introduction of the cell system. The cell idea actually went back to the continental secret societies on which James Stephens based the original Fenian organisation in the nineteenth century. The theory was that only cell members knew each other, with one member of the cell having contact with higher authority, or linking up with other cells. Another fundamentally important change in the IRA initiated by Adams was the setting up of a Northern Command. The Northern Command included both the Six Counties and the counties in the Republic along the border, and became responsible for actually prosecuting the war. A Southern Command, comprising the rest of the counties in the Republic, provided logistical support, safe houses and other services. The war was being fought in the north, and would be controlled not by the O'Bradaigh/O'Conaill wings but by northerners, specifically northerners loyal to Adams.

Adams virtually took control of the IRA after Seamus Twomey was arrested at the end of 1977, even though his tenure at the helm was short-lived. The following February, he was picked up during a wave of reaction to one of the worst atrocities of the Troubles. Bungled communications led to a delay in warning the RUC that the La Mon House Hotel in Belfast was to be blown up. The result was that 12 Protestants, seven of them women, were burned to death as they attended a dinner organised by dog-lovers. The case against Adams did not stand up in court, and he was released in September 1978. Two months later, a ferocious bombing campaign broke out across Northern Ireland, affecting 16 towns. That month also, one of the IRA's principal adversaries, General James Glover, compiled a report on the Provisionals which made a number of points conceding that the current methodology of the security forces and the propaganda effort to depict the IRA as mindless thugs were as far removed from either success or reality as they were when the same sort of label and approach were applied to Michael Collins and his colleagues in the 1920s era. Glover wrote:

> PIRA's organisation is now such that a small number of activists can maintain a disproportionate level of violence ... though PIRA may be hard hit by Security Force attrition from time to time, they will probably continue to have the manpower they need to sustain violence ... PIRA has become less dependent on public support than in the past and is less vulnerable to penetration by informers ... Our evidence of the calibre of rank-and-file terrorists does not support the view that they are mindless hooligans drawn from the unemployed and the unemployable. PIRA now trains and uses its members with some care ... They are constantly learning from mistakes and developing their expertise.
> ... There has been a marked trend towards attacks against the Security Forces and away from action which, by alienating public opinion, both within the Catholic community and outside the province is politically damaging ... The [Republican] Movement will retain popular support sufficient to maintain secure bases in the traditional Republican areas.

Just how much 'popular support' the Republicans had was about to be demonstrated and it is vital for an understanding of the political developments both within the island and between Ireland and England to further penetrate the strange 'hidden Ireland' world of prison and protest from which the Provisional IRA evolved into a position of constitutional strength and a departure from the gun. But first it is necessary to explain how the political vacuum in which the Provos grew was created.

In the wake of the fall of the power-sharing executive, Merlyn Rees had attempted to placate public opinion, particularly Irish-American opinion, which was becoming something of a factor in the situation, by setting up a convention consisting of 75 members elected by proportional representation and playing down the Council of Ireland idea. He also toyed with a proposal to increase the number of MPs who would be returned to Westminster. However, this foundered because the Unionists wanted the old Stormont restored and were only prepared to concede Catholic representation on parliamentary committees on the lines once proposed by Faulkner, whereas the SDLP wanted full-blooded power-sharing. The convention was formally dissolved in March 1976, and Rees was replaced by Roy Mason when Harold

Wilson resigned as British prime minister, to be succeeded by James Callaghan.

The Callaghan/Mason era is of significance to Irish history for two things: first, the extremely tough security policies of Mason, which were notable for a rise in the number of 'dirty tricks' and undercover operations, and coincided with a very marked rise in the number of Nationalist prisoners held in the Six Counties; and second, the frequently overlooked fact that it was the Irish situation which brought down the Callaghan government. With a slim majority in the House, Callaghan sought to bolster Labour support by reviving the Rees convention idea of increasing the number of Ulster MPs from 12 to 17 thus mainly benefiting the Unionists. Gerry Fitt, who regarded the increase as a sop to Unionist blackmail, abstained in a crucial division on 29 March 1979, and the Government was defeated by 311 votes to 310, with eight Unionists voting with their traditional allies, the Conservatives. Had Fitt, a lifelong Labour supporter, followed his normal voting pattern, the Government would have remained in office. The result would have been a tie, causing the Speaker to give his casting vote to the status quo. Thus did the election come about which brought Mrs Thatcher to power. Ominously for the character of her Irish policy, her friend Airey Neave was assassinated by a Republican group, the INLA, the day after the Fitt abstention. A bomb was detonated under his car in the House of Commons underground car park.

Mention has already been made of the battery of laws introduced by the British to curb the IRA after the ceasefire discussions. These laws were part of a triple onslaught on the IRA devised under three headings: 'Ulsterisation', 'normalisation', and 'criminalisation'. Ulsterisation was intended as an Irish version of the Americans' 'Vietnamisation' policy in Vietnam, a shifting of the burden of war from the Americans to the natives, in this case from the army to the RUC. The 'normalisation' policy meant what it said: everything possible was to be done to make the Six Counties appear 'normal'. Shortly after the bricks had stopped falling following an explosion, builders were on their way to the scene, so as to lessen the impact of the evidence of the IRA's handiwork. Money was spent on leisure centres, and a great deal of effort went into making the abnormal life of Belfast appear other than it was. 'Criminalisation', however, was the spark which really ignited the crisis that broke out in what were known as the 'H blocks', a complex of prison buildings erected at the site of the Long Kesh internment camp.

The buildings were shaped like an H, the arms on either side being filled with cells, linked in the middle by the administration offices. The internees in Long Kesh could see these structures being built as the peace talks continued in 1974 and 1975, allegedly holding out the prospect of a British withdrawal and a united Ireland. The physical presence of the buildings was one of the most telling proofs available to Adams and his cohorts that wherever the peace talks were said to be leading, it was not towards the attainment of IRA objectives. The regime in the Long Kesh compounds was quite benign. Too benign in the eyes of the Unionists and the Tories, who depicted Long Kesh –

and not without justice – as a 'Sandhurst of terror'. Jails or internment camps have traditionally formed part of the 'Republican university'. The prisoners only made contact with the authorities through their own officers, had a liberal supply of contact with the outside world, including parcels and mail of all sorts, and, a vital point, they wore their own clothes. All these conditions were part of the 'Special Category' status, which had been conceded to Billy McKee and his colleagues in order to set the scene for the 1972 talks between the Provisionals and William Whitelaw.

The failure of the 1972 talks speedily convinced the British that the concession of Special Category status had been a mistake. This was the genesis of the 'criminalisation' policy. The IRA were to be portrayed, not as a Special Category group with historical antecedents, but as a Mafia-type organisation whose brutal methods set it apart from what Merlyn Rees once described as 'ODCs' – ordinary decent criminals. The method chosen to perform this transformation was a report from the former Lord Chancellor, Lord Gardiner. After Sunningdale fell, Gardiner was asked to decide 'in the context of Civil Liberties and Human Rights, measures to deal with terrorism in Northern Ireland'. He reported (on 30 January 1975) as follows:

> The introduction of Special Category Status was a serious mistake . . . It should be made absolutely clear that Special Category prisoners can expect no amnesty and will have to serve their sentences . . . We recommend that the earliest practicable opportunity should be taken to end the Special Category.

It was Gardiner who recommended the building of the H blocks, because, he said:

> Prisons of the compound type, each compound holding up to 90 prisoners, are thoroughly unsatisfactory from every point of view; their major disadvantage is that there is virtually a total loss of disciplinary control by the prison authorities inside the compounds. The layout and construction of the compounds make close and continued supervision impossible.

Another change made by the British at this time was to rechristen Long Kesh 'The Maze'. Changes in nomenclature when dealing with unpleasant realities are a feature of Anglo-Irish relationships. The controversial nuclear facility Windscale, on the Cumbrian coast, facing Ireland across the narrow Irish Sea, was presumed to have lost its radioactive menace for the Irish by renaming it Sellafield. But there was no way in which the fallout from the decision to introduce internment could be disguised. Though the term 'internment' ceased to be used, being replaced by 'detention', the effect remained the same. Arrested prisoners were remanded in custody for indefinite periods, thereby increasing the prison problem. The early days of the civil rights movement saw an increase in the north's prison population from 727 to 2,848. Some 1,200 of these were Special Category prisoners, which had the disagreeable effect that to international opinion, the Mother of Parliaments was responsible for a large number of political prisoners, an uncomfortable position for a democratic government. But the numbers were to get larger, to approximately 3,500, because of the operation of an essential component of what became known as 'the conveyor belt' system: the Diplock courts already referred to.

Amongst the many recommendations Diplock made was one that 'A confession made by the accused should be admissible as evidence in cases involving the scheduled offences unless it was obtained by torture or inhuman or degrading treatment.'[5] The reality of what happened after the Diplock courts were set up was that brutal treatment became the order of the day. Roy Mason, who had succeeded Merlyn Rees as Secretary of State for Northern Ireland, approached the IRA in the same spirit as had the coalition in the Republic, saying that he would 'roll up the IRA like toothpaste'. In November 1977, the 30 solicitors who appeared most often in the Diplock courts wrote to Mason stating that 'Ill treatment of suspects by police officers, with the object of obtaining confessions, is now common practice, and . . . most often, but not always takes place at Castlereagh RUC station and other police stations, throughout Northern Ireland.'

The solicitors' complaint fell on deaf ears. But the publicity surrounding the use of torture in Northern Ireland led to an inquiry conducted by Lord Parker of Waddington, which found (on 31 January 1982) that the methods then in use in the 'UK overseas' were illegal under UK law. However, Lord Parker found that given the circumstances, these methods were not 'immoral'. Lord Gardiner, who had recommended the building of the H blocks, issued a minority report, disagreeing, saying that even though the prisoners involved were terrorists, the methods *were* immoral. Here, the real issue is not whether the methods were or were not immoral; the fact is that they were obviously special methods carried out as part of a special system of courts and prison building to cope with a special situation. Insofar as the average IRA volunteer was concerned, he or she was clearly in a Special Category, but the Government was attempting to deny the prisoners Special Category status.

A number of factors should be borne in mind here. One is the oft-pointed-out comparison between the number of American deaths in Vietnam, and those during the Troubles in Northern Ireland, which shows that, given the difference in the population numbers involved, the impact in percentage terms was far higher in the Six County area than was the Vietnam conflict on America, grievous though it was. What is not generally appreciated is that the impact on the Nationalist population was further magnified by the fact that most of those affected were drawn from a minority within the minority: the ghetto areas of Belfast and Derry and, to some degree, the Catholic parts of Derry, Fermanagh and Tyrone. In addition, the 'risen people' factor described by Padraig Pearse in his poem 'The Rebel' was also having an effect. Many young Nationalists saw the process they were undergoing as merely transferring them from the larger prison of their ghetto existence, with its unemployment, searches, shootings, police and army raids, and police brutality, to the smaller prison of the H blocks. All their lives they had been singled out for special treatment which they regarded as unjust, and which they were prepared to resist in order to take what would not be given.

The first prisoner to be sentenced in 1976 after Special Category status was withdrawn was Ciaran Nugent. He passed into Republican folklore by making the ringing declaration, on being offered prison clothes: 'They'll have to nail them to my back.' The conveyor belt system soon ensured that there were hundreds like him. He served his three-and-a-half year sentence naked except for a blanket. As he was in breach of prison regulations, all the furniture was removed from his cell, and he was denied visits, parcels and educational facilities. The atmosphere in the H blocks turned poisonous. The warders were Loyalist, the prisoners Nationalist. Some of the warders developed a practice of kicking over the prisoners' slop bowls in the mornings, so that the night soil spilled on the cell floors. When prisoners attempted to throw the excrement out of the windows, the warders threw it back in again. What I christened 'the battle of the bowels' in my book *On the Blanket* gradually escalated to a point where prisoners on 'the dirty protest' turned their cells into hideous, maggot-infested caves.

I came to write the book by accident. Like most people in the Republic, I was unaware of the situation building up in the H blocks, or indeed of the significance of their being built in the first place, and it was only a chance meeting with a publisher who had seen a protest by bare-footed women parading through Dublin in the month of January 1980, wrapped in prison blankets, which sparked my interest in the subject, and led me to discuss it with Father Alec Reid. He had been visiting the prison, and dealing with the blanket men's families, and was becoming progressively more worried that the situation was heading towards a hunger strike, with all its potential for serious trouble and widespread heartbreak. I discovered that his fears were well founded, and wrote the book in an effort to bring publicity to bear on the situation, and head off the hunger strike. At this stage, the IRA leadership outside the prison was also attempting to prevent a strike, because of the traditional IRA fear that if prisoners are broken inside jail, the movement outside it is broken also.

On visiting the H blocks – I have to acknowledge that I was given remarkable co-operation by the Stormont authorities – I witnessed two incidents that convinced me that the situation had advanced, or regressed, to a point where the prisoners could not be broken. The term 'cultural identity' took on a new meaning for me when in one maggot-infested cell I found a young prisoner using the crucifix of his rosary beads to help him learn Irish by cutting words into his own excrement after they had been tapped out on the heating pipes by a prisoner in another cell, who was conducting the 'Ranganna', Irish classes. In another, I found a prisoner attempting to vary the monotony by drawing sea and palm trees on the walls with his excrement. In some ways, I found the visit one of the worst experiences of my life, being appalled at the condition to which hate and history had reduced normal young men. Nevertheless, it seemed obvious that the prisoners were not going to be defeated. Nor were they. The palm tree prisoner, Martin Meehan, at the time of writing is a Sinn Féin member of the Northern Ireland Assembly. His transformation from that filthy cell to the Stormont parliament occurred as follows.

The prisoners' demands, which became known throughout the country as 'the five demands' were, with the exception of number four, basically those which had defused the Portlaoise situation:

1. The right to wear their own clothes.
2. The right not to do prison work.
3. Free association with fellow prisoners.
4. Full 50% remission of their sentences.
5. Normal visits, parcels, education and recreational facilities.

Before the Gardiner Report was adopted, the fourth demand would have been the norm for IRA prisoners. But neither it nor any of the other demands were conceded, despite the fact that both Charles Haughey and Cardinal O'Fiaich privately interceded with the British to come to an agreement along the Portlaoise lines. O'Fiaich went public on the issue in August 1980, saying:

> One would hardly allow an animal to remain in such conditions, let alone a human being. The nearest approach to it that I have seen was the spectacle of hundreds of homeless people living in the sewer pipes in the slums of Calcutta. The stench and filth in some of the cells, with the remains of rotten food and human excreta scattered around the walls, was almost unbearable. In two of them I was unable to speak for fear of vomiting.

Mrs Thatcher, however, was unmoved. The 'dirty protest' dragged on, and here it should be noticed that it affected IRA women prisoners also. Mairead Farrell, who was later assassinated by the SAS in Gibraltar, was being held in Armagh jail, where the situation was even more revolting than in the H blocks. The cells, being older, were darker, and the walls were smeared with both excreta and menstrual fluids. The effect on the prisoners' families and their supporters was, of course, upsetting in the extreme. The repercussions of the 'dirty protests' included vicious retaliation by the prisoners' comrades outside the jail, who murdered over a dozen warders as a result. Thatcher, however, publicly stuck to the view that 'crime is crime'. Apart from this being a natural expression of her 'Iron Lady' persona, she was deeply hurt and angered at the death of her friend Airey Neave. The inevitable occurred. Seven prisoners went on hunger strike on 27 October. They were Brendan Hughes, who led the strike, Tom McFeeley (with Hughes Joint OC of the Provisional prisoners), Seán McKenna, Leo Greene, Tommy McKearney, Raymond McCartney, and John Nixon, OC of the INLA prisoners. Three of the Armagh women prisoners also joined the strike: Mairead Farrell, Mairead Nugent and Mary Doyle.

The strikes, of course, produced a frenzied bout of negotiation and exchanges between Belfast, Dublin and London. It appeared that the combined efforts of the Dublin Government, Cardinal O'Fiaich, the former Irish Labour Party minister Dr John O'Connell, and a Redemptorist priest, Father Brendan Meagher, who had won the prisoners' trust, eventually produced a formula which, without overtly conceding the five demands, would yield their substance, in particular, the fact that the prisoners were to get 'clothes provided by their families', as they were described in a statement made by Mason's replacement as Northern Ireland Secretary of State, Humphrey Atkins, on 18 December 1980 in the House of Commons. I had some insights into what happened during those days, since Haughey had asked me to visit the hunger strikers earlier in the strike while he was trying to make up his mind as to the extent of the crisis: whether a genuine grievance existed, or whether it was merely an IRA propaganda event. I had some knowledge of the negotiations and I can say that the prisoners had been given reason to believe that the Atkins statement provided a basis for calling off the strike.

The prisoners' leaders may not have subjected the Atkins statement to the same rigorous analysis with which they normally examined statements by the authorities, because of the condition of one of the hunger strikers, Seán McKenna. McKenna's father had died at the age of 42 as a result of the 'deep interrogation' treatment meted out to IRA suspects after the 1971 internment swoops. Young McKenna joined the IRA and was living in the Republic near the border at Edentubber, County Louth, when he was kidnapped by the SAS in an illegal cross-border operation, and taken to Bessbrook Barracks in County Armagh, where, before being placed on the 'conveyor belt' which brought him to Long Kesh, he received some of the same treatment meted out to his father. He had begun the strike in a state of indifference as to whether he lived or died. But as it progressed, the psychological pendulum swung in the opposite direction. He went blind, and began speaking to his father and expressing a desire not to die. Of my own knowledge, I can state that one of the arguments used by the British to deflect Haughey from seeking a Portlaoise-style compromise was McKenna's condition. The authorities believed that he would crack and come off the strike, and that his comrades' resistance would then also end.

Against this background, Bobby Sands, who had succeeded Brendan Hughes as the prisoners' OC, accompanied by two of the jail chaplains, went through the prison informing the prisoners that both the 'dirty protest' and the hunger strike could be brought to an end. However, though the strike ended, it was soon clear that the authorities took a different view of the settlement terms to that of the prisoners. The issue came to a head the weekend of Friday 23 January 1981. The prisoners were given to understand that if they washed and shaved, they would then get the clothes brought in by their relatives. The washing and shaving went ahead in the expectation that at four o'clock they would get their clothes. According to the rules, normal prison work ended at four o'clock and prisoners not in breach of regulations were allowed to wear their own clothes over the weekend. However, the prisoners were not allowed their clothes, and plans were laid for a fresh hunger strike beginning on 1 March 1981. The ten hunger strikers were Sands himself, Francis Hughes, Raymond McCreesh, Patsy O'Hara (INLA), Joe McDonnell, Martin Hurson, Kevin Lynch, Ciaran Doherty, Tom McElrea and Michael Devine.

Sands's family had been driven out of their home in the then predominantly Protestant district of Rathcoole, Belfast, which meant that he lost both his home and his apprenticeship as a coach builder. He joined the IRA after the Burntollet ambush of the PD marchers, and served three years in Long Kesh, where he became fluent in Irish and a prolific writer in English. After his death, his writings were to have a particularly potent effect on young Nationalists. He was jailed again in 1976 for a fire-bomb attack on an 'economic target', a furniture company. He managed to survive a six-day interrogation period at Castlereagh without signing a statement. Apparently, he sustained himself on the example of the most famous Irish hunger-striker in history before him, Terence MacSwiney, and the words of the prophet Syrach: 'Blessed is he whose heart does not condemn him, and who does not give up hope.' A tough, argumentative personality, whom Father Meagher described to me as a 'human dynamo', Sands was to be remembered for a saying of his own: '*Tiocfaidh ár lá*', 'Our day will come.'

The hunger-striking team were chosen with care as to their character and determination, and to geographical spread. Each of the Six Counties was represented. In addition, the prisoners had learned everything that could be ascertained about the effects of hunger-striking, even going to the extent of contacting members of the PLO who had survived similar experiences. In all, the strike lasted for 217 days, with prisoners joining in at stages, until it was officially called off on 3 October 1981. It could probably have been called off a lot earlier, but the feeling of the hunger-strikers for each other was such that as each man died, those who followed were stiffened in their determination to continue, even though, under pressure from a formidable Catholic priest, Father Dennis Faul, individual hunger-strikers' families began taking their sons off the strike when they became unconscious. Although by October the strike was losing its effect on public opinion, it generated enormous publicity for the Republican cause and could fairly be regarded as having something of the same watershed effect on Sinn Féin's fortunes as had the 1916 rebellion earlier in the century.

In all, ten hunger-strikers died. The funerals of Sands and of the second man to die, Francis Hughes, were attended by something of the order of 100,000 each. After Sands died, on 5 May 1981, the Indian parliament in Delhi held a minute's silence, and in America a consciousness of being Irish was generated which had a lasting effect in bringing Irish-Americans together to further the peace process. Even before Sands died, huge publicity had been generated by visits to him by an emissary from the Pope, members of the

European parliament and the European Commission of Human Rights, and a delegation sent by Haughey which included Sile de Valera, whose grandfather had allowed hunger-strikers to die in his jails. But it was not the visits or the funerals which were of most lasting benefit to Sinn Féin. After the Nationalist Frank Maguire died in March, it was decided to nominate Sands as his successor for the Westminster constituency of Fermanagh–South Tyrone. Bernadette McAliskey (née Devlin) had announced her candidacy, but bracketed it with a statement that she would stand down in favour of an H block candidate. Accordingly, Maguire's brother Noel was talked out of going forward so late on nomination day that the SDLP candidate, Austin Currie, who had earlier withdrawn from the race in favour of Noel Maguire, had no chance of re-entering. On 9 April, Sands was duly elected. He polled 30,092 votes, and defeated the Unionist candidate, Harry West, by 1,446 votes. Afterwards, West remarked wonderingly: 'I never thought the decent Catholics of Fermanagh would vote for the gunmen.'[6]

Even though the British pushed through an amendment to the Representation of the People Act on 12 June, which prevented any more Republican prisoners from repeating Sands's success, by the result of 9 April Sinn Féin, in the words of Yeats, was 'changed, changed utterly'. First, the 'decent Catholics of Fermanagh' had shown the potential value of contesting elections. In so doing, they had energised Sinn Féin. Describing the effect on him of seeing the way the Catholics came down from the poor land on top of the hills to greet the Republican canvassers, as though they were the US cavalry coming to the rescue, Gerry Adams said, 'It was exhilarating.'[7] The party learned about the conduct of elections – the appointment of personation officers and so on – and above all that they could win them, seriously challenging the SDLP, even though at this stage the party's official line was still abstentionist. After the election, despite the censorship regulations, Adams, Martin McGuinness, Danny Morrison, Jim Gibney, Tom Hartley, Richard McAuley and other Sinn Féin activists became public figures.

A month after Sands died, the young tigers decided to extend their force field into the Republic. During the hunger strikes, Haughey's efforts to intercede had not impressed either the Sinn Féin leadership or the families of the strikers. Although he received the relatives sympathetically, he did not publicly condemn Thatcher's handling of the strike. Even if he had wanted to do so, it would have been impossible for him to clash with a British prime minister with whom he was claiming to have made a historic breakthrough on partition, and though privately he favoured the same sort of discreet 'Portlaoise solution' which had brought peace in the Republic jail conflict, he did not publicly endorse the five demands. Marcella Sands, Bobby's sister, who negotiated with Haughey, described him as an '*amadon*', the Irish for fool. The most Haughey was prepared to do was to involve the European Commission of Human Rights. In order to do this, he had to get Marcella to sign a document stating that the British were violating her brother's right to life. Though she signed reluctantly, Sands himself refused to meet the commissioners' representatives; given the labyrinthine, slow-moving procedures of the European institutions, it is reasonable to speculate that even if he had met them, he would have been long dead before the Commission took any meaningful action. The families of the other hunger-strikers were also saddened and angered at Haughey's impotence. Partly as a result of Haughey's actions, or lack of them, and partly because of the desire to extend the charge of the cavalry on to the southern hustings, it was decided to put up nine H block candidates in the general election which Haughey called in June.

These had something of the effect of Clann na Poblachta's emergence in the 1948 elections after Seán McCaughey's death in Portlaoise. Two were actually elected: Paddy Agnew, a 'blanket man', and Ciaran Doherty, who was to become the first Dail deputy to die on hunger strike since independence. Overall, the H block candidates secured 10.2% of the vote, mostly at Fianna Fáil's expense, and Garret FitzGerald succeeded Charles J. Haughey as Taoiseach.

POST H BLOCK

If history can be said to begin as tragedy, and be repeated as farce, this statement could certainly be applied to much of what passed for politics in Ireland during the 1980s. One of the factors which caused Haughey to call the general election in the summer of 1981, when the hunger strikes were so well advanced that Bobby Sands had already died, and the Republic's mood was obviously being affected by what was happening in the Six Counties, was a disastrous fire in his own constituency. This occurred at the Stardust Ballroom, in Artane, Dublin, on 14 February 1981, the eve of the Fianna Fáil Ard Fheis. Forty-eight young people were burned to death, and another 128 were injured, some of them quite horrifically so. It was a time when fire regulations were being enforced in a manner which allowed the ballroom to have barred windows and locked safety doors, and the tragedy deeply affected the Irish and particularly the Dublin public. One heard stories such as that of the fireman overheard screaming vainly through a barred window, 'Hit your head against the wall, love. Knock yourself out.' In the event, the Ard Fheis had to be postponed, and quite apart from the deterioration in Northern Ireland, the economic situation in the south went downhill also.

When Garret FitzGerald returned to the Dail having received his seal of office from President Hillery, he announced that in the few hours since he had been voted in as Taoiseach, 'even in that brief time I have learnt something of the scale of the damage done'. FitzGerald had won by 82 seats to 78, Fianna Fáil having lost six seats, Fine Gael winning 65 and Labour 15. Labour also acquired a new leader: Michael O'Leary succeeded Frank Cluskey, who had lost his seat. O'Leary became Tanaiste and Minister for Industry and Energy in the new coalition, which was sustained in power by a group of independents. To combat the economic crisis FitzGerald had discovered on the day of his appointment as Taoiseach, the new finance minister, John Bruton, introduced a tough supplementary budget, on 21 July, which raised VAT from 10% to 15% and put an embargo on pay increases and recruitment to the civil service. This went down about as well with the southern electorate as another policy initiative of FitzGerald's directed at Northern Ireland. Ignoring the reality of the depth of feelings created by the hunger strikes, he launched what he termed a 'constitutional crusade'.

FitzGerald's words deserve to be studied in some depth, because admirable though his sentiments may be judged in the abstract, the uncomfortable reality of his approach to the Unionists, which was basically the same as that of O'Neill and the IRB, who were responsible for the formation of the Volunteers in 1916, and what might be termed the Republican component of the tent-pole philosophy of the independent Irish state which subsequently emerged, was that the Unionists had so little affection either for FitzGerald or his co-religionists north and south of the border, that the open-handed approach – which of course raised huge Church–State issues for southern legislators – was almost irrelevant to the Unionist community. Almost, though possibly not quite, as the more liberal elements, such as those associated with the Alliance Party, would have supported his approach, but for a majority the most popular gesture a government in the south could have made would have been to make arrangements to have the Republic towed a little further out to sea. As we will see, this unpalatable truth was to be underlined towards the end of the century in the Unionist community's response to the Good Friday Agreement. Speaking on RTE radio, on 27 September 1981, FitzGerald said:

> Most of my relatives are in fact Northern Protestants. I was brought up with them, exchanging holidays with them, from my childhood onwards. I know their attitudes. What I want to do is, if I may borrow a phrase from someone on television the other night, I want to lead a crusade, a republican crusade, to make this a genuine republic. If I were a Northern Protestant today, I cannot see how I could be attracted to getting involved with a State that is itself sectarian – not in the acutely sectarian way that Northern Ireland was [how FitzGerald came to decide that the use of the past tense was appropriate in the context of what was happening in Northern Ireland is not known] . . . The fact is our laws and our Constitution, our practices, our attitudes, reflect those of a majority ethos, and are not acceptable to Protestants in Northern Ireland.

These sentiments had been expressed in the Ard Fheis speech which I had written for Lynch over a decade earlier. But admirable though they were, in practical terms, in 1981 they were the political equivalent of the Charge of the Light Brigade, magnificent but not war. For the moment, they had no effect on Northern Ireland, and in the Republic proved only of benefit to Charles J. Haughey. He took the opportunity of attacking FitzGerald and the crusade idea, provided by the unveiling of a memorial to de Valera at Ennis in County Clare on 11 October. He portrayed FitzGerald as giving aid and comfort to the enemies of Irish unity, and said that de Valera set no limit to the march of the Irish nation. He sought an Ireland, unified and free, which would in its constitution and its laws respect and accommodate the diverse traditions that exist in this island and he would urge us to continue to work for that objective.

He would urge us to create a just, compassionate, and tolerant society. He would glory in the fact that we have an increasing population consisting largely of a new generation of educated, talented young people and he would urge us to give them the encouragement, the support and leadership they need, to achieve their full potential. He would urge us also to have a special care of the less well off and the weaker sections of our community; to make their welfare our deep and abiding concern and to see that they are fully protected from the hazards of life and the harsh effects of economic forces.

Haughey might well have gone on to state that the record shows that after his initial burst of social commitment, de Valera did little to implement these lofty sentiments, and that the situation which had arisen under his own reign had done very little for the poor either. However, both economics and the hunger strike situation combined to render FitzGerald's crusade redundant. He found himself embroiled in attempts to get President Reagan to put pressure on Margaret Thatcher to end the hunger strikes, and on the streets of Dublin to curb repeated H block demonstrations. Fierce fighting broke out between Gardai and demonstrators seeking to vent their anger on the British Embassy during the month of July 1981.

Where domestic politics in the Republic was concerned, FitzGerald had a little more success. A Youth Employment Agency was set up, and a Combat Poverty Agency established. He had a partial success in attempting to reflect the changing status of Irish society by setting up a number of new Dail committees, concerning women's rights, marital breakdown, youth affairs, and other matters. Haughey objected to the marital breakdown committee, even though at the time, and for many years afterwards, he was involved in a well-publicised affair with Terry Keane, the wife of a prominent judge, Mr Justice Ronan Keane. FitzGerald's government collapsed over an attempt to impose VAT on children's shoes in the budget introduced on 27 January 1982. One of the independents, Jim Kemmy, a Limerick Socialist, voted against the budget, and the coalition was defeated by 82 votes to 81.

In the normal course of events, the defeated Taoiseach goes to the President, resigns his seal of office, and an election is called. This did happen in 1982, but the resignation and the calling of the election process were accompanied by some extraordinary side shows. Mention has been made of the powers of the President. These include the 'absolute discretion' to refuse a dissolution so that the Dail is forced to elect a Taoiseach and a government without an election. It subsequently emerged that Haughey had caused efforts to be made to twist Hillery's arm into doing this, even while FitzGerald was offering his resignation. Some years later, in 1990, when Brian Lenihan was running for the presidency, his campaign was destroyed when it was revealed that Lenihan himself, Haughey, and another Fianna Fáil TD, Sylvester Barrett, had all phoned the President. Some six phone calls were made, all with the shared distinction of being hotly denied. However, in 1982, all the public was aware of was that on the night in question, Haughey issued a public statement: 'It is a matter for the President to consider the situation which has arisen now that the Taoiseach has ceased to retain the support of the majority in Dail Eireann. I am available for consultation with the President should he so wish.'

The quite improper efforts made by Haughey and his cohorts to avoid the holding of an election set the tone for the administration which Haughey was to form after the election, which he won despite his efforts to prevent it being held. Fianna Fáil's total of seats increased to 81. But Haughey, having passed the test of the electorate, then had to face a contest within his own party. He fired one deputy, Charlie McCreevy, for openly criticising him for being 'against everything and for nothing', and a few weeks later, on 25 February, faced down a leadership challenge from Desmond O'Malley, whom Jack Lynch publicly supported. Haughey's control of the party on this occasion was so complete that O'Malley withdrew before the leadership issue could be voted on. Nevertheless, the era of internal Fianna Fáil 'heaves' against Haughey was under way. However, buoyed up by his success, Haughey then bought the crucial support of Tony Gregory, an effective independent TD for Dublin's badly deprived inner city, by making Gregory an offer which he had no intention of refusing – a £50 million refurbishment plan for Gregory's constituency. Haughey was also supported from the unlikely quarter of Sinn Féin, the Workers Party, which had hived itself off about ten years previously from the physical-force tradition, in this case from the Official IRA, to go constitutional.

The three Workers Party deputies followed Haughey into the lobby, but only after a scare. They had allowed themselves to be locked out of the chamber when the vote was called, and only managed to re-enter it by bursting through the press gallery, across the distinguished visitors' benches and then into the Dail chamber itself. Thus, it was said, Haughey became Taoiseach again through the influence of the media and the Marxists. His new Cabinet consisted of Ray McSharry (Tanaiste and Minister for Finance), Paddy Power (Defence), Seán Doherty (Minister for Justice), Desmond O'Malley (Industry, Commerce and Tourism), Gerard Collins (Minister for Foreign Affairs), Martin O'Donoghue (Education), Raphael Burke (Environment), Brian Lenihan (Agriculture), Michael Woods (Health and Social Welfare), Padraig Flynn (Gaeltacht), Albert Reynolds (Industry and Energy), Gene Fitzgerald (Labour and the Public Service) and John Wilson (Transport, Posts and Telegraphs).

Domestically, Haughey's short-lived administration was to preside over a series of low-grade, parish-pump activities which would have been disavowed by Tammany Hall on the grounds of inefficiency, apart from anything else. Internationally, still smarting over the H block interlude, and pressure from Neil Blaney, his anti-Thatcher stance resulted in a period during which the Anglo-Irish relationship was characterised more by brickbats than silver teapots. His domestic problems began almost immediately. His election agent, and old water-polo-playing friend, Pat O'Connor, a Dublin solicitor, was charged with impersonation, having allegedly voted twice during the general election. O'Connor got off but was known thereafter as 'Pat O'Connor, Pat O'Connor'. While the adverse publicity from the O'Connor affair was still bursting around him, Haughey then moved to improve his wafer-thin Dail majority by 'pulling a stroke', as such manoeuvres are referred to in Irish politics. He offered the post of European Commissioner to Richard Burke, who had formerly held the job but was now a Fine Gael backbencher. The idea of dispensing patronage to the opposition enraged Haughey's own supporters. Burke's acceptance of the appointment aroused wrath in Fine Gael which feared the loss of his seat in the consequential by-election (on 25 May) to the Fianna Fáil candidate, Eileen Lemass, who had married Seán Lemass's son, Noel. But the 'stroke' rebounded badly on Haughey when Lemass was unexpectedly defeated by the Fine Gael candidate, Liam Skelly.

This controversy, wounding though it was, paled into insignificance compared to what followed. A series of murders had been disturbing the public mind during the year and a sense of mingled shock and disbelief gripped the average Irish citizen when a man who was later convicted of one of them was arrested in the home of the Attorney General, Patrick Connolly, on 13 August 1982. Connolly, one of the lawyers who had defended Haughey during the Arms Trial, had nothing whatever to do with the murder, but his house guest, Malcolm MacArthur, was later shown to have fatally injured Nurse Bridie Gargan in a hammer attack in the Phoenix Park, Dublin, where he had come upon her sunbathing the previous month. Unaware of the charming MacArthur's dark side, Connolly had given the murderer lifts in his state car and even introduced him to the Garda Commissioner, Patrick McLaughlin, during a hurling match. The publicity surrounding MacArthur's arrest was heightened when, having phoned Haughey on his holiday island off the Kerry coast to inform him of what had happened, Connolly went on a pre-arranged holiday to New York the following day. Initially, Haughey did not appear to realise the enormity of Connolly's phone call and raised no objection to the Attorney General's going, with the result that no sooner had Connolly landed in New York than he was instructed to return immediately, which he did, by Concorde, to be flown to Dublin from London in an Irish air corps plane to a meeting with Haughey and resignation. At his subsequent trial on 12 January, 1983, MacArthur pleaded guilty to the Gargan murder and the state entered a *nolle prosequi* in the case of a second murder charge, that of a farmer, Donal Dunne. Thus the trial and sentencing (to life imprisonment) was over in less than ten minutes without evidence being heard in court.

This of course lay in the future. Speaking at a press conference held in the eye of the storm, Haughey described the affair as 'grotesque, unprecedented, bizarre and unbelievable'. Conor Cruise O'Brien thereupon coined the acronym 'GUBU', which was later used to characterise the Haughey administration. The Minister for Justice, Seán Doherty, himself an ex-Garda, has already been mentioned in connection with the controversy surrounding an attempt to transfer the zealous Sergeant Tully. What the public did not realise at the time of the MacArthur affair was that Doherty and Haughey were also becoming involved in what would prove to be a far more important and more frightening controversy, which would make headlines the following year when Haughey had fallen from power: the bugging of journalists' telephones and of ministerial conversations, which would lead to Commissioner McLaughlin's resignation. However, Doherty did figure prominently in another of the GUBU occurrences of the period. The so-called 'Dowra affair' became public knowledge a month after the MacArthur arrest. A brother-in-law of Doherty's, Garda Thomas Nangle, had charges of assault dismissed against him at Dowra District Court, County Cavan, on 27 September after the man whom he was accused of assaulting, James McGovern, a Six County resident from County Fermanagh, failed to turn up. It was later revealed that he had been taken into custody by the RUC, held for the day and questioned, unjustifiably, about the IRA. Moreover, though he had asked that the Gardai be informed of what had happened, the Dowra court was not told of his detention. The judge was merely informed that he would not be attending and the case was dismissed. McGovern later sued the RUC for wrongful arrest and false imprisonment and was awarded £3,000 in an out-of-court settlement.

The Dowra affair provided another brand for the burning of Haughey. Charlie McCreevy put down a motion of no confidence in his leadership at the Fianna Fáil parliamentary party meeting of 6 October. The country's political blood pressure went up considerably as a result. Colley added to the tension by announcing that two ministers, O'Malley and O'Donoghue, would be leaving the Cabinet rather than serve under Haughey. However, Haughey routed his opponents by demanding and getting an open vote, which he won by 58 to 22. Subsequently ugly scenes were witnessed on television as both McCreevy and Gibbons were jostled and had punches thrown at them by Haugheyites as they left the Dail.

Meanwhile, throughout that year, in another part of the forest, a situation had been developing wherein verbal punches were thrown between Dublin and London. The *casus belli* is probably best described as a combination of the Northern Ireland situation, and the personalities of Margaret Thatcher and Charles J. Haughey. Given the Napoleonic characteristics of the two last named, the personality differences may safely be left to the imagination, but the northern situation demands a little more explanation. Mrs Thatcher may have had Napoleonic precedent in mind, at least insofar as Elba was concerned, when she exiled James Prior to Northern Ireland to replace Humphrey Atkins during September of 1981. In economic terms, he was a leading member of the group she dismissed scornfully as 'wets'. When he got to Belfast, the hunger strikes were still in progress, the Loyalists were angered both by this and by the inter-governmental council which had emerged from the Dublin Castle summit – or, as Mrs Thatcher preferred to refer to it, the 'Dublin bi-lateral' – and Sinn Féin was commencing the wrestling match with its conscience over abstention, which it was destined to win at the expense of the SDLP.

The new leader of the SDLP, John Hume, was aware that a green tide was running in favour of his rivals for the political heart and soul of Nationalist Northern Ireland. Sinn Féin was proving itself the beneficiary of the 'risen people' syndrome. Some of the SDLP's leading personalities had dropped off the vine because of the tensions of the period. Paddy Devlin had been expelled in 1977, because of his objections to the Nationalist drift of the SDLP. Austin Currie left the party and eventually became a junior minister in the Republic, in a Fine Gael-led government. But the biggest casualty of the rise of Sinn Féin was Gerry Fitt. Hume had correctly divined that the so-called 'Irish dimension' which had emerged as a result of Humphrey Atkins's constitutional attempts was too insubstantial for the circumstances of the time. Fitt had been elected originally as a 'Republican Labour' candidate, and had become progressively uncomfortable with the increasing shift in emphasis of his constituents from the Labour component of their thinking to the Republican one. The shift was marked by a deterioration in his popularity to a point where Republican hooligans burned down his home. He had been unhappy with the Council of Ireland envisaged in the Sunningdale Agreement, arguing less from his constituents' viewpoint than from that of the Unionists. He disagreed with Hume over the Atkins proposal and resigned in 1979, leaving Hume to take over the leadership.

Prior's chances of achieving anything on the constitutional front in Northern Ireland, which have to be reckoned as being slim to start with, given Mrs Thatcher's distaste for him, were lessened by a political assassination which occurred two months after he arrived. The Reverend William Bradford was a typical Unionist cleric/politician. A good constituency representative, loud in his demands for a tougher crackdown on the IRA, he was seen by the Provisionals as having close ties to Loyalist paramilitaries, and was regarded in the words of an IRA statement issued after his murder as having helped to 'whip up anti-Nationalist murder gangs'. Paisley reacted to Bradford's death by setting up an ominously termed Third Force. The rallies and demonstrations which he led in furtherance of the Third Force's objectives were so disturbing that Irish-Americans intervened to the extent of pressurising the State Department into withdrawing his US visa. Well aware of the depth of Loyalist feeling, and the rip tide flowing in Sinn Féin's direction in the Nationalist community, Prior, who had had the ugly experience of being booed and jeered at Bradford's funeral, attempted to introduce a constitutional experiment which he termed 'rolling devolution'.

This involved setting up a local assembly with, initially, only consultative and scrutiny powers. Prior envisaged the assembly developing, getting stronger, and so requiring more devolution of powers in the governance of the north. The assembly was to consist of 78 members who, if 70% voted to agree, could apply to Westminster for the devolved powers. In effect, the 70% (or 55 of the members) proposal amounted to a weighted majority, thus preventing the Unionists from reinventing the wheel by using the numbers to restore Stormont. The Unionists rejected the idea as being the Sunningdale concept of power-sharing in a new guise. Hume and the SDLP were worried about the Prior proposals on two fronts: one, that the Unionists would prevent them from working, and two, that Sinn Féin could use elections to the assembly to further erode the SDLP's position. Hume was correct in his analysis. Provisional Sinn Féin won five seats, reducing the SDLP's overall total to 14, five fewer than it had held at the time of Sunningdale.

Even before Prior had announced his 'rolling devolution' proposals, Hume had successfully lobbied Haughey to issue a joint statement with him condemning the initiative. Where Haughey was concerned, Prior's plans for an internal settlement of course ran directly counter to his stated belief that the northern statelet was 'a failed entity'. One of his first actions on being appointed Taoiseach had been to visit Washington, for St Patrick's Day. He saw President Reagan, and tried without success to get him to pressure Mrs Thatcher to come to an agreement with Dublin. At this stage, Reagan and the State Department followed the traditional American line that the affairs of Northern Ireland were domestic to the UK, and Reagan's response was to the effect that the northerners would have to come to an agreement amongst themselves. Speaking on 23 May 1982, Haughey described the Prior plan as being one which 'will be regarded in history as one of the most disastrous things that had ever happened in Anglo-Irish relations'. By that time, other fairly disastrous situations had also arisen in Anglo-Irish relationships. For, apart from Mrs Thatcher's growing irritation with the interpretation which Haughey had placed on the Dublin Castle meeting, a fundamental dichotomy was emerging between London and Dublin over the Common Agricultural Policy.

The British, with a farm lobby which was declining in influence, as that of the Irish farmers was growing in strength – and in importance to Haughey and Fianna Fáil – were vetoing increases in farm prices in order to bring about cuts in Britain's contribution to the EEC. Ireland's position in the EEC, the Northern Ireland situation, and the Haughey–Thatcher relationship all suddenly became intertwined when Argentina invaded the Falkland Islands on 1 April 1982. Ireland initially supported the British at the UN by voting for Resolution 502 of the Security Council, which called for an Argentinian withdrawal. Although Ireland has historical links through her emigrants with Argentina, trade between the two countries was fairly small at the time. Consequently, when the British lobbied the EEC to support the UN resolution by imposing a trade embargo on Argentinian imports, the Irish beef industry, ever noted for its ethical approach, rubbed its hands at the prospect of substituting Irish meat for the embargoed Argentinian produce on the British market. However, Haughey, both because of Ireland's cultural and historical links with Argentina, whose navy was founded by an Irish man, William Brown, and because of his coolness towards Thatcher, grumbled about EEC sanctions, but eventually went along with them.

A few weeks later, on 22 April, Sile de Valera, always zealous to maintain her political legacy, issued a statement criticising the Government's policy, saying that it was a breach of Ireland's traditional neutrality. Niall Blaney added weight to the charge by stating publicly a few days later that:

> We should support Argentina for both political and economic reasons: politically, because of the continued British occupation of the Six Counties of Northern Ireland, and economically, because Argentina is one of the few countries with which we have a credit trade balance.

Haughey's tiny majority in the Dail made Blaney's vote an important one, and a combination of the Donegal deputy's intervention and Haughey's relationship with Mrs Thatcher exploded into controversy after the British sank the Argentinian battleship the *Belgrano* while it was on a bearing of 280 degrees west, already well clear of the Falklands, and obviously sailing away from any contact with British shipping. Haughey announced, at a press conference on 6 May, that Ireland would be calling on the Security Council to intervene to end hostilities, and would also be seeking an end to the EEC sanctions. He said that Ireland had voted for the sanctions unenthusiastically, but believing that they might help to bring about a diplomatic solution in accordance with the terms of Resolution 502. However, he said, 'Sanctions complementing military action are not acceptable to a neutral country.'

He had also authorised the Minister for Defence to make a speech a few days earlier (on 3 May) describing Britain as the 'aggressor' in the war. In her memoirs, Thatcher would later describe her annoyance at Haughey both for calling Northern Ireland 'an unworkable mistake', as she termed it, and for 'the thoroughly unhelpful stance taken by the Irish government during the Falklands War'. Her irritation was shared by others. David Owen, a former Labour Foreign Minister, adjudged that 'Ireland has behaved with great impertinence.' Gerry Fitt reckoned that the sanctions policy had created 'a greater degree of anti-Irish feeling in Britain than at the time of the Birmingham bombing'. Certainly something of a boycott of Irish produce and Irish holidays manifested itself for a time, and it was therefore perhaps not surprising that the British deliberately leaked a story to the papers (on 27 July) to the effect that the British Government had officially informed the Irish Ambassador to the UK that it was under no obligation to consult the Republic about Northern Ireland. Relations between the two governments had reached their nadir.

Haughey's government was also heading for the depths. Following the unsuccessful attempt on his leadership within Fianna Fáil on 6 October, Fine Gael put down a Dail motion of no confidence which was debated on 4 November, by which time Haughey's position had been weakened by the loss of two seats. One was caused by the death of Bill Loughnane on 18 October, the other through James Gibbons suffering a heart attack. Haughey lost the vote by 80 votes to 82 and a general election was scheduled for 24 November.

It says much for the calibre of Irish politics over the previous few years that one of Fine Gael's planks was an end to political interference with the Gardai. By way of illustrating the degree of hypocrisy which pervaded public morality, it should be noted, by way of binary opposition, that the influence of the Church also raised its head over the political parapet once more, resulting in the concern that both the major parties devoted to safeguarding Irish women from committing mortal sin through having abortions.

As vocations fell, it was inevitable that the geopolitical strategists in the Vatican and elsewhere in the Roman Catholic world would turn to lay organisations such as Opus Dei, the Knights of Columbanus, and others, to further their policies. The close-run competition between Irish political parties made the 1982 election an inviting battleground for Church apologists, and an organisation styling itself the Pro-Life Amendment Campaign (PLAC) ambushed Haughey successfully a couple of days before the election, with the result that he accepted the wording for a constitutional amendment which FitzGerald felt he had no option but to accept also. He would have preferred to have included an anti-abortion amendment in the constitution as part of an overall review along the lines of his 'constitutional crusade'. However, anti-abortion groups had been using the strong-arm lobbying tactics associated with such organisations on Fine Gael candidates to such demoralising effect that many of them had become seized by crozier fever.

Fever of another sort, of the anti-British variety, was also injected into the campaign by Haughey. The Northern Ireland Secretary of State, James Prior, became an object of controversy when he replied to a reporter in the US who asked him what he would like to see emerge from Fine Gael by saying that he would welcome an all-Ireland police force. Some versions of this response were transmogrified in the Irish media so that Prior was reported as saying that FitzGerald intended to introduce all-Ireland courts and an all-Ireland police force. Fianna Fáil bracketed this inaccurate report with an account which the Duke of Norfolk had given in the House of Lords of a lunch he had had with FitzGerald some time earlier.

According to the Duke, FitzGerald had told him that Prior's devolution plans were acceptable to him. Haughey made much of the fact that the Duke had been head of intelligence at the British Ministry of Defence before he retired 15 years earlier. In addition, he warned Fianna Fáil supporters that if the proposals of 'these foolish men' were adopted, Irish security policies and sovereignty would be compromised so that 'violence and bloodshed will be extended to our country as a whole, without any benefit to anybody'. Haughey interpreted the police proposals as meaning that unarmed Gardai would be sent north, and the armed RUC would operate in the south, a prospect which, whatever it did for Republican blood pressure, would certainly have had a deleterious effect on the life expectancy of members of either force. However, though blood pressures went up during the campaign, FitzGerald described Haughey's attitude as being 'indistinguishable' from that of Paisley. Haughey's ploy misfired.

Fine Gael won 70 seats, behind Fianna Fáil's 75. Labour won 16, the Workers Party dwindled to two, and there were three independents. When the new Dail met on 26 November, FitzGerald was elected Taoiseach at the head of a Fine Gael–Labour coalition. Apart from there being a new Taoiseach, there was also a new leader of Labour, Dick Spring, who was appointed Tanaiste. Spring, who was then only 32, was a former rugby international. He succeeded Michael O'Leary on the eve of the campaign's commencement (1 November 1982), as a compromise candidate between the more well-established Labour figures Michael D. Higgins and Barry Desmond. The election contest between the three had been precipitated by O'Leary's decision to quit the party and join Fine Gael. At the time of Spring's election, the party was binding up its wounds after a bout of internal warfare over the perennial question of coalition. Spring, a barrister, and the son of a popular Kerry Labour TD, Dan Spring, was an ardent coalitionist, and his espousal of this course helped to ensure that his party would have a share in government for the next five years.

The coalition government's term in office coincided with a number of important policy developments in key areas. On Northern Ireland, Anglo-Irish relationships finally and irrevocably moved from a position whereby London saw the issue as one which concerned London only, to one which could not be resolved without co-operation with Dublin. Also, although the coalition remained firmly of the view that the IRA had to be marginalised and excluded from the political process, within the IRA developments were afoot which led to an acceptance of what was to many, particularly in Fine Gael, the unacceptable fact that there could be no solution to the northern problem which excluded the Republicans. For its part, the IRA also came to an acceptance of the fact that the road towards its objectives did not lie through the barrel of a gun. The north, coupled with an on-going internal strife, by, with or from the mind and personality of Charles J. Haughey, would also result in the emergence of a new party, the Progressive Democrats, from within the ranks of Fianna Fáil, that was destined to play an important role in the political life of the country. Finally, though the flowering of the process was not seen until the year after the coalition had left office, new thinking and developments within the trade union movement were to play a role in the creation of the so-called 'Celtic Tiger' of the nineties, which deserves to be regarded as belonging to that important sequence of events – the ending of protection; free education; EEC membership, etc. – which led to the birth of contemporary Ireland.

However, before any of these important matters could be set in train, the first item on any Republican agenda had to be dealt with – the split. Once again, the split occurred within Fianna Fáil and centred on yet another challenge to Haughey's leadership. The challenge was precipitated by a startling revelation on 20 January 1983 by Michael Noonan, Minister for Justice in the new coalition government. Noonan announced that the phones of two journalists, Bruce Arnold of the *Irish Independent*, and Geraldine

Kennedy of the *Sunday Tribune*, had been tapped on Seán Doherty's instructions, but on Haughey's watch, and that for good measure, one of his ministers, Ray McSharry, had been given state-of-the-art Garda recording equipment so that he could record a conversation with another minister, Martin O'Donoghue, on 21 October 1982. The fact that one minister should feel it necessary to record the conversation of another speaks volumes for the atmosphere which the 'Haughey heaves' generated within Fianna Fáil. But readers may judge for themselves the sort of atmosphere which was generated within the police force by what followed. Noonan went on to announce that both the Commissioner of the Gardai, Patrick McLaughlin, and the Deputy Commissioner, Joseph Ainsworth, were resigning from the force.

Tapping journalists' phones is of course a reprehensible activity which should not occur in a democracy. But tapping was nevertheless a fact of Irish political life. Under the previous Fine Gael–Labour coalition, both my own phone and that of the investigative journalist Vincent Browne were tapped. Vivion de Valera, Eamon de Valera's eldest son, the controlling director and editor in chief of the *Irish Press*, a man with above-average sources of intelligence, would not even use the paper's interdepartmental phones for anything of a sensitive nature, and enjoined it on me to do likewise. Haughey's GUBU-ed career, however, made him both an enticing and a legitimate target. Under pressure, he was forced to set up a four-man committee within Fianna Fáil with James Tunney, a member of the party's oldguard, as chairman, to investigate the affair, and Desmond O'Malley, Gerard Collins and Michael O'Kennedy all began campaigning for the leadership. It appeared that the Fianna Fáil parliamentary party meeting scheduled for 27 January would see Haughey resign.

The *Irish Press*, like the other national daily papers, went to press on the morning of the meeting in this expectation, and after the 16-page country edition had been dealt with, it set about preparing a two-page résumé of Haughey's career to be cast in the stereotype department, and the plates kept in the machine room, ready for use when and if the news broke. This sort of preparation in anticipation of an important news event is standard operating procedure for newspapers. However, GUBU then struck again. The paper was beginning to experience the administrative chaos which ultimately led to the collapse of the company in 1995. Through some foul-up in communication between the various departments involved, the two pages were added to the city edition so that an 18-page paper appeared on the streets of Dublin. I will never forget the reaction of Jack Jones, the assistant editor, when we learned of the cock-up at something approaching three o'clock in the morning. 'Oh well,' smiled Jack, 'there'll be some very interesting information in today's *Irish Press*!' Thereafter, 'the *Irish Press* printed Charlie's obituary' became part of Ireland's accepted political folklore.

The 'obituary' may have helped to rally some of Haughey's supporters within the party. Certainly his own tactics did. When the meeting was convened, he failed to prevent a debate on his leadership, but announced that he would step down 'in his own time'. His adversaries, some of whom were close to weeping, took this to mean that he intended to resign in a matter of days and laid off him. One of them, Ben Briscoe, in fact announced: 'I love you, Charlie Haughey.' To which Haughey replied: 'I love you too, Ben.' The fact that Briscoe was a Jew did cause some mutterings in fundamentalist Fianna Fáil circles which may have benefited Haughey. Ironically, in view of what was later proven about Haughey's own links with big business, he was also helped by a perception that 'big business was trying to take over Fianna Fáil'. But, above all, unlike his weak-bowelled adversaries, Haughey did not rely on the power of love. Instead he began a full-blooded campaign amongst grass-roots supporters, who held a large rally outside Fianna Fáil headquarters in Dublin on 31 January. This alerted and annoyed his opponents so much that support was mobilised against Haughey to such an extent that it appeared certain that his leadership would finally end at the parliamentary party meeting scheduled to be held on Wednesday 2 February. A petition aimed at dethroning him garnered the signatures of 41 Fianna Fáil parliamentarians. Fate took a hand, however: one of the deputies opposed to him, Clem Coughlan, was killed in a car crash the day beforehand as he drove to Dublin to attend the showdown meeting.

When the meeting was called, Haughey opened the proceedings with a tribute to the dead deputy. The chairman, James Tunney, followed suit, and then, as the anti-Haugheyites swung into battle, announced in Irish that the meeting would be adjourned until the following week, and ran out of the door before anyone realised his intentions. The seething dissidents forced another meeting for the following Monday. Much of the energy of this went into dealing with Tunney's report into the phone-tapping, which, not unsur-prisingly, found that there was no evidence to link Haughey with the bugging. Haughey also gained valuable time by putting through a motion deferring the expulsion of both Doherty and O'Donoghue from the parliamentary party until the next meeting. By the time the leadership issue came to be discussed, the tide had turned in Haughey's favour. He won the vote on his leadership by a margin of seven votes. It was a narrow win, but an incredible one when it is considered that the Dublin bookmakers – who would offer odds on flies going up (or down) windows – had quoted odds of four to one against Haughey's chances of retaining the leadership, and twenty to one against ever becoming Taoiseach again. The difference was that Haughey had mobilised his support, the opposition had not. Briscoe had not even thought to arrange a seconder for his motion calling for Haughey's resignation, and it was on the point of failing when Charlie McCreevy agreed to back it.

With the Haughey issue apparently out of the way, the public's attention now turned to light matters such as the war in Northern Ireland, Church–State relationships, and the state of the economy. On the day Clem Coughlan was killed, the new Irish Foreign Minister, Peter Barry, had his first contact in office with the British, and took the opportunity, a meeting in London with James Prior, of saying that on one issue at least, Fine Gael was *ad idem* with

Haughey: the new government felt that Prior's 'rolling devolution' idea was going nowhere. Instead, while at the same time attempting to improve relations with London, FitzGerald initiated a novel constitutional dissection of the northern problem, how it had come about, and how it might be solved. In part, FitzGerald was moved by his own 'constitutional crusade' mode of thought, in part by John Hume's warnings that the wolves of Sinn Féin were gaining on the SDLP troika. Accordingly therefore, for much of 1983 and 1984, the Irish political system virtually downed tools to take part in the New Ireland Forum which FitzGerald set up in Dublin Castle.

Like much of the innovative constitutional thinking on Northern Ireland during the seventies and eighties, the forum was John Hume's idea, and Haughey had intended to announce it during the Fianna Fáil Ard Fheis in February. FitzGerald, who had to overcome some internal opposition in his own party to the proposal, however, announced it two days before the Ard Fheis was held, and all the Irish political parties and the SDLP duly came together at Dublin Castle on 30 May 1983 to decide on a formula for Nationalist Ireland which would solve the partition problem. In the event, the forum came up with not one, but three formulae: joint sovereignty, a confederal Ireland, or a united Ireland. The three had one thing in common: they were all unacceptable to the Unionists, who had boycotted the forum's proceedings. On top of this not exactly minor consideration, they were also unacceptable to Mrs Thatcher.

The forum's findings were issued a month after the Provisional IRA had attempted to kill Mrs Thatcher, and as many members of her Cabinet as possible, in the bombing of the Grand Hotel, Brighton, on 12 October. In the wake of Airey Neave and the continuing slaughter in Northern Ireland, Mrs Thatcher had obviously decided that the collective works of the Provisional IRA were reaching unacceptable proportions when she and FitzGerald met at Chequers (on 19 October 1984) to discuss the Forum Report. They had what the Irish leader obviously regarded as a friendly and constructive meeting, and then the two leaders gave separate press conferences. At hers, Mrs Thatcher delivered what entered Irish history as her 'out, out, out' speech. Each 'out' had an Exocet effect on a forum proposal. Mrs Thatcher paused deliberately after listing each of the forum's proposals before delivering her verdict: 'That is out.'

The speech went down in Ireland much as it would have done had a combined effort by the British Conservatives, Labour and Liberals produced a report on Anglo-American development, only to have it 'outed' on presentation by the White House. A similar reaction prevailed amongst Irish-Americans. Their influence had persuaded Reagan to publicly endorse the forum proceedings. Despite being humiliated, FitzGerald kept his head, although at a Cabinet meeting he described Mrs Thatcher's reaction as being 'gratuitously offensive'. Both he and the Irish Department of Foreign Affairs continued their endeavours at the coal face of Anglo-Irish relationships, in London and Washington. Finally, at an EEC meeting in Milan in June of 1985,

FitzGerald succeeded in convincing Thatcher that if something were not done, the spokespersons for the northern Nationalists with whom Dublin and London would have to deal would be not Hume and the SDLP, but Gerry Adams and Sinn Féin. The result was a series of negotiations which continued between June and November until what became known as the Hillsborough Agreement was signed at Hillsborough Castle in Belfast on 15 November 1985.

This agreement was not welcomed by Sinn Féin, the Unionists or Charles J. Haughey, but it marked an important step in the recognition of Dublin's importance to a solution of the Northern Ireland problem. It set up an inter-governmental conference, largely deriving from that envisaged in the Dublin Castle Agreement of 1980 between Haughey and Thatcher which Haughey had oversold. The remit of the conference was that it would discuss the administration of justice, and the promotion of cross-border co-operation, political affairs, and security. Under the terms of the agreement, the United Kingdom Government accepted that the Irish Government would 'put forward views and proposals on matters relating to Northern Ireland and agree to take measures both to recognise and accommodate the rights and identities of the two traditions in Northern Ireland, to protect human life and to prevent discrimination'. The agreement also stated that the conference was to have a full-time secretariat, and that it would meet 'at administerial or professional level as requested. The business of the conference will thus receive attention at the highest level.' These provisions enraged the Unionists. During the talks, both the Unionist leader, James Molyneaux, who had succeeded Brian Faulkner, and Ian Paisley had attempted unsuccessfully to pressure Thatcher into breaking off the discussions. Their wrath now centred on the fact that not only had she failed to do this, she had installed a Fenian secretariat from Dublin in Belfast (at Maryfield). The flag of the Republic, the hated tricolour, the display of which, in a dingy back-street Belfast window, had served as the pretext for Paisley's first major riot, could now fly in Belfast as a right. Dublin accents and Dublin personalities were to be seen and heard discussing the internal affairs of 'Ulster'. Shades of the unthinkable were also to be seen falling across the agreement from a Unionist perspective in the commitment that while no changes were to take place without the consent of the majority, if in the future a majority sought a united Ireland, the United Kingdom would further this aspiration rather than hinder it.

The Unionist reaction to all this took a form which actually deepened the parliamentary deficit in the Six Counties, and heightened the importance of Dublin–London co-operation. Unionist politicians withdrew from the Assembly and embarked on a large-scale programme of political protest, Belfast style. That is to say, the holding of demonstrations which showed a marked tendency to develop into riots. However, Margaret Thatcher was no Merlyn Rees, and the RUC were forced to confront the Unionist demonstrators, even though at this stage there was widespread collusion between members of the RUC and the Loyalist paramilitaries. The Unionists had been hoping that their withdrawal from the Assembly would trigger a series of by-elections, each one of which would have been in effect a mini referendum on the Hillsborough Agreement. But on 23 June 1986, just a year after FitzGerald had persuaded her to change her mind on Northern Ireland, Mrs Thatcher closed the Assembly, which had continued in being, despite the failure of Prior's 'rolling devolution' plan. The Unionists suffered the extraordinary shock of protesting Unionist politicians being carried out of Stormont by members of the Royal Ulster Constabulary. So much for notions of 'their' law and 'their' order. However, Northern Ireland was not the only place where ancestral notions were affronted.

Haughey's initial response to the Hillsborough Agreement was to reject it out of hand. On 16 November 1985 he said that if he was in power after the next election, he would repudiate the agreement. He declared himself in favour of a unitary state, claiming that the provisions stipulating that change could only come about by the consent of the majority in Northern Ireland were in conflict with Articles 2 and 3 of the Republic's constitution. In fact, the wording of the Hillsborough Agreement had taken care to closely follow that of the Dublin Castle Agreement which he had concluded with Mrs Thatcher to the accompaniment of much fanfare that it betokened the end of partition. This was also Paisley's view of the agreement. He borrowed from Prior in christening it a 'process of rolling Irish unification'. The electorate of the Republic shared Paisley's interpretation, not Haughey's, and it was generally popular, with the exception of one or two notable public figures, including Dr Conor Cruise O'Brien, who felt it unfair to the Loyalists. FitzGerald's standing in the opinion polls shot up, and Haughey's fell correspondingly, a dramatic reversal of the position which had obtained earlier in the year when Fianna Fáil had swept the boards in the local government elections. But for a time he held tenaciously to his objections before ultimately giving the agreement the nod and suggesting that in reality he had not been opposed to it; that was a media misrepresentation. When I suggested to him at a lunch in the Berkeley Court Hotel that his opposition was misplaced, his reaction was to leave his food and walk out of the restaurant. The response of some members of his party to such attitudes was to walk out of Fianna Fáil.

Mary Harney, who had voted with Fine Gael in favour of the agreement, was expelled, and her expulsion brought to a head much of the dissatisfaction in Fianna Fáil which had expressed itself in the 'heaves' against Haughey. The dissatisfaction was expressed in the creation of the Progressive Democrats, an Adam's-rib party from the body of Fianna Fáil which was launched by Harney and Desmond O'Malley, its leader, on 21 December 1985. A number of other prominent Fianna Fáilers, including Pearse Wyse and Bobby Molloy, joined the new grouping. Under O'Malley, the Progressive Democrats would be antipathetic to traditional Fianna Fáil republicanism. Apart from his own experiences with militant republicanism while Minister for Justice, the Provisional IRA had burned down a public house owned by his wife's family, the McAleers of Omagh. The premises were rebuilt, but the Provisionals burned them down a second time. The PDs, as they were popularly known, would come to stand on the right for fiscal and economic matters, be liberal where issues such as divorce and contraception were concerned, and proclaim themselves in favour of accountability and transparency in politics to such an extent that Dublin wit had it that the message on the party headquarters' answering machine was: 'Speak after the high moral tone.' In government, in coalition with Fianna Fáil, the party, jokes aside, would provide a reassurance to some sections of the electorate at least that, despite a series of scandals yet to be chronicled, the family silver was not about to be sold off.

The proceedings at the New Ireland Forum could be taken as an indication of the Republic's increasingly open attitude towards Northern Ireland, and a more pluralist view of the country as a whole. During the forum's deliberations, the Taoiseach of the country, Garret FitzGerald, had recognised publicly that 'Society in Ireland as a whole comprises a wider diversity of cultural traditions than exists in the South, and the constitution and laws of a new Ireland must accommodate these social and political realities.'[8]

However, despite these laudable sentiments, certain happenings in the sphere of liberty of conscience during the years 1982–7 could equally well be held up as examples of a more sectarian attitude on the part of the largely Roman Catholic electorate. The issues of abortion, contraception and divorce all provided Unionists with opportunities for powerful demonstrations that the 'social and political realities' of the Republic were that it still took its tone from Rome rather than Wolfe Tone. Mention has already been made of the injection of the abortion debate into the 1982 election campaign. Who exactly decided to inject the abortion issue into Irish politics, and why, cannot be said with certainty. One explanation is that developments in the European Court under the European Convention on Human Rights indicated that the Convention might be interpreted as conferring the right to have an abortion, and the Church was staging a pre-emptive strike to prevent the Convention being extended to Ireland. But certainly a number of Catholic organisations became active in the years 1980 and 1981. These included the Irish Catholic Doctors Guild, the Guild of Catholic Nurses, the Irish Association of Lawyers for the Defence of the Unborn, the Irish Pro-Life Movement, and the Society for the Protection of the Unborn Child (SPUC), which campaigned with a particular intensity and rancour. These groups amalgamated into the Pro-Life Amendment Campaign (PLAC), under the chairmanship of a Dublin doctor, Julia Vaughan, in April 1981, and, as indicated, succeeded in wresting from the politicians a commitment to amend Section 3 of Article 40 of the constitution by adding the following: 'The State acknowledges the right to life of the unborn, and, with due regard to the equal right of life of the mother, guarantees in its laws to respect and, as far as practicable, by its laws to defend and vindicate that right.'

The hierarchy had welcomed this formula, which had been provided by Fianna Fáil, and FitzGerald saw no particular reason not to accept it also. Accordingly, a Bill to permit the holding of a referendum was introduced to the Dail on 9 February 1980 by Michael Noonan, the Minister for Justice, as soon as he had dealt with the (barely) more important matter of highlighting the fact that his predecessor had been engaged in phone tapping, and decapitating the Garda Siochana in the process. However, the coalition's Attorney General, Peter Sutherland, found when he came to examine the Fianna Fáil wording that it was

> ambiguous and unsatisfactory. In particular it is not clear as to what life is being protected; as to whether 'the unborn' is protected from the moment of fertilisation or alternatively is left unprotected until an independently viable human being exists at twenty-five to twenty-eight weeks; faced with the dilemma of saving the life of the mother, a doctor knowing that to do so will terminate the life of the 'unborn' will be compelled by the wording to conclude that he can do nothing.

Sutherland went on to point out that certain contraceptives could be regarded as abortifacient if life was deemed to commence on conception. Thus, such contraceptives, or 'the morning after' pill for the treatment of rape victims, would be outlawed, as would the use of such contraceptives in other conditions affecting a woman's health such as diabetes or a heart condition.

As a result of Sutherland's objections, FitzGerald accepted an alternative abortion amendment proposed by the Attorney General: 'Nothing in this Constitution shall be invoked to invalidate any provision of the law on the grounds that it prohibits abortion.' The hierarchy greeted this by issuing a further statement saying that it was their lordship's 'earnest hope' that 'Our legislators will put before the people a form of amendment which will give them the opportunity to decide whether or not they wish to give unborn human life the full constitutional protection already guaranteed to every citizen.'

FitzGerald had hoped to explain to the hierarchy privately why Fine Gael were departing from the amendment which Haughey had proposed, before any suggestion of Church–State conflict could arise. To this end, he had called on a bishop with whom he was friendly, and asked him to convey to his fellow bishops the legal problems which had arisen, and request that a meeting be arranged between the Government and the hierarchy. Later, FitzGerald would describe what happened next:

> This courteous informal approach was flatly rejected by the hierarchy in favour of an indirect contact through an intermediary, which proved entirely abortive. I have to say that I formed the opinion at the time that this refusal stemmed from a view on the part of the hierarchy that it would be easier for them to reject any change in the wording regardless of the merits of the case if they did not have to face across the table the cogent reasons that had led to our decision.[9]

One is inclined to agree with FitzGerald's reasoning. When he went ahead with a wording proposed by Sutherland, Fine Gael was torn apart internally. FitzGerald had hoped to impose the whip on his parliamentary party to win the day for the Sutherland formula, but he had to allow eight deputies to abstain after the veteran Oliver J. Flanagan told an RTE interviewer that if anyone was to lose the whip, it should be FitzGerald, because of his failure to keep his commitments and 'his efforts to terrorise every mother, and to terrorise every woman in the country'. On 27 April, the Government had to bow to the inevitable: the Haughey wording was accepted, and a referendum set for 7 September. It was a bitter and divisive campaign. The hierarchy weighed in with further statements, culminating with one from the Archbishop of Dublin, Dermot Ryan, who had succeeded McQuaid. It wound up with a directive to 'all of you' that 'a Yes vote on Wednesday will protect the right to life of the unborn child; it will not create a threat to expectant mothers; it will block any attempt to legalise abortion in this country'.

The amendment was duly carried by a majority of over two to one, 841,233 votes to 416,136. The referendum campaign was hardly the ideal background against which to conduct a forum from which it was intended to produce a blueprint guaranteeing the north of Ireland Unionists their liberties of conscience. In addition, as we will see, the campaign was to result in the distressing 'X case' which brought much anguish to those involved, and unfavourable publicity for the country internationally. But, bloodied but unbowed, a couple of years later FitzGerald sailed again into the choppy waters of the Irish political conscience. This time the issue was divorce.

Desmond O'Malley had been breasting the waves of conscience with considerable success since February 1985, when he was finally expelled from Fianna Fáil (though he had lost the parliamentary whip, he had remained a member of the party). His offence had been to speak out in favour of an amendment to the Family Planning Bill, which at the time Haughey had termed 'an Irish solution to an Irish problem'. Barry Desmond, the Labour Minister for Health, had proposed the amendment in order to extend the benefits of the solution to unmarried people. O'Malley supported the coalition proposal in a justly praised speech in which he said that he wanted an Ireland which was truly pluralist, a state which was 'really a Republic, carrying real Republican traditions'. This was necessary, he said, to make real 'the possibility of ever succeeding in persuading our fellow Irishmen in the North to join us'. He also wanted to make it possible for young people to have the right 'to the exercise of their own private consciences'. He flatly challenged traditional hierarchical attitudes, saying:

> I have seen a Reverend Bishop saying that we can legislate for private morality. I beg to take issue with him . . . I do not believe that the interests of the State, our Constitution and of this Republic, would be served by putting politics before conscience in regard to this. There is a choice of a kind that can only be answered by saying that I stand by the Republic and accordingly I will not oppose this Bill.

Despite these ringing utterances, O'Malley did not go so far as to actually vote for the amendment, which was carried, but abstained in person by leaving the chamber when the vote was taken. However, his speech was described by Barry Desmond, the Minister for Health, as 'the finest I have heard in thirteen years in the Dail'. Haughey too felt that it merited particular recognition, and had O'Malley expelled from the party five days later, on 25 February 1985. Throughout 1985, therefore, people tended to look more towards O'Malley than FitzGerald as the standard-bearer for liberal causes. This became a real political threat after the formation of the PDs, and interacted with the divorce question. It might be noted here that where abortion was concerned, such figures as are available showing abortions carried out on women who gave Irish addresses to British clinics indicate that throughout the 1980s abortions never fell below 3,000 a year, and had reached 4,000 by 1990. The exact number may well have been far higher, but because of the shame and secrecy involved, one can only speculate here, for, as was often remarked, 'most abortions take place in order to save the life of the father'. In the case of divorce, it is estimated that the problem of broken marriages was far higher, standing at around 70,000 at the time of the divorce referendum.

The divorce saga commenced when Michael O'Leary, the ex-Labour leader, who had joined Fine Gael, introduced a private member's Bill to move the prohibition on divorce in the constitution, thus allowing divorce legislation to be introduced. A free vote was allowed, and the measure was defeated. Speaking on television in the wake of the defeat, FitzGerald said that he favoured removing the constitutional ban on divorce. This brought him into public controversy with the hard-line Minister for Defence, Patrick Cooney, who, on 6 December, told the Dail that both he and the majority in Fine Gael opposed divorce. Two days later, on the Feast of the Immaculate Conception, perhaps not the best date in the calendar for such topics, FitzGerald took issue with Cooney, saying that he spoke 'for a majority within Fine Gael, whatever anyone else may say', and wanted no delay in removing the constitutional barrier to divorce.

However, he then caused a debate himself by voting against a Labour Party Bill on the subject, on the grounds that he felt it would be wrong to change the law without obtaining the views of the churches first. As at the time the Dail Committee on Marital Breakdown had already been in existence for several years, and had obtained the views of the Catholic hierarchy, FitzGerald should have been well aware of their lordships' views on divorce: they were against it. Nevertheless, he went ahead with the consultation process, and on 23 April 1986 issued proposals for dropping the prohibition from the constitution, and allowing the courts to grant divorce. Remarriage was to be allowed in cases where there was no reasonable prospect of reconciliation, so long as dependants were provided for. There were a number of banana skins lying in wait for FitzGerald's suggestions, apart from the opposition of the Catholic Church. Probably more of his deputies were opposed to his proposals than were in favour. And Fianna Fáil ran a particularly duplicitous campaign. Publicly the party did not oppose the introduction of divorce, but privately it campaigned vigorously against the Government's proposals.

However, the public's own reaction was more encouraging than that of the politicians. The early opinion polls were in FitzGerald's favour, but he failed to capitalise on this through a series of omissions. During the abortion referendum, various pro-family measures had been promised: the introduction of family courts and conciliation services, raising the marriage age, and crucially in a country with a large peasant proprietorship, legislation to protect the entitlements of those affected by divorce. It was an era of uncertainty fuelled by rising inflation and unemployment. The questions 'What happens to the land?', 'Who gets the house?' loomed large. All these fears were exploited by the various Church groupings. The place of PLAC was taken by an organisation known as 'The Family Solidarity League'. Behind the scenes, the Knights of Columbanus and Opus Dei campaigned for the Church position, which was bolstered by funds from right-wing Catholic organisations in the US. A week before polling day, a Conservative barrister, William Binchy, a brother of the novelist Maeve Binchy, put in a compelling performance on TV in which he pointed to the lack of safeguards for everything from property entitlements to social welfare entitlements for the first family. His heightening of fears about the loss of land, or even children's allowances, may have been decisive. A week later, the referendum on deleting the divorce prohibition from the constitution was defeated by a majority of 935,843 against to 538,279 for.

An issue which has recurred throughout these pages that one might have thought should have been addressed but did not merit even one referendum question throughout this period was emigration. There was a kind of conspiracy of silence on the topic which was well summed up by two young Kerry men who attended a seminar on emigration held around this time (7 April 1987):

> Politicians *don't* like to talk about emigration because they say if you talk about it, or propose money for projects to help the emigrants, you'll only be drawing attention to the problem, or be accused of making it worse, whereas if you say nothing, there's a fair chance that the problem will solve itself. They'll go away and maybe get jobs, and either send back money, or come back some day with money made. But they won't be costing the state anything – if they stayed at home, they'd be a terrible drain.[10]

That year, around 40,000 people emigrated, and the unemployment figure stood at 250,178. The state of the economy was such that the *Economist* openly speculated on the possibility of the IMF being called in. In addition the left–right tensions between Fine Gael and Labour were driving the coalition partners apart. There were also tensions arising out of various issues and scandals. One was the winding up of the Dublin Gas Company which made over 440 permanent staff redundant. Frank Cluskey resigned in outrage at the cost to the state of the winding-up payments. Apart from repaying outstanding loans, the pension provisions for senior company executives struck a raw nerve with Labour (one executive's pension cost £600,000 to fund). But in order to save money, the Government proposed cuts in the 1986 social welfare Christmas bonus payments which would have saved only £3 million. Liam Skelly, a Fine Gael deputy, was rocking the governmental boat in an effort to get a £200 million transport development plan for Dublin approved. Another Labour deputy, Joe Bermingham, was seeking to get unemployment assistance raised to a flat rate of £60 a week. John Bruton, the finance minister, was framing his budget at a time when sterling was being devalued. Money was flowing out of the country, interest rates were rising, and the state was forced into heavy borrowing in the latter part of 1986. The Exchequer return showed that in the month of October, the country was heading for an overrun in borrowing of £180 million, contributing to a projected current budget deficit of £1,450 million, 8.5% of the nation's gross national product, the highest in the history of the state. Bruton, a man whom Barry Desmond from his Labour standpoint described as 'an idealogue of the New Right in Irish politics', was therefore faced with a budget of cuts, cuts, and still more cuts. And if he were not prepared to do it, then the PDs were.

Martin O'Donoghue, who had produced Fianna Fáil's 1977 giveaway manifesto, now wrote one for the PDs in which he proposed a take-back programme in which the PDs promised, if they achieved power, to cut public spending by £50 million in the first year, and £100 million in each succeeding year. The strong medicine was to be taken by the weak. For example, social welfare was to lose £29 million and the Department of Health £23 million. The Government squeaked through a Fianna Fáil-sponsored motion of no confidence by 83 votes to 81 on 23 October, and survived by an even narrower margin in an extraordinarily dramatic piece of political theatre on 18 December. The previous day, in rancorous circumstances, an Extradition Bill had become law, in effect allowing IRA suspects to be extradited to the UK or Northern Ireland. Alice Glenn, an ultra Catholic Fine Gael backbencher, had been at odds with the Government for some time before she was deselected by Fine Gael on 3 December because she had circulated a private newsletter in which she had attacked various people, including the leaders of the minority churches, as being 'enemies of the people' because of their stands during the abortion and divorce referenda. Though still a deputy, she resigned from the party, and voted against the Government on the Extradition Bill, citing the cases of the Birmingham Six, the Guildford Four and the Maguire family, all of whom had been wrongfully convicted, as examples of why Irish citizens should not be extradited to England. In the event, the Bill passed with the help of the Ceann Comhairle's casting vote, by 81 votes to 80 on 17 December.

The following day saw the customary adjournment debate for which Fianna Fáil put down a motion calling on FitzGerald to dissolve the Dail after the Christmas recess. Glenn announced that she would abstain in this, but the Government advantage was nullified by David Andrews of Fianna Fáil, who was recovering from a back operation, getting out of bed to vote. The Government's survival now depended on whether or not Oliver Flanagan, who was dying of cancer, would be able to travel the 60 or so miles from his

County Laois constituency to attend the Dail. With the same courageous individualism which had led him to defy his leader over the divorce issue, Flanagan supported his party by driving to Dublin in an ambulance. There was an extraordinary moment when he arrived just before the vote was taken, leaning on a stick, and had to be helped into the lobby by colleagues. Flanagan could have remained in bed, but he refused the offer of a pairing which would have allowed both himself and Andrews to stay away. As Flanagan was voting, David Andrews was being wheeled into the Fianna Fáil lobby on a stretcher. Deputies from all sides of the house congratulated Flanagan on his courage, one of the first to do so being Charles Haughey. However, Haughey knew that although Flanagan had cost him the battle – the Fianna Fáil vote was lost by 81 votes to 82 – he had won the war. Garret FitzGerald and Dick Spring duly came to an amicable arrangement whereby the Labour ministers, unable to go along with the tough budget which was clearly in prospect, resigned on 20 January 1987, and an election date was set for 17 February.

Haughey returned to power,[11] but only just. The PDs won 14 seats, a remarkable total for a new party. This left Haughey's administration dependent on the casting vote of the Ceann Comhairle, making Haughey the first Taoiseach to be confirmed in office in this way since the Captain Jinks episode in 1927, and the first Fianna Fáil Taoiseach to have failed to gain an overall majority in four successive elections. However, he proceeded to govern with considerable determination. He had said with justice during the campaign that the state was 'literally in a state of economic collapse'. The national debt had quadrupled since 1979 to £25 billion. The *Economist*'s speculation about the IMF had been prompted by the fact that the ratio of public debt to gross domestic product was one of the highest in the world – 140%. Haughey set about reforming the public finances with far more determination than he had done earlier. He appointed Ray McSharry as Minister for Finance, and began his term in office by vetoing a 15% pay rise for both politicians and members of the public service. Ministers were ruthlessly compelled to live within their budgets, and the cuts which John Bruton had envisaged, and which Labour had shrunk from, now became a reality. A factor which greatly assisted Haughey in this strategy was a change of leadership in Fine Gael.

Garret FitzGerald resigned after the election, and was succeeded by Alan Dukes, a tall, likeable economist who had spent several years in Brussels as a Eurocrat. Dukes, who defeated John Bruton for the leadership, announced what was termed 'the Tallaght strategy', after the Dublin suburb where he made his keynote speech that in the national interest, Fine Gael would continue, as it had done under FitzGerald, to support the Government in implementing its tough but necessary economic policies. For example, during the legislative year beginning in October 1998, Fine Gael voted with the Government on 42 occasions, and only 12 against.[12] It might have been better in political terms had the party turned to Peter Barry, a courtly Cork businessman who had been a successful Minister for Foreign Affairs, to succeed FitzGerald initially. Dukes, although highly intelligent and ethical in his approach, lacked political experience. While Barry might have been expected to have been equally ethical, his more streetwise leadership would both have been of more benefit to Fine Gael and allowed Dukes more time to develop his undoubted talents. As it was, Dukes's approach, coupled with that of the trade unions, did help to get the country back on its feet.

The trade union movement had been examining its position for some time prior to the 1987 election. Unlike in England, it did not have a strong Labour Party to look towards for major 'welfare state'-type improvements in society's conditions. The movement had to rely on collective bargaining for its objectives and there was a growing consciousness amongst the leadership that the times called for a new approach. Figures like Des Geraghty in the IT&GWU, and in the other, smaller unions, Phil Flynn, Bill Atley, Pat Rabbitte and Greg Maxwell realised that there was no point in wage increases which disappeared into the mists of inflation. They were impressed by the European trade union model wherein workers had a say in policy making, and the creation of social norms. The bitterness had gone out of the old rivalry between the IT&GWU and the Workers Union of Ireland, which owed its origins to the fallout between William O'Brien and Jim Larkin. But to some degree, this improvement was offset by the fact that the 'stickies', as members of the Workers Party, which had sprung from the Official IRA, were still known, had adopted a process of infiltration in both the public service and the unions as a means of gaining strength. This caused resentment, and not merely in the trade union movement. There was a proliferation of unions which impacted both on the strength of the movement as a whole, and in the number of demarcation disputes. There was also a flourishing black economy, in which employers and workers conspired in under-the-table payments out of the ken of the taxmen. Workers drew unemployment benefit, and obtained free medical cards and other benefits, while still working. Farmers used their clout to by and large evade the tax net. Department of Finance figures released on 7 April showed that in 1986 the PAYE sector paid £1,987 million in tax, whereas the farmers paid only £37 million, and received VAT returns of £79.4 million. The self-employed sector contributed only £172.7 million to the national coffers.

If the unions intended to make headway in this situation, they had a choice of either confrontation along British lines, or negotiation along those of Europe. In the event, they chose negotiation, and were encouraged to do so by Haughey, who deployed his officials to negotiate with both the unions and the employers' associations. Paddy Teohan and Padraig O'hUiginn, with a rising young star of Fianna Fáil, Bertie Ahern, the Minister for Labour, constructed a new type of deal with the unions, the Programme for National Recovery (PNR). Despite the tough stance on public service pay, the agreement embraced issues such as tax concessions, welfare provisions and job creation. The agreement provided for a shorter working week, and an annual tax increase of only 3% on the first £120 of weekly pay, and 2% over that for a three-year period. Lower-paid workers got a basic £3. The Government committed itself to tax reform, and to generating employment. One of the successful initiatives in this area was the creation of the International Financial Services Centre in Dublin.

The PNR was largely adhered to. Inflation fell to below 3% in 1991, and though changes in technology led to redundancies, the jobs target was generally met. Economic growth rose to an average of over 4% between 1987 and 1990, and GDP rose to 68% of the European Community average by 1990. The PNR was succeeded in 1990 by the Programme for Economic and Social Progress, which in turn was replaced in 1994 by the Progress for Competitiveness and Work. The improvement in industrial peace was such that the number of disputes dropped from 126 in 1985 to 85 in the first year of PNR and continued falling to a low of 32 in 1996.

Another very important development of this period was the recognition on the part of those who had inherited the mantles of Larkin and O'Brien in the trade union movement of the wasteful dissipation of energies stemming from the ancient rancours between the Workers Union of Ireland, founded by Larkin, and the Irish Transport and General Workers Union, founded originally by Connolly and Larkin, but eventually dominated by O'Brien. In 1990 the hatchet was buried and the two unions merged into a new and powerful grouping, the Services, Industrial, Professional and Technical Union (SIPTU).

Apart from the accretion of strength which the amalgamation brought to the trade union movement, SIPTU has contributed to Irish society in other ways. For example, through figures like Des Geraghty, as National Industrial Secretary (later President), and the Union's gifted Research Officer, Manus O'Riordan, several reports and research papers on economic developments, new European trends and legislation, and the changing challenges to Irish society, have enriched the national debate. Even if one takes a negative view of these developments, as some left-wing critics of the co-operative trend in Irish trade unionism do, arguing that the movement is now but a prompter sitting on a national stool whispering advice to the main players, government and industry, it cannot be denied that the trade union movement showed itself far more receptive to the idea that it should reform itself than did other sectors during the same period, including the Government, the civil service and the semi-state sector.

For example, in 1980 Charles Haughey authorised the commissioning of the Telesis Report into Irish industrial policy. The consultants' survey was completed in six months. But the report was not published until 1982 and a White Paper, Industrial Policy, a sort of denatured version of Whitaker's Economic Development, did not see the light of day for another two and a half years, and it was not until the following year (1985) that what might loosely be termed Son of Telesis emerged with the publication of a governmental national economic plan, Building on Reality 1985–87, the reality of which was that emigration would continue to be the national safety valve.

Telesis had sought to switch concentration from the multinationals to developing the indigenous sector. It urged that the Government try to overcome the perceived lack of Irish entrepreneurial talent by picking a few score of the top Irish firms, which had demonstrated managerial skills, and building them up by every means possible. It proposed that instead of having strong state agencies assisting weak private companies, the goal should be strong companies. The report also recommended that the Government should insist that foreign companies establish research and development facilities in Ireland. Possibly the most controversial Telesis recommendation was that government departments should have far more control over both the formulation and development of industrial policy. At that stage the Department of Industry only employed thirty people in its industrial policy division as opposed to 750 in the Industrial Development Authority (IDA).

The report sparked off a bureaucratic war between the IDA and the proponents of Telesis which delayed the report's publication and hindered its implementation. A Labour Party response to Telesis's criticism of the lack of Irish business initiative, a National Development Corporation, envisaged £500 million being spent on developing fishing and forestry as well as assisting industry. But this almost immediately came a cropper in the 1982 coalition's horse trading between Labour and Fine Gael being scaled down to only £200 million. The NDC was eventually formally established in 1986 to the accompaniment of what Professor Lee has termed a 'deafening public silence'.[13]

The Liam St John Devlin saga was even more protracted and not a great deal more satisfactory. It began as far back as 1966 when the Public Service Organisation Review Group was set up under the Chairmanship of the distinguished businessman Liam St John Devlin to examine the workings of the public service. It reported in 1969, but it was not until 1985 that some of Devlin's findings were acted on, in a White Paper, *Managing the Country Better*. It proposed a break with the hallowed tradition of so-called 'ministerial responsibility' for policy making. The idea was that a body known as the Aireacht, formed from the top officials in each department, should make policy in conjunction with the minister. Lower officials would have the responsibility of implementing it. Neither the politicians nor the civil servants approved of this innovation. The politicians saw it as a diminution of their powers of patronage; the civil servants as an abandonment of the system whereby they did not have to take ultimate responsibility for their decisions. Another stumbling block was Devlin's proposal that henceforth promotions within the civil service should be on merit. Accordingly his proposals were fought every step of the way at every possible level. A Department of the Public Service which owed its creation, in 1973, to his report, turned out not to be an innovating body, shaping new policies, but a review board of staff numbers and civil service pay.

Generally speaking therefore, the difference between Government and its institutions, and that of the unions, was that the former asked 'what changes are we forced to make because of EEC entry?', the latter 'What can we learn from Europe?' But between the two approaches, the realities of belonging to the European Community had, by the end of the century, forced the main interest groups in Irish society to come together to lay the building blocks for what became known as the Celtic Tiger Economy.

The Haughey administration of 1987–9 was notable for a number of fairly sizeable hiccups in the Anglo-Irish relationship, the start of what might be called 'the tribunal era', and a number of controversies which tended to overshadow the progress on the economic front. Also overshadowed, because at the time no one realised that it had occurred, was the birth of the peace process, in which Haughey had become involved in October of the previous year. The full story of the peace process is told in Chapter Twelve. Here we will turn our attention to the hiccups, and very deadly hiccups some of them were. The year 1987 saw some very grisly happenings. The Loughgall slaughter of an IRA unit occurred in May. Another blow was struck at the Provisionals on 1 November that year when a cargo of Libyan arms was seized aboard the *Eksund*, off the French coast, and a week later there was dreadful carnage at Enniskillen, when an IRA bomb was detonated during a Remembrance Day ceremony, killing 11 and badly injuring 63 others. A combination of the *Eksund* and Enniskillen prompted Haughey into an unprecedented operation on 23 November. Houses all over the country were searched in an effort to find other caches of Libyan arms known to have entered the country. Huge underground bunkers were discovered, some 40 arrests were made north and south of the border, but no arms were found. The following year, on 6 March, the SAS shot and killed an IRA team in Gibraltar as it was reconnoitring a target. It was believed in Dublin that this operation was sanctioned at Cabinet level, an extension of the 'shoot to kill' policy which had been creating considerable difficulties between Dublin and London.

As the IRA team were being buried at Milltown Cemetery in Belfast (on 16 March), a Loyalist gunman, Michael Stone, attacked the mourners with grenades and revolver fire, which killed three people. As one of these victims was being buried a little later, two British corporals in plain clothes were observed driving behind the funeral, and were set upon and lynched. Earlier in the year, the 'shoot to kill' policy had had its repercussions in Dublin and London when it was announced that 11 RUC officers who had been investigated by John Stalker, the Deputy Chief Constable of the Greater Manchester area, and later by Colin Sampson, Chief Constable of the West Yorkshire police force, were not to be prosecuted. It was Sir Patrick Mayhew, the then Attorney General, who said (on 25 January 1988) that the decision was based on reasons of 'national security'. As Stalker had been the highly publicised victim of every form of obstruction during his investigations, was taken off it, and had been made the subject of an attempt to 'fit him up' on charges of misconduct, of which he was later cleared, many people in Ireland felt that there had been a return to the days of the Black and Tans, when every atrocity was denied, every excess condoned. Such ancestral memories were heightened a little later, when the Birmingham Six had their appeal against their conviction for the 1974 pub bombings turned down. All these matters helped to raise hackles between Haughey and Thatcher, centring on the extradition issue.

Under the Haughey regime, some high-profile IRA prisoners had been returned to the UK jurisdiction. In August 1988, Gerard Harte was extradited to Northern Ireland, and a month later, Robert Russell, who had escaped from the Maze prison, was also handed over. But trouble arose over the Father Paddy Ryan case. Father Ryan, a prominent supporter of the Provisionals, was wanted by the British in connection with a series of terrorist offences. He had been arrested in Belgium, but the Belgians decided not to hand him over to the British (it is understood that a member of the Belgian royal family interceded with the Government on Father Ryan's behalf) and he was flown back to Dublin, not London, aboard a Belgian military plane. Haughey made it quite clear to Thatcher in the course of a meeting between the pair during an EC summit at Rhodes that Father Ryan could be tried in Dublin, but that the Irish Attorney General, Patrick Murray, was objecting to his being extradited in view of the massive, and highly prejudicial, publicity which the case had received in the British media and parliament. The British decided not to opt for an Irish trial, which could have been held under the Criminal Law Jurisdiction Act which allowed for trials such as Ryan's to be held in an Irish court, or, in the case of a suspect held by the British, in an English one. London was highly displeased at the Irish stance, but in view of their own position over the Stalker–Sampson affair, no further action was taken.

Haughey was also involved in domestic controversy over a number of issues which served to highlight the fragility of his government. One was the planned closure of Barrington's Hospital, Limerick, under the prevailing austerity programme. The hospital was in Desmond O'Malley's constituency, and he sponsored a Dail motion asking that it be kept open. A Fianna Fáil Limerick TD, Willie O'Dea, supported the proposal, and the Dail vote tied 79–79 with the Ceann Comhairle deciding the issue. Another was a very Irish affair, a decision to introduce rod licence fees, which almost threw Connacht into secession, and revived memories of the land war. Tourism in traditional trout and salmon fishing areas fell, but the Government held the line, to avoid setting a precedent and thereby being forced to climb down in other areas. One issue which it did have to climb down on was that of the Ombudsman, Michael Mills. Neither he nor Haughey could be regarded as each other's favourite person, and no one was surprised when Haughey used the general climate of austerity to drastically trim the staff in Mills's office. However, a lifetime in the media made Mills an effective foe when he took to the airwaves to claim that the very office of Ombudsman was in danger. Under pressure from Labour and the PDs, Haughey was ultimately forced into compromising over Mills's term in office. A deal was worked out whereby Mills was reappointed, but stepped down a few years later on reaching the mandatory retirement age of 67.

However, two other scandals proved more difficult to side-step in the early part of 1989. One involved the beef baron Larry Goodman, the other the infecting with HIV of people who had used the state's blood transfusion service. Goodman had been in the news over a row involving a figure who would loom large in the tribunal era of the latter part of the century, Liam Lawlor. Lawlor was a Fianna Fáil deputy on the Dail committee which dealt with state-sponsored bodies. One of these was the Irish Sugar Company in Tuam, which, like its sister plant in Thurles, had been closed as part of the national economy drive. At the time, Lawlor was also involved with a company owned by Goodman, who wanted to buy the Sugar Company. The opposition accused Lawlor of a conflict of interest, but he refused to leave the Dail committee until forced to step down by Haughey. This precipitated a damaging debate in the Dail which was followed by a vote that the Government lost by 69 votes to 67, because two Fianna Fáil deputies failed to turn up.

At this stage the Goodman affair was not public knowledge, only becoming so several years later after ITV's *World in Action* programme, screened on 13 May 1991, made a series of allegations that led to the Oireachtas setting up the Beef Tribunal which was to run until 29 July 1994 and cost some £38 million. The Goodman scandal had begun under the previous FitzGerald administration when it was discovered that one of his companies had been supplying meat to Egypt which was below the weight claimed when applying for EC export credit. Goodman was facing fines of the order of £10 million by January of 1988.[14] The EC gave export refunds to those who succeeded in selling intervention beef outside the EC countries. These countries included Iraq, and because it, and the Middle East, was regarded as a risky place to do business, the Irish Government provided insurance cover for Goodman's exports to the area.

In 1986, the FitzGerald administration decided that the risks were too high, and discontinued the export insurance cover. The risks were added to by some of the practices within the Goodman empire. The Garda fraud squad established that various scams involving forged meat stamps and tax evasion had taken place. (Eventually settlement terms were agreed with the Revenue Commissioners, only low-level Goodman employees were implicated and no one went to jail.) Despite this, the Fianna Fáil administration leant on the IDA (Industrial Development Authority) to provide Goodman with funds to help him improve the Irish beef industry, by way of concentrating on processing meat rather than exporting it on the hoof. When Fianna Fáil returned to power in 1987, the insurance cover was reinstated, even though the Insurance Corporation of Ireland issued a strong warning against this. In theory, the meat sent to Iraq was, as stipulated in the contracts, slaughtered by the halal method, not more than 100 days before it arrived in Iraq. Although it is said the Iraqis knew the meat was coming from intervention, was not slaughtered by the halal method, and could have been refrigerated for years, this meant that legally speaking they were free to refuse payment under the terms of their contracts. Nevertheless, despite further warnings to the contrary from the Insurance Corporation of Ireland, following a Cabinet meeting on 8 July 1988 it was decided that insurance cover should be extended. The Goodman interests had sought an additional £325 million in cover from the Department of Industry and Commerce. How much cover was actually conceded is difficult to ascertain. A subsequent Supreme Court ruling decided that the matter was covered by Cabinet confidentiality. Albert Reynolds apparently believed that he had been given sanction to lift the ceiling to £500 million. Another version of events is that the 8 July Cabinet meeting left it to Reynolds and the then Minister for Finance, Ray McSharry, to work out a new insurance figure. McSharry raised the bar to £250 million in December 1988 before departing for Europe, to be succeeded in Finance by Reynolds.

By the end of January 1989, something in excess of £60 million was overdue from Iraq, and despite the loophole provided by the non-adherence to the halal method, the state guaranteed the money owed to the banks. This was not public knowledge. Around this time, it was the haemophilia scandal which was engaging public attention, with the Labour Party seeking to force the Dail to increase the payment of £250,000 to each victim to £400,000, and Fianna Fáil lost a vote on the issue on 26 April 1989. It was not a confidence issue, but Haughey was furious at the outcome and let it be known that he planned a general election. Whether this was because he was doing well in the opinion polls at the time, or whether he was tired of having to tread a cautious financial path, so as to be certain that Fine Gael and the PDs would not ambush him, is a matter of debate. Certainly, Fine Gael were not seeking an election. Haughey's critics are inclined to suggest that neither was the case, and that he wanted to get an election out of the way before the ever-escalating Iraqi debt situation exploded. It was estimated that by the end of June 1989 Iraq could have owed as much as £160 million. At all events, Haughey called a general election to coincide with the European elections which were due to be held on 15 June.

Although the full extent of the Iraqi débâcle was not known, the election campaign was affected by rumours about the affair. Cuts in the health service also played their part, and Fianna Fáil lost four seats. This was partly balanced by the fact that the Progressive Democrats lost eight, being reduced to only six seats. A period of unprecedented manoeuvring then set in. All three of the major political party leaders were defeated when the vote for Taoiseach was called in the Dail on 28 June 1989. Dick Spring proved to have a keener instinct for the jugular than Alan Dukes when he aborted a proposal by Haughey that the Dail should adjourn until 3 July to allow him to cobble together an administration, and to permit the business of government to continue without asking the President to dissolve the Dail. Haughey informed Dukes that the Attorney General had said that this was permissible under the constitution. However, Spring, a barrister, disputed this, a recess was called, and Haughey's colleagues convinced him that in the climate of the moment, his best course was to resign. Haughey caved in, but without asking the President to dissolve the Dail, and for the next four days engaged in intensive negotiations with the other parties, from which it emerged that the only way he could hope to continue in power was by forming a coalition with the Progressive Democrats. As it was the Progressive Democrats who had weakened Fianna Fáil by leaving, this was gall and wormwood to the rank-and-file membership of Haughey's party. It was the first time in Fianna Fáil's history that the party had gone into coalition with anyone, let alone party renegades, as the PDs were still seen, although by now the party was attracting a broad-based right-wing support of its own.

The decision to form a coalition deepened divisions within Fianna Fáil, but nevertheless Haughey went ahead and formed his last administration, with two Progressive Democrats in the Cabinet (Desmond O'Malley, Minister for Industry and Commerce, and Bobby Molloy, Minister for Energy), and a PDs junior minister, Mary Harney. This meant that three former Fianna Fáil ministers lost their portfolios. There may have been a malign symbolism in the date on which Haughey announced this Cabinet on being elected Taoiseach – 12 July, the Orangemen's day of triumphalism. Almost from the formation of the Government, there were discussions about who would succeed Haughey. These discussions gathered force when Seán Doherty again figured in controversy. Though he had been given legal advice to the contrary, Doherty, who at this stage was Caithearleach of the Seánad, had presided over a hearing to suspend the popular Trinity senator David Norris, who had wrongly accused him of misconduct. Norris took his case to the courts and won, thus precipitating a vote of no confidence in Doherty which Fianna Fáil publicly successfully defended, but privately bitterly resented.

As the sparks from this row were dying out, Albert Reynolds fanned fresh flames by publicly revealing his low opinion of coalition. Speaking on 18 February 1990, Reynolds said, 'I hope that the temporary little arrangement which we have with our junior partners won't be there for all that long and that we'll be back to where we were at the start.' The shades were drawing in for Haughey. A presidential election was due in November of that year, and because of his popularity within the party, it was proving impossible to deny the nomination to Brian Lenihan, even though his candidacy would mean a dangerous by-election in the constituency of Dublin West, where Haughey had already come a cropper eight years earlier over the ill-fated attempt to 'pull a stroke' by sending Dick Burke to Europe, only to suffer the mortification of seeing Eileen Lemass fail to win Burke's seat. The one member of Fianna Fáil who could have been guaranteed to win the presidency, and quite probably without a contest as an agreed candidate, was Jack Lynch, but Haughey did not consider offering him the post. The election was to prove another disaster for Fianna Fáil.

The Labour Party candidate was Mary Robinson, who had resigned from the party at the time of the Anglo-Irish Agreement. A professor of law and a prominent barrister, prior to the campaign she had created the impression of being the rather 'jolly hockey sticks' offspring of a wealthy west of Ireland family, who campaigned for strange liberal causes such as human rights, and making contraception generally available. The Fine Gael candidate was Austin Currie, the former SDLP minister, who was not well known throughout the country. Lenihan, therefore, appeared assured of a fairly comfortable win. However, in the course of a television debate with Garret FitzGerald on 22 October, he dismissed FitzGerald's account of the phone calls he had made to President Hillery in 1982 as 'fictional'. He persisted in assuring the audience that the calls had never been made, despite FitzGerald's pointing out that he had been in the Aras at the time. Worse was to befall: a story appeared in the *Irish Times* on 24 October, saying that the paper had evidence that the calls *had* been made.

As a storm of publicity burst, the paper 'bottled out' on going it alone in printing the evidence, and instead held a press conference at which it revealed the contents of a taped interview between Lenihan and a student, Jim Duffy, in which Lenihan described phoning the President and talking to him. The tape revealed that Haughey and Sylvester Barrett had also made phone calls. However, despite this, Lenihan appeared on television on the afternoon of the press conference to give an interview to the station's political correspondent, Seán Duignan, in the course of which he said: 'From my mature recollection and discussion with other people, at no stage did I ring President Hillery on that occasion or any other time.' Lenihan had had a liver transplant, and at the time of the Duffy interview he had been on very strong medication, which was known to cause memory loss. However, when challenged on a later TV programme, he denied that he had been taking drugs and it became obvious that the affair was a disaster for him, the Government and the presidential campaign. An opinion poll in the *Irish Independent* showing him trailing Mary Robinson decided Lenihan's fate.

Under pressure from the Progressive Democrats, Haughey had already tried and failed to persuade his old friend to resign his position as Minister for Defence. He informed the Dail that he was advising the President to terminate Lenihan's appointment as a member of the Government. While it might be thought that firing his Tanaiste from a Cabinet post and at the same time asking the public to vote for him as President would be regarded as a nonsense, this proved not to be the case. Lenihan was still an immensely popular figure, and he actually headed the poll with 41.1% of the vote to Mary Robinson's 38.9%. Robinson had reinvented herself during the campaign, appearing in attractive dresses, a new hairstyle, and with an obviously genuine interest in making a go of the presidency should she win. As the campaign wore on, her natural shyness diminished, she became more at ease with people, and came across as the epitome of a modern professional Irishwoman. She faced accusations (made by her political opponents) that she was affecting an interest in maternal and domestic issues for electoral advantage, and other accusations on women's rights generally, made by Fianna Fáil campaigners who should have known better. Robinson benefited under PR from receiving a majority of Currie's transfers, and won the election.

She might have done so anyhow without the Lenihan scandal, because traditional Fine Gael voters would have found it somewhat unnatural to transfer to a Fianna Fáil candidate, but in the event her presidency was seen as a breakthrough for Irish women in public life. A constitutional lawyer, once in office she successfully resisted a number of efforts Haughey made to prevent her making public statements on issues of her choosing. She met the Dalai Lama despite Haughey's objections, which in at least one case left him open to accusations of jealousy. He summoned the chief executive of Bord Fáilte, Martin Dully, to his office to berate him for having approached Robinson to make a taped address in support of a Bord Fáilte campaign in the USA. The address had won golden opinions from everyone who saw it, except Haughey. Haughey also used the Government's power to decide whether or not the President should travel abroad to prevent Robinson giving a Dimbleby lecture on the BBC, even though her predecessor had been allowed to give one.

Haughey's decline accelerated throughout 1992. In March he became involved in controversy over that old bugbear of Irish politics, contraception, possibly because he had correctly interpreted Robinson's victory as indicating that old moulds were being broken. However, he was not to be the beneficiary of the breakage. Mary Robinson might have battled her way to the presidency, but it didn't do for the Taoiseach to espouse a liberalisation of the contraception laws, which he did at the Fianna Fáil Ard Fheis. Richard Branson's Virgin record store had been fined for selling contraceptives, and Haughey declared himself in favour of removing the prohibitions on selling condoms, because of the spread of AIDS. He proposed allowing them to be purchased by 16-year-olds, the legal age for marriage. However, predictably, members of the hierarchy opposed him, amongst them Brendan Comiskey of Wexford, who claimed that the Government was intent on creating 'a morally and spiritually bankrupt country which can only offer condoms to its young people in place of jobs'. Ironically, Haughey had once made unsuccessful overtures to the Vatican to have Comiskey appointed as Archbishop of Dublin. Comiskey would later figure in a far more 'morally and spiritually bankrupt' situation when he was forced to resign his bishopric over his handling of appalling sexual abuse scandals in his own diocese, in which one of the most notorious abusers, a Father Fortune, took his own life, but in 1992 his words still carried a certain resonance, as did those of other members of the hierarchy like Archbishop Connell of Dublin, and Cathal Daly of Down and Connor, who was soon to become a cardinal.

Much of the opposition to Haughey's proposal within his party could be stigmatised as hypocritical fear of the crozier, given what is known of the private morality of the period, including the morality of Fianna Fáil party members. But contraception was the issue on which O'Malley had been driven out of the party, and which led to the formation of the PDs, and Haughey backtracked by coming up with his own 'Irish solution to an Irish problem': he handed responsibility for the sale and distribution of condoms to the regional health boards.

The end of June saw Haughey's difficulties deepen with a bad showing in the local government elections. Fianna Fáil emerged from the election in control of only three of the country's 34 councils. The malodorous era of scandals and tribunals was dawning, the Beef Tribunal hearings were doing nothing for the Government's popularity, and other scandals were breaking with what the electorate found an enraging regularity. Two investigative journalists, Pat Brennan and Gene Kerrigan, would later produce a book which they subtitled *The A to Z of Irish Scandals and Controversies*.[15] It was a fair-sized volume. Not all of the scandals occurred during the Haughey era. It just felt as if they did at the time. One after the other they came in sleazy succession. Haughey himself was involved directly in a controversy concerning the laying of a Dublin County Council sewer pipe across his land in Kinsealy, County Dublin, which obviously increased the value of the land for building purposes. It was announced on 12 August 2003 that the property had been acquired by a property developer for €45 million. Celtic Helicopters, a company owned by his son, Ciaran, benefited from some personal lobbying by Haughey amongst wealthy friends for funds, and there was a touch of GUBU striking again when, due to a postal error, Celtic Helicopters received a confidential report destined for a rival firm owned by Aer Lingus. A number of more serious controversies came to life at around the same time, beginning with the Greencore affair. This was the name given to the old Irish Sugar Company. It emerged that four of the Greencore executives got interest-free loans from the company to buy a 49% share in one of the Sugar Company's holdings, a company called SDH. Eleven months later, the Sugar Company bought the SDH stake for £9.5 million. This occurred in 1990. The Sugar Company was privatised in April 1991, after which it became known as Greencore, and throughout September of that year the public learned not only of the huge profits made by the executives, but also, following a row between them and the chief executive, Chris Comerford, that Comerford had been given a golden handshake of £1.5 million.

Another controversy arose over the purchase of a bakery at Ballsbridge as the site of a headquarters for Telecom Eireann, who paid a company called Hoddle Investments £9.4 million for the property. It had been bought a little earlier by United Property Holdings for £4.4 million, and then sold on to Hoddle Investments. Press reports revealed that the chairman of Telecom Eireann at the time, Michael Smurfit, had a share in United Property Holdings, as did the financier Dermot Desmond, the CEO of National City Brokers. Not only had Desmond assisted Hoddle Investments in acquiring the building, he had also handled the privatisation of Greencore and was advising Telecom Eireann on how to go about its privatisation as well. Desmond, one of the best financial brains in the country; had conceived the idea of the Financial Services Centre. Smurfit was another household name through his controlling interest in the Smurfit Packaging empire. Haughey added fuel to the fires of controversy by asking both men to 'step aside' while the affair was being investigated, although he stressed that there was no indication that either they or others involved in the affair had done anything wrong, nor was any wrongdoing ever discovered. But the controversy heightened the public's perception that there was a 'golden circle' of prominent business people close to Haughey who did well out of the association. A prominent solicitor, John Glacken, was appointed to investigate the sale, and unveiled a web of companies, in Cyprus, Jersey, Dublin and the Isle of Man. His report was sent to the Director of Public Prosecutions, the Revenue Commissioners, the Dublin Stock Exchange and the Central Bank by the Minister for Enterprise, Ruairi Quinn, and though no action resulted, the rumour mill increased its speed.

Further gossip was provided by the sale of the old teacher-training college at Carysfort in Blackrock, County Dublin, for use as the site for a business college for University College Dublin. Carysfort was controversial largely only because the other issues had arisen, and because when headlines began to sprout, Haughey denied that he had been involved in any way with the sale to UCD, though he had in fact been in contact with the head of the University Business School. It later emerged that the real problem was not that anyone made a cash killing on the transaction, but that the Government had grossly underestimated the number of children who would have to be taught in future years, necessitating more, not fewer, teachers.

The barrage of controversy was making Haughey's internal critics restive, particularly Albert Reynolds, who was becoming increasingly irked with the Progressive Democrats link. A feature of the coalition deal had been an agreement to renegotiate the PDs programme for government after two years, but Reynolds walked out of the negotiations and left them to Bertie Ahern to complete. This led to rumours that yet another heave was in prospect when Haughey decided to face his parliamentary party (on 23 October 1991) full-frontally to state that he had a time frame in mind for stepping down as leader, after attending to some pending Anglo-Irish EC business, and bringing in a budget the following January. The party divided on Haughey's announcement. Ahern spoke for those who accepted his intention to step down, Reynolds those opposed. Reynolds was expected to challenge Haughey for the leadership before the week ended, but thought the matter over and announced that in order to avoid creating bitterness within the party, he was withholding his challenge in order to give Haughey 'an honourable time frame' for withdrawing. However, Reynolds reconsidered his attitude when a few days later the Greencore controversy flared up again.

Haughey had denied in the Dail that Desmond's National City Brokers and his friend, Pat O'Connor, had been appointed as advisers on the privatisation of Greencore at a meeting with the Greencore chairman, Bernie Cahill, who was also the chairman of Aer Lingus, and of a mining company called Feltrim, owned by Haughey's son, Conor. He had had no meetings with Cahill, he said. However, at an extraordinary general meeting of Greencore share-holders on 30 October, Cahill disclosed that a meeting had taken place, and that the pair had discussed a list of companies from which a broker would be chosen to advise on the privatisation. Desmond's NCB was on the list.

A Reynolds supporter, Seán Power, put down a motion calling on Haughey to step down at the next meeting of the Fianna Fáil parliamentary party, and Reynolds announced that he would support the motion. Haughey called on Reynolds to resign from the Cabinet, and when he refused was thus forced to ask the President to depose him. Padraig Flynn also backed Power, refused to resign, and fell to the presidential axe. On an open vote, Haughey won the parliamentary party battle by 55 votes to 22, and set about reshuffling his Cabinet in the wake of Flynn and Reynolds's departure. Most people are aware of Murphy's Law, that if things can go wrong, they will go wrong. Haughey was now to fall victim to its corollary: if things do go wrong, they can only get worse.

One of the new faces in his Cabinet was that of James McDaid, who became Minister for Defence. A year and a half or so earlier, McDaid had been in the Supreme Court when it ruled that a constituent of his, James Pius Clarke, a member of the Provisional IRA, was not to be extradited to the Six Counties on a charge of attempted murder. Clarke and McDaid belonged to the same GAA club, and as Clarke had been present at a club function on the night of the murder, McDaid was aware of his innocence. However, he allowed himself to be photographed outside the Four Courts, beaming happily, with his arm around Clarke. The opposition seized on the photograph, the PDs in particular judging that McDaid had compromised himself. Bobby Molloy told McDaid that someone who wished to join the army as a private would not have been accepted if he had been photographed with a member of the IRA. McDaid decided that his only course was to resign.

The resignation provoked fury within Fianna Fáil, who saw it as yet another capitulation to the PDs by Haughey. It was obvious that the Taoiseach's days were numbered. But then, on 15 January 1992, Seán Doherty struck again. On an RTE programme, he announced that other people knew about the phone tapping for which he had taken the fall in 1982. Reynolds went on another programme to suggest that Haughey was not going to step down, and that Doherty should tell what he knew. On 21 January Doherty obliged, giving a press conference at which he said that not only had Haughey been fully aware that two journalists' phones were being tapped, but that 'as soon as the transcripts from the taps became available, I took them personally to Mr Haughey in his office, and left them in his possession'.

Haughey's coalition partners left him in no doubt that he had been forced out on to a gangplank from which he had a choice of either jumping or waiting, probably for no more than a couple of days, for the PDs to see it through. On 30 January, he announced that he would retire as leader of

Fianna Fáil on 7 February. He did so, making a final speech to the Dail (on the 11th) in which he recalled the words of Othello: 'I have done the State some service, and they know't. No more of that.' There would unfortunately be more. Haughey was subsequently disgraced by revelations made about his lifestyle, and about where the money to support his lavish expenditures had come from, at a number of tribunals set up at enormous expense to the state to examine payments to politicians. But what was his contribution to Irish politics? One might sum it up by saying that it was like the curate's egg, good and bad, except that one should say that, even though Haughey was a small man – which probably accounted for his Napoleonic ego – the egg was an ostrich's, in that it was of larger proportions than anything produced by the average farmyard politician.

There really wasn't any doubt about who would succeed Haughey. Of the two likely contenders, Albert Reynolds and Bertie Ahern, Reynolds was the older man (59) by 20 years, he had been working surreptitiously to consolidate his candidacy before Haughey was pushed on to his sword by the PDs, and he was not tainted by association with Haughey. Those within the party who had shrunk from supporting him in his final abortive challenge lost their fears of joining his bandwagon once Haughey was gone. There were a few somewhat indelicate hiccups before deputies made up their minds, because of Ahern's domestic arrangements. He was separated, and living with his partner Celia Larkin, a fact which the pro-Reynoldsites made use of, both within the party and in leaks to the media. Possibly a combination of Reynolds's seniority and Ahern's worries about his own private life decided him in standing down. When the leadership vote was taken on 6 February, only two other candidates, Mary O'Rourke and Michael Woods, were left standing, neither of whom had any chance of winning. Woods got ten votes, O'Rourke six, and Reynolds 61. He used his overwhelming winning margin ruthlessly when he named his Cabinet five days later. In all, he dispensed with eight members of Haughey's Cabinet and nine of the twelve junior ministers. He was afterwards quoted as saying, 'the main thing to remember about being in this job, is that you're here to make decisions, and that involves taking risks'.

Risks Reynolds certainly took, and in his short, turbulent stay in office, it is equally certain that he achieved some spectacular successes. Possibly the economic buoyancy of the period would have happened anyhow, although his shrewd business hand at the tiller helped to keep the ship of state steady as she went. But in two areas, Albert Reynolds justifies a respected place in Irish history. One was that he did more than any other politician in the Republic of Ireland to bring about the peace process; the second was that he succeeded in extracting quite extraordinary amounts of money from the European exchequer during the Edinburgh summit which occurred on his watch. Reynolds took everyone by surprise on taking office by declaring that he would make the Northern Ireland situation a priority. He was known to the Irish public for three things: he was a dog food manufacturer, and a ballroom owner, and, early in his ministerial career, had drawn widespread ridicule for appearing on an RTE TV programme, dressed in a cowboy outfit and singing: 'Put your sweet lips a little closer to the phone . . .' The unfavourable reaction to his performance owed less to Seán Doherty's activities than to his own singing voice. However, Albert Reynolds had manufactured a very large amount of dog food, and as an impresario and ballroom owner had sold a correspondingly large number of entrance tickets. His shrewd business head saw him through most of the controversies which arose while he was Taoiseach.

One of the nastiest of these broke out on the day after he became Taoiseach. The poltroonery surrounding the abortion issue in Irish politics has already been described. What landed in Reynolds's lap was the outcome of the ill-considered abortion referendum, the so-called 'X case'. This involved a 14-year-old girl who had been raped and whose parents had taken her to England for an abortion. However, as this was aiding and abetting illegality under Irish law, the parents were forced to bring her back to Dublin. The Attorney General, Harry Whelehan, had taken out a High Court injunction to prevent the girl having an abortion. Delivering his judgment, Mr Justice Declan Costello said: 'the risk that the defendant may take her own life . . . is much less and is of a different order of magnitude than the certainty that the life of the unborn will be terminated'.[16] The court had been informed that the girl was suicidal. The case made a laughing stock out of the country, and blew gaping holes in its claim to be a modern western European democracy. Some of the attitudes thrown up were difficult to credit. I can still remember the thrill of revulsion I felt watching *The Late Late Show*, when Father Michael Cleary, who was later discovered to have fathered two children, opined that the 'X case' was a set-up to gain publicity for the pro-choice lobby. His exact words were: 'If a case was made, was planned deliberately, to test this amendment, this is it. It's the model. I honestly suspect a lot of organisation behind it.'[17]

The Supreme Court, however, did not share Father Cleary's suspicions. On appeal, the injunction was lifted, and the family travelled once again to England. Here the girl suffered a miscarriage. The PD–Fianna Fáil relationship almost terminated also. The 'X case' became interwoven with two more referenda. The first, in June, and of fundamental importance to Ireland's future, was held to ratify or reject the Maastricht Treaty. However, under pressure from right-wing Catholic opinion, which also worked upon the opposition parties, Reynolds was forced to seek a protocol to the agreement recognising the position of abortion in the Irish constitution. Without this, the Maastricht Treaty probably would not have carried. From the PDs there came pressure to recognise the rights of women either to get information about abortion or to travel to get one should they so decide. In an effort to balance the demands of the PD camp against those of the pro-lifers, Reynolds was forced to hold another referendum, which consisted of three questions: the right to information, to travel, and to make abortion illegal save in cases where the life of the mother was in danger. One and two passed, number three fell.

The abortion issue reopened old Fianna Fáil–PD tensions over coalition. During his first Ard Fheis, in March, Reynolds went out of his way to needle the PDs, saying: 'Fianna Fáil does not need another party to keep it on the right track or act as its conscience', and he sanctioned an address by his protégé, Brian Cowen, in which Cowen brought the Ard Fheis to its feet by asking: 'What about the PDs?' and then answering the question: 'When in doubt, leave out.' These hostilities were heightened immeasurably by the proceedings of the Beef Tribunal. Before becoming Reynolds's coalition partner, O'Malley had made a written statement to the tribunal in which he had said that Reynolds's operation of the export credit insurance scheme had favoured Goodman. Called to the tribunal in person, he held to this view and added that Reynolds had been 'wrong ... grossly unwise, reckless and foolish'. When Reynolds in turn took the stand, he described O'Malley's evidence as 'reckless, irresponsible, and dishonest'. Moreover, although offered the chance to do so, he refused to withdraw the word 'dishonest'.

The result was a PD-sponsored motion of no confidence in the Government of which it was an essential component, and a dissolution of the Dail on 5 November. At first the election appeared to be a disaster for Reynolds. Fianna Fáil lost 10 seats, Labour gained 17, the PDs received 10, the Democratic Left (which had grown out of the old Sinn Féin – the Workers Party) five, and others six. However, Fine Gael also dropped 10 seats and its chances of forming a coalition, because its new leader, John Bruton, had ruled out including the Democratic Left in what he called 'a rainbow coalition'. Labour let it be known that it would not ally itself with the Progressive Democrats, and Reynolds began working on the idea of going into coalition with Labour. More importantly, he began working on his European colleagues at the Edinburgh EU summit, to achieve what appeared to be the unattainable target of £6 billion in EU structural and cohesion funds. There was a good deal of scoffing at Reynolds after he publicly committed himself to the £6 billion figure before setting off to the summit, but in the event he came home, on 12 December 1992, not with £6 billion, but with £8 billion. Eight billion, whether, as became the subject of argument later, over a five-year or an eight-year period, is the sort of figure which does wonders for sensitive Labour consciences. Spring dropped a demand that he be appointed Taoiseach on a rotating basis, but in return, under a jointly accepted 'Programme for Partnership Government 1993–1997', received a commitment to a number of job-creating projects, Dail reform, increases in health and social welfare spending, the introduction of divorce, and the decriminalisation of homosexuality. Reynolds in return became Taoiseach once again on a platform which included a Labour commitment to accepting the Maastricht Treaty's obligation on countries remaining within their budgets. All this negotiation had taken time, and the new government did not take office until 12 January. Meanwhile there had been a currency crisis, largely because Britain had withdrawn from the EMS the previous September, and Irish interest rates rose as a result, but the absence of a government also played its part.

It was not the rise in the interest rates, however, but that in Reynolds's majority which was to cause difficulties for the new administration of nine Fianna Fáil and six Labour ministers. On the one hand, Reynolds now had the benefit of the largest majority in the state's history; on the other, the ordinary voters, in particular the Labour voters, now had a government which they hadn't voted for. Nor indeed had many Fianna Fáil anti-coalition supporters. This gave rise to some tensions in Government, as did the presence of a new breed of animal in Irish politics, programme managers, whose job it was to see that the 'partnership government' functioned as such. The Labour programmers were party activists; those employed by Fianna Fáil were civil servants. Inevitably, the programmers' tail began wagging the Government dog to the annoyance of both parties. A number of other issues also arose to increase disharmony between the government parties.

To begin with in the first days in power, Labour had blocked Fianna Fáil privatisation initiatives. Spring secured a commitment that the Government would not attempt to sell any more state assets after putting his foot down on a Fianna Fáil proposal to sell off a share in Telecom Eireann. The following year, Spring reacted angrily when he discovered that Fianna Fáil was proposing to include in the Finance Bill an easing of residency stipulations which would have benefited the wealthy. Reynolds appeared to back down, but the Finance Bill actually had an amendment added to it at the committee stage, which allowed the rich to spend six months of the year in Ireland while being regarded as non-residents for tax purposes. Spring and Reynolds also disagreed over a tax amnesty, the second in five years, which Fianna Fáil espoused on the grounds that it would bring in additional revenue. By now the public were becoming wary of the Government's record on what might be called 'tribunal issues', and there was widespread criticism of a proposal which appeared designed to allow wealthy tax cheats to make far more modest settlements with the Revenue Commissioners than were justifiable, and, of course, to escape without prosecution or penalties for having dodged tax in the first place. Labour benefited from the second amnesty in one sense, inasmuch as some of the money brought in went to fund Labour projects, but suffered overall for being seen to poorly discharge its role of 'keeping Fianna Fáil honest'.

Relations between the coalition partners were worsened by the operation of a scheme whereby wealthy foreigners were granted Irish citizenship if they invested in Ireland. There was widespread media comment throughout June of 1994 when it became known that Albert Reynolds's dog food firm had been thrown the substantial bone of a £1 million investment by a Saudi national who received Irish citizenship as a result, as did the investor's family. Allegations of 'passports for sale' involving a Taoiseach were not the sort of thing to endear Labour's supporters to Fianna Fáil. But all these matters paled in significance compared to the Beef Tribunal Report. It was delivered to Reynolds's office late on the Friday evening of the August bank holiday. Reynolds apparently thanked God it was Friday. After a quick perusal, he decided that the report cleared him, and issued a statement to the media to that effect, even though he had an agreement with Spring that government comment would only come when the Cabinet partners had had an opportunity to study the report. In fact, sections of the report were quite critical of Reynolds, though to nothing like the extent that his adversaries had hoped, but the quotations used in the press release glossed over the criticisms. Spring was furious, and the Fine Gael leader, John Bruton, improved the shining hour by offering a government based on Labour, Fine Gael and the Democratic Left. The offer was not proceeded with, but it remained to fester, or fructify, depending on whether or not one was a Fianna Fáil supporter.

The Dail was recalled to discuss the Beef Tribunal Report on 31 August 1994. By an extraordinary coincidence, this turned out to be a day on which history was made. At twelve midday, in large part because of Albert Reynolds's own courageous background efforts, the Provisional IRA declared a ceasefire. By common consent, the Dail turned from discussing the not very savoury meat of the tribunal report, and hearkened instead to the drumbeat of history and the issue of what lay ahead in the peace process. However, on the following day, normal parliamentary hostilities were resumed, and Spring took the opportunity to speak his mind about the way Reynolds had rushed into print on the tribunal's findings:

> The Taoiseach is aware of my strong feelings on the matter. We have discussed the leaking of sections of the Report candidly with each other. He knows that the action damaged trust. The Taoiseach knows that I am prepared to work to restore it, and I believe that he is too ... If both sides in this government are willing to see it as a genuine partnership which puts the interest of the people first, this administration will succeed in its many tasks. If delicate and sensitive situations are to be played for party or personal advantage, this government will fail.[18]

Fail it duly did. And again the Beef Tribunal played a part. Reynolds proposed to appoint the author of the report, Liam Hamilton, the President of the High Court, who had presided over the tribunal, as Chief Justice. Spring had another nominee in mind, Donal Barrington, a judge of the European Court, but a problem arose when it was discovered that there were legal difficulties in moving a judge from the European Court. These were later overcome, too late to have any bearing on what followed. The Attorney General, Harry Whelehan, who had brought the 'X case', realising that Hamilton was likely to move to the Supreme Court, threw his hat in the ring by letting it be known that he would like to succeed him. Reynolds placed the question of his nomination on the Cabinet agenda for 7 September, but agreed to withdraw it under pressure from Spring, who did not object to Whelehan's becoming a judge, but did not want him as president of the High Court. His choice was the liberal Susan Denham. The matter hung fire for the month of September, and was literally almost laughed off the political agenda by an extraordinary happening, ironically enough in the area whence came one of the Beef Tribunal's chief actors, Dessie O'Malley: Shannon Airport outside Limerick. Appropriately, the events gave rise to the following limerick:

> *There once was a silly old Yelt*
> *Who thought he could drink like a Celt*
> *But aboard an Ilyushin,*
> *He lost that illusion,*
> *The bottle hit him the hard belt.*

The Yelt was, of course, Boris Yeltsin, the Russian President, whose plane had touched down at Shannon, en route to Russia from the US, so that he could meet with Reynolds. However, the teetotaller Reynolds waited fruitlessly on the tarmac, surrounded by dignitaries, while aboard the presidential plane, panic-stricken aides tried vainly to deal with a 100% proof diplomatic crisis. The Russian Deputy Prime Minister was finally produced to meet Reynolds, who mischievously suggested that he would slip aboard the plane to greet Yeltsin there. Further panic amidst the Russians and general levity amongst the Irish public. A few days later, at another airport, Baldonnell Military Airport outside Dublin, Reynolds and Spring apparently diffused the Whelehan row at a midnight meeting at which it was agreed that the whole question of courts and judicial appointments should be gone into, and Spring agreed not to create an election issue out of Whelehan.

But then Murphy's Law set in with a vengeance. The media fastened on a story that a paedophile priest, Father Brendan Smyth, had been allowed to remain at liberty for several months while an extradition warrant issued by the RUC had lain in the Attorney General's office without being acted on. Spring's objections to Whelehan were rekindled, and he led his ministers out of a Cabinet meeting which considered the judicial appointment on 11 November. Reynolds refused to back down, and accompanied by Whelehan and the Minister for Justice, Maire Geoghegan-Quinn, went to meet President Robinson and had Whelehan's appointment officially confirmed. Frenzied efforts were made to draft a speech for Reynolds which would promise reform in the Attorney General's office, butter up Spring, and restore trust. The speech involved Reynolds in a certain amount of humiliation. But while it was being drafted, Eoghan Fitzsimons, who had succeeded Whelehan as Attorney General, discovered another case in the Attorney General's files in which there had been a delay in handling a request for extradition, involving a man called Duggan. Whelehan's report to the Cabinet on the Smyth case had been prepared on the basis that it was the only one involving a delay. As a result of the discovery, Fitzsimons was dispatched to Whelehan's home to tell him about the Duggan case, and ask him to postpone his swearing-in. Whelehan refused, and was duly sworn in. Reynolds then made a statement to the Dail in the course of which he defended the Whelehan appointment, gave a categoric assurance to the House that the Attorney General had not known of the Smyth extradition request until a few weeks earlier, and went on to say:

> It would be a great pity if a government that is achieving rapid economic progress, that has achieved the biggest breakthrough in Northern Ireland in over 25 years and that has a fine legislative programme, should be placed in jeopardy over misunderstandings surrounding a single judicial appointment. In particular, it is my profound conviction that we have to give the fragile Northern peace process the best possible chance of permanent consolidation. I believe the national interest requires continuity at this time. We must all work to restore the spirit of partnership, which is the cornerstone of this successful government. I solemnly commit myself as Taoiseach and leader of Fianna Fáil to restoring that spirit of partnership and trust.

However, Murphy's Law having come into operation, its corollary, mentioned earlier, also came into play. Fitzsimons had prepared a memorandum on the Duggan case and its implications for Reynolds before he made the speech. He had also prepared a reply should a parliamentary question be raised. But for some reason, possibly the confused, tense atmosphere of the day, although these documents were copied by Reynolds's private secretary, and were passed through several hands, ending up with Bertie Ahern, who sat beside Reynolds while he spoke, they were not shown to the Taoiseach. When he did see them late in the evening, he was incandescent. Fitzsimons was again sent out to Whelehan's house, to say that if the Government fell, the peace process might break down. Whelehan again refused to resign. His view was that his performance as Attorney General had not been wanting.

While the Government was obviously hanging by a thread, some Labour Party members began having second thoughts about precipitating a crisis, and the next day, 16 November, a speech was drafted for Reynolds by Charlie McCreevy, incorporating some Labour suggestions which might have saved the day. They read:

> I now accept that the reservations voiced by the Tanaiste are well founded and I regret the appointment of the former Attorney General as president of the High Court. I also regret my decision to proceed with the appointment against the expressed wishes of the Labour party . . .
>
> I guarantee that this breach of trust, a trust on which the partnership government was founded, will not be repeated.

Readers may remember a scene from the film *Butch Cassidy and the Sundance Kid* in which Paul Newman stuns his opponent with whom he intends having a knife fight by announcing that before the fight they must agree on a set of rules. The opponent's jaw drops, and with it his guard, as he expostulates incredulously: 'Rules! In a *knife* fight . . . ?!' Newman takes advantage of his momentary astonishment to kick him in the testicles and win the fight. With a little rewriting of the *Sundance* incident, with 'trust' substituted for 'knife', and the concept of coalition with Fianna Fáil instead of open combat, the scene might very well serve as a parable for what was to befall. On being given sight of Reynolds's proposed speech, which, it is worth repeating, was drafted by both Fianna Fáil and Labour, Spring agreed to sign a statement saying: 'On the basis of the statement prepared by me being incorporated in the Taoiseach's speech, I will lead my ministerial colleagues back into government to complete the Programme for Government.' By any reckoning, this was a remarkably large slice of humble pie for Albert Reynolds to consume. But it wasn't enough for Dick Spring. Reynolds duly delivered his *mea culpa*, but in return Spring delivered the coalition's *coup de grâce*. He had learned, after concluding the agreement, about the Duggan case being known to Reynolds the previous Monday, and after outlining the Whelehan affair as he saw it, concluded his speech by saying that neither he 'nor any of my colleagues can vote confidence in the government at the conclusion of this debate'.

The following day, 17 November, Reynolds went to relinquish his seal of office to the President. A little later, there was another resignation. Harry Whelehan stepped down as President of the High Court. Had he known about this in advance, Reynolds might have remained in office. However, on 19 November, Bertie Ahern was unanimously elected to succeed him as party leader, amidst a general expectation, from what was known of Labour's thinking, that he would then proceed to form a government with Spring. But on 5 December, press (notably the *Irish Times*) stories made it clear that Ahern, and other members of Fianna Fáil, had known about the Duggan case as far back as 14 November. Spring had pulled out of the knife fight on the grounds that Reynolds had known about the case on that day. How could he now go into the arena again with people who were in possession of that information? The answer was he couldn't, and in the small hours of 6 December (a day of portent in Irish politics; it was also in the small hours of 6 December that the treaty which enabled Ireland to have governments in the first place was originally signed), he phoned Ahern to tell him so.

Reynolds's term in office was fairly summed up by the man himself in his speech to the Dail announcing his resignation. He said:

> I set myself two political objectives, to achieve peace in Northern Ireland and on the whole island, and to turn the economy around. I was fortunate in such a short space of time to achieve those two political objectives . . . I am what I am. I do not pretend to be something that I am not. We all have human feelings. But we have a good sense of values as well . . . I was straight up; I have never hidden anything. Give it as it was; tell it as it is, that is me. That is what I have been and that is what I always will be . . . In life, in business and politics, you cannot win them all. You win some, you lose some, but throughout my life in politics, I have been delighted to be a risk-taker. If you are not a risk-taker, you will not achieve anything.[19]

On 15 December, for the first time in the history of the state, a government was formed without an election being held. It was led by John Bruton of Fine Gael, and Spring retained his old job as Tanaiste, with the assistance of the tiny Democratic Left party, the so-called Rainbow Coalition. On the face of it, the 'Fine Gabour' coalition of left and right, with Democratic Left being particularly to the left, should not have held together. But the old inside and outside factor in politics was borne out again, being very greatly assisted by the two successes alluded to by Reynolds in his valedictory speech: the improvement in the economy, and in the Northern Ireland situation. Either would have been a major plus; taken together the coalition would have almost had to take a deliberate decision to put itself out of power to have lost office before an election was due in 1997. Economic growth averaged 7% per year, inflation stayed around 2.5%. It fell to Bruton's government to introduce the new low corporate tax which heightened Ireland's attraction for investors, and (on 27 February 1997) to give effect to the divorce referendum by bringing in divorce legislation. The Rainbow Coalition also put in train the Strategic Management Initiative which introduced reforms, new management techniques and concepts of productivity to the civil service and the public sector generally.

Yet, though the Celtic Tiger continued roaring lustily for the last few years of the century, it was not a satisfactory era, although it looked like one from the outside. On the world scene, Ireland's image improved, the Celtic Tiger story being added to by the success of her popular musicians, groups like U2, the Corrs, and the musical *Riverdance*. The Irish national soccer team, under an English manager, Jack Charlton, began achieving respect in World Cup competitions. At home, some progress was made in the field of individual rights, along with divorce. An Abortion Information Bill based on the 1992 referendum was passed, as was a Freedom of Information Act, which enabled journalists to tell the public more and more about how they were governed. The old authoritarian society vanished, censorship became a thing of the past, unemployment and emigration looked like doing so also. The streets, the refurbished bars and new restaurants were increasingly filled with confident young Irish people, who either returned to the new jobs, or didn't have to go away in the first place. On skylines everywhere, the symbol of Ireland became not the steeples of the Roman Catholic churches, but the huge cranes working busily on a multitude of building sites. But increasingly, the individual also came to hear a great deal which he or she would have preferred not to know, and which made for a general conviction that there was a two-tier society: that of the man or woman in the street, and that of the charmed business elite which could buy political patronage. The increased prosperity brought in its wake opportunities for increased corruption, and these were availed of enthusiastically.

The setting up of judicial tribunals to enquire into the financial affairs of some of the leaders of the country will be detailed shortly, but there were a whole host of other scandals which helped to spread cynicism and anger throughout Irish society as the millennium approached. These touched, either directly or indirectly, almost every institution of the state. To give but a few instances: the largest Irish banking group, Allied Irish Banks (AIB), was shown to be involved in a number of malpractices involving its customers, the Revenue Commissioners, and political leaders. Deposit Income Retention

Tax (DIRT) was introduced in 1986, because many investors were not declaring interest earned from money on deposit. DIRT enjoined on the financial institutions the deduction of a percentage of interest and the remitting of it to the Revenue Commissioners. However, DIRT did not apply to non-residents with money on deposit in Irish banks. The dogs in the street were aware that the bank colluded in allowing its customers to declare themselves non-resident on a wide scale, but the authorities did not crack down on the scam until 1991, and AIB reported that of 87,000 non-resident accounts, 53,000 of them, to a value of some £600 million, were in fact held by Irish residents. A great number of these people lived in small Irish towns where every detail of their identity would be as well known to the local bank manager as it would be to, say, either the parish priest or the local Garda sergeant. The Department of Finance and the Central Bank took a blind-eye approach to the problem because of the fear of an outflow of capital from the country. It was estimated by a respected commentator, George Lee, RTE's financial expert, that the tax liability on all the hot money known to be lying in Irish banks could be in the region of £10 billion. Of course, nothing remotely like this was ever collected when the governmental blind eye finally lit up.

AIB was merely the worst offender, not the only one. It caught the public's imagination, however, because of its size, its involvement in Charlie Haughey's affairs, and public outrage at the bank's being bailed out earlier by the Government over an ill-fated venture into the insurance world in 1981. AIB had bought the Insurance Company of Ireland (ICI) and discovered in March 1984 that ICI had lost somewhere between £120 and £200 million. The Department of Industry and Commerce was directed to set up a company which acquired ICI, free of charge, from AIB. The state thus acquired ICI's liabilities. The reason given by the Government, led by Garret FitzGerald, was that had AIB gone down, it would have caused a crisis in the banking system. But in the year of the bail-out alone, AIB's profits were £84 million; by the end of the nineties, some ten times that. Thus the accident-prone bank could well have paid for its own bad investments, out of profits. It had to do so, as this was being written, for a much larger loss – revealed in February 2002 – that occasioned by a rogue currency trader, John Rusnak at the AIB's Baltimore-based subsidiary Allfirst, which cost $691 million.

The investigations into Haughey's affairs revealed that Haughey had bullied AIB into giving him extraordinarily lenient treatment. The bank allowed him to continue writing cheques, giving him new cheque-books on demand, even though he had wildly exceeded his credit limit to a point where he eventually owed £1.143 million. Eventually the bank did a deal whereby the debt was settled for £750,000. The remainder of course could be written off as a bad debt, and set against tax liabilities. The bank also wrote off approximately £170,000 owed by another ex-Taoiseach, Garret FitzGerald, who had borrowed money to buy shares in Guinness Peat Aviation, of which he was a director. The share flotation was a disaster and a number of other high-profile investors also lost money. Unlike FitzGerald, however, they had made 'non-recourse' borrowings, which meant that the bank's only redress was against the GPA shares which they had pledged. Needless to say, neither 'non-recourse' loans nor overdraft cancellations were available to ordinary members of the public.

As I have said, AIB was not the only wayward bank. For example, National Irish Bank ran a scam which again was discovered by George Lee and by RTE's special correspondent, Charlie Bird. The two journalists established that National Irish Bank induced customers to invest in something called Clerical Medical Insurance (CMI), which was based in the Isle of Man. The money from the Irish investors went into Manx numbered accounts, and was then channelled back to NIB. The bank thus got commission, and held the money on deposit, but the customer could also draw it when required, out of sight of the tax collector. Bird broke the story on 23 January 1998, and for weeks the station had to battle its way through a minefield of injunctions before the Supreme Court found (on 20 March) that the allegation was 'of serious tax evasion . . . a matter of genuine interest and importance to the general public . . . the general public should be given this information'. In the wake of this verdict, Bird then revealed that NIB had in some cases been over-charging customers, through both increased interest and fees, in order to boost profits. The story caused such shock that the Government called a special Cabinet meeting. The bank was forced to admit publicly that the report was true, although NIB claimed that the practice had long since been discontinued.

NIB interacted with the political system when the Fianna Fáil TD, Beverly Cooper-Flynn, took an action against RTE for saying that she had, in her time as an NIB employee, encouraged bank customers to evade tax. The case was the longest and most costly libel suit in the history of the state, and judgment was given against Cooper-Flynn on 3 April 2001. The opposition forced Ahern to take action against the TD, on the grounds that failure to do so would be to condone tax evasion, and she was duly expelled from the parliamentary party. In 1999, Cooper-Flynn had also been in difficulties with the party, because she refused to vote in favour of an opposition motion censuring her father, Padraig Flynn. Flynn had become involved in controversy over a payment of £50,000 alleged to have been given to him by a London property developer, Tom Gilmartin. He denied Gilmartin's allegations on the country's most popular TV show, *The Late Late Show*, which led to countrywide gossip. It also led to Gilmartin's reacting by offering to substantiate his allegations before a tribunal set up to investigate the system of granting building planning permissions in Dublin. At the time of writing, Mr Gilmartin's evidence has not yet been given.

In addition to banking and tax scandals, there were what the Minister for Defence called the 'wrong and immoral' army deafness claims which erupted in the mid-nineties. By April 1999 these had cost the state some £73 million in compensation and legal charges. They involved 2,977 soldiers who claimed

636

that they had suffered deafness because the army did not provide them with earplugs on firing ranges and so forth. In all some 14,000 soldiers lodged claims. At one stage, the Dail Committee on Public Accounts estimated that the claims could cost the state as much as £5.5 billion. The minister, Michael Smith, blamed 'a greedy minority of solicitors' for what he termed the 'compensation culture' which, he said, was 'a cancer eating at the heart of our society'.

The army was not the only arm of the state's defences to call attention to itself for dubious reasons. As this is being written, members of the Gardai are also under investigation for a variety of alleged misdemeanours. The most startling circumstances are those which ultimately (in November 2002) led to the setting up of a tribunal under Mr Justice Morris to investigate claims which include allegations that members of the force were involved in 'planting' evidence of IRA explosive caches, and, worse, in falsely accusing members of a Donegal family, the McBreartys, of causing the death of a cattle dealer, Ritchie Barron. Indeed, one of the allegations before the tribunal was that Barron had been killed by members of the Garda Siochana itself.

The Church also came badly out of the nineties. As was the case worldwide, a tide of child abuse and other sex scandals washed into public view. In addition, television programmes, such as Louis Lentin's RTE documentary, *Dear Daughters*, shown in 1996, about the treatment of little girls at an orphanage and industrial school, Goldenbridge, run by the Sisters of Mercy at Inchicore, County Dublin, underlined allegations about the harsh regimes in Church-run industrial schools, for both girls and boys, which had been gaining force for some time. The Letterfrack Industrial School in County Galway, run by the Christian Brothers, had a particularly horrific reputation, before it was eventually closed down in 1974, but nothing was ever done about it. It has been established that 100 boys died at the school between 1888 and 1974. The Brothers' statement confirming this fact pointed to 'a level of poverty that could not easily be appreciated in modern Ireland, the Great Flu of 1918 and the prevalence of tuberculosis up to the 1950s'.[20] Both Church and State were culpable in consigning unwanted, or inconvenient, children to such badly funded, draconian institutions where love, or indeed food, was often less plentiful than punishment. This factor, combined with the passage of time, has meant that physical abuse will probably never be accounted for with anything remotely approaching the retribution for sexual abuse, an ironic turn of fate for a church that for so long adjudged the sins of the bedroom as being worse than those of the boardroom, and preached a doctrine of celibacy and repressive sexuality.

Of all the child abuse scandals one could choose, that of Father Ivan Payne probably best exemplifies the combination of authoritarianism, a foetid approach to sexuality, and the deceitful *omertà* that characterised the Irish Church's approach to the problem. In July 1999, the Court of Criminal Appeal decided that Payne should serve a six-year sentence imposed on him the previous year when he pleaded guilty to 13 sample charges of sexual abuse.

Evidence was given that Payne had sexually abused sick children while a chaplain at Our Lady's Hospital for Sick Children in Crumlin, Dublin, and later in Cabra and in Sutton. Following the Church's customary 'pass the parcel' policy in Ireland, as in other countries, he was sent from Cabra to Sutton after he had been examined by a psychiatrist following a complaint by a former altar boy, Andrew Madden, that the priest had sexually abused him. In 1993 Payne received a loan of £27,000 from diocesan funds for a payment to Madden which it was hoped would prevent bad publicity. As sex abuse allegations multiplied, the Archbishop of Dublin, Desmond Connell, stated categorically (in May 1995) in response to an RTE interviewer, Joe Little: 'I have compensated nobody. I have paid out nothing whatever in compensation . . . the finances of the diocese are not in any way used to make settlements of that kind.' We will come back to the role of Dr Connell in a moment. Here it is sufficient to say that, as the facts of the accommodation with Payne became known, other cases of priestly abuse were uncovered, and calls for Dr Connell's resignation were made, casuistry was abandoned, the cardinal made what appeared to be heartfelt statements of apology and inquiries of all sorts were put in hand. However, various incidents occurred which militated against a widespread acceptance by the public that the mood of the Church either in the Dublin archdiocese, or throughout the country, was entirely one of atonement and contrition. For example, several years after the Payne scandal first became known, the RTE programme *Prime Time*, screened in October 2002, detailed some horrific stories – including one about a priest who masturbated on the altar boy who assisted him in his ordination mass – which, amongst other revelations, detailed the activities of a priestly sex ring which abused children in their respective presbyteries on alternate weekends. Writing in the aftermath of the programme's showing, Vincent Browne echoed many people's feelings when he commented:

> The yardstick of the Dublin archdiocese's 'profound regret' for all that has happened is that one of the vilest abusers, Father Frank McCarthy, who operated the sex ring with Fr Kearney, now works in the communications office of the cardinal's establishment, presumably advising on how the fallout from all this should be handled.[21]

An indemnity deal struck between the Government and 18 religious orders (as distinct from diocesan clergy) over sex abuse also aroused national indignation and was pursued vigorously but, to the time of writing, unavailingly by elements in the media and by the Labour Party. In the course of a rancorous debate on the matter, the Taoiseach, Bertie Ahern,[22] confirmed that there were approximately 3,000 possible compensation cases in the files of the Department of Education at the time of the deal, which was finally agreed on 6 June 2002, the day before the Cabinet left office to successfully contest a general election.

The amounts involved in compensation must necessarily be a matter of speculation, but few commentators have placed the final figure as being less than €500 million and some have spoken of possible liabilities of €1 billion and over. What is known is that the Department of Education initially sought a commitment from the religious to pay 50% of all compensation offered to victims, but that this demand was dropped; that the legal staff of the department were not involved[23] in the last 18 months of the protracted negotiations; and that the final settlement package was agreed at €128 million. This sum was not a straightforward cash settlement, but included components such as Church land and properties which had already been handed over to the state for educational purposes. It also included counselling and support services for victims which the Church offered to provide.

The importance of Father Payne to all this lies in the Church's attitude to control and to sex. Acquiring, say, the worldwide franchise for General Motors, McDonald's and the Iraqi oil fields pales into insignificance when compared to the clout the Vatican's allegedly celibate minions secured through assuming control over natural functions such as love, reproduction and marriage, and Catholics' thought processes affecting decisions in these areas. Marriage was Father Payne's especial responsibility. This sexual deviant was a judge in the Dublin Archdiocesan Marriage Tribunal. In this capacity he had the right to cross-examine applicants for marriage annulments on the intimate details of their relationships and to execute Vatican policy in such cases.

'Such cases' can only be understood fully by someone who has read the pathetic, embarrassed letters one is allowed to see in diocesan records. The writers are so human that they seek divorce, so conditioned that they apologise and explain and defend, against their background rearing by antiseptic nuns with scrubbed spatulate fingers, and black-robed priests whom they see as superior and impervious to their turmoil and their sinful lusts. The policy was, and to a large extent still is, to give ground grudgingly on the issue of separation, in the face of the reality of widespread marital breakdown, and growing demands amongst the laity for divorce, but to attempt to prevent remarriage. The device used to accomplish this is known by its Latin name, *veitum*, meaning veto. In relation to the overall problem of marriage breakdown prior to the introduction of divorce in Ireland, the number of people who normally applied for annulments was tiny, averaging below 700 for the first half of the 1980s for example. Of these, fewer than a fifth received decrees of nullity and of this fifth around 75% had a *veitum* attached.[24] In some cases these vetoes were positively insulting. In one annulment, conceded in Father Payne's term of office, the applicant, who had contracted an abusive relationship at 20, was informed, nearing 40, that her immature character rendered her unsuitable to remarry in the future. As the Dublin archdiocesan scandals mounted, this person, an admirable mother who had by then single-handedly established a home for her children and a career, returned her annulment certificate to Cardinal Connell with an appropriate note.

In fairness to the cardinal, it should be said that he too could be regarded as a victim of the system which extends well beyond Ireland's shores. When he was appointed he was past the normal retirement age. He had no pastoral experience, having been a professor of metaphysics at University College Dublin. But he was known as a conservative, an admirer of Pope John Paul and a friend of the Vatican conservative Cardinal Ratzinger. Following his appointment as archbishop, the red hat came, not as traditionally to Armagh, in Northern Ireland, the last place in Europe where Catholics were still literally being martyred for their faith, being murdered by Loyalists for no reason other than their religion, but to Dublin, where a number of time bombs, some of which have been indicated, were ticking away for Connell. The case of once fervent Ireland is a microcosm of the problems facing the Church in the developed world. Status and the lure of education have ensured that for the moment seminaries and churches are filled in Africa and eastern Europe, as they once were in Ireland. But Desmond Connell's troubled stay at the Irish Church helm has certainly proved the argument for those who say that the day is over when the laity are informed out of the blue that they have a new bishop for whom their duty is 100% maintenance and obedience, and their rights 0% say in his selection. The Irish experience has proved that along with the removing of the nomination of bishops from the hands of the Nuncio and the Vatican only, two other reforms are essential: the ordination of women priests and the removal of what is now a fiction for a significant percentage of clergy – clerical celibacy.

To return now from matters clerical to temporal, some might even say profane, by the mid-nineties there were ever-growing rumours about Charlie Haughey's finances. In addition, the Beef Tribunal, which, though it cost €38 million in legal fees, and at the end of the day produced no more significant change, or conclusion, than a higher profile for Liam Hamilton, leading to his subsequent installation as Chief Justice, had added its share of rumour and stories of malpractice to public discourse. The majority of this innuendo was directed at Fianna Fáil. Then, in November of 1996, it was discovered that a Fine Gael minister, Michael Lowry of Tipperary, was involved with the supermarket magnate Ben Dunne in some unorthodox business transactions. As Lowry was a particularly popular politician who had spoken out against what he termed 'cosy cartels' which operated under Fianna Fáil administrations, the revelations were extremely damaging to Fine Gael. Expensive renovations to his house were shown to have been paid for by Dunne, with whom Lowry had dealings through a refrigeration company which he owned. The leaks about the Lowry–Dunne transactions originated with Fianna Fáil, but they were to cause enormous collateral damage to Haughey. If ever there was a case of Murphy's Law setting in, this was it, and on a grand scale.

A link between Dunne, Lowry and Haughey was unearthed after a bizarre incident in Miami back in 1992, in which Ben Dunne figured in an almost stereotypical scandal of the genus Golf-Playing Businessman Away From Home. He took to the balcony of his twelfth-storey hotel room, in which a lady provided by an 'escort service' was installed, and under the influence of cocaine threatened to throw himself off. He was ultimately rescued, prosecuted on drugs charges, and treated lightly by the courts on agreeing to go into rehabilitation, appearing ultimately to have suffered no worse consequences than some family embarrassment and becoming the target of some dubious Dublin wit on the lines of: 'Have you heard the new Dunnes Stores slogan – if you spend enough, you'll get a Coke and an Escort.' However, the Miami incident triggered a ferocious row within the Dunne family, leading to litigation and Dunne's removal from the board of Dunnes Stores. In the course of the litigation, huge payments to Haughey were discovered. These led to a private confrontation between Dunne's sister, Margaret, and Haughey and, ultimately, to the establishment of the McCracken Tribunal to investigate payments to both Haughey and Lowry.

The tribunal discovered that between 1987 and 1991, Ben Dunne gave Haughey more than £1 million through what became known as the Ansbacher accounts scandal. A company called Ansbacher Cayman was set up by Haughey's friend and accountant Des Traynor. This earned interest in the Caymans while at the same time Traynor opened what were known as 'mirror' accounts for depositors in the Dublin private bank Guinness and Mahon, which he ran. Thus the depositors had access to their money in Dublin although it was technically still lodged in the Cayman Islands and therefore tax free. Some of Ireland's wealthiest people availed themselves of this scheme. As a result of the McCracken and other investigations it was established that at least £50 million was involved.

These revelations, the first of many detailing payments to Haughey, could have had a serious political implication if the Rainbow Coalition had remained in office for another few months. But Bruton called an election for 6 June 1997, before the more sensational disclosures to the tribunal were made. Ahern repeatedly declared that 'no matter how eminent the person involved', there was no place in Fianna Fáil for 'senior politicians seeking or receiving from a single donor large sums of money or services in kind'.[25] The electorate accepted that there had been a break with the past, even though the campaign was masterminded by P.J. Mara, the Fianna Fáil director of elections, who, like Ahern himself, had worked closely with Haughey. But Mara, like Ahern, was blessed with an easy-going, humorous personality, which concealed a laser-like political acuity, and a superbly run campaign resulted in Ahern's achieving the role of Taoiseach, which Spring's change of mind had denied him a few years earlier.

Once installed as Taoiseach, Ahern was able to use his position to successfully deflect brickbats thrown at him by the opposition as various matters concerning Haughey continued to force their way into public discussion. For example, when questions were asked in the Dail (10 September 1997) about Haughey's use of party funds, Ahern replied: 'In so far as I could with little available records I am satisfied, having spoken to the person who administered the account, that it was used for bona fide party purposes, that the cheques were prepared by that person and countersigned by another senior party member.'

What Ahern omitted to state in his reply was that he was the 'senior party member' who signed the cheques! Electorally speaking the difference between Reynolds's approach and Ahern's was that Fianna Fáil and the Progressive Democrats fought the election as a coalition. In percentage terms, Fianna Fáil's vote was the lowest since 1927, 39.33%, but because Fianna Fáil received PD transfers, under PR, the party won 6% more seats than votes. Labour took a hammering from those supporters who had objected to Spring's forming a coalition with Reynolds. The party lost almost half its seats, and 9% of the vote. The PDs also dropped from 10 to 4 seats. Fine Gael won 27.95% of the vote, and 54 seats. But the combined Fianna Fáil/PD total was sufficient to form a government with the aid of 3 Independents.

By now, the creation of yet another tribunal was looming. This time the subject was to be corruption in the building industry planning process, and the allegations involved a senior Fianna Fáil figure, Ray Burke, whom Ahern appointed as Minister for Foreign Affairs after conducting an investigation into the rumours without being able to substantiate them to the point of excluding Burke. For a few weeks these rumours remained in the background as Ahern sorted out a constitutional hiccup which occurred through his appointing David Andrews both as Minister of Defence and as a junior minister to Burke, without realising apparently that one minister cannot be another's subordinate. Behind the scenes Ahern, a far more welcome figure as Taoiseach to the Republicans than John Bruton, also helped to reinstate the IRA's ceasefire. (The other factor in bringing this about was the replacement of John Major's Conservative government with Tony Blair's New Labour a month earlier.) But there was to be no ceasefire in the corruption allegations. Instead there was weeping and gnashing of teeth on the opposition benches when, just over a month after the election, the proceedings at the McCracken Tribunal brought it home to the members of the former government that, had they waited a little longer, the revelations about Charlie Haughey would have ensured that they remained in government not opposition.

Haughey's strategy before the tribunal had been to say that Traynor handled all his personal affairs so as to leave him free to pursue matters of state. He knew nothing about borrowings from Dunne and had he known he would have stopped Traynor making them. But on 9 July the former Taoiseach was forced to admit he had received money from Dunne. In one case it was demonstrated that, during a chance visit to Haughey's home, Dunne handed him £200,000 in three separate cheques, because he said he felt Haughey looked a bit depressed. (Understandably, Haughey cheered up markedly thereafter, Dunne said, and pocketing the cheques replied, 'Thanks, Big Fella.') On 15 July Haughey apologised to the tribunal, saying: 'I accept that I have not co-operated with this tribunal in a manner which would have been expected of me.' But Mr Justice McCracken was not mollified. The tribunal's report, published at the end of August, referred the papers in the affair to the Director of Public Prosecutions to consider whether a prosecution could be brought. McCracken's own finding was that:

> The tribunal considers it quite unacceptable that Mr Charles Haughey, or indeed any member of the Oireachtas, should receive personal gifts of this nature, particularly from prominent businessmen within the state. It is even more unacceptable that Mr Charles Haughey's whole lifestyle should be dependent upon such gifts, as would appear to be the case. If such gifts were permissible, the potential for bribery and corruption would be enormous.

The Dáil was recalled on 10 September to debate the McCracken findings. Burke took the opportunity to make a ringing but ultimately unavailing declaration that he had not received improper gifts of money. He admitted to receiving a payment of £30,000 from a building company but claimed that this was for legitimate political expenses, part his own, part Fianna Fáil's. It then emerged that he had also received another sum of £30,000 from Rennick's, a subsidiary of Tony O'Reilly's conglomerate, Fitzwilton. A combination of the opposition before him and the PDs beside him forced Ahern to set up another tribunal headed by Justice Moriarty, to investigate whether Haughey had received money from other sources. Mary Harney, in her capacity as Minister for Industry and Enterprise, also began a separate inquiry into the Ansbacher accounts. A month later, adverse media comment forced Burke to resign. By now he was under extreme pressure, not merely from his foes in politics and the media, but because of the death of his brother. On 7 October, the day of his brother's funeral, Burke took the highly unusual step of resigning not merely his Cabinet, but his Dail seat, thus reducing Fianna Fáil's already slender majority. Burke's action heightened the opposition's demands for an investigation into his affairs and once more Ahern was driven to agree to the setting up of a tribunal, this time under the chairmanship of Mr Justice Fergus Flood, to investigate the question not merely of Burke's role, but of planning permission in County Dublin generally. At the time of writing, the Tribunal is still hearing evidence, but the revelations so far have confirmed the public perception that in Dublin the bribing of county councillors and council officials was routine and that practically no significant planning permissions were obtained without the exchange of brown envelopes filled with varying amounts of cash.

It might appear from all this that the electorate would have seized upon any opportunity to vent its wrath on the Government, but Fianna Fáil now proceeded to win an election, and an important one at that. Mary Robinson stepped down as president on completing her first seven-year term (an Irish president is allowed two) to take up a UN posting. The election for a successor was held on 30 October, and Mary McAleese, the Fianna Fáil nominee, won handsomely. Too handsomely for Dick Spring. The Labour candidate, Adi Roche, a well-respected figure for her work for the Children of Chernobyl campaign, was unable to translate her popularity into the political arena and only came fourth, behind the Fine Gael candidate Mary Banotti and, more damagingly, even the pro-life singer Rosemary Scallon. The defeat coming in the wake of Labour's heavy losses in the general election decided Dick Spring that he ought to step down, thus ensuring that Fianna Fáil benefited on two counts: it won the presidency and saw the back of a formidable Labour opponent. Labour and the other left-wing party, Democratic Left, later acknowledged their weakened position by subsuming DL into Labour under the new leader, Ruari Quinn, a prominent architect who, in his student activist days, had been known as Ho Chi Quinn. His cautious tenure at the Labour helm would demonstrate that this sobriquet belonged to his student, not his political career.

Irish public life presented a depressing picture as the end of the century neared. Pillars of society in every walk of life, the churches, the professions, politics, banking, the police, the army, whatever area one chose, validated Yeats's vision, not of a terrible beauty having been born, but of Paudeen fumbling in a greasy till, that is when he wasn't doing so in his neighbour's pocket. Some people have argued that corruption may 'loom disproportionately large in the minds of Irish commentators', and that therefore it may in turn be 'misjudged by those from abroad'.[26] This sounds suspiciously like a contemporary version of the political establishment's view in my boyhood that Ireland's ills should not be aired publicly because this would be 'letting down the country'. The contemporary argument is buttressed by a sort of league table of international corruption which in 1999 ranked Ireland nineteenth out of 25 countries in a 'corruptions perception index'.[27] Nineteenth is disturbing, but not disastrous, is the message. I, however, submit that it is disastrous, not perhaps by the standards of the popular TV crime series *The Sopranos*, or by international standards, but disastrous by the slippage in a relatively short time of Ireland's own standards. Academic criteria aside, I am driven to record, as someone who has been reporting on Irish affairs for longer than most, that as the early years of the new millennium pass, Ireland *feels* more corrupt and more dangerous than at any time in the twentieth century. And I am not talking about Northern Ireland, though the current political developments there give little ground for optimism.

A fundamental yardstick of any society is the manner in which the taking of human life is regarded. In Ireland, one has to note the growth of an appalling indifference to murder. When I began working as a journalist in 1954, and for more than a decade afterwards, until the news from Northern Ireland began to dim sensibilities, murder was such a rare occurrence that it was not merely a nine-day wonder, it was a 29-day wonder. For weeks after the event there would be follow-up stories, progress reports on the investigation, interviews with neighbours, and so forth, all of which were perused and discussed avidly by readers.

At the end of the century, a murder has to be particularly heinous to force its way on to page 1, or to receive more than a paragraph. Apart from car deaths, the Monday morning radio news bulletins routinely carry a weekend toll of murders, some drink or drugs related, some gangland slayings. Nowadays these rarely create sufficient impact to be deemed worthy of discussion later in supermarket or workplace.

Part of the reason for this is the desensitivisation created by urbanisation and the impact of the electronic media, but part too lies in the explosion of scandals and abuse of public trust indicated above. The answer to questions such as 'What is the Government doing?', 'What are the police doing ?' is so depressing that people are 'switched off'. One of the most worrying features of the 2002 general election was the fact that over half of the under-25 voters did not bother to exercise the right to vote so dearly bought by earlier generations. The economic downturn which has affected the global economy is also doing something to lessen the roar of the Celtic Tiger. There are fears that a peculiarly Irish bubble may burst, the inflated price of housing. The inflation has been such that a house in my area which would have sold for the equivalent of 6,000 euros in the mid-sixties would fetch over 700,000 today. This of course presents extraordinary challenges to the average first-home buyer, and the threat of economic chaos for banks and building societies should prices fall sharply, perhaps after another event like 11 September. But it may well be that the real challenge facing Ireland is not economic, or military, but the development of a decent sense of outrage that will lead not merely to a resuscitation of the Tiger's strength, but to a stifling of toleration for corruption, and a growth in concern for the weak, and an end to the situation wherein the law is indeed like the Ritz Hotel – open to everybody.

After the May 2002 general election had once more returned a Fianna Fáil/Progressive coalition with Ahern and Harney again at the helm as Taoiseach and Tainaiste, Quinn resigned. He was succeeded by the former Democratic Left TD, Pat Rabbitte. Fine Gael too acquired a new leader, Enda Kenny, who had succeeded John Bruton only a short time earlier. Michael Noonan resigned immediately after the election results were announced. In a catastrophic result, the party was left with only three seats in Dublin. The final tally was as follows:

PARTY	SEATS	SEATS LAST ELECTION
Fianna Fáil	81	77
Fine Gael	31	54
Labour	21	21
Democrats	8	4
GreenParty	6	2
Sinn Féin	5	1
Socialist Party	1	1
Others	13	6

Overall Fine Gael had lost 23 of its 54 seats, including those of party stalwarts such as Alan Dukes, Norah Owens, Jim Mitchell and Austin Currie. The meltdown was in part brought about by the party's increasing lack of purpose and identity. It had moved from being a law and order party under Cosgrave;

to being liberal under Garret FitzGerald; to being a mere 'me too' appendage of Fianna Fáil under Alan Dukes; to being an unlikely combination of the party of property and of socialism under John Bruton in coalition with the Democratic Left; and to campaigning on the amorphous issue of 'the quality of life' in the general election under Michael Noonan. Also, it had lost a good deal of the image of differing from Fianna Fáil in being at least a squeaky clean party through the revelations and allegations surrounding the former minister, Michael Lowry. At the time of writing Lowry has yet to appear before the Moriarty Tribunal which, amongst other matters, is expected to investigate the decision by Lowry's department to award a mobile phone licence to a company headed by the Irish businessman Denis O'Brien. Fears have been expressed in the media that, should anything improper come to light, some of the international communication giants which made unsuccessful bids for the licence might sue the state. The costs could run into hundreds of millions of euros. A combination of all these factors, combined with personality issues, had led to the vote of 'no confidence' in John Bruton which had caused him to step down as leader on 1 February 2001, being succeeded by Michael Noonan.

As the election results painfully demonstrated, there was not a great deal of public confidence in Michael Noonan either. This was largely because of the hard-line attitude he adopted as Minister for Health in defending the state's handling of the most heartbreaking scandals to come before any of the tribunals, those concerning the use of infected blood by the state agency, the Blood Transfusion Service Board (BTSB). In all some 1,600 people, men and women, but mostly mothers, were infected to a greater or lesser degree. The greatest public attention during the 'Hepatitis C scandal', as it became known, centred on the tragic and disgracefully handled case of a Donegal woman, Brigid McCole, a mother of 12, who died on 2 October 1996 of liver failure after months of agony during which, her children recalled, they lay awake listening to her scream in pain. Here it should be noted that an expert group, set up under Dr Miriam Hederman O'Brien in February 1994 to investigate the scandal after it became public knowledge in February 1991, had reported in April of 1995 criticising the BTSB's handling of the entire affair. Although the expert group was not given all the information which later became available, it became obvious that some Government reaction was called for.

Campaigners on behalf of sufferers like Brigid McCole, principally the Positive Action Group, wanted the Government to admit liability and set up a statutory body to deal with both compensation and health care issues. However, Noonan rejected this and instead set up a compensation tribunal, which came into operation in March 1996, after much controversy. The tribunal was empowered to pay compensation on an *ex gratia* basis, without admission of liability or apology, and claimants were given a month to accept an award – if one were granted. In the event the tribunal awarded £250,000 to claimants on its first day of hearing.

Brigid McCole, however, courageously decided to take her case to the courts. On 20 September, shortly before she died, lawyers for the BTSB wrote a letter to her which has passed into infamy. For the first time since 1977, when she received the fatal injection, the BTSB admitted liability and apologised, but denied liability for aggravated or exemplary damages. A sum of £175,000 had been lodged in court. If the dying woman wished to improve on this offer, she would have to pursue her case in the High Court. Should she lose, she would be responsible for the huge costs involved. On the threshold of death, desperate to leave something behind for her children, Brigid McCole accepted the BTSB offer.

In the Dail Noonan denied that he had been shown the letter before it was sent, saying that Fidelma Macken, a lawyer appointed by the state to enquire into the Government's legal strategy in the case, had made 'no such allegation'.[28] In fact Macken's report states that: 'The Department of Health was informed shortly prior to September 20th, 1996 that the letter was to be sent and given sight of it for observation.' A departmental memo of the time advises that the letter be sent 'unless the Minister disagrees'.[29] The issue of whether or not this important letter, the first admission of liability by the BTSB, was shown to Noonan before being sent is obviously a matter of debate. It is also undeniable that, as Macken pointed out, Noonan did not have control over the BTSB's activities.

However, Noonan brought the fires of controversy on his head during a Dail debate on the setting up of a tribunal of inquiry, which was announced on 15 October 1996. Speaking of the Brigid McCole case he asked: 'Could her solicitors not, in seeking a test case from the hundreds of hepatitis C cases on their books, have selected a plaintiff in a better condition to sustain the stress of a High Court case? Was it in the interest of their client to attempt to run her case, not only in the High Court but also in the media and in the Dail simultaneously?'[30]

Noonan subsequently apologised for this statement and the tribunal of inquiry went ahead under Judge Thomas Finlay the following month. It reported thoroughly, expeditiously and damningly the following March. Finlay severely criticised individual members of the BTSB. He also found that the response to the discovery by the BTSB that some of the products it was using were contaminated was 'inadequate and non-existent'. He spoke of 'failures' and 'wrongful acts'. One of the small handful of executives who retired after the tribunal's findings were made known received a golden handshake, on top of his pension, of £440,000, approximately two and half times the sum offered to Brigid McCole. However, the hepatitis C scandal became a defining moment for Irish women, heightening consciousness, producing a fine book, *Blood, Sweat and Tears*, by Glenys Spray, and seriously affecting the political fortunes of both Michael Noonan and Fine Gael.

At the time of writing the wounds inflicted by the blood scandals still fester. A section of the victims, the haemophiliacs, had walked away from the workings of the Finlay Tribunal, claiming that its terms of reference did not meet their particular concerns. Their ensuing campaign resulted in the Government's setting up yet another tribunal in 1999, this time headed by the Circuit Court Judge Alison Lindsay. By the time Lindsay reported (on 5 September 2002) it was estimated that 79 haemophiliacs had already died from being infected with the HIV and hepatitis C viruses. The tribunal found that, at a 'minimum figure', 252 haemophiliacs had contracted one or other of the viruses while receiving treatment from the BTSB. It also found that there were delays in informing victims about their condition. The results of tests for HIV on some patients taken in 1985 were not communicated to them until 1987. The tribunal found that it was 'most unfortunate' that a senior figure at the National Haemophiliac Treatment Centre, who had received the results of tests from England in March and April of 1985, had taken a sabbatical from May to October without putting in place a system for informing patients of their results.

Lindsay was critical of the 'serious failure' on the part of those concerned to act swiftly to withdraw the contaminated blood products. She also found that medical record keeping was 'unsatisfactory and incomplete' and that the treatment of haemophiliacs by doctors and hospitals was 'somewhat haphazard'. However, she turned down a request from the Irish Haemophilia Society that she formally submit a copy of her report to the Director of Public Prosecutions. The HIS remained unhappy at the fact that the role of the pharmaceutical companies in the whole affair has not yet been thoroughly explored, and it is conceivable that a further inquiry may yet be held. Prosecutions against former BTSB staff have been begun by the Government.

TWELVE

THE PEACE PROCESS

As what might be termed the 'peace process' era dawned, the Northern Ireland stage was dominated by a set of principal players: the British, the Unionists, the Republicans and, largely off-stage but willing, should the opportunity arise, to play a starring role, the Dublin Government. Also off-stage, if anything more eager to help, the Irish-Americans waited to be given a role, but their talents were largely ignored by both Dublin and London. A corollary to this last situation was that decision-taking Washington also waited in the wings for its cue. The unlikely impresario who brought all these actors together in a drama which for a time enjoyed a highly acclaimed reception was a low-sized, low-voiced, and seemingly exhausted Redemptorist priest, Father Alec Reid, who operated from the Clonard Monastery off the Falls Road, an institution of great religious and cultural significance in the life of Catholic Belfast.

Father Reid had played an active role in attempting to avert the hunger strikes, and in carrying out pastoral duties which involved him in every sort of activity, ranging from prison visitation to interceding with the authorities on behalf of people caught up in the Troubles, to comforting the victims of violence. In the course of his sojourn at the monastery, Reid had come to know and respect Gerry Adams, who attended mass there. Adams reciprocated his friendship, and when, in 1982, Reid, who had returned to Belfast following a lengthy absence occasioned by a breakdown caused by the strain of the Troubles, approached Adams with a view to seeing what might be done to end the violence, Adams was prepared to co-operate with him. At the time, Adams had been seeking to engage the Church in a dialogue on what he termed 'an alternative to the armed struggle'. The dialogue might be said to have begun with the Pope's visit to Ireland during which, as we have seen earlier, he issued a condemnation of violence, but also told politicians that it was their responsibility to indicate 'a peaceful, political way to justice. You must show that peace achieves the work of justice.'

Adams had taken up this theme with Bishop Cathal Daly, following denunciations of IRA violence by the bishop, not knowing that Daly in fact was the author of the Pope's speech. In the course of an attempt to conduct a debate with the bishop, Adams had stated publicly:

You call on Republicans to renounce violence and join in the peaceful struggle for the rights of Nationalists. What peaceful struggle? . . . those who express moral condemnation of the tactic of armed struggle have a responsibility to spell out an alternative course by which Irish Independence can be secured . . . I, for one, would be pleased to consider such an alternative . . . I know that many of my constituents, who are also lay people in your diocese, would be equally anxious to have such a strategy – that is an alternative to the arms struggle – outlined for them.

Reid referred these questions to the Redemptorists' outstanding theologian, Seán O'Riordain. He wanted to know whether they were valid queries to be addressed to a churchman by someone in Adams's position. At the time Reid had been particularly moved by the murder of a UDR man by the IRA in South Armagh, and despite his weakened health was resolved to make an effort to bring such killings to an end. But first he wanted theologically to fireproof himself with the Church authorities. O'Riordain thought that Adams's questions were valid, and that for the good of all the people involved, of whatever race or religion, the Church, despite its abhorrence of IRA violence, should become involved in trying to bring hostilities to an end. Buttressed by both O'Riordain's reply and his knowledge of Adams's character, Reid began an extraordinary campaign of underground diplomacy, in which he contacted decision-takers in the Church, London and Dublin without any word of his activities leaking out.

Simultaneously, it might be remarked, Adams was conducting an even more remarkable secret campaign within the IRA and Sinn Féin. It is quite possible that had it become known in the early eighties that he was attempting to steer the IRA towards a political path, some of his colleagues of the time would have had him shot. But he and a group of associates which included Martin McGuinness, Tom Hartley, Jim Gibney, Pat Doherty and Danny Morrison, pursued a serpentine path through the labyrinth of IRA politics which eventually saw the movement publicly recognising the logic of the electoral success achieved during the hunger strikes by dropping the abstention policy, and agreeing to favour the political over the military option. The result would be the IRA ceasefire of 31 Ausust 1994. It was achieved by an extraordinary high-wire combination of manipulation, patience, steadfastness and political guile, during which the Adams–Reid initiative gradually took root within the Republican movement, and eventually spread out to involve all the other principal actors in the drama. While Adams and his allies within the movement were arranging for secret meetings which went against them to be rescheduled, but attended by a majority in favour of their policies the second time around, while at the same time denying that anything other than an intensification of the war effort was envisaged, Reid was extending his outreach to Dublin and London. Again, it should be stressed that while he was acting on behalf of Adams, Adams was acting without the knowledge of the IRA's ruling Army Council.

A crucial year in the peace process story was 1986, the year in which both London and Dublin were each brought into the picture in a meaningful way and Adams both tightened his hold on the Republican movement and received sanction for a crucial element of his policy, the abandonment of the principle of abstention. Taking London first, most commentators date the turning point in British attitudes to the coming to Belfast of Peter Brooke as Secretary of State for Northern Ireland in 1989. Brooke ended his first hundred days in office by giving a celebrated interview in November 1989 in which he said: 'There has to be a possibility that at some stage debate might start within the terrorist community.' Should such a moment occur, Brooke said, he thought 'the Government would need to be imaginative in those circumstances as to how the process might be managed'. By that time, in fact, the debate had started. After Reid had succeeded in establishing contact with British officials, Tom King, Brooke's predecessor, had received a letter from Adams, to which the British had replied, reassuring Adams on a number of points. Firstly, although the IRA believed otherwise, Britain had no long-term interests in Northern Ireland; she would not object to any settlement arrived at peacefully and by consent; and if the IRA declared a ceasefire, Britain would raise no obstacle to Sinn Féin taking part in the settlement. Brooke gave public form to these assurances during November 1990 when, speaking in his own Westminster constituency, he said:

> The British government has no selfish, strategic or economic interests in Northern Ireland, our role is to help, enable and encourage. Britain's purpose, as I have sought to describe it, is not to occupy, oppress or exploit, but to ensure democratic debate and free democratic choice.

As this speech had been sent to the Republicans beforehand as evidence of British good intent, the words had a certain impact on Adams and his close associates, and on the wider Republican family.

They would probably have had an even greater impact if it had been realised at the time that Reid and Adams had also opened up a dialogue with Charles J. Haughey in Dublin. Reid had received encouragement in his efforts from Cardinal Thomas O'Fiaich, the Irish cardinal, who agreed to meet Adams privately. But he had drawn a blank with Dublin. It is difficult at this stage to recapture the attitude towards not only republicanism but nationalism and the Nationalist tradition which obtained in Irish decision-taking circles in 1986. Not merely politicians, but academia and the media could fairly be described as sharing the 'Dublin 4' mind-set. Dublin 4 is the postal district in which University College Dublin, RTE, and most of Dublin's embassies are situated. At the time, Garret FitzGerald's government was believed by the IRA to be engaged in secret discussions with the British on the possibility of introducing internment again, but this time on both sides of the border. FitzGerald had successfully concluded the Anglo-Irish Agreement, and he had had the dubious pleasure of being lectured by Margaret Thatcher on law and order when he raised with her the activities of the RUC Special Branch during 'interrogation' sessions at Castlereagh Barracks.

But while he was fully aware of the limitations of British policy in the Six Counties, by personal conviction and ancestral inheritance – his father had been a member of the Cumann na nGaedheal Government which ruthlessly crushed the IRA in the civil war; his mother was a north of Ireland Presbyterian – FitzGerald so loathed the IRA that the possibility of opening up a dialogue with the organisation would have been anathema to him. The attitude, though understandable, did not address the question as to how the IRA might be persuaded to abandon violence, if no one attempted to negotiate with them. However, at the time, the media in the south would have found very little to argue with in FitzGerald's position. The Section 31 mentality had ensured that although not officially applied to the newspapers, it had a *de facto* existence in the print media also. The media consensus was that talking to the IRA was akin to attempting a dialogue with the Mafia. Most political comment was of a Dail lobby correspondent nature rather than 32-county analysis, never mind Dublin/London/Washington analysis. While it might be harsh, the comment of a Nationalist friend of mine from Belfast, a supporter of the SDLP, had a certain validity: Dublin journalists, he said, could not have 'found their way up the Falls Road or down the Shankill with seeing-eye dogs'. Interest in the northern situation was low, far more people marched on a single day of the tax protests in late 1979 than appeared to demonstrate against violence in the Six Counties. Where universities were concerned, the word 'revisionism' had come to mean not the revising of facts or opinions in the light of new research, but an attempt to revise the interpretation of history in the light of contemporary politics. In a word, to so 'cleanse the culture' of Nationalist memory that it would not have surprised me to find the great famine being described not as a famine, but as a nineteenth-century precursor of the Scarsdale Diet. What all this boiled down to was a very limited set of options for political contact in the Republic.

As the leader of the more Nationalist of the two major political parties, Charles Haughey was the favoured and most obvious target for Alec Reid to contact; a direct approach by Adams was out of the question. However, efforts to get in touch with Haughey foundered. The radical priest Desmond Wilson, stationed in Ballymurphy, Adams's home turf, drew a blank in his approaches to his cousin, John Wilson, a former Fianna Fáil minister. Father Reid and I had been friends since the early days of the Troubles, and he eventually approached me to say that he thought that an opportunity existed whereby not only could the cycle of violence and death be broken, but even the achievement of Irish unity was possible. As a fighting friend for many years of Haughey's – the course of true love between journalist and politician does not, and should not, run smooth – I had no qualms about telling him about the new thinking in Republican circles. I had also known Adams for a long time and found him an impressive man.

Various accounts of the approach to Haughey have appeared in which I am supposed to have brought him a message from the IRA. I did not. At that stage, the IRA knew nothing about the meeting, and it is doubtful that the Army Council would have approved the object of the exercise had they been informed. All I ever brought with me was a letter of authorisation from Adams, which I had asked for through Father Reid in order to convince Haughey that I was not acting off my own bat. The letter simply said that I could be trusted, that I sought a meeting with Haughey, and, by way of meeting my request that some indication of the new thinking that Father Reid had spoken about be given, it indicated that talk of peace could become otiose if internment was introduced north and south. The nub of what Father Reid had told me was that Republicans were prepared to accept a negotiated settlement, involving the Unionists, which acknowledged the right of the Irish people to self-determination, and which was not dictated by the British. Immediate British military withdrawal was not sought, but political withdrawal was. Later, as matters developed, the Reid/Adams proposals expanded to include ideas such as the creation of a 'Pan Nationalist front' as it was dubbed by the talks' principal enemy, Ian Paisley. By this was meant that the Nationalists in the north, the Dublin Government, and the Irish in America should come together to develop a peace process. Other ideas which Adams put forward included putting the Government of Ireland Act 1920, which had created partition, on the table for negotiation, and by way of furthering the self-determination principle, the holding of simultaneous referenda, north and south, on the future of the Six Counties. These ideas differed very greatly from the simplistic 'Brits out' approach of traditional IRA dogma, in which the object of the struggle was sovereignty. Even at the time of writing, the fault which many Republicans find with the peace process, even though they are prepared to go along with it, is that as far as they were concerned, the struggle was not about human rights, or semantic discussions about self-determination, but about denying Britain's right to be involved in Irish affairs. Sovereignty was the key issue.

However, it was obvious that if a settlement could be achieved on the lines Father Reid outlined, then partitions of mistrust coming down would inevitably lead to Partition itself going, if for no other reason than the fact that if Nationalists were no longer driven into emigration, unemployment and political impotence, the Catholic birth rate, the pill notwithstanding, would inevitably, and rapidly, bring about political change. Accordingly, at a lunch in the Berkeley Court Hotel in October of 1986, I informed Haughey that new thinking in the IRA offered, in Father Reid's estimation, the possibility of achieving Irish unity. This thought appealed mightily to Haughey, who termed it a 'glittering prospect, if it could be had'. The 'if' was a big one. Adams wanted to meet Haughey directly, but Haughey fought shy of this in view of the climate of the time, and his own Arms Trial baggage. However, he did indicate a willingness to keep the opportunity for dialogue alive.

I thought it might die a death when Adams denounced Haughey and his government at the funeral of Jim Lynagh, who, with seven members of his active service unit, was ambushed by a British military unit which included members of the SAS, the RUC and the regular army, at Loughgall, County Armagh (the village where the Orange Order was founded), on 8 May 1987. Haughey was bracketed with FitzGerald as belonging to 'the Shoneen clan', in other words, a lackey of Britain's. A lunch I had with Haughey following this was not the most light-hearted of affairs. Not unreasonably, Haughey said that Adams's onslaught 'did not add up' with what I was telling him. But, all credit to him, he did agree with the object of the lunch, to get him to meet Father Reid, from whom I had brought a lengthy document outlining the new Republican thinking. The only stipulation he made was that Father Reid would find out for him the details of how Lynagh and so many of his colleagues came to be killed, and not long afterwards I introduced him to Father Reid at his home in Kinsealy, County Dublin. Haughey listened with interest to the story of the ambush, and how the SAS were believed to have placed the survivors face downwards and then shot them. The IRA apparently accepted this as 'fair enough'. They would probably have done the same themselves had they been in a similar situation.

By now Haughey had become Taoiseach again, and a meeting with Adams was further off than ever. But he did set up a channel of communication between his trusted adviser Martin Mansergh, the Government's expert on Northern Ireland, and Father Reid, which was to continue even after Haughey had left office. In addition, Haughey furthered what became known as the Hume–Adams dialogue. This again was initiated by Father Reid, who had worked on Hume as he was setting up the Haughey link to get him to meet Adams. Hume had been reluctant initially because a couple of years earlier an effort by him to open up a dialogue with the IRA had broken down when he discovered that the IRA intended to video the discussions. However, Haughey, having decided that he could not be discovered talking to Adams, in effect appointed Hume as his surrogate. Adams would have preferred direct contact with Haughey, but in the circumstances he and Hume commenced a dialogue, at the Clonard Monastery in January of 1988, which ultimately produced the Good Friday Agreement, ten years later. Throughout the talks, Hume, who at the time was probably the single most respected political figure in Ireland, found himself in the unfamiliar situation of being attacked both by the 'Dublin 4' circles mentioned above, whose attitudes were articulated with particular virulence in the *Sunday Independent*, and by elements within his own party who objected to the effect of his prestige rubbing off on Sinn Féin, with harmful consequences to the SDLP vote. In addition, the Hume–Adams dialogue was greeted with predictable outrage by the Unionists. But the talks, which broadened to include members of Sinn Féin and the SDLP in face-to-face discussions, continued throughout 1988 with Haughey, Mansergh and Father Reid hovering discreetly in the background.

Further talks took place at the periphery of a conference organised by German and Irish clergy in the German town of Duisburg, in October of 1988. Those present at the conference included Paisley's deputy, Peter Robinson, representatives of the Ulster Unionist Party, the SDLP and the Alliance Party, and Father Reid, who was understood to be there in his capacity as an expert on the views of Sinn Féin. Possibly with at least one eye on fireproofing himself against the discovery that his deputy had been allowed to sit in a room with someone known to be a carrier of the Sinn Féin contagion, Paisley prefaced the Duisburg Conference by getting himself thrown out of a meeting of the European Parliament addressed by the Pope three days earlier for brandishing a placard inscribed 'John Paul II, Anti-Christ'. How he would have described the Pope had he known that it was a speech of his which in a very real sense had led to Robinson's attending Duisburg, we can only speculate.

None of the foregoing discussion and political activity produced the result sought by most of the participants in the contacts generated throughout 1986 – an IRA ceasefire. There was a very good reason for this. Firstly, Adams was acutely conscious that he, Martin McGuinness and some of those he relied upon most directly would not have enjoyed their ascendancy within the Republican movement had it not been for the ceasefire of 1976, which had given the term a bad name in IRA circles. Secondly, the IRA Army Council, or most of it, was unaware of the real thrust of Adams's policy, or of Haughey's background presence, which had also been kept secret from the SDLP. However, 1986 was an important year for Adams within the Republican community. Firstly, he succeeded in getting an IRA convention, a very difficult gathering to arrange, given the exigencies of the underground movement, to back a proposal that abstention should be ended. He succeeded in convincing the gathering that the military campaign would be assisted, not hampered, by the new political development, because, as it would make for an increase in the representation in the south, the IRA would be strengthened. He was bolstered by the fact that in October, shortly after the convention was held, large consignments of Libyan weapons had been smuggled into the country. He also secured the convention's continued support for Standing Order No. 8, which forbade attacks on the Republic's army and Gardai, a reassuring signal for Haughey.

Adams publicly continued his successful campaign to get on to a political course at the Sinn Féin Ard Fheis a month later, on 2 November. He succeeded in winning a two-thirds majority of the 628 delegates for a motion to allow Sinn Féin candidates to take their seats in Dail Eireann if elected. Martin McGuinness helped to sway doubters with a ringing declaration that though Republicans might enter Leinster House, 'the war against British Rule must continue until freedom is achieved'. Prior to the holding of the Ard Fheis, the number of delegates had mysteriously mushroomed to the 628 total from only 350 at the previous year's conference, at which the abstention policy had been defeated. New Sinn Féin branches had been formed, all sympathetic to Adams. Adams's position had been further strengthened in the previous two years because two prominent Republicans who might have been powerful enough to overthrow him were sidelined. One was Kevin Mallon, a member of the Army Council, who would have been closer in outlook to his old comrades, Daithi O'Conaill, and Ruairi O'Bradaigh, than to Gerry Adams. The other was Ivor Bell, a key Belfast leader. Mallon fell from favour in the wake of controversies stemming from the kidnapping of the supermarket tycoon Don Tidey, and the stealing of the racehorse Shergar. Bell was marginalised after he mounted an unsuccessful leadership campaign against Adams.[1]

The foregoing developments within Sinn Féin give but a small taste of the complexities and dangers attendant upon the Adam–Reid initiative. For along with conducting secret negotiations both within the Republican community and with the SDLP and Haughey, Adams was also conducting *sub rosa* talks with the British, without the knowledge of the Army Council. In response to correspondence from Adams to Tom King, the then Secretary of State for Northern Ireland had given Adams the assurance, later made public by Brooke, that:

> In the second half of the 20th century no matter what has been the position in the past the British government has no political, military, strategic, or economic interest in staying in Ireland or in the exercise of authority there that could transcend respect for the wishes of the majority in Northern Ireland.[2]

However, it is not possible to point to any very startling breakthrough in the search for peace as a result of all the hugger-mugger which took place between Sinn Féin, London and Dublin for over five years from 1986 onwards. When change did come, it did so as much as a result of new personalities stepping on to the stage, as because of underground diplomacy. There were a number of reasons for this. King became enraged when a group of Republicans were arrested apparently targeting him and his family home, and broke off contact.[3] Brooke attempted to get things moving after succeeding King, but he had to contend with two factors which weighed heavily against engaging with Sinn Féin. One was the mind and personality of Margaret Thatcher, the other the outright hatred felt by many Unionists at the prospect of engaging in talks with what they regarded as a set of rebels as treacherous as they were murderous. Brooke's public statements on Sinn Féin contact, in particular his 'no selfish interests' speech, had created a red alert in the ranks of unionism, and the Orangemen seized the opportunity to call for, and get, his resignation after he appeared on RTE's *Late Late Show*, singing his party piece, 'My Darling Clementine', on the night that the IRA had blown up a van containing Protestant workmen at Trebane, County Fermanagh, on 17 January 1992. The incident illustrates the lack of empathy between north and south, and vice versa. No one connected with *The Late Late Show* linked the day's explosion, which was seen as just another northern horror story, with Brooke's position, and in the chatty, convivial atmosphere of the Dublin studio audience, Brooke, at the end of a pleasant appearance, when called upon to sing a song, agreed to do so. He departed the Cabinet on

9 April 1992, after the Tories had won the general election, but with a slim majority which left John Major, who had succeeded Thatcher in November of 1990, dependent on Unionist support when confronted by Eurosceptics within his own party.

John Major had intended to replace Brooke with Chris Patten, who had already had experience of working as a junior minister in Belfast, and who would have liked the job; instead it went to Sir Patrick Mayhew, whom Nationalists disliked because of his refusal during his period as Attorney General to prosecute RUC personnel who had been accused of involvement in shoot-to-kill policies. Mayhew, who had County Cork Anglo-Irish ancestors in his lineage, also wanted the job, and got it because he had given Major his first political promotion, as his parliamentary private secretary. In Dublin, contact with Sinn Féin continued at the level of officials. Little would have come of this, however, had not Albert Reynolds become Taoiseach after Haughey had been forced out of office. The conventional wisdom is that Haughey's background presence helped to nurture the early days of the peace process. But it is difficult to point to much of substance to show for his efforts from 1986 onwards. It is equally difficult to see what might have been accomplished given Margaret Thatcher's attitudes, and the whiff of sulphur surrounding Haughey from the days of the Arms Trial. Thatcher's views had been hardened by Republican activities such as the murder of her friend Airey Neave, and the attempt on her own life in the bombing of the Grand Hotel in Brighton. For their part, the IRA so detested Thatcher for her inflexibility during the hunger strikes that, even if matters had progressed to the point where formal negotiations involving Sinn Féin could have taken place, the possibility of a ceasefire being declared was virtually nonexistent. But a new British prime minister created new possibilities, and in addition, a new permanent secretary, John Chilcott, was appointed to take charge of the Northern Ireland Office.

Both John Hume and the Dublin bureaucracy found Chilcott intelligent, unencumbered by ideological baggage and willing to engage in the peace process. However – and this is an important point concerning the political aspic in which official British attitudes towards Ireland are concerned – Chilcott's other, and more important, role was that of Permanent Secretary to the Ministry of Defence. Indication has been given earlier of the difficulties Dublin officials encountered in dealing with London when on the face of things it would have appeared that both sides had a common interest in improving the Northern Irish situation. However, I have found privately that the oft-repeated public fulminations of Gerry Adams concerning the influence of what he and other Sinn Féin spokespersons term 'Securocrats' are replicated privately by senior Dublin officials and politicians, who frequently found that the advice given to London decision-takers by security sources did not, and at the time of writing very definitely does not, represent the reality on the ground. The influence of MI5 is frequently cited as being harmful. Another important factor is the ancestral effect of the Anglo-Irish tradition in the British army referred to in Chapter 1. To this day,[4] the Irish civil servants stationed in Belfast as a result of the various agreements concluded during the peace process remark in their reports on the difference in attitudes displayed by the army towards crowd dispersal in riots or potential riot situations on the Orange and Green sides of the interface. The general approach to potential Orange troublemakers is an attempt at reasoning and shepherding them off the streets. On the Catholic side, the approach is invariably one of baton and boot and getting the retaliation in first. Such approaches and attitudes could not and should not be attributed to a figure like Chilcott, but structurally, the fact that the top civil service post in Northern Ireland is regarded as coming under the Ministry of Defence speaks volumes for the manner in which the north is viewed strategically from London. Another factor which has to be borne in mind is the degree to which control and direction of the security forces varies between Labour and Tory administrations. It is a matter of record that huge attitudinal differences existed at crucial moments between the political arm in London and the military on the ground in Belfast, most notably in the latitude extended by the Tories to the army in the first flush of Conservative success in July 1970, and in the complete failure of the army under Labour to uphold the Sunningdale Agreement in 1974. Less chronicled, and less obvious divergences also took place throughout what might be termed the peace process era.

Prior to the coming of Chilcott, British officials had had underground contact with Sinn Féin, back in the days of the Cheyne Walk talks for which Adams had been released in 1972, during the 1976 ceasefire era, and again during the hunger strikes, when the MI6 officer Michael Oatley, who would later be referred to as Mountain Climber in the negotiations which preceded the IRA ceasefire of 1994, dealt with the IRA through the Redemptorist priest Father Brendan Meagher, known to the IRA as An Sagairt Maith, the Good Priest. Other important civil servants who had contact with the IRA through figures like Father Alec Reid were Ian Burns, who, when Tom King was Secretary of State for Northern Ireland, was the Deputy Under-Secretary of State at the Northern Ireland Office, and Mark Elliott, who was in charge of the British team which liaised with the Irish Secretariat set up after the 1985 Anglo-Irish Agreement. An important institution for British intelligence in the years before 1990 was Laneside, in Holywood, East Belfast, where a number of British military establishments are located. Figures like Elliott and Oatley met discreetly with both IRA and Unionist leaders at Laneside, which passed into Belfast folklore as a centre of intrigue and hospitality. Ultimately both MI5 and MI6 were located over the shop – in offices at Stormont – and Laneside closed down. Working with Chilcott were Sir Robin Butler, the British Cabinet Secretary, and Quentin Thomas, Chilcott's deputy.

In the wake of Thatcher's departure, Haughey decided to see what could be done to take advantage of the new arrivals in Whitehall. Martin Mansergh continued as his northern adviser. In addition, Haughey brought in his Cabinet Secretary, Dermot Nally, one of the Republic's most experienced and respected civil servants, and two of the Department of Foreign Affairs' top diplomats, Noel Dorr, who served as Irish Ambassador to the Court of St James and as Ireland's representative at the UN during the Argentine crisis, and Seán O'hUiginn, head of the Anglo-Irish division, to deal with the northern situation. There was not a great deal of substance to deal with. Brooke tried to get something going by increasing the amount of devolution available in the north, but the Unionists wanted more integration with London. Moreover, the Unionists only wished to enter talks on the basis of Sinn Féin's being excluded and the Anglo-Irish Agreement being suspended. The phrase 'talks about talks' echoed through the corridors of power in Dublin, Belfast and London. What was known as the 'three-stranded approach' emerged. This involved linkages between north and south, between Belfast, Dublin and London, and between the parties in Northern Ireland. There were internal talks amongst the northern parties involving the major Unionist groupings, the Alliance Party and the SDLP. There was also contact between Dublin and London, and between Belfast and Dublin, which Paisley boycotted but which Molyneaux supported. In fact, the 'three-stranded approach' should have been termed the 'four-stranded approach' because, unknown to the Unionists, at the same time Brooke continued with the secret Sinn Féin contacts.

In the event, all the talking culminated in a seven-week suspension of the Anglo-Irish Agreement and a series of meetings in Belfast which began on 17 June 1991 without Sinn Féin. These ended inconclusively on 3 July, being brought to a halt so as not to adversely affect Unionist blood pressure during the marching season, another indication of what is considered normal behaviour in the Six Counties. Rational political dialogue is accepted as being out of order during the annual outburst of controlled dementia sponsored by the Orange Order. Possibly unjustly, some Nationalists considered that the primary purpose of the talks had been to create an impression of a movement towards peace in Belfast aimed at preventing the Northern Ireland issue being raised during the American presidential campaign.

John Major came to Dublin at the end of the year, and he and Haughey held their first 'summit' in December, but little came of this before Reynolds replaced Haughey as Taoiseach. The conventional wisdom is that by this stage the peace process was well embedded, and that first Haughey and then Hume briefed Reynolds so that he became enthused at what was happening, and decided to run with the process. But in reality little serious political contact had occurred between Fianna Fáil and Sinn Féin prior to Haughey's departure. There were a couple of meetings involving Brian Lenihan and Dermot Ahern, who at the time was a junior minister, during 1988 at the Redemptorist monastery in Dundalk, but little of substance emerged, although Mansergh–Reid contact continued. However, Haughey steadfastly refused to meet Adams, although urged to do so by Cardinal O'Fiaich, who offered the facilities of the huge, sprawling seminary/university complex at Maynooth for the purpose. The different entrances to the colleges would have enabled several football teams to come and go unobserved, but weighed down by his Arms Trial baggage, Haughey turned down O'Fiaich's offer. For a long time, Hume was the only Irish politician of stature to openly engage with Sinn Féin, even though he attracted considerable criticism by so doing. O'Fiaich finally decided to inject momentum into the process by meeting publicly with Adams, but shortly afterwards he was struck down by a heart attack and died in Lourdes on 8 May 1990.

Where Reynolds was concerned, the record shows that on the day he became leader of Fianna Fáil, before being appointed Taoiseach a few days later, and before being briefed by anybody, he announced his intention to become involved in peacemaking, and that privately, on being appointed Taoiseach, he informed his colleagues that the north would be his main priority and that if this meant his tenure of office was to be of short duration, then so be it. Both Haughey and Hume did see him after his installation as Taoiseach, but he did not find their insights particularly earth-shattering, although they confirmed him in his belief that the time was ripe for a northern initiative.[5] Hume in particular gave him a reassuring briefing both on the calibre of the Sinn Féin leadership generally, and on Adams's willingness and, most importantly, his ability to deliver. Reynolds was moved by a number of considerations. Firstly, reading the different statements emanating from Sinn Féin, his political antennae indicated that change was afoot; secondly, coming from a county near the border (Longford), he both had dealings with people affected by the Troubles, including Unionists, with whom he did business and attended race meetings, and, as a matter of ordinary political life, had more awareness of northern issues and of grass-roots feelings concerning them than would have been the case with somebody operating in a constituency situated further from the border, in Dublin, say, or the south or west. In addition, he had developed a friendship with Major during the period when both were finance ministers on the European circuit.

Major had no Thatcher-like attitudes to Northern Ireland. In fact, he had no attitudes towards Ireland, about which he simply knew very little, his career having followed other paths. To his credit he did not allow the fact that the IRA nearly succeeded in killing him, in a mortar attack on Downing Street on 7 February 1991, not long after he had become Prime Minister, to colour his approach to the Irish issue. But, thirdly and vitally to the normal pro-Unionist patina of the Conservatives, he was at all times constrained in his freedom of manoeuvre by his slim majority and by the Eurosceptic or anti-European section of his party, which threatened to bring him down at various junctures and drove him to court support from the Ulster Unionist representatives over Maastricht, with consequent harmful implications for the Nationalist cause. His overall majority hovered at around nine seats. But, including Paisley's representatives, there were 13 Unionists in the House to be reckoned with. Moreover, his Irish Cabinet sub-committee was over-whelmingly right wing. It included such figures as Michael Portillo, Michael Howard, Sir Patrick Mayhew, and, possibly one of the most pro-Unionist figures in Westminster, Lord Cranborne. A key vote on Maastricht in the House of Commons on 22 July 1993 was only ratified with the help of James Molyneaux, the leader of the Ulster Unionists, and members of his party. Paisley and his supporters broke with the Conservatives on the issue. Although it was hotly denied at the time by the Conservatives, the price of the Unionists' support was a parliamentary select committee on Northern Ireland.

Reynolds built on his friendship with Major by making three separate gestures, each of which increased the British Prime Minister's confidence in his Irish counterpart. The first concerned a disastrous campaign which the IRA had been waging against British service and diplomatic personnel in Europe. Reynolds had learned that a group of German clergy had succeeded in both bringing an end to the campaign and, as a result, heading off a fairly ferocious counter-insurgency, counter-terrorist operation which the Germans had been about to mount. Major had heard nothing about an end to the European campaign from his own intelligence sources, and was both surprised and impressed when his subsequent enquiries proved that Reynolds's information was accurate. Reynolds also used Irish influence in Europe to lobby for European enlargement, soothing Major's fears on the issue and stiffening him to press on towards ratifying Maastricht by obtaining assurances from Helmut Kohl, the German Chancellor, that Germany was in favour of European enlargement for all its consequential increases in convergence and structural funds which Major's Eurosceptics were objecting to. After a European Summit at Birmingham went badly, Reynolds also actively lobbied for Major's position at the subsequent Edinburgh Summit, held under the British presidency, and earned Brownie points with the British premier when Edinburgh passed off far more successfully than had Birmingham. Reynolds's third olive branch was actually plucked out of the hands of the Irish-American lobby – he asked President Clinton to stay his hand on the appointment of a peace envoy. Both the Unionists and the British had regarded the peace envoy idea with anger and suspicion, to such an extent that the Conservatives briefed journalists in London on the day of Clinton's inauguration that their first priority with the new administration would be to secure an abandonment of what was seen as a Nationalist ploy to introduce an interloping America on to their turf. Agreement to appoint such an envoy had been a key factor in the decision by Niall O'Dowd and his friends, who were working for a new Irish agenda, to support Clinton, but though the Irish-Americans were initially taken aback, and Clinton himself demurred, all sides ultimately agreed with Reynolds's (correct) assessment that the gain in support from Major would outweigh the potential loss caused by the envoy idea being jettisoned.

Before the envoy issue arose (on St Patrick's Day 1993), the Americans for a New Irish Agenda (ANIA) had already made major progress with Clinton. Steps were taken which led to the National Security Council dealing with the ANIA, rather than the strongly pro-British State Department. Clinton appointed a former Ted Kennedy aide, Nancy Soderberg, as Staff Director of the NSC, where she became a principal contact for the Irish lobby. The Irish-Americans had two principal objectives, apart from the peace envoy proposal: the enticement of the British into peace talks, and the securing of a visa for Adams to visit the US, reckoning, correctly as it turned out, that the resultant publicity would help to convince the Republican movement of the worth of political as opposed to military initiative. An ANIA delegation visited Ireland in September 1993, bringing with them a letter from Clinton, which supported the peace process idea and criticised various aspects of current policy, including discrimination against Catholics in employment, and the collusion between Loyalist paramilitaries and the security forces. To mark the visit, the IRA called a seven-day ceasefire, and O'Dowd and his colleagues, drawn from a wide spectrum of corporate, political and trade union America, met with all sides in the conflict: Unionists, Nationalists, and the London and Dublin establishments. As a result of the visit, the ANIA delegation became convinced of the importance of securing the Adams visa as a method of both mainstreaming Sinn Féin and demonstrating to the Republicans that politics could work to secure their objectives.

Another vital player to enter the Irish scene in 1993 was Ted Kennedy's sister, Jean Kennedy Smith, whom Clinton appointed the American Ambassador to Ireland. Clinton and the Kennedys, the emergence of Reynolds and of the ANIA, together with the developing move towards politics within Republican circles, combined to create the most positive force brought to bear on the Northern Ireland issue throughout the entire course of the twentieth century. In fact nothing like it had been seen in Ireland since the days of Parnell, when the New Departure brought together the Land League, the Fenians, the Irish Party at Westminster and the Irish-Americans. And even then Parnell did not have the ear of an American president. Another important figure in the developing peace process was Dick Spring, who, as we have seen, became Deputy Prime Minister and Foreign Minister after the Irish general election in November 1992.

Spring began his tenure in office by making friendly noises towards the Unionists. He promised that the new government would be prepared to change Articles 2 and 3 and told a meeting of the Irish Association that 'Our besetting failure on the Nationalist side has been a persistent tendency to underestimate the depth and strength of the Unionist identity . . . we have amends to make for this failure, no less than others for theirs.'[6] But after some months fruitlessly trying to come to terms with the said 'Unionist identity', Spring changed his tune to that of John Hume, who (on 29 March 1993), in despair at the failure of Brooke's three-stranded initiative, suggested that the British and Irish governments should bypass the Unionists by agreeing a set of proposals which could be put to the Irish people north and south of the border by means of a referendum. On 8 July, Spring made the same proposal, and later in the month condemned the bargain struck by the Conservatives with the Unionists in return for Molyneaux's support over Maastricht.

The previous month, Reynolds, as part of what he termed 'a formula for peace', had given Major a draft document which incorporated the Sinn Féin position, in the belief that though some features of the document were bound to be unacceptable, nevertheless it would provide a basis for negotiation. However, it would later emerge that the British were not prepared to regard it as such. Reynolds himself had difficulties with some of the Sinn Féin approaches. One question which arose was whether 'self-determination' applied to the whole island or just to the Six Counties. The uncomfortable reality was that Sinn Féin saw it as applying to the whole island. To the Republicans, the principle of consent sounded fine in theory, but in practice translated as the Unionist veto, to which London was committed. A 'Brits Out' odour was totally unacceptable to London nostrils. Nor was there anything attractive about the Sinn Féin attempt to get London to become a 'persuader' of the Unionists on the virtues of a united Ireland. Even in the unlikely event of a Tory government deciding to follow this course, the British were bound by international agreements to respect existing boundaries, and could not enforce a vote taken in the south of Ireland on the north. To complicate matters, Hume and Adams issued a statement on 25 September which said that they had drawn up a report, which was to be forwarded to Dublin, that would both 'lead to agreement among the divided people of this island' and 'provide a solid basis for peace'. However, Hume then took off on a prearranged trade mission to America, before making a formal report to the Irish Government.

The Hume/Adams announcement helped to bring to a head all the criticisms which had been directed at the peace process, both from within the SDLP, which had not been kept informed of what was happening, and from the Unionists. It also helped to bring to a head a problem which had been simmering for several years of Dublin inactivity. Who made Northern Ireland policy, Dublin or John Hume? For years, Dublin had been content to let Hume make the running so far as policy formulation was concerned. He was prepared to come to an internal settlement in the Six Counties which would not disturb the overall status quo on the island. His was the voice of decency and sanity, and above all, he was not Sinn Féin. Now, however, with an Irish Taoiseach *in situ*, who was bringing forward policies of his own designed to entice a Tory leader who was dependent on Unionist support to settle the Irish issue, Hume suddenly became something of an embarrassment to Dublin. Reynolds agreed with Major that they would issue a joint communiqué at an EU summit in Brussels, on 29 October, distancing the two prime ministers from Hume's efforts, and promising to work together along the lines suggested by Reynolds. The communiqué said:

> The Taoiseach gave the Prime Minister an account of the outcome of the Hume/Adams dialogue in the light of the Irish Government's own assessment of these and other related matters. They acknowledge John Hume's courageous and imaginative efforts. The Prime Minister and Taoiseach agreed that any initiative can only be taken by the two Governments, and there could be no question of their adopting or endorsing the report of

the dialogue which was recently given to the Taoiseach . . . they agreed that the two
Governments must continue to work together in their own terms on a framework for
peace . . .

There could be no secret agreements or understandings between governments and
organisations supporting violence as a price for its cessation.

This was a fairly brutal public disavowal of Hume and Adams's efforts, but
Reynolds made it on the basis of what he described to me and to others as a
'firm understanding' with Major that a draft declaration on a peace formula
would be produced by the two prime ministers. Accordingly, on 1 November,
John Major informed Hume that he would not proceed along the lines of the
Hume/Adams initiative, and the following day, Hume was told by the Irish
Government that it would be preferable if he stood aside while the two
governments negotiated. It was an ironic outcome to Hume's own original
suggestion that the two governments should negotiate over the heads of the
northern parties. Understandably, after all he had been through, Hume subsequently collapsed and was taken to hospital suffering from exhaustion.

However, when Reynolds turned to Major to produce the draft declaration
envisaged, he discovered himself enmeshed in the sort of seemingly inexplicable antagonisms towards what had hitherto appeared to be eminently
reasonable goals for both Dublin and London which so often emerged
unexpectedly from the British side. Various commentators have described the
'extraordinary series of diplomatic crises' and the 'extraordinary lack of trust
and understanding' which suddenly appeared.[7] London–Dublin relations
became embroiled in the toughest set of diplomatic exchanges since Churchill
and de Valera duelled over neutrality. Reynolds traded insults with Major,
pencils were hurled across negotiating tables, and Major finally agreed to the
issuing of a draft declaration with Reynolds only after the Irishman had
threatened to appeal openly to American opinion and seek support for a
purely Irish initiative. All this of course took place behind closed doors. What
had a marked bearing on the proceedings, apart of course from the traditional
Tory–Unionist alliance, and the 'Securocrat' influence, was what had
suddenly exploded into the public domain – the revelation that the British had
been talking to Sinn Féin.

The circumstances of this disclosure raised strong suspicions in Dublin
decision-taking circles that somewhere on the other side of the Irish Sea,
someone was trying to sabotage the Reynolds initiative. For some time, Sinn
Féin had been protesting to the British about leaks concerning the talks'
existence. But on 5 November, the Sinn Féin negotiators received a message
from the British, in reply to a query from the Republicans, which quoted from
the Brussels communiqué and lowered the portcullis on further talks by
saying: 'It is the public and consistent position of the British government that
any dialogue could only follow a permanent end to violent activity.' As the
Sinn Féin talks had been going on for the previous three years, the phrase
'consistent position' rang somewhat hollow. So did the subsequent spate of

public denials which followed the disclosure of the talks by the Belfast journalist Eamon Mallie, on 8 November. On 2 December Gerry Adams released all the correspondence[8] between the British and Sinn Féin, accompanied by a statement saying that the British behaviour had been 'damnable'. This use of language becomes less surprising when it is realised that amongst other assurances given to the Republicans during the talks was one that Mayhew was in favour of a united Ireland, which was said to be inevitable in a European context anyway, and another that, unlike the Rees talks of 1976, which Rees later admitted were merely designed to 'con' the IRA, the current talks were intended to be meaningful. Mayhew then conceded that there were 'inaccuracies' in the series of denials which he had been issuing,[9] but by that time Major had also damaged his own credibility with a statement to the House of Commons (on 19 November) that not only would he not allow talks with Sinn Féin, but the prospect of talking to Adams would, he said, 'turn my stomach'.

It has to be said that the activities and personality of Sir Patrick Mayhew did not make for gastric peace on the Irish side. Like his predecessor, Peter Brooke, he had Anglo-Irish ancestors: Brooke's ancestor was the eighteenth-century poet Charlotte Brooke, Mayhew's the Lords of Fermoy, prominent Cork land owners whose family name was Roche. It would appear that the poetic gene transmitted a greater empathy with Irish Nationalist sensibilities than did that of the squirearchy. Given Brooke's ground-breaking approach, there may have been a certain symbolism in the fact that he frequently boasted that Charlotte was the first person to use the term 'Fenian' in the English language. Mayhew's approach to Fenianism, however, had raised Dublin blood pressures long before he came to Ireland. He turned down a Dublin request that cases before the Six Counties non-jury courts should be heard by three judges and supported the RUC in a number of 'shoot-to-kill' cases. In 1982 he conceded that there was a *prima facie* case against 11 members of the RUC, but refused to prosecute on grounds of 'national security'.

At one stage in the peace process negotiations, he produced his own proposals which, to Reynolds and his team, appeared to be nothing more than an effort to restore the Unionist position under the old Stormont. It became evident to Major that Reynolds was having nothing to do with his Secretary of State for Northern Ireland, and during a break in the talks one day, he asked the Irish Taoiseach if he would not have a coffee with Mayhew. To which Reynolds replied: 'Why don't you send us over a good one of your own, instead of a West Cork Brit.'[10] However, there were some influences around which were helpful to Reynolds, notably Archbishop Robert Eames, the Church of Ireland Primate of all Ireland, who was friendly with James Molyneaux, and the Presbyterian minister the Reverend Roy Magee, who enjoyed something of the same relationship with Loyalist paramilitaries as did Father Reid with Republicans. Reynolds came to have a high regard for both men, and through them Loyalist paramilitary leaders like Gusty Spence and David Irvine, who accepted that his principal motivation was not to impose joint authority on the Six Counties, but the achievement of peace as an end in itself.

This last becomes all the more remarkable when one considers that some of the worst violence of the entire Troubles was occurring in the final stages of the Reynolds–Major negotiations. As a result of a spate of Loyalist sectarian assassinations, the Provisionals, on 23 October, made an attempted attack on a meeting of Loyalist paramilitary leaders on the Shankill Road, which resulted in a bomb going off in a shop, killing ten innocent Protestants and badly injuring scores more. There was widespread public outrage when Gerry Adams helped to carry the coffin of the IRA bomber Thomas Begley, who died in the botched explosion, and further shock and outrage when the resultant spate of Protestant retaliations included an attack on a bar in Greysteel, County Derry, in which seven people died.

But despite all the mistrust, the ghastliness, and the frequent abrasiveness of their meetings, Major and Reynolds persisted until, with the aid of a last-minute phone call from Clinton to Major (prompted by Reynolds), urging the British Prime Minister to 'go the extra mile for peace', the Downing Street Declaration was signed in London on 15 December 1993. The declaration made a number of commitments on future co-operation and existing guarantees, 'including Northern Ireland statutory constitutional guarantee'. It pledged the two governments to creating 'a new political framework', both within Ireland and between the two islands. While pledging to respect the wishes of a majority in Northern Ireland as to whether or not they opted for either a continuation of the Union or a united Ireland, the document also reiterated Brooke's statement that 'the British Government . . . has no selfish, strategic or economic interests in Northern Ireland' but went on:

Their primary interest is to see peace, stability and reconciliation established by agreement . . . they will work together with the Irish Government to achieve such an agreement, which will embrace the totality of relationships. The role of the British Government will be to encourage, facilitate and enable the achievement of such agreement over a period through a process of dialogue and co-operation . . . The British Government agree that it is for the people of the island of Ireland alone, by agreement between the two parts respectively, to exercise their right of self-determination on the basis of consent, freely and concurrently given, North and South, to bring about a united Ireland, if that is their wish . . .

Sinn Féin's concept of self-determination was watered down by the qualification that

The democratic right of self-determination by the people of Ireland as a whole must be achieved and exercised with and subject to the agreement and consent of a majority of the people of Northern Ireland and must, consistent with justice and equity, respect the democratic dignity and the civil rights and religious liberties of both communities.

Reynolds also committed the Irish Government 'in the event of an overall settlement . . . as part of a balanced constitutional accommodation' to bringing about changes in the Irish constitution which would 'fully represent the principle of consent in Northern Ireland'.

Despite Sinn Féin's reservations about the Unionist veto being enshrined, the declaration was widely welcomed on both sides of the Irish Sea. Molyneaux raised no serious objection to it, and it was left to Paisley on behalf of the Unionist community to organise protest meetings at the selling of 'Ulster' to what he termed 'the fiendish Republican scum'. The putting of the next major piece of the jigsaw into place, the provision of a visa for Adams to visit the States, now took priority, both to maintain the momentum of the peace process and to soothe Sinn Féin's ruffled self-determination feathers, so that a ceasefire might be achieved to build on the commitments contained in the Downing Street Declaration. Jean Kennedy Smith and her brother, Ted Kennedy, were essential to the visa quest. A friend of the Kennedys, Bill Flynn, a central figure in the ANIA, and chairman of the Committee on American Foreign Policy, invited Adams to address a conference organised by the committee in New York on 1 February 1994, despite the fact that the British had stymied an earlier invitation, issued by Mayor Dinkins, by supplying Clinton with a dossier implicating Adams in IRA activity. On that occasion, Adams had applied for the visa in Belfast. Now Brendan Scannell, back in Dublin at the Department of Foreign Affairs, suggested that he apply via Dublin, so that the Kennedys could be brought into play.

Ted Kennedy showed his commitment to the Irish issue by coming to Dublin, at his sister's invitation, to sound out a number of people on the visa issue, including myself, and, more importantly, Albert Reynolds. Kennedy accepted the arguments that not only would the granting of the visa help to mainstream Sinn Féin, and make the Republicans convinced of the worth of political, rather than military, action, it would also enable Adams to witness at first hand the enormous wellspring of goodwill towards Ireland which existed in America, amongst Irish-Americans, as well as the equally strong desire to see violence brought to an end in the land of their ancestry. Kennedy's influence on Clinton proved to be decisive. The ANIA had come up against not only the State Department and the Justice Department, but all the other state agencies with which the British had influence through either the old 'special relationship' or on-going current shared interests in areas such as the former Yugoslavia, and the Middle East. These included the CIA, the FBI, and occasionally even the sympathetic National Security Council. But, encouraged by Kennedy, Clinton personally signed the authorisation admitting Adams to the US. In so doing, he not only overturned the influence on Irish policy which the British Government had exercised over the State Department since the days of David Gray; he also brought a storm of criticism on his head for by passing the Arafat test. This had been instituted when, in the teeth of protests from the Israeli lobby, Yasser Arafat had been admitted to New York to address the UN, after promising to renounce violence. Adams, from West Belfast, was not required to pass under the same yoke as Arafat, from the West Bank.

Adams's 48-hour visa (starting on 31 January 1994) reeled in an enormous harvest of publicity. He dominated all the major electronic and print media of America in a fashion which brought home to Republicans the fact that there were other ways of getting attention for the cause, apart from letting off bombs and killing people. His own assessment of the worth of the visit is that it advanced the peace process by about a year, although in the immediate aftermath of his triumph it was difficult to see progress. The violence continued and Sinn Féin, though anxious not to disillusion those who welcomed the Downing Street Declaration and Adams's descent on New York, made haste slowly so as not to allow divisions to develop within the movement over the direction of events. The party asked for 'clarification' of a number of points in the Downing Street Declaration, but Major refused to give these until an agreement was finally reached on 19 May that Reynolds would act as the intermediary between Major and Sinn Féin on the teasing-out process.

Privately, the IRA Army Council voted not to reject the declaration, and within the movement the debate continued. There were unrealised hopes that a special conference called by Sinn Féin at Letterkenny, County Donegal, on 24 July 1994, would result in a ceasefire, and then, towards the end of August, Niall O'Dowd, who had been shuttling back and forth across the Atlantic, was contacted by Sinn Féin and invited to return with his group to meet Adams and the Sinn Féin leadership at the Whiterock Leisure Centre in West Belfast. Prior to the meeting, the ANIA delegation saw Reynolds and Spring in Dublin, and Reynolds briefed them to simply ask whether there was going to be a ceasefire or not. He wanted no more talk about 'clarification', or about other phrases which had entered the nomenclature – 'defensive posture' or 'offensive posture'. There was none. To everyone's surprise and relief; Adams opened the meeting by telling the Irish-Americans that there was going to be a ceasefire. It was publicly announced on 31 August 1994 on RTE just before midday. But it was preceded by one of the biggest behind-the-scenes diplomatic battles of the entire peace process. It was essential that the IRA and Sinn Féin network in America was briefed before the news broke, and briefed by someone who would carry authority, if a split were to be avoided and funding kept from elements within the Republican community opposed to the process. As Joe Cahill had helped to set up NORAID in the first place, he was the obvious man to be sent. But the British objected to the Americans granting him a visa.

Both Reynolds and Sinn Féin were outraged. The British intervention at best meant a dangerous delay in the process, and could have derailed it. Worse, Washington was on holiday, so that Nancy Soderberg was nowhere to be found, and Jean Kennedy Smith had gone to the south of France. However, when Reynolds succeeded in getting word to her of the hiccup, she returned to Dublin and went into battle on behalf of the Cahill visa. Reynolds's blood pressure went up further when it was discovered at one stage in the hectic negotiations that the State Department had eventually agreed to issue Cahill with a visa, but in deference to British wishes had placed conditions on the permit which would have restricted his movements. As Cahill held an Irish passport, a furious Reynolds regarded the restrictions as an effort by Britain to infringe Irish sovereignty. Kennedy Smith got back on the phone to the White House, and at midnight Washington time, five o'clock in the morning in Dublin, Clinton okayed the visa. Later in the morning, Cahill took off for America from Dublin airport. The ceasefire announcement was made public the following day. It said:

> Recognising the potential of the current situation and in order to enhance the democratic peace process and underline our definitive commitment to its success, the leadership of *Oglaigh na hEireann* have decided that as of midnight, Wednesday 31st August, there will be a complete cessation of military operations. All our units have been instructed accordingly.[11]

It was essential that the momentum of the process be maintained. For while, apart from some Republican doubters, the announcement was greeted with relief and delight by Nationalist Ireland, and by the Irish diaspora, the Unionist community received the news of the ceasefire with anger and suspicion, believing that it had been arrived at on the basis of some secret deal which sold out the Unionist position. In an effort to reassure the Unionists, Reynolds convened a historic meeting between himself, Adams and Hume at Government Buildings on 6 September, after which the trio issued a statement saying: 'We reiterate that we cannot resolve this problem without the participation and agreement of the Unionist people.' It was also announced that, in line with the Downing Street Declaration, a Forum for Peace and Reconciliation would be set up in Dublin Castle to which all shades of political opinion would be invited. In the event, neither the British nor the major Unionist parties attended when the forum opened on 28 October. The Alliance Party did turn up – and demanded that they be given extra representation as the price of their attendance. Reynolds also put other confidence-building measures in train for the benefit of the Republicans, including the dropping of the broadcasting ban on Sinn Féin spokespersons, the formal ending of the state of emergency, which had remained on the statute books since World War II, and the release of Republican prisoners.

The British began to improve the lot of prisoners in the H blocks, but the Unionist influence, coupled with that of the Tory backbenchers, started to show within a few hours of the ceasefire being declared. Major's original reaction to the announcement was guarded but welcoming. He said that he was greatly encouraged, but added that it was necessary that it be made clear that this was a permanent renunciation of violence. Not for the first time, British and Irish intelligence sources were obviously giving different interpretations of events to their respective political masters. Then Molyneaux took a hand. He saw Major shortly after the British Prime Minister had issued his statement on the ceasefire, and emerged from the meeting to say that

Major did not accept the ceasefire statement because it did not meet the criteria of the Downing Street Declaration. Major did not contradict him, and the subsequent statements from both the Prime Minister and the Secretary of State for Northern Ireland, Sir Patrick Mayhew, incorporated the Unionist viewpoint by demanding that the IRA make it clear that the ceasefire was 'permanent', a word that was to resonate across the Irish Sea.

However, the Loyalist paramilitaries, the grouping which, apart from the IRA itself, was most directly affected by the ceasefire, had a more generous response. It was read to the world on 13 October by the Loyalist folk hero Gusty Spence, a much-matured figure compared to the man of Malvern Street in the sixties. The statement said:

> After a widespread consultative process initiated by representations from the Ulster Democratic and Progressive Unionist Parties [fringe Unionist parties representing the UDA and the UVF] and having received confirmation and guarantees in relation to Northern Ireland's constitutional position within the United Kingdom, as well as other assurances, and in the belief that the democratically expressed wishes of the greater number of people in Northern Ireland will be respected and upheld, the CLMC [the Combined Loyalist Military Council] will universally cease all operational hostilities from 12 midnight on Thursday, 13 October 1994 .[12]

Spence also expressed 'abject and true remorse' to the 'loved ones of innocent victims' for the 'intolerable suffering' they had undergone during the conflict. He included in the statement a large-minded vision of how he thought the IRA announcement could be built on:

> Let us firmly resolve to respect our differing views of freedom, culture and aspiration and never again permit our political circumstances to degenerate into bloody warfare. We are on the threshold of a new and exciting beginning with our battles in future being political battles, fought on the side of honesty, decency and democracy against the negativity of mistrust, misunderstanding and malevolence so that together we can bring forth a wholesome society in which our children and their children will know the meaning of true peace.

Unfortunately, Spence's vision was not shared in Downing Street. Yet more difficulties were put forward by the British, including one which was to bedevil the peace process from 1994 to the time of writing in 2003, and there is still no certainty of resolution of the problem on the horizon: decommissioning. Exactly how decommissioning came to be injected into the debate is not entirely clear. A generally accepted version is that during 1993, as the Maastricht debate hotted up and Major's dependence on the Unionists became more pronounced, the British Prime Minister became concerned at the prospect of the Irish issue interacting with that of Europe amongst his backbenchers. At a meeting at Chequers, British officials let it be known to their Irish counterparts in an informal way that 'the Boss' was getting concerned that the peace process was going too fast for his backbenchers, and that he needed a 'retarding factor'. The issue of what were termed the 'arsenals' would be introduced to the talks. However, it was never raised in a substantive way with either Dublin or the Sinn Féin leaders before the ceasefire. Had it been, there would have been no ceasefire.

Firstly, Republicans never willingly give up their arms. Even at the ending of the Irish civil war, Frank Aiken ordered that the IRA weapons be dumped, not handed over. For the Provisionals to have given up their weapons would have been regarded as both a surrender and an acknowledgement that they had been carrying on an illegal and unjustified war. Moreover, there was the very real possibility that the forces of British military intelligence, MI5 and the RUC, in collusion with the Loyalist death squads, might reactivate hostilities, and the prospect in Catholic ghetto areas, the bedrock of IRA support, of being left defenceless in these circumstances would have created a backlash against the peace process. Another very real circumstance was the fact that there were 160,000 licensed weapons in Protestant hands at this stage. In addition, there were huge caches of illegal arms, some of them like those smuggled into the country from South Africa by the British army intelligence agent Brian Nelson, which had been placed at the disposal of Loyalists by the security forces, of whom there were 32,000 in the Six Counties at the time of the ceasefire, all heavily armed. The underground security forces included 1,000 members of MI5, and there were huge, sophisticated computerised intelligence units scattered through the north's 135 fixed military installations. It all added up to a presence of one security force operator to every 3.7 Catholic males aged between 16 and 44. In other words, a vast security industry, which, those who controlled it were determined, should not be run down.

Of my own knowledge I can say that at the time of ceasefire, the Dublin Government had received intelligence to the effect that 45% of the total British military intelligence budget was spent in the Six Counties, and I have taken part in studio discussions about the likely impact of the fact that, post-Gorbachev, 600 MI5 operatives had been relocated from Russia to Belfast. And certainly when one gets a glimpse of the amount of money available to 'run' agents, as occurred during the revelations concerning the army's agent, 'Stakeknife', in May of 2003, the image created is one of a vast slush fund administered with doubtful accountability. One expert has written that 'even as three governments placed their faith in peace talks', senior officers were informed that a standing army of 10,000 troops or more would be required in Northern Ireland for the foreseeable future.[13] The author, a historian of the SAS, and a former chief reporter of the *Sunday Times*, wrote:

> Throughout the ceasefires of 1995 and 1997–8, the British army energetically modernized its armoury of computers. The scale of cost of this programme reflected the army's belief that it would continue to fight an intelligence war in Northern Ireland for many years ahead and that the surveillance war would increasingly become part of normal life in England.

Ireland has traditionally been the laboratory in which Britain has tried out its constitutional and military innovations for use both at home and abroad, and in the peace process era, the continuation of the military experimentation had harmful consequences for the constitutional effort, quite apart from the difficulties faced by the latter in overcoming Unionist and Tory backbench opposition. Not only did the military not scale down their presence in sensitive areas like West Belfast, huge additional barracks were built in the Falls Road, South Armagh and Tyrone. In both of the latter areas, opposition to the peace process was strong, but instead of attempting to smooth the ruffled feathers, the army increased its vehicle searches, and the stopping and harassment of young men.

Theoretically, the decommissioning argument has validity. In a democracy there should not be private armies with unlicensed weapons. But as should by now be all too apparent, the Six Counties had not been a democracy. The behaviour of the Unionists was such that the British first had to remove their parliament, then abolish their militia, the B Specials. Then they had to take control of the militia which replaced the Specials, the Ulster Defence Regiment, which was subsumed into the Royal Irish Regiment so that Unionist influence on the corps was diluted. Basic reforms such as one man one vote had to be introduced. Discrimination in housing and unemployment had to be outlawed, the Special Powers Act removed and basic rights of identity introduced, such as an entitlement to fly the Irish tricolour. The tragedy of the obtrusion of the decommissioning argument across the path of the peace process is that it retarded, rather than accelerated, the spread of democracy to a point where all the north's armed groups would have quietly disappeared and Sinn Féin would have evolved in the north as Fianna Fáil has in the south, although hopefully not to the brown envelope stage.

As to the practical merit of the decommissioning argument itself, it has to be said that there is none. Given the state of the world's armament industry, the IRA could dispose of every weapon it possesses one day, and replace them the next. As has been pointed out on more than one occasion, the main damage caused to both life and property during the Troubles has come from the use of fertiliser bombs. A 1,000lb bomb can be made up, on a schoolboy chemistry formula, by two men with shovels in a cowshed. If detection is feared, the 'bomb' can be spread harmlessly over adjoining fields, both construction and demolition taking about 12 hours. Shovels cannot be decommissioned. Mindsets, however, can, and no one has summed up the position better than a man who should know, the head of the Irish police force, Garda Commissioner Pat Byrne. Speaking at a time when the damage done by the decommissioning argument had become all too apparent, the Commissioner said:

> ... unfortunately you will always have some type of 'IRA' while you have a British presence in Northern Ireland. If we could turn the clock back I wonder would those wisest among us have insisted that this [decommissioning] issue is an issue that had to be dealt with before political progress could be continued or maintained.[14]

Well may we all wonder. However, what is known is that the Unionists took up the decommissioning issue with enthusiasm, particularly on the part of Ken Maginnis, the Unionist spokesperson on defence, who had been a member of first the B Specials and then the UDR, both of which, as we have seen, had had to be 'decommissioned' because of the behaviour of some of their members. As a result, the peace process is still stalled over the issue to the time of writing.

In October of 1994, the British attempted to have another visit by Adams to the US downgraded, by seeking not to have him received by Vice-President Al Gore at the White House. As Gore had received a Unionist delegation, barring Adams would have been seen as a significant political snub in Belfast. It took a marathon bout of diplomacy between Niall O'Dowd, Nancy Soderberg and Tony Lake, the head of the National Security Council, to work out a compromise, despite two phone calls to Clinton from John Major. Gore did not receive Adams at the White House but he did have contact with him. By prearrangement, he phoned Adams while the Sinn Féin leader was visiting Ethel Kennedy, widow of the murdered Bobby Kennedy.

The British attempted to counter this by arranging that Ken Maginnis attend a British Consulate reception in New York and attempt to match Adams's publicity by appearing with him on *The Larry King Show*, despite the fact that the Unionists refused to appear on TV with Sinn Féin spokespersons in either Ireland or England. Further hostilities broke out between London and Washington when, firstly, Clinton agreed to allow Sinn Féin to collect openly for political funds in the US, subject to the usual accountancy safeguards for such collections, and secondly, invited Adams to attend a St Patrick's Day reception in the White House on 17 March 1995. Again, both these matters were aimed at showing the Republican faithful that main-streaming and political activity could bear fruit. The fund-raising initiative, for example, meant that the NORAID connection had to be put to one side by Sinn Féin, but again, both were fought like a rearguard action in the field. Major was so enraged at Adams's admission to the St Patrick's Day gala in the White House that he refused to accept a phone call from Clinton for over a week. Prior to the St Patrick's Day event, Clinton had also delivered a rebuff to Major by telling him that if he continued in his refusal to invite Sinn Féin to a dinner which he hosted in Belfast in early December 1994, to inaugurate an investment conference, the Americans would not attend the conference either, because the object of the exercise was to end discrimination, not extend it so as to prevent the evolution of a democratic political party. The same week, on 2 December, Clinton also took the important step of appointing a Special Adviser to the President and Secretary of State on economic initiatives in Ireland. This was largely the brainchild of John Hume, who had for a long time advocated inward investment both in the Six Counties itself, and in the border counties adjoining the Six Counties, all of which had suffered economically through partition. The adviser was to prove himself one of the most significant figures to come to Ireland in decades: the former Senate majority leader, Senator George Mitchell.

These were all pluses, as it were, for the peace process. But a very large minus developed also – the fall of Albert Reynolds. The circumstances of this have already been described in a southern context. But here, both in the northern context, and in the light of what has become known about 'dirty tricks' and underground collusion between the British security forces and elements within Unionism, it is worth recording that after Reynolds had left office, because, it was claimed, the paedophile priest Father Brendan Smyth had not been proceeded against by the Irish legal authorities with due celerity, it was revealed (by Smyth's solicitor, after his sentencing) that on four separate occasions, when Smyth was allegedly being eagerly pursued by the northern authorities, he had visited the Six Counties. On each occasion, his car had been stopped by the RUC and his identity and particulars checked, and on each occasion he was allowed to proceed.

John Bruton, who succeeded Reynolds, had none of his predecessor's empathy with the northern situation, and certainly for the early part of his tenure as Taoiseach, he talked and acted in a manner which served to explain the Freudian slip of the tongue which led Reynolds to describe him as 'John Unionist'. However, Bruton, a fundamentally decent and likeable individual of wealthy Meath farming stock, learned as he went that neither the traditional Fine Gael anti-Republican outlook, nor an automatic reliance on British politicians acting as they said they would, were necessarily reliable indicators for fruitful Anglo-Irish relationships. Where Reynolds relied for guidance on the historical precedent of his own party's evolution from the days of the gun, Bruton began by sympathising with the British demand for IRA decommissioning, which, as we will see, led him to make a serious policy gaffe. Moreover, the calibre of his performance in dealing with Major was established at the outset of his tenure over the issue of the release of the British paratrooper, Private Lee Clegg, who had been jailed for shooting dead a Belfast joy-rider. His case became a *cause célèbre* when tabloids like the *Sun* began campaigning for his release and the matter was taken up by right-wing Conservatives like Lady Olga Maitland. Clegg was released on the eve of a challenge to Major's leadership, and a week before the 12 July celebrations by Orangemen. The British had refused to countenance freeing either Republican or Loyalist prisoners to improve the ceasefire climate, and outraged even moderate Irish opinion by claiming that Clegg's release had nothing to do with the leadership crisis, and the decision had been taken solely on legal grounds. Less moderate opinion responded with a ferocious outburst of Republican-inspired rioting right across the Six Counties, which, before Gerry Adams called it off as the 'twalfth' neared, caused millions of pounds' worth of damage. When Bruton attempted to raise the issue with Major at an EU meeting in Paris, he received a very public rebuke from the Prime Minister, who said, correctly, that the matter was one solely for the British to decide. However, had Reynolds still been in power, it can safely be assumed, given the relationship of the two men, that the matter would have been resolved privately, and amicably, over a phone call.

Major's declining position in the House of Commons meant that, particularly from 6 December 1994 onwards, the peace process became something of a curate's egg. On that date, the Ulster Unionists made common cause with Labour and with Tory rebels to defeat a Conservative proposal to increase VAT on fuel bills, by 319 votes to 311. The Official Unionist MPs had come to a Parnell-like realisation of their strategic worth in the House of Commons after the vote on Maastricht the previous year. Following the vote, the then Labour Party leader, John Smith, had approached Molyneaux to enquire how the Unionists would feel in the event of a similar tight situation arising with Labour in power, and a deal was struck whereby it was agreed that, given certain guarantees, the Unionists would desert their traditional Conservative allegiances and vote Labour. The principal guarantee sought, and conceded, was the head of Kevin McNamara, the Labour Party spokesperson on Northern Ireland, whom the Unionists regarded as too pro-Nationalist. Following Smith's unexpected death, McNamara was dropped by his successor, Tony Blair, and replaced by Mo Mowlam, who the Unionists also came to detest.

But though these machinations did give the Unionists a brake on the peace process, they were unable to slow it entirely. The momentum already achieved ensured that the two governments published the Framework Document on 22 February 1995. This document, which was to prove the bedrock of the Good Friday Agreement of 1998, set out to 'assist discussion and negotiation involving the Northern Ireland parties' and stated that its 'guiding principles' were:

> The principle of self-determination as set out in the Joint Declaration [Downing Street Declaration].
>
> That the consent of the governed is an essential ingredient for stability in any political arrangement.
>
> That agreement must be pursued and established by exclusively democratic, peaceful means, without resort to violence or coercion.
>
> That any new political arrangements must be based on full respect for, and protection and expression of, the rights and identities of both traditions in Ireland and even-handedly afford both communities in Northern Ireland parity of esteem and treatment, including equality of opportunity and advantage.

Goals set by the document included far-reaching changes in the structures governing relationships between the two parts of Ireland, within the north, and between Ireland and England. In other words, flesh was added to the bones of the concept of the 'three-stranded approach', which had been mooted since the days of Peter Brooke. New north–south institutions were envisaged, as well as new working relationships between the northern and southern civil services, and there was to be a new parliamentary forum. Constitutional issues were to be made subject to a 'balanced accommodation'.

Much of what was envisaged in the Framework Document did come to pass, although perhaps only temporarily, but the way towards accommodation, whether 'balanced' or not, was rocky, hard-fought, and reflected accurately the growth in strength of the Unionist position, and the weakening of Major's. There was tension between Dublin and London over the treatment of IRA prisoners in English jails, and in particular over the British decision to allow the Orange Order to march down the Garvaghy Road at Drumcree, near Portadown, against the wishes of the Catholic inhabitants of the area, which had once been filled with green fields but was now a Catholic housing estate, a microcosm of the demographic growth of Nationalist strength in the Six Counties as a whole, which underlay a good deal of Protestant fear and uncertainty. Huge concentrations of troops and police were required to cordon off the estate from gangs of drink-inflamed Loyalists who were bused and driven from all over the province to lay siege to the Catholic enclave. The Northern Ireland pressure cooker soared well above boiling point until the Republicans shifted the pressure from Drumcree by spreading the tensions right across the Six Counties by means of the widespread Republican rioting described above.

The Garvaghy march, 12 July, marked the emergence of David Trimble as a Unionist leader. He helped to broker a compromise with the police whereby the Orangemen, led by himself and Paisley, hands held aloft in triumph, marched through the Catholic area, but without bands playing, or provocation being offered to the inhabitants. This did little for his popularity amongst Catholics, but it helped with the Protestants. Trimble, who, as noted earlier, had played a part in helping the Vanguard movement to bring down the power-sharing executive in 1974, was subsequently elected leader of the Official Unionists Party (on 8 September) when Molyneaux retired.

By this time, the peace process was running into serious trouble. In Washington the previous March, John Bruton had given aid and comfort to the decommissioning lobby by making a series of speeches supporting decommissioning, in advance of Sinn Féin being admitted to talks. At the time, the Clinton White House had been swinging round to accepting the Irish-American lobbyists' view that the issue was a dangerous distraction, and that the IRA's stated intention to maintain the ceasefire so that Sinn Féin could take part in building a peace process was genuine,[15] but was being threatened by grass-roots reaction to the decommissioning proposal. The British were aware of this, and conceded privately to the Irish-Americans that decommissioning was only a red herring, and would have to be dropped. However, following the Bruton intervention, during a visit to Washington the following May, Sir Patrick Mayhew announced what became known as the 'Washington Three', a series of three tests which the Republicans would have to pass, proving that they had decommissioned, before Sinn Féin could be admitted to talks. In addition to the Washington Three departure, the British had already been making difficulties about the reason for Mayhew's visit, a White House-sponsored conference on attracting investment to Ireland. Pressed by the Unionists, the British objected to the idea of Ireland being regarded as a single unit, even for investment purposes. Apparently, though the real objection was the Unionists' abhorrence of anything which might admit the principle of a united Ireland, even if it did ameliorate the north's endemic unemployment problems, the stated reason put forward by the Northern Ireland Office was that the lion's share of investment could go to the Republic because of the attractive incentives for inward investment available in the south. The atmosphere soured considerably as a result of the Bruton/Mayhew interventions.

Gerry Adams wrote an angry article in *An Phoblacht/Republican News*, saying that the Unionists 'had not engaged at all' in the peace process, to which they were 'hostile', and he accused the British Government of being 'minimalistic, begrudging and provocatively negative in its approach'. And he issued a particularly blunt warning on decommissioning:

> The British government and others may be miscalculating the IRA's position on decommissioning or the Sinn Féin leadership's room for manoeuvre on this issue. If this is so they do so with the benefit of having heard at first hand from Sinn Féin that the IRA will not de-commission or surrender its weapons to anyone as a precondition for all-party talks. There is no room for manoeuvre . . . If a surrender of weapons had been imposed as a precondition to peace negotiations prior to the cessation, there would have been no IRA ceasefire.[16]

By 'others', Adams of course meant John Bruton, who, as time passed, began to be regarded by people not known to be overly sympathetic towards Republicans as having made a monumental blunder. Geraldine Kennedy, who later became editor of the *Irish Times*, the first woman to hold the post, later assessed Bruton's performance as follows.

> . . . an irreparable mistake was made by Mr Bruton last March when he implicitly accepted the Washington 3 test . . . Bruton said he would be telling President Clinton that they had to see some movement on the arms question so that talks could begin between British Ministers and Sinn Féin. He made statement afier statement implicitly supporting Sir Patrick's position in the US and at home . . . Either inadvertently – or worse knowingly – Mr Bruton underwrote the British demand for Washington 3, a decommissioning gesture prior to talks. He helped place it at the top of the Anglo-Irish agenda. It has dominated the agenda at heads of government, ministerial and official level ever since.[17]

Unfortunately, all I can add to Ms Kennedy's comments is that decommissioning is still dominating the agenda at the time of writing more than seven years later. Realising something of the harm that had been done, Bruton joined with Dick Spring, John Hume and Gerry Adams in issuing a statement (on 14 July 1995) declaring that the parties were 'seeking a commencement, as soon as possible, of the inclusive, all-party talks necessary to the achievement' of a revival of the peace process. The statement was issued on a day on which another difficulty had arisen: Sinn Féin's reluctance to sign up to the statement issued by the Forum on Peace and Reconciliation, which by coincidence ended its sittings for the summer on the day the joint statement was issued. The forum had found that 'the democratic right of self-determination by the people of Northern Ireland as a whole must be achieved and exercised with, and subject to, the agreement or consent of a majority of the people of Ireland'. Sinn Féin calculated, unfortunately correctly, as matters turned out, that the Unionists would translate the word 'consent' as meaning 'veto'. However, the ANIA group, led by Bruce Morrisson and Niall O'Dowd, after a fact-finding mission to Ireland, warned the White House that there was a potentially dangerous feeling of anger abroad amongst grass-roots Republicans at the slow progress of the peace process. Clinton responded by giving an interview to the Washington correspondent of the *Irish Times*, Conor O'Clery (on 3 August 1995), urging the British to move on the issues of prisoner releases and of beginning talks. By this time, the Irish Government had released 32 Republican prisoners since the calling of the ceasefire, but the British, who held a far greater number, 1,000 in all, had not released anybody. After the interview, Adams and Martin McGuinness met with Patrick Mayhew, and it was announced (on 27 July 1995) that three prisoners held in Whitemoor Prison were being sent back to the Six Counties to complete their sentences. In the circumstances, this minimalist gesture did little to improve matters, and relationships worsened between Dublin and London, to a point where 'John Unionist' was forced to demonstrate that he was not all that Unionist.

On the eve of a planned summit between Bruton and Major, a surprising statement issued from the Government Information Bureau in Dublin (on 5 September 1995) saying: 'The Taoiseach, Mr John Bruton TD, has suggested the postponement of tomorrow's Anglo-Irish Summit, and the British Prime Minister, Mr John Major, has agreed to this. The purpose for this is to allow more time to attempt to resolve outstanding differences.' Bruton followed this up two days later at a dinner in Dublin Castle, at which he announced that the two governments were working towards setting a date for talks, which he pointedly said would include 'the maximum range of parties'. Even more pointedly, he stated that all parties in the Dail, both government and opposition, accepted the IRA's *bona fides*. He added: 'The cessation of violence by the IRA is irreversible.' Following this statement, the diplomatic log jam began to loosen, culminating in a frenzied burst of negotiations timed to have something ready for Bill Clinton before he visited Belfast on 28 November. It was announced on the afternoon of the 28th that a summit was to be held between Bruton and Major in London that evening. Following the summit, the two prime ministers issued a joint communiqué. This announced that following what were diplomatically termed 'intensive' efforts by both governments, a twin-track approach was being launched to resolve both the decommissioning question and that of talks, in which all parties would be involved, by the end of the following February. One of the most significant aspects of the communiqué was its American quotient. It announced that Senator George Mitchell would chair an international commission which would advise on a suitable method for 'full and verifiable decommissioning'.

The communiqué received such heartfelt welcome that no one paid attention to the devil in the detail. It stipulated that preparatory talks to the expected all-party discussions 'could include' how those involved might 'properly take account of democratic mandates and principles, including whether and how an elected body could play a part'. This coded reference was to a proposal which Trimble had made after becoming the Ulster Unionist leader. He had suggested a new assembly for the Six Counties, which he envisaged as fostering links not between Belfast and Dublin, but between Belfast and London. As the Unionists would have controlled this, the new assembly in effect would have been the old Stormont writ small, which was not the outcome to the peace process envisaged by either Sinn Féin or the SDLP. But the assembly idea was more or less lost sight of in the welter of debate which broke out over the working of the Mitchell Commission.

The commission consisted of three members: Mitchell himself; the former Finnish Prime Minister, Mr Hari Holkari; and the distinguished diplomat and former general, John de Chastelain of Canada. It was regarded with suspicion by both sides initially, because de Chastelain's mother had worked for MI6 and Sinn Féin felt that John Bruton should have secured a balancing appointment likely to be more sympathetic to the Nationalist point of view. The Unionists simply reacted to the commission with bad manners: John Taylor said that Mitchell's presence was like having a Serb presiding over Croats. But Mitchell proved himself a model of diligence, intelligence, patience and fairness, taking submissions, talking to principals, and studying the poisoned web of Six County politics. His two colleagues too proved to be considerable figures, and on 26 January 1996, the trio produced a report which contained a formula for getting over the decommissioning crisis, which became known as the Mitchell Principles, and on which all-party talks were ultimately based. The formula in effect suggested 'parking' the decommissioning issue, saying: 'However the decommissioning issue is resolved, that alone will not lead directly to all-party negotiations. Much work remains on the many issues involved on the political track. The parties should address those issues with urgency.' The Mitchell Principles sought to commit all parties

a) To democratic and exclusively peaceful means of resolving political issues;

b) To the total disarmament of all paramilitary organisations;

c) To agree that such disarmament must be verifiable to the satisfaction of an independent commission;

d) To renounce for themselves, and to oppose any effort by others, to use force or threaten to use force, to influence the course of the outcome of all-party negotiations;

e) To agree to abide by the terms of any agreement reached in all-party negotiations and to resort to democratic and exclusively peaceful methods in trying to alter any aspect of that outcome with which they may disagree; and

f) To urge that 'punishment' killings and beatings stop and to take effective steps to prevent such actions.

The report dealt with other issues, including that of policing. It recommended that the RUC control the use of plastic bullets, and encourage more Catholic recruitment to the force, and, most significantly in the context of the decommissioning controversy, recommended that something be done about the contentious issue of legally held weapons. It was a lengthy report, containing 57 paragraphs on substantive matters, and five of what were termed 'concluding remarks'.

However, John Major greeted the report by ignoring almost all of it, with the exception of paragraph 56, which stated that 'several oral and written submissions raised the idea of an elected body if it were broadly acceptable within an appropriate mandate'. Based on this, he revivified Trimble's assembly proposal. The new Assembly was to have a 'weighted majority', code for 'controlled by Unionists', and in practice would have done little more than go back over the same issues which had already been dealt with in Dublin in the Forum on Peace and Reconciliation, with this difference – Sinn Féin were to be excluded. Remarkably, Major had a lengthy conversation with Bruton the day before he made known his decision to go ahead with the Assembly, but gave Bruton no hint of his intentions. The British followed this up by sending the Junior Minister for Northern Ireland, Michael Ancram, to Washington with the message: 'Who can be afraid of elections? Who can be afraid of democracy?' Here a comparison may fairly be drawn with the fact that, a few years later, when Tony Blair decided not to hold elections which had been scheduled for May 2003, both these questions were pointedly ignored because he feared that the outcome of the elections would be to return Ian Paisley's party as the dominant one on the Unionist side, and Sinn Féin on the Nationalist one.

Major's extraordinary decision, clearly taken under pressure from Trimble, who in those days was rarely out of the Conservative Party whips' office in the House of Commons, went down very badly on both sides of the Atlantic. Major, after all, had joined with Clinton in sponsoring the appointment of Mitchell, whose initiative he was now spurning. The White House greeted both the publication of the Mitchell Report and Major's reaction with a statement which expressed 'gratitude and appreciation' to the Mitchell Commission's members, declared the report 'helpful' on decommissioning and recommended that other ideas be 'urgently discussed'.

As indicated earlier, while preaching decommissioning, the British were also building up their military strength. A particular source of Nationalist anger was the construction of a huge new fort at the Donegal Road, a Republican heartland in which neither hearts nor minds were likely to be won by the construction of such an edifice. Nor were they. Following Major's assembly proposal, the Republicans decided that so long as the Tories continued in power, there was no point in continuing with the ceasefire. On 9 February 1996, the IRA brutally underlined the relevance of shovels to the commissioning argument by detonating a three-ton fertiliser bomb in London's Canary Wharf. It caused some £150 million worth of damage to the City of London, and claimed two lives.

The IRA statement issued after the blast contained the following:

The cessation presented a historic challenge for everyone and Oglaigh na h'Eireann commends the leadership of Nationalist Ireland at home and abroad. They rose to the challenge.

The British Prime Minister did not. Instead of embracing the peace process the British government acted in bad faith, with Mr Major and the Unionist leaders squandering this unprecedented opportunity to resolve the conflict.

Time and time again over the last eighteen months selfish party political and sectional interests in the London Parliament have been placed before the rights of the people of Ireland.

We take this opportunity to reiterate our total commitment to our Republican objectives. The resolution of the conflict in our country demands justice. It demands inclusive negotiated settlement. This is not possible unless and until the British government faces up to its responsibilities. The blame for the failure thus far of the Irish peace process lies squarely with John Major and his government.

These profoundly depressing developments were followed by a spate of other bomb attacks, of which the most destructive was that on the Arndale Centre in Manchester on 15 June, and by a series of arrests and killings. The effects of these were added to by further rioting and tension caused by the Drumcree situation, which helped to make July 1996 one of the most unpleasant months of the Troubles. The impression that the Conservatives in general, and Sir Patrick Mayhew in particular, did not inhabit the same planet shared by the rest of those involved in the Six County trauma was heightened that month when Sir Patrick Mayhew told an interviewer to 'Cheer up. No one has been killed yet.' In fact, between the calling of the ceasefire in August 1994, and the time Sir Patrick spoke, 27 people had been killed by the IRA, the British army, or the Loyalists, and the death toll would shortly escalate sharply.

However, no worthwhile political initiatives occurred until New Labour, under Tony Blair, secured its landslide majority in May of 1997. Blair, who had strong Irish connections through his mother's Donegal origins, and happy memories of his boyhood Irish holidays, interpreted his colossal mandate for change as having an urgent relevance to the Irish situation. One of his first public gestures was to make an apology for Britain's role in the great famine. The first official contacts with Dublin were extremely encouraging and Blair also sanctioned the reopening of talks with Sinn Féin, although these had to be temporarily suspended within weeks of their commencement after the IRA shot two members of the RUC in Lurgan, County Armagh, on 16 June. But despite serious rioting following the Garvaghy Road march again being forced through against the wishes of the residents in July, the Provisionals publicly announced that the ceasefire was being restored on 20 July, and a few weeks later (on 26 August), the Independent International Commission on Decommissioning was set up under General de Chastelain, to oversee the decommissioning of all paramilitary weapons. Mo Mowlam, the new Secretary of State for Northern Ireland, announced that she considered that the new ceasefire provided a basis for Sinn Féin to enter multi-party talks, and the party accordingly signed up to the Mitchell Principles and entered the talks at Stormont on 9 September. Apart from Sinn Féin, those taking part included Trimble's Ulster Unionist Party (UUP) and some of the smaller Unionist parties which had emerged from the Loyalist paramilitaries, notably the Progressive Unionist Party (PUP) led by Billy Hutchinson and David Irvine. Paisley's Democratic Unionist Party (DUP) boycotted the talks, which were strengthened, however, when, on 13 October, Gerry Adams and Martin McGuinness met Tony Blair for the first time.

The talks hit a major snag when Billy Wright, the most prominent Loyalist leader, was shot and killed by members of the INLA in Long Kesh prison. How Wright came to be murdered while in the care of the state is one of those unsolved mysteries which have their roots in the unsavoury underworld collusion between elements in the security forces and the paramilitaries.[18] What can be said with certainty is that the death almost derailed the talks, which may or may not have been its objective. The Loyalist prisoners reacted by withdrawing their support for the peace process, which could have had an effect akin to a similar withdrawal by IRA prisoners and led to another H-block-type confrontation. But in an extraordinarily daring initiative, Mo Mowlam entered the prison and successfully debated with the prisoners until they agreed to withdraw their opposition. Further problems developed in the discussions when the political offshoot of the UDA, the Ulster Democratic Party (UDP), was expelled from the talks because of the involvement of some of its cover organisation's grouping, the Ulster Freedom Fighters (UFF), in the killing of Catholics which followed Wright's murder. No sooner was the UDP readmitted than Sinn Féin had to be expelled because of two killings carried out by Republicans. Sinn Féin was readmitted on 23 March, and after a series of negotiations far more tense and intricate than those involved in the creation of the treaty of 1921, the Good Friday Agreement of Easter 1998 was concluded on 10 April.

Its difficult birth was midwifed on both sides of the Atlantic. Final corroboration of the story must await the publication of Cabinet papers, but events both during and after the negotiations would appear to bear out accounts, which I first heard from a well-placed American source close to the talks, that it was Tony Blair who mainly influenced the outcome. He is said to have called Trimble into an office a few days before the conclusion of the agreement and broken his opposition with a crisp account of the real cost to the British tax payer of maintaining the Six Counties. Outlining his own current budgetary difficulties – the Cabinet at the time had considered retrenchments which included cutting lone-parent benefit – he told Trimble that the British tax payer was prepared to continue paying for the north 'for another few years', but would require a favourable outcome to the negotiations. It is certainly worthy of note that, in the days of Sir Patrick Mayhew, Conservative references to the cost of maintaining the Six Counties ran at around £3.5 billion per year. After the Blair–Trimble confrontation, this mushroomed to between £9.5 and £14 billion.

Clinton stayed near a phone throughout the concluding stages of the talks, and Blair and the Irish Taoiseach, Bertie Ahern, intervened at crucial stages, Dublin dealing mainly, though not exclusively, with the Nationalist parties and London with the Unionists. Dublin's civil servants and the SDLP's Seamus Mallon and Mark Durkan all deserve credit for the historic document which emerged that hopeful day. The agreement provided for a new power-sharing assembly, which was to function on the basis of 'parallel consent', which meant that no measure could be enacted unless it had the agreement of a majority on either side of the political divide. It seemed that, should the occasion arise, the long-standing Unionist veto could now be nullified by an equally effective Nationalist one. There were to be new cross-border institutions, and to strengthen Anglo-Irish friendships, Dublin agreed to appoint consul generals to both Edinburgh and Cardiff. The British agreed to changes to their constitutional legislation which overrode the Government of Ireland Act so as to allow for a recognition of the will of the majority of the people living in Northern Ireland on the issue of remaining in the United Kingdom or joining with the Republic. The Anglo-Irish Agreement of 1985, which the Unionists detested, disappeared, as did the secretariat set up by the agreement at Maryfield, outside Belfast. Dublin also agreed to hold a referendum to drop Articles 2 and 3, replacing them in the constitution with a new and more generous vision of Irishness in official statements:

Article 2

It is the entitlement and birthright of every person born in the island of Ireland, which includes its islands and seas, to be part of the Irish nation. That is also the entitlement of all persons otherwise qualified in accordance with law to be citizens of Ireland. Furthermore, the Irish nation cherishes its special affinity with people of Irish ancestry living abroad who share its cultural identity and heritage.

Article 3

1. It is the firm will of the Irish nation, in harmony and friendship, to unite all the people who share the territory of the island of Ireland, in all the diversity of their identities and traditions, recognising that a united Ireland shall be brought about only by peaceful means with the consent of a majority of the people, democratically expressed in both jurisdictions in the island. Until then, the laws enacted by the Parliament established by this Constitution shall have the like area and extent of application as the laws enacted by the Parliament that existed immediately before the coming into operation of this Constitution.
2. Institutions with executive powers and functions that are shared between those jurisdictions may be established by their respective responsible authorities for stated purposes and may exercise powers and functions in respect of all or any part of the island.

The six cross-border bodies[19] were to deal with trade and business development; European matters; languages, by which was meant development of both the Irish language and the Ulster-Scots dialect; inland waterways; aquaculture; and food safety. These last three were relatively minor matters, and deliberately so intended by the Unionists, who sought to avoid giving Trimble's opponents in the UUP ammunition to bolster the charge that the cross-border bodies were a prelude to a united Ireland. One of the most protracted and heated debates concerned the Unionists' objections to having one of the most obvious areas of co-operation of all, tourism, dealt with by a cross-border body. Their preference was for an all-Ireland private company, which enabled them to claim that they had cut the number of cross-border bodies from seven to six. They also insisted that tourism should remain with the Department of Economic Development, which was to be renamed 'Enterprise, Trade and Investment', rather than move to the new Department of Culture, Arts and Leisure, where it might be construed as giving weight to innovation in the eyes of a Unionist electorate suspicious of any change. Much of the wrangling was carried out for optical reasons. Examined in the cold light of day, the cross-border bodies did not contain a great deal of substance. Their significance lay in their growth potential for the future. The shutting down of Maryfield was more than offset by the installation, in a prestigious building in the centre of Belfast, of even more Dublin civil servants from the Departments of Justice and of Foreign Affairs. The importance of these developments was underlined by the calibre of the officials selected, notably Ray Bassett, one of the Department's best men.

But of course the most important and significant undertakings of the entire agreement were the two which did not appear in it. Under the tutelage of Gerry Adams, the IRA had accepted the British presence and agreed to recognise the border, trusting that in time peaceful change, flowing from the agreement, would mean the disappearance of both. The agreement also contained the implicit understanding that, despite all the agonising over abstention, Sinn Féin would now enter Stormont. However one analyses the achievement of Good Friday 1998, the Sinn Féin commitment, combined with the changes to the Irish constitution, have to be adjudged as high-water marks in the growth of Nationalist support for conceding the principle of consent to their Orange brethren. Alas, this growth in maturity was not reciprocated by majority Unionist opinion and, as we shall see in context, important segments of republicanism also opposed the agreement, with particularly appalling results.

Paisley and his party remained opposed to the agreement, although ultimately the DUP did enter the Assembly and its elected members both drew their pay and worked with their supposedly hated Sinn Féin counterparts. A prominent rival to Trimble within the UUP, Jeffrey Donaldson, who had helped to negotiate the agreement, and who was also a Westminster MP, refused to sign the agreement because Sinn Féin were to be admitted to the Assembly in advance of decommissioning. Donaldson and David Burnside subsequently constituted the main focus of opposition to the agreement within the UUP. Burnside, a London-based public relations expert, had achieved notoriety for his role in the campaign which British Airways had conducted against Richard Branson's Virgin Airways, when the two airlines were locked in boardroom battle. Burnside was also the moving spirit in the London-based Friends of the Union, which drew support not only from backbench Tories, but from powerful Conservative figures, of whom the most notable was Viscount Cranborne, a member of the Cecil family and a direct descendant of the first Lord of the Plantation, Lord Burleigh. Cranbourne achieved a particular influence over Northern Ireland policy after he had supported John Major in his leadership battles, and he was regarded as being responsible for much of what was done, or not done, in the closing stages of John Major's regime.

However, initially, the UUP extended a welcome to the Good Friday Agreement; the Ulster Unionist Party executive voted 55 to 23 in favour of acceptance. But neither in the wake of this vote, nor subsequently, did David Trimble show the leadership or the commitment required to harness widespread Unionist support for the agreement. To further the peace process, London and Washington influence was brought to bear to ensure that the 1998 Nobel Peace Prize was not given solely to John Hume, but divided between him and Trimble. Trimble used the Oslo ceremony to attack Sinn Féin. In the midst of some high-flown rhetoric invoking the writings of Edmund Burke, he raised the subject of decommissioning, saying that delays in achieving it would reinforce suspicions that Sinn Féin was 'still drinking from the dark stream of fascism', and went back to the days of the Cold War for guidance. He said:

> What we need is George Keenan's hard-headed advice to the State Department in the 1960s for dealing with the state terrorists of his time, based on his years in Moscow. 'Don't act chummy with them, don't assume a community of aims with them which does not really exist, don't make fatuous gestures of goodwill.'[20]

Trimble might be accused of sometimes making 'fatuous gestures', but rarely of goodwill. He never came remotely near mounting the same spirited defence for the agreement which John Hume and his SDLP colleagues, or Adams and the rest of the Sinn Féin leadership, deployed in overcoming the doubts of their followers. Initially he did not have to. The executive vote was followed a week later (on 18 April 1998) by a vote in the UUP's ruling council to endorse the agreement by 540 votes to 210, which was roughly in line with what the opinion polls of the period were showing. But the council, which is largely composed of members of the Orange Order, has, to borrow the language of the Good Friday Agreement, a 'weighted majority' in favour of reaction. It has a large block vote from the Order itself. The Young Unionist Council also has a block vote on the council and it, despite the indication of its title, is a strongly reactionary and conservative grouping. In a word, the council was devised as a means of maintaining Orange Order and Unionist Party control, not of giving expression to moderate Protestant opinion.

Moderate Protestant opinion received a severe affront to its concepts of justice, in which transgressors should be punished for their deeds, when an unforeseen outburst of emotion took place at a Sinn Féin Ard Fheis, on 10 May, which voted overwhelmingly to allow Sinn Féin members to take their seats in the proposed assembly, and alter the party's constitution accordingly. But as part of the Good Friday Agreement, prominent IRA prisoners, including members of the Balcombe group, who had conducted a series of bombing attacks across London, and as part of the general thaw had been transferred to an Irish prison, were allowed out on short-term release to attend the Ard Fheis. Their appearance created a spontaneous explosion of cheering which lasted for several minutes and greatly affronted Unionist opinion. Pointedly, when the UDA's political wing, the Ulster Democratic Party, conducted a rally in favour of the agreement, also attended by a short-term release prisoner, Michael Stone, who had been jailed for his attack on the crowd attending the funeral of the IRA group cut down by the SAS in Gibraltar, Stone was not invited to speak. Apart from the prisoners' hiccup, all-Ireland sentiment in favour of the agreement was such that when the parallel referenda were held at the end of May, the results were as follows:

Northern Ireland	*Republic of Ireland*
Yes: 71.12%	Yes: 94.39%
No: 28.88%	No: 5.61%

In the euphoria which greeted the results, insufficient attention was paid to the discrepancy in 'yes' percentages north and south of the border. The 'yes' figure in the north was only achieved after a televised U2 concert in Belfast under the slogan 'Vote Yes' had had an impact on the younger voters. Trimble, who had conducted a lacklustre campaign, made a rare public appearance with Hume. However, when the result was announced, DUP propaganda immediately began to claim that it was not a true representation of opinion since a majority of Unionists had voted 'no'. This was the first all-Ireland poll since 1918, and its percentages were broadly in line with those in favour of Home Rule at that time. Unfortunately, the same disregard for the Home Rule verdict by Unionists then was shortly to be displayed towards the Good Friday Agreement by the contemporary standard-bearers of Unionism. The elections called for under the agreement were held on 25 June 1998, and resulted as follows:

Ulster Unionist Party	28
Democratic Unionist Party	20
Social Democratic and Labour Party	24
Sinn Féin	18
Alliance Party of Northern Ireland	5
United Kingdom Unionist Party	5
Progressive Unionist Party	2
Northern Ireland Women's Coalition	2
Others	3

Optimism levels continued to be high. The new Assembly met on 1 July and elected a First Minister Designate, Trimble, and a Deputy First Minister Designate, Seamus Mallon, Deputy Leader of the SDLP. But before any constructive business could be done as a result of these appointments, noises off, very terrible noises off, took centre stage.

On the Republican side, a split had developed over Adams's policy. Publicly, it became known that a new grouping had been launched (on 7 December 1997), known as the Thirty-Two County Sovereignty Committee, with whom a former leading Provisional, Michael McKevitt, and his partner, Bernadette Sands, a sister of Bobby Sands, were associated. Privately, what became known as the Real IRA was formed from the ranks of the dissidents. As I have indicated earlier, the core motivation of the IRA is sovereignty, a belief that Britain has no place in Ireland. In addition to this ancestral tenet, the Real IRA held as an article of faith that Unionists would never come to terms with Republicans, and that when the crunch came, the British would not force them to.[21] Therefore, the Good Friday Agreement was doomed to fail, and force was the only answer.

Acting on these beliefs, the Real IRA commenced a series of bombings and shootings which culminated in the carnage at Omagh on 15 August 1998, in which 29 civilians, including a woman who was expecting twins, and Spanish schoolchildren, were killed in a botched car bombing. After this atrocity, the Real IRA declared a ceasefire, assisted in coming to this decision by a series of visits paid to their former associates by members of the Provisional IRA. The INLA, which had been engaged in bloody internal feuding as much as in attacks on the security forces, also declared a ceasefire in the wake of Omagh.

Another Republican splinter group, the Continuity IRA, also commenced a series of operations from July 1996 onwards. Police activity, however, severely inhibited the activities of Continuity, one of whose most notable actions was the first publicly claimed, the bombing of a hotel near Enniskillen, County Fermanagh, on 14 July. Ruairi O'Bradaigh became the leader of a political grouping, Republican Sinn Féin (RSF), which denied that it was allied to the Continuity IRA, though RSF was supported by some Continuity members. RSF derived sufficient political support to be able to open an office in Belfast, claiming in O'Bradaigh's words to be the 'authentic Republican grouping'.

On the Loyalist side, a spate of killings and bombings also broke out from March 1997 onwards, after Billy Wright split from the Belfast-led UVF to found his own, Portadown-based, Loyalist Volunteer Force (LVF). Wright was one of those most prominently associated in the public mind with the security-force-run death squads, and is believed to have been responsible for some 30 deaths. He was also responsible for the 'muscle' behind the Drumcree protests, and the attempts by the Belfast UVF to suppress the LVF led to several killings, before Wright was picked up on what was literally a holding charge, issuing threats of death as opposed to causing them, placed in Long Kesh, and subsequently murdered.

A number of other Loyalist groupings surfaced in the late nineties. One was the Red Hand Defenders, who acknowledged their first killing, a bomb explosion, on 6 October 1998. It presented itself as a quasi-religious grouping, issuing statements which indicated that it took its inspiration from the Bible, Deuteronomy, Chapter 7, Verse 2: 'And the Lord thy God shall have delivered them to thee: thou shalt utterly destroy them. Thou shalt make no league with them, nor show mercy to them ... neither shalt thou make marriages with them.' One of those to whom the Defenders showed no mercy was Rosemary Nelson, the solicitor who acted for the Nationalist Garvaghy Road Residents Association. She was murdered by a bomb placed under her car on 15 March 1999. Another organisation which came into being, after an appeal was circulated within the Orange Order seeking volunteers, was the Orange Volunteers, whose bombings commenced on 17 December 1998. It degenerated into drug-dealing. Yet another Protestant fundamental grouping of the period was Caleb, which found its inspiration on the Internet, and modelled itself ideologically speaking on the Ku Klux Klan, the Black Israelites, and Combat Eighteen, the fascist grouping named after Hitler's birthday (18 April 1889). Caleb also threatened to exterminate the enemies of Ulster and the Protestant religion, but appears to have disappeared without causing a great deal of bloodshed, which is more than can be said for the late nineties generally. Between mid-July 1996 and the end of July 1999, there were some 70 deaths caused by either paramilitary or security force action.

None of the foregoing did anything to help resolve the developing crisis over decommissioning. The relevant paragraphs concerning the issue in the Good Friday Agreement are as follows:

Strand One. Article 25
Those who hold office should use only democratic, non-violent means, and those who do not should be excluded or removed from office under these provisions:

De-Commissioning, Paragraph 3
All participants accordingly reaffirm their commitment to the total disarmament of all paramilitary organizations. They also confirm their intention to continue to work constructively, and in good faith with the Independent Commission, and to use any influence they may have, to achieve the decommissioning of all paramilitary arms within two years following endorsement in referendums North and South of the agreement and in the context of the implementation of the overall settlement.

Adams interpreted these statements as containing nothing to prevent the immediate establishment of an Assembly executive including Sinn Féin. Trimble countered by refusing to contemplate allowing Sinn Féin into government in advance of decommissioning. But despite the yawning gap in the two positions, the two men met for the first time on 10 September 1998, which was also the first time that a Sinn Féin leader and a member of the Unionist Party had met since the foundation of the northern statelet. Other confidence-building motions continued. More prisoners were released and it was announced that some British army checkpoints and installations were to be demolished.

The putting in place of one particular confidence-building motion, however, angered the Unionists as much as it cheered the Nationalists. This was the setting up under the terms of the Good Friday Agreement of the Patten Commission, chaired by Chris Patten, to investigate the workings of the RUC to suggest reforms. The members of the commission included Dr Maurice Hayes, who had been one of Northern Ireland's top civil servants, Sir John Smith, a former Deputy Commissioner of London's Metropolitan Police, Peter Smith, QC, and another legal expert on policing, Kathleen O'Toole, from Boston. The commission took exhaustive soundings throughout the province before reporting (on 9 September 1999), a year after being set up, that what was needed was a force acceptable to both traditions which, *ipso facto*, meant increasing Catholic recruitment. Patten also recommended that the new force be called the Northern Ireland Police Service, and that its symbol, a badge showing a British crown on top of an Irish harp, should be scrapped, along with the custom of flying the Union Jack outside police stations. In addition, the overall size of the force was to be cut down.

From the time that Patten began his hearings, his operation was viewed with suspicion by the Unionists, who saw the RUC as a vital bulwark in maintaining 'our law' and 'our order'. Unionists in the Six Counties while the old Stormont still stood used to refer with confidence to 'The Orange Shamrock': the Orange Order, the Unionist Party and the RUC. Now the third leaf of the trefoil was being snipped off. This of course hardened attitudes over the decommissioning debate. In the absence of decommissioning, no executive had been formed by 31 October, which had been set as the deadline on which power-sharing was to commence. The SDLP issued a promise at its annual conference two weeks later that it would co-operate with the Unionists in removing Sinn Féin from the executive if the IRA failed to decommission, but this failed to convince Trimble and his party. The argument dragged on, and the following July, after Trimble and his party aborted an attempt to form an executive, by the simple expedient of not turning up at Stormont, the SDLP and Sinn Féin attempted to kick-start the Assembly into life by forming an executive between them. The attempt failed almost immediately because under the terms of the Good Friday Agreement, the proposed executive would not have had cross-party support. However, Seamus Mallon took a step which made a bad situation better. He resigned as Deputy First Minister Designate, which effectively created as great a crisis for the Assembly as if Trimble himself had resigned.

Once more Senator Mitchell was sent for, and he began a review of the Good Friday Agreement on 6 September 1999. The review was overshadowed by the publication of the Patten Report, which was unanimously rejected by the UUP Conference on 9–10 October 1999 as a 'threat to security'. The conference also showed itself to be strongly opposed to allowing Sinn Féin into government without decommissioning. However, the injection of a new element into the proceedings appeared to mellow Trimble somewhat. The day after the UUP Conference, Peter Mandelson was appointed to succeed Mo Mowlam as Secretary of State for Northern Ireland. Trimble had suggested that Blair appoint Mandelson, who commended himself to Unionists by virtue of the fact that it was his grandfather, Herbert Morrison, who had given legislative form to the Unionist veto after the south declared itself a republic. After talks at Stormont on 16 November, Adams and Trimble issued statements in which Adams spoke of the need to work with, not against, Unionists, and Trimble of the Nationalist goal of a united Ireland as being a 'legitimate aspiration'. He declared himself to be in favour of equality, inclusivity and mutual respect. This was greeted by the IRA the following day with an obviously prearranged statement announcing that it proposed to enter formal negotiations on decommissioning with General de Chastelain. Mitchell added his mead of sweetness and light by announcing that as a result of his review, he had decided that there was a basis for commencing devolution and forming a government. Seamus Mallon withdrew his resignation, and on 29 November 1999, for the first time in 25 years, Northern Ireland regained a power-sharing executive. Direct rule ended the following day, when Westminster approved devolution orders transferring power from London to Belfast.

It appeared that at long last, the hopes of the Good Friday Agreement were about to be realised. But in the euphoria of the moment, few people paused to analyse the significance of an action of Trimble's on 27 November. A meeting of the Ulster Unionist Council had voted two days before the formation of the power-sharing executive to accept Senator Mitchell's findings, and thus allowed Trimble to enter government with Sinn Féin. He caught the media's attention with a remark he addressed to Adams at the subsequent press conference: 'We have jumped. Now it's up to you.' Little heed was paid to the fact that the 480 to 349 vote in favour of this action was bought at the price of a letter written by Trimble announcing that he would resign as First Minister if decommissioning did not occur within months. He had also proposed a motion calling for a reconvening of the council in February 'to take a final decision'. Adams protested that Trimble's action was outside the terms of the Good Friday Agreement, but to no avail. The Assembly's long stagger towards effectiveness continued, with the Nationalists apparently gaining the most significant portfolios in the negotiations over which departments were allocated to which parties. Mark Durkan of the SLDP received Finance, and Agriculture, the north's biggest industry, went to Brid Rogers, also of the SDLP. The two biggest-spending departments went to Sinn Féin. Martin McGuinness became Minister for Education and Bairbre de Brun Minister for Health.

But again appearances were deceptive. These portfolios had an all-Ireland dimension, as their holders necessarily interfaced with their southern counterparts, particularly in the realm of agriculture, and this the Unionists shrank from. They also shrank from continuing to share power with Sinn

Féin. The following February, Trimble presented the cheque of resignation which he had written in November to Peter Mandelson, who announced in the House of Commons on 12 February 2000 that he was cashing it in. Ironically the letter was handed into the office of the Speaker of the Assembly by Sir Josias Cunningham, President of the Ulster Unionist Council and a grandson of Samuel Cunningham, the man who had signed the cheques that paid for the rifles of Carson's Ulster Volunteer Force which were illegally run into Bangor and Larne in 1914 to prevent the introduction of Home Rule to Ulster. Presumably Samuel would have looked with favour on his grandson's action. Once more a measure of Home Rule was defeated, not because the Unionists wanted guns in but because they wanted them out.

The Assembly was suspended and direct rule restored. As suspension neared, a frenetic burst of diplomatic activity occurred between Dublin, Belfast, London and Washington. At 4.30 a.m. on Friday 11 February, this appeared to have succeeded. With the assistance of three top Dublin officials, Dermot Gallagher (Foreign Affairs), Patrick Teahon (Taoiseach's office) and Tim Dalton (Department of Justice), the de Chastelain Commission managed to agree a form of words with the IRA which indicated that decommissioning would take place. The de Chastelain report said: 'The representative [of the IRA] indicated to us today the context in which the IRA will initiate a comprehensive process to put arms beyond use, in a manner to ensure maximum confidence.' De Chastelain said that his commission felt that this undertaking contained 'the real prospect of an agreement which would enable it to fulfil the substance of its mandate'.

As the organisation had also indicated that it was prepared to issue a statement saying that the war was over, a formal declaration long sought by both the Conservatives and the Unionists, Bertie Ahern was satisfied that the agreement could be used to save the power-sharing executive. Peter Mandelson, however, apparently sided with the Unionists, whose concept of decommissioning – apparently designed with a view to generating the least possible degree of support from the IRA – was that it should be carried out before TV cameras in a series of events involving ever-increasing amounts of IRA arms. Blair backed him and, on the eve of his formal announcement of suspension in the House of Commons, Mandelson made a round of Belfast's TV studios giving a series of decidedly questionable interviews. He allowed it to be thought firstly that he had not seen the IRA statement and secondly that he understood that it contained nothing of substance. However, the BBC's North of Ireland Political Editor, the experienced Sidney Grimason, said later that he had seen Mandelson receiving a copy of the report early in the evening of the 11th,[22] an assertion which the Northern Ireland Office attempted to deny, saying that the document was from a civil servant, not the IRA. The *Irish Times* reported (on 19 February) that a British Government spokesman had informed the paper that the document would have satisfied Trimble's needs and avoided the suspension 'if it had been delivered earlier'. However, Mandelson himself told Niall O'Dowd that he had been expecting the IRA to decommission in the form sought by the Unionists and that consequently when he saw their statement he had no option but to suspend the assembly.

Wherever the truth lay, it was an extraordinarily arrogant performance. The Good Friday Agreement was after all an international treaty which should not have been swept aside at the stroke of a transient British secretary of state's pen. An angry Bertie Ahern took the unusual step of writing an article in the *Irish Times* pointing out that the Irish Government had amended its written constitution, after holding a referendum, so as to include the provisions of a British–Irish agreement which did not however include provisions for a suspension.[23] Amongst the legal difficulties which Mandelson's action caused for Dublin was the fact that the Irish language body, Bord na Gaeilge, had been transferred into a cross-border body which had now been abolished, thereby undermining the legality of paying staff for working for an organisation which had officially vanished.

The subsequent enactment of the peace process drama resembles a political version of Edward Albee's play *Who's Afraid of Virginia Wolf?* in which partners, trapped in a hellish marriage they can neither love nor leave, fight, wound and scream at each other over an oft-referred-to child which, as power-sharing often appeared to be, turns out to be a figment of their imagination. Yet, as in the play, somehow dialogue and a relationship were resumed. During a visit to Washington in March, Trimble, under pressure from the Americans, made a speech at the National Press Club in which he seemed to indicate that he would be prepared to go into another assembly experiment with Sinn Féin in advance of guns being delivered up. This elicited a challenge to his leadership from the former Grand Master of the Orange Lodge, the 68-year-old Reverend Martin Smith, which Trimble defeated at a meeting of the Ulster Unionist Council on 25 March by the disturbingly small margin of 57% of the vote to Smith's 43%. His supporters had briefed the media that the indications were that Trimble would achieve at least 70%. In addition, David Burnside succeeded in adding to the decommissioning straws on the camel's back a further load. He successfully carried a motion adding another precondition for entry into government with Sinn Féin – a retention of the name and symbols of the RUC.

A further bout of negotiation involving Sinn Féin, Dublin and London finally produced a breakthrough on decommissioning. On 6 May 2000, the IRA issued a statement saying that it was prepared to allow two distinguished international observers to inspect their dumps: Cyril Ramaphosa, the ex-Secretary General of the ANC, and the former Finnish president Marti Ahtisaari. The statement also promised to re-engage with the de Chastelain Commission, with which it had broken off relations following the suspension débâcle, and stated:

> To facilitate the speedy and full implementation of the GFA and the government's measures, our arms are silent and secure. There is no threat to the peace process from the IRA.

In this context the IRA leadership has agreed to put in place within weeks, a confidence-building measure to confirm that our weapons remain secure.

The contents of a number of our arms dumps will be inspected by agreed third parties who will report that they have done so to the IICD.

The dumps will be re-inspected regularly to ensure that the weapons remain secure.

This was greeted by the two governments with a statement which in effect promised that the Assembly would not come down so easily again. It promised that difficulties would be met by conducting a review in conjunction with the executive and the Assembly, not by automatic suspension. The IRA statement enabled Trimble to secure a 53% to 47% majority in favour of going back into power-sharing at a meeting of the Ulster Unionist Council in Belfast's Waterfront Hall on 27 May 2002. There was a production of Verdi's *Aida* scheduled for that evening, and even the normally prosaic Unionists commented on the apparent symbolism of Trimble standing beside a Union Jack surrounded by mummies. Most observers concur that the occasion was one of the few in the history of the peace process when a speech of his displayed any real enthusiasm for the agreement. Nevertheless, his winning margin over Smith a short while earlier had been reduced by 4% and Jeffrey Donaldson had received a visceral roar of approval when, in the course of a highly charged speech, he reminded his audience that, when he was a member of the UDR, he had 'lain in ditches defending Ulster'. Trimble made it clear at a press conference held after the vote that his motivation in fighting off Smith and Donaldson had been to retain his leadership, not affection for Sinn Féin, of whom he said: 'As far as democracy is concerned these folk ain't house-trained yet.' However, as far as the Assembly was concerned, the power-sharing executive was back up and running. On learning the result of the Waterfront vote, Peter Mandelson signed the orders restoring the institutions.

The restoration was not long lasting. Mandelson was removed from Northern Ireland and the Cabinet by a scandal involving attempts by a wealthy Indian businessman to secure a British passport, and it fell to his successor, Dr John Reid, to suspend the Assembly once more, in October 2002, after more threats of resignation by Trimble. The principal stated reasons for the Unionist dissatisfaction which led to the suspension were threefold: the discovery (on 13 August 2001) that three Republicans had been arrested in Colombia, where it was alleged that they had been training Marxist guerrillas; a break-in at the RUC's intelligence-gathering nerve centre at Castlereagh (on 17 March 2002); and the claim that Republicans had been running an intelligence network at Stormont. This was detonated on 4 October 2002 with a raid, involving some 200 members of the RUC, under the eyes of prearranged TV cameras, on the Sinn Féin offices at Stormont, in which a couple of computer disks were seized. Subsequently, Denis Donaldson, Sinn Féin's head of administration at Stormont, was arrested and charged in connection with the affair. Reid's suspension order followed.

In Six County politics, which frequently resemble an iceberg inasmuch as there is far more beneath the surface than meets the eye, it is not possible to say with authority at this stage just what lay behind the three events, particularly as at the time of writing there are court cases involved. But it is increasingly becoming likely that at least two of the commentators on the Castlereagh break-in appear to be accurate. The *Guardian* (on 22 June 2002) said that the break-in was not carried out by the IRA but was an 'inside job'. This view was reinforced four days later in the *Irish Independent* by the paper's security correspondent, Tom Brady, who quoted Gardai sources as saying that the raid had been carried out by 'rogue special branch officers' and was part of a 'well-orchestrated security campaign aimed at blackening the Provos and forcing Sinn Féin out of Stormont'.

Though it is more likely that the 'rogue officers' were intent on preventing evidence of their own wrongdoing coming to light, rather than merely trying to damage Sinn Féin, in either event, the following April and May, the revelations of both the Stevens Inquiry and the 'Stakeknife' affair finally sealed the argument as to whether or not the security forces had been involved in murder gangs. In the former, the distinguished police officer had succeeded, after years of trying, and despite efforts to hinder his inquiries which included setting fire to his office, in establishing that there was collusion between Loyalists and the security forces in the murder of the Catholic solicitor Patrick Finucane. In the second, it was revealed that security forces had had an informer, codenamed 'Stakeknife', in the highest reaches of the IRA for over a quarter of a century, and that he had been responsible for some 40 murders. As in the case of Brian Nelson, the army, however, had rarely used advance knowledge to prevent the killings of Catholics, which sometimes involved cross-border excursions. Only in cases involving Loyalists, though not inevitably, had the authorities moved to prevent a killing taking place. As in the case of many of the horrific events of the Troubles, the real issue now is not whether or not these things occurred, but of how to deal with them. Prosecutions or tribunals of inquiry, which cost hundreds of millions of pounds, and take for ever, are not appropriate in the circumstances of Northern Ireland. It may be that, while preserving the rights of victims or their families to compensation, the best way forward is that chartered by the South African Truth and Reconciliation Commission. Few parties to the conflict in the Six Counties emerge from what happened with untarnished reputations, but all should admit what was done, so that reality can be faced up to, and progress made.

At the time of writing, the position regarding the peace process is that neither side has fully faced up to the fact that the Orange and Republican traditions are mutually antipathetic, and that on the Orange side, a leadership deficit exists. I have been studying the northern conflict for 40 years, but I am still waiting for the emergence of a Unionist leader who, instead of finding reasons why progress should not be made, makes a speech in which the following words occur: 'children', 'the future', 'investment', 'Europe', 'global economy', 'assistance from America', 'reconciliation', 'whole-hearted co-operation with the Republic'. The depressing reality is that the most likely solution to the problem lies in crude population growth. The 1991 census, when extrapolated from by two Dublin demographers, Brendan Walshe and Cormac O'Grada, both distinguished academics, showed that the true figure for Catholics was probably in excess of 43%, some 5% more than the figures shown, because during the Troubles, Catholics living in Loyalist areas had disguised their religion from the census-takers. Their findings were hotly disputed by Unionist apologists, but the surge in the Sinn Féin vote three years later bore out the findings that Catholics were in a majority in the aged-15 category, and predominated in the lower age groups. It is conceded that the number of Catholic children attending school greatly exceeds that of Protestants.

The 2001 census findings, while conceding that the Catholic population was at least 43%, presumably in an effort to avoid frightening the Unionists, presented its figures in such a way as to make extrapolation difficult. However, the indicators are that in the inter-censal period, a considerable gain in Catholic numbers has been recorded. For example, local government election returns show that the combined Nationalist vote in Belfast at the time of writing now exceeds that of the Unionists. A Sinn Féin mayor, Alex Maskey, is completing his term of office, and in Dublin Government circles it is believed that the true Catholic population now stands at around 46–7%. As there is always a cohort of 'others', foreigners, students, etc., in census returns, this would place the Unionist population as having fallen below the psychologically important threshold of 50%. It is not the vision of Wolfe Tone, or of Padraig Pearse, but it may well be the reality.

Unionism in 2003 was as disinclined to share power with Nationalists as it had been in 1974. As Trimble's position weakened within his own party, and it seemed likely that Paisley would become the dominant Unionist leader on one side, and Gerry Adams and Sinn Féin would overhaul the SDLP on the other, he became more petulant and his party less inclined to come to an accommodation with Sinn Féin. In March 2002, Trimble told a meeting of the Ulster Unionist Council that the Republic of Ireland was a 'pathetic, sectarian, mono-cultural and mono-ethnic State'. Three days later, during a visit to Washington, he defended his remarks, saying, correctly, 'the language I used was nothing new, and one I used on many occasions'.

He later told American newspaper executives that the Irish Republic would have no reason to exist 'if you took away Catholicism and anti-Britishness'. At the end of the year (on 19 December), he took advantage of a leaked Dublin official document to walk out of talks involving the current Secretary of State, Paul Murphy, and the Irish Foreign Minister, Brian Cowen, in an effort to restore the Assembly. The document, an assessment of the current situation by a highly placed official, had noted that the IRA was occupying its members by recruiting, targeting, training, and maintaining its armament as a precautionary measure, not as a prelude to returning to war. The document also, correctly in my view, described the Ulster Unionist Party as being 'dysfunctional'. The Unionists did not advert to this judgement but made use of that concerning the IRA. Here it should be noted that one of the reasons the Provisionals maintained their organisation, and continued to recruit, was out of an all too soundly based fear that the continuing dearth of political activity and constitutional progress, combined with the existence of the Real IRA, posed a credible threat that disaffected young Nationalists could end up in it, or the re-emerging INLA.

These considerations increasingly made the IRA more disinclined to be accommodating on the decommissioning issue. Exhaustive talks involving Adams, Ahern and Blair broke down early in May 2003. By now, Ahern, his party becoming hourly more unpopular in the face of a deteriorating economic situation, was increasingly aware of the electoral gains which Sinn Féin was making in the south, and showed himself less inclined to support Adams's position than of yore. Blair was becoming increasingly concerned at the likelihood that the Six County elections scheduled for 29 May were going to ensure that the Unionist leader he would shortly have to deal with would not be David Trimble, who is generally regarded as being far from being his favourite person, but Ian Paisley. Accordingly, against Ahern's wishes, Blair announced, on 5 May, that the northern elections were to be postponed. 'Who can be afraid of elections? Who can be afraid of democracy?' Someone, somewhere, decided to improve the shining hour by leaking the 'Stakeknife' story, thereby leaving Adams facing Republican upheaval, not only over the blow to his strategy that participation in politics would achieve political aims by non-violent means, but from the backlash at the revelation that for several years IRA operations had apparently been directed by a British agent.

What the outcome of all this may be cannot be forecast, but at the time of writing the only beneficiaries from what has befallen the peace process are the nay-sayers in general, and the Real IRA in particular.

THIRTEEN

CULTURE AND SOCIETY

Writing in the Ireland of 2003 one has to be conscious of the fact that, in looking back through the arches of the years at a century of development, one is doing so through a prism of irritation caused by a variety of reasons which, being neither slight nor invalid, must therefore be chronicled, but should not be allowed to obscure the achievement of substantial, tangible, meritorious progress in many areas of Irish culture and society. The terrible slum conditions of the first part of the century described in earlier chapters have vanished. The educational system has been transformed, and with it has come both an attitudinal and an economic revolution, which has brought with it, amongst other benefits, a great amelioration of the emigration plague. This last alone stands out in the century as a towering achievement. Ireland left the twentieth century looking far better than she entered it. Though certain aspects of society, such as inequality, corruption, crime, standards of design and the chronic traffic problem, affect the senses, improvements have been made to such an extent that one of the principal architects of the state, Michael Collins, would no doubt gladly rescind a judgement (an accurate one for the time and for decades afterwards) he passed not long before he died: '. . . the fine, splendid surface of Ireland is besmirched by our towns and villages – hideous medleys of contemptible dwellings and mean shops and squalid public houses'.[1]

However, as we shall see when we return to the subject shortly, the cause of the 'hideous medleys' and the remedy for them which Collins proposed was part of the reason why the squalor continued so late into the century. The complexities of life ordain that the shining vision of people like Collins, heroic in scope and in idealism, has to be adjusted to the dull realities of life as it is actually lived. It is true that in the late nineties, for the first time in centuries, the Republic's per capita GDP nudged ahead of that of Britain, and far outperformed that of Northern Ireland. It is true that with this amazing economic growth, there came an accompanying flowering of talent, not only in traditional fields of Irish self-expression such as literature, music and song, but in the newer medium of film, both in directing and in acting. But, as has happened in other countries, growth has been uneven, and the poor, particularly the unorganised poor, did not do anything like as well in the economic stakes as did the rich. In 2001, for the second year in a row, Ireland ranked as the most 'globalised' of 62 states surveyed. The survey[2] measured the depth and extent of countries' memberships of international organisations, the number of foreign embassies it hosted, its Internet use, its trade, foreign investment, payment levels and other economic indicators.

What, in the nature of things, it did not concern itself with were issues such as the quality of life, or the hammer blows to public perceptions of political institutions or the Church by the situations which led to the setting up of tribunals and the subsequent revelations at them. Radio and television programmes are filled with despairing debate over issues such as teenage drunkenness, with its attendant rise in violence and sexual crime – the Garda figures for 2002 show that rape went up by 800% between 1980 and 2002. The assault on family life by the cost of living has made it necessary for both parents to work – that is, if there are two parents. The 1996 census showed that out of 807,000 family units 129,000 were based on a lone parent. Divorce rates had risen since the 1991 census by 60% to a total of 87,000 and the marriage rate had fallen to 4.5% per thousand, from 7.4% in 1973. As in Europe generally, the number of women having babies has fallen dramatically. When I began full-time employment on the *Evening Press* in far-away 1954, incidentally the last year in which anyone was hanged for murder in the Republic, there were two murders and one manslaughter that year. By the end of the century, the total of provable murders (that is where conviction can be sustained) per year had passed the fifty mark. At the half-century mark itself (1949), indictable offences of all sorts had reached a grand total of 12,171. By the end of the century, totals had climbed to seven or eight times this figure per year. Drugs played their part, of course. But there were other factors. As the annual Garda Commissioner's Report had noted as early as 1975:

> The overall crime picture can only be described as disturbing. Substantial increases in crime, first noted in 1966 [ironically the fiftieth anniversary of the 1916 Rising, author], have continued. Criminals are becoming more vicious and mean. Attacks on old and disabled people in their homes, a type of crime practically unknown in this country some years ago, are now on the increase. The use of firearms and other offensive weapons in robberies is becoming more widespread, and menacing.

The trend identified by the Commissioner has accelerated since 1975. Gangland shootings have become commonplace in the larger cities, particularly Dublin and Limerick. As in other countries, suicide levels, particularly young male suicides, have increased, to something over 10 per 1,000.[3] Allowing for the fact that the stigma attached to suicide meant that in the earlier part of the century such deaths were not recorded, it seems that contemporary rates are more than four times those obtaining in the middle years of the century. Older males, dependent on social welfare pensions, can hardly be said to receive any wondrous inducement to hang on to life either. As the extended family becomes less extended, and the tradition of the elderly living out their lives with their children becomes attenuated, the average weekly old age pension would be sufficient to pay for approximately one and a half days in the average nursing home. Poverty is far from being eradicated; the poor have six times the disease rates of the rich.

Taking all the foregoing together, it is not to be wondered at that on a day in November 2002 the country's leading newspaper wrote: 'Few will disagree that while the quality of the things we own has improved, our quality of life is declining.'[4] The experience of being a young Irish person in 2002 was described as being one of 'personal loneliness, lack of purpose and engagement'. What at first sight is surprising, however, is that a few days later, a respected commentator, Tony Fahey, told a conference that, based on internationally accepted criteria, there was no indication of disaffection amongst the young.[5] There were high levels of national pride in Ireland, a very strong sense of being in control of one's life, coupled with a large amount of confidence in the public sphere.

But should it be surprising? Firstly, the year was a good one economically, and for the young particularly, Ireland offers much. New job creation was slowing, but the sign over the national employment situation still read 'Help Wanted'. A year later it still does in some areas, but not only is new job creation slowing, redundancies are beginning to make a reappearance at a rate of approximately 500 per week. Foreigners are being refused work permits so as to allow native Irish workers to get jobs in the service industries. Inflation is running at almost double the European average, exports are affected by the ever-growing strength of the euro, and official statistics concede that domestic Irish food prices are 9% higher than the European average. Widespread complaints about the high cost of food and drink in Dublin's bars and restaurants do not bode well for the future of the tourism industry. Some of this was inevitable. The picture of success indicated by Ireland's performance in the 'globalisation' stakes was to a degree a catching-up performance to other developed economies, based on huge export growth. But 'globalisation' means what it says, and, apart from any philosophical reservations one may hold about the process, it means that the world's economic downturn makes Ireland particularly vulnerable to the effects of decisions taken in multinational boardrooms. Obviously, therefore, the country is entering on an era of slower growth than that of its 'Celtic Tiger' performance, an era moreover in which the Brussels gravy train will have departed the station. But slower does not mean slump. For example, the pharmaceutical industry, which includes Viagra in its output, would not appear to fear the future. Nor is there a dearth of Irish entrepreneurial talent with which to adjust to changing conditions. The tough, outspoken Michael O'Leary, who has led Ryanair into becoming one of the world's most successful airlines, is certainly an outstanding figure, but by no means the only one that one could point to in Irish industry. But in concentrating on economic developments, vital though they are to either self-fulfilment or intellectual freedom, are we in some way missing the point about change and developments in Irish society over the course of the twentieth century?

Should we look more closely at the character and personality of the Irish? I believe we should. G.K. Chesterton, writing about George Bernard Shaw, once observed that the man in the street was fundamentally ignorant and fundamentally correct. He knew that George Bernard Shaw did not eat meat, did not believe in God, and did write plays. Today, a man, or woman, in the street, looking at Ireland from the outside, and basing his or her judgement on the exuberance with which Ireland revels in its popular pastimes, would probably have anticipated Fahey's judgements. The outsider would have seen on his or her TV screen the unmistakable enthusiasm with which the huge crowds of cheerful, well-behaved and obviously well-pursed Irish fans support and follow their favourite sports, be they soccer, rugby, Gaelic football, hurling or horse-racing. He or she will have noticed both the cult status accorded to, and the profusion of, singers and musicians who seem to emerge from Ireland in a never-ending flow. The stereotypical picture of the singing, partying, hard-drinking, talented, in some strange way religious Irishman, frolicking against a boggy, beautiful background, where the Quiet Man might appear at any moment, would appear to have some validity to the outsider.

And not merely to the outsider. As I was writing this, I listened to a radio interview[6] with a member of the group of fans who had accompanied the Irish entrant to the Eurovision Song Contest in Riga, Latvia, in May 2003. The singer had only come eleventh the previous night, but he might as well have won the competition to judge from the enthusiasm with which the hoarse-voiced fan, a young woman, described the trip over the phone on her way to the airport. Apart from the buzz of the actual competition, the party appeared to have majored in alcohol and minored in sleep:

> It was *great*! We had a *ball*! The average monthly wage in Latvia is two hundred euros. So at two o'clock in the morning, we took up a collection in the bar and we got a thousand euros, so we were able to hand over five months' wages to a charity. We had a lovely mass. There was a priest with us, and he was great craic. There were different performers and singers joining in the mass . . .

In its own way, the stereotype *does* have validity. Stereotypes survive not because of their hackneyed nature, but because of the quotient of truth embedded in them.

Until the era of Lemass/Whitaker and the second Vatican Council, what might be termed the Authorised Version of the thinking of the founding fathers of the Irish Republic, what Tom Garvin, in an important essay, termed the 'priests and the patriots',[7] was that the Ireland to be striven for was to be self-sufficient, Catholic and Irish-speaking. As with other anti-colonial movements, the deficiencies of the Ireland of the turn of the century were seen as those derived from the occupier and the oppressor. Given the extent of the anglicisation process described in Chapter One, it was inevitable that Irish Nationalists would attempt to swing the pendulum in the other direction. In his strictures on the appearance of Irish towns quoted above, Collins said that the reason for their ghastliness was that

> English civilisation . . . for us . . . is a misfit. The Irish . . . qualities are hidden, besmirched, by what has been imposed upon us, just as the fine splendid surface of Ireland is besmirched by our towns and villages . . . we are now free in name. The extent to which we become free, in fact, and secure our freedom, will be the extent to which we become Gaels again . . . the biggest task will be the restoration of the language.[8]

Collins and his contemporaries were building on an ideological legacy bequeathed to them by an idealised past, in which, prior to the coming of the invader, learning flourished in a prosperous land. Part of the ideological baggage they carried included an unconscious sectarianism. A much-quoted literary figure of the early century was Daniel Corkery, who wrote about *The Hidden Ireland*, the culture of the Irish-speaking Catholics of eighteenth-century Ireland, and about the poetry and poets[9] of the dispossessed, who spoke in idealised terms of the days that were, and the deliverance to come. Inevitably, such writing identified Catholicism with patriotism and Protestantism with despoliation. The actual experience of living in nineteenth-century Ireland heightened this identity. O'Connell's major success was to secure Catholic emancipation, which he followed by securing tithe reform and some improvements in municipal elections. The latter eroded Protestant hegemony and enabled him to become the first Catholic Lord Mayor of Dublin (in 1840). For those with a taste in historical parallels it might be noted that the consequences of electoral reform bear an uncanny resemblance to what is taking place in Northern Ireland as this is being written: Belfast's first Sinn Féin mayor, Alex Maskey, handed over his seal of office not to a reclaiming Unionist, but to a member of the SDLP, Martin Morgan. Morgan is the third Nationalist to wear the mayoral chain. Alban Maginness, also of the SDLP, became the city's first Nationalist mayor in 1997. O'Connell's utilisation of the Catholic clergy in his unsuccessful attempt to secure repeal of the Union further underlined the image of the superimposition of the priest upon that of the patriot, in the eyes of Protestants. Behind the demands for democracy, the Protestant saw, as he would be encouraged to see behind the demands for civil rights a hundred years later, the spectre of Rome. However, as the eye-witness account of de Tocqueville quoted in Chapter 1 illustrates, O'Connell was merely incorporating into his political machine in a formal way the energies of a clergy whose people already looked up to them as the trusted authority figures who mediated for them with an uncaring state, a process which had gone on since the Cromwellian Act of Settlement of 1652.

But Irish Protestants were further encouraged in their acceptance of a belief that Catholicism posed a threat to their way of life by what has been termed the Second Reformation in Ireland, which affected Protestants of all denominations in both Britain and Ireland in the first 50 years of the century. A proselytising zeal towards the Catholics seized Anglican, Baptist,

Methodist and Presbyterian. Biblical societies were formed, tracts poured forth, and a precursor of Ian Paisley, the Reverend Henry Cooke, (1788–1865), a Northern Ireland Presbyterian, preached a particularly efficacious brand of fundamentalism, which helped to combat the effects of the Enlightenment, and gave new life to the Orange Order. In turn, the Catholic was driven to an increased reliance on his Church by the famine, and by subsequent religious and political changes which, to a large extent, formed the type of 'traditional Irish Catholicism' which the Republic's founding fathers knew and practised. Before examining this 'traditional Catholicism', let us fast-forward for a moment to two assessments of it. One is by the respected historian Joe Lee, the other by Father Vincent Twomey, SVD, a distinguished Maynooth theologian. In 1989, Lee completed a survey of the history of Ireland in the preceding 73 years by saying of the Church:

> The Church is a bulwark, perhaps now the main bulwark, of the civic culture. It is the very opportunism of the traditional value system that leaves religion as the main barrier between a reasonably civilised civil society and the untrammelled predatory instincts of individual and pressure-group selfishness, curbed only by the power of rival predators . . . in a society where faith and culture are so intimately intertwined. It is precisely this close connection that leaves the civic culture so vulnerable to a rapid decline in the role of institutional religion. If religion were to no longer fulfil its historic civilising mission as a substitute for internalised values of civil responsibility, the consequences for the country no less than for the Church could be lethal.[10]

We will return to Lee's somewhat apocalyptic, though in the light of some of the facts stated above, understandable judgement a little later, after visiting, or perhaps more accurately revisiting, the factors already indicated in Chapter One which created for the Church the position about which Lee and Twomey wrote. Writing about the 'erosion of Catholicism's public presence in Irish life', Twomey found that 'The once powerful "traditional Irish Catholicism" marked by a close identity of being Irish and Catholic of a particular kind seems to be grinding to a halt in the face of the Celtic Tiger, and a secular "pluralist" modern Ireland.'[11] Twomey sympathised with early twentieth-century writers like Seán O'Faolain, who had found 'traditional Irish Catholicism' to be seriously flawed, 'narrow minded, anti-intellectual and rigorist on morality', and agreed with those who argue that because of post-famine developments in Ireland, that culture was not authentically Irish at all. In fact, he stated that it was his conviction that 'neither was traditional Irish Catholicism fully Catholic'.

I believe Father Twomey to be correct in his analysis. I believe that the Irish psyche took, or was pushed into taking, a wrong turning in the post-famine years. Though I do not share the Gaelic revivalists' conviction that the true mark of an Irishman is the Irish language – 'Irishness' goes deeper than that – it must be acknowledged that the loss of the Irish language did help to weaken the sense of distinctively Irish identity and culture. Much has been said in these pages about emigration and its effect on Irish life, but as the nineteenth century wore on, another type of exile became common – the internal exile – who, though he had not left his country, found that his culture was leaving him and that school, press and state agency were encouraging him to think of himself as an Englishman and become a neat, clean, well-advised chap who knew the rules of getting ahead and espoused Protestant values. These pressures helped to convince the Catholic population ever more firmly of the necessity to bandage its bleeding soul with the contents of the Church's combined first-aid and identity kit. Those bandages were of a particularly dull design and restrictive nature. They were manufactured largely by Cardinal Paul Cullen, who successfully completed the attempt begun in the twelfth century by John of Salisbury and Pope Adrian to bring the Irish Church under Rome's control by carrying out the Devotional Revolution mentioned in Chapter One. It was a revolution aimed at the mind as well as the soul. His first major act was the holding of an episcopal synod at Thurles in 1850, the first to be held in Ireland since the twelfth century. As a result, the hierarchical structure was strengthened so that power was exercised by the Roman Curia via the cardinal and the bishops to ensure that Rome's writ ran in every aspect of Irish educational and religious practice.

Prior to Cullen, who was appointed Archbishop of Armagh in 1849 and was appointed to Dublin in 1852, where he ruled until 1878, Irish religious practice tended to be celebratory and life-affirming. 'Patterns' celebrated the feast of a local saint, holy wells and shrines were visited, both individually and as a cause of annual celebration. The 'stations', masses said in remote farms, were also celebratory occasions. Even funerals were made enjoyable through the wakes custom, whereby the neighbours helped the grief-stricken to get over the loss of a loved one by sitting up all night, either with the corpse present, or in an adjoining room, drinking and playing games, some of which, it must be acknowledged, sometimes had the effect of nullifying the effect of the deceased's departure on the human race, by creating fresh pregnancies. Cullen's 'reforms', or alterations, deflected religious practice from the holy wells to church buildings. Apart from mass itself, practices such as the Adoration of the Blessed Sacrament, novenas, benedictions and processions became the norm. Parish missions became a powerful force. Missioners toured parishes, calling on homes to encourage the laiety to attend churches for the period of the missions which included mass-going, hearing of confessions, the taking of Holy Communion, and powerfully delivered lengthy sermons calling packed congregations to a sense of their duty. Paradoxically, from the time of the famine onward, as the Catholic population declined, the power of the Church to further these character-forming (or mind-bending) activities increased. The ratio of priest to population altered from approximately one in 2,600 on the eve of the famine to one in under 900 in 1900. All the great orders took part in the parish mission movement, which continued to be a feature of Irish life for many decades into the twentieth century. Redemptorists, Passionists, Dominicans, Franciscans, Cappucins, Jesuits, all descended on the parishes and towns of Ireland, giving missions and conducting retreats. In addition, the numbers of nuns shot up, ensuring that for girls as well as boys, what was imbibed by the parents from the pulpit was not lost by the children in the classroom.

The standard of morality aspired to was that laid down by a puritanical, life-denying, Jansenistic code. As one commentator has written, the training the Church imparted to its nuns and priests was

> narrow and anti-intellectual, and was as much concerned with shunning new ideas as stimulating the capacity to deal with them. Its powerful role in education was accompanied by little in the way of new educational thought; it was generally strong on instruction but weak on creativity. Its social base lay in the countryside and the middle-sized farming classes. In common with the nationalist tradition with which it was identified, it was committed ideologically to a rural fundamentalism which was suspicious and fearful of the industrial city and it glorified the family farm and the little village as the pillars of social and economic life.[12]

A certain standardisation in the type of saints who were held out as exemplars also occurred, in that Rome approved saints were elevated over those produced locally. Yet, paradoxically, though Roman instructions were followed closely, what emerged was a strongly Faith and Fatherland type of culture, rural oriented, and firmly of the opinion that things English equalled things vile, which interacted with the puritanism, parochialism, and anti-English bias of both Sinn Féin and some elements of the language revivalist movement.

By 1903, the founder of Sinn Féin, Arthur Griffith, was so uneasy about these trends that he wrote in the *United Irishman* (on 25 July 1903):

> This cocky disparagement of the work of modern thinkers is characteristic of the shoddy side of the Irish revival. According to this gospel we are to keep our eyes fixed on the Middle Ages – and then wonder we are decaying . . . The world outside has been thinking and growing, Ireland preserves her picturesque ignorance – which her smart young men, who know better themselves, tell her is more sacred than the wisdom of an infidel world – and Ireland emigrates. We require the breath of free thought in Ireland.

Alas for 'the breath of free thought'. By 1917, in the wake of the 1916 Rising, and the emotions it aroused, the official Sinn Féin pamphlet, *The Ethics of Sinn Féin*, was defining the nature of independence in the following terms:

> Independence is first and foremost a personal matter. The Sinn Féiner's moral obligations are many and restrictive. His conduct must be above reproach, his personality stainless. He must learn the Irish language, write on Irish paper, abstain from alcohol and tobacco . . . Give good example: make examples of your life, your virtues, your courage, your temperance, your manliness, which will attract your fellow countrymen to the national cause.

Irish writers like Synge, Joyce, and others who saw Irish culture in a

European tradition were inevitably decried by those who hewed to the Sinn Féin vision. Not only were the latter numerous, they eventually became the rulers of the new Irish state. Nor were they merely lip-servers; those of them who have left us memoirs, like Todd Andrews, have made it clear that that generation of Sinn Féiners practised what they preached. In what might be termed the hard man, soft man approach of differing wings of the Gaelic League, the English language and the idealised vision of an Irish speaker were set forth. Father Peadar Ua Laoghaire articulated a view shared by many revivalists: the language as bulwark. He described the language as 'the strongest shield for the faith except for the grace of God itself'.[13] Douglas Hyde, the founder of the Gaelic League, and a Protestant, went further, possibly with one eye on the hierarchy, and the other on the fact that he was addressing a largely Catholic audience:

> A pious race is the gaelic race. The Irish Gael is pious by nature. He sees the hand of God in every place, in every time and in every thing . . . The things of the Spirit . . . affect him more powerfully than the things of the body . . . What is invisible for other people is visible for him.[14]

The concept of 'Holy Ireland' was fast a-building. There was a sharp edge to this concept that what was natively Irish was pure, that which was foreign, particularly English, decidedly impure. One writer, significantly, in a pamphlet entitled *The English Language and the Faith in Ireland*, wrote:

> English is the language of infidelity. It is infidels who for the most part speak English. It is infidels who for the most part compose literature in English. Infidels have most of the power in the English-speaking world . . . The sooner we discard English and revive our own language, the better off the faith will be in Ireland.[15]

That came from the pen of a priest. But Protestant intellectuals such as Lady Gregory and W.B. Yeats also furthered the cause of the Gaelic and Catholic peasant culture. In fact, a trenchant contemporary Irish literary critic, Declan Kiberd, has trained heavy fire on Yeats as being one of Ireland's high priests of provincialism, who exalted peasant culture and struck a deadly blow for conformity and against creativity and the European dimension with his rejection of Seán O'Casey's *The Silver Tassie*. Kiberd points to Yeats's refusal to put on O'Casey's play at the Abbey Theatre in the early days of independence as one of the causative factors in the freezing of Irish freedom of expression in a stale politico-cultural aspic. This is somewhat unfair to Yeats. He did influence writers, notably J.M. Synge, to turn their backs on European civilisation, and go to the Aran Islands for inspiration. But apart from the fact that he was trying to heighten a consciousness of being Irish at a time of all-pervasive anglicisation, he was also trying to establish the authenticity of the Irish experience. While, as Kiberd points out, he did settle down comfortably enough in an Ireland more reflective of the vision of peasant, politician, priest and publican than of the poet, his advice to Synge did result in an illumination of Irish sexual realities. Synge's epiphany to the west led him to an authentic depiction of the sexuality of the Gael, in his great play *The Playboy of the Western World*, which resulted in his being declared anti-national by the conscience-keepers of nationalism. Moreover, Yeats courageously denounced these forces and went on to do something extremely rare and courageous in the Ireland of his day for the cause of diversity: he stood up for the Protestant liberty of conscience in his great Senate speech opposing divorce, pointing to its consequences for Protestant opinion, particularly northern Protestant opinion.

Nevertheless, Kiberd's basic thesis is generally correct. By the time the survivors of the Celtic Dawn emerged into the dun light of statehood, one might be forgiven for describing the situation by paraphrasing a verse from the most English, even chauvinistic, of poets, Rudyard Kipling:

> If you're a rural Catholic, and you speak Irish
> Then you're an Irishman, my son.

The only trouble was, the mass of the population did not speak Irish, were moving out of the countryside and, where possible, tended to respond to more deep-seated human impulses than the patriots and the priests acknowledged. The clue to these impulses lies not in the idealised construct of Christ and Caesar, or even in the clash of the two colonialisms, but in the phrase 'Celtic Dawn'. What Ireland might have been like in the twentieth century, had the process of invasion and cultural despoliation which began with the coming of the Normans not taken place, is a matter of speculation. It *did* take place, as did that of the Vikings before them and various contingents of English, Welsh and Scots after them. These additives to the Irish gene pool have to be acknowledged along with the Sinn Féin input. But, though scholars may dispute about inventing, or reinventing, Irish identity, the overarching truth is that the invasion process interrupted and disrupted the development of a distinctively Celtic society. Celtic precedes 'Irish' in the identity pecking order. Reading the accounts of Celts left to us by scribes of the Greek and Roman empires like Livy and Diodorus Siculus, one cannot fail to be struck by the depiction of very familiar Irish characteristics. They were noted for traits as disparate as their strong belief in the soul and an afterlife, horse-breeding, skills in agriculture, warfare, road-building, impressive physique, a fondness for the trappings of wealth, and striking design in clothing. The Celtic women were said to be often very beautiful, so much so that in AD 200 Athenaeus of Naucratis remarked in surprise at how many Celtic men seemed to prefer boys to women. Diodorus Siculus said of Celtic women that 'The women of the Celts are not only like men in their great stature, but they are a match for them in courage as well.' One may debate 'stature', but who today would dispute 'courage'?

Peter Beresford Ellis reminds us that the Celts were regarded as 'men learned in the arts of the banquet'.These arts included the allied pastimes of music, poetry and singing. The fact that these said banquets often degenerated into the sort of fatal hand-to-hand combat recorded in the Irish sagas like the Cuchulain cycle, or the Táin Bó Cúalgne, may also be explained by an uncomfortably familiar description penned by Diodorus Siculus. He found the Celts were 'exceedingly addicted to the use of wine', with which they filled themselves, 'drinking it unmixed, and since they partake of this drink without moderation, by reason of their craving for it, when they are drunken, they fall into a stupor or a state of madness'. More creditable activities attributed to the Celts were their skills in metalworking, and their hospitality. They were described as being 'very fond of strangers, and from their intercourse with foreign merchants, are civilised in their manner of life'. But they were often extremely hairy and 'different'. Characteristics which, when the Celts eventually wound up, or were pushed, into Ireland and the more remote parts of what is now the United Kingdom, easily led 'civilising' invaders to depict them as barbarous.

When, therefore, Gaelic revivalist and Irish bishop combined to create an idealised view of 'Irishness', they were air-brushing a great deal of full-blooded, hedonistic characteristics out of existence. The early Brehon laws, the laws of the Celtic, Gaelic-speaking state, which Pope Adrian and his successors destroyed, took full note of women's sexuality. A woman was entitled to divorce a husband on the grounds of impotence or homosexuality or sterility. She could not be treated cruelly, and – significant reminder that in Irish, the name MacEntegart means 'son of the priest' – she was allowed to marry a priest.

But when, in 1924, Cardinal Logue set the ground rules for public morality in the new Irish state, he included amongst the 'moral abuses which required to be condemned, the dress, or rather, the want of dress of women at the present day', which he termed 'a crying scandal'. He also declared war on dancing, the 'outcrop of the corruption of the age', which was one of the factors standing in the way of making Ireland 'what she ought to be, a good, solid, Catholic nation'. His hierarchical colleagues continued the assault the following year with a statement from Maynooth which declared that 'it is no small recommendation of Irish dances that they cannot be danced for long hours . . . they may not be the fashion in London or Paris. They should be the fashion in Ireland because Irish dances do not make for degenerates.' In fact, the Catholic hierarchy had inveighed against these very Irish dances being danced at crossroads as part of the 'devotional revolution' of the previous century, and, post the Act of Union, the Catholic bishops had been a force for the anglicisation of Ireland. The puritanisation of Ireland, which their Lordships sought in the mid-twenties to further via Irish culture, had earlier been pursued by some priests who refused the Gaelic League permission to use school classrooms for the holding of Irish classes because of the moral dangers created by such classes – they contained both young men and women.

Nor on the educational front had the Church always seen eye to eye with the Gaelic League. In 1909, the bishops opposed a proposal to have Irish made compulsory for entry to the National University of Ireland. The Church was divided on the issue between, on one side, the bishops and the president of the college, Father William Delaney, SJ, and on the other the 850 priests who had signed a petition in favour of compulsion. The hierarchy and the President were concerned that their vision of creating an international Catholic centre of excellence would be frustrated by the language requirement, which also opened the appalling vista of deflecting prospective Irish Catholic students to the Protestant Trinity College. To prove that they meant business the bishops fired the Professor of Irish at Maynooth, Father Michael O'Hickey, for persistently championing compulsion.

The flow of Catholic-inspired legislation which the hierarchy put in train in the fields of censorship, control of alcohol, dancing, divorce, etc. has already been adverted to. In the midst of this flow, there occurred, in the year after the bishops delivered their non-degenerative verdict on Irish dancing, an incident which might be construed as a parable of how the reality of Irish life continued to be lived, despite the bishops' strictures, and as an indication of how the Puritanism of Cullen's 'traditional Irish Catholicism' had helped to alter the view of Irish womanhood from that inscribed in the Brehon laws: the scandalous Honor Bright case.

Honor Bright was the professional name of a well-known Dublin prostitute called Elizabeth O'Neill, a country girl who, it is said, having become pregnant on coming to Dublin, turned to the oldest profession in order to support her illegitimate son, whom she had refused to give away at birth. Her body was found near the Lamb Doyle's pub, at Ticknock in the Dublin mountains, on 9 June 1925. She had been shot through the heart. Two men were charged with her murder on 1 February 1926. They were Garda Superintendent Leopold Dillon and Dr Patrick Purcell. Evidence of a lurid nature was given at the trial that the two men had spent the evening before Honor Bright's body was found drinking and having sex with prostitutes in various parts of Dublin. Eventually they drove with Honor Bright to the Dublin mountains where the prosecution claimed a row developed when she was refused payment for her services, culminating in her shooting. It took the jury three minutes to find Dillon and Purcell not guilty. After the trial, when the pair returned to County Wicklow they were met by crowds of well-wishers.

To return to Professor Lee's view of the Church as civic bulwark, one could find ample justification for his thesis in the fact that in the Republic, most social problems were dealt with by the Church. The Church ran the schools, hospitals, and social services such as homes for the impoverished, orphanages, refuges for unmarried mothers, and reformatories. As scandals continue to mount and a seemingly never-ending series of disclosures in books, TV documentaries and the civil courts heighten public awareness of the fact that much of what went on in these institutions was a cruel betrayal of trust, a great deal of good work has been lost sight of. In the majority of cases, these Church institutions were administered by men and women of extraordinary human goodness. The faith and dedication of people like Father Alec Reid, displayed throughout the peace process, was not unique. Like anyone who passed through the Catholic system, I can still remember with gratitude clerical teachers who had a benign and lasting effect on my life. And, as indicated earlier, no discussion of Irish society throughout the twentieth century could or should be attempted without tribute being paid to the heroism of Irish missionaries, both nuns and priests. Although the formation that these dedicated religious received, and imparted, was of a predominantly conservative character, men and women born of the race that produced Jim Larkin and James Connolly also became natural campaigners for an 'option for the poor' in Africa, Latin America and Oceania. The schools and hospitals they founded and ran in every continent on the globe were a significant plus on the side of both humanity and upward mobility. Nuns of the Sisters of Mercy order, to take but one example, have produced students who have made a measurable, significant contribution to the development of American trade union, business and professional life.

But Professor Lee's judgement might also be criticised, perhaps unfairly, for having disturbing resonances of the sermon allegedly delivered by the Church of England vicar who is said to have urged his listeners to 'pray for the squire and his relations' for showing everyone 'our proper stations'. As Mary N. Harris has pointed out, the Church was also engaged in a campaign of cultural and social protectionism to further its own ends, which may be seen as the obverse side of the medal of de Valera's self-sufficiency.[16] Harris indicates that the Church's efforts to combat poverty and operate the range of organisations it did were in large part motivated by a desire 'to prevent the more vulnerable members of Society, particularly unmarried mothers and orphans, from falling into Protestant hands'. Harris quotes a Catholic priest as pointing out in 1917 that 'The wretched economic conditions of our towns, insufficient wages, inconstant employment, bad housing, defective and unsuitable education, an iniquitous Poor-Law system, all these things have provided a superb hunting-ground for the proselytiser.'[17]

Socialism was up there with proselytisation as an evil to be resisted. The nuns and priests who worked, often quite heroically, to combat the 'wretched economic conditions' had a very different view as to how these might be alleviated to that of Connolly or Larkin. The orders and the clerical structures created in the nineteenth century were not imbued with a spirit of social radicalism. The founders of these institutions have been described with a good deal of accuracy as

religious ascetics who pursued the path of spiritual perfection through pastoral and social service work for the Church. Philanthropy did figure in their outlook, they had strong humanitarian impulses, and followed through on those impulses with remarkable energy. But philanthropy was a means to the ends of personal spiritual perfection and the winning of souls for the faith, not a primary goal in its own right.[18]

These attitudes, coupled with the fact that, as has been indicated earlier, most of Ireland's industry lay north of the border, where workers were in any case divided between Protestant and Catholic, meant that in the Republic, both the trade union movement and the Labour Party, while honouring the memory of figures like Larkin and Connolly, pursued their goals by cautious parliamentary methods. In 1925, Thomas Johnson, who at the time was both the leader of the Labour Party and the secretary of the Irish Congress of Trade Unions, set out his position, which in turn was effectively that of the two organisations he influenced so powerfully:

> Shall the aim be honestly to remove poverty . . . or are we to agitate and organise with the object of waging the 'class war' more relentlessly, and use 'the unemployed' and the 'poverty of the workers' as propagandist cries to justify our actions . . . I do not think this view of the mission of the Labour Movement has any promise of ultimate usefulness in Ireland.[19]

As Terence Browne has noted, Johnson 'knew his electorate',[20] and, bereft of an industrial base, realised, particularly after Fianna Fáil became active, how difficult it was for Labour to gain support, or even to survive without espousing ideas which Johnson described as being 'in direct conflict with the religious faith of our people'.[21] Another profoundly important consideration, bearing on the issue of restrained sexuality in late marriage, apart from Church teaching, was the economic impact of the famine, the shocking effect of what early marriages and high fertility had led to amongst an impoverished people. For over a hundred years after the famine, low marriage rates were the norm. Between 1871 and 1971, the population fell from 3.9 million to 3 million. Emigration was only part of the reason for this. The marriage rate 'remained under 5.0 per 1,000 population until the turn of this century, and then grew slowly to over 7.0 in 1971'. As Tom Inglis has noted: 'The number of bachelors and spinsters in Ireland was one of the highest in the Western world. In 1937, almost a quarter (24 per cent) of women and three in ten (29 per cent) of men aged 45 years or more had never married.'[22] Like many Irish writers, Inglis deals with the side effects of the lonely celibate picture these statistics indicate: excessive drinking, a gaucherie in the presence of the opposite sex, and a general awkwardness between the sexes which led to an emotional distancing, even in marriage. The Church's teaching on chastity and the segregation of the sexes played its part in the inculcation of these attitudes. It is difficult to argue with Inglis's conclusions that

> The control of sex helped the control of marriage. The control of marriage helped the control of population, and finally, the control of population helped improve the overall standard of living. . . . the success of the tactics used – the segregation of the sexes, the inculcation of chastity and modesty and so forth – is reflected in the demographic characteristics of the Irish population.[23]

The poet laureate of the sexually deprived Irish countryside was Patrick Kavanagh, who in his poem, *The Great Hunger*, dealt with the hunger not for the potato, but for sexual and spiritual comfort. In it, he paints an unforgettable picture of an old Irish bachelor peasant, Patrick Maguire, a man who can be neither 'damned nor glorified', and is eking out his final days with 'No hope. No lust.' There were many such Patrick and Mary Maguires throughout rural Ireland, and probably as many more living in lonely bedsitters and doss-houses in London, Manchester, Liverpool and Birmingham. But, as Terence Browne has commented, with equal mixtures of acerbity and accuracy, life was different for many middle-class people in the towns and cities, who were

content to live a comfortable, petit-bourgeois life that bore a closer relationship to the life of similarly placed people in Britain than to any vision of special destiny, gratified not that their government's diplomatic efforts were defining new forms of international relationship at the beginning of the post-colonial period but that it was people like themselves who were receiving invitations to official occasions in Dublin Castle and the Viceregal Lodge, as Dublin welcomed its new diplomatic corps.[74]

So much for the Catholic bourgeoisie, but what of those to whom the bulk of invitations used to be addressed, the Protestants? To the credit of the founders of the new state, they did attempt to make it a welcoming one for their Protestant fellow-countrymen. But politically and psychologically, the Treaty was a difficult adjustment for the southern Protestant population. A majority of them had unsuccessfully opposed Home Rule, but now they were cut off from England, and from their co-religionists in the north. They constituted a minority in the southern state which, in the census of 1911 (the only one available for this period), constituted 327,179 persons. But between 1911 and the census of 1926, this number fell by approximately one-third to 220,723. Part of the exodus was caused by the events of the Anglo-Irish war and the civil war, during which some Protestants had been attacked and killed. In addition, the disastrous practice developed by sections of the anti-Treaty-ite forces of burning historic mansions owned by scions of the Anglo-Irish ascendancy had served to heighten the sense of loss of status and security amongst this class as much as it had destroyed a valuable part of the nation's heritage in terms of architecture, works of art, and painstakingly built-up libraries, which no compensation could ever replace. Prior to independence, the various Land Acts, coupled with widespread profligate behaviour, had already eroded the Anglo-Irish economic and political base, and the destruction of the Big Houses, as they were known – thus giving a name not only to a political and ethnic class, but to a literary genre as well – served as a kind of brutal exclamation mark to an existing paragraph of Irish history.

However, the Protestants' economic position was not threatened by the new state. In 1926, the census shows Protestants to be still strong in banking, business, the professions, insurance, and the better-paid trades such as

711

printing. In farming, Protestants held a sizeable percentage of the larger holdings, 28% of those over 200 acres, for example. And numerically, there were sizeable pockets in parts of the country, particularly in the border counties such as Donegal, Cavan and Monaghan, and in areas around Dublin like Malahide, Dun Laoghaire and Greystones. Prior to the change in administration Dun Laoghaire ('The Fort of Laoire') was officially known as Kingstown, and resonances of the days of the Raj are still to be found there in the existence of clubs with names like the Royal Irish Yacht Club and the Royal St George containing imperial bric-a-brac such as royal portraits and club insignia embodying the crown. Sadder memorabilia may be seen on nearby Protestant church walls commemorating young men who gave their lives for their tradition fighting in England's wars. Sometimes the plaques can be read with the aid of the daylight filtering through stained-glass windows, showing a soldier falling '*pro patria*'.

However, the disbandment of the RIC, and the reorganisation of the civil service, caused many Protestants to either head north, to take part in the new Protestant-controlled institutions being established there, or to retreat across the Irish Sea to the metropole. Others simply left because they found the new state alien to them, and by now I trust readers will have learned enough of the hidden inter-Church warfare between the Protestants, who were once the *de jure* established Irish Church, and the Roman Catholics, who, in effect, became the *de facto* established Church, to understand why.

But, to the benefit of those who stayed, the leadership of the Church of Ireland, the principal Protestant denomination, adopted a constructive far-seeing approach to the new state. Archbishop Gregg, the Church of Ireland Archbishop of Dublin from 1920 to 1938, wrote:

> It concerns us all that we should have a strong, wise and capable government. And therefore it concerns us all to offer to the Irish Free State so shortly to be constituted our loyalty and our goodwill . . . The new Constitution will claim our allegiance with the same solemn authority as the one that is now being constitutionally annulled.[25]

His successors followed the same principles, some outstandingly so. I remember one of them, George Otto Simms, who had been translated to the See of Armagh, attending the consecration of his Roman Catholic counterpart and friend, Cardinal Thomas O'Fiaich, in Armagh Cathedral, during one of the blackest periods of the Troubles. He, and let it be said his attendant Church of Ireland bishops, was applauded enthusiastically by the Catholic crowds. Throughout the Troubles it was from the ranks of the Orange Order and from Paisley and his followers that abuse and denunciation of ecumenicalism came, not from the Catholic hierarchies. Ironically, Dr Simms was a leading exponent of one of the aspects of the new state which Protestants found it hard to come to grips with. He was a noted Irish scholar, who with a nice blend of academic ecumenicism combined expertise on the Battle of the Boyne with being an authority on the Book of Kells (the celebrated manuscript of the gospels illuminated by Irish monks, which, having escaped the attentions of the Vikings, now rests safely in Trinity College). Prior to the creation of the Free State, Irish had not been taught in Protestant schools. Now it became necessary for a career in the public service. Protestants also had to adjust to the teaching of Irish history in an Irish context – it was not taught at all in the Six Counties' Protestant schools – rather than as an aid to causing pupils to be thankful that they were happy little English children.

The crude fact that Protestant numbers continued to decline in the Republic throughout the century, falling to 111,699 in the 1991 census, would have reduced Protestant political influence in any event. As early as July 1945 Joseph Walshe was able to write to Archbishop McQuaid saying: 'From all sides I hear that the P's are very much on the run except in the higher economic spheres like the Bank of Ireland. So the time is ripe for action.' Walshe suggested to McQuaid that it would be a simple matter to supplant Protestant societies, beginning with easy targets like the Society for the Prevention of Cruelty to Children and moving on to bigger game such as the St John Ambulance Brigade.[26] But the very electoral system employed to protect Protestant rights arguably helped to reduce the influence of Protestantism as a political force. Under PR, a party needs to win approximately 25% of the votes to be certain of a seat in a three-seat constituency, and 20% in a four-seater. Constituency revisions had the effect of cutting off specifically Protestant support, both in Dublin and in Donegal, where the Protestant vote was strong. The last Protestant independent retired in East Donegal in 1961. There was of course no barrier to Protestants standing as candidates for the various political parties, and, as we have seen, Protestants were appointed presidents, but no specifically Protestant policies were pursued by Protestants as a group in the Dail, nor, given the fact that their existing economic status was preserved, and indeed, in the case of a number of well-run businesses, enhanced, was there any crying need for such a Protestant pressure group. It was in the theological realm, in the context of the conscious effort by the Catholic hierarchy to build a Catholic state, that the Protestants had legitimate cause for complaint. A number of instances may be cited: the effects of the Ne Temere decree, the Trinity ban, attitudes to divorce, the Fethard-on-Sea boycott, and the Dunbar-Harrison case.

In the last, which occurred in 1930, a Protestant graduate of Trinity College, Letitia Dunbar-Harrison, was appointed County Librarian of Mayo, by due process under the Local Appointments Commission, which sought to keep corruption and parish-pump politics out of local government appointments. However, the Mayo Library Committee objected to her appointment on the grounds that she was a Protestant and, moreover, spoke no Irish. It turned out that the candidate favoured by the Library Committee had failed her Irish exam, but this was but a venial sin compared to the mortal one of attending Trinity College. However, as the Local Government Commission had sanctioned Ms Dunbar-Harrison's appointment, the Government had no choice but to first overrule the county council decision and then dissolve the council. A right royal, or perhaps Republican, row ensued. Amongst the considered contributions to the debate was one from the Gaelic League which stated that Ms Dunbar-Harrison's appointment was 'one of the worst things done since Cromwell's day'. The Catholic Dean of Tuam, Monsignor E.A. Dalton, opined that: 'We are not appointing a washer-woman or a mechanic, but an educated girl who ought to know what books to put into the hands of the Catholic boys and girls of this country.' The Monsignor was concerned lest Ms Dunbar-Harrison start handing out books on birth control. So was Eamon de Valera, who, with his finger on the pulse of the nation, had a very shrewd idea that he was going to be the country's prime minister after the next general election. It was not a time to be flouting 'traditional Irish Catholicism' either in Mayo or anywhere else. Accordingly, in the Dail, in June 1931, he weighed in behind Monsignor Dalton:

> If it is a mere passive position of handing down books that are asked for, then the librarian has no particular duty for which religion should be regarded as a qualification . . . But if the librarian goes round to the homes of the people trying to interest them in books, sees the children in the schools and asks these children to bring home certain books, or asks what their parents would like to read; if it is active work of a propagandist educational character – and I believe it to be such if it is to be of any value at all and worth the money spent on it – then I say the people of Mayo, in a county where, I think – I forget the figures – over 98 per cent, of the population is Catholic, are justified in insisting upon a Catholic librarian.

De Valera, in fact, widened the debate by stating that Protestants should not be appointed as dispensary doctors in Catholic areas, because Catholics at the time of their deaths wanted to be attended by 'members of the same religious faith as themselves'. In fairness to de Valera, it should be said that once in power, he did not act in sectarian fashion where the appointments of county librarians and dispensary doctors were concerned, but he did extract the maximum political capital from the uproar surrounding the Dunbar-Harrison controversy. The commissioner appointed to run Mayo after the county council was dissolved duly confirmed Ms Dunbar-Harrison in her job. The result was a boycott of the county librarian services as Catholic clergy and politicians at both local and national level continued to condemn the appointment. The controversy was resolved only when the Government caved in and transferred Ms Dunbar-Harrison to the Military Library in Dublin, appointing a Catholic to the Mayo job. De Valera duly became prime minister the following year, and the dissolution of Mayo County Council was revoked.

The divorce issue continued to be a *casus belli* between Protestants and Catholics, sometimes with farcical results. In 1938, for example, the then auxiliary Bishop of Tuam, Dr Walsh, advised Catholics that they should not keep up friendships with divorced persons.[27] He took the ostracism of divorcees a stage further in 1947. A controversy had broken out because many Catholic farmers had refused to allow the Galway Blazers to hunt across their lands, because the Blazers had elected as their Joint Master a Protestant lady who had been divorced and remarried. Dr Walsh, now Archbishop of Tuam, joined with the redoubtable Bishop Michael Browne of Galway, and with Bishop Dignan of Clonfert issued a statement backing the farmers.

> ... it has been contended on the other side that divorce and remarriage are entirely the private affair of the individuals concerned; that no one has a right to show disapproval of such conduct and that Catholic farmers ought to admit over their lands whatever person the hunt committee may select as Master. Such a contention shows gross ignorance or contempt for the religious convictions and feelings of a Catholic people.
>
> The sanctity and permanence of the marriage bond are not a matter of indifference to Catholics. They are fundamental truths of their religion. They are sacred principles of Christian morality necessary for the moral health of the family and the nation. To remarry while a former spouse is living is, in Catholic eyes, contrary to the Natural Law, and, in the case of baptised persons, contrary to the Sacrament instituted by Christ.

It may well be extrapolated from the Blazer affair that the Anglo-Irish types connected with institutions like the hunt would have been better off in parts of the globe where their impious Protestant hoofs would not be accused of desecrating Catholic turnip drills. (The Joint Master involved was, in fact, forced to resign her position.)[28] But culturally speaking, such episodes, coupled with continuing economic decline, played their part in a process wherein, as the century wore on, the once all-powerful Anglo-Irish ascendancy were to be found holding out only in a handful of castles and quite often heavily mortgaged Big Houses, their memory, and decay, chronicled in the works of Anglo-Irish writers like Edith Somerville, Elizabeth Bowen and Molly Keane, or in books like Thomas Flanagan's appropriately named novel about the last days of a once great family, *The End of the Hunt*. Edith Somerville's classic novel, *The Big House of Inver*, contains the following:

> Many an ancient property foundered and sank in that storm [the famine], drawing down with it – as a great ship sucks down in her sinking those that trusted in her protection – not alone its owners, but also the swarming families of the people who, in those semi-feudal times, looked to the Big Houses for help. The martyrdoms, and the heroisms, and the devotion, have passed into oblivion, and better so perhaps, when it is remembered how a not extravagant exercise of political foresight might have saved the martyrdoms. As for other matters, it might only intensify the embittering of a now outcast class to be reminded what things it suffered and sacrificed in doing what it held to be its duty.

That passage, in particular the reference to how the Anglo-Irish might find thoughts of how they suffered for doing what they conceived of as their duty embittering, should be read in the light of what befell Somerville's own brother. As described earlier, after *Inver* appeared, in March 1936, Vice Admiral Somerville, aged 72, was shot dead at his home in Castletownsend, County Cork, because he had felt it his duty to give references to local lads who wanted to join the British navy.

The Tilson case, decided two years after the curtain was rung down on the Galway Blazer farce, had a more serious and lasting effect on Protestant–Catholic relationships in the Republic. In effect, a judgment of the High Court by Judge Gavan Duffy in 1950, later upheld by the Supreme Court, ruled that the Catholic Church's point of view in mixed marriage cases should be the law of the land. Edward Tilson had married a Catholic and signed the requisite undertaking that the children of the marriage would be brought up Catholics. However, in 1950, after the marriage had come under strain, he placed the three eldest children in a Protestant children's home, stipulating that he wanted them brought up as Protestants. The mother appealed to the High Court for their return, and Judge Duffy acceded to her request. The Tilson case and the angry reaction it provoked amongst Protestants in a Republic that was increasingly taking on a far different hue from that envisaged by Wolfe Tone, Parnell and James Connolly, to name but a few, had a bearing on the disagreeable Fethard-on-Sea boycott of 1957.

Once again, the cause of the dispute was the *Ne Temere* decree, although in this case it was the husband who was the Catholic partner. Seán Cloney, of Fethard-on-Sea, County Wexford, had married a Protestant neighbour, Sheila Kelly, in an English register office marriage, and later in both a Catholic and a Protestant church. Sheila signed the *Ne Temere* decree, but in 1957, when her eldest daughter was nearly six, began to have second thoughts. These were apparently occasioned by the visit of a Catholic priest who told her that the child would have to go to a Catholic school. In April 1957, Sheila and the children vanished without trace. The first clue as to their whereabouts came when a close associate of Ian Paisley, the lawyer Desmond Boal, travelled to Fethard-on-Sea from Belfast, and made Seán Cloney an offer he could not accept. Apart from wanting the children brought up as Protestants, the Boal formula envisaged that Cloney might change his own religion and sell his farm to emigrate to either Australia or Canada with Sheila and the children. On 13 May 1957, led by Catholic clergy, the local people began a boycott of Protestant shops and businesses, ostracising their Protestant neighbours in the wrongful belief that Sheila had been spirited out of the neighbourhood with the help of local Protestants.

The affair created controversy throughout the country and abroad. Some of the nastiness included the finding by a Protestant teacher of a note on his school door, warning him that he could expect a bullet, and the loss to a Protestant music teacher of 11 of her 12 pupils. Dr Michael Browne of Galway chose the occasion of a High Mass for the closing of the Catholic Truth Society's Annual Conference in Wexford to enquire: 'Do non-Catholics never use this weapon of boycott in the North? Here in the South, do we never hear of them supporting only their co-religionists in business and in professions?' Dr Browne went on to state that 'Those who seek the mote in their neighbour's eye, but not the beam in their own, are hypocrites or Pharisees' and warned of a 'concerted campaign to kidnap Catholic children, and deprive them of their faith, against which non-Catholics had not protested'. What they had sought to do was to make political capital from 'a peaceful and moderate protest'.

Weight was given to the Bishop's pronouncements by the fact that he delivered them in the presence of several members of the hierarchy, including Cardinal Dalton and Archbishop McQuaid. So far as can be gleaned from his papers, McQuaid did not approve of the boycott. Neither did de Valera, who replied in a manner far removed from his attitude towards the Mayo library boycott to a question from Noel Browne in the Dail, on 4 July 1957, as to whether representations had been made to him about the boycott, and whether he proposed to make a statement. De Valera said:

> Certain representations have been made to me. I have made no public statement because I have clung to the hope that good sense and decent neighbourly feeling would, of themselves, bring this business to an end. I cannot say that I know every fact, but, if, as Head of the Government, I must speak, I can only say, from what has appeared in public, that I regard this boycott as ill-conceived, ill-considered and futile for the achievement of the purpose for which it seems to have been intended; that I regard it as unjust and cruel to confound the innocent with the guilty; that I repudiate any suggestion that this boycott is typical of the attitude or conduct of our people; that I am convinced that 90 per cent of them look on this matter as I do; and that I beg of all who have regard for the fair name and good repute of our nation to use their influence to bring this deplorable affair to a speedy end.
>
> I would like to appeal also to any who might have influence with the absent wife to urge on her to respect her troth and her promise and to return with her children to her husband and her home.

The affair, which damaged Ireland's reputation internationally, gradually petered out after a local priest deliberately entered a Protestant shop to buy cigarettes, and on New Year's Eve 1957, Sheila and her children returned to Fethard-on-Sea, where the children were educated as Catholics. It seems that behind the scenes, the fine Italian hands of both Eamon de Valera and John Charles McQuaid were at work in the manoeuvrings which led to the settlement.[29] In 1998, Bishop Brendan Cumiskey, on behalf of the Wexford diocese, formally apologised and asked for forgiveness for the episode. Ironically, Cumiskey was shortly to be driven into resignation over a far worse scandal in the district, the paedophile activities of one of his priests which were a causative factor in the destruction of the sort of power which the clergy once wielded in Fethard-on-Sea.

One characteristic which Irish Protestants and Catholics shared was a willingness on the part of their men of letters to take on administrative roles, discharging them efficiently into the bargain so that the culture overall benefited on two fronts: the artistic, and that of 'bums on seats', so essential to those who would attempt artistic ventures dependent on public support. Yeats with his work for the Abbey Theatre was probably the outstanding example of this. But other noteworthy examples could also be given of men who were talented writers, poets, playwrights, but who at the same time wrestled successfully with trade unions, actors, printers and contributors. One example is Lennox Robinson, who managed the Abbey Theatre in difficult years from 1919 onward. The theatre had no subsidy until the incoming de Valera government gave it one, thus making it the first state-subsidised theatre in the English-speaking world. The Abbey's unique position in the minds of the now ageing revolutionary generation who had once been inspired by the writings of its founders, notably Yeats and Lady Gregory, was probably the deciding factor in this decision. Robinson, like Yeats a Protestant, was one of the few dramatists to successfully portray provincial Irish middle-class life. Indeed, in a very real sense he could also be taken as a symbol of the decay of the Anglo-Irish tradition. He once lived in one of the most beautifully situated houses in Ireland, set in well-cultivated gardens, overlooking Killiney Bay in County Dublin. When I knew him, he lived in a flat, large and comfortable, but still only a flat, although it also overlooked the sea, at Longford Terrace, Monkstown, some miles nearer to Dublin. One of the great sights of Monkstown in those years was Lennox, a very tall, thin, tweedy man with a distant expression, being led by a very tiny Sealyham dog, at the end of a very long lead, on his peregrinations to and from Goggins pub, the very epitome of the Irish expression 'the relics of auld decency'.

Michael MacLiammoir who was in fact born in England, and who throughout most of the thirties ran the Abbey's theatrical alter ego, the Gate Theatre, with his lover Hilton Edwards, was another example. Though often on the brink of penury and beyond, he and Edwards somehow kept the theatre open, putting on plays in the European tradition, and attracting the interest and support of, amongst others, Orson Welles. MacLiammoir also managed to make a notable contribution to the Irish language by establishing the Irish language theatre An Taibhdhearc in Galway in 1928. Another fact worth noting concerning MacLiammoir was his popularity with the ordinary man and woman in the streets of Dublin. Though his homosexuality was well known, and particularly in the latter stages of his life he heightened the atmosphere of high camp in which he moved by going about in broad daylight heavily made up, he was a popular figure who never seemed to draw the attention of the witch-hunters as did so many other Irish artists. This, considering official attitudes to homosexuality, is worth noting. One of the handful of writers of truly international standard whom Ireland produced during MacLiammoir's heyday was Kate O'Brien, whose novel *The Land of Spices* was banned on the basis of one sentence which referred to homosexuality, after a reviewer in the *Irish Independent*, having praised the book, judged 'one single sentence in the book so repulsive that the book should not be left where it will fall into the hands of very young people'.[30]

The poet Austin Clarke, who at the time was enjoying a literary career in London, returned to Dublin in 1937, saying that he was 'determined not to become an exile', despite the fact that his first novel, *The Bright Temptation*, had been banned in 1932. Even though Irish society of the time caused him much frustration and anger, he nevertheless managed a formidable output of poems, verse plays, and essays, while at the same time running the Lyric Theatre Company, which produced verse plays. George Russell (pseudonym

A.E.) was another poet (to say nothing of being a painter and a theosophist) who combined creativity with being a first-class editor. He edited the *Irish Statesman* at the behest of perhaps the leading example of benevolent unionism, Sir Horace Plunkett, who deserves to be regarded as the father both of the Irish Department of Agriculture and of the Irish co-operative movement. Theodore Roosevelt adopted Plunkett's phrase 'Better farming, better business, better living' for his rural policy. Plunkett also wanted the new state to have a journal of intellectual calibre, which A.E. provided (from 1923 to 1930) on the principles he laid down in the *Statesman* on 3 November 1923:

> It is no use reading Wolfe Tone or John Mitchel or Thomas Davis in the belief that they had a clairvoyance which pierced into our times with their complexities, or that by going back to Gaelic Ireland we shall find images upon which we can build anew. We shall find much inspiration and beauty in our own past but we have to ransack world literature, world history, world science and study our national contemporaries and graft what we learn into our own national tradition, if we are not to fade out of the list of civilised nations.

As Terence Browne wrote: 'A.E. vigorously preached a doctrine of national synthesis in which no ethnic group is predominant, no culture the assimilative one. Ireland is a fertile creation of the historic fusion of races, culture and language.'[31] Russell also published a host of the younger Irish writers, including Liam O'Flaherty and Frank O'Connor. The Dublin Magazine which carried the torch for literary journals in the Ireland of the 1930s was just that, a literary journal, edited by friends of A.E., the writer Seamus O'Sullivan and his wife Estella Solomons, a painter and a member of one of Dublin's leading Jewish families.

Another journal which deserves to be mentioned in terms of opinion-moulding is the *Irish Press* which, apart from its obvious political impact, had an important and lasting effect on Irish society through its coverage of the GAA. As the *Irish Press* pioneered the giving of substantial space to the particularly Irish sports (hurling and Gaelic football) the other two Dublin dailies, the *Irish Independent* and the *Irish Times*, began doing so also with the result that the popularity of the GAA soared and continues to do so in the era of electronic media. In the 1930s the *Irish Press* pulled off one of the great Irish journalistic achievements. Most of the staff were Republican-inclined and had a leaning towards the underdog. They worked for the worst wages in Irish journalism because most of them had joined the paper, and continued to work for it, in the belief that they were serving 'the cause'. If they were asked to define 'the cause', most of them would have said 'the republic', meaning an Ireland based on the tenets of the Proclamation of 1916. Born out of this concept, a series on the slum conditions of Dublin, which the paper's more cynical controllers disagreed with, resulted in real improvements in the living conditions of the Dublin poor. The series, which ran in October 1936, gave the Irish public a jolting insight into how people really lived, and what their priorities were as opposed to what the politicians claimed were the issues that mattered.

It was known from official statistics that at the turn of the century tenement dwellers in Dublin had the highest death rate of any city in the United Kingdom. Twice as many died of TB as in London, with 20% of all deaths in the inner city occurring amongst children less than a year old. But it was somehow either assumed, or overlooked, that these kinds of problems had gone away. If the circles within which influence was made thought at all about the slums, there was a general tendency to regard conditions therein as being the denizens' own fault. The Cumann na nGaedheal Government introduced a Housing Act in 1924, which had the effect of diverting resources into housing – for the middle classes in leafy suburbs. But Fianna Fáil's more interventionist and egalitarian policies, as exemplified by the 1932 Housing Act, did direct money into lower-income housing and slum clearance. However, the crusading *Irish Press* series shocked people into an awareness that there was such a thing as congenital debility stemming not merely from the current generation's conditions, but from the diet of decades – tea, bread (what there was of it) and margarine.

Even under native government, neither press nor pulpit had adverted to the fact that the slum child who struggled out of infancy was then subject to an onslaught of diphtheria, diarrhoeal diseases of all sorts, whooping cough, smallpox, pneumonia, typhoid, rheumatoid arthritis, and 'bronikal trouble', as the tenement dwellers referred to the host of respiratory problems to which they were prone. The nostalgic glow through which writers sometimes inspect 'dear old dirty Dublin' is a distortion akin to placing tinted lighting in a sepulchre. One might marvel at the vivacity of the barefoot children playing in the streets of tenement districts. But a closer look would have shown that the kids were probably covered in sores, bruises, chilblains, scabies, and of course the ever-present nits and lice. For these run-down districts were also chosen, because of their cheap rents and the prevailing carelessness towards the feelings of the poor, for the siting of piggeries and slaughterhouses. Flies and excrement led to the spread of disease and of rats. In his remarkable work of oral history *Dublin Tenement Life*, Kevin C. Kearns recorded a description of the presence of rats in the lives of the people in the slum district of Engine Alley, by John-Joe Kennedy, who was 18 in 1936:

> Engine Alley was *walking alive* with rats. Cause there was three slaughter houses around here and people had pigs in the yards and that drew the rats in. Oh, they were *huge* . . . Oh, I was always afraid of rats. Now there was one woman, Biddy was her name, and she woke up one morning and she was only after having a baby and the next thing the rat was *feeding off her*! The rat was at her nipple. And she rubbed the rat, she thought it was the child's head. See, they always followed the mother when the mother'd be after giving birth. Sure, me wife was giving birth to the second baby and I felt this [movement] across me feet [in bed]. So I took up the child out of the cot and the minute I put on the light the two of them hopped out of the bed. Two rats. In our bed.

In these conditions the mother was the mainstay of the family. If she died the family, devastated, was left to the inadequate mercies of an illiterate father whose main contributions to Irish society were adding to the profits of Arthur Guinness and fathering children with such frequency that while Mother Church might have approved, the actual mother lived in poverty, hysteria and bad health. Ironically, while the *Irish Press* series did achieve real social change it was always held up to me by Vivion de Valera as the type of journalism I should avoid because it cost advertising and created 'a bad image, an impression of socialism'. According to some of the older journalists, who had worked on the paper when the series ran, the problem stemmed from the fact that many of the slum properties excoriated by the series were owned by 'important personages', including those of the Church.

In neither theatre nor literary journal, prose nor poetry was there any activity in Dublin to rival the excitements of the Celtic Dawn era until one of the most remarkable of the Irish writer/manager genre, Seán O'Faolain, began *The Bell* magazine in 1940. If ever anyone illustrated the truth of Solzhenitsyn's saying that a great writer was a sort of second government, it was Seán O'Faolain, though it might be argued that one should substitute the word 'editor' for 'writer'. To produce *The Bell* at any time would have been an achievement, but to do so in censored Ireland while a world war raged was more than an achievement, it was a phenomenon. No facet of Irish life was ignored. Whether O'Faolain was attacking censorship, calling for improvements in the design of Irish furniture, or condemning poverty and/or Eamon de Valera, both of whose influences he viewed with equal distaste, *The Bell*'s coverage was conducted according to the best principles of what is now known as investigative journalism. For example, a random sampling of the magazine, chosen by no particular criteria from between 1943 and 1945, includes the following: the case of an unemployed family on outdoor relief; yacht racing; a rebuttal by the Dean of Belfast of an earlier article on 'Orange terror'; a series on favourite holiday places; the memoir of a man who had been sentenced to jail for forgery; art criticism in Dublin; a short story on a failure to sell a beast for its correct value at a fair; reflections on the BBC; an account of a visit to the islands of Connemara; an article by T.W.T. Dillon on 'What it Means to be a Catholic'; a study of the Donegal writer Patrick McGill; examinations of the state of the theatre in rural Ireland; and a broadside from the editor telling de Valera it was time to 'stop his game of trying to delude old Republicans, that the twenty-six counties is a Republic, while assuring the twenty-six counties that it is not'. O'Faolain acidly reminded his readers that at the time of the American Note crisis, Republican de Valera had unashamedly sought the assistance of the members of the Crown-acknowledging Commonwealth. In a word, it may be accepted that *The Bell* was edited according to the principles contained in a quotation from Thomas Davis which a *Bell* contributor chose as his theme: 'Knowledge, charity, and patriotism are the only powers which can loose this Promethean land.'

Even in wartime, this 'Promethean land' offered remarkable cultural attractions – for those who could afford them. Anew MacMaster's touring theatre company brought Shakespeare to rural Ireland. In the visual arts, the views of the establishment held sway in the selection of what was hung at the annual Royal Hibernian Academy Exhibition. But at the height of the war, in 1943, a group of Irish artists, inspired by European trends, founded the Irish Exhibition of Living Art. They included Louis le Brocquy, Norah McGuinness, Mainie Jellet, and Evie Hone. The Radio Eireann Symphony Orchestra drew huge audiences for a regular season of concerts staged at fortnightly interludes. However, while these developments were greeted, and fought over, in *The Bell* as elsewhere in cultivated society, the importance of *The Bell*, in addition to its raising of standards and heightening of artistic appetites, lay in the fact that it continuously brought to the attention of decision-takers in well-researched contributions the realities of life for those who lived in circumstances where Shakespeare and concert-going were unknown: the poor.

In June 1943, the month of a general election, de Valera made two statements on the subject of diet and the condition of the people. In one (*Sunday Independent*, 6 June) he claimed: 'There is no one in the country who is not getting proper food.' In the other (*Irish Press*, 16 June) he said: 'Every section of the community has had the careful consideration of the government.' O'Faolain counter-attacked savagely. He juxtaposed these statements with another from the Reverend R.J. Kerr, in the *Church of Ireland Gazette* of 4 June, who had pointed out that there were 'Over 70,000 unemployed in this state at present living with dependents on their miserable pittance provided for unemployment benefit and unemployment assistance, as a result of which malnutrition, destitution, disease and crime are widespread' by way of introduction to an article by a *Bell* contributor, Sheila May. May, who had conducted a survey of national schools, found that in one school, out of 45 children surveyed, 22 had malnutrition. O'Faolain then printed the results of an investigation by May into the conditions in which people lived in a Dublin slum. She found that they never included fruit or vegetables in their diet, which, for adults, consisted mainly of tea and bread and butter, and for children of milk and bread and butter.

The case of 'Mrs K' was not untypical. Her furniture consisted of one table, one chair and one bed, with no bedclothes. These had been pawned when Mr K became ill. At the time of May's survey, Mr K was in England, sending home £2. 10s. a week to his wife and five children. Mrs K was described as 'a pale, listless woman who could be any age, actually, she is just 30. All her teeth are gone . . . she was half hoping for, half dreading, the return of her husband. The bed was already full, and she didn't want to be seen without teeth.' Mrs K was luckier than some. The May survey included the weekly diet and its cost for 'an unemployed husband and wife with two children on outdoor relief of 18s. 6d. a week'.

<u>**Week Beginning: April 10th, 1943**</u>
Food in hand at beginning of week: 2oz butter, 1 turnover

	Breakfast	**Dinner**	**Tea**	**Extras**
Monday	3 oz tea, 9d. ½lb sugar, 2½d.	bread, 6½d. baby food 7½d.	milk, 7d. butter, 6d.	soap, 6d., society, 1s. 6d., 2 st. turf, 1s., sticks, 3d., rent, 4s. 6d., washing powder, 2½d., candles, 4½d.
Tues.		bread, 6½d. butter, 6d. milk, 3½d.		turf, 6d., sticks, 1d.
Wed.		bread, 6½d. butter, 6d. milk, 3½d.		turf, 6d., sticks, 1d.
Thurs.		bread butter } voucher milk		turf, 6d., sticks, 1d.
Friday		bread butter } voucher milk		turf, 6d., sticks, 1d.
Saturday		bread butter } voucher milk	meat, 11d. potatoes, 4d.	turf, 6d., sticks, 1d.
Sunday		bread milk } voucher	baby food 7½d. bread milk } voucher	chapel, 4d.

TOTAL OUTDOOR RELIEF   18s. 6d.
TOTAL   19s. 4d.

By way of summarising the environment in which the family eked out their existence on this diet, May noted that on her last visit she discovered that the sewer pipe under the front archway to the courtyard had burst, and 'a harassed father was urging the children not to paddle in the sewage on the ground above it'. The advances in Irish society which allowed for developments such as the Living Art exhibition and the Radio Eireann concerts have to be set against the fact that a survey of Dublin tenements conducted around this time showed that 64,940 people lived in these conditions.[32] Sixty per cent of the slum dwellings surveyed were found to be unfit for human habitation, and where the corporation had rehoused families:

> The new settlements in Crumlin and Drimnagh are without any of the essential social amenities. There are no parks, no playing fields, no town halls. No schools were provided at first . . . There are no factories, no technical schools, no secondary schools, no football grounds . . . A fine police barracks has been provided to control the unruly crowds of workless adolescents.[33]

These observations were not made by anti-clerical reds. Father John Heenan, the future Cardinal Archbishop of Westminster, visited Ireland in this period and wrote an article on his impressions for the *Catholic Herald*, in which he said of the 'appalling poverty' in Dublin that it was 'hard to believe that a Catholic government could not in twenty years have done more to put into operation the principles of rerum novarum . . . Ireland is a Catholic country and it is disturbing that in Catholic Ireland, degrading poverty should be tolerated'. Heenan's article also contained some prophetic forebodings about the lack of intellectual formation in Irish Catholicism, saying: 'in every congregation a notable percentage will go to work abroad where, without religious instruction, they will not be in a position to defend and sustain their faith'. He found when he investigated complaints from priests, and Protestant ministers, about late-night dancing and teenage drinking, that the young people were 'sullen and resentful of the attitude of the clergy. The days of the docile laity gladly accepting the dictates of the soggart aroon are surely numbered in Ireland.' Heenan's articles annoyed Archbishop McQuaid so much that he wrote to the Apostolic Delegate to Britain, Archbishop William Godfrey, complaining about the 'scandalously offensive calumny' against Catholic thought and life in his diocese.[34] Heenan's prophecies took some time to come through, but they came, though only, as we have seen, after McQuaid figured in the drama of the Mother and Child Scheme, and in a number of other lesser productions in which the power of the Church in Ireland in those years was convincingly demonstrated. A point which might be noted is that the sort of dark heart to Ireland's major city which May, and other commentators of the period, described was replicated in the other major towns and cities of the period, as for example, Frank McCourt's searing descriptions of his boyhood Limerick in *Angela's Ashes* reminds us. If it could be said of Catherine the Great's Russia that any truth in that country was like a spark hurled into gunpowder, then the effect of *The Bell* in Ireland, particularly rural Ireland, during the 1940s can readily be imagined. It had a circulation of some 3,000 copies, but as it was eagerly handed around, it may have reached as many as 30,000 readers at the time.[35] O'Faolain continued as editor until 1946 when he was succeeded by Peadar O'Donnell. During his time, O'Faolain gave a voice in *The Bell* to young writers north and south of the border. The northerners included John Hewitt and W.R. Rodgers, the southerners figure as disparate as Brendan Behan and Conor Cruise O'Brien. Curiously, under O'Donnell, the old socialist, *The Bell* developed along literary lines, rather than those of social critiques like May's. Amongst the writings he attracted were the short stories of James Plunkett Kelly, who would one day write the celebrated novel *Strumpet City*, about the role of the Avenging Angel of the slums, Jim Larkin, in the great lockout of 1913.

Those were vexatious times for writers. O'Faolain's fellow Corkonian, Michael O'Donovan, whose short stories, along with those of O'Faolain himself, entitled the pair to be regarded as the Irish de Maupassants, originally used the pseudonym by which he is best known, Frank O'Connor (Conor

Cruise O'Brien used that of Donat O'Donnell) to disguise his identity. Throughout the war, he wrote for the *Sunday Independent* as Ben Mayo, an invention of the editor, Hector Legge, who told me he used the pseudonym to prevent his ultra-Catholic management from discovering that they had an infidel in their employ. John Charles McQuaid would certainly have been displeased. Having discovered that O'Donovan, while attempting to secure an annulment for his first marriage, was, as he saw it, living in sin with his common-law wife, Evelyn, previously the wife of the actor Robert Speaight, he sent an emissary to O'Donovan, who was finding it difficult to get work with Radio Eireann at the time, offering him employment if he would part from Evelyn. Evelyn showed both diplomacy and shrewdness in avoiding an outburst of fury from O'Donovan, by promptly offering to consider a separation if she could be given work. She took up a job in Radio Eireann two days later![36] In the circumstances, it is not surprising that in the year *The Bell* closed (1954), the list of works banned by the censorship board came to a grand total of 1,034, appropriately enough the highest ever achieved (or committed). As the tolerance extended to Michael MacLiammoir indicates, left to themselves the Irish public, despite what their rulers laid down, did not necessarily respond as official directives on sexual morality suggested. This was graphically, and tragically, illustrated two years after *The Bell* closed, when the corpse of a woman, Helen O'Reilly, was discovered on the pavement in Dublin's Hume Street on 15 April 1956. There was something almost biblical in the chain of disasters that led to the tragic finding. Helen was the wife of John O'Reilly, a son of one of the RIC men who had arrested Roger Casement. O'Reilly had been in the Channel Islands when the Germans overran them during the war. He was taken to Germany, where he was trained to take part in one of the Germans' ineffectual wartime spying missions. Having parachuted into Ireland, he made his way to his father's house, where he was urged to give himself up, and spent the rest of the war in internment. The father kept the reward money which he had received for turning in his son, and handed it over to John at the end of the war to help him make a fresh start. However, the son did not appear to benefit greatly from his father's thrift, and drifted into a number of unsatisfactory ventures, amongst which must be accounted his marriage to Helen, who was living apart from O'Reilly, who was in England, with her six children in a fairly isolated cottage near Enniskerry, County Wicklow, when she became pregnant.

As in other countries, abortion is an issue concerning which heated opinion is more readily available than fact. The number of Irish women who actually seek abortions in England annually is a continuous subject of debate. The estimates, drawn from official figures, are based on the numbers of women who give Irish addresses, but it is known that another very sizeable percentage, probably as many as those listed in the official figures, give English addresses. At the time of writing, for example, pro-choice protagonists put the annual figure at around 12,000, which is double the official estimates. It is also very likely that most operations are sought by the better off, as the costs of travelling to England, paying for the procedure and the necessary accommodation would be difficult to meet for the unemployed, for example. During the war years, therefore, travel restrictions, combined with Irish prohibitions on abortion, had built up a flourishing trade for back-street abortionists, and even occasionally amongst doctors prepared to take risks with their professions and the law for money. In the hidden world of Irish abortionists, the former Nurse Cadden was one of the most prominent. She had been struck off the midwives' list for her activities, but was known to carry out her business in her flat in Hume Street. On the night of 14 April 1956, Helen O'Reilly came to her for an abortion, and died under her hand some time later.

The body was found on the pavement next morning. In the course of a trial whose every word was avidly followed by Ireland's shocked and titillated newspaper readers, it was established that Cadden had attempted to dispose of the incriminating evidence by dragging the body down the stairs and out on to the path, where either her strength gave out or she was interrupted by the milkman. She was found guilty of murder and sentenced to hang. Her sentence was later commuted to life imprisonment and she was subsequently transferred to a mental institution, where she died in 1959. The O'Reilly children were placed in care, two of them dying in early adulthood in tragic circumstances.

But life in 'holy Ireland' continued on in as holy a mould as Dr John Charles McQuaid and the religious police could make it. A series of interventions either by the Archbishop directly or through his agents punctuated the fifties and sixties in particular. Some of these will be detailed shortly. What should be noted is that while they appear on the surface to be no more than the fetid preoccupation with sex and censorship that characterised the Church at this time, largely the work of one extraordinary archbishop, they were part of a larger picture of control. McQuaid was certainly extraordinary, but the difference between himself and most of his colleagues was one of degree rather than kind.

For example, during 1944, the Easter meeting of the hierarchy was preoccupied with the possible unhealthy stimulation of young girls by the use of the sanitary tampon, Tampax, which had just come on the market. Their lordships empowered McQuaid to convey their displeasure to the Government. It was feared that if the young women's passions were aroused by the use of these new devices, the outcome might not be merely sexual activity, but *horresco referens*, the use of contraceptives. The Government bowed to their lordships' wishes, and for a time Tampax was banned. In the twenty-first century this farcical episode might almost appear funny, but there was nothing funny about the bishops' attitude towards contraception. Another manifestation of the Church's attitude towards contraception and child-bearing, which seems to have emerged in 1944 also, was the introduction of the symphysiotomy operation, which involved sawing through the woman's pelvis 'so that it opened like a hinge' and remained permanently widened.[37]

726

Apparently the introduction of the operation to Ireland was religiously motivated. While some medical apologists have claimed that symphysiotomies were carried out because Caesarean sections were deemed to be unsafe, a researcher at University College Dublin, Jacqueline Morrisey, unearthed evidence to the contrary while compiling a PhD: a letter from Dr Alex Spain, who was Master of the National Maternity Hospital from 1942–8. Under Spain use of the operation 'grew dramatically at the National Maternity Hospital' from the 1940s onwards. The letter stated that while Caesarean sections were safe, 'It will however be a long time before such a method of delivery will be accepted by the community at large . . . The result will be contraception, the mutilating operation of sterilisation and marital difficulty.'[38] Symphysiotomies were carried out in several Irish hospitals in different parts of the country, in Cork, Drogheda and in the major Dublin maternity hospitals, until the 1970s,[39] according to the Green party TD John Gormley, who raised the practice in the Dail. It left some women with permanent severe backache necessitating the extensive use of painkillers, and an understandable fear of further pregnancies. In some cases it took them a year to learn to walk again. The operation was also sometimes performed in other countries, in emergency situations, but in Ireland it was carried out on a large scale, despite the protestations of visiting doctors, who described it as 'midwifery of the dark ages'.[40] At the time of writing, survivors of this form of midwifery have joined the list of those who are trying to force the Government into carrying out an inquiry into some aspect or another of what went on in the days when Christ and Caesar were hand in (sterilised) glove, but so far without success.

John Charles McQuaid was the member of the hierarchy most likely to alert an unsuspecting rural bishop like Denis Moynihan of Kerry that moral dangers were about to befall. For example, in April of 1967 it was McQuaid who informed Moynihan that the faithful of Kerry were in imminent danger of grave moral peril because Jayne Mansfield was about to perform her cabaret act in Tralee. Moynihan immediately denounced the visit and had it cancelled. But this was more because McQuaid had the most resources and agents at his disposal to alert him of developments in Irish society, be it in the sphere of sporting, cultural or intellectual activity, which might affect the vision of the Ireland that he and a majority of his fellow bishops wished to create. (As in any human organisation, there were some exceptions, who will be adverted to shortly.)

McQuaid's general reaction to his critics reminded me of that of Rhett Butler who, when Scarlett O'Hara trained her emotional batteries on him, replied: 'Frankly, my dear, I don't give a damn.' A piece of advice he gave me once abides with me. 'Listen, my friend,' he said in that low, sibilant voice of his, a hangover of the effects of TB on his lungs (which he used to great effect as it meant that his hearer had to bend close to him, straining to catch what he was saying). 'Never let yourself become a prisoner of someone else's nerves.' John Charles McQuaid certainly practised what he preached in that regard.

The Mother and Child Scheme controversy of 1951 was a major example, but nevertheless only one example, of how throughout the decade McQuaid sought to ensure that the Ireland he wished to create actually came about.

In October of that year McQuaid presided over a ceremony in the Military Church at Arbour Hill, Dublin, in which he invited the President, Seán T. O'Kelly, the Taoiseach, Eamon de Valera, members of the Government, officers and non-commissioned officers of the army, navy and air force to take an oath dedicating themselves to Our Lady, Queen of the Holy Rosary. All present obediently rose and did so. It was not a time for considering whether a state dedicated to the Queen of the Holy Rosary was the type of society envisaged by the executed leaders of 1916. (The graves of the men lie adjacent to the church.) In the same year the textbook most frequently studied by boys and girls attending Catholic schools in Ireland was published: *The National Catechism*, sanctioned by the bishops of Ireland. McQuaid drew up this catechism; in fact, after the constitution, it was probably the document which occupied most of his attention. It stipulated that the principal dangers to the faithful were attendance at non-Catholic schools or frequenting the company of people inimical to the Church's teachings. Obviously bad books, plays, pictures and so forth had to be guarded against, as had any 'looks, words or actions' that might offend against chastity. Bad companions, drink, dancing, immodest dress or behaviour, 'occasions of sin' were all to be avoided. The *Ne Temere* decree was stitched into the teaching inasmuch as mixed marriages could only take place (provided, of course, a Church dispensation had been obtained) in a sacristy, and without mass, early in the morning. Someone marrying a non-Catholic in a register office, or before a non-Catholic minister, was living in sin.

The year after the catechism was first published, McQuaid targeted Trinity College as the bastion of the enemy. He informed Rome (in his quinquennial report) that the great enemy was liberalism.[41] Liberalism, he said, drew its power from the presence of a Protestant minority which operated from Trinity with the help of the Masons and the professions, which gave them a financial power base also, and the price of deliverance from liberalism was an unrelenting control of education. Through his influence with the Department of Education, McQuaid, or indeed any bishop, could inhibit or prevent the establishment of schools which he disapproved of in his diocese through causing the Department to withhold grants and recognition. If such methods failed, McQuaid would see to it that a clerical-run school would be established alongside, or at least in close proximity to, the offending establishment.

By the mid-fifties, McQuaid was well on his way to establishing what Seán O'Faolain termed his 'dreary Eden'. But he continuously had to do battle with a number of serpents which attempted to enter his protected garden. These included Tennessee Williams, Seán O'Casey, and Yugoslavian football players. Taking the case of the two writers first, it should be noted that the intellectual floodgates erected to keep out such creatures had, in McQuaid's eyes, suffered a grievous weakening. His man on the censorship board, the chairman, Professor J.J. Piggott, and two other Conservatives had been manoeuvred off the board, which was made up of three Conservatives and two Liberals, one of them a Protestant, R.R. Figgis, who had been appointed by the coalition administration. The coalition had compounded this error by not replacing a Catholic priest with another priest. Piggott, who was in constant touch with McQuaid, had for some time taken exception to a provision in the Censorship Act which stipulated that a book could only be banned when there were three votes in favour, and not more than one against. In practice, therefore, the two Liberals, Figgis and A.J.F. Comyn, could veto the decisions of the three Conservatives, Piggott, C.J. O'Reilly and D.J. Flynn.

It could not be argued that the liberals had succeeded in doing a great deal to prevent the censorship board making a laughing stock of itself. The list of banned publications reads like a guide to contemporary English literature. It includes names like Faulkner, Hemingway, Sartre, Ehrenburg, Tennessee Williams, Scott Fitzgerald, Beckett, Joyce, Graham Greene, Dylan Thomas, Orwell, C.P. Snow, Muriel Spark, Joseph Heller, Danilo Dolci, Frank O'Connor, John McGahern, Seán O'Faolain, Edna O'Brien, Kate O'Brien, Liam O'Flaherty and Brendan Behan. However, so far as McQuaid was concerned, the point was that the Department of Justice was frustrating the campaign he had successfully conducted through the Knights of Columbanus to keep ideas he disapproved of out of Ireland. His Knight-dominated censorship board banned twice as many books between 1950 and 1954 as had been banned between 1930 and 1945. But the move to get the Liberals off the board, which continued throughout 1957, ultimately backfired. When Piggott attempted to put a gun to the head of the Government by refusing to convene meetings of the board unless the Liberals were ousted, his resignation was sought. The two remaining Conservatives resigned with him. Three replacements were appointed by the Government the following month under the chairmanship of Judge Conroy, and as McQuaid had feared, a liberalising process commenced, albeit the process made haste slowly.

There was no official state censorship of the theatre. In fact, two years earlier, in 1955, O'Casey's distinctly anti-clerical *The Bishop's Bonfire* had run for five, rather than the planned three weeks in one of Dublin's major theatres, the Gaiety, without incurring the expected episcopal wrath. But this was to change when Tennessee Williams's play *The Rose Tattoo* was staged in the tiny back-lane theatre, the Pike, in Herbert Lane, Dublin, on 12 May 1957. The Pike, founded by an army officer, Alan Simpson, and his wife, Carolyn Swift, held only 70 people. But it achieved an impact out of all proportion to its size by putting on plays such as the first production of Brendan Behan's *The Quare Fellow,* and staging the Irish premiere of *Waiting for Godot*.

As part of his ongoing censorship campaign, McQuaid's thought police had brought the presence of Tennessee Williams's work in Dublin to the attention of the Department of Justice, with the result that a week after *The Rose Tattoo* opened, a Garda officer called at the Pike, and informed Simpson that unless certain 'objectionable passages' in the play were removed, both he and his wife could face prosecution. The objectionable passages were not specified, and Simpson and Swift decided to tough it out, continuing to stage the play to see what would happen. What happened was that Simpson was duly arrested two days later, spent a night in the Bridewell, and a year before the courts trying to find out who had briefed the police and why. Eventually, after ruinous costs, the case was dismissed, the Pike ultimately closed down, and Simpson and Swift's marriage broke up. The case aroused enormous publicity. But it did not deter McQuaid from launching an organised campaign against what were termed 'foul books' on 4 December 1957 which had the support of every imaginable Catholic society, from the Belvedere Newsboys Club to the Legion of Mary, to the Boy Scouts and even football clubs.[42] These were backed up by a letter to the Government from the hierarchy on 30 January 1958. However, though Bob Dylan was yet to be heard from, the times they were a-changing, and the campaign ground to a halt without the unhorsed Knights being returned to the saddle. The Department of Justice files for the period make it clear that the Government were aware that the onslaught was connected with the fact that Oscar Traynor, the Minister for Justice, had had the temerity to call for Piggott's resignation, and though the fact was lost sight of in the welter of controversy, the Piggott affair may be taken as the beginning of the process of a loosening of Church control over what the Republic's public could or could not read.

In the short term, however, it led to considerable uproar and to a retrograde step being taken. As a result of personal representations by McQuaid, who handed de Valera two paperback books he deemed 'highly indecent', customs officers were granted the power to seize books and forward them to the censorship board for banning. Henceforth, alerted by pre-publication publicity, the customs officials would be particularly efficacious in intercepting Irish authors. Also, the bishops issued a pastoral letter, written mainly it is thought by Bishop Browne of Galway, on 31 January 1958, calling for a 'defence of Catholic morality, especially in that sacred sphere where the health and vigour of the race, the purity of domestic life, and the sanctity of marriage are involved'. To his horror, McQuaid discovered that all of the above were likely to be seriously undermined because the organisers of the annual Tostal Spring Festival were planning to include adaptations from James Joyce's *Ulysses* and Seán O'Casey's play *The Drums of Father Ned*. He refused to allow mass to be said at the opening of the festival, and in the ensuing uproar, involving trade unionists, including journalists (McQuaid, through the Knights of Columbanus, had set up a Catholic trade union for journalists, the Guild of St Francis de Sales), Dublin Corporation threatened to withhold its grant. O'Casey withdrew his play, followed smartly by Samuel Beckett. The festival committee made a formal announcement that it would not be showing the offending plays, but this did not satisfy the hierarchy. The secretaries to the standing committee wrote to their American counterparts, explaining why McQuaid had cancelled the mass, and asking for American episcopal pressure on the Irish Government to see to it that objectionable plays did not open in Dublin.

The bishops bracketed this request with a statement that Frank Aiken's decision to vote for the admission of China to the UN 'did not reflect the views of Irish Catholics'. Cardinal Spellman confronted Aiken and Frederick Boland with this letter during a lunch given by the Cardinal. But neither man was cowed, pointing out that the Aiken vote had received an endorsement of two-thirds of the Dail membership. As a result of the Irish bishops' initiative, Spellman used his influence with the American hierarchy to secure a boycott of American pilgrimages to Ireland, which cut off some badly needed tourist revenue.

McQuaid had failed to secure a boycott of a football match between a Yugoslavian team and an Irish eleven a few years earlier, in October 1955. His papers[43] show that, with the match scheduled to be played only a few days later, he intervened with the then Taoiseach, John A. Costello, to ensure that the President, Seán T. O'Kelly, would not attend the game, because of the treatment the Communists had meted out to Archbishop Stepinac, who had been jailed after being subjected to brainwashing procedures and a show trial. Even though O'Kelly and a number of Government ministers, including the Deputy Taoiseach, Labour's William Norton, had already accepted their invitations when McQuaid's objections were made known, the politicians, with the sounds of swishing croziers still loud in their ears after the Mother and Child débâcle, promptly cancelled. But if the sound of the croziers was audible, that of the Army No. 1 Band was not. It promptly ceased its rehearsals of the Yugoslavian national anthem and cancelled also. McQuaid's Marian dedication service had had the desired effect. His opposition also caused Radio Eireann to decide not to broadcast the match. However, the Football Association of Ireland stood firm and decided for the sake of Ireland's reputation in the soccer world that the game should go ahead. Over 21,000 Irish soccer fans agreed with the decision and turned up at Dalymount Park to see the match, despite having to pass a large picket formed by Catholic actionists. Whether or not the incident stiffened Traynor's resolution that the time had come to stand up to McQuaid over the Piggot censorship issue described above cannot be said with certainty, but it is a fact that when Traynor, a former Belfast Celtic goalkeeper, in his capacity as president of the FAI, took the field to greet the team in O'Kelly's absence, he was rewarded with one of the loudest roars of approval ever heard in Dublin. Ironically, it was observed that for their part members of the Yugoslavian team, most of whom were Catholics, blessed themselves as they ran on to the pitch. Alas, Joe Wickham, the secretary of the FAI, did not receive a Traynor-like reception in his Dublin parish church at Larkhill, being denounced from the pulpit on successive Sundays for being not merely a Judas who had reneged on Christ the King for a game of football, but a 'Protestant Catholic'. But, like Traynor, Wickham did not lie down under clerical fire and registered a strong-minded protest with the Papal Nuncio, Archbishop Alberto Levame.

Against that background it is perhaps not surprising that the famous TV bishop Fulton Sheen, who was one of a host of Church dignitaries from all over the world whom McQuaid assembled to commemorate the fifteen hundredth anniversary of St Patrick in 1961, should become so overwhelmed by Irish piety that during a speech in Dublin's Theatre Royal, he inadvertently praised the 'passionate chastity of the men of Ireland'. But the background was coming increasingly to resemble an old backdrop for a long-running stage play which was now being performed by new actors in a new production. McQuaid commissioned an American Jesuit, Father Biever, to carry out a survey of public opinion in 1962, which showed that by an overwhelming majority the Catholic Church was regarded as containing the natural leadership of the people, and was the greatest force for good in Ireland. Father Biever found that the Republic was virtually a theocracy in which all significant legislation was vetted in advance by the clergy. However, the signs of what were to come were also included in the survey. The mass of those who saw the Church as the greatest force for good were the uneducated. Eighty-three per cent of the educated did not regard the Church in this light, and there was an undercurrent of criticism of the way the Church exercised its power. Moreover, in the year before Father Biever conducted his research, the very year that St Patrick was commemorated, television came to Ireland, and the Republic applied to join the Common Market. The following year Pope John declared the Second Vatican Council open, but he did not declare John Charles McQuaid a cardinal when Cardinal d'Alton died. In 1964, that honour went to William Conway, Bishop of Down and Conor.

The early sixties were of course also the Lemass era. From the time he took office, Lemass showed a disposition to resist hierarchical intervention in the legislative process. Appropriately enough for Ireland, one of his first demonstrations of independence occurred over the sale of alcohol. The hierarchy opposed Government proposals to extend the licensing laws. A statement from the bishops objected to the potential effect of the new laws on the Lord's Day and to a proposal that the pubs be allowed to remain open on weekdays until 11.30 p.m. Their lordships hoped that the new legislation would not 'weaken the moral fibre of our nation'. However, Lemass took his distance from the proposition that civil law should reflect canon law, and said in the Dail that 'drunkenness is a sin for which men are responsible to a higher court than ours'.[44] But as the decade wore on, Lemass could see merit in Church teachings in fending off hierarchical opposition to the changes he was making and wished to make. In an important speech on social and economic policy, which he delivered to a Fianna Fáil gathering on 7 October 1963, he said:

> ... the Encyclicals of Pope John are of enormous help, because they remove doubts and uncertainties, and give to all mankind the benefit of a clear guiding light. In these modern days, no nation can operate in isolation, and social progress anywhere depends in some degree on progress everywhere. It is therefore true that the universal understanding and

application of the social teachings of Pope John can help every nation, including Ireland, in their effective application. For the Irish Government, I can say that Ministers keep these Encyclicals at hand for constant inspiration and reference when working out their plan to accelerate the application of the social policy which we are seeking to develop.

Not quite the devil, but certainly the old Republican, quoting scripture for his own purposes.

The sixties were remarkable for the growth in the independence and vigour of church magazines rather than secular literary ones. Journals like *The Furrow, Christus Rex, Doctrine and Life* and *Spotlight* reflected the newer currents flowing from the Vatican Council, and a number of priests began to strike a different note from that emanating from the episcopal pastorals. Two Dominicans, Father Austin Flannery and Father Fergal O'Connor, aroused public admiration for their fresher approach not only to Church teachings, but to received political wisdom as well, attracting Charles Haughey's displeasure for their criticism of social conditions in Ireland. Father J.G. McGarry, the editor of *The Furrow*, was the guru of a number of younger priests who emerged in the wake of one of McQuaid's own initiatives. He sent some of his priests abroad, led by Father Joseph Dunn, to study the new medium of television, and Dunn, with a group of colleagues, Peter Lemass, Dermod McCarthy and Tom Stack, used the *Radharc* ('sight' or 'vision') documentary series to make a variety of challenging programmes over a wide spectrum of Church and social issues. Peter Connolly, Professor of English at Maynooth, wrote about censorship in *Hibernia* (February 1964):

> It was time to try something else. This formula was to offer positive appreciations of contemporary films and books which would simply ignore polemics about our censorship. It would demonstrate to Irish readers that in face of modern novels or films of whatever kind it was not necessary to bury one's head in the sand or, on the other hand, to sacrifice one jot of moral principle ... we hoped for a gradual growth of the climate of opinion which would make a juvenile standard of censorship – though not all censorship – untenable.

Whether it was the gradualism which Connolly advocated or the general changing intellectual climate which was responsible, one cannot say with accuracy, but not the least of Connolly's legacies was the fact that after his death, the successor appointed to his chair was not merely a woman, but a Protestant, Barbara Hayley, who had been responsible for pioneering scholarship on the nineteenth-century writer William Carleton, who to survive had had to change his religion, becoming a Protestant, but who mastered his demons so successfully that he left us the truest portraits of the Irish peasantry to survive the century.[45] A predecessor of Connolly's, Peter Birch, who became Bishop of Ossory in 1964, shared something of Connolly's approach. He told me that while he believed in censorship in certain cases to protect young people, 'the only true censorship is the judgement of the mature mind'.[46] In the social field, Birch was an important pioneering figure, who said, 'it's a pity in some ways we haven't got a Community party here, so that we would sit up and do something about the gaps in our social legislation . . . Some standards of charity are just middle-class notions that are out of date.'[47] He tried to fill the gaps by training social workers to cope with the day-to-day domestic misery caused by poverty, ignorance and drink. He used bodies like the Legion of Mary and the Society of St Vincent de Paul, who visited people in their homes, papering and decorating, teaching housewives how to cook, making furniture, and spoke openly about taboo subjects like the sexual needs of the mentally handicapped, with good reason, as we shall see. Birch was appalled by some of the conditions in orphanages. To counter the effect on children who never saw an adult eating, he got volunteers to bring children out so they could see how a cake was made, where eggs came from, what a normal home with pictures on the wall looked like. Birch was a straightforward man with no airs or graces whom one could have passed on the road as an ordinary priest. His speech reflected his lack of hauteur and eschewed pietistical rhetoric. He told me: 'There is no use preaching at a family, if the wife is sitting in squalor with eight children and the man can get more comfortable surroundings in a pub.'

The Peter Birches of the Irish Church were in a minority, but they were not unique. Years later, in conversation with Cardinal Thomas O'Fiaich, at a time of controversy caused by the perennial issue of introducing divorce to Ireland, he surprised me by saying: 'Personally I share Garret FitzGerald's approach. Let the state legislate for the state and all its citizens, and let the people follow their own consciences where Church teaching is concerned.' Like Cardinal Conway before him, O'Fiaich had the experience of living and working with Catholics, amongst Protestants, and while in public the party line had to be followed, in private both men were inclined to render unto Caesar and to Christ what each was rightfully due.

Social and cultural critiques of Ireland tend to major on aspects of culture such as the life and times of literary magazines, and these are not without importance. Light was shed on darkness after *The Bell* ceased to toll by *Irish Writing*, which was edited alongside *The Bell*, between 1946 and 1954, by David Marcus and Terence Smith, and from 1954 to 1957 by Seán J. White, and which gave several new writers a voice, amongst them Patrick Galvin, Benedict Kiely and Basil Payne, and the poets Pearse Hutchinson and Thomas Kinsella. *Poetry Ireland* and *Envoy* also made their contribution, and I am happy to say that later, from 1968 onwards, I was able to afford David Marcus the opportunity of continuing the *Irish Writing* tradition as a weekly page in the *Irish Press*, which for nearly 20 years, until 1987, gave almost every writer of stature to emerge in Ireland a shop window. But the overriding reality of Ireland in the watershed years of Lemass, the Vatican Council, increased education, the coming of television, is that (north and south) it was literally insular, poverty-stricken, drained by emigration and repressed by a great human institution, the Irish Catholic Church, which existed, particularly in the Republic, virtually without competition. In addition, there was a repression within the repression: sexual repression, which affected the nuns and priests as fiercely as it afflicted the laity. There was also downright ignorance. The industrial schools system was staffed no doubt by basically decent men and women. But they had no training in the psychology of the young, other than how to repress and mould them. A Department of Education report of 1941 illuminates much. It blames the conditions in a particularly dismal industrial school, Lenaboy, in Galway, on the nun in charge, a septuagenarian who had spent much of her life running a home for 'fallen women'. The nun was described as a 'miserly, ruthless old woman of seventy years who has as her objectives the reduction of the debt on the institution. She has been hardened by age and a lifetime spent in a Magdalene home.' We will shortly encounter more such reports and the causes of them.

Contemporary Ireland, and the Irish Church, is going through a period of exorcism, stemming from the collapse in authority and respect occasioned in part by the rebellion of the educated which Father Biever indicated, in part by the paedophile and sex scandals. These intertwine with factors such as those Peter Birch hinted at, away back in 1965: the conditions in orphanages and other institutions run by the Church. Curiously, like the Troubles in Northern Ireland, the events which provoked the exorcism process still await major literary expression. What is known comes by way of television documentaries, media interviews, and occasional books of memoir by survivors of what went on in some of these institutions.

The word 'survivor' is used advisedly. As one who grew up in Ireland, went to Catholic schools, and spent a lifetime researching and commentating on Irish society, I say in all humility that the revelations about what went on in industrial school, orphanage, and Magdalene institution, as they were known, have given me an insight into how intelligent, humane Germans could say of what befell the Jews: 'We did not know.' The public usually only saw the inmates of the reformatories and industrial schools on their Sunday walks, when crocodiles of scrubbed, cropped, and booted boys, all apparently with unusually long arms that protruded red-wristed from their shirt sleeves, clumped glumly along the roadsides in the vicinity of their institutions. There was a general widespread awareness that regimes were strict to the point of harshness in these places, to the extent that children living in an area where an industrial school or reformatory was situated would often be threatened that if they did not behave they would be sent to Letterfrack, Artane, or wherever. And pupils attending schools run by the Christian Brothers sometimes discovered that Brother X or Y, known to be particularly zealous in the use of the leather, or objectionable for some other reason, would disappear from the school, transferred, it would be learned later, without explanation to one of these institutions. In those days it should be noted corporal punishment was a feature of most schools and parental attitudes to the punishments of their children were such that many pupils would hesitate to tell that they had been beaten lest they receive another beating at home for annoying their teacher.

Even Artane did not appear too bad a place. One of the centrepiece images of Faith and Fatherland Ireland for several years after the coming of television was the spectacle of the Artane Boys Band, from the Christian Brothers Industrial School at Artane, County Dublin, in their smart, bright uniforms with their gleaming instruments, marching around the field at Croke Park before important hurling and Gaelic football matches. The boys, obviously, it seemed, trained in music by the caring brothers, and the enthusiastic crowds cheering their native sports, appeared to represent all that was best in the interaction between Church, charity, and the Irish educational tradition. When, in 1976, the brother in charge of the band, Brother Joseph O'Connor, who frequently appeared on television, was made the subject of a special programme on the bilingual RTE show *Trom agus Eadrom* ('heavy and light'), the viewing public applauded the programme, and it was generally felt that the lavish tributes paid to this good man were but his due.

In fact, it emerged more than a decade later, after Brother O'Connor had died, that the proper place for the man was not a laudatory television studio, but the lowest hell in Dante's *Inferno*. One of his victims has described how Brother O'Connor pushed his head into a drawer, and closed the drawer tight on his neck while he raped him.[48] Another told how, for some classroom misdemeanour, Brother O'Connor made him take off his clothes and

> right there in front of the whole class he sat down on the bench, on the desk with his foot on the bench where the boys would sit and write, and his other foot on the ground. He opened his cassock and put me across it and put his left hand under my private parts. He was squeezing me and beating the living hell out of my bare backside. He was foaming at the mouth, jumping and bopping. He was having a sexual orgasm in front of the whole class of boys. And I wasn't the only boy he done. He did things to me that I wouldn't even tell my wife about they were so shameful. Some of the things he did I can't talk about now. It's too painful.[49]

The Christian Brothers, like many other Irish religious orders, have since apologised for the behaviour of men like O'Connor, as has the Church. The state has added its voice to these apologies. Prompted by an extraordinary piece of investigative journalism, a series called *States of Fear*, written, directed and produced for RTE by Mary Raftery, for which she deservedly subsequently won several international awards, the Irish Government, on 11 May 1999, called a special press conference to apologise to the huge number of Irish boys and girls who were reared in hellholes like Artane. However, what the outcome of these apologies will be in terms of financial recompense for the victims of the system is not yet known. All that is certain is that, as has been indicated earlier, the many civil actions involved are being vigorously contested both by the religious orders involved and by the state. The enormity of both the hypocrisy and the criminal negligence of senior clergy, whose only response to the all too frequent discovery that a cleric was abusing children in school or parish was to transfer him to another area where his activities were not known, has not been adequately dealt with. If a lay executive knowingly spread a dangerous disease, they could be severely punished by the laws of the state. But for generations, bishops and religious superiors freely and deliberately transferred known serial predators on children to other unsuspecting parishes to prey again, in order to avoid scandal, while at the same time preaching rubbish to their flocks about keeping 'holy Ireland' safe from bad books and contraceptives. In commending a book based on Raftery and her programme consultant's research, Frank McCourt said of the work, *Suffer the Little Children*,[50] that it had 'revealed a hidden Ireland of such brutality and savagery, you wince from page to page'. McCourt's judgement was only too accurate.

For Artane was by no means the worst of these institutions. They grew up, as has been indicated earlier, because of the sectarian turf wars between the Catholic and Protestant Churches of the nineteenth century, and by the coming of independence were a part of the network of social and educational services controlled by the Church. These included orphanages, reformatories, industrial schools and 'penitentiaries', known as Magdalene laundries, wherein unmarried mothers paid for their keep, and expiated their guilt by working in seriously exploitative conditions. The children of these women were often taken for adoption, for which there was a particularly flourishing demand in America. The reformatories were institutions wherein the courts placed young offenders. Throughout the bulk of the twentieth century, the industrial schools at any one time housed thousands of boys and girls, many of whom were indeed placed there because there was nowhere else for them to go. But a large number of children also found themselves in industrial schools for very doubtful reasons. One incentive, apart from the religious factor, which churches had for getting control of these institutions was the capitation grant system, whereby the state paid the controllers of the individual institutions a grant for each child in their care.

The courts had the power to commit children being reared in what were regarded as unsuitable conditions to such institutions, and it became commonplace for children to be sent to them rather than being left to be reared by a single parent in poor circumstances. A Department of Education memorandum on the subject points out:

> . . . the fact that the Managers have an organised system for 'touting' for children. They have social workers who act as a sort of agent and get children committed to the schools. We have no means of preventing this practice but I suggest that we consult the Department of Local Government with a view to getting the assistance of the local County Managers to ensure that children are not committed without sufficient reason and to obtain periodical reports on the parents' means when children are committed on the grounds of poverty.[51]

The stated objective of these schools was to provide children with an education and a trade, and to an extent this was done. But the case histories of some of those who passed through these grim institutions show that in too many cases very little education was imparted. The trades often consisted of outdated callings such as tailoring, cobbling and farm labouring. Allegations of exploitation of child labour both by the institutions and by farmers to whom the children were sometimes sent are widespread. When they emerged from the world of strict control exercised in these schools, many of the survivors found they could not cope and drifted into a life of crime or prostitution. The state was not over-generous in its funding of industrial schools, but if one compares the grant paid for a child, 18s. 3d. per head, with that paid at the same time (*circa* 1945) for the family of four on outdoor relief described in *The Bell*, it appears that it should have been possible, given economies of scale, with several hundreds of inmates involved in each institution, particularly in institutions with their own farms, to provide children with a decent diet. (By 1970 the grant had been increased to £8 5s. a head.) However, this was not what happened. Semi-starvation was the order of the day. Memoranda from a conscientious departmental inspector in the 1940s referred to systematic underfeeding. The Secretary of the Department of Education paid a visit to Daingean Reformatory in 1955, after which he wrote an angry memo to his minister, complaining that 'the attention paid to the cattle was in marked contrast to the care for the feeding of the boys'.[52] This pattern continued late into the century. In vain did the Department circularise industrial school managers, stipulating what inmates should be fed. The reality often consisted of a breakfast of bread and dripping, two potatoes and cabbage water for lunch, and two slices of bread for tea – if the children were lucky. Authenticated accounts speak of even more attenuated diets. Children confined in places like Artane provided a virtually limitless supply of labour for the institution's farms, and survivors' accounts, with remarkable regularity, tell of eating pigs' potatoes or stealing turnips to be eaten raw in bed later that day. Grass was reportedly eaten on some occasions.

Commenting on the semi-starvation and beatings sustained by children in institutions, Father Flanagan, of Boys Town, wrote to a friend in Ireland:

> Your great country that is sending forth missionaries into foreign lands ... might well learn to begin at home to do a little missionary work among the unwanted, unloved, untrained and unfed children, who are suppressed and have become slaves because of the dictatorial policies of those in power ... I wonder what God's judgement will be with reference to those who hold the deposit of faith and who fail in their God-given stewardship of little children?

Father Flanagan was writing after a visit to Ireland in July 1946, in which he had been horrified at the conditions he found, and had spoken out publicly against them, thereby arousing the wrath of, amongst others, politicians on both sides of the political divide. The then Minister for Justice, Gerry Boland, condemned him for using 'offensive and intemperate language', and James Dillon told the Dail that Flanagan had published 'falsehoods and slanders'. He went on:

> When a Catholic Monsignor uses language which appears to give the colour of justification to cartoons in American papers where muscular warders are flogging half-naked fourteen-year-old boys with cats-of-nine-tails, I think it is right to say in public of that Monsignor that he should examine his conscience and ask himself if he has spoken the truth . . . If he finds that the substance of what he is alleged to have said is grossly untrue, then he should have the moral courage to come out in public and say so, and correct in so far as he can, the grave injustice he has done not only to the legislators of this country, but to the decent, respectable, honest men who are members of the Irish Christian Brothers.

In fact, Father Flanagan's accounts were corroborated not merely by inmates of industrial schools but by those who ran them. The beatings Father Flanagan described continued for decades.

Don Baker, who in 1963 was committed by the courts to two years in Daingean Reformatory, run by the Oblates of Mary Immaculate, has recorded:

> Shortly after that he called me down from the dormitory at night and he flogged me. They'd beat us on the stairs below the dormitories, and the sound of the strap hitting you would echo all over the place. I was stripped naked, and had to lie spread-eagled on the stairs. One Brother stood on my hands to keep me there, and another held my legs. Then the Brother who had made my life such a hell in the church flogged me with the leather. I always felt that this was his way to get me – if he couldn't get me sexually, then he could do it by beating me.

Beating was a way of life at Daingean. The Minister for Education, Michael Martin, read into the Dail record, in May 1999, the account of a Committee of Inquiry which visited Daingean three years after Baker had left. Martin was responding to questions which arose out of the publicity surrounding television disclosures of what had gone on in industrial schools and reformatories. Some of the committee members had enquired of the manager of Daingean, Father William McGonagle, OMI, how corporal punishment was administered. Father McGonagle 'replied openly and without embarrassment' that

> ordinarily the boys were called out of the dormitories after they had retired, and that they were punished here on one of the stairway landings. The boys wore nightshirts as sleeping attire when they were called for punishments. Punishment was applied to the buttocks with a leather.

When asked why he allowed boys to be stripped naked for punishment, Father McGonagle replied 'in a matter-of-fact manner that he considered punishment to be more humiliating when it was administered in that way'. Additional psychological pressure was applied by having those who were awaiting a beating stand on the stairs immediately above those who were being leathered so that they could see what was going to befall them when their turn came. Savage physical punishment was used in all industrial schools, and needless to say it sometimes drove inmates to attempt to escape. The perils of doing so are illustrated by an account of an inmate of St Joseph's Industrial School, Ferryhouse, Clonmel, run by the Rosminians, during 1951–6:

> The three lads were marched in wearing nothing but wet swimming togs. This was so it would hurt more, and so the bruising on their backsides wouldn't be as marked. Each of them was spread over a table, with Brothers holding them down. Then another Brother beat them with a thick leather strap. The head priest told us that this is what we would get if we even thought of running away. The beatings went on for about an hour, the boys were screaming and roaring. One of them fought back, and they beat him all the more.

Not surprisingly, one of the conditions which affected inmates of industrial schools was bed-wetting, for which the punishment was also beating, in addition to refinements such as the miscreants being forced to walk around the school with wet sheets on their heads. In Letterfrack, County Galway, in St Joseph's Industrial School, children who wet the bed were forced to run around a stone yard holding their wet sheets above their heads until they dried. This sometimes took an inordinately long time, as Letterfrack is subject to the heavy west of Ireland rainfall.

In the light of all this, possibly the most sinister finding by the makers of the three-part RTE documentary, *States of Fear*, which lifted the lid on the foregoing in 1999, was:

> One extraordinary absence from the Department's records relates to the deaths of children in detention. Under the 1908 Children Act, the schools had a legal duty to investigate all violent or sudden deaths of children in their care. They were obliged to furnish the state with the reports of these investigations. The published annual reports for the Department of Education up to the mid-1960s do contain figures for these deaths, and their causes. Consequently the information was centrally compiled on a yearly basis. However, these files do not exist in the Department's archive.

An inmate of St Joseph's Industrial School, Summerhill, outside Athlone, has stated:

> I remember lots of girls dying. The nuns had their own graveyard, but the children were put somewhere else. There wasn't even a flower or a cross to mark where they were buried. I can't remember any funerals or masses said for them. They weren't really recognised you know.

No, they were not recognised, by the public, the media, the politicians, anybody. One specific case described by this inmate refers to a 15-year-old girl who had an appendix operation. She died, it is alleged, because, in the days before antibiotics, the nuns forced her to return to work before she should have been allowed out of bed. Cases such as that girl's were rumoured in areas surrounding industrial schools and reformatories, but they were never followed up, and never seem to have come to the attention of medical personnel serving such institutions.

Beatings were not confined to boys; girls too were physically assaulted. An inmate of St Joseph's Industrial School, Clifden, run by the Sisters of Mercy, described eating weeds, bulbs and the tops of flowers from the nuns' garden. When she got sick after eating apples she was beaten.

> The slightest thing you'd be beaten. They used a piece of wood, like a part of an orange box. We always had splinters of wood in us, cuts all over us. They beat us on the arms, on the legs. I don't know how we didn't die. Our hands were all ripped to pieces. One of the nuns used to get two girls to hold us down. She'd pull our knickers down and she'd beat us.

Mention has been made elsewhere of the work of the swashbuckling Minister for Education, Donough O'Malley. It was he who also set in motion the process which led to the ending of the institutional system as it had been known, with the setting up of the Kennedy Committee, under the chairmanship of District Justice Eileen Kennedy, in 1967. This was a breakthrough in the culture of *omertà* as practised by both Christ and Caesar over what went on in these schools. In 1951 one of O'Malley's predecessors, General Mulcahy, had tried to set up a similar committee, but the managers of the schools simply refused to co-operate with him and the proposal withered on the vine. O'Malley died before the committee reported in 1970. Despite obstruction, and a lack of facilities, Kennedy managed to produce what has been described as 'one of the most damning indictments of the operation of any State system ever produced in this country'. It criticised every aspect of the system, particularly the tendency to place people in charge of the institutions because they were surplus to requirements in other areas, rather than because they had an interest in childcare. Lack of funding and the conditions which obtained in places like Daingean were also criticised, as was the attitude of the Department of Education, which was condemned for not fulfilling its statutory obligation of inspecting what went on in industrial schools.

However, though the report led to a gradual improvement and, over the years, the closure of these institutions, one could not say that the conscience of the public was stirred in any significant way. The Church fought a protracted rearguard action along the lines that the report had overlooked the magnificent work done by the Church in caring for the poor and the vulnerable. It took the making of the *States of Fear* documentary, coupled with the impact of an earlier programme, *Dear Daughters*, to bring about the setting up of the Laffoy Commission under a Circuit Court judge to inquire into child abuse. *Dear Daughters*, made in 1996, looked at the case of Christine Buckley, who had been abused at Goldenbridge Industrial School in

Dublin, run by the Sisters of Mercy. Some of the incidents described in the programme included beatings, the use of boiling water as a punishment, children being forced to stand all night in a corridor, and, particularly disturbing, toilet training routines which involved so much squatting on chamber pots that the children's rectums collapsed. In addition, police inquiries have led to hundreds of religious being interviewed, resulting in there being close to 200 cases pending, before the courts, or awaiting a verdict from the Director of Public Prosecutions as to whether there is sufficient evidence to proceed with prosecution. In a few cases jail sentences have been imposed.

Child abuse has not and will not be eradicated in Ireland, or in any other country for that matter, but the norm nowadays is for sustainable allegations to be followed by prosecutions, whether of lay or religious perpetrators. Moreover, institutionalised childcare is increasingly child-centred, rather than directed at exerting authority, inculcating a certain type of religious mindset, or securing increased funding.

Interestingly, the foregoing facets of the Irish Church rarely formed the subject matter of critiques by Irish intellectuals, who mainly trained their fire on censorship or the attitude of the hierarchy on the given issue of the day. This should probably not be put down to cowardice or similar motives, but simply to the fact that most people were not aware of what went on behind those high walls. The darkest place is under the light. But I feel that it cannot be without significance that one of the few writers to produce an outstanding novel on the Troubles, Bernard MacLaverty, a Belfast Catholic, whose *Cal* (1983) was made into a successful film starring Helen Mirren, was also the writer of *Lamb*, a tragic account of the abuse in a Christian Brothers-run institution. This was also made into a successful film, starring Liam Neeson, in 1980. The best-known voice from the Gulag itself is that of Mannix Flynn, whose Stations of the Cross included Letterfrack and several other places of detention as he collided abrasively with the system. His *James X* is a theatrical account, a one-man show, of what that process meant in practice which left packed audiences both shaken and stirred. His novels *The Liberty Suit* (written in collaboration with Peter Sheridan) and *Nothing to Say* are both a terrible indictment of a sick system that institutionalised ritual physical and sexual abuse, and a tribute to the human spirit which enabled Flynn to survive not merely the enclosed trauma, but the alcohol abuse which followed his emergence from the 'corrective' system.

Since the deaths of Patrick Kavanagh (in 1967) and Brian O'Nolan (in 1965), Irish writing has taken a different curve from that of Kavanagh's preoccupation with religion and the life of the countryman – O'Nolan's phantasmagorical, maniac world of satire and comic genius, and Behan's experience of borstal, prison and the IRA. The three outstanding writers of the latter part of the century fit neatly into the categories of novel, theatre and poetry. John McGahern, in his literally dark, unflinching dissections of rural Irish adolescence and parenthood, *The Dark* and *Amongst Women*, in particular, reached heights that very few of his contemporaries come near.

Brian Friel, for both the quality and the extraordinary range of his plays, from *Off to Philadelphia in the Morning*, to *Translations*, to *Dancing at Lughnasa*, deserves to be regarded as the Irish Chekhov, exploring issues of identity, emigration, a son's isolation from place and parenthood, and the tragedy and the fire that underlie the seemingly dull, sexless lives of a group of spinster countrywomen disturbed by the return of their missionary priest brother from Africa. In poetry, Seamus Heaney shines by his own light, a lamp of talent burnished by the winning of the Nobel Prize for Literature in 1995. Again, his range and versatility, apart from the quality of his work, are remarkable. Whether musing on the secrets of the bogs, the place of pilgrimage in Irish life, occasionally a glancing look at the Troubles or translations from the Greek classics, Heaney's quiet style gently brings the reader on a journey of insight without polemic. It might also be remarked that his equitable temperament, and attractive personality, his ability to move easily into chairs at Harvard or Oxford, make him the archetypical figure of the Artist Accepted as opposed to that of Outcast during the mid-century. In shaping his career, Heaney has shown a Yeatsian managerial talent, somehow making clear where his ancestral national sympathies lie, without overidentification with cause or 'ism'. The playwright Thomas Murphy, whose status is such that the Abbey devoted an entire season to his work in 2002, has also produced a distinguished oeuvre, ranging from depictions of violence amongst the emigrant Irish, *A Whistle in the Dark*, to the effects of the famine, to the pathos of ordinary men under stress in the *Gigli Concert*.

Beneath, or perhaps simply apart from, the heights occupied by the fore-going, a number of Irish writers occupy what might be termed the specialist niches of some significance. Given the productivity of Irish writers, an in-depth explanation of all would require a book in its own right, but one or two should be alluded to, for differing reasons. Edna O'Brien, for example, stirred up extraordinary controversy with her early work during the sixties. *The Country Girls*, *The Lonely Girl*, *Girl with Green Eyes*, *August is a Wicked Month* and *Casualties of Peace* dealt with issues of female sexuality and joyless marriage in far too authentic a fashion for the censors. Her work was both an exercise in liberation and a target for the establishment unwilling to see the old ways change and give way to the new. Although banned, she was the most read and most talked-of woman writer of the period, incurring a quite remarkable degree of hostility from those who objected to her depiction of the fact that where the official image of Irish marriage was concerned, the Emperor, very definitely, had no clothes.

Inevitably, the passage of time, and the coming of a generation attuned not to the teachings of clergy seeking to prevent Irish womanhood from the lustful side effects of tampons, but to scandals about paedophilia and the luridities of the Internet, lessened O'Brien's impact in the eighties and nineties. The newer generation of readers hearkened to the irreverent, working-class tones of the characters in Roddy Doyle's fictional Barrytown. Film and the inspired directorship of Alan Parker brought his work to a world stage. In particular, *The Commitments* and *The Snapper*, the former dealing with the tragic hilarity of an effort to found a soul band in Barrytown, the latter with the impact on a family of discovering that a daughter has been impregnated by a neighbour, a family man, accurately portrayed the manner in which life was (and is) really lived in contemporary working-class Dublin housing estates.

The film culture, that is, making as opposed to going to movies, took its time coming to Dublin. After the war, Emmet Dalton, Michael Collins's colleague, was responsible for a venture which transferred many of the Abbey's classics to the cinema screen. But this worthy effort, though not without a certain attraction, remained just that, a somewhat pedestrian transfer from stage to film. Ardmore Studios outside Bray also attracted international film companies to Ireland before running into financial diffi- culties, and there were a few curiosities like Peter Ustinov's *The Purple Taxi*. But remarkably, for a country with the acting, writing and technical talents of the Irish, to say nothing of the scenery, the film culture took a long time to put down roots in Ireland. It took works like *The Commitments*, and Jim Sheridan's *My Left Foot*, in which Daniel Day-Lewis played Christy Brown, the working-class Dubliner affected from birth by cerebral palsy who learned how to type out his story with his left foot, thanks to the dedication of his mother, to, as it were, place Irish film-making on the international map. This process was subsequently aided by the work of Neil Jordan (*Mona Lisa*, *Angel* and *The Crying Game*), Peter Sheridan's *Some Mothers' Sons*, Paddy Brenacht's *I Went Down* and several other films, some, like *Into the West*, starring Gabriel Byrne, displaying that incorrigibly romantic vision of the country that stubbornly continues to defy the reality of life in Ireland.

A remarkable feature of the period under review is the limited extent to which the Troubles impacted on the Irish creative mind, be it in film, prose or poetry. A group of intellectuals which included Seamus Heaney, Brian Friel, Seamus Deane and Tom Paulin did make an attempt at a response to the Troubles which resulted in the founding of the Field Day Theatre Company, a series known as the Field Day Pamphlets, and later the Field Day Anthology. This huge compendium of Irish writing over the centuries ran into critical difficulties over its first edition, not because of any perceived Nationalist bias, but because it outraged the feminists for its lack of female contributors. Even in the north, where the traditional Irish seedbed of literature, war, jail, the clash of identities, sprouted all too actively and virulently for over 30 years, no Behan or O'Casey, Frank O'Connor or Seán O'Faolain germinated. Possibly the major literary work to emerge was John Montague's long poem, *The Rough Field*, which came relatively early in the conflict. The two major plays of the latter part of the twentieth century which related to Northern Ireland dealt with aspects of sectarianism and the Loyalist mind, but not with the Troubles directly. These were Sam Thompson's play depicting sectarianism in the shipyards, *Over the Bridge*, and Frank McGuinness's *Observe the Sons of Ulster Marching to the Somme*, in which the playwright explores the lives and attitudes of a group of Ulster Protestant soldiers on the eve of the great World War I battle.

The Ulster Protestant, or to be more precise the northern Unionist tradition, has not proved to be the greatest wellspring of literary talent thrown up in Ireland by the twentieth century. There have been some notable exceptions to this what some will no doubt deem opprobrious judgement. The poetry of Louis MacNeice comes to mind, as does the work of John Hewitt and of W.R. Rodgers. The stage has called forth some notable contemporary talent also: the actor Kenneth Branagh and, in popular music, the iconic figure of Van Morrison. It would be true to say that while Northern Ireland has obviously produced some notable poets and writers, as the existence, to name but a few, of a Heaney, a Friel or a Montague more than adequately demonstrates, to say nothing of poets like Derek Mahon and Michael Longley, nevertheless the Troubles themselves were curiously meagre in their contribution to Irish literature. Inevitably, there was some writing, in fact a great deal of it, but quality was more difficult to observe than bulk. The already mentioned short novel by Bernard MacLaverty, *Cal*, about a star-crossed love affair across the religious and terrorist divide, and Seamus Deane's *Reading in the Dark*, which is as much the story of childhood in Derry as of the Troubles, deserve to be remembered, but not a great deal else. It was as if the writers felt uneasy about this brutal eruption in their lives, part irrelevant and part central to much of contemporary Ireland.

While the impact on the Six County area itself, in percentage terms, was far greater than the impact of the Vietnam War on America, south of the border writers, like historians, were troubled and uneasy about what was happening. They opted either to ignore the Troubles or to concentrate solely on condemning terrorism. The problem for some intellectuals was largely one of what the Nationalist identity was, or rather how to fashion a construct of Nationalist identity that would somehow include in its lineage the Celtic Dawn, and the early Abbey Theatre, without adverting to the Irish physical-force tradition or sectarianism, save in a manner acceptable to the arbiters of Section 31 and to that frequently observed offspring of the Troubles, Conference-Going Man.

Occasionally one came across a writer confident enough to break away from the issues of identity and concentrate on a universal phenomenon: Michael O'Siadhail, in his long poem on the Holocaust, for example. There is no shortage of Irish poetical talent. One thinks of poets like Thomas Kinsella, Brendan Kenneally and Derek Mahon as indications that the Irish poetic wellsprings are far from drying up. But in general, if one may dare to generalise where such a dangerous subject is concerned, one could say that Irish writing today tends to be concerned with the individual rather than the epic. Some of the more interesting work has been on the theme of childhood: Seamus Deane and John McGahern, Frank McCourt, Nuala O'Faolain and Hugo Hamilton have fashioned more from childhood trauma than any contemporary on Northern Ireland. Perish the thought that one would wish poverty on the writer, but it is interesting that from the time of what some have called the 'Haughey Bounty', Irish writing would be more accurately described as being mannered and low key, rather than characterised by any great originality or fire in the belly. Haughey both symbolised and helped to accentuate the change in official Irish attitudes to the writer with the introduction first of his artist tax exemption measure, and then the creation of the Aosdana. Members of this organisation elect each other and are paid a state bounty which has moved with inflation to a contemporary €11,000 per year. These were enlightened and welcome policies, good in themselves, and a kind of atonement for the attitudes towards O'Casey, O'Nolan, Kavanagh, Edna O'Brien and the others.

Irish publishing is in a better state than I can ever recall despite the competition from abroad, which has been met in several cases by linkages with international publishers. O'Brien Press, Poolbeg, Wolfhound, Blackstaff, Appletree (located in Belfast), Townhouse, Mercier are but a few of the imprints which spring to mind. But for sheer durability in the maintenance of standards in the fields of biographical, historical and political publishing – the roots of the firm go back to the nineteenth century – the palm has to go to Gill and Macmillan, still run by a Gill, Michael, a descendant of the founder.

Obviously one still hears the distinctive voice of talent in the ranks of the younger Irish school of playwrights; for instance, Martin McDonagh, who portrays his troubling west of Ireland characters in the authentic dialogue he learned from his Connemara grandmother while he was growing up in London. Marina Carr finds her inspiration in everything from incest to Medea. Bernard Farrell's quiet humour and accurate depiction of lower middle-class Dublin life has won him a distinctive following. But we are in the days of the Internet, film and the electronic media. As in the world generally, the talent that would once have been geared to the stage alone, like that of Conor MacPherson, for example, now turns its eyes towards television and film-making.

The facet of Irish culture which has undergone most transformation is the Irish language. Polemics have died down, and as the twentieth century ended, one no longer heard debate between binary opposites such as, on the one hand, 'Irish is the authentic mark of an Irishman' as opposed to 'It's a waste of time learning Irish'. Possibly a factor in arriving at a less contentious position in Irish society concerning the language was the ending of compulsion in the 1980s. But what is certain is that alongside a growing Europeanisation and recognition of the values of other cultures, there has come a growth in the appreciation of Ireland's own heritage in language, sport and music. A tradition has grown up wherein people tend to play to enjoy themselves in an Irish milieu, rather than argue rancorously. One of the significant developments in Irish education has been the growth of the Gael scoileanna, in which Irish is the sole medium of instruction. It is commonplace for middle-class families to send their children to Gaeltacht districts, principally in the west of Ireland, for summer immersion courses in the language, music and dancing. What the real strength of the language is it is hard to gauge, but the census returns show that over the century the percentage of those claiming an ability to speak some Irish has grown from a low of 18% in 1911 to a current figure of around 30%, roughly 350,000 people. Although the purists decried it, the extraordinary success of the musicals *Riverdance* and *Lord of the Dance* has helped the development of dancing in particular. All over the world I have found parents going to considerable expense and trouble to provide classes and expensive costumes so that their children can learn Irish dancing. A particularly good television channel, Telefís na Gaeilge, and a radio station, Radio na Gaeltachta, have helped to bolster the image of the native Irish culture. In general, writers in the Irish language must do so in the knowledge that they are largely writing for each other. They can read English writers; the average Irish writer in the English language is not likely to be able to read the work of his Irish-speaking counterpart. Nevertheless, the major annual Irish music and literary competitions, the Feis Ceoil and the Oireachtas, continue to flourish and grow, and purely sporting contests like the all-Ireland Gaelic football and hurling championships each put up national interest (and blood pressure) to at least the equivalent levels of a general election.

Anthony Cronin, who delivered the gloomy mid-century judgement on the Irish artistic scene which I have already quoted, and in the same year helped to launch Bloomsday, would later influence Charles Haughey in the introduction of the imaginative Aosdona scheme, which gives a state income to a selected group of writers. He was taking a far more emollient view of the position of an Irish artists at the end of the twentieth century than he was in the middle of it:

> Ireland became a place worth writing about. Time was when most great interesting issues were English issues. English novels dealt with things like wills, money, power. Things of importance, Society mattered. There wasn't enough circumstance to keep things going in Ireland. Two things happened. It became accepted that it was right and proper to have the analysis that artists provided. We needed them and there was provision made for them. So instead of being suppressed and forced out artists began a dialogue with society, though I don't think that society understood the vast energy, the care and time artists devote to their work.
>
> However on a political level arts, literature, ceased to be dirty words, became words to brandish. Charlie [Haughey, author] understood something about the creative process. He would have announced the Aosdana earlier than he did but the Stardust fire cancelled the Ard Fheis at which the Aosdana was announced. It started with a lower scale of payments than would have been possible had the scheme been announced with the backing of a supportive Ard Fheis. The £3,000 to £4,000 levels could have been £10,000 to £15,000. Artists need a sympathetic mileau to operate in and Ireland today has become a mecca of artists.[53]

Cronin's view might be taken as neo-Marxist. Society becomes interesting when there's a bit of money about. But given his background this is understandable. His book *Dead as Doornails*, which amongst other things contains hilarious accounts of the escapades of himself and Brendan Behan in their early days, is rightly regarded as one of great Irish comic works. But one of the things which influenced Haughey into accepting Cronin's thesis that artists should be given state encouragement was a recognition of the fact that the facade of drinking and hilarity masked a distinctly unfunny, enervating poverty. It's too early to say what the lasting impact of state encouragement as opposed to state oppression on Irish writing will be. To me much of what is currently produced appears bland and lacking in passion. Dermot Bolger's *The Journey Home* is one of the few novels one can mention which has anything of the once commonly met with savage indignation of the Irish writer towards unjust authority and corruption. But obviously encouragement has to be regarded as a great improvement on suppression.

To sum up then. How stands Ireland as the twentieth century recedes into the mist of history? Probably the appropriate answer is that, given the climate, mist is the operative word. Ireland as a society stands socio-religiously and economically as it does geographically and geologically: surrounded by powerful currents, sturdy enough in its underpinnings, but with large boggy areas and a somewhat uncertain climate. The institutional Church has unquestionably been buffeted by severe storms, and it is probably true to say that its contemporary esteem in the eyes of the public is somewhat below that of the GAA. But man is mortal, and given this realisation and the historic background to the Church in Ireland, it is likely that Catholicism will continue to be the bandage wrapped around the bleeding soul of a majority of the people. Practices such as confession and mass-going seem certain to continue to decline, but, per contra, other sacramental occasions which have an impact on the family would appear set to continue and even to grow in popularity, e.g. first Holy Communion, baptism, confirmation, and, despite growing divorce rates, marriage. As on the continent of Europe and in North America, Irish Catholics like to mark these milestones in a church, and to depart this life from a church also.

And the Church still possesses sizeable bulwarks. Lay organisations such as Opus Dei and the Knights of Columbanus help to make up in influence what the Church is losing in clerical numbers. While the scandals have weakened the authority of individual bishops and clergy, and numbers of priests and nuns are declining drastically, it is not without significance that the Church's income for the archdiocese of Dublin rose by 6% for the year 2002. And though newer irritations at Church teachings in areas like divorce and abortion increasingly make themselves felt, older attitudes still have substantial numbers of adherents. The 1997 general election returned a number of independents who supported the Government. All three secured a promise for another pro-life referendum as the price of their support. One independent, Harry Blaney, condemned a proposal to site a vasectomy clinic in Donegal. In the Euro-elections of 1999, the successful Connacht West candidate, the singer Dana (Rosemary Brown), talked equally of those excluded from the benefits of the Celtic Tiger and the need to continue to keep abortion from Ireland. In the years 2002 and 2003, extraordinary scenes of old-style devotion were witnessed as particles of bone, the relics of St Theresa of Lisieux and of St Anthony of Padua, were put on display in various churches. In both cases, worshippers thronged in such numbers as to cause huge traffic jams. A tendency to shoot what might be thought of as unsatisfactory messengers, therefore, would not appear to indicate an equivalent distaste for the message.

In the national school system, the government-backed rules still stipulate that:

> Of all parts of a school curriculum, Religious Instruction is by far the most important, as its subject matter, God's honour and service, includes the proper use of man's faculties, and affords the most powerful inducements to their proper use. Religious instruction is, therefore a fundamental part of the school course, and a religious spirit should inform and vivify the whole school's work.

The desire to maintain this ethos is unchanging and occasionally unjust. For example in 1965 this mentality led to the young John McGahern being sacked from his job as a primary schoolteacher, paid by the state, because he had published a banned book, *The Dark*. The teachers' union did not dare to attempt to protect him. Nor did unions, employment tribunals or the courts uphold the plea of Eileen Flynn, a secondary schoolteacher, also paid by the state, who was fired by the Holy Faith nuns from her teaching post in their school in New Ross in 1981. Flynn had had a baby out of wedlock by a man, with whom she had been living, who had been separated from his wife. Delivering his judgment, Judge Noel Ryan said:

> Times are changing and we must change with them, but they have not changed that much in this or the adjoining jurisdiction with regard to some things. In other places women are being condemned to death for this sort of offence. They are not Christians in the far East. I do not agree with this, of course. Here people take a serious view of this and it is idle to shut one's eyes to it.[54]

During 2002, Tomas O'Dulaing, a teacher at an all-Irish primary, inter-denominational school in Dunboyne, County Meath, paid for by the state, was fired because, as the school was all-denominational, he had attempted to ensure that Protestant pupils should not have to remove themselves when their Catholic classmates were being taught about Holy Communion. The Board of Management insisted that all religious instruction take place within school hours. O'Dulaing had attempted to give religious instruction to Catholic children outside teaching hours.

At the time of writing, therefore, religious instruction still takes up a sizeable portion of the children's study time, even though no foreign language is taught at primary level, a circumstance which obviously affects the poorer classes more than the rich, who can better afford extra-curricular classes. In addition, the Church enjoys other advantages, such as the fact that the state, even in second- and third-level state-controlled educational institutions, continues to pay the salaries of chaplains. Church influence may also be seen in the hospital sector. Twenty-six of the 63 hospitals in the Republic are Catholic voluntary hospitals, wherein an ethics committee seeks to ensure that the Church ethos is maintained, meaning that in effect procedures such as artificial fertilisation and sterilisation are not available. Since abortion is banned, amniocentesis tests are supposedly banned also (because there is no point in finding out about deformities in the foetus), but anecdotal evidence suggests that in some cases at least, an Irish solution to this particular Irish problem has been found. If therefore the Church acts wisely in the future, and for example desists from policies of parsimony where compensation for victims of physical or sexual abuse are concerned, it has a position of strength from which to maintain a significant presence in Irish society, albeit this would be far from the role ascribed to it by Professor Lee, for example. It would also presuppose that under a new Pope, the Church will make alterations in the areas of clerical celibacy, women priests and lay involvement in the selection of bishops.

In the politico-economic sphere, one would also expect to see certain fundamental changes. For example, Ireland still has one of the lowest representations of women parliamentarians in the world, ranking below Angola, Eritrea, and Rwanda, in only having 14.6% women in parliament.[55] This of course places it ahead of America, which has only 12%, but it's a long way below the percentage of women employed in Ireland, 46%, and ludicrously out of line with the fact that Ireland has 100% female enrolment in secondary education. However, in this regard, it is not without significance that Ireland has both a woman president, Mary McAleese, and a female deputy prime minister, Mary Harney. It was Harney who (on 21 July 2000) defined the Republic's political, economic and even geographical situation as the century closed in a much-quoted speech:

> History and geography have placed Ireland in a very special position between America and Europe . . . Geography has placed this country on the edge of the European continent. One of our most significant achievements as an independent nation was our entry, almost thirty years ago, into what is now the European Union. Today, we have strong social, economic and political ties with the EU.
>
> As Irish people our relationships with the United States and the European Union are complex. Geographically we are closer to Berlin than Boston. Spiritually we are probably a lot closer to Boston than Berlin.
>
> . . . What really makes Ireland attractive to corporate America is the kind of economy which we have created here. When Americans come here they find a country that believes in the incentive power of low taxation. They find a country that believes in economic liberalisation. They find a country that believes in essential regulation but not over-regulation. On looking further afield in Europe they find also that not every European country believes in all of these things.
>
> The figures speak for themselves. It is a remarkable fact that a country with just 1% of Europe's population accounts for 27% of US Greenfield investment in Europe.

... Look at what we have done over the last ten years. We have cut taxes on capital. We have cut taxes on corporate profits. We have cut taxes on personal incomes. The result has been an explosion in economic activity and Ireland is now the fastest-growing country in the developed world.

And did we have to pay some very high price for pursuing this policy option? Did we have to dismantle the welfare state? Did we have to abandon the concept of social inclusion? The answer is no: we didn't.[56]

Many people would question Harney's analysis. While her figures are indisputable, it is also true that the ratio of earnings between top management and workers at the bottom level has increased from 3.5 to 5 times between 1987 and 1994. The Celtic Tiger's record on levelling off earnings is not a good one. One critic of the Boston rather than Berlin approach, Kieran Allen, has called the Republic's performance 'one of the worst records on earnings dispersion in the developed industrial world'.[57] In the two years which have elapsed since Harney delivered her speech, Allen's strictures, and those of people like him, have gained strength from the softening in the global economy. Job losses are currently running at an average of 500 a week. At a time of economic downturn, the public are becoming increasingly aware of, and angry at, deficiencies in the system. It is a demonstrable fact that people in the last stages of terminal cancer have been left for up to 15 hours lying on hospital trolleys. The Republic has not merely a two-tier, but a three-tier hospital service. Apart from the obvious gap between what is available to the better-off with private health insurance, and those relying on state services, people in rural Ireland relying on local hospitals can hardly be claimed to have the same facilities as those in Dublin. Hospital beds are being closed, public transport is a shambles, the road system is in chaos as patchwork alterations and improvements are attempted, with varying degrees of success.

The social partnership is creaking under the strain of trying to cope with both the economic downturn and Government attempts to correct inefficiencies. Severe unrest has occurred, and more is threatened in the agricultural sector, transport, and other areas, particularly medicine, wherein both public service doctors and nurses have taken strike action. However, Ireland has seen similar situations before, as by now should have been made clear in these pages, and the celebrated Irish solution to Irish problems was somehow found. The new, and worrying, ingredient in the Irish political stew is corruption. In the days of John Charles McQuaid, people were clear about what they were either for or against. Those who opposed the system naively thought that once clerical power was lessened all would be well. Now the enemies are hidden, behind phalanxes of spin-doctors, lawyers, and the New Elite, the brass-necked men who have done well out of the boom. These are the builders, the developers, the lawyers, architects and accountants who colluded with the corrupt planners, the venal politicians, the bribable officials to make the Golden Calf a more appropriate symbol for modern Ireland than the Celtic Tiger. They spawned the tribunals, but they also spawned intangible

751

evils like cynicism and mistrust, along with the badly built, amenity-deprived housing estates, which are the most tangible sign of their activities.

Even the tribunals may not provide answers to these evils. Their costs have been so astronomic that the public, incensed by the sight of so many lawyers enriching themselves out of the public purse, are murmuring against them. Most, apparently, have many more years' sittings ahead before conclusions can be arrived at on a variety of issues. For instance, delaying tactics have so slowed down the work of the Flood Tribunal that there is currently a debate in official circles centring on how to deal with the fact that it might have to sit for another 15 years. Mr Justice Flood retired in his middle seventies and was succeeded by Mr Justice Mahon. A senior journalist who has covered Flood's work closely, Paul Cullen, of the *Irish Times*, has written:

> On dozens of occasions, the tribunal was forced to traipse through the High Court and the Supreme Court. It won most of the time, but the loss of time and momentum was immense. In a game with no give-and-take, opponents insisted on using every legal route possible to defend their interests.
>
> The response of many parties to requests for information could be described as leisurely at best. Deadlines came and went, correspondence flew back and forth. Information was drip-fed to the tribunal. The documents sought always seemed to arrive at the last minute, just before a witness was due to enter the box. There were endless earnest protestations of how anxious people were to cooperate, but usually the bare minimum was done to avoid being dragged down to the High Court like Liam Lawlor.[58] Records and receipts were frequently non-existent, and memories were blank.

And these were not the only methods used. As Cullen has noted:

> This was often a dirty war and some individuals have not shied away from using more irregular stratagems. Fear, intimidation, obstruction, time-wasting and spin-doctoring were the weapons of choice of some of those anxious to keep out of the limelight.
>
> I have heard credible allegations about the intimidation of potential witnesses. Attempts have been made to buy the silence of would-be whistle-blowers. Unsolicited presents have been delivered to people in the hope that they might be persuaded to give evidence critical of others.[59]

But despite these and other pressures, Mr Justice Flood persisted, and, as he said in his second interim report to the Oireachtas, published in September 2002, the Revenue and Criminal Assets Bureau to that date had received €34,500,000 as a result of 'compliance issues' arising directly from the tribunal's work. Flood commented that 'certain parties who appeared before me chose not to co-operate with the Tribunal . . . and further, having been duly sworn, did not tell the truth'. The interim report itself was also sent to the Director of Public Prosecutions.

One of the many pieces of fallout from the torrent of rumour and scandal which the tribunals have elicited was a totally unfounded allegation that the Taoiseach, Bertie Ahern, had received a £50,000 bribe from a Cork builder,

Denis 'Starry' O'Brien. Ahern successfully sued O'Brien for libel in the Dublin Circuit Civil Court in July of 2001, being awarded the maximum damages the court could give, £30,000. Judge O'Hagan found O'Brien's allegation 'utterly, completely and absolutely false and untrue'. Apart from the intrinsic unfairness of the allegation, which initially exposed Ahern to what he later said was more criticism on the day of the story's breaking than in his previous 25 years in politics, it also had the effect of involving the Taoiseach in what might be taken as a symbolic Irish morality play for the end of the twentieth century. The story broke during April 2000 just before Easter Monday, on which he attended the annual Fianna Fáil commemoration for the Easter Rising, and walked into a barrage of questions from journalists about the accusation. As a result, on the eighty-fourth anniversary of the day the men of 1916 marched into the GPO, the images on television were not of idealistic endeavour extolled, but of the men's spiritual successor dealing with charges of corruption.

If the 1916 men could have foreseen that their action would lead to an Ireland in which such an almost sacrilegious situation could arise, would they have marched? The question is rhetorical. What did happen has been chronicled in these pages. What will happen is unknowable. But, based on the experience of the twentieth century, it would seem that the Irish tent-pole philosophy for the twenty-first should be based on a combination of mastering the destructive components of their distinctive Celtic ancestry, while at the same time using their love of education to help them develop their great constructive energies in a contemporary version of Sinn Féin, this time really meaning Ourselves Alone, and not a hybrid construct based on a combination of a denatured linguistic identity and an obsessively sex-centred, authoritarian religion. If they can do this, while avoiding the bogs of corruption, and learning something from past wrong turnings, then it seems reasonable to speculate that the Irish, with their attractive personality, love of sport – not necessarily confined to the varieties found on playing fields – drinking and singing, will, in their own inimitable style, find their way safely through the mists of the future.

There are slight but significant signs that they may be so doing. I normally like, if it is possible to do so without distorting reality, to end my books on an up-beat note, but candidly I was somewhat at a loss as to how to do it in the present Irish climate, until the opening of the Special Olympics was staged at Croke Park at the end of June 2003, attended by Irish icons like the organisers, the Kennedy family, particularly Eunice Shriver, by native film and rock stars, like Bono and Colin Farrell and, above all, by Nelson Mandela. The spectacular pageantry was a fitting tribute to the heroism of the contestants themselves, and the fact that the country had rallied to supporting the event, the first time it had been held outside the United States, to such an extent that 34,000 people in every part of the country, north and south, including the Aran Islands, had given their services free to host and care for the contestants. It was immediately obvious that the carnivorous Celtic Tiger had not devoured the Irish caring tradition. But there were other highly significant examples of what is going on beneath the surface of Irish life. The Olympic Flame itself was preceded into Croke Park, the citadel of Irish national sporting self-expression – so much so that it was shot up by the Black and Tans on Bloody Sunday – not only by, as might be expected, a Garda motor-cycle escort, but also a corps from the Police Service of Northern Ireland. This gesture of co-operation would have been unthinkable a few years ago. That traditional Irish sympathy for the underdog was also still alive and well was graphically illustrated in the two greatest outbursts of cheering for the national delegations.

As might be expected, given the close shared history with Ireland, the huge US contingent received an enormous welcome, but so too did the relatively tiny contingent which had managed to get to Dublin from Iraq. The fact that, the evidence of 'tribunalitis' nothwithstanding, the Irish public is still not prepared to take everything that is thrown at them was also demonstrated. Booing broke out on two occasions: once, when the soccer star Roy Keane was introduced, the other while Bertie Ahern spoke. In the case of the former, some people were registering disapproval of the fact that Keane had pulled out of the Irish squad during the previous year's World Cup, thereby ruining the team's chances of progress, and triggering a huge media feeding frenzy which ultimately led to the resignation of the popular team manager, Mick McCarthy. In the second case, people were showing their annoyance at the fact that Ahern should derive publicity by speaking at the event at a time when his government was cutting back on the monies available to help people like those taking part in the Olympics. No doubt the moment was hurtful for both men. But the memories of the booing will die away, and on the present trends in Irish politics, the weakened state of the opposition would appear to indicate that Ahern, Fianna Fáil and the Progressive Democrats could continue in government for the foreseeable future, possibly even beyond the next general election. Meanwhile it is good to know that the Irish still possess their traditional Celtic attributes of hospitality, and a talented independence of spirit.

The Irish have successfully negotiated the difficult, lengthy transition from one form of colonialism, that of Mother England, to arrive at a position of independence and co-existence. They must now complete the equally difficult task of developing an efficient and a caring society by similarly freeing themselves of the constraints of – while not being unmindful of the benefits of – that other form of colonialism: Mother Church.

NOTES

1. Churchill addressed his audience in an artfully duplicitous manner which became the leitmotiv of the Conservatives' utilisation of the Irish question for domestic political gain. He told his audience of Belfast Unionists that he was with them, as was his ancestor, the Duke of Marlborough, who had been a general of William of Orange, the Orangemen's icon, but neglected to remind them that the Duke had also been a general of William's enemy, the Catholic James II, whom William defeated at the Battle of the Boyne in 1690.

2. Quoted in Dorothy Macardle, *The Irish Republic*, Irish Press, Dublin, 1951 edition.

3. Thomas Pakenham, *The Year of Liberty*, Hodder & Stoughton, London, 1969.

4. Ibid.

5. Macardle, op. cit.

6. Quoted in Carty, James (ed.), *Ireland from the Great Famine to the Treaty*, C.J. Fallon, Dublin, 1951.

7. Emmet Larkin (trans. and ed.), *Alexis de Tocqueville's Journey in Ireland, July–August 1835*, Wolfhound Press, Dublin, 1990.

8. Ibid.

9. For an examination of anti-Irish prejudice, see L.P. Curtis, *Anglo-Saxons and Celts: a Study of Irish Prejudice in Victorian England* (New York, 1968); T. Carlyle, *Reminiscences of my Irish Journey* (London 1882); C. Kingsley, *Letters and Memories* (London, 1877); and an article in *Eire – Ireland* (September, 1981) by D.T. Dorrity, '"Monkeys in a Menagerie", the Imagery of Unionist Opposition to Home Rule, 1886–1903'.

10. Barry Coldrey, *Faith and Fatherland*, Gill & Macmillan, Dublin, 1988.

11. Larkin, *De Tocqueville's Journey*, op. cit.

12. Tomas de Bhaldraithe (trans.), *The Diary of Humphrey O'Sullivan, 1827–35*, Mercier, Dublin and Cork, 1979.

13. P.S. O'Hegarty, *A History of Ireland Under the Union*, Methuen, London, 1952.

14. Coldrey, op. cit.

15. C.S. Andrews, *Dublin Made Me*, Dublin, 1979.

16. F.X. Martin, *Leaders and Men of the Easter Rising*, Dublin, 1967.

17. Donald R. Pearce (ed.), *The Senate Speeches of W.B. Yeats*,

Prenderville, London, 2001.

18. Kevin C. Kearns, *Dublin Tenement Life*, Gill & Macmillan, Dublin, 1994.

19. Paul Bew, *Ideology and the Irish Question, Ulster Unionism and Irish Nationalism, 1912–1916*, Clarendon Press, Oxford, 1994.

20. Paul Dubois, *Contemporary Ireland*, Maunsel, Dublin. Translated from *L'Irlande Contemporaire, La Tragedie Irelandaise*, Perrin, Paris, 1907.

21. Bew, op. cit.

22. Jeremy Smith, *The Tories and Ireland*, Irish Academic Press, Dublin, 2000.

23. Quoted in Bew, op. cit.

24. Patrick Buckland, *Ulster Unionism and the Origins of Northern Ireland*, Gill & Macmillan, Dublin, 1973.

25. Ibid.

26. Ibid.

27. Ibid.

28. Margaret Macmillan, *Peacemakers*, John Murray, London, 2002.

29. Ibid.

30. John Campbell, *F.E. Smith*, Jonathan Cape, London, 1983.

31. Piaras Béaslaí, *Michael Collins and the Making of a New Ireland*, Vol. 1, Phoenix, Dublin, 1926.

32. Macardle, op. cit.

33. Ward's important, perspective-altering article, 'Marginality and Militancy, Cumann na mBann, 1914–36' originally appeared in *Ireland: Divided Nation, Divided Class*, eds. Austen Morgan and Bob Purdie, London, 1980. An extract from it appears in the invaluable guide to the role of women in 20th-century Ireland, *The Irish Women's History Reader*, eds. Alan Hayes and Diane Urquhart, Routledge, London, 2001.

34. It included besides the O'Rahilly, Padraig Pearse, Seán MacDermott, Eamonn Kent, Bulmer Hobson, Piaras Béaslaí, W. J. Ryan, Colm O'Lochlainn, Seamus O'Connor, Seán Fitzgibbon, J.A. Deakin, and the poet Joseph Campbell.

35. Macardle, op. cit.

36. Ibid.

37. Quoted in Seán Cronin, *The McGarrity Papers*, Anvil, Tralee, 1972.

38. *Irish Citizen*, 23 October 1915.

39. Lord Longford and T.P. O'Neill, *Eamon de Valera*, Hutchinson, London, 1970.

40. T.P. Coogan, *Long Fellow, Long Shadow*, Hutchinson, London, 1993, for further information on de Valera's origins and the nature of his baptismal and birth certificates.

41. R. Blake, *The Unknown Prime Minister, The Life and Times of Andrew Bonar Law, 1858–1923*, Eyre & Spottiswood, 1955.

42. Ian F.W. Beckett, *The Army and the Curragh Incident*, Army Records

Society, Bodley Head, London, 1986.

43 . Blake, op. cit.

44. Ibid.

45. Quoted in Beckett, op. cit.

46. Brigadier General Frank Crozier was particularly explicit in *Ireland for Ever*, Jonathan Cape, 1932.

47. A.T.Q. Stewart, *The Ulster Crisis*, Faber & Faber, London, 1967 and Beckett's work are excellent accounts of the mutiny.

48. Quoted in Macardle, op. cit.

49. The O'Connor incident is described in Coogan, op. cit.

50. Asquith, Earl of Oxford, *50 Years of Parliament,* Cassell, London, 1926.

51. Lord Riddell, *War Diary, 1914–1918*, Nicholson and Watson, London.

52. *Collected Works of Padraig Pearse*, Maunsel & Co., Dublin, 1917.

53. Macardle, op. cit.

54. Béaslaí, op. cit.

55. For Birrell's Irish career, see Leon Ó'Broin, *The Chief Secretary*, Chatto & Windus, London, 1969; and *Dublin Castle and the 1916 Rising*, Sidgwick & Jackson, London, 1910.

56. W.B. Yeats, *Senate Speeches*, ed. Donald R. Pearce, Prendeville, London, 2001.

57. O'Broin, *The Chief Secretary*, op. cit.

58. Béaslaí, op. cit.

59. Macardle, op. cit.

60. Stewart, op. cit.

61. For accounts of what passed between the Volunteer leaders before the Rising, and the subsequent fighting, readers are recommended to Max Caulfield, *The Easter Rebellion*, Heron Books, London, 1963; and to Edgar Holt, *Protest in Arms*, Putnam, 1960.

62. This measure was larger than a barrel, but smaller than a hogshead.

63. William Redmond-Howard, *Six Days of the Irish Republic*, Dublin, 1916.

64. WO 141/21 and WO 141/27, PRO, London.

65. MacLochlainn, Piaras, *Last Words,* Kilmainham Jail Restoration Society, Dublin, 1971.

CHAPTER 2 (PAGE 60 TO 141)

1. Frank Thornton, memoir for the Irish Bureau of Military History, Dublin.

2. Quoted by O'Broinn, Leon, *Dublin Castle and the 1916 Rising*, Sidgwick & Jackson, London, 1970.

3. MacLochlainn, Piaras, *Last Words*, Kilmainham Jail Restoration Society, Dublin, 1971.

4. Quoted in Coogan, T.P. *Michael Collins*, Hutchinson, London, 1990.

5. Hansard, 27 July 1916.

6. Lloyd George to Carson, 29 May 1916, quoted by Macardle, op. cit.
7. Lord Longford and T.P. O'Neill, *Eamon de Valera*, Hutchinson, London, 1970.
8. As this election was of such historic importance, it is worth retelling an anecdote told to me by Alex MacCabe. On the first count, the Irish parliamentary candidate was declared elected. But MacCabe, then a prominent Sinn Féiner and a Volunteer, jumped up on the platform in full Volunteer uniform and, placing a .45 revolver between one and one and a half inches from the returning officer's head, suggested that the worthy gentleman think again. In the circumstances, the returning officer decided to fall in with his suggestion, another bundle of 'uncounted votes', all of them for McGuinness, was then discovered, and he was declared elected by a margin of 37 votes.
9. Thornton, op. cit.
10. Longford and O'Neill, op. cit.
11. Coogan, op. cit.
12. CAB 24, No. 89, PRO, London.
13. Ibid.
14. The Irish Committee of the British Government met for the first time on 15 April 1918, under the chairmanship of Walter Long. At various times luminaries in the British political firmament, such as Austen Chamberlain, Lord Curzon, Arthur Balfour, Lord Birkenhead, Winston Churchill and Lloyd George, took part in its deliberations.
15. CAB 24, No. 193, PRO, London.
16. Ibid.
17. Callwell, C.E., *Field Marshal Sir Henry Wilson, His Life and Diaries*, 2 vols., Cassell, 1927.
18. Alexis de Tocqueville, Journey in Ireland, op. cit.
19. Coogan, op. cit.
20. Ibid.
21. Quoted in Coogan, op. cit.
22. Macmillan, Margaret *Peacemakers*, John Murray, London, 2002.
23. Creel's mission is described in Francis M. Carroll, *American Opinion and the Irish Question, 1910–23*, Gill & Macmillan, Dublin, 1978.
24. Lavelle, Patricia, in *James O'Mara*, Clonmore and Reynolds, 1961.
25. Quoted in Coogan, op. cit.
26. Carroll, op. cit.
27. Ibid.
28. CAB 24/92. Quoted in Coogan, op. cit.
29. CAB 103. Quoted in Coogan, op. cit.
30. Callwell, op. cit.
31. Coogan, op. cit.
32. Ibid.
33. Carroll, op. cit.
34. Quoted in Coogan, op. cit.

35. Quoted in Coogan, op. cit.
36. Coogan, op. cit.
37. Several authors have written extensively on the various peace initiatives, the truce and the treaty negotiations which followed, culminating in civil war. These include the author's biographies of Collins and de Valera, Dorothy Macardle, Longford and O'Neill's biography of de Valera and Lord Longford's *Peace by Ordeal*.
38. Coogan, op. cit.
39. Ibid.
40. Ibid.
41. Seán Dowling, quoted in Uinseán MacEoin, *Survivors*, Argenta Press, 1987.
42. Coogan, op. cit.
43. CAB 23/18 PRO, London.
44. Apart from the work of the authors cited earlier for obtaining information on the creation of the six-county state, readers are recommended to Michael Farrell, *Arming the Protestants*, Pluto, London, and Brandon, Tralee, simultaneously, 1983.
45. Quoted in Coogan, op. cit.
46. Ibid.
47. The original 'Notes for a Lecture' is in the National Archives, Dublin.
48. O'Broin, Leon, *Michael Collins*, Gill & Macmillan, London, 1980.
49. Etienne Rynne to author, 7 December 2001.
50. Quoted by T. Ryle Dwyer, *Michael Collins*, Mercier Press, 1982.
51. Quoted by Donal O'Sullivan, *The Irish Free State and its Senate*, Faber & Faber, London,1940.
52. The Brugha quotation is taken from the author's *Michael Collins*, as are many of the statements emanating from both official sources and individuals which occur throughout this chapter. Readers wishing to study the period in more detail are recommended to the work of Dr T. Ryle Dwyer, Dorothy Macardle and de Valera's own official biography.
53. Patrick Murray, *Oracles of God*, University of Dublin Press, Dublin, 2000.
54. Quoted by Leon O'Broin, *In Great Haste*, Gill & Macmillan, 1983.
55. The account of the meeting also appears in Maryann Valuisis's biography of Mulcahy, *Portrait of a Revolutionary*, Irish Academic Press, Dublin, 1992.
56. Quoted in Murray, op. cit.
57. A.T.Q. Stewart, *Edward Carson*, Gill & Macmillan, Dublin, 1981.
58. Quoted in Macardle, *The Irish Republic*, Irish Press, Dublin, 4th edition, 1950.
59. CAB 23/23, PRO, London, quoted in Coogan, op. cit.
60. Hardy's activities are described in the author's *Michael Collins*, op. cit.
61. Craig to Cabinet, CAB 5/1, PRONI.
62. Intelligence Report, 3rd Northern Division, 26/10/21, Mulcahy Papers,

UCD, P7/2/26.

63. See Michael Farrell, *Northern Ireland – The Orange State*, Pluto, 1992.

64. Cited in Intelligence Report to Free State Government, 20/2/24, Blythe Papers, UCD, P24/176.

65. Evidence given to the committee may be examined in boxes S10111 and S11195 in the National Records Office, Dublin. MacRory's contribution was made a day after the committee first met, on 12 April 1922.

66. Pg. No. 45, 30-1-22, National Records, Dublin.

67. Collins's policy towards Northern Ireland is extensively discussed in the author's *Michael Collins*, op. cit. See Chapter 11, 'Setting up the Six'.

68. Quoted in Coogan, op cit.

69. Ibid.

70. Collins to Churchill, 24.3.22, CAB 6/75, PRONI.

71. Mulcahy Papers, UCD, P7/1a/47l.

72. The evidence came from a commission appointed by Belfast Catholics investigating a series of murders in Belfast during 1922. The report of the commission and other similar documents form part of a large collection detailing the work of the Northern Advisory Committee. Some of the most relevant of these are contained in boxes S10111 and S11195, National Archives, Dublin.

73. Callwell, op. cit.

74. The names of the dead were Thomas Crozier and his wife; James Heaslip and Robert Heaslip, his son; James Lockhart; James Gray. Serious injuries were sustained by John T. Gray, William Lockhart, Joseph and Edward Little. The atrocities took place in the townlands of Altanaveigh and Lisdrumliska.

75. Hansard, 26 June 1922.

76. CAB 16/42, PRO, London.

77. Wilson's speech to diehards at Caxton Hall, 9 May 1922.

78. CO 906/25, PRO, London.

79. Dawson Bates to Craig, 15.6.22, CO 906/29.

80. The Tallents Report is contained in CO 906/30, PRO, London.

81. Included with text of the report in CO 906/24, PRO, London.

82. Tallents to Sir James Masterson Smith, Under-Secretary at the Colonial Office, 4.7.22, CO 906/30.

83. One of Dawson Bates's bodyguards and general factotums was a man known as 'Buck Alex', who was regarded by Nationalists as one of the leading Loyalist murderers of the period. Buck Alex used to keep a toothless circus lion in the yard of his terraced Belfast 'kitchen house', which had an outside lavatory to which he delighted in directing uninitiated visitors, without informing them what lay in their path. Buck Alex's reputation was such that the neighbours on either side of the yard raised no objection to the stench from the lion's accumulated dung.

84. Wilson's death and its sequel are described in the author's *Michael Collins*, op. cit., pp. 373–7.

85. S1570, National Records, Dublin.
86. Affidavit of Thomas Kelly, quoted in author's *Michael Collins*, op. cit.
87. Coogan, op. cit.
88. Mulcahy Papers, UCD.
89. P94, 19/8/22.
90. Quoted by Patrick Murray, *Oracles of God*, University College Dublin Press, Dublin, 2000.
91. Ibid.
92. O'Donoghue, Florence, quoted in T.P. Coogan, *de Valera*, Hutchinson, London, 1993.
93. Quoted in Coogan, *de Valera*, op. cit.
94. Coogan, *de Valera*, op. cit.
95. The account of the ending of the civil war draws largely on the author's own writings, notably the Eamon de Valera biography, but readers are also recommended to Michael Hopkinson's *Green against Green*, Macmillan, Dublin, 1988; Dorothy Macardle's *The Irish Republic*, Irish Press, Dublin, 1951; and T. Ryle Dwyer, *de Valera's Darkest Hour*, Mercier, 1982.

CHAPTER 3 (PAGE 142 TO 229)

1. Thomas Garvin, *1922: The Birth of Irish Democracy*, Dublin, 1996.
2. Quoted in Patrick Murray, *Oracles of God*, University College Dublin Press, Dublin, 2000.
3. T.K. Whitaker, in *Commemorative Essays, Bank of Ireland, 1973–83*, ed. F.S. Lyons, Gill & Macmillan, Dublin, 1983.
4. The figures are taken from a number of works, *vide* Dorothy Macardle, *The Irish Republic*, Irish Press, Dublin, 4th edition 1950; Dermot Keogh's *20th Century Ireland Nation and State*, Macmillan, Michael Hopkinson's *Green Against Green*, Gill and Macmillan, and T.P. Coogan, *de Valera*, Hutchinson, London, 1993.
5. W.T. Cosgrave to Judge Cohalan, 11 September 1924, D/T S11724, National Archives of Ireland.
6. Keogh, op. cit.
7. The Oranmore anecdote is substantiated by records in the possession of Conneally's daughter, Maureen Conneally, generally known by the anglicised form of the name Connolly, a retired civil servant who was interviewed by the author at her home, on a number of occasions, the last being 31 December 2002.
8. Stephens Papers, MS 4240, Trinity College, Dublin, quoted by Keogh, op. cit.
9. The oversight over the Boundary Commission clause wording is dealt with by Griffith's biographers, Padraig Colum, *Arthur Griffith*, Dublin, 1959; and Brian Maye, *Arthur Griffith*, Griffith College Publications Ltd., 1997.

10. Quoted both by Macardle, op. cit., and by Coogan, op. cit.
11. Mary E. Daly, *The Buffer State, The Historical Roots of the Department of the Environment*, IPA, Dublin, 1997.
12. Quoted in Keogh, op. cit.
13. Minutes of Comhairle na dTeachtai, 7 August 1924, quoted in Coogan, op. cit.
14. Diary of Frank Gallagher, Gallagher Papers, Trinity College Dublin, quoted in Coogan, op. cit.
15. Dail Eireann, Vol. 9, Col. 562.
16. Daly, op. cit.
17. Dail Eireann Local Government Department files (DELG, 6/44 Cork County Council, 11.10.21), quoted in Daly, op. cit.
18. The foregoing is described in DELG 12/16, Inspectors' Reports, 12 and 13 January 1922.
19. Ibid.
20. J.H. Whyte, *Church and State in Modern Ireland, 1923–1970*, Gill & Macmillan, Dublin, 1971.
21. Aine McCarthy, 'Hearts, Bodies and Minds: Gender Ideology and Womens's Committal to Enniscorthy Lunatic Asylum, 1916–25', in *Female Experiences: Essays in Irish Women's History*, eds. Alan Hayes and Diane Urquhart, Dublin, 2000.
22. T.P. Coogan, *Wherever Green is Worn, The Irish Diaspora*, Hutchinson, London, 2000.
23. The text of Bishop O'Doherty's sermon is contained in the Irish Catholic Directory, 1925. According to the *Irish Independent* of 9 April 1924, the Bishop disposed of the argument that dancing was good physical exercise by suggesting that it would be better for dancers to get their exercise by going outside and skipping with a rope.
24. Report of the Registrar General, quoted by Whyte, op. cit.
25. Dail Debates, 11 February 1925.
26. Mary Clancy, 'Aspects of Women's Contribution to the Oireachtas Debate in the Irish Free State, 1922–1937', in *Women Surviving: Studies in Irish Women's History in the 19th and 20th Centuries*, eds. Maria Luddy and Cliona Murphy, Dublin, 1989.
27. Whyte, op. cit., was informed by a successor to the relevant Minister for Education, John Marcus O'Sullivan, that O'Sullivan put his guarantee to the bishops in writing.
28. Edward Cahill SJ, 'Notes on Christian Sociology', *Irish Monthly*, December 1924.
29. Hansard, Col. 303.
30. Dail Eireann, Vol. 36, Cols. 1229–30, and 1620–1, and Vol. 39, Col. 2360.
31. Anthony J. Butler, quoted in T.P. Coogan, *The IRA*, HarperCollins, 2000.
32. Coogan, *de Valera*, op. cit.

33. *Irish Times*, 13 February 1929.
34. Coogan, *de Valera*, op. cit.
35. Hugh Kennedy to de Valera, 1.11.1932., D/T/S8532, NAI.
36. Kennedy to de Valera, D/T S10550, NAI.
37. Coogan, *The IRA*, op. cit.
38. Ibid.
39. When interviewing IRA men of the period for my book on the IRA, many of those I spoke to, particularly those who did not have civil war experience and joined after the war ended, told me that the de Valera statement gave the IRA a patina of legitimacy in their eyes.
40. Conor Foley, *Legion of the Rear Guard*, Pluto, London, 1992.
41. Gallagher Papers, MS 18, 375 (2), NLI.
42. Quoted in Coogan, *de Valera*, op. cit.
43. *Irish Press*, 3 September 1933.
44. Quoted in Foley, op. cit.
45. Ramsay MacDonald papers, 30/69/678/782, PRO, London.
46. Ryan had given evidence in a prosecution for illegal drilling.
47. Quoted in Coogan, *The IRA*, op. cit.
48. *Irish Press*, 13 October 1937.
49. *Irish Times*, 6 March 1932.
50. Dail Eireann, 11 May 1937.
51. Ibid.
52. Quoted in T.Ryle Dwyer, *de Valera, the Man and the Myths*, Poolbeg, 1991.
53. Deirdre MacMahon, *Republicans and Imperialists*, Yale University Press, New Haven and London, 1984.
54. PRO PREM 3/131/2, de Valera to Chamberlain, 4.7.40.

CHAPTER 4 (PAGE 230 TO 297)

1. Quoted in T.P. Coogan, *de Valera*, Hutchinson, London, 1993.
2. Robert Fisk, *In Time of War*, Andre Deutsch, London, 1983.
3. Ibid.
4. As late as 21 August 1941, Roosevelt was still referring to de Valera as 'my old friend' in a letter to the American Ambassador in Dublin, David Gray. Quoted in T.P. Coogan, *Long Fellow, Long Shadow*, Hutchinson, London, 1993.
5. Quoted in Joseph T. Carroll, *Ireland in the War Years, 1939–45*, David & Charles, Newton Abbot, Devon, 1975.
6. Quoted in T.P. Coogan, *The IRA*, HarperCollins, London, 2000.
7. John P. Duggan, *Neutral Ireland and the Third Reich*, Lilliput, Dublin, 1989.
8. Carroll, op. cit.
9. John P. Duggan, *A History of the Irish Army*, Gill & Macmillan, Dublin, 1991.

10. Malkin Memorandum, 19.10.39, FO800/310, PRO.
11. Churchill to Halifax, 23.10.39, FO800/310, PRO.
12. Eden to Malkin, 20.10.39, 900/310, PRO.
13. Government Minutes, 27.9.39, G3/2, 2nd Govt. G2/56–113, NAI.
14. Maffey Minute, 14.9.39, CAB 6/1, PRO.
15. CAB 66/8, PRO.
16. DFA A/3, NAI.
17. Ibid.
18. T.P. Coogan, *de Valera*, Hutchinson, London, 1993, Appendix 2.
19. Memo to Churchill from Desmond Morton, 10.6.40, PREM. 3/131/2, PRO.
20. Cabinet record, 20.6.40, CAB 66/9, PRO.
21. MacDonald Minute, 21.6.40. PREM. 3/131/1, PRO.
22. Chamberlain Memo, 25.6.40, CAB 66/9, PRO.
23. Roosevelt Papers, Roosevelt Library, Hyde Park, New York.
24. Roosevelt to Gray, 6.3.41, Roosevelt Papers, Roosevelt Library, Hyde Park, New York.
25. Assessment by a State Department Official to the author in the wake of 11 September 2001.
26. Morgenthau papers, Book 433, p.92, Roosevelt Papers, Roosevelt Library, Hyde Park, New York, memo to Harry Hopkins from Oscar Cox.
27. Spender to Hankey, 9.11.40, D715/15, Spender Diaries, PRONI.
28. Ibid. 2.12.40.
29. Wood Memorandum, 16.12.40.
30. Memorandum headed 'War, Essential Materials', dated 4.12.35, is available in the National Archives of Ireland (S28208) and is quoted by Fisk in *In Time of War*, op. cit.
31. The story may have a basis in truth as the incident is recorded in Frank Aiken's private papers, Aiken Collection, U.C.D. archives.
32. Carroll, op cit.
33. Brian Farrell, *Seán Lemass*, Gill & Macmillan, Dublin, 1983.
34. 'Neutrality, Censorship and Democracy', 23 January 1940, quoted extensively in Appendix 1, Fisk, op. cit., and available in the National Archives of Ireland (S115868).
35. Cabinet Minutes, 11.12.39, NAI.
36. Fisk, op. cit.
37. Carroll, op. cit.
38. Quoted in Coogan, *de Valera*, op. cit.
39. Quoted in Farrell, op. cit.
40. Hempel to Foreign Ministry, 31 July 1940, Documents on German Foreign Policy, 1918–45.
41. FO371, 29108, quoted by Carroll, op. cit.
42. Described in Coogan, *de Valera*, op. cit.
43. Apart from the version of the entire Aiken mission episode given in

Coogan, *de Valera*, op. cit., Gray has left an extensive account of his meeting with de Valera in *Through the Green Curtain* (University of Wyoming, Laramie), and in a document, Notes for conversation with the Irish Prime Minister, delivered 26 April 1941. His despatches are also available in Foreign Relations of the United States, Diplomatic Papers, 1941.

44. PRO CAB 27/528, Re-Armament work in Northern Ireland, 1938 (Appendix C).
45. Civil Defence Memo, 19.6.39, CAB 4/408/12, PRONI.
46. CAB 4/441/3, 1.6.40, PRONI.
47. Fisk, op. cit.
48. Dawson Bates memo, 15.5.41, CAB 4/473/8, PRONI.
49. Fisk, op. cit.
50. Congregational Union of Ireland to Stormont Government, 8.5.40, CAB 9CD/171, PRONI.
51. Blake Papers, CAB 3/A/49 BTNI, War Diary, February 1942, PRONI.
52. Protest by General Sir Hubert de la Poer Gough and others to Churchill, 23.9.40, CAB 9CD/169/2, PRONI.
53. Wilson Report on Northern Ireland's manpower resources, 17.12.40, COM61/440, PRONI.
54. Censorship Intercepts COM61/861, PRONI.
55. Ibid 27.2.42.
56. Fisk, op. cit.
57. Northern Ireland Cabinet to Herbert Morrison, 21.5.41, CAB 4/475/15, PRONI.
58. Walshe memorandum to de Valera, 22 May 1941. Quoted in Lord Longford and T.P. O'Neill, *Eamon de Valera*, Hutchinson, 1970.
59. Gray to Roosevelt, 28 May 1941. Gray's telegrams of this period, his memoranda, and diary entries are quoted extensively in *Through the Green Curtain*.
60. Quoted in Coogan, *de Valera*, op. cit.
61. *Through the Green Curtain*.
62. Ibid.
63. Wickham memorandum original, 24.5.41, is in the PRO, London, CAB 66/16. Quoted in Coogan, *de Valera*, op. cit., and Fisk, op. cit.
64. Winant to Hull, quoted in T.P. Coogan, *The IRA*, HarperCollins, London, 2000.
65. Longford and O'Neill, op. cit.
66. Roosevelt to Gray, 21.8.41, Roosevelt Papers, Roosevelt Library, Hyde Park, New York.
67. Longford and O'Neill, op. cit.
68. Ibid.
69. Ibid.
70. Sumner Wells draft to Roosevelt, 24.2.42, Roosevelt Papers, Roosevelt Library, Hyde Park, New York.

71. Ibid.
72. Ibid.
73. Roosevelt to Cordell Hull, 15.6.43, Roosevelt Papers, Roosevelt Library, Hyde Park, New York.
74. Quoted in Martin Quigley, *Peace without Hiroshima*, Madison Books, New York, 1991.
75. Gray to Acting Secretary of State, 1.11.43, Roosevelt Papers, Roosevelt Library, Hyde Park, New York.
76. Hempel to Berlin, 12 May 1941.
77. In the Chanak incident of 1922 Lloyd George, Churchill etc unsuccessfully attempted to involve the Dominions in a war against the Turks over Kemal Pasha's threat to reclaim a former Turkish enclave, Chanak, held by a British force, during his war with the Greeks. On the ground, good sense prevailed and, despite being ordered to by London, the British commander refused to attack the Turks. Nor did the Turks attack the British. The affair generated an explosion of publicity which probably helped to cost Lloyd George his premiership. But there is no doubt that a lasting effect of Chanak was to demonstrate that the Dominions' refusal to join in war against Turkey illustrated that Dominion status also meant Dominion independence. By using the Chanak precedent de Valera was reminding the Canadians that it was from Mackenzie King's Canada had come the firmest refusal to become involved against Turkey.
78. Quoted in Coogan, *de Valera*, op. cit.
79. Quoted in Coogan, *de Valera*, op. cit.
80. Quoted by Carroll, op. cit.
81. Cordell Hull to Roosevelt, 24 March 1944.
82. Quoted in Coogan, *de Valera*, op. cit.
83. Coogan, de Valera, op. cit.
84. Ibid.
85. Dermot Keogh, *Twentieth-Century Ireland: Nation and State*, Gill & Macmillan, Dublin, 1994.
86. 'The Ireland that we dreamed of', quoted in *Speeches and Statements by Eamon de Valera, 1917–73*, ed. Maurice Moynihan, Gill & Macmillan, and St Martin's Press, New York, 1980.
87. J. Lee, *Ireland, 1912–1985*, Cambridge University Press, 1989.
88. Gray to State Department, 3 May 1945.
89. Ibid.
90. Quoted in Longford and O'Neill, op. cit.
91. Maffey to Dominions Office, 21.5.45, DO 35/1229/WX 910/3, PRO.
92. Quoted in Coogan, *de Valera*, op. cit.
93. Coogan, *de Valera*, op. cit.
94. Quoted in M. Elsasser, *Germany and Ireland, 1000 Years of Shared History*, Brookside, Dublin,1987.
95. Ibid.

96. Coogan, *de Valera*, op. cit.

97. These orders were only discovered towards the end of the war after a German U-boat had scuttled itself off the Cork coast. They represented one of the first 'scoops' by the distinguished journalist Douglas Gageby, at the time a German-speaking intelligence officer under Colonel Dan Bryan in charge of Irish counter-intelligence, who on inspection of some canisters containing the submarine's documents realised the significance of what they contained. Gageby later became editor of the *Evening Press* and of the *Irish Times*.

98. Duggan, *Neutral Ireland*, op. cit.

99. *Irish Press*, 12 December 1940.

100. 'Fuehrer's Conferences on Naval Affairs', 3 December 1940, *Brassey's Naval Annual*, 1948.

101. Carroll, op. cit.

102. The Creagh affair is discussed at length in Dermot Keogh, *The Jews in Ireland, Refugees in Ireland, Anti-semitism and the Holocaust*, Cork University Press, 1998.

103. I conducted a long interview with him for my book *The Irish, a Personal View*, Phaidon, London, 1975, in which I used him as an example of a quintessential Irish rural TD.

104. For departmental memoranda and the quotations describing de Valera's refugee policy, see Keogh, *The Jews in Ireland*, op. cit.

105. Quoted in John Cooney, *John Charles McQuaid, Ruler of Catholic Ireland*, O'Brien Press, Dublin,1999.

106. Keogh, *The Jews in Ireland*, op. cit.

107. Dail Debates, Vol. 91, Col. 2126.

108. A.J.P. Taylor, *English History,1914–1945*, Oxford University Press, 1965.

Chapter 5 (page 298 to 325)

1. Marianne Elliott, *The Catholics of Ulster*, Penguin, London, 2001.

2. *Northern Whig*, 2 April 1925.

3. G.C. Duggan was writing in the *Irish Times* of 4 May 1967. He was a former top North of Ireland civil servant, comptroller and auditor general.

4. *Londonderry Sentinel*, 20 March 1934.

5. Hansard, Northern Ireland, Vol. 16, Cols. 1091, 1095.

6. The transcripts of the committee's proceedings have been transferred from the State Paper Office (S1011) to the National Records.

7. Memo from District Inspector Spears to the Minister of Home Affairs, Dawson Bates, PRONI T2258, quoted by Michael Farrell, *Northern Ireland – The Orange State*, Pluto, London, 1992.

8. Farrell, op. cit.

9. Denise Kleinrichert, *Republican Internment and the Prison Ship* Argenta,

Irish Academic Press, Dublin, 2001.

10. *Belfast Newsletter*, 13 July 1923.
11. The incident was verified by researchers for the Mansion House anti-partition conference in a pamphlet published in Dublin in 1949 entitled 'One Vote Equals Two' and is quoted in Farrell, op. cit.
12. Farrell, op. cit.
13. Elliott, op. cit.
14. *Northern Whig*, 28 August 1933.
15. Hansard, Northern Ireland, Vol. 8, Col. 2276.
16. Ibid., Vol. 14, Col. 103
17. *Irish News*, 2 November 1932.
18. *Belfast Newsletter*, 21 March 1933.
19. Hansard, Northern Ireland, Vol. 16, Col. 1095.
20. *Belfast Newsletter*, 24 June 1935.
21. Kidd's letter was circulated to British MPs in a memorandum describing the 1935 riots, drawn up by a Catholic committee.
22. The letter, taken from an article by T.J. Campbell, in the *Cappucin Annual*, 1943, is quoted by Farrell, op. cit.
23. Hansard, Northern Ireland, Vol. 16, Col. 1078.
24. J.F. Harbinson, *The Ulster Unionist Party 1882–1973: Its Development and Organisation*, Blackstaff Press, Belfast, 1973.
25. Patrick Buckland, *James Craig: Gill's Irish Lives Series*, Gill & Macmillan, Dublin, 1980.

CHAPTER 6 (PAGE 326 TO 418)

1. Quoted in T.P. Coogan, *The IRA*, HarperCollins, London, 2000.
2. There were in fact six more deaths from 1936 until 1940, beginning with the suicide of Seán Glynn in Arbour Hill Prison, Dublin. One was shot by the police in 1937, three died in an accidental explosion in 1938 and one was accidentally shot in training in 1939.
3. I interviewed Hayes in the course of my researches for my book on the IRA, and he gave me a point-by-point written refutation of his confession. Some of the charges brought against him are obviously groundless. Others could only be substantiated by third parties who had either died, or refused to talk. Hayes, by the late 1960s, was a figure who was obviously borne down by his experiences, and by alcohol. He told me that he only wrote the confession under extreme duress over a long period in which he said he was 'thunder struck and gun struck'.
4. Sir Arthur Hezlet, *The 'B' Specials – A history of the Ulster Special Constabulary*, Tom Stacey, London, 1972.
5. Quoted in Michael Farrell, *Northern Ireland – the Orange State*, Pluto, 1992.
6. Quoted in Coogan, *De Valera*, op. cit.
7. George Kerr, who later became news editor of the *Irish Press*, and

described the incident to the author.

8. Quoted in T. J. O'Connell, *One Hundred Years of Progress: the story of the Irish National Teachers Organisation, 1868–1968.*
9. Department of Foreign Affairs Memo, 6.5.48, FAS 14319, NAI.
10. T.P. Coogan, *de Valera*, Hutchinson, London, 1993.
11. Ibid.
12. Quoted in Coogan, *de Valera*, op. cit.
13. James Meenan, 'Irish Industry and Industrial Policy', *Studies*, Vol. 32, p. 126.
14. S12888B; Smiddy to de Valera, General comments on agricultural policy, 4.12.44.
15. De Valera delivered a vast, sprawling address to the Dail on 6 and 7 July, 1939 during a debate on the Banking Commission and economic policy which covered many aspects of Fianna Fáil and government policy.
16. The development and course of the Clonlast experiment and of the Children's Allowances scheme are chronicled by Eamonn McKee in his PhD thesis 'From Precepts to Praxis: Irish Governments and Economic Policy, 1939 to 1952', submitted to UCD in 1987.
17. GC2/55, 14/3/39, NAI. The scheme was drawn up by the secretary of the Government's Economic Planning Committee, Hugo Flinn.
18. S10 927, SWP/OPW, 4/6//40, NAI.
19. Dail Reports, Vol. 80, Cols. 1349–50, 29.5.40.
20. McKee, who at the time of writing was one of Ireland's senior diplomats, based his opinion on research, and interviews with Turf Development Board personnel, whom he consulted for his PhD thesis.
21. Smiddy to de Valera, 26/5/39, S11 265 B, NAI.
22. Second children became eligible in 1952 and the scheme was extended to cover all children in 1963. The amounts payable grew with the years.
23. J.J. Lee, *Ireland, 1912–1985, Politics and Society*, Cambridge University Press, 1989.
24. Interdepartmental Committee on Family Allowances, 19.10.42, S12 117B, NAI.
25. Unsigned memorandum in S11 265A, Office of the Minister for Finance to the Taoiseach's secretary, 29.9.39, NAI.
26. MacEntee to de Valera, 14.8.39, D/T S11265A, NAI.
27. Cabinet Minutes, 14.11.39, S12 117A, Department of Finance Memo, Par. 10, NAI.
28. Department of Finance memo, 11.3.43, Par. 6. S12 117A, NAI.
29. MacElligott to Moynihan, 14.12.42, S12 117B, NAI.
30. Moynihan to MacElligott, 21.12.42, ibid.
31. Dail Reports, 23.11.43, Vol. 92, Col. 24.
32. Lee, op. cit.
33. Quoted by Lee, op. cit.
34. Memo to Taoiseach, 19.1.48, D/TS.13866B, NAI.
35. D/TS 14153C, NAI.

36. Dail Reports, 9.5.50.
37. Coogan, *De Valera*, op. cit.
38. *Sunday Independent*, 29 January 1984.
39. *Irish Times*, 8 September 1967, and McGilligan Papers, P.35a/C/5c, UCD Archives, Dublin.
40. Dail Reports, 3/5/50, Vol. 120, Col. 1639.
41. Ibid.
42. Dail Reports, 2/5/49, Vol. 120, Col 1460.
43. Ibid, Col. 1647.
44. Dail Reports, 21/3/1950, Vol. 19, Col. 2098.
45. Brennan Papers, MS26 383, handwritten note, 25/4/50, quoted by McKee in PhD thesis, op. cit.
46. Noel Browne, *Against the Tide*, Gill & Macmillan, Dublin, 1986.
47. Boland to MacElligott, 14.1.48, F121/3/48, D/F.
48. Whitaker to Hogan, 26.10.48, F121/3/48, D/F.
49. Ibid.
50. *Irish Independent*, 18 May 1948.
51. S14 106C: 'Discussion in Washington regarding terms of aid to Ireland', D/EA, NAI.
52. 4.5.48, 841d, 00/3, 2448, National Archives, Washington.
53. Memo of conversation, 10.1.50, 6/66/48/6, Federal Records Centre, Maryland.
54. Hickerson to Secretary of State, 18.5.48; 841d, 021/5–1848, National Archives, Washington.
55. Department of Industry and Commerce Memo, 4.3.49, GC5/74, NAI.
56. Hogan to MacElligott, 2.9.49, McGilligan Papers, MSP35 C/9, UCD Archives.
57. Ronan Fanning, *The Irish Department of Finance 1922–58*, Dublin, 1978.
58. Lynch memo to Department of Taoiseach, 15.6.51, and Cabinet Minutes, 21.8.51, S14 818B/1, NAI.
59. Fanning, op. cit.
60. Whitaker to Secretary, Department of Finance, 18/9/51, F200/18/51, Dept of Finance.
61. The original letter from MacBride is among the McQuaid papers in the Archdiocesan records at Archbishop's House, Drumcondra, Dublin.
62. Walshe to Boland, 25.2.48, DFA P140, Secretary's Files, NAI.
63. John Cooney's biography of John Charles McQuaid (The O'Brien Press, Dublin, 1999) gives a graphic account of the Irish contribution to the Christian Democrats.
64. Cooney, op. cit.
65. Browne, op. cit.
66. Lee, op. cit.
67. Ibid.
68. MacEntee wrote to de Valera on 13 October 1944 (S10949A, NAI)

asking him without success to at least attempt reform of the cultural panel. Ryan had equal lack of success the previous year (27 October, SI0949A, NAI) when he urged a reform of the Senate election system which 'would have the merit of preventing corruption'.

69. *Irish Independent*, 12 October 1945.
70. Lee, op cit.
71. Cooney, op. cit.
72. Archbishop McQuaid to de Valera, 23.1.46, Cabinet Files, S13444C, NAI.
73. Browne, op. cit.
74. Ibid.
75. During an interview with me in 1965 for my first book, *Ireland Since the Rising*, Pall Mall, London, 1966.
76. Gospel of St Matthew, Chap. VIII, Verses 27–8.
77. Browne, op. cit.
78. Eamonn McKee, 'Church State relations and the Development of Health Policy, the Mother and Child Scheme, 1944–53,' Irish Historical Studies, Dublin.
79. Ibid.
80. Thanks to the courtesy of Mr David Sheehy, the archivist of the Dublin Archdiocese, I have been given access to the McQuaid papers and other archival material for over a decade. I have refreshed this research for my other books with added delvings for this one into McQuaid's correspondence, more and more of which is being released with the passage of time. For easier access to the life of this extraordinary man readers are recommended to John Cooney's fascinating biography of McQuaid which deals extensively with the Mother and Child Scheme controversy.
81. Dr Patrick Dargan, selected by McQuaid's aide, Monsignor Richard Glennon.
82. Although it was for many years the custom to refer to the Archbishop's headquarters as 'the Palace', the place always seemed to me to be nothing more than a large and rather gloomy house, set in large grounds which accommodated some agricultural land and Clonliffe College, which prepared priests for the archdiocese.
83. Lord Longford and T.P. O'Neill, *Eamon de Valera*, Hutchinson, London, 1970.
84. Cooney, op. cit.
85. Ibid.
86. Browne, op. cit.
87. Father Dan O'Connell SJ to McQuaid, 14.10.53, AB8/B/XVI/20, DDA.
88. Quoted in Dermot Keogh, *Ireland and the Vatican*, Cork University Press, 1995, p. 310, n.66; Walshe to MacBride, D/FA, 6.9.45, p/126/1, NAI.
89. Longford, O'Neill, op. cit..

90. Moynihan Memo, 14.3.52, S15 221A, NAI.
91. Ibid.
92. Dail Reports, 23.4.52.
93. O'Donovan interview with John McCarthy, quoted in *Planning Ireland's Future*, ed. John McCarthy, Glendale Press, Dublin, 1990.
94. Whitaker interview with Bruce Arnold, quoted by McCarthy, op. cit.
95. Whitaker to McCarthy, op. cit.
96. Interview with John McCarthy, op. cit.
97. *Irish Times*, 28 February 1957.
98. Carter Script, Dept of Taoiseach, S16211, NAI.
99. By way of assessing de Valera's continuing influence it is worth recording that Whitaker himself stressed the importance of his role in various interviews with the author.
100. Whitaker to Bruce Arnold, quoted by McCarthy, op. cit.
101. *Economic Development*, Government Publications, Dublin, 1958.
102. The inscription on the title page read: 'This study of national development problems and opportunities was prepared by the Secretary of the Dept of Finance with the cooperation of others in, or connected with, the public service.'
103. Maurice Moynihan to author, 11 June 1991.
104. Dail Report, 12 December 1958.
105. Maurice Moynihan, who was aware of what was happening, witnessed the scene and described it to the author. Quoted in Coogan, *de Valera*, op. cit.
106. A list of Irish diplomatic missions established since 1923 appears in the appendices.
107. During a visit to Washington in March 1951, MacBride spoke to leading American decision-takers, including President Truman, and Dean Acheson, saying that Ireland would like to join NATO but could not because of partition. The American response was the standard one that the matter was between the two countries involved, but that all the NATO countries would be glad to see Ireland join. MacBride's request for arms so that Ireland might be able to defend itself from any Communist invasion was also stalled on the grounds that the needs of America's other allies were greater than those of Ireland. Volume 6, Part 1, FRUS, 1951.
108. Taoiseach's Department, S13570C, NAI.
109. Paul Sharp, *Irish Foreign Policy and the European Community*, Dartmouth Publishing Company, Vermont, 1980.
110. Aiken Papers, P104/6912, UCD Archives, 6.5.68.
111. I interviewed him for my book *Ireland Since the Rising*, Pall Mall, London, 1966.
112. Aiken Papers, P104/5637, UCD Archives.
113. T.P. Coogan, *Wherever Green is Worn*, Hutchinson, London, 2000.
114. Quoted on BBC news, 9 June 2001.

115. At the Meteor Ireland Music Awards, 3 March 2003.
116. *Challenges and Opportunities Abroad*, White Paper on Foreign Policy, Stationery Office, Dublin, 1996.
117. Sir Auckland Geddes to Earl Curzon of Kedleston, 16 June 1920, quoted in T.P. Coogan, *de Valera*, Hutchinson, London, 1993.
118. Coogan, *Wherever Green is Worn*, op. cit.
119. Coogan, *de Valera*, op. cit.
120. Script issued by Government Information Bureau, 1 March 1985.
121. Jack Holland, *The American Connection*, Poolbeg, Dublin, 1989.
122. *Irish Times*, 25 January 1993.
123. Holland, op. cit.
124. For this and other examples of Dublin's policy at the time, see T.P. Coogan, *The Troubles*.
125. Notably, *The IRA*, published by HarperCollins, and *The Troubles*, op. cit.
126. Coogan, *Wherever Green is Worn*, op. cit.

CHAPTER 7 (PAGE 419 TO 458)

1. Ryan funded a number of literary ventures including the magazine *Envoy* (1949–51), which gave a voice to most of the outstanding Irish writers of the day.
2. In recent years, clips from the interview have been shown in various documentaries made about the great writer's life. In my view, these screenings can only be described as Glimpses of the Artist as a Sick Man.
3. Dail Reports, 7 November 1951.
4. Dillon memo, 30.8.47, External Affairs, S11 582B, NAI.
5. Both the results of the author's interviews, and the researches of other writers are quoted in T.P. Coogan, *Wherever Green is Worn*, Hutchinson, 2000, a study of the Irish diaspora.
6. James Meenan, *The Irish Economy Since 1922*, Liverpool, 1970.
7. Commission on Emigration Report, Department of Taoiseach, S14249 A/2, NAI.
8. Caroline Woodstock, *An Officer's Wife in Ireland*, Parkgate Publications, Dublin, 1994. Caroline's husband, who served with the 1st Lancashire Fusiliers, was one of the British officers attacked and wounded, though not killed, in Michael Collins's strike against the British secret service network on "Bloody Sunday", in November 1920. At the time Caroline was mistaken for an emigrant, in the summer of 1920, the IRA were attempting to dissuade Irish people from emigrating and had agents placed in ports and railway stations charged with preventing emigrations.
9. Government minute, 22.8.51, D/T S11582A-F, NAI.
10. Boland to Secretary, Department of Foreign Affairs, 11 November 1952, NAI.

11. Childers to Tommy Mullins, 10.2.48, P67/299 MacEntee Papers, UCD.
12. Quoted in Seamus O'Buachalla, *Education Policy in 20th Century Ireland*, Wolfhound Press, Dublin, 1988.
13. Statistics supplied by the Central Statistics Office. It might be noted that to mark its 50th anniversary, the CSO produced a valuable account of change in Ireland during the latter half-century, *That was then, this is now*, published by the Stationery Office, Dublin, in 2000.
14. Lynch to author, quoted in T.P. Coogan, *The Irish, a Personal View*, Phaidon, London, 1975.
15. O'Buachalla, op. cit.
16. Ibid.
17. Letter from Mulcahy to McGilligan,11.4.51, Mulcahy Papers, P7/C/152, UCD Archives.
18. Maurice Manning, *James Dillon, A Biography*, Wolfhound Press, Dublin, 1999.
19. John Horgan, *Seán Lemass, The Enigmatic Patriot*, Gill & Macmillan, 1997.
20. O'Buachalla, op. cit.
21. Horgan, op. cit.
22. Brian O'Farrell, *Seán Lemass*, Gill & Macmillan, 1983, describes having been told by five members of the Cabinet that they understood that Lemass vetted the speech in advance.
23. Horgan, op. cit.
24. O'Farrell, op. cit.
25. *Irish Press*, 16 October 1959.
26. *Irish Press*, 21 October 1959.
27. Quoted in T. Ryle Dwyer, *Short Fellow – A Biography of Charles J. Haughey*, Marino Books, an imprint of Mercier Press, Dublin, 1999-2001.
28. The most famous late-night drinking club in Dublin in the sixties and seventies was Groome's Hotel, owned by the Fianna Fáil stalwart, Joe Groome, which was frequented by politicians, actors and Fianna Fáil deputies and ministers, including Donough O'Malley, Charlie Haughey and Brian Lenihan, the latter of whom vouched for this account of what happened and said he had heard it in Groome's from O'Malley himself, as did O'Malley's confidant, the journalist John Healy.
29. Quoted by Ryle T. Dwyer, op. cit.
30. *Irish Press*, Dail report 28 October 1964.
31. Lemass Policy on Partition, 7.10.60, DFA 3305/14/341, NAI.
32. *Irish Press*, 16 October 1959.
33. Maurice Manning's account of a Just Society debate within Fine Gael is comprehensive and fair to both the conservative and progressive wings of the party. See Manning, op. cit.
34. *Irish Times*, 19 March 1965.
35. Whitaker letter, 22.10.65, D/T, 17.8.72, C/65, NAI.

36. Ambassador's Report, 18.8.65, DFA 96/3 210.
37. *Irish Times*, 9 November 1966.
38. MacEntee Papers, P67/734, UCD Archives.
39. Horgan, op. cit., p. 325.

CHAPTER 8 (PAGE 459 TO 510)

1. Quoted in T.P. Coogan, *The IRA*, HarperCollins, London, 2000.
2. Ibid.
3. Ibid.
4. *Irish News*, 2 March 2003.
5. Andrew Boyd, *Brian Faulkner and the Crisis of Ulster Unionism*, Anvil, Tralee, 1972.
6. CAB 4/1115, 2.2.60, PRONI.
7. *Irish Press* 2 April 1960.
8. Sir Graham Larmor to author, quoted in T.P. Coogan, *Ireland Since the Rising*, Pall Mall, London, 1966.
9. T.P. Coogan, *The Troubles*, Hutchinson, London, 1995.
10. *The Future of Northern Ireland, A Paper for Discussion*, Northern Ireland Office, Her Majesty's Stationery Office, October 1972, N7, Part IV, 'The Way Forward', quoting from 'Disturbances in Northern Ireland', CMD 532 of 1969.
11. Farrell, Michael, *Northern Ireland: the Orange State*, Pluto, 1992.
12. Both Faulkner and Paisley's quotations are taken from Boyd, op. cit.
13. Quoted in Barry White, *John Hume, Statesman of the Troubles*, Blackstaff, Belfast, 1984.
14. The Witness Seminar on British Policy in Northern Ireland involved several decision-takers on a Chatham House rules basis. However, some of the contributions were given to the present author, and reproduced in *The Troubles*, op. cit.
15. Hansard, House of Commons, Vol. 728, Cols. 721–2.
16. Terence O'Neill, *Autobiography of Terence O'Neill*, Rupert Hart Davis, London, 1972.
17. Interview with Michael Farrell, quoted in Coogan, *The Troubles*, op. cit.
18. Quoted by Paul Bew and Gordon Gillespie, *Northern Ireland Chronology, 1968–93*, Gill & Macmillan, Dublin, 1993.
19. The considerations and personalities which affected the British Cabinet's decisions are described, and interviewed, in some detail in the author's *The Troubles*, op. cit.
20. Ibid.
21. Ibid.
22. Father Egan gave his account in an address from the pulpit of the Clonard Monastery church to a packed congregation of the Men's Confraternity. It was recorded and with the permission of the monastery's archivist, Father O'Donnell, reproduced by the author in

full in *The Troubles*, op. cit.

23. Flackes, *Northern Ireland: A Political Directory, 1968–79*, Gill & Macmillan, Dublin, 1980.

24. T. Ryle Dwyer has an excellent description of the arms trial saga in his biography of Haughey, *Short Fellow*, published by Marino Books, 2001, and apart from Captain Kelly's own memoir, published by himself because of legal difficulties put in his way, *Orders for the Captain*, the saga has been described by the present author in *The Troubles*, op. cit., and in Kevin Boland's biography, *Up Dev*, published by the author, Dublin, 1977.

25. Lurid tales circulated in Dublin for months afterwards that Haughey's injuries were sustained in a brawl with any one of a number of allegedly disgruntled husbands, lovers or rivals of one sort or another.

26. Ed Moloney, *A Secret History of the IRA*, Allen Lane, The Penguin Press, London, 2002.

27. Colonel Jackson was giving evidence on 21 January 2003 before the Saville Inquiry into the shooting dead of unarmed civilians by British paratroopers in Derry in January 1972, 'Bloody Sunday'.

28. *Irish Times*, 25, 26 and 27 December 2002.

CHAPTER 9 (PAGE 511 TO 543)

1. Copy in author's possession.

2. McMahon, Bryan, ME, *Developments in the Irish Legal System since 1945, Ireland, 1945–70*, ed. J.J. Lee, Gill and Macmillan, Dublin, ????.

3. Keogh, Dermot, *Twentieth Century Ireland*, Gill & Macmillan, Dublin, 1994.

4. Amongst the voluminous journalistic output on the subject are two authorative books, *Blind Justice*, Poolbeg, Dublin 1984, by Joe Joyce and Peter Murtagh and *Round Up the Usual Suspects, Nicky Kelly and the Cosgrave Coalition* by Derek Dunne and Gene Kerrigan, Magill, Dublin1984.

5. Quoted in Coogan, T.P., *The Troubles*, Hutchinson, London, 1995.

6. Bishop, Patrick and Mallie, Eamon, *The Provisional IRA*, Heinemann, London,1987.

7. Quoted by T.K. Whitaker in *Financial Turning Points, Interests*, Institute of Public Administration, Dublin 1983.

8. Ibid.

9. Ibid.

10. Ibid.

11. Quoted in Keogh, op. cit.

12. Quoted in Coogan, *Disillusioned Decades*, Gill & Macmillan, Dublin, 1987.

13. Ibid.

14. *Irish Press*, 30 July 1969.

15. Quoted in Dwyer, T. Ryle, *Short Fellow, a Biography of Charles J. Haughey*, Marino Books, Dublin, 1999.
16. Arnold, Bruce, *Haughey, His Life and Unlucky Deeds*, HarperCollins, London, 1993.
17. *Irish Times*, 19 March 2003.
18. O'hAnrachain intended to write his memoirs which, had they been published, would have been the equivalent of the *Whitehall Diaries* of the British civil servant, Tom Jones, who served under Lloyd George. However, he died before the project came to fruition. I helped him in the production of early drafts of the manuscript, and it was during the preparation of these that O'hAnraichain told me the provenance of the 'totality of relationships' phrase.

CHAPTER 10 (PAGE 554 TO 577)

1. It is sometimes very difficult to be specific about either IRA or Loyalist casualties. Both sides have a tradition of burying their dead secretly, so as to either minimise losses, or avoid revealing embarrassing information about the deceased.
2. Martin Dillon, *The Enemy Within*, Doubleday, 1994.
3. Moloney, op. cit.
4. Brian Faulkner, *Memoirs of a Statesman*, Weidenfeld and Nicolson, London, 1978.
5. Command Paper 4823, 16.11.71, HMSO, London.
6. Volume 826, Col. 1584.
7. An eye-witness account of what happened at Magilligan by the *Daily Telegraph* journalist Nigel Wade, which was not published at the time, appears in Coogan, *The Troubles*, op. cit.
8. *Irish News*, 21 January 2003.
9. Dillon, op. cit.
10. To the Bloody Sunday Inquiry, Friday 22 November 2002, Guardian Unlimited Special Reports, guardian.co.uk/bloodysunday.
11. Contained in the British Cabinet State Papers for 1972, released on 1 January 2003.
12. Including to the present author.
13. The chairman of the inquiry was The Rt. Hon. Lord Saville of Newdigate. The other members were the Hon. Mr William L. Hoyt, and the Hon. Mr John L. Toohey. Prime Minister Blair told the House of Commons, on 29 January 1998, that the government had decided 'that a Tribunal be established for inquiring into a definite matter of urgent public importance, namely the events on Sunday 30 January 1972 which led to loss of life in connection with the procession in Londonderry on that day, taking account of any new information relevant to events on that day'.
14. Details of these papers were carried at considerable length in the

broadsheets for the first few days of January 2003, particularly the *Irish Times*, the *Irish Independent* and the *Examiner*. Shorter versions appeared in the British press and on various websites, particularly on Guardian Unlimited at www.guardian.co.uk/bloodysunday/article.

15. Report of British Cabinet Papers disclosures, *Irish Times*, 1 and 2 January, 2003.
16. White, op. cit. See also Coogan, *The Troubles*, op. cit.
17. Ibid.
18. Ibid.
19. Shevlin subsequently gave the author a copy of the minutes. An extended account of the meeting based on these appears in Coogan, *The Troubles*, op. cit.
20. The Lynch note details a conversation with Peck on 6 January 1972, and is contained in the State Papers published in the *Irish Times* on 1 and 2 January 2003.
21. Ibid.

CHAPTER 11 (PAGE 578 TO 648)

1. Adams, Gerry, *Cage 11*, Brandon Books Ltd., Dingle,1990.
2. Ibid.
3. Ibid.
4. Ibid.
5. T.P. Coogan, *The IRA*, HarperCollins, London, 2000.
6. Patrick Bishop, and Eamonn Mallie, *The Provisional IRA*, Heinemann, London, 1987.
7. T.P. Coogan, *The Troubles*, Hutchinson, London, 1995.
8. New Ireland Forum report, 21 May 1984.
9. Garret FitzGerald, *Reflections on the Irish State*, Irish Academic Press, Dublin, 2003.
10. Quoted in T.P. Coogan, *Disillusioned Decades*, Gill & Macmillan, Dublin, 1987.
11. His cabinet was Brian Lenihan, Tanaiste and Minister for Foreign Affairs; Ray McSharry, Finance and Public Service; Gerard Collins, Justice; Michael O'Kennedy, Agriculture; Michael Woods, Social Welfare; Albert Reynolds, Industry and Commerce,;Ray Burke, Energy; Brendan Daly, Tourism, Fisheries and Forestry; Padraig Flynn, Environment; Bertie Ahern, Labour; Rory O'Hanlon, Health; Michael J. Noonan, Defence; Mary O'Rourke, Education; John Wilson, Communications; and John Murray, Attorney General.
12. T. Ryle Dwyer, *Short Fellow*, Marino Books, Dublin, 1990.
13 J.J. Lee, *Ireland 1912–1985*, Cambridge University Press, Cambridge 1989.
14. Dwyer, op. cit.
15. Gene Kerrigan and Pat Brennan, *This Great Little Nation, The A to Z of*

Irish Scandals and Controversies, Gill & Macmillan, Dublin, 1999.

16. Ibid.
17. Ibid.
18. Dail debates, 1 September 1994.
19. Ibid., 17 December 1994.
20. *Irish Times*, 5 November 2002.
21. Ibid., 23 October 2002.
22. Dail debates, 11 February 2003.
23. *Irish Times*, 12 February 2003.
24. Dermot Keogh, *Twentieth Century Ireland: Nation and State*, Macmillan, 1994.
25. *Irish Independent*, 4 June 1997.
26. Neil Collins and Mary O'Shea, 'Political Corruption in Ireland', in *Irish Politics Today*, ed. Neil Collins and Terry Cradden, 4th edition, 2001.
27. Ibid.
28. Quoted in Spray, Glenys, *Blood, Sweat and Tears*, Wolfhound Press, Dublin, 1998.
29. Ibid.
30. Quoted in Kerrigan and Brennan, op. cit.

CHAPTER 12 (PAGE 649 TO 696)

1. Both the Bell and Mallon controversies are well described in Ed.Moloney, *A Secret History of the IRA*, Penguin, Allen Lane, London, 2002.
2. Ibid.
3. Described in T.P. Coogan, *The Troubles*, Hutchinson, London, 1995, and in *The IRA*, HarperCollins, London, 2000.
4. The first time that the differing attitudes of the British Army towards Unionists and Nationalists was brought to public attention was in the days of the *Sunday Times* Insight team's early coverage of the Troubles which was later made the subject of a book: *Ulster*, Insight Team, Sunday Times, Penguin, London, 1972. It was still in evidence 30 years later.
5. I interviewed Reynolds on a number of occasions concerning developments in the peace process, particularly for the works mentioned above, and at other times enjoyed informal chats with him on the topic. For the purposes of this work, I saw him again for a substantial conversation on 7 May 2003, during which he went back over the peace process, and the influences which played upon it, in some detail.
6. The Irish Association meeting was held in Dublin on 5 March 1993.
7. Quoted in Coogan, *The Troubles*, op. cit.
8. This correspondence is quoted at some length in Coogan, *The IRA*, op. cit.
9. The discrepancies between Mayhew's account of the talks, and the

documentary evidence produced to the contrary are detailed in *The Troubles*, op. cit.

10. Reynolds interview with author, 7 May 2003.
11. Quoted in Coogan, *The Troubles*, op. cit.
12. Ibid.
13. Tony Geraghty, *The Irish War*, HarperCollins, London, 1999.
14. *Irish News*, 31 March 2000. Quoted in *Irish Times*, 14 March 2000.
15. Interview between author and Bruce Morrisson, quoted in *The IRA*, op. cit.
16. *An Phoblacht/Republican News*, 27 July 1995.
17. *Irish Times*, 17 February 1996.
18. Chris Anderson, a North of Ireland investigative journalist with first-hand experience of RUC/UDA collusion, has described the circumstances of Wright's death in *The Billy Boy*, Mainstream, Glasgow, 2002.
19. The Unionists' position on the cross-border bodies is described in Brendan de Breadun, *The Far Side of Revenge*, The Collins Press, Cork, 2001.
20. A full text of Trimble's speech was carried in the *Irish Times* the day after it was delivered in Oslo, on 10 December 1998, and on the Cain website: www.cai.ulst.ac.uk.
21. Author's interview with Real IRA spokesperson.
22. On *Spotlight* programme, 22 February 2002.
23. *Irish Times*, 14 February 2002.

CHAPTER 13 (PAGE 697 TO 754)

1. Michael Collins, *The Path to Freedom*, Talbot Press, Dublin, 1922.
2. The survey is conducted by the *A.T. Kearney/Foreign Policy* magazine. Quoted in the *Irish Times*, 8 January 2003.
3. Figures supplied by the Central Statistics Office.
4. *Irish Times*, 1 November 2002.
5. Tony Fahey, addressing the Ceifinn Conference, Ennis, on 7 November 2002. Fahey, a senior research officer with the Economic & Social Research Institute in Dublin, kindly supplied the author with the data on which he based his judgements.
6. On Newstalk 106, Dublin, 26 May 2003.
7. Tom Garvin, *Patriots and Republicans: An Irish Evolution in Ireland and the Politics of Change*, eds. William Crotty and David E. Schmitt, Addison Wesley Longman Ltd., Essex, 1998.
8. Collins, op. cit.
9. The major poets cited were Aodhgan O'Rathaille (1670–1726), Eoghan Ruadh O'Suilleabhain (1748–84), and Seán Clarach Mac Domnhaill (1691–1754). They included in their repertoire both satirical and Aisling (a dream or vision) poetry in which Ireland appears to a sleeper in the guise of a beautiful woman, speaking of her hopes for deliverance from

bondage by the return of the Stuarts and, later, by French intervention.

10. J.J. Lee, *Ireland 1912–1985*, Cambridge University Press, Cambridge, 1989.

11. Father Twomey, editor of the *Irish Theological Quarterly*, was dealing with the subject matter of his book *The End of Irish Catholicism?*, Veritas, Dublin, 2003, in the *Irish Times*, 14 April 2003.

12. Tony Fahey, 'Catholicism and Industrial Society in Ireland', in J.H. Goldtherpe and C.T. Whelan (eds.), *The Development of Industrial Society in Ireland*, Oxford University Press, 1992.

13. Father Peadar Ua Laoghaire, quoted by Mary M. Harris, in *Christianity in Ireland, Revisiting the Story*, ed. Brendan Bradshaw and Daire Keogh, The Columba Press, Dublin, 2002.

14. In his translation from the Irish: 'Religious Songs of Connacht', quoted by Richard Kearney in *Faith and Fatherland*, ed. Mark Patrick Hederman and Richard Kearney, Cranebag, Vol. 8, No. 1, Dublin, 1984.

15. Father Cathaoir O'Braonain, quoted by Harris, op. cit.

16. Ibid.

17. L. McKenna, 'The Relations of Catholics to Protestants in Social Work', *The Irish Monthly*, 45 (July 1917).

18. Tony Fahey, 'Money, Spirituality, and the Religious Congregations', in *A Fire in the Forest, Religious Life in Ireland*, ed. Michael J. Breen, Veritas, 2001.

19. Terence Browne, *Ireland – A Social and Cultural History, 1922–1985*, Fontana, London, 1981.

20. Ibid.

21. Ibid.

22. Tom Inglis, *Lessons in Irish Sexuality*, University College Dublin Press, Dublin, 1998.

23. Ibid.

24. Browne, op. cit.

25. Quoted by G. Seaver in *John Allen Fitzgerald Gregg, Archbishop*, Dublin, 1963, and by Kenneth Milne, 'The Church of Ireland since Partition', in Harris, op. cit.

26. Walshe to McQuaid, July 1945, S/Files DEA, NAI.

27. *Irish Weekly Independent*, 5 February 1938.

28. Ibid., 3 January 1948.

29. There are several accounts of the Fethard-on-Sea controversy available. See T.P. Coogan, *de Valera*, Hutchinson, London, 1993; John Cooney, *John Charles McQuaid*, The O'Brien Press, Dublin, 1999; and J.H. Whyte, *Church & State in Modern Ireland 1923–1970*, Gill & Macmillan, Dublin, 1971. There was also a film about the boycott, *A Love Divided*, released in 1999.

30. Quoted by O'Faolain in 'Standards and Taste', *The Bell*, Vol. 2, No. 3, 1941.

31. Browne, op. cit.
32. Ibid.
33. T.W.T. Dillon, 'Slum Clearance: Past and Present', *Studies*, Vol. XXXIV, No. 133, March 1945, quoted by Browne, op. cit.
34. The incident is described in McQuaid's papers and recounted in Cooney, op. cit. The phrase 'Sagairt aroon' is misspelt, it is the Gaelic term of affection and respect for priests during the penal times.
35. O'Faolain, quoted by Browne, op. cit.
36. Cooney, op. cit.
37. Statement to the Dail by John Gormley, Dail Debates, 3 May 2001.
38. Ibid.
39. Claire Kavanagh, a mother of five, who suffers from continuous backache, told the *Irish Times* (on 11 June 2003) that her operation was performed on 20 August 1972.
40. Jacqueline Morrissey, who researched the subject for a PhD, quoted in the *Irish Times*, 11 June 2003.
41. Cooney, op. cit.
42. The Piggott affair and its consequences are dealt with in Department of Justice, memoranda, D/T S2321B, NAI and in Coogan, op. cit.
43. The Yugoslav affair is dealt with both in McQuaid's own papers and in the Irish State papers released under the 30-year rule on 1 January 1991 and published in the Irish daily newspapers. It is also treated extensively in Cooney, op. cit.
44. Dail Debates, 25 November 1959, and correspondence between Lemass and McQuaid, D/TS16524D, NAI.
45. William Carleton, *Traits and Stories of the Irish Peasantry*, first published in 23 parts,1842, republished in 1844 by Colin Smythe Ltd. with a foreword by Barbara Haley, Gerrards Cross, Buckinghamshire,1990
46. Interview with author, *Ireland Since the Rising*, Pall Mall Press, London, 1966.
47. Ibid.
48. Mary Raftery, and Eoin O'Sullivan, *Suffer the Little Children*, New Island, Dublin, 1999.
49. Ibid.
50. Ibid.
51. SpEd G001/e Daingean Reformatory, Department of Education, NAI, quoted by Raftery and O'Sullivan, op. cit.
52. Ibid.
53. In discussion with the author, 17 July 2003.
54. Quoted in Gene Kerrigan and Pat Brennan, *This Great Little Nation*, Gill & Macmillan, Dublin, 1999.
55. Figures supplied by the UN Women's Fund, UNIFEM, *Irish Times*, 11 June 2003.
56. Speech to American Bar Association, 21 July 2000. Text supplied to

author by Progressive Democratic Party.

57. Kieran Allen, *The Celtic Tiger, the Myth of Social Partnership in Ireland*, Manchester University Press, Manchester, 2000.

58. Lawlor, a former Fianna Fáil TD, actually went to jail for short spells, for obstructing the work of the tribunal.

59. Paul Cullen, *With a Little Help from my Friends, Planning Corruption in Ireland*, Gill & Macmillan, Dublin, 2000.

ACKNOWLEDGEMENTS AND SOURCES

I am indebted to many people who helped me with this work, either with assistance and the provision of material or by facilitating my consultation of archival material. I would particularly like to thank Anthony Cronin, Alan Gray, Tom Garvin, Desmond Geraghty, Eamonn McKee, Michael MacEvilly, Micheal O'Siadhail, Marcus O'Riordan, and Albert Reynolds for direct help with this book, as I would important figures of the Irish twentieth century like Kenneth Whitaker, who, whenever I approached him for information for earlier works, some of which is incorporated in this book, was unfailingly candid and helpful. Michael MacEvilly generously opened his huge collection of Irish books to me, as did John O'Mahony, and both were kind and efficient in their checking and provision of source material, as was my daughter, Jackie and my son, Tom. I must also thank Muiris MacCartaigh of the Department of Politics, UCD and Anna Bryson of the Department of Modern History, TCD, for reading the ms. Opinions and mistakes remain my own.

Amongst the many archivists and library staffs who have helped me, I would like to particularly thank David Sheehy, archivist of the Dublin Arch-Diocesan records, and the staffs at the National Archives of Ireland, the National Library, and at UCD Archives. Although lengthy, the Bibliography which follows literally covers only a fraction of the vast output of books, pamphlets, and memoirs which the turbulent events of twentieth century Ireland elicited. However, if readers wish to be directed to more extensive collections of private papers and other material, I would suggest that they consult the bibliographies of my earlier works, particularly for material dealing with the Irish diaspora. Last, but far from least, I would like to acknowledge the care and attention with which the manuscript was shepherded through the press by a prince among editors, my friend, Tony Whittome, Commissioning Editor, Hutchinson, and the courtesy and kindly efficiency with which Liam Mulcahy, Group Photographic Manager, Independent Newspapers (Ireland) Limited, provided the illustrations used in this book.

BIBLIOGRAPHY

Adams, Gerry, *Falls Memories*, Brandon, Dingle, County Kerry, 1982
———, *Free Ireland; Towards a Lasting Peace*, Brandon, Dingle, County Kerry, 1986
———, *Cage Eleven*, Brandon, Dingle, County Kerry, 1990
———, *The Street, and other stories*, Brandon, Dingle, County Kerry, 1992
———, *An Irish Voice – the Quest for Peace*, Mount Eagle, County Kerry, 1997
Adams, Michael, *Censorship – the Irish Experience*, University of Alabama Press, Alabama, 1968
Akenson, Harman, D., *Conor – A biography of Conor Cruise O'Brien*, McGill-Queens University Press, Montreal, 1995
Akenson, Donald H., *If the Irish Ran the World, Montserrat 1630–1730*, McGill-Queens University Press, Montreal, 1997
Allen, Kieran, *The Celtic Tiger, The Myth of Social Partnership in Ireland*, Manchester University Press, 2000
Andrews, C.S., *Dublin Made Me*, Lilliput Press, Dublin, 2001
———, *Man of No Property*, Lilliput Press, Dublin, 2001
Arthur, Paul, *Government and Politics of Northern Ireland*, Longman, Essex, 1980
Barkey, John M., *Blackmouth and Dissenter*, The White Row Press, Belfast, 1991
Barrit, Denis P. and Carter, Charles F., *The Northern Ireland Problem*, Oxford University Press, London, 1962
Béaslaí, Piaras, *Michael Collins and the Making of a New Ireland*, Phoenix, Dublin, 1926
Beckett, J.C., *The Anglo-Irish Tradition*, Faber & Faber, Belfast, 1976
Bell, Geoffrey, *The Protestants of Ulster*, Pluto Press, London, 1987
Bew, Paul, *The State in Northern Ireland 1921–72*, Manchester University Press, Manchester, 1979
———, *Ideology and the Irish Question*, Clarendon Press, Oxford, 1994
Birrell, Derek, *Policy and Government in Northern Ireland*, Gill & Macmillan, Dublin, 1980
Bishop, Patrick and O'Malley, Eamonn, *The Provisional IRA*, William Heinemann Ltd, London, 1987

Blake, Robert, *The Conservative Party from Peel to Thatcher*, Fontana, London, 1985

Bloch, J., *British Intelligence and Covert Action*, Brandon, Dingle, County Kerry, 1983

Boland, Kevin, *The Rise and Decline of Fianna Fáil*, Mercier Press, Dublin, 1982

———, *Under Contract with the Enemy*, Mercier Press, Dublin, 1988

———, *Up Dev!*, Kevin Boland, Rathcoole

———, *Fine Gael: British or Irish*, Mercier, 1988

Bolton, Roger, *Death on the Rock, and other stories*, W.H. Allen & Co., London, 1990

Boulton, D., *The UVF, 1966–1973, An Anatomy of Loyalist Rebellion*, Torc, Dublin, 1973

Bourke, Marcus, *John O'Leary*, Anvil Books Ltd, Tralee, County Kerry, 1967

Bowyer Bell, J., *The IRA – From 1916*, The Academy Press, Dublin, 1970

———, *The Secret Army*, Sphere Books, London, 1972

———, *The Gun in Politics*, Transaction Publishers, New Brunswick, 1991

———, *The Irish Troubles – A Generation of Violence*, St Martin's Press, New York, 1993

Boyd, Andrew, *Brian Faulkner and the Crisis of Ulster Unionists*, Anvil Books, County Kerry, 1972

———, *The Rise of the Irish Trade Unions*, Anvil Books, 1972

———, *How the Trade Unions Failed the North*, Mercier, Dublin, 1984

Boylan, Henry, *A Dictionary of Irish Biography*, Gill & Macmillan, Dublin, Third Edition, 1998

Bradshaw, Brendan and Keogh, Daire, *Christianity in Ireland*, The Columba Press, Dublin, 2002

Brady, Ciaran, *Interpreting Irish History*, Irish Academic Press, Dubln, 1994

Breadun de, Deaglan, *The Far Side of Revenge*, The Collins Press, Cork, 2001

Breen, Dan, *My Fight for Irish Freedom*, The Talbot Press, Dublin, 1926

Broderick, Joe, *Fall from Grace, the Life of Eamon Casey*, Brandon, Dingle, County Kerry, 1992

Brogan, Hugh de, *Tocqueville*, Collins/Fontana, UK, 1973

Bromage, Mary C., *De Valera and the March of a Nation*, Hutchinson, London, 1956

———, *Churchill and Ireland*, University of Notre Dame Press, Indiana, 1964

Brown, Terence, *Ireland – A Social and Cultural History*, Fontana Press, London, 1981

Browne, Noel, *Against the Tide*, Gill & Macmillan, Dublin, 1986

Bruce, Steve, *The Edge of the Union*, Oxford University Press, London, 1994

———, *The Red Hand*, Oxford University Press, London, 1992

Buckland, Patrick, *Irish Unionism 2 – Ulster Unionism and the Origins of Northern Ireland, 1886 to 1922, The Factory of Grievances*, Gill & Macmillan, Dublin, 1979

———, *Gill's Irish Lives – James Craig*, Gill & Macmillan, Dublin, 1980

————, *A History of Northern Ireland*, Gill & Macmillan, Dublin, 1981

Burnes-Bisogno, L., *Censoring Irish Nationalism, The British-Irish and American Suppression of Republican Images in Film and Television, 1909–1995*, McFarland & Co., North Carolina, 1997

Burton, Frank, *The Politics of Legitimacy*, Routledge & Kegan Paul Ltd, London, 1978

Cafferky, John, *Scandal and Betrayal*, Collins Press, Cork, 2002

Cahill, Thomas, *How the Irish Saved Civilization*, Hodder & Stoughton, London, 1995

Cairns, Ed, *Caught in Crossfire*, Appletree Press, Belfast, 1987

Callaghan, Hugh, *Cruel Fate, One Man's Triumph over Injustice*, Poolbeg, Dublin, 1993

Campbell, Brian, *Nor Meekly Serve My Time, The H-Block Struggle 1976–1981*, Beyond the Pale, Belfast

Campbell, John, *F.E. Smith – First Earl of Birkenhead*, Jonathan Cape Ltd, London, 1983

Canning, P., *British Policy towards Ireland, 1921–1941*, Clarendon, Oxford, 1985

Carey, Tim, *Mountjoy – The Story of a Prison*, The Collins Press, Cork, 2003

Carleton, William, *The Autobiography*, preface by Patrick Kavanagh, MacGibbon & Kee, London, 1968

————, *Traits and Stories of the Irish Peasantry*, ed. Barbara Hayley, Cullen Smythe, Buckinghamshire, 1990

Carroll, Denis, *The Man From God Knows Where, Thomas Russell*, The Columban Press, Dublin, 1995

Carroll, Francis M., *American Opinion and the Irish Question 1910–23*, Gill & Macmillan, Dublin, 1978

Carroll, Joseph T., *Ireland in the War Years, 1939–1945*, David & Charles (Holdings) Ltd, Devon, 1975

Central Statistics Office, *That Was Then, This Is Now, Change in Ireland 1949–99*, Dublin, 2000

Chubb, Basil, *A Source Book of Irish Government*, Institute of Public Administration, Dublin, 1964

————, *Cabinet Government in Ireland*, Institute of Public Administration, Dublin, 1974

————, *The Government and Politics of Ireland*, Oxford University Press, Oxford, 1974

————, *Politics of the Irish Constitution*, Institute of Public Administration, Dublin, 1991

Clark, Alan, *Diaries*, Weidenfeld & Nicolson, London, 1993

Clarke, W., *Guns in Ulster*, Constabulary Gazette, Belfast, 1967

Clayton, P., *Enemies and Passing Friends, Settler Ideologies in Twentieth-Century Ulster*, Pluto, London, 1996

Clinch, Peter, Convery, Frank, Walshe, Brendan, *After the Celtic Tiger*, The O'Brien Press, Dublin, 2002

787

Coakley, John and Gallagher, Michael, *Politics in the Republic of Ireland*, Routledge, London and New York, 1992

Coates, Tom, ed., *The Irish Uprising, 1914–21*, HMSO, London, 2000

Collins, E., *Killing Rage*, Granta, London, 1997

Collins, M., *An Outline of Modern Irish History (1850–1951)*, Education Co., Dublin, 1974

Collins, Michael, *The Path to Freedom*, Talbot Press, Dublin, 1922

Collins, Neil, *Irish Politics Today*, Manchester University Press, Manchester and New York, 1989

Collins, Peter, *Nationalism and Unionism*, Institute of Irish Studies, Queens University, Belfast, 1994

Collins, Stephen, *The Power Game – Ireland under Fianna Fáil*, The O'Brien Press, Dublin, 2001

Comerford, James L., *My Kilkenny IRA Days 1916–22*, Dinan Publishing Co., Kilkenny, 1978

Comerford, M., *The First Dail: January 21st 1919*, Joe Clarke, Dublin, 1969

Condren, Mary, *The Serpent and the Goddess*, New Island Books, Dublin, 2002

Conlon, Gerry, *Proved Innocent*, Penguin, London, 1991

Conlon, L., *Cumann na mBan and the Women of Ireland 1913–1925*, Kilkenny, 1969

Connolly, C., *Michael Collins*, Weidenfeld and Nicolson, London, 1996

Connolly, N., *The Irish Rebellion of 1916 or the Unbroken Tradition*, Boni & Liveright, New York, 1919

Connolly, S.J., *The Oxford Companion to Irish History*, Oxford University Press, Oxford, 1999

Connor, R., *Shake Hands with the Devil*, Panther, London, 1959

Coogan, O., *Politics and War in Meath 1913–1923*, Dublin, 1930

Coogan, T.P., *Ireland Since the Rising*, Pall Mall Press, London, 1966

———, *The Irish – A Personal View*, Phaidon Press, London, 1975

———, *Disillusioned Decades – Ireland 1966–87*, Gill & Macmillan, Dublin, 1987

———, *Michael Collins: A Biography*, Hutchinson, London, 1990

———, *De Valera, Long Fellow, Long Shadow*, Hutchinson, London, 1993

———, *The Troubles, Ireland's Ordeal 1966–1996 and the Search For Peace*, Hutchinson, London, 1995

———, *The Irish Civil War*, Macmillan, London, 1998

———, *The IRA*, HarperCollins, London, 2000

———, *Wherever Green is Worn*, Palgrave, New York, 2001

Cooney, John, etc., *Ireland and Europe – in Times of World Change*, Humbert International School Publication, 2002

Cooney, John, *Race for Europe*, Dublin University Press, Dublin, 1979

———, *The EEC in Crisis*, Dublin University Press, Dublin, 1979

———, *John Charles McQuaid – Ruler of Catholic Ireland*, The O'Brien Press, Dublin 1999

Corfe, T., *The Phoenix Park Murders. Conflict Compromise and Tragedy in Ireland 1879–1882*

Corkery, Daniel, *The Hidden Ireland*, Gill & Son, Dublin, 1924

Cosgrove, Art, *A New History of Ireland 11*, Oxford University Press, Oxford, 1987

Costello, C., *A Most Delightful Station*, Collins Press, Cork, 1996

Costello, F., *Michael Collins, In His Own Words*, Gill & Macmillan, Dublin, 1997

Costello, F.J., *Enduring the Most. The Life and Death of Terence MacSwiney*, Brandon, County Kerry, 1995

Costello, Francis, *The Irish Revolution and its Aftermath, 1916–1923*, Irish Academic Press, Dublin, 2003

Cowell, John, *Where They Lived in Dublin*, The O'Brien Press Ltd, Dublin, 1980

Cox. T., *Damned Englishman. A Study of Erskine Childers (1870–1922)*, Expositon Press, New York, 1975

Coxhead, Elizabeth, *Lady Gregory*, Macmillan & Co., London, 1961

———, *Daughters of Erin*, New English Library, London, 1965

Coyle, A., *Evidence on Conditions in Ireland Presented to the American Commission of Inquiry*, Washington, 1921

———, Final Report, Carty, Washington, 1921.

Crawford, Robert, *Loyal to King Billy*, Gill & Macmillan, Dublin, 1987

Creel, G., *Ireland's Fight for Freedom*, Harper, New York, 1919

Cronin, M., etc., *Ireland: The Politics of Independence, 1922–1949*, Macmillan, London, 2000.

Cronin, Seán, *Resistance, the Story of the Struggle in British Occupied Ireland*, Irish Freedom Press, Dublin, 1957

———, *The Revolutionaries: The Story of Twelve Great Irishmen*, Republican Publications, Dublin, 1971

———, *The McGarrity Papers: Revelations of the Irish Revolutionary Movement in Ireland and America*, Anvil, County Kerry, 1972

———, *Freedom The Wolfe Tone Way*, Anvil, County Kerry, 1973

———, *Irish Nationalism*, The Academy Press, Dublin, 1980

———, *Washington's Irish Policy 1916–1986*, Anvil Books, Dublin, 1987

Cross, I.B., *Frank Roney, Irish Rebel and Californian Labour Leader*, University of California Press, California, 1931

Crotty, Raymond, *Ireland in Crisis*, Brandon, County Kerry, 1986

Crotty, William and Schmitt, David E., *Ireland and the Politics of Change,* Longman, Essex, 1998

Crozier, F.P., *Ireland for Ever*, Jonathan Cape, London, 1932

Cruickhank, Charles, *The Fourth Arm*, Oxford University Press, Oxford, 1981

Cu Uladh, *Blian na hAiseiri*, Coisceim, Dublin, 1992

Cullen, L.M., *An Economic History of Ireland since 1660*, Batsford Ltd, London, 1972

———, *Life in Ireland*, B.T. Batsford, London, 1968

Cullen, M., *Female Activists, Irish Women and Change, 1900–1960*, Woodfield Press, Dublin, 2001

Cullen, Paul, *With a Little Help From My Friends*, Gill & Macmillan, Dublin, 2002

Cunningham, Peter, *Who Trespass Against Us*, Random House, London, 1992

Curran, J.M., *The Birth of the Irish Free State 1921–1923*, University of Alabama Press, Alabama, 1980

Curran, James, *The British Press – A Manifesto*, Macmillan Press, London, 1978

Curry, C.E., *Sir Roger Casement's Diaries*, Munich, 1922

Curtis, L., *Ireland – The Propaganda War*, Pluto Press, London and Sydney, 1984

———, *Nothing But the Same Old Story, The Roots of Anti-Irish Racism*, Information on Ireland, London, 1988

———, *The Cause of Ireland. From the United Irishmen to Partition*, Beyond the Pale, Belfast, 1994

Czira, S.G., *The Years Flew By: The Recollections of Mme Sydney Czira*, Gifford & Craven, Dublin, 1974

Darby, J., *Northern Ireland. The Background to the Conflict*, Appletree Press, Belfast, 1983

———, *Political Violence, Ireland in a Comparative Perspective*, Appletree, Belfast, 1990

D'Arcy, Fergus, *Workers in Union*, The Stationery Office, Dublin, 1988

Daiken, L.H., *Goodbye Twilight – Songs of the Struggle in Ireland*, Lawrence & Wishart, London, 1936

Dalta, *An Irish Commonwealth*, Talbot Press, Dublin, 1920

Dalton, C., *With the Dublin Brigade 1917–1921*, Peter Davies, London, 1929

Daly, Leo, *Aran Island*, Hayden House Publications, Mullingar, 1986

Daly, Mary E., *The Buffer State*, Institute of Public Administration, Dublin, 1997

Dangerfield, G., *The Damnable Question, 120 years of Anglo-Irish Conflict*, Little Brown & Co., Boston, 1976

Davis, R., *Arthur Griffith and Non-Violent Sinn Féin*, Anvil, County Kerry, 1974

Davitt, M., *The Fall of Feudalism in Ireland*, Harpur, London, 1904

Dawson, R., *Red Terror and Green*, New English Library, London, 1972

De Baroid, C., *Ballymurphy and the Irish War*, Pluto, London, 1990

De Blacam, A., *What Sinn Féin Stands For*, Mellifont, Dublin, 1921

De Blaghd, E., *Slan le hUltaigh, Vol. 2*, Sairseal & Dill, Dublin, 1970

———, *Gaeil A Muscailt, Vol. 3*, Sairseal & Dill, Dublin, 1973

De Burca, P., *Free State or Republic*, Talbot Press, Dublin, 1922

De Burca, S., *The Soldiers Song. The Story of Peadar O'Cearnaigh*, P.J. Burke, Dublin, 1955

De Paor, Liam, *Divided Ulster*, Pelican, Middlesex, 1970

————, *Portrait of Ireland*, Rainbow, Bray, County Wicklow, 1985

————, *On the Easter Proclamation and other Declarations*, Four Courts Press, Dublin, 1997

Deasy, L., *Brother against Brother*, Mercier, Cork, 1982

————, *Towards Ireland Free: The West Cork Brigade in the War of Independence, 1917–1921*, Mercier, Cork, 1973

Devlin, Denis, *Collected Poems*, Dolmen Press, Dublin, 1963

Devlin, Bernadette, *The Price of My Soul*, Knopf, New York, 1969

Devlin, Paddy, *The Fall of the North of Ireland Executive*, Private, Belfast, 1975

————, *Yes We Have No Bananas*, Blackstaff Press, Belfast, 1981

————, *Straight Left – An Autobiography*, Blackstaff Press, Belfast, 1993

Devoy, J., *Recollections of an Irish Rebel, A Personal Narrative*, New York, 1929

Dickson, David, *New Foundations Ireland 1660–1800*, Helicon Ltd, Dublin, 1987

Dillon, Eilis, *The Head of the Family*, Faber & Faber, London, 1960

Dillon, Martin, *The Dirty War*, Hutchinson, London, 1990

————, *Stone Cold*, Hutchinson, London, 1992

————, *The Enemy Within*, Doubleday Ltd, London, 1994

Doerries, R., *Prelude to the Easter Rising*, Frank Cass, London, 2000

Doheny, M., *The Felons' Track or History of the Attempted Outbreak in Ireland*, M.H. Gill & Son

Doherty, G., *Michael Collins and the Making of the Irish State*, Mercier, Cork, 1998

Doherty, P., *An Autobiography of a Leitrim Freedom Fighter*, London, 1977

Donnelly, James, *The Land and the People of Nineteenth-Century Cork*, Routledge & Kegan Paul, London and New York, 1975

Dorril, Stephen, etc., *Smear! Wilson and the Secret State*, Grafton, London, 1992

Douthwaite, Richard, *The Growth Illusion*, Lilliput Press, Dublin, 1992

Drower, George, *John Hume Peacemaker*, foreword by Albert Reynolds, Gollancz, London, 1995

Drummond, M., *The Riddle*, Nautical, London, 1985

Duff, C., *Six Days to Shake an Empire*, J.M. Dent, London, 1966

Duggan, J.P., *Neutral Ireland and the Third Reich*, Lilliput Press, Dublin, 1975

————, *A History of the Irish Army*, Gill & Macmillan, Dublin, 1991

Duignan, S., *One Spin on the Merry-go-Round*, Blackwater, Dublin, 1995

Dunleavey, G.W., *Douglas Hyde*, Bucknell, Louisburg, 1974

Dunleavy, J.E., *Douglas Hyde, A Maker of Modern Ireland*, University of California Press, California, 1991

Dunne, Derek, *Round up the Usual Suspects*, Magill, Dublin, 1984

Dunne, Joseph, *No Tigers in Africa*, Columban Press, Dublin, 1986

Dunne, Seamus, *Ireland's Field Day*, Hutchinson, London, 1985

Dunne, Tom, *Theobald Wolfe Tone*, Colonial Outsider, Cork, 1992

Dwane, D., *Early Life of Eamon de Valera*, Talbot Press, Dublin, 1922

Dwyer, T. Ryle, *Michael Collins and the Treaty, His Differences with de Valera*, Mercier, Cork, 1981

———, *De Valera's Darkest Hour*, Mercier, Cork, 1982

———, *Strained Relations*, Gill & Macmillan, Dublin, 1988

———, *Michael Collins 'The Man who won the War'*, Mercier, Dublin, 1990

———, *De Valera – The Man and the Myths*, Poolbeg Press, Dublin, 1991

———, *Short Fellow – A Biography of C.J. Haughey*, Marino Books, Dublin, 1999

———, *Tans, Terror and Troubles. Kerry's Real Fighting Story 1913–1923*, Mercier, Cork, 2001

Earl of Longford and O'Neill, Thomas P., *Eamon de Valera*, Hutchinson, London, 1970

Edmonds, S., *The Gun, the Law and the Irish People*, Anvil, Tralee, County Kerry, 1971

———, *Eamon De Valera*, GPC Books, Cardiff, 1987

———, Edwards, R.D., *Patrick Pearse. The Triumph of Failure*, Victor Gollancz, London, 1977

Elliott, Marianne, *Partners in Revolution, The United Irishman and France*, Yale University Press, 1982

———, *The Catholics of Ulster, A History*, Allan Lane, London, 2000

———, *Wolfe Tone, Prophet of Irish Independence*, Yale, London, 1989

Ellis, Peter Berresford, *James Connolly, Selected Writings*, Monthly Review Press, New York, 1973

———, *Celt and Greek, Celts in the Hellenic World*, Constable, London, 1997

Elsasser, Martin, *Germany and Ireland – 1000 Years of Shared History*, Brookside, Dublin, 1997

Ely, R.F., *Soldier of Ireland*, Dorrance Publishing Co., Pittsburg, 1998

English, Richard, *Ernie O'Malley, IRA Intellectual*, Clarendon, Oxford, 1998

———, *Armed Struggle – A History of the IRA*, Macmillan, London, 2003

Fairfield, Leticia, *The Trial of Peter Barnes and Others*, William Hodge, London, 1953

Fallon, C., *Soul of Fire: A Biography of Mary MacSwiney*, Mercier, Cork, 1986

Fannin, A., *Letters for Dublin, Easter 1916, Diary of the Rising*, Irish Academic Press, Dublin, 1995

Fanning, R., *The Irish Department of Finance, 1922–1958*, Irish Academic Press, Dublin, 1978

———, *Independent Ireland*, Helicon, Dublin, 1983

———, *Documents on Irish Foreign Policy, Vol. 1*, Royal Irish Academy, Dublin, 1998

———, *Documents on Irish Foreign Policy, Vol. 2*, Royal Irish Academy, Dublin, 2000

Farragher, S.P., *Dev and his Alma Mater*, Paraclete Press, Dublin, 1984

Farrell, B., *The Founding of Dail Eireann*, Gill & Macmillan, Dublin, 1971

————, *Chairman or Chief? The Role of Taoiseach in Irish Government*, Gill & Macmillan, Dublin, 1971

————, *The Irish Parliamentary Tradition*, Gill & Macmillan, Dublin, 1973

————, *The Irish Parliamentary Division*, Gill & Macmillan, Dublin, 1973

————, *Seán Lemass*, Gill & Macmillan, Dublin, 1983

————, *The Creation of the Dail*, Blackwater Press, Dublin, 1994

Farrell, Michael, *Northern Ireland – The Orange State*, Pluto Press, London, 1976

————, *Arming the Protestants*, Brandon, County Kerry, 1983

Farry, M., *Sligo 1914–1921. A Chronicle of Conflict*, Killoran Press, Trim, 1992

————, *The Aftermath of Revolution, Sligo 1921–1923*, University College Dublin Press, Dublin, 2000

Feehan, John M., *The Shooting of Michael Collins*, Royal Carbery Books, Cork, 1987

Feeney, P.J., *Glory O, Glory O, Ye Bold Fenian Men*, Cork, 1996

Fennell, Desmond, *Beyond Nationalism*, Ward River Press, Dublin 1985

————, *A Connacht Journey*, Gill & Macmillan, Dublin, 1987

Ferguson, J., *The Curragh Incident*, Faber, London, 1964

Fetherstone Haugh, Neil and McCullagh, Tony, *They Never Came Home – The Stardust Story*, Merlin, Dublin, 2001

Fields, R., *Society Under Siege, A Psychology of Northern Ireland*, Temple University Press, Philadelphia, 1976

Figgis, D., *A Chronicle of Jails*, Talbot Press, Dublin, 1919

————, *A Second Chronicle of Jails*, Talbot Press, Dublin, 1919

————, *Recollections of the Irish War*, Bouverie House, London, 1927

'Fighting Story', *Dublin's Fighting Story 1916–1921*, Kerryman, Tralee, 1949

————, *Kerry's Fighting Story, 1916–1921*, Kerryman, Tralee, 1949

————, *Limerick's Fighting Story 1916–1921*, Kerryman, Tralee

————, *Rebel Cork's Fighting Story*, Anvil, Tralee, 1935

Finlay, Fergus, *Mary Robinson, A President with a Purpose*, O'Brien Press, Dublin, 1990

Finnegan, R.B., *Ireland, Historical Echoes*, Contemporary Politics, Westview, Colorado, 2000

Fischer, J., *The Correspondence of Myles Dillon 1922–1925*, Four Courts, Dublin, 1998

Fisk, Robert, *The Point of No Return, the Strike Which Broke the British in Ulster*, André Deutsch, London, 1975

————, *In Time of War*, André Deutsch Ltd, London, 1983

FitzGerald, Garret, *All in a Life*, Gill & Macmillan, Dublin, 1989

————, *Reflections on an Irish State*, Irish Academic Press, Dublin, 2003

Fitzgerald, R., *Cry Blood, Cry Eireann*, Barrie & Rockcliff, London, 1966

Fitzgibbon, C., *Out of the Lions Paw: Ireland Wins Her Freedom*, Macdonald, London, 1969

————, *The Life and Times of Eamon de Valera*, Macmillan, New York, 1973

Fitzpatrick, D., *Politics and Irish Life, 1913–1921*, Gill & Macmillan, Dublin, 1977

———, *Revolution: Ireland 1917–1923*, Trinity History Workshop, Dublin, 1990

———, *The Two Irelands 1912–1939*, Oxford University Press, Oxford, 1998

Fitzpatrick, David (ed) *Revolution? Ireland 1917–1923*, Trinity History Workshop, Dublin, 1990

Flood, M., *Soldier of the Rearguard: The Story of Matt Flood*, Eigse, Fermoy, 1977

Foley, Conor, *Legion of the Rearguard, the IRA, and the Modern Irish State*, Pluto, Dublin, 1992

Follis, B., *A State Under Seige*, Clarendon, Oxford, 1995

———, *For God and Ulster, An Alternative Guide to the Loyal Orders*, Pat Finucane Centre, 1997

Foot, Paul, *Who Framed Colin Wallace?*, Macmillan, London, 1989

Forester, Margery, *Michael Collins: The Lost Leader*, Sidgwick & Jackson, London, 1971

Foster, R., *Modern Ireland 1600–1972*, Allen Lane, London, 1988

Fox, R.M., *Rebel Irishwomen*, Talbot Press, Dublin, 1935

———, *Green Banners, the Story of the Irish Struggle*, Secker & Warburg, London, 1938

———, *The History of the Irish Citizen Army*, James Duffy, Dublin, 1943

———, *James Connolly – the Forerunner*, Kerryman, Tralee, 1946

———, *Jim Larkin, Irish Labor Leader*, International Publishers, New York, 1957

Foy, M., *The Easter Rising*, Sutton Publishing, Gloustershire, 1999

Freedman, Victoria, *The Cities of David, the Life of David Norris*, Basement Press, Dublin, 1995

Freine de, Seán, *The Great Silence*, Mercier Press, Dublin, 1965

Freyer, G., *Peader O'Donnell*, Bucknell University Press, New Jersey, 1973

Gageby, Douglas, *The Last Secretary General, Seán Lester and the League of Nations*, Townhouse Press, Dublin, 1999

Gallagher, F., *The Four Glorious Years*, Irish Press, Dublin, 1953

———, *The Indivisible Island*, Victor Gollancz, London, 1957

———, *The Anglo-Irish Treaty*, Hutchinson, London, 1965

Gallagher, Thomas, *Paddy's Lament*, Poolbeg, Dublin, 1982

Gallivan, G.P., *Dev* (play), Co-op Books, Dublin, 1978

Galvin, M., *Kilmurry Volunteers 1915–1921*, Cork, 1996

Garnett, Mark, *Splendid! Splendid! The Authorized Biography of William Whitelaw*, Jonathan Cape, London, 2002

Garvaghy Residents, *Garvaghy, A Community Under Siege*, Beyond the Pale Press, Belfast, 1999

Garvin, Tom, *1922, The Birth of Irish Democracy*, Gill & Macmillan, Dublin, 1996

————, *Nationalist Revolutionaries in Ireland 1858–1928*, Clarendon, Oxford, 1987

————, *The Evolution of Irish Nationalist Politics*, Gill & Macmillan, Dublin, 1981

Gates, P.S., *The Black Diaries*, The Olympia Press, Paris, 1959

Gaughan, J.A., *Listowel and its Vicinity*, Dublin, 1974

————, *Memoirs of Constable Jeremiah Mee, R.I.C.*, Anvil, Dublin, 1975

————, *Austin Stack, Portrait of a Separatist*, Kingdom Books, Dublin, 1977

————, *Thomas Johnson 1872–1963*, Kingdom Books, Dublin, 1980

————, *Alfred O'Rahilly, Vol. I, Academic*, Kingdom Books, Dublin, 1980

————, *A Political Odyssey*, Kingdom Books, Dublin, 1983

————, *Alfred O'Rahilly, Vol. II, Public Figure*, Kingdom Books, Dublin, 1989

————, *Alfred O'Rahilly, Vol. III, Controversialist*, Kingdom Books, Dublin, 1992

————, *Memoirs of Senator Joseph Connolly: A Founder of Modern Ireland*, Irish Academic Press, Dublin, 1996

————, *Memoirs of Senator James G. Douglas 1887–1954*. University College Dublin Press, Dublin, 1998

Gavin, J. and O'Sullivan, Harold, *Dundalk – A Military History*, Dundalgen Press, Dundalk, 1987

Geraghty, Tony, *The Irish War*, HarperCollins, London, 1998

Gilbert, Martin, Gill & Macmillan, Dublin, 1973

————, *World in Torment, Winston S. Churchill, 1916–22*, Minerva, London, 1990

Gillespie, Paul, *Blair's Britain, England's Europe, A View from Ireland*, Institute of European Affairs, Dublin, 2000

Girwin, Brian, *From Union to Union*, Gill & Macmillan, Dublin, 2002

Gleeson, J., *Bloody Sunday*, Peter Davies, London, 1962

Glynn, A., *High Upon the Gallows Tree*, Anvil, Tralee, 1967

Golden, P., *The Voice of Ireland*, New York, 1921

Goldring, M., *Faith of our Fathers*, Repsol, Dublin, 1987

Good, J., *Enchanted by Dreams, The Journal of a Revolutionary*, Brandon, Dingle, County Kerry, 1996

Government Publications (British), *The Royal Commission on the Rebellion in Ireland*. HMSO, London, 1916

Government Publications (Ireland), *Minutes of the First Dail 1919–1921*, Dublin

————, *The Second Dail – Private Sessions, 1921–1922*, T.P. O'Neill

————, *Debate on the Treaty between Great Britain and Ireland*, Official Report, Dublin

————, *Official Correspondence relating to the Peace Negotiations June–September 1921*, Dail Eireann, Dublin, 1921

————, *Dail Eireann, Standing Orders (with) Constitution of the Irish Free State*, Dublin, 1923

————, *Cuimhneachain, 1916–1966, a Record of Ireland's Commemoration of the 1916 Rising*, Dept. of External Affairs, Dublin, 1966

Granville, G., *Dublin 1913 – A Divided City*, O'Brien, Dublin, 1972

Gray, Alan W., *The Economic Consequences of Peace in Ireland*, Indecon International Economic Consultants, Dublin, 1995

————, *International Perspectives on the Irish Economy*, Indecon Economic Consultants, Dublin, 1997

Greaves, C.D., *The Life and Times of James Connolly*, Lawrence & Wishart, London, 1961

————, *Liam Mellows and the Irish Revolution*, Lawrence & Wishart, London, 1971

————, *The Easter Rising in Song and Ballad*, Workers Music Association, London, 1980

————, *The Irish Transport and General Workers Union. The Formative Years, 1909–1923*. Gill & Macmillan, Dublin, 1982

————, *Theobald Wolfe Tone and the Irish Nation*. Fulcrum, Dublin, 1991

Griffith, K., and O'Grady, Tim, *Curious Journey, An Oral History of Ireland's Unfinished Revolution*, Hutchinson, London, 1982

Gwynn, D., *De Valera*, Jarrolds, Plymouth, 1933

————, *The History of Partition 1912–1925*, Brian & Nolan, Dublin, 1950

Hachey, T.E., *Perspectives on Irish Nationalism*, University of Kentucky, Lexington, 1989

Haddick-Flynn, K., *Orangeism, The Making of a Tradition*, Wolfhound Press, Dublin, 1999

Haicead, P., *In Bloody Protest: North Tipperary's IRA Roll of Honour 1916–1926*, Tipperary, 1996

Hall, Mr and Mrs S.C., *Hall's Ireland, Mr and Mrs' Tour of 1840*, Sphere Books, London, 1984

Haltzel, Michael H. and Keogh, Dermot, (ed.) *Northern Ireland and the Politics of Reconciliation*, Cambridge University Press, 1993

Hamill, Desmond, *Pig in the Middle, the Army in Northern Ireland, 1969–84*, Methuen, London, 1985

Hamilton Norway, M., *The Sinn Féin Rebellion as They Saw it*, Irish Academic Press, Dublin, 1999

Hamrock, Ivor, *The Famine in Mayo 1845–1850*, Mayo County Council, 1998

Hand, G., *Report of the Irish Boundary Commission 1925*, Irish University Press, Shannon, 1969

Hanley, Brian, *The IRA 1926–1936*, Four Courts Press, Dublin, 2002

Harkness, David, *The Restless Dominion*, New York University Press, 1970

————, *Northern Ireland since 1920*, Helicon, Dublin, 1983

Harnden, Toby, *Bandit Country, The IRA and South Armagh*, Hodder & Stoughton, London, 1999

Harrington, Niall C., *Kerry Landing, August 1922*, Anvil Books, Dublin, 1992

Harris, A., *The Easter Rising*, Dryad Press, London, 1987

Harris, M., *The Catholic Church and the Foundation of the Northern Irish State*, Cork University Press, Cork, 1993

Hart, P., *The IRA and its Enemies. Violence and Community in Cork 1916–1923*, Clarendon, Oxford, 1998

Hartley, S., *The Irish Question as a Problem in British Foreign Policy 1914–1918*, Macmillan, London, 1987

Hartnett, N., *Prison Escapes*, Pillar Publicity, Dublin, 1945

Harvey, D., *The Barracks, A History of Victoria/Collins Barracks, Cork*, Mercier, Cork, 1997

Hastwell, J., *Citizen Armies*, History Book Club, London, 1973

Haverty, A., *Constance Markiewicz: An Independent Life*, Pandora Press, London, 1988

Hawthorne, J., *Two Centuries of Irish History*, BBC, London, 1966

Hayden, Tom, *Irish on the Inside*, Verso, London and New York, 2003

Hayes, Alan, *The Irish Women's History Reader*, Routledge, London, 2001

Hayes, K.E., *A History of the RAF and US Naval Air Service in Ireland 1913–1923*, Irish Air Letter, Dublin, 1988

Healy, John, *Nineteen Acres*, Kennys Bookshop & Art Galleries Ltd, Galway, 1978

Hegarty, P., *Peadar O'Donnell*, Marino Books, Dublin, 1999

Henry, R.M., *The Evolution of Sinn Féin*, Talbot, Dublin

Herlihy, J., *Peter Golden. The Voice of Ireland*, Local Committee, Cork, 1994

Herlihy, J., *The Royal Irish Constabulary, A Short History and Genealogical Guide*, Four Courts Press, Dublin, 1997

Herlihy, Jim, *The Dublin Metropolitan Police, A Complete Alphabetical List of Officers and Men, 1936–1925*

Heskin, Ken, *Northern Ireland, A Psychological Analysis*, Gill & Macmillan, Dublin, 1980

Hezlet, Sir Arthur, *The 'B' Specials*, Tom Storey Ltd, London, 1972

Hill, Paul, with Bennett, Ronan, *Stolen Years*, Corgi, London, 1991

Hobson, B., *Ireland Yesterday and Tomorrow*, Anvil, Tralee, 1968

Hodges, J.G., *Report of the Trial of William Smith O'Brien for High Treason at Clonmel 1848*, Alexander Thom, Dublin, 1849

Holland, Jack, *The American Connection*, Poolbeg, Dublin, 1989

Holland, Jack and McDonald, Henry, *INLA, Deadly Divisions*, Torc, Dublin, 1994

Holroyd, F., *War Without Honour*, Medium, Hull, 1989

Holt, E., *Protest in Arms: The Irish Troubles 1916–1923*, Putnam, London, 1960

Hopkinson, Michael, *Green Against Green: The Irish Civil War*, Gill & Macmillan, Dublin, 1988

———, *Frank Henderson's Easter Rising*, Cork University Press, Dublin, 1998

———, *The Last Days of Dublin Castle*, Irish Academic Press, Dublin, 1999

———, *The Irish War of Independence*, Gill & Macmillan, Dublin, 2002

Hoppen, K.T., *Ireland Since 1800, Conflict and Conformity*, Longman, London, 1989

Horgan, John, *Seán Lemass, The Enigmatic Patriot*, Gill & Macmillan, Dublin, 1997

Hostettler, J., *Sir Edward Carson, A Dream too Far*, Barry Rose, Chichester, 1997

Howard, L., Red, *Six Days of the Irish Republic*, J.W. Luce, Boston, 1916

Hull, Mark M., *Irish Secrets, German Espionage in Wartime Ireland 1939–1945*, Irish Academic Press, Dublin

Hume, John, *A New Ireland*, with introductions by Senator Edward M. Kennedy, and Tom McEnery, Reinhardt, Colorado

Hussey, C.M., *The Mountain Can Move*, Dunesk Press, Dublin, 1985

Hussey, Gemma, *Ireland Today, Anatomy of a Changing State*, Townhouse, Dublin, 1993

Hyde, H.M., *Carson*, Constable, London, 1953

———, *Famous Trials, Roger Casement*, Penguin, Middlesex, 1964

Hyland, J.L., *James Connolly*, Historical Association of Ireland, Dublin, 1997

Inglis, B., *Roger Casement*, HBJ, New York, 1973

Inglis, Tom, *Lessons in Irish Sexuality*, University College Press, Dublin, 1998

———, *Moral Monopoly: The Rise and Fall of the Catholic Church in Modern Ireland*, University College Dublin Press, Dublin, 1998

Irish Times, *Sinn Féin Rebellion Handbook*, Irish Times, Dublin, 1916

Irish Times, *1916 Rebellion Handbook*, Mourne River Press, Dublin 1998

Irvine, Maurice, *Faith and Faction, Northern Ireland*, Routledge, London, 1991

Irwin, W., *Betrayal in Ireland: A Record of Revolution and Civil War in Ireland 1916–1924*, Dublin

Jackson, T.A. (ed), and with an Epilogue by C. Desmond Greaves, *Ireland Her Own*, Lawrence & Wishart, London, 1971

Joannon, Pierre, *L'Historie Politique et Constitutionnelle de l'Irlande*, University of Nice, Nice, 1972

———, *Ireland, Land of Troubles*, Book Club, London, 1982

———, *Michael Collins*, La Table Ronde, Paris, 1996

Johnston, A., *Connolly, A Marxist Analysis*, Irish Workers Group, Dublin, 1990

Jones, F.P., *History of the Sinn Féin Movement and the Irish Rebellion of 1916*, P.J. Kennedy & Sons, New York, 1917

Jones, T., *Whitehall Diary Vol. III, Ireland 1918–1925*, Oxford University Press, London, 1971

Jordan, A., *Willie Yeats and the Gonne-MacBrides*, Dublin, 1997

Jordan, A.J., *Major John MacBride, 1865–1916*, Westport Historical Society, Westport, 1991

———, *Seán MacBride*, Blackwater Press, Dublin, 1993

———, *Churchill – A Founder of Modern Ireland*, Dublin, 1995

———, *The Yeats, Gonne, MacBride Triangle*, Westport Books, Dublin, 2000

Joy, M., *The Irish Rebellion of 1916 and its Martyrs: Erin's Tragic Easter*, Devin Adair, New York, 1916

Joyce, Joe, *The Boss – Charles J. Haughey in Government*, Poolbeg Press, Dublin, 1983

Kautt, W.H., *The Anglo-Irish War 1916–1921*, Praeger, Connecticut, 1999

Kearns, Kevin C., *Stoneybatter, Dublin's Inner Urban Village*, Glendale, Dublin, 1989

———, *Dublin Tenement Life – An Oral History*, Gill & Macmillan, Dublin, 1994

Kearns, L., *In Times of Peril*, Talbot Press, Dublin, 1922

Keatinge, Patrick, *A Place Among the Nations, Issues of Irish Foreign Policy*, Institute of Public Administration Dublin, 1978

———, *A Singular Stance, Irish Neutrality in the 1980s*, Institute of Public Administration, Dublin, 1984

Kee, R., *The Green Flag, A History of Irish Nationalism*, Weidenfeld & Nicolson, London, 1972

, *The Laurel and the Ivy, the Story of Charles Stewart Parnell*, Hamish Hamilton, London, 1993

Keena, Colm, *A Biography of Gerry Adams*, Mercier, Dublin, 1990

Kehoe, A.M., *History Makers of Twentieth-Century Ireland, Collins, MacBride, etc.*, Mentor, Dublin, 1989

Kellegher, G.D., *Gunpowder to Guided Missiles: Ireland's War Industries*, Cork, 1993

Kelly, B., *Sworn to be Free: The Complete Book of IRA Jailbreaks*, Anvil, Tralee, 1971

Kelly, Freida, *A History of Kilmainham Gaol*, Mercier, Dublin, 1988

Kelly, Henry, *How Stormont Fell*, Gill & Macmillan, Dublin, 1972

Kelly, Capt. James, *Orders for the Captain*, Kelly Kane Ltd, County Cavan, 1971

Kendle, J., *Walter Long, Ireland, and the Union, 1905–1920*, Glendale, Dublin, 1992

Kenny, Ivor, *Government and Enterprise* in Ireland, Gill & Macmillan, Dublin, 1984

Kenny, Mary, *Goodbye to Catholic Ireland*, New Island Books, Dublin, 2000

Kenny, Shane, *Irish Politics Now*, Bandon, Dingle, County Kerry, 1987

———, *Go Dance on Somebody Else's Grave, Kildanore, The Inside Story of the Haughey Coalition*, Dublin, 1990

Keogh, Dermot, *Twentieth-Century Ireland – Nation and State*, Gill & Macmillan, Dublin, 1994

———, *Ireland and the Vatican*, Cork University Press, Cork, 1995

———, *Jews in Twentieth-Century Ireland*, Cork University Press, Cork, 1998

Kerrigan, Gene and Brennan, Pat, *This Great Little Nation*, Gill & Macmillan, Dublin, 1999

Kerryman, *Rebel Cork's Fighting Story 1916–21*, Kerryman Ltd, Tralee, County Kerry, 1947

Key, Robert, *The Green Flag, Vols 1, 2, and 3*, Quartet, London, 1976.

Kiberd, Damien (ed.), *Media in Ireland, Studies in Broadcasting*, Four Courts Press, Dublin, 2002

Kiberd, Declan, *Inventing Ireland*, Jonathan Cape, London, 1995

Kineally, Christine, *This Great Calamity*, Roberts Reinhardt, Colorado, 1995

Kitson, Frank, *Gangs and Countergangs*, Barry & Rockliff, London, 1960

———, *Low Intensity Operations*, Faber, London, 1971

Kleinrichert, Denise, *Argenta 1922*, Irish Academic Press, Dublin, 2001

Knott, George H., *Trial of Sir Roger Casement*, William Hodge & Co., Edinburgh and London

Kotsonouris, Mary, *Retreat from Revolution, The Dail Courts 1920–24*, Irish Academic Press, Dublin, 1994

Laffan, Michael, *The Partition of Ireland 1911–1925*, Dublin Historical Association, Dundalgan Press, 1983

Langan Egan, Maureen, *Women in Mayo 1821–1851*, Maureen Langan Egan, Galway, 1986

Larkin, Emmet, *James Larkin, Irish Labour Leader, 1876–1947*, Routledge & Keegan Paul, London, 1965

———, *Alexis de Tocqueville's Journey in Ireland, July–August 1835*, Wolfhound Press, Dublin, 1990

Lavelle, P., *James O'Mara*, Clonmore & Reynolds, Dublin, 1961

Lee, J.J., *The Modernisation of Irish Society, 1848–1918*, Gill & Macmillan, Dublin, 1973 and 1989

———, *Ireland 1945–70*, Gill & Macmillan, 1979

———, *Ireland Towards a sense of Place, the UCC-RTE Lectures*, Cork University Press, 1985

———, *Ireland 1912–1985, Politics and Society*, Cambridge University Press, Cambridge, 1989

Lee, Joseph and O'Tuathaigh, Gearóid, *The Age of de Valera*, based on the RTE series, Ward River Press, Dublin, 1982

Litton, Helen, *The Irish Famine*, Wolfhound Press, Dublin, 1994

Lloyd George, David, *War Memoirs, Vols 1 and 2*, Odhams Press, London, 1938

Logan, Patrick, *Fair Day, The Story of Irish Fairs and Markets*, Appletree Press, Belfast, 1986

Lucey, Charles, *Ireland and the Irish, Cathleen Ni Houlihan is Alive and Well*, Doubleday, New York, 1970

Lynch, Diarmuid, *The IRB and the 1916 Insurrection*, ed. Florence O'Donoghue, Mercier, Dublin (nd)

Lyons, F.S.L. and Hawkins, R.A.J. (ed.), *Ireland under the Union*, Clarendon Press, Oxford, 1980

Lyons, F.S.L., *Ireland since the Famine*, Clarendon, Oxford, 1979

Lyons, J.B., *Oliver St John Gogarty*, Blackwater, Dublin, 1980

———, *The Enigma of Tom Kettle*, Glendale, 1983

Macardle, Dorothy, *The Irish Republic*, Irish Press, Dublin, 1951

MacBride, Seán, (ed.), *Crime and Punishment*, Ward River Press, Dublin, 1982

MacCaffrey, L. J., *The Irish Question, 1800–1922*, University of Kentucky Press, 1968

MacClean, Dr Raymond, *The Road to Bloody Sunday*, Ward River Press, Dublin, 1983

MacCoole, Sinead, *Hazel, A Life of Lady Lavery*, Lilliput, Dublin, 1996

———, *Guns and Chiffon, Women Revolutionaries in Kilmainham Jail, 1916–1923*, Stationery Office, Dublin, 1997

MacCurtain, Margaret (ed.), *Women in Irish Society, The Historical Dimension*, The Women's Press, Dublin, 1978

MacDonagh, Oliver, *Ireland, the Union and its Aftermath*, Allen & Unwin, London, 1979

MacDonald, Darach, *The Chosen Few – Exploding Myths in South Armagh*, Mercier Press, Dublin, 2001

MacDonnell, Kathleen, *There is a Bridge at Bandon*, Mercier, Cork, 1972

MacEntee, Seán, *Episode at Easter*, Gill & Macmillan, Dublin, 1966

MacEoin, Uinseánn, *Survivors*, Argenta Publications, Dublin, 1980

———, *Harry, the Story of Harry White*, Argenta Publications, Dublin, 1985

———, *The IRA in the Twilight Years, 1923–1948*, (nd)

MacGuffin, J., *Internment*, Anvil, Tralee, County Kerry, 1973

MacGuinness, C.J., *Nomad*, Methuen, London, 1934

MacGuire, M., *To Take Arms, A Year in the Provisional IRA*, Macmillan, London, 1973

MacInerney, Michael, *Peadar O'Donnell*, O'Brien Press, Dublin, 1974

MacIntyre, T., *Through the Bridewell Gate, the Diary of the Dublin Arms Trial*, Faber & Faber, London, 1971

MacLochlainn, P.F., *Last Words, Letters and Statements of the Leaders Executed After the Rising at Easter 1916*, Kilmainham Jail Society, Dublin, 1971

MacMahon, D., *Republicans and Imperialists, Anglo-Irish Relations in the 1930s*, Yale University Press, 1984

MacManus, Francis (ed.), *The Years of the Great Test 1926–39*, Mercier, 1967

Macready, N., *Annals of an Active Life, Vol. 2*, Hutchinson, London, 1924

MacSweeney, Terence, *Principles of Freedom*, Talbot, Dublin, 1921

MacThomais, E., *The Lady at the Gate*, Joe Clarke, Dublin, 1971

Maher, Jim, *The Flying Column, West Kilkenny, 1916–1921*, Geography Publications, Dublin, 1987

Malcolmson, A.P.W., *The Politics of the Anglo-Irish Ascendancy*, Oxford, 1978

Malone, T., *Alias, Seán Forde*, Danesfort Publications, Limerick, 2000

Manning, Maurice, *The Blueshirts*, Gill & Macmillan, Dublin, 1970

———, *Irish Political Parties*, Gill & Macmillan, Dublin, 1972

———, *James Dillon – a Biography*, Wolfhound Press, Dublin, 1999

Mansergh, Nicholas, *The Irish Free State, its Government and Politics*, George Allen, London, 1934

———, *The Unresolved Question, the Anglo-Irish Settlement and its Undoing, 1912–1972*, Yale University Press, Newhaven, 1991

———, *Nationalism and Independence, Selected Irish Papers*, ed. Diana Mansergh, foreword, J.Lee, Cork University Press, 1997

Marcus, David, *Oughto, Leaves From the Diary of a Hyphenated Jew*, Gill & Macmillan, Dublin, 2001

Marrinan, P., *Paisley: Man of Wrath*, Anvil, Tralee, 1973

Mansfield, Michael, QC, and Wardell, Tony, *Presumed Guilty, the British Legal System Exposed*, Heinemann, London, 1993

Marjoribanks, Edward, *The Life of Lord Carson*, Gollancz, London, 1932

Martin, F.X., *Leaders and Men of the Easter Rising: Dublin 1916*, Methuen, London, 1967

Maume, Patrick, *The Long Gestation, Irish Nationalist Life, 1891–1918*, Gill & Macmillan, Dublin, 1991

Maye, Brian, *Arthur Griffith*, Griffith College Publication, Dublin, 1997

McCaffrey, Laurence, *Ireland from Colony to Nation State*, Prentice Hall, New Jersey, 1979

McCann, Eamonn, *War and an Irish Town*, 4th edition, Pluto, London, 1993

McCann, John, *War by the Irish*, The Kerryman, Tralee, 1946,

McCarthy, John F., *Planning Ireland's Future – the Legacy of T.K. Whitaker*, The Glendale Press Ltd, Dublin, 1990

McCartney, Donal, *The Dawning of Democracy, Ireland 1800–1870*, Helicon, Dublin, 1987

McColgan, John, *British Policy and the Irish Administration, 1920–22*, Allen & Unwin, 1983

McConville, Michael, *Ascendancy into Oblivion, the Story of the Anglo-Irish*, Quartet, London, 1986

McCracken, Donal, *MacBride's Brigade*, Four Courts Press Ltd, Dublin, 1999

McCracken, J.L., *Representative Government in Ireland*, Oxford University Press, London, 1958

McDonald, Henry, *Trimble*, Bloomsbury, London, 2001

McDonnell, Kathleen Keyes, *There is a Bridge at Bandon*, Mercier, Dublin, 1972

McGarry, John and O'Leary, Brendan, *Explaining Northern Ireland, Broken Images*, Blackwell, Oxford, 1995

McGee, John, *Northern Ireland Crisis and Conflict*, Routledge and Kegan Paul, London, 1974

McKay, Susan, *Northern Protestants – an Unsettled People*, The Blackstaff Press Ltd, Belfast, 2000

McKittrick, David, *End Game*, Blackstaff Press, 1994

McLoone, Martin and McMahon, John (ed.), *Television and Irish Society*, RTE, Dublin, 1984

McMahon, Seán, *Rich and Rare, A Book of Ireland*, Ward River, Dublin, 1984

Metress, Seamus P., *Outlines in Irish History, 800 Years of Struggle*, Connolly Books, Detroit, 1995

Miller, David W., *Church State, A Nation in Ireland 1898–1921*, Gill & Macmillan, Dublin, 1973

———, *Queen's Rebels, Ulster Loyalism in Historical Perspective*, Gill & Macmillan, Dublin, 1978

Mitchell, Arthur, *Revolutionary Government in Ireland, Dail Eireann, 1919–22*, Gill & Macmillan, Dublin, 1995

Moloney, Ed, *A Secret History of the IRA*, London, Penguin, 2002

Moody, T.W. and Martin, F.X., *A New History of Ireland IV*, Clarendon Press, Oxford, 1986

Moody, T.W., *The Ulster Question, 1603–1973*, Mercier, Dublin, 1974

Moore, Chris, *The Kincora Scandal*, Marino Books, 1996

Moynihan, Daniel, *Pandaemonium*, Oxford University Press, New York, 1993

Moynihan, Maurice, *Speeches and Statements by Eamon de Valera*, Gill & Macmillan, Dublin, 1980

Mullan, Don (ed.), *Eye Witness Bloody Sunday, the Truth*, Wolfhound, Dublin, 1997

———, *The Dublin and Monaghan Bombings*, Wolfhound, Dublin, 2000

Mullen, Pat, *Man of Aran*, MIT Press, New York, 1935

Mullin, Chris, *Error of Judgement, the Truth About the Birmingham Bombings*, Poolbeg, (pb) Dublin, 1990

Murphy, Brian P., *Patrick Pearse and the Lost Republican Ideal*, James Duffy, Dublin, 1991

Murphy, John A., *Ireland in the Twentieth Century*, Gill & Macmillan, Dublin, 1975

Murray, P. and L., *Dictionary of Art and Artists*, Penguin, London, 1959

Murray, Patrick, *Oracles of God*, University Press, Dublin, 2003

Murray, Raymond, *The SAS in Ireland*, Mercier, Dublin, 1990

Murray, Raymond, (ed.), *Irish Church History Today*, Armagh Diocesan Historical Society, (nd)

National Graves Association, *The Last Post, Details and Stories of Irish Republican Dead 1916–85*, Dublin, 1985

Neeson, Eoin, *The Civil War in Ireland*, Poolbeg, Dublin, 1989

Nelligan, David, *The Spy in the Castle*, MacGibbon & Kee, London, 1968

Nevin, Donal (ed.), *1913: Jim Larkin and the Dublin Lockout*, Workers Union of Ireland, Dublin, 1964

———, *James Larkin, Lion of the Fold*, Gill & Macmillan, Dublin, 1998

Ni Dhonnchadha, Mairin and Dorgan, Theo, *Revising the Rising*, Field Day, Derry, 1991

Nixon, W.M. and Healy, Eric, *Asgard*, Cioste an Asgard, Dublin, 2000

O'Bradaigh, R., *The Story of Commdt. General Tom Maguire and the Second (All-Ireland) Dail*, Irish Freedom Press, Dublin, 1997

O'Brien, Conor Cruise, *The Shaping of Modern Ireland*, Routledge & Kegan Paul Ltd, London, 1960

O'Brien, Conor Cruise and Maire, *Ireland – A Concise History*, Thames and Hudson, London, 1992

O'Brien, Eileen, *Modern Ireland 1868–1966*, Mentor Publications, Dublin, 1995

O'Brien, Jack, *British Brutality in Ireland*, Mercier Press, Dublin, 1989

O'Brien, Justin, *The Arms Trial*, Gill & Macmillan, Dublin, 2000

O'Broin, Leon, *Dublin Castle and the 1916 Rising*, Helicon, Dublin, 1966

———, *The Chief Secretary, Augustin Birrell in Ireland*, Chatto & Windus, London, 1969

———, *The Prime Informer, A Suppressed Scandal*, Sidgwick & Jackson, London, 1971

———, *Revolutionary Underground*, Gill & Macmillan, Dublin, 1976

———, *Michael Collins*, Gill & Macmillan, Dublin, 1980

———, *No Man's Man*, Institute of Public Administration, Dublin, 1982

———, *In Great Haste, The Letters of Michael Collins and Kitty Kiernan*, Gill & Macmillan, Dublin, 1983

O'Byrnes, Stephen, *Hiding Behind a Face, Fine Gael Under FitzGerald*, Gill & Macmillan, Dublin, 1986

O'Buachalla, Seamas, *Education Policy in Twentieth-Century Ireland*, Wolfhound, Dublin, 1988

O'Clery, Conor, *Phrases Make History Here, 1886–1987*, O'Brien Press, Dublin, 1986

———, *The Greening of the White House*, Gill & Macmillan, Dublin, 1996

———, *Ireland in Quotes*, O'Brien Press, Dublin, 1999

O'Connell, Michael, *Truth, the First Casualty*, Riverstone Ltd, Ireland, 1993

O'Connor, Frank, *The Big Fellow*, Poolbeg, Dublin, 1979

O'Connor, Ulick, *Oliver St John Gogarty*, New English Library, London, 1963

———, *A Terrible Beauty is Born*, Hamish Hamilton, London, 1975

———, *Executions*, Brandon, Tralee, County Kerry, 1992

O'Cuinneagain, Michael, *Partition – from Michael Collins to Bobby Sands, 1922–81*, O'Cuinneagain, Donegal, 1986

O'Day, Alan, *A Survey of the Irish in England (1872)*, Hambledon Press, London, 1990

O'Donnell, James, *How Ireland is Governed*, Institute of Public Administration, Dublin, 1974

O'Donnell, Peadar, *The Gates Flew Open*, Jonathan Cape, London, 1932

———, *There Will Be Another Day*, Dolmen, Dublin, 1963

O'Donoghue, Florence, *No Other Law, the Story of Liam Lynch and the Irish Republican Army, 1916–1923*, Irish Press, Dublin, 1954

O'Donovan, Donal, *Kevin Barry and His Time*, Glendale, Dublin, 1989

O'Driscoll, Robert and Reynolds, Lorna (ed.), *The Untold Story: The Irish in Canada*, Celtic Arts of Canada, Toronto, 1988 (2 vols)

O'Dwyer, William, *Beyond the Golden Door*, ed. Paul O'Dwyer, St John's University, New York, 1987

O'Faolain, Seán, *Constance Markievicz, or the Average Revolutionary*, Jonathan Cape, London, 1938

O'Farrell, Patrick, *Ireland's English Question*, Schocken Books, New York, 1971

——, *England and Ireland Since 1800*, Oxford University Press, 1975

O'Halloran, C., *Partition and the Limits of Irish Nationalism, an Ideology Under Stress*, Gill & Macmillan, Dublin, 1987

O'Hanlon, Thomas, *The Irish, Portrait of a People*, André Deutsch, London, 1976

O'Hegarty, P.S., *The Indestructible Nation*, Monsell, Dublin, 1918

O'Leary, Brendan, *Northern Ireland Sharing Authority*, IPPR, London, 1993

O'Mahony, Seán, *Frongoch, University of Revolution*, FDR Teoranta, Dublin, 1987

O'Malley, Ernie, *Army without Banners*, Riverside Press, Massachusetts, 1937

——, *The Singing Flame*, Anvil, Dublin, 1978

——, *On Another Man's Wound*, Anvil, Kerry, 1979

——, *Raids and Rallies*, Anvil, Kerry, 1982

O'Malley, Padraig, *The Uncivil Wars*, Blackstaff, Belfast, 1983

O'Murchu, Liam, *Hindsights*, Gill & Macmillan, Dublin, 2000

O'Neill, Marie, *From Parnell to de Valera, a Biography of Jennie Wyse Power*, Blackwater Press, Dublin, 1991

O'Neill, Timothy, *Merchants and Mariners in Medieval Ireland*, Irish Academic Press, Dublin, 1987

O'Neill, T.P. and Lord Longford, *De Valera*, Gill & Macmillan and Hutchinson, Dublin and London, 1970

O'Suilleabhain, M., *Where Mountainy Men have Sown*, Anvil, Tralee, County Kerry, 1965

O'Sullivan, Donal, *The Irish Free State and its Senate*, Faber & Faber, London, 1950

O'Sullivan, Harold and Gavin, Joseph, *Dundalk, A Military History*, Dundealgan Press, Dundalk, 1987

Oliver, John A., *Working at Stormont*, Institute of Public Administration, Dublin, 1978

Pakenham, F., *Peace by Ordeal*, Jonathan Cape, London, 1935

Pakenham, Thomas, *The Year of Liberty*, Hodder & Stoughton, London, 1969, Paris, 1995

Parker, Tony, *May the Lord in His Mercy be Kind to Belfast*, Jonathan Cape, London, 1993

Partington, Angela, *The Oxford Dictionary of Quotations*, new edition, Book Club Associates, London, 1992

Patterson, H., *The Politics of Illusion, Republicanism and Socialism in Modern Ireland*, London, 1989

Peck, J., *Dublin from Downing Street*, Gill & Macmillan, Dublin, 1978

Phoenix, Eamon, *Northern Nationalism*, Ulster Historical Foundation, Belfast, 1994

Pimlott, Ben, *Harold Wilson*, HarperCollins, London, 1993

Pine, Richard, *2RN and the Origins of Irish Radio*, Four Courts Press, Dublin, 2002

Pringle, Peter, *Those Are Real Bullets, Aren't They?*, Fourth Estate, London, 2000

Quinn, Antoinette, *Patrick Kavanagh*, Gill & Macmillan, Dublin, 2001

Rafter, Kevin, *Neil Blaney, A Soldier of Destiny*, Blackwater, Belfast, 1993

———, *Martin Mansergh*, New Island, Dublin, 2002

Raftery, Mary and O'Sullivan, Eoin, *Suffer the Little Children, Story of the RTE Series*, New Island, Dublin, 1999

Redmond, Adrian, *That Was Then, This Is Now – Change in Ireland 1949–1999*, Stationery Office, Dublin, 2000

Rice, Charles E., *Divided Ireland, A Cause for American Concern*, Tyholland Press, Notre Dame, Indiana, 1985

Robinson, Philip, *The Plantation of Ulster*, Gill & Macmillan, Dublin, 1984

Rose, Richard, *Governing Without Consensus, An Irish Perspective*, Faber & Faber, London, 1971

Roth, A., *Mr Bewley in Berlin, Aspect of the Career of an Irish Diplomat, 1933–39*, Four Courts, Dublin, 2000

Ryan, Desmond, *James Connolly*, Talbot Press, Dublin, 1924

———, *Michael Collins*, Anvil, Kerry, (nd)

———, *Remembering Sion*, Barker, London, 1934

———, *Unique Dictator*, Barker, London, 1936

Ryan, Mark, *War and Peace in Ireland*, Pluto, London, 1994

Ryan, T., *Albert Reynolds, The Longford Leader*, Blackwater, Dublin, 1994

Ryder, Chris, *The RUC, A Force Under Fire*, Mandarin, London, 1990

———, *The Ulster Defence Regiment, An Instrument of Peace?*, Mandarin, London, 1991

———, *Inside the Maze, the Untold Story of the Northern Ireland Prison Service*, Methuen, London, 2000

Salvidge, Stanley, *Salvidge of Liverpool: Behind the Political Scene, 1890–1928*, Hodder & Stoughton, London, 1934

Scheper-Hughes, Nancy, *Saints, Scholars and Schizophrenics*, University of California Press, Los Angeles and London, 2001

Scott, C.P. (ed.), *Wilson, The Political Diaries, 1911–28*, Collins, London, 1970

Selwin, F., *Hitler's Englishman, the Crime of Lord Haw Haw*, Routledge & Kegan Paul, London, 1987

Senior, Hereward, *Orangeism in Ireland and Britain*, Routledge & Kegan Paul, London, 1966

Shakespeare, Sir G., *Let Candles be Brought In*, MacDonald, London, 1949

Shannon, E., *I am of Ireland*, Little Brown, Boston, 1989

Shannon, William, *The American Irish*, Collier Macmillan, New York, 1963

Sharnock David, *Man of War – the Unauthorised Biography of Gerry Adams*, Macmillan, London, 1997

Shaw, G.B., *Autobiography 1898–1950*, Reinhardt Books, London, 1970

———, *Collected Letters, Vol. III*, Reinhardt Books, London, 1985

———, *How to Settle the Irish Question*, Talbot Press, Dublin, 1917

Sheedy, Kieran, *The Clare Elections*, Bouroe Publications, Dun Laoghaire, 1993

Sherman, Hugh, *Not an Inch*, Faber, London, 1942

Sloan, Barry, *The Pioneers of Anglo-Irish Fiction: Smythe*, Buckinghamshire, 1986

Smith, Jeremy, *The Tories and Ireland, 1910–1914*, Irish Academic Press, Dublin, 2000

Smith, Raymond, *Haughey and O'Malley, The Quest For Power*, Aherlow Publishers, Dublin, 1986

Soukhand, Anne, *The American Heritage Dictionary of English Language*, 3rd edition, Houghton Mifflin Co.

Spray, Glenys, *Blood, Sweat and Tears: The Hepatitis C Scandal*, Wolfhound, Dublin, 1998

Stalker, J., *The Stalker Affair*, Penguin, London, 1989

Steele, E.D., *Irish Land and British Politics*, Cambridge University Press, 1974

Stevenson, Francis (ed.), *Lloyd George: a Diary*, Hutchinson, London, 1971

Stewart, A.T.Q., *The Ulster Crisis*, Faber, London, 1967

———, *Edward Carson*, Gill & Macmillan, Dublin, 1981

Stradling, R.A., *The Irish and the Spanish Civil War, 1936–39, Crusades and Conflict*, Mandolin, Manchester, 1999

Street, Major C.J., *The Administration of Ireland, 1920*, Philip Allen, London, 1921

———, *Ireland in 1921*, Philip Allen, London, 1922

Stuart, Francis, *Black List, Section H*, Feffer & Simons Inc., USA, 1971

Sweetman, R., *On Our Knees*, Pan, London, 1972

Swift, John P., *John Swift: an Irish Dissident*, Gill & Macmillan, Dublin, 1991

Tansill, Charles, *America and the Fight for Irish Freedom*, Devin-Adare, New York, 1957

Tarpey, Marie V., *The Role of Joseph McGarrity in the Struggle for Irish Independence*, Arno Press, New York, 1976

Taylor, A.J.P., *English History, 1914–1945*, Oxford University Press, 1965

Taylor, P., *Beating the Terrorists?* Penguin, Middlesex, 1980

———, *Provos, the IRA and Sinn Féin*, Bloomsbury, London, 1997

———, *Loyalists*, Bloomsbury, London, 1999

———, *Brits*, Bloomsbury, London, 2001

Taylor, Rex, *Michael Collins*, Four Square, London, 1958

———, *Assassination, the Death of Sir Henry Wilson*, Hutchinson, London, 1961

Toolis, K., *Rebel Hearts*, Picador, London, 1995

Townsend, Charles, *The British Campaign in Ireland, 1919–1921, and Britain's Civil Wars Counterinsurgency in the Twentieth Century*, Faber & Faber, Cambridge, 1986

———, *Ireland, the Twentieth Century*, Arnold, London, 1999

Trollope, Anthony, *Phineas Finn*, J.M. Dent & Sons, London,1929

Urban, Mark, *Big Boys' Rules*, Faber & Faber, London, 1992

Valarasan-Toomey, M., *The Celtic Tiger – From the Outside Looking In*, Blackhall Publishing, Dublin, 1998

Valuilis, Maryanne G., *Portrait of a Revolutionary – General Richard Mulcahy*, Irish Academic Press, Dublin, 1992

Waldron, Jarlath, *Mamtrasna – the Murders and the Mystery*, Edmond Bourke Publisher, Dublin, 1992

Walshe, Dick, *The Party Inside Fianna Fáil*, Gill & Macmillan, Dublin,1986

Walter, Bronwen, *Outsiders Inside, Whiteness, Place and Irish Women*, Routledge, London, 2001

Ward, A.J., *Ireland and Anglo-American Relations, 1899–1921*, London School of Economics, London, 1969

Ward, M., *In Their Own Voice, Women and Irish Nationalism*, Attic Press, Dublin, 1995

Warner, Alan, *A Guide to Anglo-Irish Literature*, Gill & Macmillan, 1981

Waters, John, *Jiving at the Crossroads*, The Blackstaff Press, Belfast, 1991

Weitzer, Ronald, *Transforming Settler States, Communal Conflict and Internal Security in Northern Ireland and Zimbabwe*, University of California Press, 1990

West, Rebecca, *The Meaning of Treason*, Virago Press, London, 1982

Whelan, Gerard with Carolyn Swift, *Spiked, Church–State Intrigue and The Rose Tattoo*, New Island, Dublin, 2002

Whelan, Thomas R., *The Stranger in our Midst*, Kimmage Mission Institute of Theology and Cultures, Dublin, 2001

———, *Statesman of the Troubles*, White, Barry, Blackstaff, 1984

Whitaker, T.K., *Interests*, Institute of Public Administration, Dublin, 1983

Whyte, J.H., *Church and State in Modern Ireland 1923–1970*, Gill & Macmillan, Dublin, 1971

Winter, Orde, *Winter's Tale, An Autobiography*, Richards Press, London, 1955

Williams, Paul, *Evil Empire*, Merlin Publishing, Dublin, 2001

Wilson, A.J., *Irish America and the Ulster Conflict, 1968–1995*, Blackstaff, Belfast, 1995

Woodcock, C., *An Officer's Wife in Ireland*, Parkgate, Dublin, 1994

Woodham Smith, Cecil, *The Great Hunger*, Penguin, London, 1991

Younger, Calton, *Ireland's Civil War*, Muller, London, 1968

———, *A State of Disunion, Four Studies – Griffith, Collins, Craig, de Valera*, Muller, London, 1972

———, *Arthur Griffith*, Gill & Macmillan, Dublin, 1981

DICTIONARIES AND CHRONOLOGIES

American Heritage Dictionary of the English Language, 3rd edition, Houghton Mifflin, Boston, 1992

Annual Register, Longmans, Harlow

Keesing's Contemporary Archives, Keesings, London

Bew, Paul and Gillespie, Gordon, *Northern Ireland, A Chronology of the Troubles*, Gill & Macmillan, Dublin, 1993

Boylan, Henry, *A Dictionary of Irish Biography*, Gill & Macmillan, Dublin, 1999

Connolly, S.J., *The Oxford Companion to Irish History*, Oxford University Press, 1998

Deutsch, Richard and Magowan, Vivien, *Northern Ireland, A Chronology of Events, Vols, 1–3 (1968–75)*, Blackstaff, Belfast,

Flackes, W.D., *Northern Ireland, A Political Directory, 1968–79*, Gill & Macmillan, Dublin, 1980

Flackes, W.D. and Elliott, Sydney, *Northern Ireland: a Political Director, 1968–1993*, Blackstaff, Belfast, 1994

Webster, 2 vols, Bell, 2nd edition, London, Springfield, 1932

PARLIAMENTARY RECORDS

Dail Debates – Official Reports, Stationery Office, Dublin

House of Commons Reports, Hansard, HMSO, London

Northern Ireland Assembly Debates, Official Report, HMSO, Belfast

REPORTS AND OFFICIAL DOCUMENTS

Amnesty International, *UK Killings by Security Forces in Northern Ireland* (update), London, 1990

Bloody Sunday and the Report of the Widgery Tribunal: Irish Government assessment presented to the British Government, 1997

Cameron Report into Disturbances in Northern Ireland, Cmnd 532, HMSO, Belfast, 1969

Hunt Report on Police in Northern Ireland, Cmnd 535, HMSO, Belfast, 1969

Macrory Report on Local Government in Northern Ireland, HMSO, Belfast, 1970

Report on Reform Programme: A Record of Constructive Change, Cmnd 558, HMSO, Belfast, 1971

Scarman Report on Northern Violence in 1969, Cmnd 566, HMSO, Belfast, 1971

Compton Report into Security Force Behaviour in August 1971, Cmnd 4823, HMSO, London, 1971

Parker Report into Interrogation Procedures of Suspected Terrorists, Cmnd 4901, HMSO, London, 1972

Diplock Report of Commission on New Legal Procedures to Deal With Suspected Terrorists, Cmnd 5185, HMSO, London, 1972

Widgery Report into Bloody Sunday, January 30th, 1972, HC220 1971–72, HMSO, London, 1972.

Anglo-Irish Law Enforcement Commission Report, Cmnd 5627, HMSO, London, 1974

Gardiner Report on Counter-Insurgency Methods [recommended H blocks],. *Cmnd 5847*, HMSO, London, 1975

Bennett Report on RUC Interrogation Methods, Cmnd 7497, HMSO, London, 1979.

European Parliament Report on Discrimination in Northern Ireland, issued by Committee on Social Affairs, Employment and the Working Environment, 18 March 1994 (English edition)

Opsahl Report, A Citizens' Inquiry on Northern Ireland, Lilliput, Dublin, 1993

NEWSPAPERS AND PAMPHLETS

An Phoblacht/Republican News, Belfast Telegraph, Economist, Fortnight, Guardian, Independent, Irish Independent, Irish News, Irish Press, Irish Times, News Letter, Observer, Sunday Press, Sunday Tribune, Sunday Independent, Sunday Times, New Statesman, Spectator

APPENDIX 1

TRIBUNALS

The following, necessarily abbreviated, list of Tribunals was originally drawn up by Carol Coulter, Legal Affairs Correspondent of the *Irish Times* on 23 November 2002 as part of an important investigation into the problems confronting – and raised by – the Tribunals. The Lindsay Tribunal has since reported, and the costs have obviously increased greatly between 2002 and the time of publication. But the list does give an indication of some of the issues, and their implications, which were troubling the Irish public as one century ended and another began.

ANSBACHER INSPECTION

Set up: 1999
Chairman: There was no chairman, as this was a High Court inspection under Section 8 of the Companies Act, where inspectors were asked to examine the affairs of Ansbacher (Cayman) Limited.
Inspectors: Judge Seán O'Leary; Noreen Mackey BL; Paul Rowan FCA; and Michael Cush SC; along with former Inspector, Justice Declan Costello, former President of the High Court, who retired from the inspection on health grounds.
Terms of Reference: These were set up by the Companies Act, and based on the Tanaiste's belief that an inspection was the only way to investigate the affairs of the company, which she believed were carried out in a fraudulent or unlawful manner. A High Court inspection allows inspectors to interview various parties under oath.
Pay: Not available
Cost to date: €3.5 million, approximately
Completion: The report was published on 6 July 2002

BARRON INQUIRY

Set up: January 2000 under Justice Liam Hamilton, who died and was replaced by Justice Henry Barron, retired judge of the Supreme Court, in October 2000.
Chairman: Justice Henry Barron, retired Supreme Court Judge
Terms of Reference: To be an independent commission of inquiry into the

Dublin, Monaghan and Dundalk bombings of 1974
There have been no public hearings
Pay: Justice Barron is paid the difference between his pension and salary as judge of the Supreme Court
Costs so far: €1,690,577, which includes payments made to the late Justice Liam Hamilton, Justice Henry Barron, miscellaneous expenses, as well as costs associated with the legal engagement of Justice for the Forgotten.
Expected date of completion: Early in 2003 (had not reported before this book was published)

BARR TRIBUNAL

Set Up: 2002
Chairman: Justice Robert Barr
Terms of Reference: Set up after the Supreme Court ruled that the Oireachtas Committee on Justice could not inquire into the shooting in Abbeylara of John Carthy by members of the Garda Emergency Response Unit. This offended the constitutional rights of people not members of the Oireachtas, as their reputations could be damaged without recourse to natural justice.
Pay: As for the Morris Tribunal
Cost so far: €225,000
Expected date of completion: Not known

DUNNE INQUIRY

Set up: April 2000
Chairman: Anne Dunne SC
Terms of Reference: A private (not statutory) inquiry into the retention of organs by certain hospitals, in light of fears following a report into a Bristol hospital in the UK
Pay: Senior Counsel: €1,904.61 a day
Junior Counsel: €1,206.25 a day
Cost so far: €5.3 million. This includes €1,189 million paid to the campaigning group, Parents for Justice, and their legal advisers
Expected date of completion: No definite date

FLOOD TRIBUNAL [now known as Mahon Tribunal]

Set up: 1997
Chairman: Justice Feargus Flood, retired High Court Judge, succeeded in 2003 by Mr Justice Mahon
Terms of Reference: To inquire into planning matters in certain parts of Dublin; the allocation of the broadcasting licence to Century Radio, and related allegations of payments to politicians.
Pay: Justice Flood was paid the difference between his pension and a High

Court Judge's salary of €172,409
Senior Counsel: €2,250 a day
Junior Counsel: €1,500 a day
Cost so far: €22.7 million
Expected date of completion: Not known

LAFFOY COMMISSION

Set up: 1999
Chairman: Justice Mary Laffoy, Judge of the High Court, who retired just before this book went to press.
Terms of Reference: To inquire into the physical, sexual and emotional abuse of children in institutions, seeking both personal testimonies and attempting to identify those responsible and examining the supervisory role of the State.
Pay: High Court Judge's salary of €172,409
Senior Counsel: €2,159–€1,905 a day, declining as the commission continues
Junior Counsel: €1,4399–1,270 a day, as above
Cost so far: €5.46 million
Expected date of completion: Recently extended to May 2005

LINDSAY TRIBUNAL

Set up: 1999
Chairman: Judge Alison Lindsay
Terms of Reference: To inquire into the infection of haemophiliacs with AIDS and hepatitis C through contaminated blood products
Pay: Circuit Court Judge's salary of €125,933
Senior Counsel: €1,841 a day
Junior Counsel: €1,206 a day
Cost: Not available
Date of Completion: Reported in 2002,. On 23 July 2003, Gardai launched a series of arrests and prosecutions against IBTB personnel arising out of Hepatitis C infections caused to women by contaminated blood products. At the time of going to press, these cases had yet to be heard

THE MORIARTY TRIBUNAL

Set up: ???
Chairman: Justice Michael Moriarty
Terms of Reference: To inquire into payments to Charles Haughey and Michael Lowry
Pay: High Court Judge's salary of €172,409
Senior Counsel: €2,500 a day
Junior Counsel: €2,000 a day
Cost so far: Almost €11 million

Expected date of completion: Work is ongoing

MORRIS TRIBUNAL

Set up: July 2002
Chairman: Justice Frederick Morris, retired President of the High Court
Terms of Reference: To inquire into various allegations of corruption against certain members of the Donegal Division of the Garda Siochana
Pay: Judge Morris is paid the difference between his pension and his salary as President of the High Court, €172,409 a year
Senior Counsel: €2,250 a day
Junior Counsel: €1,500 a day
Cost so far: €999,054
Expected date of completion: The tribunal is expected to last at least two years

MURPHY TRIBUNAL

Set up: October 2002
Chairman: Justice Frank Murphy, retired judge of the Supreme Court
Terms of Reference: Following a recommendation from George Birmingham SC, it was decided to set up a non-statutory inquiry into the treatment of allegations of child sex abuse by clergy of the Ferns diocese.
Cost so far: The Birmingham preliminary investigation cost €423,861
Expected date of completion: Not known

(Reproduced courtesy of the
Irish Times)

APPENDIX 2

IRISH GENERAL ELECTIONS RESULTS 1923 TO 1997

Year of Election	Fianna Fáil	Fine Gael (Cumann na nGaedheal to 1937)	Labour	Farmers	Other Parties
	seats % vote % seats	seats % vote % seats	seats % vote % seats	seats % seats	seats % seats
1923	44 27.6 28.75	63 38.9 41.17	14 12.4 9.15	15 9.8	17 11.1
June 1927	44 26.1 28.75	47 27.5 30.71	22 13.8 14.37	11 7.18	29 18.9
Sept 1927	57 35.2 37.25	62 38.7 40.52	13 9.5 8.49	6 3.92	15 9.8
1932	72 44.5 47.05	57 35.3 36.30	7 7.7 4.57	4 2.61	13 8.4
1933	77 49.7 50.30	48 30.5 31.37	8 5.7 5.23	–	20 13.1
1937	69 45.2 50	48 34.8 34.78	13 10.3	–	8 5.7
1938	77 51.9 55.79	45 33.3 32.6	9 10.0 6.52	–	7 5.0
1943	67 41.9 48.55	32 23.1 23.18	17 15.7 12.31	14 10.14	8 5.8
1944	76 48.9 55.07	30 20.5 22.22	12 11.5 8.69	11 7.97	9 6.5
1948	68 41.9 46.25	31 19.8 21.08	19 11.3 12.92	7 4.76	22 14.9
1951	69 46.3 46.93	40 25.7 27.21	16 11.4 10.88	6 4.08	16 10.8

815

Year of Election	Fianna Fáil	Fine Gael (Cumann na nGaedheal to 1937)	Labour	Farmers	Other Parties
	seats % vote % seats	seats % vote % seats	seats % vote % seats	seats % seats	seats % seats
1954	65 43.4 44.21	50 32 34.01	19 12 12.92	5 3.4	8 5.4
1957	78 48.3 53.06	40 26.6 27.21	12 9.1 8.16	3 2.04	14 9.5
1961	70 43.8 48.61	47 32.0 32.63	16 11.6 11.11	2 1.38	9 6.2
1965	72 47.8 50	47 33.9 32.63	22 15.4 15.27	–	3.21
1969	75 45.7 52.08	50 34.1 34.72	18 17 12.5	–	1.69
1973	69 46.2 47.91	54 35.1 37.5	19 13.7 13.9	–	2 1.3
1977	84 50.6 56.75	43 30.5 29.05	17 11.6	–	4 2.7
1981	78 45.3 46.98	65 36.5 39.15	15 9.9 9.03	–	7 4.2
Feb. 1982	81 45.3 48.79	63 37.3 37.95	15 9.1 9.03	–	4 2.4
Nov. 1982	75 45.2 45.18	70 39.2 42.16	16 9.4 9.63	–	3 1.8
1987	81 44.2 48.79	51 27.1. 30.72	12 6.4 7.22	–	4 2.4
1989	77 44.2 46.38	55 29.3 33.13	15 9.5 9.03	–	6 3.6
1992	68 39.1 40.96	45 24.5 27.1	33 19.3 19.8	–	6 3.6
1997	77 39.3 46.38	54 28 32.53	17 10.4 10.2	–	18 10.8

The results of the 2002 General Election would be obtained in the above format because this would yield 34 'Others', thus masking the shifts which occurred. Accordingly they are given as follows:

Seats	*Percentages*
Fianna Fáil 80	Fianna Fáil 41.5
Fine Gael 31	Fine Gael 22.5
Labour 21	Labour 10.8
Green Party 6	Green Party 3.8
Sinn Féin 5	Sinn Féin 6.5
Socialist Party 1	Others and
Independents 14	Independents 11

Turn-out   63%

(Tables above for the 2002 Election results
courtesy Electoral Reform Society)

APPENDIX 3

PERCENTAGE DISTRIBUTION OF OUTPUT EXPORTED

1986	UK	Other EU	USA	Elsewhere
Irish	55.2	16.5	11.5	16.7
Foreign	23.1	46.0	12.7	18.2
Total	30.9	38.9	12.4	17.8
1988				
Irish	41.6	19.8	9.7	28.9
Foreign	25.3	48.1	8.5	18.1
Total	29.5	40.9	8.8	20.8
1990				
Irish	42.8	23.8	8.1	25.3
Foreign	22.6	49.4	9.9	18.1
Total	27.6	43.2	9.4	19.9
1995				
Irish	42.1	32.2	7.3	18.4
Foreign	22.6	50.9	10.8	15.7
Total	26.0	47.6	10.2	16.2
1996				
Irish	42.2	32.2	8.2	17.3
Foreign	22.6	50.0	10.7	16.8
Total	25.7	47.1	10.3	16.9
1998				
Irish	41.1	32.3	10.9	15.7
Foreign	17.8	47.9	13.9	20.4
Total	20.7	46.0	13.5	19.8
1999				
Irish	40.2	35.3	9.4	15.0
Foreign	17.7	47.4	16.8	18.2
Total	19.9	46.2	16.0	17.9

The latest figures for 1999 are for the distribution of output by market between the Irish- and foreign-owned industrial sectors.

Figures show that while only 19.9% of industrial output is sold to the UK, for Irish-owned firms it remains the Republic's largest market and still accounts for over 40% of exports of the Irish owned industrial sector.

Levels:

	Gross National Product (Constant 1995 Prices) – IR£	Gross Domestic Product (Constant 1995 Prices) – IR£	Gross National Product (Constant 1995 Prices) – Euro	Gross Domestic Product (Constant 1995 Prices) – Euro
1990	29,513	32,986	37,474	41,884
1991	30,187	33,623	38,330	42,692
1992	30,888	34,744	39,220	44,116
1993	31,934	35,681	40,548	45,306
1994	33,950	37,735	43,108	47,914
1995	36,723	41,408	46,629	52,578
1996	39,432	44,594	50,069	56,623
1997	43,106	49,383	54,734	62,704
1998	46,485	53,610	59,024	68,071
1999	50,119	58,876	63,638	74,757
2000	55,061	65,174	69,913	82,754
2001	58,380	68,758	74,128	88,574
2002 (f)	59,442	71,057	75,476	90,223

Growth Rates:

	GDP	GNP	GDP per Head	GNP per Head
1990	6.8	6.9	6.9	7.1
1991	1.9	2.3	1.4	1.7
1992	3.3	2.3	2.5	1.5
1993	2.7	3.4	2.1	2.8
1994	5.8	6.3	5.4	5.9
1995	9.7	8.2	9.3	7.7
1996	7.7	7.4	7.0	6.6
1997	10.7	9.3	9.7	8.3
1998	8.6	7.8	7.3	6.5
1999	9.8	7.8	8.7	6.7
2000	10.7	9.9	9.5	8.6
2001	7.0	6.0	5.9	4.9
2002 (f)	1.9	1.8	1.0	0.9

(figures supplied courtesy of
Alan Gray, Indecon Consultants)

APPENDIX 4

YEAR ESTABLISHED	MISSIONS
1923	United Kingdom
1924	U.S.A.
1929	Boston (Consulate)
	Holy See
	France
1930	New York (Consulate)
1932	Belgium (Embassy)
1933	Chicago (Consulate)
	San Francisco (Consulate)
1935	Spain
1938	Italy
1939	Canada
1940	Switzerland
1941	Portugal
1946	Australia
	Sweden
1947	Argentina
1950	The Netherlands
1951	Germany
1955	Strasbourg (Council of Europe)
1956	Permanent Mission to the UN – New York
1960	Nigeria
1961	Denmark
1964	India
1965	Geneva
1966	Brussels (Perm. Rep. to the EU)
1973	Japan
	Luxembourg
1974	Beirut (closed 1982)
	USSR (now Russia)
	Austria
1975	Egypt
1976	Saudi Arabia
	Iran

1977	Greece
1978	Lesotho DCO
1979	Kenya (closed 1988)
	China
	Tanzania DCO
1980	Zambia DCO
1984	Iraq (temporarily closed 14 January 1990)
1989	Republic of Korea (South Korea)
1990	Poland
1992	Finland
1994	Ethiopia
1995	South Africa
	Uganda
	Czechoslovakia (now Czech Republic)
	Hungary
	Malaysia
1996	Mozambique
	Israel
1998	Cardiff Con. Gen.
	Edinburgh Con. Gen.
	Turkey
1999	Mexico
2000	Sydney Con. Gen.
	Shanghai Con. Gen.
	Singapore
	Palestinian National Authority – Ramallah
2001	Norway
	Slovakia
	Cyprus
	Slovenia
	Brazil
	Estonia

APPENDIX 5

The following table extracted from the Department of Education's revised list of payments after the 1946 teachers' strike was settled gives an indication of the levels of teachers' pay obtaining before and after the strike. The system of calculating differential between teachers with varying lengths of service – and between women teachers and men – was extremely complicated, but it can be taken that it took over a decade to reach the upper levels.

New Single men's scale	New Married men's scale	New Salary rate on 31/10/46 – Single man's rate, Col. (2), + £50 or married man's rate, Col. (3), whichever is the higher.	Former salary rate. 1934 scale	New Single men's scale.	New married men's scale.	New salary rate on 31/10/46 – Single man's rate, Col. (2), + £50 or married man's rate, Col. (3), whichever is the higher.
£	£	£	£	£	£	£
288	350	350	268	342	440	440
297	365	365	277	351	455	455
306	380	380	286	360	470	470
315	395	395	295	369	{ 485	485
324	410	410	303	380		
333	425	425	–	–	–	–

INDEX

Friel, Brian 743, 744
Friend, Major-General L. B. 47, 56
Friends of Fianna Fáil 412
Friends of Soviet Russia 180, 209,
212
Froude, James 8
FUE *see* Federation Union of
Employers
Furrow, The (journal) 733

GAA *see* Gaelic Athletic
Association
Gaelic American (newspaper) 86,
253
Gaelic Athletic Association (GAA)
16, 27, 67, 183, 273, 459, 511,
537, 719, 748
Gaelic League 16, 26, 27, 30, 32, 41,
63, 168, 183, 225, 274, 707–8,
714
Gaffney, Joseph 49
Gageby, Douglas 447
Gallagher, Denis 539
Gallagher, Dermot 415, 417, 691
Gallagher, Frank 183–4
Gallagher, Thomas 78
Galvin, John 445
Galvin, Patrick 734
Galway 57, 84
Galway Blazers (hunt) 714–15
Gandon, James 92
Garda Siochana 122, 126, 146, 151,
184, 195, 196–7, 207, 247,
446–7, 460–1, 479, 520, 529–31,
637
Gardiner, Lord: Report (1975) 583,
584, 586
Gargan, Bridie 594
Garrett, George 360
Garvey, Edmund 529–30
Garvin, Professor Tom 142, 700
Gaughan, Michael 518–19
Gaulle, Charles de 443
Gedda, Dr Luigi 358
Geddes, Sir Auckland 410, 411

Geehan, Tommy 318, 320
GEN 42 committee 551, 553, 554
Geoghegan, James 185, 194, 195
George V 22, 38–9, 78, 89–90, 96,
102, 176, 190, 322
George VI 323
Geraghty, Des 613, 614
German-Irish Association 49, 50,
279
Germans/Germany 35, 47–51,
233–6, 241, 255, 269–70, 276–7,
278–94, 296–7, 408, 654–5; *see
also* U-boats
Gibbons, James 503, 506, 507, 508,
509, 510, 512, 595, 598
Gibney, Jim 589, 650
Gifford, Grace 59, 62
Gildernew, Anne-Marie 485
Gildernew, Geraldine 485
Gill and Macmillan (publishers) 746
Gilmartin, Tom 636
Gilmore, Charlie 212, 213, 214
Gilmore, George 195, 207, 215
Gilmore, Harry 212, 213
Glacken, John 624
Gladstone, William Ewart 1, 13, 14
Glasgow Observer 61
Glencree (ship) 289
Glencullen (ship) 289
Glenn, Alice 611
globalisation 697–8
Glover, General James 581
Glynn, Seán 216–17, 326
Gneisenau (warship) 269
Godfrey, Archbishop William 724
Goertz, Hermann 285, 287–8, 333
Goldenbridge Industrial School,
Dublin 637, 741–2
Gonne, Maud *see* MacBride,
Maud
Good Friday Agreement (1998) xiii,
xiv, 91, 213, 218, 245, 396, 523,
536, 591, 654, 675, 681–6, 688,
689–90, 692–3
Goodman, Larry 618–19

unions *see* trade unions
United Ireland Party *see* Fine Gael
United Irishman 198, 294, 460, 461,
    704
United Kingdom Unionist Party
    523
United Nations 255, 394–5, 396,
    397–8, 399–400, 401, 407–8,
    409, 410, 502, 523, 731
United States of America 9, 29, 38,
    63–4, 88–9, 190–1, 397,
    398–400, 411–18, 431, 463, 536,
    668–9
  investment in Ireland 402, 527
  Irish-Americans xiv, 11–12, 13,
    66, 77, 79, 408, 409, 410–11,
    414, 416–18, 588, 661–2, 667
  in World War II 242, 243–5, 252,
    253–5, 264–9, 270–1, 272,
    333
  see also Carter, Jimmy; Clinton,
    Bill; Cohalan, Judge; de Valera,
    Eamon; Marshall Aid; Wilson,
    Woodrow
United Ulster Unionist Council
    (UUUC) 572, 574, 575
University College Dublin (UCD)
    311, 335, 438, 439, 440–1, 651,
    624
UPA *see* Ulster Protestant Action
    Group; Ulster Protestant
    Association
UPL *see* Ulster Protestant League
Urban, Mark 416
UUUC *see* United Ulster Unionist
    Council
UVF *see* Ulster Volunteer Force

Vaizey, John 389
Valeros, Vivion de 32
Vanguard Movement 676
Vanguard Unionist Progressive
    Party 570, 572
Vanier, Jean 448
Vatican, the 12, 13, 281, 358–9, 371,

380, 430, 447, 456–7; *see also*
    Catholic Church
Vaughan, Dr Julia 606
Veesenmayer, Dr Edmund 284, 286
Vincentians, Castleknock, County
    Dublin 15
Virgin Airways 684–5
Volunteers *see* Irish Volunteers;
    Ulster Volunteers
Vorster, John 303

Walsh, Dr Joseph, Archbishop of
    Tuam 714–15
Walshe, Brendan 695
Walshe, Frank P. 78, 79
Walshe, J.J. 167
Walshe, Joseph P. 177, 219, 220,
    221, 226, 234, 235, 240–1, 252,
    257, 276, 278, 286, 291, 357–8,
    359, 380, 713
Walshe, Dr Tom 404
Ward, Dr F. Con 345, 364, 365
Ward, Margaret 29
Ware, John 416
Waring, Colonel 305
Warlimont, General Walter 292, 293
Warnock, Edmund 256
Warnock, William 282, 285, 289
Washington Post 524
Watson, Colonel Edwin 253
Webber-Drohl, Ernest 288
Weisbach, Lieutenant Julius 51
Welles, Orson 718
West, Harry 550, 551, 570, 572, 574,
    576, 589
Westminster Gazette 86
Wexford 57, 84, 293, 716
Wheelwright, Catherine (*née* Coll)
    32–3
Whelehan, Harry 627, 630, 631–3
Whitaker, T.K. xiii, 172, 342, 353,
    356, 382, 384–5, 386, 387, 388,
    389, 390–2, 438–9, 452, 453,
    456, 526, 528, 529
White, General Sir George 30

Also available in Arrow
Order further *Tim Pat Coogan* titles from
your local bookshop, or have them delivered
direct to your door by Bookpost

☐	**Michael Collins**	0099685809	£10.00
☐	**De Valera**	0099958600	£11.99
☐	**The Troubles**	009946571X	£10.00
☐	**Wherever Green is Worn**	0099958503	£10.00

Free post and packing
Overseas customers allow £2 per paperback

Phone: 01624 677237

Post: Random House Books
c/o Bookpost, PO Box 29, Douglas

Isle of Man, IM99 1BQ

Fax: 01624 670923

email: bookshop@enterprise.net

Cheques and credit cards accepted

Prices and availability subject to change without notice
Allow 28 days for delivery

www.randomhouse.co.uk

arrow books